The Handbook of Economic Sociology

The Handbook of Economic Sociology

SECOND EDITION

Neil J. Smelser and
Richard Swedberg EDITORS

PRINCETON UNIVERSITY PRESS
PRINCETON AND OXFORD

RUSSELL SAGE FOUNDATION
NEW YORK

ISBN: 0-691-12125-7
ISBN (pbk.): 0-691-12126-5

Library of Congress Cataloging-in-Publication Data

The handbook of economic sociology / Neil J. Smelser
and Richard Swedberg, editors.—2nd ed.
p.   cm
Includes bibliographical references and index.
ISBN 0-691-12125-7 (cl : alk. paper)—
ISBN 0-691-12126-5 (pbk. : alk. paper)
1. Economics—Sociological aspects.   I. Title:
Economic sociology.   II. Smelser, Neil J.
III. Swedberg, Richard.

HM548.H25 2005
306.3—dc22   2004050524

British Library Cataloging-in-Publication Data is available

This book has been composed in ITC Galliard

Printed on acid-free paper. ∞
www.pupress.princeton.edu
www.russellsage.org

Printed in the United States of America

10 9 8 7 6 5 4 3 2 1

Contents

Preface

IN THE FIRST EDITION of the *Handbook*, published in 1994, we as editors ventured the judgment that, in the previous 15 years, economic sociology had enjoyed a remarkable renaissance, following on a season of relative quiescence. This led us to believe that the time was ripe for a consolidating publication that told about the past, assessed the present, and looked toward the future.

The decade following that volume's appearance seemed to validate those assessments, if the amount of critical attention given, sizable and sustained sales, and course adoptions are taken as measures. If anything, the book's fortunes surpassed our expectations. Furthermore, the momentum of economic sociology as an enterprise has accelerated in the meantime. The quality and quantity of research have remained high; new and young talent continues to flow into the field; sociology departments in half a dozen or more leading research universities have established centers of excellence in economic sociology; courses in economic sociology have become standard fare in the curricula of most colleges and universities; and a section on economic sociology has formed and now thrives in the American Sociological Association.

All these circumstances have convinced us that a second, fully updated edition of the *Handbook* is needed, and we are more confident of this judgment than we were the first time around. While the first edition still contains much of value to scholars and students, the knowledge it contains has in some cases been superseded by advances in the meantime. To take these into account—and also to accelerate the development of economic sociology—we had to undertake a wholesale revamping of the first edition. Fully two-thirds of the chapters in this second edition are either new or have authors different from those in the first.

Despite this transformation, we found that the general intellectual architecture of the first edition remained a good organizing framework for the second. Thus, part I (chapters 1–6) is a series of general considerations of the field from a variety of different perspectives; part II (chapters 7–21), which we call the economic core, deals with economic systems, economic institutions, and economic behav-

ior. Part III (chapters 22–30) concerns a number of intersections among the economy and various noneconomic sectors of the society.

Within this general frame the reader will find the following substantial thematic changes:

- Two chapters on international and global concerns (contrasted with the single chapter in the first edition), with international aspects covered in other chapters as well
- A chapter on behavioral economics, which continues as a vibrant subfield of economics
- A chapter by Pierre Bourdieu on economic anthropology; Bourdieu had agreed to write such a chapter but his untimely death in 2002 prevented this; still wishing to have him represented, we are printing the English translation of "Principes d'une anthropologie économique," which is published on pp. 233–70 in *Les structures sociales de l'économie* (Paris: Seuil, 2000)
- A chapter on new lines of institutional analysis in economics and sociology
- A chapter on the transitions from socialist economies (replacing the earlier chapter on socialist economies themselves)
- A chapter on labor markets and trade unions
- A chapter on the sociology of work and the professions
- A chapter on culture and consumption
- A chapter on the sociology of money and credit
- A chapter on law and the economy
- A chapter on technology and the economy
- A chapter on emotions and the economy

We regard these changes as reflecting recent shifts in emphasis and active lines of research in economic sociology.

We now provide a brief supplement to the table of contents, intended as a guide to readers wishing to delve selectively into the volume according to their specific interests. For those interested in learning about the scope of sociology we recommend chapter 1 ("Introducing Economic Sociology"). The remainder of part I contains chapters on comparative and historical treatments of economy and society in chapter 2 ("Comparative and Historical Approaches to Economic Sociology," by

Frank Dobbin), recent developments in institutional analysis of the economy in chapter 3 ("The New Institutionalisms in Economics and Sociology" by Victor Nee), Pierre Bourdieu's critical anthropological formulations in chapter 4 ("Principles of an Economic Anthropology"), developments in behavioral economics, which has made its main business the modification of the psychological assumptions of neoclassical economics and tracing the implications of these modifications (chapter 5, "Behavioral Economics," by Roberto Weber and Robyn Dawes), and an assessment of the scattered literature on the role that emotions play in economic life (chapter 6, "Emotions and the Economy," by Mabel Berezin).

The first section of part II takes a look at sociological aspects of economies at the macroscopic—including the global—level. We introduce the section with the chapter by Ian Morris and J. G. Manning on the economic sociology of the classical civilizations of Egypt, Greece, and Rome (chapter 7, "The Economic Sociology of the Ancient Mediterranean World"). Next comes a general chapter on the international economy (chapter 8, "The Global Economy: Organization Governance, and Development," by Gary Gereffi), and one on its governance (chapter 9, "The Political and Economic Sociology of International Economic Arrangements," by Neil Fligstein). Finally, Lawrence King and Iván Szelényi develop a distinctive perspective on the varieties of transition from socialist to post-socialist economies (chapter 10, "Post-Communist Economic Systems").

The second section of part II—"The Sociology of Economic Institutions and Economic Behavior"—reaches to the heart of economic activity itself. The section begins with three chapters on markets, the core economic institutions. Richard Swedberg (chapter 11, "Markets in Society") treats the subject from a sociological and historical point of view. Wolfgang Streeck (chapter 12, "The Sociology of Labor Markets and Trade Unions") concentrates on the market for labor services, and Linda Brewster Stearns and Mark Mizruchi (chapter 13, "Banking and Financial Markets") deal with a range of markets that have only recently commanded significant sociological attention. The sociology of the production side of the economic process is the topic of Andrew Abbott's contribution (chapter 14, "Sociology of Work and Occupations"). Viviana Zelizer explores the diversity of ways in which cultural factors infuse consumption (chapter 15, "Culture and Consumption"), and Bruce Carruthers synthesizes

past and present literature on the social aspects of money and credit (chapter 16, "The Sociology of Money and Credit"). Two additional chapters deal with the less formal aspects of economic life. The important work on networks in the economy is covered in chapter 17 ("Networks and Economic Life," by Laurel Smith-Doerr and Walter Powell); and the complex and seemingly contradictory nature of the informal economy is analyzed in chapter 18 ("The Informal Economy," by Alejandro Portes and William Haller).

The third secion of part II—"The Sociology of Firms, Organizations, and Industry"—draws mainly from organization theory and general economic sociology. Mark Granovetter updates and reassesses the character of business groups in a comparative context (chapter 19, "Business Groups and Social Organization"). Howard Aldrich examines the nature of entrepreneurial activity and entrepreneurs in chapter 20 ("Entrepreneurship"), and Gerald Davis examines a number of environments of business firms—especially other business firms—in chapter 21 ("Firms and Environments").

Part III—"Intersections of the Economy"—deals with the mutual penetration of economic activity and many "noneconomic" sectors of society. Three chapters address the most important aspects of the economy and the polity. The first is on the state in general (chapter 22, "The State and the Economy," by Fred Block and Peter Evans). Lauren Edelman and Robin Stryker focus on law as a special aspect of state activity (chapter 23, "A Sociological Approach to Law and the Economy"), while Evelyne Huber and John Stephens assess recent developments in the welfare state and a number of assessments of those developments (chapter 24, "Welfare States and the Economy"). Two additional chapters deal with economic intersections with the institutions of education (chapter 25, "Education and the Economy," by Mary Brinton) and religion (chapter 26, "New Directions in the Study of Religion and Economic Life," by Robert Wuthnow). Chapters 27 ("Gender and Economic Sociology," by Paula England and Nancy Folbre) and 28 ("The Ethnic Economy," by Ivan Light) deal with the embeddedness of the socially constructed dimensions of gender and ethnicity in economic life. The volume is rounded out by a chapter on technology (chapter 29, "Technology and the Economy," by Giovanni Dosi, Luigi Orsenigo, and Mauro Sylos Labini), and one on economic-environmental relations (chapter 30, "The Economy and the Environment," by Allan Schnaiberg). Both these final topics have significant international aspects.

We conclude with the hope that the stocktaking of economic sociology contained in this *Handbook*, as well as its attempts to drive the field forward by selecting a few new important areas, will be successful. Economic sociology, we are convinced, currently represents one of the leading edges of sociology, as well as one of its most important interdisciplinary adventures.

Acknowledgments

THE RUSSELL SAGE FOUNDATION once again figures at the head of the list of those to whom we are grateful for facilitating the appearance of this *Handbook*. As he did a decade ago, Eric Wanner, its president, secured the support of his board of trustees to finance all the activities necessary for creating the volume, including the all-important conference among authors at the foundation in September 2002, where first drafts were circulated and benefited from the comments and criticisms from all the other contributors. Eric was supportive of our efforts throughout; we would like to record our more general appreciation for his encouragement of economic sociology during the past two decades.

Bindu Chadaga at Russell Sage was the staff person designated to shepherd the project from beginning to end. Her work in processing correspondence and manuscripts and in organizing the authors' conference was a model of efficiency. There was not one flaw or snag under her management. At the early stages of organizing the project, Julie Schumacher, Smelser's assistant at the Center for Advanced Study in the Behavioral Sciences (Stanford) deftly orchestrated our work and handled the complex process of inviting and signing authors.

Without editors authors are lost, and we happily acknowledge a multitude of debts to Suzanne Nichols of Russell Sage and Peter Dougherty of Princeton University Press.

It is not customary for editors to thank their authors in notes of acknowledgment, but we were given such excellent intellectual effort, responsiveness, and cooperation that we must make public our debt to them. We would like to single out Mark Granovetter in particular, who was a valued advisor throughout, and put us on to lines of research that we ourselves might have missed or neglected. In particular, he suggested both the topic and the authors for the chapter on the economic sociology of the ancient world, which we believe is one of the most interesting and ingenious applications of economic sociology in the volume.

Part I

General Concerns

1   Introducing Economic Sociology

Neil J. Smelser and Richard Swedberg

As A DESIGNATED FIELD of inquiry, economic sociology is not much more than a century old, even though its intellectual roots are identifiable in older traditions of philosophical and social thought.[1] During the past quarter-century it has experienced an explosive growth, and now stands as one of the most conspicuous and vital subfields of its parent discipline. In this introduction we first define the field and distinguish it from mainstream economics. Next we trace the classical tradition of economic sociology, as found in the works of Marx, Weber, Durkheim, Schumpeter, Polanyi, and Parsons-Smelser. Finally, we cite some more recent developments and topics of concern in economic sociology. Throughout our discussion in this chapter we emphasize the importance of paying attention to economic interests *and* social relations.

THE DEFINITION OF ECONOMIC SOCIOLOGY

Economic sociology—to use a term that Weber and Durkheim introduced[2]—can be defined simply as *the sociological perspective applied to economic phenomena*. A similar but more elaborate version is *the application of the frames of reference, variables, and explanatory models of sociology to that complex of activities which is concerned with the production, distribution, exchange, and consumption of scarce goods and services*.[3] One way to make this definition more specific is to indicate the variables, models, and so on, that the economic sociologist employs. When Smelser first put forth that definition (1963, 27–28; 1976, 37–38), he mentioned the sociological perspectives of personal interaction, groups, social structures (institutions), and social controls (among which sanctions, norms, and values are central). Given recent developments, we would add that perspectives of social networks, gender, and cultural contexts have also become central in economic sociology (e.g., Granovetter 1974, 1985a, 1995; Zelizer 1988). In addition, the international dimension of economic life has assumed greater salience among economic sociolo-

gists, at the same time as that dimension has come to penetrate the actual economies of the contemporary world (Makler, Martinelli, and Smelser 1982; Evans 1995).

MAINSTREAM ECONOMICS AND ECONOMIC SOCIOLOGY COMPARED

We now compare economic sociology and mainstream economics as a way of further elucidating the sociological perspective on the economy. This is a useful exercise only if qualified by the caution that both bodies of inquiry are much more complex than any brief comparison would suggest. Any general statement almost immediately yields an exception or qualification. To illustrate the caution on each side of the comparison:

1. In economics the classical and neoclassical traditions have enjoyed a certain dominance—hence the label *mainstream*—but the basic assumptions of those traditions have been modified and developed in many directions. In a classic statement, Knight ([1921] 1985, 76–79) stressed that neoclassical economics rested on the premises that actors have complete information and that information is free. Since that time economics has developed traditions of analysis based on assumptions of risk and uncertainty (for example, Sandmo 1971; Weber 2001) and information as a cost (for example, Stigler 1961; Lippmann and McCall 2001). In addition, numerous versions of economic rationality—for example, Simon's (1982) emphasis on "satisficing" and "bounded rationality"—have appeared. Still other variations on rational behavior have been developed in behavioral economics, which incorporates many psychological assumptions at variance with the mainstream (Mullainthan and Thaler 2001; Camerer, Loewenstein, and Rabin 2004). Looking in the direction of sociology, some economics now incorporates "norms" and "institutions," though with meanings different from those found in the sociological tradition.

2. Sociology lacks one dominant tradition. Various sociological approaches and schools differ from and compete with one another, and this circumstance has affected economic sociology. For example, Weber was skeptical about the notion of a social "system," whether applied to economy or society, while Parsons viewed society as a system and economy as one of its subsystems. Furthermore, even if all economic sociologists might accept the definition of economic sociology we have offered, they focus on different kinds of economic behavior. Some do so following Arrow's hint (1990, 140) that sociologists and economists ask different questions—about consumption, for example. Others, including what is called new economic sociology (see Granovetter 1990 for a programmatic statement), argue that sociology should concentrate directly on core economic institutions and problems.

These caveats recorded, a comparison between the central features of mainstream economics and economic sociology will clarify the specific nature of the sociological perspective. The following differences are most salient.

The Concept of the Actor

To put the matter baldly, the analytic starting point of economics is the individual; the analytic starting points of economic sociology are typically groups, institutions, and society. In microeconomics, the individualistic approach finds its origins in early British utilitarianism and political economy. This orientation was elucidated systematically by the Austrian economist Carl Menger and given the label *methodological individualism* by Schumpeter (1908, 90; for a history of methodological individualism, see Udehn 2001). By contrast, in discussing the individual, the sociologist often focuses on the actor as a socially constructed entity, as "actor-in-interaction," or "actor-in-society." Often, moreover, sociologists take the group and the social-structural levels as phenomena sui generis, without reference to the individual actor.

Methodological individualism need not be logically incompatible with a sociological approach. In his theoretical chapter introductory to *Economy and Society,* Weber constructed his whole sociology on the basis of individual actions. But these actions are of interest to the sociologist only insofar as they are *social* actions or "take account of the behavior of other individuals and thereby are oriented in their course" (Weber [1922] 1978, 4). This formulation underscores a second difference between microeconomics and economic sociology:

the former generally assumes that actors are not connected to one another; the latter assumes that actors are linked with and influence one another. We argue below that this difference has implications for how economies function.

The Concept of Economic Action

In micoeconomics the actor is assumed to have a given and stable set of preferences and to choose that alternative line of action which maximizes utility. In economic theory, this way of acting constitutes economically rational action. Sociology, by contrast, encompasses several possible types of economic action. To illustrate from Weber again, economic action can be either rational, traditional, or affectual (Weber [1922] 1978, 24–26, 63–68). Except for residual mention of "habits" and "rules of thumb," economists give no place to traditional economic action (which, arguably, constitutes its most common form; see, however, Akerlof 1984; Schlicht 1998).

Another difference between microeconomics and economic sociology in this context concerns the scope of rational action. The economist traditionally identifies rational action with the efficient use of scarce resources. The sociologist's view is, once again, broader. Weber referred to the conventional maximization of utility, under conditions of scarcity, as *formal rationality*. In addition, however, he identified *substantive rationality*, which refers to allocation within the guidelines of other principles, such as communal loyalties or sacred values. A further difference lies in the fact that economists regard rationality as an *assumption,* whereas most sociologists regard it as a *variable* (see Stinchcombe 1986, 5–6). For one thing, the actions of some individuals or groups may be more rational than others (cf. Akerlof 1990). Along the same lines, sociologists tend to regard rationality as a phenomenon to be explained, not assumed. Weber dedicated much of his economic sociology to specifying the social conditions under which formal rationality is possible, and Parsons ([1940] 1954) argued that economic rationality was a system of norms—not a psychological universal—associated with specific developmental processes in the West.

Another difference emerges in the status of *meaning* in economic action. Economists tend to regard the meaning of economic action as derivable from the relation between given tastes, on the one hand, and the prices and quantities of goods and services, on the other. Weber's conceptualization has a different flavor: "the definition of economic action [in sociology] must . . . bring out the fact that all 'economic' processes and objects are characterized as such entirely by the *meaning* they have for human action" ([1922] 1978, 64). Meanings are historically constructed and must be investigated empirically, and are not simply to be derived from assumptions and external circumstances.

Finally, sociologists tend to give a broader and more salient place to the dimension of *power* in economic action. Weber ([1922] 1978, 67) insisted that "[it] is essential to include the criterion of power of control and disposal (*Verfügungsgewalt*) in the sociological concept of economic action," adding that this applies especially in the capitalist economy. By contrast, microeconomics has tended to regard economic action as an exchange among equals, and has thus had difficulty in incorporating the power dimension (Galbraith 1973, 1984). In the tradition of perfect competition, no buyer or seller has the power to influence price or output. It is also true that economists have a tradition of analyzing imperfect competition—in which power to control prices and output is the core ingredient—and that the idea of "market power" is used in labor and industrial economics (e.g., Scherer 1990). Still, the economic conception of power is typically narrower than the sociologist's notion of economic power, which includes its exercise in societal (especially political and class), as well as market, contexts. In a study of the power of the U.S. banking system, for example, Mintz and Schwartz (1985) analyze how banks and industries interlock, how certain banks cluster into groups, and how banks sometimes intervene in corporations in order to enforce economic decisions. More generally, sociologists have analyzed and debated the issue of the political implications of wealth inequality and the extent to which corporate leaders constitute a "power elite" in the whole of society (e.g., Mills 1956; Dahl 1958; Domhoff and Dye 1987; Keister 2000).

Constraints on Economic Action

In mainstream economics, actions are constrained by tastes and by the scarcity of resources, including technology. Once these are known, it is in principle possible to predict the actor's behavior, since he or she will always try to maximize utility or profit. The active influence of other persons and groups, as well as the influence of institutional structures, is set to one side. Knight codified this in the following way: "Every member of society is to act as an individual only, in entire independence of all other persons" ([1921] 1985, 78). Sociolo-

gists take such influences directly into account in the analysis of economic action. Other actors facilitate, deflect, and constrain individuals' action in the market. For example, a friendship between a buyer and a seller may prevent the buyer from deserting the seller just because an item is sold at a lower price elsewhere (e.g., Dore 1983). Cultural meanings also affect choices that might otherwise be regarded as "rational." In the United States, for example, it is difficult to persuade people to buy cats and dogs for food, even though their meat is as nutritious and cheaper than other kinds (Sahlins 1976, 170–79). Moreover, a person's position in the social structure conditions his or her economic choices and activity. Stinchcombe (1975) evoked the principle that structural constraints influence career decisions in ways that run counter to considerations of economic payoff. For example, for a person who grows up in a high-crime neighborhood, the choice between making a career stealing and getting a job has often less to do with the comparative utility of these two alternatives than with the structure of peer groups and gangs in the neighborhood.

The Economy in Relation to Society

The main foci for the mainstream economist are economic exchange, the market, and the economy. To a large extent, the remainder of society lies beyond where the operative variables of economic change really matter (see Quirk 1976, 2–4; Arrow 1990, 138–39). Economic assumptions typically presuppose stable societal parameters. For example, the long-standing assumption that economic analysis deals with peaceful and lawful transactions, not with force and fraud, involves important presuppositions about the legitimacy and the stability of the state and the legal system. In this way the societal parameters—which would surely affect the economic process if the political legal system were to disintegrate—are frozen by assumption, and thus are omitted from the analysis. In recent times economists have turned to the analysis of why institutions arise and persist, especially in the new institutional economics and game theory. They have varied the effects of institutional arrangements in various logical experiments (see, e.g., Eggertsson 1990; Furubotn and Richter 1997). Nevertheless, the contrast with economic sociology remains. When economists talk about institutions, norms, and the like, their vocabulary is identical to that of sociologists, but they often mean something quite different. It is still very common, for example, for economists to treat the economic arena as lacking norms and institutions. The latter only emerge when markets cannot be constructed or when traditional rational choice analysis fails. Economic sociology, on the other hand, has always regarded the economic process as an organic part of society. As a consequence, economic sociology has usually concentrated on three main lines of inquiry: (1) the sociological analysis of economic process; (2) the analysis of the connections and interactions between the economy and the rest of society; and (3) the study of changes in the institutional and cultural parameters that constitute the economy's societal context.

Goals of Analysis

As social scientists, both economists and sociologists try to explain phenomena encompassed by their respective subject matters. Within this common interest, however, different emphases emerge. Economists tend to be critical of descriptions—they condemn traditional institutional economics as too descriptive and atheoretical. Instead they stress the importance of prediction. Sociologists, by contrast, offer fewer formal predictions, and often find sensitive and telling descriptions both interesting in themselves and essential for explanation. As a result of these differences, sociologists often criticize economists for generating formal and abstract models and ignoring empirical data, and economists reproach sociologists for their "*post factum* sociological interpretations" (Merton 1968, 147–49). Though these differences have become part of the professional cultures of economists and sociologists, it should be noted that the last 10 years have seen a new interest for model building and game theory among sociologists, and a new interest in culture and use of empirical material among economists (e.g., Greif 1998, forthcoming; Swedberg 2001). It is also possible that the fields of economics and economic sociology may one day agree on some methodological compromise, say along the lines of "analytic narratives" (Bates et al. 1998).

Models Employed

The emphasis on prediction constitutes one reason why mainstream economists place such high value on expressing hypotheses and models in mathematical form. Though the advantages of this formal theorizing are readily apparent, economists themselves have at times complained that it tends to become an end in itself. In his presidential address to the American Economic Association in 1970, Wassily Leontief criticized his profession's "uncritical enthusiasm for mathematical formulation" (1971, 1). When economists do turn to empirical data, they tend to rely mainly on those generated for them by economic processes themselves (for example, aggregated market behavior, stock exchange transactions, and official economic statistics gathered by governmental agencies). Sample surveys are occasionally used, especially in consumer economics and in labor economics; archival data are seldom consulted, except by economic historians; and ethnographic work is virtually nonexistent. By contrast, sociologists rely heavily on a great variety of methods, including analyses of census data, independent survey analyses, participant observation and fieldwork, and the analysis of qualitative historical and comparative data.

Intellectual Traditions

Sociologists not only rely on different intellectual traditions that overlap only slightly, but they also regard those traditions differently. Evidently influenced by the natural science model of systematic accumulation of knowledge, economists have shown less interest than sociologists in study and exegesis of their classics (with notable exceptions such as Adam Smith and David Ricardo). Correspondingly, economics reveals a sharp distinction between current economic theory and the history of economic thought. In sociology these two facets blend more closely. The classics are very much alive, and are often required reading in theory courses.

Despite these differences, and despite the persisting gulf between the traditions of economics and economic sociology, some evidence of synthesis can be identified. Major figures such as Alfred Marshall, Vilfredo Pareto, and Talcott Parsons have attempted theoretical syntheses. Certain other figures, notably Weber and Schumpeter, have excited interest among both economists and sociologists. In addition, economists and sociologists find it profitable to collaborate in specific problem areas such as poverty and labor markets. Later in the chapter we will reraise the issue of intellectual articulation among economists and sociologists.

THE TRADITION OF ECONOMIC SOCIOLOGY

There exists a large and rich tradition of economic sociology, which roughly begins around the turn of the twentieth century. This tradition has generated both important concepts and ideas and significant research results, which we now present and set in perspective. Economic sociology has peaked twice since its birth: in 1890–1920 with the classic theorists (who were all interested in and wrote on the economy), and today, from the early 1980s onwards. A small number of important works in economic sociology—by economists as well as sociologists—were also produced during the period in between. A major thread in the tradition of economic sociology is that investigation must *combine the analysis of economic interests with an analysis of social relations*.

Classical Economic Sociology and Its Predecessors

The first use of the term *economic sociology* seems to have been in 1879, when it appears in a work by British economist W. Stanley Jevons ([1879] 1965). The term was taken over by the sociologists and appears, for example, in the works of Durkheim and Weber during the years 1890–1920 (*sociologie économique*, *Wirtschaftssoziologie*). It is also during these decades that classical economic sociology is born, as exemplified by such works as *The Division of Labor in Society* (1893) by Durkheim, *The Philosophy of Money* (1900) by Simmel, and *Economy and Society* (produced 1908–20) by Weber. These classics of economic sociology are remarkable for the following characteristics. First, Weber and others shared the sense that they were pioneers, building up a type of analysis that had not existed before. Second, they focused on the most fundamental questions of the field: What is the role of the economy in society? How does the sociological analysis of the economy differ from that of the economists? What is an economic action? To this should be added that the classical figures were preoccupied with understanding capitalism and its impact on society—"the great transformation" that it had brought about.

In hindsight it is clear that several works published before the 1890–1920 period in one way or another prefigure some of the insights of economic sociology. Important reflections on, for example, the role of trade can be found in *The Spirit of the Laws* by Montesquieu, as well as a pioneer comparative analysis of the role of various economic phenomena in republics, monarchies, and despotic states (Montesquieu [1748] 1989). The role of labor in society is emphasized in the work of Saint-Simon (1760–1825), who also helped to popularize the term *industrialism* (cf. Saint-Simon 1964). That the work of Alexis de Tocqueville (1805–1859) is full of sharp, sociological observations is

something that most sociologists would agree on. That he also made contributions to economic sociology is, however, less known (Tocqueville [1835–40] 1945, [1856] 1955; cf. Swedberg 2003, 6–8). Of these various precursors we will concentrate only on Karl Marx, a towering figure in nineteenth-century thought, even though he was active before the birth of modern sociology.

Karl Marx

Karl Marx (1818–1883) was obsessed with the role of the economy in society and developed a theory according to which the economy determined society's general evolution. What drives people in their everyday lives, Marx also argued, are material interests, and these also determine the structures and processes in society. While Marx wanted to develop a strictly scientific approach to society, his ideas were equally infused by his political desire to change the world (e.g., [1843] 1978, 145). The end result was what we know as "Marxism"—a mixture of social science and political statements, welded into a single doctrine.

For a variety of reasons much of Marxism is erroneous or not relevant to economic sociology. It is far too tendentious and dogmatic to be adopted as a whole. The task that confronts economic sociology today is to extract those aspects of Marxism that are useful. In doing so, it is useful to follow the suggestion of Schumpeter, and distinguish between Marx as a sociologist, Marx as an economist, and Marx as a revolutionary (Schumpeter [1942] 1994, 1–58). We now turn to a preliminary effort to pull out the relevant ingredients for economic sociology.

Marx's point of departure is labor and production. People have to work in order to live, and this fact is universal (Marx [1867] 1906, 50). Material interests are correspondingly universal. Labor is social rather than individual in nature, since people have to cooperate in order to produce. Marx severely criticized economists for their use of the isolated individual; and he himself sometimes spoke of "social individuals" (e.g., [1857–58] 1973, 84–85). The most important interests are also of a collective nature—what Marx calls "class interests." These interests will, however, only be effective if people become aware that they belong to a certain class ("class for itself," as opposed to "class in itself"; Marx [1852] 1950, 109).

Marx severely criticized Adam Smith's idea that individual interests merge and further the general interest of society ("the invisible hand"). Rather, according to Marx, classes typically oppress and fight each other with such ferocity that history is as if written with "letters of blood and fire" ([1867] 1906, 786). Bourgeois society is no exception on this score since it encourages "the most violent, mean and malignant passions of the human heart, the Furies of private interest" ([1867] 1906, 15). In various works Marx traced the history of the class struggle, from early times into the future. In a famous formulation from the 1850s, Marx states that at a certain stage the "relations of production" enter into conflict with "the forces of production," with revolution and passage to a new "mode of production" as a result ([1859] 1970, 21). In *Capital* Marx writes that he has laid bare "the economic law of motion of modern society" and that this law works "with iron necessity towards inevitable results" of revolutionary change ([1867] 1906, 13–14).

A positive feature of Marx's approach is his insight into the extent to which people have been willing to fight for their material interests throughout history. He also contributed to understanding how large groups of people, with similar economic interests, under certain circumstances can unite and realize their interests. On the negative side, Marx grossly underestimated the role in economic life of interests other than the economic ones. His notion that economic interests in the last hand always determine the rest of society is also impossible to defend; "social structures, types and attitudes are coins that do not readily melt," to cite a famous quote from Schumpeter ([1942] 1994, 12).

Max Weber

Among the classics in economic sociology Max Weber (1864–1920) occupies a unique place. He proceeded furthest toward developing a distinct economic sociology, laying its theoretical foundation and carrying out empirical studies (Swedberg 1998). The fact that he had worked as a professor of economics was no doubt helpful in these efforts to build bridges between economics and sociology. Also helpful was the major research task that occupied Weber throughout his career, which was economic as well as social in nature: to understand the origin of modern capitalism. Weber drew heavily on the theoretical work on interests of his time and extended that line of work by making it more sociological.

Weber's academic training was broad in nature, and its main emphasis was on law, with the history of law as his specialty. His two dissertations—one on medieval trading corporations (lex mercatoria) and the other on the sale of land in early Rome—

were relevant topics for understanding the rise of capitalism: the emergence of private property in land and of property in the firm (as opposed to individual property). Those works, in combination with a commissioned study of rural workers, earned him a position in economics ("political economy and finance") in the early 1890s. In this capacity he taught economics but published mainly in economic history and in policy questions. Weber wrote, for example, voluminously on the new stock exchange legislation.

Toward the end of the 1890s Weber fell ill, and for the next 20 years he worked as a private scholar. In these years he produced his most celebrated study, *The Protestant Ethic and the Spirit of Capitalism* (1904–5), as well as studies of the economic ethics of the world religions. In 1908 Weber accepted a position as chief editor of a giant handbook of economics. From the very beginning Weber set aside the topic of "economy and society" for himself. The work that today is known as *Economy and Society* consists of a mixture of material that Weber had approved for publication and of manuscripts found after his death (see, e.g., Mommsen 2000). In 1919–20 Weber also taught a course in economic history, which, pieced together a few years later on the basis of students' notes, was published posthumously as *General Economic History*. Though primarily a work in economic history, it contains much interesting material for the economic sociologist.

Much of what Weber wrote in economic sociology can be found in *Collected Essays in the Sociology of Religion* (1920–21) and *Economy and Society* (1922). The former contains a revised version *The Protestant Ethic*, "The Protestant Sects and the Spirit of Capitalism" (1904–5; revised 1920) and voluminous writings on the economic ethics of the Chinese, Indian, and Judaic world religions and a few other texts (for the latter see Weber [1920] 1958, [1915] 1946a, [1915] 1946b). According to Weber, the material in *Collected Essays* concerns mainly the sociology of religion but is also of interest to economic sociology.

The most influential study is *The Protestant Ethic*. This work is centered around Weber's general preoccupation with the articulation of ideal and material interests and ideas. The believer in ascetic Protestantism is driven by a desire to be saved (a religious interest) and acts accordingly. For various paradoxical reasons the individual eventually comes to believe that secular work, carried out in a methodical manner, represents a means to salvation—and when this happens, religious interest is combined with economic interest. The result of this combination is a release of a tremendous force, which shattered the traditional and antieconomic hold of religion over people and introduced a mentality favorable to capitalist activity. The thesis in *The Protestant Ethic* has led to an enormous debate, with many scholars—probably a majority—arguing against Weber (for an introduction to this debate, see especially Marshall 1982).

While he was writing *The Protestant Ethic* Weber published an essay, " 'Objectivity' in Social Science and Social Policy," that summarized his theoretical views on economic sociology. In this work he argued that the science of economics should be broad and umbrella-like (*Sozialökonomik;* Weber [1904] 1949, 64–65). It should include not only economic theory but also economic history and economic sociology. Weber also proposes that economic analysis should cover not only "economic phenomena" but also "economically relevant phenomena" and "economically conditioned phenomena" (64–65). Economic phenomena consist of economic norms and institutions, often deliberately created for economic ends—for example, banks and stock exchanges. Economically relevant phenomena are noneconomic phenomena that under certain circumstances may have an impact on economic phenomena, as in the case of ascetic Protestantism. Economically conditioned phenomena are those that to some extent are influenced by economic phenomena. The type of religion that a group feels affinity for is, for example, partly dependent on the kind of work that its members do. While economic theory can only handle pure economic phenomena (in their rational version), economic history and economic sociology can deal with all three categories of phenomena.

A somewhat different approach, both to economic sociology and to interests, can be found in *Economy and Society.* The first chapter of this work contains a general sociological analysis. Two concepts are important building blocks: "social action" and "order" (*Ordnung*). In the former, "action," defined as behavior invested with meaning, is qualified as "social" if it is oriented to some other actor. An "order" is roughly equivalent to an institution, and it comes into being when social actions are repeated over a period, regarded as objective, and surrounded by various sanctions. Economists study pure economic action, which is action exclusively driven by economic interests (or "desire for utilities," in Weber's formulation; [1922] 1978, 63). Economic sociologists, however, study *social* economic action, which is driven

not only by economic interest but also by tradition and emotions; furthermore, it is always oriented to some actor(s).

If one disregards single actions, Weber says, and instead focuses on empirical uniformities, it is possible to distinguish three different types: those inspired by "convention," by "custom" (including "habit"), and by "interest" ([1922] 1978, 29–36). Most uniform types of action presumably consist of a mixture of all three. Actions that are "determined by interest" are defined by Weber as instrumental in nature and oriented to identical expectations. An example would be the modern market, where each actor is instrumentally rational and counts on everybody else to be so as well.

Weber emphasized that interests are always subjectively perceived; no "objective" interests exist beyond the individual actor. In a typical sentence Weber speaks of "[the] interests of the actors as they themselves are aware of them" ([1922] 1978, 30). He also notes that when several individuals behave in an instrumental manner in relation to their individual interests, the typical result is collective patterns of behavior that are considerably more stable than those driven by norms imposed by an authority. It is, for example, very difficult to make people do something economic that goes against the individual's interest.

A sketch of Weber's economic sociology in *Economy and Society* yields the following main points. Economic actions of two actors who are oriented to one another constitute an economic relationship. These relationships can take various expressions, including conflict, competition, and power. If two or more actors are held together by a sense of belonging, their relationship is "communal"; and if they are held together by interest, "associative" (Weber [1922] 1978, 38–43). Economic relationships (as all social relationships) can also be open or closed. Property represents a special form of closed economic relationship.

Economic organizations constitute another important form of closed economic relationships. Some of these organizations are purely economic, while others have some subordinate economic goals or have as their main task the regulation of economic affairs. A trade union is an example. Weber attaches great importance to the role in capitalism of the firm, which he sees as the locus of entrepreneurial activity and as a revolutionary force.

A market, like many other economic phenomena, is centered around a conflict of interests—in this case between sellers and buyers (Weber [1922] 1978, 635–40). A market involves both exchange and competition. Competitors must first fight out who will be the final seller and the final buyer ("competition struggle"); and only when this struggle has been settled is the scene set for the exchange itself ("exchange struggle"). Only rational capitalism is centered around the modern type of market (Weber [1922] 1978, 164–66). In so-called political capitalism the key to profit making is rather the state or the political power that grants some favor, supplies protection, or the like. Traditional commercial capitalism consists of small-scale trading, in money or merchandise. Rational capitalism has emerged only in the West.

Émile Durkheim

As compared to Weber, Émile Durkheim (1858–1917) knew less economics, wrote less about economic topics, and in general made less of a contribution to economic sociology (e.g., Steiner 2004). While none of his major studies can be termed a work in economic sociology, all of them nonetheless touch on economic topics (see also Durkheim [1950] 1983). Durkheim also strongly supported the project of developing a *sociologie économique* by encouraging some of his students to specialize in this area and by routinely including a section on economic sociology in his journal *L'année sociologique*. At one point he gave the following definition of economic sociology:

> Finally there are the economic institutions: institutions relating to the production of wealth (serfdom, tenant farming, corporate organization, production in factories, in mills, at home, and so on), institutions relating to exchange (commercial organization, markets, stock exchanges, and so on), institutions relating to distribution (rent, interest, salaries, and so on). They form the subject matter of *economic sociology*. (Durkheim [1909] 1978b, 80)

Durkheim's first major work, *The Division of Labor in Society* (1893), has most direct relevance for economic sociology. Its core consists of the argument that social structure changes as society develops from its undifferentiated state, in primordial times, to a stage characterized by a complex division of labor, in modern times. Economists, Durkheim notes, view the division of labor exclusively as an economic phenomenon, and its gains in terms of efficiency. What he added was a sociological dimension of the division of labor—how it helps to integrate society by coordinating specialized activities.

As part of society's evolution to a more advanced division of labor, the legal system changes. From being predominantly repressive in nature, and having its center in penal law, it now becomes restitutive and has its center in contractual law. In discussing the contract, Durkheim also described as an illusion the belief, held by Herbert Spencer, that a society can function if all individuals simply follow their private interests and contract accordingly (Durkheim [1893] 1984, 152). Spencer also misunderstood the very nature of the contractual relationship. A contract does not work in situations where self-interest rules supreme, but only where there is a moral or regulative element. "The contract is not sufficient by itself, but is only possible because of the regulation of contracts, which is social in origin" (Durkheim [1893] 1984, 162).

A major concern in *The Division of Labor in Society* is that the recent economic advances in France may destroy society by letting loose individual greed to erode its moral fiber. This problematic is often cast in terms of the private versus the general interest, as when Durkheim notes that "subordination of the particular to the general interest is the very well-spring of all moral activity" ([1893] 1984, xliii). Unless the state or some other agency that articulates the general interest steps in to regulate economic life, the result will be "economic anomie," a topic that Durkheim discusses in *Suicide* ([1897] 1951, 246ff., 259). People need rules and norms in their economic life, and they react negatively to anarchic situations.

In many of Durkheim's works, one finds a sharp critique of economists; and it was Durkheim's conviction in general that if economics was ever to become scientific, it would have to become a branch of sociology. He attacked the idea of *homo economicus* on the ground that it is impossible to separate out the economic element and disregard the rest of social life ([1888] 1978a, 49–50). The point is not that economists used an analytical or abstract approach, Durkheim emphasized, but that they had selected the wrong abstractions (1887, 39). Durkheim also attacked the nonempirical tendency of economics and the idea that one can figure out how the economy works through "a simple logical analysis" ([1895] 1964, 24). Durkheim referred to this as "the ideological tendency of economics" ([1895] 1964, 25).

Durkheim's recipe for a harmonious industrial society is as follows: each industry should be organized into a number of corporations, in which the individuals will thrive because of the solidarity and warmth that comes from being a member of a group ([1893] 1984, lii). He was well aware of the rule that interest plays in economic life, and in *The*

Elementary Forms of Religious Life he stresses that "the principal incentive to economic activity has always been the private interest" ([1912] 1965, 390). This does not mean that economic life is purely self-interested and devoid of morality: "We remain [in our economic affairs] in relation with others; the habits, ideas and tendencies which education has impressed upon us and which ordinarily preside over our relations can never be totally absent" (390). But even if this is the case, the social element has another source other than the economy and will eventually be worn down if not renewed.

Georg Simmel

Simmel's works typically lack references to economics as such. Simmel (1858–1918), like Durkheim, usually viewed economic phenomena within some larger, noneconomic setting. Nonetheless, his work still has relevance for economic sociology.

Much of Simmel's most important study, *Soziologie* (1908), focuses on the analysis of interests. He suggested what a sociological interest analysis should look like and why it is indispensable to sociology. Two of his general propositions are that interests drive people to form social relations, and that it is only through these social relations that interests can be expressed:

> Sociation is the form (realized in innumerable different ways) in which individuals grow together into a unity and within which their interests are realized. And it is on the basis of their interests—sensuous or ideal, momentary or lasting, conscious or unconscious, causal or teleological—that individuals form such units. (Simmel [1908] 1971, 24)

Another key proposition is that economic interests, like other interests, can take a number of different social expressions (26).

Soziologie also contains a number of suggestive analyses of economic phenomena, among them competition. In a chapter on the role of the number of actors in social life, Simmel suggests that competition can take the form of *tertius gaudens* ("the third who benefits"). In this situation, which involves three actors, actor A turns to advantage the fact that actors B and C are competing for A's favor—to buy something, to sell something, or the like. Competition is consequently not seen as something that only concerns the competitors (actors B and C); it is in addition related to actor A, the target of the competition. Simmel also distinguishes competition from conflict. While a conflict typically means a confrontation between two actors, competition rather implies parallel efforts, a circumstance in which society can benefit from the actions of both the actors. Instead of destroying your opponent, as in a conflict, in competition you try to do what your competitor does—but better.

Philosophy of Money (1900), Simmel's second major sociological work, has always enjoyed a mixed reputation. Durkheim disapproved of it for its mix of genres, and according to Weber economists detested Simmel's way of dealing with economic topics (e.g., Frisby 1978; Durkheim ([1902] 1980; Weber 1972). Simmel does mix philosophical reflections with sociological observations in an idiosyncratic manner, but *Philosophy of Money* has nonetheless much to give if it is read in its own frame. Simmel's main point is that money and modernity belong together; in today's society there does not exist one exclusive set of dominant values but rather a sense that everything is relative (cf. Poggi 1993). Simmel's work also contains a myriad of insightful sociological reflections on the connections of money with authority, emotions, trust, and other phenomena. The value of money, Simmel observed, typically extends only as far as the authority that guarantees it ("the economic circle"; [1907] 1978, 179ff.). Money is also surrounded by various "economically important sentiments," such as "hope and fear, desire and anxiety" ([1907] 1978, 171). And without trust, Simmel argues, society could simply not exist; and "in the same way, money transactions would collapse without trust" (179). In relation to money, trust consists of two elements. First, because something has happened before—for example, that people accept a certain type of money—it is likely to be repeated. Another part of trust, which has no basis in experience and which can be seen as a nonrational belief, Simmel calls "quasi-religious faith," noting that it is present not only in money but also in credit.

After the Classics

Despite its foundation in the classics, economic sociology declined after 1920 and would not return to full vigor before the 1980s. Exactly why this happened is still not clear. One reason is probably that neither Weber nor Simmel had any disciples. Durkheim did, however, and the study of Marcel Mauss, *The Gift* (1925), should be singled out. It rests on the argument that a gift typically implies an obligation to reciprocate and should not be mistaken for a one-way act of generosity. *The Gift* also contains a number of interesting observations on credit, the concept of interest, and the emergence of *homo economicus*. Evenually, however, Durkheimian economic sociology declined.

Despite the slowing in economic sociology during the years 1920–80, there were several noteworthy developments, especially the theoretical works of Joseph Schumpeter, Karl Polanyi, and Talcott Parsons (for contributions by other sociologists during this period, see Swedberg 1987, 42–62). All three produced their most important works while in the United States, but had roots in European social thought.

Joseph Schumpeter

We preface our notes on Schumpeter (1883–1950), an economist, by noting some contributions by economists more generally to economic sociology. One example is Alfred Marshall (1842–1924), whose analyses of such topics as industries, markets, and preference formation often are profoundly sociological in nature (Marshall [1920] 1961, 1919; cf. Aspers 1999). Vilfredo Pareto (1848–1923) is famous for his sociological analyses of rentiers versus speculators, business cycles, and much more (Pareto [1916] 1963; cf. Aspers 2001a). The work of Thorstein Veblen (1857–1929) sometimes appeared in sociological journals, and his analyses include such topics as consumer behavior ("conspicuous consumption"), why industrialization in England slowed down ("the penalty of taking the lead"), and the shortcomings of neoclassical economics (Veblen [1899] 1973, [1915] 1966, [1919] 1990; cf. Tillman 1992). Final mention should also be made of Werner Sombart (1863–1941), who wrote on the history of capitalism, on "the economic temper of our time," and on the need for a "*verstehende* economics" (1902–27, 1930, 1935).

The contributions of Schumpeter are especially noteworthy (see, e.g., Swedberg 1991b). His life spanned two periods in modern economics—the period around the turn of the century, when modern economics was born, and the period of a few decades later when it was mathematized and secured its place as "mainstream." Schumpeter similarly spanned two distinct periods in sociology—from Max Weber in the first decade of the 20th century through Talcott Parsons in the 1930s and 1940s. Schumpeter is also unique among economists for trying to create a place for economic sociology next to economic theory. In this last effort Schumpeter was clearly inspired by Weber and, like the latter, referred to this type of broad economics as *Sozialökonomik*, or "social economics." Schum-

peter defines economic sociology as the study of institutions, within which economic behavior takes place (e.g., 1954, 21).

Schumpeter produced three studies in sociology. The first is an article on social classes that is of interest because of his distinction between economists' and sociologists' use of the concept of class. While for the former, he argues, class is a formal category, for the latter it refers to a living reality. The second study is an article about the nature of imperialism that can be compared to the equivalent theories of Hobson, Lenin, and others. Schumpeter's basic idea is that imperialism is precapitalistic and deeply irrational and emotional in nature—essentially an expression for warrior nations of their need to constantly conquer new areas or fall back and lose their power. The third study is perhaps the most interesting one from the viewpoint of contemporary economic sociology, "The Crisis of the Tax State" (1918). Schumpeter characterizes this article as a study in "fiscal sociology" (*Finanzsoziologie*); its main thesis is that the finances of a state represent a privileged position from which to approach the behavior of the state. As a motto Schumpeter cites the famous line of Rudolf Goldscheid: "The budget is the skeleton of the state stripped of all misleading ideology (Schumpeter [1918] 1991, 100).

Schumpeter did not regard *Capitalism, Socialism, and Democracy* (1942) as a work in sociology, but its main thesis is nonetheless sociological in nature: the motor of capitalism is intact but its institutional structure is weak and damaged, making it likely that socialism will soon replace it. On this point Schumpeter was evidently wrong. His analysis of the forces that are undermining capitalism may seem idiosyncratic at times. Nonetheless, Schumpeter should be given credit for suggesting that the behavior of intellectuals, the structure of the modern family, and so on, do affect capitalism. Of special importance are his insights about economic change or, as Schumpeter phrased it with his usual stylistic flair, "creative destruction."

Entrepreneurship is at the heart of Schumpeter's treatment of economic change (1912, chap. 2; 1934, chap. 2; 2003). He himself saw his theory of entrepreneurship as falling in economic theory, more precisely as an attempt to create a new and more dynamic type of economic theory. Nonetheless, many of his ideas on entrepreneurship are sociological in nature. His central idea—that entrepreneurship consists of an attempt to put together a new combination of already existing elements—can be read sociologically, as can his idea that the main enemy of the entrepreneur is the people who resist innovations.

Karl Polanyi

Trained in law, Polanyi (1886–1964) later taught himself Austrian economics as well as economic history and economic anthropology. Though he was interdisciplinary in approach, his main specialty was economic history, with an emphasis on nineteenth-century England and preindustrial economies.

Polanyi's most famous work is *The Great Transformation* (1944), conceived and written during World War II (e.g., Block 2001, 2003). Its main thesis is that a revolutionary attempt was made in nineteenth-century England to introduce a totally new, market-centered type of society. No outside authority was needed; everything was automatically to be decided by the market ("the self-regulating market"). In the 1840s and 1850s a series of laws was introduced to turn this project into reality, turning land and labor into common commodities. Even the value of money was taken away from the political authorities and handed over to the market. According to Polanyi, this type of proceeding could only lead to a catastrophe. When the negative effects of the market reforms became obvious in the second half of the nineteenth century, Polanyi continues, countermeasures were set in to rectify them ("the double movement"). These measures, however, only further unbalanced society; and developments such as fascism in the twentieth century were the ultimate results of the ill-fated attempt in mid-nineteenth-century England to turn everything over to the market.

Polanyi also cast his analysis in terms of interests and argued that in all societies, before the nineteenth century, the general interests of groups and societies ("social interests") had been more important than the money interest of the individual ("economic interest"). "An all too narrow conception of interest," Polanyi emphasizes, "must in effect lead to a warped vision of social and political history, and no purely monetary definition of interest can leave room for that vital need for social protection" ([1944] 1957, 154).

The theoretical part of *The Great Transformation* is centered around Polanyi's concepts of "embeddedness" and "principles of behavior" (later changed to "forms of integration"). The fullest elaboration of this line of work is to be found in *Trade and Market in the Early Empires* (Polanyi, Arensberg, and Pearson [1957] 1971), and especially in Polanyi's essay "The Economy as Institut-ed Process" ([1957] 1971). Polanyi criticized economic theory for being essentially "formal"—a kind of logic focused on choice, the means-end relationship, and the alleged scarcity of things that people want. There is also "the economistic fallacy," or the tendency in economics to equate the economy with its market form ([1944] 1957, 270). To the formal concept of economics Polanyi counterposes a "substantive" concept, grounded in reality and not in logic. "The substantive meaning of economic derives from man's dependence for his living upon nature and his fellows" ([1957] 1971b, 243). While the notion of economic interest is directly linked to "the livelihood of man" in substantive economics, it is only an artificial construction in formal economics (Polanyi 1977).

The most famous concept associated with Polanyi's work is "embeddedness," which, however, he used in a way different from its contemporary use. According to the current use, an economic action is in principle always "embedded" in some form of social structure. According to Polanyi, economic actions become destructive when they are "disembedded," or not governed by social or noneconomic authorities. The real problem with capitalism is that instead of society deciding about the economy, it is the economy that decides about society: "instead of the economic system being embedded in social relationships, these relationships were now embedded in the economic system" ([1947] 1982, 70).

Another set of conceptual tools for economic sociology is Polanyi's "forms of integration." His general argument is that rational self-interest is too unstable to constitute the foundation for society; an economy must be able to provide people with material sustenance on a continuous basis. There are three forms of integration, or ways to stabilize the economy and provide it with unity. These are *reciprocity*, which takes place within symmetrical groups, such as families, kinship groups, and neighborhoods; *redistribution*, in which goods are allocated from a center in the community, such as the state; and *exchange*, in which goods are distributed via price-making markets (Polanyi [1957] 1971b). In each economy, Polanyi specifies, there is usually a mixture of these three forms. One of them can be dominant, while the others are subordinate.

Talcott Parsons

Talcott Parsons (1902–79) was educated as an economist in the institutionalist tradition and taught economics for several years before he switched to sociology in the 1930s. At this time he developed the notion that while economics deals with the means-end relationship of social action, sociology deals with its values ("the analytical factor view"). In the 1950s Parsons recast his ideas on the relationship of economics to sociology, in a work coauthored with Neil Smelser, *Economy and Society* (1956). This work constitutes Parsons's major contribution to economic sociology, but both before and after its publication Parsons produced a number of studies relevant to economic sociology (Camic 1987; Swedberg 1991a).

In *The Structure of Social Action* (1937) Parsons launched a forceful attack on utilitarian social thought, including the idea that interests represent an Archimedean point from which to analyze society. Interest theorists, Parsons notes, cannot handle the Hobbesian problem of order; they try to get out of this dilemma by assuming that everybody's interests harmonize (what Elie Halévy referred to as "the natural identity of interests"; Parsons [1937] 1968, 96–97). What is not understood by the utilitarians is that norms (embodying values) are necessary to integrate society and provide order. Interests are always part of society, but a social order cannot be built on them (405).

In *Economy and Society* (1956) Parsons and Smelser suggested that both sociology and economics can be understood as part of the general theory of social systems. The economy is a subsystem, which interchanges with the other three subsystems (the polity, the integrative subsystem, and the cultural-motivational subsystem). The concept of a subsystem is reminiscent of Weber's notion of sphere, but while the latter refers only to values, the economic subsystem also has an adaptive function as well as a distinct institutional structure. It may finally be mentioned that *Economy and Society* got a negative reception by economists and failed to ignite an interest in economic sociology among sociologists. Smelser's attempt to consolidate economic sociology in the next decade helped fix economic sociology as a subfield in the minds of scholars and in the curricula of colleges and universities, but did not spawn distinct new lines of research (see especially Smelser 1963, 1965, 1976).

THE CURRENT REVIVAL OF ECONOMIC SOCIOLOGY (1980s–)

Despite the efforts of Parsons and Smelser in the mid-1950s and the 1960s to revive economic sociology, it attracted little attention, and by the 1970s the field was somewhat stagnant. A number of

works inspired in one way or another by the Marxist tradition—and its general revival in the late 1960s and the early 1970s—made their appearance in this period. Among these were Marxist analyses themselves (e.g., Gorz 1977), dependency theory (Frank 1969; Cardoso and Faletto 1969), world systems theory (Wallerstein 1974), and neo-Marxist analyses of the workplace (Braverman 1974; Burawoy 1979).

In the early 1980s, a few studies suggested a new stirring of interest (e.g., White 1981; Stinchcombe 1983; Baker 1984; Coleman 1985). And with the publication in 1985 of a theoretical essay by Mark Granovetter—"Economic Action and Social Structure: The Problem of Embeddedness"—the new ideas came into focus. The same year Granovetter spoke of "new economic sociology"—yielding a tangible name.

Why economic sociology, after decades of neglect, suddenly would come alive again in the mid-1980s is not clear. Several factors may have played a role, inside and outside sociology. By the early 1980s, with the coming to power of Reagan and Thatcher, a new neoliberal ideology had become popular, which set the economy—and the economists—at the very center of things. By the mid-1980s economists had also started to redraw the traditional boundary separating economics and sociology, and to make forays into areas that sociologists by tradition saw as their own territory. It is also during this period that Gary Becker, Oliver Williamson, and others came to the attention of sociologists. Likewise, sociologists began to reciprocate by taking on economic topics.

To some extent this version of what happened resembles Granovetter's version in 1985. He associated "old economic sociology" with the economy and society perspective of Parsons, Smelser, and Wilbert E. Moore, and with industrial sociology—two approaches, he said, that had been full of life in the 1960s but then "suddenly died out" (Granovetter 1985b, 3). Parsons's attempt to negotiate a truce between economics and sociology had also been replaced by a more militant tone. According to Granovetter, new economic sociology "attacks neoclassical arguments in fundamental ways," and it wants to take on key economic topics, rather than focus on peripheral ones.

Since the mid-1980s new economic sociology has carved out a position for itself in U.S. sociology. It is well represented at a number of universities. Courses are routinely offered in sociology departments. A section in the American Sociological Association has been formed. A number of high-quality monographs have been produced, such as *The Transformation of Corporate Control* (1990) by Neil Fligstein, *Structural Holes* (1992) by Ronald Burt, and *The Social Meaning of Money* (1994) by Viviana Zelizer. These three works draw on the insights of organization theory, networks theory, and cultural sociology, respectively. The subfield has also seen the appearance of several anthologies, readers, a huge handbook, a textbook, and a general introduction to the field (Zukin and DiMaggio 1990; Guillén et al. 2002; Dobbin 2003; Granovetter and Swedberg 1992, 2001; Biggart 2002; Smelser and Swedberg 1994; Carruthers and Babb 2000; Swedberg 2003).

Granovetter on Embeddedness

While several attempts have been made to present general theories and paradigms in new economic sociology, the perspective that continues to command most conspicuous attention is Granovetter's theory of embeddedness. Since the mid-1980s Granovetter has added to his argument and refined it in various writings that are related to his two major projects since the mid-1980s: a general theoretical work in economic sociology entitled *Society and Economy: The Social Construction of Economic Institutions,* and a study (together with Patrick McGuire [1998]) of the emergence of the electrical utility industry in the United States.

The most important place in Granovetter's work where embeddedness is discussed is his 1985 article, which operated as a catalyst in the emergence of new economic sociology and which is probably the most cited article in economic sociology since the 1980s. His own definition of embeddedness is quite general and states that economic actions are "embedded in concrete, ongoing systems of social relations" (Granovetter 1985a, 487). Networks are central to this concept of embeddedness (491). An important distinction needs also to be drawn, according to Granovetter, between an actor's immediate connections and the more distant ones—what Granovetter elsewhere calls "relational embeddedness" and "structural embeddedness" (1990, 98–100; 1992, 34–37).

The most important addition to the 1985 article has been connecting the concept of embeddedness to a theory of institutions. Drawing on Berger and Luckmann (1967) Granovetter argues that institutions are "congealed networks" (1992, 7). Interaction between people acquires, after some time, an objective quality that makes people take it for granted. Economic institutions are characterized by "the mobilization of resources for collective action" (Granovetter 1992, 6).

Granovetter's argument on embeddedness has been widely discussed and sometimes criticized. An attempt to elaborate it can be found in the work of Brian Uzzi, who argues that a firm can be "underembedded" as well as "overembedded," and that a firm is most successful when it balances between arm's-length market ties and more solid links (Uzzi 1997). Several other critics have pointed out that Granovetter omits consideration of many aspects of economic action, including a link to the macroeconomic level, culture, and politics (e.g. Zukin and DiMaggio 1990; Zelizer 1988; Nee and Ingram 1998). Zukin and DiMaggio suggest that to remedy this lacuna, one should not only talk of "structural embeddedness," but also of "political," "cultural," and "cognitive embeddedness."

Contributions Using Structural Sociology and Networks

Structural sociology has played a crucial role in promoting and adding to network analysis in sociology, including economic socioloy. This approach is centered around the proposition that the relations of persons and positions are crucial to the social process (Mullins and Mullins 1973, 251–69). Its practitioners often use a mathematical approach, focus on social mechanisms, and avoid regression analysis and similar quantitative methods. Its most prominent scholars are Harrison White and his students, such as Mark Granovetter, Scott Boorman, and Michael Schwartz. White's work in economic sociology has concerned networks, vacancy chains, and markets. He begins his analysis from people's physical dependence on their surroundings but notes that interests are soon embedded in social relations (White 1970, 1981, 1992, 24).

Network studies have been at the center of the new economic sociology. Many studies have been made of the links between corporations and, more generally, within so-called industrial districts (Ebers 1997; Saxenian 1994). Burt (1992) analyzes competition by drawing on Simmel's idea that you are in a good position if you can play out two competitors against one another (*tertius gaudens*, or "the third who benefits"). Brian Uzzi's study of embeddedness from 1997 also makes use of networks, as does Granovetter's essay (1994) on business groups. A multitude of other fine studies could be mentioned (see, e.g., Powell and Lisa-Doerr 1994, this volume). One criticism of the network approach is that it has ignored the role in economic life of politics and culture (Fligstein 1996, 657).

Contributions Using Organization Theory

New economic sociology has been very successful in using organization theory to explore a number of important topics, such as the structure of firms and the links between corporations and their environments. One fine example is Nicole Woolsey Biggart's *Charismatic Capitalism* (1989), which deals with a very special type of organization: direct selling organizations, such as Tupperware and Mary Kay Cosmetics. Three theoretical approaches in organization theory have been especially important for the development of new economic sociology: resource dependency, population ecology, and new institutionalism.

Resource dependency, as its name suggests, rests on the postulate that organizations are dependent on their environments to survive. An example of this approach is work by Burt (1983), who suggests that three important factors that affect profits are the number of suppliers, competitors, and customers. The more "structural autonomy" a firm has, the higher its profits; that is, a firm with many suppliers, few competitors, and many customers will be in a position to buy cheaply and sell expensively.

In population ecology the main driving force of organizations is survival. It has been shown that the diffusion of an organizational form typically passes through several distinct stages: a very slow beginning, then explosive growth, and finally a slow settling down (e.g., Hannan and Freeman 1989). Individual studies of this process in various industries, such as railroads, banks, and telephone companies, fill a void in economic sociology (e.g., Carroll and Hannan 1995).

New institutionalism is strongly influenced by the ideas of John Meyer and is centered around what may be called cultural and cognitive aspects of organizations (see Powell and DiMaggio 1991). Meyer argues that organizations seem much more rational than they actually are, and that specific models for organizing activities may be applied widely—including to circumstances they do not fit. It has been argued that the strength of new institutionalism is its exploration of "factors that make actors unlikely to recognize or to act on their interests" and its focus on "circumstances that cause actors who do recognize and try to act on their interests to be unable to do so" (DiMaggio 1988, 4–5). The possibility of uniting a more traditional interest analysis with new institutionalism is exemplified by Fligstein's (1990) study of the large corporation in the United States. Fligstein notes that the multidivisional form of organization spread for mimetic reasons—but also because this organizational form made it easier for firms to take advantage of new technology and the emerging national market.

Contributions Using Cultural Sociology

A group of economic sociologists is committed to a cultural approach, and a substantial number also refer to symbols, meaning structures, and the like in their studies of the economy. Cultural economic sociology owes much to the work of its two most prominent representatives, Viviana Zelizer and Paul DiMaggio. In a programmatic statement Zelizer criticized contemporary economic sociology for its tendency to reduce everything to social relations and networks—"social structural absolutism" (1988, 629). She also rejected the alternative of reducing everything in the economy to culture ("cultural absolutism"). The goal should be to take economic *and* cultural factors into account. DiMaggio has been similarly skeptical of a full-scale cultural analysis of the economy, but argues that it should include a "'cultural' component"—but not more (DiMaggio 1994, 27; cf. Zukin and DiMaggio 1990, 17–18). According to DiMaggio, culture can be either "constitutive," referring to categories, scripts, and conceptions of agency, or "regulative," referring to norms, values, and routines.

Viviana Zelizer's work on culture occupies a central position (however, see also Dobbin 1994; Abolafia 1998). Her first major work (1979) was a study of life insurance in the United States, with special emphasis on the clash between sacred values and economic values. Over time the economic emphasis came to dominate. Later Zelizer published *Pricing the Priceless Child* (1985), which describes a similar movement, but this time in reverse. Children, who in the nineteenth century had had an economic value, would in the twentieth century increasingly be seen in emotional terms and regarded as "priceless." In her most recent major study (1994), Zelizer argues that money does not constitute a neutral, nonsocial substance, but appears in a variety of culturally influenced shapes ("multiple monies").

Contributions Building a Historical and Comparative Tradition

A number of comparative and historical studies, bringing Max Weber's monumental works to mind, have been an ingredient of recent economic sociology (see Dobbin, chap. 2 in this volume). A few of the works already mentioned draw on historical material (e.g. Granovetter and McGuire 1998; Zelizer 1979, 1985, 1994). To this list should be added Bruce Carruthers's study of finance in seventeenth- and eighteenth-century England, and several attempts by economic sociologists to challenge Alfred Chandler's account of the rise of the large industrial corporation in the United States. Carruthers is interested in showing that not only do economic interests influence politics, but also the opposite: "political interests influence economic action" (1996, 7). Using primary material on the trade in shares in the East India Company in the early 1700s, he establishes that political ambitions clearly influenced the choices of buyers and sellers. The critique of Chandler has similarly emphasized the state's role in the emergence of the large industrial corporation. Chandler's key idea—that recent advances in technology had made it necessary around the turn of the last century to reorganize the large corporation as a multidivisional unit—has also been criticized (e.g. Fligstein 1990; Roy 1990, 1997; Freeland 1996, 2001).

Explicitly comparative studies are fewer in number. One notable work is *Forging Industrial Policy: The United States, Britain, and France in the Railway Age* (1994) by Frank Dobbin (see also Evans 1995). The author argues that industrial policy in these three countries between 1825 and 1900 differed on important points. In the case of the United States, local self-rule and a weak federal state meant that railway regulation translated into antimonopoly policy and attempts to safeguard private initiatives. The tradition of a centralized state in France inspired strong interference from the authorities in the planning and running of the railroads. And the tradition of safeguarding elite individuals in Britain helped to bring about an industrial policy that shielded the small, entrepreneurial firm.

The Contribution by James Coleman and Interest-Based Sociology

The most radical attempt during the last few decades to develop a sociological interest analysis is that of James Coleman (1926–1995). His efforts were initiated in the early 1960s and found final expression in *Foundations of Social Theory* (1990). Coleman's intention was to use interest as the foundation for *all* of sociology, and initially he paid little attention to economic sociology (see, how-

ever, Coleman 1994). It should be mentioned, however, that in the same year Granovetter's essay on embeddedness appeared, Coleman published a brief article in which he developed the parallel argument that economists have failed to introduce social relations into their analysis (1985, 85).

The key theoretical chapter in *Foundations of Social Theory* is entitled "Actors, Resources, Interest, and Control" (chap. 2); it attempts to reconceptualize interest theory and to make it sociological. Coleman's point of departure is that it is not sufficient to speak of actors and their interests; "resources" and "control" must be considered. Coleman argues that if an actor has something of interest to another, the two will interact and thereby create a social system. In Coleman's terminology, if actor A has control over a resource that is of interest to actor B, they will interact.

Foundations, as well as other works by Coleman, contains a number of analyses of much relevance to economic sociology. Three subjects of particular importance are trust, social capital, and the modern corporation. Trust is conceptualized by Coleman in a manner very different from Simmel. While the latter emphasized trust as unthinking belief, Coleman characterizes trust as a conscious bet: you calculate what you can win and lose by trusting someone. Social capital is any social relation that can be of help to an individual in realizing an interest. "The function identified by the concept 'social capital' is the value of those aspects of social structure to actors, as resources that can be used by the actors to realize their interests" (Coleman 1990, 305). A firm represents, for example, a form of social capital—even if social capital is usually the unintended result of some action, undertaken for a different purpose. Finally, Coleman emphasizes that once people have created a firm to realize their interests, the firm can develop interests of its own (see especially Coleman 1974). To Coleman, the firm is basically a social invention, and agency theory is particularly useful for analyzing it.

Bourdieu and Other European Contributions to Economic Sociology

New economic sociology is primarily a U.S. phenomenon and has only recently begun to spread to Europe. Many of the major European sociologists have, however, written on the economy as part of their general concern with society. This is not only true of Raymond Aron, Michel Crozier, and Ralf Dahrendorf, but also of major sociologists with notable contemporary influence, such as Niklas

Luhmann, Jürgen Habermas, and Pierre Bourdieu (cf. also Giddens 1973, 1987). Luhmann (1927–1998), for example, has written a number of essays on the economy, which, however, have been somewhat neglected in the current debate. His consistent thesis is that "economic sociology can only develop if its approach is overhauled and it sets out . . . from the concept of the economy as a subsystem of society" (Luhmann [1970] 1982, 221–22; cf. 1988; Beckert 2002, 201–40). Habermas has written much less on the economy than Luhmann and has not shown any interest in economic sociology. Nonetheless, his general thesis that in modern society the lifeworld of the individual has been uncoupled from the system world, including the economic subsystem, has been much discussed (e.g. Habermas 1984–87; cf. Sitton 1998; for knowledge-constitutive interests, see Habermas [1968] 1971).

Of the major European sociologists Pierre Bourdieu (1930–2002) has shown the most interest in the economy, from his studies of Algeria in the 1950s to a recent work on the housing market in *Les structures sociales de l'économie* (2000b). Bourdieu has also devoted issues of his journal *Actes de la recherche en sciences sociales* to economic topics, such as "social capital" (no. 31, 1980), "the social construction of the economy" (no. 65, 1986), and "the economy and the economists" (no. 119, 1997). Most importantly, however, he has developed an important theoretical alternative to the model of embeddedness and its offshoots, namely the idea of the economy as a field, with all that this implies.

Bourdieu's foremost empirical study of interest to economic sociology—*Travail et travailleurs en Algérie* (*Work and workers in Algeria*; 1963)—can be described as a rich ethnographic study (for a shortened version in English, see Bourdieu 1979). Some of its strength comes from the author's juxtaposition of the traditionalistic worldview of the Algerian peasants with the capitalist worldview of modern people. While the peasant in Algeria has an intensely emotional and nearly mystical relationship to the land, this is not the case in a society dominated by wage labor and capital. Work is not directly related to productivity in Algeria; one tries to keep busy all the time. Institutions such as money and credit are seen in a different light. Money and exchange are seen as inferior to barter; and credit—which, as opposed to assets, is tied to the person—is resorted to only in rare circumstances such as personal distress. In Algeria commercial ventures are preferred to industrial ones, since the risk involved is much smaller.

In economic sociology Bourdieu has also developed a general approach; an application of his general sociology, which is centered around the concepts of the field, habitus, and different types of capital. In 1997 he published an article entitled "The Economic Field," which was revised and given the new title of "Principles of an Economic Anthropology" a few years later (Bourdieu 1997, 2000a; see chap. 4 in this volume). Since Bourdieu is very critical of Granovetter's approach—for ignoring the structural dimension embodied in the notion of the field—one may well be justified in speaking about two different approaches in contemporary economic sociology: that of embeddedness and that of fields.

According to Bourdieu, the economy can be conceptualized as a field (as can an industry and a firm), that is, as a structure of actual and potential relations (Bourdieu and Wacquant 1992, 94–120; Bourdieu 1997; cf. Fligstein 2001). Each field has its own logic and its own social structure. The structure of a field can also be understood in terms of its distribution of capital. Besides financial capital, three other forms of capital are especially important: social, cultural, and symbolic. Social capital is one's connections of relevance to economic affairs; cultural capital comes from one's education and family background; and symbolic capital has to do with various items with a cognitive basis, such as goodwill and brand loyalty (Bourdieu 1997; for a general account of the different types of capital, see Bourdieu [1983] 1986). The individual actors in the economic field bring with them their "economic habitus" (or "economic predispositions"), which relates their future actions to their past experience. *Homo economicus,* Bourdieu says, is "a kind of anthropological monster" (1997, 61). Bourdieu's economic actor does not act in a *rational* way but in a *reasonable* way.

In addition to the three concepts of field, capital, and habitus important in Bourdieu's general sociology, there exists a fourth concept that is equally important but often ignored: *interest,* or that which drives the actor to participate in a field. "*Interest* is to 'be there,' to participate, to admit that the game is worth playing and that the stakes that are created in and through this fact are worth pursuing; it is to recognize the game and to recognize its stakes" (1998a, 77; cf. Bourdieu and Wacquant 1992, 115–17). The opposite of interest (or *illusio*) is indifference (or *ataraxia*). Each field has its own interest, even if it masquerades as disinterestedness. Bourdieu criticizes the economists' version of interest as ahistorical—"far from being an anthropological invariant, interest is a *historical arbitrary*" (Bourdieu and Wacquant 1992, 116). The economists are also wrong in thinking that "economic interest" drives everything; "anthropology and comparative history show that the properly social magic of institutions can constitute just about anything as an interest" (Bourdieu and Wacquant 1992, 117). The error of assuming that the laws of the economic field are applicable to all other fields in society Bourdieu terms "economism" (1998a, 83).

Bourdieu's analysis has been discussed in only limited ways in contemporary economic sociology. *Distinction* (Bourdieu [1979] 1986), for example, has much to say on preference formation and also contains a new approach to consumption. Bourdieu's emphasis on economic suffering and his attempt to tie it to the problematic of theodicy is also of much interest (e.g., Bourdieu et al. 1999). So is his related effort to discuss the normative aspect of economic sociology, for example, in his recent little book on "the tyranny of capital" (1998b; see also Bourdieu 2002).

It would, however, be incorrect to give the impression that Bourdieu is the only economic sociologist of interest in contemporary France. Luc Boltanski and Laurent Thévenot's work ([1987] 1991) on the different ways that an action can be justified or legitimized is of potential relevance to economic sociology (e.g., Stark 2000). Their ideas about the way that people legitimize their actions by referring to different "worlds" of justification are hard to summarize, and one example will have to suffice. A person who works for a firm may justify his behavior by referring either to efficiency ("the world of the market") or to loyalty ("the domestic world")—with very different results (Boltanski and Thévenot [1987] 1991). Boltanski has also criticized the network approach as ideological and procapitalistic (Boltanski and Chiapello 1999). In speaking of networks, it must also be mentioned that Michel Callon has added to network theory by arguing that not only individuals and organizations, but also *objects*, can be actors (e.g., Law and Hassard 1999; cf. Callon 1998). A machine, for example, can determine what kinds of actions a machine operator has to perform and also how she is connected to other people in the process of production. According to another important argument of Callon, economic theory often fits reality so well because it has helped to create this reality in the first place (so-called *performivity*).

Outside of the United States, France has become something of a center for innovative economic sociology, and to the work just mentioned one should

also add the studies of Frédéric Lebaron on French economists, Emmanuel Lazeaga on work in a law firm, and Philippe Steiner on different types of economic knowledge (Lebaron 2000; Lazega 2000; Steiner 1998, 2001, 2004). There is considerable research in economic sociology in other European countries as well. Sociology of money and finance has, for example, several skillful practitioners in England and Spain (e.g., Dodd 1994; Ingham 1998, 2004; Izquierdo 2001). An innovative study of inheritance has just been published in Germany, where the sociology of finance is also very strong (Beckert, forthcoming; see also Beckert 2002; Knorr Cetina and Preda, forthcoming; cf. Zuckerman 1999). Industrial districts are being studied in Italy (e.g., Trigilia 2001). Finally, Knorr Cetina in Germany and Aspers in Sweden have independently of one another embarked on the project of applying phenomenology to economic sociology (Knorr Cetina and Brügger 2002; Aspers 2001b). A few general introductions to economic sociology have been published in Europe; there also is a newsletter exclusively devoted to economic sociology in Europe (Steiner 1999; Trigilia 2002; see *Economic Sociology. European Electronic Newsletter*, 1999–; see http://econsoc.mfipg.de).

A Concluding Note

Space has constricted our review of both historical developments and contemporary highlights (the latter are amply covered in the chapters that follow). We have seen enough, however, to permit a few, equally brief, evaluative comments on the field of economic sociology today, and more particularly on the relations between economics and sociology.

What is unique about the situation, as it has developed through the 1990s, is that for the first time since the nineteenth century, mainstream economics has begun to analyze economic institutions again. This has already led to a number of interesting developments within economics proper as well as to a tentative dialogue with sociology and other social sciences, such as psychology and history. It is important that efforts be made, by sociologists as well as by economists, to deepen this dialogue since both disciplines are needed to fill the void created by nearly a century of neglect of economic institutions. As an example of cooperation between the economic and the sociological approach that has occurred since the first edition of the *Handbook*, we cite the important work of Avner Greif (e.g., 1994, forthcoming).

The "imperialistic" mode, whether in its sociological form or in its economic form, seems unpromising as a way of dealing with either economic behavior or economic institutions (or for that matter, behavior and institutions in general). The complexity of determinants bearing on every kind of behavior suggests the greater scientific utility of approaches that are less monolithic. It is true that "imperialistic" works have greatly stimulated the debate over economy and society. Eventually, however, this approach becomes counterproductive scientifically, tending to excite territorial battles rather than dispassionate inquiry.

Correspondingly, it is, in our opinion, more fruitful to pursue the kind of approach to economic sociology taken by Weber and Schumpeter in their social economics, or *Sozialökonomik*. Such an approach is broad-based and multidisciplinary. Economic sociology, in other words, should have its own distinct profile as well as cooperate and coexist with economic theory, economic history, and economic anthropology. We also hope that departments of economics will include economic sociology among their courses and hire economic sociologists, as business schools currently do in the United States.

While the current pluralistic approach has given economic sociology richness and vitality, the bolder, creatively synthesizing efforts of the classics are notably missing. Without that complementary line of theorizing, the field of economic sociology—like any area of inquiry that specializes and subspecializes—tends to sprawl. Continuing efforts to sharpen the theoretical focus of economic sociology and to work toward synthetic interpretations of its findings are essential.

One promising model of relating the fields of economics and sociology might be termed "complementary articulation." Of necessity, any line of disciplined inquiry focuses on certain operative variables and determinants, and "freezes" others into parametric assumptions. Often the ground thus frozen is that very territory which is problematical from the standpoint of some other line of social science inquiry. This dialogue about the precise role of operative variables and the conceptual status of parameters holds out the promise for communication and theoretical development in both economics and sociology. This strategy appears much more engaging than several others we have identified in this overview—imperialism, polemical hostility, mutual separation and toleration, or shapeless eclecticism.

Given the void after a century's neglect of eco-

nomic institutions, we also expect that new questions will be raised that cut across the conventional boundaries between economics and sociology. For this reason it is essential that economists as well as sociologists be willing to entertain new and unfamiliar ideas. An opportunity, such as the current one, to pull economics and sociology closer to each other is rare and should not be neglected.

NOTES

1. While this chapter covers much of the same ground as our chapter in the first edition of the *Handbook* ("The Sociological Perspective on the Economy"), it has been completely rewritten and revised for the current edition. We have also introduced a new theme: the need to pay more attention to interests in economic sociology. For helpful comments we would like to thank Fred Block, Robyn Dawes, Frank Dobbin, and Viviana Zelizer.

2. The field has been called "the sociology of economic life," as in Smelser 1976 and in Granovetter and Swedberg 1992, 2001; Fred Block's (1990) preferred term is *sociology of economies*. We find little if any difference in denotation between these terms and *economic sociology*. For convenience we stay with the term that emerged in the classical literature. As a term for all social science analysis of the economy—economic theory plus economic history, economic sociology, and so on—we agree with Weber, Schumpeter, and Etzioni (1988) that *social economics* (*Sozialökonomik*) is an appropriate term.

3. The term *economic sociology* has also been used to denote a rational choice perspective as applied to social behavior in general (see Becker 1990). This usage is, to us, too broad since it encompasses practically all of sociology (*minus* the analysis of the economy proper).

REFERENCES

Abolafia, Mitchel. 1998. "Markets as Culture: An Ethnographic Approach." Pp. 69–85 in *The Laws of the Markets*, ed. Michel Callon. Oxford: Blackwell.

Akerlof, George. 1984. "A Theory of Social Custom, of Which Unemployment May Be One Consequence." *Quarterly Journal of Economics* 44:749–75.

———. 1990. "Interview." Pp. 61–78 in *Economics and Sociology*, ed. Richard Swedberg. Princeton: Princeton University Press.

Arrow, Kenneth. 1990. "Interview: Kenneth Arrow." Pp. 133–51 in *Economics and Sociology*, ed. Richard Swedberg. Princeton: Princeton University Press.

Aspers, Patrik. 1999. "The Economic Sociology of Alfred Marshall: An Overview." *American Journal of Economics and Sociology* 58:651–67.

———. 2001a. "Crossing the Boundary of Economics and Sociology: The Case of Vilfredo Pareto." *American Journal of Economics and Sociology* 60: 519–46.

———. 2001b. *A Market in Vogue: A Study of Fashion Photography in Sweden*. Stockholm: City University Press.

Babb, Sarah. 2001. *Managing Mexico: Economists from*

Nationalism to Neoliberalism. Princeton: Princeton University Press.

Baker, Wayne. 1984. "The Social Structure of a National Securities Market." *American Journal of Sociology* 89:775–811.

Bates, Robert, Avner Greif, Margaret Levi, and Jean-Laurent Rosenthal. 1998. *Analytic Narratives.* Princeton: Princeton University Press.

Becker, Gary. 1990. "Interview: Gary Becker." Pp. 27–46 in *Economics and Sociology,* ed. Richard Swedberg. Princeton: Princeton University Press.

Beckert, Jens. 2002. *Beyond the Market: The Social Foundations of Economic Efficiency.* Princeton: Princeton University Press.

———. Forthcoming. *Unearned Wealth: Inheritance in France, Germany, and the United States since 1800.*

Berger, Peter, and Thomas Luckmann. 1967. *The Social Construction of Reality: A Treatise in the Sociology of Knowledge.* New York: Doubleday.

Biggart, Nicole Woolsey. 1989. *Charismatic Capitalism: Direct Selling Organizations in America.* Chicago: University of Chicago Press.

———, ed. 2002. *Readings in Economic Sociology.* Oxford: Blackwell.

Block, Fred. 1990. "Economic Sociology." Pp. 21–45 in *Post-industrial Possibilities: A Critique of Economic Discourse.* Berkeley and Los Angeles: University of California Press.

———. 2001. Introduction. Pp. xviii–xxxviii in *The Great Transformation,* by Karl Polanyi. Boston: Beacon Press.

———. 2003. "Karl Polanyi and the Writing of *The Great Transformation.*" *Theory and Society* 32:275–306.

Boltanski, Luc, and Eve Chiapello. 1999. *Le nouvel esprit du capitalisme.* Paris: Gallimard.

Boltanski, Luc, and Laurent Thévenot. [1987] 1991. *De la justification. Les economies de la grandeur.* Paris: Gallimard.

Bourdieu, Pierre. 1963. "Travail et travailleurs en Algérie: Étude sociologique." Pp. 257–389 in *Travail et traveilleurs en Algérie,* by Pierre Bourdieu et al. Paris: Mouton.

———. 1979. "The Disenchantment of the World." Pp. 1–91 in *Algeria, 1960.* Trans. Richard Nice. Cambridge: Cambridge University Press.

———. [1979] 1986. *Distinction: A Social Critique of the Judgment of Taste.* Trans. Richard Nice. London: Routledge.

———. [1983] 1986. "The Forms of Capital." Pp. 241–58 in *Handbook of Theory and Research in Education,* ed. John Richardson. Westport, Conn.: Greenwood Press.

———. 1997. "Le champ economique." *Actes de la recherche en sciences sociales* 119:48–66.

———. 1998a. "Is a Disinterested Act Possible?" Pp. 75–91 in *Practical Reason: On the Theory of Action.* Trans. Richard Nice, et al. Stanford: Stanford University Press.

———. 1998b. *Acts of Resistance: Against the Tyranny of the Market.* Trans. Richard Nice. New York: New Press.

———. 2000a. "Principes d'une anthropologie economique." Pp. 233–70 in *Les structures sociales de l'économie.* Paris: Seuil.

———. 2000b. *Les structures sociales de l'économie.* Paris: Seuil.

———. 2002. *Interventions, 1961–2001. Science sociale & action politique.* Marseille: Agone.

Bourdieu, Pierre, and Loïc Wacquant. 1992. *An Invitation to Reflexive Sociology.* Chicago: University of Chicago Press.

Bourdieu, Pierre, et al. 1999. *The Weight of the World: Social Suffering in Contemporary Society.* Trans. Priscilla Parkhurst Ferguson. Stanford: Stanford University Press.

Burawoy, Michael, 1977. *Manufacturing Consent: Changes in the Labor Process under Monopoly Capitalism.* Chicago: University of Chicago Press.

Burt, Ronald. 1983. *Corporate Profits and Cooptation: Networks of Market Constraints and Directorate Ties in the American Economy.* New York: Academic Press.

———. 1992. *Structural Holes: The Social Structure of Competition.* Cambridge: Harvard University Press.

Braverman, Harry. 1974. *Labor and Monopology Capital: The Degradation of Work in the Twentieth Century.* New York: Monthly Review Press.

Callon, Michel, ed. 1998. *The Laws of the Markets.* Oxford: Blackwell.

Camerer, Colin, George Loewenstein, and Matthew Rabin, eds. 2004. *Advances in Behavioral Economics.* Princeton: Princeton University Press.

Camic, Charles. 1991. "Introduction: Talcott Parsons before *The Structure of Social Action.*" Pp. ix–lxix in *The Early Essays,* by Talcott Parssons. Chicago: University of Chicago Press.

Cardoso, Fernando H., and E. Faletto. 1979. *Dependency and Development in Latin America.* Berkeley and Los Angeles: University of California Press.

Carroll, Glenn, and Michael Hannan, eds. 1995. *Organizations in Industry.* Oxford: Oxford University Press.

Carroll, Glenn, R., and Michael T. Hannan. 2000. *The Demography of Corporations and Industries.* Princeton: Princeton University Press.

Carruthers, Bruce. 1996. *City of Capital: Politics and Markets in the English Financial Revolution.* Princeton: Princeton University Press.

Carruthers, Bruce, and Sarah Babb. 2000. *Economy/Society: Markets, Meanings, and Social Structure.* Thousand Oaks, Calif.: Pine Forge Press.

Coleman, James. 1974. *Power and the Structure of Society.* New York: W. W. Norton.

———. 1985. "Introducing Social Structure into Economic Analysis." *American Economic Review* 74(2): 84–88.

———. 1990. *Foundations of Social Theory.* Cambridge: Harvard University Press.

———. 1994. "A Rational Choice Perspective on Economic Sociology." Pp. 166–80 in *The Handbook of*

Economic Sociology, ed. Neil Smelser and Richard Swedberg. New York: Russell Sage Foundation; Princeton University Press.

Dahl, Robert. 1958. "A Critique of the Ruling Elite Model." *American Political Science Review* 52: 436–69.

DiMaggio, Paul. 1988. "Interest and Agency in Institutional Theory." Pp. 3–21 in *Institutional Patterns and Organizations*, ed. Lynn Zucker. Cambridge: Ballinger.

———. 1994. "Culture and Economy." Pp. 27–57 in *The Handbook of Economic Sociology*, ed. Neil Smelser and Richard Swedberg. New York: Russell Sage Foundation; Princeton University Press.

Dobbin, Frank. 1994. *Forging Industrial Policy: The United States, Britain, and France in the Railroad Age*. Cambridge: Cambridge University Press.

———, ed. 2003. *The Sociology of the Economy*. New York: Russell Sage Foundation.

Dodd, Nigel. 1994. *The Sociology of Money: Economics, Reason, and Contemporary Society*. Cambridge: Polity Press.

Domhoff, William G., and Thomas Dye, eds. 1987. *Power Elites and Organizations*. London: Sage.

Dore, Ronald. 1983. "Goodwill and the Spirit of Capitalism." *British Journal of Sociology* 34:459–82.

Durkheim, Émile. 1887. "La science positive de la morale en Allemagne." *Revue philosophique de la France et de l'étranger* 24:33–58, 113–42, 275–84.

———. [1897] 1951. *Suicide: A Study in Sociology*. Glencoe, Ill.: Free Press.

———. [1895] 1964. *The Rules of Sociological Method*. New York: Free Press.

———. [1912] 1965. *The Elementary Forms of Religious Life*. New York: Free Press.

———. [1888] 1978a. "Course in Sociology: Opening Lecture." Pp. 43–70 in *On Institutional Analysis*, by Émile Durkheim, ed. Mark Traugott. Chicago: University of Chicago Press.

———. [1909] 1978b. "Sociology and the Social Sciences." Pp. 71–90 in *On Institutional Analysis, by* Emile Durkheim, ed. Mark Traugott. Chicago: University of Chicago Press.

———. [1902] 1980. "Georg Simmel, *Philosophie des Geldes*." Pp. 94–98 in *Contributions to l'Année Sociologique*. New York: Free Press.

———. [1950] 1983. *Professional Ethics and Civic Morals*. Westport, Conn.: Greenwood Press.

———. [1893] 1984. *The Division of Labor in Society*. New York: Free Press.

Ebers, Mark, ed. 1997. *The Formation of Inter-organizational Networks*. Oxford: Oxford University Press.

Economic Sociology: European Electronic Newsletter. 1999–. http://econsoc.mpifg.de.

Eggertsson, Thráinn. 1990. *Economic Behavior and Institutions*. Cambridge: Cambridge University Press.

Etzioni, Amitai. 1988. *The Moral Dimension: Towards a New Economics*. New York: Free Press.

Evans, Peter. 1995. *Embedded Autonomy: State and Industrial Transformation*. Princeton: Princeton University Press.

Fligstein, Neil. 1990. *The Transformation of Corporate Control*. Cambridge: Harvard University Press.

———. 1996. "Markets as Politics: A Political-Cultural Approach to Market Institutions." *American Sociological Review* 61:656–73.

———. 2001. *The Architecture of Markets: An Economic Sociology of Twenty-First Century Capitalist Societies*. Princeton: Princeton University Press.

Frank, Andre Gunder. 1967. *Capitalism and Underdevelopment in Latin America*. New York: Monthly Review Press.

Freeland, Robert. 1996. "The Myth of the M-Form? Governance, Consent, and Organizational Change." *American Journal of Sociology* 102:483–526.

———. 2001. *The Struggle for Control of the Modern Corporation: Organizational Change at General Motors, 1924–1970*. Cambridge: Cambridge University Press.

Frisby, David. 1978. Preface to the 2d ed. Pp. xv–xlii in *The Philosophy of Money*, by Georg Simmel. London: Routledge.

Furubotn, Eirik, and Rudolf Richter. 1997. *Institutions and Economic Theory: The Contribution of New Institutional Economics*. Ann Arbor: University of Michigan Press.

Galbraith, John Kenneth. 1973. "Power and the Useful Economist." *American Economic Review* 63:1–11.

———. 1984. *The Anatomy of Power*. London: Hamilton.

Giddens, Anthony. 1983. *The Class Structure of Advanced Societies*. London: Hutchinson.

———. 1987. "Social Theory and the Problems of Macroeconomics." Pp. 183–202 in *Social Theory and Modern Sociology*. Stanford, Calif.: Stanford University Press.

Gorz, André. 1977. *Capitalism in Crisis and Everyday Life*. Trans. John Howe. Atlantic Highlands, N.J.: Humanities Press.

Granovetter, Mark. 1974. *Getting a Job: A Study of Contacts and Careers*. Cambridge: Harvard University Press.

———. 1985a. "Economic Action and Social Structure: The Problem of Embeddedness." *American Journal of Sociology* 91:481–510.

———. 1985b. "Luncheon Roundtable Talk on the 'New Sociology of Economic Life.'" American Sociological Association Meeting, August 26. Washington, D.C.

———. 1990. "The Old and the New Old Economic Sociology: A History and an Agenda." Pp. 89–112 in *Beyond the Marketplace: Rethinking Economy and Society*, ed. Roger Friedland and A. F. Robertson. New York: Aldine de Gruyter.

———. 1992. "Economic Institutions as Social Constructions: A Framework for Analysis." *Acta Sociologica* 35:3–11.

———. 1994. "Business Groups." Pp. 453–75 in *The Handbook of Economic Sociology*, ed. Neil J. Smelser and Richard Swedberg. New York: Russell Sage Foundation; Princeton University Press.

———. 1995. *Getting a Job: A Study of Contacts and Careers.* 2d ed. Chicago: University of Chicago Press.

Granovetter, Mark, and Patrick McGuire. 1998. "The Making of an Industry: Electricity in the United States." Pp. 147–73 in *The Laws of the Market*, ed. Michel Callon. Oxford: Blackwell.

Granovetter, Mark, and Richard Swedberg, eds. 1992. *The Sociology of Economic Life.* Boulder, Colo.: Westview Press.

———, eds. 2001. *The Sociology of Economic Life.* 2d ed. Boulder, Colo.: Westview Press.

Greif, Avner. 1994. "Cultural Beliefs and Organization of Society: Historical and Theoretical Reflections on Collectivist and Individualist Societies." *Journal of Political Economy* 102:912–50.

———. 1998. "Historical and Comparative Institutional Analysis." *American Economic Review* 88(2): 80–84.

———. Forthcoming. *Institutions: Theory and History. Comparative and Historical Analysis.* Cambridge: Cambridge University Press.

Guillén, Mauro, et al., eds. 2002. *The New Economic Sociology: Developments in an Emerging Field.* New York: Russell Sage Foundation.

Habermas, Jürgen. [1968] 1971. *Knowledge and Human Interest.* Trans. Jeremy J. Shapiro. Boston: Beacon Press.

———. 1984–87. *The Theory of Communicative Action.* 2 vols. Cambridge: MIT Press.

Hannan, Michael, and John Freeman. 1989. *Organizational Ecology.* Cambridge: Harvard University Press.

Ingham, Geoffrey. 1998. "On the Underdevelopment of 'The Sociology of Money.'" *Acta Sociologica* 41:3–18.

———. 2004. *The Nature of Money.* Cambridge: Polity Press.

Izquierdo, A. Javier. 2001. "Reliability at Risk: The Supervision of Financial Models as a Case Study for Reflexive Economic Sociology." *European Societies* 3(1): 69–90.

Jevons, W. Stanley. [1879] 1965. Preface to the 2d ed. Pp. xi–liii in *The Theory of Political Economy.* 5th ed. New York: Augustus M. Kelley.

Keister, Lisa. 2000. *Wealth in America: Trends in Wealth Inequality.* Cambridge: Cambridge University Press.

Knight, Frank. [1921] 1985. *Risk, Uncertainty, and Profit.* Chicago: University of Chicago Press.

Knorr Cetina, Karin, and Urs Brügger. 2002. "Global Macrostructures: The Virtual Societies of Financial Markets." *American Journal of Sociology* 107:905–50.

Knorr Cetina, Karin, and Alex Preda, eds. Forthcoming. *The Sociology of Financial Markets.* Oxford: Oxford University Press.

Law, John, and John Hassard, eds. 1999. *Actor Network Theory and After.* Oxford: Blackwell.

Lazega, Emmanuel. 2000. *The Collegial Phenomenon: Social Mechanisms of Cooperation among Peers.* Oxford: Oxford University Press.

Lebaron, Frédéric. 2000. *La croyance économique. Les économistes entre science et politique.* Paris: Seuil.

Leontief, Wassily. 1971. "Theoretical Assumptions and Nonobserved Facts." *American Economic Review* 61(1): 1–7.

Lippmann, S. A., and J. J. McCall. 2001. "Information Economics." Pp. 7480–86 in vol. 11 of *International Encyclopedia of the Social and Behavioral Sciences*, ed. Neil J. Smelser and Paul B. Baltes. Oxford: Elsevier.

Luhmann, Niklas. [1970] 1982. "The Economy as a Social System." Pp. 190–225 in *The Differentiation of Society.* New York: Columbia University Press.

———. 1988. *Die Wirtschaft der Gesellschaft.* Frankfurt am Main: Suhrkamp.

Makler, Harry, Alberto Martinelli, and Neil Smelser, eds. 1982. *The New International Economy.* London: Sage.

Marshall, Alfred. 1919. *Industry and Trade.* London: Macmillan.

———. [1920] 1961. *Principles of Economics.* 9th (variorum) ed. 2 vols. London: Macmillan. The first edition appeared in 1890.

Marshall, Gordon. 1982. *In Search of the Spirit of Capitalism: Max Weber's Protestant Ethic Thesis.* London: Hutchinson.

Marx, Karl. [1867] 1906. *Capital: A Critique of Political Economy.* New York: Modern Library.

———. [1852] 1950. *The Eighteenth Brumaire of Louis Bonaparte.* New York: International Publishers.

———. [1859] 1970. *A Contribution to the Critique of Political Economy.* New York: International Publishers.

———. [1857–58] 1973. *Grundrisse: Foundations of the Critique of Political Economy.* New York: Vintage Books.

———. [1843] 1978. "Theses on Feuerbach." Pp. 143–45 in *The Marx-Engels Reader*, ed. Robert C. Tucker. 2d ed. New York: W. W. Norton.

Mauss, Marcel. [1925] 1990. *The Gift: The Form and Reason for Exchange in Archaic Societies.* New York: W. W. Norton.

Merton, Robert K. 1968. *Social Theory and Social Structure.* Enlarged ed. New York: Free Press.

Mills, C. Wright. 1956. *The Power Elite.* Oxford: Oxford University Press.

Mintz, Beth, and Michael Schwartz. 1985. *The Power Structure of American Business.* Chicago: University of Chicago Press.

Mommsen, Wolfgang. 2000. "Max Weber's 'Grand Sociology': The Origins and Composition of *Wirtschaft und Gesellschaft. Soziologie.*" *History and Theory* 39:364–83.

Montesquieu, Charles de Secondat, baron de. [1748] 1989. *The Spirit of the Laws.* Trans. and ed. Anne M. Cohler, Basia Carolyn Miller, and Harold Samuel Stune. Cambridge: Cambridge University Press.

Mullainthan, S., and R. H. Thaler. 2001. "Behavioral Economics." Pp. 1094–1100 in vol. 2 of *International Encyclopedia of the Social and Behavioral Sciences*, ed. Neil J. Smelser and Paul B. Baltes. Oxford: Elsevier.

Mullins, Nicholas, and Carolyn Mullins. 1973. *Theories and Theory Groups in Contemporary American Sociology*. New York: Harper and Row.

Nee, Victor, and Paul Ingram. 1998. "Embeddedness and Beyond: Institutions, Exchange, and Social Structure." Pp. 19–45 in *The New Institutionalism in Sociology*, ed. Mary C. Brinton and Victor Nee. New York: Russell Sage Foundation.

Pareto, Vilfredo. [1916] 1963. *The Mind and Society: A Treatise on General Sociology*. 2 vols. New York: Dover.

Parsons, Talcott. [1940] 1954. "Motivation of Economic Activities." Pp. 50–68 in *Essays in Sociological Theory*. New York: Free Press.

———. [1937] 1968. *The Structure of Social Action*. 2 vols. New York: Free Press.

Parsons, Talcott, and Neil J. Smelser. 1956. *Economy and Society: A Study in the Integration of Economic and Social Theory*. New York: Free Press.

Poggi, Gianfranco. 1993. *Money and the Modern Mind: Georg Simmel's* Philosophy of Money. Berkeley and Los Angeles: University of California Press.

Polanyi, Karl. [1944] 1957. *The Great Transformation*. Boston: Beacon Hill.

———. [1957] 1971. "The Economy as Instituted Process." Pp. 243–69 in *Trade and Market in the Early Empires*, ed. Karl Polanyi, Conrad Arensberg, and Harry Pearson. Chicago: Henry Regnery.

———. 1977. *The Livelihood of Man*. New York: Academic Press.

———. [1947] 1982. "Our Obsolete Market Mentality." Pp. 59–77 in *Primitive, Archaic, and Modern Economies: Essays of Karl Polanyi*, ed. George Dalton. Boston: Beacon.

Polanyi, Karl, Conrad Arensberg, and Harry Pearson, eds. [1957] 1971. *Trade and Market in the Early Empires*. Chicago: Henry Regnery.

Powell, Walter, and Paul DiMaggio, eds. 1991. *The New Institutionalism in Organizational Analysis*. Chicago: University of Chicago Press.

Powell, Walter, and Laurel Smith-Doerr. 1994. "Networks and Economic Life." Pp. 368–402 in *The Handbook of Economic Sociology*, ed. Neil Smelser and Richard Swedberg. New York: Russell Sage Foundation; Princeton Princeton University Press.

Quirk, James. 1976. *Intermediate Microeconomics*. Palo Alto, Calif.: Science Research Associates.

Roy, William. 1990. "Functional and Historical Logic in Explaining the Rise of the American Industrial Corporation." *Comparative Social Research* 12:19–44.

———. 1997. *Socializing Capital: The Rise of the Large Industrial Corporation in America*. Princeton: Princeton University Press.

Sahlins, Marshall. 1976. *Culture and Practical Reason*. Chicago: University of Chicago Press.

Saint-Simon, Henri de. 1964. *Social Organization, The Science of Man, and Other Writings*. New York: Harper and Row.

Sandmo, Agnar. 1971. "On the Theory of the Competitive Firm under Price Uncertainty." *American Economic Review* 61(1): 65–73.

Saxenian, AnnaLee. 1994. *Regional Advantage: Culture and Competition in Silicon Valley and Route 128*. Cambridge: Harvard University Press.

Scherer, F. M. 1990. *Industrial Market Structure and Industrial Performance*. 3d ed. Boston: Houghton Mifflin.

Schlicht, Ekkehart. 1998. *On Custom in the Economy*. Oxford: Clarendon Press.

Schumpeter, Joseph A. 1908. *Das Wesen und der Hauptinhalt der theoretischen Nationalökonomie*. Leipzig: Duncker and Humblot.

Schumpeter, Joseph A. 1912. *Theorie der wirtschaftlichen Entwicklung*. Leipzig: Duncker and Humblot.

Schumpeter, Joseph A. 1934. *The Theory of Economic Development*. Cambridge: Harvard University Press.

Schumpeter, Joseph A. 1954. *History of Economic Analysis*. London: Allen and Unwin.

Schumpeter, Joseph A. [1918] 1991. "The Crisis of the Tax State." Pp. 99–140 in *The Economics and Sociology of Capitalism*, by Joseph A. Schumpeter, ed. Richard Swedberg. Princeton: Princeton University Press.

Schumpeter, Joseph A. [1942] 1994. *Capitalism, Socialism, and Democracy*. London: Routledge.

Schumpeter, Joseph A. 2003. "Unternehmer [Entrepreneur]." *Annual Review of Austrian Economics* 6:235–66.

Simmel, Georg. [1908] 1955. "Competition." Pp. 57–85 in *Conflict and the Web of Group-Affiliation*. New York: Free Press.

———. [1908] 1971. "The Problem of Sociology." Pp. 23–35 in *On Individuality and Social Forms*, by Georg Simmel, ed. Donald Levine. Chicago: University of Chicago Press.

———. [1907] 1978. *The Philosophy of Money*. London: Routledge. The first edition appeared in 1900.

Simon, Herbert. 1982. *Models of Bounded Rationality*. 2 vols. Cambridge: MIT Press.

Sitton, John. 1998. "Disembodied Capitalism: Habermas' Conception of the Economy." *Sociological Forum* 13:61–83.

Smelser, Neil. 1963. *The Sociology of Economic Life*. Englewood Cliffs, N.J.: Prentice-Hall.

———. 1976. *The Sociology of Economic Life*. 2d ed. Englewood Cliffs, N.J.: Prentice-Hall.

———, ed. 1965. *Readings on Economic Sociology*. Englewood Cliffs, N.J.: Prentice-Hall.

Smelser, Neil, and Richard Swedberg, 1994. *The Handbook of Economic Sociology*. New York: Russell Sage Foundation; Princeton: Princeton University Press.

Sombart, Werner. 1902–27. *Der Moderne Kapitalismus*. 3 vols. Leipzig: Duncker und Humblot.

———. 1930. *Die Drei Nationakökonomien. Geschichte und System der Lehre von der Wirtschaft*. Leipzig: Duncker und Humblot.

———. 1935. *Das ökonomische Zeitalter.* Berlin: Buchholz und Weisswange.

Stark, David. 2000. "The Sociology of Wealth." Department of Sociology, Columbia University.

Steiner, Philippe. 1998. *Sociologie de la connaissance économique.* Paris: Presses Universitaires de France.

———. 1999. *La sociologie économique.* Paris: Éditions la Découverte.

———. 2001. "The Sociology of Economic Knowledge." *European Journal of Social Theory* 4:443–58.

———. 2004. *L'école durkheimienne et l'économie, sociologie, religion, et connaissance.* Geneva: Droz.

Stigler, George. 1961. "The Economics of Information." *Journal of Political Economy* 69:213–25.

Stinchcombe, Arthur. 1975. "Merton's Theory of Social Structure." Pp. 11–33 in *The Idea of Social Structure,* ed. Lewis Coser. New York: Harcourt Brace Jovanovich.

———. 1983. *Economic Sociology.* New York: Academic Press.

———. 1986. "Rationality and Social Structure." Pp. 1–29 in *Stratification and Organization.* Cambridge: Cambridge University Press.

Swedberg, Richard. 1987. "Economic Sociology: Past and Present." *Current Sociology* 35 (spring): 1–221.

———. 1991a. "Thematic Introduction [to Parsons' Marshall Lectures]—Guest Editor's Introduction." *Sociological Inquiry* 61(1): 2–9.

———. 1991b. *Schumpeter—a Biography.* Princeton: Princeton University Press.

———. 1998. *Max Weber and the Idea of Economic Sociology.* Princeton: Princeton University Press.

———. 2001. "Sociology and Game Theory: Contemporary and Historical Perspectives." *Theory and Society* 30:301–35.

———. 2003. *Principles of Economic Sociology.* Princeton: Princeton University Press.

Tillman, Rick. 1992. *Thorstein Veblen and His Critics, 1891–1963.* Princeton: Princeton University Press.

Tocqueville, Alexis de. [1835–40] 1945. *Democracy in America.* Trans. Henry Reeve. 2 vols. New York: Vintage Books.

——— [1856] 1955. *The Old Régime and the French Revolution.* New York: Doubleday.

Trigilia, Carlo. 2001. "Social Capital and Local Development." *European Journal of Social Theory* 4: 427–42.

———. 2002. *Economic Sociology: State, Market, and Society in Modern Capitalism.* Oxford: Blackwell.

Udehn, Lars. 2001. *Methodological Individualism: Background, History, and Meaning.* London: Routledge.

Uzzi, Brian. 1997. "Social Structure and Competition in Interfirm Networks: The Paradox of Embeddedness." *Administrative Science Quarterly* 42:35–67.

Veblen, Thorstein. [1915] 1966. *Imperial Germany and the Industrial Revolution.* Ann Arbor: University of Michigan Press.

———. [1899] 1973. *The Theory of the Leisure Class.* Boston: Houghton Mifflin.

———. [1919] 1990. *The Place of Science in Modern Civilization and Other Essays.* New Brunswick, N.J.: Transaction Publishers.

Wallerstein, Immanuel. 1974. *The Modern World System.* Vol. 1, *Capitalist Agriculture and the Origins of the European World Economy.* New York: Academic Press.

Weber, M. 2001. "Risk: Theories of Decision and Choice." Pp. 13364–68 in vol. 24 of *International Encyclopedia of the Social and Behavioral Sciences,* ed. Neil J. Smelser and Paul B. Baltes. Oxford: Elsevier.

Weber, Max. [1915] 1946a. "Religious Rejections of the World and Their Directions." Pp. 323–59 *From Max Weber,* ed. and trans. Hans Gerth and C. Wright Mills. Oxford: Oxford University Press.

———. [1915] 1946b. "The Social Psychology of the World Religions." Pp. 267–301 in *From Max Weber,* ed. Hans Gerth and C. Wright Mills. Oxford: Oxford University Press.

———. [1920] 1946c. "The Protestant Sects and the Spirit of Capitalism." Pp. 302–22 in *From Max Weber,* ed. Hans Gerth and C. Wright Mills. Oxford: Oxford University Press.

———. [1904] 1949. "'Objectivity' in Social Science and Social Policy." Pp. 49–112 in *The Methodology of the Social Sciences.* New York: Free Press.

———. [1904–5] 1958a. *The Protestant Ethic and the Spirit of Capitalism.* Trans. Talcott Parsons. New York: Charles Scribner's Sons.

———. [1920] 1958b. "Author's Introduction." Pp. 13–31 in *The Protestant Ethic and the Spirit of Capitalism.* New York: Charles Scribner's Sons.

———. 1972. "Georg Simmel as Sociologist." *Social Research* 39:155–63.

———. [1922] 1978. *Economy and Society: An Outline of Interpretive Sociology.* 2 vols. Berkeley and Los Angeles: University of California Press.

White, Harrison. 1970. *Chains of Opportunity: System Models of Mobility in Organizations.* Cambridge: Harvard University Press.

———. 1981. "Where Do Markets Come From?" *American Journal of Sociology* 87:517–47.

———. 1992. *Identity and Control: A Structural Theory of Social Action.* Princeton: Princeton University Press.

Zelizer, Viviana. 1979. *Morals and Markets: The Development of Life Insurance in the United States.* New York: Columbia University Press.

———. 1985. *Pricing the Priceless Child: The Changing Social Value of Children.* New York: Basic Books.

———. 1988. "Beyond the Polemics of the Market: Establishing a Theoretical and Empirical Agenda." *Sociological Forum* 3:614–34.

——— 1994. *The Social Meaning of Money.* New York: Basic Books.

Zuckerman, Ezra. 1999. "The Categorical Imperative: Securities Analysts and the Illegitimacy Discount." *American Journal of Sociology* 104:1398–1438.

Zukin, Sharon, and Paul DiMaggio, eds. 1990. *Structures of Capital: The Social Organization of the Economy.* Cambridge: Cambridge University Press.

2 Comparative and Historical Approaches to Economic Sociology

Frank Dobbin

INTRODUCTION

Students of economic behavior have long subscribed to the commonsense view that natural laws govern economic life. In the discipline of economics, the prevailing view is that economic behavior is determined exogenously, by a force outside of society, rather than endogenously, by forces within. Self-interest is that force, and it is exogenous to society because it is inborn—part of human nature. Self-interest guides human behavior toward the most efficient means to particular ends. If economic behavior is instinctual, the reasoning goes, we need to know little about society to predict behavior.

Sociologists have always found this approach appealing, not least because it supports the Enlightenment view that the universe is knowable—that it can be understood by science. There is something inherently attractive about cogent mathematical formulas that can explain the velocity of light, or the price people pay for coffee.

However, sociologists have always made comparisons across societies and over time, and they invariably come to the conclusion that the lion's share of economic behavior can only be explained by society itself—by context. Whether you are running a farm in Croatia or in Sicily matters quite a bit for how you will behave. We cannot predict much about how you will run a railroad in Cleveland without knowing whether the year is 1880 or 1980. Historical and comparative studies illuminate the role of society in shaping economic behavior like nothing else can.

The discipline of sociology was launched by men who sought to understand modernity. How did societies come to be organized around progress, rationality, and science, when for so long they had been organized around tradition, myth, and ritual? Sociologists grappled with this question by making comparisons across societies and over time. These comparisons were driven by the observation that

social context shapes economic behavior—that modern rational behavior is learned, not innate.

The comparative and historical method is one of sociology's comparative advantages. Sociologists more frequently use this method than do economists, and the method itself tends to highlight contextual differences in economic behavior. This difference between the disciplines emerged only gradually, for the two disciplines began as one. As economics moved toward highly stylized rational-actor models and away from comparative and historical studies, early analysts who emphasized the role of social institutions in shaping economic behavior, including Karl Marx and Max Weber, were rejected by economists and embraced by sociologists.

Marx, Weber, and Émile Durkheim sought to understand the rise of modern economic behavior by comparing precapitalist societies to capitalism. Marx explored the transition from feudalism to capitalism; Weber the capitalist impulse that arose with Protestantism; and Durkheim the rise of capitalism's division of labor. As capitalism was in its infancy, none was certain that modern industrial capitalism would take widely different forms, though Weber described a number of different forms, including booty, political, imperialist, colonial, adventure, and fiscal capitalism (1978, 164–67; see also Swedberg 1998, 47). The comparative and historical methods these men developed were designed to explain why human behavior varied over time and across contexts.

Historical analysts often build directly on the problematic that Marx, Durkheim, and Weber sketched—how did modern economic practices come about? Comparative analysts often take another tack, trying to understand the social forces that cause modern economic systems to differ so dramatically. If human nature drives the evolution of economic systems and if human nature is universal, why do economic systems take such different forms? Historical and comparative works in economic sociology point to society itself, suggesting that societies develop along different trajectories for reasons having to do with history and happenstance.

In this chapter I review historical and comparative works in economic sociology that seek to explain the substantial variation found in economic behavior across time and space. While most sociologists share the view that economic behavior patterns are driven by social processes rather than by instinct alone, they have argued that different sorts of social processes are primary. Some focus on power relations, others on institutions and social conventions, and still others on social networks and roles. Comparative and historical sociologists once treated these perspectives as alternatives, but they increasingly treat them as complementary.

Next I review the theoretical underpinnings of power, institutional, and network approaches. Then I sketch the analytic methods used by historical and comparative sociologists before turning to a review of empirical studies.

How Power, Institutions, and Networks Shape Economic Behavior

Most economic sociologists proceed inductively, looking at how economic behavior varies over time or across countries and tracing that variation to something about social context. This is quite different from the approach of most neoclassical economists, who proceed deductively from the premise that individual self-interest explains economic behavior. Studies of investment among early Protestants, management of new enterprises in China's market-oriented sector, and business strategy among Argentine wine producers have produced myriad insights about the forces that shape economic behavior. But one of three different social processes is usually at the heart of the matter, and these processes have been spelled out in power, institutional, and network theories.

Power

Power relations shape economic behavior, both directly, as when a powerful firm dictates to a weak supplier, and indirectly, as when a powerful industry group shapes regulation to its own advantage. The structural theory of power is the direct inheritor of Marx's ideas, even if not all of its practitioners would call themselves Marxists. They include Neil Fligstein (1990), William Roy (1997), Beth Mintz and Michael Schwartz (1985), Michael

Useem (1996), and Charles Perrow (2002). Their concern is with how powerful groups succeed in promoting practices and public policies that are *in their interest* as being *in the common interest*. Marx described the capitalist state as a tool of the capitalist class, which justified its existence under the guise of political liberalism. His idea was that modern states serve one group while claiming to embody principles that benefit everyone. Structural theorists of power explore the role that power plays in determining the state policies, corporate strategies, and individual behaviors that we take to be transparently rational. When a particular group succeeds in promoting its favorite public policy or business strategy—in making that approach the new convention—that group can reinforce its own power or wealth without having to exercise constant coercion.

Institutions

Social institutions—conventions and the meanings they have for people—shape economic action. Weber (1978) argued that social conventions must be understood in terms of their subjective meaning to individuals because we behave in ways that are meaningful to us—that we understand (see Swedberg 1998). Sociological institutionalists understand economic behavior to be regular and predictable not because it follows universal economic laws, but because it follows meaningful institutionalized scripts (Meyer and Rowan 1977; Scott 1995; Powell and DiMaggio 1991). The meaning underlying modern behavior patterns is highly rationalized. We know what the decision to downsize the workforce might mean—that the workforce is larger than need be, or that the stock market expects higher returns from the firm. Economic customs thus carry meaning, and economic customs often spread as fads spread. The fad of downsizing appeared on the horizon, and suddenly firms were doing it whether they needed to or not (Budros 1997). Since the time of Weber, institutionalists have also pointed to the ways in which wider social institutions—religious, educational, labor market—constrain and shape economic behavior.

Social Networks

Your social network—what sociologists used to call your peer group and role models—influences your behavior by providing concrete examples of how to behave and by enforcing sanctions for misbehavior. Network theory builds on Simmel's and Durkheim's ideas about how the individual's position in a social milieu shapes both his behavior and his underlying identity. For Durkheim, social networks shape the actions of individuals not merely in a negative sense, of undermining antisocial behavior, but in a positive sense, of establishing accepted behavior patterns. Mark Granovetter (1985) spells out the implications of the network approach in an article challenging transaction-cost economists' understanding of price gouging, in which gouging occurs when a supplier finds that she is the sole seller of a needed good. Granovetter argues that the norm against price gouging is enforced informally by members of an industry network; a seller who price gouges in times of scarcity will find that buyers turn elsewhere in times of plenty. Interpersonal networks thus enforce norms by sanctioning members who do not follow them. Development theorists find that societies with strong social networks have an advantage in development, in part because they can effectively carry out both positive and negative sanctioning.

These three camps are in the process of developing an integrated approach to historical and comparative economic sociology, as people in each camp employ ideas from the others. The camps agree on much. Economic practices—behavior patterns such as pricing strategies and firm structures—emerge in networks of actors, via the institutionalization of scripts for how to behave in order to achieve particular ends. Powerful actors try to shape the scripts that are constructed, and to shape the rules of the game that become institutionalized in public policy. The economic practices, or scripts, that emerge shape individual cognition, and determine how individuals will respond to situations in the future. In other words, economic practices emerge through distinctly social processes in which social networks and power resources play roles in the definition of certain practices as rational. Many of the studies reviewed below synthesize ideas from two or all three of these approaches.

The Comparative Method in Economic Sociology

If you begin with the assumption that "history is efficient," the (economic) world is your oyster. Economies develop in a single direction, toward some optimal form; any change is a change for the better; and any change reveals the character of natural economic laws. Present practices are by definition more efficient than past practices. Advanced societies are closer to the ideal than less advanced societies, and in consequence, the problem of modernization is just a problem of how you get

from Warsaw to New York—how Poland becomes more like the United States.

If you begin with the assumption that history is not always efficient, as historical and comparative economic sociologists do, you are left with a lot to explain. You have to explain not only why countries vary today in their economic practices, but why they have varied in so many different ways in the past. If we cannot assume that the conglomerate replaced the single-industry firm because it was more efficient, then we have to go back to the drawing board.

What kind of scientific method does this approach imply? Three points are important. First, sociologists of science suggest that we should reserve judgment about the efficiency of practices whose practitioners make efficiency claims. Second, Max Weber suggests that we should try to understand the meaning of behavior to the actor. This seems a trivial point, but the deductive method favored by many economists suggests that people's understandings of their own actions are irrelevant. Third, Émile Durkheim and John Stuart Mill counsel that we should use analytic comparisons to single out the causal factors underlying human behavior.

Economic sociologists have built on some of the ideas of sociologists of science. They reserve judgment about whether a new scientific claim, or economic practice, is superior to that which it replaced. Bloor (1976) argued that sociological explanations of science should be *causal*, in that they should analyze the origins of knowledge; *impartial* vis-à-vis the truth of scientific claims; and *symmetrical*, in that they should use the same approach to analyze both "true" and "false" knowledge claims. The idea is that scientific claims, and economic claims, emerge and are institutionalized through a social process, whether they are eventually proven "right" or "wrong."

Max Weber insisted that we seek to understand what Clifford Geertz would later call the "native's point of view." For most economists, people can behave in ways that are rational without knowing they are doing so. They can believe they are doing something for religious reasons, for instance, while behaving perfectly rationally from the perspective of economists. Weber, like Marx, believed that the consequences of an individual's actions often occurred "behind the back" of the actor—were obscure to her. But he insisted that it was important to understand the subjective meaning of behavior to the individual (Weber 1978, 4). People only follow an economic convention because of their understanding of that convention, and so to grasp why economic conventions persist, we have to grasp what they mean to people.

John Stuart Mill (1974) and Émile Durkheim ([1938] 1982) argued that the comparative method is the only valid method in the social sciences. They followed the earliest precept of the scientific method, which suggested that to establish causality one must at least show that a causal condition is present where its purported effect is found and absent where its purported effect is not found. This requires a comparison of two cases. In large-scale statistical studies, we sort out the causes of social phenomena by looking for correlation across many cases. In laboratory studies, we identify causal relations through randomization, comparing subjects exposed to a particular stimulus with those not exposed. As Smelser (1976) has pointed out, however, we seldom have such laboratory-like conditions in comparative analysis. Countries typically vary on many dimensions of relevance. Most analysts try, at the minimum, to show that a cause and its consequence coexist in one situation (one country, or one time frame) and that neither exists in another. Skocpol and Somers (1980) advise comparing countries that are alike on most dimensions. Charles Ragin (1987) advises drawing multiple countries into an analysis to try to control for possible alternative causes.

Many studies make comparisons both across countries and over time, to rule in certain explanations and rule out others. For instance, to understand the new industrial policies that the United States, Britain, and France adopted during the Great Depression, I compared industrial policies before and during the depression across the three countries, to find that in each case, the downturn caused nations to try to reverse the decline by reversing their industrial policies (Dobbin 1993). Roosevelt tried to build cartels. The depression was a common shock, and each country could be compared with its predepression self as well as with the others. All of the studies reviewed here use comparisons over time and/or space to demonstrate causality.

The Behavior of Firms and Nations

Most of the comparative studies I review address differences in the behavior of firms, national institutions, or nations. This institutional focus distinguishes economic sociology from economics, where the focus is more often on the behavior of institutions. I review studies in three groups, which vari-

ously emphasize the causal role of power, of institutions, and of networks and roles. Many of the studies could be grouped differently, because many emphasize more than one of these processes. It is a huge field, and rather than touching on every important work in a word or two, I have chosen to cover works that exemplify important approaches, while trying to avoid duplication with the other chapters in this volume. Thus I have sacrificed breadth for depth.

POWER: THE LEGACY OF MARX

Karl Marx pioneered the historical approach to economic sociology in his studies of the rise of capitalism. Marx reacted against Hegel's view that human history, including economic history, was driven by the dialectical evolution of ideas. For Hegel, ideas were translated into ways of living and of organizing the economy. Marx saw the world in quite the opposite way, believing that economic relations shape the ideas of the day.

While Marx's prophecy that communism would triumph over capitalism died with the breakup of the Soviet Union, his method and core insights are very much alive in economic sociology. His method of tracing the factors that lead to changes in economic behavior patterns over time has shaped all brands of historical economic sociology. His main insight was that it is not merely abstract ideas that drive economic history, but production processes and social relations. Like neoclassical economists, Marx argued that self-interest shapes economic behavior. But for Marx, individual self-interest leads people to try to shape the world to their advantage rather than to simply achieve the best price in every transaction, as neoclassical economic theory suggests. Marx's focus on power is reflected in a number of recent historical studies of the evolution of business practices.

Marx produced reams of material about economic life. Economic sociologists focusing on labor-management relations, such as Burawoy (1979) and Biernacki (1995), often build on his final work and magnum opus, *Das Kapital* (1994). But Marx's early writings on the transition from feudalism to capitalism have been more widely influential, including *The German Ideology* (1974), *The Eighteenth Brumaire of Louis Bonaparte* (1963), *The Communist Manifesto* (Marx and Engels [1872] 1972), and the wide-ranging notes for *Das Kapital*, *The Grundrisse* (1971).

How did changes in production alter the relative

power of the aristocracy and the bourgeoisie, giving the latter the upper hand in shaping the economy and the capacity to promote capitalism? In *The German Ideology*, Marx chronicles the history of class conflict in Europe. Under feudalism a nascent class of craftspeople and manufacturers grew by actively selling their wares and building their production capacity. They challenged the traditional political rights and privileges of feudal lords, encouraging policies that favored industry, such as free labor and free elections. As they gained resources, they gained the capacity to shape the political and economic realm to their own advantage.

Both feudalism and capitalism were designed to suit the classes that controlled the means of production—the aristocracy and the bourgeoisie, respectively—and the interesting question for Marx was how these classes managed to legitimate economic institutions that favored themselves. Marx argued that the modern state imposed capitalist rules of economic behavior on a society in which the vast majority were not capitalists, and it did so under the rhetoric of political liberalism rather than under that of capitalist domination. In so doing, modern states made capitalism itself seem natural and inevitable, and Marx did not see it as either. Recent power theorists have taken from this analysis the idea that modern states impose a particular set of rules, regulations, and institutions shaping economic life. Citizens of any state tend to see state policies that create the ground rules for economic competition as neutral and as conforming to economic laws rather than as the consequence of a series of power struggles. Modern power theorists point to the role of conflict and power in creating these ground rules, and in forming conventional business practices.

Power and Change in the Corporate Form in America

Next I review the arguments of historical sociologists about four important changes in the organization of American firms since the mid–nineteenth century. In each case, sociologists have shown that a change that others explain in terms of efficiency can be traced to power dynamics among different groups. Why did the huge manufacturing firm arise in the early textile industry, and later become dominant? Why were so many manufacturing industries consolidated in short order at the beginning of the twentieth century? Why did the diversified conglomerate become the dominant large corporate form after World War II? Why did

the conglomerate give way to the single-industry behemoth by the end of the 1990s?

In each case, a particular group (textile mill owners, Wall Street financiers, finance-trained executives, and institutional investors respectively) changed the strategies of American firms, and the structure of American industry, because they saw it as in their own interest to do so. In each case, the group institutionalized a new model of how to run a business that would soon become taken for granted, and that would be backed up by a powerful rhetoric of efficiency.

Charles Perrow: The Rise of Giant Firms

Charles Perrow (2002) traces the early rise of huge textile mills and gigantic railroads in America not to their greater efficiency but to the fact that the Constitution gave state officials little power to regulate industry. The American state, designed as the antithesis of tyrannical European states, had meager administrative capacities and was deliberately opened to influence by the very groups it might have sought to control. This invited the powerful to reshape property rights—the laws that govern trade and corporate form—to their own taste. The American business elite changed property rights to the advantage of big corporations early in the nineteenth century. Wealthy industrialists won court and legislative decisions giving big corporations all kinds of new advantages over small ones. In Europe, states protected small firms and regulated large ones. The result in textiles was that American mill owners preferred to use capital-intensive rather than labor-intensive production methods, even when returns were the same, because capital-intensive methods made them less dependent on workers—made them more powerful. In moving to capital-intensive methods, textile mills became larger and more powerful, but in the process they obliterated a vibrant alternative source of efficiency—entrepreneurialism. Efficiency arguments thus do not explain the rise of America's first big businesses.

William Roy: Financiers and the Rise of Manufacturing Oligopoly circa 1900

How did the oligopolistic manufacturing firm become the dominant model after the beginning of the twentieth century? William Roy, in *Socializing Capital: The Rise of the Large Industrial Corporation in America* (1997), argues that power was key. The initial enforcement of antitrust in 1897 had an unanticipated effect on the balance of power between small and large firms. While antitrust was designed to prevent the concentration of economic power, by preventing collusion among firms, it gave big firms an advantage over small ones. Under antitrust a group of small firms could not set prices together, but if they merged, the resulting large firm could set a single price. Roy argues that the advantage big firms had over small firms was not one of scale economies, *pace* America's preeminent business historian, Alfred Chandler (1977), who contends that firms combined around the turn of the century because it was cheaper to produce things in large numbers. Roy shows that the merger wave also swept across industries that could not have benefited from scale economies. When antitrust prevented firms from joining cartels to set prices, large firms demanded that smaller competitors sell out or face certain death in price wars. The ensuing mergers had little to do with manufacturing efficiency, and much to do with the fact that antitrust law put an end to the refuge of small firms, the cartel. The huge concentrated firm was born, then, of an unanticipated coincidence of public policy and private power.

Timothy Dowd and I (Dobbin and Dowd 2000) found that antitrust enforcement and a power play also stimulated a merger wave in railroading. By 1880, American railroads had organized themselves into cartels that forestalled destabilizing price wars. When the Supreme Court enforced antitrust law in 1897, financiers, who typically held stock in many different railroads, decried price wars and heralded amicable mergers that would sustain the value of the railroads they held. J. P. Morgan led financiers in threatening to withhold future financing from firms that engaged in price wars. Thus, powerful financiers made amicable mergers customary, and quashed price wars.

Neil Fligstein: Finance-Trained Executives and the Rise of the Diversified Conglomerate

Why did the large single-industry companies that resulted from the processes Perrow and Roy outline transform themselves into diversified conglomerates between 1950 and 1975? Neil Fligstein's *The Transformation of Corporate Control* (1990) traces competition between three different management factions for the leadership of American corporations: production, marketing, and finance managers. Fligstein's story of competing elite factions is reminiscent of Marx's arguments about struggles among French elite groups in *The Eighteenth Brumaire of Louis Bonaparte* (1963). In *The Visible Hand* (1977), Chandler had argued that management naturally became focused on finance

and on conglomeration, once they had solved the problems of marketing.

Fligstein shows instead that a power play by finance managers was at the heart of the matter. After the Celler-Kefauver amendments to antitrust in 1950, which made it more difficult for firms to expand into related businesses, finance experts sketched a new theory of the firm in which large firms should act like investors with diversified portfolios. Portfolio theory in economics reinforced the idea that firms should spread their risk and should invest profits in industries with high growth potential. Finance managers succeeded largely by force of argument—by convincing boards and investors that the diversified conglomerate was the way of the future and that they, finance managers, were uniquely qualified to pursue this model of growth. This group came to hold most CEO positions. What makes Fligstein's argument about power and propaganda compelling, in the context of Chandler's pure efficiency arguments, is that the diversification model has since given way to the core-competence model. New groups have succeeded in promoting a corporate form that looks suspiciously like the preconglomerate form.

Davis, Fligstein, and Colleagues: Institutional Investors and the Rise of the Focused Firm

Why did the diversified conglomerate firm give way to the focused firm, operating under the theory of core competence, sometime after 1975? By 1990, the pattern of corporate mergers and acquisitions had changed radically from that which Fligstein described. In 1970, big firms were buying firms in other industries to diversify their assets. General Electric bought NBC, and R. J. Reynolds bought Nabisco. By 1990, big firms were buying others in the same industry to take advantage of their own core competence—of their core managerial abilities. Now Daimler bought Chrysler. What happened? As Davis, Diekmann, and Tinsley (1994) and Fligstein and Markowitz (1993) have argued, this new model arose because institutional investors and securities analysts found the diversified conglomerate difficult to place a value on, and assigned higher values to single-industry firms. As institutional securities holdings rose, institutional investors and analysts had increasing influence over how firms behaved, through their power to determine the value of stock. At the same time, firms were compensating executives based on stock performance rather than profits, and this gave executives an incentive to cater to investors and analysts. Meanwhile the invention of the hostile takeover gave a new group—takeover specialists—the power to break up diversified firms that investors and analysts assigned low values to. The result was a change in corporate strategy, as diversified firms struggled to please the market—meaning these analysts and investors. This explanation emphasizes the power of some actors to shape the behavior of others and particularly the power to define what rational behavior is.

From the muckraking stories of the abuse of power among early railway barons and oil magnates to the stories of the accounting scandals at the dawn of the twenty-first century, most stories of power in economic relations are stories of abuse—of individuals who subvert the rules for their own purposes. Marx, Perrow, Roy, Fligstein, and Davis, by contrast, show that power shapes the rules of the game and prescriptions for how firms should behave. Power is endemic in these accounts. Powerful industries often shape their own regulations (Useem 1984), and it is often power struggles among management factions that determine what is defined as rational firm behavior. The studies of Perrow, Roy, Fligstein, and Davis also use ideas from the institutional and network camps in economic sociology. In each account, changes in public policy are important. In each account, a network of managers, institutional investors, or financiers plays a big role in defining what is rational.

Power and the Labor Process

Marx was concerned with how power operated in the modern factory, in no small part because he thought that the downfall of capitalism would come as workers recognized that power and exploitation were at the center of the factory production system. For Marx, physical coercion and the threat of dismissal gave capitalists the power to dictate to workers and prevent insurgency. Burawoy, Biernacki, Kimeldorf, and Shenhav are interested in why workers resist capitalist class power, and why they fail to resist.

Michael Burawoy: How Factory Production Absorbs Class Conflict

Burawoy's *Manufacturing Consent* (1979) is an ethnography of factory production, but it is a work of historical sociology because Burawoy compares his experiences with those of Donald Roy, who conducted a similar study in the same factory 30 years earlier. In both cases, workers were drawn into the game of increasing production by the character of the labor process. This machine shop operated on a piece rate system, and "making out" under this system was a game that workers played eagerly. What changed over this period, and what appeared to Burawoy to have dampened class conflict and undermined worker resistance and activism, was the way in which work was directed. When Roy was there, time-and-motion men walked the floor of the factory, and dissent was political in nature and was directed directly at these management surrogates. By the time Burawoy arrived, engineering studies were done by men in faraway offices, and in consequence the workers were less likely to develop politically motivated complaints against management. When the shop seemed to operate as an agent-less abstract game, the class conflict that Marx had predicted evaporated.

Richard Biernacki: The Cultural Construction of Labor

In *The Fabrication of Labor* (1995), Biernacki tries to understand why German unions developed a more Marxian critique of capitalism than did British unions, which focused on negotiating a good deal for workers rather than on changing the capitalist system. Biernacki traces these differences to different labor institutions and views of the role of labor in the production process. In Britain, textile workers were paid for their output and generally treated as independent contractors. In Germany, workers thought they were being paid for the labor itself—for each pass of the shuttle through the loom—and they were held under the close tutelage of managers. British workers thus came to see themselves as independents who contracted with capitalists, whereas German workers saw themselves as the servants of the capitalist class. Biernacki traces differences in working conditions to the timing of the rise of markets for commodities and for labor. In Britain, the market for commodities arose first, and when a free labor market emerged, workers saw themselves as producers of commodities. In Germany, the two markets arose at the same time, and workers came to view the labor market as a place to sell their labor power rather than as a place to sell the products of their labor. In Biernacki's account, the capitalist class gained power in the British case from a happenstance of history as it shaped collective understandings of the factory.

Howard Kimeldorf: When Does the Working Class Act as a Class?

In *Reds or Rackets?* (1989), Kimeldorf takes a comparative tack on what was in some ways Marx's central question: what would cause the working class to see that they are being exploited and to act as a class? Kimeldorf compares the postdepression West Coast longshoremen's union, which became radicalized, with its East Coast counterpart, which did not. On the West Coast, longshoremen had been recruited from autonomous occupations—seamen and foresters—made up of liberal northern European immigrants. On the East Coast, longshoremen had been recruited from among new, conservative Catholic, Irish, and then Italian immigrants with no tradition of independent work. Shipping was also organized more monopolistically on the West Coast, facilitating concerted labor action. For Kimeldorf, class interest resulted from a convergence of the past experience of workers and the structure of the labor market.

Yehouda Shenhav: Engineers and the Depoliticization of Management

Yehouda Shenhav's *Manufacturing Rationality: The Engineering Foundations of the Managerial Revolution* (2000) explores how between 1875 and 1925, American managers came to define their role not as the suppression of labor but as the technical coordination of workers and work processes. They did this in a quest for legitimacy, given the political activism of the working class. Engineers translated their expertise in systematization and rationalization into a management rhetoric, and in the process they won an increasing share of major management positions. They spread the word through their journals that the engineering function could be extended from the design of machines to the design and rationalization of the work process itself and that management would thus come to be based in science rather than in politics. Shenhav carries on the tradition of Marx, in *Das Kapital*, by exploring the ideological underpinnings of the labor process. By basing management in abstract engineering science, engineers made it seem less of a political enterprise to managers and workers alike.

Burawoy, Biernacki, and Kimeldorf find that in the modern factory it is not capitalists' coercive power that caused workers to reject radical unionism, but something about the organization of the factory floor, the timing of industrialization, or the origins of the working class. In all three cases, it is not power per se that shapes the economic behavior of the working class. Shenhav traces the decline of working-class activism to an active engineering movement to depoliticize management. From studies focusing on how power shapes economic behavior, we now turn to studies focusing on how social institutions shape behavior.

INSTITUTIONS: THE LEGACY OF WEBER

Marx's work inspired many of the historical studies of how power and politics shape economic behavior. Weber's work inspired many comparative studies of how social institutions, customs, and conventions determine economic behavior. In *The Protestant Ethic*, in his various studies of the world religions ([1916] 1951, [1917] 1952, [1916] 1958, 1963), and in his opus on capitalism, *Economy and Society* (1978), Weber tried to understand the actual customs of different societies, the thinking behind those customs, and the forces that lead to changes in customs. For Weber, it is the beliefs underlying customs that sustain them. Thus he argued for the importance of understanding the meaning of an action to the actor. Rationality is not in the eye of the beholder, but in the mind of the actor. Institutions are carried forward by the shared meaning they embody. Weber also argued for a broad view of the causes of economic behavior. In his comparative studies of the world religions, Weber argued that economic behavior is influenced by social institutions in different realms—law and the state, the religious system, the class system (Swedberg 1998). In those studies, a society's different institutional realms are integrated—under Hinduism as under Protestantism, these systems operate in conjunction. They reinforce one another and follow a common logic, of tradition or of progress, for instance.

Weber's work inspired studies that look beyond the focal economic interaction to understand the institutional framework within which it occurs. These studies explore the character of societal institutions, and the meanings that underlie and uphold social conventions.

National Economic Institutions

Max Weber: Protestantism, Catholicism, and the Rise of Capitalism

Max Weber was a professor of economics in Germany, but with the publication of *The Protestant Ethic and the Spirit of Capitalism* ([1905] 2002) he became one of the founders of economic sociology. Weber traces modern ("rational") capitalist customs to the rise of a particular brand of early Protestantism. By contrast to Marx, who always saw class relations behind economic conventions, Weber thought that economic customs could be shaped by class, tradition, or ideology. In this case, religious sects with a new ethic gave capitalism an unexpected boost (on Weber, see also chapter 1 by Smelser and Swedberg, and chapter 26 by Wuthnow). A decade after writing *The Protestant Ethic*, Weber began work on three thick volumes on the world religions and economies. In *The Religion of China* ([1916] 1951), *The Religion of India* ([1916] 1958), and *Ancient Judaism* ([1917] 1952) Weber traced economic systems to religious ethics and to social institutions more broadly.

Weber saw in Protestantism a religious ideology that was compatible with capitalism, and wondered why such an ethic had appeared under Protestantism alone among the world religions. Early Calvinism taught predestination, or the idea that one's destiny in the afterlife was fixed at birth. While one could not earn a place in heaven, God gave everyone an earthly calling, and for the anxious, working hard and achieving success in business might at least signal divine approval. Calvin's God also demanded self-denial and asceticism. The idea of God's calling led Protestants to devote themselves to their work, and the idea of asceticism led them to save. Some argue that Catholicism promoted the same kinds of behavior (e.g., Novak 1993), and others argue that Protestantism's main effect was to promote bureaucratization of the state (Gorski 1993), but what is novel about Weber is not so much this particular argument as his vision of how economy and society were intertwined.

In comparing the world's religions, Weber found that others were oriented to salvation but that they preached very different routes (Swedberg 1998, 138). In Protestantism salvation was signaled (if not earned) through piety, asceticism, and devotion to one's calling. In Chinese Confucianism and Indian Hinduism alike, salvation was achieved by accepting one's given station and withdrawing from the world in prayer. These religious ethics fostered traditionalism and complacency rather than activism and entrepreneurialism. Ancient Judaism discouraged rational capitalism by favoring the life of religious scholarship over that of entrepreneurialism. What Weber demonstrated in these comparative studies, and what he argued in *Economy and Society*, was that economic customs were related to wider social institutions—the law and the state, religion, class—and that to understand economic conventions one must understand their links to these other institutions.

Richard Whitley: Parsing National Business Systems

Richard Whitley's national business systems approach does for the varieties of capitalism what Max Weber did for the world religions, sketching the logic underlying each form of capitalism to grasp the meaning of conventions for actors and linking economic conventions to the wider institutional milieu. Weber had shown that different religious ideas about salvation correspond to different prescriptions for how to behave in this world. Whitley finds that different national ideas about efficiency, as institutionalized in national business systems, correspond with different prescriptions for economic behavior. Whitley finds that a number of different economic systems appear to be about equally effective. Weber did not judge the efficacy of the different roads to salvation.

Whitley begins with national economic and political institutions, which offer a particular understanding of the relationships between state and industry, buyer and supplier, finance and industry. Institutions arise for reasons of history and happenstance, but over time ancillary customs and conventions emerge that hold them in place—a process that Brian Arthur (1988) terms "lock-in." In a famous illustration, Paul David (1985) shows that while the typewriter keyboard layout was designed to slow typists to the speed of the early typewriter, once people learned the arrangement of the keys it became impossible to introduce a new arrangement of keys. Once in place, the original system was difficult to displace because typists learned it and found that it proved effective enough. Whitley and other comparativists argue that economic conventions become similarly institutionalized, as people come to take them for granted and learn how to operate with them.

Whitley (1992a) first set his sights on East Asian business systems. In Japan, the large corporation, or *kaisha*, dominates; the bank-dominated business group, the descendent of the prewar *zaibatsu*, brings together large diverse firms; the state actively promotes exports and plans industry expansion. In Korea, the family-controlled conglomerate, or *chaebol*, dominates; symbiotic relationships among conglomerate members characterize interfirm relations; and the state actively promotes the rise and expansion of huge and stable empires. In Taiwan and Hong Kong, smaller Chinese family businesses dominate; interfirm relations are relatively unstructured, with a few medium-sized family business groups (*jituanqiye*); and the state leaves firms largely to their own devices. These different systems influence all kinds of economic behavior. For instance, they influence market entry in new export sectors, with new firms sponsored by business groups in Japan; new firms sponsored by families that own small businesses in Taiwan and Hong Kong; and new firms subsidized by the central state under the auspices of existing *chaebol* in Korea. What is rational under one system—starting up a company with family backing—would be folly in another. Whitley argues that the Asian Miracle is built on at least three different systems (see Johnson 1982; Cumings 1987; Westney 1987), and in subsequent studies has found just as much diversity in European business systems (Whitley 1992b; Whitley and Kristensen 1996).

Frank Dobbin: How the Economy Came to Resemble the Polity

Weber shows that across different societies, early religious institutions shaped economic practices. In *Forging Industrial Policy: The United States, Britain, and France in the Railway Age* (1994), I show that across different societies, early political institutions shaped government industrial strategies, and industry itself. Modern industrial strategies were based on the logic of state–private sector relations. In the United States, the polity was organized around self-governing communities with a federal state in the role of umpire. Americans applied the same principles to railroading, and so the federal government became referee in a free market of self-governing enterprises. In France, the polity was organized through a strong central state designed to dominate intermediate groups that could threaten its sovereignty—theirs was a form of democracy antithetical to the American form. The French applied the principle of central coordination to railroading, with the state becoming the ultimate planner and ruler of the system of private railroads. Britain's polity produced yet a third form of democracy, based on the idea of affording maximum autonomy to the citizen. When the British considered the railroads, they could not imagine that the state would regulate markets as the American state did or plan routes as the French state did. The British state left railroaders to their own devices, and to protect them from other railroads, they created cartels that would quell cutthroat competition.

In each country, the structure of the polity had shaped the understanding of social order, and thereby shaped the ideas that emerged for organizing industry. The economy thus came to reflect the polity, with the federal state as market umpire in the United States, the central government as the guardian and planner of key industries in France, and a state committed to maximizing individual initiative in Britain.

Agency and Economic Institutions

Many neo-Weberian institutional analyses neglect interest and agency in the formation of institutions, and that is certainly true of the studies reviewed above (Swedberg 2001). Others emphasize that the agency of individuals shapes, or is shaped by, economic institutions. Hamilton and Biggart argue that in the years after World War II, political leaders in Japan, South Korea, and Taiwan chose industrial strategies that built on traditional authority systems—but they emphasize that these leaders did *choose*, and could have chosen other alternatives. Guillén shows that politicians, entrepreneurs, and managers make use of idiosyncratic industrial patterns, building strategies based on their comparative advantages and thereby reinforcing idiosyncrasies. Kiser and Schneider use agency theory to explain the particular efficiency of the Prussian tax system. Carruthers shows how early British stockholders used trading to further their political aims.

Hamilton and Biggart: Asian Business and Precapitalist Social Relations

Gary Hamilton and Nicole Biggart (1988; Orrù, Biggart, and Hamilton 1991) explain the origins of different Asian economic systems in terms of tradition and agency. They trace these systems to the actions of postwar politicians, who pursued strategies of legitimation that built on certain aspects of traditional authority structures. For Hamilton and Biggart, postwar state-industry relations arose by design, but history provided the alternatives from which designers chose.

Japan has powerful intermarket industry groups under a state that helps them to plan and coordinate. After the American occupying regime dissolved the prewar *zaibatsu*, politicians built directly on the Tokugawa and Meiji authority system, in which the shogun, or emperor, was "above politics" and provided a weak center surrounded by strong but loyal independent powers (Hamilton

and Biggart 1988, S81). The postwar Taiwanese
and South Korean states built on two different legitimating aspects of the Confucian political system. When Korea was embroiled in a civil war, the
state directed industrial growth, and presidential
cronies became leaders of huge empires. The Rhee
and Park regimes drew on the imagery of the
strong, centralized Confucian state, with weak intermediate groups. The result was large family-
dominated business groups beholden to the state.
In Taiwan, Chiang Kai-shek modeled the state on
the late imperial Confucian state's principle of fair
treatment of the population. The postwar Taiwanese state allowed private parties to pursue their
own projects. The resulting system mirrored late
imperial China, with small family-run firms that
had direct contacts with suppliers and buyers. In
each case, politicians who were determined to
build new economic institutions that would have
some legitimacy in terms of tradition deliberately
employed aspects of traditional authority structures that suited their own goals. Old political institutions shaped new economic institutions, but
only through the agency of calculating politicians.

Mauro Guillén: Constructing Advantages from National Differences

Mauro Guillén's (2001) *The Limits of Convergence* explores the very different firm and industry
strategies found in the emerging economies of Argentina, South Korea, and Spain. Guillén challenges the conventional wisdom about convergence, which is that countries will converge on one
set of "best practices" for making each and every
product. Instead, Guillén finds politicians, entrepreneurs, and managers relishing and building on
their industrial idiosyncrasies as a means to distinguish themselves and to develop unique market
niches. Far from converging, these economies
build on their perceived strengths—trying to remain different.

What is striking about these countries is that
across industries—wine making, banking, automobiles—broad public policy strategies have advantaged different sorts of industry structures and
owners. But each of these public policy strategies
has proven highly profitable under the right conditions. South Korea's ardently nationalistic and
centralized growth policies have favored huge integrated business groups over multinationals and
smaller firms. Spain's pragmatic and flexible approach to regulation has resulted in a large presence of multinationals, a wide range of smaller

domestic firms, and huge domestic firms in traditionally oligopolistic sectors. Argentina's populist
policy orientation has discouraged foreign multinational penetration in some sectors, but has promoted business groups that can provide stability
and the economic basis for wider competition.
Across these countries, parallel industries are organized quite differently. To be sure, there is more
than one effective way to organize these industries.
Once established, a particular system becomes self-
reinforcing, as individuals develop economic strategies that build up its strengths. In these cases, states
and legal institutions shape economic behavior as
Weber anticipated they would, but individuals built
on the idiosyncrasies that state policies produced.

Kiser and Schneider: Agency and Efficiency in Early Prussian Taxation

Edgar Kiser and Joachim Schneider (1995) take
a very different tack on Weber, and a very different
tack on agency. Weber had much to say about the
efficiency of the bureaucratic form, and he distilled
an ideal type of modern bureaucracy from the
nation-states of the early twentieth century. He
was interested in what made formal bureaucracy
efficient, and he argued that the early Prussian
state was particularly efficient at collecting taxes
because it was so bureaucratic. Kiser and Schneider
show that the Prussian state was an efficient tax
collector even before it became bureaucratic, and
they use agency theory to show that it was efficient
because it diverged from the bureaucratic ideal in
ways that were particularly effective given the situation. Agency theory suggests that rulers seek to
maximize tax revenues, their agents (tax collectors)
seek to maximize their own take from taxes collected, and taxpayers seek to minimize payments.
Prussia developed a system that aligned interests to
maximize the take of the ruler, by, for instance, establishing long-term conditional contracts for tax
farming that could minimize the cost of rent collection. Kiser and Schneider are part of a small
group of economic sociologists who apply rational
choice principles from agency theory.

Bruce Carruthers: How Politics Shapes Stock Trades

Bruce Carruthers's analysis of early British stock
trading exemplifies a related tradition in historical
economic sociology, by showing that politics, and
not narrow self-interest alone, drives economic behavior. Weber had argued that political institutions
often shape economic behavior. Carruthers finds

that stock trades were driven by politics as well as by price. *City of Capital: Politics and Markets in the English Financial Revolution* (1996) questions a central tenet of price theory in economics, namely that sellers choose the buyer offering the highest price. There were strong political battle lines in place in the early 1700s, and large companies exercised significant influence over political decision-making. Who controlled the East India Trading Company was of some importance, and major stockholders were aware of this. In consequence Carruthers finds that, in the case of important companies, stockholders with clear political leanings were significantly more likely to sell to members of their own political party. This did not go for professional traders so much as for private stockholders. Sellers might lose money by constraining their sales to members of their own party, but they were more likely to sell to party members nonetheless. Carruthers shows that purely political ideals can influence economic behavior, even in such seemingly pristine economic realms as stock trading.

Change in National Economic Institutions

The institutional studies reviewed up to this point echo two of Weber's points: economic institutions follow logics that are meaningful to the participants who enact them; and economic institutions are shaped by surrounding institutions, particularly political institutions. Others take up Weber's task of explaining change in economic institutions, which is exemplified in *The Protestant Ethic*. Bai Gao looks at how economic thought influenced the development of Japan's modern industrial strategy. Gao's books build on the Weberian insight that new ideals can alter economic institutions. John Campbell and colleagues look at how changes in one part of an institutional configuration led to new governance regimes in American industries. Their study builds on Weber's insight that economic institutions are integrated with surrounding institutions.

Bai Gao: The Rise of Japan's Modern Industrial Policy

In *Economic Ideology and Japanese Industrial Policy* (1997) and *Japan's Economic Dilemma* (2001), Bai Gao asks how Japan's unique industrial strategy emerged in the years after 1930. That strategy emphasized strategic planning of the economy, the restraint of competition through the

governance of markets, and the suppression of short-term profit orientation in favor of long-term orientation. The approach was influenced by economic thought from Europe: Marx's ideas about the downside of unbridled competition, Schumpeter's ideas about innovation, and Keynes's ideas about state management of economic cycles. Japanese policymakers and capitalists who favored economic stability and industry self-governance (as opposed to cutthroat competition) used these ideas to formulate Japan's unique industrial policy stance.

In *Japan's Economic Dilemma* Gao traces the consequences of this system in the 1990s. Industry self-governance had worked well when the economy was booming, but in an economic downturn firms were free to engage in cutthroat competition and to make ill-conceived investments to counter declining profits. If *Economic Ideology* supports the Weberian notion that ideas can shape economic institutions, *Japan's Economic Dilemma* supports the Weberian notion that institutions become resilient to change. Japan found it hard to change its industrial policy midstream, even when the old policy had clearly gone awry.

Campbell, Hollingsworth, and Lindberg: Changes in Industry Structure

John Campbell, Rogers Hollingsworth, and Leon Lindberg's *Governance of the American Economy* (1991) shows the diversity of industry governance structures found in the United States, and develops a Weberian approach to explaining change in governance. In studies of eight industries, contributors identify a series of different industry configurations—markets, mergers, monitoring systems, obligational networks, promotional networks, and associations. Historical change in industry governance follows a common pattern. Governance institutions tend to be stable when surrounding institutions (state regulation, economic theory, supplier institutions, the practices of consumers) are stable. But external shocks can destabilize the existing structure, whether it is a cartel or a competitive market, leading different groups to vie to define a new structure. Power is key at critical moments of change. Campbell et al. challenge the prevailing view from transaction cost economics (Williamson 1985), which suggests that firms change governance forms when it is efficient to do so. Campbell and colleagues show that poor profitability may stimulate a search for new governance mechanisms, but many other kinds of shocks can stimulate change as well. And it is typically power that determines which alternative will prevail.

National Management Institutions

Now I turn to comparative studies of internal management systems. These systems are subordinate to the broad economic systems discussed above. Weber's arguments suggest that differences in internal management systems will be related to differences in wider institutions, and this is what many studies find.

Reinhard Bendix: Social Structure and Management Ideology

Reinhard Bendix's sweeping *Work and Authority in Industry: Ideologies of Management in the Course of Industrialization* (1956) traces the roots of management practice and ideology in four settings. Why does management vary across countries? Bendix looked at countries that differed on two dimensions, early versus mature industry, and independent versus state-subordinated management. His two-by-two table includes early English industry (independent management), early czarist Russian industry (state-subordinated management), mature American industry (independent management), and mature East German industry (state-subordinated management).

Successful management practices emerged where industry was autonomous, not where it was merely mature. It was in the two settings where management was autonomous, mature America and early Britain, rather than in the two where management was mature, America and East Germany, that managers developed ideologies that co-opted workers by suggesting to them that they too could benefit from social mobility, as current managers had. In czarist Russia and Communist East Germany, where managers were not autonomous, they did not succeed in countering the idea that managers' positions were undeserved and that management was a function of state oppression. In all four settings, the legacy of old ideas about class relations, and the reality of present class-state relations, shaped management patterns. For instance, in early England, the aristocracy's power vis-à-vis the state, and its antipathy toward industry, meant that the state left capitalist enterprises alone. In czarist Russia, by contrast, the state fostered early entrepreneurial activities and held early capitalists in its grasp, just as it held agricultural aristocrats in its grasp. In the wake of the collapse of Communism, an important punch line is that where the

state subordinates entrepreneurs and industry to rule workers directly, the chances for the development of a successful managerial ideology are weak.

Like Weber, Bendix was interested in the articulation between ideas and economic practices. He found that broadly similar economic practices could attain legitimacy in one setting, but not in another, largely on the basis of how effective the ideology of management was.

Wolfgang Streeck: Industrial Relations in Developed Countries

Wolfgang Streeck's comparative studies of industrial relations systems build on Weber's insight that economic conventions are embedded in a broad set of societal institutions. *Social Institutions and Economic Performance* (1992) compares industrial relations systems across countries and links those systems to success in the global economy. For Streeck, history has produced different sorts of institutional configurations—labor markets, public employment policies, educational institutions—in each country, and these institutional configurations shape the industrial relations system. But what are the comparative advantages of different industrial relations systems? Nations with strong institutions (Germany and Japan) can make choices about how industry and training will be configured, and those choices can give them a comparative advantage over more marketized nations (Britain and the United States) where decisions are left to individuals—where the collective is the sum of individual decisions.

Germany's strong labor unions and rich educational system have allowed it to choose to produce high-value-added products that require skilled employees. Britain and the United States simply do not have the institutional capacity to make the same decision. The German and Japanese cases suggest that competitiveness in the modern economy depends on social institutions that permit countries to pursue collective goals through their industrial relations systems, educational systems, and corporations.

Geert Hofstede: Culture and Work Values

Geert Hofstede (1980) has taken the Weberian task of characterizing the work orientation of individuals to its logical conclusion, developing a scheme for understanding values in 40 different countries. His study is based on a survey of employees of a single multinational corporation with offices in 40 countries. In describing authority relations and work values across countries, he identifies four dimensions: power distance (acceptable degree of supervisory control), uncertainty avoidance (degree to which people avoid the unknown to manage stress), individualism (importance of the individual versus the group), and masculinity (relative importance of earning and achievement versus cooperation and atmosphere). Hofstede correlates cultural types with societal institutions, arguing that the psyche is shaped by those institutions. One implication is that rational action takes very different forms across contexts, depending on whether close supervision is seen as improper, whether uncertainty elicits stress, whether individuals are valued over and above the group, and whether achievement is valued over cooperation. Hofstede thus fleshes out dimensions of the work ethic that Weber describes in *The Protestant Ethic*, and like Weber he identifies societal institutions as the ultimate cause of differences.

Japanese Management Institutions

Since the postwar Japanese miracle caught the attention of economic sociologists, many have sought to bring Weber's comparisons of East and West up to date, to understand the characteristics of Japanese society and workplace that produced unparalleled growth rates after World War II.

Ronald Dore: Factory Organization in Japan and Britain

Ronald Dore's *British Factory—Japanese Factory* (1973) pioneered factory comparisons in the two hemispheres, showing dramatic differences between Britain's market-oriented management system and Japan's welfare corporatism. In Britain, Dore found high labor mobility between firms, wages set by the external market, weak employee loyalty, paltry fringe benefits, and poor integration of unions. In Japan he found low external labor mobility but an elaborate internal labor market with extensive training; wages set under the internal career system; high employee loyalty; elaborate fringe benefits; and enterprise unions that play an integral role in the workplace.

Dore rejected the idea that culture explains these differences, tracing them instead to the timing of industrialization and to the conditions under which industrialization occurred. Japan's industrial form was forged in the postwar period, with the most advanced management thinking available at the time—ideas about worker involvement and long-term incentives to orient employees' goals to the firm's goals. In addition the American occupying forces encouraged a collaborative relationship between management and labor. Britain's factory conditions were forged in a much earlier era, before modern ideas about employee motivation were developed and before the idea that union-management collaboration could be effective was popular. Dore was one of the first sociologists to argue that countries would sustain their unique organizational characteristics, and his recent work (Dore 2000) suggests that countries have converged little. William Ouchi (1981) brought the case of Japanese management practices to a much wider audience, showing that the same practices that worked well in Japan could have a positive effect on American firms.

Lincoln and Kalleberg: Comparing Work Systems in the United States and Japan

Weber suggested that the spirit of capitalism was fueled by Calvinism, but is work ethic also shaped by concrete workplace conventions? James Lincoln and Arne Kalleberg's (1985) study of some 8,000 workers in the United States and Japan suggests that work practices are important. While corporatist practices are more common in Japan, they increase worker commitment in both countries. The Japanese wage system presumes the absence of an external labor market—wages are shaped by tenure in the firm's career system. In the United States, the wage system presumes competition across firms, and thus wages reflect job characteristics, position in the hierarchy, and union representation (Kalleberg and Lincoln 1988; Lincoln et al. 1990). The received wisdom about differences between Japan and the United States was that they were cultural—that both worker commitment and employer commitment (to the worker) were part of a broader cultural system. Lincoln and Kalleberg's findings show that work practices themselves shape commitment. They build on Weber's foundation to suggest that local conventions are as important as broader cultural systems in shaping work ethic.

The Diffusion of Management Institutions

While Weber was most interested in how customs differ among societies, recent works in economic sociology have focused on the factors that facilitate diffusion across organizations or across societies (Meyer and Rowan 1977; Powell and DiMaggio 1991). How do social institutions mediate the successful diffusion of an economic convention from one society to another?

Mauro Guillén: The Spread of Management Paradigms

Mauro Guillén's *Models of Management: Work, Authority, and Organization in a Comparative Perspective* (1994) charts the spread of three important management paradigms in the United States, Britain, West Germany, and Spain. Guillén stands on Bendix's and Weber's shoulders, exploring the social structural and ideological factors that shape ideas about management. What determines the successful spread of scientific management, with its time-and-motion studies and focus on the engineering of work; the human relations school, with its emphasis on treating workers humanely; and structural analysis, with its focus on the link between technical demands and the human factor? What matters most is the institutionalization of large, bureaucratized firms that can put a new management technique into practice when they truly want to.

Religion plays an interesting role that is typically neglected. In Spain, the Catholic Church supported the human relations school for its humane treatment of workers. In Germany, Protestants supported the scientific management movement for its emphasis on individualism and self-reliance. New practices do not diffuse universally; rather, they diffuse where existing social institutions are compatible with them and where systems have the capacity to effect change. This finding supports Weber's notion that societal institutions reinforce one another when they share an "elective affinity."

Marie-Laure Djelic: Copying the American Model of Capitalism

Marie-Laure Djelic's *Exporting the American Model: The Postwar Transformation of European Business* (1998) explores why France and Germany succeeded in importing American-style capitalism after World War II and why Italy failed. What mattered most was the character of institutions, both international institutions and national political institutions. France and Germany adopted the corporate structure (rather than independent ownership), the multidivisional form (rather than the simple unitary form), and enforced price competition (rather than cartels). Support from international institutions, in the form of the Marshall Plan; from the local political system; and from the business community mattered. In the case of Italy, industry resistance to change, the emphasis of Marshall Plan administrators on infrastructure over

industry, and the disarticulation of the recovery plan worked against the American model.

Weberian comparative and historical studies share a focus on the meanings of social conventions to actors and on the articulation of different social institutions. Economic conventions are only replicated to the extent that those who enact them understand them, so understanding is key to the persistence of conventions. Diverse social institutions must reinforce economic conventions, and where they do not, conventions tend to change. These insights were not Weber's alone, but his work brought them to the forefront of economic sociology more than the work of any other single author.

NETWORKS AND ROLES: THE LEGACY OF DURKHEIM

Changes in Networks and Roles

Economic behavior is fundamentally role-oriented behavior, in the view of most economic sociologists. Whereas neoclassical economists tend to see economic behavior as driven by individual calculations, economic sociologists tend to view it as driven by norms about social roles. Émile Durkheim explored how social networks and social roles varied across different societies, and much of the comparative and historical work in economic sociology builds on his insights. The network approach in economic sociology also carries forward his insights about the role of concrete social connections in shaping economic behavior.

Émile Durkheim: The Division of Labor

Durkheim tried to understand the emergence of industrial capitalism through the concrete social networks that gave rise to an increasing division of labor. For Durkheim, social networks gave to individuals the roles and scripts they followed in economic life. Interpersonal networks varied dramatically among the societies Durkheim studied, from the totemic, tribal societies of the South Pacific to the complex industrial societies of early-twentieth-century Europe.

The division of labor, where the tasks of sustaining life were divided up, set modern societies apart. Durkheim's *The Division of Labor in Society* (1933) explores how social attachment was restructured with industrialization, as individuals developed primary attachments to their occupational or professional groups rather than simply to their local communities. In Durkheim's view, economic behavior was shaped by social role, and in modern societies role identity was formed increasingly by occupation. People identify with those in their occupations, behaving according to occupational scripts and norms. One implication is that executives, physicians, accountants, and janitors follow economic customs rather than making rational calculations about how to behave in every situation they face. Occupational conventions may be based on rational ideas, but day-to-day behavior is guided by tradition rather than by active rational choice.

Viviana Zelizer: The Changing Role of Children in Industry

How do social roles change in modern society? Viviana Zelizer (1987) shows how a network of social reformers altered the role of children under capitalism, redefining rationalized roles and changing behavior. With the advent of the custom of selling labor by the hour under early industrial capitalism, the labor of children was bought and sold just like the labor of adults. In realms ranging from factory production to life insurance to foster care to litigation, children were treated as laborers. Life insurance for children was designed to replace children's income. Foster parents favored older boys because of their earning potential. The courts awarded the parents of children killed in accidents remuneration based on the child's lost wages.

A network of social reformers sought to protect children from the industrial labor market by changing society's understanding of their role. They described childhood as a sacred category and defined children's value to parents as primarily emotional rather than economic. Their successes could be counted in institutional changes. Most forms of child labor were outlawed. Life insurance for children was transformed to provide parents with compensation for their grief over the loss of a child. Adoptive parents came to favor baby girls, who were inferior workers but superior objects of emotional attachment. The courts awarded grieving parents compensation for their emotional loss. Between 1870 and 1930, new norms about the role of children in capitalism were institutionalized. Employers themselves came to argue that children's time was better spent in schooling that would prepare them for the workforce. This change was the result of a social movement that promoted a new theory of the role of children—a new rationalization of childhood centered around education rather than labor.

Julia Adams: The Principal-Agent Problem in Dutch Colonial Networks

Like Kiser and Schneider, Julia Adams (1996) is interested in the problem of agency and revenue collection among early European states. She combines network and agency approaches, arguing with Durkheim that identity often causes individuals to conform to economic norms. But identity, in this case as honorable members of the Dutch colonial empire, was not always enough. The Dutch East India trading network brought revenues back to Holland, and in its early stages it did so quite successfully. Adams shows that this was the case largely because Dutch agents abroad had no alternative network through which to move goods and receive payments. With the growth of Britain's parallel East India trading network, Dutch agents found an alternative trading route, and many of them became free agents, acting for their own enrichment rather than for the good of their principal, the empire. The weak incentives to stick with the Dutch network were to blame. The British Empire reduced disincentives to leave the network, and its agents were less likely to defect. The structure of the social network, and its efficacy at binding individuals, were key to predicting whether agents would stick with their empires.

Networks and Economic Development

Network position also shapes the roles that different nations play in the international order. Marx recognized this, and so especially did Lenin ([1916] 1976) in his work on imperialism. Neo-Durkheimian studies (Putnam 1993) that emphasize the positive effects of strong social networks on development have come to play an important role in recent studies, and hence I discuss networks and development under the heading of Durkheim.

Immanuel Wallerstein: The World System

Immanuel Wallerstein's (1976–80) sweeping historical studies of the evolution of the world system suggest that late developers will follow a different pattern than early developers, in part because their profits will be drawn toward early developing countries rather than remaining at home. Core countries, in Wallerstein's model, will buy raw materials and agricultural goods from peripheral countries at low prices. Power, in terms of core countries' capacity to make war and control technology, keeps peripheral countries in subordinate positions. Wallerstein's studies built directly on the work of Paul Baran (1957; Baran and Sweezy 1966), who similarly contended that differences in a country's location in the global trade network would shape the pattern of development, and that power was the key factor that permitted developed nations to extract value from underdeveloped nations.

Cardoso and Faletto: Economic Dependence and Industrialization

Cardoso and Faletto's *Dependency and Development in Latin America* (1979) took on the problem of the economic dependency of underdeveloped nations on developed nations. Cardoso is best known for his stint as Brazil's president from 1994 to 2002, but he was also arguably the most important scholar of development in the 1980s. Baran (1957) had argued that development would be stalled in underdeveloped nations by the fact that developed nations extract value from them— by the fact that they pay little for raw materials— farm products, wood, oil, minerals. But Baran's argument was something of a blunt instrument.

Cardoso and Faletto refine the idea, arguing that class characteristics of developing countries shape their relations of dependency with core countries, thereby influencing industry structure. The power of different domestic elite groups is key. Cardoso and Faletto describe different patterns of local class incorporation in the international economy, representing typical phases in the evolution of dependency. At first commercial groups are involved in the transfer of raw materials. Later the urban middle classes and the industrial bourgeoisie play roles, as countries begin to trade in manufactured goods. When a country starts to substitute local products for imports, a wider range of social groups becomes involved in manufacturing. At each stage, the collaboration of local elites helps to shape the kind of relationship a dependent country will have with the core, with export platform manufacturing requiring a very different pattern of cross-national class relations than, say, mining and lumbering. Here, international cross-class networks shape the pattern of development.

Gary Gereffi: Multinational Strategy and Dependent Development

Whereas Cardoso and Faletto find that the international network shapes how export industries will be structured in developing countries, Gary Gereffi's (1983) systematic analysis of a single industry in 14 countries shows a similar pattern based on the strength of multinationals. Using J. S. Mill's comparative method, Gereffi shows that powerful multinationals producing steroids suppress the development of domestically owned competitors in all of these settings—multinational power trumps all kinds of domestic configurations. It is their market power and their willingness to bend the rules, rather than their efficiency, that keep multinationals in charge of this industry.

Gereffi and colleagues (Gereffi and Korzeniewicz 1994) have refocused comparative studies of development, turning away from the dependent nation to the production network, or the "commodity chain." They trace goods from the extraction of raw materials to the consumer. As transnational corporations made the production process truly global in many industries, commodity chains became increasingly complex, wending through many countries. Case studies of different industries reveal that transnational corporations make use of unregulated extractive industries in one location, low wages in another, and advanced manufacturing techniques in a third. They practice the concept of comparative advantage, shopping for the best wages, environmental regulations, and so on for each stage in the production process.

Peter Evans: State Strategies and Elite Networks in Development

Whereas comparative studies of developed economic systems suggest that there are many ways to skin a cat—that different configurations of state and industry can produce growth—comparative studies of developing countries typically focus on the forces that spur development. Peter Evans has focused on how networks of bureaucrats, multinationals, and local capitalists can foster development. Conventional wisdom suggests that laissez-faire state policies produce growth. In two books, one principally on Brazil (*Dependent Development* [1979]) and one comparing Brazil with South Korea and India (*Embedded Autonomy* [1995]) Evans amends this wisdom. First, he finds that in virtually all successful cases of development, the state takes an active role in the promotion of industry. Comparisons across industries in Brazil make this clear. Second, he suggests that states need to be *autonomous*—they need to have bureaucratic insulation from the military and from other societal groups—to develop successful growth strategies. Weberian norms of rationality make states effective managers of the economy. Where capitalists hold state bureaucrats in their pockets, dynamic growth rarely ensues. Third, in successful cases of development, states need to be embedded in societal networks in order to gain information on industry and to be able to influence industry. A comparison of the information technology industries in Brazil, South Korea, and India provides evidence: South Korea best exemplified embedded autonomy and had the greatest success, but in Brazil and India, segments of the sector where the state got it right saw significant successes. For successful development, bureaucratic rules must contain the power of societal groups over the state, but the state must play an active role in development, and to do so effectively, state elites must be involved in networks of entrepreneurs and financiers.

Development studies have increasingly emphasized the importance of strong social networks to the successful pursuit of economic growth. Societies without adequate "social capital" are disadvantaged compared to their peers with rich and dense networks (Woolcock 1998).

Roles and Institutions in the Transition to Capitalism

The transition to capitalism has provided a sort of natural laboratory for analyzing rapid shifts in economic practices in Eastern Europe, in the former Soviet Republics, and in China. In the short run, the plans for transition via "shock therapy" sketched by economists such as Jeffrey Sachs (1989) appeared to have failed, and this brought greater interest in sociological analyses of the transition. Followers of shock therapy believed that by destroying socialist economic forms, such as collective ownership, they would unleash the power of markets. Sociological analyses suggest that no one particular system fills the void—not American-style neoliberalism, but certainly not Japanese-style state-industry collaboration either. As Weber would predict, institutions do not change so easily. As Durkheim would suggest, social roles and social networks often explain how systems change. Here I review only a handful of studies, as the lion's share are reviewed by King and Szelényi in chapter 10.

Iván Szelényi: The Rise of a Bourgeoisie under Communism

Iván Szelényi documented the emergence of protocapitalist enterprises even before socialism fell, abruptly, in Eastern Europe in 1989. In *The Intellectuals on the Road to Class Power*, Konrád and Szelényi (1979) showed that intellectuals were becoming the ruling class under modern socialism. Yet by the late 1980s, Szelényi and colleagues (1988) found that a new bourgeois elite was rising in Hungary, contrary to all expectations. It was a farming elite, producing agricultural goods for sale in private markets. Szelényi found that the participants were typically from families that had been entrepreneurial even before the advent of Communism in Hungary. Some 40 years later the entrepreneurial inclination survived in these families, and some developed active and quite successful businesses targeting unmet demand for agricultural goods in private, unregulated, markets. Szelényi proposes an argument about the continuity of social roles at the level of the family. In Hungary, those whose families were on the path to embourgeoisement in 1944 put their ambitions on hold, but revived those ambitions as a private, secondary economy emerged that allowed them to behave as entrepreneurs.

David Stark: Path Dependence in Postsocialism

David Stark's (1992a, 1992b; Stark and Bruszt 1998) laboratory is Eastern Europe after the fall of Communism. His comparative studies of the transition to capitalism lend support to the idea that economic institutions are built on the foundation of previous institutions. Stark finds that the transition to capitalism is mediated by the economic and political institutions of Communism. Tradition matters even when nations are deliberately trying to shed the old. In the final analysis, societies with strong social networks that encourage political participation have the greatest potential for growth.

Stark's study of post-1989 privatization strategies challenges the idea of "cookbook capitalism"— the idea that one can use a single recipe to create identical capitalist systems everywhere. Countries pursuing the recipe for privatization built very different systems, based on pre-1989 institutions and assumptions (1992b). States chose either corporations or individuals to acquire stock in state-owned firms, and they distributed stock either to those who could buy it or to those who, they deemed, had a right to it. Czechoslovakia and Poland chose citizens to acquire stock, the former selling it in a voucher auction and the latter distributing it through citizen grants. East Germany and Hungary both chose corporations to acquire stock, the former selling it and the latter reorganizing enterprises that would own themselves. The form of public ownership of corporations under Communism, and the structure of elite networks, account for these differences.

Which kinds of transitions produce growth? Stark and Bruszt's *Postsocialist Pathways* (1998) shows that the structure of social ties matters more than the extent to which nations have approximated the neoliberal model of the market. Consistency in the property rights regime is a precondition to success, and consistency is a consequence of a society's network structure. Where there is a "deliberative association" of producers that generates a market that is open and participatory, policy continuity and growth ensue. The Czech Republic's consistent policies are one result, and they contrast starkly with Hungary's policy vacillations.

Victor Nee: Social Roles and Economic Incentives in the Chinese Market Transition

Victor Nee (1989, 1991, 1992, 1996) studies the ways in which policy institutions have shaped the interests of elites in the Chinese transition to capitalism, and the implications for the transition. The implicit story is that economic practices and structures persist because they produce a sort of equilibrium of interests, but that change in policy can alter interests and economic patterns. When public policy encouraged entrepreneurialism, government officials were the first out of the gate because they had the requisite knowledge and access to resources (Nee 1991). Yet when state cadres used privileges of position to build enterprises, they created a crisis of legitimacy in party socialism that further hastened the move toward capitalism (Nee 1996). Here a change in the incentives created by public policy brought about a new set of economic behaviors that fed back into the political system. Policy incentives can also shape the form of enterprises that emerge under capitalism. In "Organizational Dynamics of Market Transition" (1992) Nee shows that China's transformation did not spawn a single enterprise form, because public policy continued to support hybrid forms such as cooperatives and enterprises owned by local governments. These forms were not inherently uncompetitive when they came head-to-head with private enterprises organized on the Western model. Their competitiveness depended on whether public policy encouraged efficiency in the particular form. Nee's rich analyses point to the importance of long-standing social networks among elite cadres for the transition to capitalism.

Douglas Guthrie: American Management Practices Spread to China

Douglas Guthrie's *Dragon in a Three-Piece Suit: The Emergence of Capitalism in China* (1999)

charts changes in Chinese management practices during the 1990s, as a growing number of enterprises adopted Western management conventions. The need to reform is not what determines which enterprises move toward the Western conventions of bureaucratic wage and promotion systems, market pricing, diversification into the profitable service sector, and adoption of company law as a governance form. Two other factors determine which enterprises reform. Networks matter, and specifically links to Western ideas, through the training of managers or through joint contracts with Western firms. And enterprises that had received significant public subsidies in the past change quickly after being cut off from the public trough. Guthrie thus finds that institutional theory, with its emphasis on crises catalyzing change and its emphasis on the spread of new strategies through networks, better explains new corporate strategies in China than does efficiency theory.

Comparative and historical studies of the transition to capitalism may best exemplify the promise of economic sociology, because they tend to draw on all of its best ideas, bringing insights from the Marxist, Weberian, and Durkheimian traditions to bear.

CONCLUSION

Karl Marx, Max Weber, and Émile Durkheim observed that economic institutions and customs vary significantly across time and space. All three were intrigued by what set modernity apart—by what made modern societies different from traditional societies. Thus all three compared modern societies to traditional societies, seeking clues about what made rational economic behavior patterns emerge. Historical economic sociology was born of this search for what made modernity different. Although they arrived at very different conclusions about where modern economic customs came from—from class struggle under feudalism, from the norms of Protestantism, or from population density and the division of labor—they began with a common insight, that economic behavior must be explained by social context. Given the same set of economic options, people from different societies will make very different choices, for society conditions economic choices.

Economic sociologists have moved from the question of what produced modern economic behavior patterns to that of why people exhibit such different sorts of economic behavior across modern societies. Whereas Marx, Weber, and Durkheim could not be certain that modern societies would take as many different forms as ancient societies, time has shown that nations develop a wide range of economic behavior patterns. Not only are Japan, Taiwan, and South Korea quite different from the West, they are different from one another. And the West is not of a piece when it comes to economic institutions, customs, and behaviors. Germany, France, Britain, Sweden, the United States—in these countries we find fundamentally different labor management systems, corporate strategies, intraindustry firm relations, supplier-buyer relations, interindustry relations, and state-industry relations. Modern common sense suggests that there must be "one best way" to organize each of these domains. Comparative economic sociologists demonstrate that there are many different ways of organizing these domains—and many that appear to be about equally efficient. If these countries do not represent different steps on the stairway to heaven, or to perfect rationality, then what explains their differences?

Economic sociologists address this question in studies that are inductive and comparative. Their method is inductive because they start out with a tool-kit of theoretical ideas, but with no firm conviction that a single process shapes economic behavior. Many of the studies reviewed here are thus hard to categorize because they use insights from more than one tradition. Their method is comparative, because only through comparisons can they discern what it is about a society that produces one pattern of economic behavior or another—that produces intermarket business groups, cartels, or vertically integrated firms. The comparisons can be over time, with an eye to identifying the factors that precede changes in economic behavior, or across space, with an eye to identifying the factors that covary with different economic behavior patterns.

It is worth noting that as a group, economic sociologists do not reject the idea that efficiency plays a role in shaping economic behavior. But the empirical fact of the matter is that many different kinds of economic systems operate effectively today, and so for economic sociologists the problem is to explain this diversity. The question of what kinds of economic behavior patterns are actually extinguished by their inefficiency is an important one, but it is remarkable how many different behavior patterns are not extinguished, or have not yet been.

For well over a century, economic sociologists have undertaken these inductive and comparative studies, and they have identified three broad mechanisms that shape economic behavior. First, power shapes economic institutions and conventions. Marx found that the emerging bourgeoisie under late feudalism used their newfound economic resources to move public policy in their direction, so that policy favored capitalist activities. The modern state professes neutrality in matters economic, but Marx found that it pursues policies that favor particular groups in the name of the collective good. Under democratic regimes, the powerful often win the right to establish the rules by which firms play, but the state and corporations depict those rules as oriented to efficiency and progress rather than as oriented to the interests of particular groups. By analogy, Fligstein shows that as finance-trained managers sought to win control of American corporations, they did so with the claim that their particular form of expertise was uniquely well suited to the problems of modern firms. And Roy shows that the legal rules that made the corporation the most profitable governance structure were backed by a particular group of capitalists, who succeeded in convincing society at large that limited liability and kindred legal forms were good not only for the owners of corporations but for society. Power often influences the evolution of economic institutions and customs, and what makes power effective is the capacity to frame its exercise as an exercise in pursuing the good of the nation or firm.

Second, existing economic institutions and customs shape the new institutions and customs that emerge. This happens in part because existing institutions provide models of how the world should be organized and resources for organizing new fields of activity in the way that old fields were organized. Historical studies find dramatic shifts in economic behavior and institutions over time, but they also find that countries build on past experience. Hamilton and Biggart trace the modern industrial strategies of Japan, South Korea, and Taiwan not to postwar innovations in industrial policy, but to the strategic use of traditional forms of state–private sector relations. Cardoso and Faletto find that the pattern of export-sector development in emerging markets depends on the character of preexisting class relations. And I find that the logics of state-society relations in the preindustrial polities of the United States, Britain, and France informed later state-industry relations.

Finally, networks are the conduits through which new economic customs diffuse, and through which power is exercised. Social networks take very different forms, and concrete networks determine what is possible in economic life and what is not. Thus as Davis and colleagues have shown, a network of institutional investors changed the rules of the corporate game sometime after 1970, making it difficult for diversified firms to maintain high stock prices and thereby encouraging their breakup. For Nee, the network of state cadres (officials) shaped the transition to capitalism in China by jumping into the fray as entrepreneurs. For Gao, the close ties between state officials and corporations in Japan, and the resulting absence of formal controls over corporate activity, played a role in the economic collapse of the 1990s. Networks also define social roles for their members, and many studies have shown that individuals follow social norms unthinkingly in economic life rather than making rational calculations at every crossroad they meet.

Comparative and historical economic sociologists may emphasize one process or another when they are trying to explain new business practices or public coordination of industry, but increasingly they find all three of these processes at work (Fligstein 2001). Once a national economic institution or a business practice is put into place, and becomes taken for granted as the most efficient way to organize a particular domain, some kind of shock is usually required to displace it. The shock typically sets off a contest among different groups, with different ideas about what the new policy or practice should look like. At this point power comes into the equation, as groups try to use rhetoric and resources to ensure that their favored solution is adopted. Networks often provide the conduits through which new practices are tested out, and through which the word is spread. As powerful agents use their networks to try to convince others of the efficacy of the economic policy or business practice they favor, a new policy or practice becomes institutionalized, often eliminating competitors in the process. Thus begins a new cycle, in which taken-for-granted policies and practices are eventually undermined by challenges, and in which groups vie to define what will replace them.

NOTE

Thanks to Richard Swedberg, Neil Smelser, Joseph Manning, Bruce Carruthers, and Fred Block for comments and suggestions.

REFERENCES

Adams, Julia. 1996. "Principals and Agents, Colonialists and Company Men: The Decay of Colonial Control in the Dutch East Indies." *American Sociological Review* 61:12–28.

Arthur, W. Brian. 1988. "Self-Reinforcing Mechanisms in Economics." Pp. 9–33 in *The Economy as an Evolving Complex System*, ed. Philip W. Anderson, Kenneth J. Arrow, and David Pines. New York: Wiley.

Baran, Paul A. 1957. *The Political Economy of Growth*. New York: Monthly Review Press.

Baran, Paul A., and Paul M. Sweezy. 1966. *Monopoly Capital*. New York: Modern Reader.

Bendix, Reinhard. 1956. *Work and Authority in Industry: Ideologies of Management in the Course of Industrialization*. New York: John Wiley and Sons.

Biernacki, Richard. 1995. *The Fabrication of Labor: Germany and Britain, 1640–1914*. Berkeley and Los Angeles: University of California Press.

Bloor, David. 1976. *Knowledge and Social Imagery*. London: Routledge.

Budros, Art. 1997. "The New Capitalism and Organizational Rationality: The Adoption of Downsizing Programs, 1979–1994." *Social Forces* 76:229–49.

Burawoy, Michael. 1979. *Manufacturing Consent: Changes in the Labor Process under Monopoly Capitalism*. Chicago: University of Chicago Press.

Campbell, John L., J. Rogers Hollingsworth, and Leon N. Lindberg, eds. 1991. *Governance of the American Economy*. Cambridge: Cambridge University Press.

Cardoso, Fernando Henrique, and Enzo Faletto. 1979. *Dependency and Development in Latin America*. Berkeley and Los Angeles: University of California Press.

Carruthers, Bruce. 1996. *City of Capital: Politics and Markets in the English Financial Revolution*. Princeton: Princeton University Press.

Chandler, Alfred D., Jr. 1977. *The Visible Hand: The Managerial Revolution in American Business*. Cambridge: Harvard University Press.

Cumings, Bruce. 1987. "The Origins and Development of the Northeast Asian Political Economy: Industrial Sectors, Product Cycles, and Political Consequences." Pp. 44–83 in *The Political Economy of the New Asian Industrialism*, ed. Frederick C. Deyo. Ithaca, N.Y.: Cornell University Press.

David, Paul. 1985. "Clio and the Economics of QUERTY." *American Economic Review* 75:332–37.

Davis, Gerald F., Kristina A. Diekmann, and Catherine H. Tinsley. 1994. "The Decline and Fall of the Conglomerate Firm in the 1980s: The Deinstitutionalization of an Organizational Form." *American Sociological Review* 59:547–70.

Djelic, Marie-Laure. 1998. *Exporting the American Model: The Postwar Transformation of European Business*. Oxford: Oxford University Press.

Dobbin, Frank. 1993. "The Social Construction of the Great Depression: Industrial Policy during the 1930s in the United States, Britain, and France." *Theory and Society* 22:1–56.

———. 1994. *Forging Industrial Policy: The United States, Britain, and France in the Railway Age*. Cambridge: Cambridge University Press.

Dobbin, Frank, and Timothy Dowd. 2000. "The Market

That Antitrust Built: Public Policy, Private Coercion, and Railroad Acquisitions, 1825–1922." *American Sociological Review* 65:635–57.

Dore, Ronald. 1973. *British Factory—Japanese Factory*. Berkeley and Los Angeles: University of California Press.

———. 2000. *Stock Market Capitalism: Welfare Capitalism—Japan and Germany versus the Anglo-Saxons*. Oxford: Oxford University Press.

Durkheim, Émile. 1933. *The Division of Labor in Society*. Trans. George Simpson. New York: Free Press.

———. [1938] 1982. *The Rules of Sociological Method*. Trans. W. D. Halls. New York: Free Press.

Evans, Peter. 1979. *Dependent Development: The Alliance of Multinational, State, and Local Capital in Brazil*. Princeton: Princeton University Press.

———. 1995. *Embedded Autonomy: States and Industrial Transformation*. Princeton: Princeton University Press.

Fligstein, Neil. 1990. *The Transformation of Corporate Control*. Cambridge: Harvard University Press.

———. 2001. *The Architecture of Markets: The Economic Sociology of Twenty-first-Century Capitalist Societies*. Princeton: Princeton University Press.

Fligstein, Neil, and Linda Markowitz. 1993. "Financial Reorganization of American Corporations in the 1980s." Pp. 185–206 in *Sociology and the Public Agenda*, ed. William Julius Wilson. Beverly Hills, Calif.: Sage.

Gao, Bai. 1997. *Economic Ideology and Japanese Industrial Policy: Developmentalism between 1931 and 1965*. Cambridge: Cambridge University Press.

———. 2001. *Japan's Economic Dilemma: The Institutional Origins of Prosperity and Stagnation*. Cambridge: Cambridge University Press.

Gereffi, Gary. 1983. *The Pharmaceutical Industry and Dependency in the Third World*. Princeton: Princeton University Press.

Gereffi, Gary, and Miguel Korzeniewicz, eds. 1994. *Commodity Chains and Global Capitalism*. New York: Praeger.

Gorski, Philip S. 1993. "The Protestant Ethic Revisited—Disciplinary Revolution and State Formation in Holland and Prussia." *American Journal of Sociology* 99:265–316.

Granovetter, Mark. 1985. "Economic Action and Social Structure: The Problem of Embeddedness." *American Journal of Sociology* 91:481–510.

Guillén, Mauro F. 1994. *Models of Management: Work, Authority, and Organization in a Comparative Perspective*. Chicago: University of Chicago Press.

———. 2001. *The Limits of Convergence: Globalization and Organizational Change in Argentina, South Korea, and Spain*. Princeton: Princeton University Press.

Guthrie, Douglas. 1999. *Dragon in a Three-Piece Suit: The Emergence of Capitalism in China*. Princeton: Princeton University Press.

Hamilton, Gary G., and Nicole Woolsey Biggart. 1988. "Market, Culture, and Authority: A Comparative Analysis of Management and Organization in the Far East." *American Journal of Sociology* 94: S52–S94.

Hofstede, Geert. 1980. *Culture's Consequences: International Differences in Work Values*. Beverly Hills, Calif.: Sage.

Johnson, Chalmers. 1982. *MITI and the Japanese Miracle: The Growth of Industrial Policy, 1925–1975*. Stanford, Calif.: Stanford University Press.

Kalleberg, Arne L., and James R. Lincoln. 1988. "The Structure of Earnings Inequality in the United States and Japan." *American Journal of Sociology* 94:S121–S153.

Kimeldorf, Howard. 1989. *Reds or Rackets: The Making of Radical and Conservative Unions on the Waterfront*. Berkeley and Los Angeles: University of California Press.

Kiser, Edgar, and Joachim Schneider. 1995. "Bureaucracy and Efficiency: An Analysis of Taxation in Early Modern Prussia." *American Sociological Review* 59: 187–204.

Konrád, George, and Ivan Szelényi. 1979. *The Intellectuals on the Road to Class Power*. Brighton: Harvester Press.

Lenin, V. I. [1916] 1976. "Imperialism, the Highest Stage of Capitalism." Pp. 169–263 in *Selected Writings*. New York: International Publishers.

Lincoln, James R., and Arne L. Kalleberg. 1985. "Work Organization and Workforce Commitment: A Study of Plants and Employees in the U.S. and Japan." *American Sociological Review* 50:738–60.

Lincoln, James R., and Arne Kalleberg, with Mitsuyo Hanada and Kerry McBride. 1990. *Culture, Control, and Commitment: A Study of Work Organization and Work Attitudes in the United States and Japan*. Cambridge: Cambridge University Press.

Marx, Karl. 1994. *Das Kapital*. 3 vols. New York: International Publishers.

——— 1963. *The Eighteenth Brumaire of Louis Bonaparte*. New York: International Publishers.

——— 1971. *The Grundrisse*. Ed. and trans. David McLellan. New York: Harper and Row.

———. 1974. *The German Ideology*. New York: International Publishers.

Marx, Karl, and Friedrich Engels. [1872] 1972. "Manifesto of the Communist Party." Pp. 331–62 in *The Marx-Engels Reader*, ed. Robert C. Tucker. New York: W. W. Norton.

Meyer, John W., and Brian Rowan. 1977. "Institutionalized Organizations: Formal Structure as Myth and Ceremony." *American Journal of Sociology* 83: 340–63.

Mill, John Stuart. [1888] 1974. *A System of Logic*. Ed. J. M. Robson. Toronto: University of Toronto Press.

Mintz, Beth, and Michael Schwartz. 1985. *The Power Structure of American Business*. Chicago: University of Chicago Press.

Nee, Victor. 1989. "A Theory of Market Transition: From Redistribution to Markets in State Socialism." *American Sociological Review* 54:663–81.

———. 1991. "Social Inequalities in Reforming State

Socialism: Between Redistribution and Markets in China." *American Sociological Review* 56:267–82.

———. 1992. "Organizational Dynamics of Market Transition: Hybrid Forms, Property Rights, and Mixed Economy in China." *Administrative Science Quarterly* 37:1–27.

———. 1996. "The Emergence of a Market Society: Changing Mechanisms of Stratification in China." *American Journal of Sociology* 101:908–49.

Novak, Michael, ed. 1993. *The Catholic Ethic and the Spirit of Capitalism*. New York: Free Press.

Orrù, Marco, Nicole Woolsey Biggart, and Gary G. Hamilton. 1991. "Organizational Isomorphism in East Asia." Pp. 361–89 in *The New Institutionalism in Organizational Analysis*, ed. Walter Powell and Paul DiMaggio. Chicago: University of Chicago Press.

Ouchi, William G. 1981. *Theory Z: How American Business Can Meet the Japanese Challenge*. Reading, Mass.: Addison-Wesley.

Perrow, Charles. 1992. "Organizational Theorists in a Society of Organizations." *International Sociology* 3:371–80.

———. 2002. *Organizing America: Wealth, Power, and the Origins of Corporate Capitalism*. Princeton: Princeton University Press.

Powell, Walter W., and Paul J. DiMaggio, eds. 1991. *The New Institutionalism in Organizational Analysis*. Chicago: University of Chicago Press.

Putnam, Robert D. 1993. *Making Democracy Work: Civic Traditions in Modern Italy*. Princeton: Princeton University Press.

Ragin, Charles. 1987. *The Comparative Method: Moving Beyond Qualitative and Quantitative Strategies*. Berkeley and Los Angeles: University of California Press.

Roy, William G. 1997. *Socializing Capital: The Rise of the Large Industrial Corporation in America*. Princeton: Princeton University Press.

Sachs, Jeffrey. 1989. "My Plan for Poland." *International Economy* 3: 24–29.

Scott, W. Richard. 1995. *Institutions and Organizations*. Thousand Oaks, Calif.: Sage.

Shenhav, Yehouda. 2000. *Manufacturing Rationality: The Engineering Foundations of the Managerial Revolution*. Oxford: Oxford University Press.

Skocpol, Theda, and Margaret Somers. 1980. "The Uses of Comparative History in Macrosocial Inquiry." *Comparative Studies in Society and History* 22:174–97.

Smelser, Neil. 1976. *Comparative Method in the Social Sciences*. Englewood Cliffs, N.J.: Prentice-Hall.

Stark, David. 1992a. "From System Identity to Organizational Diversity: Analyzing Social Change in Eastern Europe." *Contemporary Sociology* 21:299–304.

———. 1992b. "Path Dependence and Privatization Strategies in East Central Europe." *East European Politics and Societies* 6:17–51.

Stark, David, and Laszlo Bruszt. 1998. *Postsocialist Path-* *ways: Transforming Politics and Property in East Central Europe*. Cambridge: Cambridge University Press.

Streeck, Wolfgang. 1992. *Social Institutions and Economic Performance: Studies of Industrial Relations in Advanced Capitalist Economies*. Newbury Park, Calif.: Sage.

Swedberg, Richard. 1998. *Max Weber and the Idea of Economic Sociology*. Princeton: Princeton University Press.

———. 2001. "Max Weber's Vision of Economic Sociology." Pp. 77–95 in *The Sociology of Economic Life*. Boulder, Colo.: Westview.

Szelényi, Iván. 1983. *Urban Inequalities under State Socialism*. Oxford: Oxford University Press.

Szelényi, Iván, with Robert Manchin, Pál Juhász, Bálint Magyar, and Bill Martin. 1988. *Socialist Entrepreneurs: Embourgeoisement in Rural Hungary*. Madison: University of Wisconsin Press.

Useem, Michael. 1984. *The Inner Circle*. Oxford: Oxford University Press.

———. 1996. *Investor Capitalism: How Money Managers Are Changing the Face of Corporate America*. New York: Basic Books.

Wallerstein, Immanuel. 1976–80. *The Modern World-System*. Vols. 1–2. New York: Academic.

Weber, Max. [1916] 1951. *The Religion of China: Confucianism and Taoism*. Glencoe, Ill.: Free Press.

———. [1917] 1952. *Ancient Judiasm*. Glencoe, Ill.: Free Press.

———. [1916] 1958. *The Religion of India: The Sociology of Hinduism and Buddhism*. Glencoe, Ill.: Free Press.

———. 1963. *The Sociology of Religion*. Trans. Ephriam Fischolff. Boston: Beacon.

———. 1978. *Economy and Society*. 2 vols. Ed. Guenther Roth and Claus Wittich. Berkeley and Los Angeles: University of California Press.

———. [1905] 2002. *The Protestant Ethic and the Spirit of Capitalism*. Trans. Stephen Kalberg. Los Angeles: Roxbury.

Westney, Eleanor. 1987. *Imitation and Innovation: The Transfer of Western Organizational Forms to Meiji Japan*. Cambridge: Harvard University Press.

Whitley, Richard. 1992a. *Business Systems in East Asia: Firms, Markets, and Societies*. London: Sage.

———, ed. 1992b. *European Business Systems: Firms and Markets in Their National Contexts*. London: Sage.

Whitley, Richard, and Peer Hull Kristensen, eds. 1996. *The Changing European Firm: Limits to Convergence*. New York: Routledge.

Williamson, Oliver E. 1985. *The Economic Institutions of Capitalism*. New York: Free Press.

Woolcock, Michael. 1998. "Social Capital and Economic Development: Toward a Theoretical Synthesis and Policy Framework." *Theory and Society* 27:151–208.

Zelizer, Viviana A. 1987. *Pricing the Priceless Child: The Changing Social Value of Children*. New York: Basic.

3 The New Institutionalisms in Economics and Sociology

Victor Nee

THE FOCUS on institutions as a foundational concept in the social sciences has given rise to a variety of new institutionalist approaches. Not since the behavioral revolution of the 1950s has there been so much interest in a cross-disciplinary concept, one that offers a common theme for exchange and debate. The writings of Ronald Coase, Douglass North, and Oliver Williamson on the endogenous emergence and evolution of economic institutions have inspired a broadly based movement in economics. In sociology, neoinstitutionalists—principally John Meyer, Richard Scott, Paul DiMaggio, and Walter Powell—have redirected the study of organizations by analyzing how institutional environment and cultural beliefs shape their behavior. In a parallel shift of analytic attention, economic sociologists—Peter Evans, Neil Fligstein, Richard Swedberg, and myself—argue for a new focus to explain how institutions interact with social networks and norms to shape and direct economic action. The common starting point of these approaches is the claim that institutions matter and that understanding institutions and institutional change is a core agenda for the social sciences.

This chapter does not seek comprehensiveness in its coverage of the new institutionalisms in the social sciences.[1] Instead I focus selectively on the new institutionalisms in economics and sociology as a means to lay out core features of a new institutional economic sociology, which brings back into the research agenda a crucial focus on explaining the workings of shared beliefs, norms, and institutions in economic life. My aim is to integrate a focus on social relations *and* institutions into a modern sociological approach to the study of economic behavior by highlighting the mechanisms that regulate the manner in which formal elements of institutional structures in combination with informal social organization of networks and norms facilitate, motivate, and govern economic action.[2] Thus both distal and proximate causal mechanisms are addressed and incorporated into a comparative institutional analysis of economic life. This entails revisiting Weber's ([1904–5] 2002; [1922] 1968) view that rationality is motivated and guided by systems of shared beliefs (religious and cultural), custom, norms, and institutions. A conceptual framework underscoring such context-bound rationality serves as the foundation for examining the emergence, persistence, and transformation of institutional structures.

NEW INSTITUTIONAL ECONOMICS

In the view of new economic institutionalists, the old institutionalism offered penetrating and insightful descriptions of economic institutions (Veblen 1909 [1899], 1934; Mitchell 1937; Commons 1934, 1957), but ultimately failed in the bid to shape the direction of modern economics. Instead, it remained a dissident movement within economics, which, Coase (1984, 230) quipped, produced a "mass of descriptive material waiting for a theory, or a fire." With the limitations of the old economic institutionalism in mind, he noted that 'what distinguishes the modern institutional economists is not that they speak about institutions . . . but that they use standard economic theory to analyze the working of these institutions and to discover the part they plan in the operations of the economy." Kenneth Arrow (1987, 734) offers a similar assessment in his answer to his rhetorical question, "Why did the older institutionalist school fail so miserably, though it contained such able analysts as Thorstein Veblen, J. R. Commons, and W. C. Mitchell?" The new institutional economics has been influential, he thinks, not because it offers "new answers to the traditional questions of economics—resource allocation and the degree of utilization," but because it uses economic theory to answer "new questions, why economic institutions emerged the way they did and not otherwise."

Without question new economic institutionalists

have sought to differentiate themselves from the old institutional economics by adapting, rather than rejecting, as did the earlier institutionalists, neoclassical economic theory. First, Coase's theory of transaction cost corrected an important omission in neoclassical economics, and shows that Pigou was wrong in arguing that taxation and regulation are the only effective way to deal with negative externalities.[3] His use of transaction cost reasoning is not essentially different from Stigler's adding information costs to correct neoclassical theory. Second, the idea that human agency is "intendedly rational, but limitedly so" (Simon 1957, xxiv) can be incorporated into a "thick" view of rational choice as context-bound; as Posner (1993, 80) points out, "rationality is not omniscience."[4] Third, through concepts like "asset specificity" and "opportunism," Williamson extended microeconomic reasoning to understudied topics in economics such as vertical integration, corporate governance, and long-term contracts to show that transaction cost economizing can generate predictions about the organizational boundaries and governance structures of firms competing for survival and profit in a competitive environment. Fourth, North's account of institutional change views organizations as rational actors in pursuing marginal gains stemming from changes in relative prices.

The differences between the old and new institutionalisms may have been overstated, however (Rutherford 1994).[5] The old economic institutionalists were not as lacking in theory as Coase's quip suggests. Veblen's concept of cumulative causation is consistent with modern ideas about explanation and path dependence. Mitchell (1927), who founded the National Bureau of Economic Research (NBER), was not a dust-bowl empiricist, but espoused the idea of research driven by middle-range theory. Both old and new economic institutionalisms argue that the mathematical formalism of neoclassical economics has contributed little to understanding real-world economic behavior. Both espouse a realist orientation, which, as Coase (1984, 230) writes, seeks to study economic behavior "within the constraints imposed by real institutions."[6]

Figure 1 provides a schematic view of the causal model posited by the new institutional economics, as adapted by Williamson (1994, 80) from Richard Scott. In this model, the institutional environment is shaped by the rules of the game (see North 1981). The downward arrow indicates that if shifts in the broad parameters of the institutional

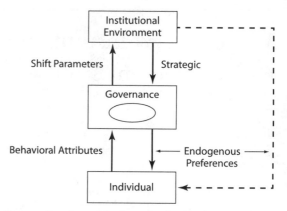

FIGURE 1.   A model of new institutional economics

environment—property rights, legal change, and norms—result in altering the relative prices for firms, this induces changes in governance structures or efforts by the firm to lobby government. The model includes a purposive actor whose behavioral attributes—"self-interest seeking with guile"—lie behind many of the transaction costs that governance structures are designed to address.

The Place of Transaction Cost Reasoning

The core concept of the new institutional economics is transaction cost—the cost of negotiating, securing, and completing transactions in a market economy. In Coase's (1988, 15) view, neoclassical economics "is incapable of handling many of the problems to which it purports to give answers" because it assumes a world of zero transaction cost in which institutions are superfluous to economic analysis:

> In order to carry out a market transaction it is necessary to discover who it is that one wishes to deal with, to inform people that one wishes to deal and on what terms, to conduct negotiations leading up to a bargain, to draw up the contract, to undertake the inspection needed to make sure that the terms of the contract are being observed, and so on. These operations are often extremely costly, sufficiently costly at any rate to prevent many transactions that would be carried out in a world in which the pricing system worked without cost. (Coase 1960, 15)

Hence in contrast to the world of zero transaction costs assumed in neoclassical economics, transaction cost reasoning provides a method enabling economists to "study the world that exists."

In "The Nature of the Firm" (1937) Coase applied transaction cost reasoning to explain the endogenous existence of the firm in a competitive market economy. If market transactions were costless, Coase argued, then there would not be sufficient motivation for entrepreneurs to operate firms. But, in fact, all solutions to the problem of measuring the performance of agents and enforcing contracts are costly. Information asymmetry and uncertainty are found in all institutional environments; hence the same agency problems found in markets also apply to the firm. The distinguishing characteristic of the firm is the suspension of the price mechanism. The entrepreneur has the power and authority within the limits set by the employment contract to direct workers from one part of the firm to another. Thus "firms will emerge to organize what would otherwise be market transactions whenever their costs are less than the costs of carrying out the transactions through the market" (1988, 7). In other words, the reason for the firm's existence is that the "operation of a market costs something," and the firm saves on this cost.

The new institutional economics includes a diverse group of economists with important differences and ongoing debates.[7] I focus here on three distinctive approaches—pioneered by Williamson, North, and Greif—that are of interest to a new institutional economic sociology. The unifying theme of all three is the proposition that social institutions matter to economic actors because they shape the structure of incentives.

Williamson builds on Coase's insight that information asymmetry and uncertainty make credible commitment to agreements difficult to secure, integrating this insight with other literatures.[8] His synthesis emphasizes that corporate governance is principally concerned with addressing the problem of opportunism and reducing the risk of malfeasance in agents' performance.[9] By examining the comparative costs of planning, adapting, and monitoring agents' performance, Williamson derives testable predictions about alternative governance structures. His prediction turns on three types of asset specificity—site, physical, and human—that firms encounter. Because firms compete in Darwinian-like selection in markets to survive and remain profitable (Hayek 1945), they are under continuous pressure to adapt by economizing on transaction costs. Hence, where asset specificity is greater, principals and agents "will make special efforts to design" a governance structure with "good continuity properties" to reinforce incentives for credible commitments to agreements. By contrast, if "assets are nonspecific, markets enjoy

advantages in both production cost and governance cost respects" Williamson (1981, 558).[10] Williamson's contribution has been to build a theory-driven research program in which core hypotheses derived from Coase have been empirically verified.

A second research program stimulated by Coase's seminal essays emphasizes the importance of property rights in shaping the incentive structure (Cheung 1970, 1974; North and Thomas 1973; Alchian and Demsetz 1973; North 1981). Cheung showed that in a neoclassical world of zero transaction costs, private property rights can be dropped without negating the Coase theorem, an insight that North extended to develop a new institutionalist property rights approach to explain economic performance. Because transaction costs make up a significant part of the cost of production and exchange, North reasoned that alternative institutional arrangements can make the difference between economic growth, stagnation, or decline. The first of the new institutionalists to explicitly disavow the efficiency assumption of the functionalist theory of institutions (Schotter 1981), North asserts that because incentives are structured in institutional arrangements, perverse incentives abound and give rise to property rights that discourage innovation and private entrepreneurship. It is frequently profitable and more rewarding for political actors to devise institutions that redistribute wealth, which can dampen incentives for innovation and private enterprise.

North's approach is state-centered in that it focuses analytic attention on the role of the state in devising the underlying structure of property rights in society.[11] In his view, the central task in explaining economic growth is to specify the events and conditions that provide incentives for political actors to establish formal institutional arrangements supporting efficient property rights.[12] In the rise of the West, this entailed the dilution of state control over resources and the emergence of some form of political pluralism.[13]

Conceived as "humanly devised constraints that structure political, economic and social interactions," institutions in North's view (1991, 97) consist of formal rules like constitutions, laws, and property rights and also informal elements such as "sanctions, taboos, customs, traditions and codes of conduct." Although he was among the first to point to the informal elements of institutions, North has consistently emphasized the "fundamental rules of the game" or the basic ground rules provided by constitutions and law. These are the rules that govern political actors and shape the structure of property rights that define and specify the rules for competition and cooperation in markets. The importance of formal rules is amplified in modern market economies, where, North argues, the growth of long-distance trade, specialization, and division of labor contributes to agency problems and contract negotiation and enforcement problems. Though interpersonal ties, social norms, and sanctions such as ostracism are very important elements of institutional arrangements, they are not sufficient in themselves to enforce credible commitments to agreements, because "in the absence of effective impersonal contracting the gains from defections are great enough to forestall the development of complex exchange" in modern economies (North 1991, 100).

North's theory of institutional change applies standard marginalist theory in its emphasis on changing relative prices. His economic history of the rise of the West showed that institutional change "comes from a change in the relative bargaining power of rulers versus constituents (or rulers versus rulers), and, broadly speaking, changes arise because of major, persistent changes in relative prices" (1984, 260). Changes in relative prices are in turn often driven by demographic change, change in the stock of knowledge, and change in military technology. The dynamics of institutional change in North's theory stem from a continuous interaction between institutions and organizations within the context of competition over scarce resources. Because institutions are self-reinforcing, vested interests in the existing stock of institutions reinforce path dependence in efforts to revise the rules. Institutional innovations will come from states rather than constituents because states generally do not have a free-rider problem (except sometimes in international affairs), whereas individuals and organizational actors are limited in their capacity to implement large-scale changes due to the problem of free riding.[14] Entrepreneurs are the agents of change, and organizations are the players who respond to changes in relative prices, which include changes in the ratio of factor prices, changes in the cost of information, and changes in technology. Organizations are agents of change when they lobby the state to initiate institutional innovations that enable economic actors to survive and profit from changes in relative price.[15]

Critical of North's approach, Greif (forthcoming) argues that its focus on formal rules and state power does not illuminate why economic actors follow some rules but not others. Although North acknowledges the role of ideology, cultural beliefs, norms, and conventions, Greif contends that his approach to institutional analysis does not provide an appropriate framework to study how actors are endogenously motivated to follow rules not enforced by the state. North relegates beliefs and norms to a black box of informal constraints, and is unable to show how informal rules and their enforcement combine with formal rules to enable, motivate, and guide economic behavior. Greif's own approach, applying game theory to examine how cultural beliefs shape the principal-agent relationship, giving rise to and sustaining distinct economic institutions, is discussed below, in the section on the sociological turn in new institutional economics.

A COUNTERPERSPECTIVE FROM ECONOMIC SOCIOLOGY

In his influential article "Economic Action and Social Structure" (1985) Granovetter points out that "Actors do not behave or decide as atoms outside a social context, nor do they adhere slavishly to a script written for them by the particular intersection of social categories that they happen to occupy. Their attempts at purposive action are instead embedded in concrete, ongoing systems of social relations" (487). He proffers the view that "social relations, rather than institutional arrangements or generalized morality [e.g. shared beliefs and norms], are mainly responsible for the production of trust in economic life" (491). He criticizes Williamson's use of transaction cost reasoning in explaining the boundaries of firms for what he views as unrealistic assumptions of under- and oversocialized conceptions of human action, "both hav[ing] in common a conception of action and decision carried out by atomized actors" (485). Williamson's "state of nature" view of markets, Granovetter contends, is devoid of reference to the history of concrete relationships and network structures, failing to take into account "the extent to which concrete personal relations and the obligations inherent in them discourage malfeasance, quite apart from institutional arrangements" (489). Williamson's Hobbesian conception of hierarchical authority is also on shaky ground, given the extent to which congealed social networks in firms structure power relations; hence, "Williamson vastly overestimates the efficacy of hierarchical power ('fiat,' in his terminology) within organizations" (499).

Granovetter thus contributed the seminal theme of *embeddedness* to the revitalization of the sociological study of economic life. Asserting that even when economics tries to take into account social factors, its conception of human action remains deeply flawed, since both the under- and over-socialized versions commonly found in economic analysis assume atomized actors, Granovetter's argument tended to frame this revitalization of economic sociology in terms of a disciplinary-based competition with economics. In contrast to transaction cost economics' emphasis on hierarchies in solving the problem of trust, economic sociologists guided by the embeddedness approach "pay careful and systematic attention to the actual patterns of personal relations by which economic transactions are carried out" (504). The focus on concrete interpersonal ties is likely to show "that both order *and* disorder, honesty *and* malfeasance have more to do with structures of such relations than they do with organizational form" (502–3). Interpersonal ties play a crucial role in both markets and firms in securing trust and serving as a conduit for useful information.[16]

We must note, however, that interpersonal ties entail costs, whether in avoiding and resolving conflict, or in the accumulation of obligations. Indeed, social relations can be very costly when conflict, disorder, opportunism, and malfeasance erupt in networks. Transaction cost analysis suggests that entrepreneurs will take such costs into account in considering alternative forms of economic organization, including network-based quasi firms. Despite the contrast in focus, the transaction cost and the embeddedness approaches appear to agree that firms generally prefer social contexts where negotiating agreements is less problematic and costly. In essence, the embeddedness approach differs from transaction cost economics in its emphasis on informal solutions to address the problem of trust, as opposed to formal institutional arrangements. Not surprisingly therefore, Williamson's (1994, 85) response to Granovetter's essay was, "Transaction cost economics and embeddedness reasoning are evidently complementary in many respects."

While Granovetter's embeddedness approach laid the basis for the revitalization of the sociological study of economic life, his sole emphasis on the nature of interpersonal ties and the structure of networks contributed to a narrowing of the scope of economic sociology from the broader institutional canvas pioneered by its founders. The causal imagery of the embeddedness approach, positing variation in the underlying structure of concrete social relationships to explain the workings of markets and firms, relies on a conceptual framework that limits economic sociology's explanatory power to proximate causes.[17] Moreover, the approach requires the construction of a taxonomy of structural contexts as a necessary step to become sufficiently abstract to generate a powerful analytical framework.[18] By contrast, the classical sources of economic sociology in the writings of Weber, Schumpeter, and Polanyi outlined analytical approaches that pointed to a broad institutional canvas of distal and deeper causal forces.

Another limitation is the absence of a clear specification of mechanisms that explain why economic actors sometimes decouple from ongoing networks to pursue economic interests. If, as Granovetter asserts, a dense network of personal ties does more than institutional arrangements to secure trust and useful information crucial for complex transactions, then why do economic actors routinely decouple from interpersonal ties to transact in market exchanges? A defining feature of an advanced twenty-first-century market economy as an institutional order is its capacity to enable economic agents to switch virtually seamlessly between transactions within close-knit networks and with strangers. In sum, the social relations rather than institutions orientation of this embeddedness approach introduced an element of indeterminacy in the new economic sociology, especially in the context of a global market economy where the volume of cross-national transactions has increased through innovations in information technology enabling complex transactions between strangers (Kuwabara, forthcoming).

THE SOCIOLOGICAL TURN IN NEW INSTITUTIONAL ECONOMICS

Central among sociology's concerns from its origins as a social science has been the goal of explaining institutions, as exemplified in Max Weber's and Émile Durkheim's seminal works on the subject. It is not surprising, therefore, that there has been something of a "sociological turn" in economics, motivated by difficulties in explaining institutions and institutional change within the framework of economic theory (Furubotn and Richter 1993). If a sociological turn is in progress, how is it manifested in the recent work of new institutional economists? To what extent has economic sociology influenced their thinking?

In his article "The New Institutional Economics: Taking Stock, Looking Ahead," Williamson (2000, 595) confesses that "we are still very ignorant about institutions" despite the progress made over the past quarter-century. "Chief among the causes of ignorance is that institutions are very complex. . . . pluralism is what holds promise for overcoming our ignorance." Williamson's multi-level causal model of the economy outlines "four levels of social analysis" in which the higher level imposes constraints on the lower level. "The top level," he writes, "is the social embeddedness level. This is where the norms, customs, mores, traditions, etc. are located. . . . North poses the query, 'What is it about informal constraints that gives them such a pervasive influence upon the long-run character of economies?' (1991, 111). North does not have an answer to that perplexing question, nor do I." This embeddedness level influences the lower three levels: level 2, institutional environment; level 3, governance; level 4, resource allocation and employment.[19] Hence it is important to identify and explicate "the mechanisms through which informal institutions arise and are maintained" (596). Thus the embeddedness perspective now is in the process of being incorporated into the new institutional economics. But Williamson acknowledges that though level 1 shapes the parameters of what economists study, it "is taken as given by most institutional economists."

A sociological turn is apparent in the influence of Weber, Marx, Polanyi, and Parsons on North's conception of institutions as elaborated in *Structure and Change in Economic History* (1981). More recently, in response to confronting the difficulties of implementing institutional change as an economic advisor to reformers in the transition economies of Eastern Europe, North acknowledges a greater interest in understanding the informal elements of institutions embedded in social relations. Devising new formal rules to institute market economies in Eastern Europe and the former Soviet Union has had only limited success; this has pointed to the intractable nature of social arrangements embedded in interpersonal ties, cultural beliefs, norms, and old regime institutional arrangements studied by economic sociologists.[20] Clearly, "Formal rules are an important part of the institutional framework but only a part. To work effectively they must be complemented by informal constraints (conventions, norms of behavior) that supplement them and reduce enforcement costs. If the formal rules and informal constraints are inconsistent with each other the resulting tension is going to induce political instability. But we know very little about how informal norms evolve" (North 1993, 20).

A sociological turn is further evident in new theorizing on the importance of cognitive mechanisms. Because beliefs and norms are unobservable, Greif argues, integrating social variables has been hampered by the fact that any behavior can be explained by ad hoc assertions about the beliefs and norms that motivate it. The integration of social variables in a manner consistent with economic methodology requires an analytical framework that can reconcile two seemingly contradictory views of institutions: the view of institutions common in economics as constraints created by individuals and the structural view of institutions as social facts external to the individuals common in sociology. Organizational new institutionalists focus on diffusion of rules, scripts, and models (Meyer and Rowan 1977), whereas some new institutional economists offer game theoretic models of endogenous motivation stemming from systems of shared beliefs and norms (Greif [1994] 1998).[21] Although game theory does not offer a theory of institutions, Greif argues that it does offer an appropriate analytical framework to incorporate sociological variables into economic analysis of institutions. It does not provide a theory of the constraints defining the parameters of strategic interaction, but it offers deep insights on the dynamics of choice within constraints. It provides a theory of social behavior in which actors' optimal course of behavior depends on the behavior and expected behavior (cultural beliefs and social norms) of others.[22] It also incorporates a realistic view of the social world in which information is asymmetric and actors are interdependent and motivated to act in a particular manner. It offers a method to examine how strategic interactions give rise to and sustain self-enforcing institutions. Greif ([1994] 1998) has extended its application to the comparative institutional analysis of economic behavior using cases studies drawn from medieval European and Mediterranean economic history. He models the recurrent strategic social interactions that sustain institutions in equilibrium.[23]

Overall, economists interested in studying social institutions have found that the more they come to understand the workings of institutions as endogenous to social processes in society, the more their work must address questions that lead them to turn to sociology for answers. New institutional economists apparently agree that advances in understanding institutions requires integrating sociological variables—shared beliefs, norms, and social relationships—to understand motivation to follow rules.

NEW INSTITUTIONALISM IN ECONOMIC SOCIOLOGY

In 1898 Émile Durkheim founded the *Année sociologique*, establishing modern sociology as a discipline dedicated to the comparative study of institutions. Since then, Durkheim's conception of institutions as systems of shared beliefs, norms, and collective sentiments has persisted to shape the sociological approach to their study. Max Weber similarly pioneered the interpretive study of societal institutions through his comparative analysis of cultural beliefs, economy, and polity. Reinterpreting the classics of European sociology, Talcott Parsons later synthesized the institutionalist ideas associated with Durkheim, Weber, Pareto, and Tönnies into a structural-functionalist framework for modern sociology. He too conceived of institutions as organized systems of cultural beliefs, norms, and values common to most individuals in a society, systems giving rise to socially structured interests that organize incentives for individuals. His outline of a theory of institutions adumbrated the idea of choice within institutional constraints. Parsons's *Economy and Society* (1956), coauthored with Neil Smelser, established economic sociology as a subfield in American sociology. Like Parsons, Robert K. Merton viewed institutions as structures of opportunity, shaping the interests and strategic action of individuals.

The new sociological institutionalism reformulates the earlier European and American institutionalist approaches in sociology through the lens of a different generation of American sociologists. Sociological new institutionalism has been closely identified with the perspective on organizational analysis pioneered by Meyer and Rowan (1977) and many other organizational theorists of the Stanford "legitimacy" school, and canonized in a widely used anthology, *The New Institutionalism in Organizational Analysis,* edited by Powell and DiMaggio (1991). DiMaggio and Powell (1983) introduce into neoinstitutional theory the influence of Max Weber's and Herbert Simon's ideas, evident in their treatment of how organizational fields emerge and then constrain the action of agents under conditions of uncertainty. The elements of a new institutional economic sociology I lay out below include ideas and insights from this organizational research program, which are inte-

grated into a framework of sociological research that examines context-bound rationality shaped by custom, networks, norms, cultural beliefs, and institution arrangements, as in *The New Institutionalism in Sociology,* edited by Brinton and Nee (1998). The new institutional economic sociology builds on the pioneering work of Barnard ([1938] 1964), Homans (1950), and Blau (1955), analyzing the manner in which interpersonal ties in firms and markets interact with formal institutional arrangements (Nee and Ingram 1998).

For a new institutional economic sociology to make advances in explaining the role of institutions and institutional change, it is important to have a definition of institutions appropriate for analysis from the sociological perspective that emphasizes the causal effect of social structures. Institutions are not simply the formal and informal constraints that specify the structure of incentives, as defined by North (1981), or discrete institutional elements—beliefs, norms, organizations, and communities—of a social system (Greif, forthcoming), but fundamentally they involve actors, whether individuals or organizations, who pursue real interests in concrete institutional structures. An institution in this view is defined as *a dominant system of interrelated informal and formal elements—custom, shared beliefs, conventions, norms, and rules—which actors orient their actions to when they pursue their interests.* In this view, institutions are social structures that provide a conduit for collective action by facilitating and organizing the interests of actors and enforcing principal-agent relationships. It follows from this interest-related definition that institutional change involves not simply remaking the formal rules, but fundamentally requires the realignment of interests, norms, and power.[24]

As economic sociology moves beyond the earlier perspective on embeddedness, the challenge is to specify and explicate the social mechanisms determining the relationship between the informal social organization of close-knit groups and the formal rules of institutional structures monitored and enforced by organizations and states. The new institutional economics has contributed to explaining the emergence and maintenance of formal institutional arrangements that shape economic behavior. However, as North (1993, 12) acknowledges, economics has largely "ignored the informal constraints of conventions and norms of behavior." Economists pose probing questions about the social dimensions of economic life as they encounter the limits of economic analysis of institutions (North 1991; Williamson 2000). Their questions address the manner in which informal social organization and formal rules *combine* to shape the performance of organizations and economies. With recent advances in application of game theory, economists recently have begun to incorporate informal institutional elements into their models of economic performance (Greif, forthcoming). While economic sociologists may not have all the answers, clearly in cross-disciplinary research aimed at explaining the capacity of social institutions to facilitate, motivate, and govern economic behavior, sociology's comparative advantage is to address questions that focus on the social mechanisms that shape economic behavior. As Smelser and Swedberg point out, "the concept of embeddedness remains in need of greater theoretical specification" (1994, 18).

Figure 2 provides a schematic representation of the multilevel causal model for the new institutionalism in economic sociology, which is related to, but different from, the new institutionalist models proposed by Williamson (1994). The institutional environment—the formal regulatory rules monitored and enforced by the state that govern property rights, markets, and firms—imposes constraints on firms through market mechanisms and state regulation, thus shaping the incentives structure. The *institutional mechanisms* operating at this level are distal, as opposed to the proximate network mechanisms at the micro- and meso-levels of individuals and their interpersonal ties. Institutional mechanisms encompass the deeper causes because they shape the incentive structure for organizations and individuals, and thereby the *contexts* in which proximate mechanisms operate. The institutional-level mechanisms posited by economists and sociologists, despite differences in behavioral assumptions and conceptual language, are not as far apart as is commonly perceived. New institutional economists emphasize incentives structured by the monitoring and enforcement of formal rules, a mechanism widely accepted by both political economy and sociology. The new institutionalism in economic sociology specifies the manner in which the norms of close-knit groups interact with formal rules in the realization of interests. The variety of market mechanisms schematically represented in the downward arrow from the institutional environment to the organizations includes those embedded in labor markets, capital markets, raw material markets, and so on. Surprisingly perhaps, economists generally do not focus on markets as such, but just assume their existence in the neoclassical view of perfect competition in markets

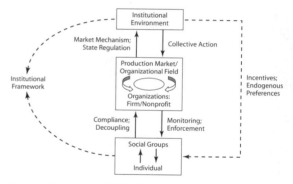

FIGURE 2. A model for the new institutionalism in economic sociology

underlying the supply-demand curve. The institutional framework encompasses formal rules of the institutional environment and informal rules embedded in ongoing social relations, which interact to shape economic behavior.

Organizations through collective action lobby for changes in the formal rules to make them in closer accord with their interests. Industry-based associations and professional lobbyists act as agents representing their interests. Groups of organizations are arrayed in an *organizational field*. The production market is a close-knit network of firms in an industrial sector arrayed in a status hierarchy of perceived quality.[25] In White's (2001) model of the production market, firms compete and maneuver for advantage and status with peer firms in a market niche. They are guided by the signals they read from the operations of their peers. In competitive markets, pressures on firms stemming from Darwinian selection processes necessitate an *interest-related* logic of strategic action, differing in emphasis from the *legitimacy-centered* orientation of nonprofit organizations—public schools, museums, day-care centers—which are dependent on state and federal government and philanthropy for resources. Legitimacy is also important for enterprises, as manifest in firms' investments in promoting brand-name recognition, reputation for reliability and quality service or product, and compliance with federal and state laws, but legitimacy-seeking is driven mainly by the firm's interest in its survival and profitability in competitive markets. For nonprofit organizations, especially, legitimacy is essential social capital, increasing the chances for optimizing access to scarce resources. In both for-profit firms and nonprofit organizations, legitimacy can be viewed as a condition of fitness that enables them to enhance their survival chances and secure advantages in economic and political markets. Processes of conformity with the rules of the game and cultural beliefs in organizational fields—*isomorphism*—motivate and guide organizations, endogenously giving rise to increasing homogeneity within an organizational field (DiMaggio and Powell 1983).[26]

The social mechanisms facilitating, motivating, and governing the action of organizations in organizational fields or production markets are not dissimilar from those influencing strategic action of individuals in close-knit groups. Mechanisms of conformity in close-knit groups have coercive, normative, and mimetic aspects (Homans [1961] 1974). Actors are motivated by interests and preferences, often formed and sustained within such groups. Rationality is context-bound and embedded in interpersonal ties. Individual interests and preferences are enfolded in "welfare-maximizing" norms, which, depending on the incentives structured in the institutional environment, reinforce compliance to formal rules through self-monitoring or give rise to decoupling arising from opposition norms (as discussed below).

Informal Institutional Elements

The bottom box of our causal model overlaps with the earlier embeddedness concept, which argues that the *nature* and *structure* of social relationships have more to do with governing economic behavior than do institutional arrangements and organizational form. Specifically, Granovetter (1985, 490) refers to the "role of concrete personal relations and structures (or 'networks') of such relations in generating trust and discouraging malfeasance," which he attributes to the human preference for transacting with individuals known to be trustworthy and for abstention from opportunism. But what explains motivation for trustworthiness and abstention from opportunism in ongoing social relationships? Why is trustworthiness found more commonly in ongoing social relationships than in transactions between strangers?

The answer is found in specifying the *mechanisms* intrinsic to social relationships that develop and maintain cooperative behavior within close-knit groups, enabling actors to engage in collective action to achieve group ends. These mechanisms are rewards and punishment in social exchange and their use in the *enforcement* of social norms—shared beliefs and statements about expected behavior.[27] Social exchange theorists have explicated the mechanisms involved, empirically in Blau's (1955) classic study of social exchange and net-

works in a federal bureaucracy, *The Dynamics of Bureaucracy,* and theoretically in the network exchange literature pioneered by Homans ([1961] 1974), Emerson (1962), and Blau (1964). Numerous studies in natural settings and in laboratory experiments confirm the efficacy of social rewards and punishment in facilitating, motivating, and governing trustworthy behavior and abstention from opportunism with respect to the norms of the group.[28] Enforcement of norms within close-knit groups occurs spontaneously in the course of social interaction among members through the exchange of social rewards (i.e., esteem and status) for behavior that conforms to the group's norms, and punishment (i.e., disapproval and ostracism) for violating them. As Homans ([1961] 1974, 76) perspicaciously points out: "The great bulk of controls over social behavior are not external but built into the relationship themselves." Frequency of interaction, a characteristic feature of close-knit networks, lowers the cost of monitoring members of the group, assuming they are in close enough contact with one another that information about members' conduct is common knowledge. Axelrod (1984) effectively simulated the operation of network mechanisms in his tit-for-tat model, showing that reward and punishment in repeated exchanges—when actors take into account the weight of the future, as in ongoing relationships—motivate cooperative behavior. In sum, trustworthiness and reliability as forms of cooperative behavior arise from rational action responding to social rewards and punishment in networks or close-knit groups.

In his detailed account of the interactions in the work group he studied made up of a supervisor, 16 agents, and one clerk, Blau (1955) provides a rare illustration of how self-interested action of individuals endogenously produces the informal social organization of a close-knit work group. In the work group Blau studied, agents consulted fellow agents about the appropriate legal rules that applied to their case, rather than bring their questions to the attention of the supervisor who evaluated their work. Blau observed that the informal interactions between agents involved a *social exchange* similar in logic to a decentralized market exchange:

A consultation can be considered an exchange of values; both participants gain something, and both have to pay a price. The questioning agent is enabled to perform better than he could otherwise have done, without exposing his difficulties to the supervisor. By asking for advice, he implicitly pays his respect to the superior proficiency of his colleague. This acknowledgement of inferiority is the cost of receiving assistance. The consultant gains prestige, in return for which he is willing to devote some time to the consultation and permit it to disrupt his own work. The following remark of an agent illustrates this: "I like giving advice. It's flattering, I suppose, if you feel that the others come to you for advice." (Quoted in Homans 1974, 343)

Blau found that the more competent the agent, the more contacts she had with other agents, and the higher the esteem in which she was held. A few agents who were perceived as competent but who discouraged others from consulting them were disliked and had fewer contacts. These findings highlight the importance of social rewards and sanctions (e.g., esteem and disapproval) in the normative regulation of informal social organization. Routine social exchanges, such as the one described by Blau, comprise the informal social organization that emerges and sustains the performance of formal organizations (Nee and Ingram 1998).

Norms are the informal rules that facilitate, motivate, and govern joint action of members of close-knit groups. They arise from the problem-solving activity of individuals as rule-of-thumb guidelines for expected behavior. Throughout history, norms have coordinated group action to improve the chances for success—the attainment of rewards—through cooperation. As statements of shared beliefs about expected behavior, norms evolved together with language, as in the norms uttered by early hunting parties to coordinate action during the course of the expedition. Norms probably evolved through trial and error, with success the arbiter of why a particular norm persists in equilibrium across generations and diffuses to different groups.[29] Members of close-knit groups cooperate in enforcing norms because not only their interests are linked to the group's success, but their identity as well (White 1992).

The Relationship between Informal and Formal Institutional Elements

In uncovering the social norms of Shasta County, a sparsely settled rural county of northern California, where local ranchers and suburbanites maintain ongoing multiplex relationships, Ellickson "was struck that they seemed consistently utilitarian"; from which he inferred that "members of a close-knit group develop and maintain norms whose content serves to maximize the aggregate welfare that members obtain in their workaday affairs with one another" (1991, 167).[30] Norms coordinating individuals' activities, as in the convention of arriving in a timely fashion at an agreed-upon social engagement, are not difficult to explain since it is easy to show that self-interested individuals share a common interest in complying with this convention. But the prisoner's dilemma norm is more difficult to explain since self-interested individuals derive a greater payoff for opportunism in a prisoner's dilemma game. What makes this game so interesting is that this type of dilemma is such a common feature of social and economic life. It is the prisoner's dilemma aspects of human interaction that give rise to opportunism in contractual agreements and in ongoing social relationships. To a degree, all social exchange resembles the prisoner's dilemma game insofar as there is always a temptation not to reciprocate a good turn provided by a friend or acquaintance (Hardin 1988). The prisoner's dilemma norm involves higher costs of monitoring and enforcement than coordination norms because it is always in the self-interest of individuals to free ride or defect. Hence, prisoner's dilemma norms must be welfare-maximizing in terms of the Kaldor-Hicks criterion in order to create sufficient rewards to individuals to overcome the temptation to do so (Ellickson 1991, 171; Posner 1986, 11–15).[31]

The nature of the relationship between informal social groups and formal organizations can substantially affect the cost of monitoring and enforcement of formal rules in institutional and organizational environments. The norms of close-knit groups can contribute to the realization of the organization's goal if the interests embedded in welfare-maximizing norms are, broadly speaking, congruous with the incentives embedded in the formal rules. This condition is met when members of close-knit groups or networks perceive that their preferences and interests are aligned with the organization's capacity to survive and profit. It is strengthened when members of networks identify with the organization's goals. This gives rise to endogenous motivation in networks to enforce formal rules, which substantially lowers the cost for organizations to monitor and enforce through formal sanctioning mechanisms, providing the necessary and sufficient conditions for high-level group performance in line with formal organizational goals. However, close coupling between informal and formal rules does not necessarily give rise to efficiency and high organizational performance. Indeed, population ecologists argue that the environment selects adaptive organizational forms independent of the collective will and effort of individuals acting within the organization (Hannan and Freeman 1989). For example, many high-technology firms renowned for the high morale and commitment of management and employees to achieve corporate goals have fallen by the wayside.

In contrast, when the formal rules are at odds with the interests and identity of individuals in close-knit groups, the welfare-maximizing hypothesis predicts the rise of opposition norms that facilitate, motivate, and govern the action of individuals in those groups. Opposition norms enable networks to coordinate action to resist either passively, through slowdown or noncompliance, or actively, in manifest defiance of formal rules and the authority of organizational leaders. This leads to increase in the cost of monitoring and enforcing formal rules as the incidence of opportunism and malfeasance increases. There is also a higher level of uncertainty and information asymmetry as members of close-knit networks collectively withhold information that might lead to discovery of opportunism and malfeasance. When group performance facilitated, motivated, and governed by opposition norms reaches a tipping point, the necessary and sufficient conditions for demoralization and oppositional movements at the organizational and institutional levels are met. *The incentives and disincentives emanating from the institutional environment, in combination with interests, needs, and preferences of individuals, influence whether norms and networks give rise to a close coupling of informal and formal rules, or decoupling through opposition norms.*[32]

In the new institutional economic sociology purposive action by corporate actors and individuals (usually in close-knit networks) cannot be understood apart from the institutional framework within which incentives—including legitimacy—are structured.

Despite differences in local and regional history and culture, the laws and regulations monitored and enforced by the federal government apply to all regions of the United States, with very few exceptions. Variations in locality and region may limit the effectiveness of monitoring and enforcement, but they do not give rise to different underlying rules. Not only is the constitutional framework invariant, but federal rules aim to extend the power of the central state uniformly. As North's (1981) theory emphasizes, the state is the sovereign actor specifying the framework of rules that governs competition and cooperation in a society. The state has the power to enact and enforce laws and initiate institutional innovations to secure and uphold public goods and respond to changing relative prices (Stiglitz 1989).

Laws, like norms, are statements of expected behavior, ideas framed with moral and ethical authority backed by state power. Whether as ideology or as cultural beliefs, they define the parameters of legitimate behavior to which organizations and individuals adapt. In keeping with disciplinary traditions, economists emphasize the costs of opposing the coercive forces of the state, and organizational sociologists emphasize the value of legitimacy gained through compliance with the state's rules. But in actuality, whether the price of noncompliance is perceived as costs imposed by fines and penalties or as a loss of legitimacy is moot since both are costly to the firm.

The institutional mechanisms of monitoring and enforcement operate directly on firms and nonprofit organizations through the costs of penalties and withholding of federal grants and contracts, but also have indirect effects. The increase in costs of discrimination—loss of legitimacy and financial penalty—following institutional changes during the civil rights era decisively opened American mainstream organizations to formerly excluded ethnic and racial groups (Alba and Nee 2003). The civil rights movement and the legislative changes enacted by Congress created a normative environment in which legitimacy was conditioned on fair governance through formal protections of the principle of equality of rights (Edelman 1990, 1992). Equal employment opportunity law (EEO) defined broad parameters and guidelines of legitimate organizational practices with respect to minorities and women. Because the civil rights laws have weak enforcement features and are ambiguously stated, organizations construct the meaning of compliance "in a manner that is minimally disruptive of the status quo" (Edelman 1992, 1535). This enables organizations to gain legitimacy and hence resources through the appearance of abiding by civil rights legislation. However, "once in place, EEO/AA [affirmative action] structures may produce or bolster internal constituencies that help to institutionalize EEO/AA goals" (1569). The civil rights laws may have their largest impact indirectly through professionals who generate "ideologies of rationality" or cultural beliefs about how organizations should respond to the law. Not only do high-profile landmark court cases (e.g., Texaco, Coca-Cola)[33] impose direct costs through penalties and loss of legitimacy to specific firms, but a more far-reaching effect of these court decisions, along with legal advice about what organizations can do to insulate themselves from costly litigation, is to generate cultural beliefs about the rationality of self-monitored compliance with antidiscriminatory laws. This is manifested in the diffusion of EEO-specified grievance procedures in organizations (Edelman, Uggen, and Erlanger 1999). Thus ideologies of rationality and cultural beliefs have combined with the incentives and disincentives of the institutional environment, mediated by state regulation and market mechanism. This is consistent with the causal model in figure 2, suggesting that mechanisms of isomorphism align with the structure of incentives stemming from formal rules of the institutional environment.[34]

ILLUSTRATIVE STUDIES IN NEW INSTITUTIONAL ECONOMIC SOCIOLOGY

The causal model in the new institutional economic sociology integrates a micro-foundation based on an account of the rational pursuit of interests, influenced by social relations and norms, with the idea that each economy has an institutional framework. As figure 2 indicates, causal mechanisms operate in both directions, from macro to micro and micro to macro levels of analysis. The multilevel causal model moves beyond the earlier embeddedness perspective toward a social relations *and* institutions approach to explanation of the emergence, persistence, and transformation of economic institutions and behavior. As a conceptual framework, the new institutionalism in economic sociology offers an open architecture for generating theories at the middle range extending the sociological approach to understanding economic behavior. The central challenge in new institutional economic sociology is to specify and explicate the nature of the relationships between elements at different levels of the multilevel causal model to explain how informal social organizations interact with large institutional structures. Here are four illustrations of such use of a multilevel causal model.

Weberian Model of Economic Growth

Evans and Rauch (1999) specify a three-level causal model to examine the effect of Weberian state structures on economic growth in developing economies. They argue that the characteristic feature of the institutional framework of the develop-

ment state, as opposed to the predatory state, is the presence of relatively well developed bureaucratic forms of public administration. As Weber argued in his theory of bureaucracy, the introduction of merit-based recruitment offering predictable career ladders established the basis for long-term commitments to bureaucratic service. Whether in the Meiji bureaucracy in Japan or in late-developing industrial economies like China, the development of modern bureaucratic capacity at the service of reform politicians was critical to government's ability to monitor and enforce rules oriented toward promoting economic development. At the level of individual action, close-knit groups of elite bureaucrats share norms and goals shaped by meritocratic rules for recruitment and promotion, which reduces the attractiveness of corruption. This Weberian model provides an alternative to Shleifer and Vishny's (1994, 1023) "grabbing hand of the state" model that conflates bureaucrats and politicians, showing that politicians invariably "try to influence firms to pursue political objectives" inconsistent with the objective of economic growth. In the Weberian model, bureaucrats are distinct from politicians insofar as they are vested with long-term careers governed by meritocratic rules of recruitment and promotion. Norms, shared belief in meritocratic service, and national development goals not only reduce the temptation of corruption but over time give rise to competence and credibility of commitment to civil service dedicated to the public good. The result is increased organizational capacity of the state, which in turn enables and motivates reform-minded rulers to increase revenues through economic growth rather than predation.

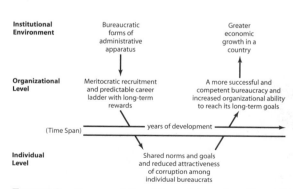

FIGURE 3.   Evans and Rauch's model on the effects of Weberian state structure on economic growth

A Dynamic Game-Theoretic Model of Deinstitutionalization

A multilevel causal model provides analytic leverage in understanding the emergence of market economies in postsocialist China, Eastern Europe, and the former Soviet Union. When Western economists traveled to Eastern Europe and the former Soviet Union to advise reformers at the onset of market reforms, their advice consistently emphasized big-bang approaches to instituting a market economy by designing sweeping changes in the formal rules governing property rights and markets. They assumed that formal rules—that is, constitution, civil law, and other regulations—instituted by administrative fiat would establish a modern capitalist economy (Sachs 1995). Such efforts at capitalism by design overlooked the realities of power and interests vested in the ruins of Communism.[35] By contrast, the incremental reform approach taken by reformers in China allowed economic actors to base their choices of institutions on trial and error that balanced speed with a credible record of success. This more evolutionary approach to market transition soon gave rise to the most dynamic economy in the world. In China, institutional change was driven not so much by top-down changes in the formal rules, but by bottom-up realignment of interests and power as new organizational forms, private property rights, and market institutions evolved in an economy shifting away from central state control over economic activity to market-driven firm performance.[36] Changes in formal rules governing the emerging market economy tended to follow *ex post* changes in the informal business practices, and were therefore more in keeping with the real interests of political and economic actors.[37] As in the former Soviet Union, however, efforts to reform state-owned enterprises through formal rule changes in China also proved largely ineffectual because, in part, *ex ante* changes in formal rules often ran counter to the vested interests and conflicting sources of legitimacy of the Communist Party organization entrenched in state-owned firms.

Nee and Lian's dynamic game theory model (1994) of declining ideological and political commitment helps to explain deinstitutionalization of the Communist Party in departures from central planning in transition economies. The technological and military gap that grew during the Cold War between the advanced market economies and state socialist countries precipitated reform efforts by Communist elites to narrow the gap through innovations

that sought to incorporate in the institutional framework of central planning increased reliance on the market mechanism. But at the individual level of party bureaucrats and officials, the growth of economic and political markets increased the payoff for opportunism and malfeasance, which in turn sparked within close-knit groups of party members a group-based social dynamic leading to declining ideological and political commitment to the Communist Party. This is demonstrated in a tipping point model wherein opportunism and malfeasance among party members, initially small, eventually reaches a critical mass. The reform leaders in the party attempt to address the problem through campaigns aimed at punishing malfeasance. Over time, however, declining commitment reaches a critical tipping point, precipitating demoralization and collapse of the Communist Party as an effective ruling organization. This in turn paves the way for deinstitutionalization of the party and far-reaching change in political institutions, including political revolution, in reforming state socialism. This game-theoretic model provides an explanation for declining organizational performance, highlighting the embedded nature of ideological commitment among party members and specifying the social dynamics that produce the tidal shift from commitment to the party's rules and goals to widespread opportunism and defection. The model links change in the incentive structure of the institutional environment—from redistribution to market—to the emergence in close-knit party networks of belief in opportunism as the expected behavior, presently, in a ruling party founded on an ideology opposed to such behavior. This sociological explanation for the rapid and relatively nonviolent collapse of Communist polities in Eastern Europe and the

FIGURE 4. Nee and Lian's dynamic model of declining political commitment in state socialism

former Soviet Union is an alternative to standard economic and political interpretations (Aslund 1995; Beissinger 2002). In China and Vietnam, where Communist parties still retain power, the model predicts a cumulative decline of ideological and organizatonal commitment to the party.

A Signaling Model of the Market Mechanism

White's (2001) theory of production markets portrays them as social structures constructed by producers in response to uncertainty arising upstream and downstream in particular market niches. When a new market niche emerges, new and established firms gear up production as they enter the market. Inevitably they must make investment and production decisions in a state of uncertainty with respect to upstream suppliers and downstream buyers. Applying Spence's (1974) signaling theory and Burt's (1992) model of rational action in networks, White argues that firms watch for cues and clues emitted by rival firms, as each firm adapts products for the market niche.

Thus the social construction of a market comprised of producers in a niche stems from the attempts by firms to interpret and use information from signals emitted by peers, as they maneuver and compete for position in the production market. Firms watch each other, and use signals from other firms to guide their choices and action. They search for their identity through the signals from competitor firms about the quality of their products or services. A firm's reputation for quality is crucial to its survival. Through mutual signaling of perceived quality, firms order themselves in a pecking order—their market profile—in the niche. In the production market firms may form strategic alliances to strengthen ties or decouple from specific ties with member firms to disengage from dependencies. The outcome over time is an institutional framework of stable industrial sectors comprised of networks of firms. White's model specifies and explicates a market mechanism arising endogenously from producers signaling each other in the production market. The identity of member firms in that market is framed by its roles and norms. White proffers a sociological view of markets as social structures in which producers act as the interface between upstream suppliers and downstream buyers—an alternative model of markets as a social institution, differing from the neoclassical economic assumption of perfect competition in markets.

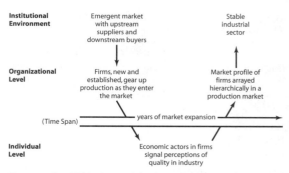

FIGURE 5.   White's model of production markets

A Study of Close Coupling between Informal Norms and Formal Organizational Goals

In a classic ethnography of shop-floor work norms and the emergence of institutionalized rules of advanced capitalism, Burawoy (1979) integrates insights from the Marxist theory of the firm with the context-bound utilitarian view of rational action of managers and employees in a large industrial firm. His organizational analysis shows that the emergence of internal labor markets and the shift of management styles to the image of an internal state grew out of the firm's strategy of adaptation to competition arising from global markets. Introducing these characteristic institutional features of advanced capitalist firms induced a rise of individualism among employees competing in internal labor markets for advancement and promotion. Self-organized activity among employees also increased. Burawoy maintains that the informal games and norms of close-knit shop-floor work groups led to norm-based consent between employees and managers supporting the goals of management. The informal employee consent in

FIGURE 6.   Burawoy's model of shop-floor work norms and monopoly capitalism

turn gave rise to the institutional environment of advanced capitalism characterized by industrial peace and high productivity.

SUMMARY COMPARISON

Overall, the new institutionalisms in economics and sociology are unified around the view that neoclassical economics is limited by its unrealistic behavioral assumption of individual utility maximization, its conception of *homo economicus*, and its unrealistic assumption of zero transaction costs, as if institutions, social relations, and cultural beliefs were superfluous to understanding economic

and organizational life. Notwithstanding this shared viewpoint, these institutionalist approaches should be viewed as distinct but related research programs with overlapping assumptions and shared concepts. Table 1 offers a summary comparison between them.

Durkheim's methodological holism has had a powerful influence on institutional theory in organizational analysis, as has its origins in studies of nonprofit organizations. This is evident in its behavioral assumption emphasizing nonrational action molded by codified and legitimated beliefs, scripts, myths, rituals, and rationalized stories. In the foundation essay by Meyer and Rowan (1977), there is little mention of the pressures imposed on

TABLE 1. The New Institutionalisms in Sociology and Economics

	New Institutionalism in Organizational Analysis	*New Institutionalist Economic Sociology*	*New Institutional Economics*
Behavioral assumption	Emphasis on nonrational action oriented to cultural beliefs constitutive of the institutional environment	Rationality is context bound; actors motivated by interests, usually shaped by shared beliefs, norms, and network ties	"Intendedly rational, but limitedly so"; information asymmetry and uncertainty give rise to hazards accruing to opportunism
Actors	Professionals serve as the agents of institutionalization	Organizations are actors; individuals articulate interests within organizations and networks	Organizations and individuals are actors
Definition of institution	Rationalized myths and routines, conformity to which confirms legitimacy	Interrelated system of institutional elements—informal and formal—facilitating, motivating, and governing social and economic action	Humanly constructed constraints—the formal and informal rules that structure incentives; discrete governance structures as contracting units
Macro-level mechanisms	State regulation, coercive and normative isomorphism	State regulation, market mechanism, collective action	States seek revenue maximization; transaction cost economizing by firms
Micro-level mechanisms	Action oriented to mimicking, conformity, and decoupling	Interest-driven action within organizations and networks	Self-interested principal/agents; calculating hazards of opportunism
Sources	Durkheim, Weber, Berger and Luckmann	Weber, Marx, Polanyi, Homans	Smith, Knight, Commons, Coase

organizations by the motive to survive and profit in competitive markets. Rather, the organization's practical action and strategy are principally motivated by concern for securing and maintaining legitimacy. Organizational neoinstitutionalists tend to reject utilitarian conceptions of purposive action to embrace what they perceive as a cultural turn in social theory. The behavioral assumption emphasizing the nonrational cultural basis of social action integrates Durkheim's conception of institutions as social molds with insights from ethnomethodology (Garfinkel 1967; Cicourel 1974; Giddens 1979) and social theorists who are leading the cultural turn in sociology (Goffman 1967; Berger and Luckmann 1967; Douglas 1986; Bourdieu [1972] 1977; Swidler 1986). Notwithstanding, DiMaggio and Powell (1983) incorporate bounded rationality in their conception of organizational actors, and hence their seminal essay provides a useful bridge linking new institutional economic sociology with organizational theory.

At the other end of the continuum, new institutional economics explicitly assumes bounded rationality: individuals intend to be utility maximizing, but are limitedly so, due to uncertainty, information asymmetry, and imperfect cognitive ability. Its basic underlying view of human agency—"self-interest seeking with guile"—is, despite Posner's (1993) remarks to the contrary, distinct from and not readily incorporated into the neoclassical view of *homo economicus,* who is wholly rational, having complete information and perfect computational skills.

New institutional economic sociology stands at the center, between the economists' assumption of bounded rationality and the cultural turn in organizational sociology. Despite differences in emphasis, its conception of organizational action is complementary with core arguments advanced by DiMaggio and Powell (1983) on interest-driven aspects of *isomorphic* adaptation by organizations to their institutional environment. Despite similarities in emphasis, it differs from economics in building on "a broader formulation of rational choice" (Granovetter 1985, 506), in which rationality is viewed as context-bound—often decisively influenced by shared beliefs and norms monitored and enforced by mechanisms arising from social interactions in close-knit networks and groups. Thus rational action in economic life is facilitated, motivated, and governed by shared beliefs, social relations, norms, and institutions—a view that is inconsistent with neoclassical economics' assumption of an atomistic, utility-maximizing *homo economicus.*

Although transaction cost economics assumes individual opportunistic actors, its unit of analysis—economic transactions—is operationalized at the organizational and institutional levels. Individual-level action is seldom a focus of analytic attention. Economists unproblematically extend their conception of individual-level action to corporate actors in a conceptual framework that views institutions as the rules of the game and organizations as the players. North's (1990) theory of institutional change turns on the assumption that organizations respond efficiently, even when gradually, as rational actors to changing relative prices, mounting collective action to pressure for changes in the formal rules of the game that enable them to adapt to the new price structure. North's theory of institutional change, however, overlooks the powerful inertial forces within organizations stemming from past investments in stable formal rules, informal social organization, and opposition norms (Stinchcombe 1965).

Organizational new institutionalists emphasize professionals as actors driven by concern for legitimacy in their relationship to particular organizational fields and to the broader institutional environment. Rules, scripts, myths, stories, and menus provide the rationalized guidelines for strategic and practical action. But as in transaction cost economics, individual-level action is implicit in neoinstitutional organizational theory, and is uncommonly a focus of empirical attention, except by reference to the role of professionals as occupational groups. Neoinstitutional theory shifts attention away from informal social structures and processes inside the organization, emphasized by old institutionalists like Barnard, Selznick, and Blau, to focus on actors at the levels of the organizational field and the institutional environment. The actors that matter are external to the organization, in professional associations and legitimacy-monitoring agencies.

In accord with the embeddedness perspective's emphasis on proximate causes embedded in networks, new institutional economic sociologists often focus on individual-level actors, whether entrepreneurs or employees. Agency and the pursuit of interests are facilitated, motivated, and governed by social relations, shared beliefs, norms, and institutions. Established organizations often appear inert, from this perspective, because they face powerful inertial forces; instead new organizational forms generate the pressures for institutional change (Ingram 1998). In this respect economic sociologists agree with organizational sociologists that rational action by organizational actors is problematic, not only because it is difficult to measure, but because unintended consequences of individual-level rational action and path dependence at the institutional level greatly complicate matters at the organizational level.

As DiMaggio and Powell (1991) point out, there are many more definitions of institutions than there are new institutionalisms in the social sciences, because scholars have been casual in defining them. Despite the profusion of definitions, there is an underlying consensus about this matter in economic and sociological new institutionalisms. Organizational new institutionalists conceive of institutions as systems of rationalized myths and routines, conformity to which confers legitimacy upon organizations. While their conceptual language may differ, the underlying theme of institutions as rule-governed social constructions is consistent with new institutionalist economics and economic sociology, which share similar definitions of institutions as dominant systems of interrelated formal and informal rules that facilitate, motivate, and govern social and economic behavior. Economic sociology differs from economics, however, in the view that institutions are not simply the formal and informal constraints that specify incentives and disincentives, as in North (1981), but fundamentally encompass socially constructed arenas in which actors identify and pursue interests. Although economists acknowledge the importance of informal social organization, their analysis emphasizes the role of the state in enforcing formal rules. Economic sociologists emphasize the norms produced and maintained in close-knit groups that comprise the informal social organization in firms. As they see it, ongoing interpersonal ties and networks are crucial to understanding the nature of the relationship between informal social organization and formal rules.

New institutionalists in economics and sociology concur that regulatory rules monitored and enforced by the state and statelike organizations frame the underlying social structure of the institutional environment. Formal rules are important in economic analysis insofar as they define the incentive structure for organizations and firms, as in the rules governing property rights. Economists emphasize the monitoring and enforcement of formal rules by the state as the crucial macro-level mechanism. They simply *assume* markets and instead focus explanatory attention on changes in the relationship between the economic and political actors (e.g., North and Weingast 1989). Organizational

analysts, in turn, highlight organizations' quest for legitimacy as the motor that drives conformity to institutionalized rules and practices through coercive, normative, and mimetic mechanisms. The mechanisms of isomorphism operate within the organizational field, promoting increasing homogeneity among organizations. New institutional economic sociology once again occupies the center, drawing on insights on the role of the state in implementing institutional innovations and on legitimacy as a motivating interest of organizations. Economic sociologists borrow insights from organizational research on the importance of isomorphism as a macro-level causal mechanism, but their focus on firms and entrepreneurs as opposed to nonprofit organizations (i.e., public schools, local government, museums, hospitals) imparts greater attention to specifying and explicating how market mechanisms and state regulation shape the way economic actors compete for survival and profits.[38]

With respect to specification of micro-level mechanisms, organizational sociologists emphasize organizational action oriented to mimicking, conformity, and decoupling. New institutional economists build on a modified version of the maximizing assumption of neoclassical economics. The integration of information asymmetry and uncertainty confers a greater level of realism on bounded rationality. New institutional economic sociology conceives of micro-level mechanisms as stemming from the interest-driven action of individuals influenced by ongoing social relations, shared beliefs, norms, and institutions.

The sources of the new institutionalisms in economics and sociology are diverse, reflecting differences in emphasis, behavioral assumptions, and core organizing concepts. Economic new institutionalists extend the Smithian classical tradition of economic reasoning through the writings of Coase, Knight, Commons, North, and Williamson, but they also borrow key insights from Weber, Marx, and Polanyi in their understanding of institutions and institutional change. In organizational analysis, institutional theorists extend Durkheim's view of institutions as "social facts" that mold social behavior and Weber's view of the importance of cultural beliefs in motivating social and economic action. New institutionalists in economic sociology extend insights from Weber's methodological individualism and pioneering work in comparative institutional analysis focusing on systems of shared beliefs, law, bureaucracy, markets, and the state; from Marx's theory of capitalist economic institutions, which anticipated the concept of transaction costs in analyzing the nature of the relationship between capitalists and workers; and from Polanyi's concept of social embeddedness and analysis of the institutional mechanisms giving rise to and maintaining modern market economies. They also draw on insights from economics, especially following the recent sociological turn in economics that has increased the areas of overlapping concerns.

CONCLUSION

Sociological analysis of the nature of the relationships between networks, norms, and large institutional structures in economic life is at an early stage. As economic sociology refines and deepens its explanation of the nature of these relationships, it will necessarily draw on a variety of methodological and theoretical tools. Insights from cognitive science, behavioral economics, game theory, and computer simulation of the emergence, diffusion, and transformation of norms and beliefs can contribute to deepening understanding of the micro-macro links (Marsh 2002). These methods can also contribute to understanding the stability of customs, conventions, norms, and beliefs.

Central to the research agenda of a new institutional approach is to bring comparative institutional analysis back into economic sociology. Much of this work to date has involved qualitative historical analysis of one or two case studies. While such work has led to advances in understanding the relationship between institutions and economic behavior, the use of quantitative methods moving beyond case studies to engage systematic cross-national firm-level studies can specify and explicate how variable features of the institutional environment affect firms' behavior in the global economy. Comparative institutional analysis of firm-centric data on sources of perceived costs in the institutional environment offers a promising approach to the measurement of transaction costs. Though transaction cost is the core theoretical concept of new institutional economics, economists have yet to measure this concept in a manner useful for empirical analysis.[39] As it refers to the costs stemming from uncertainty and information asymmetry embedded in social relations (e.g., the principal-agent relationship), it is a concept of significant interest to sociologists as well. The development of standardized indexes of transaction costs arising from a variety of institutional sources (i.e., property rights, uncertainty, transparency of rules, resource

dependence, bureaucracy, government regulation, state predation) using firm-centric data opens the way for a more differentiated account of how the institutional environment influences economic behavior.[40] Economic sociologists, for example, can fruitfully extend the ecological reasoning of organizational sociology to examine discrete patterns in institutional environments that support distinct organizational forms. For example, what features of the institutional environment—"institutional ecology"—support modern public-owned corporations as opposed to the traditional family-owned firms in the global economy?

The idea of path dependence, imported into economics from the physical sciences, has deepened social science understanding of institutional change (Nelson and Winter 1982; David 1986; Arthur 1988). Path dependence refers to the lock-in effects stemming from initial conditions on subsequent development and change in the institutional environment. Economic historians have used the idea productively to explain the stability of institutions and the persistence of institutional arrangements that may later be inefficient for economic actors, given changes in relative prices (North 1990; Greif [1994] 1998). Hamilton and Feenstra (1998, 173) show that the idea of path dependence is adumbrated in Weber's theory of economic rationalization, which maintains that "entrepreneurial strategy is necessarily embedded in an array of existing economic interactions and organizations." Further research is needed to deepen understanding of path-dependent institutional change and especially of the relationship between the persistence of informal institutional elements and change in formal rules (Nee and Cao 1999). It is the stability of informal institutional elements—customs, networks, norms, cultural beliefs—that disproportionately accounts for path dependence in institutional arrangements.

Just as economists find it useful to incorporate the idea of embeddedness in their models of the economy, so economic sociology can benefit from integrating economic ideas that are complementary to the modern sociological approach. Economic exchange is a specialized form of social exchange (Homans 1974, 68); hence the mechanisms facilitating, motivating, and governing social processes extend to economic behavior. Cross-disciplinary trade with economics has been useful to sociology in the past, as evident in the extensive borrowing from economics by the founders of modern sociology, and in the influence of imported ideas such as human capital, social capital, and path dependence. New institutional economic sociology is well positioned to benefit from, and contribute to, intellectual trade with economists, especially in light of their turn to sociology for understanding about the social dimension of economic life.

NOTES

I am very appreciative of the careful reading of an earlier draft, and excellent comments generously provided by Rachel Davis, Paul DiMaggio, Oliver Williamson, Paul Ingram, Sonja Opper, Rudolf Richter, Richard Swedberg, and Brett de Bary. Thanks to Wubiao Zhou and Suzanne Wright for their research assistance.

1. Recent reviews provide overviews of the new institutionalisms in economics (Eggertsson 1990; Williamson 1994; Furubotn and Richter 1997), in organizational analysis (DiMaggio and Powell 1991; Ingram and Clay 2000), in rational choice political science (Ordeshook 1990; Weingast 2003), and in historical institutionalism (Thelen and Steinmo 1992; Hall and Taylor 1996; Pierson and Skocpol 2003). Scott (2001) offers a useful conceptual inventory of advances in organizational new institutionalism.

2. See Granovetter 1992 for an application of a social constructionist approach to the study of economic institutions. Granovetter offers an interpretive account of institutions amenable to historical studies of institutions and institutional change.

3. Coase believes nonetheless that state intervention can be effective, but not always or automatically.

4. Furubotn and Richter (1997) show, however, that bounded rationality cannot be incorporated in neoclassical economics as such.

5. A thoughtful review of the old economic institutionalism by Hodgson (1998) argues that habitual behavior was the starting point of its institutional analysis. The old institutional economist examined patterns and regularities of human behavior—habits—as the basis for the approach to macroeconomic systems. It was not that the old institutionalists failed to generate important findings, but they were displaced by the rise of mathematical economics. See also Yonay 1998 for an examination of the conflict between the old institutionalists and neoclassical economists.

6. Stinchcombe (1997) in fact views Coase's "The Nature of the Firm" (1937) as an important contribution to the old economic institutionalism's core research agenda, identifying the institutional elements making possible the competitive structure of capitalism. According to Stinchcombe, Coase's analysis of the nature of firm boundaries complements Commons's work on the noncontractual basis of the contracts that constitute the firm. Williamson (1981, 549–50) explicitly acknowledges his own intellectual debt to Commons (1934), who "recognized that there were a variety of governance structures with which to mediate the exchange of goods or services between technologically separable entities. Assessing the capacities of different structures to harmonize relations between parties and recognizing that new structures arose in the service of these harmonizing purposes were central to the study of institutional economics as he conceived it."

7. Significant early writings of the new institutional economists influenced by Coase's classic essays include Alchian 1950; Alchian and Demsetz 1972, 1973; Cheung 1970,

1974; Davis and North 1971; Demsetz 1967, 1968, 1983; North and Thomas 1973; Barzel 1982, 1989; Williamson 1975, 1985; and Ostrom 1990. In a recent review, Williamson (2000) includes six Nobel laureates among key figures in the new institutional economics: Kenneth Arrow, Friedrich Hayek, Gunnar Myrdal, Herbert Simon, Ronald Coase, and Douglass North. The founding of the International Society for New Institutional Economics by Coase, North, and Williamson in 1996 has provided an annual forum for new work, much of it empirical, and has greatly expanded the scope of research addressed by new institutional economists.

8. Specifically, Williamson makes use of the contract law literature and the organization literatures of Barnard ([1938] 1964) and especially the Carnegie school (Simon 1957; March and Simon 1958, Cyert and March 1963).

9. "Problems of contracting are greatly complicated by economic agents who make 'false or empty, that is, self-disbelieved threats or promises' (Goffman 1959, p. 105), cut corners for undisclosed personal advantage, cover up tracks, and the like" (Williamson 1981, 554).

10. Transaction cost economics concurs with population ecology's core assumption that competition in a market economy is the driving mechanism of adaptive fitness of organizational forms (Hannan and Freeman 1989) and offers a firm-level answer to their question, "Why are there so many kinds of organizations?" Its predictions have been confirmed in empirical tests (Joskow 1988; Shelanski and Klein 1995; Masten 1993).

11. Because the essence of property rights is the right to exclude, North (1981) reasoned that the state, which has a comparative advantage in violence, plays a key role in specifying and enforcing property rights. North's theory of the state is neoclassical insofar as it assumes that rulers seek to maximize revenue through an exchange of protection and justice for revenue from constituents. Although the ruler has an interest in devising property rights to maximize state revenues, the existence of rivals capable of providing the same services constrains the state. Because the free-rider problem limits the ability of constituents to carry out society-wide institutional change, the state, which as a monopolist does not face a free-rider problem, is the source of institutional innovations.

12. Campbell and Lindberg (1990) analyze how a weak state structure like the United States derives enormous power through its control of formal rules governing property rights.

13. North and Weingast (1989) argue that in the English case, the key events and conditions stemmed from the eruption of the tension between ruler and constituent that gave rise to institutions limiting the capacity of the state to expropriate resources from producers, and hence the needed incentives to fuel economic growth through innovation and private enterprise.

14. Libecap (1994) integrates public choice theory with new institutional economics to develop a property rights approach to institutional change that takes into account political and economic interests.

15. For example, the demise of China's planned economy led to a change in the structure of industrial production and an increase in labor demand (changing relative prices). The state's response was to liberalize rules on internal migration and household registration in rural areas.

16. A second prong of Granovetter's critique was to point to the limitations of the functionalist claim that institutions and generalized morality are solutions to problems in economic life, a claim that "fails the elementary tests of a sound

functional explanation laid down by Robert Merton in 1947" (1985, 488–89). In orienting economic sociology to study the effect of interpersonal ties and network structures on economic performance, Granovetter is well aware of a slippery slope leading to functionalism within a social relations approach. It is not uncommon in the embeddedness literature, for example, to uncover arguments positing the advantages of networks as (1) solving efficiently the problem of trust, (2) providing ready access to fine-grained, timely, and reliable information, and (3) allowing collective problem solving by entrepreneurs. This leads to his methodological emphasis on the need for economic sociology to study the history of concrete interpersonal relations.

Because "enormous trust and enormous malfeasance may follow from personal relations" (492), Granovetter argues it is impossible to determine *ex ante* whether reliance on interpersonal ties will cement trust or give rise to opportunities for malfeasance *ex post*. It is necessary therefore to examine through historical case studies how specific interpersonal ties and network structures evolve (McGuire, Granovetter, and Schwartz 1993). To succeed in its competition with new institutional economics, the embeddedness approach needs to demonstrate that interpersonal ties have more to do with shaping economic behavior and performance in markets and hierarchies than do organizational forms. Along these lines, Granovetter has proposed a rival hypothesis to transaction cost economics, which asserts that variation in the structure and nature of interpersonal ties explains vertical integration of firms: "we should expect pressures towards vertical integration in a market where transacting firms lack a network of personal relations that connects them or where such a network eventuates in conflict, disorder, opportunism, or malfeasance. On the other hand, where a stable network of relations mediates complex transactions and generates standards of behavior between firms, such pressures should be absent" (1985, 503).

17. As Richard Miller (1987) points out, proximate causes are often shallow when contrasted with the deep determinative causes identified with large structures and processes.

18. Here I use virtually verbatim a comment provided by Paul DiMaggio.

19. Williamson's multilevel model in which a higher level constrains the lower level differs from the multilevel model I propose in figure 2 for new institutional economic sociology, where each level is in mutual dependence with the other. As Paul DiMaggio has pointed out to me in a personal communication, the latter approach offers a "co-evolutionary model, with phenomena at different levels mutually constituting contexts within which each evolves."

20. See Rona-Tas 1994; Eyal, Szelényi, and Townsley 1998.

21. New institutional organizational analysis represents more diversity in viewpoints on agency than is often acknowledged. For example, DiMaggio, Powell, and Scott differ with Meyer and Rowan in their interest in taking into account agency—actors who share beliefs and norms; hence the former are closer to the position articulated by Greif than to the structuralism of Meyer and Rowan.

22. Its use is restricted to analyzing social interactions in equilibrium, a situation in which each player's behavior is optimal given the perceived and expected behavior of others in the game.

23. In his influential study of the Maghrebi and Genoese traders in late medieval economic history, Greif ([1994] 1998) demonstrated the use of game theory to explicate the manner in which social variables such as beliefs, norms, and networks motivate economic action. Both groups of traders relied on community-based social institutions to solve principal-agent issues: the problem of negotiating and securing contracts *ex ante* and ensuring their compliance *ex post* given asymmetric information, partial contracting, and uncertainty. Genoese traders guided by individualist cultural beliefs constructed formal institutional structures that enabled them to employ nonkin agents. The Maghrebi traders were collectivist in their cultural beliefs and relied on ethnically bounded institutional arrangements to organize long-distance trade. Greif points out that although the historical record does not allow a test of relative efficiency between the two trading systems, the Maghrebis eventually disappeared from the Mediterranean world, whereas Genoese traders flourished in late medieval Europe. Greif ([1994] 1998, 96–97) observes that "it is intriguing that the Maghribis' societal organization resembles that of contemporary developing countries, whereas the Genoese societal organization resembles the developed West, suggesting that the individualistic system may have been more efficient in the long run. . . . To the extent that the division of labor is a necessary condition for long-run sustained economic growth, formal enforcement institutions that support anonymous exchange facilitate economic development."

24. Development of an interest-related approach to comparative institutional analysis is being pursued by Nee and Swedberg at the Center for the Study of Economy and Society at Cornell University (see www.economyandsociety .org). The views expressed by Scott and Meyer (1983) are complementary to an interest-related approach to institutional analysis.

25. Clearly, organizational field and production markets are overlapping and redundant concepts with respect to for-profit firms. Mechanisms of conformity to group norms and beliefs about expected behavior operate in all close-knit groups, whether of firms or individuals. Given the emphasis on for-profit firms in economic sociology, production market, as opposed to organizational field, is the more useful concept.

26. An early focus on nonprofit organizations may account for why organizational sociologists specify legitimacy-seeking as the driving mechanism of organizational behavior. DiMaggio and Powell (1983) specify three mechanisms—coercive, normative, and mimetic—promoting isomorphism in organizational fields. They integrate their mechanisms of isomorphism with resource dependence theory to specify hypotheses predicting the extent of isomorphism at the organization and field levels. Coercive isomorphism integrates resource dependence theory into organizational analysis; normative isomorphism specifies how professional associations influence organizational behavior under conditions of uncertainty; and mimetic isomorphism, as DiMaggio writes in a personal communication, "is about how . . . intendedly rational actors, facing uncertainty under high stakes, satisfice by identifying successful peers and making reasonable but incorrect attributions about the causes of their success."

27. Social ties and norms do not themselves constitute mechanisms insofar as they are concepts referring to elements of social structure—the relationship connecting two or more actors and the informal rules governing the relationship.

28. See Roethlisberg and Dickson 1939; Whyte 1943; Festinger, Schachter, and Back 1950; Schachter et al. 1951; Jennings 1950; Seashore 1954; Bott 1957; Riley and Cohn 1958; Walker and Heyns 1962; Cook et al. 1983; Ellickson 1991; Petersen 1992; Kollock 1994; Lawler and Yoon 1996.

29. Shibutani (1978) provides detailed observations about the emergence and maintenance of norms of a close-knit group of Japanese American soldiers in a military base,

documenting norm emergence as a product of collective problem-solving as members of the group socially construct a definition of the situation and course of action that optimizes their welfare.

30. Ellickson's analysis of conflict arising from damage to property caused by trespassing cattle showed that the residents of Shasta County commonly resorted to informal norms of cooperation to settle disputes. Ellickson reports that ranchers and residents have only a vague grasp of the formal litigation procedures involved in resolving disputes over trespassing. Moreover, litigation is viewed as a costly way to settle property disputes, both financially and with respect to long-standing relationships in a close-knit community. Ellickson's narrative of the incidents of disputes between ranchers and suburbanites shows that despite their cultural differences, a common identity as residents of Shasta County sustains a live-and-let-live philosophy that enables parties to practice mutual restraint. As long as accounts balanced along multiple dimensions of interpersonal relations, parties in disputes settled informally:

> The landowners who were interviewed clearly regard their restraint in seeking monetary relief as a mark of virtue. When asked why they did not pursue meritorious legal claims arising from trespass or fence-finance disputes, various landowners replied: "I'm not that kind of guy", "I don't believe in it"; "I don't like to create a stink"; "I try to get along." The landowners who attempted to provide a rationale for this forbearance all implied the same one, a long-term reciprocity of advantage. Ann Kershaw: "The only one that makes money [when you litigate] is the lawyer." Al Levitt: "I figure it will balance out in the long run." Pete Schultz: "I hope they'll do the same for me." Phil Ritchie: "My family believes in 'live and let live.'" (1991, 61)

31. Ellickson's specification of welfare-maximization is not Pareto-superior insofar as its criterion focuses on the question, do most people derive a net benefit from the norm? According to the prisoner's dilemma game, $T > R > P > S$, where T is the temptation to defect, R is the reward for mutual cooperation, P is punishment for mutual defection, and S is the sucker's payoff. The condition for the prisoner's dilemma norm to be in equilibrium is that the total payoff for cooperation, after deducting the cost of monitoring and enforcement (C), must be greater than the payoff for defection (T) and the sucker's payoff (S) : $2R - C > T + S$ (Nee and Ingram 1998).

32. Nee and Ingram (1998) specify how informal norms emerge and interact with formal institutional elements, permitting predictions about organizational and economic performance that can be empirically tested.

33. For example, in 1997 the landmark federal discrimination case against Texaco imposed a costly settlement of $175 million to minority employees, and the publicity arising from the case also damaged the firm's reputation. Texaco was compelled to carry out extensive organizational changes in personnel policy and practices in making credible commitment to eliminating racial discrimination to avoid further fines and restore its legitimacy. The federal discrimination case against Coca-Cola was resolved at a cost of $192 million to the firm. Coca-Cola's management, moreover, agreed to ongoing external monitoring of its progress in eliminating bias in all aspects of the firm's operation. As with the public response to the landmark Texaco discrimination case, both damage to Coca-Cola's brand name and the financial and organizational penalties of the settlement had the effect of reinforcing other firms' belief in self-monitoring for compliance with EEO/AA guidelines.

34. In their study of the history of personnel practices in 279 firms in California, Virginia, and New Jersey—localities with different institutional contexts— Sutton and Dobbin (1996) confirm an endogenous motivation of personnel professionals and affirmative action officers to develop strategies for compliance with EEO guidelines. Federal activism through expanded legal and political pressures on firms increased the rate of adoption of legalization within the firm of due-process governance. In general, the diffusion of legalized governance structures demonstrating compliance with EEO/AA guidelines shows time-trends corresponding to ups and downs of federal EEO/AA enforcement activities. Firms that contracted with the federal government were more likely to file annual EEO reports to demonstrate good faith in compliance with federal guidelines. Organizations closer to the public domain more readily complied with federal EEO/AA rules and guidelines. Significantly, findings by Sutton et al. "suggest that legalization is not aimed inward, toward specific employee demands or organizational requirements, but outward at the shifting concerns of regulators and courts" (1994, 996). In a follow-up study using a different data set of 154 for-profit firms, Sutton and Dobbin (1996) confirm the close coupling of state regulation of formal rules and the normative pressures on management from human resource professionals inside the firm to institute proactive governance strategies (i.e., formal lawlike rules governing grievance procedures and internal labor markets to protect equality of rights) in order to comply with federal EEO/AA guidelines.

35. For analyses of how institutional change by administrative design and formal rule change faltered in Eastern Europe and Russia, see Stark 1996; Gray and Hendley 1997; Hellman 1997; Varese 2001.

36. For analyses by economic sociologists of realignment of power and interests favoring economic actors in market transitions and institutional change in China, see Walder 1995; Nee 1996; Cao 2001; Guthrie 1999; Keister 2000.

37. See Shirk 1993; Naughton 1995; and Opper, Wong, and Hu 2002 for analyses of how economic and political actors benefited from institutional change.

38. Economic sociologists whose work examines the effect of markets include Saxenian (1994); Swedberg (1994); Abolafia (1996); Uzzi (1997); Guillén (2001); White (2001); Baron and Hannan (forthcoming); Freeman (forthcoming); and Davis and Marquis (forthcoming). Those examining the effect of both market and state regulation on economic actors include Nee (1992, 1996, 2000); Nee, Sanders, and Sernau (1994); Walder (1995); Fligstein (1996, 2001); and Guthrie (1999).

39. North and Wallis (1986) estimated the size of the transaction sector of the American economy; however, their aggregate data is not useful for empirical analysis.

40. Firm-centric data, rather than aggregate national-level data, is needed to measure transaction costs, which are the costs to firms of negotiating, securing, and completing economic transactions. The problem with national-level aggregate data is that it does not measure the effect of variation in institutional conditions on the firm and entrepreneur.

REFERENCES

Abolafia, Mitchell Y. 1996. *Making Markets: Opportunism and Restraint on Wall Street*. Cambridge: Harvard University Press.

Alba, Richard, and Victor Nee. 2003. *Remaking the*

American Mainstream: Assimilation and Contemporary Immigration. Cambridge: Harvard University Press.

Alchian, Armen A. 1950. "Uncertainty, Evolution, and Economic Theory." *Journal of Political Economy* 59:211–221.

Alchian, Armen A., and Harold Demsetz. 1972. "Production, Information Costs, and Economic Organization." *American Economic Review* 62:777–95.

———. 1973. "The Property Right Paradigm." *Journal of Economic History* 33:16–27.

Arrow, Kenneth J. 1987. "Reflections on the Essays." Pp. 727–34 in *Arrow and the Foundations of the Theory of Economic Policy,* ed. George Feinel. New York: New York University Press.

Arthur, Brian W. 1988. "Self-Reinforcing Mechanisms in Economics." Pp. 9–32 in *The Economy as an Evolving Complex System,* ed. Philip W. Anderson, Kenneth J. Arrow, and David Pines. Menlo Park, Calif.: Addison-Wesley.

Aslund, Anders. 1995. *How Russia Became a Market Economy.* Washington, D.C.: Brookings Institution Press.

Axelrod, Robert. 1984. *The Evolution of Cooperation.* New York: Basic Books.

Barnard, Chester I. [1938] 1964. *The Functions of the Executive.* Cambridge: Harvard University Press.

Baron, James, and Michael T. Hannan. Forthcoming. "The Economic Sociology of Organizational Entrepreneurship: Lessons from the Stanford Project on Emerging Companies." In *Economic Sociology of Capitalism,* ed. Victor Nee and Richard Swedberg. Princeton: Princeton University Press.

Barzel, Yoram. 1982. "Measurement Cost and the Organization of Markets." *Journal of Law and Economics* 25:27–28.

———. 1989. *Economic Analysis of Property Rights.* Cambridge: Cambridge University Press.

Beissinger, Mark R. 2002. *Nationalist Mobilization and the Collapse of the Soviet State.* Cambridge: Cambridge University Press.

Berger, Peter L., and Thomas Luckmann. 1967. *The Social Construction of Reality.* New York: Doubleday.

Blau, Peter. 1955. *The Dynamics of Bureaucracy.* 2d ed. Chicago: University of Chicago Press.

———. 1964. *Exchange and Power in Social Life.* New York: John Wiley and Sons.

Bott, Elizabeth. 1957. *Family and Social Network.* London: Tavistock.

Bourdieu, Pierre. [1972] 1977. *Outline of a Theory of Practice.* Cambridge: Cambridge University Press.

Brinton, Mary C., and Victor Nee, eds. 1998. *The New Institutionalism in Sociology.* New York: Russell Sage Foundation.

Burawoy, Michael. 1979. *Manufacturing Dissent: Changes in the Labor Process under Monopoly Capitalism.* Chicago: University of Chicago Press.

Burt, Ronald. 1992. *Structural Holes: The Social Struc-*

ture of Competition. Chicago: University of Chicago Press.

Campbell, John L., and Leon N. Lindberg. 1990. "Property Rights and the Organization of Economic Activity by the State." *American Sociological Review* 55:634–47.

Cao, Yang. 2001. "Careers inside Organizations: A Comparative Analysis of Promotion Determination in Reforming China. *Social Forces* 80:683–712.

Cheung, Steven N. S. 1970. "The Structure of a Contract and the Theory of a Non-exclusive Resource." *Journal of Law and Economics* 13:49–70.

———. 1974. "A Theory of Price Control." *Journal of Law and Economics* 12:53–71.

Cicourel, Aaron. 1974. *Cognitive Sociology.* New York: Free Press.

Coase, Ronald H. 1937. "The Nature of the Firm." *Economica* 4:386–405.

———. 1960. "The Problem of Social Cost." *Journal of Law and Economics* 3:1–44.

———. 1984. "The New Institutional Economics." *Journal of Institutional and Theoretical Economics* 140:229–31.

———. 1988. *The Firm, the Market, and the Law.* Chicago: University of Chicago Press.

Commons, John R. 1934. *Institutional Economics: Its Place in Political Economy.* New York: Macmillan.

———. 1957. *Legal Foundations of Capitalism.* Madison: University of Wisconsin Press.

Cook, Karen S., Richard M. Emerson, Mary R. Gillmore, and Toshio Yamagishi. 1983. "The Distribution of Power in Exchange Networks: Theory and Experimental Results." *American Journal of Sociology* 89:275–305.

Cyert, Richard M., and James G. March. 1963. *A Behavioral Theory of the Firm.* Englewood Cliffs, N.J.: Prentice-Hall.

David, Paul. 1986. "Understanding the Economics of QWERTY: The Necessity of History." Pp. 30–49 in *Economic History and the Modern Economist,* ed. William N. Parker. Oxford: Blackwell.

Davis, Gerald, and Christopher Marquis. Forthcoming. "The Globalization of Stock Markets and Convergence in Corporate Governance." In *Economic Sociology of Capitalism,* ed. Victor Nee and Richard Swedberg. Princeton: Princeton University Press.

Davis, Lance E., and Douglass C. North. 1971. *Institutional Change and American Economic Growth.* Cambridge: Cambridge University Press.

Demsetz, Harold. 1967. "Toward a Theory of Property Rights." *American Economic Review* 57:347–59.

———. 1968. "Why Regulate Utilities." *Journal of Law and Economics* 11:55–66.

———. 1983. "The Structure of Ownership and the Theory of the Firm." *Journal of Law and Economics* 26:375–93.

DiMaggio, Paul J., and Walter W. Powell. 1983. "The Iron Cage Revisited: Institutional Isomorphism and

Collective Rationality in Organizational Fields." *American Sociological Review* 48:147–60.

Douglas, Mary. 1986. *How Institutions Think.* Syracuse, N.Y.: Syracuse University Press.

Edelman, Lauren B. 1990. "Legal Environments and Organizational Governance: The Expansion of Due Process in the American Workplace." *American Journal of Sociology* 95:1401–40.

———. 1992. "Legal Ambiguity and Symbolic Structures: Organizational Mediation of Civil Rights Law." *American Journal of Sociology* 97:1531–76.

Edelman, Lauren B., Christopher Uggen, and Howard S. Erlanger. 1999. "The Endogeneity of Legal Regulation: Grievance Procedures as Rational Myth." *American Journal of Sociology* 105:406–54.

Eggertsson, Thráinn. 1990. *Economic Behavior and Institutions.* Cambridge: Cambridge University Press.

Ellickson, Robert. 1991. *Order without Law.* Cambridge: Harvard University Press.

Emerson, Richard. 1962. "Power-Dependence Relations." *American Sociological Review* 22:31–41.

Evans, Peter, and James E. Rauch. 1999. "Bureaucracy and Growth: A Cross-National Analysis of the Effects of 'Weberian' State Structures on Economic Growth." *American Sociological Review* 64:748–65.

Eyal, Gil, Ivan Szelényi, and Eleanor Townsley. 1998. *Making Capitalism without Capitalists: The New Ruling Elites in Eastern Europe.* London: Verso.

Festinger, Leon, Stanley Schachter, and Kurt Back. 1950. *Social Pressures in Informal Groups.* New York: Harper.

Fligstein, Neil. 1996. "Markets and Politics: A Sociological View of Market Institutions." *American Sociological Review* 61:656–73.

———. 2001. *The Architecture of Markets: An Economic Sociology of Twentieth-first-Century Capitalist Societies.* Princeton: Princeton University Press.

Freeman, John. Forthcoming. "Venture Capital and Modern Capitalism." In *Economic Sociology of Capitalism,* ed. Victor Nee and Richard Swedberg. Princeton: Princeton University Press.

Furubotn, Eirik G., and Rudolf Richter. 1993. "The New Institutional Economics: Recent Progress; Expanding Frontiers." *Journal of Institutional and Theoretical Economics* 149:1–10.

———. 1997. *Institutions and Economic Theory: The Contribution of the New Institutional Economics.* Ann Arbor: University of Michigan Press.

Garfinkel, Harold. 1967. *Studies in Ethnomethodology.* Englewood Cliffs, N.J.: Prentice-Hall.

Giddens, Anthony. 1979. *Central Problems in Social Theory: Action, Structure, and Contradictions in Social Analysis.* Berkeley and Los Angeles: University of California Press.

Goffman, Erving. 1959. *The Presentation of Self in Everyday Life.* Garden City, N.Y.: Doubleday Anchor Books.

———. 1967. *Interaction Ritual.* Garden City, N.Y.: Anchor.

Granovetter, Mark. 1985. "Economic Action and Social Structure: The Problem of Embeddedness." *American Journal of Sociology* 91:481–510.

———. 1992. "Economic Institutions as Social Constructions: A Framework for Analysis." *Acta Sociologica* 35:3–11.

Gray, Cheryl W., and Kathryn Hendley. 1997. "Developing Commercial Law in Transition Economies: Examples from Hungary and Russia." Pp. 139–64 in *The Rule of Law and Economic Reform in Russia,* ed. Jeffrey Sachs and Katharina Pistor. Cambridge, Mass.: Westview.

Greif, Avner. [1994] 1998. "Cultural Beliefs and the Organization of Society: A Historical and Theoretical Reflection on Collectivist and Individualist Societies." *Journal of Political Economy* 102:912–50. Adapted for *The New Institutionalism in Sociology,* ed. Mary Brinton and Victor Nee (New York: Russell Sage Foundation), 77–104.

———. Forthcoming. *Institutions: History and Theory: Comparative and Historical Institutional Analysis.* Cambridge: University of Cambridge Press.

Guillén, Mauro F. 2001. *The Limits of Convergence: Globalization and Organizational Change in Argentina, South Korea, and Spain.* Princeton: Princeton University Press.

Guthrie, Doug. 1999. *Dragon in a Three-Piece Suit: The Emergence of Capitalism in China.* Princeton: Princeton University Press.

Hall, Peter A., and Rosemary Taylor. 1996. "Political Science and the Three New Institutionalisms." *Political Studies* 44:936–57.

Hamilton, Gary D., and Robert Feenstra. 1998. "The Organization of Economies." Pp. 153–80 in *The New Institutionalism in Sociology,* ed. Mary Brinton and Victor Nee. New York: Russell Sage Foundation.

Hannan, Michael T., and John Freeman. 1989. *Organizational Ecology.* Cambridge: Harvard University Press.

Hardin, Russell. 1988. *Morality within the Limits of Reason.* Chicago: University of Chicago Press.

Hayek, Friedrich. 1945. "The Use of Knowledge in Society." *American Economic Review* 35:519–30.

Hellman, Joel S. 1997. "Constitutions and Economic Reform in the Post-Communist Transitions." Pp. 55–78 in *The Rule of Law and Economic Reform in Russia,* ed. Jeffrey Sachs and Katharina Pistor. Cambridge, Mass.: Westview.

Hodgson, Geoffrey M. 1998. "The Approach of Institutional Economics." *Journal of Economic Literature* 36:166–92.

Homans, George C. 1950. *The Human Group.* New York: Harcourt Brace Jovanovich.

———. [1961] 1974. *Social Behavior: Its Elementary Forms.* New York: Harcourt Brace Jovanovich.

Ingram, Paul. 1998. "Changing the Rules: Interests, Organizations, and Institutional Change in the U.S. Hospitality Industry." Pp. 258–76 in *The New In-

stitutionalism in Sociology, ed. Mary Brinton and Victor Nee. New York: Russell Sage Foundation.

Ingram, Paul, and Karen Clay. 2000. "The Choice-within-Constraints New Institutionalism and Implications for Sociology." *Annual Review of Sociology* 26:525–46.

Jennings, Helen Hall. 1950. *Leadership and Isolation.* 2d ed. New York: Longmans, Green.

Joskow, Paul L. 1988. "Asset Specificity and the Structure of Vertical Relationships: Empirical Evidence." *Journal of Law, Economics, and Organization* 4: 95–117.

———. 1991. "The Role of Transaction Cost Economics in Antitrust and Public Utility Regulatory Policies." *Journal of Law and Economic Organization* 7:53–83.

Keister, Lisa. 2000. *Chinese Business Groups: The Structure and Impact of Interfirm Relations during Economic Development.* Oxford: Oxford University Press.

Knight, Frank H. 1921. *Risk, Uncertainty, and Profit.* Boston: Houghton Mifflin.

Kollock, Peter. 1994. "The Emergence of Exchange Structures: An Experimental Study of Uncertainty, Commitment, and Trust." *American Journal of Sociology* 100:315–45.

Kuwabara, Ko. Forthcoming. "Affective Attachment in Electronic Markets: A Sociological Study of eBay." In *Economic Sociology of Capitalism,* ed. Victor Nee and Richard Swedberg. Princeton: Princeton University Press.

Lawler, Edward J., and Jeongkoo Yoon. 1996. "Commitment in Exchange Relations: Test of a Theory of Relational Cohesion." *American Sociological Review* 61:89–108.

Libecap, Gary D. 1994. *Contracting for Property Rights.* Cambridge: Cambridge University Press.

Lin, Justin Yifu, Fang Cai, and Zhou Li. 1996. *The China Miracle: Development Strategy and Economic Reform.* Hong Kong: Hong Kong University Press.

March, James, and Herbert Simon. 1958. *Organizations.* New York: John Wiley and Sons.

Marsh, Barnaby. 2002. "Heuristics as Social Tools." *New Ideas in Psychology* 20:49–57.

Masten, Scott. 1993. "Transaction Costs, Mistakes, and Performance: Assessing the Importance of Governance." *Management and Decision Sciences* 14: 119–29.

McGuire, Patrick, Mark Granovetter, and Michael Schwartz. 1993. "Thomas Edison and the Social Construction of the Early Electricity Industry in America." Pp. 213–48 in *Explorations in Economic Sociology,* ed. Richard Swedberg. New York: Russell Sage Foundation.

Merton, Robert K. 1947. "Manifest and Latent Functions." Pp. 19–84 in *Social Theory and Social Structure.* New York: Free Press:

Meyer, John, and Brian Rowan. 1977. "Institutionalized Organizations: Formal Structure as Myth and Ceremony." *American Journal of Sociology* 93:340–63.

Miller, Richard W. 1987. *Fact and Method: Explanation, Confirmation, and Reality in the Natural and the Social Sciences.* Princeton: Princeton University Press.

Mitchell, Wesley C. 1927. *Business Cycles: The Problem and Its Setting.* New York: National Bureau of Economic Research.

———. 1937. *The Backward Art of Spending Money and Other Essays.* New York: Augustus M. Kelley.

Naughton, Barry. 1995. *Growing out of the Plan: Chinese Economic Reform, 1978–1993.* Cambridge: University of Cambridge Press.

Nee, Victor. 1992. "Organizational Dynamics of Market Transition: Hybrid Forms, Property Rights, and Mixed Economy in China." *Administrative Science Quarterly* 37:1–27.

———. 1996. "The Emergence of a Market Society: Changing Mechanisms of Stratification in China." *American Journal of Sociology* 101:908–49.

———. 2000. "The Role of the State in Making a Market Economy." *Journal of Institutional and Theoretical Economics* 156:64–88.

Nee, Victor, and Yang Cao. 1999. "Path Dependent Societal Transformations." *Theory and Society* 28: 799–834.

Nee, Victor, and Paul Ingram. 1998. "Embeddedness and Beyond: Institutions, Exchange, and Social Structure." Pp. 19–45 in *The New Institutionalism in Sociology,* ed. Mary Brinton and Victor Nee. New York: Russell Sage Foundation.

Nee, Victor, and Peng Lian. 1994. "Sleeping with the Enemy: A Dynamic Model of Declining Political Commitment in State Socialism." *Theory and Society* 23:253–96.

Nee, Victor, Jimy M. Sanders, and Scott Sernau. 1994. "Job Transitions in an Immigrant Metropolis: Ethnic Boundaries and Mixed Economy." *American Sociological Review* 59:849–72.

Nelson, Richard, and Sidney Winter. 1982. *An Evolutionary Theory of Economic Change.* Cambridge: Cambridge University Press.

North, Douglass C. 1981. *Structure and Change in Economic History.* New York: W. W. Norton.

———. 1984. "Government and the Cost of Exchange in History." *Journal of Economic History* 44: 255–64.

———. 1990. *Institutions, Institutional Change, and Economic Performance.* Cambridge: Cambridge University Press.

———. 1991. "Institutions." *Journal of Economic Perspectives* 5:97–112.

———. 1993. "Institutions and Credible Commitment." *Journal of Institutional and Theoretical Economics* 149:11–23.

North, Douglass C., and Robert Paul Thomas. 1973. *The Rise of the Western World: A New Economic History.* Cambridge: Cambridge University Press.

North, Douglass C., and John J. Wallis. 1986. "Measuring the Transaction Sector in the American Economy, 1870–1970." Pp. 95–161 in *Long-Term Factors in American Economic Growth*, ed. Staley L. Engerman and Robert E. Gallman. Chicago: University of Chicago Press.

North, Douglass C., and Barry R. Weingast. 1989. "Constitutions and Commitment: The Evolution of Institutions Governing Public Choice in Seventeenth-Century England." *Journal of Economic History* 49:803–32.

Opper, Sonja, Sonia M. L. Wong, and Ruyin Hu. 2002. "Party Power, Market, and Private Power: Chinese Communist Party Persistence in China's Listed Companies." In "The Future of Market Transition," ed. K. Leicht, special issue of *Research in Social Stratification and Mobility* 19:105–38.

Ordeshook, Peter. 1990. "The Emerging Discipline of Political Economy." Pp. 9–30 in *Perspectives on Positive Political Economy*, ed. James Alt and Kenneth Shepsle. Cambridge: Cambridge University Press.

Ostrom, Elinor. 1990. *Governing the Commons: The Evolution of Institutions for Collective Action*. Cambridge: Cambridge University Press.

Parsons, Talcott, and Neil J. Smelser. 1956. *Economy and Society: A Study in the Integration of Economic and Social Theory*. Glencoe, Ill.: Free Press.

Petersen, Trond. 1992. "Individual, Collective, and Systems Rationality in Work Groups." *Rationality and Society* 4:332–55.

Pierson, Paul, and Theda Skocpol. 2003. "Historical Institutionalism in Political Science." In *The State of the Discipline*, ed. Ira Katznelson and Helen Milner. New York: W. W. Norton.

Posner, Richard A. 1986. *Economic Analysis of Law*. Boston: Little, Brown.

———. 1993. "The New Institutional Economics Meets Law and Economics." *Journal of Institutional and Theoretical Economics* 149:73–87.

Powell, Walter W., and Paul J. DiMaggio, eds. 1991. *The New Institutionalism in Organizational Analysis*. Chicago: University of Chicago Press.

Riley, M. W., and R. Cohn. 1958. "Control Networks in Informal Groups." *Sociometry* 21:30–49.

Roethlisberger, F. J., and William J. Dickson. 1939. *Management and the Worker*. Cambridge: Harvard University Press.

Rona-Tas, Akos. 1994. "The First Shall Be Last? Entrepreneurship and Communist Cadres in the Transition from Socialism." *American Journal of Sociology* 100:40–69.

Rutherford, Malcolm. 1994. *Institutions in Economics: The Old and the New Institutionalism*. Cambridge: Cambridge University Press.

Sachs, Jeffrey D. 1995. "Consolidating Capitalism." *Foreign Policy* 98:50–64.

Saxenian, Annalee. 1994. *Regional Advantage: Culture and Competition in Silicon Valley and Route 128*. Cambridge: Harvard University Press.

Schachter, Stanley, Norris Ellertson, Dorothy McBride, and Doris Gregory. 1951. "An Experimental Study of Cohesiveness and Productivity." *Human Relations* 4:229–38.

Schotter, Andrew. 1981. *The Economic Theory of Social Institutions*. Cambridge: Cambridge University Press.

Scott, Richard W. 2001. *Institutions and Organizations*, 2d ed. Thousand Oaks, Calif.: Sage.

Scott, Richard W., and John W. Meyer. 1983. "The Organization of Societal Sectors." Pp. 129–54 in *Organizational Environments: Rituals and Rationality*, ed. John Meyer and Richard W. Scott. Beverly Hills, Calif.: Sage.

Seashore, Stanley E. 1954. *Group Cohesiveness in the Industrial Work Group*. Ann Arbor: Institute for Social Research, University of Michigan.

Selznick, Philip. 1949. *TVA and the Grass Roots*. Berkeley and Los Angeles: University of California Press.

Shelanski, Howard A., and P. G. Klein. 1995. "Empirical Research in Transaction Cost Economics: A Review and Assessment." *Journal of Law, Economics, and Organization* 11:335–61.

Shibutani, Tomatsu. 1978. *The Derelicts of Company K: A Study of Demoralization*. Berkeley and Los Angeles: University of California Press.

Shirk, Susan L. 1993. *The Political Logic of Economic Reform in China*. Berkeley and Los Angeles: University of California Press.

Shleifer, Andrei, and Robert W. Vishny. 1994. "Politicians and Firms." *Quarterly Journal of Economics* 109:995–1025.

Simon, Herbert A. 1957. *Models of Man: Social and Rational*. New York: John Wiley and Sons.

Smelser, Neil J., and Richard Swedberg, eds. 1994. *Handbook of Economic Sociology*. New York: Russell Sage Foundation; Princeton: Princeton University Press.

Spence, Michael A. 1974. *Market Signaling: Informational Transfer in Hiring and Related Screening Processes*. Cambridge: Harvard University Press.

Stark, David. 1996. "Recombinant Property in Eastern European Capitalism." *American Journal of Sociology* 101:993–1027.

Stiglitz, Joseph E. 1989. *The Economic Role of the State*. Oxford: Basil Blackwell.

Stinchcombe, Arthur. 1965. "Social Structure and Organizations." Pp. 142–93 in *Handbook of Organizations*, ed. James G. March. Chicago: Rand McNally.

———. 1997. "On the Virtues of the Old Institutionalism." *Annual Review of Sociology* 23:1–18.

Sutton, John R., and Frank Dobbin. 1996. "The Two Faces of Governance: Responses to Legal Uncertainty in U.S. Firms, 1955 to 1985." *American Sociological Review* 61:794–811.

Sutton, John R., Frank Dobbin, John W. Meyer, and W. Richard Scott. 1994. "The Legalization of the Workplace." *American Journal of Sociology* 99:944–71.

Swedberg, Richard. 1994. "Markets as Social Structures." Pp. 255–82 in *The Handbook of Economic*

Sociology, ed. Neil J. Smelser and Richard Swedberg. New York: Russell Sage Foundation; Princeton: Princeton University Press.

———. 1998. *Max Weber and the Idea of Economic Sociology*. Princeton: Princeton University Press.

———. 2003. *Principles of Economic Sociology*. Princeton: Princeton University Press.

Swidler, Ann. 1986. "Culture in Action: Symbols and Strategies. *American Sociological Review* 51:273–86.

Thelen, Kathleen, and Sven Steinmo. 1992. "Historical Institutionalism in Comparative Politics." Pp. 1–32 in *Structuring Politics: Historical Institutionalism in Comparative Analysis*. Cambridge: Cambridge University Press.

Uzzi, Brian. 1997. "Social Structure and Competition in Interfirm Networks: The Paradox of Embeddedness." *Administrative Science Quarterly* 42: 35–67.

Veblen, Thorstein. 1909. "The Limitations of Marginal Utility." *Journal of Political Economy* 17:620–36.

———. [1899] 1934. *The Theory of the Leisure Class: An Economic Study of Institutions*. New York: Modern Library.

Varese, Fedrico. 2001. *The Russian Mafia: Private Protection in a New Market Economy*. Oxford: Oxford University Press.

Walder, Andrew G. 1995. "Local Government as Industrial Firms: An Organizational Analysis of China's Transitional Economy." *American Journal of Sociology* 101:263-301.

Walker, Edward L., and Roger W. Heyns. 1962. *An Anatomy for Conformity*. Englewood Cliffs, N.J.: Prentice-Hall.

Weber, Max. [1922] 1968. *Economy and Society: An Outline of Interpretive Sociology*. Ed. Guenther Roth and Claus Wittich. Berkeley and Los Angeles: University of California Press.

———. [1904–5] 2002. *The Protestant Ethic and the Spirit of Capitalism*. Los Angeles: Roxbury.

Weingast, Barry. 2003. "Rational Choice Institutionalism." Pp. 660–92 in *The State of the Discipline,* ed. Ira Katznelson and Helen Milner. New York: W. W. Norton.

White, Harrison. 1992. *Identity and Control: A Structural Theory of Social Action*. Princeton: Princeton University Press.

———. 2001. *Markets from Networks: Socioeconomic Models of Production*. Princeton: Princeton University Press.

Whyte, William Foote. 1943. *Street Corner Society*. Chicago: University of Chicago Press.

Williamson, Oliver E. 1975. *Markets and Hierarchies: Analysis and Antitrust Implications*. New York: Free Press.

———. 1981. "The Economics of Organization: The Transaction Cost Approach." *American Journal of Sociology* 87:548–77.

———. 1985. *The Economic Institutions of Capitalism*. New York: Free Press.

———. 1994. "Transaction Cost Economics and Organization Theory." Pp. 77–107 in *The Handbook of Economic Sociology,* ed. Neil J. Smelser and Richard Swedberg. New York: Russell Sage Foundation; Princeton: Princeton University Press.

———. 2000. "The New Institutional Economics: Taking Stock, Looking Ahead." *Journal of Economic Literature* 38:595–613.

Yonay, Yuval P. 1998. *The Struggle over the Soul of Economics: Institutionalist and Neoclassical Economists in America between the Wars*. Princeton: Princeton University Press.

Zucker, Lynne G. 1977. "The Role of Institutionalization in Cultural Persistence." *American Sociological Review* 42:726–43.

4 Principles of an Economic Anthropology

Pierre Bourdieu

To BREAK with the dominant paradigm [in economics], we must attempt to construct a realist definition of economic reason as an encounter between dispositions that are socially constituted (in relation to a field) and the structures, themselves socially constituted, of that field. In doing so, we need to take note, within an expanded rationalist vision, of the historicity constitutive of agents and of their space of action.

THE STRUCTURE OF THE FIELD

Agents, that is to say, in this case firms, create the space, that is to say, the economic field, which exists only through the agents that are found within it and that deform the space in their vicinity, conferring a certain structure on it. In other words, it is in the relationship between the various "field sources," that is to say between the different production firms, that the field and the relations of force that characterize it are engendered.[1] More concretely, it is the agents, that is to say, the firms, defined by the volume and structure of specific capital they possess, that determine the structure of the field that determines them, that is, the state of the forces exerted on the whole set of firms engaged in the production of similar goods. These firms, which exert potential effects that are variable in their intensity and direction, control a section of the field ("market share"), the size of which increases with the size of their capital. As for consumers, their behavior would be entirely reduced to the effect of the field if they did not have a certain interaction with it (as a function of their—quite minimal—inertia). The weight (or energy) associated with an agent, which undergoes the effects of the field at the same time as it structures that field, depends on all the other points and the relations between all the points, that is to say, on the entire space.

Though we are here stressing the constants, we do not overlook the fact that capital in its various species varies depending on the particularity of each subfield (corresponding to what is ordinarily referred to as a "sector" or a "branch" of industry), that is, depending on the history of the field, on the state of development (and, in particular, on the degree of concentration) of the industry considered and on the particularity of the product. At the end of the huge study he conducted of the pricing practices of various American industries, W. H. Hamilton related the idiosyncratic character of the different branches (that is to say, of the different fields) to the particularities of the histories of their emergence,[2] each being characterized by its own mode of functioning, its specific traditions, and its particular way of making pricing decisions.[3]

The force attached to an agent depends on its various "strengths," sometimes called "strategic market assets," differential factors of success (or failure), which may provide it with a competitive advantage, that is to say, more precisely, on the *volume and structure of the capital* the agent possesses in its different species: financial capital (actual or potential), cultural capital (not to be confused with "human capital"), technological capital, juridical capital and organizational capital (including the capital of information about the field), commercial capital, social capital, and symbolic capital. Financial capital is the direct or indirect mastery (through access to the banks) of financial resources, which are the main condition (together with time) for the accumulation and conservation of all other kinds of capital. Technological capital is the portfolio of scientific resources (research potential) or technical resources (procedures, aptitudes, routines, and unique and coherent know-how, capable of reducing expenditure in labor or capital or increasing its yield) that can be deployed in the design and manufacture of products. Commercial capital (sales power) relates to the mastery of distribution networks (warehousing and transport), and marketing and after-sales services. Social capital is the totality of resources (financial capital and also information, etc.) activated through a more or less extended, more or less mobilizable network of relations that procures a competitive advantage by providing higher returns on investment.[4] Symbolic capital resides in the mastery of symbolic resources based on knowledge and recognition, such as "goodwill investment," "brand loyalty," and so on; as a power that functions as a form of credit, it presupposes the trust or belief of those upon whom it bears because they are disposed to grant it credence (it is this symbolic power that Keynes invokes when he posits that an injection of money is effective if agents believe it to be so).[5]

The structure of the distribution of capital and the structure of the distribution of costs, itself linked mainly to the scale and degree of vertical integration, determine the structure of the field, that is to say, the relations of force among firms: the mastery of a very large proportion of capital (of the overall energy) in effect confers a power over the field, and hence over the firms least well endowed (relatively) in terms of capital; it also governs the price of entry into the field, and the distribution of the opportunities for profit. The various species of capital do not act only indirectly, through prices; they exert a structural effect, because the adoption of a new technique or the control of a larger market share, et cetera, modifies the relative positions and the yields of all the species of capital held by other firms.

By contrast with the interactionist vision, which knows no other form of social efficacy than the "influence" directly exerted by one enterprise (or person entrusted with representing it) over another through some form of "interaction," the structural vision takes account of effects that occur outside of any interaction: the structure of the field, defined by the unequal distribution of capital, that is, the specific weapons (or strengths), weighs, quite apart from any direct intervention or manipulation, on all the agents engaged in the field; and the worse placed they are within that distribution, the more it restricts the *space of possibles* open to them. The dominant is the one that occupies a position in the structure such that the structure acts on its behalf. It is through the weight they possess within this structure, more than through the direct interventions they may also make (in particular through the "interlocking directorates" that are a more or less distorted expression of it),[6] that the

dominant firms exert their pressure on the dominated firms and on their strategies: they define the *regularities* and sometimes the *rules* of the game, by imposing the definition of strengths most favorable to their interests and modifying the entire environment of the other firms and the system of constraints that bear on them or the space of possibles offered to them.

The tendency for the structure to reproduce itself is immanent to the very structure of the field: the distribution of strengths governs the distribution of chances of success and of profits through various mechanisms, such as the economies of scale or "barriers to entry" resulting from the permanent disadvantage with which new entrants have to cope or the operating costs they have to meet or the action of all kinds of "uncertainty-reducing institutions," to use Jan Kregel's expression,[7] such as wage and debt contracts, controlled prices, supply and trading agreements, or "mechanisms which provide information on the potential actions of the other economic agents." It follows that, by virtue of the regularities inscribed in the recurrent games that are played out in it, the field offers a predictable and calculable future and agents acquire in it transmissible skills and dispositions (sometimes called "routines") that form the basis of practical anticipations that are at least roughly well founded.

Because it is a particularity of the economic field that it authorizes and fosters the calculating vision and the strategic dispositions that go with it, one does not have to choose between a purely structural vision and a strategic vision: the most consciously elaborated strategies can be implemented only within the limits and in the directions assigned to them by the structural constraints and by the practical or explicit knowledge—always unequally distributed—of those constraints (the informational capital afforded to the occupants of a dominant position—particularly through presence on company boards or, in the case of banks, through the data provided by those requesting credit—is, for example, one of the resources that make it possible to choose the best strategies for capital management). Neoclassical theory, which refuses to take structural effects and, a fortiori, objective power relations into account, is able to explain the advantages accorded to those with the highest capital by the fact that, being more diversified, having greater experience and a greater reputation (and hence more to lose), they offer the guarantees that enable capital to be provided to them at a lower cost, all simply for reasons of economic calculation. And it will no doubt be objected that it is more parsimonious and rigorous to invoke the "disciplinary" role of the market as an agency ensuring optimal coordination of preferences (by virtue of individuals being forced to submit their choices to the logic of profit maximization on pain of being eliminated) or, more simply, the price effect.

Now the notion of the field breaks with the abstract logic of the automatic, mechanical, and instantaneous determination of prices in markets in which unfettered competition prevails:[8] it is the structure of the field, that is to say, the structure of relations of force (or power relations) among firms that determines the conditions in which agents come to decide (or negotiate) purchase prices (of materials, labor etc.) and selling prices (we see also in passing that, overturning entirely the usual image of "structuralism," conceived as a form of "holism" implying adherence to a radical determinism, this vision of action restores a certain free play to agents, without forgetting, however, that decisions are merely choices among possibles, defined, in their limits, by the structure of the field, and that actions owe their orientation and effectiveness to the structure of the objective relations between those engaging in them and those who are the objects of those actions). The structure of the relations of force among firms, which do not just interact indirectly, by way of prices, contributes, in most essential respects, to determining prices by determining, through the position occupied within this structure, the differential chances of influencing price-formation—for example, through the economy-of-scale effect resulting from the fact that bargaining positions with suppliers improve with size, or investment costs per unit of capacity diminish as total capacity increases. And it is this specific social structure that governs the trends immanent to the mechanisms of the field and, thereby, the degrees of freedom left for the strategies of the agents. It is not prices that determine everything, but everything that determines prices.

Thus, field theory stands opposed to the atomistic, mechanistic vision that hypostasizes the price effect and that, like Newtonian physics, reduces agents (shareholders, managers, or firms) to interchangeable material points, whose preferences, inscribed in an exogenous utility function or even, in the most extreme variant (formulated by Gary Becker, among others), an immutable one, determine actions mechanically. It also stands opposed, though in a different way, to the interactionist vision, which is, by virtue of the representation of the agent as a calculating atom, able to cohabit with the mechanistic vision, and according to which the economic and social order can be reduced to a host of interacting individuals, most often interacting on a contractual basis. Thanks to a series of postulates fraught with consequences, notably the decision to treat firms as isolated decision-makers maximizing their profits,[9] some industrial organization theorists transfer to the collective level, such as that of the firm (which, in reality, itself functions as a field) the model of individual decision-making on the basis of a conscious calculation, consciously oriented toward profit maximization (some readily accept that the model is unrealistic, recognizing, for example, that the firm is a "nexus of contract," though without deriving any consequences from this). In this way, industrial organization theory reduces the structure of the relations of force constitutive of the field to a set of interactions that in no respect transcend those engaged in the field at a particular moment and can therefore be described in the language of game theory. Being perfectly congruent in its basic postulates with the intellectualist theory that also underlies it, neoclassical theory, which, as is often forgotten, was explicitly and expressly constructed against the logic of practice—on the basis of postulates lacking any anthropological underpinning, such as the postulate that the system of preferences is already constituted and transitive[10]—tacitly reduces the effects that take place in the economic field to a play of reciprocal anticipations.

Similarly, those who, in order to avoid the representation of the economic agent as an egoistic monad confined to the "narrow pursuit of his interests" and as an "atomized actor taking decisions outside of any social constraints," remind us, as Mark Granovetter does, that economic action remains embedded in networks of social relations "generating trust and discouraging malfeasance,"[11] avoid "methodological individualism" only to fall back into the interactionist vision that, ignoring the structural constraint of the field, will (or can) acknowledge only the effect of the conscious and calculated anticipation each agent may have of the effects of its actions on the other agents (precisely what a theorist of interactionism, like Anselm Strauss, referred to as "awareness context");[12] or the effect, conceived as "influence," that "social networks," other agents, or social norms have on it. These are so many solutions that, eliminating all structural effects and objective power relations, amount to proposing a false supersession of the (itself spurious) alternative between individualism and holism.[13] Though there is no question here of denying the economic efficacy of "networks" (or, better, of social capital) in the functioning of the economic field, the fact remains that the economic practices of agents and the very potency of their "networks," which a rigorously defined notion of social capital takes into account, depend, first and foremost, on the position these agents occupy in those structured microcosms that are economic fields.

> It is not certain, then, that what is usually called the "Harvard tradition" (that is to say, the industrial economics developed by Joe Bain and his associates) does not deserve better than the somewhat condescending attitude "industrial organization theorists" usually accord it. It is perhaps better to move in the right direction with "loose theories," stressing the empirical analysis of industrial sectors, than to go off, with all the appearances of rigor, down a cul-de-sac, from a concern to present an "elegant and general analysis." I refer here to Jean Tirole, who writes: "The first wave, associated with the names of Joe Bain and Edward Mason and sometimes called the 'Harvard tradition,' was empirical in nature. It developed the famous 'structure-conduct-performance paradigm' according to which market structure (the number of sellers in the market, the degree of product differentiation, the cost structure, the degree of vertical integration with suppliers and so on) determines conduct (which consists of price, research and development, investment, advertising and so forth) and conduct yields market performance (efficiency, ratio of price to marginal cost, product variety, innovation rate, profits and distribution). This paradigm, although plausible, often rested on loose theories, and it emphasized empirical studies on industries."[14]
>
> Edward Mason does indeed have the merit of laying the foundations of a true structural (as opposed to interactionist) analysis of the functioning of an economic field: first, he argues that only an analysis capable of taking account both of the structure of each firm, which underlies the disposition to react to the particular structure of the field, and the structure of each industry, both of which are disregarded by advocates of game theory (a theory that, in passing, he criticizes in advance of its actual emergence: "Elaborate speculation on the probable behavior of A on the assumption that B will act in a certain way, seems particularly fruitless"), can account for all the differences between firms in terms of competitive practices, particularly in their pricing, production, and investment policies.[15] He subsequently strives to work out, both theoretically and empirically, the factors that determine the rela-

tive strength of the firm within the field: absolute size, number of firms, and product differentiation. Reducing the structure of the field to the space of possibles as they appear to the agents, he attempts, lastly, to draw up a "typology" of "situations" defined by "all those *considerations* which . . . [the seller] takes into account in determining his business policies and practices."[16]

THE ECONOMIC FIELD AS A FIELD OF STRUGGLES

The field of forces is also a field of struggles, a socially constructed field of action in which agents equipped with different resources confront each other in order to gain access to exchange and to preserve or transform the currently prevailing relation of force. Firms undertake actions there that depend, for their ends and effectiveness, on *their position in the field of forces*, that is to say, in the structure of distribution of capital in all its species. Far from being faced with a weightless, constraint-free world in which to develop their strategies at leisure, they are oriented by the constraints and possibilities built into their position and by the representation they are able to form of that position and the positions of their competitors as a function of the information at their disposal and their cognitive structures. The amount of free play afforded to them is undoubtedly greater than in other fields, on account of the particularly high degree to which the means and ends of action, and hence strategies, are made explicit, avowed, declared, if not indeed cynically proclaimed, particularly in the form of "native theories" of strategic action (management) expressly produced to assist the agents, and particularly business leaders, in their decisions, and explicitly taught in the schools where they are trained, such as the major business schools.[17] ("Management theory," a literature produced by business schools for business schools, fulfills a function identical to that of the writings of the European jurists of the sixteenth and seventeenth centuries who, in the guise of describing the state, contributed to building it: being directed at current or potential managers, that theory oscillates continually between the positive and the normative, and depends fundamentally on an overestimation of the degree to which conscious strategies play a role in business, as opposed to the structural constraints upon, and the dispositions of, managers.)

This kind of instituted cynicism, the very opposite of the denial and sublimation that tend to predominate in the worlds of symbolic production, means that in this case the boundary between the native representation and the scientific description is less marked: for example, one treatise on marketing refers to the "product market battlefield."[18] In a field in which prices are both stakes and weapons, strategies, both for those who produce them and for others, have spontaneously a *transparency* they never achieve in such worlds as the literary, artistic, or scientific fields, where the potential sanctions remain largely symbolic, that is to say, both vague and subject to subjective variations. And, in fact, as is attested by the work that the logic of the gift has to perform to mask what is sometimes known in French as *la vérité des prix* [literally: the truth of prices] (for example, price tags on presents are always carefully removed), the money price has a kind of brutal objectivity and universality that allows little scope for subjective appreciation (even if one can say, for example: "It's expensive for what it is" or "It's well worth the price you paid for it"). It follows that conscious or unconscious bluffing strategies, such as strategies of pure pretension, have less chance of succeeding in economic fields—though they also have their place in those fields, but rather as strategies of deterrence or, more rarely, strategies of seduction.

Strategies depend, first, on the particular configuration of powers that confers structure on the field and that, defined by the degree of concentration, that is to say, the distribution of market share among a more or less large number of firms, varies between the two poles of perfect competition and monopoly. If we are to believe Alfred D. Chandler, between 1830 and 1960 the economies of the large industrialized countries saw a process of concentration (particularly through a wave of mergers) that gradually eliminated the world of small competing firms to which the classical economists referred: "The profile of American industry delineated in the McLane Report and other sources is, then, one of production being carried out by a large number of small units employing less than fifty workers and still relying on traditional sources of energy. . . . Investment decisions for future output, as well as those for current production, were made by many hundreds of small producers in response to market signals, in much the way Adam Smith described."[19] Now, at the end of a period of development characterized, particularly, by a long series of mergers and a profound transformation of corporate structures, we see that, in most fields of industry, the struggle is confined to a small number of powerful competing firms that, far from pas-

sively adjusting to a "market situation," are able to shape that situation actively.

These fields are organized in a relatively invariant manner around the main opposition between those who are sometimes called "first movers" or "market leaders" and the "challengers."[20] The dominant firm usually has the initiative in terms of price changes, the introduction of new products, and distribution and promotion; it is able to impose the representation most favorable to its interests of the appropriate style of play and rules of the game, and hence of participation in the game and the perpetuation of that game. It constitutes an essential reference point for its competitors, who, whatever they do, are called upon to position themselves, either actively or passively, in relation to it. The threats it constantly faces—either of the appearance of new products capable of supplanting its own or of an excessive increase in costs such as to threaten its profits—force it to be constantly vigilant (particularly in the case of shared market dominance, where coordination designed to limit competition is the order of the day). Against these threats, the dominant firm has a choice of two quite different strategies: it can work to improve the overall position *of* the field, by attempting to increase overall demand; or it can defend or improve its established positions *within* the field (its market share).

The interests of the dominant are indeed bound up with the overall state of the field, defined, in particular, by the average opportunities for profit it offers, which also define the attraction it exerts (by comparison with other fields). It is in their interest to work for increased demand, from which they derive a particularly substantial benefit, since it is proportionate to their market share, by attempting to recruit new users, and stimulate new uses or a more intensive utilization of the products they offer (by acting, where applicable, on the political authorities). But, above all, they have to defend their position against the challengers by permanent innovation (new products and services, etc.) and by price reductions. By virtue of all the competitive advantages they enjoy (foremost among them the economies of scale linked to their size), they can lower their costs and, at the same time, reduce their prices, while limiting any reduction in their margins, making life very difficult for new entrants and eliminating the least well equipped competitors. In short, by virtue of the determining contribution they make to the structure of the field (and the price-formation in which that structure expresses itself), a structure whose effects manifest themselves in the form of barriers to entry or economic constraints, the "first movers" enjoy decisive advantages both in relation to already established competitors and to potential new entrants.[21]

The forces of the field orient the dominant toward strategies whose end is the perpetuation or reinforcement of their domination. In this way, the symbolic capital they have at their disposal, by virtue of their preeminence and also their seniority, enables them successfully to resort to strategies intended to intimidate their competitors, such as putting out signals to deter them from attacking (for example, by organizing leaks about price reductions or the building of a new factory)—strategies that may be pure bluff but that their symbolic capital renders credible and hence effective. It may even happen that these dominant firms, confident in their strength and aware they have the resources to sustain a long offensive that puts time on their side, choose to abstain from any riposte and allow their opponents to mount attacks that are costly and doomed to failure. Generally speaking, the hegemonic firms have the capacity to set the tempo of transformation in the various areas of production, marketing, research, and so on, and the differential use of time is one of the main levers of their power.

The appearance of a new, effective agent modifies the structure of the field. Similarly, the adoption of a new technology or the acquisition of a greater market share modifies the relative positions and field of all the species of capital held by the other firms. But the second-rank firms in a field can also attack the dominant firm (and the other competitors), either frontally, for example, by attempting to reduce their costs and prices (particularly by technological innovation), or laterally, by attempting to fill the gaps left by the action of the dominant firm and to occupy niches at the cost of a specialization of their production, or by turning the dominant firm's strategies back against it. In this case, success seems to depend on the relative position in the structure of capital distribution and, thereby, in the field: whereas very large firms can make high profits by achieving economies of scale, and small firms can obtain high profits by specializing to devote themselves to a limited market segment, medium-size firms often have low rates of profit because they are too big to benefit from tightly targeted production and too small to benefit from the economies of scale of the largest firms.

Given that the forces of the field tend to reinforce the dominant positions, one might well wonder how real transformations of relations of force within a field are possible. In fact, *technological capital* plays a crucial role here, and we may cite a number of cases in which dominant firms have been supplanted through a technological change that, thanks to ensuing cost reductions, handed the advantage to smaller competitors. But technological capital is effective only if it is associated with other kinds of capital. This no doubt explains the fact that victorious challengers are very seldom small, emerging firms and that, where they are not the product of mergers between existing firms, *they originate in other nations or, particularly, from other subfields.* It most often falls to the large firms to effect revolutions—firms that, by diversifying, can take advantage of their technological competences to present a competitive proposition in new fields. So, the changes within a field are often linked to changes in the relations with the exterior of that field.

To these boundary-crossings must be added also *redefinitions of boundaries* between fields: some fields may find themselves segmented into smaller sectors, the aeronautics industry dividing up, for example, into producers of airliners, fighter planes, and tourist aircraft; or, conversely, technological change may lower the barriers between industries that were previously separated: for example, computing, telecommunications, and office technology are increasingly coming to be merged, with the result that firms previously present in only one of the three subfields are increasingly tending to find themselves in competition in the new space of relationships that is forming—the field of the audiovisual industry undergoing drastic change as a result of new entrants breaking into it from telecommunications and computing, where firms have resources greatly exceeding those of the traditional agents. In this case, a single firm may come into competition not merely with other firms in its field, but also with firms belonging to various other fields. We can see, in passing, that in economic fields, as in all other categories of field, the *boundaries* of the field are at stake in the struggles within the field itself (most notably, through the question of possible substitutes and the competition they introduce); and that, in each case, empirical analysis alone can determine these. (It is not uncommon for fields to have a quasi-institutionalized existence in the form of branches of activity equipped with professional organizations functioning as clubs for the managers of the industry, defense groups for the prevailing boundaries, and hence for the principles of exclusion underlying them; and as representative bodies for dealing with the public authorities, trade unions, and other similar bodies, in which capacity they are equipped with permanent organs of action and expression.)

However, of all exchanges with the exterior of the field the most important are those established with the state. Competition among firms often takes the form *of competition for power over state power*—particularly over the power of regulation and property rights[22]—and for the advantages provided by the various state interventions: preferential tariffs, trade licenses, research and development funds, public sector contracts, funding for job-creation, innovation, modernization, exports, housing, and so on. In their attempts to modify the prevailing "rules of the game" to their advantage, and thereby to exploit some of their properties that can function as capital in the new state of the field, dominated firms can use their social capital to exert pressures on the state and to have it modify the game in their favor.[23] Thus, what is called the market is the totality of relations of exchange between competing agents, direct interactions that depend, as Simmel has it, on an "indirect conflict" or, in other words, on the socially constructed structure of the relations of force to which the different agents engaged in the field contribute to varying degrees through the modifications they manage to impose upon it, by drawing, particularly, on the state power they are able to control and guide. The state is not simply the regulator put there to maintain order and confidence, the arbiter responsible for "overseeing" firms and their interactions, as commonly conceived. In the quite exemplary case of the field of production of single-family houses, as in many other fields, it contributes, quite decisively, to the construction of both demand and supply, each of these two forms of intervention occurring under the direct or indirect influence of the parties most directly concerned.[24]

Other external factors capable of contributing to a transformation of relations of force within the field include transformations of sources of supply (for example, the great petroleum finds of the early twentieth century) and changes in demand determined by demographic changes (such as the fall in the birthrate or increased life expectancy) or in lifestyles (women's increased participation in the labor force, which leads to a fall in demand for certain products linked to the traditional definition of women's roles and creates new markets, such as those for frozen foods and microwave ovens). In fact, these external factors exert their effects on the relations of force within the field only through the logic of those re-lations of force, that is to say, only to the extent that they provide an advantage to the challengers: they enable the challengers to gain a position in specialized niche-markets when it is difficult for "first movers," focused on standardized, volume production, to satisfy the very particular demands of these markets—those of a particular category of consumer or a specific regional market—and the footholds gained by the challengers may constitute bridgeheads for subsequent development.

THE FIRM AS A FIELD

It is clear that decisions on prices or in any other area of activity do not depend on a single actor, a myth that conceals the power games and stakes within the firm functioning as a field or, to put it more precisely, within the field of power specific to each firm. In other words, if we enter the "black box" that is the firm, we find not individuals, but, once again, a structure—that of the firm as a field, endowed with a relative autonomy in respect of the constraints associated with the firm's position within the field of firms. Though the surrounding field affects its structure, this embedded field, as a specific relation of force and area of free play, defines the very terms and stakes of the struggle, giving a particular cast to them that often renders them unintelligible, at first sight, from the outside.

If the strategies of firms (most notably with regard to prices) depend on the positions they occupy within the structure of the field, they depend also on the structure of power positions constitutive of the internal governance of the firm or, more exactly, on the (socially constituted) dispositions of the directors [*dirigeants*] acting under the constraint of the field of power within the firm and of the field of the firm as a whole (which may be characterized in terms of indices such as the hierarchical composition of the labor force, the educational and, in particular, scientific capital of the managerial staff, the degree of bureaucratic differentiation, the weight of the trade unions, etc.). The system of constraints and inducements that is built into the position within the field and inclines the dominant firms to act in the direction most likely to perpetuate their domination, has nothing inevitable about it, nor does it even represent a kind of infallible instinct orienting firms and managers toward the choices most favorable to the maintenance of acquired advantages. Reference is often made, in this connection, to the example of Henry Ford, who, after his brilliant success in production and distribution had made him the manufacturer of the world's cheapest automobiles, destroyed his firm's competitive capacities in the period after the First World War by driving out almost all his most experienced and competent managers, who subsequently brought about the success of his competitors.

This being said, though it enjoys relative autonomy from the forces of the overall field, the structure of the field of power within the firm is itself closely correlated with the position of the firm in that field, principally through the *correspondence* between, on the one hand, the volume of the firm's capital (itself linked to the age of the firm and its position in the life cycle—hence, roughly speaking, to its size and integration) and the structure of that capital (particularly, the relative proportions of financial, commercial, and technical capital) and, on the other, the structure of the distribution of the capital among the various directors [*dirigeants*] of the firm, that is, between owners and "functionaries"—managers—and, among these latter, between the holders of different species of cultural capital: predominantly financial, technical, or commercial, that is to say, in the French case, between the various elite corps and the schools where they received their training: the École Nationale d'Administration, the École Polytechnique, or the École des Hautes Etudes Commerciales.[25]

Undeniable trends can be identified over the long term in the evolution of the relations of force between the major agents in the field of power within firms: most notably one sees, first, a preeminence of entrepreneurs with a mastery of new technologies, capable of assembling the funds required to exploit them, then the increasingly inevitable intervention of bankers and financial institutions, and finally the rise of managers.[26] However, apart from the fact that one must analyze the particular form the configuration of the distribution of powers among firms assumes at each state of each field, it is by analyzing, for each firm at every moment, the form of the configuration of powers within the field of power *over* the firm that one can fully understand the logic of the struggles in which the firm's goals are determined. It is, in fact, clear that these goals are the stakes in struggles and that, for the rational calculations of an enlightened "decision maker," we have to substitute the political struggle among agents who tend to identify their specific interests (linked to their position in the firm and their dispositions) with the interests of the firm and whose power can no doubt be measured by their capacity to identify, for better or for worse (as the Henry Ford example shows), the interests of the firm with *their interests within* the firm.

STRUCTURE AND COMPETITION

To take into account the structure of the field is to say that competition for access to exchange with clients cannot be understood as being oriented solely by conscious, explicit reference to direct competitors or, at least, to the most dangerous of them, according to Harrison White's formula: "Producers watch each other within a market."[27] The same point is made even more explicitly by Max Weber, who sees here a "peaceful conflict" to seize "chances or advantages also wanted by others." He writes: "the potential partners are guided in their offers by the potential action of an indeterminately large group of real or imaginary competitors rather than by their own actions alone."[28] Weber is here describing a form of rational calculation, but a calculation quite different in its logic from that of economic orthodoxy: not agents who make their choices on the basis of information furnished by prices, but agents taking account of the actions and reactions of their competitors and "evolv[ing] roles on the basis of each other's behavior"; hence they are equipped with information about their competitors and capable of acting with or against them, as in the action of bargaining, the "most consistent form of market formation," and the "compromise of interests" that seals it. However, though he has the virtue of substituting the *relationship with the totality of producers* for the transaction with the partner or client alone, he reduces that relationship to a conscious, considered interaction between competitors investing in the same object ("all parties potentially interested in the exchange"). And it is the same with Harrison White, who, though he sees the market as a "self-reproducing social structure," seeks the underlying principle behind the strategies of the producers not in the constraints inherent in their structural position, but in the observation and deciphering of signals given out by the behavior of other producers: "Markets are self-reproducing social structures among specific cliques of firms and other actors who evolve roles from observations of each other's behavior."[29] Or elsewhere: "Markets are tangible cliques of producers watching each other. Pressure from the buyer side creates a mirror in which producers see themselves, not consumers."[30] The producers, armed with the knowledge of the cost of production, attempt to maximize their income by determining the right volume of production "on the basis of observed positions of all other producers" and seek a niche in the market.

The point is, in fact, to subordinate this "interactionist" description of strategies to a structural analysis of the conditions that delimit the space of possible strategies—while, at the same time, not forgetting that competition among a small number of agents in strategic interaction for access (for some of them) to exchange with a particular category of clients is also, and above all, an encounter between producers occupying different positions within the structure of the specific capital (in its different species) and clients occupying positions in social space homologous to the positions those producers occupy in the field. What are commonly called *niches* are simply those sections of the clientele that structural affinity assigns to the different firms, and particularly to second-rank firms: as I have shown for cultural goods and goods with a high symbolic content such as clothes or houses, one can probably observe in each field a homology between the space of the producers (and products) and the space of the clients distributed according to the pertinent principles of differentiation. We may note, in passing, that this amounts to saying that the sometimes lethal constraints the dominant producers impose on their current or potential competitors are invariably mediated by the field: consequently, competition is never other than an "indirect conflict" (in Simmel's sense) and is not targeted directly against the competitor. In the economic field, as elsewhere, the struggle does not need to be inspired by any intention to destroy for it to produce destructive effects. (We may deduce an "ethical" consequence from the vision of the worlds of production as fields: just as we can say with Harrison White that "each firm is distinctive," as a position in a field, a point in a space, without being obliged to suppose that all its strategies are inspired by a pursuit of distinction—the same thing being true of every undertaking of cultural production, for example on the part of an artist, a writer, or a sociologist—so we can assert that every agent committed to a field is engaged in an "indirect conflict" with all those engaged in the same game: his/her actions may have the effect of destroying them, without being in the least inspired by any destructive intent, or even any intention to outdo them or compete with them.)

THE ECONOMIC HABITUS

Homo economicus, as conceived (tacitly or explicitly) by economic orthodoxy, is a kind of anthropological monster: this theoretically minded man of practice is the most extreme personification of the scholastic fallacy,[31] an intellectualist or intellectualocentric error very common in the social sciences (particularly in linguistics and ethnology), by which the scholar puts into the heads of the agents he is studying—housewives or households, firms or entrepreneurs, et cetera—the theoretical considerations and constructions he has had to develop in order to account for their practices.[32] It is one of the virtues of Gary Becker, who is responsible for the boldest attempts to export the model of the market and the (supposedly more powerful and efficient) technology of the neoclassical firm into all the social sciences, that he declares quite openly what is sometimes concealed within the implicit assumptions of scholarly routine:

"The economic approach . . . now assumes that individuals maximize their utility from basic preferences that do not change rapidly over time and that the behavior of different individuals is coordinated by explicit or implicit markets. . . . The economic approach is not restricted to material goods and wants or to markets with monetary transactions, and *conceptually* does not distinguish between major or minor decisions or between 'emotional' and other decisions. Indeed, the economic approach provides a framework applicable to all human behavior—to all types of decisions and to persons from all walks of life."[33]

Nothing now escapes explanation in terms of the maximizing agent—structural organizations, firms or contracts, parliaments and municipal authorities, marriage (conceived as the economic exchange of services of production and reproduction) or the household, and relations between parents and children or the state. This mode of universal explanation by an explanatory principle that is itself universal (individual preferences are exogenous, ordered, and stable and hence without contingent genesis or evolution) no longer knows any bounds. Gary Becker does not even recognize those bounds Pareto himself was forced to assume in the founding text in which, identifying the rationality of economic behavior with rationality as such, he distinguished between strictly economic behavior, which is the outcome of "a series of logical reasonings" based on experience, and behavior determined by "custom," such as the act of raising one's hat on entering a room[34] (thus acknowledging another principle of action—usage, tradition, or custom—unlike methodological individualism that recognizes only the alternative between conscious and deliberate choice, satisfying certain conditions of efficacy and coherence, and the "social norm,' which also requires a choice for it to become effective.

It is perhaps by recalling the arbitrary nature of the founding distinction (a distinction still present today in the minds of economists, who leave the *curiosa* or failings of economic operations to sociologists) between the economic order, governed by the effective logic of the market and a place of logical behaviors, and the uncertain "social" order, shot through with the "nonlogical" arbitrariness of custom, passions, and powers, that we can best contribute to the integration, or "hybridization," of the two disciplines of sociology and economics—disciplines that have undergone a dramatic separation, in spite of the efforts to the contrary on the part of some of their great founders (Pareto and Schumpeter, for example, in the direction of sociology, and Durkheim, Mauss, Halbwachs, and, above all, Weber, in the direction of economics).[35] One can reunify an artificially divided social science only by becoming aware of the fact that economic structures and economic agents or, more exactly, their dispositions, are social constructs, indissociable from the totality of social constructs constitutive of a social order. But this reunified social science, capable of constructing models that cannot easily be assigned to either of the two disciplines alone, will undoubtedly find it very hard to win acceptance, for both political reasons and reasons relating to the specific logic of scientific worlds. There are undoubtedly many who have an interest in obscuring the connections between economic policies and their social consequences or, more precisely, between so-called economic policies (the political character of which asserts itself in the very fact of their refusing to take account of the social) and the social, and economic, costs—which would not be so difficult to calculate if there were any will to do so—of their short- and long-term effects (I have in mind, for example, the increase in economic and social inequalities resulting from the implementation of neoliberal policies, and the negative effects of those inequalities on health, delinquency, crime, etc.). But if strong reasons exist for the cognitive hemiplegia currently afflicting sociologists and economists to perpetuate itself, in spite of the increasing efforts to overcome it, this is also because the social forces that weigh on the supposedly pure and perfect worlds of science, particularly through the systems of penalties and rewards embodied in scholarly publications, caste hierarchies, and so on, promote the reproduction of separate spaces, associated with different, if not indeed irreconcilable dispositions and structures of opportunity, which are the product of the initial separation.

It is the primary function of the concept of habitus to break with the Cartesian philosophy of consciousness and thereby overcome the disastrous mechanism/finalism alternative or, in other words, the alternative of determination by causes and determination by reasons; or, to put it another way, between so-called methodological individualism and what is sometimes called (among the "individualists") holism—a semiscientific opposition that is merely the euphemistic form of the alternative (undoubtedly the most powerful in the political order) between, on the one hand, individualism or liberalism, which regards the individual as the ultimate autonomous elementary unit, and, on the other, collectivism or socialism, which are presumed to regard the collective as primary.

Insofar as he/she is endowed with a habitus, the social agent is *a collective individual or a collective individuated by the fact of embodying objective structures*. The individual, the subjective, is social and collective. The habitus is socialized subjectivity, a historic transcendental, whose schemes of perception and appreciation (systems of preferences, tastes, etc.) are the product of collective and individual history. Reason (or rationality) is "bounded" not only, as Herbert Simon believes, because the human mind is generically bounded (there is nothing new in that idea), but because it is socially structured and determined, and, as a consequence, limited. Those who will be first to point out that this, too, is nothing new should ask themselves why economic theory has remained so solidly deaf to all reminders of these anthropological findings. For example, even in his day Veblen defended the idea that the economic agent is not a "bundle of desires," but "a coherent structure of propensities and habits,"[36] and it was James S. Duesenberry who observed that the explanation for consumer choices was to be found not in rational planning, but rather in "learning and habit formation" and who established that consumption was as dependent on past income as on present.[37] And it was Veblen again, anticipating the idea of "interactive demand," who, like Jevons and Marshall, long ago enunciated the effects of structure, or of position within a structure, on the definition of needs and hence on demand. In short, if there is a universal property, it is that agents are not universal, because their properties and, in particular, their preferences and tastes, are the product of their positioning and movements within social space, and hence of collective and individual history. The economic behavior socially recognized as rational is the product of certain economic and social conditions. It is only by relating it to its individual and collective genesis that one can understand its economic and social conditions of possibility and, consequently, both the necessity and the sociological limits of economic reason and of apparently unconditioned notions such as needs, calculation, or preferences.

This said, habitus is in no sense a mechanical principle of action or, more exactly, of reaction (it is not a "reflex"). It is *conditioned and limited spontaneity*. It is that autonomous principle which means that action is not simply an immediate reaction to a brute reality, but an "intelligent" response to an actively selected aspect of the real: linked to a history fraught with a probable future, it is the inertia, the trace of their past trajectory, that agents set against the immediate forces of the field, that means that their strategies cannot be deduced directly either from the immediate position or situation. It produces a response, the directing principle of which is not pregiven in the stimulus and that, without being entirely unpredictable, cannot be predicted on the basis of knowledge of the situation alone; a response to an aspect of reality that is distinguished by a selective and (in both senses of the term) partial—but not strictly "subjective"—apprehension of certain stimuli, by an attention to a particular side of things of which it can be said, without distinction, either that it "arouses interest" or that interest arouses it; an action that one can describe noncontradictorily as being both determined and spontaneous, since it is determined by *conventional, conditional* stimuli that exist as such only for an agent disposed to perceive them and capable of perceiving them.

The screen that the habitus introduces between stimulus and reaction is a screen of time insofar as, being itself the product of a history, it is relatively constant and durable, and hence *relatively* independent of history. As a product of past experiences and a whole collective and individual accumulation, it can be understood adequately only by a genetic analysis applying both to collective history—with, for example, the history of tastes, as illustrated by Sidney Mintz's demonstration of how the taste for sugar, originally an exotic luxury product reserved for the well-to-do, gradually became an indispensable element in the ordinary diet of the working classes[38]—and to individual history—with the analysis of the economic and social conditions of the genesis of individual tastes in terms of diet, decoration, clothing and also songs, theater, music or cinema, et cetera,[39] and, more generally, of the *dispositions* (in the dual sense of capacities and propensities) to perform economic actions adapted to an economic order (for example, calculating, saving, investing, etc.).

The concept of habitus also enables us to escape the dichotomy between finalism—which defines action as determined by the conscious reference to a deliberately set purpose and which, consequently, conceives all behavior as the product of a purely instrumental, if not indeed cynical, calculation—and mechanism, which reduces action to a pure reaction to undifferentiated causes. The orthodox economists and philosophers who defend rational action theory swing, sometimes in the space of a single sentence, between these two logically incompatible theoretical options: on the one hand, a finalist decisionism, in which the agent is a pure rational consciousness acting in complete awareness of the consequences, the principle of action being a reason or rational decision determined by a rational evaluation of probable outcomes; and on the other hand, a physicalism that regards the agent as an inertia-less particle, reacting mechanically and instantaneously to a combination of forces. But the task of reconciling the irreconcilable is made easier here by the fact that the two branches of the alternative are really only one: in each case, yielding to the scholastic fallacy, the scientific subject, endowed with a perfect knowledge of causes and probable outcomes, is projected into the active agent, presumed to be rationally inclined to set as his goals the opportunities assigned to him by the causes (it hardly needs saying that the fact that economists subscribe quite consciously to this fallacy in the name of "the right to abstraction" is not sufficient to obviate its effects).

Habitus is a highly economical principle of action, which makes for an enormous saving in calculation (particularly in the calculation of costs of research and measurement) and also in time, which is a particularly rare resource when it comes to action. It is, therefore, particularly well suited to the ordinary conditions of existence, which, either because of time pressure or an insufficiency of requisite knowledge, allow little scope for the conscious, calculated evaluation of the chances of profit. Arising directly out of practice and linked to it in both its structure and functioning, this practical sense cannot be assessed outside of the practical conditions of its implementation. This means that the tests to which "judgmental heuristics"[40] subjects individuals are doubly inadequate, since they attempt, in an artificial situation, to assess an aptitude to conscious and calculated evaluation of probable outcomes, the implementation of which itself presupposes a break with the inclinations of practical sense (this is, in fact, to forget that the calculus of probabilities was developed to counter the spontaneous tendencies of primary intuition).

The relation of the habitus to the field—a relationship that is obscure in practice because it lies below the level of the dualism of subject and object, activity and passivity, means and ends, determinism and freedom—in which the habitus determines itself in determining what determines it, is a calculation without calculator and an intentional action without intention, for which there is much empirical evidence.[41] In the particular (and particularly frequent) case in which the habitus is the product of objective conditions similar to those under which it operates, it generates behaviors that are particularly well suited to those conditions without being the product of a conscious, intentional search for adaptation (it is for this reason that we should beware of taking Keynes's "adaptive expectations" for "rational expectations," even if the agent with a well-adjusted habitus is, in a sense, a replica of the agent as producer of rational expectations). In this case, the effect of the habitus remains, so to speak, invisible, and the explanation in terms of habitus may seem redundant in relation to explanation in terms of the situation (one may even have the impression that we are dealing with an ad hoc explanation along the lines of the explanation of sleep by some "dormitive property"). But the specific efficacy of habitus can be clearly seen in all the situations in which it is not the product of the conditions of its actualization (increasingly frequent as societies become differentiated): this is the case when agents formed in a precapitalist economy run up, in some disarray, against the demands of a capitalist cosmos;[42] or when old people quixotically cling to dispositions that are out of place and out of time; or when the dispositions of an agent rising, or falling, in the social structure—a nouveau riche, a parvenu, or a déclassé—are at odds with the position that agent occupies. Such effects of hysteresis, of a lag in adaptation and counteradaptive mismatch, can be explained by the relatively persistent, though not entirely unchangeable, character of habitus.

To the (relative) constancy of dispositions there corresponds a (relative) constancy of the social games in which they are constituted: like all social games, economic games are not games of chance; they present regularities, and a finite number of similar patterns recur, which confers a certain monotony on them. As a result, the habitus produces *reasonable* (not rational) expectations, which, being the product of dispositions engendered by the im-

perceptible incorporation of the experience of constant or recurring situations, are immediately adapted to new but not radically unprecedented situations. As a disposition to act that is the product of previous experiences of similar situations, habitus provides a practical mastery of situations of uncertainty and grounds a relation to the future that is not that of a project, as an aiming for possible outcomes that equally well may or may not occur, but a relation of *practical anticipation*: discovering in the very objectivity of the world what is, apparently, the only course of action, and grasping time-to-come as a quasi present (and not as a contingent future), the anticipation of time-to-come has nothing whatever in common with the purely speculative logic of a calculus of risk capable of attributing values to the various possible outcomes. But habitus is also, as we have seen, a principle of differentiation and selection that tends to conserve whatever confirms it, thus affirming itself as a potentiality that tends to ensure the conditions of its own realization.

Just as the intellectualist vision of economic orthodoxy reduces the practical mastery of situations of uncertainty to a rational calculus of risk, so, drawing on game theory, it construes the anticipation of the behavior of others as a kind of calculation of the opponent's intentions, conceived hypothetically as intentions to deceive, particularly with regard to intentions themselves. In fact, the problem that economic orthodoxy resolves by the ultraintellectualist hypothesis of "common knowledge" (I know that you know that I know) is resolved in practice by the *orchestration of habitus* that, to the very extent that they are congruent, permits a mutual anticipation of the behavior of others. The paradoxes of collective action have their solution in practices based on the implicit assumption that others will act responsibly and with that kind of constancy and truth-to-self which is inscribed in the durable character of habitus.

A Well-Founded Illusion

Thus, the theory of habitus allows us to *explain the apparent truth of the theory that it shows to be false*. If a hypothesis as unrealistic as the one that founds rational action theory or rational expectation theory may seem to be validated by the facts, this is because, by virtue of an empirically established statistical correspondence between dispositions and positions, in the great majority of cases (the most noticeable exceptions being subproletarians, déclassés, and renegades, which the model does in fact enable us to explain nonetheless) agents form reasonable expectations, that is to say, expectations matching up to the objective probabilities—and almost always adjusted and reinforced by the direct effect of collective controls, particularly those exercised by the family. And the theory of habitus even enables us to understand why a theoretical construct such as the "representative agent," based on the hypothesis that the choices of all the different agents in a single category—consumers, for example—can, in spite of their extreme heterogeneity, be treated as the choice of a standard "representative individual" maximizing his utility, is not visibly invalidated by the evidence. Alan Kirman has shown not only that this fiction rests on very restrictive and special hypotheses, but that there are no grounds for asserting that the aggregated set of individuals, even if they were all maximizers, itself behaves as an individual maximizing its utility and, conversely, that the fact that a community presents a certain degree of rationality does not entail that all the individuals are acting rationally; Kirman consequently suggests that we may found a global demand function not on the homogeneity, but the heterogeneity, of agents, as highly dispersed demand behavior on the part of individuals is capable of producing very unified and highly stabilized overall aggregated demand behavior.[43] Now, there is a realist grounding for such a hypothesis in the theory of habitus and in the representation of consumers as a set of heterogeneous agents with dispositions, preferences, and interests that are very different (just as they have very different conditions of existence), but adjusted, in each case, to conditions of existence involving different chances, and subject, as a result, to the inbuilt constraints of the structure of the field—the structure of the overall economic field—and also of the more or less limited subspaces in which they interact with a limited subgroup of agents. There is little room in the economic field for "madcap behavior," and those who indulge in it pay the price for defying the immanent rules and regularities of the economic order by failure or disappearance.

In giving an explicit, systematic form to the philosophy of the agent and of action that economic theory most often accepts tacitly (because, among other reasons, with notions such as "preference" or "rational choice," economic orthodoxy is merely rationalizing a commonsense "theory" of decision making), the advocates of rational action theory (which includes a number of economists such

as Gary Becker) and of methodological individualism (such as James Coleman, Jon Elster, and their French epigones) will undoubtedly have rendered a great service to research: by its very excess and its unconcern for experience, their narrowly intellectualist (or intellectualocentric) ultrarationalism directly contradicts the best-established findings of the historical sciences of human practices. If it has seemed necessary to demonstrate that many of the established findings of economic science are perfectly compatible with a philosophy of agents, action, time, and the social world quite different from the one normally accepted by the majority of economists, this has, therefore, not been done here to satisfy some philosophical point of honor, but solely in an attempt to reunify the social sciences by working to restore economics to its true vocation as a historical science.

NOTES

This text was originally published as "Principes d'une anthropologie économique (in *Les structures sociales de l'économie*. Paris: Seuil, 2000). It has been translated by Chris Turner and checked by Richard Nice. For help with this chapter, we also thank Jerome Bourdieu, Johan Heilbron, and Loïc Wacquant. Printed with permission of Polity Press.

Paragraphs above that are indented and marked by a line on the left are, in the French original, printed in a smaller typeface (to indicate subordinate status).

1. In the absence, as yet, of any formalization along the lines laid down by these principles, we can call on correspondence analysis (the theoretical foundations of which are very similar) to help us bring out the structure of the economic field or, in other words, the true *explanatory principle* of economic practices.

2. Walton H. Hamilton et al., *Price and Price Policies* (New York: McGraw Hill, 1938).

3. Marc R. Tool, "Contributions to an Institutional Theory of Price Determination," in *Rethinking Economics: Markets, Technology, and Economic Evolution*, ed. Geoffrey M. Hodgson and Ernesto Screpanti (Hants: E. Elgar, 1991), 29–30.

4. This conception of social capital differs from the definitions that have subsequently been given in American sociology and economics in that it takes into account not only the network of relations, characterized as regards its extent and viability, but also the volume of capital of different species that it enables to be mobilized by proxy (and, at the same time, the various profits it can procure: promotion, participation in projects, opportunities for participation in important decisions, chances to make financial or other investments). See Bourdieu, "Le capital social. Notes provisoires," *Actes de la recherche en sciences sociales* 31 (January 1980): 2–3.

5. Cultural capital, technical capital, and commercial capital exist both in objectivized form (equipment, instruments, etc.) and in embodied form (competence, skills, etc.). One can see an anticipation of the distinction between the two states of capital, the objectivized and the embodied, in the

work of Thorstein Veblen, who criticizes the orthodox theory of capital for overestimating tangible assets to the detriment of intangible ones. See Thorstein Veblen, *The Instinct of Workmanship* (New York: Augustus Kelley, 1964).

6. Beth Mintz and Michael Schwartz, *The Power Structure of American Business* (Chicago: University of Chicago Press, 1985).

7. Jan A. Kregel, "Markets and Institutions as Features of a Capitalistic Production System," *Journal of Post-Keynesian Economics* 3, no. 1(1980): 32–48.

8. As R. H. Coase has pointed out, it is on the basis of the assumption, tacitly made in orthodox theory, of zero transaction costs that acts of exchange can be rendered instantaneous: "Another consequence of the assumption of zero transaction costs, not usually noticed, is that, when there are no costs of making transactions, it costs nothing to speed them up, so that eternity can be experienced in a split second." R. H. Coase, *The Firm, the Market, and the Law* (Chicago: University of Chicago Press, 1988), 15.

9. Jean Tirole, *The Theory of Industrial Organization* (Cambridge: MIT Press, 1988), 4.

10. The classic work of Amos Tversky and Daniel Kahneman has shown up the shortcomings of agents, and the mistakes they make, with regard to probability theory and statistics. See A. Tversky and D. Kahneman, "Availability, a Heuristic for Judging Frequency and Probability," *Cognitive Psychology* 2(1973): 207–32; see also Stuart Sutherland, *Irrationality, the Enemy Within* (London: Constable, 1992). There is a danger that the intellectualist assumption that underlies this research may lead us to miss the fact that the logical problem one infers from a real situation is not posed as such by the agents (friendship as a social relation is not informed by the principle that "my friends' friends are my friends") and the logic of dispositions means that agents are capable of responding in practice to situations involving problems of anticipation of opportunity that they cannot resolve abstractly. See Pierre Bourdieu, *The Logic of Practice* (Cambridge: Polity Press, 1990).

11. Mark Granovetter, "Economic Action and Social Structure: The Problem of Embeddedness," *American Journal of Sociology* 91(1985): 481–510.

12. Anselm L. Strauss, *Continual Permutations of Action* (New York: Aldine de Gruyter, 1993).

13. See Mark Granovetter, "Economic Institutions as Social Constructions: A Framework for Analysis," *Acta Sociologica* 35(1992): 3–11. Granovetter presents here a modified version of the alternative between "individualism" and "holism," which is rampant in economic (and sociological) orthodoxy, in the form of the opposition, borrowed from Dennis Wrong ("The Oversocialized Conception of Man in Modern Sociology," *American Sociological Review* 26[1961]: 183–93) between the "undersocialized view" dear to economic orthodoxy and the "oversocialized view," which assumes that agents are "so sensitive to the opinions of others that they automatically [obey] commonly held norms for behavior" (Granovetter, "Economic Action," 5) or that they have so profoundly internalized the norms or constraints that they are no longer affected by existing social relations (wholly erroneously, the notion of habitus is sometimes understood in this way). Hence the conclusion that, ultimately, this oversocialization and undersocialization have much in common, both of them regarding agents as closed monads, uninfluenced by "concrete, ongoing systems of social relations" (6) and "social networks." ·

14. Tirole, *Theory of Industrial Organization*, 2–3. A little further on, the author gives some hints regarding the costs

and benefits associated with the different categories of product (mainly, theoretical and empirical) on the economics market, which enables us to understand the comparative destinies of the "Harvard tradition" and the "new theory of industrial organization" he is defending: "Until the 1970s, economic theorists (with a few exceptions) pretty much ignored industrial organization, which did not lend itself to elegant and general analysis the way the theory of competitive general equilibrium analysis did. Since then, a fair number of top theorists have become interested in industrial organization."

15. Edward S. Mason, "Price and Production Policies of a Large-Scale Enterprise," *American Economic Review* 29(1939), supplement, 61–74 (esp. 64).

16. "The structure of a seller's market includes all those *considerations* which he takes into account in determining his business policies and practices." Mason, "Price and Production Policies," 68 (my italics, to point up the oscillation between the language of structure and structural constraint and that of consciousness and intentional choice).

17. Max Weber observes that commodity exchange is quite exceptional in that it represents the most instrumental, most calculating of all forms of action, this "archetype of rational action" representing "an abomination to every system of fraternal ethics." *Economy and Society*, ed. Guenther Roth and Claus Wittich, trans. Ephraim Fischoff et al., vol. 1 (Berkeley and Los Angeles: University of California Press, 1978), 637.

18. Philip Kotler, *Marketing Management, Analysis, Planning, Implementation, and Control* (Englewood Cliffs, N.J.: Prentice Hall, 1988), 239.

19. Alfred D. Chandler, *The Visible Hand: The Managerial Revolution in American Business* (Cambridge: Harvard University Press, 1977), 62.

20. Although this vision has sometimes been contested in recent years on the grounds that the recession has seen a constant overturning of hierarchies, and that mergers and acquisitions allow small firms to buy up large ones, or to compete effectively with them, the world's two hundred largest firms have nonetheless remained relatively stable.

21. Alfred D. Chandler, *Scale and Scope: The Dynamics of Industrial Capitalism* (Cambridge: Harvard University Press, 1990), 598–99.

22. See John L. Campbell and Leon Lindberg, "Property Rights and the Organization of Economic Action by the State," *American Sociological Review* 55(1990): 634–47.

23. Neil Fligstein has shown that one cannot understand the transformation of corporate control without dissecting the state of firms' relations over the long term with the state. And he has done this in the case most favorable to liberal theory, that of the United States, where the state remains a decisive agent in the structuring of industries and markets. See Neil Fligstein, *The Transformation of Corporate Control* (Cambridge: Harvard University Press, 1990). Further evidence of the decisive importance of central regulation is provided by the organized lobbying activity European firms carry on in Brussels.

24. The state, which plays a clear role in the case of the economy of house building, is far from being the only mechanism for coordinating supply and demand. Other institutions, such as networks of interpersonal relations in the case of crack cocaine, the "communities" formed by auctiongoers, or "matchmakers" in the economy of boxing, also play their part in the creative regulation of markets. See Phillippe Bourgois, *In Search of Respect: Selling Crack in El Barrio* (Cambridge: Cambridge University Press, 1996); Charles W. Smith, *Auctions* (Berkeley and Los Angeles: University of

California Press, 1990); and Loïc Wacquant, "A Flesh Peddler at Work: Power, Pain, and Profit in the Prizefighting Economy," *Theory and Society* 27, no. 1(1998): 1–42.

25. Among France's major employers I have elsewhere demonstrated a close homology between the space of firms and the space of their directors, as characterized by the volume and structure of their capital. See Pierre Bourdieu, *The State Nobility: Elite Schools in the Field of Power*, trans. Lauretta C. Clough (Cambridge: Polity Press, 1996), 300–335.

26. See Fligstein, *Transformation of Corporate Control*, which describes how the control of firms comes successively under the sway of the directors in charge of production, marketing, and, ultimately, finance. See also Neil Fligstein and Linda Markowitz, "The Finance Conception of the Corporation and the Causes of the Reorganization of Large American Corporations, 1979–1988," in *Sociology and Social Policy*, ed. William Julius Wilson (Beverly Hills, Calif.: Sage, 1993); Neil Fligstein and Kenneth Dauber, "Structural Change in Corporate Organization," *Annual Review of Sociology* 15 (1989): 73–96; and Neil Fligstein, "The Intraorganizational Power Struggle: The Rise of Finance Presidents in Large Corporations," *American Sociological Review* 52 (1987): 44–58.

27. Harrison White, "Where Do Markets Come From?" *American Journal of Sociology* 87(1981): 518.

28. Weber, *Economy and Society*, 636.

29. White, "Where Do Markets Come From?" esp. 518.

30. Ibid., 543.

31. Phrase in English in original [Trans.].

32. See Pierre Bourdieu, *Pascalian Meditations*, trans. Richard Nice (Cambridge: Polity Press, 2000), 49–50.

33. Gary S. Becker, *Treatise on the Family* (Cambridge: Harvard University Press, 1981), ix. See also *The Economic Approach to Human Behavior* (Chicago: University of Chicago Press, 1976).

34. Vilfredo Pareto, *Manual of Political Economy*, ed. Ann S. Schweir and Alfred N. Page, trans. Ann S. Schweir (London: Macmillan, 1972), 29–30.

35. See J.-C. Passeron, "Pareto, l'économie dans la sociologie," in *Economia, sociologia e politico nell'opera di Vilfredo Pareto*, ed. Corrado Malandrino and Roberto Marchionatti (Florence: Leo S. Olschki, 2000), 25–71.

36. Thorstein Veblen, "Why Is Economics Not an Evolutionary Science?" *Quarterly Journal of Economics*, July 1898, 390.

37. James S. Duesenberry, *Income, Saving, and the Theory of Consumer Behavior* (Cambridge: Harvard University Press, 1949).

38. Sidney Mintz, *Sweetness and Power: The Place of Sugar in Modern History* (New York: Penguin, 1985).

39. Pierre Bourdieu, *Distinction: A Social Critique of the Judgement of Taste*, trans. Richard Nice (London: Routledge and Kegan Paul, 1986); Lawrence W. Levine, *Highbrow/Lowbrow: The Emergence of Cultural Hierarchy in America* (Cambridge: Harvard University Press, 1988). As we see from the analysis of the economic and social determinants of preferences for buying a house or renting, we may repudiate the ahistorical definition of preferences without condemning ourselves to a relativism—which would rule out all rational knowledge—of tastes consigned to pure social arbitrariness (as the old formula *de gustibus non est disputandum*, invoked by Gary Becker, suggests). We are led, rather, to establish empirically the necessary statistical relations that form between tastes in the various fields of practice and the economic and social conditions of the formation of those tastes, that is to say, the present and past position of the agents in (or their trajectory through) the structure of the distribution of economic and cultural capital (or, if the reader prefers, the state at the given moment and the development over time of the volume and structure of their capital).

40. See Tversky and Kahneman, "Availability."

41. We may call in evidence here the findings of the behaviorist tradition, represented most notably by Herbert Simon, though without accepting this philosophy of action. Herbert Simon has stressed, on the one hand, the degree of uncertainty and incompetence that affects the process of decision making, and, on the other, the limited capacity of the human brain. He rejects the general maximization hypothesis, but retains the notion of "bounded rationality": agents may not be capable of gathering and processing all the information required to arrive at overall maximization in their decision making, but they can make a rational choice within the bounds of a limited set of possibilities. Firms and consumers do not maximize, but, given the impossibility of gathering and processing all the information required to achieve a maximum, they do seek to achieve acceptable minima (a practice Simon calls "satisficing"). Herbert Simon, *Reason in Human Affairs* (Stanford, Calif.: Stanford University Press, 1984).

42. See Pierre Bourdieu, *Algeria, 1960*, trans. Richard Nice (Cambridge: Cambridge University Press, 1979).

43. Alan P. Kirman, "Whom or What Does the Representative Individual Represent?" *Journal of Economic Perspectives*, 6(spring 1992): 117–36.

5 Behavioral Economics

Roberto Weber and Robyn Dawes

WHILE RESEARCH in behavioral economics goes back to at least the middle of the twentieth century (e.g., Herb Simon's [1955] work on bounded rationality), it is largely in the last decade of the twentieth century that behavioral economics developed from a vague and broad research area pursued by a small number of researchers at an even smaller number of academic institutions to a large, widely recognized subfield within economics. Over the last few years of the century, the standing and acceptance of behavioral economics changed considerably as many economists took notice of behavioral work and began to accept it as valid economic research. In fact, the change was so sudden and significant that, while at the beginning of the 1990s at most one or two of the top 10 economics departments had a behavioral economist, by the end of the decade at most one or two did not. The rise in publication of behavioral economics papers in the top research journals was similarly striking. Perhaps the clearest indication of the acceptance of behavioral economics as a valid area of economic research by most mainstream economists is the awarding of the 2002 Nobel Prize in economics to two pioneers of behavioral work, Daniel Kahneman and Vernon Smith.

The purpose of this chapter is to introduce briefly some of the areas of work in behavioral economics, and to tie the work together by noting common aspects. We do not attempt a comprehensive survey of all (or even a large part) of the work in behavioral economics. As a consequence of the growth of the area, it is impossible to cover in one chapter all the work in economics that falls under the behavioral label—in fact, there are entire books devoted to subareas of behavioral economics (e.g., Thaler 1993; Camerer 2003a). Specifically, we will provide an introduction to the history and development of three of the more important areas of behavioral work. These subareas are (1) nonegoistic preferences, which is concerned with relaxing the assumption of narrow self-interest underlying most economic theory, (2) intertemporal choice, which addresses problems with the discounted utility model, and (3) reference-dependence in preferences, which allows for the possibility that reference levels (such as the status quo and expectations) affect preferences. Each of these areas will be defined and discussed in detail in later sections, and we will briefly describe some of the key work, both empirical and theoretical, in each of them.

Of course, work in behavioral economics extends well beyond these areas. In fact, different forms of behavioral research are present in most areas of economics, such as labor economics (Camerer et al. 1997), law and economics (Sunstein 2000), financial economics (Schleifer 2000; Shiller 2000), and macroeconomics (Akerlof 2002). However, the three topics selected above represent areas of behavioral research that directly question some of the most basic assumptions on which traditional economics is built and are therefore likely to have a broad and important impact on economic research.

After introducing and describing work in the three areas, we bring them together by pointing to a common thread in behavioral economic research. Specifically, we argue that one common element of this work, and one of its key differences from traditional economics, is that it takes into account *trajectories*. Whereas traditional theoretical work in economics has a static view of preferences in which they are rarely directly affected by what occurred previously or what will happen in the future, behavioral economists have recognized that trajectories—of consumption, of action, and so on—matter. For instance, when considering the possibility of a person eating an apple in a given month, traditional economic analysis rests on the assumption that there is an implicit (or explicit) value a decision maker places on the consumption or use of the apple and that he or she will experience this value in one month's time (which may lead to valuing it less than the value of an apple in the present, but only because consumption in the future is always valued less than in the present). Behavioral economics, however, notices that other factors might make a difference. Specifically, decision makers might derive pleasure from the anticipation of receiving the apple, or might care about what things they get to eat before or after the apple, or might care about if and when others get their apple. Therefore, the main argument with, and difference from, the traditional approach is that how we get somewhere often matters almost as much as what is there. This argument will be presented in more detail following a discussion of behavioral economics and some of its areas of research.

Following this argument, we discuss the links between behavioral economics and economic sociology. We note that—though not immediately transparent—these links are nonetheless present and provide fruitful avenues for future research.

Finally, we conclude with discussion of specific contributions behavioral economics has made to the field of economics, and we point to possible future work in the area. To begin, however, we will attempt to define behavioral economics and the approach used by its researchers.

What Is Behavioral Economics?

Behavioral economics is the combination of economics and other, more behaviorally descriptive, social sciences. More precisely, behavioral economics results when economists combine research and methods from economics and other social sciences with the goal of improving the descriptive value of economic theory.[1] The result is an area of research in social science that relies on the theoretical and methodological approaches of economics, but carefully observes actual behavior and uses the results of such observation to modify existing theory.

A key aspect of behavioral economics is that, while it is an area of research that brings together work in several of the social sciences, it is still primarily focused on doing so within the field of economics. The main goal of behavioral economists is to change the way that economics is done by replacing behaviorally unrealistic assumptions of economic theory and analysis, while keeping the approach of economic research that has proved valuable. Therefore, the goal of most behavioral economists is not to tear down economics and replace it with something else, but rather to improve the existing economic approach to increase its

value as a descriptive and positive science.[2] Behavioral economists are interested in disciplining the basic assumptions of economic models (such as the rational choice framework that underlies expected utility maximization, the cornerstone of traditional microeconomics and decision theory) with behavioral observation. The main contention of behavioral research is that many of the basic assumptions in standard economic models (e.g., self-interest, optimization) are not based on how people actually make economic decisions, and that they therefore lead to a descriptively worse theory than one based on more behaviorally correct assumptions. To achieve a better theory, behavioral economists argue, it is necessary to look at how real people actually behave and decide, and then use observed regularities to inform the basic elements of a theory of behavior.

This desire to work within economics, rather than from outside it, has important implications for behavioral economics and its researchers. First, most behavioral economists are *economists*. Consequently, they have realized that the best way to win arguments with economists over economic assumptions is by doing careful, convincing economic research, and that to do this it is necessary to use the tools and standards of economic research (e.g., the rigor of formal theory and the statistical methods of econometrics). Therefore, most research in behavioral economics is done by researchers with a solid training in economics, and the most convincing research is done by people who are as well trained in the tools of economic research as the best "traditional" economists.

Stages of Development of Behavioral Research

Research in several subareas within behavioral economics usually progresses toward improving the descriptive value of economic theory through similar stages of research. These stages are (1) the demonstration of a behavioral result anomalous with traditional economic theory, (2) the replication, collection, and synthesis of a behavioral regularity, and (3) the development of behavioral theory incorporating the regularity.[3] In most cases, one stage naturally leads to the next. Of course, categorizing the complex and often haphazard process of scientific discovery in these three simple stages simplifies a progression that is inherently much messier in reality. However, this categorization traces the path of most areas of behavioral work, progressing from initial empirical demonstrations of anomalies (often viewed with skepticism by mainstream economists) to the development of behaviorally based economic theory—built on well-established regularities.

The first stage of research is the observation of behavior. Much of this observation is motivated by work in other social sciences demonstrating behavior that is systematically inconsistent with traditional economics. Behavioral economists then attempt to demonstrate these behavioral results using approaches and settings that are both convincing and important to other economists. To do this, behavioral economists often rely on the methods and sources of observation used by traditional economists. A large amount of behavioral "observation" is done using the same real-world empirical data used by traditional economists (e.g., large longitudinal surveys; data on employment, prices, and consumption; data from financial markets). When using these data, behavioral researchers typically look for reliable patterns of deviations from the predictions of traditional economic models.

An equally important part of this observation comes from a method borrowed from other social sciences (notably psychology): the laboratory experiment. Experiments present an almost ideal way to test basic assumptions of behavior. The control in a laboratory setting allows an experimenter to explore the source and causes of behavior carefully, while eliminating many possible confounds. Economists have designed experiments similar to those in other social sciences: subjects are brought into a "laboratory" where they are presented with a task, problem, or artificial environment (e.g., a market), and then their decisions and actions are recorded and analyzed.

However, when using experiments as a tool for research, behavioral economists have distinguished themselves from other social scientists by focusing on experiments that are likely to be convincing to traditional economists skeptical of experimental research. As a result, most experimental work in economics has followed certain guidelines that may seem odd and overly restrictive to other social scientists. For instance, experimental economists avoid all deception in experiments (the tests are intended to study basic processes that should surface even when subjects are aware of what is being tested), they pay subjects for their decisions (if the tests do not provide an incentive to behave rationally, then subjects may have no reason to do so), they use experiments in which the main task is repeated several times (if subjects behave irrationally

in only one or two trials, this does not mean they would not quickly adjust with experience),[4] and until recently they have avoided context in experiments (the basic processes being tested should be apparent in the most basic situations when interfering elements have been stripped away). While the merit of these guidelines is open to debate—particularly from researchers in other social sciences—they have allowed behavioral research to preemptively address several of the concerns that might have been raised by traditional economists in response to the results.

Another important criticism by traditional economists of experiments in economics (and the usual last resort that skeptical traditional economists use to argue that experimental research is not valid for informing economics) is that they are often done using an unsophisticated subject pool (college students) making decisions for small stakes (e.g., Aumann 1990). This criticism has been addressed by collecting additional data demonstrating that behavior anomalous with traditional economic theory persists even when decision makers are experienced and dealing with high stakes (Lichtenstein and Slovic 1973; Shefrin and Statman 1985; Hoffman, McCabe, and Smith 1996). The effect of increasing incentives in experiments is typically negligible, and, more importantly, no regularly observed behavioral result has been overturned by raising incentives (Camerer and Hogarth 1999).

The second common stage in research in behavioral economics is the collection and synthesis of evidence supporting a particular behavioral phenomenon. This means both that behavioral results are replicated and carefully tested across manipulations, researchers, and sources of data, and that this evidence is then collected and synthesized by those most familiar with the area. To clearly establish and understand a behavioral regularity, behavioral economists have relied on the collection of a large body of evidence demonstrating and dissecting a phenomenon—and on someone familiar with the research area synthesizing the evidence supporting the phenomenon (e.g., Thaler 1992; Camerer and Thaler 1995; Babcock and Loewenstein, 1997).

Most behavioral regularities have been demonstrated in several independent studies. Because the goal of behavioral economists is to convince even the most skeptical traditional economists of the robustness of these behavioral regularities, it is necessary to build a solid case with as many separate pieces of evidence as possible. In addition, in several areas of behavioral research, the empirical demonstration of an anomaly often encounters alternative explanations that are consistent with traditional models. (For example, demonstrations of nonegoistic behavior in experiments were often met with the criticism that subjects may be affected by reputation and repeated interaction effects since their actions were observable by the experimenters.) To address these possible alternative explanations (no matter how ludicrous), behavioral economists have countered with more data and studies that control for these possibilities. (In the example above, experimental economists demonstrated that nonegoistic behavior persists even in "double blind" experiments in which the actions of a participant are not known even by the experimenter [Berg, Dickhaut, and McCabe, 1995; Hoffman et al. 1994].) Once a behavioral regularity has been clearly established and synthesized, it is possible to begin to develop economic theory that includes the regularity.

The third stage in the development of an area within behavioral economics, and perhaps the most important, is the development of behavioral economic theory incorporating the behavioral phenomenon. Once a result has been firmly established and enough work done that it is possible to synthesize and understand the regularity, behavioral economists typically turn to developing modifications to traditional economic theory that rely on assumptions consistent with the behavioral phenomenon. This work has proceeded mainly by researchers asking two questions: "What part of the traditional theory is inconsistent with the behavior?" and "How can this part be modified to produce predictions consistent with the behavioral phenomenon?" For example, one of the first areas of research in behavioral economics was in altruism and nonegoistic behavior (see the next section). After first demonstrating that people do not always behave in the narrow, self-interested manner predicted by traditional economic theory and then collecting a large body of evidence supporting, and providing insights into, the phenomenon, behavioral economists turned their attention to developing an economic theory that incorporates this behavior. By asking the above two questions, behavioral theorists first noted that the narrow definition of self-interest in traditional economic theory was leading to incorrect predictions, and then created models replacing this assumption with others in which individuals can derive welfare from the outcomes experienced by others and from the actions of these others (e.g., Andreoni and Miller 2002; Rabin 1993).

While behavioral theory is the product of empirical observation, the creation of behavioral theory—or sometimes competing behavioral theories by different researchers—often produces the need for more behavioral observation. This need arises because the new theories make predictions that can then be tested to determine their descriptive validity. As a result, behavioral theory is sometimes produced, demonstrated to be incorrect by empirical testing, and then replaced with new theory that takes into account the additional evidence.[5] However, it is important to draw a distinction between areas of economic research that have reached the stage where economic theory is being produced and those that have not, because the development of theory usually marks a point at which traditional economists begin to take the associated behavioral regularity seriously.

As the following sections of this chapter will indicate, research in several areas of behavioral economics has gone through each of the three steps indicated above: after the behavioral anomaly is first demonstrated, it is explored and better understood through further observation and synthesis, leading to the final stage when its key elements are incorporated into formal economic theory. The growth of behavioral economics means that a review of the whole field is beyond the scope of this chapter. However, we hope that the presentation of the development of some of the key areas of research will leave the reader with an understanding of the kind of work done by researchers in the field, and of the type of conclusion that results from this work.

BEHAVIORAL RESEARCH ON NONEGOISTIC PREFERENCES

While some of the first empirical demonstrations of nonegoistic behavior in economics came from laboratory experiments in public goods games (see below) economists have long recognized the possibility that people may care about things other than their direct, personal, material gains. For instance, even the earliest economists, such as Adam Smith and Francis Edgeworth, wrote about sympathy and altruism as important elements of economic decision making [6] In fact, while traditional economic theory has largely focused on the self-interest of the butcher, the brewer, and the baker in Adam Smith's *The Wealth of Nations* (1776), it has largely ignored the same author's writings in *The Theory of Moral Sentiments* ([1759] 2000) on the lack of self-interest:

How selfish soever man may be supposed, there are evidently some principles in his nature, which interest him in the fortunes of others, and render their happiness necessary to him, though he derives nothing from it, except the pleasure of seeing it. (3)

Overlooking Smith's argument created a need, centuries later, to reexplore the possibility of more than narrow self-interest in preferences.

The earliest domain in which the self-interest assumption was carefully examined in economics was in experiments testing public goods problems. Public goods problems—which share the same underlying structure as social dilemmas, the tragedy of the commons, and collective action problems—are those in which an individual's marginal benefit of contributing to the production of the good is negative, but the impact on social welfare (the sum of all individuals' benefits) of contributions is positive. The problem is the same one as in the well-known prisoner's dilemma, in which there is one action that is socially optimal (cooperate), but another that makes an individual better off (defect). Public goods have long interested economists (e.g., Samuelson 1954), because of the prediction that no one should ever take the action that is socially optimal at a cost to themselves. Doing so, according to traditional economic theory, is irrational.

Careful demonstration of nonegoistic behavior began with the work of social psychologists. Dawes and Orbell and colleagues, who were familiar with the traditional economic assumption of self-interest, studied subjects' decisions in social dilemmas.[7] Several studies (e.g., Dawes, McTavish, and Shaklee 1977; Van de Kragt, Orbell, and Dawes 1983; Dawes et al. 1986) investigated the effects of manipulating payoffs, communication, and group identity on behavior in social dilemma and public goods games. While they found several interesting results related to the effects of group identity and communication (see Dawes and Messick 2000), the main result of interest to economists was the presence of high levels of cooperation inconsistent with the assumption of self-interest. Similar work by sociologists (Marwell and Ames 1981) led economists to take interest in exploring cooperation and non-self-interested behavior in public goods games.

In reaction to the above work indicating that subjects may contribute to public goods, experimental economists began exploring the extent to which similar behavior would arise in experiments that conformed to the guidelines of economics experiments, such as repetition (Isaac, Walker, and Thomas 1984; Kim and Walker 1984; Isaac, McCue, and Plott 1985). While most of these early experiments were intended to see if cooperation would go away in more carefully controlled (e.g., economics) experiments, the results were very similar to the previous ones in that subjects initially contributed substantially to the public good, foregoing self-interest.

While the results of these first experiments indicated that cooperation decreased with repetition, several subsequent studies showed that this was not simply the result of initial confusion by subjects in an experiment, and that cooperation persisted even with experience. For instance, Isaac and Walker (1988) and Andreoni (1988) found high degrees of cooperation among subjects with previous experience in public goods games when they played a new game. Therefore, while cooperation and giving decrease when the same public goods game is repeated with the same people, it goes back up when people start the game over with different people, or even when it is restarted with the same people.

The laboratory evidence invalidating the assumption of narrow self-interest goes beyond experiments on public goods. While there are many experiments that demonstrate this behavioral phenomenon, perhaps the most convincing series of studies are on ultimatum, trust, and dictator games. Ultimatum games are simple games in which there is a very clear prediction that follows from the self-interest assumption. In these two-player games, one player proposes a division of an original fixed amount of money, and the other player either accepts (in which case the allocation stands) or rejects (in which case both players receive nothing). If players care only about personal monetary outcomes, then the second player should accept any allocation greater than zero, and, knowing this, the first player should propose the allocation that gives the second player the smallest possible amount that is better than nothing. Across several studies, this prediction is wrong (Güth, Schmittberger, and Schwarze 1982; Kahneman, Knetch, and Thaler 1986a; Hoffman et al. 1994). The second player almost always rejects unfair divisions (e.g., anything less than 30 percent of the initial allocation), and the first player rarely makes offers that are too small to be accepted. The model offer is often 40 to 50 percent of the original amount.

Trust games measure the extent to which a player is willing to commit resources to a second player, who must then be trusted to return some of the surplus generated by the commitment. Specifically, one player decides how much of an original amount to send to a second player, and this second player then receives this amount multiplied by a constant (usually three). The second player then decides how much of this amount received to send back to the first player. Similarly to the prisoner's dilemma and public goods games, there is a socially optimal outcome (player 1 sends everything, player 2 returns half) that is not the equilibrium predicted by traditional theory. The traditional economic prediction is again clear: the second player should never return anything, and given this possible decision, the first player should never send anything. This prediction is again wrong. Even when actions are completely secret (even to the experimenters), subjects in the role of the second player typically return some portion of the increased amount, and subjects in the role of the first player typically send amounts greater than zero (Berg, Dickaut, and McCabe 1995).

Perhaps the clearest laboratory test of the self-interest assumption is the dictator game. While not precisely a game, it closely captures the decision to give some amount of money to another. In the dictator game, one subject is given a fixed amount of money and told to decide how much, if any, of this amount to send to another "player." Even in situations where choices are completely anonymous, the player who decides how much to give frequently leaves a significant amount for the other person (Forsythe et al. 1994; Hoffman et al. 1994; Hoffman, McCabe, and Smith 1996). When actions are completely anonymous, this result is inconsistent with the self-interest assumption.

An important regularity arising out of the several studies demonstrating other-regarding preferences is that people do not only care about the welfare of others or their own standing relative to others. Instead, it is often the case that what these others did previously directly impacts social preferences. Therefore, rather than always being kind or unkind toward others in a particular situation, people are likely to reciprocate kindness with kindness and unkindness with unkindness. This reciprocation occurs even in situations absent of reputation or other ways in which kindness may lead to greater personal rewards in the future—occurring, for example, in the anonymous, one-shot trust games discussed above. While evidence consistent with this regularity is found in several kinds of experiments (e.g., in both ultimatum and trust games the second mover is more likely to respond "kindly" to a "kind" action), perhaps the clearest demonstration of this phenomenon is in the work of Fehr and colleagues using the "gift exchange" game (e.g., Fehr, Kirchsteiger, and Riedl 1993, 1998). In this game, subjects in one group offer contracts to subjects in another, who then each decide whether or not to accept a contract and, if accepting one, whether to take a costly action that benefits the specific subject who offered that contract. This game models situations such as an employment market where a group of employers offers job contracts that are then possibly accepted by prospective employees, who then decide how much to work or shirk. The important finding across several experiments is that subjects in the second group, who have no incentive to exert costly "effort," respond more kindly (with more effort) to more generous contract offers.

While most of the evidence of social and other-regarding preferences comes from laboratory experiments, some studies demonstrated similar results outside of the laboratory. Using household survey responses, Kahneman, Knetsch, and Thaler (1986b) found that people have clear and consistent concerns about fairness and believe that these concerns are likely to influence behavior in the real world. In other work outside of the laboratory, Frank, Gilovich, and Regan (1993) report survey responses from college professors in which an overwhelming majority of respondents (more than 90 percent) reported giving some money to charity. Interestingly, even 90 percent of economics professors reported giving money. Yezer, Goldfarb, and Poppen (1996) used a field experiment in which unsealed, addressed envelopes containing $10 were left in undergraduate classrooms. The results again provided evidence against the self-interest hypothesis: over 40 percent of the envelopes were returned. These studies, together with the myriad everyday decisions people make that are inconsistent with the self-interest assumption in traditional economics (e.g., anonymous charitable donations, tipping on the last day of vacation, costly acts of vengeful vandalism), provide convincing evidence that reciprocity and other-regarding behavior are not just artifacts of the laboratory.

Research on the behavioral incorrectness of the self-interest assumption reached the second stage of behavioral economics research when researchers in the field began summarizing and synthesizing the key points of the above research and other work demonstrating the incorrectness of the self-interest assumption (e.g., Ledyard 1995; Dawes and Thaler 1988). Once these review pieces brought together the existing work and pointed out the key behavioral regularities, attention turned to incorporating the regularities into formal economic theory.

In early work that introduced nonselfish motives into economic theory, Akerlof (1982) introduced a model of reciprocal fairness in employment relationships similar to the gift-exchange experiments used subsequently by Fehr. In the model, workers may choose to behave in a non-self-interested manner due to norms to reciprocate kindness.

In other, more general, early work, Andreoni (1989, 1990) presented a model of individual utility in which decision makers derive "consumption" from the amount that they give to others. Andreoni and Miller (2002) showed that such models of utility-from-giving are consistent with the behavior of subjects in experiments and with a generalization of traditional economic theory that includes preferences for giving as a consumption good.

Since this early work, several other theoretical models have been proposed that relax the self-interest assumption (e.g., Rabin 1993; Fehr and Schmidt 1999; Bolton and Ockenfels 2000). The goal of most of these models has been to capture and describe the key feature of behavior discussed above—that reciprocity matters more than pure altruism. For example, in the theoretical contribution that perhaps best captures this feature, Rabin (1993) presents a model in which players care not just about outcomes, but about what others did and why they did so. This model captures a key feature of reciprocity: I am kind to those who do something good for me, especially if they are doing it to be kind. Rabin's model, which is an equilibrium model for games, therefore posits that players take into account not only what others did, but that individuals' beliefs about why others did what they did also matter. This accounting often results in situations where the predicted behavior is that people are mutually nice or mutually spiteful to each other (for instance, in the well-known prisoner's dilemma game, Rabin's model predicts equilibria where both players cooperate and where both players defect).

In other recent work modeling social, nonegoistic preferences, Akerlof and Kranton (2000) introduced the notion of identity to economic theory and modeled how it can affect preferences. Specifically, in their model, decision makers derive utility from behaving according to certain norms prescribed by their identity as members of particular groups. Thus, membership in a group associated with a particular behavior can increase the utility derived from such behavior.

The self-interest assumption underlying traditional economics seems unreasonable to most people outside the field. However, the amount of behavioral work summarized in this section reveals that convincing traditional economists of its lack of validity has been a long process. Significant advances in relaxing the assumption in economic models were begun only after decades of empirical demonstration both within and outside of the laboratory. Even now, the work is incomplete. While formal economic theory relaxing self-interest now exists, the models are often specific to a particular type of problem. More importantly, and partly because of the lack of a general model, the traditional approach is still the basis for an overwhelming majority of research within economics.

BEHAVIORAL RESEARCH ON INTERTEMPORAL CHOICE

Intertemporal choice is the area of research that deals with decisions that have consequences at other points in time. In economics, a large body of research deals with how individuals should and do make these types of decisions. For instance, saving is an important topic of economic theory and research that deals specifically with choices (how much to save) that impact future welfare (how much consumption is available in the future). Other important economic behaviors that fall within the area of intertemporal choice are addiction (drug use has potential future health consequences) and preventive health care (preventive actions involve a cost today that will likely produce a positive future consequence). These types of decisions boil down to one key question: how do individuals decide when considering delaying present gratification against the prospect of future rewards?

The traditional approach in economics—following largely from the work of Fisher (1930) and Samuelson (1937)—has been to assume that all of these choices simply involve weighing the benefit or cost of the present action versus the future consequences. The basis of the economic approach, the discounted utility model, simply assumes that there is a discount—or weighting—function that measures how valuable future welfare is relative to present welfare, when deciding in the present. When evaluated from today, a certain amount of welfare at a future point in time is worth some fraction $(0 < \delta < 1)$ of that same amount of welfare today. According to this approach, individuals discount the future consequences by this fraction and then choose the action that maximizes their welfare. This discount rate is applied to discrete periods of time (e.g., days, years), so that—from today's perspective—welfare one period from now (holding everything else constant) is worth δ times what it would be today, welfare two periods from now is worth δ^2, and welfare t periods from now is worth δ^t. An important assumption of this model is that future consumption only matters to the extent that an individual in the present weighs his or her welfare that far into the future.

This model produces strong implications about how individuals should consider temporal trade-offs. First, the model assumes that individuals are aware—at least implicitly—of the value of this discount rate at all points in time. Therefore, it must be the case that individuals know how much they will value trade-offs in the future. Second, as a consequence of this knowledge, people should display dynamic consistency, meaning that they should not make decisions that they later regret simply because they were unable to control themselves. Third, individuals should make the same trade-offs across decisions. This constancy means that discount rates for an individual should not vary across decision-making domains (i.e., one cannot be incredibly patient for some types of decisions and incredibly impatient for others). Finally, when choices over time involve monetary decisions, the discount rate used by individuals to decide should be close to the discount rate in financial markets.

As with the self-interest assumption, very early work in economics did not impose such restrictive assumptions on the way people made choices involving self-control and delayed gratification. For instance, in *The Theory of Moral Sentiments* ([1759] 2000), Adam Smith wrote:

At the very time of acting, at the moment in which passion mounts the highest, he hesitates and trembles at the thought of what he is about to do: he is secretly conscious to himself that he is breaking through those measures of conduct which, in all his cool hours, he had resolved never to infringe, which he had never seen infringed by others without the highest disapprobation, and of which the infringement, his own mind forebodes, must soon render him the object of the same disagreeable sentiments. Before he can take the last fatal resolution, he is tormented with all the agonies of doubt and uncertainty; he is terrified at the thought of violating so sacred a rule, and at the same time is urged and goaded on by the fury of his desires to violate it. He changes his purpose every moment; sometimes he resolves to adhere to his principle, and

not indulge a passion which may corrupt the remaining part of his life with the horrors of shame and repentance. (227)

In particular, Smith wrote of an important duality within an individual between an "indifferent spectator" who makes coolly calculated decisions and the "fury of his desires," when deciding whether to take actions with negative future consequences. This conflict is inconsistent with the discounted utility model where individuals simply maximize their lifetime welfare—weighing future experiences less than present ones—and have no self-control problems.

In contrast with research on nonegoistic preferences, early behavioral work on intertemporal choice began outside of the laboratory. In particular, the first work demonstrating anomalies that caught the attention of economists was empirical work analyzing household consumption and savings decisions. Some of these early studies (e.g., Hausman 1979; Gateley 1980) found individual discount rates exhibiting extremely present-favoring preferences. Specifically, when choosing appliances with varying prices and energy efficiency, consumers appeared to be much more concerned with lower present prices, as against future energy cost savings, than would a rational decision maker with access to financial markets.

Another demonstration of behavior inconsistent with the traditional model dealt with the pattern of lifetime savings and consumption. One of the applications of the discounted utility model to savings is the "life-cycle" model (see Modigliani and Brumberg 1954; Ando and Modigliani 1963), which predicts that consumption will be generally smooth over time and that the effects on consumption of unanticipated changes in income will also be spread over time. This model predicts that individuals will borrow to consume more during periods when their income is lower (youth, old age) and will save to finance this consumption when income is higher. Moreover, a sudden surprise windfall (such as winning the lottery) will be consumed at a constant rate over the remaining years of an individual's life. However, empirical studies have turned up behavioral results inconsistent with the life-cycle model. For instance, consumption is not smooth over time, but instead is very elastic with respect to income and events such as retirement (e.g., Mankiw, Rotemberg, and Summers 1985; Carroll and Summers 1991; Stephens 2003). Moreover, drops in consumption resulting from expected events such as retirement are unexpected; not only do people not smooth consumption over their lifetime, but they are frequently surprised by the extent to which their disposable income falls following retirement (Bernheim, Skinner, and Weinberg 2001; Loewenstein, Prelec, and Weber 1999).

Another domain of intertemporal choice that has long posed problems for traditional economic theory is addiction. Addictive goods are problematic because they involve decisions that individuals typically regret—either because past consumption strongly affects current preferences in an unpredicted way or because they were aware of future consequences but were unable to control themselves. This produces situations where individuals either do not correctly anticipate their preferences or where they take actions they know are suboptimal. As a consequence, observed behavior—such as that addicts try to quit but cannot, and that they regret past consumption—is difficult to explain using the traditional economic approach (see, for instance, Goldstein 1994). Becker and Murphy (1988) proposed a model of addiction that works within the traditional framework (i.e., addicts are rational and forward looking) and is consistent with some behavior typically associated with addiction—such as withdrawals and bingeing. However, one problem with addiction that is not explained by the model is the key fact that addicts typically regret their addiction and their level of consumption of the addictive substance. This dynamic inconsistency is difficult—if not impossible—to explain using modifications of the discounted utility model such as that of Becker and Murphy.

As in the behavioral economics research on nonegoistic preferences, the behavioral regularities inconsistent with the traditional model were explored in experiments, as well as in the field. Early experimental work in the area demonstrated a behavioral regularity problematic for traditional theory. One implication of the traditional approach is that the discount rate should remain the same, regardless of when the delayed gratification takes place or how long the delay is. However, experiments by Benzion, Rapoport, and Yagil (1989) and Thaler (1981) demonstrated that discount rates decrease for longer waiting periods, indicating that it becomes less costly to tack on additional delays in the future than it is to have to wait initially. While these experiments did not use monetary rewards as incentives, similar results were produced by Horowitz (1991) and Holcomb and Nelson (1992) using monetary incentives.

In several experiments, Loewenstein and colleagues found that intertemporal preferences varied depending on aspects of consumption profiles that should not matter, such as which option is presented first. For instance, Loewenstein (1988) found a "delay versus speed-up" asymmetry in which subjects exhibited different discount rates when deciding how much to pay to move a future reward forward (from one week to four weeks) than they did when deciding how much to accept to move the same reward back (from four weeks to one week). Subjects were overwhelmingly more patient when it came to moving the reward forward from the original date than they were when it came to delaying it further.

Other experimental studies obtained results indicating that subjects valued specific patterns of consumption over time, directly contradicting the predictions of the discounted utility model. For instance, in one study (Loewenstein 1987), subjects preferred to delay receiving a pleasant experience (a kiss from their favorite movie star) and to move up a negative one (an electric shock).[8] In a similar study, most subjects preferred to put off receiving a dinner at a fancy French restaurant and instead first receive dinner at a local Greek diner, which was less preferred in a direct comparison between the two options (Loewenstein and Prelec 1991). These results call into question an important implication of the traditional model—that people should always want to delay negative experiences and speed up positive ones.

Behavioral economic research on intertemporal choice reached the second stage of development—summary and synthesis—with the publication of several chapters and volumes collecting the evidence against the assumptions of the discounted utility model and proposing alternative principles guiding choice over time (e.g., Loewenstein and Thaler 1989; Loewenstein and Elster 1992).[9]

As with other areas of behavioral research, behavioral economic theory developed to explain the behavioral regularities inconsistent with the discounted utility model. For instance, one kind of model (e.g., Ainslie and Haslam 1992; Laibson 1997; Rabin and O'Donoghue 1999) assumes that individuals have "present-biased" preferences. That is, while the discounted utility model assumes that the discount rate is the same independent of when the delay is (in the present or in the future), these models assume there is a different discount rate for any decisions that involve delaying reward or pain from the present, meaning it is always harder to delay gratification for one day when that day is now. If decision makers are unaware of this bias, the model predicts behavior consistent with several empirical regularities, such as the tendency to be extremely impatient in the present but to believe that one will be more patient in the future (a common source of procrastination). These models also explain the empirical regularity that elicited discount rates (measured for a particular period of time) decrease when the time horizon is longer.

Another category of models builds on the assumption that there are, in a sense, two decision makers responsible for every individual's choices (see Schelling 1984; Thaler and Shefrin 1981). One of these decision makers is farsighted and takes into account the effect of actions on future welfare, similar to the single rational planner in the discounted utility model. The other decision maker is impulsive and myopic, seeking only to maximize current welfare without regard for future consequences. Intertemporal choice then involves a limited degree of restriction, by the first decision maker, of the second decision maker's ability to act. Using this kind of model, one can explain, for instance, why individuals may take the seemingly irrational decision to limit their future behavior (such as putting money in low-interest-bearing accounts with withdrawal penalties to prevent themselves from spending money, or preferring to receive a fixed salary spread out evenly rather than in a single payment up front).

Finally, some models directly include preferences for such things as anticipation and increasing welfare (e.g., Loewenstein and Prelec 1992; Prelec and Loewenstein 1998). In these "savoring" models, individuals choose rationally and are aware of their future preferences. However, they do not only weigh the utility of outcomes at the point in time at which they are to be consumed (as in the discounted utility model), but also derive benefit from knowing that there are as yet unexperienced future benefits and from simply being better off than they were before. These models are consistent with the behavior of subjects who frequently decide to delay the consumption of positive experiences and speed up negative experiences.

Behavioral economics research on intertemporal choice has reached a similar point as the work on relaxing the self-interest assumption. Much evidence now exists that the traditional theory is descriptively wrong, and behavioral researchers have a good understanding of several aspects of how actual choice differs from the traditional model. In addition, several competing theories have been presented that account for different aspects of this behavior. Moreover, in some instances these theories have impacted policy related to intertemporal choice (e.g., Aaron 1999). In spite of this impact, however, none of the behavioral theories of intertemporal choice has achieved wide acceptance within the field of economics as the correct theory of intertemporal choice, or replaced the traditional approach as the tool of choice of most economists, meaning there is still work to do.

BEHAVIORAL RESEARCH ON REFERENCE-DEPENDENT PREFERENCES

Traditional economic theory assumes that the value individuals place on an item is not very easily changed, particularly by things that should not affect the pleasure derived from consuming the good. Therefore, the fact that an individual possesses a good should not make it more or less valuable, and other individuals' consumption should not affect the value an individual places on a good (unless it makes the good more or less "useful," as in certain types of communication technology where the good becomes more valuable when others are using it). This section, the last of our examples of areas of research in behavioral economics, reviews evidence to the contrary. The conclusion of this research is that reference levels (such as the status quo or individuals' expectations) do affect preferences.

Among the first results revealing reference-dependent preferences were experimental results demonstrating "loss aversion." Loss aversion (or the endowment effect) refers to the tendency to place greater value on an item when an individual possesses (or is endowed with) that item than when he or she does not. Some of the pioneering work demonstrating this phenomenon was done by Kahneman and Tversky (1979), who showed that gambles involving losses weighed more heavily (were associated with higher absolute monetary values) than gambles involving identical gains. Similarly, Thaler (1980) showed that how much individuals were willing to accept ("willingness to accept") for a loss was greater than the amount individuals were willing to pay ("willingness to pay") for an equivalent gain.

While the above work involved hypothetical choices, the same effect was also found in experiments using monetary incentives. These early experiments simply demonstrated that subjects who were given an item, such as a coffee mug or a lottery ticket, required more money to give up the item than subjects who had not been endowed with the item were willing to pay for it (Knetsch and Sinden 1984). This phenomenon persisted even when subjects were placed in a market environment, countering one early criticism by traditional economists arguing that the effect was unimportant because it would disappear with market forces and repetition (Kahneman, Knetsch, and Thaler 1990).

If gains are weighed less than losses, individuals should be less likely to take courses of action that might produce either gains or losses than they would under traditional economic theory, where the two are weighed equally. This tendency, referred to as the "status quo bias," follows from loss aversion: possible losses loom larger than possible gains and therefore impact decisions more than they would in the absence of loss aversion. Samuelson and Zeckhauser (1988) demonstrated such a bias. In experiments, they found that choices became more attractive and were therefore more likely to be selected, simply by being the status quo.

The result that reference levels matter has also been demonstrated using field data. For instance, the discrepancy between willingness to accept and willingness to pay was found in a market environment to decide tree planting for a park (Brookshire and Coursey 1987).

In addition, behavior consistent with the gain/loss asymmetry in loss aversion is found in financial markets. For instance, people sell stocks that have risen in value too early and hold on to stocks that have declined in value too long (Shefrin and Statman 1985; O'Dean 1998). This pattern is inconsistent with traditional economic theory, which predicts that differences in decisions to buy or sell stock will be based solely on expectations about their future value, and will be independent of whether a particular stock has increased or decreased in value since being purchased.

The status quo bias has also been demonstrated outside of the laboratory. In one example, Hartman, Doane, and Woo (1991) examined choices of utility service plans by residential consumers in California and found a discrepancy between the amounts consumers were willing to accept for service disruptions and the amount they were willing to pay to avoid them. They also found a tendency for consumers to select options simply because they were the status quo. In another study, Johnson, Hershey, Meszaros, and Kunreuther (1993) found that residents in New Jersey and Pennsylvania chose different insurance options from very similar sets of choices, based simply on which option was presented as the default one.

As with other areas of behavioral research, the development of behavioral theory attempting to account for the discrepancy between observed phenomena and traditional economic theory followed the collection and synthesis of the evidence demonstrating reference-dependence in preferences (e.g., Kahneman, Knetsch, and Thaler 1991). However, unlike most other areas where several competing models were developed that accounted for different aspects of the behavioral phenomenon, the behavioral theory developed to account for loss aversion was simple and much less fragmented.

The main theoretical contributions to modeling loss aversion using economic theory were remarkably similar. The first theory that incorporated the concept of loss aversion in an economic decision model was Kahneman and Tversky's (1979) "prospect theory," applied to decision making under risk. In prospect theory, outcomes are not evaluated in absolute terms, as they are in expected utility theory, but instead are evaluated relative to a reference point. The key aspect of prospect theory that accounts for loss aversion is that the function representing values in the domain of losses is steeper than the function representing values for gains. Therefore, the decision weight associated with losses and gains (defined relative to the reference point) are unequal, and losses have a greater impact on decision making than comparable gains.

The work of both Tversky and Kahneman (1991) and Monro and Sugden (1998) built on prospect theory in an attempt to generalize reference-dependence to a model of consumer choice. In both models, the key modification from the traditional approach is also the introduction of a reference point (for instance, the status quo) relative to which outcomes are evaluated. In both of these models, the acquisition of a particular good makes that good more valuable relative to others. The nice property of these models is they involve only a small modification to the traditional economic theory, meaning that these models can often be used in the same way as traditional theory. This correspondence means that the usefulness of introducing reference levels to economic models is testable; we can directly compare the behavioral and traditional models across several decisions for descriptive validity (see Harless and Camerer 1994). Moreover, while the introduction of a reference point at the status quo makes it easy to model loss aversion—distinguishing gains from losses—the concept can be extended to include other types of reference levels that might affect decisions (e.g., aspiration levels, security levels, social comparisons, etc.).[10]

BEHAVIORAL ECONOMICS: RECOGNIZING THE IMPORTANCE OF TRAJECTORIES

The main contribution of behavioral economics is pointing out that traditional economic theory is a descriptively incomplete theory of human behavior. From the work of independent researchers conducting studies demonstrating the existence of behavioral regularities inconsistent with traditional theory, to the collection and synthesis of these results, and to the subsequent development of behavioral theory that accounts for these regularities, the ultimate goal of all behavioral research is to make economic analysis more descriptively complete.

One common thread in much of behavioral economics research lies in a common source of incompleteness in the traditional model—it ignores the importance of trajectories. Trajectories in this case mean paths or histories of consumption and action that impact the way decisions are made. One of the main shortcomings of traditional economics is that it is a static theory in this sense. It typically considers only outcomes and experiences at the point in time at which they are encountered, and ignores that how we get to these outcomes and what happens before and after them have strong effects on the desirability of these outcomes. However, as much research in behavioral economics shows, how we get to the point of making a decision has almost as much of an effect on choice as the consequences of the decision.

For example, one of the key findings in the study of violations of the self-interest assumption is that people care about reciprocity. The finding is that people are not only not self-interested, but that they also do not have consistent preferences for the welfare of others independent of what has happened previously. In particular, people prefer to be kind to those who have been kind to them in the past and unkind to those who have been unkind. Therefore, what happened previously matters significantly for current preferences and behavior. Traditional economics, however, takes this history into account only to the extent that reciprocity can act as a social mechanism enhancing expected gains (through processes like enhanced reputation), but does not include the possibility that it may exist otherwise.

The behavioral research on intertemporal choice similarly points to the importance of trajectories. One key finding is that people have preferences for increasing consumption profiles and that they derive pleasure from waiting for good things. Also, for goods such as addictive goods individuals experience unanticipated changes to their preferences based on previous consumption. All of these behavioral regularities fail to be predicted by traditional theory. This failure occurs mainly because the theory assumes that future experiences only affect decision making in the present by a weight equal to the discounted welfare they will produce at the point in time at which they are experienced. Behavioral models that allow past and future experiences to directly or indirectly affect present welfare are therefore much more descriptively valid.

The research on loss aversion and reference-dependence similarly indicates that traditional economics has failed to take into account trajectories. While traditional economic theory assumes that decisions are not be affected by historical accident, research on the status quo bias indicates that this is not the case. The fact that something was previously chosen makes it more attractive, and this path dependence is similarly true for loss aversion. Again, the main flaw in the traditional approach is to neglect the importance of how we got somewhere.

We should note that it is not our argument that everything that happened before and after a decision should be taken into account by a model of decision making. Such a model would likely lack both parsimony and predictive ability. Instead, if a modification that takes into account trajectories is possible, creates an improvement in descriptive ability, and does not sacrifice too much else, then theoretical economics should attempt to include such a modification. The theoretical work on loss aversion and reference-dependent preferences serves as an example of how following such a principle can produce a descriptively better model.

BEHAVIORAL ECONOMICS AND ECONOMIC SOCIOLOGY

An economic sociologist reading our chapter up to this point will no doubt wonder about the apparent relative absence of economic sociology—and sociology more generally—from the work of behavioral economists. It is certainly true that an overwhelming majority of work in behavioral economics is rooted in psychology, perhaps reflecting the contributions of several prominent early behavioral "economists" (e.g., Daniel Kahneman, Amos Tversky, Robyn Dawes) whose primary training was in psychology. This emphasis is manifested in the topics (e.g., fairness and cognitive biases) and methods (e.g., experiments) of behavioral research. To date, the topics and methods of areas such as economic sociology have had a significantly smaller impact in behavioral economics and economics more generally. Thus, topics that seem important for mainstream economic research such as culture, institutions, organizational environment, and social networks appear to have received scant attention even among behavioral economists.

However, a closer examination of behavioral economics reveals two sources of optimism for those who would like to see a stronger connection with economic sociology.

The first source of optimism is that a closer examination of existing work in behavioral economics reveals a significant amount of work that directly addresses topics or relies on methods from economic sociology. While this work lies outside of the mainstream of behavioral economics research—compared with topics such as fairness, reference-dependent preferences, or biased time preference—it nonetheless certainly lies within its boundaries.

For instance, following the demonstration that individuals' preferences are affected by the welfare of others, an important question for behavioral economists is how to explain variance in such preferences. The work of a few researchers looks at the role of culture, institutions, and social networks in determining preferences for things like fairness or equity. As an example, the work of Henrich et al. (2001) explored how varying economic and social environments in 15 relatively small primitive societies affected behavior in the ultimatum game. Another set of studies (Babcock, Engberg, and Greenbaum 1999; Greenbaum 2002) explores how teachers' salaries in Pennsylvania are determined, showing that social comparisons with teachers in other "similar" districts have an important effect on wage levels and negotiations. Note that studies of both kinds are important for economics because they raise the possibility that even things as basic as preferences are affected by the institutions, culture, and social networks that surround an individual or society.

Another area of research recognizes that much economic interaction takes place through relationship networks, relaxing the usual assumption in economics that economic actors are linked in "complete" networks. Recent theoretical (e.g., Allen and Gale 2000; Jackson and Watts 2002) and experimental (e.g., Berninghaus, Ehrhart, and Keser 2002; Corbae and Duffy 2002) work studies how different network configurations affect economic outcomes. Note that this emphasis on network structure and the importance of social links is something that economic sociologists have long argued plays an important role in economic activity (Granovetter 1985; Davis 1991). While the work above represents only a small step by economists in the direction of accounting for the importance of the relationship networks, it nonetheless represents an important "behavioral" modification to the traditional approach.

The second source of optimism for those who would like to see more economic sociology in behavioral economics lies not in existing work, but rather in promising potential future work. While this chapter has indicated the considerable advances made by behavioral economists, there remain many areas in which (even behavioral) economic theory is still incomplete. Much of this work has to do with filling in gaps in the theory that limit its ability to correctly predict outcomes and behavior. Behavioral economics has resulted in a better, though still incomplete, theoretical tool for such prediction. In these likely future areas of research exists considerable promise for incorporating the work of economic sociologists.

As an example, consider the work in economics on coordination and coordination games (e.g., Van Huyck, Battalio, and Beil 1990; Mehta, Starmer, and Sugden 1994). Coordination refers to situations where there are multiple possible equilibrium outcomes (where no individual actor wants to change her behavior given what others are doing). Examples of such situations include several individuals deciding whether to exert costly effort when the reward to such effort is only achieved if others exert it as well, or where units in the same firm all need to adopt a communication technology but the value of the technology depends on that adopted by others (see Schelling 1960). These situations pose a problem for economic theory because of its inability to predict which of the several possible equilibrium outcomes will result, and experiments have demonstrated that otherwise identical groups of people will converge on different outcomes (Van Huyck, Battalio, and Beil 1991; Bacharach and Bernasconi 1997).

It is for this kind of prediction that behavioral economists might benefit by turning to economic sociology and sociology more generally. Given that economic theory fails to predict why identical groups of economic actors may arrive at entirely different equilibrium outcomes, a solution to this problem may lie in looking at the way economic sociologists might argue the individuals (or their surroundings) differ. For instance, some economists have already recognized that culture may play a significant role in determining which of the several outcomes results in a situation involving coordination (Kreps 1990; Weber and Camerer 2003). However, other topics of interest to economic sociologists, such as social environments and networks, social comparisons, and institutional forces, may equally well explain the different outcomes. It is in such a combination of economic sociology and economic theory, using the former to fill in the gaps of the latter, where exists perhaps the greatest potential for future work in behavioral economics.

Conclusion

The goal of this chapter is to introduce the approach to research in the social sciences known as behavioral economics. By describing the methodology and a few important areas of research, we hope to have left the reader with an improved understanding of what behavioral economists do and why they do it. Moreover, we have attempted to link much of the research in behavioral economics together under a common theme: the taking into account of trajectories. To conclude this chapter, we turn to more general statements about what behavioral economics has accomplished and might still accomplish.

First, however, it is important that we reiterate a point from our introductory discussion, one that addresses a common concern of traditional economists in accepting behavioral work. This point has to do with the goal of behavioral economics. As we have previously stated, the goal of researchers in this area is not to tear down economic theory and replace it with theory borrowed from other social sciences. Instead, the goal is to improve economics as a descriptive and positive social science and make traditional economic theory richer and descriptively more accurate, while retaining many of the goals of traditional economic theorists such as parsimony and formalism. The work in each of the areas discussed above has proceeded toward this goal—usually through carefully observation of how people actually behave and the incorporation of this observation into formal economic theory.

The main contribution of behavioral economics is the recognition that traditional economic theory is an incomplete story. It omits important characteristics of decisions and situations that enter into an individual's decision process. Behavioral economics recognizes the importance of things such as trajectories that play an important role in decision making but are not part of traditional models.

The demonstration of results inconsistent with traditional economic theory and improvements to the theory are not the only benefits that behavioral economics has produced. For example, due to the willingness of behavioral economists to borrow research tools from the other social sciences, behavioral economics has introduced new research methods—such as laboratory experiments—to traditional economic research. Some of these methods are now used by economists not doing specifically behavioral work (e.g., experimental economics testing mechanism design). In addition, behavioral economics has created a link with research in other social sciences and given economics more credibility among researchers in other areas who previously dismissed all of economics due to its reliance on the rational choice model.

Aside from these benefits, behavioral economics has also resulted in an economic theory better suited for positive analysis. Even the slight improvements to economic theory discussed in the previous sections have produced a theory more likely to correctly predict important behavior such as consumption of addictive substances, bargaining impasse, retirement savings, and donations to charity. Armed with this better understanding, policy interventions are much more likely to succeed than if they are based on a simpler, but unrealistic, model.

In addition to creating a theory better suited for predicting behavior, recognition of deviations from the traditional model points us to some important sources of error that decision makers routinely make (for instance, see Kahneman and Tversky 1974). Once aware of and familiar with these mistakes, economists can look for ways to help people avoid them when making important decisions.[11]

While our goal in this chapter is not to predict the future of research in behavioral economics, we believe some directions are likely to prove fruitful. One such direction is work aimed at bringing together different strands of behavioral economics by finding links between basic processes underlying behavioral results (such as the connection between loss aversion and a preference for improving consumption paths). To the extent that researchers are able to link behavioral phenomena by understanding how they operate more similarly at a basic level, the result is a better understanding likely to be reflected in a better theory. Similarly, work using the observation of neuropsychology to understand how humans make economic decisions is also likely to prove fruitful (see, for instance, Camerer 2003b; and Camerer, Loewenstein, and Prelec 2003). Work in these directions may result in a fourth stage in the development of behavioral economic research: the linking of all behavioral regularities to form a single behavioral economic theory.

NOTES

Many thanks to participants at the Russell Sage conference on the *Handbook of Economic Sociology* for helpful comments and suggestions. Thanks especially to Paula England and George Loewenstein for carefully reading and commenting on the chapter.

1. While behavioral economists have typically focused on methods (such as experiments) and assumptions (such as cognitive biases) from psychology, recent behavioral work more broadly encompasses other social sciences. For instance, Henrich et al. (2001) combine experiments and anthropological research to study the impact of culture on economic decisions. Moreover, recent theoretical and experimental work (e.g., Berninghaus, Ehrhart, and Keser 2002; Jackson and Watts 2002) emphasizes the importance of (simple forms of) social networks in determining group outcomes.

2. In fact, this goal of working within economics and making progress through incremental improvements to neoclassical economics often results in a negative view of behavioral economics from researchers in other disciplines, who view the improvements as insufficient and question the validity of relying on economic methods such as formal theory. At the same time, many behavioral economists argue that the ultimate goal of behavioral research must be to completely change the way economics research is done (e.g., replacing all of the current assumptions with a new set of behaviorally realistic assumptions). The view of this group is that incremental changes will never allow economics to fully incorporate important aspects of economic decision-making learned from areas such as neuroscience and social psychology.

3. The last stage could be divided into two separate stages: (1) the development of individual choice models that incorporate the behavioral anomaly, and (2) the incorporation of these models into behavioral macroeconomic models. This is an important distinction because economists largely value a new theory based on the extent to which it can be modified to achieve the latter. However, since there are several areas of behavioral research that have thus far not reached this stage—though most have reached the first stage of theoretical development—we pool the two while noting the distinction (and the ultimate goal of having four, instead of three, stages).

4. Unfortunately, however, the repetition of choice with the same incentives may also be "sending a message" to subjects about what we expect them to do, with the result that the subjects may be responding to this inferred expectation

as much as to whatever external (usually monetary) payoffs are involved (see Dawes 1999).

5. As Camerer (2003a) points out, this is how the physical sciences typically rely on observation and proceed differently than does economics: theory is developed from observation, tested using observation, and then improved to account for new observation. This point, however, is not new, as Von Neumann and Morgenstern noted over half a century ago that "the empirical background of economic science is definitely inadequate. . . . It would have been absurd in physics to expect Kepler and Newton without Tycho [Brahe],—and there is no reason to hope for an easier development in economics" (1944, 4).

6. In the seminal book *Mathematical Psychics* ([1881] 1995), Edgeworth wrote of a weighted sympathy component in individual utility functions by which the welfare of others counts for some fraction of our own welfare. Edgeworth even noted that this fraction decreases with "social distance" (see also Collard 1975).

7. The first experiment involving production of public goods is believed to be by Bohm (1972), but his experiments do not clearly demonstrate that subjects are foregoing self-interest to contribute to the public good. For a discussion of these experiments and an excellent survey of the experimental literature on public goods, see Ledyard 1995.

8. These experiments represent a rare departure for economists from the usual requirement in laboratory studies that subjects' choices somehow be tied to their payoffs. Perhaps these results are so consistent with our intuition about everyday intertemporal choice ("save the best for last" and "get it over with") that the hypothetical choices are sufficient to convince most economists.

9. For an excellent and concise summary of behavioral work on delayed gratification, see Fehr 2002.

10. See Markowitz 1952 for an early theoretical discussion of the possibility that people evaluate wealth relative to a reference level such as the status quo.

11. For instance, the dynamic inconsistency common to decisions involving intertemporal choice means that we end up with economically inefficient outcomes and the need for entire industries to help avoid these outcomes (the dieting industry, rehab clinics). Being able to correct these "mistakes" in decision making before they happen would lead to better economic outcomes in which the resources devoted to these industries are used elsewhere.

REFERENCES

Aaron, Henry J., ed. 1999. *Behavioral Dimensions of Retirement Economics.* Washington, D.C.: Brookings Institution Press.

Ainslie, George, and Nick Haslam. 1992. "Hyperbolic Discounting." In *Choice over Time*, ed. George Loewenstein and Jon Elster. New York: Russell Sage Foundation.

Akerlof, George A. 1982. "Labor Contracts as Partial Gift Exchange." *Quarterly Journal of Economics* 87:543–69.

———. 2002. "Behavioral Macroeconomics and Macroeconomic Behavior." *American Economic Review* 92(3): 411–33.

Akerlof, George A., and Rachel Kranton. 2000. "Economics and Identity." *Quarterly Journal of Economics* 115:715–53.

Allen, Franklin, and Douglas Gale. 2000. "Financial Contagion." *Journal of Political Economy*, 108: 1–33.

Ando, Albert, and Franco Modigliani. 1963. "The Life Cycle Hypothesis of Saving: Aggregate Implications and Tests." *American Economic Review* 53:55–84.

Andreoni, James. 1988. "Why Free Ride? Strategies and Learning in Public Goods Experiments." *Journal of Public Economics* 37:291–304.

———. 1989. "Giving with Impure Altruism: Applications to Charity and Ricardian Equivalence." *Journal of Political Economy* 97:1447–58.

———. 1990. "Impure Altruism and Donations to Public Goods: A Theory of Warm-Glow Giving." *Economic Journal* 100:464–77.

Andreoni, James, and John H. Miller. 2002. "Giving According to GARP: An Experimental Test of the Consistency of Preferences for Altruism." *Econometrica* 70:737–53.

Aumann, Robert A. 1990. Foreword to *Two-Sided Matching: A Study in Game-Theoretic Modeling and Analysis*, by Alvin E. Roth and Marilda A. Sotomayor. Cambridge: Cambridge University Press.

Babcock, Linda, John Engberg, and Robert T. Greenbaum. 1999. "Wage Spillovers in Public Sector Contact Negotiations: The Importance of Social Comparisons." Unpublished manuscript.

Babcock, Linda, and George Loewenstein. 1997. "Explaining Bargaining Impasse: The Role of Self-Serving Biases." *Journal of Economic Perspectives* 11(1): 109–26.

Bacharach, Michael, and Michele Bernasconi. 1997. "The Variable Frame Theory of Focal Points: An Experimental Study." *Games and Economic Behavior* 19:1–45.

Becker, Gary S., and Kevin M. Murphy. 1988. "A Theory of Rational Addiction." *Journal of Political Economy* 4:675–700.

Benzion, Uri, Amnon Rapoport, and Joseph Yagil. 1989. "Discount Rates Inferred from Decisions: An Experimental Study." *Management Science* 35: 270–84.

Berg, J., J. Dickhaut, and K. McCabe. 1995. "Trust, Social History, and Reciprocity." *Games and Economic Behavior* 10(1): 122–42.

Bernheim, B. Douglas, Jonathan Skinner, and Steven Weinberg. 2001. "What Accounts for the Variation in Retirement Savings across U.S. Households?" *American Economic Review* 91:832–57.

Berninghaus, Siegfried K., Karl-Martin Ehrhart, and Claudia Keser. 2002. "Conventions and Local Interaction Structures: Experimental Evidence." *Games and Economic Behavior* 39(2): 177–205.

Bohm, Peter. 1972. "Estimating Demand for Public Goods: An Experiment." *European Economic Review* 3:111–30.

Bolton, Gary E., and Axel Ockenfels. 2000. "ERC: A Theory of Equity, Reciprocity, and Competition." *American Economic Review* 90:166–93.

Brookshire, David S., and Don L. Coursey. 1987. "Measuring the Value of a Public Good: An Empirical Comparison of Elicitation Procedures." *American Economic Review* 77:554–66.

Camerer, Colin F. 2003a. *Behavioral Game Theory: Experiments in Strategic Interaction*. Princeton: Princeton University Press.

———. 2003b. "Strategizing the Brain." *Science* 300: 1673–75.

Camerer, Colin F., Linda Babcock, George Loewenstein, and Richard H. Thaler. 1997. "Labor Supply of New York City Cab Drivers: One Day at a Time." *Quarterly Journal of Economics* 112:407–41.

Camerer, Colin F., and Robin M. Hogarth. 1999. "The Effects of Financial Incentives in Experiments: A Review and Capital-Labor-Production Framework." *Journal of Risk and Uncertainty* 19(1): 7–42.

Camerer, Colin F., George Loewenstein, and Drazen Prelec. 2003. "Neuroeconomics: How Neuroscience Can Inform Economics." Typescript.

Camerer, Colin, and Richard H. Thaler. 1995. "Ultimatums, Dictators, and Manners." *Journal of Economic Perspectives* 9(2): 209–19.

Carroll, Christopher D., and Lawrence H. Summers. 1991. "Consumption Growth Parallels Income Growth: Some New Evidence." Pp. 305–43 in *National Saving and Economic Performance*, ed. B. Douglas Bernheim and J. Shoven. Chicago: University of Chicago Press.

Collard, David. 1975. "Edgeworth's Propositions on Altruism." *Economic Journal* 85:355–60.

Corbae, P. Dean, and John Duffy. 2002. "Experiments with Network Economies." Unpublished manuscript.

Davis, Gerald F. 1991. "Agents without Principles? The Spread of the Poison Pill through the Intercorporate Network." *Administrative Science Quarterly* 36:583–613.

Dawes, Robyn M. 1999. "Experimental Demand, Clear Incentives, Both, or Neither?" Pp. 21–28 in *Games and Human Behavior: Essays in Honor of Amnon Rapoport*, ed. David V. Budescu, Ido Erev, and Rami Zwick. Mahwah, N.J.: Laurence Erlbaum Associates.

Dawes, Robyn M., Jeanne McTavish, and Harriet Shaklee. 1977. "Behavior, Communication, and Assumptions about Other People's Behavior in a Commons Dilemma Situation." *Journal of Personality and Social Psychology* 35(1): 1–11.

Dawes, Robyn M., and David Messick. 2000. "Social Dilemmas." *International Journal of Psychology* 35(2): 111–16.

Dawes, Robyn M., John M. Orbell, Randy Simmons, and Alphons Van de Kragt. 1986. "Organizing Groups for Collective Action." *American Political Science Review* 8:1171–85.

Dawes, Robyn M., and Richard H. Thaler. 1988.

"Cooperation." *Journal of Economic Perspectives* 2: 187–97.

Edgeworth, F. Y. [1881] 1995. *Mathematical Psychics and Other Essays*. Mountain Center, Calif.: James and Gordon.

Fehr, Ernst. 2002. "The Economics of Impatience." *Nature* 415:269–72.

Fehr, Ernst, Georg Kirchsteiger, and Arno Riedl. 1993. "Does Fairness Prevent Market Clearing? An Experimental Investigation." *Quarterly Journal of Economics*, 108:437–60.

———. 1998. "Gift Exchange and Reciprocity in Competitive Experimental Markets." *European Economic Review* 42:1–34.

Fehr, Ernst, and Klaus M. Schmidt. 1999. "A Theory of Fairness, Competition, and Cooperation." *Quarterly Journal of Economics* 114:817–68.

Fisher, Irving. 1930. *The Theory of Interest*. New York: Macmillan.

Forsythe, Robert, Joel L. Horowitz, N. E. Savin, and Martin Sefton. 1994. "Fairness in Simple Bargaining Experiments." *Games and Economic Behavior* 6:347–69.

Frank, Robert H., Thomas Gilovich, and Dennis T. Regan. 1993. "Does Studying Economics Inhibit Cooperation?" *Journal of Economic Perspectives* 7: 159–71.

Gately, Dermot. 1980. "Individual Discount Rates and the Purchase and Utilization of Energy-Using Durables: Comment." *Bell Journal of Economics* 11:373–74.

Goldstein, Avram. 1994. *Addiction: From Biology to Drug Policy*. New York: W. H. Freeman.

Granovetter, Mark. 1985. "Economic Action and Social Structure: The Problem of Embeddedness." *American Journal of Sociology* 91:481–570.

Greenbaum, Robert T. 2002. "A Spatial Study of Teachers' Salaries in Pennsylvania School Districts." *Journal of Labor Research* 23(1): 69–86.

Güth, Werner, Rolf Schmittberger, and Bernd Schwarze. 1982. "An Experimental Analysis of Ultimatum Bargaining." *Journal of Economic Behavior and Organization* 3:367–88.

Harless, David W., and Colin F. Camerer. 1994. "The Predictive Utility of Generalized Expected Utility Theories." *Econometrica* 62:1251–90.

Hartman, Raymond S., Michael J. Doane, and C. K. Woo. 1991. "Consumer Rationality and the Status Quo." *Quarterly Journal of Economics* 106:141–62.

Hausman, Jerry A. 1979. "Individual Discount Rates and the Purchase and Utilization of Energy-Using Durables." *Bell Journal of Economics* 10:33–54.

Henrich, Joseph, Robert Boyd, Samuel Bowles, Colin F. Camerer, Herbert Gintis, Richard McElreath, and Ernst Fehr. 2001. "In Search of Homo-economicus: Experiments in 15 Small-Scale Societies." *American Economic Review* 91(2): 73–79.

Hoffman, Elizabeth, Kevin McCabe, Keith Shachat, and Vernon L. Smith. 1994. "Preferences, Property Rights, and Anonymity in Bargaining Games." *Games and Economic Behavior* 7:346–80.

Hoffman, Elizabeth, Kevin McCabe, and Vernon L. Smith. 1996. "On Property Rights and the Monetary Stakes in Ultimatum Game Bargaining." *International Journal of Game Theory* 25:289–301.

Holcomb, James H., and Paul S. Nelson. 1992. "Another Experimental Look at Individual Time Preference." *Rationality and Society* 4:199–220.

Horowitz, Joel L. 1991. "Discounting Money Payoffs: An Experimental Analysis." In vol. 2B of *Handbook of Behavioral Economics*, ed. Benjamin Gilad and Stanley Kaish. Greenwich, Conn.: JAI Press.

Isaac, R. Mark, Kenneth F. McCue, and Charles R. Plott. 1985. "Public Goods Provision in an Experimental Environment." *Journal of Public Economics* 26:51–74.

Isaac, R. Mark, and James M. Walker. 1988. "Group Size Effects in Public Goods Provision: The Voluntary Contributions Mechanism." *Quarterly Journal of Economics* 103:179–99.

Isaac, R. Mark, James M. Walker, and Susan H. Thomas. 1984. "Divergent Evidence on Free Riding: An Experimental Examination of Possible Explanations." *Public Choice* 43:113–49.

Jackson, Matthew O., and Alison Watts. 2002. "On the Formation of Interaction Networks in Social Coordination Games." *Games and Economic Behavior* 41(2): 265–91.

Johnson, Eric J., John C. Hershey, Jacqueline R. Meszaros, and Howard Kunreuther. 1993. "Framing, Probability Distortions, and Insurance Decisions." *Journal of Risk and Uncertainty* 7:35–53.

Kahneman, Daniel, Jack L. Knetsch, and Richard H. Thaler. 1986a. "Fairness and the Assumptions of Economics." *Journal of Business* 59(4:2): S285–S300.

———. 1986b. "Fairness as a Constraint on Profit Seeking: Entitlements in the Market." *American Economic Review* 76:728–41.

———. 1990. "Experimental Tests of the Endowment Effect and the Coase Theorem." *Journal of Political Economy* 98:1325–48.

———. 1991. "Anomalies: The Endowment Effect, Loss Aversion, and Status Quo Bias." *Journal of Economic Perspectives* 5(1): 193–206.

Kahneman, Daniel, and Amos Tversky. 1974. "Judgment under Uncertainty: Heuristics and Biases." *Science* 185:1124–31.

———. 1979. "Prospect Theory: An Analysis of Decision under Risk." *Econometrica* 47:263–91.

Kim, Oliver, and Mark Walker. 1984. "The Free Rider Problem: Experimental Evidence." *Public Choice* 43:3–24.

Knetsch, Jack L., and J. A. Sinden. 1984. "Willingness to Pay and Compensation Demanded: Experimental Evidence of an Unexpected Disparity in Measures of Value." *Quarterly Journal of Economics* 99: 507–21.

Kreps, David M. 1990. "Corporate Culture and Economic Theory." In *Perspectives on Positive Political Economy*, ed. J. E. Alt and K. A. Shepsle. Cambridge: Cambridge University Press.

Laibson, David. 1997. "Golden Eggs and Hyperbolic Discounting." *Quarterly Journal of Economics* 112: 443–77.

Ledyard, John O. 1995. "Public Goods: A Survey of Experimental Research." Pp. 111–94 in *The Handbook of Experimental Economics*, ed. J. Kagel and A. Roth. Princeton: Princeton University Press.

Lichtenstein, Sarah, and Paul Slovic. 1973. "Response-Induced Reversals of Preferences in Gambling: An Extended Replication in Las Vegas." *Journal of Experimental Psychology* 101:16–20.

Loewenstein, George. 1987. "Anticipation and the Valuation of Delayed Consumption." *Economic Journal* 97:666–84.

———. 1988. "Frames of Mind in Intertemporal Choice." *Management Science* 34:200–214.

Loewenstein, George, and Jon Elster, eds. 1992. *Choice over Time*. New York: Russell Sage.

Loewenstein, George, and Drazen Prelec. 1991. "Negative Time Preference." *American Economic Review* 82(2): 347–52.

———. 1992. "Anomalies in Intertemporal Choice: Evidence and an Interpretation." *Quarterly Journal of Economics* 107:573–97.

Loewenstein, George, Drazen Prelec, and Roberto A. Weber. 1999. "What, Me Worry? A Psychological Perspective on Economic Aspects of Retirement." In *Behavioral Dimensions of Retirement Economics*, ed. Henry J. Aaron. Washington, D.C.: Brookings Institution Press.

Loewenstein, George, and Richard H. Thaler. 1989. "Anomalies: Intertemporal Choice." *Journal of Economic Perspectives* 3:181–93.

Mankiw, N. Gregory, Julio J. Rotemberg, and Lawrence H. Summers. 1985. "Intertemporal Substitution in Macroeconomics." *Quarterly Journal of Economics* 100:225–51.

Markowitz, Harry. 1952. "The Utility of Wealth." *Journal of Political Economy* 60:151–58.

Marwell, Gerald, and Ruth Ames. 1981. "Economists Free Ride, Does Anyone Else?" *Journal of Public Economics* 15:295–310.

Mehta, Judith, Chris Starmer, and Robert Sugden. 1994. "The Nature of Salience: An Experimental Investigation of Pure Coordination Games." *American Economic Review* 84:658–74.

Modigliani, Franco, and Richard Brumberg. 1954. "Utility Analysis and the Consumption Function: An Interpretation of Cross-Section Data." Pp. 388–436 in *Post-Keynesian Economics*, ed. K. Kurihara. New Brunswick, N.J.: Rutgers University Press.

Monro, A., and Robert Sugden. 1998. "A Theory of General Equilibrium with Reference-Dependent Preferences." University of East Anglia School of Economic and Social Studies Working Paper No. 9803.

O'Dean, Terry. 1998. "Are Investors Reluctant to Realize Their Losses?" *Journal of Finance* 53:1775–98.

Prelec, Drazen, and George Loewenstein. 1998. "The Red and the Black: Mental Accounting of Savings and Debt." *Marketing Science* 17(1): 4–28.

Rabin, Matthew. 1993. "Incorporating Fairness into Game Theory and Economics." *American Economic Review* 83:1281–1302.

Rabin, Matthew, and Ted O'Donoghue. 1999. "Doing It Now or Later." *American Economic Review* 89(1): 103–24.

Samuelson, Paul. 1937. "A Note on Measurement of Utility." *Review of Economic Studies* 4(11): 155–61.

———. 1954. "The Pure Theory of Public Expenditure." *Review of Economics and Statistics* 36(4): 350–56.

Samuelson, William, and Richard Zeckhauser. 1988. "Status Quo Bias in Decision Making." *Journal of Risk and Uncertainty* 1:7–59.

Schelling, Thomas C. 1960. *The Strategy of Conflict*. Cambridge: Harvard University Press.

———. 1984. "Self-Command in Practice, in Policy, and in a Theory of Rational Choice." *American Economic Review* 74(2): 1–11.

Schleifer, Andrei. 2000. *Inefficient Markets: An Introduction to Behavioral Finance*. Oxford: Oxford University Press.

Shefrin, Hersh M., and Meir Statman. 1985. "The Disposition to Sell Winners Too Early and Ride Losers Too Long: Theory and Evidence." *Journal of Finance* 40:777–90.

Shiller, Robert J. 2000. *Irrational Exuberance*. Princeton: Princeton University Press.

Simon, Herbert A. 1955. "A Behavioral Model of Rational Choice." *Quarterly Journal of Economics* 69: 99–118.

Smith, Adam. [1776] 1994. *An Inquiry into the Nature and Causes of the Wealth of Nations*. New York: Random House.

———. [1759] 2000. *The Theory of Moral Sentiments*. Amherst, N.Y.: Prometheus Books.

Stephens, Melvin Jr., 2003. "'3rd of Tha Month': Do Social Security Recipients Smooth Consumption between Checks?" *American Economic Review* 93:406–22.

Sunstein, Cass R., ed. 2000. *Behavioral Law and Economics*. Cambridge: Cambridge University Press.

Thaler, Richard H. 1980. "Toward a Positive Theory of Consumer Choice." *Journal of Economic Behavior and Organization* 1:39–60.

———. 1981. "Some Empirical Evidence on Dynamic Inconsistency." *Economic Letters* 8:201–7.

———. 1992. *The Winner's Curse*. New York: Free Press.

———, ed. 1993. *Advances in Behavioral Finance*. New York: Russell Sage Foundation.

Thaler, Richard H., and Hersh M. Shefrin. 1981. "An Economic Theory of Self-Control." *Journal of Political Economy* 89:392–406.

Tversky, Amos, and Daniel Kahneman. 1991. "Loss Aversion in Riskless Choice: A Reference-Dependent Model." *Quarterly Journal of Economics* 106: 1039–61.

Van de Kragt, Alphons, John M. Orbell, and Robyn M. Dawes. 1983. "The Minimal Contributing Set as a Solution to Public Goods Problems." *American Political Science Review* 77:112–22.

Van Huyck, John B., Raymond C. Battalio, and Richard O. Beil. 1990. "Tacit Coordination Games, Strategic Uncertainty, and Coordination Failure." *American Economic Review* 80:234–48.

———. 1991. "Strategic Uncertainty, Equilibrium Selection, and Coordination Failure in Average Opin-

ion Games." *Quarterly Journal of Economics* 106: 885–911.

Von Neumann, John, and Oskar Morgenstern. 1944. *Theory of Games and Economic Behavior.* Princeton: Princeton University Press.

Weber, Roberto A., and Colin F. Camerer. 2003. "Cultural Conflict and Merger Failure: An Experimental Approach." *Management Science* 49: 400–415.

Yezer, Anthony, Robert Goldfarb, and Paul Poppen. 1996. "Does Studying Economics Discourage Cooperation? Watch What We Do, Not What We Say or How We Play." *Journal of Economic Perspectives* 10(1): 177–86.

6   Emotions and the Economy

Mabel Berezin

THE RETURN OF EMOTION

"Emotion and economy" describes a relation that social scientists have recently begun to acknowledge and valorize. Outside of various fields of psychology, sociologists and economists often treat emotions as residual categories. It is arguable that the project of modern social science from its European nineteenth-century origins to its contemporary variations defines emotion out of social action in general and economic action in particular. In contrast to other contributions to this volume that discuss more or less established literatures, this chapter suggests plausible analytic frames that reinscribe emotion in social and economic action. Even though strong, let alone competing, paradigms have not developed around emotion and economy, this pairing does not constitute an uncharted terrain.

Emotions, rather than gone from sociological and economic analysis, have been, to put it more aptly, in disciplinary exile. Multiple signs suggest that emotions are reentering sociological and economic analysis. In the last few years, interest in emotions has flourished among sociologists who usually place their work on the macro rather than the micro level of analysis. In his now classic article, Collins (1981) argued that interactions on the ritual and social level were marketplaces where emotional and cultural resources provided the media of exchange. Repeated positive interactions within a group produced emotional solidarity and positive currency; conversely, negative interactions devalued currency. Collins was theorizing the emotional mechanisms that bridged the micro and macro level of analysis. He was among the first in a theoretical field that others are joining. The return of emotion is, in part, an attempt to counter the growing salience of rational choice and formal economic models in both political science and sociology; and is, in part, fueled by real-world problems

such as ethnic cleansing, addiction, greed, and (a theoretical problem but welcome in the real world) altruism. Theories that exclude the affective dimension of social life have difficulty explaining individual or collective behaviors that rationality does not appear to govern.

In his 1997 presidential address to the American Sociological Association, Neil Smelser (1998) focused upon the psychological state of ambivalence to underscore the salience of emotion for thick social analysis. A mere four years later, Douglas Massey's (2002) presidential address to the 2001 American Sociological Meetings called for a reappraisal of the role of emotions in social life. Even more surprising than his subject matter was Massey's quasi-essentialist argument that emotions are so intrinsic to human life that they should be at the core of any meaningful sociology—no matter what the subdisciplinary interest.

Smelser's address offered a perspective that countervailed the rational choice theories and formal models that had burgeoned in political science and were gaining ground in sociology. Smelser argued that the problem with rational choice is its assumption that individuals experience social life as a series of either/or or zero-sum choices in a series of atemporal and ahistorical contexts. Choices can only be rational in those limited instances where the choice context is stable. In general, both rationality and choice recede before empirical reality. The ideal type of contemporary rational choice theory fails to take affect, emotion, and "valence" into account.

According to Smelser, *ambivalence,* the state of holding "opposing affective orientations towards the same person, object or symbol" (1998, 5) is more characteristic of how individuals experience social life than *certainty.* Smelser provides numerous observations of states that generate ambivalence. For example, bonding with others creates dependence that can be positive but can also signal a loss of freedom; parents are both happy and sad when their children grow up and leave home; consumers are both attracted to and feel guilty about the pursuit of status goods. Smelser argues that institutions both mediate ambivalence and provide a context in which behaviors based upon rational choice make sense. In short, Smelser does not completely dismiss rational choice, but takes a grounded approach to it. He argues that rational choice is useful in those contexts in which choice is institutionalized.

In the last few years, historians (Reddy 2001), philosophers (Nussbaum 2001; Pizarro 2000), natural scientists (Damasio 1994, 1999), as well as social scientists (Loewenstein 2000; Elster 1999b; Turner 2000; Barbalet 1998) have all affirmed the importance of emotion in social life. While there is a growing recognition that emotions matter for social science analysis, questions remain as to *how* they matter—that is, *how* emotional responses are transposed from physical states to particular forms of individual or collective social actions. Kemper (1987) numbers 27 emotions in his work and identifies a range of social actions that might channel them. While the process of identifying emotions is seemingly infinite, the mechanisms that transpose an emotion to an action are relatively restricted and in general underspecified.[1]

EMOTION AND ECONOMY: CORE PROBLEMS AND RELEVANT DISTINCTIONS

As there is currently no firmly marked disciplinary path through the fields of emotion and economy, this chapter aims to forge one. In so doing, it attempts to synthesize a large array of literature in a relatively compressed framework—covering aspects of history, sociology, economics, psychology, and philosophy. As this author is not an expert in any of these disciplines except sociology, the article is schematic and lays out possibilities rather than prescriptions.

The principal assumption that governs the discussion is that individual and collective action is central to social analysis. While it is hardly novel to underscore the importance of action—after all, it is central to Parsons's ([1937] 1968) as well as Coleman's (1990) work—emotion is crucial for interpreting both the *means* and *ends* of action. Except for rational choice theories, action is often underemphasized in discussions of emotion. This chap-

ter divides into three broad segments: first, a segment on relevant distinctions that specifies various disciplinary modes of theorizing the relation between emotion and action; second, a more standard review of the literature that groups works around similar themes and issues; and third, an analytic typology that recalibrates the literature in terms of events and emotions. The second section will begin first with Adam Smith's *The Theory of Moral Sentiments* ([1759] 2000) and address various exigeses of the argument; then move on to explore the contemporary social science debate about rationality; and lastly discuss work that has developed in emotion management.

Four relevant distinctions emerge from parsing the contradictions, as well as points of agreement, among the various literatures of emotion. These distinctions are as follows.

1. *Emotion is a physical not a psychological state.* Neuroscience (Frijda 1993; Mendoza and Ruys 2001) is the disciplinary site of much innovative contemporary work on emotion. Neuroscientist Antonio Damasio (1994, 1999) the most compelling theorist (whom I rely on, as do scholars such as Jon Elster), makes the important point that emotion is first a physical feeling that we secondarily articulate as a cognition. Cognition, the second step in emotion, is where culture and historical specificity as well as institutional realms matter. We experience emotion as a physical state—elation, weeping, nausea. Even autoimmune disease, in which the body literally turns upon itself, plausibly signals the repression of emotion. The physical experience of emotion is ontologically different from the interpretation (cognition) of emotion and the actions that we take in response to our experienced emotions. Social scientists frequently conflate this distinction, and it attenuates the strength of their arguments because it bypasses the physical dimension of emotion.

2. *Emotion is constitutive of human nature and by inference constitutive of social life.* Charles Darwin ([1872] 1998) made the classic argument that even animals have emotions. Classical studies of human nature beginning in the eighteenth century understood that absence of emotion and affect is moral and social death. Emotion's relation to ethics or morality and human nature persists to this day, as emotion remains the province of moral philosophy and psychology (for example, De Sousa 1980; Middleton 1989; Pizarro 2000; D'Arms and Jacobson 2000; Greenspan 2000; Nussbaum 2001). *Having emotions is natural; channeling emotions is social.* An emotionless person would

exist in a state of perfect equilibrium. While individuals would not want to live in a state of continuing emotional upheaval, perfect equilibrium (an economist's and rational choice theorist's heaven) would be equally dysfunctional. Economist Robert Frank's (1988, 1993) arguments that emotions are rational are based on the unstated assumption that social equilibrium takes away from, rather than enhances, social and economic innovation. The creative (i.e., innovative and productive) social and economic actor follows his or her passions beyond reason.

3. *Emotion is not culture and vice versa.* Emotion and culture are interconnected, but they should be kept analytically distinct even if they cannot be so in real life. Culture, norms, and values affect the expression of emotion but not the reality of the emotion, or norms or values (Shweder 1993). Culture affects practices within different economic institutions, as well as the organization and practice of economic life (Middleton 1989).

4. *Trust and risk are perceptions not emotions.* Trust is a perception or a cognitive act. Emotion may influence the formation of those cognitions and the resultant mental state of trust, but emotion and trust are not coterminous entities. It is important to make this distinction early on because trust, in the literature on economics and society, is sometimes treated (erroneously, according to this author) as an emotion (for example, Pixley 1999a, 1999b, 2002a, 2002b). This chapter follows Coleman (1990), whose discussion of trust and risk clearly links them to the problem of action, even though emotions may be built into the action. Coleman argues that trust is a "bet on the future" that we place with respect to knowledge that we have about past actions. Past experience both with our own internal psyches as well as with others determines our assessment of trust and risk in various situations.

Trust is a judgment that we make about actions.[2] Culture influences how we make those judgments. All actions have a degree of uncertainty built into them—even the most routine. The concept of *accident* is the recognition of the uncertainty that underlies even the most mundane and routine situations. Trust and risk are directly proportional to each other. Generalized trust informs actions that individuals and collectivities repeat day after day because they are in quotidian low-risk situations. In the absence of information, we may decide to act on little or no information and follow what Elster (1996) describes as "gut feelings." According to Coleman (1990), time is constitutive of trust.

Misplaced trust is an error that results from the failure to give adequate time to decision making. Coleman's example of a young woman who does not allow sufficient time to investigate a young man who offers to walk her home and subsequently attacks her (91–108) underscores the relation between time and trust.

In its purist form, emotion and economy should focus on the noncognitive dimension of economic action. The analytic line is emotion—cognition—action. Much of the social science literature that focuses on emotion focuses on its cognitive dimension. Arlie Hochschild's (1979, 1983, 1990) work on emotion rules and management is seminal in this area. The cognitive perspective does not adequately acknowledge that individuals have experiential and physical knowledge of the emotions that they manage or the rules that they follow. Culture and cognition are of course crucial but so is the physical experience of emotion. Culture and cognition intervene between emotion and action.

Recognizing that emotion is a physical state, that it is about the body rather than the mind, is central to theorizing the link between emotion and economic action. Absence of emotion is equilibrium in both physical and economic life. Emotion disequilibrates, and it is in moments of disequilibration and reequilibration that innovation occurs in social and economic life. Sociology's contribution to the study of emotions and the economy will lie in its ability to map the steps between emotion and action.

Figure 1 provides a preliminary diagram of the preceding discussion.

EMOTION AND ECONOMY: HISTORICAL ANTECEDENTS

The study of emotion as analytic object dates to antiquity. Aristotle's *Rhetoric* (1991) explored emotion as ontology and teleology. Emotion as a problem of modernity (the emphasis in this review) emerged in the eighteenth century with the burgeoning of market society. As Elias's (1994) magisterial study of the "civilizing process" demonstrates, the disciplining of affect was a constitutive feature of the transition from feudal to modern society. In England and Scotland and to a lesser degree on the continent, philosophers were pondering the ontology of human nature and the passions at the same moments, if we accept Elias's account, as the passions were in the process of being institutionally tamed. In the eighteenth century, tam-

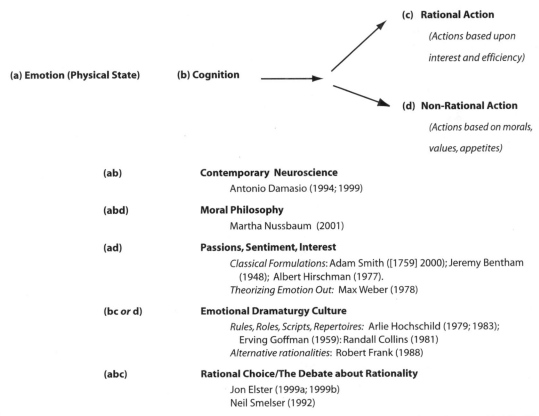

FIGURE 1. Relating emotion and action: disciplinary paths. Max Weber's forms of social action (1978, 22–26) suggest, but do not define, the distinctions outlined in this figure. Authors cited serve as selective examples within a category.

ing the passions was a problem of moral philosophy that became a problem of political economy and capitalism in the nineteenth century.

Eighteenth-century England was the stage for many of the ideas that became commonplace on the continent as well as the site of a burgeoning and vibrant bourgeoisie society. Sentiments and sensibilities, passions and appetites were problems of a new market society as well as moral philosophy (Rothschild 2001). Hirschman (1977) provides the classic account of how passions were repressed with the help of interests in the service of the emerging market economy. Hirschman points out that moneymaking from classical antiquity to the Renaissance always carried a social stigma. Passions, the appetites (Hirschman draws heavily on Machiavelli), were the motor forces behind the constant warfare of the Renaissance princes. But passion was disruptive to the development of the mature statecraft that market society required. Beginning in the late Renaissance, *interests* emerged as the term for conducting a more balanced public

and private life (Hirschman 1977, 42). The passions did not serve either political or economic interests. But the passions were constitutive of human nature and, in Freudian terms, needed an object of sublimation. The object was the formerly vulgar and immoral pursuit of money that became coterminous with interest. Moneymaking became the "calm passion." Commerce, depending upon which side of the English Channel one was on, was called "innocent" or "doux." Vice became virtue in the service of a new economic order. These ideas diffused in intellectual circles as well as through the popular culture. For example, Molière wrote *The Miser* as well as *The Bourgeois Gentleman*.

Markets and commercial society required freedom to thrive (laissez-faire as metaphor and practice), yet individuals could not be completely unfettered if a capitalist system were to develop. Capitalism, as Weber ([1920] 1976) argues in *The Protestant Ethic and the Spirit of Capitalism*, required discipline as well as desire to thrive. Barbalet (2000) makes the argument that the concept of vocation, *Beruf*, rationalized in the notion of career, was the institutional vehicle that contained the emotive and the rational. It is no accident that novelistic narrative fiction began to develop during this period (Watt [1957] 2001). The heroes and heroines of the new novel genre (remember Moll Flanders as well as Robinson Crusoe) graphically capture the tension between exuberance, passion and appetite, and discipline that would characterize emerging capitalist economy.

The focus on sentiment and sensibility in French and English eighteenth-century moral philosophy adjudicated the tension between unruly passion and cold interest in the language of domesticated emotion. Within the realm of economics and emotion, Adam Smith's *The Theory of Moral Sentiments* is a core book.[3] Published in 1759, it predates the *Wealth of Nations* by 17 years. Although sentiment is in the title, Smith does not write in the mode of a Shaftesbury, his contemporary and fellow partisan of emotion. *The Theory of Moral Sentiments* expounds a political economy of emotion that shifts scarcity from the productive to the interior psychological realm.

In the main, Smith argues that "fellow feeling," or sympathy, is the core of social life. Smith suggests that we are moved by our imaginative engagement with the suffering of others. Human suffering generates an unspoken moral calculus. Human beings have the capacity to sympathize and to be the object of sympathy. Although the former is preferable to the latter, the fungibility of sympathy serves as a moral glue of social, and by extension, productive life. Underlying this argument is a notion of appropriate and inappropriate objects of sympathy. The concept of appropriateness emerges at the beginning of the work as well as in the chapters on merit, demerit, and utility. Smith argues that gratitude and resentment are the core affects of empathy ([1759] 2000, 94–111). Those who are objects of gratitude are those whom we see as worthy of reward; those who are objects of resentment we see as deserving punishment. Close reading reveals some ambiguity as to who is the subject and who is the object of gratitude and resentment. Deference and jealousy can as easily replace gratitude and resentment. To put it in other words, we see as worthy of their good fortune those who have been deferent to us and with whom we can identify; we view as worthy of bad fortune those who have an independent relation to us and whose actions appear foreign to us.

A large literature exists on Adam Smith that this chapter only touches upon. While a commonly accepted notion is that there are two Adam Smiths, the empathetic moralist of *The Theory of Moral Sentiments* and the calculating capitalist of *Wealth of Nations,* revisionist approaches are suggesting that the two works are more intricately connected than scholars had previously understood. While there are an infinite number of objects to trade in the marketplace, there is a far more limited supply of sympathy. More importantly, as critics are beginning to point out, no one can really be the other person—that is, the person who requires the sympathy. In fact, though it might appear that Adam Smith is an early advocate of "feeling another's pain," the more likely response to the suffering of others is relief that we are not the sufferer. This logic yields an unstated next step, that contempt, rather than pity or sympathy, is the natural response to the suffering of others. In short, sympathy is an emotional draping on the secure feeling that we ourselves are intact.[4]

Agnew (1986) in a historical analysis argues that the development of the theater and market in precapitalist England are two sides of the same coin. Drawing upon Adam Smith, Agnew argues that mutual sympathy comes from the recognition of mutual inaccessibility. What is created is an imaginative, not an emotional, identification with others. Imagination is also a function of cognition or rationality—that is, we have to imagine an agreeable story about another person in order to identify or sympathize with him or her. The more affluent persons or societies become, the more time they have for sympathy or empathy. A thin line separates sympathy, jealousy, and disapproval. Paradoxically, we would rather sympathize with those who are graced than with those who have fallen from grace. Sympathy is a frail rather than robust force. In the theater, no matter how emotionally engaged we are, we go home at the end of the performance. The "bottom line" of sympathy is parallel to leaving the theater: whether fortune is good or bad, it is always experienced by someone other than ourselves.

Agnew (1986, 186) makes the argument that emotional isolation lies at the heart of Smith's system because scarcity exists in the emotional as well as economic realm. Individuals compete for limited supplies of social attention—whether as givers or as objects of sympathy. Those who are not competitive in the attention sphere simply drop off the social and economic radar screen. Unstated but implicit in Agnew's argument is that the poor and socially marginal are most likely to suffer physically as well as psychologically if they lose in the sympathy, or attention, market. Thompson (1971) shifts this valence in his study of bread riots in eighteenth-century England as part of a "moral economy" of the crowd. Aneurin Bevan, one of the architects of the British postwar welfare state, entitled his treatise on the subject *In Place of Fear* (1952). Bevan argued that a welfare state would provide the security that would break the link between emotional and material deprivation.

Offer (1997), drawing upon *The Theory of Moral Sentiments*, formulates a concept of the "economy of regard" that follows from where Agnew leaves off. Offer argues that there is a tension between the gift relation as described by Marcel Mauss and the market. The "economy of regard" attempts to resolve this tension. Offer argues that with respect to sympathy, individuals crave *approbation* or *regard*. The "gift relationship" elucidates the scarcity *and* social significance of regard—the gift of attention. The social function of regard, as with gifts, is to enter into an exchange relation. The currency of the gift is usually some type of material object; the currency of regard is status and deference. The economy of regard operates wherever personal relations affect incentives (471).

While the market, to borrow from Bentham, may ultimately provide the greatest good for the greatest number, *it cannot provide the best goods for the greatest number.* As Max Weber recognized, the best societal goods combine money and status, or in Adam Smith's terms, the positive approbation of one's fellow men. Similar to gifts with rules of engagement and prestige hierarchies, approbation or regard is a scarce commodity and is more akin to competition than emotional empathy. Offer's argument, coupled with Agnew's, points to the rational rather than emotional dimension of sympathy—because sympathy is about competition for place *and* position (i.e, to be worthy of regard) and not charity.

Rothschild's *Economic Sentiments* (2001) focuses on Smith and Condorcet, underscoring the essential modernity of *uncertainty* as a social fact (51). Feeling emotions that one can be aware of and reflect upon requires a modern perception of time. Premodern men and women perceived and experienced time as nonlinear. Experiencing time synchronically and not diachronically, premodern men and women lived in the moment. Feudal hierarchies and nature regulated social life. Peasants and lords did not need highly refined time sensibilities. Barring natural disasters, their production systems reduced uncertainty to virtually zero. For peasants and lords, tomorrow offered few surprises. Capitalist production systems required planning. Modern economic men and women, in contrast to their predecessors, required a finely calibrated sense of time—to think and to plan.[5] It is no accident that, like economics, the study of the mind and human understanding is an eighteenth-century obsession.

Market capitalism gave birth to the recognition of uncertainty. Along with the perception of uncertainty came social groups who could imagine a future and who had an expanded time horizon. Rothschild (2001) argues that the capacity to imagine a future was a feature of Enlightenment thought that penetrated the collective modern psyche more deeply than standard philosophical accounts suggest. Futurity and uncertainty meant that one could pursue different paths of action. Choice, as well as its kinship concept rationality, is a feature of modernity itself. In premodern, or precommercial, societies, choice was not an option, and the ethics or moral sentiments required to make normative distinctions and choices were not social or political requisites.

THE DEBATE ABOUT RATIONALITY AND EMOTION IN SOCIOLOGY AND ECONOMICS

History reveals that utility proved a more attractive concept than sentiment. In the nineteenth century, the boundary between moral philosophy and practical life was drawn sharply and gave birth to the full-blown science of, first, political economy and, then, modern economics. It is axiomatic in economic history that rationality and rational man are products of the eighteenth and nineteenth centuries (see Persky 1995 for a brief history of the concepts). Jeremy Bentham introduced the concept of utility in *An Introduction to the Principles of Morals and Legislation* (1948), and his foremost student John Stuart Mill continued to develop it in a series of books and treatises.

According to Bentham, "An action . . . may be said to be conformable to the principle of . . . utility (meaning with respect to the community at large), when the tendency it has to augment the happiness of the community is greater than any it has to diminish it" (1948, 127). As utility applies to any action that accords the greatest good to the greatest number, the individual pursuing his or her self-interest will increase the level of general happiness in the community.

Nineteenth-century political economy (with the

exception of Marx's critique) is synonymous with rationality and the corresponding process of rationalization. Twentieth-century economists built upon nineteenth-century theories to mathematize economics and to drain it of historical and cultural context. John Stuart Mill's two-volume *Principles of Political Economy* established him as the father of modern political economy. On the strength of this volume, theorists of all stripes overlook Mill's commitment to emotion as well as his position as a public figure within the age of English romanticism and early Victorianism. Among his voluminous writings, Mill's *Autobiography* ([1873] 1969) and his twin essays on Bentham and Coleridge remind us that the nineteenth century was the highpoint of sensibility, what English poet William Wordsworth characterized as "emotion reflected in tranquility," as well as market capitalism. Mill's awakening to the value of emotion that he so resonantly describes in his *Autobiography* is widely known among intellectual historians. Contemporary political economists and sociologists have for the most part neglected this aspect of Mill's thought and writings.

Mill's twin essays on Bentham and Coleridge are instructive (Mill 1950). Mill identifies Bentham's greatest contribution to modern political thought as his insistence on the necessary relation between means-ends rationality and law. Mill finds Bentham's vision of human nature deficient. Mill argues that Bentham recognized that men (and women) were capable of self-interest and even a form of sympathy but failed to understand the deeper principles that govern human nature: "Man is never recognized by him [Bentham] as a being capable of pursuing spiritual perfection as an end; of desiring, for its own sake, the conformity of his own character to his standard of excellence, without hope of good or fear of evil from a source other than his own inward consciousness" (Mill 1950, 66). Mill continued his critique: "Even under the head of *sympathy*, his recognition does not extend to the more complex forms of the feeling—the love of *loving*" (68). Mill juxtaposed Bentham with his contemporary, the poet and essayist Samuel Taylor Coleridge. According to Mill, Coleridge was more capable than Bentham of comprehending the immanent nature of human and social life because he took emotion into account. Mill found that the distinction between sentiment and reason, or between emotion and rationality, was ultimately false. Mill's final point was that the truly rational life combined emotion and reason—the "training by the human being himself,

of his affections and will" and "[in] co-equal part, the regulation of his outward actions" (71).

Rationality and its contradictions, the tension between reason and emotion, was an underlying concern of classical social theory (Barbalet 1998). Pareto's concept of nonlogical conduct (1935) and Weber's (1978) forms of social action that include a category of nonrational action indirectly incorporate the issue of emotion. Weber's ([1920] 1976) *Protestant Ethic* thesis as well as James's (1956) concept of the "sentiment" of rationality both point to the fact that emotion was never far from the minds of those who on the surface appeared to have been explaining it away. Parsons ([1940] 1954b) in an essay on "motivation" and economy pointed out that "self-interest," which economists assume governs economic choice, is a complicated social phenomenon replete with emotions such as satisfaction, recognition, need, pleasure, and even affection (57–59). Smelser in a prescient discussion in *The Sociology of Economic Life* (1963) built upon Parsons's work to argue that rationality should be understood as an institutionalized feature of the economy that has psychological and cultural valence (34). Smelser later expanded this point (1992), arguing that rationality should be viewed as an independent rather than a dependent variable in economic analysis. Despite this early notice, it was not until formal modeling and rational choice began to make inroads into both political science and sociology that rationality returned to the sociological agenda.

The publication of James Coleman's *The Foundations of Social Theory* in 1990, coupled with the founding of his journal *Rationality and Society* in 1988 at the University of Chicago, marked the explicit turn toward rational choice in sociology. While rational choice evokes strong passions pro and con, a large literature that challenges it has not emerged.[6] Paradoxically, as sociologists were beginning to concern themselves with rationality, the economists and political scientists who were associated with rational choice theory became interested in emotions. Three distinct and overlapping discussions of rationality and emotion can be identified: first, the discussion within sociology itself; second, the interest in emotions among those who are otherwise partial to rational choice theories (this is, principally, the work of Jon Elster and Robert Frank, a political scientist and an economist); and third, an emerging focus on emotion within the area of behavioral economics and cognitive psychology.

In a theme issue of *Sociological Forum* devoted

to the issue of rationality, Amatai Etzioni (1987) began by questioning the idea of collective rationality. Focusing on the concept of human nature, Etzioni argued that rational choice was a binary system that overlooked human complexity as a factor in the choices that social actors individually and collectively make. Etzioni's article foreshadowed the more extended analysis he offered in his full-length study of the moral dimension of the economy (1988). In the same issue of *Sociological Forum*, economist Robert Frank (1987) argued that economists who have had an interest in non-rational dimensions of action have mistakenly focused on "habits" that are neither rational nor irrational but simply efficient. Frank argued that a calculus of rationality could be found in rage, love, and sympathy. Frank described these "non-self-interested" behaviors as "shrewdly irrational." Frank's idea that emotions are strategic has antecedents in recent work in moral philosophy and psychology (for example, De Sousa 1980; Solomon 1980; Greenspan 2000). While Frank is an economist by training, he has addressed a series of issues in books and articles that are as sociological as they are economically oriented. These include studies of excessive consumption, or "luxury fever," and tailoring expectations to possibilities, or "fishing in the right pond."

Passions within Reason: The Strategic Role of the Emotions (1988) contains Frank's principal statement on emotion and economics. He develops a perspective on economics and emotion concerning the "commitment problem." Frank begins with the famous Hatfield and McCoy feud in Appalachia, which lasted for 35 years and killed off numerous members of both families before the participants decided to call it to a halt. The essence of the "commitment problem" is that on the surface it appears irrational to commit to any actions or relationships that appear to be based solely on emotions such as love or anger. Marriage is among the institutional examples that Frank uses to expound his argument. Marriage as an institution is irrational because it requires individuals to make a long-term commitment to another before sampling the universe of all possible mates. A better spouse may always be just over the horizon. Love, an emotion, provides the push that enables individuals to commit to a marriage. Once an emotion has catapulted us into a commitment, we tend to honor those commitments because of our memberships in groups.

Frank (1993) argues that we choose our commitments based on social interactions within and among groups. Within a group, individuals have the same repertoire of emotions and, most importantly, ways of discerning them. Frank uses the term *norms* for this similarity of discernment, but *culture* or Bourdieu's (1977) now familiar concept of *habitus* would serve as well. Sometimes we make commitments because they are costless, but the more basic reason we make them is because norm breakers, that is, those who violate prevailing conceptions of commitments, are excluded from valuable social networks. Therefore, it is in one's interest to engage in certain actions that appear irrational because to do otherwise would lessen one's position in a reference group.

Within sociology, Smelser (1992, 1995) has led the current critical discussion of rationality and emotion, beginning with his review in *Contemporary Sociology* (1990) of Coleman's *Foundations of Social Theory* and culminating in his 1997 address to the American Sociological Association (1998). In his review (1990), Smelser criticizes Coleman for attempting to construct a general sociology from the position of methodological individualism. He correctly points out that Coleman's theory fails to take either culture or emotions into account. A novelty in Smelser's critique is his observation that Coleman's valorization of primordial social ties lends a conservative, and even reactionary, cast to his arguments.

In a review article prepared for *Rationality and Society* (1992), Smelser argued that while the rational choice model is elegant as an economic model of human behavior, it leaves much of social life unexplained because it fails to resolve the tension between analytic simplicity and social realism. The rational man model is anchored in the social and productive relations of eighteenth-century Britain—the historical context where it first emerged. Rationality as a postulate does have analytic utility. In the same article, Smelser argues that scarcity, the core of economics, may apply to the nonmaterial dimensions of social life.[7] Theoretical and empirical difficulties for rational choice theory arise when its practitioners attempt to extend it beyond its appropriate ranges of applicability. Smelser advocates solving the problem of rational choice by treating "maximization and rational calculations as variables rather than postulates" (404). This allows the analyst to introduce questions of context such as information, culture, institutions, and motive, as well as rationality, into analysis of choice or purposive action.

In 1993, the editors of *Rationality and Society* devoted a special issue to the study of emotions and rational choice. According to the editor of the issue (Heckathorn 1993), three ways to think about emotion and rational action emerged from the articles: first, emotions are derived from rational action, and they permit us to act in ways compatible with our long-term interests (Frank 1993; Hirshleifer 1993; Smith-Lovin 1993); second, rationality derives from group solidarity and the emotion of social interaction (Collins 1993); and third, rationality and emotion are linked in an underlying process that permits emotion to follow a judgment of rationality (Jasso 1993).

In addition to Heckathorn's summary, certain arguments merit further discussion. Kemper's argument (1993) that emotion operates as a form of self-interest complements Frank's contribution (1993) to the debate. Hirshleifer (1993) argues that there is an economic logic to emotion that might cause a person to override what would appear to be his material interests. Distinguishing between the passions and the affections, Hirshleifer points out that affections are stable, whereas passions are reactive. Emotions or passions are nature's tricks (underscoring their physiological components) and suggest that our material goals are better served when they are not intentionally pursued. Hirshleifer's argument recalls Goethe's bon mot—one never goes further than when one does not know where one is going.

In the same volume of *Rationality and Society,* Collins (1993) develops his concept of "emotional energy." He argues that it is necessary to establish interaction rituals centered within the economic sphere. These interaction rituals point to a kind of paradox in contemporary society. All work and no play, as well as all play and no work, leads to a social anomie that is dysfunctional for society. The modern occupational structure demands excessive work that curtails leisure and its accompanying solidarity rituals. If we expend all our emotional energy in work, we sacrifice solidarity among persons for solidarity among things—that is, the items we consume serve as codes that signal our place within specific material solidarity circles. For example, if you own a Porsche and I own a Porsche, we are the same kind of person (solidaristic) even if we have never met.

During the same period that the debate on rationality emerged in sociology, political scientist Jon Elster produced a corpus of work on emotions. In an essay on norms and economic theory (1989), Elster's arguments are similar to the ideas that Collins (1993) expresses. Elster argues that norms are multiple and that in any given situation an individual might appeal to any given set of norms. All norms, according to Elster, have "emotional tonality" because they are not, strictly speaking, useful. Elster's principal point is that social norms differ from moral and legal norms because the "informal community" and not institutions enforce them. Elster's argument recalls Collins (1993) on "solidarity" and Offer (1997) on "regard."

Elster draws a distinction between social and moral norms. According to Elster, guilt and shame follow the violation of social norms; legal punishment follows the violation of moral norms. Social norms inspire fear. For example, *if* I drink too much in public and babble indiscriminately, I will be socially ostracized *if* my reference community values propriety and discretion. Social norms in the strictest sense do not benefit, or harm, anyone. Rather, they define the boundaries of the community. My drinking and babbling may leave me socially ostracized, but my neighbors cannot take my house away for verbal indiscretion! Where Elster's analysis falls short is in his effort to make the case that norms are a product of emotion rather than rationality; he does not recognize that social norms determine who receives attention, who commands more of the scarce social resource—regard.

Throughout the 1990s, Elster was deeply engaged in the study of emotions and rationality. In an article titled "Rationality and Emotions," published in an economics journal, Elster (1996) argued that economists have neglected the relation between "gut feelings" and maximizing utility. In a later article, Elster (1998) attempted to make an explicit link between emotions and economic theory. He argued that emotions help us to explain behavior that appears to lack a good (i.e., rational) explanation. Elster develops a typology of emotions (1998, 53) that relates emotions to interests. In Elster's view, interests by definition are rational and economic in the broadest sense of that term. As in much of Elster's work, he proceeds by way of fictitious examples. He has drawn up a table of characteristics of emotions that includes such features as these: first, to have an emotion you have to see the object of emotion (out of sight, out of mind); second, intentionality (emotions are about something); third, volatility, physiological arousal (screaming, weeping); and fourth, expressivity (sour face, scowling mouth, drooping eyes).

Elster believes that individuals need emotions to act judiciously. Yet, despite his multitude of writings on the subject, it is hard to identify a specific mechanism that links emotion to action in Elster's work. If anything, Elster's principal point is that emotions shape both our choices and rewards—what he calls the "dual role of emotions" (1998, 73). Elster's articles were prolegomena to two book-length treatises, *Alchemies of the Mind: Rationality and the Emotions* (1999a) and *Strong Feelings: Emotion, Addiction, and Human Behavior* (1999b), as well as an anthology, *Addiction* (1999c). *Alchemies of the Mind* is Elster's summary statement on emotions. The book is five interconnected sections that stand very much on their own. The first chapter, "A Plea for Mechanisms," raises the central dilemma that confronts every social scientist who studies emotions. As a social scientist, one wants to be able to map triggering events, or sequences of events, that invariably give rise to particular emotions. While Elster provides an exhaustive and learned account of emotions from Aristotle through the French moralists up to contemporary rational choice theories, the specification of a mechanism eludes him. Romer (2000) solves some of the problems that mechanisms pose by breaking decision mechanisms into four categories: autonomous (natural), feeling-based (emotional and reactive), thought-based (cognitive and decision based), and hybrid (future oriented) mechanisms. The principal problem that Elster and others face in identifying a mechanism that links emotion to action lies within the nature of emotions themselves. That is, the moment that one is conscious of an emotion and attempts to control it, emotion becomes a cognition and is no longer, strictly speaking, an emotion. This dilemma suggests why Elster and others have turned to studies of addiction. If one characterizes addiction as complete absence of control when confronted with an object of desire, then it is an ideal venue for studying the tension between rationality and emotion or appetite.

EMOTION, ECONOMY, AND THE BODY

Much of the literature thus far discussed focuses on the necessity of acknowledging emotions. A parallel theme is emerging that addresses the role of "visceral" factors in economic action. In general, this view focuses upon the physiological dimension of emotions. Metaphors of the body, rather than the mind, define this perspective, such as Elster's (1996) idea that "gut feelings" are a credible part of economic analysis. George Loewenstein in a seminal article (2000) argues that Bentham originally theorized a relation between both utility and emotion and that modern economics missed the

point by making utility an index of preference. Loewenstein argues that economists have worked on anticipatory emotions such as regret and disappointment but have paid too little attention to immediate emotions, which he labels "visceral factors."[8] Following the recent trend in neuroscience that emphasizes the physiological component of emotion, Loewenstein argues that emotions, while normally viewed as destructive, are crucial for survival. Although visceral factors are erratic and unpredictable, they are superior to cognitive functions. Consciousness that makes us stop and think gets in the way of survival. Visceral factors increase marginal utility because they help us resolve the tension between what one feels driven to do and what is best to do. Addictive behavior (intertemporal behavior—can you or can you not control yourself) is a physical state where visceral factors have blunted cognitive factors that facilitate control.

DiMaggio (2002) picks up this thread when he points to "animal spirits" as a factor that should be "endogenized" in economic analyses. DiMaggio takes the concept of "animal spirits" from British economist John Meynard Keynes, who argued that in the last analysis "animal spirits" did much to contribute to the ups and downs of the economy. Affective or emotional states become important to decision making in the absence of information. DiMaggio argues that the diffusion of economic confidence and willingness to assume risk is the product of emotion, not rationality. DiMaggio draws upon Shiller's *Irrational Exuberance* (2000) to underscore the emerging interest in emotion among mainstream economists. Shiller predicted the downturn in American stocks that began in fall 2000. Shiller argued that the precipitous rise in stock prices that began in the early 1990s led to a market that was vastly overvalued—that is, the price-to-earnings ratios of stocks were disproportionately high. Yet investors, or more precisely, small investors, continued to pour money into the market, even when it became clear that a bubble was forming. Shiller provides a historical analysis of rises and falls in the American stock market. After factoring in a number of "rational" explanations, such as baby boomer investors and the popularization of finance in the mass media, he concludes that investors for emotional reasons became overconfident in markets and eventually this overconfidence worked against their own overall financial advantage.[9]

The strength of DiMaggio's article comes from its ability to demarcate the particular disciplinary insights that sociology might bring to bear on the study of emotion and economy. He argues that sociologists are conceptually equipped to study emotions and economics because they focus upon collective action, or as DiMaggio labels it, "interdependent action." He develops a set of hypotheses about markets as social movements that borrows from both sociology and cognitive psychology. From sociology, DiMaggio draws on Robert Merton's idea of the "self-fulfilling prophecy" and Mark Granovetter's theories of "threshold" and "diffusion models" of collective action. To his arsenal of concepts DiMaggio adds Randall Collins on interaction rituals and Harrison White on collective identity. To buttress his sociological theory, DiMaggio adds Kahneman and Twerksy's work on "decision heuristics." DiMaggio combines these concepts to form several hypotheses: when animal spirits are high, participants in a commercial transaction are more likely to define themselves as sharing a common identity; animal spirits covary with generalized trust; shared identity and generalized trust lead to the purchase of optional objects.

DiMaggio's article captures a trend that had appeared in the literature under a variety of labels (Archer 2000; Abelson 1996). For example, in 1986 Conover and Feldman described a phenomenon of "anger" at the economy and an attempt (not particularly rational) to get even that parallels Shiller's notion of exuberance. Nye (1991) argued that, in contrast to received perception of entrepreneurs as rational plodders, careful analysis of economic history suggests that successful entrepreneurs are "lucky fools"—people who pursue some idea based on a feeling or attraction—and then just happen to hit it right. The economy, according to Nye's argument, needs people with this sort of offbeat tunnel vision for innovation to occur. Although 99 out of 100 "fools" fail, it is the one hundredth, the "lucky fool," who keeps the economy vigorous. Pixley (1999a, 2002a, 2002b) in a series of articles focuses upon modern corporations or financial organizations as collective structural actors and argues that emotion as well as rationality governs monetary and macro-level financial policy decisions.

EMOTION AS CULTURAL PERFORMANCE

The work of Arlie Russell Hochschild (1979, 1983, 1990, 2003) and the research genre that followed from it is the most explicit sociological contribution to the study of emotion and economy. Erving Goffman's (1959) emphasis upon the performative aspects of modern cultural interaction and the importance of "impression management" underlies much of Hochschild's work. Although he uses other terminology, much of Goffman's work focuses on the suppression of emotion in the service of status ends. Hochschild develops the twin concepts of "feeling rules" and "emotion management." Her principal point is that while individuals may experience a myriad of emotions in any given situation, "social rules" govern when it is appropriate to express emotions. "Emotion management" of ourselves as well as of others is the task of controlling inappropriate affect.

While "emotion management" may appear to be merely the observance of social norms, what makes Hochschild's analysis remarkable is that she was the first sociologist to argue that these rules and norms also applied to labor market transactions (i.e., jobs) and that emotions were a constitutive part of economic life. *The Managed Heart: Commercialization of Human Feeling* (1983) is Hochschild's initial and perhaps major statement on this process. *The Managed Heart* is principally a study of the training of flight attendants at Delta Airlines. Hochschild interviewed flight attendants as well as the personnel who hired and trained them; she attended training sessions and immersed herself in airline culture. In-flight service is a good occupational site to explore the role of emotions in the market. Flight attendants were originally women (the first flight attendants were supposed to be nurses). As flying became more commercial after World War II, flying and the women who served passengers in the cabin acquired an aura of glamor—carefully nurtured by the airlines. Despite its past image, flight attending is hard work, and safety and evacuation procedures today take precedence over the weight or gender of the persons in the role.

Hochschild found that flight attendants' training included the management of feelings. This emotional training added to the exploitation of workers (the first chapter of the book opens with a reference to *Das Kapital*) by forcing flight attendants to suppress emotions (fear, anger) and to enact emotions that they do not feel (care, cheerfulness). Hochschild did her fieldwork in the middle to late 1970s when in-flight service as an occupation and the structure of the airlines were changing. Yet she identifies a process that is a constant in all service sector work by nurses, social workers, home health aids, hospice workers, and child care workers. The concept of emotional labor is widely diffused in the literature on gender. If one does a search on JSTOR under Arlie Hochschild's name 80 percent of the articles that appear relate to issues of gender, *not* to work and occupations per se. Much of what Hochschild and those who have turned to her research to model their own studies are describing is emotion as a cultural performance. In all of these instances emotions are suppressed and rechanneled into culturally acceptable behavior in a particular situation. This tells us what anthropologists have always known, that while emotions are universal, their expression is context dependent.[10]

RECALIBRATING ACTION AS EMOTION AND EVENT: AN ANALYTIC TYPOLOGY

The existing literature on emotion and economy poses more questions than it provides answers, and suggests fundamental problems that require solution. The path from feeling an emotion (the physical and the cognitive) to action is both undertheorized and underempiricized. What are the social mechanisms that transpose a feeling state into an emotional action? One way to get analytic purchase on this problem is to theorize the possible ways that emotions and events interact.[11] This chapter concludes by developing a typology based upon my reading in the literature. At the core of this analysis is a distinction between predictability and unpredictability in social life. Some aspects of social and emotional life are ordinary and expected; some are extraordinary. Predictability and unpredictability, juxtaposed with events and emotions, reveal that different ontologies of emotion and as well as epistemologies characterize approaches to emotion within the social and natural sciences. Table 1 summarizes the discussion that follows.

Emotion is natural and innate. This is an uncontroversial statement no matter what body of literature one looks to. History and culture, time and space, determine the expression of emotion and provide the epistemological categories by which we classify the varieties of appropriate and inappropriate affect. While the distinction between the ontological and epistemological dimensions of emotion may blur *empirically*, it is necessary to maintain the distinction for *analytic* purposes. The formal analysis that follows is transhistorical and transcultural. The specific examples I give are Western and Eurocentric.

The problem of action is at the core of all social analysis no matter what theoretical perspective one holds (Alexander 1982). Traditional rational choice theories strip action of context, that is, culture and history. Action is usually discussed in terms of means and ends—as if all the things about which individuals take action were discrete units. But actions only take place in the context of events that are historically and culturally situated. Events range from the micro-level of dyadic interaction to the macro-level of collective action. Emotions as well as temporal and spatial phenomena (history and culture) of more or less complexity constrain decisions or choices about action. I sit at my desk writing this chapter. My emotions are in equilibrium. I want to finish. I type away. Sitting at my desk writing is an event. Everything that happens in between is a choice about an unpredictable event—what words will appear next on the page![12]

Predictable Emotions and Predictable Events

The old aphorism, the only thing we can be sure of in life is death and taxes, has the ring of truth to it. Even though this is a chapter on economy and emotion, for present purposes we will overlook the

TABLE 1. Action as Emotion and Event: An Analytic Typology

Emotions	Events	
	Predictable	*Unpredictable*
Predictable		
Ontology	Nature	Equilibrium
Epistemology	Ethics	Calculus of rationality
Discipline	Moral philosophy	Economics/mathematics
Unpredictable		
Ontology	Culture	Emotion as physical state
Epistemology	Institutions	Appetite, aggression, fear
Discipline	Sociology	Interdisciplinarity; Natural and social sciences

taxes. In truth, birth and death are the only truly predictable human events—although the timing of these events is deeply contextual. The transcultural presence of birth and death rituals attests to the emotional significance of these events. Sadness at the death of a loved one and joy at the birth of a child are predictable emotions no matter how they are culturally mediated. In practice, of course, if one harbored negative feelings for a family member or was confronted with an unwanted child, one might feel joy at death and sorrow or anger at birth, but the principal point is that it is virtually impossible to feel no emotion in the presence of birth and death. In general, people cry at funerals, and mothers report love at the first glimpse of their offspring. Birth and death represent the realm of *emotion and nature* that has most appropriately engaged *moral philosophy*. How *ought* we feel in the face of the great existential events? What actions *ought* we take? This value-ridden sphere lies outside the realm of sociological analysis, which in general does not take moral issues into account.[13]

Predictable Emotions and Unpredictable or Contingent Events

Even in a stable society, everything that happens is a contingent event. Individuals make a hundred minor decisions every day about actions. It would be counterproductive and inefficient if they stopped to think about each of these minor decisions. Frank describes these minor decisions as *habits* and argues that they are important for the smooth functioning of social life (1987). One could argue that rational choice is a predictable emotion (or nonemotion) in the face of an unpredictable or contingent event. In the face of these unpredictable events, individuals make choices based on the principal of maximizing *utility*. Preferences exist independently of emotions, and what is predictable is nonemotionality and rational outcome. The goal is the optimum means to the desired ends. At the extremes, the ends justify the means and *efficiency* trumps ethics. This is the realm of *economics and mathematical reasoning.*

Unpredictable Emotions and Predictable Events

Predictable events are those structured by institutions—institutions as defined by Parsons ([1942] 1954c, 1951) as values embedded in mediating structures.[14] Institutions that pattern events may be private, such as the family (patterning love and marriage); or public, such as the market (jobs and organizations) or the polity (the states and citizenship). The legal system regulates criteria of participation or membership in these various institutional arenas. What is unregulated in the legal sphere is the range of emotional responses and correspondingly appropriate actions that individuals may take within those institutional settings. This is where culture and emotion management come in. Certain emotions are appropriate to each institutional setting. *Culture* is the governing frame and *institutions* are the structural support. Arlie Hochschild's work falls squarely within this category, as does much of the research on sociology and emotion that her research influenced.

From the vantage point of many of the issues raised in this chapter, emotion managed is emotion short-circuited. Emotions are only expressed if they are the appropriate to the institutional framework in which they occur. Workers in the emotion industries, flight attendants, salespersons, caregivers have to display emotion that is appropriate to their social role. They cannot dislike their clients, and emotion management is a coterminous part of all service industries. It is also increasingly a part of (a now familiar term) *corporate culture*, which may require all members of the organization to behave in emotionally pleasing ways (Flam 1990).

In most market situations, for example, jobs, one is required to keep emotions (and the appetites) out, what Parsons ([1939] 1954) described as "affective neutrality." This is one of the reasons that nepotism and love at the office, not to mention sexual harassment, are out of bounds. Although political and moral arguments are offered against these behaviors, they actually violate institutional norms because they mix public and private spheres, leading to conflicts of interest and institutional disarray. They represent inappropriate affect in a market situation. This is why coordinating home and work is more than simply a technical and legal decision about hours worked or dividing the household labor. These different institutional spheres have different cultural rules about emotion. This area has been explored, but not as a discussion of feeling versus nonfeeling realms.

This is why the debate about women and women's work is so profound. Culture defines women as emotional and men as rational—despite empirical evidence to the contrary. In practice, we have all encountered rational women and emotional men; men who nurtured at home and women who climbed the corporate ladder. It is nonetheless important not to forget that it is institutional arrangements, with their culturally proscribed emotional rules, that have created what is recalibrated as gender inequality.

Unpredictable Emotions and Unpredictable Events

As methodological individualists, rational choice theorists tend to gloss over the institutional patterning of affect. Emotion, as unpredictable feeling state, is troubling to their calculations because it introduces the possibility of instability and disequilibria. There is no easy way to predict how emotions will pattern action when both emotions and events are unpredictable. Yet whether or not one subscribes to rational choice models, much of the current interdisciplinary social research is occurring in the area of unpredictable emotions and events. When unpredictable emotions and events occur simultaneously, a state of disequilibrium occurs between the agent and his or her environment. This is the state of uncertainty in which "gut feelings" or "visceral" reactions govern actions.

Within politics, violence is the core subject. Within economics, appetites construed broadly from their benign manifestations in consumption to their more malign forms, greed and addiction, are the core subjects.[15] Appetites govern "irrational exuberance" as well as drug addiction. Appetites may be large or small but in general are unpredictable. I am 50 pounds overweight and diabetic but I cannot control my desire for cake. I go into a store—I cannot resist buying my one hundredth pair of shoes even though my credit cards are maxed out. These are not unreasonable scenarios in the United States. Manning (2000) provides poignant narratives of consumers who lost the capacity to control their credit card purchasing and had to declare personal bankruptcy. This is of course also the realm of love and erotic attraction (not marriage, which falls into the preceding category). Popular culture of all stripes suggests that love, disequilibria, and uncertainty are of a piece. Popular music of past eras says so clearly, "who knows where or when," "some enchanted evening"—and the common Mediterranean European metaphor for falling in love—the thunder bolt.

Appetites—whether for food, sex, or money; consumption items (news junkies); or even power—can be large or small, disciplined or undisciplined (Watson 1999). To return to Frank's example, the Hatfields and McCoys could have hired a negotiator and dealt in a rational manner with their antipathies, sparing lives on both sides. Every divorce lawyer knows that there is money to be made in irrational anger. Excessively controlled appetites are as socially dysfunctional as those that are excessively uncontrolled—although the latter are more attractive subjects of research as well as popular interest. The miser is no more socially attractive than the profligate. Mean-spiritedness destroys the fabric of society by attenuating the possibilities of both cooperative and altruistic behavior (Monroe 1996).

CONCLUSION: THE FUTURE OF EMOTION AND THE ECONOMY

The growing realization that emotions matter for economic life is fueling a resurgence of interest in emotion in the social sciences. To understand how emotions matter in sociologically useful ways, economic sociologists must design empirical research on economic actions that do not appear to be governed by a calculus of rationality. Several topic areas present themselves.

Wills and inheritance. Fiction abounds with examples of anger and preference determining the bestowing of money through wills (for example, Titus, Rosenblatt, and Anderson 1979; Silverstein, Parrott, and Bengston 1995). The empirical evidence is much slighter, but we know that inheritance law varies culturally and historically. The United States is one of the few countries where you can dispose of your property in any way you wish after death. A built-in irrationality of American inheritance law is that it protects spouses and not offspring. If you are married and die without a will in the United States, your estate automatically goes to your surviving spouse. This is irrational in a society with the highest divorce rate in the world. It also paradoxically protects the less stable institution, marriage, at the expense of the family. In America, you can disinherit your kin and marry for money—in the name of love![16]

Compensation studies. These studies take up the issue of economic compensation in the face of moral wrongs. Wrongful-death suits, medical malpractice, all forms of victim compensation fall into this category, including recent claims about economic compensation for historical injustices. There is a literature on these subjects, but with the exception of Zelizer's work (1985) it does not address the fundamental moral question: Can you put a price on injustice, family ties, or, in some cases, sheer bad luck? Data from the claims made by victims of the World Trade Center attacks would provide a source for the language and reasoning that governs thinking about economics and emotion.

Consumption. While there is a huge literature on consumption (see Zelizer, this volume), much of it does not examine how emotions affect what should be rational purchase decisions. The literature on addiction covers the shop-till-you-dropism that contributes to credit card debt. There is another realm of consumption, such as home buying and automobile purchases, that strictly speaking concerns necessities but in which strict rationality does not govern the decision. Buying a new car, for example, is an irrational economic act because a car loses value as soon as you drive it out of the dealership. Yet buying a new car is the dream and reality of Americans. To what extent obsessions with cars and real estate are manifestations of what Leibenstein (1950) identified long ago as "bandwagon" effects, and to what extent they represent deeper emotional needs, is an empirical question (O'Shaughnessy and O'Shaughnessy 2003).

Commodifying emotional objects. This relatively new area focuses on love and money (Zelizer 2002) or religion and money (Friedland 2002).

The literature on emotion and macrosociology suggests that sociologists need to recalibrate their analytic questions so as to sharpen their sociological focus. Social scientists of all stripes need to factor into their analyses the recognition that emotions are as much physiological as psychological, and it is by no means clear that they should be controlled. With respect to the economy, we would gain analytic purchase if we assumed emotionality just as economists, and even sociologists, have always assumed rationality. There is a degree of unpredictability to both individual and collective emotion. Not all individuals respond in the same ways to the same external stimuli. If individual emotion is somewhat unpredictable, collective emotion is even more so. If this were not the case, advertising campaigns would not fail, and there would be no surprise "best-sellers."

The *New York Times* recently reported that the Federal Reserve Bank of Boston invited a group of behavioral economists (many of them cited in this chapter and this volume) to a conference on Cape Cod, the focus being "How Humans Behave." The point was to get input on the "irrational" from experts that would be useful in planning macroeconomic policy. The words that the chief economist for the State Street Corporation used to summarize the rationale of the conference are an apt conclusion to the issues that this chapter has

taken up: "We're looking outside the box because the box we've been looking inside is empty."[17]

Notes

1. For a quick view of the difficulties that this project encounters, see the collection of essays in Barbalet 2002. My own contribution (Berezin 2002) to that volume on politics and emotions developed an argument that the feeling of security is the mechanism that links emotion and political action. When security is threatened, emotions of love, hate, and anger will be transposed into collective political action. The "state" refers to both the physicality of emotion as well as the institution of the state that embeds emotion. I made the argument by recalibrating standard literatures on the state, rationalism, and collective action.

2. See for example, the collection of essays in Cook 2001.

3. Camic (1979) departs from this position in his discussion of utilitarianism, arguing that David Hume is a more important predecessor than Adam Smith.

4. Clark's (1987) discussion of sympathy norms is congruent with this argument.

5. See Landes 2000 for a discussion of the development of clocks.

6. Karl Polanyi's essays (1971) offer an early critique of rationality from the perspective of comparative historical economic sociology. More recently, scholars have incorporated rational choice theory into other modes of analysis. For a cogent example, see Adams 1999 on culture, rational choice, and state formation.

7. See Stanley 1968 for an early discussion of "scarcity" within sociology.

8. The emerging literature on regret covers a multitude of areas. For philosophical theorizing see Rorty 1980; Bell 1983 on decisions and risk; Engelbrecht-Wiggans 1989 on auctions; on consumption Simonson 1992; Tsiros and Mittal 2000; Inman, Dyer, and Jia 1997; on addiction Orphanides and Zervos 1995.

9. See Campbell and Cochrane 1999 for a counterargument that puts habit at the core of stock market behavior.

10. Space constraints do not permit me to address the large literature in anthropology that addresses the issue of the cultural specificity of economic transactions. Recent analytic summaries of that literature include Gudeman 2001 and Carrier 1997.

11. In using the term *event*, I follow Abbott's (2001, 161–205) discussion.

12. Writing is an event because presumably there will be an audience for this chapter.

13. See Fontaine 2001 for a discussion of empathy and social welfare.

14. Camic (1990) published a historical account of Parsons's "Prolegomena to a Theory of Social Institutions." As the literature on institutions in general is voluminous (see Nee this volume), this chapter follows Parsons's discussion in his 1942 essay "Propaganda and Social Control" as well as chapter 2 of *The Social System* (1951).

15. The essays in Loewenstein, Read, and Baumeister 2003 discuss appetite on a variety of levels from the neurological to the legal and take up issues of consumption, weight management, drug dependence, and even patience.

16. Jens Beckert's forthcoming study of inheritance law will provide us with one of the first systematic comparisons of inheritance in different historical and cultural instances

when it is completed. For a preliminary report, see Beckert 2003.

17. Stephen J. Dubner, "Calculating the Irrational in Economics," *New York Times*, June 28, 2003.

REFERENCES

Abbott, Andrew. 2001. *Time Matters*. Chicago: University of Chicago Press.

Abelson, Robert P. 1996. "The Secret Existence of Expressive Behavior." Pp. 25–36 in *The Rational Choice Controversy: Economic Models of Politics Reconsidered*, ed. Jeffrey Friedman. New Haven: Yale University Press.

Adams, Julia. 1999. "Culture in Rational Choice Theories of State Formation." Pp. 98–122 in *State/Culture*, ed. George Steinmetz. Ithaca, N.Y.: Cornell University Press.

Agnew, Jean Christophe. 1986. *Worlds Apart*. Cambridge: Cambridge University Press.

Alexander, Jeffrey C. 1982. *Theoretical Logic in Sociology*. Vol. 1. Berkeley and Los Angeles: University of California Press.

Archer, Margaret S. 2000. "*Homo Economicus, Homo Sociologicus*, and *Homo Sentiens*." Pp. 36–56 in *Rational Choice Theory: Resisting Colonization*, ed. Margaret S. Archer and Jonathan Q. Tritter. London: Routledge.

Aristotle. 1991. *The Art of Rhetoric*. London: Penguin.

Barbalet, Jack. M. 1998. *Emotion, Social Theory, and Social Structure: A Macrosociological Approach*. Cambridge: Cambridge University Press.

———. 2000. "*Beruf*, Rationality, and Emotion in Max Weber's Sociology." *Archives Européennes de Sociologie* 41:329–51.

———, ed. 2002. *Emotions and Sociology*. Oxford: Basil Blackwell.

Beckert, Jens. 2003. "Unearned Wealth: Discursive Structures and the Regulation of Wealth Transmission in France, Germany, and the United States." Paper presented to the Meetings of the American Sociological Association, Atlanta, August 16–19.

Bell, David E. 1983. "Risk Premiums for Decision Regret." *Management Science* 29:1156–66.

Bentham, Jeremy. 1948. *A Fragment on Government* and *An Introduction to the Principles of Morals and Legislation*. Oxford: Basil Blackwell.

Berezin, Mabel. 2002. "Secure States: Towards a Political Sociology of Emotion." Pp. 33–52 in *Emotions and Sociology*, ed. Jack Barbalet. Oxford: Basil Blackwell.

Bevan, Aneurin. 1952. *In Place of Fear*. New York: Simon and Schuster.

Bourdieu, Pierre. 1977. *Outline of a Theory of Practice*. Trans. Richard Nice. Cambridge: Cambridge University Press.

Camic, Charles. 1979. "The Utilitarians Revisited." *American Journal of Sociology* 85:516–50.

———. 1990. "'Prolegomena to a Theory of Social Institutions' by Talcott Parsons, with Prologue and Commentary." *American Sociological Review* 55: 313–45.

Campbell, John Y., and John H. Cochrane. 1999. "By Force of Habit: A Consumption-Based Explanation of Aggregate Stock Market Behavior." *Journal of Political Economy* 107(2): 205–51.

Carrier, James, ed. 1997. *Meanings of the Market: The Free Market in Western Culture*. New York: Berg.

Clark, Candace. 1987. "Sympathy Biography and Sympathy Margin." *American Journal of Sociology* 93: 290–321.

Coleman, James. 1990. *The Foundations of Social Theory*. Cambridge: Harvard University Press.

Collins, Randall. 1981. "On the Microfoundations of Macrosociology." *American Journal of Sociology* 86: 984–1014.

———. 1993. "Emotional Energy as the Common Denominator of Rational Action." *Rationality and Society* 5(2): 203–30.

Conover, Pamela Johnston, and Stanley Feldman. 1986. "Emotional Reactions to the Economy: I'm Mad as Hell and I'm Not Going to Take It Anymore." *American Journal of Political Science* 30(1): 50–78.

Cook, Karen S., ed. 2001. *Trust in Society*. New York: Russell Sage Foundation.

D'Arms, Justin, and Daniel Jacobson. 2000. "Sentiment and Value." *Ethics* 110:722–48.

Damasio, Antonio R. 1994. *Descartes' Error: Emotion, Reason, and the Human Brain*. New York: Harper-Collins.

———. 1999. *The Feeling of What Happens: Body and Emotion in the Making of Consciousness*. New York: Harcourt Brace.

Darwin, Charles. [1872] 1998. *The Expression of the Emotions in Man and Animals*. New York: Harper-Collins.

De Sousa, Ronald. 1980. "The Rationality of Emotions." Pp. 125–51 in *Explaining Emotions*, ed. Amelie Rorty. Berkeley and Los Angeles: University of California Press.

DiMaggio, Paul. 2002. "Endogenizing 'Animal Spirits': Toward a Sociology of Collective Response to Uncertainty and Risk." Pp. 79–100 in *The New Economic Sociology: Developments in an Emerging Field*, ed. Mauro F. Guillén, Randall Collins, Paula England, and Marshall Meyer. New York: Russell Sage Foundation.

Elias, Norbert. 1994. *The Civilizing Process*. Trans. Edmund Jephcott. Oxford: Basil Blackwell.

Elster, Jon. 1989. "Social Norms and Economic Theory." *Journal of Economic Perspectives* 3(4): 99–117.

———. 1996. "Rationality and Emotions." *Economic Journal* 106:1386–97.

———. 1998. "Emotions and Economic Theory." *Journal of Economic Literature* 36:47–74.

———. 1999a. "Emotion and Addiction: Neurobiology, Culture, and Choice." Pp. 239–76 in *Addiction:*

Entries and Exits, ed. Jon Elster. New York: Russell Sage Foundation.

———. 1999b. *Alchemies of the Mind: Rationality and the Emotions*. Cambridge: Cambridge University Press.

———. 1999c. *Strong Feelings: Emotion, Addiction, and Human Behavior*. Cambridge: MIT Press.

———, ed. 1999d. *Addiction: Entries and Exits*. New York: Russell Sage Foundation.

Engelbrecht-Wiggans, Richard. 1989. "The Effect of Regret on Optimal Bidding in Auctions." *Management Science* 35:685–92.

Etzioni, Amitai. 1987. "How Rational Are We?" *Sociological Forum* 2(1): 1–20.

———. 1988. *The Moral Dimension: Towards a New Economics*. New York: Free Press.

Flam, Helena. 1990. "Emotional 'Man': II. Corporate Actors as Emotion-Motivated Emotion Managers." *International Sociology* 5(2): 225–34.

Fontaine, Philippe. 2001. "The Changing Place of Empathy in Welfare Economics." *History of Political Economy* 33(3): 387–409.

Frank, Robert H. 1987. "Shrewdly Irrational." *Sociological Forum* 2(1): 21–41.

———. 1988. *Passions within Reason: The Strategic Role of the Emotions*. New York: W. W. Norton.

———. 1993. "The Strategic Role of Emotions: Reconciling Over- and Undersocialized Accounts of Behavior." *Rationality and Society* 5(2): 160–84.

Friedland, Roger. 2002. "Money, Sex, and God: The Erotic Logic of Religious Nationalism." *Sociological Theory*. 20(3): 381–425.

Frijda, Nico H. 1987. *The Emotions*. Cambridge: Cambridge University Press.

———. 1993. "Moods, Emotion Episodes, and Emotions." Pp. 381–403 in *Handbook of Emotions*, ed. Michael Lewis and Jeannette M. Haviland. New York: Guilford.

Goffman, Erving. 1959. *The Presentation of Self in Everyday Life*. New York: Anchor.

Greenspan, Patricia. 2000. "Emotional Strategies and Rationality." *Ethics* 10:469–87.

Gudeman, Stephen. 2001. *Anthropology of Economy: Community, Market, and Culture*. Malden, Mass.: Basil Blackwell.

Heckathorn, Douglas D. 1993. "Emotions and Rational Choice: Introduction." *Rationality and Society* 5(2): 157–59.

Hirschman, Albert O. 1977. *The Passions and the Interests: Political Arguments for Capitalism before Its Triumph*. Princeton: Princeton University Press.

Hirshleifer, Jack. 1993. "The Affections and the Passions: Their Economic Logic." *Rationality and Society* 5(2): 185–202.

Hochschild, Arlie Russell. 1979. "Emotion Work, Feeling Rules, and Social Structure." *American Journal of Sociology* 85:551–75.

———. 1983. *The Managed Heart: The Commercialization of Human Feeling*. Berkeley and Los Angeles: University of California Press.

———. 1990. "Ideology and Emotion Management: A Perspective and Path for Future Research." Pp. 117–42 in *Research Agendas in the Sociology of Emotions*, ed. Theodore Kemper. Albany: State University of New York Press.

———. 2003. *The Commercialization of Intimate Life: Notes from Home and Work*. Berkeley and Los Angeles: University of California Press.

Inman, J. Jeffrey, James S. Dyer, and Jianmin Jia. 1997. "A Generalized Utility Model of Disappointment and Regret Effects on Post-choice Valuation." *Marketing Science* 16(2): 97–111.

James, William. 1956. "The Sentiment of Rationality." Pp. 63–110 in *The Will to Believe and Other Essays in Popular Philosophy*. New York: Dover.

Jasso, Guillermina. 1993. "Choice and Emotion in Comparison Theory." *Rationality and Society* 5(2): 231–74.

Kemper, Theodore D. 1987. "How Many Emotions Are There? Wedding the Social and the Autonomic Components." *American Journal of Sociology* 93: 263–89.

———. 1993. "Reason in Emotions or Emotions in Reason." *Rationality and Society* 5(2): 275–82.

Landes, David S. 2000. *Revolution in Time: Clocks and the Making of the Modern World*. 2d ed. Cambridge: Harvard University Press.

Leavis. F. R. 1950. Introduction to *Mill on Bentham and Coleridge*. London: Chatto and Windus.

Leibenstein, Harvey. 1950. "Bandwagon, Snob, and Veblen Effects in the Theory of Consumers' Demand." *Quarterly Journal of Economics* 64:183–207.

Loewenstein, George. 2000. "Emotions in Economic Theory and Economic Behavior." *American Economic Review* 90:426–32.

Loewenstein, George, Daniel Read, and Roy Baumeister, eds. 2003. *Time and Decision: Economic and Psychological Perspectives on Intertemporal Choice*. New York: Russell Sage Foundation.

Manning, Robert D. 2000. *Credit Card Nation*. New York: Basic Books.

Massey, Douglas S. 2002. "A Brief History of Human Society: The Origin and Role of Emotions in Social Life." *American Sociological Review* 67:1–29.

Mendoza, Sally P., and John D. Ruys. 2001. "The Beginning of an Alternative View of the Neurobiology of Emotion. *Social Science Information* 40(1): 39–60.

Middleton, Dwight R. 1989. "Emotional Style: The Cultural Ordering of Emotions." *Ethos* 17(2): 187–201.

Mill, John Stuart. 1950. *Mill on Bentham and Coleridge*. With an introduction by F. R. Leavis. London: Chatto and Windus.

———. [1873] 1969. *Autobiography*. Ed. Jack Stillinger. Boston: Houghton Mifflin.

Monroe, Kristen. 1996. *The Heart of Altruism: Perceptions of a Common Humanity*. Princeton: Princeton University Press.

Nussbaum, Martha C. 2001. *Upheavals of Thought: The Intelligence of Emotions*. Cambridge: Cambridge University Press.

Nye, John Vincent. 1991. "Lucky Fools and Cautious Businessmen: On Entrepreneurship and the Measurement of Entrepreneurial Failure." *Research in Economic History*, suppl. 6:131–52.

O'Shaughnessy, John, and Nicholas Jackson O'Shaughnessy. 2003. *The Marketing Power of Emotion*. Oxford: Oxford University Pres.

Offer, Avner. 1997. "Between the Gift and the Market: The Economy of Regard." *Economic History Review* 50:450–76.

Orphanides, Athanasios, and David Zervos. 1995. "Rational Addiction with Learning and Regret." *Journal of Political Economy* 103:739–58.

Pareto, Vilfredo. 1935. *The Mind and Society*. Ed. Arthur Livingstone. Trans. Andrew Bongierno and Arthur Livingstone. New York: Harcourt, Brace.

Parsons, Talcott. 1951. *The Social System*. New York: Free Press.

———. [1939] 1954a. "The Professions and Social Structure." Pp. 34–49 in *Essays in Sociological Theory*. Rev. ed. Glencoe, Ill.: Free Press.

———. [1940] 1954b. "The Motivation of Economic Activities." Pp. 50–68 in *Essays in Sociological Theory*. Rev. ed. Glencoe, Ill.: Free Press.

———. [1942] 1954c. "Propaganda and Social Control." Pp. 142–76 in *Essays in Sociological Theory*. Rev. ed. Glencoe, Ill.: Free Press.

———. [1937] 1968. *The Structure of Social Action*. New York: Free Press.

Persky, Joseph. 1995. "The Ethology of Homo Economicus." *Journal of Economic Perspectives* 9(2): 22–31.

Pixley, Jocelyn. 1999a. "Beyond Twin Deficits: Emotions of the Future in the Organizations of Money." *American Journal of Economics and Sociology* 58:1091–1118.

———. 1999b. "Impersonal Trust in Global Mediating Organizations." *Sociological Perspectives* 42:647–71.

———. 2002a. "Emotions and Economics." Pp. 69–89 in *Emotions and Sociology,* ed. Jack Barbalet. Oxford: Basil Blackwell.

———. 2002b. "Finance Organizations, Decisions, and Emotions." *British Journal of Sociology* 53(1): 41–65.

Pizarro, David. 2000. "Nothing More Than Feelings? The Role of Emotions in Moral Judgment." *Journal for the Theory of Social Behavior* 30(4): 355–75.

Polanyi, Karl. 1971. *Primitive, Archaic, and Modern Economics: Essays of Karl Polanyi*. Ed. George Dalton. Boston: Beacon Press.

Reddy, William M. 2001. *The Navigation of Feeling*. Cambridge: Cambridge University Press.

Romer, Paul M. 2000. "Thinking and Feeling." *American Economic Review* 90:439–43.

Rorty, Amelie. 1980. "Agent Regret." Pp. 489–506 in *Explaining Emotions*, ed. Amelie Rorty. Berkeley and Los Angeles: University of California Press.

Rothchild, Emma. 2001. *Economic Sentiments: Adam Smith, Condorcet, and the Enlightenment*. Cambridge: Harvard University Press.

Shiller, Robert J. 2000. *Irrational Exuberance*. Princeton: Princeton University Press.

Shweder, Richard A. 1993. "The Cultural Psychology of the Emotions." Pp. 417–31 in *Handbook of Emotions*, ed. Michael Lewis and Jeannette M. Haviland. New York: Guilford.

Silverstein, Merril, Tonya M. Parrott, and Vern L. Bengston. 1995. "Factors That Predispose Middle-Aged Sons and Daughters to Provide Social Support to Older Parents." *Journal of Marriage and the Family* 57:465–75.

Simonson, Itamar. 1992. "The Influence of Anticipating Regret and Responsibility on Purchase Decisions." *Journal of Consumer Research* 19:105–18.

Smelser, Neil J. 1963. *The Sociology of Economic Life*. Englewood Cliffs, N.J.: Prentice-Hall.

———. 1990. "Can Individualism Yield a Sociology?" *Contemporary Sociology* 19:778–83.

———. 1992. "The Rational Choice Perspective: A Theoretical Assessment." *Rationality and Society* 4(4): 381–410.

———. 1995. "Economic Rationality as a Religious System." Pp. 73–92 in *Rethinking Materialism*, ed. Robert Wuthnow. Grand Rapids, Mich.: William Eerdmans.

———. 1998. "The Rational and the Ambivalent in the Social Sciences." *American Sociological Review* 63: 1–15.

Smith, Adam. [1759] 2000. *The Theory of Moral Sentiments*. New York: Prometheus Books.

Smith-Lovin, Lynn. 1993. "Can Emotionality and Rationality Be Reconciled?" *Rationality and Society* 5(2): 283–93.

Solomon, Robert C. 1980. "Emotion and Choice." Pp. 251–80 in *Explaining Emotions*, ed. Amelie Rorty. Berkeley and Los Angeles: University of California Press.

Stanley, Manfred. 1968. "Nature, Culture, and Scarcity: Foreward to a Theoretical Synthesis." *American Sociological Review* 33:855–70.

Sutton, Robert I. 1991. "Maintaining Norms about Expressed Emotions: The Case of Bill Collectors." *Administrative Science Quarterly* 36:245–68.

Thompson, E. P. 1971. "The Moral Economy of the English Crowd in the Eighteenth Century." *Past and Present* 50:76–136.

Titus, Sandra L., Paul C. Rosenblatt, and Roxanne M. Anderson. 1979. "Family Conflict over Inheritance of Property." *Family Coordinator* 28(3): 337–46.

Tsiros, Michael, and Vikas Mittal. 2000. "Regret: A Model of Its Antecedents and Consequences in Consumer Decision Making." *Journal of Consumer Research* 26:401–17.

Turner, Jonathan H. 2000. *On the Origins of Human Emotions*. Stanford, Calif.: Stanford University Press.

Watson, Gary. 1999. "Disordered Appetites: Addiction,

Compulsion, and Dependence. Pp. 3–28 in *Addiction: Entries and Exits*, ed. Jon Elster. New York: Russell Sage Foundation.

Watt, Ian. [1957] 2001. *The Rise of the Novel*. Berkeley and Los Angeles: University of California Press.

Weber, Max. [1920] 1976. *The Protestant Ethic and the Spirit of Capitalism*. Trans. Talcott Parsons. New York: Charles Scribner's Sons.

———. 1978. *Economy and Society*. Ed. Guenther Roth and Claus Wittich. Vol. 2. Berkeley and Los Angeles: University of California Press.

Zelizer, Viviana A. 1985. *Pricing the Priceless Child*. New York: Basic Books.

———. 2002. "Intimate Transactions." Pp. 274–300 in *The New Economic Sociology: Developments in an Emerging Field*, ed. Mauro F. Guillén, Randall Collins, Paula England, and Marshall Meyer. New York: Russell Sage Foundation.

Part II

The Economic Core:
Economic Systems,
Institutions, and Behavior

Section A: The Economy in a Macrosociological Perspective

7 The Economic Sociology of the Ancient Mediterranean World

Ian Morris and J. G. Manning

INTRODUCTION

Issues and Goals

In this essay we review the economic sociology of the ancient Mediterranean world (roughly 3000 B.C.–A.D. 700). The ancient Mediterranean has held a privileged place in the history of economic sociology. For Marx ([1857–58] 1964), an ancient slave mode of production played a vital part in the development toward capitalism and communism; for Weber ([1921] 1958, [1909] 1976), contrasts between ideal types of ancient Mediterranean and medieval west European societies were important in explaining the capitalist takeoff; for Polanyi (Polanyi, Arensberg, and Pearson 1957), ancient Babylon and Athens were key case studies in redistribution and early markets; and more recently Michael Mann (1986, 73–340) made the ancient Mediterranean central to the first volume of his *Sources of Social Power*. Some sociologists look to antiquity to show the deep historical roots of contemporary social formations, while others do just the opposite, contrasting the ancient Mediterranean world with our own times to highlight the peculiarities of modernity. But for both groups, the ancient Mediterranean's rich documentation, institutional variety, and importance in European and Middle Eastern history have, since the discipline's creation, made it a valuable resource for comparative sociology (e.g., Swedberg, this volume). A century ago higher education in Europe, North America, and other parts of the world influenced by these regions routinely exposed the adolescent sons of middle- and upper-class families to both Greek and Latin languages and classical history, and since most sociologists were drawn from their ranks, it is hardly surprising that they turned readily to classical antiquity as a comparison case. But class and educational changes in the last 40 years have made this practice less common (Phinney 1989). Some scholars also worry that mainstream social scientists are turning away from history toward more formal models, while humanists are losing interest in causation and explanation. But while sociologists certainly illustrate their arguments with ancient case studies less often than they did a century ago, a minority of sociologists do see great value in long-term historical comparisons; and far more professional ancient historians look toward the questions and methods of economic sociology today than has been the case in the past. Our goal in this essay is to set out some of the major issues in the study of the ancient Mediterranean and their links to the broader field of economic sociology.

We spend most of this first section defining our key terms. But before doing so, we want to draw attention to an important difference between the ways that ancient historians and economic sociologists present their work, which often sets up barriers to understanding. Scholars in the two fields tend to write for very different audiences, framing their arguments within entirely different assumptions about whom they are arguing with. Economic sociologists tend to define their work against mainstream economics, the leading rival explanation for the same phenomena, which would disembed economic action from its larger social context (Smelser and Swedberg, this volume; Dobbin, this volume). In ancient history, though, the leading rival is a liberal humanities tradition, emphasizing philology and empirical details over model building, and sidelining economic phenomena altogether (Morris 2001a; Morris and Manning 2004). Much of the scholarship by historians who could reasonably be called ancient economic sociologists is directed toward persuading humanists of the importance of economic phenomena, rather than of persuading economists of the importance of sociological phenomena. While economic sociologists challenge economists to think about economic structures as well as performance, ancient economic historians challenge mainstream scholars to think about economic structures as well as elite literary culture, while performance has hardly been studied at all. Differences in intended audiences, tone, and style can make it difficult for economic sociologists and ancient historians to communicate. We hope that this chapter will do something to reintroduce the fields.

After we define our terms in the next section, there follows a section that describes the parameters of the ancient Mediterranean world (the nature of our evidence, the basic historical narrative, the environment, and technology). Some readers will already be familiar with these topics and may wish to skip over this section; but it might be difficult for economic sociologists who have had little exposure to ancient Mediterranean history to contextualize the debates we review in subsequent sections and without this background material. The third part of the chapter describes the main models of ancient economic sociology, and the fourth part focuses on three major areas of debate—the state, cities, and economic growth.

Definitions

First, we take economic sociology to mean a way of looking at the world that assumes that (1) economic action is a form of social action; (2) economic action is socially situated; and (3) economic institutions are social constructions (Granovetter and Swedberg 1992, 6). In a classic statement, Neil Smelser (1963, 27–28) defined the field's core concerns as being the place in economic phenomena of personal interaction, the actions of groups and institutions, and norms and values. All have been central to scholarship in ancient economic sociology. Some well-established sociological methods, most obviously network analysis, have played almost no role in ancient studies, while others, such as gender and household labor, are only beginning to receive serious attention (Saller, forthcoming).

By *ancient*, we mean here the period from the emergence of complex society around 3000 B.C. through the division of the Mediterranean into Christian and Islamic spheres in the seventh–eighth centuries A.D. By *Mediterranean* we mean those areas bordering on the sea and characterized by (*a*) hot, dry summers and cool, wet winters, (*b*) the juxtaposition of plains, hills, and mountains or

deserts within very short distances, and (*c*) the cultivation of the "Mediterranean triad" of grains, olives, and wine (fig. 1). These definitions of both *ancient* and *Mediterranean* crosscut conventional academic divisions of labor, and immediately embroil us in controversies (Manning and Morris 2004). Since the eighteenth century ancient historians normally split the Mediterranean geographically into a northwestern Greco-Roman civilization, studied by classicists, and southeastern Egyptian and Near Eastern civilizations, studied by orientalists. The idea behind this division (fully shared by Marx and Weber) was that modern Europe grew organically out of ancient Greece and Rome. European and American classicists therefore study the origins of us, orientalists the origins of the other (analyses in Said 1978; Bernal 1987; Morris 1994). This model rested on a highly ideological assumption that Europe's differences from the rest of the world must go far back in time. In the late twentieth century, though, more and more scholars rejected this model as Eurocentric (see Blaut 2000), and historical sociologists of the self-styled "California School" have argued that until A.D. 1700, the similarities between the major Eurasian civilizations massively outweighed the differences, meaning that we should seek explanations for the Euro-American takeoff on a time scale of few centuries, not millennia (e.g., Frank 1998; Goldstone 1998, 2000; Wong 1998, 2001; Stokes 2001).

These arguments raise fundamental questions about appropriate analytical units. For most nineteenth- and twentieth-century comparativists, the major question was the relationship between Greco-Roman civilization and modern western Europe and North America, while for adherents of the California School, the main units of analysis are all premodern advanced organic/agrarian economies, from Neolithic times through the seventeenth or eighteenth century, as opposed to post-eighteenth-century mineral-energy economies (we take these terms from Wrigley 1988). Yet neither group has subjected their core categories to very sustained analysis. In the 1990s, more and more ancient historians have argued that the Mediterranean Sea made interconnections between the societies around its shores so easy that it makes most sense to treat all these communities together, rather than imposing a distinction between Greco-Roman culture and the Near East. This argument often draws on Fernand Braudel's classic treatment of the Mediterranean in the sixteenth century ([1949] 1972). In the most developed version of

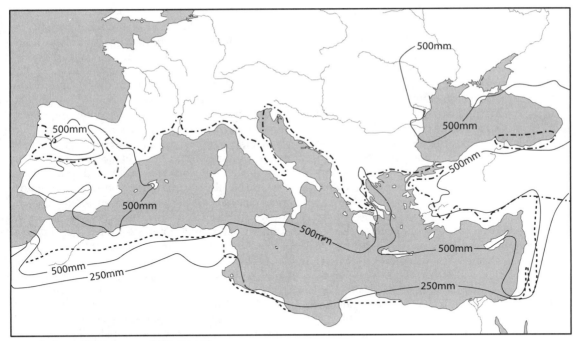

—— Isohyets (250 mm p.a. and 500mm p.a.)
·–·– Northern limit of the olive
----- Southern limit of Mediterranean vegetation

FIGURE 1.   Ecological boundaries of the Mediterranean region. After Horden and Purcell 2000, map 1.

this approach, Peregrine Horden and Nicholas Purcell (2000) argue that neither geographical nor spatial divisions within the premodern Mediterranean are helpful.

We believe that some aspects of Horden and Purcell's position are overstated (Morris, forthcoming a), but share in the growing consensus that for many cultural and economic questions—and particularly for an overall sketch of ancient economic sociology—the Mediterranean basin is an appropriate analytical unit. For other questions, we can clarify our understanding by looking at individual parts of the Mediterranean, or by lumping together all premodern societies.

That said, acute definitional issues remain. Just as Braudel could not write the history of the early modern Mediterranean without looking at Antwerp and London, we cannot make sense of the Mediterranean in the last three millennia B.C. without Mesopotamia and Iran, or of the first millennium A.D. without the northern provinces of the Roman Empire. Setting the geographical boundaries also raises chronological issues: the old classical/oriental distinction went hand-in-hand with a chronological classical/nonclassical boundary, defining "classical" in terms of a literary tradition in

Greek and Latin, normally said to begin with Homer (ca. 700 B.C.) and end with Augustine (ca. A.D. 400). The chronological distinction makes little sense if we bypass the geographical one. We start instead from social-economic categories, beginning not with Homer but with the earliest states, around 3000 B.C., and ending not with Augustine but with a demographic, economic, and intellectual transformation that was already under way in his lifetime, leading by the eighth century to a divided Mediterranean world (see Hodges and Whitehouse 1983; Haldon 1997).

PARAMETERS

Evidence

The evidence that survives from this ancient Mediterranean world is very different from what economic sociologists of the modern world are used to, and also varies enormously through time and space within the Mediterranean (Manning and Morris 2004). The main problems are, first, that few ancient organizations collected systematic data on economic questions; and, second, that accidents of preservation and discovery have made our evidence even more fragmentary. Only one long-run price series survives from the entire Mediterranean basin across these 3,500 years. These texts are astronomical diaries from Babylon, which for the years 454–73 B.C. give monthly prices for barley, dates, *cuscuta* (something like mustard), cardamom, sesame, and wool, in addition to observations on the moon and stars (Slotsky 1997). But even these unique documents pose acute problems of interpretation (e.g., Grainger 1999; Aperghis 2001; Temin 2002). We get occasional flashes of illumination, as from the Ahiqar Scroll, a Roman-era papyrus text from the Jewish community at Elephantine in southern Egypt that turned out to have been written over a partially erased tax document from an Egyptian port, probably dating to 475 B.C. The original text listed the contents of 36 ships, importing wine, oil, wood, wool, and jars, and exporting mineral soda (Porten and Yardeni 1993, 82–195). This is a remarkable document, but we do not know how typical these ships were, or whether the (unknown) harbor was itself typical; and, as with the Babylonian prices, there are major interpretive problems (Briant and Descat 1998). The same kinds of problems apply to spectacular archaeological discoveries like the two Phoenician ships of about 750 B.C. found in deep water off the Israeli coast (Ballard et al. 2002): by definition, we lack the contextual information necessary to interpret unique discoveries.

The most important evidence comes not from outstanding one-off finds, but from the painstaking collection of large numbers of references to economic matters in humbler documents. In Mesopotamia, incised clay tablets recording inventories, transactions, and business dealings begin about 2500 B.C. They have an uneven chronological and geographical distribution, and most come from large institutions like temples and palaces. However, 15,000 tablets from private trading companies dealing between Kanesh and Assyria in the nineteenth century B.C. (Özgüç 1959, 1986) and another large archive from the fifth-century-B.C. Mûrashû family in Babylon (Stolper 1985) reveal other sectors of the economy. In the first millennium B.C. Mesopotamians generally shifted to papyrus, which survives less well. In the Egyptian desert, however, papyri do survive, often dealing with day-to-day transactions. Some form what Egyptologists call "archives"—although they are not organized as systematic business records—and often have serious gaps. The 1,700 third-century-B.C. records of Zenon are the best-known such

archive (Orrieux 1985). In Greece and Rome, by contrast, few actual business documents survive, but rich literary traditions attest to elite attitudes and ideologies, and inscriptions record some state activities. Enough scattered references survive from Roman Egypt (Rathbone 1997) and fourth-century-B.C. Athens (http://nomisma.geschichte.uni-bremen.de) that we can assemble rough series for prices and wages, but they remain fragmentary and biased toward urban centers. Starting in the fifth century A.D., the evidence is increasingly dominated by church records and the lives of saints. Finally, there is a huge body of archaeological data, again unevenly distributed in time and space and shaped by varied processes of formation and recovery, but potentially more generalizable than the written record (Morris 2004).

Overall, the evidence is fragmentary, ambiguous, and difficult to decipher. Controversies rage over general interpretations and points of minute detail. We are well informed about some things (e.g., the palace in nineteenth-century-B.C. Mari) but almost completely ignorant about others (e.g., wages in the private sector in classical Athens). Few points of importance can be settled by direct appeal to the supposed facts; more often, ancient historians devote considerable ingenuity to finding proxy data, or elaborating on the implications of hypotheses that might be testable when the hypothesis itself is not.

A Basic Political Narrative, 3000 B.C.–A.D. 800

As we pointed out in the introduction, some readers interested in using the ancient Mediterranean world as a comparative case may find a summary of the basic narrative history useful.

Settled agriculture began around 8500 B.C. in the hilly flanks of Mesopotamia (fig. 2), which were uniquely well endowed with cultivable grains and domesticable large animals. Mesopotamia itself was peripheral until circa 5500 B.C., when its population harnessed irrigation. This required much labor, but produced huge yields. By 3000 B.C., southern Mesopotamia (Sumer) was dotted with city-states with populations of 10,000 or more, practicing irrigation agriculture, casting in bronze, building temples, and employing scribal bureaucracies with simple writing systems.

There were similar developments in the Nile, Indus, and Yellow River basins, but Egypt diverged from Mesopotamia early on. Around 3100 Menes united the Nile valley into a single kingdom; and where Mesopotamian elites claimed special access

FIGURE 2. Main sites and regions mentioned in this chapter

to the gods, Egyptian pharaohs actually claimed to be gods. In Mesopotamia city-states were the norm. Around 2300 Sargon of Akkad built an empire from the Persian Gulf to the Mediterranean, and his grandson Naram-Sin claimed divinity. But after 2200 invasions from the deserts broke up the empire. A century later the city of Ur built up another great empire, but invaders overthrew it around 2000.

Despite the rise and fall of individual empires, the Near Eastern system expanded relentlessly. Similar palaces, scripts, and art appear in the Levant and southwest Iran before 2500; by 2000, they were established on the Iranian plateau, down the Persian Gulf, across Anatolia, and on Crete. By 1600 there were palaces in mainland Greece, and by 1400 Aegean goods reached the west Mediterranean. This was a dynamic, expansionist system; peripheral societies were either drawn into its orbit or adapted its institutions to resist it. It was also an "international age": long-distance trade flourished, art styles were widely diffused, and royal families intermarried.

There were independent moves toward complex society in the west Mediterranean, but these all collapsed into more egalitarian forms. The most

successful examples were in southeast Spain, which had an arid climate and required irrigation. Possibly would-be elites could only overcome opposition when there was sufficient geographical caging.

Expansion ended around 1200 B.C. From Greece to Syria, palaces burned to the ground. We do not know why, although Egyptian texts from the 1180s speak of wars with the "Peoples of the Sea," and Assyrian and later Greek texts mention invasions. There is evidence for earthquakes, climatic change, and economic stress. In Greece palaces disappeared, along with the Linear B syllabic script. The Hittite kingdom fell in 1200, the Assyrian soon after 1100, and Egypt broke up in the 1060s. Population fell, long-distance trade withered, and states dissolved. The west Mediterranean, where palaces had not taken hold before 1200, did not go through a comparable Dark Age, but contact with the east almost vanished after 1050.

Starting on Cyprus around 1100 and reaching the west Mediterranean by 900, iron replaced bronze for weapons. No one has yet shown that this had major social consequences, but signs of revival appear in the east Mediterranean in the tenth century Phoenician traders sailed to the Aegean and the west, and Assyria became a major power. Its kings staged massive raids for plunder, from Iran to Syria. Pressed for tribute, many city-states and tribes in their path collapsed into anarchy; others organized and fought back, creating new states.

The eighth century saw a major population increase all around the Mediterranean, and great expansion of long-distance contact. By 700 B.C. interregional trade almost certainly surpassed pre-1200 levels, as Phoenicians and Greeks settled in the west Mediterranean. Eighth-century Greece experienced particularly rapid population growth and major social changes as city-states formed out of simpler Dark Age societies. The Greek settlements in Sicily and southern Italy were independent city-states, which seized the coastal plains. This landgrab more than doubled the amount of arable land under direct Greek control. Phoenician settlers, by contrast, rarely conquered the hinterland, and may have been driven west by increasing Assyrian pressure for tribute from the Phoenician homeland. Assyrian kings were always desperate for funds; they had to reward their nobles in order to get troops, which meant that if their raids faltered—as in the 780s—central authority weakened. Provincial governors broke away, and there were frequent coups. But when Tiglath-Pileser III seized power in 744 in one of these coups, he gained the upper hand over the nobility, centralizing power, strengthening the army, and systematizing taxes. Assyriologists often say that a true empire only began now, and Tiglath-Pileser's demands for tribute probably ratcheted up pressure on the Phoenician cities, giving them incentives to intensify trade. This neo-Assyrian empire marked a break: from this point until the twentieth century A.D. large empires dominated the Near East.

Assyria conquered Babylon (which had at least 100,000 residents) and Egypt, perhaps the richest parts of the ancient world. It absorbed Israel and made Judah a client state, and opposition to the Assyrian god Ashur played a large role in shaping Jewish monotheism and identity. By 650 the Assyrian Empire was the largest yet seen, but was suffering from imperial overreach. Its grandest monuments date to the 630s, but it abruptly collapsed before a rebel alliance in 615–612. The Medes and Babylonians then divided up the empire between them. In 550 the province of Persis rebelled against Media. The Persian Cyrus seized the Median Empire in a single campaign, then took Babylon, conquered Anatolia, and marched into central Asia, where he met his death in 530. His son took Egypt in 525, making Persia the largest empire the world had seen, with perhaps 35 million subjects. This rapid expansion worked largely through elite replacement: the Persians changed little of what they found after defeating other kings, either putting their own men in the places formerly occupied by native aristocrats or (better still) persuading local elites to switch allegiance. A famous statue base set up in Egypt by a certain Udjahorresnse shortly before 500 illustrates well how the Persian system could work to the advantage of these local elites. In the 510s Darius I reformed the empire's organization, making Persia the richest and most efficient empire yet seen, as well as the largest.

Darius moved into Europe, annexing parts of the Balkans and subduing many Greek city-states. By 500 some of the Greek city-states were populous and rich. They developed different forms of capital-intensive power. Sparta invested heavily in one kind of human capital; Spartan citizen-soldiers were a full-time army who suffered no defeats in major battles between the seventh century and 371 B.C. Other Greek communities decided to invest in human capital in different ways, having much higher literacy rates (perhaps reaching 10 percent in Athens), and experimenting with *dēmokratia,* in which free adult male citizens (usually 10–20 percent of the resident population) decided the major issues in open votes. After a revolt of subject Greeks within his empire in 499–494, Darius sent a small force to punish Athenian support for the rebels. To everyone's surprise Athens defeated them at Marathon in 490; and in 480 the Greeks defeated a much larger attack. This left Athens the greatest naval power in the Mediterranean. Fifth-century Athens concentrated capital in new forms, and invested in ships and fortifications; but Sparta's victory in the Peloponnesian War (431–404) cut off Athenian development, and no other Greek city came close to transcending the city-state network.

Through much of the fourth-century-B.C. Persia manipulated the Greeks through finance, even though Egypt broke away and the western provinces were in open revolt. But the balance of power was shifting. As in the Bronze Age, the expansive east Mediterranean system created a penumbra of formative states, adapting institutions to their own needs. In the fourth century, the periphery proved stronger than the core. Carthage became a major economic power; Rome conquered peninsular Italy; and Macedon subdued the Balkans, the Greek cities, and then in just a decade the whole Persian Empire. Alexander wanted to fuse the Macedonian and Persian ruling elites, but in 301 his warring successors divided the empire into three kingdoms, which historians call "Hellenistic." Down to 250, there was steady emigration from Greece to the East, and Alexandria in Egypt grew to perhaps 200,000 people. Greek cities in Mesopotamia and Syria also reached six figures.

But the outer periphery, in the west Mediterranean, was already outstripping the Hellenistic kingdoms in manpower, wealth, and organization. Between 264 and 201 Rome defeated Carthage in two terrible wars, then in 200 attacked Macedon. Romans pressed into the Near East, shattering the Seleucid kingdom in Syria in 188. At the same time Parthians infiltrated Iran from central Asia, breaking down the Seleucid realm from the other direction. Rome also fought a guerrilla war in Spain through most of the second century, and probably had the highest military participation ratio of any state until seventeenth-century Prussia. According to Polybius, writing in Rome around 150 B.C., "the Romans succeeded in less than 53 years [220–167 B.C.] in bringing under their rule almost the whole of the inhabited world, an achievement which is without parallel in human history" (1.1). This involved millions of deaths, mass deportations, and the collapse of the Hellenistic kingdoms into financial crises, revolutions, and virtual anarchy.

The net results were destabilization and the biggest transfer of resources in ancient history. The city of Rome grew to a million inhabitants, with much of the Mediterranean supplying its food through taxes, rents, and trade. By the 130s B.C. an agrarian crisis gripped Italy; with so many men in the legions, aristocrats made rich by their victories could buy up the land and work it with millions of slaves captured in the wars, growing food for the city, and leaving dispossessed farmers little choice but to move to Rome, expanding the urban market still further, or to join the army. Some ancient historians call this the "war-slave-war loop": it created a feedback process enriching the aristocracy and driving the Italian free peasantry into ruin. But as dispossession accelerated, fewer men met the property qualification for military service, starving Rome of soldiers and bringing on a crisis. Rome's oligarchs murdered the Gracchus brothers when they tried to hijack state institutions to redistribute land in 133 and 122. Abolishing property requirements for the army in 107 solved some problems, but created new ones: soldiers now looked to their generals for land grants when they were demobilized, and the army became an independent force. Political legitimacy broke down as generals, backed by virtual private armies, dictated terms to the Senate, which increasingly provoked overseas wars simply to keep its generals and their land-hungry men busy. In 60, Pompey, Crassus, and Caesar—three of the richest and most prominent generals—formed a secret coalition and subverted the constitution by using money and threats to divide all the key offices among themselves. Caesar was authorized to conquer Gaul in the 50s to maintain this alliance, but this only created yet another great army. Caesar and Pompey fought another civil war in 49–45. Caesar won, but his murder in 44 unleashed another set of wars, ending with Octavian's victory in 31 B.C.

Octavian took the name Augustus and the functions but not the form of a sole ruler. Millions had died, and the devastation was beyond measure, but the combination of elite exhaustion and Augustus's clever manipulation of military and financial offices and imperial symbolism ushered in two centuries of *pax romana* for the Mediterranean basin. Population grew; cities thrived; tax rates were sustainable; there was some standardization of measures, language, and law; and communications improved. The empire had 50–60 million inhabitants in A.D. 200, perhaps 15 percent of them living in cities of more than 20,000 people, and the average tax burden was something like 2–3 percent. Monuments all over the empire attest to wealthy aristocracies, but average standards of living also improved perhaps nearly doubling across the first two centuries A.D. At no point did economic growth in the Roman Empire or any other ancient Mediterranean society match levels in early modern Holland or England, let alone those of industrialized economies, but Rome nevertheless ranks alongside cases like Sung China as a major example of sustained premodern per capita economic growth.

The years since about 1000 B.C. had been good for the Mediterranean: there were many internal wars, but few major population movements out of central Asia. That changed in the second century A.D. Nomads entered China and Iran, and pressed German tribes in central Europe. Some of these tribes crossed the Rhine and Danube into the empire. Often Rome welcomed them as recruits and taxpayers, but large groups caused chaos. In the 160s major invasions and plague reached the empire at the same time. The situation held until the 230s, but then the frontiers collapsed. German bands plundered Athens and Italy. Twenty emperors reigned in 50 years. Unable to pay large armies, they debased the coinage. Despairing of the central government, Gaul and Syria broke away. And to make matters worse, Sapor I established an aggressive Sassanid dynasty in Persia, killing a Roman emperor in 244 and capturing another in 260. The slowing of population movements, remission of the plague, and military reforms allowed recovery in the 270s–280s, but a gap opened between the largely rural western Roman Empire and the more urban east. Local power increased as aristocrats increasingly had to usurp the state's role of providing security. They increased rents at the expense of centralized taxes.

In the 290s Diocletian expanded the army and taxes, and tried to control inflation. He also persecuted the growing minority of Christians, but in another civil war in 312 Constantine declared himself a Christian. After he took the throne, the church became the richest institution in the empire. Constantine continued military and fiscal reforms and moved the capital from Rome, now too distant from the eastern centers, to the well-placed Greek city Byzantium, which he renamed Constantinople. The empire flourished in the fourth century, but the underlying problems remained. Around 370 the Huns left central Asia and drove the Goths west, pushing the Germans ahead of them. Much of the empire was "Germanized": armies of Germans under German generals fought for Rome against Germanic invaders who often saw themselves as simply wanting to become Romans. Still larger armies were needed, but population was declining, and the church and great landowners could not be taxed. Elite culture changed too, as Christianity replaced Romanness at the core of identity. In 378 a large group of Goths got out of control, destroyed a Roman army, and ran amok in the Balkans. Constantine's reformed empire, which had looked so strong around 350, now unraveled. In 406 Gaul was overrun; in 410 the Goths sacked Rome. The western empire broke up into smaller kingdoms, still nominally Roman, but de facto German.

In 476 Odoacer the Goth deposed Romulus Augustulus, officially ending the western empire, though in most ways this was not a major transition. Trends in place since the third century continued, with declining population, state power, and cities, and exchange increasingly local and nonmonetized. The eastern (usually called Byzantine) empire recovered, and in the 530s Justinian even reconquered part of the west. However, this effort exhausted Byzantine resources just as new invasions began, and by the 580s most of the gains were lost. An even more serious collapse hit the entire Mediterranean: plagues returned, population shrank, large areas were abandoned, and trade collapsed.

This demographic-economic collapse was one part of the ancient-medieval transition; the Arab conquests provided the other, creating a tripartite political/religious division of the Mediterranean into Islamic, Orthodox Christian, and Catholic spheres in the eighth century. Just as the western empire was "Germanized" in the fourth century, the eastern empire was "Arabized," with both the Byzantine and Persian states settling Arabs in their territories and using them in their armies. Unable to cope with the late-sixth-century crises, Byzantium almost collapsed before Persian attacks, which overran Syria, Palestine, and Egypt, and in 626 threatened Constantinople. Byzantium rebounded, but when Mohammed died in 632, there was a power vacuum in the Near East. As had happened to Sargon of Akkad's empire nearly 3,000 years earlier, migrations out of the desert toppled a weakened institutional structure. The initial Arab conquests saw Islamic Arabs fighting against Arabs in the service of Byzantium and Persia. The Moslems destroyed the Byzantine army, probably in 636. Jerusalem fell in 638, Egypt in 641, and Sassanid Persia in 642. These successes unleashed huge population movements. Constantinople was besieged from 674 through 678 and again in 717–18, by which time Islamic forces had reached India, Samarkand, and Spain. They were only stopped near Paris in 732 and deep in central Asia in 751, but went on in the ninth century to occupy Sicily and Crete.

The trials of the seventh and eighth centuries transformed Byzantium. Feudal relations were established on the land, and the savage iconoclast controversy effectively ended elite classical culture. By 800 the Mediterranean world had broken into three camps: the dynamic, creative Islamic east and south; a harried, struggling Byzantine Orthodox Christian center; and a backward, impoverished, and depopulated Catholic Christian west.

Natural Environment

We have defined our analytical unit as the societies clustered around the shores of the Mediterranean—"like frogs around a pond," as Plato put it in fourth-century-B.C. Athens (*Phaedo* 109B). One of its unifying features was a shared climate. As in all preindustrial societies, ecology was the single most important factor structuring economic life.

We therefore describe the basic ecological parameters in this section.

The modern Mediterranean has hot, dry summers. Temperatures can reach 40°C at sea level in July and August, with little or no rain between May and September. The cool, wet winters sometimes reach freezing point at sea level, and typically get 250–500 millimeters of rain between October and April. Texts and pollen evidence suggest that this was broadly true in antiquity, though there were important changes. In particular, the shift from sub-Boreal to sub-Atlantic climates around 800 B.C. lowered typical temperatures by up to 2°C, and increased the amount and reliability of winter rainfall, producing a climate like that of the recent past (Lamb 1972–77). There were drier episodes 1500–900 B.C. and 200 B.C.–A.D. 350, then more rain and cold after 350. Climate may be linked to disease, which drives mortality and demography (Galloway 1986). In temperate zones, where winter respiratory diseases were the main premodern killers, warm phases coincide with population growth; in Mediterranean zones, where summer intestinal diseases and malaria were the main killers, cooler weather coincides with population growth. The hot, dry twelfth through ninth centuries B.C. saw demographic growth in temperate Europe, but decline in the Mediterranean; the cooler, wetter period from the eighth century on saw the opposite (Bouzek 1997). Similarly, population grew in the Mediterranean (particularly the east) from A.D. 350 on, as the climate cooled, but declined in England (Greene 1986, 81–86; M. Jones 1996, 186–243; Scheidel 2001a, 78–79).

Short-term variations are also important. The great problem for Mediterranean farmers is interannual variability in rainfall: while the average rainfall may support crops, it fluctuates from year to year. In Athens rainfall varied so much between 1931 and 1960 that barley failed one year in 20, wheat one in four, and legumes three in four. Pollen data, tree rings, and texts suggest that these figures too are broadly applicable to antiquity (Garnsey 1988, 8–16). According to a third-century-B.C. Greek proverb, "The year makes the crop, not the soil" (Theophrastos, *History of Plants* 8.7.6). The sub-Atlantic climate regime, with its more reliable winter rains, was good for Mediterranean farmers, while drier phases were better in temperate Europe into which the Roman Empire expanded, where more rain made potentially fertile bottom lands too heavy to plow.

Most Mediterranean landscapes include plains, hills, and mountains within short distances of the sea, and the interleaving of diverse microecologies is typical (Horden and Purcell 2000). On the whole, plains were used for grains, hills for vines, olives, and winter pasture, and mountains for summer pasture. The plains are generally small, broken up by chains of hills; the larger plains of Sicily and Thessaly were famous as breadbaskets. The coastline is heavily indented, and probably 90 percent of ancient people lived on plains within two or three days' walk of the sea. The sea united this world: sea travel was far faster and cheaper than land. According to Diocletian's Price Edict of A.D. 301, it cost as much to move a load of grain 10 miles inland as to ship it halfway across the Mediterranean.

There were also geographical variations. The earliest civilizations emerged in river valleys with very low rainfall. Even the toughest ancient crop, barley, needs 200 millimeters of winter rain, which the Euphrates, Tigris, and Nile valleys do not get. Summer rains in the Ethiopian mountains caused the Nile to flood, bringing rich silt to Egypt just in time for farmers to plant crops. The limited winter rains then fertilized the crops, and after the spring harvest the sun dried and cracked the ground, aerating it and preventing salinization. Irrigation allowed farmers to extend the flooded area, retain water, and fertilize a second crop in the summer. In Mesopotamia, however, the rivers flood in spring, exactly the wrong time. Farmers there had to store water much longer, which raised many technical problems. But once these were mastered, in the fourth millennium B.C., yields of 25:1 were possible, five or six times as high as in most rainfed agriculture. Egypt and Mesopotamia therefore had unusual settlement patterns, concentrated in strips just a kilometer or two wide but hundreds of kilometers long; outside this cultivated strip was desert. Only in a few places, like the Nile delta and the Fayyum depression, was this rule broken.

In the last few years, ancient historians have recognized the importance of interrelations between climate, ecology, and the disease pool in driving demography and larger economic structures (particularly Scheidel 2001b; Sallares 2002). Research is still at an early stage, but there are signs that malaria played a much larger role in the Mediterranean basin's economic history than has hitherto been realized.

Technology

Technology was simple. All ancient societies were what E. A. Wrigley (1988) called advanced organic economies, relying on plants, trees, and animals for materials and power. In a famous essay, Finley (1965) argued that the only important technological advances took place early on, or in the Middle Ages. Through most of antiquity, he concluded, technology stagnated, because slave labor was so cheap that it did not pay to invent or buy machines.

This is only partly true. We will take three examples.

1. In agriculture, after the domestication of crops and animals (starting ca. 8500 B.C.) and development of irrigation (ca. 5000), there was a "secondary products revolution" (Sherratt 1997, 158–248) exploiting animal power and by-products. Animals were harnessed to scratch plows in Sumer by 4500. By 3500 this practice had reached Poland and England, and wheeled vehicles were used by 3000. But the cart and plow that the Greek poet Hesiod described around 700 B.C. (*Works and Days* 423–38) sound quite like these prehistoric examples. Heavy wheeled plows able to turn wet clay soils, crucial in temperate Europe, only came in the sixth century A.D. (L. White 1962, 39–69). There were changes in the intensity of manuring, and some Romans bred special cattle for fertilizer. But progress consisted of adapting very ancient Mediterranean techniques to local conditions and the gradual accumulation of capital in the form of tools and animals (especially during the long Roman peace).

2. In metallurgy, bronze- and ironworking were mastered around 3000 and 1100 B.C. respectively. Each diffused widely, though the process took centuries. The Mediterranean civilizations never mastered high-quality steel, which had to be imported from India. Chinese blacksmiths had cast iron since the third century B.C., but European bellows could not raise temperatures high enough until the eighteenth century. As with agriculture, there were incremental improvements, including a massive increase in the amount of metal available, but no fundamental technological changes.

3. In shipbuilding, again, the main advances came early. The basic pattern of building shell-first hulls from edge-jointed planks with internal braces had been worked out by 2500 B.C. Bronze Age ships, like the Ulu Burun wreck (ca. 1300 B.C.), were small, displacing no more than 30 tons. Greeks added heavy wooden keels. The Alonnisos wreck (ca. 400 B.C.) displaced 120-plus tons, but most wrecks dating 500–100 B.C. were in the range of 30–50 tons (Gibbins 2001). By the first century B.C. Roman merchantmen were mostly 100–150 tons. Five hundred tons was not unusual, and one second-century-A.D. ship reached 1,200 tons (Greene 1986, 20–28; Parker 1992). Roman ships were the largest built in Europe until the fifteenth century, but their rigging remained primitive. Fore-and-aft sails were known, but most ships probably relied on a single square mainsail. As in agriculture and metallurgy, advances were small and incremental.

There were a few remarkable inventors, like the third-century-B.C. Ktesibios of Alexandria, credited with the hydraulic organ, metal springs, the water clock, and the force pump; or the first-century-A.D. Hero, also of Alexandria, inventor of a steam engine that opened temple doors, a coin-operated vending machine for holy water, and a surveying instrument like a transit. The ancient world had skilled engineers, as is shown by the Antikythera mechanism, a first-century-B.C. astronomical machine found in a shipwreck, which used complex gears and applied geometry to reproduce the movements of the sun, moon, and planets. But as Finley stressed (1965), the most striking things are (*a*) that most of these inventions were toys for the amusement of the elite, and (*b*) that the few with practical uses, like the transit, force pump, and Archimedes' screw, were ignored. Ancient Greece ranks along with China in having the most creative premodern scientific elites (Lloyd 2002), and was one of the most numerate ancient cultures (Netz 2002); but it differed fundamentally from western Europe during the scientific revolution in the narrowness of channels of communication between the scientific elites and the vast mass of producers (cf. Mokyr 2002).

Finley (1965) suggested that there were no incentives to spread innovations, repeating a famous story (Suetonius, *Vespasian* 18) that when an inventor in the 70s A.D. showed the Roman emperor a machine for moving columns, the emperor sent him away, saying it would cause the Roman poor to starve. Finley took Roman failure to capitalize on water mills, making a first step away from an organic economy, as his test case. The data then available suggested that water mills were invented around 100 B.C., but not widely diffused till the fifth century A.D. But new finds have changed this picture (Wikander 1984; Oleson 1984; K. White 1984; Lewis 1997; Wilson 2002). There was a wave of water-powered inventions in Alexandria between about 260 and 230 B.C., including lifting devices, pumps, and mills. A water mill was built at Chaplis in Switzerland in A.D. 57–58, and the huge complex at Barbegal in France, formerly dated to the late third century A.D., was in fact built in A.D. 100–120 (Leveau 1996, 145–49). A still larger complex was built in Rome in the third century (Wilson 2000). Excavations have also confirmed Pliny the Elder's claims (*Natural History* 33.21.72–77) that waterpower was used to lower the water table in Spanish mines in the first century A.D. and to expose ores. Water-powered devices were probably common throughout the empire by A.D. 150, perhaps spread by the army.

Finley was wrong to speak of stagnation (Greene 2000). The accumulation of small improvements and the first steps toward nonanimal sources of power were very important in Europe's economic development (Greif 2004). But that does not mean that there was a technological revolution in antiquity: compared to contemporary China or to the European Middle Ages, levels were low (see Mokyr 1990, 19–30, 193–208; Angresano 1991, 29–56).

Performance

Agricultural yields set the basic parameters for ancient economic sociology. We have few direct figures. The best come from the Roman Empire, and are controversial. Much of the rest of the time, we rely on comparative evidence and the archaeological analysis of bone and seed remains.

The major distinction is between irrigation and rain-fed agriculture. From at least 3000 B.C., the former could generate crop-to-seed yields of between 12:1 and 24:1 in Egypt and Mesopotamia, but only at the cost of high capital investments and labor inputs. Mesopotamia and Egypt both supported high populations throughout antiquity. Egypt probably had at least 5 million people under the Roman Empire, which was not reached again till the nineteenth century (Scheidel 2001b), and was a major grain exporter. Roman historians conventionally assume yields in Egypt around 10:1 (Rathbone 1991, 242–44), although local crop yields could be much higher (Rowlandson 1996, 247–52).

Varro (*On Agriculture* 1.44.1), Columella (3.3.4), and Cicero (*2nd Verrine* 3.112) provide some figures for yields in Italy in the first centuries B.C. and A.D. Varro says that in Etruria, yields could vary from 10:1 to 15:1, and Cicero that in Sicily at a sowing rate of 160 kilograms of seed per hectare, wheat yielded 8:1 (1,300 kg/ha) in a good year, and 10:1 (1,625 kg/ha) in an excellent year. Columella, however, says that in most of Italy yields of 4:1 on cereals were rare, implying that

they were normally lower. Varro's and Cicero's figures seem very high, but most historians have favored their testimony over Columella's. Garnsey and Saller (1987, 82) remark, "There is nothing we can do about Columella except distrust him," and Harry Pleket (1993, 323) comments that Roman agriculture was so successful that "the early medieval growth meant a return to a 'normal level' after the period of the Dark Ages, rather than an alleged agricultural revolution." Keith Hopkins (2002, 197–203), on the other hand, argues on broad comparative grounds for yields closer to Columella's figure. At present, there seems to be no obvious way to resolve the question.

Our data for Greece are poor: relying heavily on comparative evidence, Garnsey (1992, 148) estimated typical yields of up to 4.8:1 on wheat and 6:1 on barley (625 and 770 kg/ha at 130 kg/ha seed) in fourth-century-B.C. Attica. By 500 B.C. at the latest, major Greek cities were permanently reliant on imported grains.

So far as we can tell, food shortages were unpredictable but common throughout antiquity, although actual famines, in which significant numbers of people died of malnutrition, were rare, and usually had political causes (Garnsey 1988). But while people rarely starved, most were poorly fed. Skeletal evidence shows that chronic malnutrition in childhood was normal, and that periods of severe deprivation were quite common (Garnsey 1999, 34–61). Age-specific stature correlates tightly with nutritional levels in modern samples (Floud, Wachter, and Gregory 1990); skeletal studies show relatively stable stature in antiquity. Rick Steckel is now producing a systematic data set for Europe like that he and Rose built for the Americas (Steckel and Rose 2002), but it is already clear that most ancient Mediterranean samples produce average adult male heights in the 163–68 cm range, close to the 168 cm cutoff that Robert Fogel (1993) has used to define "short" populations. Most ancient people were stunted and wasted, suffered frequently from disease, were often hungry, and carried heavy parasite loads.

In the section below on cities we will present evidence for economic growth in antiquity. Arguments about per capita growth, what Eric Jones ([1988] 2000) calls "intensive" growth, are controversial; but some aggregate or extensive growth is undeniable. By nineteenth- and twentieth-century standards, ancient growth was so slow as to be imperceptible, but compared to most other preindustrial societies, some periods—such as Greece between 550 and 300 B.C., or the western

Roman Empire between 200 B.C. and A.D. 200—saw major improvements (Saller 2002; Morris 2003). Through much of antiquity, per capita consumption was probably not far above subsistence level, but by the second century A.D. it may have been 50 percent higher in most of the Mediterranean. Robert Lucas (2002) has recently argued that through most of agrarian history, per capita consumption has been something like the equivalent of $550–600 (1985 U.S.) per capita; if it reached $800 at some points in Mediterranean antiquity, then the performance of the ancient economy fell not far short of that of seventeenth-century western Europe.

Models of Ancient Economic Sociology

There was little systematic analysis of ancient economies before the 1890s, when historians in Germany began to take exception to evolutionary schemes that placed Greece at the bottom of a ladder that reached from closed, household economies to modern industrial ones. The so-called primitivist-modernist debate raged for a dozen years, with professional ancient historians generally concluding that Greece and Rome were basically like modern Europe, but on a somewhat smaller scale (Finley 1979). Finley (1965, 12) dismissed this consensus among ancient historians as "a schoolboy version of Adam Smith," and tried to improve on it by drawing historians' attention to a tradition of ancient economic sociology going back to Weber. Hopkins (1983a, xi) probably exaggerated when he called Finley's version of Weber model "a new orthodoxy," but by the time Finley died in 1986 the substantivism that he had developed from Weber's and Polanyi's contributions was probably the most influential approach among those historians who sought a consistent theoretical framework. In this section we describe the development and success of substantivist models, and responses to these models in the 1990s.

Max Weber

Ancient economic sociology began in just the same period that the primitivist-modernist debate was preoccupying professional ancient historians, with Weber's attempts to show that antiquity did not really belong on a primitive-modern scale (Weber [1891] 1962; [1909] 1976; [1922] 1968, 1212–1372). Weber ([1909] 1976, 69–79) sketched a seven-part evolutionary typology of ancient states. He saw types I (simple unwalled villages with free, independent farmers) and II (small cities with rulers, sometimes grouped into larger kingdoms) as common to the whole Mediterranean. In the Near East and Egypt these evolved into types IV and V. In type IV kings first of all made themselves semi- or wholly divine and developed bureaucracies and taxes, and in type V they created forced labor systems, state monopolies, and administered trade. In the Mediterranean, however, types I and II developed into type III, in which kings were replaced by aristocratic families monopolizing war and extracting labor from the poor through debt-bondage. Type VI evolved out of III, with the mass of farmers taking on military responsibilities and abolishing the aristocratic clans; and in some cases IV evolved into VII, the democratic city-state, in which political and military participation was completely separate from land ownership. What interested Weber about types IV–VII was the ways they differed from medieval European cities, where capitalism developed. In his later essay on the city ([1922] 1968, 1212–1372), Weber argued that all ancient cities were consumer cities, in which urban elites exploited the countryside through various forms of tax and rent, which they then spent on the urban poor who supported their lifestyles. Medieval cities, on the other hand, were producer cities, feeding themselves by exchanging manufactured goods or exotic imports for food produced in the countryside. Ancient types VI and VII (the Greco-Roman cities) were the most advanced cities in antiquity, but even so, they did not hold the seeds of capitalism, because economic activity was subordinated to more profitable military/political rent-seeking. This meant that Greek and Roman men saw themselves chiefly as members of warrior brotherhoods, and cared most about maintaining their standing within the military community: "in Antiquity the polis preserved during its heyday its character as the technically most advanced military association: The ancient townsman was a *homo politicus*" ([1922] 1968, 1354). In such a situation, economic relationships could not be placed on a primitive-modern continuum. They simply worked differently: "where stratification by status permeates a community as strongly as was the case in all political communities of Antiquity and the Middle Ages, one can never speak of genuinely free market competition as we understand it today" (937). Only in situations of debt crisis did social relations break free of status considerations and coalesce around market relations, creating genuine class groups (303–4, 931). To understand the ancient economy, Weber argued, we must first understand ancient politics.

Karl Polanyi

Weber's account of Mesopotamia ([1909] 1976, 83–104) was out-of-date almost as soon as it was written, because of the rapid pace of publication of new tablets, and it had little influence on Near Eastern historiography. His discussion of Greece and Rome fell afoul of ancient historians' awareness of the limits of Weber's empirical knowledge and their inability to distinguish between his subordination of economics to politics and the recently discredited primitivist positions. For a generation, the few Greco-Roman historians who took Weber's arguments seriously, like Johannes Hasebroek (1926, 1928 [1933]), were either pilloried or ignored (see Cartledge 1983). Nearly 50 years passed before there was much serious development in ancient economic sociology, and then it came not from a professional ancient historian, but from Karl Polanyi, a consummate outsider. Like Weber, Polanyi insisted that in precapitalist societies economics were embedded in larger sets of social relations, and could not be analyzed in neoclassical terms. He proposed a three-part typology of forms of exchange. In some societies, reciprocity is the rule: items are moved around mainly as gifts, creating obligations to repay, without money or markets playing a major role. In others, redistribution is the major institution, with central authorities pooling resources and dividing them up, again leaving little scope for money and markets. Only in western Europe since about A.D. 1800, he argued, had market exchange broken loose from social constraints, disembedding exchange and subordinating all relationships to the pursuit of profit (Polanyi 1944).

In the late 1940s Polanyi became convinced that the only way to advance his substantivist agenda (see Smelser and Swedberg, this volume) was through historical comparisons, showing that there had been large, complex economies that were neither capitalist nor communist. Polanyi rarely cited Weber, but his treatment of antiquity generally took Weber's types and exaggerated them. Believing that in Bronze Age Mesopotamia all land had belonged to temples that fed their workers with rations, he took Babylon as a perfect example of a redistributive economy. In Athens, on the other hand, he saw reciprocity within the citizen community giving way in the fourth century B.C. to a nascent market economy (Polanyi 1957a, 1957b).

Leo Oppenheim

In 1953–55 Polanyi attracted talented specialists to his seminar at Columbia University on the institutionalization of the economic process (Polanyi and Arensberg 1957). The ancient historians were generally critical of Polanyi's cavalier use of evidence, but two of them—Leo Oppenheim and Moses Finley—went on to introduce more nuanced versions of Polanyi's categories into their fields. By the 1950s the older Marxist models that represented Near Eastern societies as statist, redistributive command economies were giving way to images of an Asiatic mode of production in which the state coexisted with village communities tributary to the temple and palace (see Liverani 2003). Oppenheim (1957, [1964] 1977) positioned himself between these models and liberal theories that saw a large, private market sector beyond the palaces. He argued that Mesopotamian city-dwellers were mainly free citizens who fed themselves by keeping farms going in the countryside. This urban-rural interpenetration prevented markets from developing, and coexisted in symbiosis with the command economy (1977, 114). Oppenheim's Mesopotamia was a mix of redistribution and reciprocity, and remained stable for three millennia (1977, 95).

In the 1970s–1980s, versions of substantivism were the main rivals to Marxism in Near Eastern history. Most scholars accepted a much larger role for markets than Polanyi had given them, developing a picture in which temple- and palace-based redistribution, craft production, and administered trade existed alongside local reciprocity, individual entrepreneurs, and free markets, but with markets in a decidedly subordinate position (e.g., Lipinski 1979; Briant 1982; Renger 1984, 1994, 1995; Liverani 2004; Bedford 2004). Egyptologists were even warier than Assyriologists about constructing ideal types, but in that field, too, substantivism made progress against older statist theories in the 1970s and 1980s (e.g., Janssen 1975, 1981; Kemp 1989, 232–60; Warburton 1997).

Moses Finley

Finley was even more critical of Polanyi than Oppenheim had been, declining to contribute to *Trade and Market in the Early Empires* and trying to persuade Harry Pearson, Polanyi's literary executor, to omit the Greek material from Polanyi's 1951 manuscript *The Livelihood of Man* (published in 1977). Finley's vision was more Weberian than Polanyian (Morris 1999), but like Oppenheim, he brought Polanyi's core typology of reciprocity, redistribution, and market exchange into the center of ancient history. In his first book, *Studies in Land and Credit in Ancient Athens, 500–200 B.C.* (1952), Finley argued that the inscribed mortgage stones called *horoi* recorded elite attempts to raise cash for consumption purposes, such as weddings and funerals, not to create capital for investment. He claimed that Athenian capital, land, and credit markets were crude. When Athenians needed cash, they went to kin and friends for interest-free loans, and felt obligated to lend within these circles. Athenians wanted to be rich, but status overrode market considerations. Like Weber and Polanyi before him, he concluded that the sophisticated Athenian economy was noncapitalist; the Parthenon was built in a world where reciprocity dominated.

Finley rejected class as a useful analytical category, preferring "the word 'status,' an admirably vague word with a considerable psychological element," adding that Greeks and Romans "were, in the nature of things, members of criss-crossing categories" (1973, 51). Markets certainly existed, but they were less important mechanisms for moving goods around than reciprocal relationships between citizens or political relationships between rulers and ruled. Market exchange was inconsistent with membership in an egalitarian community of citizen-warriors: "the citizen-élite were not prepared, *in sufficient numbers,* to carry on those branches of the economy without which neither they nor their communities could live at the level to which they were accustomed. . . . They lacked the will; that is to say, they were inhibited, as a group (whatever the responses of a minority), by over-riding values" (Finley 1973, 60).

Like Weber, Finley saw Greco-Roman and Near Eastern civilization as evolving out of similar social forms. When Weber wrote, very little was known about the Bronze Age palaces of the Aegean, but the decipherment of the Linear B script in 1953 made it clear that redistributive palaces something like Weber's type IV had flourished in the Aegean before 1200 (Finley [1957–58] 1981, 199–232). This raised the obvious question of how the Greeks got from Weber's type IV to types III, VI, and VII, rather than moving to type V. Finley suggested in his second book, *The World of Odysseus* (1954), that Homer's epic poetry reflected real aristocratic societies of type III that had existed around 900 B.C., after the collapse of 1200 and an intervening dark age had destroyed all traces of type IV society. In this world, competitive gift-giving created hierarchy among chiefs, who won prestige, followers, and wealth through success in war. Beginning in 1959, Finley published a series of essays addressing what seemed to him the still more pressing question of how Greece moved from the hierarchical reciprocity of the Homeric age to the egalitarian reciprocity of classical Athens. His answer was simple: slavery (essays collected in Finley 1981, 97–175, plus Finley 1968). He argued that debt crises in the seventh and sixth centuries B.C. swept away the Homeric system of graded hierarchical statuses, polarizing men (women are conspicuously absent from Finley's accounts) into two groups, one of citizens practicing reciprocity, and the second of imported chattel slaves. Status concerns set the parameters of the economy, rather than vice versa: only reputable sources of wealth were acceptable for citizens, which ruled out direct exploitation of other members of the warrior fraternity, and inhibited the development of price-setting markets in land, labor, or credit. Only outsiders should be exploited, in the extreme but common case through commoditizing their very bodies. Where Polanyi had seen Aristotle struggling to understand the rise of market exchange in the 320s B.C., Finley (1970) saw him trying to theorize the exchange of goods without markets in a community of equals.

The ancient economy was thus a matter for the historical sociologist, not the economist. Finley offered a grand theory of a

> highly schematic model of ancient society. It moved from a society in which status ran along a continuum to one in which statuses were bunched at the two ends, the slave and the free—a movement which was most nearly completed in the societies which most attract our attention for obvious reasons [i.e., classical Greece and late republican/early imperial Rome]. And then, under the Roman Empire, the movement was reversed; ancient society gradually returned to a continuum of statuses and was transformed into what we call the medieval world. ([1957–58] 1981, 132)

Responses

We identify seven main responses to the 1970s substantivist interpretations since Finley's death in 1986.

Response 1: Substantivism as Normal Science

Many historians have found substantivism broadly satisfactory, and have set about filling in the details that Finley, Oppenheim, and others neglected (e.g., Garnsey and Saller 1987; Jongman 1988; Millett 1991; Whittaker 1993; Renger 1994, 1995; Warburton 1997; Möller 2000). This position is particularly common among Greek and Near Eastern historians.

Response 2: Empirical Critique

Second, a much larger group of scholars, closely familiar with the details of a particular part of the ancient world, sees sins of both omission and commission in the general statements by Finley, Oppenheim, and others. They have produced a steady stream of critiques detailing these errors (e.g., Frederiksen 1975; Parkins 1997; Parkins and Smith 1998). We see two trends within this scholarship. First, some studies contain valuable scholarship but seem not to understand fully the substantivists' use of ideal types. Rather than attempting to falsify a high-level model, the critics are more interested in reiterating the obvious truth that a very abstract model (e.g., the consumer city) is not much help in answering much narrower historical questions than it was ever meant to illuminate. A second group, though, raises more serious issues. At a certain point (which is hard to specify in models that cannot be expressed quantitatively) a model must be judged a failure if there are too many data that it cannot accommodate. Some of the more sophisticated empirical critiques, particularly from the Saint-Bertrand-des-Comminges group (Andreau, Briant, and Descat 1994, 1997; Bresson 2000), have shown that there are crucial points in the substantivist model, such as the density and scale of market places (de Ligt 1993) or banks (Cohen 1992; Andreau 1999), where the data do not seem to fit the substantivist model well. However, even these studies often seem to overlook the fact that no model can be judged good or bad in the abstract; it can only be evaluated relative to some other model, and so far no coherent alternative has been forthcoming from these critics.

Response 3: Substantivism and Primitivism

A third group confuses substantivism with primitivism. Some substantivists could perhaps be accused of also being primitivists, and Hopkins (1983a) identified a focus on "cellular self-sufficiency" as being at the heart of the models developed by A.H.M. Jones and Finley. But too often, historians act as if showing that cities were large (Engels 1990), that agricultural production sometimes went beyond local needs (Mattingly 1995), that there was extensive nonagricultural ac-

tivity (Mattingly and Salmon 2001) and a lot of trade (Burke 1990) falsifies the substantivist model. But despite the undertheorization of these critiques, the data they provide have sometimes been very useful in illustrating the oversocialization critiques discussed below.

Response 4: Eurocentrism

Fourth, the reaction since the 1980s against Eurocentrism has encouraged some historians to question the way the substantivists framed their research. Finley was at pains to insist that the Greco-Roman and Near Eastern/Egyptian worlds were very distinct, so much so that "were I to define 'ancient' to embrace both [the Near Eastern and the Greco-Roman] worlds, there is not a single topic I could discuss without resorting to disconnected sections, employing different models and concepts" (1973, 28). This went beyond Weber and Oppenheim, who seem to have seen the different Mediterranean societies as local variations evolving out of common ancestors. As Bedford suggests in a forthcoming essay, "The two regions do not belong to completely separate and unrelated worlds; they have produced distinct yet historically and typologically related forms of social organization" (2004). If we reject the idea that we study ancient sociology in order to explain the roots of European superiority to the rest of the world, we must also question the analytical value (which seemed obvious to Weber and Finley) of lumping all of Greco-Roman history and all of Near Eastern/Egyptian history together into two contrasted ideal types. Liverani (2004) and Bedford (2004) emphasize the huge variety of Near Eastern socioeconomic formations, from nomadic tribes through mercantile city-states to theocratic empires; while at the other extreme, Horden and Purcell (2000) have questioned the value of drawing any strong boundaries between regions in the Mediterranean, or even between distinct periods in the past three millennia.

Response 5: The Oversocialization Critique

The fifth and sixth responses exemplify some of the ideas in Mark Granovetter's (1985) classic essay on embeddedness in economic sociology. These seem to us to be the most important new directions, and we spend most time on them. A growing number of historians, particularly Romanists, criticize substantivism for oversocializing economic activity (although they do not use that term). They have done this in a variety of ways. One of the major debates concerns Roman estate management. Dominic Rathbone (1991) suggests that the detailed calculations of expenses and profit rates in the estate records of one Appianus, from third-century-A.D. Egypt, reveal attitudes very similar to the instrumental rationalism assumed by neoclassical economics, directly contradicting Weber's vision of *homo politicus*. But as is usually the case with the fragmentary evidence from antiquity, other readings are possible, and Dennis Kehoe (1993; cf. 1988, 1997) has argued that we cannot assume that Appianus made investment choices after weighing up the profitability of alternatives; given the small scale of commercial activity and the huge size of some men's fortunes in Roman Egypt, Appianus simply did not have much choice. There were few outlets for capital other than investment in land. Forced to invest heavily in land, he then tried to maximize his revenues within a narrow set of parameters. More recently, though, Paul Christesen (2003) has suggested that in fourth-century-B.C. Athens we can actually see rich men weighing up the risks and likely profits involved in a range of outlets for their capital, from farming to mining and maritime loans, and choosing rationally between them without regard for social norms. He further shows that typical rates of return on different forms of investment broadly correlated with the level of risk involved.

Keith Hopkins pioneered another approach, building models that could be assessed on their logical consistency, and which had implications that could sometimes be tested empirically (1978, 1980, 2002). He assumed that the Roman Empire levied taxes in coin in the provinces and spent these taxes mostly to feed the population of the great cities and the army along the frontiers. If these assumptions are correct, then taxpayers had to sell agricultural produce to generate coin, and the city and army had to buy this produce with coin to stay alive. There would have been large movements of food from the coin-paying agricultural provinces to the coin-spending regions at the empire's core and peripheries. The city of Rome had a million residents by the first century B.C., who would have consumed so much food that most of the west Mediterranean would have been involved in supplying it. We have no evidence that could directly test this theory, but the sharp increase in the number of shipwrecks from the Mediterranean and coin hoards from the provinces between 200 B.C. and A.D. 200 seem consistent with Hopkins's theory that monetization was far-reaching and that the volume of trade increased. Finley had insisted that "ancient society did not

have an economic system which was an enormous conglomeration of interdependent markets" (1973, 22–23); Hopkins went some way toward showing the opposite. Further, he pointed out that Roman grain ships were so large, and their cargoes so expensive, that many members of Rome's elite must have been heavily involved in the grain trade, whatever Cicero might say (Hopkins 1983b). Some historians dispute Hopkins's initial assumptions, suggesting that Rome in fact raised much tax revenue in kind, making it more a redistributive than a market economy (e.g., Garnsey and Saller 1987, 50–54); but arguing in a similar manner to Hopkins, economist Peter Temin (2001) points out that the logical consequence of the tax-in-kind model is that Rome would have needed a much bigger bureaucracy than we know that it had (Hopkins [1983b, 186] points out that person-for-person, Rome employed only one-twentieth as many bureaucrats as the Chinese empire).

The most aggressive oversocialization critiques have come from outsiders to ancient history. In a series of books, Morris Silver (1983, 1985, 1994) has attacked substantivism and used selections from Near Eastern primary sources to claim that markets heavily dominated economic life in this region, but has persuaded few specialists (e.g., Renger 1994). Ellickson and Thorland (1995) have provided a more sustained and influential critique in their law-and-economics treatment of Near Eastern land law, which suggested that a rational-actor approach "can be a timelessly valuable heuristic for analyzing human affairs." They claimed that their position is necessary to counterbalance historians' exaggerations of the "friction" that culture and ideology exacted on market forces in antiquity (1995, 411). They predicted that "changes in economic conditions will prompt residents of a society to alter their property institutions so as to minimize the sum of: (1) transaction costs; and (2) the costs of coordination failures" (1995, 324–25). After reviewing evidence from Mesopotamia, Egypt, and Israel, they concluded,

> Much of the evidence adduced seems consistent with our initial hypothesis that a small, close-knit social group will typically succeed in devising land-tenure institutions that maximize the welfare of the group's members. When free from outside coercion, ancient villagers appear to have adopted the marble-cakes of land-tenure arrangements that law-and-economics theory predicts: private ownership of houses, gardens, and small arable lands plots; communal or institutional ownership of arable and grazing lands where that

arrangement was necessary to exploit efficiencies of scale or spread risks; and network of open-access lands. The record suggests that the social impetus toward these arrangements was universal—i.e., present regardless of a society's religion, ethnic make-up, and other cultural features. (Ellickson and Thorland 1995, 408–9)

Reviewing recent debates in Near Eastern economic history, Granovetter has suggested that the nature of the evidence simply does not allow us to choose between such extreme positions as law-and-economics and substantivism.

In the absence of hard evidence on the costs of transactions or of coordination, it is all too tempting to examine the data at hand and assert that they show such costs to have been minimized. This can only be argued after the fact, by stretching the definitions of such costs, or of social welfare, to fit what has been found. Such hidden tautology is the only way to preserve what is more an article of faith than an empirical hypothesis. (Granovetter, forthcoming 2004)

Response 6: The Undersocialization Critique

In the 1990s, just as oversocialization critiques became standard fare in Roman history, undersocialization critiques also began, this time concentrated in Greek history. Since the 1960s, Michel Foucault had argued that the history of thought could be divided into roughly successive *épistèmes*, regimes of truth in which all forms of knowledge cohered into a dominant, diffuse, and controlling discourse, from which escape was impossible (Sheridan [1980] summarizes Foucault's thought). Some literary critics suggested that far from being a scientific discovery of the logic of the desire for gain, classical economics was but one dimension of a new set of subjectivities, narrativities, and gender relations, with political economy operating in the male sphere in the same way that the realist novel operated in the female (e.g., Nicholson 1994; Sherman 1996). The implication is that economic categories, like all other categories, are cultural constructions. Cultural analysis can show what interests were represented by these constructions, what interests contested them, and how such cultural conflicts were negotiated.

These ideas won a ready audience in classics, a field dominated by literary criticism (e.g., Dougherty and Kurke 1993). Like scholars of eighteenth-century English literature, specialists in Greek literature reinterpreted what had previously been seen as "economic" issues, outside the proper sphere of humanistic inquiry, as questions about the formation of subjectivities; thus economic history became the study of the economic passions (e.g., Cozzo 1991; Davidson 1997; Balot 2001). The major debate grew up around the origins and functions of coinage. The "new historicists" took a 50-year-old thesis that the Greeks first coined metal, probably early in the sixth century, for political rather than economic reasons, and linked coinage to larger shifts in self-fashioning. Sitta von Reden (1997, 155) stresses "the ideological constraints of money use created by the ethical frame of the polis and the uneasy fit of coinage with honour, the body and 'Self,' which were part of that frame," and Leslie Kurke (1999, 12, 35) sees "an alternative narrative behind the development of various money forms in Greece: an ongoing struggle over the constitution of value and who controlled the highest spheres of exchange, between the traditional elite and the emerging city-state," adding that this "argument about political and economic contestation . . . is strangely shadowed by the tropes and troubles of identity-formation." Both von Reden and Kurke find inspiration in Jonathan Parry and Maurice Bloch's (1989) model of "transactional orders," with money taking on different meanings depending on whether it is perceived as being used to promote the long-term good of the community or the short-term gain of the individual. But whereas Kurke concludes from this that different interest groups reacted to the device of coined money in different ways, von Reden suggests that archaic Greece had an "embedded money economy," in which "money does not by nature signify anything in particular—economic relationships, egalitarianism, the market, etc.—but is symbolised by its repeated usage in particular institutions" (1997, 154). Kurke responds that "Von Reden's argument . . . tends to suppress all trace of conflict in the momentous political and conceptual shift she documents" (1999, 18), and ties the differences in the ways Greeks responded to coined money to clashes between what one of the authors of the present chapter has called "middling" and "elitist" ideologies (Morris 2000, 109–91).

The strength of the undersocialization critique is that it draws attention to the subtleties of the texts that most economic sociologists have missed. The weakness is that it seems to leave us trapped in a bloodless, intellectualized realm of competing discourses, where our data always come to us already implicated in elite acts of representation. Kurke explains that

Because coinage is a polyvalent symbol within a complex symbolic system, the struggle I endeavor to reconstruct is a struggle fought *over* and *in* representation. At issue is who controls signification and who has the power to constitute the culture's fundamental hierarchies of value. While these issues have "real life" implications—for example, in the sociological basis of citizenship and relative status of citizens—such a struggle over fundamental hierarchies of value can only be a discursive one, fought out in the codes of our texts, visual images, and signifying practices over the constitution of the cultural imaginary. Thus, it is not as if there is some "reality" we are struggling to get to behind the texts, images, and practices, if we can just break through their screen by patient source criticism and sifting of "facts." In this "contest of paradigms," the discursive structures of our texts (literary and visual) *are* the "facts" at issue. (1999, 23)

Response 7: Alternative Frameworks

In Near Eastern history, a strong Marxist tradition existed alongside substantivism, and some scholars (particularly in Italy: e.g., Liverani 1988; Zaccagnini 1989) even moved back and forth between the two. Like Weber, Marxists tended to see strong similarities between the Near East and the Aegean in early times, with ecological and class differences leading to separate evolutionary strands in the Bronze Age. In Igor Diakonoff's sophisticated version (1991), the Near East had upper, middle, and lower classes, made up respectively of the state's ruling elite, free farmers and craftsmen, and serfs or slaves. The economy consisted of two sectors, the state's command economy and traditional village or extended-family communes. Greco-Roman societies, on the other hand, were one-sector economies, in which the state's role was minimal (Diakonoff 1982). The Asiatic mode of production achieved a relatively stable form in the third millennium B.C., and thereafter changed little, because it did not have the potential for revolutionary transformation, unlike the classical (or slave) mode of production.

English-language Greco-Roman historians have always been more cautious about Marxism (in the former Soviet bloc it was, of course, a different story). Continental neo-Marxists often found substantivism useful (e.g., the papers published in the Italian journal *Opus*), but in the United States and Britain the relationship was more antagonistic. The most sustained attempt to develop a Marxist analysis is Geoffrey de Ste. Croix's *The Class Struggle in the Ancient Greek World* (1981), but this depended on tendentious redefinitions of key terms (class, struggle, exploitation). By collapsing chattel slavery and serfdom-type relationships such as Spartan helotage into a single category of "unfree labor," Ste. Croix effaced the very redistribution/market distinction that most historians influenced by substantivism thought was central to Greek social history. Ste. Croix only engaged very briefly with substantivism (1981, 58–59, 91–94), suggesting that status was a useful descriptive category, but not useful analytically. The book won high praise from Marxist theorists, including Perry Anderson (1983), but Anderson's own book *Passages from Antiquity to Feudalism* (1974), which owed as much to Finley as to Marx, was both theoretically and empirically more coherent.

Mediterranean archaeology developed along very different theoretical lines than Mediterranean ancient history. Most archaeologists practiced forms of connoisseurship and art history, more connected to the museum world than to economics or sociology. But prehistoric archaeology was very different, and in the 1960s–1970s some fields, particularly Aegean and Near Eastern prehistory, engaged heavily with the contemporary North American "New Archaeology" (see Adams 1966, 1981; Renfrew 1972). The new archaeologists emphasized ecology, social evolution, and systems theory. Their social evolution drew on 1960s neoevolutionary anthropology (Service 1962; Fried 1967; see Trigger 1998), and their systems theory partly on the Parsonian tradition in sociology and partly on cybernetics. In the 1980s similar analyses were extended to the end of the ancient world (Hodges 1982; Hodges and Whitehouse 1983). Given the nature of the data, the sociological models involved were rather schematic, and despite ancient historians' repeated demands for quantitative archaeological studies, the new archaeology generally failed to impress scholars used to more nuanced textual sources (e.g., Humphreys 1978, 109–29; Finley 1975, 87–101). In the 1980s archaeology went through a second theoretical revolution, drawing particularly on social scientists like Bourdieu and Giddens interested in more reflexive approaches (see Hodder 1982, 1991, 1992). This led Mediterranean archaeologists to shift their focus to ideology and class, and in the 1990s to gender, ethnicity, and identity (e.g., Hall 1997; Woolf 1998; Morris 2000; Whitley 2001; Meskell 2002). Much of this work simply bypassed substantivist questions about status structures.

Conclusion

Ancient economic historians have generally been cautious about ideas and methods developed outside their own fields. The profession firmly rejected large-scale evolutionary models in the 1890s and ignored Weber. Polanyi's substantivism made serious gains only in the 1970s, after Oppenheim, Finley, and others had been pushing versions of it for 20 years. Since then, it has dominated discussion; even though the questions it was designed to answer rarely coincide with those that ancient historians seem to find interesting, few of the critics have developed coherent, properly theorized alternatives. Some classicists have found the cultural and literary approaches to economics pioneered in the 1980s useful, but there has been less interest in the ideas developed in the past 20 years among social scientists, such as the new economic sociology, new institutional economics, law and economics, and development economics (Morris, Saller, and Scheidel, forthcoming).

But that said, some of the debates in ancient history have the potential to bring the field closer to economic sociology in the next decade. In the final section, we look at three of these in more detail.

THREE CORE QUESTIONS IN ANCIENT ECONOMIC SOCIOLOGY

The State and the Emergence of Markets

The role of the state as an economic actor, particularly with respect to markets, is one of the oldest concerns in economic sociology (see Block and Evans, this volume; Swedberg 1994). Marx, Weber, and Polanyi made the state central to their sociologies of antiquity. Near Eastern and Egyptian historians put particular emphasis on the early twentieth century, developing strongly statist models. While the connection between the structure of states and their environmental base has been treated before, most importantly in the overdetermined "oriental despotism" model of the hydraulic civilizations of Egypt and the Near East, the role of the environment and the natural endowments of particular civilizations in state structure has not been of major importance in historical analysis (Berger 1994). Bronze Age royal ideology often represented all good as coming from the king, and some of the earliest major finds of tablets, such as those dating circa 2500 B.C. from Lagash, seemed to imply that all land was owned by the temple-state. In the most developed statist model, Karl Wittfogel (1957) suggested that only divine kings had the power to organize the labor needed to build irrigation systems, and so Mesopotamian and Nile societies were necessarily highly central-

ized. It has been clear since the 1970s that irrigation preceded centralized states by many centuries in both these regions, and that control of irrigation works generally remained in the hands of local authorities. The interannual variability of floodwater in the Nile valley was, however, one important cause for state intervention in local economies, but the mix between "public" mechanism of distribution and more diffused "private" transaction made through local state institutions such as temples demonstrates quite clearly that the interaction of the state with the individuals was complex (see Kemp 1989, 232–60). The contrast that Finley (1973) drew between the classical world and the Near East described in terms of the centralizing role of the temple in the latter is too stark and ignores the extensive evidence of individual economic actors. Strongly statist models remain popular, though, particularly in Egyptian history (see Manning 2002, 2003).

Polanyi emphasized the Near Eastern states' role as agents of redistribution: they constructed centralized command economies, while classical Greek city-states did not. However, it might be more fruitful to conceptualize all ancient states in this role, as groups of officeholders seeking to expand their power both inside and outside the polity, as well as to meet ideological goals. Greek city-states and Rome redistributed resources just as Babylon did, but did so in different ways, such as pay for poor citizens to hold office, or hand out free grain. We might see the issue as being less a contrast between classical and Near Eastern/Egyptian ideal types as a variety of balances between state officeholders and civil society. On the whole, officeholders were very weak by the standards of modern bureaucracies. Many ancient historians have found Ernest Gellner's (1983, 8–18) well-known model of agro-literate states useful (fig. 3). Gellner suggested that "the ruling class forms a small minority of the population, rigidly separated from the great majority of direct agricultural producers, or peasants." Members of this group control state institutions, are internally stratified, and use cultural artifacts like writing and religion to underwrite social structure, distancing themselves from nonmembers of the national elite. "Below the horizontally stratified minority at the top," Gellner continued, "there is another world, that of the laterally separated petty communities of the lay members of the society . . . the state is interested in extracting taxes, keeping the peace, and not much else" (1983, 9, 10). On the whole, the holders of state institutions tried to grab up what resources they could at as low a cost as possible, spending

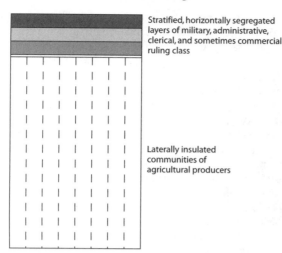

Stratified, horizontally segregated layers of military, administrative, clerical, and sometimes commercial ruling class

Laterally insulated communities of agricultural producers

FIGURE 3.   Ernest Gellner's model of the "agro-literate polity." The diagram shows with broken lines how distance, geography, and culture effectively isolate peasant communities from one another, inhibiting collective action on a large scale. The elite groups, on the other hand, share a Great Tradition that unites them across the whole polity, but may be divided from one another by very rigid status and occupational boundaries. After Gellner 1983, fig. 1.

chiefly on ceremony and defense against other states' elites.

It was not easy for ancient state elites to capture a large percentage of the wealth of their societies. The basic parameters of ecology and technology described previously meant that the bulk of all production was consumed by the primary producers themselves; production beyond subsistence may often have been as low as 20 percent. The best estimates suggest that even in the Roman Empire, probably the richest ancient economy, central and local government combined captured no more than 5 percent of the revenue generated (Hopkins 1980; Goldsmith 1984; Duncan-Jones 1994; Lo Cascio, forthcoming). In the fifth-century-B.C. Athenian empire, the figure was about the same (Morris 2001b, n. 1). Because revenues were small, bureaucracies were also small; and because bureaucracies were small, it was hard to trap more revenue. Many ancient states relied on tax farming, self-assessment, or voluntary contributions from the rich to ease the costs of tax collection. Indirect taxes (particularly market and harbor dues) often drove out poll taxes and land taxes (income taxes were virtually unheard of), presumably because they were easier to assess and collect (Goldsmith 1987). In large empires, tax collection was also usually decentralized, forcing the central state to delegate powers and a share of the proceeds to numerous governors, satraps, and so on. This could create serious principal-agent problems and profound structural weaknesses (Manning 2003). Hopkins (2002) has suggested that in the Roman Empire's third-century-A.D. crisis, local action was much more effective than central efforts, and that the share of surplus captured by the rural aristocracy through rent bit so deeply into what was available for the center that tax receipts plummeted to dangerously low levels. He sees this as one of the main economic reasons for the western empire's decline in the fifth century.

The behavior of the ruling elites often seems almost consciously designed to interfere with economic health, and neoclassical models of state behavior (e.g., Olson 2000) are chiefly of interest for the ways in which they break down, and fail to account for the tremendous duration of very suboptimal equilibria (cf. North 1981, 20–32). However, there are cases of officeholders acting (perhaps unconsciously) to reduce transaction costs and defend property rights, sometimes even cutting into the ability of the state itself to act rapaciously. The early Roman Empire is perhaps the best example: the army along the frontiers provided internal security and uniform weights and measures, and to some extent language made transactions easier, state investments in harbors and roads improved transport, and Roman law sometimes afforded protection to buyers and sellers (Hitchner, forthcoming). Imperial coinage speeded up transactions. There is considerable disagreement on the volume of coinage in circulation (Duncan-Jones's estimate [1994, 178] is four times as high as Hopkins's [2002, 226]), but even by the lowest estimates, parts of the Roman Empire were as highly monetized as any society before nineteenth-century western Europe and North America.

Eric Jones ([1988] 2000) has suggested that the major factor restraining economic growth in premodern societies was predatory behavior by elites. On occasion, though, states enter what he calls an "optimality band," in which they are strong enough to enforce property rights and provide security, but not strong enough to act as predators. In such cases (like Sung China), standards of living can rise. Early imperial Rome may have been another case; and perhaps also classical Greece.

Growth

The issue of growth, long ignored in ancient economic history, underlies much of these discussions of the state and cities. Substantivism gave studies of economic performance a bad name; and that, combined with the problematic nature of the evidence, deterred much serious discussion until recently, when Roman archaeologists in particular began to argue that the sheer scale of industrial activity in the early empire seemed inconsistent with Finley's characterization of the economy. This point now seems well established (e.g., Mattingly and Salmon 2001).

Hopkins (2002) is the only Romanist to have ventured quantitative estimates of per capita growth, based on prior probabilities. He suggests that per capita output in the western Mediterranean rose from something fairly near subsistence before the Roman conquest to perhaps 40–50 percent above subsistence by A.D. 200. Saller (2002) has shown that this is a plausible estimate, and growth at a slower rate (because beginning from a higher level) in the first two centuries A.D. can also be documented in the eastern empire (Alston 2002). As we noted in our discussion of the role of the state, Rome's ability to provide low-cost security, stable markets and (much of the time) currency, and lower transport costs contributed much to this process. Twenty years ago (1983b) Hopkins had noted that the quantity of artifacts on sites is larger in the Roman period than earlier or later, but did not develop this fact into an empirical method for quantifying standards of living and consumption. In fact, the categories of evidence available from archaeology—the stature of skeletons, the size and quality of houses, the quantity of domestic goods, public amenities—overlap substantially with those used by historians debating the "standard-of-living question" in the industrial revolution. One of us has argued elsewhere (Morris 2004) that these indices can be quantified, and that we can extrapolate from them that there was a similar increase of roughly 50 percent in per capita consumption in Greece between 800 and 300 B.C. Averaged out across the whole half-millennium, this would represent 0.07 percent per annum. In fact, the increase was probably concentrated in two spurts, 800–700 and 550–350 B.C., but even if per capita growth reached 0.1 percent per annum in these phases, that would still be just half of the growth rate in the sixteenth- and seventeenth-century Netherlands (but about the same rate that Saller [2002, 258] suggests for early imperial Rome).

Life may have been nasty, poor, brutish, and short, but it was not uniformly so. Eric Jones ([1988] 2000) and Jack Goldstone (2002) have suggested that the performance of premodern economies was anything but static, and the Mediterranean provides important empirical support for their theories. There were cycles of improvement and decline. The ancient Mediterranean saw very long-term, very slow growth between 3000 B.C. and A.D. 500, but also relatively shorter cycles. Interestingly, both the classical Greek and early imperial phases of improvement coincide with episodes of population growth; and within Greece, other periods of improving standards of living in the mid-second-millennium B.C. and fourth and fifth centuries A.D. also coincide with population growth. Contrary to what is often assumed, output could increase faster than population even without major technological revolutions. Aggregate growth in output grew impressively, probably quadrupling in the western Mediterranean in the first two centuries A.D., and increasing 15- to 20-fold in Greece between 800 and 300 B.C. The Greek case averages out to 0.5 percent per annum aggregate growth, which compares favorably to early modern Holland; but again we should remember that Dark Age Greece began from unnaturally depressed levels, creating convergence problems for comparative assessments of performance (Morris, forthcoming b).

Just what caused the periods of ancient growth and decline remains unclear. The sociology and governmental structures of Minoan Crete, classical Greece, and the early and late Roman empires were wildly different (redistributive palaces, independent peasant farmers, flourishing urban aristocracies, and a theocratic empire). Some theories of growth stress the need for representative institutions, encouraging the ruling group not to tax itself into stagnation. This might apply to classical Greece, but not to the other cases. Nor is there much support for the common contention that strong structures of egalitarian citizenship acted as a brake on economic performance. The recurrence of growth within very different sociological settings will repay further study (cf. Scheidel, forthcoming a).

Cities

The ancient Mediterranean is often called a world of cities. The world's first centers of 10,000 or more people probably formed in third-millennium river valleys in Mesopotamia and Egypt, and by the second century A.D. perhaps 10–20 percent of the basin's population was living in cities of 20,000 or more residents. However, as Weber saw ([1922]

1968, 1212–1372), percentages and sizes are not the only issue: the economic sociology of cities is decisive. Through most of the twentieth century, ancient historians produced almost nothing resembling the urban sociology of more recent periods. There were certainly accounts of individual cities, which Finley characterized as "pseudo-histories . . . in which every statement or calculation to be found in an ancient text, every artefact finds a place, creating a morass of unintelligible, meaningless, unrelated 'facts'" (1985, 61). Instead of reducing ancient urbanism to "the mere arithmetical total of layout and drains and inhabitants," Finley (1981, 8) insisted, we should return to Weber's lines of inquiry. Agreeing with Weber, Finley argued that on the whole, ancient cities were consumer cities. That is, they were the homes of elites who controlled most of the countryside, and drew its wealth into the city as tax and rent. They then spent this wealth in the cities, paying large numbers of servants and workers. Medieval cities, on the other hand, were often politically separate from the countryside. They survived either by importing exotic goods and selling them to country-dwellers so that they could buy food, or by manufacturing goods and selling those. The ancient city was a consumer city; the medieval, a producer city. A capitalist takeoff was possible in late medieval producer cities, but not in ancient consumer cities.

Finley drew ancient historians' attention to Weber's thesis in a 1977 essay (Finley 1981, 3–23), which generated a huge literature (see particularly Andreau and Hartog 1987–89). The quality of this scholarship is mixed: ancient historians generally recognized that Finley's critique of the "tell-all-you-know" approach to cities was valid, but few ancient historians were very interested in Weber's macrosociological questions, and so found the consumer/producer city debate limited (e.g., Parkins 1997; Parkins and Smith 1998). Like the response to substantivism as a whole, much of the time ancient historians concentrated on arguing that Weber's high-level ideal type did not account for all the facts known about this or that particular city. Some critics believe that showing that there were markets in which farmers and townsfolk directly exchanged goods disproves Weber's claim that ancient cities were essentially consumer cities. But this misses the most important point. The first really large cities (with populations over 100,000) were Babylon and Ashur, which were the administrative centers of major empires. The great ancient cities sucked in wealth from the country through political means. In Mesopotamia this was often through a command economy bringing in tribute or rent in kind (van de Mieroop 1997), while in other parts of the Mediterranean it was more commonly through market mechanisms as wealth and high prices attracted sellers. The second of these models describes classical Greek cities well: Athens reached a population of 40,000 or more by the 430s B.C. and Syracuse about 100,000 in the early fourth century because they were centers into which imperial tribute flowed. This money was redistributed to poorer male citizens as pay for political office and military service; so long as their spending power drove prices high enough to attract sellers, the cities could continue to grow (Morris, forthcoming c). Greek cities in the second millennium B.C., by contrast, were much smaller: they extracted wealth from quite small territories through centralized redistribution, and none grew above 15,000 or so residents (Whitelaw 2001; Bennet, forthcoming).

Alexander the Great's conquests in the 330s–320s B.C. grafted Greek-style institutions onto Near Eastern cities. Linking the Mediterranean market system with older command systems allowed even larger cities to develop—Alexandria in Egypt probably had 250,000 people by 200 B.C. (Scheidel, forthcoming b), and Antioch and Seleukeia probably over 100,000 each. But the real urban giant was Rome: as revenues from conquest flowed into the city, it grew to probably a million people in the first century B.C. To be able to support such urban giants, rural life must have changed significantly in most areas within easy reach of harbors or navigable rivers (Morley 1996). Braudel said of early modern Europe, "Towns are like electric transformers. They increase tension, accelerate the rhythm of exchange and constantly recharge human life" (1981, 479). This was equally true in the ancient Mediterranean.

While some ancient historians have tried to break down Weber's consumer/producer distinction by claiming that there were producers in ancient cities, Alberto Ades and Edward Glaeser (1995) have made a very different claim with equally important implications for Weber's theories. Asking why the capitals of some countries (e.g., Argentina, Japan, Mexico) contain 35 percent or more of the country's total population while the capitals of other states (e.g., the United States) have less than 10 percent, they tried to isolate the relevant variables through a survey of 85 contemporary cases and 5 more detailed studies, including ancient Rome. They concluded that "Urban giants ultimately stem from the concentration of power in the hands of a small cadre of agents living in the capital. This power allows the leaders to extract wealth out of the hinterland and distribute it in the capital. Migrants come to the city because of the demand created by the concentration of wealth, the desire to influence the leadership, the transfers given by the leadership to quell local unrest, and the safety of the capital. This pattern was true in Rome, 50 B.C.E., and it is still true in many countries today" (1995, 224). In a survey of Greek cities in the first millennium B.C., one of us (Morris, forthcoming c) found that contrary to Ades and Glaeser's findings for the twentieth century, it made little difference in antiquity whether the ruling elite was a democracy (Athens), an oligarchy (Rome), or a god-king (Alexandria); in the first millennium B.C., as now, the decisive factor (in the absence of major changes in transport technology) was the total population within a political unit that a ruling elite concentrated in a capital city could tax and charge rent.

The consumer-city debate is mostly concerned with the largest cities, but most people lived in much smaller settlements. Archaeological surface surveys have made an important contribution here, showing that many parts of the Mediterranean went through long-term cycles, with each phase lasting hundreds of years, between nucleated and dispersed settlement (see Bintliff and Sbonias 1999 and Bintliff, Kuna, and Venclová 2000 on the nature of the evidence and its problems). In Aegean Greece, the period of highest population and prosperity in the fourth century B.C. coincided with both large urban concentrations and the greatest degree of dispersion, with perhaps 20 percent or more of the population living in isolated farmsteads. Pollen evidence and potsherds scattered over the countryside, probably indicating the extent of manuring, suggest that in these periods the countryside was more intensively farmed than ever before (Zangger et al. 1997; Snodgrass 1991; Ault 1999). Comparative evidence from the Ottoman era shows that the factors behind dispersed versus nucleated settlement could be complex (Davis 1991), and research on this aspect of rural settlement has much to offer.

Finally, we should note Horden and Purcell's recent argument (2000, 89–122) that instead of Weberian typologies and more precise definitions of city types, we should dissolve the very notion of the city, thinking instead of a rural-urban settlement continuity, formed through constant mobility. This does not seem very helpful to us (cf. Shaw 2001;

Morris, forthcoming a), in that it renders the growth of progressively larger cities inexplicable.

CONCLUSION

The founding fathers of sociology turned regularly to the ancient Mediterranean to illustrate their claims about the interrelations of economy and society. Marx, Engels, and Weber all scrutinized it closely. The decline of grand evolutionary theories reduced sociological interest in antiquity, but when Polanyi developed his macrosociological models in the 1940s–1950s, the ancient Mediterranean was once again an obvious place to look. Polanyi attracted professional ancient historians in a way that Weber had not, and by the 1970s substantivism was the best-theorized framework for thinking about economy and society in most branches of ancient Mediterranean history. But in the past 30 years, as the new economic sociology has emerged as a research field in its own right, ancient historians have not kept up with sociological thinking. Polemics against substantivism have too often substituted for serious analyses of ancient economic sociology. We suggested here that this situation is beginning to change. Some aspects of the oversocialization critique of substantivism are forcing ancient historians to think more seriously about the roles of the state, cities, and growth in antiquity; and in doing so they are engaging with a variety of social-scientific approaches. The 3,500 years covered in this review provide one of the greatest resources available to historical sociologists, and the models and methods developed by economic sociologists provide organizing principles that will continue to reveal unsuspected patterns in the ancient data.

REFERENCES

Adams, Robert McCormick. 1966. *The Evolution of Urban Society*. Chicago: Aldine.

———. 1981. *Heartland of Cities*. Chicago: University of Chicago Press.

Ades, Alberto, and Edward Glaeser. 1995. "Trade and Circuses: Explaining Urban Giants," *Quarterly Journal of Economics* 110:195–227.

Alston, Richard. *The City in Roman and Byzantine Egypt*. London: Routledge.

Anderson, Perry. 1974. *Passages from Antiquity to Feudalism*. London: NLB.

———. 1983. "Geoffrey de Ste. Croix and the Ancient World." *History Workshop Journal* 16:163–87.

Andreau, Jean. 1999. *Banking and Business in the Roman World*. Trans. Janet Lloyd. Cambridge: Cambridge University Press.

Andreau, Jean, Pierre Briant, and Raymond Descat, eds. 1994. *Économie antique. Les échanges dans l'antiquité: Le rôle de l'état*. Saint-Bertrand-des-Comminges: Musée archéologique départemental.

———. 1997. *Économie antique. Prix et formation des prix dans les economies antiques*. Saint-Bertrand-des-Comminges: Musée archéologique départemental.

Andreau, Jean, and François Hartog, eds. 1987–89. "La cite antique? A partir de Moses I. Finley." *Opus* 6–8 (special edition).

Angresano, James. 1991. *Comparative Economics*. Englewood Cliffs, N.J.: Prentice-Hall.

Aperghis, M. 2001. "Population—Production—Taxation—Coinage: A Model for the Seleukid Economy." Pp. 69–102 in *Hellenistic Economies*, ed. Zofia H. Archibald, John Davies, Vincent Gabrielson, and Graham J. Oliver. London: Routledge.

Ault, Bradley. 1999. "Koprones and Oil Presses at Halieis: Interactions of Town and Country and the Integration of Domestic and Regional Economies." *Hesperia* 68:549–73.

Balot, Ryan K. 2001. *Greed and Injustice in Classical Athens*. Princeton: Princeton University Press.

Ballard, Robert, Lawrence Stager, Daniel Master, Dana Yoerger, David Mindell, Louis Whitcomb, Hanumant Singh, and Dennis Piechota. 2002. "Iron Age Shipwrecks in Deep Water off Ashkelon, Israel." *American Journal of Archaeology* 106:151–68.

Bedford, P. 2004. "The Economy of the Near East in the First Millennium B.C.: Evidence and Models." In *The Ancient Economy: Evidence and Models*, ed. J. G. Manning and Ian Morris. Stanford, Calif.: Stanford University Press.

Bennet, J., forthcoming. "The Aegean Late Bronze Age." In *The Cambridge Economic History of the Greco-Roman World*, ed. Ian Morris, Richard Saller, and Walter Scheidel. Cambridge: Cambridge University Press.

Berger, J. 1994. "The Economy and the Environment." Pp. 766–97 in *The Handbook of Economic Sociology*, ed. Neil J. Smelser and Richard Swedberg. New York: Russell Sage Foundation; Princeton: Princeton University Press.

Bernal, Martin. 1987. *Black Athena*. Vol. 1, *The Fabrication of Ancient Greece, 1785–1985*. New Brunswick, N.J.: Rutgers University Press.

Bintliff, John, Martin Kuna, and Natalie Venclová, eds. 2000. *The Future of Surface Artefact Survey in Europe*. Sheffield: Sheffield Academic.

Bintliff, John, and Kostas Sbonias, eds. 1999. *Reconstructing Past Population Trends in Mediterranean Europe*. Oxford: Oxbow.

Blaut, James M. 2000. *Eight Eurocentric Historians*. New York: Guilford Press.

Bouzek, Jan. 1997. *Anatolia and Europe: Cultural Interrelations in the Early Iron Age*. Studies in Mediterranean Archaeology 122. Jonsered: Astroms Forlag.

Braudel, Fernand. [1949] 1972. *The Mediterranean and the Mediterranean World in the Age of Philip II*. Trans. Siân Reynolds. 2 vols. New York: Harper and Row.

———. 1981. *Civilization and Capitalism*. Vol 2, *The Wheels of Commerce*. London: Collins.

Bresson, Alain. 2000. *La cité marchande*. Paris: Ausonius.

Briant, Pierre. 1982. *Rois, tributs et paysans*. Paris: Les Belles Lettres.

Briant, Pierre, and R. Descat. 1998. "Un register douanier de la satrapie d'Égypte à l'époque achéménide (*TAD* C3,7)." Pp. 59–104 in *Le commerce en Égypte ancienne*, ed. N. Grimal and B. Menu. Cairo: IFAO.

Burke, Edmund. 1990. "The Economy of Athens in the Classical Era: Some Adjustments to the Primitivist Model." *Transactions of the American Philological Association* 122:199–226.

Cartledge, P. 1983. "'Trade and Politics' Revisited: Archaic Greece." Pp. 1–15 in *Trade in the Ancient Economy*, ed. Peter Garnsey, Keith Hopkins, and C. R. Whittaker. Berkeley and Los Angeles: University of California Press.

Christesen, Paul. 2003. "Economic Rationalism in Fourth-Century B.C.E. Athens." *Greece and Rome* 50:31–56.

Cohen, Edward E. 1992. *Athenian Economy and Society: A Banking Perspective*. Princeton: Princeton University Press.

Cozzo, Andrea. 1991. *Le passioni economiche nella Grecia antica*. Palermo: Sellerio.

Davidson, James. 1997. *Courtesans and Fishcakes: The Consuming Passions of Classical Athens*. New York: St. Martin's Press.

Davis, Jack. 1991. "Contributions to a Mediterranean Rural Archaeology: Historical Case Studies from the Ottoman Cyclades." *Journal of Mediterranean Archaeology* 4:131–215.

de Ligt, L. 1993. *Fairs and Markets in the Roman Empire*. Amsterdam: J. C. Gieben.

Diakonoff, Igor. 1982. "The Structure of Near Eastern Society before the Middle of the 2nd Millennium B.C." Pp. 7–100 in vol. 3 of *Oikumene*, ed. István Hahn. Budapest: Akad. Kiadó.

———, ed. 1991. *Early Antiquity*. Chicago: University of Chicago Press.

Dougherty, Carol, and Leslie Kurke, eds. 1993. *Cultural Poetics in Archaic Greece*. Oxford: Oxford University Press.

Duncan-Jones, Richard. 1994. *Money and Government in the Roman Empire*. Cambridge: Cambridge University Press.

Ellickson, Robert, and Charles Thorland. 1995. "Ancient Land Law: Mesopotamia, Egypt, Israel." *Chicago-Kent Law Review* 71:321–411.

Engels, Donald. 1990. *Roman Corinth*. Chicago: University of Chicago.

Finley, Moses I. 1952. *Studies in Land and Credit in Ancient Athens, 500–200 BC* New Brunswick, N.J.: Rutgers University Press.

———. 1954. *The World of Odysseus*. New York: Viking Press.

———. 1965. "Technical Innovation and Economic Progress in the Ancient World." *Economic History Review* 2d ser. 18:29–45.

———. 1968. "Slavery." Pp. 307–13 in vol. 14 of *International Encyclopedia of the Social Sciences*, ed. David L. Sills. New York: Macmillan.

———. 1970. "Aristotle and Economic Analysis." *Past and Present* 47:3–25.

———. 1973. *The Ancient Economy*. Berkeley and Los Angeles: University of California Press.

———. 1975. *The Use and Abuse of History*. London: Chatto and Windus.

———. [1957–58] 1981. *Economy and Society in Ancient Greece*. Ed. Brent Shaw and Richard Saller. London: Chatto and Windus.

———. 1985. *Ancient History: Evidence and Models*. London: Chatto and Windus.

———, ed. 1979. *The Bücher-Meyer Controversy*. New York: Arno Press.

Floud, Roderick, Kenneth Wachter, and Annabel Gregory. 1990. *Height, Health, and History: Nutritional Status in the United Kingdom, 1750–1980*. Cambridge: Cambridge University Press.

Fogel, Robert. 1993. "New Sources and New Techniques for the Study of Secular Trends in Nutritional Status, Health, Mortality, and the Process of Aging." *Historical Methods* 26:5–43.

Frank, Andre G. 1998. *ReOrient: Global Economy in the Asian Age*. Berkeley and Los Angeles: University of California Press.

Frederiksen, M. 1975. Review of Finley 1973. *Journal of Roman Studies* 55:170–71.

Fried, Morton H. 1967. *The Evolution of Political Society*. New York: Random House.

Galloway, Patrick. 1986. "Long-Term Fluctuations in Climate and Population in the Preindustrial Era." *Population and Development Review* 12: 1–24.

Garnsey, Peter. 1988. *Famine and Food Supply in the Graeco-Roman World*. Cambridge: Cambridge University Press.

———. 1992. "Yield of the Land." Pp. 147–53 in *Agriculture in Ancient Greece*, ed. Berit Wells. Stockholm: The Institute.

———. 1999. *Food and Society in Classical Antiquity*. Cambridge: Cambridge University Press.

Garnsey, Peter, and Richard Saller. 1987. *The Roman Empire*. London: Duckworth.

Gellner, Ernest. 1983. *Nations and Nationalism*. Ithaca, N.Y.: Cornell University Press.

Gibbins, David. 2001. "Shipwrecks and Hellenistic Trade." Pp. 273–312 in *Hellenistic Economies*, ed. Zofia H. Archibald, John Davies, Vincent Gabrielson, and Graham J. Oliver. London: Routledge.

Goldsmith, Raymond. 1984. "An Estimate of the Size and Structure of the National Product of the Early Roman Empire." *Review of Income and Wealth* 30: 263–88.

———. 1987. *Premodern Financial Systems*. Cambridge: Cambridge University Press.

Goldstone, Jack. 1998. "The Problem of the 'Early Modern' World." *Journal of the Economic and Social History of the Orient* 41:249–84.

———. 2000. "The Rise of the West—or Not? A Revision to Socio-economic History." *Sociological Theory* 18:175–92.

———. 2002. "Efflorescences and Economic Growth in World History: Rethinking the 'Rise of the West' and the Industrial Revolution." *Journal of World History* 13:323–89.

Grainger, John D. 1999. "Prices in Hellenistic Babylonia." *Journal of the Economic and Social History of the Orient* 42:303–50.

Granovetter, Mark. 1985. "Economic Action and Social Structure: The Problem of Embeddedness." *American Journal of Sociology* 91:481–510.

———. 2004. "Comment on Liverani and Bedford." In *The Ancient Economy: Evidence and Models*, ed. J. G. Manning and Ian Morris. Stanford, Calif.: Stanford University Press.

Granovetter, Mark, and Richard Swedberg, eds. 1992. *The Sociology of Economic Life*. Boulder, Colo.: Westview Press.

Greene, Kevin. 1986. *The Archaeology of the Roman Economy*. London: B. T. Batsford.

———. 2000. "Technical Innovation and Economic Progress in the Ancient World: M. I. Finley Reconsidered." *Economic History Review* 53:29–59.

Greif, Avner. 2004. "Comment on Saller and Hitchner." In *The Ancient Economy: Evidence and Models*, ed. J. G. Manning and Ian Morris. Stanford, Calif.: Stanford University Press.

Haldor, John. 1997. *Byzantium in the Seventh Century*. Rev. ed. Cambridge: Cambridge University Press.

Hall, Jonathan. 1997. *Ethic Identity in Greek Antiquity*. Cambridge: Cambridge University Press.

———. 2002. *Hellenicity: Between Ethnicity and Culture*. Chicago: University of Chicago Press.

Hasebroek, Johannes. 1926. *Die Imperialistic Gedanke in Altertum*. Stuttgart: Kohlhammer.

———. [1928] 1933. *Trade and Politics in Ancient Greece*. Trans. L. M. Fraser and D. C. Macgregor. London: G. Bell and Sons.

———. [1931] 1966. *Griechische Wirtschafts- und Gesellschaftsgeschichte*. Hildesheim: Georg Olms.

Hitchner, R. Forthcoming. *The First Globalization*.

Hodder, Ian. 1982. *Symbols in Action*. Cambridge: Cambridge University Press.

———. 1991. *Reading the Past*. 2d ed. Cambridge: Cambridge University Press.

———. 1992. *Practice and Theory in Archaeology*. Cambridge: Cambridge University Press.

Hodges, Richard. 1982. *Dark Age Economics*. London: Duckworth.

Hodges, Richard, and David Whitehouse. 1983. *Mohammed, Charlemagne, and the Origins of Europe. London: Duckworth.

Hopkins, Keith. 1978. *Conquerors and Slaves*. Cambridge: Cambridge University Press.

———. 1980. "Taxes and Trade in the Roman Empire." *Journal of Roman Studies* 70:101–25.

———. 1983a. Introduction to *Trade in the Ancient Economy*, ed. Peter Garnsey, Keith Hopkins, and C. R. Whittaker. *Trade in the Ancient Economy*. London: Chatto and Windus.

———. 1983b. "Models, Ships, and Staples." Pp. 84–109 in *Trade and Famine in Classical Antiquity*, ed. Peter Garnsey and C. R. Whittaker. Cambridge: Cambridge Philological Society.

———. 2002. "Rome, Taxes, Rents, and Trade." Pp. 190–230 in *The Ancient Economy*, ed. Walter Scheidel and Sitta von Reden. Edinburgh: Edinburgh University Press.

Horden, Peregrine, and Nicholas Purcell. 2000. *The Corrupting Sea: A Study in Mediterranean History*. Oxford: Blackwell.

Humphreys, S. C. 1978. *Anthropology and the Greeks*. London: Routledge.

Janssen, J. J. 1975. "Prolegomena to the Study of Egypt's Economic History during the New Kingdom." *Studien zur Altägyptischen Kultur* 3:127–85.

———. 1981. "Die Struktur der pharaonischen Wirrschaft." *Göttingen Miszellen* 48:59–77.

Jones, Eric. [1988] 2000. *Growth Recurring: Economic Change in World History*. Oxford: Clarentun; repr. Ann Arbor: Univeristy of Michigan Press.

Jones, Michael E. 1996. *The End of Roman Britain*. Ithaca, N.Y.: Cornell University Press.

Jongman, Willem. 1988. *The Economy and Society of Pompeii*. Amsterdam: J. C. Gieben.

Kehoe, Dennis. 1988. "Allocation of Risk and Investment on the Estates of Pliny the Younger." *Chiron* 18:15–42.

———. 1993. Review of Rathbone 1991. *Journal of Roman Archaeology* 6:476–84.

———. 1997. *Investment, Profit, and Tenancy*. Ann Arbor, Mich.: University of Michigan Press.

Kemp, Barry. 1989. *Ancient Egypt: Anatomy of a Civilization*. London: Routledge.

Kurke, Leslie. 1999. *Coins, Bodies, Games, and Gold: The Politics of Meaning in Archaic Greece*. Princeton: Princeton University Press.

Lamb, H. H. 1972–77. *Climate: Present, Past, and Future*. 2 vols. London: Methuen.

Leveau, Phillipe. 1996. "The Barbegal Water Mill in Its Environment." *Journal of Roman Archaeology* 9: 137–53.

Lewis, M. 1997. *Millstone and Hammer: The Origins of Water Power*. Hull: University of Hull.

Lipinski, Edward, ed. 1979. *State and Temple Economy in the Ancient Near East*. 2 vols. Leuven: Departement Oriëntalistick.

Liverani, M. 1988. *Anticó Oriente: Storia, società, economia*. Rome: Laterza.

———. 2004. "The Near East: The Bronze Age." In *The Ancient Economy: Evidence and Models*, ed. J. G. Manning and Ian Morris. Stanford, Calif.: Stanford University Press.

Lloyd, G. 2002. *The Ambitions of Curiosity: Understanding the World in Ancient Greece and China*. Cambridge: Cambridge University Press.

Lo Cascio, Elio, forthcoming. "State and Army." In Morris et al., forthcoming.

Lucas, Robert. 2002. *Lectures on Economic Growth*. Cambridge: Harvard University Press.

Mann, Michael. 1986. *The Sources of Social Power*. Vol. 1 Cambridge: Cambridge University Press.

Manning, J. 2002. "Irrigation et état en Égypte antique." *Annales. Histoire, Sciences Sociales* 57:611–23.

———. 2003. *Land and Power in Ptolemaic Egypt*. Cambridge: Cambridge University Press.

Manning, J. G., and Ian Morris, eds. 2004. *The Ancient Economy: Evidence and Models*. Stanford, Calif.: Stanford University Press.

Marx, Karl. [1857–58] 1964. *Pre-capitalist Economic Formations*. Ed. E. J. Hobsbawn. Trans. Jack Cohen. London: Lawrence and Wishart.

Mattingly, David. 1995. *Tripolitania*. London: B. T. Batsford.

Mattingly, David, and John Salmon, eds. 2001. *Economies beyond Agriculture in the Classical World*. London: Routledge.

Meskell, Lynn. 1999. *Archaeologies of Social Life*. Oxford: Blackwell.

———. 2002. *Private Life in New Kingdom Egypt*. Princeton: Princeton University Press.

Millett, Paul. 1991. *Lending and Borrowing in Ancient Athens*. Cambridge: Cambridge University Press.

Mokyr, Joel. 1990. *The Lever of Riches*. Oxford: Oxford University Press.

———. 2002. *The Gifts of Athena: Historical Origins of the Knowledge Economy*. Princeton: Princeton University Press.

Möller, Astrid. 2000. *Naukratis: Trade in Archaic Greece*. Oxford: Oxford University Press.

Morley, Neville, 1996. *Metropolis and Hinterland*. Cambridge: Cambridge University Press.

Morris, Ian. 1994. "Archaeologies of Greece." Pp. 8–47 in *Classical Greece: Ancient Histories and Modern Archaeologies*, ed. Ian Morris. Cambridge: Cambridge University Press.

———. 1999. Foreword to reprint of 2d. ed. Pp. ix–xxxvi in *The Ancient Economy*, by Moses I. Finley. Berkeley and Los Angeles: University of California Press.

———. 2000. *Archaeology as Cultural History*. Oxford: Blackwell.

———. 2001a. "Hard Surfaces." Pp. 8–43 in *Money, Labour, and Land*, ed. Paul Cartledge, Edward E. Cohen, and Lin Foxhall. London: Routledge.

———. 2001b. "The Athenian Empire (478–404 B.C.)." http://www.stanford.edu/group/sshi/empires2 .html.

———. 2004. "Archaeology and Greek Economic History." In *The Ancient Economy: Evidence and Models*, ed. J. G. Manning and Ian Morris. Stanford, Calif.: Stanford University Press.

———. Forthcoming a. "Mediterraneanization." In *Mediterranean Paradigms and the Study of Antiquity*, ed. I. Malkin. Tel Aviv.

———. Forthcoming b. "Economic Growth in Ancient Greece." *Journal of Institutional and Theoretical Economics*.

———. Forthcoming c. "The Growth of Greek Cities in the First Millennium B.C." In *The Archaeology of Preindustrial Cities*, ed. G. Storey.

Morris, Ian, and J. Manning. 2004. Introduction. In *The Ancient Economy: Evidence and Models*, ed. J. G. Manning and Ian Morris. Stanford, Calif.: Stanford University Press.

Morris, Ian, Richard Saller, and Walter Scheidel, eds. Forthcoming. *The Cambridge Economic History of the Greco-Roman World*. Cambridge: Cambridge University Press.

Netz, Reviel. 2002. "Counter Culture: Towards a History of Greek Numeracy." *History of Science* 40: 321–52.

Nicholson, Colin. 1994. *Writing and the Rise of Finance: Capital Satires of the Early Eighteenth Century*. Cambridge: Cambridge University Press.

North, Douglass. 1981. *Structure and Change in Economic History*. New York: W. W. Norton.

Oleson, John. 1984. *Greek and Roman Mechanical Water-Lifting Devices*. Toronto: University of Toronto Press.

Olson, Mancur. 2000. *Power and Prosperity*. New York: Basic Books.

Oppenheim, A. Leo. 1957. "A Bird's-Eye View of Mesopotamian Economic History." Pp. 27–37 *Trade and Market in the Early Empires*, ed. Karl Polanyi, Conrad M. Arensberg, and Harry W. Pearson. Glencoe, Ill.: Free Press.

———. [1964] 1977. *Ancient Mesopotamia*. Rev. ed. completed by Erica Reiner. Chicago: University of Chicago Press.

Orrieux, Claude. 1985. *Zénon de Caunos, parépidèmos et le destin grec*. Paris: Les Belles-Lettres.

Özgüç, Tahsin. 1959. *Kültepe-Kanis I: New Researches at the Center of the Assyrian Trade Colonies*. Ankara: Türk Tarih Kurumu.

———. 1986. *Kültepe-Kanis II: New Researches at the Trading Center of the Ancient Near East*. Ankara: Türk Tarih Kurumu Basimevi.

Parker, A. J. 1992. *Ancient Shipwrecks of the Mediterranean and the Roman Provinces*. Oxford: Tempus Reparatum.

Parkins, Helen M., ed. 1997. *Roman Urbanism*. London: Routledge.

Parkins, Helen M., and Christopher Smith, eds. 1998. *Trade, Traders, and the Ancient City*. London: Routledge.

Parry, Jonathan, and Maurice Bloch. 1989. "Introduction: Money and the Morality of Exchange." Pp. 1–32 in *Money and the Morality of Exchange*, ed. Jonathan Parry and Maurice Bloch. Cambridge: Cambridge University Press.

Phinney, Edward. 1989. "The Classics in American Education." Pp. 77–87 in *Classics: A Discipline and Profession in Crisis?* ed. Phyllis Culham and Lowell Edmunds, technical ed. Alden Smith. Lanham, Md.: University Press of America.

Pleket, H. 1993. "Agriculture in the Roman Empire in Comparative Perspective." Pp. 317–42 in *De agricultura: In memoriam Pieter Willem de Neeve*, ed. H. Sancisi-Weerdenburg. Amsterdam: J. C. Gieben.

Polanyi, Karl. 1944. *The Great Transformation: The Political and Economic Origins of Our Time*. Boston: Beacon Press.

———. 1957a. "Marketless Trading in Hammurabi's Time." Pp. 12–56 in *Trade and Markets in the Early Empires*, ed. Karl Polanyi, Conrad M. Arensberg, and Harry W. Pearson. Glencoe, Ill.: Free Press.

———. 1957b. "Aristotle Discovers the Economy." Pp. 64–94 in *Trade and Markets in the Early Empires*, ed. Karl Polanyi, Conrad M. Arensberg, and Harry W. Pearson. Glencoe, Ill.: Free Press.

Polanyi, Karl, and Conrad M. Arensberg. 1957. Preface. Pp. v–xi in *Trade and Markets in the Early Empires*, ed. Karl Polanyi, Conrad M. Arensberg, and Harry W. Pearson. Glencoe, Ill.: Free Press.

Polanyi, Karl, Conrad M. Arensberg, and Harry W. Pearson, eds. 1957. *Trade and Market in the Early Empires*. Glencoe, Ill.: Free Press.

Porten, Bezald, and Ada Yardeni, eds. and trans. 1993. *Textbook of Aramaic Documents from Ancient Egypt*. Vol. 3, *Literature, Accounts, Lists*. Jerusalem: Hebrew University, Dept. of the History of the Jewish People.

Rathbone, Dominic. 1991. *Economic Rationalism and Rural Society in Third-Century A.D. Egypt: The Heroninos Archive and the Appianus Estate*. Cambridge: Cambridge University Press.

———. 1997. "Price and Price Formation in Roman Egypt." Pp. 183–244 in *Économie antique. Prix et formation des prix dans l'économie antiques*. Saint-Bertrand-de-Comminges: Musée archéologique départemental.

Renfrew, Colin. 1972. *The Emergence of Civilisation*. London: Methuen.

Renger, Johannes. 1984. "Patterns of Non-institutional Trade and Non-commercial Exchange in Ancient Mesopotamia at the Beginning of the Second Millennium B.C." Pp. 31–123 in *Circulation of Goods in Non-palatial Context in the Ancient Near East*, ed. Alfonso Archi. Rome: Edizioni dell'Ateneo.

———. 1994. "On Economic Structures in Ancient Mesopotamia." *Orientalia* n.s. 63:157–208.

———. 1995. "Institutional, Communal, and Individual Ownership or Possession of Arable Land in Ancient Mesopotamia from the End of the Fourth to the

End of the First Millennium B.C." *Chicago-Kent Law Review* 71:269–319.

Rowlandson, Jane 1996. *Landowners and Tenants in Roman Egypt: The Social Relations of Agriculture in the Oxyrhynchite Nome.* Oxford: Clarendon Press.

Said, Edward. 1978. *Orientalism.* New York: Pantheon.

Ste. Croix, Geoffrey E. M. de. 1981. *The Class Struggle in the Ancient Greek World.* Ithaca, N.Y.: Cornell University Press.

Sallares, Robert. 2002. *Malaria and Rome: A History of Malaria in Ancient Italy.* Oxford: Oxford University Press.

Saller, Richard. 2002. "Framing the Debate on the Ancient Economy." Pp. 251–69 in *The Ancient Economy,* ed. Walter Scheidel and Sitta von Reden. New York: Routledge.

———. Forthcoming. "Gender and Labor in the Household." In *The Cambridge Economic History of the Greco-Roman World,* ed. Ian Morris, Richard Saller, and Walter Scheidel. Cambridge: Cambridge University Press.

Scheidel, Walter. 2001a. "Progress and Problems in Roman Demography." Pp. 1–81 in *Debating Roman Demography,* ed. Walter Scheidel. Leiden: Brill.

———. 2001b. *Death on the Nile: Disease and the Demography of Roman Egypt.* Leiden: Brill.

———. Forthcoming a. "Demographic and Economic Development in the Ancient Mediterranean World." *Journal of Institutional and Theoretical Economics.*

———. Forthcoming b. "Creating a Metropolis: A Comparative Demographic Perspective."

Service, Elman R. 1962. *Primitive Social Organization.* New York: Random House.

Shaw, B. 2001. "Challenging Braudel: A New Vision of the Mediterranean." *Journal of Roman Archaeology* 14:419–53.

Sheridan, Alan. 1980. *Michel Foucault: The Will to Truth.* London: Tavistock.

Sherman, Sandra. 1996. *Finance and Fictionality in the Early Eighteenth Century: Accounting for Defoe.* Cambridge: Cambridge University Press.

Sherratt, Andrew. 1997. *Economy and Society in Prehistoric Europe.* Princeton: Princeton University Press.

Silver, Morris. 1983. *Prophets and Markets: The Political Economy of Ancient Israel.* Boston: Kluwer-Nijhoff.

———. 1985. *Economic Structures of the Ancient Near East.* London: Croom Helm.

———. 1994. *Economic Structures of Antiquity.* Westport, Conn.: Greenwood Press.

Slotsky, Alice. 1997. *The Bourse of Babylon: Market Quotations in the Astronomical Diaries of Babylonia.* Bethesda, Md.: CDL Press.

Smelser, Neil J. 1963. *The Sociology of Economic Life.* Englewood Cliffs, N.J.: Prentice-Hall.

Snodgrass, Anthony. 1991. "Archaeology and the Study

of the Greek City." Pp. 1–24 in *City and Country in the Ancient World,* ed. John Rich and Andrew Wallace-Hadrill. London: Routledge.

Steckel, Richard H., and Jerome C. Rose, eds. 2002. *The Backbone of History.* Cambridge: Cambridge University Press.

Stokes, Gale. 2001. "The Fates of Human Societies." *American Historical Review* 106:508–25.

Stolper, Matthew W. 1985. *Entrepeneurs and Empire: The Murašû Archive, the Murašû Firm, and Persian Rule in Babylonia.* Leiden: Nederlands Historisch-Archaeologisch Instituut te Istanbul.

Swedberg, Richard. 1994. "Markets as Social Structures." Pp. 255–82 in *The Handbook of Economic Sociology,* ed. Neil J. Smelser and Richard Swedberg. New York: Russell Sage Foundation; Princeton: Princeton University Press.

Temin, Peter. 2001. "A Market Economy in the Early Roman Empire." *Journal of Roman Studies* 91: 169–81.

———. 2002. "Price Behavior in Ancient Babylon." *Explorations in Economic History* 39:46–60.

Trigger, Bruce. 1998. *Sociocultural Evolution.* Oxford: Blackwell.

van de Mieroop, Mare. 1997. *The Ancient Mesopotamian City.* Oxford: Clarendon Press.

von Reden, Sitta. 1997. "Money, Law, and Exchange: Coinage in the Greek Polis." *Journal of Hellenic Studies* 107:154–76.

Warburton, David A. 1997. *State and Economy in Ancient Egypt: Fiscal Vocabulary of the New Kingdom.* Fribourg: University Press.

Weber, Max. [1921] 1958. *The City.* Ed. and trans. Don Martindale and Gertrud Neuwirth. Glencoe, Ill: The Free Press.

———. [1891] 1962. *Die römische Agrargeschichte in ihrer Bedeutung für das Staats- und Privatrecht.* Amsterdam: P. Schippers.

———. [1922] 1968. *Economy and Society.* Ed. Guenther Roth and Claus Wittich. Trans. Ephraim Fischoff et al. 2 vols. Berkeley and Los Angeles: University of California Press.

———. [1909] 1976. *The Agrarian Sociology of Ancient Civilizations.* Trans. R. I. Frank London: NLB.

White, K. D. 1984. *Greek and Roman Technology.* Ithaca, N.Y.: Cornell University Press.

White, Lynn. 1962. *Medieval Technology and Social Change.* Oxford: Clarendon Press.

Whitelaw, Todd. 2001. "From Sites to Communities: Defining the Human Dimensions of Minoan Urbanism." Pp. 15–37 in *Urbanism in the Aegean Bronze Age,* ed. Keith Branigan. Sheffield: Sheffield Academic Press.

Whitley, James. 2001. *The Archaeology of Ancient Greece.* Cambridge: Cambridge University Press.

Whittaker, C. R. 1993. *Frontiers of the Roman Empire: A Social and Economic Study.* Baltimore: Johns Hopkins University Press.

Wikander, Örjan. 1984. *Exploitation of Water-Power or Technological Stagnation? A Reappraisal of the Productive Forces in the Roman Empire*. Lund: CWK Gleerup.

Wilson, Andrew. 2000. "The Water-Mills on the Janiculum." *Memoirs of the American Academy in Rome* 45:185–223.

———. 2002. "Machines, Power, and the Ancient Economy." *Journal of Roman Studies* 92:1–32.

Wittfogel, Karl. 1957. *Oriental Despotism: A Study of Total Power*. New Haven: Yale University Press.

Woolf, Greg. 1998. *Becoming Roman: The Origins of Provincial Civilization in Gaul*. Cambridge: Cambridge University Press.

Wong, Roy. B. 1998. *China Transformed: Historical Change and the Limits of European Experience*. Ithaca, N.Y.: Cornell University Press.

———. 2001. "Entre monde et nation: Les régions braudéliennes en Asie." *Annales Histoire Sciences Sociales* 56:5–41.

Wrigley, E. A. 1988. *Continuity, Chance, and Change*. Cambridge: Cambridge University Press.

Zaccagnini, Carlo. 1989. "Asiatic Mode of Production and Ancient Near East: Notes towards a discussion." Pp. 1–126 in *Production and Consumption in the Ancient Near East*, ed. Carlo Zaccagnini. Budapest: University of Budapest.

Zangger, Eberhard, Michael Timpson, Sergei Yazvenko, Falco Kuhnke, and Jost Knauss. 1997. "The Pylos Regional Archaeological Project, Part II: Landscape Evolution and Site Preservation." *Hesperia* 66:549–641.

8   The Global Economy: Organization, Governance, and Development

Gary Gereffi

THE GLOBAL ECONOMY has changed in very significant ways during the past several decades, and these changes are rooted in how the global economy is organized and governed. These transformations affect not only the flows of goods and services across national borders, but also the implications of these processes for how countries move up (or down) in the international system. The development strategies of countries today are affected to an unprecedented degree by how industries are organized, and this is reflected in a shift in theoretical frameworks from those centered around the legacies and actors of nation-states to a greater concern with supranational institutions and transnational organizations. Policymakers, managers, workers, social activists, and many other stakeholders in developed as well as developing nations need a firm understanding of how the contemporary global economy works if they hope to improve their position in it, or forestall an impending decline.

The topic of the global economy is inherently interdisciplinary. No single academic field can encompass it, nor can any afford to ignore it. Because of its vast scope, those pundits who focus on the global economy are likely to be classified as academic interlopers; they run the risk of being too simplistic if they advance forceful hypotheses and too eclectic if they try to capture the full complexity of their topic. Scholars in this field thus have to master what economist Albert Hirschman has popularized as "the art of trespassing" (Hirschman 1981; Foxley, McPherson, and O'Donnell 1986).

The global economy can be studied at different levels of analysis. At the *macro* level are international organizations and regimes that establish rules and norms for the global community. These include institutions like the World Bank, the International Monetary Fund, the World Trade Organization, and the International Labor Organization, as well as regional integration schemes like the Eu-

ropean Union and the North American Free Trade Agreement. These regimes combine both rules and resources, and hence they establish the broadest parameters within which the global economy operates.

At the *meso* level, the key building blocks for the global economy are countries and firms. Those scholars who take countries as their main analytical unit (as in the varieties-of-capitalism literature) provide an *institutional* perspective on the main, enduring features of national economies. The global economy is seen as the arena in which countries compete in different product markets. An alternative approach is to focus on firms and interfirm networks as the central units of analysis, and analyze these actors in a global industry or sectoral framework (as in the global commodity chains or industrial districts approaches). These scholars typically take a more *organizational* approach. In both the institutional and the organizational perspectives on the global economy, we tend to get a top-down focus on leading countries and firms as drivers of change.

Institutionalists like those in the varieties-of-capitalism school tend to focus on developed or industrialized countries. Alternatively, one can take a development-oriented perspective with regard to countries, and ask how the economic prospects of developing nations are shaped by their position in the global economy. These questions help to bridge the concerns of economic sociologists and development specialists because the theories of industrial upgrading that have emerged in the last couple of decades have been shaped very closely by several of the organizational and institutional theories mentioned above.

At a *micro* level, there is a growing literature on the resistance to globalization by consumer groups, activists, and transnational social movements (such as those dealing with labor issues and environmental abuses). This research is relevant to a chapter titled "The Global Economy" because the very same perspectives used to understand how the global economy is organized are being employed by social and environmental activists to challenge the existing order.

Many theories related to economic sociology incorporate the global economy in their frameworks, but they differ in the degree to which it is conceptualized as a system that shapes the behavior and motivation of actors inside it, or as an arena where nationally determined actors meet, interact, and influence each other (Therborn 2000). This chapter identifies how the global economy has been constructed analytically by a wide range of social scientists. The first task is to define what is really "new" about the global economy in the last half of the twentieth century, which is the main temporal focus of this chapter. The increasingly seamless web of international production and trade networks that girdle the globe appears to be a distinctive feature of the last several decades, and it requires a new kind of organizational perspective that has been growing rapidly. The second section of this chapter takes a closer look at how and why production and trade have been reorganized in the global economy in the contemporary era. Research by a diverse group of scholars from economics, business schools, sociology, and economic geography, among other fields, has contributed to a reconceptualization of the key actors that make up the global economy, and to a realization that the integration of trade and the disintegration of production on a global scale are fundamentally altering our ideas about what connects national economies, firms, places, and people. The third section reviews selected institutional and organization perspectives on the global economy. We will highlight the competing and complementary claims of various approaches, such as the varieties-of-capitalism literature, national business systems, and global commodity chains.

The last two sections of the chapter offer "bottom up" perspectives on the global economy to complement the "top down" views on the reorganization of global industries. The fourth section takes a country perspective, and asks how a focus on global production networks allows us to understand the process of industrial upgrading, whereby economic actors try to move to higher-value activities in the global economy. The fifth and concluding section of the chapter examines several of the emerging challenges and dilemmas for governance and development in the contemporary global economy.

HOW NEW IS THE GLOBAL ECONOMY?

Much of the globalization debate has been fueled by different conceptions of what is happening "out there" in the global economy, and whether it really represents something new. We need to distinguish the process of *internationalization*, which involves the mere extension or geographic spread of economic activities across national boundaries, from *globalization*, which is qualitatively distinct because it involves the functional integration of internationally dispersed activities (Dicken 2003, 12). How functional integration occurs is a topic that we will deal with in more detail below in terms of the governance structures in the global economy. However, one of the key actors that distinguishes the global economy of the latter half of the twentieth century from its predecessors is the transnational corporation (TNC), which we will discuss in this section.[1]

The origins of a global economy can be traced back to the expansion of long-distance trade during the period of 1450–1640, which Wallerstein (1979) has labeled the "long sixteenth century." From the fifteenth century onward, a number of chartered trading companies emerged in Europe, such as the East India Company and the Hudson's Bay Company, which created vast international trading empires. Although their activities were worldwide in scope, their main purpose was trade and exchange, rather than production. The development of a world trading system over a period of several centuries helped to create the tripartite structure of core, semiperipheral, and peripheral economic areas. According to world-systems theory, the upward or downward mobility of nations in the core, semiperiphery, and periphery is determined by a country's mode of incorporation in the capitalist world-economy, and these shifts can only be accurately portrayed by an in-depth analysis of the cycles of capitalist accumulation in the *longue durée* of history (Wallerstein 1974, 1980, 1989; Arrighi 1994).

The dynamics of the capitalist world-system laid the foundation for a process of industrialization and new international divisions of labor on a global scale. Originally, as defined by the eighteenth-century political economist Adam Smith ([1776] 1976), the "division of labor" referred simply to the specialization of workers in different parts of the production process, usually in a factory setting. Quite early in the evolution of industrial economies, the division of labor also acquired a geographical dimension. Different areas began to specialize in particular types of economic activity. At the global scale, the "classic" international division of labor was between the industrial countries producing manufactured goods, and the nonindustrialized economies that supplied raw materials and agricultural products to the industrial nations and that became a market for basic manufactures. This relatively simple pattern no longer applies. During the decades following the Second World War, trade flows have become far more complex, and so have the relationships between the developed and developing nations of the global economy.

The foundations of the contemporary economic order were established in the late 1940s by the system of financial and trade institutions that were set up at an international conference in Bretton Woods, New Hampshire, in 1944. The principal institutions that constitute the Bretton Woods system are the International Monetary Fund (IMF), the International Bank for Reconstruction and Development (later renamed the World Bank), and the General Agreement on Tariffs and Trade (GATT) (see Held et al. 1999, chaps. 3 and 4). Unlike the classical gold standard system, which collapsed during the First World War, the Bretton Woods financial system required that every currency had a fixed exchange rate vis-à-vis the U.S. dollar, with the dollar's value pegged to gold at $35 an ounce. In practice, Bretton Woods became a dollar system because the United States was the leading economy and the only major creditor nation in the first 25 years following the Second World War. While the rise of the Eurocurrency market in the 1960s placed increasing strain on the Bretton Woods financial order, its actual demise came on August 15, 1971, when President Nixon announced that the U.S. dollar was no longer freely convertible into gold, effectively signaling the end of fixed exchange rates.

Notwithstanding these changes, the legacy of the Bretton Woods system remained powerful throughout the latter decades of the twentieth century. The IMF has policed the rules of the international financial order, and intervened in national economies (especially in developing countries) to impose stabilization programs when balance-of-payments crises were deemed structural rather than cyclical. Following the postwar reconstruction of Europe and Japan, the World Bank increasingly became a development agency for third world nations (Ayres 1983). Its policy recommendations were closely tied to those of the IMF, especially after the neoliberal agenda (dubbed the

Washington Consensus) became established in the 1980s (Gore 2000). GATT, a multilateral forum for trade negotiations, became the primary international trade agency by default when the International Trade Organization, provided by the 1947 Havana Charter, was abandoned by President Truman after it was staunchly opposed in the U.S. Congress. In 1995, the GATT was superseded by the much more powerful World Trade Organization (WTO), which sought to reduce or eliminate a whole range of nontariff barriers and uneven trading conditions between countries.

Distinctive Features of the Contemporary Global Economy, 1960s to the Present

There is considerable controversy over how to characterize the distinctive aspects of the global economy in the postwar period. Wallerstein (2000, 250) argues that the period from 1945 to the present corresponds to a typical Kondratieff cycle of the capitalist world-economy, which has an upward and a downward swing: an A-phase of economic expansion from 1945 to 1967–73, and a B-phase of economic contraction from 1967–73 to the present day. While the evolution of the capitalist world-economy stretches from 1450 to the contemporary era, in world-systems theory it is marked by periods of genesis, normal development, and the current phase of "terminal crisis" (Wallerstein 2000, 2002).

From a trade perspective, the level of economic integration in the latter half of the twentieth century is not historically unprecedented. The decades leading up to 1913 were considered a golden age of international trade and investment. This was ended by the First World War and the Great Depression, when most of the world's economies turned inward. Merchandise trade (imports and exports) as a share of world output did not recover its 1913 level until sometime in the mid-1970s (Krugman 1995, 330–31).[2] If we take 1960 as the baseline, interconnectedness through trade has vastly increased in recent decades, and furthermore trade has grown consistently faster than output at the world level. Among the OECD[3] nations (the 24 richest industrial economies), the ratio of exports to gross domestic product (GDP) roughly doubled from 1960 to 1990, rising from 9.5 percent to 20.5 percent in this period, and world merchandise trade grew at an average of one and a half times the rate of growth of world GDP from 1965 to 1990 (Wade 1996, 62).

International trade, investment, and finance

have become the hallmarks of economic globalization. Global interconnectedness through foreign direct investment grew even faster than trade during the 1980s, and the most dynamic multinationalization of all has come in finance and in technology. Flows of foreign direct investment grew three times faster than trade flows and almost four times faster than output between 1983 and 1990 (Wade 1996, 63), and according to one estimate, TNCs control one-third of the world's private sector productive assets (UNCTAD 1993, 1). Globalization appears to have gone furthest in the area of finance. The stock of international bank lending (cross-border lending plus domestic lending, denominated in foreign currency) rose from 4 percent of the GDP of OECD countries in 1980 to an astonishing 44 percent in 1990, and foreign exchange (or currency) trading was 30 times greater than and quite independent of trade flows in the early 1990s (Wade 1996, 64). Global financial flows accelerated in considerable measure because of the growing popularity in the 1980s and 1990s of new financial instruments, such as international bonds, international equities, derivatives trading (futures, options, and swaps), and international money markets (Held et al. 1999, 205–9).

This quantitative assessment of the growth in international trade, investment, and financial flows is one side of the story, but it is challenged by the notion that the nature of global economic integration in the recent era is qualitatively different than in the past. Before 1913, the world economy was characterized by *shallow integration* manifested largely through *trade* in goods and services between independent firms and through international movements of portfolio capital. Today, we live in a world in which *deep integration*, organized primarily by TNCs, is pervasive and involves the *production* of goods and services in cross-border value-adding activities that redefine the kind of production processes contained within national boundaries (UNCTAD 1993, 113). There is little consensus, however, over what kind of framework to use in analyzing the contemporary global economy because of the breadth and rapidity of change, and the fact that countries, firms, workers, and many other stakeholders in the global economy are affected by these shifts.

A global manufacturing system has emerged in which production and export capabilities are dispersed to an unprecedented number of developing as well as industrialized countries. Fröbel, Heinrichs, and Kreye (1980) likened the surge of manufactured exports from labor-intensive export platforms in low-wage economies to a "new international division of labor" that used advanced transport and communication technologies to promote the global segmentation of the production process. The OECD coined the term *newly industrializing countries* and reflected the concern of advanced capitalist nations that the expanding share of these emergent industrializers in the production and export of manufactured goods was a threat to slumping Western industrial economies (OECD 1979). World-systems theorists argued that the gap between core and periphery in the world economy had been narrowing since the 1950s, and by 1980 the semiperiphery not only caught up with but also overtook the core countries in their degree of industrialization (Arrighi and Drangel 1986, 54–55; Arrighi, Silver, and Brewer 2003).

In retrospect, the assembly-oriented export production in the newly industrializing countries was merely an early stage in the transformation of the global economy into "a highly complex, kaleidoscopic structure involving the *fragmentation* of many production processes, and their *geographical relocation* on a global scale in ways which slice through national boundaries" (Dicken 2003, 9). Expanded niches for labor-intensive segments have been created by splitting the production of goods traditionally viewed as skill-, capital-, or technology-intensive and putting the labor-intensive pieces of the value chain in low-wage locations.

In Mexico, for example, the booming export-oriented maquiladora program[4] has engaged in more sophisticated kinds of manufacturing operations over time. First-generation maquiladoras were labor-intensive with limited technology, and they assembled export products in industries like apparel using imported inputs provided by U.S. clients (Sklair 1993). In the late 1980s and early 1990s, researchers began to call attention to so-called second- and third-generation maquiladoras. Second-generation plants are oriented less toward assembly and more toward manufacturing processes that use automated and semiautomated machines and robots in the automobile, television, and electrical appliance sectors. Third-generation maquiladoras are oriented to research, design, and development, and rely on highly skilled labor such as specialized engineers and technicians. In each of these industries, the maquiladoras have matured from assembly sites based on cheap labor to manufacturing centers whose competitiveness derives from a combination of high productivity, good quality, and wages far below those prevailing north of the border (Shaiken and Herzenberg 1987;

Carrillo and Hualde 1998; Bair and Gereffi 2001; Cañas and Coronado 2002).

A cover story in the February 3, 2003, issue of *Business Week* highlighted the impact of global outsourcing over the past several decades on the quality and quantity of jobs in both developed and developing countries (Engardio, Bernstein, and Kripalani 2003). The first wave of outsourcing began in the 1960s and 1970s with the exodus to developing countries of jobs making shoes, clothes, cheap electronics, and toys. After that, simple service work, like processing credit-card receipts and airline reservations in back-office call centers, and writing basic software code, went global. Today, driven by digitization, the Internet, and high-speed data networks that circle the world, all kinds of "knowledge work" that can be done almost anywhere are being outsourced. Global outsourcing reveals many of the key features of contemporary globalization: it deals with international competitiveness in a way that inherently links developed and developing countries; a huge part of the debate centers around jobs, wages, and skills in different parts of the world; and there is a focus on value creation in different parts of the value chain. There are enormous political as well as economic stakes in how global outsourcing evolves in the coming years, particularly in well-endowed and strategically positioned economies like India, China, the Philippines, Mexico, Costa Rica, Russia, parts of eastern Europe, and South Africa—that is, countries loaded with college grads who speak Western languages and can handle outsourced information-technology work. India seems particularly well positioned in this area.

However, these shifts reveal a sobering globalization paradox: the dramatic expansion of production capabilities reflected in global outsourcing across a wide range of industries does not necessarily increase levels of development or reduce poverty in the exporting nations. As more and more countries have acquired the ability to make complex as well as standard manufactured goods, barriers to entry have fallen and competitive processes at the production stage of value chains have increased. This has resulted in a pattern that Kaplinsky (2000, 120), following Bhagwati's (1958) original use of the term, has dubbed "immiserizing growth," in which economic activity increases in terms of output and employment, but economic returns fall. The emergence of China and, to a lesser extent, India has expanded the global labor force so significantly that the likely consequence of globalization is to bid down living standards not only for unskilled work and primary products, but increasingly for skilled work and industrial products as well (Kaplinsky 2001, 56). The only way to counteract this process is to search for new sources of dynamic economic rents (i.e., profitability in excess of the competitive norm), which are increasingly found in the intangible parts of the value chain where high-value, knowledge-intensive activities like innovation, design, and marketing prevail (Kaplinsky 2000).

These trends raise fundamental questions about winners and losers in the global economy, and also about the forces and frameworks needed to understand why these changes are occurring, and what their impact is likely to be. In the next section of this chapter, we will review how and why new patterns of international production and trade are emerging. In the subsequent section, we will examine some of the major theoretical perspectives in economic sociology and related fields that seek to account for these institutional and organization features of the global economy.

THE REORGANIZATION OF PRODUCTION AND TRADE IN THE GLOBAL ECONOMY

The Role of Transnational Corporations

While the postwar international economic order was defined and legitimized by the United States and the other core powers that supported it in terms of the ideology of free trade, it was the way in which TNCs linked the production of goods and services in cross-border, value-adding networks that made the global economy in the last half of the twentieth century qualitatively distinct from what preceded it. Transnational corporations have become the primary movers and shakers of the global economy because they have the power to coordinate and control supply chain operations in more than one country, even if they do not own them (Dicken 2003, 198). Although they first emerged in the late nineteenth and early twentieth centuries in the natural resource (oil, mineral, and agricultural) sectors, TNCs did not play a central role in shaping a new global economic system until after the Second World War.

To the neoclassical economists of the 1950s, the postwar world economy was constituted by international capital flows, which were viewed at the country level as foreign direct investment (FDI). The United States was the main source of outward FDI, and the first empirical studies of U.S. FDI at the country level were carried out by Dunning (1958) on the United Kingdom and Safarian (1966) on Canada. Both of these studies were interested in the public policy question of the benefits that U.S. FDI had for a host economy (Rugman 1999), and thus they did not really think about transnational corporations as an institutional actor. The Multinational Enterprise Project at Harvard Business School, which began in 1965 under the direction of Raymond Vernon and lasted for 12 years, tried to remedy the economists' relative neglect of the TNCs. Despite being out of step with its academic brethren in economics departments and business schools, who were using general equilibrium models and rational choice to study the properties of efficient markets, the Harvard Multinational Enterprise Project was distinguished by its emphasis on the strategies and activities of TNCs at the micro level of the firm, rather than as merely one more form of international capital movement (Vernon 1999).

In the 1960s and 1970s, the key players in most international industries were large, vertically integrated TNCs, whose use and abuse of power in the global economy were chronicled by numerous authors (e.g., Sampson 1973; Barnet and Müller 1974). The overseas activities of these firms were primarily oriented toward three main objectives: the search for raw materials; finding new markets for their products; and tapping offshore sources of abundant and relatively low-cost labor (Vernon 1971).[5] In developing countries, which were attractive to TNCs for all three of these reasons, the predominant model of growth since the 1950s was import-substituting industrialization. This development strategy used the tools of industrial policy, such as local-content requirements, joint ventures, and export-promotion schemes, to induce foreign firms that had established local subsidiaries inside their borders to transfer the capital, technology, and managerial experience needed to set up a host of new industries. In return, TNCs could make and sell their products in the relatively protected domestic markets of Latin America, Asia, and Africa, and even in the socialist bloc connected with the former Soviet Union (see Bergsten, Horst, and Moran 1978; Newfarmer 1985).

By the mid-1980s, several significant shifts were transforming the organization of the global economy. First, the oil shock of the late 1970s and the severe debt crisis that followed it were the death knell for import-substituting industrialization in many developing countries, especially in Latin America. The import-substitution approach had found no way to generate the foreign exchange needed to pay for increasingly costly imports, and escalating debt service payments led to a net outflow of foreign capital that crippled economic growth.[6] Second, the "East Asian miracle," based on the rapid economic advance of Japan and the so-called East Asian tigers (South Korea, Hong Kong, Taiwan, and Singapore) since the 1960s, highlighted a contrasting development model: export-oriented industrialization. Buttressed by the neoliberal thrust of the Reagan and Thatcher governments in the United States and the United Kingdom, respectively, export-oriented development soon became the prevailing orthodoxy for developing economies around the world.[7] Third, the transition from import-substituting to export-oriented development strategies during the 1980s in many industrializing countries was complemented by an equally profound reorientation in the strategies of TNCs. The rapid expansion of industrial capabilities and export propensities in a diverse array of newly industrializing economies in Asia and Latin America allowed TNCs to accelerate their own efforts to outsource relatively standardized activities to lower-cost production locations worldwide.

One of the central questions that generated great interest in TNCs was this: To what extent have TNCs supplanted national governments, and in what areas? The attitude of many researchers was that TNCs had the power, the resources, and the global reach to thwart the territorially based objectives of national governments in both developed and developing countries (see Bergsten, Horst, and Moran 1978; Barnet and Müller 1974). This was a key tenet of dependency theory, one of the most popular approaches in the 1970s, which argued that TNCs undercut the ability of nation-states to build domestic industries controlled by locally owned firms (Sunkel 1973; Evans 1979; Gereffi 1983). Even the most balanced scholarly approaches reflected the challenge to national autonomy captured by the title of Raymond Vernon's best-known book, *Sovereignty at Bay* (1971). The large size of TNCs, whether measured in sales or by more sophisticated calculations of value added, still leads to the conclusion that many TNCs are bigger than countries.[8] However, the concentrated power of vertically integrated, industrial TNCs has been diminishing for the past couple of decades as a result of the tendency toward both the geographic and the organizational outsourcing of production. Thus, the original concern with how TNCs affect the sovereignty and effectiveness of national governments needs to be reframed in light of the current shift to a more network-centered global economy, which will be discussed below.

The Emergence of International Trade and Production Networks

The growth of world trade has probably received the most attention in the globalization literature because of its direct relevance to employment, wages, and the rising number of free trade agreements around the world. The most common causes usually given to explain expanding world trade are technological (improvements in transportation and communication technologies) and political (e.g., the removal of protectionist barriers, such as tariffs, import quotas, and exchange controls, which had restricted world markets from 1913 until the end of the Second World War).[9] It is also important to acknowledge that the volume of international trade depends to a considerable degree on how boundaries are drawn, both for different geographies of production[10] and according to whether trade covers final products only or whether it also includes intermediate inputs. However, even though the share of trade in world output surpassed its 1913 peak in the 1980s and 1990s, the sheer volume of trade is probably not sufficient to argue for a qualitative break with the past.

Of far greater significance are several novel features in the *nature* of international trade that do not have counterparts in previous eras. These suggest the need for a new framework to understand both patterns of competition among international firms and the development prospects of countries that are trying to upgrade their position in diverse global industries. The three new aspects of modern world trade relevant here are (1) the rise of intraindustry and intraproduct trade in intermediate inputs; (2) the ability of producers to "slice up the value chain," in Krugman's (1995) phrase, by breaking a production process into many geographically separated steps; and (3) the emergence of a global production networks framework that highlights how these shifts have altered governance structures and the distribution of gains in the global economy.

Intraindustry Trade in Parts and Components

Arndt and Kierzkowski (2001) use the term *fragmentation* to describe the international division of labor that allows producers located in different countries and often with different ownership structures to form cross-border production networks for parts and components. Specialized "production blocks" are coordinated through service links, which include activities such as transportation, insurance, telecommunications, quality control, and management specifications. Yeats (2001), analyzing detailed trade data for the machinery and transport equipment group (SITC 7),[11] finds that trade in components made up 30 percent of total OECD exports in SITC 7 in 1995, and that trade in these goods was growing at a faster pace than the overall SITC 7 total. Similarly, Hummels, Rapaport, and Yi (1998, 80–81) argue that the "vertical specialization" of global trade, which occurs when a country uses imported intermediate parts to produce goods it later exports, accounted for about 14.5 percent of all trade among OECD countries in the early 1990s. Vertical specialization captures the idea that countries link sequentially in production networks to produce a final good, although vertical trade itself does not require the vertical integration of firms.

Feenstra (1998) takes this idea one step further, and explicitly connects the "integration of trade" with the "disintegration of production" in the global economy.[12] The rising integration of world markets through trade has brought with it a disintegration of the production process of multinational firms,[13] since companies are finding it profitable to outsource (domestically or abroad) an increasing share of their noncore manufacturing and service activities. This represents a breakdown of the vertically integrated mode of production—the so-called Fordist model, originally exemplified by the automobile industry—on which U.S. industrial prowess had been built for much of the twentieth century (Aglietta 1980). The success of the Japanese model of "lean production" in the global economy since the 1980s, pioneered by Toyota in automobiles, reinforces the central importance of coordinating exceptionally complex interfirm trading networks of parts and components as a new source of competitive advantage in the global economy (Womack, Jones, and Roos 1990; Sturgeon and Florida 2000).

Slicing Up the Value Chain

The notion of a value-added chain has been a useful tool for international business scholars who have focused on the strategies of both firms and countries in the global economy. Bruce Kogut (1984, 151), a professor at the Wharton School of Business, University of Pennsylvania, was one of the first to argue that value chains are a key element in the new framework of competitive analysis that is needed because of the globalization of world markets: "The formulation of strategy can be fruitfully viewed as placing bets on certain markets and on certain links of the value-added chain. . . . The challenge of global strategy formulation is to differentiate between the various kinds of economies, to specify which link and which factor captures the firm's advantage, and to determine where the value-added chain would be broken across borders." In a subsequent paper, Kogut (1985) elaborates the central role of the value-added chain[14] in the design of international business strategies, which are based upon the interplay between the comparative advantage of countries and the competitive advantage of firms. While the logic of comparative advantage helps to determine *where* the value-added chain should be broken across national borders, competitive (or firm-specific) advantage influences the decision on *what* activities and technologies along the value-added chain a firm should concentrate its resources in.[15]

Michael Porter of Harvard Business School also developed a value-chain framework that he applied both at the level of individual firms (Porter 1985) and as one of the bases for determining the competitive advantage of nations (Porter 1990). At the firm level, a value chain refers to a collection of discrete activities performed to do business, such as the physical creation of a product or service, its delivery and marketing to the buyer, and its support after sale.[16] On the basis of these discrete activities, firms can establish two main types of competitive advantage: low relative cost (a firm's ability to carry out the activities in its value chain at lower cost than its competitors); or differentiation (performing in a unique way relative to competitors). While competitive advantage is determined at the level of a firm's value chain, Porter argues, "The appropriate unit of analysis in setting international strategy is the industry because the industry is the arena in which competitive advantage is won or lost" (1987, 29).

The pattern of competition differs markedly across industries: at one extreme are "multidomestic" industries, in which competition in each country is basically independent of competition in other countries; and at the other end of the spectrum are "global industries," in which a firm's competitive position in one country is significantly impacted by its position in other countries. Since international competition is becoming the norm, Porter believes that firms must adopt "global strategies" in order

to decide how to spread the activities in the value chain among countries.[17] A very different set of scholars, studying the political economy of advanced industrial societies, highlighted the transformation from "organized capitalism" to "disorganized" or "competitive" capitalism. This approach is based on dramatic shifts in the strategic and institutional contexts of the global economy in the 1980s toward deregulated national markets and unhampered international exchanges (Offe 1985; Lash and Urry 1987). According to Schmitter (1990, 12), sectors or industries are the key unit for comparative analysis in this setting because they represent a meso level where a number of changes in technology, market structure, and public policy converge.

Our review of the contemporary global economy thus far has highlighted two distinctive shifts: the unparalleled fragmentation and reintegration of global production and trade patterns since the 1970s; and the recognition by Kogut and Porter, among others,[18] of the power of value-chain or industry analysis as a basis for formulating global strategies that can integrate comparative (location-specific) advantage and competitive (firm-specific) advantage. However, the third transformation in the global economy that needs to be addressed as a precursor to the global value chain perspective is the remarkable growth of manufactured exports from low-wage to high-wage nations in the past several decades. This phenomenon has produced a range of reactions—from anxiety by producers in developed countries who believe they cannot compete with the flood of low-cost imports, to hope among economies in the South that they can catch up with their neighbors in the North by moving up the ladder of skill-intensive activities, to despair that global inequality and absolute levels of poverty have remained resistant to change despite the rapid progress of a relative handful of developing nations.

Production Networks in the Global Economy

In the 1990s, a new framework, called global commodity chains (GCC), tied the concept of the value-added chain directly to the global organization of industries (see Gereffi and Korzeniewicz 1994. Gereffi 1999, 2001). This work was based on an insight into the growing importance of global buyers (mainly retailers and brand companies, or "manufacturers without factories") as key drivers in the formation of globally dispersed production and distribution networks. Gereffi (1994a) contrasted these buyer-driven chains to what he termed producer-driven chains. The latter are the production systems created by vertically integrated transnational manufacturers, while the former term recognizes the role of global buyers, highlighting the significance of design and marketing in initiating the activities of global production systems.[19] The GCC approach drew attention to the variety of actors that could exercise power within global production and distribution systems. It was the field-based methodology of GCC research, in particular, that provided new insights into the statistics showing an increase in trade involving components and other intermediate inputs. The trade data alone mask important organizational shifts because they differentiate neither between intrafirm and interfirm trade nor between the various ways in which global outsourcing relationships were being constructed.

A variety of overlapping terms has been used to describe the complex network relationships that make up the global economy. Each of the contending concepts, however, has particular emphases that are important to recognize for a chain analysis of the global economy:

Supply chains. A generic label for an input-output structure of value-adding activities, beginning with raw materials and ending with a finished product

International production networks. A focus on the international production networks in which TNCs act as "global network flagships" (Borrus, Ernst, and Haggard 2000)

Global commodity chains. An emphasis on the internal governance structure of supply chains (especially the producer-driven vs. buyer-driven distinction) and on the role of diverse lead firms in setting up global production and sourcing networks (Gereffi and Korzeniewicz 1994)

French "filière" approach. A loosely knit set of studies that used the *filière* (i.e., channel or network) of activities as a method to study primarily agricultural export commodities such as rubber, cotton, coffee, and cocoa (Raikes, Jensen, and Ponte 2000)

Global value chains. Emphasis on the relative value of those economic activities that are required to bring a good or service from conception, through the different phases of production (involving a combination of physical transformation and the input of various producer services), delivery to final consumers, and final disposal after use (Kaplinsky 2000; Gereffi and Kaplinsky 2001)

The "value chain" concept has recently gained popularity as an overarching label for this body of research because it focuses on value creation and value capture across the full range of possible chain activities and end products (goods and services), and because it avoids the limiting connotations of the word *commodity*, which to some implies the production of undifferentiated goods with low barriers to entry. Like the GCC framework, global value chain (GVC) analysis accepts many of the observations made previously on geographical fragmentation, and it focuses primarily on the issues of industry (re)organization, coordination, governance, and power in the chain (Humphrey and Schmitz 2001). Its concern is to understand the nature and consequences of organizational fragmentation in global industries. The GVC approach offers the possibility of understanding how firms are linked in the global economy, but also acknowledges the broader institutional context of these linkages, including trade policy, regulation, and standards.[20] More generally, the global production networks paradigm has been used to join scholarly research on globalization with the concerns of both policymakers and social activists, who are trying to harness the potential gains of globalization to the pragmatic concerns of specific countries and social constituencies that feel increasingly marginalized in the international economic arena.[21]

The next section of this chapter looks at different perspectives on governance at the meso level of the global economy, and it will be followed by a discussion of industrial upgrading, which analyzes the trajectories by which countries seek to upgrade their positions in the global economy.

GOVERNANCE IN THE GLOBAL ECONOMY: INSTITUTIONAL AND ORGANIZATIONAL PERSPECTIVES

Scholars who study the global economy at the meso level form distinct camps in terms of their units of analysis, theoretical orientations, and methodological preferences. The two main units of analysis at the meso level are countries and firms. In the 1970s and 1980s, political economy perspectives dealing with nations and TNCs in the global economy tended to predominate, fueled by dependency theory (Cardoso and Faletto [1969] 1979; Evans 1979), world-systems theory (Wallerstein 1974, 1980, 1989), and statist approaches (Amsden 1989; Wade 1990; Evans 1995), among others. During the last decade, however, research on the global economy has shifted toward institutional and organizational theories. The choice of countries or firms as empirical units has a striking affinity with the researcher's primary theoretical

TABLE 1. Comparison of Varieties of Capitalism and Global Production Networks

Dimension	Varieties of Capitalism	Global Production Networks
Theoretical orientation	Institutional analysis	Organizational analysis
Unit of analysis	Countries	Interfirm networks
Empirical focus	Advanced industrial economies/ capitalist democracies	Linkages between developed and developing countries
Methodological preference	Rational actor; multivariate analysis	Comparative/historical analysis across industries, firms, and countries
Research style	Quantitative, cross-national; country case studies	International, industry-based field research; political economy interpretations
Ideal types	Liberal and coordinated market economies	Producer-driven and buyer-driven commodity chains
Main challenges/ collective action problems	Coordination problems in developed countries	Industrial upgrading in developing countries
Key concepts	Institutional complementarities	Lead firms; economic rents; learning through networks

orientation: those who study countries tend to adopt institutional perspectives, while those who work with firms favor organizational frameworks.[22]

This paradigm divide at the meso level of the global economy is revealed by looking at two broad literatures, which we label "varieties of capitalism" and "global production networks." The former is closely associated with institutional analysis, and the latter with diverse organizational perspectives. Both approaches tend to focus on governance structures in the global economy, but the scope and content of what is being governed differ greatly. The varieties-of-capitalism literature looks primarily at coordination problems and institutional complementarities in advanced industrial economies, where the nation-state is the explicit unit of analysis. This research is comparative, but not transnational, in orientation. By contrast, the research on global production networks highlights the linkages between developed and developing countries created by TNCs and interfirm networks. Governance in this context is typically exercised by lead firms in global industries, and one of the key challenges addressed is industrial upgrading—that is, how developing countries try to improve their position in the global economy, which is characterized both by power asymmetries and by opportunities for learning through networks. International and industry-based field research is a requisite in the study of global production networks because publicly available and detailed information at the level of firms is gener-

ally lacking. The main dimensions of this comparison are outlined in table 1.

The institutionalist paradigm encompasses several related approaches that deal with the governance of modern capitalist economies, including regulation theory (Aglietta 1980; Boyer 1989), national systems of innovation (Lundvall 1992; Nelson 1993), social systems of production (Campbell, Hollingsworth, and Lindberg 1991; Hollingsworth, Schmitter, and Streeck 1994; Hollingsworth and Boyer 1997), and varieties of capitalism (Berger and Dore 1996; Kitschelt et al. 1999; Hall and Soskice 2001). All of the authors in this field focus on the "institutional foundations of comparative advantage" in the advanced capitalist democracies, with an emphasis on topics like business-government relations, labor markets and collective bargaining, the welfare state, the internationalization of capital, and innovation systems. A key unifying concept is institutional complementarity, which rests on "multilateral reinforcement mechanisms between institutional arrangements: each one, by its existence, permits or facilitates the existence of the others" (Amable 2000, 656). Complementary institutions and other forms of path dependency lead most scholars in the varieties-of-capitalism genre to argue vociferously against convergence, given their belief that unique and valued institutions will sustain national diversities despite the withering pressures of international competition in an increasingly open global economy. Actually, the paradigm does allow for a limited form of convergence in the sense that advanced market economies are organized into three broad types: liberal market economies, which adopt laissez-faire, probusiness policies (United States, United Kingdom, Canada, and Australia); and coordinated market economies, with their corporatist (strong state—Germany and Japan) and welfare state (strong trade unions—Scandinavian and northern European) variants. However, there is no serious effort to extend this paradigm to address the varieties of capitalism in the vast majority of countries that are in the developing world.[23]

The global production networks paradigm provides a very different perspective on the global economy because its organizational lens focuses on transnational linkages between developed and developing nations. The central questions deal with the kinds of governance structures that characterize global industries, how these governance arrangements change, and what consequences these shifts have for development opportunities in rich and poor countries alike. International institutionals, such as trade and intellectual property regimes, clearly shape inclusion and exclusion of countries and firms in global production networks, but this approach tends to focus on the strategies and behavior of the players (firms), while the rules of the game (regulatory institutions) are taken as an exogenous variable.

Notwithstanding the potential complementarities between institutional and organizational perspectives on the global economy, there has been virtually no dialogue between these two literatures. They do not cite one another's research or engage in collaborative projects, despite the fact that both are concerned with the international forces shaping countries and firms in the global economy.

There are several hybrid approaches that seek to bridge this gap between organizational and institutional frameworks. One of these is the business systems perspective, pioneered by Whitley (1992a, 1992b). As defined by Whitley (1996, 412), "Business systems are particular forms of economic organization that have become established and reproduced in certain institutional contexts—local, regional, national or international. They are distinctive ways of coordinating and controlling economic activities which developed interdependently with key institutions which constitute particular kinds of political, financial, labor and cultural systems. The more integrated and mutually reinforcing are such institutional systems over a particular territory or population, the more cohesive and distinctive will be its business system." While firms presumably are central to business systems, Whitley's framework shares the institutionalist paradigm's emphasis on institutional complementarities and cohesion, and national or culturally proximate regions. However, the business systems approach seems relatively ill equipped to deal with the question, How do U.S., European, or Asian business systems respond to globalization? While the business systems logic would lead us to expect that firms of the same nationality maintain their distinctive features in the face of international competition, findings from research on global production networks indicate that the competition among firms from different business systems in overseas markets tends to diminish the influence of national origins on firms' behavior (Gereffi 1996, 433).[24]

Sociologists have looked at a range of other actors in the global economy. "Business groups," defined as a collection of firms bound together in persistent formal or informal ways, are a pervasive phenomenon in Asia, Europe, Latin America, and elsewhere (Granovetter 1994; "Business Groups and Social Organization," this volume). Business groups may encompass kinship networks, but they are not delimited by family boundaries because the goals of families can conflict with the principles of profit maximization that characterize firms in these groups. Business groups play a role in the global economy through their impact on national market structures, and on product variety and product quality in international trade (Feenstra, Yang, and Hamilton 1999). Transnational business networks based on family or ethnic ties are another form of economic organization that shapes global production and trade (Hamilton, Zeile, and Kim 1989; Yeung 2000). Japanese *sogo shosha*, British trading companies, and Chinese and Indian merchants laid the social groundwork for the long-distance supply routes between Asian producers and their export markets (Gereffi 1999, 60–61). For Castells (1996), the universality of network society in the information age is a defining feature of the modern era. Others argue that the global system is now ruled by a transnational capitalist class, which is more interested in building hegemony than in domination and control (Sklair 2001; Carroll and Fennema 2002).

At a more micro level, phenomena within nation-states can also reflect globalization processes. Meyer (2000) defines modern actors on the global stage as entities with rights and interests that create and consult collective rules, that often enhance their legitimacy by adopting common forms, and that exercise agency through moral action. From Meyer's "world society" perspective, the modern world is stateless; it is based on shared rules and models, and made up of strong, culturally constituted actors. Sassen (2000) also detaches sovereignty from the national state. She emphasizes the role of global cities as strategic sites for the production of specialized functions to run and coordinate the global economy, and posits that financial and investment deregulation are driving the geographic location of strategic institutions related to globalization deep inside national territories.

INDUSTRIAL UPGRADING AND GLOBAL PRODUCTION NETWORKS

Major changes in global business organization during the last several decades of the twentieth century have had a significant impact on the upgrading possibilities of developing countries. This section will illustrate how the reorganization of international trade and production networks affects the capability of developing countries in different regions of the world to improve their positions in the value chains of diverse industries.

Industrial upgrading refers to the process by which economic actors—nations, firms, and workers—move from low-value to relatively high-value activities in global production networks. Different mixes of government policies, institutions, corporate strategies, technologies, and worker skills are associated with upgrading success. However, we can think about upgrading in a concrete way as linked to a series of economic roles associated with production and export activities, such as assembly, original equipment manufacturing (OEM), original brand name manufacturing (OBM), and original design manufacturing (ODM) (Gereffi 1994b, 222–24). This sequence of economic roles involves an expanding set of capabilities that developing countries must attain in pursuing an upgrading trajectory in diverse industries. In the remainder of this section, we will look at evidence from several sectors to see how global production networks have facilitated or constrained upgrading in developing nations.

Apparel

The global apparel industry contains many examples of industrial upgrading by developing countries.[25] The lead firms in this buyer-driven chain are retailers (giant discount stores like Wal-mart and Target, department stores like J.C. Penney and Marks & Spencer, specialty retailers like The Limited and Gap), marketers (who control major apparel brands, such as Liz Claiborne, Tommy Hilfiger, Polo/Ralph Lauren, Nike), and brand name manufacturers (e.g., Wrangler, Phillips–van Heusen). These lead firms all have extensive global sourcing networks, which typically encompass 300 to 500 factories in various regions of the world. Because apparel production is quite labor intensive, manufacturing is typically carried out in countries with very low labor costs.

The main stages for firms in developing countries are first, to be included as a supplier (i.e., exporter) in the global apparel value chain; and then to upgrade from assembly to OEM and OBM export roles within the chain. Because of the Multi-Fiber Arrangement (MFA) associated with the GATT, which used quotas to regulate import shares for the United States, Canada, and much of Europe, at least 50 to 60 different developing countries have been significant apparel exporters since the 1970s, many just assembling apparel from imported inputs using low-wage labor in local export-processing zones.

The shift from assembly to the OEM export role has been the main upgrading challenge in the apparel value chain. It requires the ability to fill orders from global buyers, which includes making samples, procuring or manufacturing the needed inputs for the garment, meeting international standards in terms of price, quality, and delivery, and assuming responsibility for packing and shipping the finished item. Since fabric supply is the most important input in the apparel chain, virtually all countries that want to develop OEM capabilities need to develop a strong textile industry. The OBM export role is a more advanced stage because it involves assuming the design and marketing responsibilities associated with developing a company's own brands.

East Asian newly industrializing economies (NIEs) of Hong Kong, Taiwan, South Korea, and Singapore, which are generally taken as the archetype for industrial upgrading among developing countries, made a rapid transition from assembly to OEM production in the 1970s. Hong Kong clothing companies were the most successful in making the shift from OEM to OBM production in apparel, and Korean and Taiwanese firms pursued OBM in other consumer goods industries like appliances, sporting goods, and electronics.[26] After mastering the OEM role, leading apparel export firms in Hong Kong, Taiwan, and South Korea began to

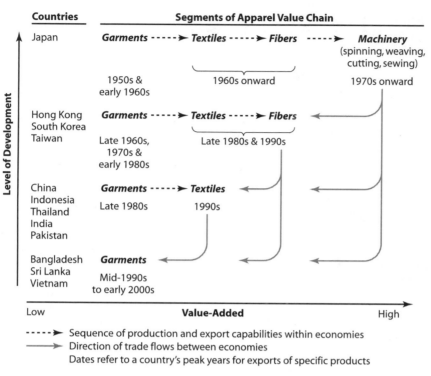

FIGURE 1. Industrial upgrading in the Asian apparel value chain. Dotted arrows refer to the sequence of production and export capabilities within economies. Solid arrows refer to the direction of trade flows between economies. Dates refer to a country's peak years for exports of specific products.

set up their own international production networks in the 1980s, using the mechanism of "triangle manufacturing" whereby orders were received in the East Asian NIEs, apparel production was carried out in lower-wage countries in Asia and elsewhere (using textiles from the NIEs), and the finished product was shipped to the United States or other overseas buyers using the quotas assigned to the exporting nation (Gereffi 1999).

Thus, international production networks facilitated the upgrading of East Asian apparel firms in two ways: first, they were the main source of learning from U.S. and European buyers about how to make the transition from assembly to OEM and OBM; and second, the East Asian NIEs established their own international production networks when faced with rising production costs and quota restrictions at home, and in order to take advantage of lower labor costs and a growing supply base in their region. Asian apparel manufacturers thus made the coordination of the apparel supply chain into one of their own core competences for export success.

Figure 1 presents a stylized model of industrial upgrading in the Asian apparel value chain. The main segments of the apparel chain—garments, textiles, fibers, and machinery—are arranged along the horizontal axis from low to high levels of rela-

tive value added in the production process. Countries are grouped on the vertical axis by their relative level of development, with Japan at the top and the least-developed exporters like Bangladesh, Sri Lanka, and Vietnam at the bottom.

Figure 1 reveals several important dynamics about the apparel value chain in Asia, and the GVC approach more generally. First, individual countries progress from low- to high-value-added segments of the chain in a sequential fashion over time. This reinforces the importance in GVC research of looking at the entire constellation of value-added steps in the supply chain (raw materials, components, finished goods, related services, and machinery), rather than just the end product, as traditional industry studies are wont to do. Second, there is a regional division of labor in the apparel value chain, whereby countries at very different levels of development form a multitiered production hierarchy with a variety of export roles (e.g., the United States generates the designs and large orders, Japan provides the sewing machines, the East Asian NIEs supply fabric, and low-wage Asian economies like China, Indonesia, or Vietnam sew the apparel). Industrial upgrading occurs when countries change their roles in these export hierarchies.[27] Finally, advanced economies like Japan and the East Asian NIEs do not exit the industry when the finished products in the chain become mature, as the "product cycle" model (Vernon 1966; 1971, chap. 3) implies, but rather they capitalize on their knowledge of production and distribution networks in the industry and thus move to higher-value-added stages in the apparel chain. This strategic approach to upgrading requires that close attention be paid to competition within and between firms occupying all segments of global value chains.

It is important to note, in closing this section, the key role played by international regulation in the organization of the apparel value chain. The MFA and its apparel quotas will be eliminated in 2005 as a result of the Agreement on Textiles and Clothing in the WTO, and many of the smaller apparel exporters that only do assembly will probably be forced out of the world export market. This should greatly increase export concentration in the global apparel industry, with China likely to be the major winner, along with other large countries such as Mexico, India, Turkey, Romania, and Vietnam that have developed considerable expertise in OEM production. Mexico's rapid move in the 1990s to the top of list as the leading apparel exporter to the United States owes a great deal to the passage of NAFTA in 1994, which allowed the creation of textile production and other backward linkages in Mexico, and thereby facilitated the entry of the U.S. retailers and apparel marketers that previously shunned Mexico in order to import apparel from Asia. In addition, employment in the apparel export industry increased in Mexico from 73,000 in 1994 to nearly 300,000 in 2000, mainly because Mexico coupled its relatively low wage rates with its recently acquired ability to carry out "full-package" (or OEM) production (Bair and Gereffi 2001; Gereffi, Spener, and Bair 2002). However, China regained the lead from Mexico in 2001 and 2002, as Mexico has been unable to match the volume and low price of Chinese apparel exports, and because of the intense competition from new suppliers that continue to enter the U.S. market.[28]

Electronics

Global production networks have been a central feature in the development and upgrading of Asia's large, dynamic electronics sector. In the case of electronics, there have been competing cross-border production networks set up by U.S., Japanese, and European firms, led by TNCs that span the entire value chain in various industries. For high-tech industries like electronics, these producer-driven chains must combine cost competitiveness with product differentiation and speed to market. Cross-border networks not only allow firms to combine these very different market demands effectively, but they also permit the integration of Asia's four distinct development tiers: Japan occupies the first tier; the East Asian NIEs are in the second tier; the major Southeast Asian countries of Malaysia, Thailand, the Philippines, and Indonesia are in the third tier; and the fourth tier contains China and late-late developers such as Vietnam. While the economic crisis of 1997 called East Asia's economic miracle into question, it appears that the structural changes associated with recovery from the crisis will reinforce and increase the opportunities for networked production, as the process of corporate restructuring leads firms to focus on core activities and supplement these with the increasingly specialized technology, skills, and know-how that are located in different parts of Asia (Borrus, Ernst, and Haggard 2000).

The diverse upgrading dynamics in Asian electronics can best be seen by contrasting the U.S. and Japanese production networks. In the mid-1990s, U.S. networks were considered to be relatively open and conducive to local development in host countries, while Japanese networks were perceived as closed and hierarchical with activities confined within affiliates that were tightly controlled by the parent company (Borrus 1997). U.S. electronics multinationals typically set up Asian networks based on a complementary division of labor: U.S. firms specialized in "soft" competencies (the definition of standards, designs, and product architecture), and the Taiwanese, Korean, and Singaporean firms specialized in "hard" competencies (the provision of components and basic manufacturing stages). The Asian affiliates of U.S. firms in turn developed extensive subcontracting relationships with local manufacturers, who became increasingly skilled suppliers of components, subassemblies, and even entire electronics systems. Japanese networks, by contrast, were characterized by market segmentation: electronics firms in Japan made high-value, high-end products, while their offshore subsidiaries in Asia continued to make low-value, low-end products. In terms of Asian upgrading, the U.S. production networks were definitely superior: U.S. networks maximized the contributions from their Asian affiliates, and Japanese networks minimized the value added by their regional suppliers. Although there is some evidence that Japanese firms tried to open up their production networks in the late 1990s, at best there has been partial convergence, with persistent diversity (Ernst and Ravenhill 2000).

Taiwan's achievements in electronics are especially notable for several reasons. During the 1990s, Taiwan established itself as the world's largest supplier of computer monitors, main boards, mouse devices, keyboards, scanners, and notebook personal computers (PCs), among other items. About 70 percent of the notebook PCs sold under OEM arrangements to American and Japanese computer companies, which resell them under their own logos, have been designed by Taiwanese firms. Acer, Taiwan's leading computer maker, is successful at both OEM and OBM production. Progress has been equally remarkable in the field of electronic components, and Taiwan also boasts one of the world's leading silicon foundry companies, the Taiwan Semiconductor Manufacturing Corporation (Ernst 2000). What is especially impressive about these accomplishments is that small and medium enterprises have played a central role as a source of flexibility in Taiwan's production networks. The role of small and medium enterprises as engines of growth and industrial transformation sets Taiwan apart from South Korea, which has relied extensively on huge, diversified conglomerates (*chaebol*) as the cornerstone of its electronics sector. The Taiwanese model in the computer industry draws on a combination of several factors: government policies that facilitated market entry and upgrading; strong linkages with large Taiwanese firms and business groups; and organizational innovations, such as the shift from relatively simple, production-based OEM to more complex "turnkey production" arrangements that encompass a wide variety of high-end support services, including design and global supply chain management (Poon 2002).

One of the most striking features of the electronics industry in recent years has been the rise of global contract manufacturers (Sturgeon 2002). A significant share of the world's electronics manufacturing capacity is now contained in a handful of huge contractors, such as Solectron, Flextronics, and Celestica. These firms are pure manufacturers. They sell no products under their own brand names and instead focus on providing global manufacturing services to a diverse set of lead firms, such as Hewlett Packard, Nortel, and Ericsson. All have operations that are truly global in scope, and all have grown dramatically since the early 1990s. Solectron, the largest contractor, expanded from a single Silicon Valley location with 3,500 employees and $256 million in revenues in 1988 to a global

powerhouse with more than 80,000 employees in 50 locations and nearly $20 billion in revenues in 2000. Although they have global reach, all of the largest contract manufacturers are based in North America. Except for the personal computer industry, Asian and European contract manufacturers have not developed, and the few that did were acquired by North American contractors during their buying spree fueled by the inflated stock prices of the 1990s. Global contract manufacturers introduce a high degree of modularity into value chain governance because the large scale and scope of their operations create comprehensive bundles of standardized value chain activities that can be accessed by a variety of lead firms through modular networks.

Fresh Vegetables

A final example of the role of global production networks in promoting industrial upgrading involves the production of fresh vegetables in Kenya and Zimbabwe for export to U.K. supermarkets.[29] Africa has very few success stories in the realm of export-oriented development, but some countries of sub-Saharan Africa seem to have found a niche in the fresh vegetables market. Several factors tie this case to our previous examples. First, fresh vegetables are a buyer-driven value chain, albeit in the agricultural sector. As with apparel, there is a high level of concentration at the retail end of the chain. The largest U.K. supermarkets and other food retailers control 70 to 90 percent of fresh produce imports from Africa. These retailers have avoided direct involvement in production; they just specialize in marketing and in the coordination of their supply chains.

Second, a major stimulus for local upgrading in Africa comes from U.K. retailers ratcheting up the standards that exporters must meet. U.K. supermarkets have moved beyond compliance with product quality and legislative (or due diligence) requirements for how produce is grown, processed, and transported. They now are focusing on broader standards that exporters must meet, such as integrated crop management, environmental protection, and human rights. In addition, retailers are beginning to use third-party auditors paid for by producers to ensure compliance with these standards.

Third, more stringent U.K. requirements have led to a decline in the market share of smallholder production and small export firms, which have been excluded from the supermarket supply chain. The horticulture industry in sub-Saharan Africa is dominated by a few large exporters that source predominantly from large-scale production units. In both Kenya and Zimbabwe, the top five exporters controlled over three-quarters of all fresh vegetable exports in the late 1990s.[30]

Fourth, as in apparel and electronics, market power in the horticultural chain has shifted from those activities that lower production costs to those that add value in the chain. In fresh vegetables, the latter include investing in postharvest facilities, such as cold storage; barcoding products packed in trays to differentiate varieties, countries, and suppliers; moving into high-value-added items such as ready-prepared vegetables and salads; and treating logistics as a core competence in the chain in order to reduce the time between harvesting, packing, and delivery. Pushing back these functions into Africa can reduce the cost for U.K. supermarkets because adding value to vegetables is labor-intensive and African labor is relatively cheap, but taken together these high-end services can become a new source of competitiveness and an opportunity to add value in Africa.

THE GLOBALIZATION BACKLASH: DILEMMAS OF GOVERNANCE AND DEVELOPMENT

In recent decades, a strong antiglobalization movement has emerged. As markets have gone global, many people sense that globalization means greater vulnerability to unfamiliar and unpredictable forces that can bring economic instability and social dislocation, as well as a flattening of culture in the face of well-financed global marketing machines and "brand bullies" (Rodrik 1997; Klein 2000; Ritzer 2000). The so-called Battle of Seattle, the massive protest against WTO trade talks in late 1999, was triggered not only by a lack of accountability and transparency in the deliberations of dominant global economic institutions like the WTO and the IMF, but also by a sense of outrage that corporate-sponsored international liberalization was moving full steam ahead, while the social safety nets and adjustment assistance traditionally provided by national governments were being removed. The historic compromise of "embedded liberalism," characterized by the New Deal in the United States and social democracy in Europe, whereby economic liberalization was rooted in social community, was being undone (Ruggie 2002a).

A major problem is that the purported benefits of globalization are distributed highly unequally. The IMF's managing director, Horst Köhler, has conceded that "the disparities between the world's richest and poorest nations are wider than ever."[31] Of the world's 6 billion people, almost half (2.8 billion) live on less than two dollars a day, and a fifth (1.2 billion) live on less than one dollar a day, with 44 percent of them living in South Asia. In East Asia the number of people living on less than one dollar a day fell from 420 million to 280 million between 1987 and 1998, largely because of improvements in China. Yet the numbers of poor people continue to rise in Latin America, South Asia, and sub-Saharan Africa (World Bank 2001, 3). What forces might be able to ameliorate these problems in both governance and development in the global economy?

In the 1990s, there was a sharp escalation in social expectations about the role of corporations in society, both in developed and developing nations (Ruggie 2002b). One reason is that individual companies have made themselves, and in some cases entire industries, targets by engaging in abusive or exploitative behavior. As a result, trust in the corporate sector has been eroded. In addition, there is a growing imbalance in global rule-making: on the one hand, the rules favoring market expansion have become stronger and more enforceable (such as intellectual property rights for software and pharmaceutical companies, or the restrictions on local content provisions and export performance requirements in the WTO); on the other hand, rules that favor other valid social objectives, such as human rights, labor standards, environmental sustainability, or poverty reduction, are lagging behind. These perceived problems and others have provided the fuel for anticorporate campaigns worldwide.

Government policy alone is inadequate to handle these grievances: they are transnational in scope, and they deal with social demands in areas where regulations are weak, ill defined, or simply absent. A variety of new "private governance" responses or certification institutions are emerging (Gereffi, Garcia-Johnson, and Sasser 2001), such as individual corporate codes of conduct; sectoral certification schemes involving nongovernmental organizations (NGOs), firms, labor, and other industry stakeholders; third-party auditing systems, such as SA 8000 for labor standards or the Forest Stewardship Council (FSC) certification for sustainable forestry practices; and the United Nations' Global Compact, an initiative that encourages the private sector to work with the United Nations, in partnership with international labor and civil society organizations, to move toward "good practices" in human rights, labor standards, and environmental sustainability in the global public domain. While skeptics claim there is little evidence to show that these codes have significant impact on corporate behavior (Hilowitz 1996; Seidman 2003), proponents generally argue that new systems of certification, enforced either by global consumers or by institutional actors such as the United Nations, can provide the basis for improved regulatory frameworks (Fung, O'Rourke, and Sabel 2001; Williams 2000).

Although there is enormous variation in the character and purpose of different voluntary regulatory schemes—with some schemes created by activists in response to global concerns, and others implemented by corporations as a preemptive effort to ward off activist pressure—certification institutions have gained a foothold in both Europe and North America. In the apparel industry, a variety of certification and monitoring initiatives were established in the latter half of the 1990s.

> Clean Clothes Campaign (CCC), a consumer coalition in Europe that aims to improve working conditions in the worldwide garment industry
>
> Social Accountability 8000 (or SA 8000), a code of conduct verification and factory certification program launched in October 1997 by the New York–based Council on Economic Priorities
>
> Fair Labor Association (FLA), which includes major brand merchandisers such as Nike, Reebok, and Liz Claiborne
>
> Worldwide Responsible Apparel Production (WRAP), an industry-initiated certification program designed as an alternative to the FLA and representing the large U.S. apparel manufacturers that produce for the discount retail market
>
> Workers Rights Consortium (WRC), developed by the United Students Against Sweatshops in cooperation with apparel unions, universities, and a number of human rights, religious, and labor NGOs (see Maquila Solidarity Network 2002)

In Mexico, the FLA and WRC collaborated in settling a strike and gaining recognition for the workers' union in the Korean-owned Kukdong factory, which made Nike and Reebok sweatshirts for the lucrative U.S. collegiate apparel market (Gereffi, Garcia-Johnson, and Sasser 2001, 62–64). In the coffee sector, the Fair Trade movement has worked with small coffee growers in Costa Rica and elsewhere to get above-market prices for their organic and shade-grown coffees distributed by Starbucks and other specialty retailers (Fitter and Kaplinsky 2001; Ponte 2002).

Private governance in multistakeholder arrangements seeks to strengthen oversight in global supply chains by charting a course that goes beyond conventional top-down regulation based on uniform standards, on the one hand, and reliance on voluntary initiatives taken by corporations in response to social protest, on the other. Some argue that a continuous improvement model based on "ratcheting labor standards" upward would work well in a highly competitive, brand-driven industry such as apparel (Fung, O'Rourke, and Sabel 2001). Others propose a "compliance plus" model that pushes beyond the basic floor of minimum standards set by most codes, and seeks an "inside-out" approach to ethical sourcing based on training and empowerment initiatives that address the needs and interests of factory-based stakeholders (Allen 2002). In either instance, sustainable and meaningful change requires a shift in organizational cultures and expectations regarding improvement of social and environmental conditions.

Governance has become a central theoretical issue in the global economy. Institutional paradigms and local or regional frameworks centered on the nation-state are being superseded by approaches that emphasize transnational governance structures, with an emphasis on power, networks, and the uneven distribution of gains from globalization. Much still needs to be done in this area. The inability of the neoliberal agenda to redress the most serious development problems in the world is leading to fresh thinking on the role of the state and civil society institutions in developing nations (Wolfensohn 1998; IDB 1998, 2000; Garretón et al. 2003). Transnational corporations are being pressured to comply with a broad range of social objectives in multistakeholder institutions of private governance that can have an impact on public policies in the developed as well as the developing world. The challenge in research on the global economy is to create theory and carry out insightful empirical studies that provide tools to understand the constantly changing reality we seek to apprehend and change.

Notes

I am grateful to Giovanni Arrighi, Fred Block, Frank Dobbin, Mark Granovetter, Evelyne Huber, Larry King, Victor Nee, Gay Seidman, Neil Smelser, and Richard Swedberg for their helpful comments on an earlier draft of this chapter.

1. Another key actor in the contemporary global economy is the state. While the role of the state is an important as-

pect in many of the institutional perspectives we will review, a more comprehensive discussion of this topic can be found in the chapter "The State and the Economy" by Fred Block and Peter Evans (this volume).

2. Because the services component of GDP in industrial countries has grown substantially relative to "merchandise" trade like manufacturing, mining, and agriculture, the merchandise component of GDP is shrinking. Thus Feenstra (1998, 33–35) uses the ratio of merchandise trade to merchandise value-added to measure the significance of trade for industrial economies between 1890 and 1990. He finds that this ratio doubled for France, Germany, Italy, and Sweden between 1913 and 1990, and nearly tripled for the United States.

3. Organization for Economic Co-operation and Development.

4. The maquiladora program in Mexico, initially called the Border Industrialization Program, was created in 1965 after the United States terminated the bracero program, whose main objective had been to bring in Mexican workers to fulfill the demand for agricultural labor. The end of the bracero program left thousands of unemployed farmworkers in Mexican border cities, and the maquiladora program was set up to alleviate the resultant unemployment and growing poverty. The growth of the maquiladora program has been spectacular, especially in the 1990s. In 1991, Mexico's maquiladora industry generated $15.8 billion in exports and employed 466,000 Mexicans; by 2000, it had grown to $79.5 billion in exports with nearly 1.3 million employees. Around 15 percent of Mexico's GDP corresponded to maquiladora exports in 2001, and the main destination for these products is the United States (Cañas and Coronado 2002).

5. These three motives for investing abroad subsequently became popularized as distinct forms of foreign direct investment: resource-seeking FDI, market-seeking FDI, and efficiency-seeking FDI (Beviglia Zampetti and Fredriksson 2003, 406).

6. The debt crisis hit all of Latin America very hard. The high external debt burden required the allocation of 25 percent to 30 percent of the region's foreign exchange proceeds merely to cover interest payments, which prompted scholars to refer to the 1980s as Latin America's "lost development decade" (Urquidi 1991).

7. The World Bank's (1993) overview of the East Asian development experience attributes the region's sustained international competitiveness largely to the application of market-friendly policies, including stable macroeconomic management, high investments in human capital (especially education), and openness to foreign trade and technology. For a critique of this "Washington consensus" model, see Gore 2000. For a detailed comparison of the import-substituting and export-oriented development strategies in Latin America and East Asia, see Gereffi and Wyman 1990.

8. UNCTAD's *World Investment Report, 2002* contains a table of the largest 100 "economies" in the world in 2000, using a value-added measure for firms that is conceptually comparable to the GDP calculation used for countries. There were 29 TNCs in the top 100 entities on this combined list of countries and nonfinancial companies. The world's largest TNC was ExxonMobil, with an estimated $63 billion in value added in 2000; it ranked forty-fifth on the country-company list, making the company approximately equal in size to the economies of Chile or Pakistan (UNCTAD 2002a, 90–91).

9. For OECD countries, falling tariffs were twice as important as falling transport costs in explaining the growth of trade relative to income between 1958 and 1988 (Feenstra 1998, 34).

10. The European Union is a case in point. Taken individually, European Union economies are very open, with an average trade share of 28 percent in 1990, but more than 60 percent of their trade is with each other. Taken as a unit, the European Union's merchandise trade with the rest of the world is only 9 percent of GDP, which is similar to that of the United States (Krugman 1995, 340).

11. SITC refers to Standard International Trade Classification, which is the United Nations' system of trade categories. One-digit product groups, such as SITC 7, are the most general. Components are reported at the level of three-, four-, and five-digit product groups.

12. Feenstra's focus on linkages between the integration of trade and the disintegration of production in the current trade-based era calls to mind a similar duality in Osvaldo Sunkel's classic article "Transnational Capitalism and National Disintegration in Latin America." Writing 25 years before Feenstra in a TNC-based world economy, Sunkel (1973) argued that vertically integrated TNCs were generating international polarization as they used direct foreign investment (rather than trade) to integrate the global economy and simultaneously disintegrate national and regional economies. Thus, we have a curiously reversed image of TNCs moving from being highly integrated to disintegrated actors in the last quarter of the twentieth century, while the economic context shifts from transnational capitalism (based on closed domestic economies) in the 1970s to global value chains (based on specialized economic activities in relatively open economies) in the 1990s.

13. Actually, the disintegration of production through outsourcing of specific activities by large corporations itself leads to more trade, as intermediate inputs cross borders several times during the manufacturing process. This is part of the boundary problem in measuring international trade noted by Krugman (1995).

14. Kogut (1985, 15) defines the value-added chain as "the process by which technology is combined with material and labor inputs, and then processed inputs are assembled, marketed, and distributed. A single firm may consist of only one link in this process, or it may be extensively vertically integrated."

15. The main sources of a firm's competitive advantage that can be transferred globally are several economies that exist along and between value-added chains: economies of scale (related to an increase in market size); economies of scope (related to an increase in product lines supporting the fixed costs of logistics, control, or downstream links of the value-added chain); and learning (based on proprietary knowledge or experience). "When these economies exist, industries are global in the sense that firms must compete in world markets in order to survive" (Kogut 1985, 26).

16. A firm's value chain is nested in a larger stream of activities Porter calls a "value system," which include the separate value chains of suppliers, distributors, and retailers (Porter 1990, 40–43).

17. There are two distinct dimensions in how a firm competes internationally: the *configuration* of a firm's activities worldwide, which range from concentrated (performing an activity, such as research and development, in one location and serving the world from it) to dispersed (performing every activity in each country); and the *coordination* of value chain activities, which range from tight to loose structures (Porter 1987, 34–38).

18. Reich (1991) says that core corporations in the United States at the end of the twentieth century have moved from high-volume production of standard commodities to high-value activities that serve the unique needs of particular customers. This requires an organizational shift from vertical coordination (represented as pyramids of power, with strong chief executives presiding over ever-widening layers of managers, atop an even larger group of hourly workers) to horizontal coordination (represented as webs of high-value activities connected by networks of firms).

19. The GCC approach adopted what Dicken et al. (2001, 93) call "a network methodology for understanding the global economy." The objective is "to identify the actors in these networks, their power and capacities, and the ways through which they exercise their power through association with networks of relationships."

20. One of the key findings of value chain studies is that access to developed country markets has become increasingly dependent on participating in global production networks led by firms based in developed countries. Therefore, how value chains function is essential for understanding how firms in developing countries can gain access to global markets, what the benefits from such access might be, and how these benefits might be increased. A GVC research network has formed to study these issues (see http://www.globalvaluechains.org).

21. Several international organizations have featured the global production networks perspective in recent reports, including UNIDO (2002, chap. 6), UNCTAD (2002a, chap. 5; 2002b, chap. 3), the World Bank (2003, 55–66), and the International Labor Organization's program "Global Production and Local Jobs" (see the April 2003 issue of *Global Networks* for several articles from this project).

22. These distinctions are not ironclad. Often they reflect primary versus secondary research orientations. The scholars who adopt an institutional perspective at the national level can still look at the diversity of firm strategies within national contexts (e.g., Morgan, Kristensen, and Whitley 2001). Similarly, those who use organizational perspectives to understand the evolution of firm strategies and interfirm networks within global industries may ground their generalizations in diverse institutional contexts at the regional, national, and local levels of analysis (e.g., Bair and Gereffi 2001; Gereffi, Spener, and Bair 2002).

23. Guillén (2001) offers a very insightful sociological perspective on the limits of convergence in his systematic comparison of organizational change in Argentina, South Korea, and Spain since 1950. Guillén uses a comparative institutional approach to show that "the emergence of a specific combination of organizational forms in a given country enables it to be successful in the global economy at certain activities but not others" (2001, 16).

24. Indeed, companies from the *same* national business system may show contradictory patterns as they confront global markets. A careful study of seven German transnational companies in three of Germany's core industries—Hoechst, Bayer, and BASF in the chemical/pharmaceutical industries; Volkswagen, Mercedes-Benz, and BMW in the automobile industry; and Siemens in electrical/electronic engineering—reveals that strikingly different strategies exist within and between these industries, resulting from a mixture of traditional German ways of doing business and bold global moves (Lane 2001). This departs markedly from Whitley's classification of firms in the German business system as "collaborative hierarchies."

25. This analysis of industrial upgrading in apparel draws mainly from Gereffi (1999) and Gereffi and Memodovic (2003).

26. However, a number of OBM companies have returned to OEM because it capitalizes on East Asia's core competence in manufacturing expertise. Some East Asian companies pursue a dual strategy of doing OBM for the domestic and other developing country markets, and OEM production for the United States and other industrial country markets.

27. By contrast, the popular "flying geese" model of Asian development assumes that countries industrialize in a clear follow-the-leader pattern (Akamatsu 1961), and no attention is paid to the kind of international production networks that may emerge between the lead economies and their followers.

28. A prime example is sub-Saharan Africa, which, under the African Growth of Opportunity Act of October 2000, has been granted quota-free and duty-free access to the U.S. market for products that meet specified rules of origin (see http://www.agoa.gov).

29. See Dolan and Humphrey 2000 for the facts relevant to this case.

30. The one exception to this high level of concentration is organic produce, for which there is both a price premium and a significant unmet market demand in the United Kingdom because local production is very fragmented. Smaller African exporters still have an opportunity to penetrate this market because organics do not presently require the scale and investment of more exotic forms of produce.

31. "Working for a Better Globalization," remarks by Horst Köhler at the Conference on Humanizing the Global Economy, Washington, D.C., January 28, 2002. Cited in Ruggie 2002a, 3.

REFERENCES

Aglietta, Michel. 1980. *A Theory of Capitalist Regulation*. London: New Left Books.

Akamatsu, K. 1961. "A Theory of Unbalanced Growth in the World Economy." *Weltwirtschaftliches Archiv* 86(1): 196–217.

Allen, Michael. 2002. "Analysis: Increasing Standards in the Supply Chain." *Ethical Corporation*, October 15.

Amable, Bruno. 2000. "Institutional Complementarity and Diversity of Social Systems of Innovation and Production." *Review of International Political Economy* 7:645–87.

Amsden, Alice H. 1989. *Asia's Next Giant: South Korea and Late Industrialization*. Oxford: Oxford University Press.

Arndt, Sven W., and Henryk Kierzkowski, eds. 2001. *Fragmentation: New Production Patterns in the World Economy*. Oxford: Oxford University Press.

Arrighi, Giovanni. 1994. *The Long Twentieth Century*. London: Verso.

Arrighi, Giovanni, and Jessica Drangel. 1986. "The Stratification of the World-Economy: An Exploration of the Semiperipheral Zone." *Review* 10: 9–74.

Arrighi, Giovanni, Beverly J. Silver, and Benjamin D.

Brewer. 2003. "Industrial Convergence, Globalization, and the Persistence of the North-South Divide." *Studies in Comparative International Development* 38(1): 3–31.

Ayres, Robert L. 1983. *Banking on the Poor: The World Bank and World Poverty.* Cambridge: MIT Press.

Bair, Jennifer, and Gary Gereffi. 2001. "Local Clusters in Global Chains: The Causes and Consequences of Export Dynamism in Torreon's Blue Jeans Industry." *World Development* 29:1885–1903.

Barnet, Richard J., and Ronald E. Müller. 1974. *Global Reach: The Power of the Multinational Corporations.* New York: Simon and Schuster.

Berger, Suzanne, and Ronald Dore, eds. 1996. *National Diversity and Global Capitalism.* Ithaca, N.Y.: Cornell University Press.

Bergsten, C. Fred, Thomas Horst, and Theodore H. Moran. 1978. *American Multinationals and American Interests.* Washington, D.C.: Brookings Institution Press.

Beviglia Zampetti, Americo, and Torbjörn Fredriksson. 2003. "The Development Dimension of Investment Negotiations in the WTO: Challenges and Opportunities." *Journal of World Investment* 4: 399–450.

Bhagwati, Jaqdish. 1958. "Immiserizing Growth: A Geometrical Note." *Review of Economic Studies* 25: 201–5.

Borrus, Michael. 1997. "Left for Dead: Asian Production Networks and the Revival of U.S. Electronics." Pp. 139–63 in *The China Circle*, ed. Barry Naughton. Washington, D.C.: Brookings Institution Press.

Borrus, Michael, Dieter Ernst, and Stephan Haggard, eds. 2000. *International Production Networks in Asia.* London: Routledge.

Boyer, Robert. 1989. *The Regulation School: A Critical Introduction.* Trans. Craig Charney. New York: Columbia University Press.

Campbell, John L., J. Rogers Hollingsworth, and Leon N. Lindberg, eds. 1991. *Governance of the American Economy.* Cambridge: Cambridge University Press.

Cañas, Jesus, and Roberto Coronado. 2002. "Maquiladora Industry: Past, Present, and Future." *Business Frontier*, issue 2. El Paso Branch of the Federal Reserve Bank of Dallas.

Cardoso, Fernando Henrique, and Enzo Faletto. [1969] 1979. *Dependency and Development in Latin America.* Trans. Marjory Mattingly Urquidi. Expanded ed. Berkeley and Los Angeles: University of California Press.

Carrillo, Jorge, and Alfredo Hualde. 1998. "Third Generation Maquiladoras: The Delphi-General Motors Case." *Journal of Borderlands Studies* 13(1): 79–97.

Carroll, William K., and Meindert Fennema. 2002. "Is There a Transnational Business Community?" *International Sociology* 17(3): 393–419.

Castells, Manuel. 1996. *The Rise of the Network Society.* Oxford: Blackwell.

Dicken, Peter. 2003. *Global Shift: Reshaping the Global Economic Map in the 21st Century.* 4th ed. London: Sage.

Dicken, Peter, Philip F. Kelly, Kris Olds, and Henry Wai-Chung Yeung. 2001. "Chains and Networks, Territories and Scales: Towards a Relational Framework for Analysing the Global Economy." *Global Networks* 1(2): 89–112.

Dolan, Catherine, and John Humphrey. 2000. "Governance and Trade in Fresh Vegetables: The Impact of UK Supermarkets on the African Horticulture Industry." *Journal of Development Studies* 37(2): 147–75.

Dunning, John H. 1958. *American Investment in British Manufacturing Industry.* London: Allen and Unwin.

Engardio, Peter, Aaron Bernstein, and Manjeet Kripalani. 2003. "Is Your Job Next?" *Business Week*, February 3, 50–60.

Ernst, Dieter. 2000. "What Permits David to Grow in the Shadow of Goliath? The Taiwanese Model in the Computer Industry." Pp. 110–40 in *International Production Networks in Asia*, ed. Michael Borrus, Dieter Ernst, and Stephan Haggard. London: Routledge.

Ernst, Dieter, and John Ravenhill. 2000. "Convergence and Diversity: How Globalization Reshapes Asian Production Networks." Pp. 226–56 in *International Production Networks in Asia*, ed. Michael Borrus, Dieter Ernst, and Stephan Haggard. London: Routledge.

Evans, Peter B. 1979. *Dependent Development: The Alliance of Multinationals, State, and Local Capital in Brazil.* Princeton: Princeton University Press.

———. 1995. *Embedded Autonomy: States and Industrial Transformation.* Princeton: Princeton University Press.

Feenstra, Robert C. 1998. "Integration of Trade and Disintegration of Production in the Global Economy." *Journal of Economic Perspectives* 12(4): 31–50.

Feenstra, Robert C., Tzu-Han Yang, and Gary G. Hamilton. 1999. "Business Groups and Product Variety in Trade: Evidence from South Korea, Taiwan, and Japan." *Journal of International Economics* 48(1): 71–100.

Fitter, Robert, and Raphael Kaplinsky. 2001. "Who Gains from Product Rents as the Coffee Market Becomes More Differentiated? A Value-Chain Analysis." *IDS Bulletin* 32(3): 69–82.

Foxley, Alejandro, Michael S. McPherson, and Guillermo O'Donnell, eds. 1986. *Development, Democracy, and the Art of Trespassing: Essays in Honor of Albert O. Hirschman.* Notre Dame, Ind.: University of Notre Dame Press.

Fröbel, Folker, Jürgen Heinrichs, and Otto Kreye. 1980. *The New International Division of Labor.* Cambridge: Cambridge University Press.

Fung, Archon, Dara O'Rourke, and Charles Sabel. 2001. "Realizing Labor Standards: How Transparency, Competition, and Sanctions Could Improve Working Conditions Worldwide." *Boston Review*, February–March.

Garretón, Manuel Antonio, Marcelo Cavarozzi, Peter Cleaves, Gary Gereffi, and Jonathan Hartlyn. 2003. *Latin America in the Twenty-First Century: Toward a New Sociopolitical Matrix.* Miami: North-South Center Press.

Gereffi, Gary. 1983. *The Pharmaceutical Industry and Dependency in the Third World.* Princeton: Princeton University Press.

———. 1994a. "The Organization of Buyer-Driven Global Commodity Chains: How U.S. Retailers Shape Overseas Production Networks." Pp. 95–122 in *Commodity Chains and Global Capitalism*, ed. Gary Gereffi and Miguel Korzeniewicz. Westport, Conn.: Praeger.

———. 1994b. "The International Economy and Economic Development." Pp. 206–33 in *The Handbook of Economic Sociology*, ed. Neil J. Smelser and Richard Swedberg. Princeton: Princeton University Press.

———. 1996. "Global Commodity Chains: New Forms of Coordination and Control among Nations and Firms in International Industries." *Competition and Change* 1(4): 427–39.

———. 1999. "International Trade and Industrial Upgrading in the Apparel Commodity Chain." *Journal of International Economics* 48(1): 37–70.

———. 2001. "Shifting Governance Structures in Global Commodity Chains, with Special Reference to the Internet." *American Behavioral Scientist* 44: 1616–37.

Gereffi, Gary, Ronie Garcia-Johnson, and Erika Sasser. 2001. "The NGO-Industrial Complex." *Foreign Policy* 125:56–65.

Gereffi, Gary, and Raphael Kaplinsky, eds. 2001. "The Value of Value Chains: Spreading the Gains from Globalisation." Special issue of the *IDS Bulletin* 32(3).

Gereffi, Gary, and Miguel Korzeniewicz, eds. 1994. *Commodity Chains and Global Capitalism.* Westport, Conn.: Praeger.

Gereffi, Gary, and Olga Memodovic. 2003. "The Global Apparel Value Chain: What Prospects for Upgrading by Developing Countries?" Vienna: UNIDO, Strategic Research and Economy Branch.

Gereffi, Gary, David Spener, and Jennifer Bair, eds. 2002. *Free Trade and Uneven Development: The North American Apparel Industry after NAFTA.* Philadelphia: Temple University Press.

Gereffi, Gary, and Donald L. Wyman, eds. 1990. *Manufacturing Miracles: Paths of Industrialization in Latin America and East Asia.* Princeton: Princeton University Press.

Gore, Charles. 2000. "The Rise and Fall of the Washington Consensus as a Paradigm for Developing Countries." *World Development* 28:789–804.

Granovetter, Mark. 1994. "Business Groups." Pp. 453–75 in *The Handbook of Economic Sociology*, ed. Neil J. Smelser and Richard Swedberg. New York: Russell Sage Foundation; Princeton: Princeton University Press.

Guillén, Mauro F. 2001. *The Limits of Convergence: Organization and Organizational Change in Argentina, South Korea, and Spain.* Princeton: Princeton University Press.

Hall, Peter A., and David Soskice, eds. 2001. *Varieties of Capitalism: The Institutional Foundations of Comparative Advantage.* Oxford: Oxford University Press.

Hamilton, Gary G., William Zeile, and Wan-Jin Kim. 1989. "The Network Structure of East Asian Economies." Pp. 105–29 in *Capitalism in Contrasting Cultures*, ed. Stewart Clegg and Gordon Redding. Berlin: Walter de Gruyter.

Held, David, Anthony McGrew, David Goldblatt, and Jonathan Perraton. 1999. *Global Transformations.* Stanford, Calif.: Stanford University Press.

Hilowitz, Janet. 1996. *Labelling Child Labour Products: A Preliminary Study.* Geneva: International Labor Organization.

Hirschman, Albert O. 1981. *Essays in Trespassing: Economics to Politics and Beyond.* Cambridge: Cambridge University Press.

Hollingsworth, J. Rogers, and Robert Boyer, eds. 1997. *Contemporary Capitalism: The Embeddedness of Institutions.* Cambridge: Cambridge University Press.

Hollingsworth, J. Rogers, Philippe Schmitter, and Wolfgang Streeck, eds. 1994. *Governing Capitalist Economies: Performance and Control of Economic Sectors.* Oxford: Oxford University Press.

Hummels, David, Dana Rapaport, and Kei-Mu Yi. 1998. "Vertical Specialization and the Changing Nature of World Trade." *Federal Reserve Bank of New York Economic Policy Review*, June, 79–99.

Humphrey, John, and Hubert Schmitz. 2001. "Governance in Global Value Chains." *IDS Bulletin* 32(3): 19–29.

Inter-American Development Bank (IDB). 1998. *Facing Up to Inequality in Latin America: Economic and Social Progress in Latin America, 1998–99 Report.* Washington, D.C.: IDB.

———. 2000. *Development beyond Economics: Economic and Social Progress in Latin America, 2000 Report.* Washington, D.C.: IDB.

Kaplinsky, Raphael. 2000. "Globalisation and Unequalisation: What Can Be Learned from Value Chain Analysis?" *Journal of Development Studies* 37(2): 117–46.

———. 2001. "Is Globalization All It Is Cracked Up to Be?" *Review of International Political Economy* 8(1): 45–65.

Kitschelt, Herbert, Peter Lange, Gary Marks, and John D. Stephens, eds. 1999. *Continuity and Change in Contemporary Capitalism.* Cambridge: Cambridge University Press.

Klein, Naomi. 2000. *No Logo: Taking Aim at the Brand Bullies.* New York: Picador.

Kogut, Bruce. 1984. "Normative Observations on the International Value-Added Chain and Strategic Groups." *Journal of International Business Studies,* fall, 151–67.

———. 1985. "Designing Global Strategies: Comparative and Competitive Value-Added Chains." *Sloan Management Review* 26(4): 15–28.

Krugman, Paul. 1995. "Growing World Trade." *Brookings Papers on Economic Activity* 1:327–77.

Lane, Christel. 2001. "The Emergence of German Transnational Companies: A Theoretical Analysis and Empirical Study of the Globalization Process." Pp. 69–96 in *The Multinational Firm: Organizing across Institutional and National Divides,* ed. Glenn Morgan, Peer Hull Kristensen, and Richard Whitley. Oxford: Oxford University Press.

Lash, Scott, and John Urry. 1987. *The End of Organized Capitalism.* Oxford: Polity Press.

Lundvall, Bengt-Ake, ed. 1992. *National Systems of Innovation: Towards a Theory of Innovation and Interactive Learning.* London: Pinter.

Maquila Solidarity Network. 2002. "Memo: Codes Update." No. 12, November.

Meyer, John W. 2000. "Globalization: Sources and Effects on National States and Societies." *International Sociology* 15(2): 233–48.

Morgan, Glenn, Peer Hull Kristensen, and Richard Whitley, eds. 2001. *The Multinational Firm: Organizing across Institutional and National Divides.* Oxford: Oxford University Press.

Nelson, Richard R., ed. 1993. *National Innovation Systems: A Comparative Analysis.* Oxford: Oxford University Press.

Newfarmer, Richard, ed. 1985. *Profits, Progress, and Poverty: Case Studies of International Industries in Latin America.* Notre Dame, Ind.: University of Notre Dame Press.

Offe, Claus. 1985. *Disorganized Capitalism.* Ed. John Keane. Cambridge: Polity Press.

Organization for Economic Cooperation and Development (OECD). 1979. *The Impact of the Newly Industrializing Countries on Production and Trade in Manufactures.* Paris: OECD.

Ponte, Stefano. 2002. "The 'Latte Revolution'? Regulation, Markets, and Consumption in the Global Coffee Chain." *World Development* 30:1099–1122.

Poon, Teresa Shuk-Ching. 2002. *Competition and Cooperation in Taiwan's Information Technology Industry: Inter-firm Networks and Industrial Upgrading.* Westport, Conn.: Quorum Books.

Porter, Michael E. 1985. *Competitive Advantage.* New York: Free Press.

———. 1987. "Changing Patterns of International Competition." Pp. 27–57 in *The Competitive Challenge: Strategies for Industrial Innovation and Renewal,* ed. David J. Teece. Cambridge, Mass.: Ballinger.

———. 1990. *The Competitive Advantage of Nations.* New York: Free Press.

Raikes, Philip, Michael Friis Jensen, and Stefano Ponte. 2000. "Global Commodity Chain Analysis and the French *Filière* Approach: Comparison and Critique." *Economy and Society* 29:390–417.

Reich, Robert B. 1991. *The Work of Nations: Preparing Ourselves for 21st-Century Capitalism.* New York: Alfred A. Knopf.

Ritzer, George. 2000. *The McDonaldization of Society.* Thousand Oaks, Calif.: Pine Forge Press.

Rodrik, Dani. 1997. *Has Globalization Gone Too Far?* Washington, D.C.: Institute for International Economics.

Ruggie, John G. 2002a. "Taking Embedded Liberalism Global: The Corporate Connection." Paper presented at the 98th Annual Meeting of the American Political Science Association, Boston, August 26–September 1.

———. 2002b. "The New World of Corporate Responsibility." *Financial Times,* October 25.

Rugman, Alan M. 1999. "Forty Years of the Theory of the Transnational Corporation." *Transnational Corporations* 8(2): 51–70.

Safarian, A. Edward. 1966. *Foreign Ownership of Canadian Industry.* Toronto: McGraw-Hill.

Sampson, Anthony. 1973. *The Sovereign State of ITT.* New York: Stein and Day.

Sassen, Saskia. 2000. "Territory and Territoriality in the Global Economy." *International Sociology* 15(2): 372–93.

Schmitter, Philippe C. 1990. "Sectors in Modern Capitalism: Modes of Governance and Variation in Performance." Pp. 3–39 in *Labour Relations and Economic Performance,* ed. Renato Brunetta and Carlo Dell'Aringa. New York: New York University Press.

Seidman, Gay. 2003. "Monitoring Multinationals: Lessons from the Anti-apartheid Movement." *Politics and Society* 31(3): 381–406.

Shaiken, Harley, and Stephen Herzenberg. 1987. *Automation and Global Production: Automobile Engine Production in Mexico, the United States, and Canada.* La Jolla, Calif.: Center for U.S.-Mexican Studies, University of California, San Diego.

Sklair, Leslie. 1993. *Assembling for Development: The Maquila Industry in Mexico and the United States.* La Jolla, Calif.: Center for U.S.-Mexican Studies, University of California, San Diego.

———. 2001. *The Transnational Capitalist Class.* Oxford: Blackwell.

Smith, Adam. [1776] 1976. *An Inquiry into the Nature and Causes of the Wealth of Nations.* 2 vols. Oxford: Clarendon Press.

Sturgeon, Timothy. 2002. "Modular Production Networks. A New American Model of Industrial Organization." *Industrial and Corporate Change* 11(3): 451–96.

Sturgeon, Timothy, and Richard Florida. 2000. "Globalization and Jobs in the Automotive Industry." Final report to the Alfred P. Sloan Foundation. International Motor Vehicle Program, Center for

Technology, Policy, and Industrial Development, Massachusetts Institute of Technology.

Sunkel, Osvaldo. 1973. "Transnational Capitalism and National Disintegration in Latin America." *Social and Economic Studies* 22(1): 132–76.

Therborn, Göran. 2000. "Globalizations: Dimensions, Historical Waves, Regional Effects, Normative Governance." *International Sociology* 15(2): 151–79.

United Nations Conference on Trade and Development (UNCTAD). 1993. *World Investment Report: Transnational Corporations and Integrated International Production.* New York: United Nations.

———. 2002a. *World Investment Report: Transnational Corporations and Export Competitiveness.* New York: United Nations.

———. 2002b. *Trade and Development Report, 2002: Developing Countries in World Trade.* New York: United Nations.

United Nations Industrial Development Organization (UNIDO). 2002. *Industrial Development Report 2002/2003: Competing through Innovation and Learning.* Vienna: UNIDO.

Urquidi, Victor L. 1991. "The Prospects for Economic Transformation in Latin America: Opportunities and Resistances," *LASA Forum* 22(3): 1–9.

Vernon, Raymond. 1966. "International Investment and International Trade in the Product Cycle." *Quarterly Journal of Economics* 80:190–207.

———. 1971. *Sovereignty at Bay: The Multinational Spread of U.S. Enterprises.* New York: Basic Books.

———. 1999. "The Harvard Multinational Enterprise Project in Historical Perspective." *Transnational Corporations* 8(2): 35–49.

Wade, Robert. 1990. *Governing the Market: Economic Theory and the Role of Government in East Asian Industrialization.* Princeton: Princeton University Press.

———. 1996. "Globalization and Its Limits: Reports of the Death of the National Economy Are Greatly Exaggerated." Pp. 60–88 in *National Diversity and Global Capitalism*, ed. Suzanne Berger and Ronald Dore. Ithaca, N.Y.: Cornell University Press.

Wallerstein, Immanuel. 1974. *The Modern World-System.* Vol. 1, *Capitalist Agriculture and the Origin of the European World-Economy in the Sixteenth Century.* New York: Academic Press.

———. 1979. *The Capitalist World-Economy.* Cambridge: Cambridge University Press.

———. 1980. *The Modern World-System.* Vol. 2, *Mercantilism and the Consolidation of the European World-Economy, 1600–1750.* New York: Academic Press.

———. 1989. *The Modern World-System.* Vol. 3, *The Second Era of Great Expansion of the Capitalist World-Economy, 1730–1840s.* New York: Academic Press.

———. 2000. "Globalization or the Age of Transition? A Long-Term View of the Trajectory of the World-System." *International Sociology* 15(2): 249–65.

———. 2002. "The Eagle Has Crash Landed." *Foreign Policy* 131:60–68.

Whitley, Richard. 1992a. *Business Systems in East Asia: Firms, Markets, and Societies.* London: Sage.

———. 1996. "Business Systems and Global Commodity Chains: Competing or Complementary Forms of Economic Organisation?" *Competition and Change* 1(4): 411–25.

———, ed. 1992b. *European Business Systems.* London: Sage.

Williams, Oliver F., ed. 2000. *Global Codes of Conduct: An Idea Whose Time Has Come.* Notre Dame, Ind.: University of Notre Dame Press.

Wolfensohn, James D. 1998. "The Other Crisis." Speech by the president of the World Bank Group to the Board of Governors, October 6. http://www.worldbank.org/html/extdr/am98/jdw-sp/am98-en.htm.

Womack, James P., Daniel T. Jones, and Daniel Roos. 1990. *The Machine That Changed the World.* New York: Macmillan.

World Bank. 1993. *The East Asian Miracle.* Oxford: Oxford University Press.

———. 2001. *World Development Report, 2000/2001: Attacking Poverty.* Oxford: Oxford University Press.

———. 2003. *Global Economic Prospects and the Developing Countries, 2003.* Washington, D.C.: World Bank.

Yeats, Alexander J. 2001. "Just How Big Is Global Production Sharing?" Pp. 108–43 in *Fragmentation: New Production Patterns in the World Economy*, ed. S. W. Arndt and H. Kierzkowski. Oxford: Oxford University Press.

Yeung, Henry Wai-chung. 2000. "Economic Globalization, Crisis, and the Emergence of Chinese Business Communities in Southeast Asia." *International Sociology* 15(2): 266–87.

9 The Political and Economic Sociology of International Economic Arrangements

Neil Fligstein

THE GOVERNANCE (or some would say, the lack of governance) of the global economy is one of the key issues in the fields of international relations, political economy, and comparative politics. So far, little of the "new" economic sociology has taken up this question. The purpose of this chapter is to consider what positive agenda might be carved out for economic sociology in helping to make sense of the expansion and governance of the global economy. The sociology of markets provides us with a theoretical understanding of the institutional underpinnings of markets and the dynamics by which new markets are created. The globalization of markets can be reconceptualized as a process of market integration whereby new markets emerge where more localized markets previously existed. Once these markets come into existence, there is a demand by market participants for more global governance, that is, more institutional underpinnings. The issues at stake, property rights, governance structures, and rules of exchange, are at the core of the types of agreements that have been reached in the World Trade Organization, the North American Free Trade Agreement, and the European Union. In this way, economic sociology can provide for an important and interesting research agenda that adds to the existing literature and points to research areas that have so far been underexploited.

Economic globalization is a somewhat vague idea that refers to at least three related phenomena. First, there has been tremendous growth in world trade in the past 50 years. In 1950, about 5 percent of the world GDP crossed national borders. By 2001, this figure had risen to 17 percent (World Trade Organization 2002). World trade grew 1,400 percent even as world economic output rose over 400 percent for the same period. Second, there has been increased expansion and integration of the world's various financial markets as a cause and consequence of this increase in trade. There is a huge and expanding world mar-

ket for currencies, equities, government bonds, and other financial instruments such as derivatives. Fund managers move money across countries and instruments with the push of a computer key. Finally, the world has witnessed tremendous economic development in Asia, in particular, Japan, Korea, Thailand, Indonesia, the Philippines, and most recently China and India. These countries' economic development has been driven by production for the world market, particularly the U.S. market.

Historically, trade relations were governed by governments. Given the huge increase in trade that has occurred, it is not surprising that policymakers and scholars are concerned to understand how this control has changed. A useful approach is to consider the governance of international markets as a question of the role of positive and negative integration in creating international markets for goods and services (Scharpf 1996). Many of the changes in trade regulation around the world have involved the tearing down of trade barriers erected by governments to promote national economic development. These barriers consist of tariffs on imported goods, capital controls, rules governing the amount of foreign goods allowed in the country (such as quotas on imported steel), rules that make it hard for foreign companies to do business without national partners, or rules that force foreign companies to change their products in order to meet local standards.

The removal of these barriers without producing new regulation to guide trade is termed *negative integration*. Generally, free trade has produced positive outcomes for most participants. But there can be negative effects as well. Depending on the economic mix, both countries can lose jobs, have decreased economic security and increased income inequality, face higher odds of financial meltdowns, and face negative environmental or health consequences (particularly in less developed countries). There can also be disadvantages for firms in competing across national borders. Firms that try to take advantage of new market openings can find themselves at the mercy of national governments and local courts that make it difficult to enforce contracts. Firms that cannot compete with new entrants face bankruptcy and dissolution. These bad effects of negative integration drive the international search for new mechanisms of governance. Rules that guide trade across national boundaries are termed *positive integration* when they specify how exchange will be governed (Scharpf 1996).

An important insight provided by economic sociology is that the problems facing actors in international markets are very similar to the problems facing actors in national markets. As Polanyi (1944) noted long ago, as national markets integrate, they cause dislocation and disorganization. Firms worry about how to organize, gain access to capital, engage in competition, and exchange with workers, customers, and suppliers. Workers find themselves being exploited by working long hours, sometimes under unsafe and unhealthy conditions. Consumers also worry about the safety and usefulness of products. As a result, in most national economies governments intervene with rules and laws to make markets operate and protect workers, firms, and consumers (Fligstein 2001).

It is useful to consider the economic history of the United States as a case in point. The state governments were larger and more powerful than the federal government from 1789 to 1860. The state governments, controlled by local economic elites, tried to use their power to prevent out-of-state corporations from competing with local business interests. But the commerce clause of the U.S. Constitution implies that states could not prevent corporations (or any other kind of economic actor) from competing with local firms. The U.S. Supreme Court consistently ruled against states that tried to pass and enforce laws barring out-of-state firms, and in favor of so-called foreign corporations (Friedman 1973). The nineteenth century also produced the limited liability joint stock corporation as the main vehicle to organize large capitalist enterprise (Roy 1998). At the beginning of the nineteenth century, incorporation required an act of state legislatures. By the end of the century, incorporation could be done by anyone. Over the 100 years, the corporation as a legal form changed from being a "creature of the state," a circumstance in which state legislatures appeared to have total control over corporations, to an entity with the same rights as individuals (Horwitz 1977). During the period from 1870 to 1920, the issue of fair and

unfair forms of competition arose as a central focus for government policy. The United States created modern antitrust (or as it is sometimes called, competition) policy with the Sherman Act and the Federal Trade Commission. These laws and the organizations that enforced them came to govern corporations through the extensive interaction of firms, courts, and government. Finally, investor and consumer protection was extended during the depression of the 1930s. The process by which these legal vehicles evolved was contentious. There were winners and losers along the way. These same issues have been faced and resolved within all of the main capitalist societies. While their solutions have reflected the unique politics of each society, they have crafted rules that helped solve collective problems of organizing markets.

The main difference between solutions to national problems and solutions to international market problems, of course, is that in national markets, there is a government to which firms, workers, and other organized social actors can appeal. In international markets, the political arenas are less well formed and there are great barriers to cooperation across societies with different interests and different legal and political institutions. There is also the problem that most nation-states take the issue of state sovereignty as quite important. This creates a dilemma that is at the heart of making international economic agreements. It is relatively easy for governments to produce negative integration. But to agree to positive rules of market integration, governments have to accept supranational political arenas where rules are made and courts or mediators will make binding decisions against national firms or governments. The United States is the most vocal among nation-states in invoking sovereignty to avoid international oversight. The U.S. government's official policy on most issues of trade is that negative integration (i.e., the tearing down of trade barriers) is good and that positive integration, which might interfere with the sovereignty of the U.S. government, is bad. Still, even the United States agreed to the WTO's arbitration process.

There are two main theoretical schools of thought about how these processes of national and international market integration should work. The dominant view is the neoclassical theory of regulation that has by now come to be called "neoliberalism." Economists generally think that regulation of markets should be undertaken only after extensive market failure. For them, deregulation is a form of negative integration. Tearing down market barriers will make firms compete harder and force them to allocate their capital more efficiently. Economists are always skeptical of regulation because of the possibility of rent seeking either on the part of governments or a subset of firms (see Noll 1989 and Peltzman 1989 for reviews). Governments will want to keep control over economic actors and keep tax revenues high. The largest and most powerful firms will push to have laws written to protect them. Regulatory bodies are also more subject to takeover by incumbent firms that will make regulation work for them at the expense of others. The long-term effect of regulation for either governments or firms will be to produce less economic growth. So most economists favor negative integration projects and deregulation of industries because they push firms to compete directly on the price and quality of their goods.

The opposite point of view is that markets cannot function without formal and informal institutions (North 1990; Fligstein 2001; Vogel 1996; Weiss 1998; Rodrik 1997; Dezalay and Garth 1996; see the papers in Dezalay and Garth 2002a). Market actors need rules to guide their interactions and exchanges, and without these rules, they may fail to make investments. The issue is not whether to have rules guiding economic exchange, but how to create the right kind of rules to promote economic exchange and allow for the rule of law. For institutionalists, the negative integration project is only one step toward market building. It unleashes demands by market actors (firms, workers, consumers, and governments) for positive integration to insure that markets function properly and that their potentially negative effects are mitigated (Fligstein and Stone-Sweet 2002).

This debate has played out in interesting ways in discussions of globalization. For most of those (and they are mainly economists) who dominate the economic policymaking of the U.S. government, the Organization for Economic Cooperation and Development, the World Bank, and the International Monetary Fund, deregulation and negative integration (particularly the reduction of tariff barriers) are good things. National government interventions into capital, product, and labor markets are bad things. The main recommendation by economic policymakers to governments around the world is to deregulate markets and resist national appeals to do otherwise.

But it is here that the empirical literature shows curious results. Instead of getting weaker or less involved with their economies, governments have actually increased their involvement even as they have embraced free trade (see the papers in Berger and Dore 1996 and Crouch and Streeck 1997; Weiss 1998; Vogel 1996; Smelser 1995). Rodrik (1995) shows that as national economies have become more open to trade, governments have tended to spend more money to equalize the bad distributional effects of trade. Garrett (1998) has shown that national political coalitions based on center-left parties have preserved the ability of governments to redistribute income and regulate labor markets even as trade has increased.

Moreover, the literature shows positive integration projects often follow on the heels of negative integration projects (for a partial review, see Berger 2000). So, for example, the European Union has moved from fundamentally a negative integration project in the 1960s and 1970s to a more positive integration project in the 1980s and 1990s (Fligstein and Stone-Sweet 2002). The General Agreement on Tariffs and Trade, the basic framework for reducing tariffs around the world, started out as a negative integration project. But in the last round of trade negotiations, governments decided to form a more permanent organization, the World Trade Organization, and a dispute-settling mechanism to resolve trade disputes under WTO rules. The various trade agreements between the United States, Canada, and Mexico that evolved over the twentieth century culminated in an extensive and ambitious agreement, the North American Free Trade Agreement, that also contains transnational mechanisms to enforce it. Indeed, it will be argued that globalization via negative integration will not produce an integrated world economy. The most integrated regional economy is the European Union, and it is no surprise that it has the most extensive system of positive trade rules, a court that handles disputes, and now, a single currency.

The increase in global governance over time is what institutionalists of all varieties would predict. But there has been a great deal of unevenness in what sort of projects have been undertaken. It is obvious that international trade agreements have favored traders. It is here that economic sociology may shed some light. Among the questions one can pose are the following: Where does the demand for international governance come from? What kind of governance do actors seek? How do they enforce the rules they collectively create? Why is it easier to get international agreements for producers, but much harder to get agreements for other groups, such as labor and the environment? Under what conditions are governments prepared to give up sovereignty in international economic agreements?

This chapter first considers the extant theoretical background in political science, sociology, and economics. Then it provides a critique of these perspectives, focused primarily on what they leave out. Next comes a consideration of how economic sociology can help by offering a conception of markets, their institutions, and their links to governments. A typology of international economic arrangements is suggested. Then an extensive discussion of one case, the European Union, illustrates these various principles. Finally, some possible research agendas are proposed.

BACKGROUND

The literature on international economic agreements is dominated by research in political science and economics, although sociologists have contributed in their work on political economy (Block 1977; Wood 1986), world systems (Wallerstein 1984; Arrighi 1994), neo-Marxist approaches (Streeck and Schmitter 1991; Murphy 2000; Robinson 2001), and world culture (Meyer et al. 1997; Boli and Thomas 1998). The classic literature on international relations was dominated by the realist school of thought. Here the world of states was depicted as an anarchic realm where power and interest dominated. Military might and security were the central concerns of states. International agreements were seen as derivative from the larger power dynamics of states and therefore as inconsequential (Waltz 1979).

A number of schools of thought that have evolved over the past 30 years have taken issue with the realist point of view: neorealism or liberalism, political economy from an interest group and a neo-Marxist perspective, constructivism, world systems, and world culture. All begin with the idea that international institutions produce constraints on states and shape their subsequent behavior. In this way, these arrangements have consequence for the sovereignty claims of states. One of the core features of modern states is their claim to control everything that goes on within their borders. This claim of absolute sovereignty is, of course, just a claim, and the sovereignty that states actually have depends on their capacity and politics (Krasner 1988). The interesting question that each of the postrealist perspectives poses is why states enter into international economic arrangements if they may lose control over some aspect of sovereignty.

NEOREALISM

The neorealist perspective sticks with the idea that states are unitary actors with interests (Keohane 1984; for a recent interesting updating of this perspective see Koremenos, Lipson, and Snidal 2001). Instead of seeing an anarchic world where military power dominates, neorealists view states as willing to cooperate with other states when it serves their interests. States are prepared to trade off sovereignty if they can make arrangements that have tangible benefits. So, for example, states are prepared to lower tariffs in an international agreement, thereby making it harder for subsequent governments to raise those tariffs. This decrease in sovereignty is acceptable because of the societal gains from free trade. International organizations are viewed in a similar light. States give power to international organizations in order to attain joint gains from cooperation. Moreover, the particular institutional design of an international organization is thought to precisely reflect the willingness of states to cede such sovereignty in order to capture gains. So some international organizations are "talk shops," while others have more bite. What explains states' willingness to participate in either is the size of positive gain (Koremenis, Libson, and Snidal 2001). Neorealism makes one strong prediction: states will not enter into binding agreements or set up international organizations unless the benefits outweigh the potential costs (in both harm to national interests and declines in national sovereignty). An international economic agreement requires states be willing to cede sovereignty to an international governmental organization (IGO). The unevenness of current international systems of governance suggests that it is difficult to get states to make these kinds of agreements.

Scholars in this tradition have viewed the international arenas where trade agreements have been hammered out and enforced as important to pushing governments toward freer trade. The General Agreement on Tariffs and Trade (GATT), World Trade Organization (WTO), European Union (EC), North American Free Trade Agreement (NAFTA), "Market of the South" (MERCOSUR), Association of Southeast Asian Nations (ASEAN), and APEC (Asian Pacific Economic Cooperation) all have reinforced cooperation between governments on issues of trade and seemed to push the possibility of cooperation. The main mechanism by which increases in cooperation over time occur is positive feedback. Governments that participate get increased economic growth as free trade works for their society. This makes them more likely to open more markets. It is also the case that some international governmental organizations have been less successful in pushing free trade (e.g., APEC and ASEAN) and been more like "talk shops." A neorealist explanation of this pattern would focus on the lack of payoff perceived by national governments.

POLITICAL ECONOMY

In the political economy perspective, states' interests are less unitary and more subject to internal and external political pressures (for recent reviews, see Milner 1999 and Berger 2000). Its views are related to the general model of regulation that comes from economics. Economics starts out from the position that free trade is always good because of the theory of comparative advantage. Adherents to this theory wonder why governments ever undertake protectionist measures. Political scientists and sociologists generally start with the opposite view: that various constituencies in society prevent state actors from entering into free trade agreements centered on negative integration. Scholarly attention has focused on which national interest groups favor of trade and which oppose it.

In the case of international economic agreements, exporters (i.e. multinational corporations, or as some call them, transnational corporations [hereafter TNCs]) generally favor more open markets, and local producers who are totally dependent on the national market favor closed markets. The relative size and weight of these groups in a particular society affect the ability of governments to enter into international economic agreements. There are two basic variants of this thesis. One emphasizes that sectoral interests predominate, while the other views class interests as pivotal. In the former approach, firms in particular sectors, like steel and sugar, that have been negatively affected by opening up boundaries to imports oppose participation by their governments in trade pacts. Similarly, those that would benefit from exporting, like airplane manufacturers and computer firms, favor such pacts. Governments may pursue trade openings for their major exporters and protectionism for those that might be hurt by open markets (for empirical examples in this literature, see Irwin 1994, 1996; Frieden 1990).

Another approach focuses attention on capital and labor, seeing firms and workers as pitted against one another. Capital would theoretically prefer to have open product and capital markets so it can seek out the highest possible returns. Labor would prefer to keep capital captive. Since labor is the least mobile of resource endowments, it is the most likely to pressure governments to protect industry. Evidence exists to support this division of interests (Rogowski 1989; Midford 1993; Scheve and Slaughter 1998). One way to bring both theories together is to recognize that sector and factor interests could coincide. So, low-skill, labor-intensive industries confronted with high and rising import penetration would mobilize both firms and workers to support protection. There are research results that support this view (Baldwin 1986; Trefler 1993).

The political economy literature has also been interested in why the past 20 years have witnessed such a huge global expansion of world trade and of world trade agreements. Theorists who begin with the idea that a particular country has a trade regime because of its mix of economic activities have to consider how those activities have changed in order to explain why governments have shifted policies. A number of provocative arguments have been made. One argument is that as trade barriers have decreased (with the GATT and the European Union), both capitalists and skilled workers view exporting as an opportunity and therefore press their governments for more trade agreements. This produces a kind of "virtuous circle" for support of free trade (Frieden and Rogowski 1996). This argument seems of greater relevance to more developed than to less developed countries.

In the case of less developed countries, another set of arguments has been made. Scholars argue that governments have taken the relative failure of import substitution strategies and the relative success of the open Asian countries as impetus to shift from trade protectionism to trade openness (Krueger 1997; Rodrik 1994, 1995; Bates and Krueger 1993). It turns out that there is little evidence to support this view. Most less developed countries still have organized opposition to such shifts in policy among both capital and labor. Their governments often changed policies in the face of substantial opposition.

A more promising line of research to explain the interest in open trade among less developed countries looks at political factors. Some of these are domestic, like the capacity of the local bureaucracy to act autonomously from key interest groups and the existence of democracy. Others are international. Here, scholars have emphasized the role of

U.S. hegemony, the fall of communism, and the push to economic liberalization by IGOs like the Organization for Economic Cooperation and Development, the World Bank, and the International Monetary Fund (Krasner 1976; Lake 1988; Gowa 1994; Russett 1985; Haggard 1995; Evans 1996, 1997). The international economic environment has provided ideological and material support to push free trade and financial deregulation. The epistemic community of international aid and economics organizations has pushed the view that the path to economic growth is more market and less regulation. Both carrots (i.e., trade access to developed countries and international investment) and sticks (requirements from the IMF and the World Bank to open markets in exchange for aid) are used to open markets.

NEO-MARXIST AND WORLD SYSTEMS APPROACHES

Several other related literatures, located mostly in sociology, try to understand the link between international economic arrangements and global economic activity: neo-Marxist approaches and world systems theory. Both of these schools of thought view the dynamics of capitalism as driving world economic integration and producing economic governance on a world scale. Their main similarity is to posit that the world system of states and the world economy are mutually constituted. This means that the dynamics of the economy (both national and international) will have direct effects on the types of international governance that are possible. They differ in emphasizing different political and economic forces in the construction of global governance. Unlike political economy approaches in political science, they assume that capitalism is a system. Neo-Marxists and world systems theorists view the forms of regulation that emerge less as a product of bargaining processes and more as a product of systemic imperatives.

One approach is to focus on how the United States as the hegemonic economy and military power has pushed its "liberal" agenda through its design of and control over international organizations. Block (1977) documents the U.S. attempt to produce an international financial architecture following World War II that would promote a free trade agenda. But Block concludes that the IMF and the World Bank (and by implication, the U.S. government) were ultimately unsuccessful in this

effort. The financial architecture could not contain crises, and this inability produced the collapse of the Bretton Woods system in 1973. Wood (1986) shows that the U.S. government dictated policies to developing countries and used the international financial system to force countries to pursue free trade and deregulation. Some political scientists have noted these processes. Helleiner (1994) considers the pressure on developing countries to pursue financial liberalization during the 1980s. Recently, studies of the Asian financial crisis of the late 1990s have focused on the role of the IMF and the World Bank in promoting financial liberalization around the world. Most scholars agree that this intervention set up the financial meltdowns of the late 1990s (Stiglitz 2002; see the papers in Jackson 1999 and Pempel 1999).

While some neo-Marxists believe the international apparatus is fragile and generally not up to the task of regulating the world economy, others have viewed the forms of global governance in more functionalist terms. World systems theory starts with the premise that the world economy has been evolving since at least 1450 (Wallerstein 1974). During this time, there have been waves of economic growth that were presided over by hegemonic powers, first in Italy, then the Netherlands, then Great Britain, and finally, the United States (Arrighi 1994, 6; Wallerstein 1984). World systems theory argues that the rise and fall of these hegemons follows an economic cycle that involves expansion of the existing capitalist world system under their direction, the maturing of that expansion, and an eventual decline. The old hegemon is replaced by a new one with a new set of strategies and tactics to dominate the world.

In the most current cycle, the hegemon is the United States. The United States was able to assume this political role after World War II because it was the largest economy and had the strongest military apparatus. The United States produced a world order that reflects its attempt to maintain power. From the world system perspective, the world division of labor between developed and developing societies is reinforced by this order, keeping the world safe for development by American economic interests, primarily TNCs (see Arrighi 1994; McMichael 1996; Chase-Dunn 1998). From this point of view, the IMF, World Bank, GATT, and WTO are all outgrowths and representatives of U.S. hegemony. The main current concern in the world systems literature is that the United States is in decline economically (Wallerstein 1984;

Boswell and Chase-Dunn 2000; Arrighi 1994). This implies that there will be a resurgence of conflict in the world system and that U.S.-inspired IGOs will fall as the hegemon they support falls.

Another perspective on the global economy and international governance is neo-Marxist in its orientation. Instead of locating the structure of the world economy and polity in the interests of the United States, this literature views the global system as an outgrowth of the emergence of a global capitalist class. The strongest statement of this perspective is Robinson's (1996, 2001). Robinson argues that the world economy has moved to become a global economy. This implies an emerging worldwide capitalist class made up of the owners of multinational corporations. These corporations are now transnational; that is, they organize their activities on a worldwide scale in order to take advantage of differences in regulation and the price of labor.

From Robinson's perspective, this transnationalist capitalist class wants to undermine the power of traditional states in order to force those states to deregulate their markets, tear down tariff barriers, and generally lower social protection of workers. They also have set up a transnational state that consists of the international organizations that enforce fiscal, monetary, and regulatory discipline on countries around the world, such as the World Bank, the IMF, the OECD, and the WTO. These organizations help push forward a neoliberal state at the national level and prevent international regulation of capital.

Robinson (2001) and Murphy (1994) argue that a large number of international nongovernmental organizations (INGOs) have emerged to help firms coordinate their production. Murphy (1994) views these INGOs as creating a kind of international civil society that promotes the interests of corporations. He shows that the growth of these international organizations over the past 150 years reflects the concerns of capital over labor. Most of these organizations promote international trade by guaranteeing the standardization of products. Murphy argues that while other kinds of issues have been put on the international agenda (i.e., health, safety, the environment, and to a lesser degree, labor standards), labor has lost the most in the past 30 years. He believes that eventually transnational interest groups, in the forms of INGOs, can have influence over this emerging polity. But he recognizes that this emergence is fraught with difficulties.

CONSTRUCTIVISM

Constructivism is an umbrella term for approaches emphasizing that the arenas of international agreements are social constructions and that the interests and identities of states are endogenously determined in the process of making such agreements (for recent reviews, see Finnemore 1996; Finnemore and Sikkink 2001; Jacobson 2000). This point of view encompasses a number of positions. John Meyer and his colleagues (for a review, see Boli and Thomas 1998) have undertaken a research program in what they call "world culture." Other scholars have studied how international norms are formed in particular domains. Still others have studied international law and international intergovernmental organizations (see Dezalay and Garth 1996; and the papers in Dezalay and Garth 2002a). Finally, epistemic communities and NGOs are viewed as agents who have affected the evolution of various agreements. It is useful to briefly review these arguments.

The constructivists pick up where the neorealists leave off. Neorealists believe that international organizations can help states cooperate by providing arenas where governments can learn more about each other and gain trust that collective agreements will be enforced (Keohane 1984; Yarbrough and Yarbrough 1992). Constructivists believe that under some circumstances, international organizations and the nongovernmental actors that populate the fringe of international politics can affect the preferences, identities, and actions of states (Finnemore and Sikkink 2001; Jacobson 2000). "Constructivism focuses on the role of ideas, norms, knowledge, culture, and argument in politics, stressing in particular the role of collectively held or 'intersubjective' ideas and understandings on social life" (Finnemore and Sikkink 2001, 392). Its theorists hold that human interaction is shaped primarily by ideas, not just material interests; these ideas are not reducible to individual interests, and they shape the identity and interests of actors (Ruggie 1998; Wendt 1999).

In the context of international relations, scholars have spent a great deal of energy trying to demonstrate that such factors have independent causal effects on outcomes of interest. So, for example, Katzenstein and colleagues tried to show the effectiveness of internationally held norms on security issues like slavery, piracy, the trafficking of women, foreign aid, and the rules of war (see the papers on national security in Katzenstein 1996). Checkel (1997, 1998) has focused on how particular international norms have been interpreted and used in domestic politics of states.

The constructivist approach suggests a laundry list of mechanisms by which ideas and norms might be consequential for the organization of international activities like trade. One idea that has come out of this literature is that of a norm entrepreneur; that is, a person, an organization, or even a set of organizations that works to change some aspect of international rules or laws. Klotz (1995) and Thomas (2001) show how these activists work within countries and across them. Keck and Sikkink (1998) and Risse, Ropp, and Sikkink (1999) look at cases in which activist groups use the media, symbolic politics, and issue framing to get national governments to engage in international negotiations.

Scholars have identified several kinds of organizations here: national nongovernmental organizations (NNGOs), international nongovernmental organizations (INGOs), international governmental organizations, epistemic communities, transnational issue networks, and transnational social movements (for reviews, see Tarrow 2001; Jacobson 2000). Scholars have shown that the coordination of efforts at the national and international levels can lead to more significant outcomes. This mechanism (the coordination of efforts) allows environmental and labor groups to have an effect on international economic agreements. Many scholars are convinced that "rational discourse" can have pivotal effects in particular situations. It is, perhaps, possible for Habermasian "communicative action" to change minds and worldviews (Risse 2000).

Another constructivist interest is the spread of formal laws and informal dispute-settling mechanisms across societies. Slaughter (2002) argues that the proliferation of actors in the global economy has produced a proliferation of laws and jurisdictions. NGOs, TNCs, and IGOs have found ways to create their own laws and settle their disputes in private courts or through mediation that takes place outside the boundaries of nation-states. Dezalay and Garth (1996) show that this has occurred in the world of international commercial arbitration, where courts in London and other places have created an international law outside of the jurisdiction of nation-states. Dezalay and Garth (2002b) argue that the model for much of this jurisprudence is U.S. law, and that the driving force for the spread of dispute mechanisms is U.S.-based transnational corporations.

The main contribution in sociology to this constructivist position comes from the world culture perspective usually associated with Meyer and his collaborators. This school of thought is interested in how the culture of modernity is created and spread. Meyer and his collaborators characterize world culture as a "relatively unified cultural system and a densely linked economy without a centralized political system" (Meyer and Hannan 1978, 298). Meyer argues that states and markets were embedded in a larger common culture that emphasized the construction of actors as individuals, rights, and laws and prescribed to states what it took to embody modern forms (2000). Such forms included constitutions, educational systems, and specific practices like censuses.

Meyer, Boli, Thomas, and Ramirez (1997) consolidated this view. They argued that the main agents of the propagation of modernity were IGOs, NGOs, epistemic communities of experts, and activist networks. Meyer et al. showed empirically the expansion of these groups in time, space, and function. They also argued that the world culture was selling a standard model of actorhood and citizenship. Boli and Thomas (1998) expand on this thesis by analyzing data on the expansion of NGOs from the nineteenth century on.

CRITIQUE

The preceding review of theories seems to imply a cacophony of voices without much agreement. But there are many stylized facts on which all perspectives agree. Over time, there has been an expansion in the number and intensity of international economic agreements. This pattern is roughly related to the growth of international trade and the expansion of international finance (although most scholars do not try to theorize the dynamic character of this process). Governments, transnational corporations, NGOs (both national and international), and IGOs have all participated in producing these agreements. They have also helped construct international standards that are informally adopted by transnational corporations. They have participated in the creation of private courts. Within countries, labor and businesses oriented toward the local market have tried to prevent these agreements or at least worked to get their governments to put into place forms of social protection in the face of free trade. Social movement NGOs focused on the environment, human rights, and women's rights have all pushed governments to sign agreements that address social justice in the context of market-opening projects. Many theories highlight the role of the United States because it is the leading military and economic power and its banks and transnational corporations are among the main actors in world trade. Most of the theories assume that the economic agreements that have been reached are "functional"; that is, they serve the interests of those who set them in place, reflecting current distributions of power within and across societies.

The major source of disagreement is that neo-Marxism and world systems theory see the world economic governance structures as a direct outcome of either the U.S. government or the needs of TNCs, while political scientists and economists generally see these agreements as the outcome of bargaining processes. The result is that neo-Marxism and world systems theory tend to view the lack of extensive governance of the world economy as benefiting the key actors, the U.S. government and TNCs. Political scientists and economists are likely to view the current level of governance as possibly suboptimal and ineffective because governments, firms, and labor from different countries can block forms of economic governance that would increase trade and economic growth. Neo-Marxism and world systems theory suggest that the United States and TNCs get the system they want. Other perspectives see existing arrangements as suboptimal because potential gains cannot be achieved for lack of governance.

It seems pretty obvious that there is a lack of governance in the world economy. The endemic crises of the financial system, the degradation of the environment, and the incidence of poverty and war (Evans and Rausch 1999) suggest that we do not have enough governance. Firms' opportunities to earn profits are affected by bad politics and lack of governance. With more and better national and international global economic governance, the possibilities for economic growth increase. The lack of economic governance is harmful not just to the interests of firms and the sovereignty of governments, but to the greater welfare of the citizens of various societies.

Much of the current discussion omits important elements. First, the degree to which changes in international trade drive agreements is not well specified. Second, almost no attention is given to what is or is not contained in agreements. Third, it is difficult to develop a typology of such agreements because what they are used for is not clear. Finally, the dynamics of such agreements, once in place,

are poorly understood. The political economy approach has put the idea of feedback between agreements and the likelihood of subsequent agreements on the research agenda, but it needs more development. These are questions that the sociology of markets and economic sociology are prepared to help answer. Economic sociology gives us insight into how these various approaches might be linked and suggests research agendas that have been barely begun.

There is a kind of "chicken and egg" problem in linking international economic agreements to domestic actors in various countries who might favor them. If there are substantial trade barriers in a particular sector or if one factor is able to block the mobility of others (i.e., labor over capital), then actors who want a different trade regime have no opportunity to put that issue on the agenda. Indeed, the status quo in a particular government tends to stay in place. The real issue to explain is why trade openings occur. Indeed, in a world where one actor wanted protection everywhere where another wanted open trade, the possibility for new trade deals does not exist. One of two things has to happen. One possibility is that my traders are in the same business as your traders and both are arrogant enough to believe they will dominate. Another is that we have perfectly complementary traders, so that my gain will be yours. This logic suggests that the substance of trade agreements is a good clue as to which groups are powerful across societies and why.

A related issue is the already existing degree of market openness. We know that some products and services (investment banking, automobiles, petroleum) are widely traded across international borders, while others are not (home mortgages, retail trade). One would expect the existing level of integration of markets to identify which market actors favor international agreements. To put the matter another way, we do not have a definition of a single world market for a product. In order to make sense of which markets include actors who demand for rules and which do not, it is important to know which goods and services are highly traded across societies and which are not. Part of the problem is that our theories begin with governments and national markets and then extrapolate to international markets without governments. In reality, some markets are more, and other markets less, national. It is this difference (and changes in integration) that drives expansion in trade regimes.

One reason to pay attention to the content of trade agreements has already been mentioned (i.e., which sectors are affected tells us who is interested in such rules). But there is a deeper theoretical problem. Most economic literature is about creating open markets, that is, markets without rules governing who gets to be a producer and what is produced and its price. This is what we have termed negative integration. But such a focus takes us away from interesting issues that all sorts of trade agreements raise: that is, what are the institutional conditions necessary to produce an integrated market? One part of such an agreement would be the ease of entry of actors. But that is only one issue. Once trade begins on a routine basis, producers face decisions and dilemmas in order to make a real integrated market sustainable. They must have rules of exchange that allow them to write and enforce contracts, insure their products meet health and safety standards of whichever country is involved, allow them to seek out financing, and insure their products can work in any country. Producers also want to enforce property rights governing their investments, allowing them to partner with locals and protecting intellectual property. Finally, they want to avoid unfair competition. The existing literature says little about how market-opening projects that provide positive market integration will look and the conditions under which such rules will occur.

Finally, the problem of dynamics haunts most social science arguments. We understand why an existing order is likely to remain in place. After all, rules are written to favor the most organized, who have resources to ensure that if situations change, new rules will help them adjust. It is much harder to make sense of the direction of social change in the world economy. There are more international organizations and agreements today than 40 years ago. A feedback mechanism whereby the existence of agreements empowers actors, stimulating the demand for more agreements, is the best explanation of changes that have occurred.

CONTRIBUTIONS OF THE SOCIOLOGY OF MARKETS

The sociology of markets can be used to make more sense of international economic agreements. My basic view is that the sociology of markets conceives of a market as an organizational field in which a self-reproducing role structure of firms reflects a system of power (i.e., it contains a set of challenger and incumbent firms) that operates with a conception of control (i.e., collective un-

derstandings about what the actions of other market actors mean) (Fligstein 1996, 2001). Markets depend on extensive societal infrastructure in order to exist. They need stable states and currency, the rule of law, functioning property rights, governance structures, and rules of exchange. Markets depend greatly on states, courts, and rules. States, too, can be conceived of as organizational fields (Laumann and Knoke 1987). States develop regulatory capacity for particular issues and industries. They produce laws and rules. They also produce courts that enforce rules. Thus, the sociology of markets proposes that to make markets, you need participants (i.e., firms), rules, and usually, governments to create and enforce rules.

Four main conceptual understandings relevant to understanding international economic agreements can be derived from the literature. First, the theory provides an account of how markets come into existence, stabilize, and are transformed. This can be used as a way to understand if markets are becoming globalized and how many such markets exist. Second, the sociology of markets implies that actors frequently seek out states to help them produce rules to guide their actions. It follows that firms in more globalized markets desire international rules more than firms in markets protected by national governments. If we know which markets are being globalized, we can predict the nature and direction of rules. Third, the sociology of markets specifies the social institutions that are necessary to produce stable markets. It follows that if global markets are to work, firms will push states to make rules to create stable market interactions. More extensive market integration projects require more extensive rule making of the positive integration variety. The content of international economic agreements can be analyzed in terms of the types of rules they produce (for an example, see Fligstein and Mara-Drita 1996). Finally, these relationships are about power. Firms prefer rules that they themselves write and enforce. But barring that, they probably prefer no rules (i.e., negative integration). States try to maintain sovereignty, and the most powerful state, the United States is one of the main obstacles to international agreements.

The first step in developing a sociology of markets is to propose what rules and understandings are necessary to make structured exchange (i.e., markets as fields) possible. Four types of rules or institutions are relevant to producing social structures in markets: property rights, governance structures, rules of exchange, and conceptions of control. Property rights are rules that define who has claims on the profits of firms (akin to what agency theorists call "residual claims" on the free cash flow of firms [Jensen and Meckling 1976; Fama 1980]). This leaves open the issues of the different legal forms that exist (i.e., corporations vs. partnerships); the relationship between shareholders and employees, local communities, suppliers, and customers; and the role of the state in directing investment, owning firms, and preventing owners from harming workers. The holders of property rights are entitled to dispose of property or earn income from it. Patents and credentials are forms of property rights that entitle their holder to earn profits by claiming to use a resource. The constitution of property rights is a continuous and contestable political process, not the outcome of an efficient process (for a similar argument, see Roe 1994). Organized groups from business, labor, government agencies, and political parties try to affect the constitution of property rights.

Governance structures refer to the general rules in a society that define relations of competition and cooperation, and the organization of firms. These rules define the legal and illegal forms of firms' control over competition. The rules can be (1) laws or (2) informal institutional practices. Laws, called antitrust, competition, or anticartel laws, exist in most advanced industrial societies. The passage, enforcement, and judicial interpretation of these laws is contested (Fligstein 1996), and the content of such laws varies widely across societies. Some societies allow extensive cooperation between competitors, particularly when foreign trade is involved, while others tend to reduce the effects of barriers to entry and promote competition. Competition is regulated not just within societies, but across societies. Countries have tariffs and trade barriers to help national industry compete with foreign firms. These laws often benefit particular sectors of the economy.

Rules of exchange define who can transact with whom and under which conditions. Rules must be established regarding weights, common standards, shipping, billing, insurance, the exchange of money (i.e., banks), and the enforcement of contracts. Rules of exchange regulate health and safety standards of products and the standardization of products more generally. For example, pharmaceutical products undergo extensive testing. Health and safety standards help both buyers and sellers and facilitate exchange between parties who may have only fleeting interactions.

Product standardization has become increasingly important in the context of rules of exchange, particularly in the telecommunications and computer industries. National and international bodies agree on standards for products across many industries. Standard settings produce shared rules that guarantee that products will be compatible. This facilitates exchange by making it more likely that products will work as intended. Rules of exchange help stabilize markets by insuring that exchanges occur under rules that apply to everyone. If firms that ship their goods across a particular society do not have rules of exchange, exchanges will be haphazard at best. Making these rules has become even more important for trade across societies. Many of the newest international trade agreements, including the European Union's Single Market Program and the last round of GATT, focus on producing and harmonizing practices connected to rules of exchange.

Conceptions of control reflect market-specific agreements between actors on principles of internal organization (i.e., forms of hierarchy), tactics for competition or cooperation (i.e., strategies), and the hierarchy or status ordering of firms in a given market. A conception of control is a form of "local knowledge" (Geertz 1983). Conceptions of control are historical and cultural products, specific to a certain industry in a certain society. They are cultural in that they form a set of understandings and practices about how things work in a particular market. A stable market is a social field with a conception of control that defines the social relations between incumbent and challenger seller firms whereby the incumbent firms reproduce those relations on a period-to-period basis.

A set of rules under which stable markets can operate helps to structure exchange in particular product fields in a particular society. To move from unstructured to structured exchange in a market implies that actors have become aware of systematic problems in stabilizing exchange. Their awareness stimulated them to search for social-organizational solutions to their problems. But this awareness did not come all at once. The emergence of the general social technologies that help actors to produce and maintain modern markets depended on solving the problems presented by property rights (i.e., who owned what), governance structures (i.e., ways to organize, including fair and unfair forms of competition), rules of exchange (i.e., making exchanges), and conceptions of control (i.e., producing local status hierarchies within markets to stabilize the situation of dominant players).

One way to partially understand modern governments is to view them as organized entities that produce and enforce market (and other) rules.

There was no necessity for this historical development. It is theoretically possible for firms to routinize exchange with one another without the benefit of rules or governments. After all, most trade before the eighteenth century took place in the absence of strong states and legal systems (Spruyt 1994). Before modernity, the problems posed by unstable exchange were solved by private parties to those exchanges.

There was a very practical reason for developing more general rules for markets. North and Thomas (1973) noted long ago that social institutions have made entrepreneurs richer, their firms bigger and more stable. But in spite of the fact that rules encouraged markets as fields, entrepreneurs, managers, and governments did not comprehend that creating governmental capacity to make rules would help create wealth. So, for example, Carruthers (1996) shows that the first modern capital market in England was organized along political party lines. People traded only with those with whom they agreed on politics. One of the purposes of the markets was to reward people in the party, by giving them access to friendly pools of capital.

North, in his later work (1990), realized that modern economic history cannot be read as the gradual reduction of transaction costs for markets by the production of rules that facilitate trade. Entrepreneurs and government officials were entirely unaware that their actions were producing positive consequences. Their actions were not framed in these terms; indeed, they were often framed in terms that tended to benefit the friends of the rulers and cut out their enemies. Moreover, the rulers of premodern European states had time horizons that were far too short to understand what produced long-term economic growth. Most market institutions were the outcome of political struggles whereby one group of capitalists captured government and created rules to favor itself over political opponents. This central insight is the basis of the theory of market governance presented here.

As one problem was solved and one set of markets stabilized, another set of problems emerged. The increasing scale of production, and the growth of markets and the growing awareness of entrepreneurs and managers of their common problems pushed the search for new common understandings and new rules.

GLOBALIZATION AND MARKET PROCESSES

These insights can be used to understand globalization. The only difference between a global market and a local one is geographic spread. A market is "globalized" if a small number of participants form an incumbent-challenger structure and operate across countries with a common conception of control. It is an empirical question as to how many world markets are truly global in this sense. Moreover, it may be the case that some markets are partially globalized in that regions are dominated by firms that know each other, but some part of the world market is protected or local. How many globalized markets are there? Given that 83 percent of world economic activity is national, it is safe to say that there are fewer than many observers believe. Of course, many of these markets are for important products like automobiles, chemicals, airframe manufacturers, computers, software, pharmaceuticals, and business services like accounting and consulting. Industries that are partially global include telecommunications and some financial services like investment banking.

How can we tell if a market is being globalized? Obviously as the share of the world market for the product that crosses national borders increases and as firms in different countries increasingly orient their activities toward one another, a global market is emerging. The process by which foreign firms enter a stable national market begins when invaders arrive with a new conception of control. When this happens, the market model predicts that incumbents will respond (1) by reinforcing the old conception of control, (2) by getting their governments to intervene to protect their local market, (3) by co-opting invaders by forming alliances or joining marketing or production arrangements. If these efforts fail, the national market may be absorbed into the international market, with firms adopting the new conception of control either by employing the "new" methods for competition or through merger.

Firms that are not exporting and are not threatened by exporters do not pressure their governments to regulate trade. Firms that are exporting and are not threatened by other firms (i.e., firms already in globalized markets under my definition) are also unlikely to pressure their governments to exclude foreign firms. Firms that are not exporting but find themselves under assault by invaders in their home market try to get protectionist measures passed by their governments. Firms that are exporting and feeling pressure from other exporters may pressure their governments to help open up foreign markets, particularly those of their main competitors. This set of responses implies that governments will simultaneously pursue the opening of some markets abroad while protecting

TABLE 1. A Typology of International Economic Agreements with Examples of Existing Agreements

Dominant Actors in Negotiations	Enforcement of Rules	
	Hard Law	Soft Law
States	NAFTA, WTO, IMF	ASEAN, OECD, APEC
States plus NGOs and firms	European Union	Basle Accords for banking
Firms and NGOs	London Court of International Arbitration	ISO 2000

some of their own markets at home. So, for example, the U.S. government supports the textile and sugar industries domestically while it tries to force the internal market in Japan open for cars and other American products.

The European Union, the North American Free Trade Agreement, and the recently completed GATT treaty that founded the World Trade Organization can be analyzed according to whether or not they address property rights, governance structures, and rules of exchange. They can also be broken down by sectors that do or do not involve exporters, to see if rules apply more or less exclusively to those sectors (Fligstein and Mara-Drita 1996). These agreements have so far been mostly concerned with rules of exchange that facilitate more trade.

One arena in which agreements have not occurred is the creation of a world market for corporate control (Blair and Roe 1999). It is relatively difficult to engage in hostile takeovers in any society except the United States and Great Britain. Most national elites have resisted the transfer of property rights to the highest bidder because they thereby would lose power. States remain players in the creation of the global economy because their elites depend on them to preserve their power and guarantee entry to global markets. This is prima facie evidence that a world capitalist class does not exist. National economic elites have jealously hung onto their local bases of power.

A TYPOLOGY OF INTERNATIONAL ECONOMIC AGREEMENTS

The sociology of markets offers good suggestions as to the link between the creation of global markets and the creation of international economic agreements. As producers come to compete with each other on a global basis, they encounter prob-

lems in protecting property rights, issues of competition and cooperation, and the need for rules of exchange that facilitate trade. The demand for global market rules thus comes from global firms trying to create and stabilize regional or worldwide markets. Governments play two roles in this process. They facilitate the opening of, and rule making in, global markets by negotiating rules affecting market access and processes. But they can also protect their internal market, or worry about rules that undermine their sovereignty. This forces firms to consider forms of governance alternative to state-created supranational structures. If firms can create private governance arrangements that work for them, they avoid the costs associated with courts and nation-states.

Table 1 encapsulates this argument.[1] There are two dimensions of international economic agreements: the parties to the agreement, and the kind of rules and enforcement that come out of the agreements. There are two main sorts of parties to agreements: states and private organizations such as NGOs, including corporations. Two kinds of agreements can be reached: those that involve hard laws that nations are supposed to incorporate into their national law and those that involve agreements over general rules or principles.

An unexplored issue is the conditions under which nongovernmental organizations, including corporations, are allowed to enter into international trade agreements. Sometimes firms prefer not to have governments involved in attempts to establish general rules of trade. The London Court of International Arbitration, for example, is a private court where firms and governments can litigate their contracts (Dezalay and Garth 1996; Mattli 2001). In this instance, firms select a private court precisely because they do not want to be subject to the judgments of public courts. Many international firms sign contracts specifying that disagreements over fulfilling the terms of the contract will be settled by private arbitration. Private courts develop their own case law, and their decisions are viewed as binding by the participants. While private courts were never directly the focus of international economic agreements, they form one way in which corporations address possible contract disputes. They are private international legal arenas that produce "law" and binding outcomes.

Similarly, firms have a great deal of interest in standards of different kinds. ISO 2000 (International Standards Organization) is an organization that helps promote standard setting in technical products. It also certifies that firms have met those standards in their products. This standard setting can take on many issues. First, it can be concerned with health and safety standards. It can insure that products are compatible with existing technical requirements. Software, for example, is often certified to be able to run on particular operating systems. These are clear cases of soft law. The rules created by ISO 2000 are not enforceable in national law. They only signal to potential buyers that the technology has been certified to meet certain agreed-upon standards. In both the ISO 2000 and private courts cases, corporations have found means of collective governance without state actors. Private courts help facilitate exchange by guaranteeing to firms that contracts are enforced. They rely mostly on enforcing rules of exchange. ISO 2000 also promotes exchange by providing buyers with information about the technical standards of particular products.

At the opposite end are formal international economic agreements among states. NAFTA was negotiated by the American, Mexican, and Canadian governments. While the agreement had extensive input from interested groups, such as bankers, it was a treaty. The GATT and later the WTO were negotiated by representatives of states. Both agreements produced treaties that are hard law. Signatory governments agree to give the provisions of the treaties the rule of law. Governments also engage in creating agreements that do not have the force of law. ASEAN and APEC are organizations that bring together leaders of Asian and Pacific Rim countries to discuss economic issues of mutual benefit. Such organizations are often "talk shops" where viewpoints are exchanged with little implication for policy.

In a third category fall instances in which both states and nonstate organizations are privy to negotiations. The cell in table 1 that contains hard law as output and states and nonstate organizations as actors identifies the way that most govern-ments operate within their national jurisdiction. The interests of both state and nonstate actors figure into economic policymaking. The output of that policymaking is hard law enforceable in courts. It is not surprising that the international economic agreement in this cell of the table is the European Union. The EU has pushed supranational governance farther than any other international agreement. It has set in place a permanent legislative function complete with lobbying groups, a court, and a monetary system. This extensive political apparatus produces the most integrated transnational market in the world.

There are also arenas of international economic cooperation where states and nonstate organizations gather to produce soft law agreements. Perhaps the most important site for this kind of action is the Basle Accords. The Basle Accords are both an agreement and an organization that works to provide rules governing international banking and finance. Bank supervisors from around the world meet to determine standards for such things as capital reserve requirements. The goal is to establish international standards for banks that will help guarantee their solvency and signal to potential investors that banks have met those standards. Frequently, governments make these standards part of national rules. But the accords themselves do not have the force of law. Instead, they are goals and common rules that are meant to guide banks, investors, and governments. These kinds of standards do not just cover such issues as rules of exchange. They also govern property rights because they specify how to evaluate the fiscal soundness of banks and other financial institutions.

This plethora of international economic agreements shows clearly the limits of thinking about such agreements from either the narrow perspective of trade, or alternatively, the perspective of international relations theory in political science. It is the sociology of markets that pushes us to consider what the relevant field of international economic agreements consists of and what the underlying dimensions of the structuring of that field are. This orientation means that those actors will need rules to govern their interactions. They will need rules to govern property rights and competition and cooperation, and need rules of exchange. These rules can be hard or soft. They can be made with or without governments.

There are two interesting questions on which to speculate: how are we to understand when states include nonstate actors in their negotiations (and similarly, when do nonstate actors avoid states)?

When do actors choose hard over soft law? It is useful to envision a continuum of arenas that runs from talk shops to agreements with both governments and nonstate organizations that produce hard law. In table 1, ASEAN is one extreme, while the EU is the other. The WTO and the London Court of International Arbitration are closer to the EU, and the Basle Accords and ISO 2000 closer to ASEAN.

It is here that the existing literature on political economy and international relations provides us with hypotheses. The attaining of agreements rests on the ability of disparate organizations (be they states or nonstate organizations) to accept binding results in order to further their interests at an acceptable cost. If some states or organizations will inevitably lose by international agreements, we can expect them to favor soft over hard agreements. The constructionist view that existing agreements and organizations can work to persuade either governments or nonstate organizations to participate in new agreements seems plausible as well. To the degree that such existing organizations can convince other actors that going along with more agreements (particularly of the hard law variety) is in their interest, they will form. This is an important future avenue of research.

One can speculate that the main mechanism by which agreements become more binding is through a process of ratcheting up or imitation. If groups find that cooperation is of mutual benefit, they may be inclined to enter into new arrangements. They may also find that current agreements do not produce enough or the right kind of collective governance and act to improve them. As international economic arrangements appear to be effective in producing collective gains, they will be expanded. This appears to be the case with the GATT, which morphed into the WTO and the current round of trade negotiations (the so-called Doha round). Successful negotiations may also give other parties the idea of imitating such agreements. For example, the success of the EU inspired Latin American countries to undertake the MERCOSUR agreement. NAFTA is currently being touted as a model for a Free Trade Agreement for the Americas (FTAA).

THE CASE OF THE EUROPEAN UNION

It is useful to apply insights from the sociology of markets to a particular case, the European Union. The underlying logic of the sociology of markets model can be stated simply. As problems and new circumstances arise, firms and other market actors press governmental organizations, including legislators and courts, for rules to govern markets. As these organizations respond to these demands, new opportunities to expand markets emerge. If market actors adapt their activities to exploit new opportunities, they will, as a result, push new demands. The feedback loop is completed, and the cycle begins anew.

The EU provides an extraordinary example of this process. The EU is a unique polity. Some observers characterize it as an intergovernmental organization, an interstate "regime," constituted by a voluntary pooling of sovereignty (Keohane and Hoffmann 1991). Others see it as a quasi-federal statelike structure (Sbragia 1992), or as a "multilevel" polity (Marks et al. 1996). Wessels describes the EU as a "fusionist" state, in which national governments have fused some of their functions (1997). Still other observers see it as a complex blend of supranational and intergovernmental modes of governance that varies across time and policy arenas (Sandholtz and Stone Sweet 1998).

The Treaty of Rome, which initiated the European Union, provided a blueprint for a complex set of organizations with jurisdiction over economic exchange defined very broadly. The issues on the table have been primarily concerned trade and, much less so, labor, the welfare state, and the environment (Streeck and Schmitter, 1991). Over time, EU-regulated policy domains for these issues have widened, but many have remained in the purview of member states. The EU was built from provisions, more or less vague and in need of concretizing, contained in the treaty. The EU has four major organizations: the Council of Ministers, the Commission, the European Court of Justice (ECJ), and the European Parliament (EP). The Council, made up of government ministers from each country, votes on new rules for the whole of Europe. Once a new piece of legislation has been adopted, each nation-state is obligated to transpose it into national law. The member states maintain permanent representatives in Brussels, who are in continuous contact with each other and with the Commission; and heads of government meet semi-annually to consider more ambitious initiatives and to discuss the overall direction of the EC. The European Commission produces legislative proposals for the Council and the EP to consider, either at its own initiative or upon request from the latter. The Commission was created to help states solve their bargaining problems. It does so by producing policy studies, proposing new measures, negotiating draft legislation with social actors (organized interests), and shepherding bills through the Council and the EP. New measures are usually not considered by the Council until extensive negotiations with relevant lobby groups have already taken place. The Commission is divided into directorates, each in charge of a competence delineated by the Rome treaty. There are always a great number of proposals, large and small, floating around the Commission, and much political activity among people who work for the directorates and lobbying groups (Mazey and Richardson 1993). This complicated structure organizes multiple, nested games in which various actors in the Commission build coalitions in support of divergent agendas (Peters 1992).

The ECJ is the authoritative interpreter of EU law. It enforces the treaties and secondary legislation pursuant to litigation brought by private organizations, individuals, and states. These decisions are binding on all parties involved, including nation-states. In the 1960s, the Court established the principle that EU rules supersede national law when the two conflict. This is called the doctrine of "supremacy."[2] The ECJ also decided that, under certain conditions, EC law confers judicially enforceable rights and duties on all subjects of EU law, including firms and individuals, rights that national law and courts are obliged to protect. This is called the doctrine of "direct effect."[3] Taken together, these decisions transformed the Treaty of Rome and the EU from an international organization to a vertically integrated, quasi-federal, rule-of-law polity (Stein 1981; Slaughter, Stone Sweet, and Weiler 1998; Weiler 1990). The EP is directly elected. It sets the budget and advises the Commission. Until the 1980s, its powers were mostly advisory in nature. With the Single Act and the Treaty of European Union, the EP accrued broad agenda-setting powers and, under some conditions, veto authority in the legislative process. Thus, after 1986, the Council of Ministers legislates with the EP, while the Commission retains its powers of legislative initiative.

This complex mix of organizational competences, decision rules, and legislative procedures can be confusing to participants and analysts. National governments often seek to maintain power through their control of the Council, and through the activities of their permanent representatives in processes otherwise managed by the Commission. But with qualified majority voting and the enhanced role of the EP, governments can find themselves having to accept legislation they voted

against. Monitoring and controlling the Commission is a costly and difficult proposition, especially when it has an activist agenda. Finally, governments do not control the interpretation or enforcement of EU law. The Commission or a private party may attack them in court for noncompliance with EU rules, and it is usually the case that national courts and the ECJ rule against the governments (see Stone Sweet and Brunell 1998).

The institutionalization of the Rome Treaty has been driven by the construction of feedback loops and other connections between relatively autonomous fields in the EU. Three such fields are the most important (Fligstein and Stone Sweet 2002): between firms engaged in cross-border trade (seeking to expand markets); between litigants (seeking to vindicate their rights under EU law), national judges (seeking to effectively resolve disputes to which EU law is material), and the ECJ; and between lobbying groups (seeking to influence EU regulation) and EU officials in Brussels. European integration occurred in three periods.[4] From 1958 to 1969, actors were engaged in building its main organizations and figuring out how to make the Treaty of Rome work. The pivotal event during this period was the Court's "constitutionalization" of the treaty through the doctrines of supremacy and direct effect. During the second period, 1970–85, the Commission and ECJ dismantled barriers to intra-EU trade and other kinds of transnational exchange (negative integration). At the same time, the Commission and the Council replaced the disparate regulatory regimes at the national level with harmonized regulatory frameworks (positive integration). Although the data (Fligstein and Stone Sweet 2002) show that positive integration proceeded more steadily than is often appreciated, many important harmonization projects stalled in the Council, in part because more ambitious initiatives required the unanimous vote of national ministers. The unanimity rule, a product of the Luxembourg compromise in the 1960s, made agreements difficult to forge, at a time when the cumulative impact of negative integration was to raise the costs of intergovernmental deadlock for an increasing number of social and economic actors who wanted wider and deeper integration. This period ended with the passage of the Single European Act, which altered the voting rules for adopting legislation pertaining to the Single Market Program, from unanimity to qualified majority voting in most cases. The final period, from 1986 to the present, can be characterized as the most active from the perspective of institutionalizing European market and governance structures through positive integration.

During all of these periods trade within the EU expanded. It expanded most dramatically following the announcement of the completion of the Single Market in 1985 (Fligstein and Stone Sweet 2002). In 1992, the EU agreed to form a monetary union, and in January 2002, most of the EU member states adopted the euro as their currency. National markets are now highly integrated in Europe, and exports are now critical to economic growth. Almost half of world trade occurs within the borders of the EU, making it virtually a single economy. Transnational networks of producers and public interest groups have oriented their activities toward Brussels. The EU's political organizations govern by making, applying, and interpreting rules that are authoritative throughout the territory of the EU. National courts routinely enforce European law, coordinating EU rules with national rules, and national bureaucracies incorporate EU legislation into their procedures and practices. European law now includes competition policy, attempts to create a single system of property rights, an integrated financial system, and extensive rules of exchange. European governments have facilitated integration, sometimes proactively, sometimes by being dragged along.

THE FUTURE OF GLOBAL GOVERNANCE: HOW MUCH? WHAT KIND? WHY NOT MORE?

The European Union is an extreme case of international economic cooperation. Its very success and its uniqueness suggest the limits of current economic international arrangements. Existing arrangements tend to be piecemeal and focused on particular firms or industrial sectors. They frequently lack strong enforcement mechanisms or hard law. What general lessons can be learned from the EU? Perhaps the most important is that governments have to be prepared to give up some sovereignty if they expect to produce extensive agreements that will lead to more market integration. While national governments did not always agree with the ECJ's decisions, they eventually concluded that attaining agreements was more important than maintaining either veto power or preventing those agreements from overriding national law. Marketing opening increased trade across Europe. The largest producers were the winners in this market-opening project. These producers convinced their national governments that pooling sovereignty was a good thing. Not surprisingly, the EU subsequently proved to be a useful vehicle for economic cooperation that produced rules to favor traders, often the largest multinational producers.

It is useful to consider an analogous process in the world today. The GATT lowered tariff barriers around the world. This had the effect of increasing world trade substantially. Nonstate actors, including multinational corporations, convinced their governments that increased cooperation and the removal of nontariff trade barriers was a good idea. They also convinced their governments that there needed to be a procedure whereby trade disputes involving the GATT and WTO rules could be arbitrated. This produced the dispute resolution mechanism of the WTO (described in Block and Evans, this volume). The WTO dispute resolution mechanism is somewhere between court and mediator. A ruling by the WTO that a trade violation has occurred implies only that the aggrieved parties should negotiate a settlement. If a settlement is not reached, then the WTO suggests that trade sanctions can be used to collect damages. The WTO has no independent enforcement mechanism.

The evolution of the WTO has a limited similarity to the EU. The WTO, for example, has no ability to continuously engage in the creation of new trading rules. Its dispute resolution mechanism allows only states to sue each other and does not allow nonstate organizations to participate. These limits mean that the creation and enforcement of WTO rules is fixed unless renegotiated. One can predict if the nations who have signed onto the WTO believe that additional trade has been useful and if they feel pressure by firms to continue market-opening projects, then more market rules and more extensive enforcement will be created.

The world economy is nowhere near a single market. There are multiple currencies, limited courts, an unintegrated system of property rights, and no policy on international competition. There are many mechanisms to facilitate exchange (like standard settings and removal of tariff barriers). One can argue that one of the main (although not the only) impediments to a single market is the U.S. government. In protecting the interests of the largest economy and the military hegemon, U.S. policymakers are not likely to tie themselves to international agreements that restrict their freedom. The largest American corporations use the U.S. political system to their advantage, and it is difficult to see the conditions under which they might get a better deal from an international trade organization. They are among the leaders in proposing private forms of governance that involve firms in the making and enforcing of rules. By keeping negotiations like the Basle Accords, for instance, outside of the public eye, they make results favorable to corporations more likely to appear in rule making. In sum, the American government's globalization project with its exclusive focus on negative integration is unlikely to result in a single world market. This means that the potential economic gains to increased trade are limited.

Ironically, the institutionalist sociology of markets implies that if firms really want access to worldwide market opportunities, they need to get states to help them make rules about positive integration. There is evidence this has occurred both in the EU and in the WTO. But these forces do not necessarily lead to a globalized form of governance that is more "democratic." Instead, large corporations can be as satisfied with private forms of hard and soft law. This keeps large governmental organizations from interfering too readily in corporate affairs. This restraint produces the mixed system of international economic agreements that we observe.

Most international economic agreements begin and end with governments and nonstate actors that primarily reflect the interests of corporations. It is very difficult for consumers, labor, or environmentalist groups to place their concerns on the agendas of international economic talks. If corporations can move to systems of private governance to settle contract disputes or produce common rules of property rights, governance, or rules or exchange, then they make difficult targets for anyone else to rule over. If states protect their sovereignty and view economic agreements as narrowly concerning issues of interest to exporters, then they too will not be useful vehicles to press other interests. This leaves more local national interest groups with their national governments as the main place to express their grievances. National governments continue to be the providers of environmental, labor, health, safety, and consumer protections. As constructivist research has shown, however, the successes of interest groups depend on their organization, the existence of transnational activist networks, and the pressure brought to bear at multiple points in the system (i.e., on national governments and in international arenas).

RESEARCH AGENDAS SUGGESTED BY THE SOCIOLOGY OF MARKETS

The sociology of markets can offer conceptual and theoretical tools that imply interesting and innovative research projects. The sociology of markets helps conceptualize markets and their links to systems of governance. It provides conceptual tools to figure out which markets are "globalized," how long they have been that way, and which markets are in the process of being globalized. It also provides a framework for understanding where the demand for global rules will emerge. Generally, one expects global governance where markets exist, and the push for new governance where market openings have occurred. Comprehensive analysis of markets and global governance is a large-scale project that has yet to be undertaken.

A second group of projects suggested by this perspective is to evaluate what types of governance have actually emerged and why. Projects would address who participates in these discussions, why, and whether they produce hard or soft law. It would also be important to make sense of which forces push actors toward one system or another. Finally, it is important to assess the dynamics of these kinds of arrangements.

Finally, a frontier issue is if and how labor, environmental, and consumer groups can become part of discussions. In the EU, environmental and consumer groups have done fairly well in getting their issues on the agenda. Labor has done less well and remained more attached to national political parties (see the papers in Stone Sweet, Sandholtz, and Fligstein 2001; Cichowski 1998). Such groups have been vocal in telling their national governments that their issues need a place on the EU agenda. By exploring this process in the EU, one could get a better sense of whether such groups can get a hearing at other organizations like the WTO and the NAFTA. The NAFTA has labor and environmental side agreements that provide the opening for discussion of these issues (Evans 2002). Groups pushing these agreements succeeded by building a transnational political coalition, focused on labor and the environment, in Canada, the United States, and Mexico. These issues have been put into play in subsequent trade negotiations involving the United States.

CONCLUSION

International economic agreements have proliferated in the past 40 years. They have brought together governments, nongovernmental organizations, and corporations. The agreements have covered a large number of issues in a large part of the world. The most extensive of these agreements are regional, the EU and the NAFTA. This implies that international economic agreements are relatively hard to attain. Our review highlighted the political factors that produce this pattern. National governments seek to preserve their sovereignty. They also come under pressure from organized groups that seek to protect their current advantages. Nonetheless, these agreements have grown more extensive over time.

The sociology of markets has several important concepts to add to discussions. It offers a way to understand the structure of global markets. It also offers insight into the important link between markets and governance. Its conceptual tools suggest that there will be an increased demand for global governance in industries or sectors where trade expands. Through a feedback process, as firms meet in a more globalized market, they come to prefer more extensive rules. The sociology of markets also suggests why it is difficult for labor, environment, and consumer groups to participate in discussions over international economic agreements. Corporations can engage in the private production of some forms of governance and avoid states entirely. Other groups have to pressure their governments to include them in international economic arrangements. If corporations think these groups will have too much influence, they may opt out of negotiation altogether.

Finally, the sociology of markets suggests a number of research projects that so far have been underexploited. By using the sociology of markets, we can learn much more about how globalized markets are, the process by which they become so, and the process of creating international forms of governance. Much interesting work remains to be done.

Notes

I would like to thank Fred Block, Paula England, Wolfgang Streeck, and the editors, Neil Smelser and Richard Swedberg, for comments on an earlier draft. I would also like to acknowledge Christopher Chase-Dunn and Ron Jepperson, who alerted me to some literature I had neglected in an earlier draft.

1. The figure does not include another dimension of interest: whether or not the agreement results in the creation of a permanent organization. Most international economic agreements tend to produce at least some organizational residue in which discussions are ongoing. But some, such as bilateral trade agreements or the meetings of the G-7 (heads of the seven most developed economies in the world) do not generate formal organizations.

2. First articulated in the Costa judgment (ECJ 1964).

3. First announced in the Van Gend en Loos judgment (ECJ 1963).

4. For different purposes and with somewhat different results, Weiler (1999, chap. 2) analyzes the EC as a sequence of equilibria, stages that map onto our periodization scheme.

References

Arrighi, Giovanni. 1994. *The Long Twentieth Century.* London: Verso.

Baldwin, Robert E. 1986. *The Political Economy of U.S. Import Policy.* Cambridge: MIT Press.

Bates, Robert H., and Anne O. Krueger. 1993. *Political and Economic Interactions in Economic Policy Reform.* Cambridge, Mass.: Blackwell.

Berger, Suzanne. 2000. "Globalization and Politics." *Annual Review of Political Science* 3:43–62.

Berger, Suzanne, and Ronald Dore. 1996. *National Diversity and Global Capitalism.* Ithaca, N.Y.: Cornell University Press.

Blair, Margaret M., and Mark J. Roe. 1999. *Employees and Corporate Governance.* Washington, D.C.: Brookings Institution Press.

Block, Fred L. 1977. *The Origins of International Economic Disorder.* Berkeley and Los Angeles: University of California Press.

Boli, John, and George M. Thomas. 1998. *Constructing World Culture: International Intergovernmental Organizations since 1875.* Stanford, Calif.: Stanford University Press.

Boswell, Terry, and Christopher Chase-Dunn. 2000. *The Spiral of Capitalism and Socialism.* Boulder, Colo.: Lynne Reimer.

Carruthers, Bruce. 1996. *City of Capital.* Princeton: Princeton University Press.

Chase-Dunn, Christopher. 1998. *Global Formation: Structures of the World Economy.* Lanham, Md.: Rowman and Littlefield.

Checkel, Jeffrey T. 1997. "International Norms and Domestic Politics." *European Journal of International Relations* 3:473–95.

———. 1998. "The Constructivist Turn in International Relations." *World Politics* 50:324–48.

Cichowski, Rachel. 1998. "Integrating the Environment: The European Court and the Construction of Supranational Policy." *Journal of European Public Policy* 5(1): 66–97.

Crouch, Colin, and Wolfgang Streeck. 1997. *The Political Economy of Modern Capitalism.* London: Sage.

Dezalay, Yves, and Bryant G. Garth. 1996. *Dealing in Virtue: International Commercial Arbitration and the Construction of an International Commercial Order.* Chicago: University of Chicago Press.

———. 2002a. *Global Prescriptions.* Ann Arbor: University of Michigan Press.

———. 2002b. "Legitimating the New Legal Orthodoxy." Pp. 306–34 in *Global Prescriptions,* ed. Yves Dezalay and Bryant G. Garth. Ann Arbor: University of Michigan Press.

European Court of Justice (ECJ). 1963. Van Gend en Loos, Case 26/62. *European Court Reports* 1963:1.

———. 1964. Costa, Case 6/64. *European Court Reports* 1964:585.

Evans, Peter. 1996. *Embedded Autonomy*. Princeton: Princeton University Press.

———. 1997. "The Eclipse of the State?" *World Politics* 50:62–87.

Evans, Peter, and J. Rauch. 1999. "Bureaucracy and Economic Growth." *American Sociological Review* 64:187–214.

Evans, Rhonda. 2002. "The Rise of Ethical Trade Advocacy: NAFTA and the New Politics of Trade." Ph.D. diss., Department of Sociology, University of California.

Fama, Eugene F. 1980. "Agency Problems and the Theory of the Firm." *Journal of Political Economy* 88(2): 288–307.

Finnemore, Martha. 1996. *National Interests in International Society*. Ithaca, N.Y.: Cornell University Press.

Finnemore, Martha, and Kathryn Sikkink. 2001. "Taking Stock: The Constructivist Research Program in International Relations and Comparative Politics." *Annual Review of Political Science* 4:391–416.

Fligstein, Neil. 1996. "Markets as Politics: A Political-Cultural Approach to Market Institutions." *American Sociological Review* 61:656–73.

———. 2001. *The Architecture of Markets*. Princeton: Princeton University Press.

Fligstein, Neil, and Iona Mara-Drita. 1996. "How to Make a Market: Reflections on the European Union's Single Market Program." *American Journal of Sociology* 102:1–33.

Fligstein, Neil, and Alec Stone Sweet. 2002. "Constructing Markets and Politics: An Institutionalist Account of European Integration." *American Journal of Sociology* 107:476–511.

Frieden, Jeffry A. 1990. *Debt, Development, and Democracy*. Princeton: Princeton University Press.

Frieden, Jeffry A., and Ronald Rogowski. 1996. "The Impact of the International Community on National Domestic Politics." Pp. 25–47 in *Internationalization and Domestic Politics*, ed. Robert O. Keohane and Helen V. Milner. Cambridge: Cambridge University Press.

Friedman, Lawrence M. 1973. *The History of American Law*. New York: Simon and Schuster.

Garrett, Geoffrey. 1998. *Partisan Politics in the Global Economy*. Cambridge: Cambridge University Press.

Geertz. Clifford. 1983. *Local Knowledge*. New York: Basic Books.

Gowa, Joanne. 1994. *Allies, Adversaries, and International Trade*. Princeton: Princeton University Press.

Haggard, Stephan. 1995. *Developing Nations and the Politics of Global Integration*. Washington, D.C.: Brookings Institution Press.

Helleiner, Eric. 1994. *States and the Reemergence of Global Finance*. Ithaca, N.Y.: Cornell University Press.

Horwitz, Morton J. 1977. *The Transformation of American Law, 1780–1860*. Cambridge: Harvard University Press.

Irwin, Douglas A. 1994. "The Political Economy of Free Trade." *Journal of Law and Economics* 37:75–108.

———. 1996. "Industry or Class Cleavages over Trade Policy?" Pp. 53–75 in *The Political Economy of Trade Policy*, ed. Robert C. Feenstra, Gene M. Grossman, and Douglas A. Irwin. Cambridge: MIT Press.

Jackson, Karl D. 1999. *Asian Contagion*. Boulder, Colo.: Westview Press.

Jacobson, Harold K. 2000. "International Institutions and System Transformation." *Annual Review of Political Science* 3:149–66.

Jensen, Michael C., and William H. Meckling. 1976. "Theory of the Firm: Managerial Behavior, Agency Costs, and Ownership Structure." *Journal of Financial Economics* 3:305–40.

Katzenstein, Peter J. 1996. *The Culture of National Security Norms and Identity in World Politics*. Ithaca, N.Y.: Cornell University Press.

Keck, Margaret E., and Kathryn Sikkink. 1998. *Activists beyond Borders*. Ithaca, N.Y.: Cornell University Press.

Keohane, Robert O. 1984. *After Hegemony*. Princeton: Princeton University Press.

Keohane, Robert O., and Stanley Hoffman. 1991. "Institutional Change in Europe in the 1980s." Pp. 1–40 in *The New European Community*, ed. Robert O. Keohane and Stanley Hoffman. Boulder, Colo.: Westview Press.

Klotz, Audie. 1995. *Norms in International Relations: The Struggle against Apartheid*. Ithaca, N.Y.: Cornell University Press.

Koremenos, Barbara, Charles Lipson, and Duncan J. Snidal. 2001. "The Rational Design of International Institutions." *International Organizations* 55: 761–99.

Krasner, Stephen D. 1976. "State Power and the Structure of International Trade." *World Politics* 28: 317–47.

———. 1988. "Sovereignty: An Institutionalist Perspective." *Comparative Political Studies* 21:66–94.

Krueger, Anne O. 1997. "Trade Policy and Economic Development." *American Economic Review* 87: 1–22.

Lake, David A. 1988. *Power, Protection, and Free Trade*. Ithaca, N.Y.: Cornell University Press.

Laumann, Edward O., and David Knoke. 1987. *The Organizational State*. Madison: University of Wisconsin Press.

Marks, Gary, Liesbet Hooghe, and Kermit Blank. 1996. "European Integration from the 1980s: State Centric vs. Multilevel Governance." *Journal of Common Market Studies* 34:341–78.

Mattli, Walter. 2001. "Private Justice in a Global Economy: From Litigation to Arbitration." *International Organization* 55:919–47.

Mazey, Sonia, and Jeremy Richardson, eds. 1993. *Lobbying in the European Community*. Oxford: Oxford University Press.

McMichael, Philip. 1996. *Development and Social Change*. Thousand Oaks, Calif.: Pine Forge Press.

Meyer, John W. 2000. "Globalization: Sources and Effects on National States and Society." *International Sociology* 15:233–49.

Meyer, John W., John Boli, George M. Thomas, and Francisco O. Ramirez. 1997. "World Society and the Nation State." *American Journal of Sociology* 103:144–81.

Meyer, John W., and Michael T. Hannan, eds. 1979. *National Development and the World System: Educational, Economic, and Political Change, 1950–1970*. Chicago: University of Chicago Press.

Midford, Paul. 1993. "International Trade and Domestic Politics." *International Organization* 47:535–64.

Milner, Helen V. 1999. "The Political Economy of International Trade." *Annual Review of Political Science* 2:91–114.

Murphy, Craig. 1994. *International Organization and Industrial Change*. Cambridge: Polity Press.

———. 2000. "Global Governance: Poorly Done and Poorly Understood." *International Affairs* 76: 789–803.

Noll, Roger G. 1989. "Economic Perspectives on the Politics of Regulation." Pp. 1257–87 in *Handbook of Industrial Organization*, ed. Richard Schmalensee and Robert D. Willig. New York: Elsevier.

North, Douglass C. 1990. *Institutions, Institutional Change, and Economic Performance*. Cambridge: Cambridge University Press.

North, Douglass C., and Robert Paul Thomas. 1973. *The Rise of the Western World*. Cambridge: Cambridge University Press.

Peltzman, Sam. 1989. "The Economic Theory of Regulation after a Decade of Deregulation." Pp. 1–59 in *Brookings Papers in Microeconomics*. Washington, D.C.: Brookings Institution Press.

Pempel, T. J. 1999. *The Politics of the Asian Economic Crisis*. Ithaca, N.Y.: Cornell University Press.

Peters, B. Guy. 1991. "Bureaucratic Politics and the Institutions of the European Community." Pp. 75–122 in *Euro-politics*, ed. Alberta M. Sbragia. Washington, D.C.: Brookings Institution Press.

Polanyi, Karl. 1944. *The Great Transformation*. Boston: Beacon Press.

Risse, Thomas. 2000. "Let's Argue: Communicative Action in World Politics." *International Organization* 54:1–40.

Risse, Thomas, Stephen C. Ropp, and Kathryn Sikkink. 1999. *The Power of Human Rights: International Norms and Domestic Change*. Cambridge: Cambridge University Press.

Robinson, William I. 1996. *Promoting Polyarchy*. Cambridge: Cambridge University Press.

———. 2001. "Social Theory and Globalization: The Rise of a Transnational State." *Theory and Society* 30:157–200.

Rodrik, Dani. 1994. "The Rush to Free Trade in the Developing World." Pp. 61–88 in *Voting for Reform*, ed. Stephen Haggard and Steven B. Webb. New York: Oxford University Press, for the World Bank.

———. 1995. "Political Economy of Trade Policy." Pp. 1457–95 in vol. 3 of *Handbook of International Economics*, ed. Gene M. Grossman and Kenneth Rogoff. New York: Elsevier.

———. 1997. *Has Globalization Gone Too Far?* Washington, D.C.: Institute for International Economics.

Roe, Mark J. 1994. *Strong Managers, Weak Owners: The Political Roots of American Corporate Finance*. Princeton: Princeton University Press.

Rogowski, Ronald. 1989. *Commerce and Coalitions*. Princeton: Princeton University Press.

Roy, William G. 1998. *Socializing Capital*. Princeton: Princeton University Press.

Ruggie, John G. 1998. "What Makes the World Hang Together?" *International Organization* 52:855–87.

Russett, Bruce M. 1985. "The Mysterious Case of Vanishing Hegemony." *International Organization* 39: 207–32.

Sandholtz, Wayne, and Alec Stone Sweet. 1998. *European Integration and Supranational Governance*. Oxford: Oxford University Press.

Sbragia, Alberta M. 1992. "Thinking about the European Future." Pp. 257–91 in *Europolitics*, ed. Alberta M. Sbragia. Washington, D.C.: Brookings Institution Press.

Scharpf, Fritz W. 1996. "Negative and Positive Integration in the Political Economy of European Welfare States." Pp. 15–39 in *Governance in the European Union*, ed. Guy Marks, Fritz W. Scharpf, Philippe C. Schmitter, and Wolfgang Streeck. London: Sage.

Scheve, Kenneth F., and Matthew J. Slaughter. 1998. "What Determines Individual Trade Policy Preferences?" NBER Working Paper No. 6531.

Slaughter, Anne-Marie. 2002. "Breaking Out: The Proliferation of Actors in the International System." Pp. 12–36 in *Global Prescriptions*, ed. Yves Dezalay and Bryant G. Garth. Ann Arbor: University of Michigan Press.

Slaughter, Anne-Marie, Alec Stone Sweet, and J.H.H. Weiler, eds. 1998. *The European Court and the National Courts—Doctrine and Jurisprudence: Legal Change in Its Social Context*. Oxford: Hart Press; Evanston, Ill.: Northwestern University Press.

Smelser, Neil J. 1995. *Problematics of Sociology*. Berkeley and Los Angeles: University of California Press.

Spruyt, Hendrik. 1994. *The Sovereign State and Its Competitors*. Princeton: Princeton University Press.

Stein, Eric. 1981. "Lawyers, Judges, and the Making of a Transnational Constitution." *American Journal of International Law* 75:1–27.

Stiglitz, Joseph E. 2002. *Globalization and Its Discontents*. New York: W. W. Norton.

Stone Sweet, Alec, and Thomas L. Brunell. 1998. "Constructing a Supranational Constitution: Dispute Resolution and Governance in the European Community." *American Political Science Review* 92: 63–81.

Stone Sweet, Alec, Wayne Sandholtz, and Neil Fligstein, eds. 2001. *The Institutionalization of Europe*. Oxford: Oxford University Press.

Streeck, Wolfgang, and Philippe C. Schmitter. 1991. "From National Corporatism to Transnational Pluralism." *Politics and Society* 19:133–64.

Tarrow, Sidney. 2001. "Transnational Politics: Contention and Institutions in International Politics." *Annual Review of Political Science* 4:1–20.

Thomas, Daniel C. 2001. *The Helsinki Effect*. Princeton: Princeton University Press.

Trefler, Daniel. 1993. "Trade Liberalization and the Theory of Endogenous Protection." *Journal of Political Economy*, 101:138–60.

Vogel, Steven C. 1996. *Freer Markets, More Rules*. Ithaca, N.Y.: Cornell University Press.

Wallerstein, Immanuel. 1974. *The Modern World System*. Vol. 1. New York: Academic Press.

———. 1984. "The Three Instances of Hegemony in the History of the Capitalist World System." Pp. 100–108 in *Current Issues and Research in Macrosociology*, ed. Gerhard Lenski. Leiden: E. J. Brill.

Waltz, Kenneth N. 1979. *Theory of International Politics*. Reading, Mass.: Addison-Wesley.

Weiler, J.H.H. 1990. "The Transformation of Europe." *Yale Law Review* 100:2403–83.

———. 1999. *The Constitution of Europe: "Do the New Clothes Have an Emperor?" and Other Essays on European Integration*. Cambridge: Cambridge University Press.

Weiss, Linda. 1998. *The Myth of the Powerless State*. Ithaca, N.Y.: Cornell University Press.

Wendt, Alexander. 1999. *Social Theory of International Politics*. Cambridge: Cambridge University Press.

Wessels, Wolfgang. 1997. "An Ever Closer Fusion: A Dynamic Macro-political View of Integration Processes." *Journal of Common Market Studies* 35:267–99.

Wood, Robert E. 1986. *From Marshall Plan to Debt Crisis*. Berkeley and Los Angeles: University of California Press.

World Trade Organization. 2002. *World Trade Statistics*. Geneva: World Trade Organization.

Yarbrough, Beth V., and Yarbrough Robert M. 1992. *Cooperation and Governance in International Trade*. Princeton: Princeton University Press.

10 Post-Communist Economic Systems

Lawrence P. King and Iván Szelényi

IN THE FIRST EDITION of this *Handbook* we wrote a chapter under the title "The Socialist Economic System." This chapter can be read as a follow-up to, or a new section of, the previous one since our aim now is to describe the economic systems that have emerged with the sudden collapse (as happened in Eastern Europe) or gradual erosion (as is currently the case in East Asia) of the socialist economic system. The chapter in the first edition was about the emergence of a distinctive social structure and economy that accompanied development under the Soviet model of total state ownership and "rational redistribution," whereby party bureaucrats setting a plan moved resources (especially capital and labor) around the economy (Kornai 1980). This produced a tendency toward a shortage economy, and the formation of a privileged class of intellectuals (composed of bureaucrats, technocrats, and humanistic intellectuals) that disproportionately benefited from state redistribution relative to workers (Konrád and Szelényi 1979). The chapter in this second edition describes the new systems that have emerged in the post-Communist world and the reform Communist systems of East Asia, which all have developed increasingly capitalist social structures based on the growing dominance of private property and market integration, above all in capital and labor markets.

Our analysis demonstrates the overwhelming conditioning power of social structures—including intraelite structures—in processes of economic change.

The emergent post-Communist systems have several features that distinguish them from capitalist systems we know from East Asia, from the North Atlantic region, or from the old periphery of the capitalist system before the fall of Communism. Whether the unique features identified below are only transition phenomena, and eventually post-Communist capitalisms will merge with the rest of the capitalist world into one unified system, remains to be seen. A growing literature has detailed the persistent differences between capitalist systems, most typically the differences between East Asian "state-led" capitalism, Anglo-Saxon "market-led" forms, and northern European "coordinated, negotiated or consensual" capitalisms (see Thurow 1992; Hart 1992; Marquand 1997; Coates 2000; Hall and Soskice 2001). It is reasonable to assume, therefore, that the rather different trajectories former Communist societies take during the process of transition may be consequential for the structure of their socioeconomic systems once they are consolidated.

Whether the post-Communist world is converging toward a single form of capitalism under the impact of strong forces of globalization, or the future is a multiplicity of capitalist socioeconomic organizations, is in itself an intriguing question. Some observers (Fligstein 1996; Stark and Bruszt, 1998, 2001; Nee 1998; Eyal, Szelényi, and Townsley 1998, 2001; King 2001a, 2001b, 2002) have suggested that the core of the classical concern of comparative macrosociology, namely the cross-systemic comparison between capitalism and socialism, should be substituted by a "neoclassical"[1] research program, which focuses on "comparative capitalisms." Michael Burawoy (2001a) challenged this position, seeing capitalism as a unitary system. Indeed, both from world system theory and neoclassical economics the multiplicity of capitalisms makes little sense (ironically, these otherwise so different approaches seem to converge when it comes to the characteristics of contemporary capitalism). From this perspective, there is a single logic of capitalism, since, as Burawoy puts it, capitalism "erases the past." From this perspective, path dependency in the transition to capitalism may be real, but it is relatively unimportant and will vanish with the consolidation of capitalism.

One also may wonder whether all former Communist states can be simply called "capitalist," or whether some or even all constitute a new form of socioeconomic organization somewhere between capitalism and socialism. Some scholars, most prominently David Stark (1992), insist that the term *transition* is inaccurate. From this perspective, the reality of post-Communism is not that capitalism is being built *on* the ruins of socialism. Rather, a new system is emerging built *with* the ruins of socialism, combining features of socialism and capitalism. Stark argued that individual private property has not been sufficiently formed in central Europe, creating a system dominated by what he calls "recombinant property," which is neither private property nor state ownership, and which is integrated by networks, as opposed to markets (Stark 1996; Stark and Bruszt 1998). While the evidence indicates that Stark was too hasty to pass judgment (see Hanley, King, and Toth 2002), this implies that there are limitations to the extent that the new post-Communist economies are indeed capitalist. Many observers (including Burawoy and Krotov [1992]) have pointed out how poorly market institutions have developed in Russia, drawing attention to the pervasive role of barter in economic exchange. Andrew Walder (1995) criticized the market transition theory of Victor Nee (1989), for not realizing that in China, redistribution, rather than being replaced by markets, is decentralized to the local level. As a result, the continuity with the Communist economic system is much stronger than market transition theory implies. Nee himself slightly revised his 1989 market transition thesis by pointing out the "hybrid" character of Chinese economy (Nee 1992), although he maintained that China was moving in the direction of full capitalism.

Some, however, argue that none of the post-Communist systems approximate the "ideal type" of modern rational capitalism (see Eyal, Szelényi, and Townsley 1998; King 2002). In central Europe individual private property may not have been formed to the extent we know it from the West (Eyal and coauthors call it "capitalism without capitalists"). In Russia and some other post-Soviet states the market institutions may be rather underdeveloped (Eyal and coauthors labeled this "capitalists without capitalism"). In China, given the political monopoly of the Communist Party, and lack of progress made in privatizing state and collectively owned industries, it may be problematic to talk about capitalism at all. Rather, China may have a "socialist mixed economy," in which capitalism is primarily being built from "below."

In this chapter we bracket these two issues. While none of the former Communist systems offers a close approximation to the ideal type of cap-

italism, they certainly are on their way from socialist redistributive economies to market capitalist systems. In all countries (arguably with the exception of North Korea) we see clear trends of the formation of private property, the making of market institutions, and the emergence of stratification systems based on class. While we believe the post-Communist economies can be analyzed as examples of capitalism, we do not accept Burawoy's critique. While the Communist systems were undergoing convergence with each other, the post-Communist world is undergoing a clear divergence—both politically and economically (see EBRD 1999). However, even if world system theory or neoclassical economics are right, and eventually capitalism will converge into one single system, the process of such convergence will last long enough to make the study of diverse trajectories or pathways from Communism to capitalism of sufficient intellectual interest.

Instead of dealing with these two interesting, but metatheoretical questions, this chapter will focus on two sets of issues. First, we review the unique features of the transition from Communism to capitalism; to what extent and in what ways is this transition different from previous historical instances of transitions to market economies? Second, we will offer an attempt to develop a comparative political economy of various forms of post-Communist capitalism.[2]

In this analysis, we describe three ideal-typical paths by which capitalism has emerged from Communism. In some countries capitalism emerged "from below," by the creation of a new, market-integrated private (and "hybrid") sector in the shadow of the old socialist redistributive economy. In this scenario, a new capitalist class emerges from actors that emerged in the nonplanned sector of the economy. China is the most obvious example. In other countries, capitalism is created with a revolution "from above," in a process where state elites try to transform the old socialist redistributive economy into a market capitalist system by following the neoliberal economist's "blueprint" (see Stark 1992). In this path, the new capitalist class emerges "from above" to the extent that neoliberal policy enables the nomenklatura (and its clients) to transform itself into a grand bourgeoisie. This is Russia's path. Finally, there have been attempts to make capitalism "from without." In these systems elites also try to follow the neoliberal blueprint with a major exception; rather than allowing the nomenklatura (or its clients) to privatize large state-owned enterprises (SOEs), they rely on foreign ownership and cooperation with multinationals. Hungary is the exemplar of this path.

These pathways produce different outcomes. Those countries that followed "capitalism from without" have created an economy where market institutions are highly developed and economies are well integrated into the world economy. We call this system *liberal capitalism*. "Capitalism from below" also creates market-integrated systems, but they rely more on relatively small domestic capitalist (or "hybrid") enterprises coexisting with a large state-owned sector, which is increasingly market-dependent (and thus "state capitalist"). Because of the existence of noncapitalist property forms integrated by markets (hybrid and state capitalist), we call this *hybrid capitalism*. "Capitalism from above" results in a *patrimonial* system. In such systems patron-client relationships pervade the economy: between the state and enterprises, as well as between management and labor. In patrimonial systems, the redistributive institutions are destroyed, to be replaced by economic activity deeply embedded in reciprocity and networks in addition to market integration. Businesses cancel each other's debts, use local monies, and engage in barter.

We believe it is far from accidental that countries built capitalism in these different ways. The path taken can be explained by the divergent constellation of class forces and inter- and intraclass struggles (Eyal, Szelényi, and Townsley 1998; King 2001a, 2001b, 2002). The pattern of class conflict and constellations are significantly affected by historical and cultural heritages, as well as by differences in the level of economic development, the geographic proximity to the core capitalist economies, and especially the timing of industrialization and its articulation with the development of nationalism (see King 2001b). These factors can be thought of as creating the opportunity structure in which class formation, coalition building, and conflict take place.

Unique Features of the Transition from Communism to Capitalism

Arguably, the transition from Communism to capitalism is strikingly different from all previous transitions to capitalism in two ways. It is the first case in history when capitalism emerged from a system that did not know the institution of private ownership and in which a class of private proprietors did not exist. It is also the first instance in history when capitalism emerged from a noncapitalist economy where capital accumulation had already taken place, and in which industrialization was more or less completed.

Making Capitalism without Capitalists

Karl Marx was arguably quite correct when he suggested that "within the wombs" of a decaying mode of production, the "embryo" of the new mode of production is already formed. While it can be debated whether this proposition holds for all transitions,[3] it certainly seems to be true—prior to the fall of Communism—for all instances of transition to capitalism. Indeed, in the classical case of transition, the transition from feudalism to capitalism in Europe, private ownership emerges first. Feudal lords often gradually transform themselves into private landlords, and a propertied bourgeois class emerges (in England, of capitalist tenant farmers), and market integration of the economy gradually gains ground. Even the French revisionist historians, who challenge the Marxian thesis that the French Revolution can be accurately understood as the struggle of the bourgeoisie against the aristocracy, do not doubt that a propertied bourgeoisie and the institution of private ownership existed well before the revolution.

Socialism, however, was conceived as a negation of capitalism. Therefore, actually existing socialist societies were great experiments in operating a socioeconomic system without the basic institution of capitalism: private ownership. In *all instances* the transition to socialism occurred in societies that had eliminated some time ago the institution of private property, and eliminated the class of the propertied grand bourgeoisie as well. All major—and often not only the major—means of production were nationalized. Former owners were sent into reeducation camps, jailed, killed, sent into exile, or in the best-case scenario tolerated at the very margins of the society, stripped of their private wealth. Even the middle and small bourgeoisie was usually eliminated, or at least greatly constrained. Few of the shopkeepers, merchants, and artisans could continue their individual businesses. They were forced to become state employees and work in government-owned and -managed large operations, or they were forced to join so-called producers cooperatives. In most countries the same thing happened even to the peasantry.

In terms of property and class relations, actually existing socialism was indeed a radical negation of any form of known capitalism. Markets were less radically erased. After initial attempts to get rid of markets and monetary institutions, most socialist economies did allow some room for the operation of market mechanisms. As socialism progressed from Stalinism to reform Communism, market forces began to gain some ground. Market forces, however, were typically limited to the sphere of consumption and not the allocation of capital goods. Preciously little or no price-regulating markets were allowed to operate. For example, the "nonmarket trade of labor" was a widely known phenomenon. Thus labor power did take the form of a commodity, but its price was administratively set and was sheltered in this way from the forces of supply and demand. With rare exceptions socialist economies were economies of "shortage" (Kornai 1980). This was observable in the nonmarket trade for labor: unemployment was the exception, and labor shortage was the rule.

Even in the most reform-oriented countries, Hungary and Poland, and even until the very fall of Communism, private ownership was limited to consumer goods, and markets to the sphere of consumption. There was no capitalist class in the making, and no signs of accumulation of private capital. This is not to say that there were no differences in terms of wealth across groups or classes of the population. As reform progressed, the bureaucratic estate, or "caste," began to "commodify" its bureaucratic privileges (Manchin and Szelényi 1987). Real estate may have been the most important vehicle to accumulate some private wealth. Members of the nomenklatura began to build privately owned housing—usually of modest, but occasionally of high quality—with government subsidies for themselves or for their children. One also can find evidence of other instances of such protoaccumulation of private capital: the purchase of luxury cars, the collection of valuable artwork, the opening of secret bank accounts in Western countries. Some "proper" capital accumulation also took place in the "second economy" by the emergent new socialist petty bourgeoisie in some reform Communist countries (more in Hungary than elsewhere). Finally, during the terminal illness of state socialism some of the smartest members of the nomenklatura tried to find ways to transform their "right to control" into individual private property. In Hungary and Poland in 1988 a process of "spontaneous" privatization got under way (Voszka 1993; Hankiss 1990; Staniszkis 1991). In Russia, during the perestroika period, the nomenklatura attempted to accumulate wealth by funneling state resources to the newly legalized cooperative sectors, especially new banks (often established by Komsomol members [the future oligarchs] and older Communist Party aparatchiks [see Hoffman 2002]). If the collapse of Communism had not occurred in 1989 and the system had continued functioning for a few more decades, the nomenklatura may have undergone a transformation similar to the one experienced by the feudal aristocracy in western Europe.

But the fall of Communism came far too fast. Most of the economy was not affected by spontaneous privatization. With very few exceptions the reform Communist new petty bourgeoisie did not have enough time and opportunity to accumulate enough private ownership to become major players after the fall of Communism. The individual wealth accumulated in consumer goods (or smuggled into Western bank accounts) typically also remained rather trivial and hardly was enough to qualify its possessor as a new "grand bourgeoisie." Thus it is reasonable to claim that it was during the transition from Communism to capitalism that capitalism was made on the ruins (or with the ruins) of a system that did not know the institution of private ownership and in which no propertied bourgeoisie existed.

But is this of any significance? Does it matter what the precapitalist class relations were for the development of capitalism? Contra Burawoy and neoclassical economic accounts, we believe it has a major impact on the kinds of trajectories countries take after the fall of Communism. Because of the exceptional weakness of the bourgeoisie during late state socialism, the early stages of post-Communist capitalism has to operate with some sort of "substitute bourgeoisie." We will argue in the second half of this chapter that what kind of substitute bourgeoisie becomes hegemonic has a major impact on which of the three trajectories to capitalism post-Communist countries follow.

In countries that follow "capitalism from above" the former Communist nomenklatura is likely to be such a substitute bourgeoisie. This segment of the post-Communist power elite allies with elements of the technocracy (firm managers) and to a substantial degree uses its political office to convert public goods into its individual private ownership. In regimes that pursue "capitalism from without" the trend toward such political capitalism is weak. Civil society is relatively strong, and an alliance of technocrats and dissident intellectuals blocks the nomenklatura in its bid to gain possession of the commanding heights of the economy. Instead, the hegemonic role is played by foreign investors, who rely on domestic expert-managers to run their local operations. In regimes that build "capitalism from below," the technocracy remains hegemonic, but does not overthrow the political bureaucracy. Thus the nomenklatura remains in power. However, it must come to accommodate and eventually share power with a group of emerging domestic capitalists (such as has occurred in China, where the Communist Party recently welcomed capitalists into its ranks). At any rate, the nomenklatura will eventually become "structurally dependent" on the rate of investment of this class of private capitalists.

Thus, the path traveled will determine the nature of the emergent capitalist systems (liberal, patrimonial, or hybrid), and thus their propensity for economic growth (see King 2001a, 2001b, and 2002 for applications of this argument). How long lasting this effect will be is difficult to predict, but more than a decade after the transition process began, it seems to be quite consequential for the way post-Communist capitalism operates.

Making Capitalism after Industrialization

The "historic mission" of capitalism was to separate the producers from the means of production, accumulate capital, and launch and complete industrialization. Since actually existing socialism was implemented only in countries that did not complete capitalist development, socialism performed the same historic functions. Socialism, as reinterpreted by Lenin, became an ideology of modernization (Lane 1981). The task was to catch up and overtake the capitalist world. As a result, state socialism proved to be a strategy of accelerated industrialization and accumulation. At least in its "classical epoch," during the 1930s in Russia, the late 1940s and early 1950s in Eastern Europe and China, what distinguished socialism from capitalism most was its capacity to invest a larger proportion of GNP into the productive sphere compared to consumption. In addition, there was a tendency to concentrate development more in the secondary and less in the tertiary sector, and to create monopolistic industrial structures, as these priorities tendencies maximized what was redistributed, thereby facilitating control by the bureaucracy (Kornai 1992).

This massive industrialization and capital accumulation was accomplished by an incomplete, contradictory separation of the producers from the means of subsistence and production. In one respect socialism went even further than capitalism. While there were country-by-country variations, it almost completely eliminated self-employment and universalized wage labor. At the same time, given the economics of shortage, socialism could only operate by allowing massive subsistence production (which occasionally resulted in massive starvation). There were other limits on the separation of producers from the means of production, also resulting from the economics of shortage. Workers could hardly be laid off, and, as a result, they had certain property rights in the means of production (because the full set of capitalist property rights—the right to residual income, the right to transferability, and the right to control—are limited by the de facto right that workers have to some income from the firm, since they cannot practically be excluded from all benefits even if they do nothing). Therefore, the income of workers under socialism could be understood as composed of wages, which reflected the compensation for their wage labor, and "rent," which they collected as co-owners of the means of production.

The transition from Communism to capitalism therefore does not lead to industrialization and capital accumulation. In fact, in some respects, exactly the opposite is happening: "capitalism from above" and "capitalism from without" result in a massive deindustrialization and substantial destruction of the previously accumulated capital, thus in deaccumulation. In the latter path, however, foreign direct investment (FDI) leads to reindustrialization. Nonetheless, during the process of transition the former Communist economies are massively reconfigured as they are integrated into the world economy.

Socialism also led to "overindustrialization"—no capitalist country ever achieved as high a proportion of the labor force employed in manufacturing industry as typically found in socialist economies. Since socialism was a strategy of accelerated economic growth, in particular during the classical epoch, "department one" (heavy industry) grew faster than it ever did under the conditions of a market economy. Socialism turned out to be "production for production's sake" (Heller, Fehér and Markus 1983), with excessive concentration of production in mining and heavy industry. The fact that socialism fell when world manufacturing already suffered from excess capacity contributed to the destruction of the productive capacities of former socialist economies.

This is much less the case in China and Vietnam, where the agrarian sector remained dominant through the whole socialist epoch, though China in particular also created a large heavy industrial capacity, which has proved dysfunctional as China is integrated into the world economy. In East Asia, socialism did not finish the task of industrialization and accumulation; therefore the transition to capitalism follows the more traditional pattern. Anywhere from 100 to 150 million people are underemployed in the Chinese countryside.[4] As migrant workers, they move first to rural industry, but also to urban industrial centers as a supply of cheap labor, not unlike the rise of rural protoindustrialization and then the massive rural-urban migration in early capitalist development. This is different from the European post-Communist transition, where the transition leads to a deurbanization and in some cases reruralization and even repeasantization.

With the deindustrialization and deaccumulation cycle completed—by the year 2000 this was achieved everywhere in Europe—the post-Communist capitalist economies have joined the global capitalist system in different ways. For those that followed "capitalism from without," a substantial reindustrialization, primarily through foreign direct investment, is under way. Given the high human capital resources, and low wage levels and transportation costs in the region, high-tech industries often move in to create new industrial capacities oriented toward the international market (see King 2001a, 2001b, 2002). The second half of the 1990s for these regimes was an epoch of growth, which occasionally was rather dynamic. But much of this growth took place in the sector that is owned by, or linked with, foreign capital, and that is primarily export-oriented.[5] It remains to be seen whether recession or weak recovery in the core countries will lead to an even sharper decline in these regimes, or whether they will now be able to develop their domestic markets and compensate for the declining demands for their products on foreign markets by a growth in domestic consumption.

While it is premature to describe the post-Communist "capitalism from without" as being trapped in "dependent development" (Evans 1979), it is clear that these countries are more dependent on foreign investments than any of the "dependent" Third World countries during the 1960s, when dependency theory most accurately captured the socioeconomic condition in Latin America or Southeast Asia. Nevertheless, the Czech Republic, Hungary, or Poland is not the replay of Brazil, Colombia, Malaysia, or Thailand during the 1960s. The post-Communist liberal regimes are not only rich in human capital and in close geographic proximity to major capital and commodity markets

of the core of the capitalist system, but they are also about to join the European Union. It remains to be seen whether there will be convergence with the core in the long run. It is not possible to tell whether the fate of post-Communist liberal capitalism will be similar to the kind of partial convergence with the capitalist core experienced by southern Europe, but it would not be surprising.

Regimes created by capitalism from above, however, follow a rather different trajectory. In these countries foreign capital is far more modest, and their development shows a closer resemblance to what one would expect from "the development of underdevelopment" (Frank 1969). These countries also experienced substantial deindustrialization and deaccumulation, but so far there are no signs of a similar reindustrialization. There was a massive resurgence of the subsistence economy (in Russia or Romania for instance), and exportable raw materials have become the most important sector in the economy. Burawoy's notions of nonproductive merchant capital (Burawoy and Krotov 1992) and "economic involution" (1996, 2001b) capture these processes.

In brief, capitalism from without means that post-Communist semiperipheral regimes may be moving toward the core (though they may be locked in their semiperipheral position—only the future can tell), while capitalism from above seems to be heading toward the periphery of the capitalist world system. Capitalism from below, because its most important cases were in primarily agrarian countries, has led to a move up in the world system, from the ranks of the superpoor to the poor, with the future an open book.[6]

DIVERSE DESTINATIONS AFTER THE FALL OF COMMUNISM

In the previous discussion we suggested that post-Communist socioeconomic systems were moving along different trajectories. These trajectories lead to three different destinations, or three big families of post-Communist capitalism. These are ideal types: concrete paths taken by various post-Communist countries always combine elements from all three, and thus the emergent capitalist systems will combine elements of all three types as well.

China and Vietnam are the best empirical examples of capitalism from below leading to hybrid capitalism. Arguably Hungary was also along that path between the mid-1970s and mid-1980s, and there were signs of similar development in Poland, Estonia, and to a lesser extent in some other socialist countries of Europe. Capitalism from below occurred only in countries where the Communist Party was able to retain its political monopoly: the power of the apparatus and the force of socialist ideology remained strong enough to offer a lasting defense of the public sector against privatization. Under these circumstances capitalism is developing in "new spaces" created next to the planned public sector. At some point the privatization of the public sector inevitably comes on the agenda, as happened in China in 1994. But it will happen once a market-integrated private sector is already quite established, and privatization will also likely be rather gradual and occur through fair auctions with the participation of many homegrown domestic capitalists. As a result, it will not result in massive unemployment and deaccumulation.

Capitalism from below most naturally begins in the agricultural sector. First, collective farms are either dismantled—as in China—or they are loosened up sufficiently to allow private farming activity by individual peasants, initially part time, and eventually even full time, as happened in the later stages of reform Communism in Hungary (Szelényi 1988). Capitalism from below may also coincide with an influx of foreign capital. However, since the public sector is defended, this did not open the doors wide for giant multinationals, but rather attracted smaller investors in the Chinese case, or paved the road toward capitalism by creating a debt trap, as happened in Hungary or Poland.

To what extent capitalism from below coincides with "political capitalism" is debatable, and it is one of the central contested issues in the so-called market transition debate. In his seminal article Victor Nee (1989) insisted that capitalism from below benefits the "direct producers" and undermines the power of redistributors, while others (e.g., Walder [1995], Rona-Tas [1994], and Staniszkis [1991])[7] insisted that cadres benefit from the transition. We do not have the definite data to adjudicate between the competing claims. However, in the context of capitalism from below, especially in comparison with the other trajectories, Nee had a good point. In China the central bureaucracy retains its political monopoly, and therefore has neither the motivation nor (in absence of mass privatization) the opportunity to convert public goods into their individual private wealth. In the case of capitalism from below, local apparatchiks may take advantage of new rural industries, camouflaged

often as "collective" firms, but in practice operating as private enterprises (so called red cap enterprises). Nevertheless, the space exists for noncadre entrepreneurs to start businesses and be successful, which is far from the case in strategies of capitalism from above.

It is also likely that China has experienced a rise in political capitalism as the private sector has grown in importance. After the private economy becomes so large that its reversal seems impossible, it becomes increasingly rational for the nomenklatura to hedge its bets and get involved in the private economy, often through their children (thus the social category of HCC, high-cadre children).

Capitalism from below resembles the "classical road" to capitalism, the road we are familiar with especially in the United States or in the other "white colonies." (This is very different, of course, from the European "classical" transition, where capitalism emerges both from below and from above, by feudal relations turning into capitalist relations.) In capitalism from below a propertied bourgeoisie is created rather gradually, and market institutions are similarly established in a gradualist way (see Barry Naughton's analysis of "growing out of the plan" [1995]). Given the existence of a sizable public sector and the political domination of the Communist Party with its anticapitalist ideology, capitalism from below is still a unique post-Communist way of creating capitalism. This eventually creates a hybrid capitalist system where small and medium private (and mixed property) enterprises coexist with state-owned enterprises, which also begin to behave like capitalist firms. This is not just a socialist mixed economy, because the state-owned enterprises represent a form of state capitalism, as they are increasingly integrated by the market and seek to maximize profits.

Diametrically opposed to capitalism from below is capitalism from above. This strategy opened up rather unexpectedly when in 1988–91 European Communist regimes "melted down." Until the mid-1980s no one seriously considered this a possibility. During this time, no scenario was developed for a way to turn an economy based exclusively on public ownership into a system of private property. East European economists, speculating about ways to escape the deepening economic crisis of state socialism, threw their hands up and said jokingly, "We know how to make fish soup out of fish (thus how to nationalize private property), but we do not have the faintest idea how to make fish from a fish soup (thus how to convert a socialist system into a liberal market economy)." The recipe for this culinary miracle was discovered during the second half of the 1980s, and it was called "shock therapy" and "mass privatization."[8] The key idea was that a modern capitalist economy could be created with one bold move in which the public sector is offered en masse for privatization. All firms will be transferred to identifiable private owners, without much worry about the price paid for these firms. This strategy represented a coalition of elements of the Communist-era bureaucracy with elements of the technocracy, mostly enterprise directors.[9]

The creation of private property from above either took the form of voucher privatization schemes where property was distributed to all citizens, or firms were essentially given to their employees and managers. In practice most countries implemented a mass privatization based on both of these strategies (Liberman, Nestor, and Desai 1997). This was of course possible only if the Communist Party was ready to give up its power and the ideology of socialism could be delegitimated. Until mid-1988 or early 1989 this sounded like an unrealistic scenario. However, as we know, socialism melted down during the fall of 1989. Either a new elite grabbed political power, or the old elite changed its ideological colors over night. In both cases they decided to build capitalism in exactly the same way that socialism was built, by a blueprint, led from above, by modernizing elites. This transformation would again be led by a "vanguard" with privileged theoretical knowledge (this time neoclassical economics instead of Marxist-Leninism). Sachs, possibly the most influential neoliberal ideologue, even entitled a very influential article in the *Economist* "What Is to Be Done" (1990), deliberately invoking Lenin's famous language. The message was clear: there is nothing inherently wrong with vanguardism; only the end of history changed.[10]

In capitalism from above, the emergent socioeconomic system has a distinctive patrimonial character. In patrimonial regimes "political capitalism" reigns supreme. Communist apparatchiks manage to exchange their political capital into private property, frequently using management buyouts to achieve these aims (see Freedland 2000; Klebnikov 2000). This creates a group of owners of giant corporations with no experience as capitalists, typically without international contacts, and with no capital for restructuring. This significantly contributed to a sharp drop in demand and the supply of key investment inputs, resulting in generalized economic stagnation (see King 2002, 2003b for the

development of this argument linking mass privatization to enterprise failure).

Those regimes in which the technocracy and humanistic intellectuals form an alliance against the party bureaucrats pursue capitalism from without, ultimately creating a liberal capitalist system, which relies on Western multinationals. It is "liberal" in the sense that it is dominated by legal-rational authority. In these regimes privatization is a reasonably transparent process. Public firms are auctioned off at public auctions, or ownership is transferred to workers or citizens via vouchers, which are traded on the market place. There is limited political capitalism—former Communist apparatchiks are rarely able to manipulate the process sufficiently to acquire massive private wealth. It typically only happens in small or medium-sized firms, and large corporations virtually never become the private property of individual Communist apparatchiks or even groups of former Communist apparatchiks.[11]

In the early stages of the transition the privatization of large enterprises creates a certain amount of "quasi-private property" or "recombinant property" (Stark 1996). Under these circumstances governments retain substantial indirect control, mainly through the banking system (as long as banks are not privatized and as long as they own substantial stocks in privatized firms). Evidence from Hungary indicates that recombinant property was never dominant (King 2001a, 32–34) and was a transitory phenomenon limited to the very largest enterprises in capital-intensive sectors (Hanley, King, and Toth 2002).[12] Over a relatively brief period of time, by the middle to late 1990s, ownership tended to shift into the hands of foreign investors. Market institutions are created in these regimes fairly early in the game. Prices are deregulated, currency is made convertible, the banking system is modernized and eventually some or most of it privatized, capital imports are deregulated, and so on. Under such circumstances, even if corporate management is able to acquire controlling private ownership in firms, managers still have incentives to bring in foreign investors in order to attract capital for restructuring and secure access to export markets.

Table 1 summarizes the overall argument relating class coalitions to the development of three distinct types of capitalism. The remainder of this chapter will explain this table, with examples from Russia, China, and central Europe.

Exogenous and endogenous factors may help explain why some countries followed a liberal, or

TABLE 1.   Varieties of Post-Communist Capitalism

	Capitalism from Without	Capitalism from Above	Capitalism from Below
Transitional political strategy/elite struggle/class and intradominant class alliance	Technocracy defeats bureaucracy and struggles with former dissidents for hegemony	Bureaucracy retains power, uses office to acquire private property, allies with technocracy	Technocracy hegemonic, allies with domestic bourgeoisie, but bureaucracy retains political power
Type of capitalism	Liberal systems (Czech Republic, Hungary, Poland)	Patrimonial systems (Russia, Ukraine, Rumania, Serbia under Milošević)	Hybrid systems (China, Vietnam)
Dominant class formation	Multinationals, some domestic capitalists	Patron-client ownership networks; parasitic financial-industrial groups	Domestic ownership class; marketized hybrid property forms
Extent of class formation	Under way, but dual structure, with patron-client relations	Dominant estate structure, mainly patron-client relations	Some class formation, but great deal of patron-client relations
Foreign capital	Dominant	Very limited	Supplementary, smaller investors
Political capitalism	Little	Lot, dominant	Some
Domestic (petty, or middle) bourgeoisie	Some	Little	Lot
Firm integration	Markets with low levels of nonmarket horizontal coordination (barter, debt-swaps, arrears)	Markets and high levels of nonmarket horizontal coordination (barter, debt-swaps, arrears)	Markets and central plan (and the barter associated with planning)
Economic dynamism	Some	Little or none	A great deal
Leading sector	Manufacturing exports	Raw materials export	Manufacturing exports
Dynamic of accumulation	FDI; importing capital; export driven, some technological upgrading; financial fragility	Political accumulation; capital flight; technological downgrading	State-led development of SOEs, technological upgrading; growth of new private sector
Size of the state	Medium	Large	Large
State capacity/formal bureaucracy	Modest/very	Little/almost none	Great/very
State-economy interaction	State provides adequate public goods (e.g., stock of human capital); some personalistic enforcement of laws; state implements an industrial policy; medium informal sector	State does not provide adequate public goods (e.g., stock of human capital); extensive personalistic enforcement of laws by patrons to benefit clients; huge informal sector	State provides public goods (e.g., infrastructure); state implements industrial policy; small informal sector
Political institutions	Liberal democracy	Multiparty authoritarianism (unfree and unfair elections or "norpolyarchy")	Selective and partial process of liberalization of totalitarian regime

patrimonial, path and why some managed to go a long way by building capitalism from below. In this chapter we will focus our attention on the endogenous factors, which are rooted in the class structure, the dynamics of struggles among different factions of elites.

It would be foolish, however, to deny that exogenous factors are consequential. Most importantly, the level of economic development countries achieved prior to Communism and, to some degree, were able to retain under Communism, and the proximity of markets in core countries are likely to play an important role. It cannot be accidental that only countries bordering the European Union, and which were traditionally more developed, created liberal capitalism. One possible argument is that the more developed countries were able to adopt neoliberal policies, since they could afford to pay the rather high price of neoliberal shock therapy. Less developed countries, however, may have experimented with some shock, but they had to suspend it before it could work since their population could not tolerate more pain (hence shock without therapy—see Gerber and Hout 1998; but see Murrell 1993; and King 2002, 2003b for a different interpretation of Russia's "neoliberalness.") Thus, the argument could be made that the better economic performance in central Europe may have nothing to do with economic policies, or the path capitalist development took there, but can be explained simply by the fact that they were stronger economies and closer to Western markets.

This exogenous explanation is not without merit, but it has limits. First of all, during the socialist epoch the gap in the level of economic development among the socialist countries narrowed and just began to grow again after the fall of Communism. And there are also curious exceptions to such economic determinism. For instance, how can one explain the unusual success of the Baltic states, which were for half a century parts of the Soviet Union. Sure, they were relatively better developed regions of the USSR; nevertheless they were within the USSR, and during the 1990s they comfortably outperformed the countries of the Balkans. China is also an important exception to economic determinism. What made it possible for China to advance toward market institutions more effectively than some of the patrimonial regimes of Eastern Europe?

In addition to geography and prior level of development, let us add a possible cultural explanation to the different routes various societies took.

We do not know how far this analysis can be pushed, but the reconfiguration of post-Communist states along religious lines certainly deserves attention. It may be just an artifact, or it may have something to do with elective affinities between religion and modernization, but the three types of capitalisms correspond to various great world religions. All liberal regimes are dominated by Western Christianity; patrimonial states are Orthodox (or Islamic); while hybrid capitalism happened to be in the Confucian and Taoist part of the world. It is beyond our competence to assess how important this fact may be; we just have to note that an affinity between religion and type of modernization might exist.

We argue that the pattern of class conflict and intraclass alliance (or interelite struggle) determines which path to capitalism is selected. This does not have to be thought of as an explanation alternative to geography, prior level of development, or culture. These factors affect the opportunity structure of the different segments of the class structure. For example, the fact that a country is closer to Western Europe and more culturally similar may make an alliance of technocrats and multinationals seem much more possible. At a microlevel, it is likely to result in networks linking socialist managers with foreign managers. This seems to have occurred in Hungary, and then translated into an early lead in FDI resulting from the formation of small joint ventures joining up former socialist era managers with often small and medium-sized enterprise actors in the core (e.g. Germany, Austria) (see King and Varadi 2002; King 2001a, 55–58).

The fact that a county industrialized prior to the imposition of socialism means that its middle classes (its technocrats and cultural intellectuals) have memories and a set of internalized myths about the "nation" that weaken their enthusiasm for Communism (King 2001b; see Darden's [2002] excellent study on nationalism in the former Soviet Union). Thus, these exogenous factors are important most of all because they affect the pattern of intra- and interclass conflict and alliance.

In the remainder of this chapter, we will discuss the different paths to, as well as different resulting types of, capitalism. It must be kept in mind that these three paths are ideal types, and thus features of the three resultant styles of capitalism are found in all post-Communist countries. There are some multinationals and modern capitalist markets in Russia, while in Hungary, the archetype of capitalism from without, paternalism plays an important role not only in the political-cultural sphere, but even in the economy. Barter is not unknown in the central European economies, and some degree of capitalism from below can be found in the Czech Republic and Hungary as well. Indeed, in Poland and Slovenia there were strong elements of this path, because these countries severely delayed the privatization of very large state-owned enterprises. Thus, they created a space for more capitalism from the ground up, even as they pursued capitalism from without through strategic foreign investment.[13] Political capitalism (thus the use of political office to acquire private wealth), which is a central feature of patrimonial regimes, is far from nonexistent in systems that build capitalism from below, such as in China (as executions for corruption attest). Similarly, China has seen a great deal of FDI (in fact, it has been the biggest recipient in the world since the late 1990s, but its levels are still modest on a per capita basis).

Capitalism from Above Leading to Patrimonial Capitalism

In those countries that wound up with patrimonial systems, a fraction of the Communist political apparatus was able to retain its power and defend the privileges of its clients as well. While the momentum of technocratic reforms and intellectual challenges in central Eastern Europe in the late 1960s might have been able to radically transform the power structure if not for Soviet military might, the bureaucratic estate in Russia was never seriously challenged. Indeed, the collapse of Communism cannot be seen as a defeat of the Communist Party bureaucracy by outside forces. While Russia had dissident intellectuals (such as Solzhenitsyn) who, as in central Europe, had a role to play in delegitimizing the regime (see Shlapentokh 1990), they were not nearly as powerful as the nomenklatura. That is, the key players in this transition were members of the political bureaucracy itself (Linz and Stepan 1996; Garcelon 1997; and the authoritative Reddaway and Glinski 2001). The driving force of change was the party's growing recognition that it could not compete economically and militarily with Western capitalism (Szelényi and Szelényi 1995). Gorbachev should be seen as a technocratic reformer who opened up to intellectuals as ammunition against the Brezhnev-era hardliners whom he viewed as standing in the way of necessary reforms (see Shlapentokh 1990). At the same time, the perestroika reforms that legalized individual profitable activity and cooperatives (in 1986 and 1987) created vast opportunities for elites in managerial and ministerial positions to profit as middlemen—enabling them to accumulate personal wealth (the most outstanding journalistic account is Klebnikov's *The Godfather of the Kremlin* [2000]). This gave at least some partocrats the ability to see a future for themselves in a post-Communist world.

Gorbachev's move was initially successful, as he managed to replace much of the top Brezhnev-era elite whom he saw as corrupt and inefficient bureaucratic obstacles to reform (Hanley, Yershova, and Anderson 1995, 647). However, these reforms started to get out of control as activists in the Baltics and Armenia used glasnost to espouse anti-Russian nationalism. Soon, the partocracy realized they could survive on the regional level, drawing their attention away from the center, and initiating the disintegration of the Soviet Union (Helf and Hahn 1992; Linz and Stepan 1996).

In the Russian Federation, 1988 saw the emergence of "civil society" in the form of Democratic Russia (DR). A full 80 percent of respondents in one survey of DR's Moscow activists were technocrats, or "specialists," holders of technical and professional degrees and skills (whereas 28 percent of those employed in the Russian Republic fit this definition). While this movement mobilized the real discontent and grievances of the intelligentsia, it was nonetheless "launched from within the highest echelons of the Soviet-Party state. This movement against the party's political monopoly was part of, and contributed to, a struggle of technocratic reformers against party conservatives. This essentially split the party internally, creating two warring factions (the Democratic Platform and the Russian Communist Party)" (Garcelon 1997, 39, 47, 49).

When Gorbachev tried to use limited elections against party conservatives, his strategy backfired. Yeltsin rose to prominence through his control over the Moscow Association of Voters, which provided leadership for the mass-based DR movement. The fact that this was a section of the Communist Party coming to power (and not a non-Communist elite, as in Poland) is clear. A full 86 percent of DR's deputies were party members, and Yeltsin himself had been a member of the Politburo (Garcelon 1997, 64).

In June the Russian Supreme Soviet declared its "sovereignty" from the USSR, and a dual-power structure emerged. After the failed coup of 1991, Yeltsin assumed full power over Russian territory. DR, having always been a top-down product of a section of the bureaucratic estate, soon withered into irrelevance. Yeltsin chose instead to align with enterprise managers and implement shock therapy from above. Indeed, a full 74 percent of Yeltsin's appointees were members of the nomenklatura (Garcelon 1997, 70).

In January 1992, the radical transformation of the Russian economy began. With the help of a team of Western economists headed by Jeffrey Sachs, "a radical reform package focusing on economic liberalization and privatization was adopted" (EBRD 1996, 169; see Wedel 2001). Six months of this shock therapy led to unprecedented hyperinflation and a fall in living standards. To shore up support, Yeltin incorporated into his regime representatives of enterprise directors, such as Chernomyrdin, chairman of the board of Gazprom (Russia's giant natural gas monopoly), who was made vice premier of the fuel and energy sector, and later replaced Gaidar as prime minister when the public outcry against shock therapy forced his ouster (Reddaway and Glinski 2001). At the same time that Chernomyrdin joined the government, a privatization plan relying on a combination of citizen vouchers and giveaways to managers and employees was launched in June 1992. This was easily the largest, most rapid transformation of ownership in world history. "By July of 1994, 15,052 medium- and large-scale enterprises, employing more than 80 per cent of the industrial workforce, had been privatized" (EBRD 1996, 169). Thus, in Russia, a self-re-created bureaucratic estate, in coalition with elements of the technocracy in charge of large enterprises, unleashed capitalism from above via a full dose of shock therapy.

In these systems, Communist ideology was of course instantly abandoned, but the former Communist parties were not taken over by technocrats and transformed into centrist or even right-wing social democratic movements, as happened in the liberal regimes. Instead the core of the political apparatus retained control over the successor parties and turned the Communist ideology into nationalist, often xenophobic, ideology. Iliescu in Romania (at least during the early 1990s—less so after his return to power) and Milošević in Serbia are prime examples. The transformation was more complex in Russia, where the successor party lost political power, but Yeltsin followed policies that were quite similar to those of Iliescu and Milošević. In those countries where working-class resistance, political or economic, did not weaken the political apparatus, the technocratic and intellectual opposition could not smash the political

bureaucracy. Instead, it adapted a nationalistic, xenophobic rhetoric and the practices of political capitalism.

The Economic Institutions of Post-Communist Patrimonial Capitalism

Because part of the "blueprint" for creating capitalism includes rapidly liberalizing prices, eliminating trade barriers, and drastically curtailing the money supply (by reducing monetary emissions, raising interest rates, and curtailing subsidies), post-Communist firms confront a harsh new environment. Rapid price deregulation, given the monopolistic structure of Soviet-style economies, leads to a jump in the price of inputs. The wholesale liberalization of imports creates an enormous drop in aggregate demand for domestic producers, as they must face global competition.[14] With monetary emissions severely limited, government subsidies drastically curtailed, and credit dramatically more expensive, most firms run into severe cash flow problems and a shortage of capital for restructuring and even day-to-day transactions. Similarly, there was also the devastation resulting from the political destruction of the old Warsaw Pact Council for Mutual Economic Aid (COMECON, also called the Council of Mutual Economic Assistance, or the CMEA) trading system. For many states, a vast majority of exports and imports were from the COMECON, accounting for a huge amount of economic activity. The breakdown of this trading system therefore disrupted supply chains and created a gigantic loss of markets.[15]

In addition to these shocks, many firms suffered shocks associated with mass privatization (King 2002, 2003a). While the rapid privatization of small and some medium-sized businesses is beneficial because it provides a superior incentive structure for those in control of these enterprises, large SOEs cannot be rapidly privatized without unacceptable costs. Most importantly, mass privatization means that the resulting private corporation will not have an owner or owners with sufficient resources to restructure the company. Without any capital to carry out desperately needed restructuring, and without the injection of any new managerial talent, many firms found themselves in untenable positions. Mass privatization also frequently created outside owners, with very poor arrangements to monitor managers or even to monitor other (typically inside) owners. This outcome was virtually inevitable, as these economies lacked a developed business information infrastructure or effective legal protection of shareholder rights, which help "make markets" in advanced capitalist systems.

The combination of these two conditions led to massive amounts of asset stripping in the post-Communist economy, wreaking havoc on the functioning of many firms.[16] This is a paradox from the neoliberal perspective—while involving the state in the economy is allegedly a recipe for rent-seeking behavior, not involving the state in the transition creates an environment that encourages corruption (see King 2001a, 2001b).

Only those firms with privileged access to raw materials, or those that enjoy "natural protection" as a result of prohibitive shipping costs (e.g., makers of furniture), are likely to be able to successfully restructure (King 2002, 2003a; for useful reviews of sectoral change in the Russian economy see Vorobyov and Zhukov 2000 and Schroeder 1998). This creates what Gustafson (1999, 219) calls a "barbell economy" to indicate the hollowing out of the manufacturing sector, leaving only a significant raw materials sector and a financial services sector (the sphere of "merchant capital" [Burawoy and Krotov 1992] or financial clientelism [King 2001a]).

These structural challenges are exacerbated by the habitus of former Communist officials turned private owners. They are likely to be less entrepreneurial, and more inclined to be paternalistic toward their business partners and employees (one may also call this corruption if one wants to use value-burdened labels). Communist apparatchiks turned capitalists might ruin the emerging capitalist system just as much as they ruined socialism. In regimes "from without," the domestic expert-managers carry a habitus as well, and are not immune to paternalism either. Such actors are used to operating within the system of a paternalistic state and are likely to continue their state-dependent, deferential role. Paradoxically, multinational investors need these local experts exactly because they are well networked and have local social and political know-how. Nevertheless, with capitalism from without, foreign owners call the shots, and this, together with the existence of liberal press and democratic parliamentary institutions that guarantee some degree of transparency, limits paternalism (and corruption).

In regimes of capitalism from above, the combination of massive structural challenges facing enterprises led by "inappropriate" agents typically results in economic disaster. Asset stripping typically becomes the most "rational" way to respond, fur-

ther exacerbating the precarious position of most firms (see King 2003a, 2003b).

In this situation, firms frequently cannot afford to pay wages. This contributes to labor markets remaining underdeveloped, and paternalism frequently characterizes the relationship between workers and managers. This retreat from labor markets leads firms to aid workers in gaining access to the means of subsistence. Workers typically must resort to food grown on garden plots or collective potato farming to survive, and they are thus increasingly reunited with the means of their subsistence (Burawoy and Krotov 1992; Southworth 2001; King 2002). This means that the enterprise and the household become increasingly merged. As vertical patron-client relations grow in importance, workers are also separated from each other, and their "classness" decreases.

As firms entered into financial crisis and technical bankruptcy, they frequently could not pay taxes, which at any rate were drastically contracting along with the economy.[17] This loss of revenues, when combined with the antistatist ideology of the neoliberals, quickly led to a lack of state support for the basic institutions that enable firms to successfully restructure by raising their quality and changing their product line to compete on the world market. An important instance of this occurs when the state stops supporting the educational institutions that turn out skilled manpower, leading to a crisis for many firms. Of particular importance is the production of experts with scientific credentials by local polytechnic institutes. While some of this is brain drain, case study data indicates that much is also the result of a shortage of new technicians (see McDermott 2002 for the Czech Republic, and King 2002 for Russia). Furthermore, because the crisis of education also affects primary educational institutions, the shortage of skilled manpower will only intensify in the future (UNDP 1999, 58).

As a result of widespread financial crises, firms up and down commodity chains are unable to get the money or credit they need to continue production. Rather than go out of business, however, managers reactivate old "horizontal" ties (or generate new ones) to managers at other firms that functioned to compensate for the scarcity of inputs in the shortage economy. These networks now function to aid in production given the absence of money and credit in the new capitalist economy. These network ties allow the firms to withdraw from the market through interenterprise arrears, debt swaps, and barter (see Woodruff 1999 for an outstanding account of these processes in Russia). Barter decreases the efficiency of transactions (because a middleman typically must be used), shields firms from market pressures (because business partners are selected on network ties, not price considerations), and makes taxation highly problematic (because transactions can be concealed from the state, and because in-kind taxes are easy to overvalue when they are paid, and are difficult and expensive to collect anyway).

The loss of tax revenue from enterprise failure, exacerbated by the rise of hard-to-tax barter, inevitably weakens the state. As the state is increasingly unable to meet its formal obligations, it begins to break down. Poorly paid (or unpaid) state officials are easily corrupted, and the bureaucratic nature of the state decomposes. It becomes riddled by reactivated (as well as new) patron-client ties between government officials and businessmen. Private market success comes to depend to a high degree on arbitrary political decisions and the exercise of private force. As the state both weakens and loses its bureaucratic character, "mafias" rise to fulfill some of the functions of the state—such as contract enforcement (Varere 2001).

Over time, the politically constituted ownership groups will spread throughout the economy—swallowing up the shares of insider-dominated firms that can be stripped of their assets in one way or the other. Therefore, the compromise between the bureaucratic estate and enterprise managers will not result in equal gains for both segments of the former elite in the long run. In Russia, the eventual takeover of insider-owned firms by politically connected financial groups, who then typically fail to make any investment in restructuring the enterprise, is quite common.

Capitalism from above is also not conducive to the development of domestic small business. Since in both trajectories there was the massive privatization of the public sector, starting small and growing bigger was very difficult. The ensuing economic collapse and state disintegration (which includes an increase in the size of mafia groups to fill the void), and inability of banks to provide loans to new enterprises mean that new enterprises face incredible odds (banks funnel money out of the system; they do not turn savings into investments [see Popov 1999 for an insightful discussion of the specificity of the Russian banking system in comparative postcommunist perspective]).

Finally, the economic changes that result from following the path of capitalism from above will have inevitable political consequences. Specifically,

the existence of a large class of political capitalists who owe their very ownership of property to particular patrons in political office means that there will be enormous pressure to erode the institutions of democracy. For owners in Russia—unlike those in Hungary or Poland—may lose their property rights if their patron loses office. Thus, what results are systems in which elections matter, but they are neither particularly free nor fair.[18]

Capitalism from Without Leading to Liberal Capitalism

On the whole classes were not particularly well formed under state socialism. Socialist society can be better described as a rank order, rather than a class-stratified society. Nevertheless, classes were in formation and in particular the strength of the working class had far-reaching consequences for how intraclass struggles among various factions of the ruling elites unfolded. Arguably, in central Europe, in particular in Hungary and Poland, the power monopoly of the political apparatus had been challenged for quite some time by an emerging alliance between enlightened technocrats, usually operating within the Communist Party, and critical intellectuals (Kennedy 1992).

This alliance was based on common interest. Politically, both wanted freedom from the bureaucratic estate. Economically, both believed they could do just as well in a capitalist system by becoming professionals and selling their relatively scarce labor power on the market or by becoming entrepreneurs. A major factor in this notion was the possibility of working for a large multinational corporation.

The formation of the working class was most advanced in Poland, of course, where the collective action of workers in 1980 almost brought down the rule of the Communist political apparatus, which was only saved by the military dictatorship of Jaruzelski. In the summer of 1981, sudden price hikes precipitated strikes throughout the country, but particularly in the Baltic cities. In August, general strikes in Gdansk and Szczecin spread through the country, ending with government recognition of the right to form independent unions (Kramer 1995, 673). The working class entered into an alliance with a group of dissident intellectuals that had defended worker strikes in 1976 (Kennedy 1987; Bernhard 1993). The workers and intellectuals picked up the support of disaffected technocrats and professionals (Kubic 1994; Kennedy 1992, 1987; Karabel 1993), culminating in the 10 million–strong Solidarity Union (which was four times larger than the Communist Party, and 10 times larger than the official trade unions [Ost 1990, 139–40]). From this movement an anti-Communist political counterelite was created, bent on abolishing the nomenklatura and wresting control from the bureaucratic estate (Wasilewski and Wnuk-Lipinski 1995, 674).

For the rest of 1981, Solidarity tried to negotiate the institutionalization of its power to determine and implement economic policy. Ultimately, the government would not agree to share its economic power. Massive strikes continued throughout the year, precipitating Jaruzelski's imposition of martial law, during which he outlawed Solidarity and arrested many of its leaders (Ost 1990, 113–48). The threat of Soviet intervention was crucial in this process.

In an effort to restore some legitimacy, Jaruzelski sought to drive a wedge between intellectuals and workers, to make concessions to the church, and even to open up to a small class of "socialist entrepreneurs" as in Hungary (Kennedy 1992, 55–56; Ost 1990, 155; Korbonski 1999, 146). While Solidarity was thereby weakened, Jaruzelski never won any measure of legitimacy, and Poland continued to undergo serious economic problems and the buildup of international debt (partially to bolster consumption, and partially to try to invest its way out of the slump) (Korbonski 1999, 143). Unable to garner support for his 1987 economic plan, and with the additional blow of the new Polish pope (John Paul II) calling for the relegalization of Solidarity, the party teetered near collapse. As a result of declining living standards, a new round of strikes started in Gdansk and Kraków in April 1988. In August, strikes started in Silesia and began to spread northward. That same month, Jaruzelski initiated roundtable meetings with the opposition, which would lead, in short order, to the decisive defeat of the government in semifree elections, ending Communist rule.

Hungary followed a somewhat similar pattern. While the Hungarian working class never engaged in the kind of collective action taken by the Polish working class, it was sufficiently a threat to the Communist apparatus that it had to try to buy political peace by opening up the second economy to workers and peasants. The resulting petty bourgeoisification in Hungary played a substantial role in eroding the ideological hegemony of the Communist bureaucracy and laid the groundwork for the Hungarian technocratic-intellectual alliance to defeat the bureaucracy (Rona-Tas 1997). In both

countries the political apparatus was wiped out in 1989. It lost political power altogether, and therefore had neither the will nor the capacity to carry out a project of political capitalism. It did, however, have an ideology. The ideology of the victorious technocratic-intellectual elite by 1989 was neoliberalism (see Eyal, Szelényi, and Townsley 1998; Eyal 2000). However, the technocratic-intellectual alliance did not last long. The intellectual elite turned against the technocracy, which was now seen as part of the former Communist establishment.

In 1990, in both Poland and Hungary the newly formed Socialist Party suffered humiliating defeat. The intellectuals themselves were split into liberal and patriotic-Christian wings, and the last decade of the century can be described as struggles among these various political forces. Nevertheless, despite the political differences among all of these intellectual and technocratic elites, they favored neoliberal policies, and in particular, cooperation with foreign investors. Hungary and Poland are in many respects the purest types—the alliance of classes or elites may have been somewhat different in the other liberal regimes, but our key hypothesis is that in all of these regimes the Communist bureaucracy was unseated by an alliance between reform-minded technocrats with liberal and patriotic-Christian intellectuals. This alliance received some initial support from the working class, though for the most part it was demobilized after the defeat of the Communist bureaucracy.

In these regimes, neoliberalism served as the ideological cement to the alliance of the technocracy and the political dissidents (the humanistic intellectuals). Its chief appeal was its radical antistatism (see Eyal 2000 for a more elaborate analysis of the role of monetarism). However, because these systems were functioning democracies, political elites abandoned strict adherence to neolibreal precepts (see Kolodko and Nuti 1997; Snadjer and King 2002; King 2003b), especially ideas favoring the quick "mass" privatization of the SOE sector. First, direct sales to foreigners were prevalent everywhere in central Europe. The Hungarians privatized relatively rapidly via auctions, which frequently resulted in FDI. Slovakia, Slovenia, and Poland delayed the privatization of many large SOEs, choosing to first restructure them and then privatize them through competitive auctions (often to multinationals [MNCs]).[19] Only the Czech Republic managed to implement a significant mass privatization program—which most analysts now acknowledge led to major problems in governance. Only the Czech Republic's very high level of FDI has kept this country out of the patrimonial camp.[20]

The Economic Institutions of Post-Communist Liberal Capitalism

To the extent that the central European cases pursued the neoliberal transition strategy, and to the extent that they were dependent on imports from and exports to the former COMECON system (the economic counterpart to the Warsaw Pact), they suffered deindustrialization just as in the former Soviet Union. However, FDI partially compensates for the problems created by shock liberalization and stabilization, as it leads to reindustrialization. Multinationals provide capital and technology, expertise, and access to world markets. This allows more firms in non-resource-based manufacturing to restructure to enable their survival on the market—and to export to Western Europe without massive technological downgrading and occasionally with substantial upgrading (see case studies in King 2001a, 2001b; King and Varadi 2002; King 2002). Taxes from these restructured privatized firms, as well as continued revenues from large SOEs and their domestic suppliers, allow the economy to avoid the vicious circle of declining state capacity and market withdrawal that follows from "capitalism from above." The presence of high levels of FDI also reduces the level of nonmarket survival strategies like barter and inter-enterprise arrears, as well as reducing wage arrears.

The new private economy will be strengthened, as large greenfields and small joint ventures emerge. Domestically owned small and medium-sized businesses, however, are likely to suffer in at least the short and medium term because of foreign competition in consumer markets, and the replacement of industrial input producers with the suppliers from elsewhere in the global empires of MNCs. Basically, there will be capitalist growth, but it will depend on the investment strategy of particular MNCs, the lending decisions of foreign-owned banks, and the ability to import industrial inputs and capital from, and export manufactured goods to, the core of the capitalist world economy. Because there is capital account liberalization, and because these economies are so sensitive to the cost of currencies and external markets, they will be "fragile"—or prone to devaluation (which partially restores the market for some domestic companies, even as it results in much less consumption for those with savings or on fixed incomes).

Finally, democracy is consolidated because relatively little political capitalism exists, resulting in little pressure to manipulate elections.

Capitalism from Below Leading to Hybrid Capitalism

Arguably, China followed most closely the script described by Konrád and Szelényi (1979). In 1978 the political bureaucracy formed an alliance with the technocratic intelligentsia, and in fact accepted the leadership of the technocratically minded faction of the party elite during the years of Teng Hsiao-ping.[21]

The rise of the technocracy can be traced to the disastrous policies of the political/ideological hardline faction of the party during the Great Leap Forward and Cultural Revolution. On the one hand, these policy failures greatly undermined the legitimacy of the political bureaucracy and forced it to give leadership to the technocratic faction. On the other hand, these disasters emboldened, if not empowered, the dominated class, who had no choice but to abandon central policies and experiment with reform on their own. Yang's (1996) historical study shows that in regions more heavily affected by the Great Leap Forward, spontaneous reforms started earlier and took more radical forms. Another study (Zhou 1996) also shows that many of the initial agricultural reform measures were actually spontaneously taken by local peasants, without the government's approval. The central government only sanctioned them as faits accomplis. Teng Hsiao-ping himself acknowledges that the success of village township enterprises (VTEs) is completely unexpected (Chen 1989).

The bureaucracy and technocracy keep each other under control to the present day.[22] The technocracy did not allow the political apparatus to implement a political capitalist scenario (it had little incentive to do so anyway, since it was not deprived of its political power or many of its economic privileges). The Communist bureaucracy, on the other hand, put strict limits on how far the technocracy could go in its attempts to ally with the intelligentsia and to pursue a liberal policy. This is seen most clearly in the events of Tiananmen Square, where the intelligentsia and workers were repressed; the former much less severely than the latter (see Walder and Xiaoxia 1993).

Workers and peasants could take advantage of the resulting balance of power. Thus, Nee is probably correct to a large extent when he sees the "direct producers" benefiting from transition in China, while they proved to be the losers in the two other systems.[23]

It is in this sense that the path to capitalism was from below. Economists (Jiang 2001; Naughton 1992, 1994) have found that China's transition first started with the opening up of the large domestic markets, giving small firms an enormous space to grow in the production of consumer products, an area where SOEs were less concentrated. While many markets remain regulated and the national consumer market is largely segregated, small local-based firms, supported by local governments, often gain advantages over large state-owned firms (and foreign firms for that matter) in accessing local resources and materials.

The Economic Institutions of Hybrid Capitalism

Since Nee's agenda-setting article in 1989, studies done by both sides of the market transition debate have consistently shown both substantial numbers of noncadre entrepreneurs in rural China and substantial positive returns to household incomes produced as a consequence (Nee 1989, 1996; Walder 2002).

However, a recent study by Walder and Zhao (2002) of rural China shows that the emergence of capitalism in China can be divided into two periods. During the first full decade of economic reform (the 1980s), nonelites with nonagricultural jobs were most likely to become private entrepreneurs. In the second decade, however, when public enterprises began to be privatized, public enterprise managers and relatives of cadres were more likely to become new private entrepreneurs. Therefore, it seems plausible that there is a growing "political capitalism" problem.

Thus, China's hybrid capitalist system still has a great many patrimonial relationships that mirror processes observed in Eastern Europe and the former Soviet Union. Steinfeld's case study (1998) shows that among many Chinese SOEs the exchange of products is often not accompanied by monetary transaction, instead resulting in accumulation of unpaid intercorporate debts—known as "triangular debts." Other elements of Russia's patrimonial system are present. Wank (1999) finds that patron-client relationships also survived the transition and became commodified—because private entrepreneurs still need to have resourceful patrons in the bureaucracy to get deals done.[24] Indeed, the worst inefficiencies of patrimonialism can be identified. Ding (2000) reports on how offshore businesses have become a major channel for the Chinese nomenklatura to turn state assets into private wealth. Lin and Zhang (1999) study how

subsidiaries to urban SOEs have been used as a vehicle to transfer state assets into private or corporate wealth.

Even if it is empirically true that cadres in China benefit more from the transition than noncadres, the situation is still very different from the political capitalism in Eastern Europe, where the apparatchiks simply directly sell off state assets and accumulate private wealth that is then channeled out of the local economy. Thus far, cadres help their children, but refrain from becoming capitalists themselves. In China, because a thriving private economy exists, political capitalists are likely to reinvest pilfered funds in the domestic economy, where their political connections can help them get high returns. Moreover, private entrepreneurs thus far have not entered into cadre positions (Walder and Zhao 2002).

All these changes considered, we believe China's and Vietnam's economic systems can best be described as hybrid capitalist systems. While China is moving in the direction of a full-fledged capitalist system, it has not arrived there yet. Most crucially, there is no clear dominance of private property. For although the state has decentralized, the most dynamic sector of the Chinese economy, the VTEs, are still not privately owned, although they are market dependent. These locally owned firms outperform SOEs, and between 1985 and 1996 they increased from 14.6 percent of gross industrial output to 27.8 percent, while SOEs fell from 65 percent to 28.5 percent (see Peng 2001). Nan Lin (1995) proposes a "local market socialism" perspective to understand the hybrid nature of the Chinese political economy. He claims that this perspective integrates socialism as the political axis, market-oriented reform as the economic axis, and locally embedded social networks as the social axis. Similar to Walder (1995) and Oi (1999), he argues that decentralization does not mean abandoning the command system. Instead, the command system and newly emerged market mechanisms are both incorporated and embedded in local sociocultural networks.[25]

However, there is no doubt that China is moving in the direction of capitalism. First, many VTEs are "red caps"—in which local state ownership is legal cover for what are really private businesses (see Liu 1992; Nee and Su 1996). Moreover, privatization has finally started to make headway in China, which up until the late 1990s mostly "grew out of the plan" without actively dismantling state ownership (Naughton 1995). The privatization of state and collectively owned industries has been greatly accelerated in recent years. Lin and Zhu (2001) use a 1998 national survey to show that by that year private ownership in SOEs was already quite substantial. Cao, Qian, and Weingast (1999) study the accelerated privatization process since 1995 and argue that it is helped by the federalist structure of the Chinese political economy: regions with larger private economies are more likely to privatize their SOEs (because the newly unemployed will be more likely to find jobs). On the other hand, many collectively owned enterprises are also being aggressively privatized by their local governments. By 2002, the massive rural VTE sector, which had employed more than 80 million people at its zenith, underwent significant privatization, shrinking to half its former size (Walder and Zhao 2002, 5; Li and Rozelle [2000] also report empirical evidence of the privatization of VTEs).

Another factor pushing in the direction of capitalist property relations is the importance of foreign direct investment in China's economy. While per capita levels of FDI remain modest compared to central Europe, as a percentage of total investment they are quite high, and absolute levels are enormous. Of particular importance have been Taiwanese and Hong Kong capital investments in southern China, creating what Naughton calls the second China Circle (1997, 7). This investment has lead to explosive export growth, especially in electronics.

Furthermore, the SOEs that do exist have become increasingly marketized. Guthrie (1997) studies asset diversification of Chinese SOEs and finds that they respond to market instability and exhibit increasingly market-oriented behaviors. Keister (1998, 2001) shows that Chinese SOEs adopt capitalist-like intercorporate structures—business groups and interlocking directorates—that have effects on firms' performance similar to that in capitalist economies. Nee (2001) shows that from 1978 to 1991, the investment capital provided to SOEs came increasingly from non-central-state sources (retained earnings, loans from state-owned banks, and foreign sources). Over this period, the percentage provided by state redistributors fell from 62 percent to under 7 percent.[26] Other studies (Groves et al. 1994; Huang and Kalirajan 1998) have found that many SOEs are subjected to market competition and are market integrated. Furthermore, market integration leads to improved performance: greater technical efficiency (Huang and Kalirajan 1998) and higher productivity (Groves et al. 1994). Another study (Groves et al. 1995) also finds that a managerial

labor market is emerging in the state sector and that the allocation of managerial resources is increasingly governed by the market. Because these firms remain state owned, but are increasingly market integrated (must buy inputs and sell products on markets) and behave like capitalist firms, we can call this type of property state capitalism.

The Chinese system is hybrid because it is still a long way from becoming dominated by capitalist private property. However, it is capitalist to the extent that markets have flourished, and the private economy continues to expand, while the SOEs decline but behave increasingly like capitalist firms (see Nee 1992, 2001). By 1993, SOE employment in urban areas declined from 75 percent to 60 percent, and in rural areas to around 30 percent (Cao, Qian, and Weingast 1999). This should not be taken to imply that China is particularly neoliberal (see King 2003a). The Chinese transition has been overseen by a strong state (see Nee 2000), which continues to promote "national champions" from the SOEs that constitute Chinese business groups (see Keister 2000).[27] More important for Chinese growth, however, has been the state's massive infrastructural investments, which provide support for new private enterprise formation and growth.

These economic changes have political effects as well. The Communist Party loses its ideological commitment, replaced by a pragmatic approach that emphasizes growth and increasing living standards. China looks less and less like a totalitarian system, and more and more like a bureaucratic authoritarian regime—although it is still clearly totalitarian (because the Communist Party maintains its political monopoly).

Conclusions

The transition to capitalism from Communism is different from earlier transitions to capitalism. First, capitalism was formed on the ruins of a society that did not have even in embryonic form the institution of private property and therefore did not have a propertied bourgeoisie. Second, socialism had accomplished some of the "historic missions" of capitalism: it completed the process of capital accumulation and industrialization and, though in contradictory ways, separated the producers from the means of subsistence and production.

These features are consequential, though in different ways, for the nature of capitalism that emerges from Communism. Post-Communist capitalisms constitute an "extended family" of capitalisms. In some countries the alliance of the technocracy and intellectuals could smash the power of the Communist political apparatus, preventing the development of political capitalism and implementing a post-Communist liberal system that is highly dependent on foreign direct investments and foreign demand and is sensitive to currency fluctuations. In countries where the technocratic-intellectual alliance and the working class were weaker, the political apparatus retained its power, abandoned the Communist ideology and substituted nationalism, and implemented political capitalism. Finally, in some countries the bureaucracy and technocracy arrived at a balance of power, and under these circumstances capitalism develops from below: the technocracy delays the political capitalism project of the political bureaucracy, while the Communist political bureaucracy limits the liberal reform attempts of the technocracy.

NOTES

1. It is "neoclassical" because it is concerned with the origin and functioning of capitalism, the questions that occupied the "founding fathers" of sociology (Marx, Weber, and Durkheim) and is inspired by Weber's emphasis on the multiplicities of capitalist forms. In this respect neoclassical sociology is the polar opposite of neoclassical economics, which operates with the assumption of a unified capitalist system.

2. The transition from Communism to capitalism, from socialist-redistributive economies to market-integrated systems, is largely uncharted territory. This chapter does not offer a review of every important piece of research in these areas, although it does make reference to many of the most influential works. This chapter can therefore be complimented by a review of the publications of the World Bank and the European Bank for Reconstruction and Development on the transition, most prominently the latter's editions of the *Transition Report,* as well as its newsletter (*Transition Newsletter*) put out jointly with the William Davidson Institute at the University of Michigan Business School. The latter also has hundreds of very useful working papers, almost all using original data (see http://www.wdi.bus.umich.edu). Of course, as social scientists we should keep in mind the basic facts of the sociology of knowledge; the EBRD is both a member bank of the World Bank and a fairly substantial investor in the transition economies. In the official publications of the World Bank and the EBRD, much of the analysis is cast from a clearly discernable perspective: it is a financial investor's point of view (which, according to Nobel laureate Joseph Stiglitz [2002] among many others [e.g., Gowan 1995], has a bias in favor of preserving the value of money and the repayment of loans over other features of transition, such as the minimization of poverty or unemployment). The excellent but far less numerous publications of the United Nations Development Program (especially the Human Development Reports on the former Soviet Union and East Europe) offer a very useful contrasting perspective. Similarly, social scientists should be even more careful than usual in using post-Communist

official statistics (see the very useful paper by Filer and Hanousek [2001] for an extended discussion of reliability and validity issues, as well as a compilation of country websites and a list of firm-level data sets).

Finally, for those wishing to use this chapter as a reference to all of the economic sociology of post-Communist society, there is a good deal that we do not address, such as comparative welfare institutions (Haney 2002), gender and racial stratification and poverty (Kligman and Szelényi 2002; Fodor 2002), and patterns of consumption (Davis 2000). A more comprehensive typology of post-Communist capitalism might well incorporate these dimensions.

3. Perry Anderson for instance—under some Weberian influence—in *Passages from Antiquity to Feudalism* (1974) considers the possibility that feudalism may not have been born "within the wombs" of antiquity, but rather can be best understood as some sort of merger of the Germanic form with antiquity.

4. The key to the surplus relationship between the peasantry and the rational redistributers in the past until this day is that they could not buy subsidized state grain but had to grow their own. The system still disadvantages the rural population by requiring them to pay higher taxes (the so-called agricultural tax) and provides subsidized health and education systems to the urban population. Some say that 150 million are underemployed. Others estimate the number at only 100 million. In terms of possession of the land, all rural people regardless of their jobs or degree of underemployment have lifelong claim to village land. The exact size of their fields (and thus their expected grain deliveries and taxes) was set by the size of the household 15 years ago. The state's policy is to have no redistributions for 30 years, in order to encourage residents to use the land wisely. However, many places redistribute every two to three years to keep up with changes in the household size of the villagers, while other places do not. Already in 1984 the Communist Party let rural residents sign long-term leases with nonvillagers for right to farm land (and take up tax and grain quotas); but even in this situation the ownership remains with the village, and the villager is entitled to the return of his land after the lease is up. We are not aware of any research indicating how widespread these arrangements are, but to the extent that it has caught on, it is probably in the wealthiest areas. China clearly will not allow a landless rural mass to emerge. This is one of the impetuses for the VTE reforms, which diversified employment in rural areas; VTEs did so successfully from 1985 to 1996, although since then the picture is less rosy. Thus, virtually every rural resident is guaranteed access to land, both as a place to build a house (which is owned as private property) and as a place to till the soil. Because farming is often so poorly remunerated, most people want at least one member of the household in a nonfarm job, and the route to high incomes, not to mention wealth, is outside farming (Deborah Davis personal communication 2003).

5. For an analysis of the developmental impact of FDI using firm-level data in Hungary, see Toth 2001; King 2000; King and Varadi 2002. For the Czech Republic see Djankov and Hoekman 2000; for Poland see Liberska 1997; Kaminski and Smarzynska 2001; for China see Kinoshita 1999. While these studies describe foreign-owned firms as more efficient and dynamic than domestically owned firms, they do point out that the spillover effects (the use of domestic suppliers) are less than anticipated. This means that the beneficial effects of FDI might not be truly long-lasting, for firms might stop investing once they establish themselves

as monopolists or oligopolists, and begin pumping surplus out of the domestic economy by repatriating profits. If they are not contributing to the domestic economy by making purchases from domestic firms, the developmental benefit will indeed be less than many anticipated. Furthermore, foreign-owned firms contribute to trade deficits because of their very high level of imports. Finally, studies have found that in both Poland (Dyker and Kubielas 2000) and Hungary (Toth 2001) firms exporting to Western Europe have a low level of technological upgrading, casting further doubt on the transformative power of FDI. Clearly, the empirical question on the role of FDI in the transition is far from resolved—despite the correlation between high levels of FDI and post-Communist performance. It is quite possible that the effects of FDI are different in the various environments in different countries. Only longitudinal, cross-country, firm-level surveys will shed light on the question of origin of ownership and performance. Thus far, one of the thorniest issues in the literature on firm performance and property change is how to deal with endogeneity. That is, how do we know whether foreign firms perform better because they are foreign owned, or are foreign owned because they are better firms (the jewels of the industrial structure are privatized by foreigners, and the inefficient firms are left for domestic owners). It is by no means an easy task to fully control for this possibility. Selection bias issues are equally relevant in evaluating other property forms, such as state ownership.

6. Most agree that China's continued success hinges on the health of the banking sector, where state-owned banks channel the very high savings rate of the population into the SOE sector. If the Chinese population ever lost confidence in state-owned banks, a major crisis for the SOE sector would follow.

7. Although Rona-Tas really speaks to another historical context, to what we call here "capitalism from without."

8. See Lipton and Sachs 1990 for possibly the most influential statement of this position. See also Murrell 1993; Gowan 1995; King 2002, 2003b; and Stiglitz 2002 for a discussion of this theory. See anthropologist Janine Wedel 2001 for an excellent discussion of the role of Western economic advisors in the post-Communist transition.

9. The only major exception is the Czech Republic, where the technocracy and dissident intellectuals implemented a substantial mass privatization program. But even this program covered a much smaller proportion of the economy than in Russia, since it included a much larger portion of firms that were sold through direct sales to foreign investors (FDI per capita was almost an order of magnitude greater in the Czech Republic than in Russia). Mass privatization programs can also benefit enterprise managers (a fraction of the technocracy) because it can fragment outside owners, leaving control to enterprise insiders. In the Czech case, mass privatization was also used by Vaclav Klaus, a technocrat, to boost his political popularity (the citizen vouchers bore his name). While the implementation of this program boosted the Czech Republic's claim to be the most neoliberal post-Communist country in the first half of the 1990s, it ironically blocked substantial amounts of FDI (McDermott 2002), which only later grew to very high levels (surpassing the early leader Hungary in the late 1990s).

10. Of course, this time around the vanguard paid lip service to representative democracy. Sachs himself admitted that the "ideal" democratic system was one in which the executive was elected and then allowed to act without constraints until the next election (see Rodrik 1996, 32 n. 30).

Sachs and other prominent neoliberals offered a political economy that emphasized the dangers of "losers" and "winners" in "partial" reform systems reversing the transition or locking in "incomplete" reforms. We believe this danger is overemphasized, as suggested by reforms in China, Poland (see King 2002), and elsewhere (see King 2003b for a 14-country comparison that covers the vast majority of the post-Communist population).

11. Elite survey data backs up this claim. According to Szelényi and Szelényi (1995), more than twice as many former members of nomenklatura made it into the new economic elite in Russia than in Poland (629).

12. It seems more likely that what Stark labeled "recombinant property" in most cases was simply an attempt by the state to break up huge horizontally and vertically integrated industrial firms (such as steel and aluminum producers) so that their individual pieces could be more easily privatized.

13. In these countries "capitalism from above" was slowed by resistance from workers and other political groups as well as the legacy of worker's self-management (for Polish workers see Kramer 1995, 654; also see Ekiert 2001; for Slovenia see Mencinger 1996; Gligorov 1995).

14. Theoretically, firms should be able to import these inputs. However, firms cannot instantly find inputs, and may not be able to afford them.

15. For a discussion of these points see Stiglitz 2002; Amsden, Kochanowicz, and Taylor 1994; Gowan 1995, 1999; Andor and Summers 1998; Chussodovsky 1997; and UNDP 1999.

16. In Russia, for example, capital flight in all its forms has averaged about $40 billion a year (Golovachev 2002).

17. In Russia, for example, receipts of the consolidated state budget declined from 41 percent of GDP in 1990 to only 26.8 percent in 1997, even though GDP was only about 50 percent of its prior level (Vorobyov and Zhukov 2000, 5).

18. The most infamous example was the "loans for shares" program, in which a handful of politically connected businessmen gained control of Russia's oil companies for a small fraction of what they were worth, in exchange for ensuring Yeltsin's 1996 reelection (see Wolosky 2000; Klebnikov 2000; Freedland 2000; Hoffman 2002; and the authoritative account in Reddaway and Glinski 2000).

19. In 1995 a small program covering some small and medium enterprises was implemented. These firms constituted only about 10 percent of the productive capacity of the SOE sector (Baltowski and Mickanwicz 2000).

20. And indeed, the Czech Republic has low state capacity and weak security of property rights compared to its liberal neighbors, despite its privileged starting point (King 2003a). There also seemed to be quite a bit of political capitalism around the Klaus administration.

21. A study (Li 2001) of the "fourth generation" of Chinese leaders—those who will succeed the current leadership of Jiang Zemin—has confirmed the technocratic background of this elite group. Most of these leaders have an educational background in technology and started their career either as technocrat-managers in the state industrial sector or as professionals.

22. Walder and associates have long studied the dual career paths and bifurcated elite structure in China (Li and Walder 2001; Walder 1995; Walder, Li, and Treiman 2000). Basically the findings are (1) there are two distinctive paths into the Chinese elite: prestigious administrative positions within the bureaucracy and professional positions; (2) there is considerable circulation between the two (the

study on the fourth-generation leaders [Li 2001] attests to this too); and (3) the dual career paths create a bifurcated elite structure.

23. For a useful review of the rather large body of stratification literature in China, see Bian 2002.

24. Wank (1999) argues that Chinese cadres, rich in networked social capital, play a crucial *functional* role as the brokers between private firms and the state, between the coexisting market and redistributive systems, and provide the institutional infrastructure for markets and reduce transaction costs.

25. See Nee and Cao 1999 on the implications of a hybrid mixed economy for social stratification.

26. The OECD (2000) provides some recent data on this process. For instance, in 1999 the central government made the decision to withdraw state control from small and medium-sized SOEs. The number of industrial SOEs is expected to fall from the existing 75,000 to at most 1,000 or 2,000.

27. See Zhou 2001 for an analysis of the state-led process of constructing a national grain market.

REFERENCES

Amsden, Alice H., Jacek Kochanowicz, and Lance Taylor. 1994. *The Market Meets Its Match.* Cambridge: Harvard University Press.

Anderson, Perry. 1974. *Passages from Antiquity to Feudalism.* London: NLB.

Andor, Lazlo, and Martin Summers. 1998. *Market Failure: Eastern Europe's 'Economic Miracle.'* London: Pluto Press.

Baltowski, Maciej, and Tomasz Mickanwicz. 2000. "Privatization in Poland: Ten Years After." *Post-Communist Economies* 12(4): 425–43.

Bernhard, Michael H. 1993. *The Origins of Democratization in Poland: Workers, Intellectuals, and Oppositional Politics, 1976–1980.* New York: Columbia University Press.

Bian, Yanjie. 2002. "Chinese Social Stratification and Social Mobility." *Annual Review of Sociology* 28(1): 91–117.

Burawoy, Michael. 1996. "The State and Economic Involution: Russia through a Chinese Lens." *World Development* 24:1105–17.

———. 2001a. "Neoclassical Sociology: From the End of Communism to the End of Classes." *American Journal of Sociology* 106:1099–1120.

———. 2001b. "Transition without Transformation: Russia's Involutionary Road to Capitalism." *East European Politics and Society* 15(2): 269–92.

Burawoy, Michael, and Pavel Krotov. 1992. "The Soviet Transition from Socialism to Capitalism: Worker Control and Economic Bargaining." *American Sociological Review* 57:16–38.

Burawoy, Michael, Pavel Krotov, and Tatyana Lytkina. 2000. "Domestic Involution: How Women Organize Survival in a North Russian City." Pp. 231–61 in *Russia in the New Century*, ed. Victoria Bonnell and George Breslauer. Boulder, Colo.: Westview Press.

Cao, Y. Z., Y. Y. Qian, and Barry R. Weingast. 1999. "From Federalism, Chinese Style to Privatization, Chinese Style." *Economics of Transition* 7(1): 103–31.

Chen, Yaobang. 1989. "Tongyi Sixiang, Jiji Tiaozheng, Cujin Xiangzhen Qiye Chi xu Xietiao Jiankang Fazhan." *Chinese Township-Village Enterprises (Zhongguo Xiangzhen Qiye)* 9 (September): 1–8.

Chussodovsky, Michel. 1997. *The Globalization of Poverty: Impacts of IMF and World Bank Reform.* London: Zed.

Coates, David. 2000. *Models of Capitalism.* Cambridge: Polity Press.

Darden, Keith A. 2002. "The Scholastic Revolution: Explaining Nationalism in the USSR." Paper presented at Workshop on Postcommunism, Yale University, Fall.

Davis, Deborah, ed. 2000. *The Consumer Revolution in China.* Berkeley and Los Angeles: University of California Press.

Ding, X. L. 2000. "Informal Privatization through Internationalization: The Rise of Nomenklatura Capitalism in China's Offshore Businesses." *British Journal of Political Science* 30:121–46.

Djankov, Simeon, and Bernard Hoekman. 2000. "Foreign Investment and Productivity Growth in Czech Enterprises." *World Bank Economic Review* 14(1): 49–64.

Donnithorne, Audrey. 1972. "China's Cellular Economy: Some Economic Trends since the Cultural Revolution." *China Quarterly* 52:605–19.

Dyker, David A., and Stanislaw Kubielas. 2000. "Technology and Structure in the Polish Economy under Transition and Globalization." *Economic Systems* 24(1): 1–24.

European Bank for Reconstruction and Development (EBRD). 1996, 1999, 2001. *Transition Report.* London: EBRD.

Ekiert, Grzegorz. 2001. "The State after State Socialism: Poland in Comparative Perspective." Center for European Studies, Harvard University, February 1. Photocopy.

Evans, Peter. 1979. *Dependent Development: The Alliance of Multinational, State, and Local Capital in Brazil.* Princeton: Princeton University Press.

Eyal, Gil. 2000. "Anti-politics and the Spirit of Capitalism: Dissidents, Monetarists, and the Czech Transition to Capitalism." *Theory and Society* 29:49–92.

Eyal, Gil, Ivan Szelényi, and Eleanor Townsley. 1998. *Making Capitalism without Capitalists.* New York: Verso.

———. 2001. "The Utopia of Postsocialist Theory and the Ironic View of History in Neoclassical Sociology." *American Journal of Sociology* 106:1121–28.

Filer, Randall K., and Jan Hanousek. 2001. "Data Watch: Research Data from Transition Economies." William Davidson Working Paper No. 416., William Davidson Institute at the University of Michigan Business School.

Fligstein, Neil. 1996. "The Economic Sociology of the Transition of from Socialism to Capitalism." *American Journal of Sociology* 101:1074–80.

Fodor, Eva. 2002. "Introduction: Gender and the Experience of Poverty in Eastern Europe and Russia after 1989." *Communist and Post-Communist Studies* 35(4): 369–83.

Frank, Andre. 1969. *Capitalism and Underdevelopment in Latin America: Historical Studies of Chile and Brazil.* New York: Monthly Review Press.

Freedland, Chrystia. 2000. *Sale of the Century.* New York: Crown.

Garcelon, Marc. 1997. "The Estate of Change: The Specialist Rebellion and the Democratic Movement in Moscow, 1989–1991." *Theory and Society* 26: 39–85.

Gerber, Theodore P., and Michael Hout. 1998. "More Shock Than Therapy: Market Transition, Employment, and Income in Russia, 1991–1995." *American Journal of Sociology* 104:1–50.

Gligorov, Vladimir. 1995. "Republic of Slovenia: Country Report." Vienna Institute for Comparative Economic Studies, December.

Golovachev, Vitaly. 2002. "Russian Money Goes Around the World." WPS Monitoring Agency, September 13. www.wps.ru/e_index.html.

Gowan, Peter. 1995. "Neoliberal Theory and Practice for Eastern Europe." *New Left Review* 213:3–60.

———. 1999. *The Global Gamble: Washington's Faustian Bid for World Domination.* London: Verso.

Granick, David. 1990. *Chinese State Enterprises: A Regional Property Rights Analysis.* Chicago: University of Chicago Press.

Groves, Theodore, Yongmiao Hong, John McMillan, and Barry Naughton. 1994. "Autonomy and Incentives in Chinese State Enterprises." *Quarterly Journal of Economics* 109(1): 183–209.

———. 1995. "China's Evolving Managerial Labor Market." *Journal of Political Economy* 103:873–92.

Gustafson, Thane. 1999. *Capitalism Russian-Style.* Cambridge: Cambridge University Press.

Guthrie, Douglas. 1997. "Between Markets and Politics: Organizational Responses to Reform in China." *American Journal of Sociology* 102:1258–1304.

Hall, Peter A., and David Soskice. 2001. *Varieties of Capitalism: The Institutional Foundations of Comparative Advantage.* Oxford: Oxford University Press.

Haney, Lynne. 2002. *Inventing the Needy.* Berkeley and Los Angeles: University of California Press.

Hankiss, Elemer. 1990. *East European Alternatives.* Oxford: Clarendon Press.

Hanley, Eric, Lawrence King, and Istvan Janos Toth. 2002. "The State, International Agencies, and Property Transformation in Post-Communist Hungary." *American Journal of Sociology* 108:129–67.

Hanley, Eric, Natasha Yershova, and Richard Anderson. 1995. "Russia—Old Wine in a New Bottle? The Circulation and Reproduction of Russian Elites, 1983–1993." *Theory and Society* 24:639–68.

Hart, Jeffrey A. 1992. *Rival Capitalists: International Competitiveness in the United States, Japan, and Western Europe.* Ithaca, N.Y.: Cornell University Press.

Helf, Gavin, and Jeffrey Hahn. 1992. "Old Dogs and New Tricks: Party Elites in the Russian Regional Elections of 1990." *Slavic Review* 51:511–30.

Heller, Agnes, Ferenc Fehér, and György Márkus. 1983. *Dictatorship over Needs.* Oxford: Basil Blackwell.

Hoffman, David. 2002. *The Oligarchs: Wealth and Power in the New Russia.* New York: Public Affairs.

Huang, Yasheng. 1995. "Information, Bureaucracy, and Economic Reforms in China and the Soviet Union." *World Politics* 47:102–34.

Huang, Yiping, and K. P. Kalirajan. 1998. "Enterprise Reform and Technical Efficiency of China's State-Owned Enterprises." *Applied Economics* 30:585–92.

Jiang, Xiaojuan, ed. 2001. *China's Industries in Transition: Organizational Change, Efficiency Gains, and Growth Dynamics.* Huntington, N.Y.: Nova Science Publishers.

Kaminski, Bartlomiej, and Beata Smarzyńska. 2001. "Foreign Direct Investment and Integration into Global Production and Distribution Networks: The Case of Poland." Working Papers—International Economics, Trade, Capital Flows No. 2646, World Bank.

Karabel. Jerome. 1993. "Polish Intellectuals and the Origins of Solidarity: The Making of an Oppositional Alliance." *Communist and Post-Communist Studies* 26(1): 25–46.

Keister, Lisa A. 1998. "Engineering Growth: Business Group Structure and Firm Performance in China's Transitional Ecoonomy." *American Journal of Sociology* 104:404–40.

———. 2000. Chinese Business Groups: *The Structure and Impact of Interfirm Relations during Economic Development.* Oxford: Oxford University Press.

———. 2001. "Exchange Structures in Transition: Lending and Trade Relations in Chinese Business Groups." *American Sociological Review* 66:336–60.

Kennedy, Michael D. 1987. "Polish Engineers' Participation in the Solidarity Movement." *Social Forces* 65:641–69.

———. 1992. "The Intelligentsia in the Constitution of Civil Societies in Post-Communist Regimes in Hungary and Poland." *Theory and Society* 21:29–76.

King, Lawrence P. 2000. "Foreign Direct Investment and Transition." *European Journal of Sociology* 41(2): 189–224.

———. 2001a. *The Basic Features of Post-Communist Capitalism: Firms in Hungary, the Czech Republic, and Slovakia.* Westport, Conn.: Praeger Press.

———. 2001b. "Making Markets: A Comparative Study of Postcommunist Managerial Strategies in Central Europe." *Theory and Society* 30:494–538.

———. 2002. "Postcommunist Divergence: A Comparative Analysis of the Transition to Capitalism in Poland and Russia." *Studies in Comparative International Development* 37(3): 3–35.

———. 2003a. "Shock Privatization: The Effects of Rapid Large Scale Privatization on Enterprise Restructuring." *Politics and Society* 31:3–34.

———. 2003b. "Explaining Postcommunist Economic Performance." William Davidson Working Paper No. 559, William Davidson Institute at the University of Michigan Business School.

King, Lawrence P., and Balasz Varadi. 2002. "Beyond Manichean Economics: Foreign Direct Investment and Growth in the Transition from Capitalism." *Communist and Post-Communist Studies* 2(3): 1–22.

Kinoshita, Yuko. 1999. "Technology Spillovers through Foreign Direct Investment." Working Paper No. 221, William Davidson Institute at the University of Michigan Business School.

Klebnikov, Paul. 2000. *The Godfather of the Kremlin.* New York: Harcourt.

Kligman, Gail, and Iván Szelényi. 2002. *Poverty and Social Structure in Transitional Economics.* Berlin: Max-Planck-Institut für Bildung und Forschung.

Kojima, Reeitsu. 1992. "The Growing Fiscal Authority of Provincial-Level Governments in China." *Journal of Developing Economies* 30(4):315–46.

Kolodko, Grzegorz, and D. Mario Nuti. 1997. *The Polish Alternative: Old Myths, Hard Facts, and New Strategies in the Successful Transformation of the Polish Economy.* Helsinki: UNU World Institute of Development Economics Research.

Konrád, George, and Iván Szelényi. 1979. *Intellectuals on the Road to Class Power.* Trans. Andrew Arato and Richard E. Allen. New York: Harcourt Brace Jovanovich.

Korbonski, Andrzej. 1999. "East Central Europe on the Eve of the Changeover: The Case of Poland." *Communist and Post-Communist Studies* 32: 139–52.

Kornai, János. 1980. *The Economics of Shortage.* Amsterdam: North Holland.

———. 1992. *The Socialist Economic System.* Princeton: Princeton University Press.

Kramer, Mark. 1995. "Polish Workers and the Post-Communist Transition, 1989–93." *Europe-Asia Studies* 47:669–713.

Kubik, Jan. 1994. "Who Done It: Workers, Intellectuals, or Someone Else? Controversy over Solidarity's Origins and Social Composition." *Theory and Society* 23:441–66.

Lane, David Stuart. 1981. *Leninism: A Sociological Interpretation.* Cambridge: Cambridge University Press.

Li, Bobai, and Andrew G. Walder. 2001. "Career Advancement as Party Patronage: Sponsored Mobility into the Chinese Administrative Elite, 1949–1996." *American Journal of Sociology* 106:1371–1408.

Li, Cheng. 2001. *China's Leaders: The New Generation.* Lanham, Md.: Rowman and Littlefield.

Li, H. B., and Scott Rozelle. 2000. "Saving or Stripping Rural Industry: An Analysis of Privatization and Efficiency in China." *Agricultural Economics* 23(3): 241–52.

Liberman, Ira, Stilpon Nestor, and Raj Desai, eds. 1997. *Between State and Market: Mass Privatization in Transition Economies.* Studies of Economies in Transformation 23. Washington, D.C.: World Bank.

Liberska, Barbara. 1997. "Foreign Direct Investment in Poland." Working Paper No. 7, Polish Academy of Sciences, Institute of Economics, Warsaw.

Lin, Nan. 1995. "Local Market Socialism: Local Corporatism in Action in Rural China." *Theory and Society* 24:301–54.

Lin, Yi-Min, and Zhanxin Zhang. 1999. "Backyard Profit Centers: The Private Assets of Public Agencies." Pp. 203–25 in *Property Rights and Economic Reform in China,* ed. Jean C. Oi and Andrew G. Walder. Stanford, Calif.: Stanford University Press.

Lin, Yi-Min, and Tian Zhu. 2001. "Ownership Restructuring in Chinese State Industry: An Analysis of Evidence on Initial Organizatioonal Changes." *China Quarterly* 166:305–341.

Linz, Juan, and Alfred Stepan. 1996. *Problems of Democratic Transition and Consolidation: Southern Europe, South America, and Post-Communist Europe.* Baltimore: Johns Hopkins University Press.

Lipton, David, and Jeffrey D. Sachs. 1990. "Creating a Market Economy in Eastern Europe: The Case of Poland." *Brookings Papers on Economic Activity* 1: 75–133.

Liu, Yia-Ling. 1992. "Reform from Below: The Private Economy and Local Politics in the Rural Industrialization of Wenzhou." *China Quarterly* 130: 293–316.

Lyons, Thomas P. 1986. "Explaining Economics Fragmentation in China: A Systems Approach." *Journal of Comparative Economics* 10(3): 209–36.

Manchin, Róbert, and Iván Szelényi. 1987. "Social Policy under State Socialism." Pp. 102–39 in *Stagnation and Renewal in Social Policy,* ed. Gøsta Esping-Anderson, Lee Rainwater, and Martin Rein. White Plains, N.Y.: M. E. Sharpe.

Marquand, David Ramsay MacDonald. 1997. *New Reckoning: Capitalism, States, and Citizens.* Malden, Mass.: Polity Press.

McDermott, Gerald. 2002. *Embedded Politics: Industrial Networks and Institutional Change in Postcommunism.* Ann Arbor: University of Michigan Press.

Mencinger, Joze. 1996. "Privatization Experiences in Slovenia." *Annals of Public and Cooperative Economics* 67:415–28.

Montinola, Gabriella, Yingyi Qian, and Barry R. Weingast. 1996. "Federalism, Chinese Style: The Political Basis for Economic Success." *World Politics* 48(1): 50–81.

Murrell, Peter. 1993. "What Is Shock Therapy? What Did It Do in Poland and Russia?" *Post-Soviet Affairs* 9:111–40.

Naughton, Barry. 1992. "Implications of the State Monopoly over Industry and Its Relaxation." *Modern China* 18(1): 14–41.

———. 1994. "Chinese Institutional Innovation and

Privatization from Below." *American Economic Review* 84:266–70.

——. 1995. *Growing Out of the Plan: Chinese Economic Reform, 1978–1993* Cambridge: Cambridge University Press.

Nee, Victor. 1989. "A Theory of Market Transition: From Redistribution to Markets in State Socialism." *American Sociological Review* 54:663–81.

——. 1992. "Organizational Dynamics of Market Transition: Hybrid Forms, Property Rights, and Mixed Economy in China." *Administrative Science Quarterly* 37:1–27.

——. 1996. "The Emergence of a Market Society: Changing Mechanisms of Stratification in China." *American Journal of Sociology* 101:908–49.

——. 1997. "The Emergence of the China Circle." Pp. 3–40 in *The China Circle: Economics and Technology in the PRC, Taiwan, and Hong Kong*, ed. Barry Naughton: Washington, D.C.: Brookings Institution Press.

——. 1998. "Sources of the New Institutionalism." Pp. 1–16 in *The New Institutionalism in Sociology*, ed. Mary C. Brinton and Victor Nee. New York: Russell Sage Foundation.

——. 2000. "The Rule of the State in Making a Market Economy." *Journal of Institutional and Theoretical Economics* 156(1): 64–94.

——. 2001. "North's Theory of Institutional Change and State Capitalism in China." Paper presented at the conference "Economic Sociology of Capitalism," Center for the Study of Economy and Society, Cornell University.

Nee, Victor, and Shijin Su. 1996. "Institutions, Social Ties, and Commitment in China's Corporatist Transformation." Pp. 111–34 in *Reforming Asian Socialism: The Growth of Market Institutions*, ed. John McMillan and Barry Naughton. Ann Arbor: University of Michigan Press.

Nee, Victor, and Yang Cao. 1999. "Path Dependent Societal Transformation: Stratification in Hybrid Mixed Economies." *Theory and Society* 28:799–834.

Nolan, Peter, and Robert F. Ash. 1996. "China's Economy on the Eve of Reform. " Pp. 18–36 in *China's Transitional Economy*, ed. Andrew G. Walder. Oxford: Oxford University Press.

Organization for Economic Cooperation and Development (OECD). 2000. *Reforming China's Enterprises*. Paris: OECD.

Oi, Jean. 1999. Rural *China Takes Off: Institutional Foundations of Economic Reform*. Berkeley and Los Angeles: University of California Press.

Ost, David. 1990. *The Politics of Anti-Politics*. Philadelphia: Temple University Press.

Pearson, Margaret M. 1997. *China's New Business Elite: The Political Consequences of Economic Reform*. Berkeley and Los Angeles: University of California Press.

Peng, Yusheng. 2001. "Chinese Villages and Townships as Industrial Corporations: Ownership, Gover-

nance, and Market Discipline." *American Journal of Sociology* 106:1338–70.

Popov, Vladamir. 1999. "The Financial System in Russia Compared to Other Transition Economies: The Anglo-American versus the German-Japanese Model." *Comparative Economic Studies* 41(1): 1–41.

Qian, Yingyi, and Barry Weingast. 1997. "Federalism as a Commitment to Preserving Market Incentives." *Journal of Economic Perspectives* 11(4): 83–92.

Reddaway, Peter, and Dmitri Glinski. 2001. *The Tragedy of Russia's Reforms: Market Bolshevism against Democracy*. Washington, D.C.: United States Institute of Peace Press.

Rodrik, Dani. 1996. "Understanding Economic Policy Reform." *Journal of Economic Literature* 34:9–41.

Rona-Tas, Akos. 1994. "The First Shall Be Last: Entrepreneurship and Communist Cadres in the Transition." *American Journal of Sociology* 100:40–69.

——. 1997. "The Czech Third Wave." *Problems of Post-Communism* 44(6): 53–63.

Sachs, Jeffrey D. 1990. "What Is to Be Done." *The Economist*, January 13, 19–24.

Sachs, Jeffrey D., and Wing Thye Woo. 1994. "Structural Factors in the Economic Reforms of China, Eastern Europe, and the Former Soviet Union." *Economic Policy* 18:102–45.

Schroeder, Gertrude. 1998. "Dimensions of Russia's Industrial Transformation, 1992 to 1998: An Overview." *Post-Soviet Geography and Economics* 39(5): 243–70.

Shlapentokh, Vladimir. 1990. *Soviet Intellectuals and Political Power*. Princeton: Princeton University Press.

Snadjer, Aleksandra, and Lawrence King. 2002. "Controlled Liberalism: Poland's State Led Transition to Capitalism." Paper presented at the Yale Workshop in Comparative Studies.

Southworth, Caleb. 2001. "How Russian Industry Works: Worker and Firm Survival Strategies in Six Enterprises in Bashkortosan." Ph.D. diss., University of California, Los Angeles.

Staniszkis, Jadwiga. 1991. "Political Capitalism in Poland." *East European Politics and Societies* 5(1): 127–41.

Stark, David. 1992. "Path Dependence and Privatization Strategies in East Central Europe." *East European Politics and Society* 6(1): 15–51.

——. 1996. "Recombinant Property in East European Capitalism." *American Journal of Sociology* 101: 993–1027.

Stark, David Charles, and Laszlo Bruszt. 1998. *Postsocialist Pathways: Transforming Politics and Property in East Central Europe*. Cambridge: Cambridge University Press.

——. 2001. "One Way or Multiple Paths? For a Comparative Sociology of East European Captialism." *American Journal of Sociology* 106:1129–37.

Steinfeld, Edward S. 1998. *Forging Reform in China: The Fate of State-Owned Industry*. Cambridge: Cambridge University Press.

Stiglitz, Joseph. 2002. *Globalization and Its Discontents*. New York: W. W. Norton.

Szelényi, Iván. 1988. *Socialist Entrepreneurs*. Madison: University of Wisconsin Press.

Szelényi, Iván, and Balasz Szelényi. 1995. "Why Socialism Failed." *Theory and Society* 23:211–31.

Thurow, Lester. 1992. *Head to Head: The Coming Economic Battle among Japan, Europe, and America*. New York: William Morrow.

Toth, Janos Istvan. 2001. "Market Environment and Production of Hungarian Manufacturing Firms." http://www.econ.core.hu/.

United Nations Development Program (UNDP). 1999. *Human Development Report for Europe and the CIS*. New York: UNDP.

Van de Lippe, Tanja, and Eva Fodor. 1998. "Changes in Gender Inequality in Six Eastern European Countries." *Acta Sociologica* 41(2): 131-50.

Varese, Federico. 2001. *The Russian Mafia: Private Protection in a New Market Economy*. Oxford: Oxford University Press.

Vorobyov, Alexander, and Stanislav Zhukov. 2000. "Russia: Globalization, Structural Shifts, and Inequality." CEPA Working Paper Series 1, No. 19.

Voszka, Eva. 1993. "Spontaneous Privatization in Hungary." Pp. 89–107 in *Privatization in the Transition to a Market Economy: Studies in Preconditions and Policies in Eastern Europe*, ed. John S. Earl, Roman Frydman, and Andrzej Rapaczynski. New York: St. Martin's Press

Walder, Andrew G. 1995. "Career Mobility and the Communist Political Order." *American Sociological Review* 60:309–28.

———. 2002. "Markets and Income Inequality in Rural China: Political Advantage in an Expanding Economy." *American Sociological Review* 67:231–53.

Walder, Andrew G., Bobai Li, and Donald J. Treiman. 2000. "Politics and Life Chances in a State Socialist Regime: Dual Career Paths into the Urban Chinese Elite, 1949–1996." *American Sociological Review* 65:191–209.

Walder, Andrew G., and Gong Xiaoxia. 1993. "Workers in the Tiananmen Protests: The Politics of the Beijing Workers' Autonomous Federation." *Australian Journal of Chinese Affairs* 29:1–29.

Walder, Andrew G., and Litao Zhao. 2002. "Political Office, Kinship, and Household Wealth in Rural China." Working paper, Asia/Pacific Research Center, Stanford University, December.

Wank, David L. 1999. *Commodifying Communism: Business, Trust, and Politics in a Chinese City*. Cambridge: Cambridge University Press.

Wasilewski, Jacek, and Edmund Wnuk-Lipinski. 1995. "Poland: Winding Road from the Communist to the Post-Solidarity Elite." *Theory and Society* 24:669–96.

Wedel, Janine. 2001. *Collision and Collusion: The Strange Case of Western Aid to Eastern Europe*. New York: Palgrave.

Wolosky, Lee. 2000. "Putin's Plutocrat Problem." *Foreign Affairs* 70(2): 18–31.

Wong, Christine. 1988. "Interpreting Rural Industrial Growth in the Post-Mao Period." *Modern China* 14:3–30.

———. 1992. "Fiscal Reform and Local Industrialization: The Problematic Sequencing of Reform in Post-Mao China." *Modern China* 18:197–227.

Woo, W. T. 1994. "The Art of Reforming Centrally Planned Economies—Comparing China, Poland, and Russia." *Journal of Comparative Economics* 18(3): 276–308.

Woodruff, David. 1999. *Money Unmade: Barter and the Fate of Russian Capitalism*, Ithaca, N.Y.: Cornell University Press.

Yang, Dali L. 1996. *Calamity and Reform in China: State, Rural Society, and Institutional Change since the Great Leap Famine*. Stanford, Calif.: Stanford University Press.

Zhou, Kate Xiao. 1996. *How Farmers Changed China: Power of the People*. Boulder, Colo.: Westview Press.

Zhou, Wubiao. 2001. "The Making of an Integrated National Grain Market in China." William Davidson Working Paper No. 397, William Davidson Institute at the University of Michigan Business School.

Zhou, Xueguang. 1993. "Unorganized Interests and Collective Action in Communist China." *American Sociological Review* 58:54–73.

Part II

The Economic Core: Economic Systems, Institutions, and Behavior

Section B: The Sociology of Economic Institutions and Economic Behavior

11 Markets in Society

Richard Swedberg

COMPARED to economic theory, economic sociology has a very short tradition of studying the market, and one that is considerably less known.[1] A small number of attempts have been made to construct a theory of markets—by Max Weber, Harrison White, Neil Fligstein, Pierre Bourdieu, and a few others—and these have neither been fully explored nor very much discussed by economic sociologists themselves. Much work remains to be done before a reasonably complete theory has come into being. In this chapter I will try to pull the different pieces together and add some ideas about the role of interests in markets.

One strength of economic sociology in the analysis of markets is that sociologists are skillful at uncovering the social structure of a phenomenon. As I will discuss later in this chapter, sociologists have suggested new ways of conceptualizing how markets operate in social terms. But as the work on a sociological theory of markets has advanced, new problems have emerged. This is especially true for the attempt to view the market *exclusively* in social terms ("markets as social structures"). While it is possible to find references in this type of analysis to resources and profits, not enough attention is paid to them. The key role of interests more generally in the functioning of markets is rarely discussed or theorized by sociologists.

While it represents a serious error not to deal with interests in the sociological analysis of markets, including them can be done in different ways. My own suggestion is that the following five propositions are helpful in developing a sociology of markets.

- The market's unique strength is that actors use it *voluntarily,* and they do so because it offers both parties the possibility of getting something better than what they had before the exchange.
- An actor's degree of interest in a market depends on her degree of dependence on it.
- The kind of interest that an actor has in the market depends largely on whether she defines this interest as economic, as political, and so on.

- Economic power represents the likelihood that an actor can make other actors *voluntarily* devote their energies to some task, through the offer of money (in contrast to other forms of power that operate by authority or *coercion*).
- The interest that political actors have in a market depends on the amount of resources that pass through it and how dependent society as a whole is on the market.

The usefulness of these propositions in illuminating how markets operate will be shown in the next section, which presents important types of markets that can be found throughout history. This is followed by a presentation and discussion of attempts by sociologists to construct a theory of markets. Conclusions as well as some remarks on the role of money and prices, from the perspective of a sociology of markets, can be found in the last part of the chapter. Readers interested in a detailed account of the analysis of markets in economic theory, from Adam Smith till the twentieth century, are referred to the chapter on markets in the first edition of the *Handbook.*[2]

THE STARTING POINT: REAL MARKETS IN HISTORY

At this point in its attempt to develop a theory of markets, economic sociology should as I see it, take concrete markets as its point of departure— how they work in real life and what their consequences are, for the economy as well as society at large. This is not the only way to proceed, but it will help break with the artificiality that characterizes the concept of the market in economic theory as well as in social science discourse in general. It should also inspire novel conceptualizations of markets, which are precisely what is needed today. Much of the relevant material for these efforts will naturally come from historians, who have produced a huge number of studies on markets. A much-recommended introduction to this historical material can be found in volume 2 of Fernand Braudel's giant work *Civilization and Capitalism, Fifteenth–Eighteenth Century* ([1979] 1985), one of very few attempts to write a history of markets and survey the existing literature.

In what follows I present general types of markets from different historical periods in order to indicate what issues, in my view, a sociology of markets should work with. I start with markets at the dawn of history and then move on to markets for merchants, national markets, and so on. In each case, I try to show how different interests have been involved in different social configurations—and how these variations have resulted in markets that operate in very different ways and have a very different impact on society at large.

External Markets

Trade goes far back in human history, though it is impossible to set a date for its original appearance (Weber [1923] 1981; Curtin 1984; Clarke 1987). People engaged in trade early in human history because resources, such as salt, minerals, and obsidian (black volcanic glass that is ideal for making tools with sharp edges), are unevenly distributed in nature. Communities that live on an ecological boundary have tended to trade with one another, say a nomadic tribe in a desert trading with a sedentary tribe living in an adjacent area. This early trade was clearly local, not conducted across long distances.

According to Weber, the earliest type of market also had a very distinct sociological structure. "In the beginning commerce is an affair between ethnic groups; it does not take place between members of the same tribe or of the same community but is in the oldest social communities an external phenomenon, being directed only toward foreign tribes" ([1923] 1981, 195). The fact that trade could only be entered into with persons other than those from one's own local community in these "external markets" (as I shall call them) is highly significant from a sociological point of view:

> We find everywhere a primitive, strictly integrated internal economy such that there is no question of any freedom of economic action between members of the same tribe or clan, associated with absolute freedom of trade externally. Internal and external [economic] ethics are distinguished, and in connection with the latter there is complete ruthlessness in financial procedure. (Weber [1923] 1981, 312–13)

The level of trust in these earliest markets may have been low, but it is also possible that stable norms for the conduct of exchange did develop—we simply do not know (cf. Simmel [1907] 1978, 94–97; Benet [1957] 1971). The earliest form of trade was barter; it took some time before money came into being and was used as payment to people living *outside* of one's own community ("external money" as opposed to "internal money"; cf. Weber [1923] 1981, 237–39).

With respect to interests, it is likely that the value of the items exchanged in external markets was fairly insignificant and that society did not depend on this type of trade, either for survival or for the generation of wealth. No group devoted itself exclusively to trade, and trade was primarily engaged in because of use value, not profit. As specialization grew, however, so did trade. Longer distances were covered and the range of traded objects increased. Certain tribes began to specialize in trade; riches were made; and groups of merchants began to emerge. As markets grew in wealth, they also began to attract the interest of political rulers. For a long time to come, however, rulers would show disdain for the economic ethic of the merchants and find violence a much more honorable means to acquire wealth than haggling in the market.

Internal Markets

As an example of the internal market I will use the Athenian agora, one of the best-researched markets in antiquity (e.g. Thompson and Wycherley 1972; Camp 1986). This market illustrates a more general point, namely that markets soon came to acquire a complex social structure and needed political as well as legal regulation. Internal markets, as opposed to external markets, are first and foremost characterized by the fact that they are situated inside the community. Another defining feature is that community members trade with one another, not only with foreigners. This represents an important change in the economic ethic, even if fixed prices (which mean that foreigners and members of the community are treated in the same way) were still far away. Money was also used, which facilitated trade and dramatically increased the scope of items that could be traded.

All Greek city-states had an agora, or a central public area where trade, politics, worshipping, and socializing took place. The agora is often called the living heart of the Greek city and essentially consisted of an open square, marked off from the rest of the city through boundary stones. Typical buildings included market booths, public buildings, and a stoa, that is, an open colonnade that could be used for different purposes. Temples and religious statues could be found all over the area. Some of the economic features of the agora come out in the following description of the Greek agora, by a British historian:

> Marketing "when the agora was full," i.e. in the morning, must have been a noisy and nerve-racking business, with much haggling. The fishmongers has a particularly bad reputation: according to the comic poets they used the Greek equivalent of "Billingsgate" [coarse language, so called after a famous fish market in London], glared at their customers like Gorgons, asked exorbitant prices with a take-it-or-leave-it air, and faked rotten fish. Most cities had officials called *agoranomoi* to exercise control and ensure fair dealing. Athens had, in addition, corn-inspectors for a particularly vital trade and inspectors of weights and measures. We read in inscriptions of the agoranomoi seeing that agora and streets are kept clean and tidy and watching relations between employers and employed. (Wycherley 1976, 66)

Archaelogical evidence supplies a picture of the Athenian agora around 400 B.C. (see, e.g., Camp 1986, 89). Commercial activities took place all over the agora, in the temporary booths, at the tables (where money changers and bankers could be found), and in the shops. The South Stoa at the southern boundary appears to have been a commercial center. Next to it was the mint, where the bronze coins of the city were produced. The political authorities, it should be noted, checked the weights and the measures that were used in the market as well as the quality of the coins. Inscriptions also describe what happened if someone used false weights or coins of too low quality: the items were destroyed or confiscated. Crimes, including breaches of the market law, were handled by the many courts in the agora.

The Athenian agora did not only hold buildings that were directly or indirectly related to the economy. The Athenian senate, for example, and its executive committee used two of the buildings along the western boundary (the *bouleuterion* and *tholos*). At the center of the agora was an area for the spectators of various contests and similar amusements (the orchestra). In general the Athenians enjoyed going to the agora, the way people today take pleasure in going downtown or to a shopping mall. Of the religious statues and shrines in the agora, some were devoted to Hermes, the god of the market.

Even if the citizens of Athens to some extent depended on the market for their economic survival, they basically relied on farming. The impact of the market on the relations within the community was nonetheless visible, such as in the appearance of wealthy merchants and bankers testified to. The Athenian market also played an important role in financing the city-state and its foreign policy. The merchants and bankers had mainly made their money through trade, not through manufacture; and the predominant economic ideal was still the independent farm. The merchants and the haggling in the market were looked down on by many citizens, including Aristotle, whose hostility to moneymaking is well known. Hermes, according to Greek mythology, not only protected the market but was also the patron god of the thieves (e.g., Brown 1947).

Markets for Merchants (the European Fair)

Internal markets were local markets in the sense that they supplied people with items from their immediate surroundings. At a very early stage in history, however, long-distance trade appeared. The Athenian agora, for example, got much of its economic vitality from contacts with other markets in the Mediterranean. While the difference between local trade and long-distance trade may seem mainly to be one of geographic distance, their social structure was very different. Long-distance trade could be extremely profitable; hence the actors differed as well as the level of investment. Once the merchant left his community, the risk for attacks increased and special protection was needed. The interaction with foreign buyers and sellers typically took place in an area under foreign rule, which led to various complications. If the merchant decided to stay abroad, special living arrangements had to be made, which usually meant physical segregation from the native population. Markets for long-distance trade, in brief, were often organized as external markets.

One very special type of market that involved long-distance trade was the *fair*, which played a key role in Europe from the eleventh to the fourteenth centuries (e.g., Huvelin 1897; Verlinden 1963; Lopez 1976). The fair is often defined as a marketplace where merchants from a whole region met at periodic intervals. Weber specifies that "the first form of trade between merchant and merchant is met at the [European] fairs" ([1923] 1981, 220). The name *fair*, it can be added, comes from *feria*, meaning "feast" or "holiday," and is a reminder that the merchants were not the only participants in this type of market; it was also open to common people. Fairs constituted huge and festive occasions: "fairs meant noise, tumult, music, popular rejoicing, the world turned upside down, disorder and sometimes disturbances" (Braudel [1979] 1985, 2:85).

Most of the European fairs were situated in the area between Italy and Flanders, and they exchanged goods from the south, including spices from Asia, against goods from the north, especially wool products from England and Flanders. The fairs, especially the ones in Champagne, were also extremely important money markets. A fair typically took place on the land of a feudal lord, in a specially designated area where stalls were erected and tents pitched. Fairs, in other words, are closer to external than to internal markets. The lord guaranteed the safe conduct of the merchants and typically provided an escort for them, once they arrived on his land with their merchandise. For this service a fee was charged, and fairs also presented many other opportunities for the lord to make money. He could mint new coins, grant the right to gamble, and give permission to trade without regard to the prohibition of usury. Inside the market area the international law of the merchants (the lex mercatoria, or law merchant) was valid, and the merchants also had their own court with elected judges. Many ordinary people came to the fairs to enjoy themselves, to drink, and to gamble. Order was upheld by special guards.

The bill of exchange was perfected at the fairs. Soon it could also be discounted and pass more easily from hand to hand. Bills of exchange, it should be emphasized, represented a form of credit especially tailored to the needs of merchants. Similarly, the lex mercatoria consisted of legal rules adopted to the needs of the merchants in their business (Berman 1983). Of special importance was the introduction of bona fides in the law merchant; that is, an item acquired in good faith could not be reclaimed by the original owner. It has often been noted that merchants lacked a coercive apparatus to enforce their legal decisions. To compensate, they screened merchants, allowing to participate only those in good standing. If someone broke the law, the judges' main recourse was to destroy the credibility of the merchant. In recent scholarship this is referred to as enforcing the rules of the market with "the reputation mechanism" (e.g. Milgrom, North, and Weingast 1990; cf. Barzel 2002).

The most important of all the fairs were the ones that took place from the twelfth to the fourteenth centuries in the province of Champagne. Here the merchants met in four small cities at six fairs that each lasted 50 days. By far the most important business was the trade in money and credit. While other fairs typically covered a region, the fairs in Champagne covered all of western Europe. Their importance in financial matters was enormous, and they essentially operated as a clearinghouse for much of Europe.

After the fourteenth century the fairs in Champagne and elsewhere started to decline, for a number of reasons. The expansion of trade in Europe made permanent markets necessary. The Italians had by now begun to sail straight to Flanders, and this made them less dependent on the inland fairs. The fairs in Champagne also were incorporated into the kingdom of France and became heavily taxed. Finally, a new type of market for merchants had emerged at the end of the Middle Ages, taking over some of the functions of the fair: the exchange (bourse). This institution differed on especially two points from the fair: it was continuous, and the merchants did not bring their goods to it, just samples.

The fair of the Middle Ages represents a much more powerful type of market than the internal or local market that we met in Athens. The reason for this difference does not have to do with the dependence of ordinary people on the goods that were traded at the fairs; common people still lived mainly from agriculture, and what was sold at the market were basically agricultural and artisanal products. Manufacture, which would revolutionize everyday life for ordinary people, had not yet become dominant. What gave the fairs a great deal of power was the concentration of money that came with the trade between merchants. By this time in Western history, merchants had established themselves as a distinct group with their own identity and also started to develop their own financial instruments and their own commercial law. The feudal lords were well aware of this economic power and tried to control and tap into it. One way to do so was by imposing taxes and fees on the fairs; another was to borrow money from merchants and bankers (e.g., Coser 1972). The constant need of the feudal lords to finance wars against their neighboors made them directly dependent on merchants and bankers.

National Markets

If one takes a quick look at the early history of markets, one may sense that there is a natural progression from small and simple markets to large and complex ones, and that the key to this development is to be found in the activities of the merchants. A version of this view can be found in *The Wealth of Nations,* where Adam Smith states that there exists "a certain propensity in human nature . . . to truck, barter, and exchange one thing for another" ([1776] 1976, 25). Another version of this view can be found in the works of some economists, who have argued that the development of markets is primarily due to economic causes, especially the activities of the merchants (e.g. Sombart 1902–27; Hicks 1969). To create national markets was, however, anything but automatic; it could only be done, as we soon shall see, with the help of political actors, especially the state (e.g. Braudel [1979] 1985, 1:277–385).

The development of huge markets faced enormous obstacles in Europe during the Middle Ages. Travel along roads and rivers required constant payment of tolls. In the 1400s there were, for example, more than 60 different customs along the Rhine (Heckscher [1931] 1994, 1:57). To participate in a city market, nonresidents also had to pay a fee. The city population forbade peasants to trade anywhere but inside the city, at prices advantageous to the city. Guilds closely controlled who was allowed to produce a large range of products. The only huge markets that existed during this period—the fairs—did not challenge this situation so much as adapt to it. They were not permanent, and they often took place in the countryside, far away from the cities.

One of the forces that helped to counter this fragmentation and bring about national markets were the mercantilist statesmen. The view that mercantilism was nothing but a fetter on the economy and blocked all economic development was popularized by Adam Smith in *The Wealth of Nations.* Historians, however, led by Gustav Schmoller, soon developed a different view. According to Schmoller, mercantilism is to be understood as the ruler's means to counter medieval localism and construct a modern state, including a national economy.

> What was at stake was the creation of real *political* economies as unified organisms, the center of which should be, not merely a state policy reaching out in all directions, but rather the living heartbeat of unified sentiment. Only he who thus conceives of mercantilism will understand it; in its innermost kernel it is nothing but state making—not state making in a narrow sense, but state making and national-economy

making at the same time; state making in the modern sense, which creates out of the political community an economic community, and so gives it a heightened meaning. (Schmoller [1884] 1902, 50–51)

Today Schmoller's argument is more or less accepted by historians. Alexander Gerschenkron, for example, similarly notes in his critique of *A Theory of Economic History* (Hicks 1969) that the author exclusively addresses the role of the merchant in the creation of markets, ignoring the fact that "mercantilist statesmen from Colbert to Peter the Great were first of all the great unifiers . . . it was at least just as much the policies of the state as the activities of the merchants that laid the ground both for subsequent great spurts of industrial development (metaphorically described as revolutions) and for the advent of *laissez-faire* policies" (Gerschenkron 1971, 665).

The measures that mercantilist rulers carried out to combat medieval localism can be exemplified by the case of France (Schmoller [1884] 1902; Heckscher [1931] 1994). Louis XI (1461–1483) fought against local interests and tried to unify weights and measures in his kingdom. In the early 1500s freedom of trade in corn was introduced, and Richelieu tried to launch a large national market through various measures. It was during the administration of Colbert (1662–83), however, that a concerted effort was made to bring about a uniform market within France. Colbert developed efficient roads and canals; he reformed the river tolls; and, most importantly, in 1664 he eliminated the customs in about half of France.

But much more was needed to create national markets than could be accomplished by the mercantilist rulers themselves. Through the great political revolutions in the seventeenth and eighteenth centuries were introduced free trade as well as freedom of movement and settlement, which advanced the creation of national markets (Hintze [1929] 1975). In the United States the second revolution of 1787 and the Constitution helped to bring about a unified American market. Interstate trade, for example, was assigned to the jurisdiction of Congress, not to the individual states. The founders of the Constitution, many of whom were big landowners and merchants, also advanced markets in other ways. Otto Hintze concludes that "the great national markets . . . were brought about not only by economic developments but also by political actions intimately tied to the great revolutions in England, America, and France" ([1929] 1975, 442).

The establishment of true national markets would not be complete until much later, when means of communication such as the telegraph, the telephone, and the railroads, could tie together even the most distant localities. In the United States, for example, the modern national market came into being around the turn of the last century (Chandler 1977). Nonetheless, the foundations of the national markets were laid much earlier; and to understand the evolution of this type of market fully, it is essential to take political as well as economic interests into account. In the Middle Ages local interests in the cities had the upper hand and held the countryside in an iron grip. In Schmoller's words: "what . . . we have before our eyes in the Middle Ages are municipal and local economic centers whose whole economic life rests upon this—that the various local interests have, for the time, worked their way into agreement, that uniform feelings and ideas have risen out of common local interests, and that the town authorities stand forward to represent these feelings with a complete array of protective measures" ([1884] 1902, 11–12).

No economic power could break the local interests' hold on the economy; only political force could accomplish this. The successful activities of political powers in this situation does not, however, mean that the actions of the mercantilist state were invariably beneficial to the creation of the national market. Adam Smith has much to say on this point and notes, for example, that the bureaucratic mentality of Colbert made it impossible for him to conceive of a truly free market (Smith [1776] 1976, 663–64). Part of the mercantilist project was to create colonies, where independent economic development was effectively stifled since manufacture was allowed only in the home country.

Modern Mass Markets

The Industrial Revolution, which first occurred in England (circa 1760–1830), also initiated a new and crucial stage in the history of markets. The Industrial Revolution is conventionally defined in terms of what happened to production: a series of key inventions were made; the modern factory was introduced; and new types of fuel, especially fossil fuel, began to be used. All of these changes, however, occurred in a capitalist society, which means that the role of markets in the economy was dramatically changed. According to a famous statement by the historian who popularized the term *Industrial Revolution*, "the essence of the Indus-

trial Revolution is the substitution of competition for the medieval regulations which had previously controlled the production and distribution of wealth" (Toynbee [1884] 1969, 58).

Another way of putting this would be to say that from now on markets began to encompass most of production and most of consumption. For this to be possible, not only new production and consumption markets had to be developed but also new financial markets and new markets in distribution. In addition, all of these markets had to be coordinated. The Industrial Revolution, according to Karl Polanyi in *The Great Transformation*, set off a development in which the traditional economy was replaced by a whole new type of economy:

> A market economy is an economic system controlled, regulated, and directed by markets alone; order in the production and distribution of goods is entrusted to this self-regulating mechanism. . . . Self-regulation implies that all production is for sale on the market and that all incomes derive from such sales. Accordingly, there are markets for all elements of industry, not only for goods (including services) but also for labor, land, and money. ([1944] 1957, 68–69)

Before the Industrial Revolution, markets were typically defined in terms of a specific place; a market took place in a clearly delineated area—say in a special square in a city or on a designated piece of land belonging to a lord. Now, however, markets were no longer confined to distinct areas but spread out geographically, a change reflected in the definitions of markets that we find in the nineteenth century. According to Cournot, for example, "it is well understood that by *market* economists mean, not a certain place where purchases and sales are carried on, but the entire territory of which the parts are so united by the relations of unrestricted commerce that prices there take the same level throughout, with ease and rapidity" (Cournot 1838 as cited in Marshall [1920] 1961, 1:325).

The "market economy" that now began to emerge was centered on the modern mass market. First of all there was the mass market in consumption, which soon was to provide the great majority of the population with what they needed in their everyday lives. There also existed mass markets in production, distribution, and finance. A prerequisite for the smooth functioning of all of these markets, Weber notes, was stability and order in society. Enormous amounts of capital were needed for this type of economy to operate, and the capitalists had to be able to count on a steady demand as well as predictable behavior by the state and the legal system (Weber [1923] 1981, 161, 276–77).

At the center of this new system of markets was the modern consumer market, usually traced to England in the second half of the eighteenth century. Its full appearance, however, came roughly a century later, as part of what Douglass North has called "the second economic revolution" (1981, 171–86). The role of consumption in eighteenth-century England has been much debated in recent economic history (e.g. McKendrick 1982; Mokyr 1993; Brewer and Porter 1993). What has mainly been discussed, however, is whether the Industrial Revolution was primarily caused by consumption (demand) or by technological and related factors (supply). A growing amount of empirical material has become available through this debate, and it is today possible to say something about early mass consumption—what items were consumed, by which kind of people, and how these goods were distributed. Information about the financial side of this development—minor borrowing, credit, and the like—is considerably less known.

A common means of distribution during this period was via single stores—an institution that has its origin in eleventh-century cities (for the history of the store, see Braudel [1979] 1985, 2:60–75). By the eighteenth century the first shop windows of glass had been installed in London, to the amazement of foreign visitors, and a crude form of advertisement had come into being, which supplemented the information on shop signs and the traditional crying of goods. The two social groups that sustained the emerging mass market were the middle strata and the laboring poor; the rich preferred items made by hand and were in any case too few to matter in this context (e.g., Fine and Leopold 1990; Styles 1993). The laboring poor bought such items as cotton gowns, breeches, earthenware teapots, and watches. They also consumed an increasing amount of coal. The middle strata bought household items such as clothes, prints, cutlery, and window curtains. Ready-made clothing was marginal, and the great majority of clothes were still made by hand. The level of standardization was far from modern standards:

In a purely numerical sense, none the less, there was in the eighteenth century a kind of mass market. Hundreds of thousands of humble consumers bought a wide range of goods from distant producers with some regularity. But caution needs to be exercised regarding the implications of a mass market in this lim-

ited sense for product design and particularly product differentiation. (Styles 1993, 540)

The first real mass markets came into being in the second half of the nineteenth century. This development took place more or less simultaneously in several countries, including the United States. The system of distribution also changed around this time, and new economic institutions to handle mass consumption emerged. Single stores, which were supplied by wholesalers, from now on increasingly had to compete with chain stores and department stores. It was during this time that Macy's was founded in New York and Bon Marché in Paris—two of the world's first department stores (Miller 1981). Advertising greatly advanced, and brand names began to appear for the first time (e.g. Schudson 1984, 147–77). The shipping of goods was much quicker than during the eighteenth century, mainly due to railroads and steamships. Customers started to travel quite far in order to shop, using trams and later automobiles. In the 1910s Henry Ford installed a moving assembly line in one of his Detroit factories; he also created the first truly standardized consumer item with the Model T automobile. Ready-to-wear clothing began to replace handmade clothing, a development set off by the invention of the sewing machine in the 1850s. Finally, science was increasingly used in production, leading to the creation of many new products.

A novel type of firm emerged around the turn of the last century—the so-called multidivisional firm—which had the administrative capacity to handle the production of enormous amounts of goods. In many cases these giant corporations also took care of the marketing of their goods since it was difficult to move huge amounts of merchandise through the existing system of distribution. According to the main historian of the multidivisional firm, Alfred Chandler, it was especially hard to market machines that had been produced for the mass market:

The mass marketing of new machines that were mass produced through the fabricating and assembling of interchangeable parts required a greater investment in personnel to provide the specialized marketing services than in product-specific plant and equipment. The mass distribution of sewing machines for households and for the production of apparel; typewriters, cash registers, adding machines, mimeograph machines, and other office equipment; harvesters, reapers and other agricultural machines; and, after 1900, automobiles and the more complex electrical appliances all called for demonstration, after-sales service, and consumer credit. As these machines had been only recently invented, few existing distributors had the necessary training and experience to provide the services, or the financial resources to provide extensive consumer credit. (Chandler 1984, 489–90)

Around 1900 modern mass markets had begun to dominate the economy in the United States. As part of this process, everyday life became increasingly dependent on the mass market. By 1790, for example, 80 percent of all clothing in the United States was made in the home, while a century later 90 percent was made outside the home (Boorstin 1974, 97–99). The number of people getting their livelihood from agriculture also steadily declined during the same time. This naturally changed the food habits of people as well as the number of items that had to be bought. The canning of food and refrigerated railroad cars, for example, made it possible to transport food from one part of the country to another.

All of this naturally increased the dependence of the average American on getting a wage, that is, on an employer. The owners of the factories and their managers were at the same time becoming more powerful through their control of ever larger amounts of capital. In this process they were helped not only by the emergence of national markets but by the creation of new capital markets that allowed enormous amounts of capital to be concentrated. In the late 1890s U.S. manufacturers increasingly started to use stock exchanges, and the aggregate value of stocks and bonds had by 1903 jumped from one to seven billion dollars (Roy 1997, 4–5).

International Markets

Like national markets, international markets have their own distinct social structure: a certain type of actor, a certain type of social control and regulation, and a certain type of financial order (Braudel [1979] 1985, vol. 2; Curtin 1984; Cameron 1993, 275ff.). They can also be the result of conscious political design, just like national markets; the current international market is, for example, a case in point (Bourdieu 2001, 93–108; Fligstein 2001). The embryo of international trade can be traced far back in time, more precisely to Mesopotamia circa 3500 B.C., when surplus from agriculture allowed a small part of the population to devote itself to something other than farming. The earliest forms of trade were local and long dis-

tance. The latter was often carried out with the help of so-called trade diasporas, or networks of traders who lived abroad and operated as brokers between two communities (Curtin 1984, 1–3; cf. Greif 1989).

From 500 B.C. to the time of Christ, long-distance trade typically took place within regions such as the Hellenic world, India, or China. Soon, however, the area widened, and from around 200 B.C. the Mediterranean was connected to China, through trade on land as well as by sea. The earliest long-distance trade was in luxury goods, but from the thirteenth century and onward the evolution of ship technology made long-distance trade in bulk merchandise profitable. A few centuries later, the so-called maritime revolution took place, helping Europeans to take over much of world trade through their superior knowledge of the world winds. The trade diasporas, which represented a peaceful form of trade, were now replaced by trading posts, backed up by force. A very different type of international market had come into being.

The Industrial Revolution led to an explosion in international trade and strengthened European domination. During 1780–1880 world trade increased by 20 times, and by the mid–nineteenth century some people began to speak of the "world market" (Marx and Engels [1848] 1978, 475; Kuznets 1966, 306–7). Advances in weapons technology allowed the Europeans to strengthen their hold on world trade, and the trading post system was now replaced by direct territorial control, made possible by new and superior means of communication. In the 1830s, for example, a letter took five to eight months to reach London from India, by sailing ship; in the 1850s it took 45 days, by train and steamer; and in the 1870s a message could be sent and received the same day, with the help of the telegraph (Curtin 1984, 252). A free trade ideology was formulated in England in the early 1800s and quickly spread throughout Europe, even if protectionist sentiments still were strong. "By the beginning of the twentieth century," economic historian Rondo Cameron concludes, "it was possible to speak meaningfully of a world economy, in which virtually every inhabited portion participated at least minimally, though Europe was by far the most important" (1993, 275).

It is often noted that the world market that existed around the turn of the nineteenth century did not find its equal until after World War II. The world economy started to disintegrate after World War I for a number of reasons, leading to the creation of different currency blocs as well as the introduction of autarchy by Nazi Germany (Hirschman [1945] 1980). The depression also slowed international trade. After World War II the United States rebuilt world trade, with the help of such institutions as the International Monetary Fund, the World Bank, and the General Agreement on Tariffs and Trade (GATT) (Block 1977; Shoup and Minter 1977; Wood 1986). In the 1950s national European currencies were strengthened and the foundations laid for the European Union. By the mid-1960s an international capital market had begun to emerge, thanks to the so-called Euromarkets, and soon it had grown enormously in size. The turnover in the global foreign exchange market was $1.5 trillion per day in 1998 (up from $36.4 billion in 1974; Knorr-Cetina and Brügger 2002, 905). According to some globalization theorists, the traditional world economy has been replaced by a fully integrated global economy (Castells 1996, 92; for the traditional concept of the world economy, see Braudel [1979] 1985, 3:21–22).

What is characteristic of a fully developed international market is, first of all, that people in different countries are to a large extent dependent on what happens in the economies of other countries. This goes for consumer items—food, clothes, and so on—as well as for their jobs and income. Already by the end of the nineteenth century, the exports of such countries as Great Britain, Germany, and France amounted to between 15 and 20 percent of their total national income (Cameron 1993, 283). Transborder ownership grew rapidly during the twentieth century and led to new forms of economic and political dependencies. Local capitalist elites have been challenged and sometimes replaced. The existence of a giant international market in currencies has not only tied the value of national currencies to forces outside individual countries but also decreased the power of their central banks to intervene. International corporations are also beginning to operate outside the jurisdiction of national governments.

Labor Markets

It is possible to create a typology of markets by focusing on the kind of merchandise that is traded: money, consumer goods, machines to be used in production, and so on. This division has not been done in this chapter, however, where the main concern is rather with the different social configurations that markets have assumed throughout his-

tory. Nonetheless, an exception needs to be made for labor markets, which are a unique species. According to Robert Solow, everybody except mainstream economists believes that "there is something special about labor as a commodity and therefore about the labor market too" (1990, 3). Marx's view of labor as different from other commodites is well known, including his attempt to unlock the secrets of capitalism by analyzing the values created by "this peculiar commodity" ([1867] 1906, 189). According to Marx in *Capital*, "the capitalist epoch . . . is characterized by this, that labor power takes in the eyes of the laborer himself the form of a commodity which is his property" (189).

Polanyi was as incensed as Marx by labor's being treated as a commodity to be bought and sold like any other object. *The Great Transformation* is filled with outrage over the attempt in nineteenth-century England to turn labor into a commodity. According to Polanyi, "labor is only another name for a human activity which goes with life itself, which in turn is not produced for sale but for entirely different reasons, nor can that activity be detached from the rest of life, be stored or mobilized" ([1944] 1957, 72).

The earliest labor markets appeared in the thirteenth and fourteenth centuries, when small groups of men would gather at some public place in a village or a city and offer their services for sale (Braudel [1979] 1985, 2:49–54; cf. Weber [1922] 1978, 679). Labor markets, however, did not advance in tandem with capitalism, since early capitalist production often took place in the homes of peasants and craftsmen. From the Industrial Revolution and onward, however, practices changed dramatically, and work was now transferred to the factories, where it could be better organized (and monitored) by the capitalists. The disorder and poverty created by this change in production was classically described by Engels in *The Condition of the Working Class in England* (1845). It is during this period as well that the concept of unemployment emerges. During the twentieth century it became common not only to hire people from outside the corporation, but also to promote those who already worked there (internal labor markets). Personnel departments began to emerge around the turn of the twentieth century, at which time categorization of workers into different occupations became common (Tilly and Tilly 1994).

In today's society some types of work are bought in labor markets, while others are not. Voluntary work, work in the household, and some of the activities that take place in the so-called informal economy are typically unpaid. Crafts and professions have labor markets with distinct features. Professions, for example, control the number of practitioners and often the price and quality of the services that they offer. Buyers and sellers in ordinary labor markets typically locate each other with the help of advertisements, placement agencies, and personal connections. Networks play an important role in transmitting knowledge about vacancies (Granovetter 1995; see later in this chapter). A common career pattern in the United States is that workers explore different jobs till their mid-30s and then settle down. While some employers, such as the military and the church, exclusively rely on internal labor markets, most employers use both.

According to mainstream economics, it is the productivity of the worker that decides her salary, who gets hired and who gets promoted. Productivity, however, is notoriously hard to measure; and it is clear that many other factors play a role, such as seniority, ethnicity, gender, and whether one works in an expanding or in a contracting firm (e.g. Granovetter 1986, 1988; Farkas and England 1988; Berg and Kalleberg 2001). The number of openings that exist in one part of the economy may also be affected by the number of openings in some other part, due to so-called vacancy chains, that is, the fact that when someone gets a job, she leaves a position that needs to be filled by someone else, who in her turn leaves a job, and so on (White 1970; see also later in this chapter).

It is obvious that interests play a very special role in labor markets. The average person in modern society is totally dependent on his or her wage; and a person's status as well as personality are also deeply influenced by what he or she does at work. It is furthermore very difficult to understand such phenomena as unionization and strikes without the concept of interest. Labor history is full of events that testify to the strength with which employers and employees have defended and advanced their interests (see also the discussion of free riding in Olson 1965 for a different approach to an interest analysis of trade unions). Interest is at the very heart of what makes labor markets so different from all other markets, since what is sold are the activities of human beings with interests of their own. What is traded in labor markets also differs from inert objects through human subjectivity and through links to other people. A person's perception of what is fair pay may, for example, affect her productivity, and so may her links to other people.

Before leaving this discussion of various types of markets, it may be useful to sum up what a historical typology of markets may teach us. The material presented here shows that the role of markets in human communities has varied over time. Some markets have been located in a specific place, while others have covered a more diffuse area. The earliest markets were apparently situated at the margin of a community, while later markets are to be found at its very center. Whether located in a specific place or in a general area, markets require order, kept through norms and laws, and quite a bit of variation exists on this point as well. The act of exchange has to be regulated through norms and laws (for a discussion of the role of law in the economy, see Swedberg 2003a; Edelman and Stryker, this volume).

What can be exchanged in different types of markets has also varied throughout history. Labor is, as I have discussed, a very special commodity and demands a very special type of market. As for nonhuman goods, these come in different kinds: luxury goods, everyday items, mass-produced items, and so on. Political authorities may encourage markets and help to construct them—but they may also block them under certain circumstances since markets can upset the status quo or otherwise threaten political interests (Sachs 2000, 36). As to the role of money, there are first of all markets where barter takes place and markets where money is used. Money can be internal, external, local, national, or international, and a huge variety of credit instruments have gradually come into being. Interest, finally, highlights the importance of markets to individuals, political authorities, and society at large, by emphasizing the extent to which all of them are dependent on markets to properly function. The dependence of all of these actors on the market has increased significantly through history—and continues to grow even stronger. Interest also helps to elucidate the economic power that accumulates through markets and the economic resources that different actors command.

Several other market types could be added to the ones that have just been presented. A look at what can be called electronic markets would, for example, highlight the crucial role that communication and related technology have begun to play in the modern economy (Knorr-Cetina and Bruegger 2002; DiMaggio and Cohen, forthcoming). It would also be possible to argue that a change in the mentality of people toward markets took place in the 1500s and 1600s, along the lines described in *The Protestant Ethic and the Spirit of*

Capitalism. Whether it would make sense to speak of rational markets in a Weberian sense is arguable. Nonetheless, the general point—that a sociology of markets, at this stage of its development, would do well to start from empirical, historical material as opposed to some preconceived model of *the* market—should by now be clear. I would also argue that general insight into what accounts for the diversity of markets can be acquired by going through the historical literature on markets. Indicating what economic sociology can add to theoretical insights produced in this manner is the task to which the rest of this chapter is devoted.

SOCIOLOGISTS ON MARKETS

The lack of communication between economists and sociologists in the twentieth century led to Schumpeter's quip, that economists have created their own "primitive sociology," and sociologists their own "primitive economics" (1954, 21). But there is more to the story than this; and just as it is possible to find a multitude of valuable observations in the economics literature on the social dimension of markets, one can also find interesting attempts by sociologists to understand the general operation of markets (for the former, see Swedberg 2003a). To this should be added that since the sociological literature on markets is so much smaller than the economic literature, it is considerably easier to present and evaluate the contribution by sociologists.

In what follows I have singled out the most important and useful attempts by sociologists to understand the workings of markets. These are Weber's approach, Harrison White's $W(y)$ model, and what I call "markets as networks," and "markets as parts of fields." Other possible candidates are the efforts by Parsons and Smelser in *Economy and Society* to provide "starting-points for a systematic development of a sociology of markets," Karl Polanyi's analysis of markets, and the attempt to view markets from a cultural-sociological perspective (Parsons and Smelser 1956, 143–75; Polanyi [1944] 1957, [1947] 1971a, [1957] 1971b; Zelizer 1979; Abolafia 1996, 1998). All of these approaches have contributed to the sociological analysis of markets. Parsons and Smelser, for example, show very clearly that markets are part of the larger social system, and so do the sociologists who draw on a cultural approach. Karl Polanyi's argument that one should not use the modern theory of the market to analyze markets in precapitalist societies is also well taken (see the long and heated debate in economic anthropology over the status of economic analysis in early societies, as summarized in Orlove 1986). There also exist valuable studies that focus on some special aspect of markets, without suggesting a full theory of markets. There are, for example, analyses of the role of status in markets and of the formation of market identities (Abolafia 1984, 1996; Callon 1998; Garcia 1986; Collins 1990; Lie 1997; Podolny 1992; Aspers 2001a, 2001b).

Weber on Markets

Of the early sociologists Weber was by far the one most interested in markets, and especially during his last years he tried to develop a "sociology of 'the market'" ([1922] 1978, 81; see also Swedberg 2000). Also during his presociological period, Weber paid quite a bit of attention to markets. As a young scholar and professor of economics, Weber, for example, wrote voluminously on the stock exchange (1999, [1894–96] 2000; see Lestition 2000). From the writings that resulted, it is clear that Weber was convinced that stock exchanges filled a crucial role in the modern capitalist machinery and that they could be organized in different ways, depending on the attitude of the state, how experienced the local businessmen were in operating on stock exchanges, and so on. Weber emphasized the legal and ethical dimension of the dealings in the modern stock exchange but was also fascinated by its political role–its role as "a means to power" in the economic struggle between nations ([1894–96] 2000, 369).

This emphasis on struggle is also evident in Weber's lectures a few years later as a professor in economics. In the 1890s Weber lectured on economic theory in Freiburg and Heidelberg and followed primarily Menger when it came to markets. Weber, however, added his own distinct touch to these lectures by emphasizing that "the price on the market is a result of economic struggle (price struggle)" ([1898] 1990, 45). The struggle over prices, he explained, had two aspects that should be separated. On the one hand, there is a "struggle of competition" between all those who are potentially interested in an exchange; and on the other hand there is an "interest struggle" between the two parties who end up by engaging in an exchange. Weber also argued that when "the empirical price," as opposite to "the theoretical price," was to be determined in an analysis, several new factors had to be taken into account, such as the actors' lack of perfect information.

When Weber started to define himself as a sociologist about a decade later, he reworked his analysis of the market from the viewpoint of social action. Some results of this effort can be found in *The Protestant Ethic*, with its emphasis on the creation of a rational attitude towards profit making, work, and the market more generally. Weber's sociological theory of markets, however, came to its fullest expression in *Economy and Society,* where one of the key passages reads as follows:

> A market may be said to exist wherever there is competition, even if only unilateral, for opportunities of exchange among a plurality of potential parties. Their physical assemblage in one place, as in the local market square, the fair (the "long distance market"), or the exchange (the merchants' market), only constitutes the most consistent kind of market formation. It is, however, only this physical assemblage which allows the full emergence of the market's most distinctive feature, viz. dickering. ([1922] 1978, 635)

As he had earlier done in his lectures on economic theory, Weber made a conceptual distinction between exchange and competition. Social action in the market begins, according to Weber, with competition but ends up as exchange. In phase 1, "the potential partners are guided in their offers by the potential action of an indeterminate large group of real or imaginary competitors rather than by their own actions alone" ([1922] 1978, 636). Here, in other words, there is orientation to others rather than direct social interaction. Phase 2, the final phase, is structured differently; and here the only actors involved are the two parties who end up making the exchange (635). As Weber saw it, exchange in the market was also exceptional in that it represented the most instrumental and calculating type of social action possible between two human beings. In this sense, he said, exchange represents "the archetype of all rational social action" and constitutes, as such, "an abomination to every system of fraternal ethics" (635, 637). While classes thrive on markets, they represent a threat to status groups.

In his sociology of markets, Weber also emphasized the element of struggle or conflict. He used terms such as "market struggle," and he spoke of "the battle of man against man in the market" ([1922] 1978, 93, 108). Competition, for example, is defined as "a 'peaceful' conflict . . . insofar as it consists in a formally peaceful attempt to attain control over opportunities and advantages which are also desired by others." Exchange, on the other hand, is defined as "a compromise of interests on the part of the parties in the course of which goods or other advantages are passed as reciprocal compensation" (38, 72).

Weber was furthermore very interested in the interaction between the market and the rest of society. Weber's analysis on this point can be approached through his analysis of the role that regulation (including legal regulation) plays. A market, Weber explains in *Economy and Society,* can either be free or regulated ([1922] 1978, 82–85). In precapitalistic societies there typically exists quite a bit of "traditional regulation" of the market. The more rational a market is, however, the less it is formally regulated. The highest degree of "market freedom" or "market rationality" is reached in capitalistic society, where most irrational elements have been eliminated. In order for the market to be this rational and predictable, however, several conditions have to be fulfilled, including the expropriation of the workers from the means of production and the existence of calculable law (161–62). Capitalist markets, in other words, are the result of a long historical process. How Weber envisioned the historical evolution of the market can be gleaned from *Economy and Society* as well as from *General Economic History*.

Harrison White on the Market: The W(y) Model

Since the mid-1980s sociologists have become more interested in the market than they have ever been before, and if one person deserves credit for having helped to ignite this interest, it is Harrison White (see especially 1981; for brief introductions to White's ideas on the market, see White and Eccles 1987; Aspers 2001b; Azarian 2003). White's research on markets, which began in the mid-1970s, represents a bold attempt to create a totally new and a totally sociological theory of markets, the so-called $W(y)$ model. This theory has been shaped by White's deep dissatisfaction with neoclassical economics. Contemporary economics, according to White, has no interest in concrete markets and is mainly preoccupied with exchange markets, as opposed to production markets (or markets where the actors produce goods). As a result, White says, "there does not exist a neoclassical theory of the market—[only] a pure theory of exchange" (1990, 3).

But even if White breaks with economists' theory of the market, he has been deeply influenced by a few select economists. He refers repeatedly to the analyses of Marshall and Chamberlain, and he makes extensive use of Michael Spence's theory of signaling (e.g. White 1990; cf. Spence 1974). Spence influences one of the key features of White's theory, namely the notion that markets consist of social structures that are partly produced and reproduced through signaling between the participants. In a production market, firms constantly check what the other firms do and adjust their actions accordingly.

White is mainly interested in production markets because they constitute the backbone in an industrial economy. In a production market the actor is either a buyer or a seller of a specific good, while in an exchange market the actor is a buyer as well as a seller. The stock exchange is the archetype of an exchange market. Being a seller *or* a buyer versus a buyer *and* a seller has, according to White, important consequences, both for the social structure of the market and the identities of the market actors. The exchange market, for example, is much closer to the neoclassical ideal of a market in which demand and supply decide the price.

Production markets, on the other hand, typically consist of about a dozen of firms that view each other as constituting a market and are also perceived as such by the buyers. The central mechanism in the social construction of a market is its "market schedule," operationalized by White as $W(y)$, where W stands for revenue and y for income. This schedule, according to White, is considerably more realistic than the economists' demand-supply analysis. Businessmen know what it costs to produce something and try to maximize their income by determining a certain volume for their product. On the other hand, they do *not* know how the consumers view their product—all they know is what items sell in which volumes and at which price. If businessmen are correct in their calculations, they will be able to locate a niche in the market for their products, which their customers acknowledge by buying a certain volume at a certain price. Depending on its structure, a market can be one of the following four types: "paradox," "grind," "crowded," and "explosive." The closest to a definition of a (production) market that can be found in White's work may well be the following:

> Markets are tangible cliques of producers watching each other. Pressure from the buyer side creates a mirror in which the producers see themselves, not consumers. (1981, 543)

Having devoted several years exclusively to markets, White shifted to other concerns in the late 1980s and early 1990s. In *Identity and Control* (1992), for example, he presents a general theory of action. Insofar as markets are concerned, this work is primarily interesting in that his earlier research on markets is integrated into a larger theoretical whole. Production markets are seen as an example of "interfaces," defined as a certain way of achieving control in a "social molecule" (White 1992, 41–43). In the interface, the individual identities of the actors (such as firms) come into being through continuous production. But control can also be achieved in a different manner; in the so-called arena it comes about via the creation of a very different and more general type of identity that is essentially interchangeable. Exchange markets are typical examples of what White here terms "arena markets" (1992, 51–52).

In a recent work entitled *Markets from Networks* White further develops his theory of production markets and also broadens its scope. Instead of focusing exclusively on individual production markets, White attempts to see how they fit into the larger whole of an industrial economy. Three different "layers of action" are distinguished: "upstream," "producers," and "downstream" (White 2001). The upstream firms basically supply the input to producers whose output goes to the downstream firms. According to White, there also exists a dynamic relationship between markets with goods that can substitute for each other.

Markets as Networks

Using networks to analyze markets appears to be more popular than any other perspective in current economic sociology (see, e.g., the studies cited in Smith-Doerr and Powell, this volume; Lie 1997). The main reason for this may well be that analysis of networks is a very flexible method, which allows the researcher to both keep close to the empirical reality and to theorize freely. On the negative side, the networks approach does not come with a theory of markets, but constitutes a general method for tracing relationships. Why people engage in an exchange, and under what circumstances a market can be established, are not part of the theory but something that has to be added—and rarely is. Harrison White's $W(y)$ model, with its explicit focus on terms of trade that decide whether a market can exist and under what conditions an actor can become part of a market, can be used as a contrast to markets as networks. As indicated by its title, White's *Markets from Networks* includes a network approach; this part of the analysis, however, is secondary to the idea of terms of trade and basically used to add to it.

Mark Granovetter's *Getting a Job* (1974) may be the most successful networks study of a market and constitutes, more generally, an exemplary study in economic sociology. It is innovative, meticulously researched, and analytically sharp. Although *Getting a Job* was written in the 1970s, its author has claimed it for "new economic sociology" with the following motivation: "In retrospect, *GAJ* was one of the first exemplars of what I have called the 'new economic sociology,' which differed from older work in its attention to a core rather than a peripheral aspect of the economy, and in its willingness to challenge the adequacy of neoclassical economic theory in one of its core domains" (Granovetter 1995, vii).

Getting a Job represents an attempt to analyze the social mechanisms through which people find employment, and is based on a study of professional, technical, and managerial workers in Newton, a small suburb to Boston. A random sample was taken; some 280 people filled in a questionnaire, and of them 100 were interviewed. The questions tried to establish the source of information that led to new employment. Are economists correct in seeing the labor market as a place where information about jobs reaches all the participants? Is the person who gets a new job best understood as someone who engages in a job search, according to utility-maximizing principles?

Granovetter's conclusion is that "perfect labor markets exist only in textbooks" and that the idea of a rational job search does not capture what actually happens when people find jobs (1974, 25). Some people do indeed engage in a job search—but this is not necessarily the key to getting a job. For example, a sizable number of people apply for a job only if they are approached by someone with a concrete proposal ("quasi-searchers"; about 20 percent). Furthermore, those who actively look for a job are not the ones who are likely to end up with the best jobs. The job search theory of the economists misses one very important fact, namely that "much labor-market information actually is transmitted as a byproduct of other social processes" (52). What matters in many cases is *contacts*—so much so, the author concludes, that "regardless of competence or merit, those without the right contacts are penalized" (100).

What Granovetter's research showed is the following: almost 56 percent of the respondents got their jobs through contacts, 18.8 percent through direct application, 18.8 percent through formal

means (half of this portion through advertisements), and the rest through miscellaneous means. The economists' assumption that information about new jobs spreads evenly throughout the labor market was clearly invalidated (39.1 percent got information directly from the employer, 45.3 percent got it via one contact, 12.5 percent through two contacts, and only 3.1 percent through more than two contacts). Of special importance to Granovetter was also the fact that in the great majority of the cases, the person who got the job associated only "occasionally" or "rarely" with the person who supplied the information (27.8 percent "rarely," 55.6 percent "occasionally," and 16.7 percent "often"). This situation was theorized by Granovetter in the following way: people whom you know intimately ("strong ties") tend to share the same limited information and are therefore rarely able to help you. But people you know casually ("weak ties"), on the other hand, have by definition access to much more distant and varied information—and can therefore be of much more help in finding a job (for a full presentation of the strength-of-weak-ties thesis, see Granovetter 1973). People who stay very long in one job, Granovetter also noted, have much more difficulty in finding a new job than those who change jobs often.

Granovetter's analysis of the labor market differs quite a bit from that of his thesis adviser, Harrison White, in *Chains of Opportunity* (1970). White's argument is that when someone gets a new job, an opening is created that has to be filled—which results in a new vacancy, which also has to be filled, and so on. When a person gets a new job, in brief, a movement is set off that traverses the labor market and which the individual is unaware of. Tested against Granovetter's results in *Getting a Job*, it is clear that White's ideas about "vacancy chains" do capture some of the dynamics in the labor market—but by no means all (in 44.9 percent of all cases, the person who got a new job was replacing a particular person; in 35.3 percent, on the other hand, the position was totally new, and in 19.9 percent the job was new but of a type that had existed before).

It should also be mentioned that in 1995, when Granovetter's study was reissued, the author noted that new evidence was now available that confirmed his assessment from 1974 that finding a job via information supplied in a network was widespread (one figure from the United States is 45 percent, one from Japan 70–75 percent; cf. Granovetter 1995, 139–41). He also noted that economists during the last few decades have continued to ignore this fact and stuck to their theory of the job search.

Among the early network studies of markets one by Wayne Baker deserves to be singled out. In his doctoral dissertation, called "Markets as Networks" (1981), Baker presented both a general theoretical argument for a sociological theory of markets and an empirical analysis. Economists, according to Baker, have developed an implicit rather than an explicit analysis of markets: "Since 'market' is typically assumed—not studied—most economic analyses implicitly characterize 'market' as a 'featureless plane'" (Baker 1981, 211). In reality, however, markets are not homogenous but socially constructed in various ways. To analyze this structure constitutes the main task for "a middle-range theory of 'markets-as-networks'" (183).

How this can be done with the help of networks analysis is clear from the empirical part of Baker's thesis, which has been published separately (1984; see also Baker and Iyer 1992 for a mathematical rendition). Using empirical material from a national securities market, Baker showed that at least two different types of market networks could be distinguished: a small, rather dense network and a larger, more differentiated and looser one. On this ground Baker argued that the standard economic view of the market as an undifferentiated whole was misleading.

But Baker also wanted to show that the social structure of a market has an impact on the way that the market operates; and to do this he looked at volatility in option prices. He found that the fragmented, larger type of network caused much more volatility than the smaller, more intense networks. "Social structural patterns," he concluded, "dramatically influenced the direction and the magnitude of price volatility" (1984, 803). Baker's study also contradicted the idea in mainstream economics that a huge number of actors results in a perfect market.

A third important network study of the operation of markets can be found in Brian Uzzi's "Social Structure and Competition in Interfirm Networks: The Paradox of Embeddedness" (1997; cf. Uzzi 1996). Drawing on an ethnographic study of some 20 firms in the apparel industry in New York, the author found that the firms tended to divide their market interactions into what they call "market relationships" and "close or special relationships" (Uzzi 1997, 41). The former more or less matched the kind of relationships that can be found in standard economic analysis, while the lat-

ter were close to Granovetter's notion of embeddedness. Market relationships tended to be more common than close or special relationships, but also to be considerably less important. Embedded relationships were especially useful in the following three cases: when trust was important, when fine-grained information had to be passed to the other party, and when certain types of joint problem-solving were on the agenda.

Uzzi interpreted his results in the following manner. For a business to operate successfully, it cannot exclusively rely on market ties (as the economists claim), or exclusively on embedded ties (as some sociologists claim); it needs a mixture of the two. The ideal is a balance between market ties and embedded ties—an "integrated network." Too many market ties makes for an "underembedded network," and too many embedded ties for an "overembedded network." A firm with an over-embedded network, for example, has difficulty in picking up new information.

Uzzi's interpretation of his findings, in terms of interest analysis, is that the actors in his firms were neither selfish nor altruistic; they rather switched forward and backward between self-interest and cooperation. "[S]tringent assumptions about individuals being either innately self-interested or cooperative are too simplistic, because the same individuals simultaneously acted 'selfishly' and cooperatively with different actors in their network" (1997, 42). The author adds complexity to this analysis by arguing that cooperative behavior can sometimes be a way of satisfying interests that are difficult to satisfy in arm's-length deals: "multiplex links among actors enable assets and interests that are not easily communicated across market ties to enter negotiations" (50). This does not mean, however, that the actor simply can switch from one way of satisfying her interests to another, from market ties to embedded ties. One of the cases Uzzi discusses, in which the owner of a firm that had decided to move his business to Asia nonetheless carried out his contractual obligations in New York, clearly shows that embedded ties can acquire a dynamic of their own in which self-interest is held back.

Markets as Parts of Fields (Bourdieu and Others)

One theory of how markets behave that has not received the discussion it deserves is that of Pierre Bourdieu, most succinctly outlined in "Principles of an Economic Anthropology" (2000, 233–70 and chapter 4 of this volume; for an earlier version, see

Bourdieu 1997). Bourdieu's key idea is that economic life is largely the result of the encounter between actors with a special disposition (habitus) in the economic field; and that the market is deeply influenced by the nature of the field. The economic field can be a firm, an industry, a country, or the whole world. Its structure, if we use an industry as our example, consists of the power relations between the firms, which are maintained through capitals in various combinations (financial capital, technological capital, social capital, and so on). There are dominant firms as well as dominated firms, and a constant struggle goes on between them. What happens outside the field also plays an important role in the struggles within an industry; the state especially has the power to influence what happens in a field.

The market is conceptualized as part of a field and dominated by its dynamic. Prices, for example, are determined by the structure of the field, and not the other way around. "The whole is not the result of prices; it is the whole that decides the prices" (Bourdieu 2000, 240). Mark Granovetter's and Harrison White's theories of the market are mistaken, according to Bourdieu, because they ignore the impact of the structure of the field on the market; they express an "interactionist vision," as opposed to a "structural vision." Bourdieu's own view of the market is well captured by the following statement from "Principles of an Economic Anthropology":

> What is called the market is the totality of relations of exchange between competing agents, direct interactions that depend, as Simmel has it, on an "indirect conflict," or, in other words, on the socially constructed structure [of the field] of the relations of force to which the different agents engaged in the field contribute to varying degrees, through the modifications they manage to impose upon it, by drawing, particularly, on the state power they are able to control and guide. (Bourdieu this volume, 81)

In "Principles of an Economic Anthropology" Bourdieu refers to the work of Neil Fligstein, and there exist significant parallels between their views. At one point in "Markets as Politics"—Fligstein's most important theoretical statement on markets—the author says, for example, that "my view of markets is roughly consistent with the idea of organizational fields, in that a market consists of firms who orient their actions toward one another" (1996, 663; cf. Fligstein 2001, 67–78). Fligstein also agrees with Bourdieu that the attempt to use networks analysis to study markets is unsatisfactory since it exclusively focuses on social interaction.

Networks analysis fails to consider the role of politics, the view of the actors, and what characterizes markets as social institutions.

In Fligstein's view, markets are social situations in which goods are exchanged for a price in money; and these situations can only come into being if three elements exist: "property rights," "governance structures," and "rules of exchange." Property rights are defined as social relations that determine who is entitled to the profit of a firm; governance structures consist of rules for how to organize a firm as well as competition and cooperation; and rules of exchange determine under what conditions exchange can take place and who can participate in it.

Like Bourdieu and Weber, Fligstein emphasizes the role of struggles in the market. But Fligstein adds to this analysis by proposing that what drive individual firms and characterize modern production markets are "attempts to mitigate the effects of competition with other firms" (1996, 657). This search for stability represents the basic principle of Fligstein's theory of markets (see also Fligstein, this volume). In "Markets as Politics" Fligstein suggests a number of propositions for empirical verification, all related to this principle. He proposes, for example, that the state typically tries to stabilize markets and eliminate competition—but also that its actions can inadvertently bring about disorder (and restore competition). When the largest firms in a field fail to reproduce themselves, a market crisis ensues, with interorganizational power struggles as a result. Existing markets can also be transformed through exogenous factors, such as economic crises and invasions by other firms.

The theories of Bourdieu and Fligstein may seem somewhat schematic as described here; and it should therefore be noted that these authors have made empirical studies of concrete markets. Bourdieu has, for example, analyzed the markets for individual homes in France (Bourdieu 2000). In the studies of both of these writers, the relevant field is presented in rich empirical detail, which makes Bourdieu's scheme come alive and show its potential as a tool to analyze markets. Fligstein has shown the importance of looking at property rights, governance structures, and rules of exchange, by using the Single Market of the European Union as a case study (Fligstein and Mara-Drita 1996; Fligstein and Stone Sweet 2001). How firms try to control competition and how the state can shape the market also come out with great force in Fligstein's study of the evolution of the huge firm during the twentieth century in the United States (Fligstein 1990).

CONCLUDING REMARKS ON STRENGTHS AND WEAKNESSES IN THE SOCIOLOGY OF MARKETS

This chapter starts out with the observation that neither economists nor sociologists currently have a satisfactory theory of markets, and that one way of advancing the discussion is to bring in historical material on markets. When one studies concrete markets, it soon becomes clear that markets have been structured in very different ways throughout history. There are external as well as internal markets; national as well as international markets; and markets for the elite as well as for the masses. Political authorities early in history began to keep an eye on the markets in their territories, and the modern state is deeply committed to keep the economy going. The concept of interest, as it turns out, can elucidate aspects of the structure and functioning of markets.

Sociologists have studied markets since the early 1980s, and it is today possible to summarize what has been accomplished and what still remains to be done. The idea that social relations are crucial to the existence of markets has, for example, been amply proven. Networks analysis, in particular, is a very useful tool in this context, even if Bourdieu and Fligstein are correct in their argument that studies of this type tend to ignore the role of the state as well as structural forces in general. Sociologists such as Weber, Bourdieu, and Fligsetin have paid attention to the concept of interest. By contrast, in the work of White and Granovetter, for example, the concept of interest is implicit rather than explicit.

But sociologists have barely explored some aspects of markets. One of these has to do with the popular or ideological view of markets, another with how prices are set. Markets have had their ups and downs in official economic ideologies ever since Adam Smith's attack on mercantilism in *The Wealth of Nations*. A few sociological studies of more recent economic ideologies, such as neoliberalism, can also be found (e.g., Campbell and Pedersen 2001; Babb and Fourcade Gourinchas 2003). Totally missing from the current sociological literature, however, are studies of representations of markets in the media and in schoolbooks, and, more generally, studies of what role they play in the process of economic socialization in modern capitalist society.

Similarly, few sociological studies of how prices are set exist. Here, however, there are some instructive exceptions. As to the classics, Weber notes, for example, that the fixed price was pioneered by the Baptists and the Quakers (Weber [1920] 1946, 312; cf. Kent 1983). One can also find the evocative statement in *Economy and Society* that "money prices are the product of conflicts of interest and of compromises; they thus result from power constellations" (Weber [1922] 1978, 108). Weber adds that prices result from "struggle" and that prices "are instruments of calculations only as estimated quantifications of relative chances in this struggle of interests" (108). One contemporary attempt to draw on these ideas can be found in a study of price setting in the American electrical utility industry in the nineteenth century (Yakubovich and Granovetter 2001). In this study, Weber's suggestion that prices are the result of power constellations and struggle is fleshed out in an exemplary manner.

Granovetter has also used the embeddedness approach to analyze the "stickiness" of prices (e.g., Granovetter and Swedberg 2001, 13–14; see also Uzzi and Lancaster 2004). Economic sociologists have in addition begun to study price-fixing, how status affects price, and how prices are determined in different types of auctions (e.g., Smith 1989; Podolny 1992; Baker and Faulkner 1993). It has furthermore been noted that for a long time a simple rule of thumb was used to determine prices in the U.S. computer industry: three times the manufacturing cost (MacKenzie 1996, 53).

Finally, it seems that the current sociology of money, which has made many interesting advances, nonetheless needs to be much more firmly linked to the analysis of markets (cf. Dodd 1994; Ingham 1998; Zelizer 1994, 2001). Money and related financial instruments—such as bills of exchange, shares, options, and so on—have emerged in close connection to various markets. The step from barter to exchange, with the help of money, deeply affected the structure of markets, and so have many other financial innovations. The current sociology of money, however, is much too focused on money as such, and has little to say about the relationship of money to markets. What needs to be looked into, for example, is the way that new forms of money have helped to create new markets and how money itself has been transformed into new forms, from primitive forms of credit to ever new financial instruments with varying degrees of liquidity (see, e.g., Baker 1987; Stinchcombe and Carruthers 1999). To express this last point another way, the sociology of money should not only study the impact of (conventional) money on social relations, but also pay attention to money as a dynamic and ever changing instrument used to acquire economic power. Money and markets, in brief, belong together.

NOTES

1. This chapter is different from "Markets as Social Structures" (which appeared in the first edition of *The Handbook of Economic Sociology*) primarily in that it pays much more attention to the role of markets throughout history. It also argues that a sociological theory of markets needs to address not only social structures but also interest. Finally, much less space is devoted to economists' theory of markets. For helpful comments I especially would like to thank Neil Smelser, Alejandro Portes, and William Haller.

2. See Swedberg 1994; and for an updated version of this account, see chapter 5 in *Principles of Economic Sociology* (Swedberg 2003b).

REFERENCES

Abolafia, Mitchel. 1984. "Structured Anarchy: Formal Organization in the Commodity Futures Industry." Pp. 129–50 in *The Social Dynamics of Financial Markets*, ed. Patricia Adler and Peter Adler. Greenwich, Conn.: JAI Press.

———. 1996. *Making Markets: Opportunism and Restraint on Wall Street*. Cambridge: Harvard University Press.

———. 1998. "Markets as Culture: An Ethnographic Approach." Pp. 69–85 in *The Laws of the Markets*, ed. Michel Callon. Oxford: Blackwell.

Arrow, Kenneth. 1998. "What Has Economics to Say about Racial Discrimination?" *Journal of Economic Perspectives* 12(2): 91–100.

Aspers, Patrik. 2001a. "A Market in Vogue: Fashion Photography in Sweden." *European Societies* 3:1–22.

———. 2001b. *A Market in Vogue: A Study of Fashion Photography in Sweden*. Stockholm: City University Press.

Azarian, Reza. 2003. "The General Sociology of Harrison White." Ph.D. diss., Department of Sociology, Stockholm University.

Babb, Sarah, and Marion Fourcade Gourinchas. 2003. "Neoliberalism in Four Countries." *American Journal of Sociology* 108:533–79.

Baker, Wayne. 1981. "Markets as Networks: A Multimethod Study of Trading Networks in a Securities Market." Ph.D. diss., Department of Sociology, Northwestern University.

———. 1984. "The Social Structure of a National Securities Market." *American Journal of Sociology* 89: 775–811.

———. 1987. "What Is Money? A Social Structural Interpretation." Pp. 85–108 in *Intercorporate Relations*, ed. Mark Mizruchi and Michael Schwartz. Cambridge: Cambridge University Press.

Baker, Wayne, and Robert Faulkner. 1993. "The Social Organization of Conspiracy: Illegal Networks in the Heavy Electrical Equipment Industry." *American Sociological Review* 58:837–60.

Baker, Wayne, and Ananth Iyer. 1992. "Information Networks and Corporate Behavior." *Journal of Mathematical Sociology* 16:305–32.

Barber, Bernard. 1977. "The Absolutization of the Market: Some Notes on How We Got from There to Here." Pp. 15–31 in *Markets and Morals*, ed. Gerald Dworkin, Gordon Bermant, and Peter G. Brown. New York: John Wiley and Sons.

Barzel, Yoram. 2002. *A Theory of the State*. Cambridge: Cambridge University Press.

Benet, Francisco. [1957] 1971. "Explosive Markets: The Berber Highlands." Pp. 188–217 in *Trade and Market in the Early Empires*, ed. Karl Polanyi, Conrad Arensberg, and Harry Pearson. Chicago: Henry Regnery.

Berg, Ivar, and Arne Kalleberg, eds. 2001. *Sourcebook of Labor Markets: Evolving Structures and Processes*. New York: Kluwer.

Berman, Harold. 1983. "Mercantile Law." Pp. 333–56 in *Law and Revolution: The Formation of the Western Legal Tradition*. Cambridge: Harvard University Press.

Block, Fred. 1977. *The Origins of International Economic Disorder: A Study of the United States International Monetary Policy from World War II to the Present*. Berkeley and Los Angeles: University of California Press.

Boorstin, Daniel. 1974. *The Americans: The Democratic Experience*. New York: Vintage.

Bourdieu, Pierre. 1997. "Le champ économique." *Actes de la recherche en sciences sociales* 119:48–66.

———. 2000. *Les structures sociales de l'économie*. Paris: Seuil.

———. 2001. *Contre-feux 2. Pour un mouvement social européen*. Paris: Raisons d'Agir Editions.

Braudel, Fernand. [1979] 1985. *Civilization and Capitalism, Fifteenth–Eighteenth Century*. 3 vols. London: Fontana Press.

Brewer, John, and Roy Porter, eds. 1993. *Consumption and the World of Goods*. London: Routledge.

Brown, Norman O. 1947. *Hermes the Thief: The Evolution of a Myth*. Madison: University of Wisconsin Press.

Callon, Michel, ed. 1998. *The Laws of the Markets*. Oxford: Blackwell.

Cameron, Rondo. 1993. *A Concise Economic History of the World: From Paleolithic Times to the Present*. 2d ed. Oxford: Oxford University Press.

Camp, John. 1986. *The Athenian Agora: Excavations in the Heart of Classical Athens*. London: Thames and Hudson.

Campbell, John, and Ove Pedersen, eds. 2001. *The Rise*

of Neoliberalism and Institutional Analysis. Princeton: Princeton University Press.

Castells, Manuel. 1996. *The Rise of the Networks Society.* Oxford: Blackwell.

Chandler, Alfred. 1977. *The Visible Hand: The Managerial Revolution in American Business.* Cambridge: Harvard University Press.

———. 1984. "The Emergence of Managerial Capitalism." *Business History Review* 58:473–503.

Clarke, David. 1987. "Trade and Industry in Barbarian Europe till Roman Times." Pp. 1–70 in vol. 2 of *The Cambridge Economic History,* ed. M. M. Postan and Edward Miller. Cambridge: Cambridge University Press.

Collins, Randall. 1990. "Market Dynamics as the Engine of Historical Change." *Sociological Theory* 8:111–35.

Coser, Lewis. 1972. "The Alien as a Servant: Court Jews and Christian Renegades." *American Sociological Review* 37:574–81.

Curtin, Philip. 1984. *Cross-Cultural Trade in World History.* Cambridge: Cambridge University Press.

DiMaggio, Paul, and Joseph Cohen. "Information Inequality and Network Externalities: A Comparative Study of the Diffusion of the Television and the Internet." Forthcoming. In *The Economic Sociology of Capitalism,* ed. Victor Nee and Richard Swedberg.

Dodd, Nigel. 1994. *The Sociology of Money: Economics, Reason, and Contemporary Society.* Cambridge: Polity Press.

Farkas, George, and Paula England, eds. 1988. *Industries, Firms, and Jobs: Sociological and Economic Approaches.* New York: Plenum Press.

Fine, Ben, and Ellen Leopold. 1990. "Consumerism and the Industrial Revolution." *Social History* 15:151–79.

Fligstein, Neil. 1990. *The Transformation of Corporate Control.* Cambridge: Harvard University Press.

———. 1996. "Markets as Politics: A Political-Cultural Approach to Market Institutions." *American Sociological Review* 61:656–73.

———. 2001. *The Architecture of Markets: An Economic Sociology of Twenty-first-Century Capitalist Societies.* Princeton: Princeton University Press.

Fligstein, Neil, and Iona Mara-Drita. 1996. "How to Make a Market: Reflections on the Attempt to Create a Single Unitary Market in the European Community." *American Journal of Sociology* 102: 1–33.

Fligstein, Neil, and Alec Stone Sweet. 2001. "Institutionalizing the Treaty of Rome." Pp. 29–55 in *The Institutionalization of Europe,* ed. Alec Stone Sweet, Wayne Sandholtz, and Neil Fligstein. Oxford: Oxford University Press.

Garcia, Marie-France. 1986. "La construction sociale d'un marché parfait: Le marché au Cadran de Fontaines-en-Sologne." *Actes de la recherche en sciences sociales* 65:2–13.

Gerschenkron, Alexander. 1971. "Mercator Gloriosus." Review of John Hicks, *A Theory of Economic History. Economic History Review* 24:653–66.

Granovetter, Mark. 1973. "The Strength of Weak Ties." *American Journal of Sociology* 78:1360–80.

———. 1974. *Getting a Job: A Study of Contacts and Careers.* Cambridge: Harvard University Press.

———. 1986. "Labor Mobility, Internal Markets, and Job Matching: A Comparison of Sociological and Economic Approaches." *Research in Social Stratification and Mobility* 5:3–39.

———. 1988. "The Sociological and Economic Approaches to Labor Market Analysis: A Social Structural View." Pp. 187–216 in *Industries, Firms, and Jobs: Sociological and Economic Approaches,* ed. George Farkas and Paula England. New York: Plenum Press.

———. 1995. *Getting a Job: A Study of Contacts and Careers.* 2d ed. Chicago: University of Chicago Press.

Granovetter, Mark, and Richard Swedberg, eds. 2001. *The Sociology of Economic Life.* 2d ed. Boulder, Colo.: Westview Press.

Greif, Avner. 1989. "Reputation and Coalitions in Medieval Trade: Evidence on the Maghribi Traders." *Journal of Economic History* 49:857–82.

Heckscher, Eli. [1931] 1994. *Mercantilism.* 2 vols. London: Routledge.

Hicks, John. 1969. *A Theory of Economic History.* Oxford: Oxford University Press.

Hintze, Otto. [1929] 1975. "Economics and Politics in the Age of Modern Capitalism." Pp. 422–52 in *The Historical Essays of Otto Hintze,* ed. Felix Gilbert. Oxford: Oxford University Press.

Hirschman, Albert O. [1945] 1980. *National Power and the Structure of Foreign Trade.* Berkeley and Los Angeles: University of California Press.

Huvelin, P. 1897. *Essai historique sur le droit des marchés et foirs.* Paris: Arthur Rousseau.

Ingham, Geoffrey. 1998. "On the Underdevelopment of 'The Sociology of Money.'" *Acta Sociologica* 41: 3–18.

Kent, Stephen. 1983. "The Quaker Ethic and the Fixed Price Policy: Weber and Beyond." *Sociological Inquiry* 53 (winter): 16–32.

Knorr-Cetina, Karin, and Urs Brügger. 2002. "Global Macrostructures: The Virtual Societies of Financial Markets." *American Journal of Sociology* 107: 905–50.

Kuznets, Simon. 1966. *Modern Economic Growth: Rate, Structure, and Spread.* New Haven: Yale University Press.

Lestition, Steven. 2000. "Historical Preface to Max Weber, 'Stock and Commodity Exchanges.'" *Theory and Society* 29:289–304.

Lie, John. 1997. "Sociology of Markets." *Annual Review of Sociology* 23:341–60.

Lopez, Robert. 1976. *The Commercial Revolution of the Middle Ages, 950–1350.* Cambridge: Cambridge University Press.

MacKenzie, Donald. 1996. "Economic and Sociological Explanations of Technological Change." Pp. 49–65 in *Knowing Machines: Essays on Technical Change*, ed. Donald MacKenzie. Cambridge: MIT Press.

———. 2000. "Fear in the Markets." *London Review of Books*, April 13, 31–32.

Macneil, Ian. 1978. "Contracts: Adjustment of Long-Term Economic Relations under Classical, Neoclassical, and Relational Contract Law." *Northwestern University Law Review* 72:854–905.

Marshall, Alfred. [1920] 1961. *Principles of Economics.* 9th (variorum) ed. 2 vols. London: Macmillan.

Marx, Karl. [1867] 1906. *Capital: A Critique of Political Economy.* New York: Modern Library.

Marx, Karl, and Friedrich Engels. [1848] 1978. "Manifesto of the Communist Party." Pp. 473–500 in *The Marx-Engels Reader*, ed. Robert C. Tucker. 2d ed. New York: W. W. Norton.

McKendrick, Neil. 1982. "The Consumer Revolution of Eighteenth-Century England." Pp. 9–196 in *The Birth of a Consumer Society*, by Neil McKendrick, John Brewer, and J. H. Plumb. London: Europa.

Milgrom, Paul, Douglass North, and Barry Weingast. 1990. "The Role of Institutions in the Revival of Trade: The Law Merchant, Private Judges, and the Champagne Fairs." *Economics and Politics* 2:1–23.

Miller, Michael. 1981. *The Bon Marché: Bourgeois Culture and the Department Store, 1869–1920.* Princeton: Princeton University Press.

Mokyr, Joel. 1993. "Editor's Introduction: The New Economic History and the Industrial Revolution." Pp. 1–131 in *The British Industrial Revolution: An Economic Perspective*, ed. Joel Mokyr. Boulder, Colo.: Westview Press.

North, Douglass. 1981. *Structure and Change in Economic History.* New York: W. W. Norton.

Olson, Mancur. 1965. *The Logic of Collective Action: Public Goods and the Theory of Groups.* Cambridge: Harvard University Press.

Orlove, Benjamin. 1986. "Barter and Cash Sale on Lake Titicaca: A Test of Competetive Approaches." *Current Anthropology* 27:85–106.

Parsons, Talcott, and Neil J. Smelser. 1956. *Economy and Society: A Study in the Integration of Economic and Social Theory.* New York: Free Press.

Podolny, Joel. 1992. "A Status-Based Model of Market Competition." *American Journal of Sociology* 98:829–72.

Polanyi, Karl. [1944] 1957. *The Great Transformation.* Boston: Beacon Press.

———. [1947] 1971a. "Our Obsolete Market Mentality." Pp. 59–77 in *Primitive, Archaic, and Modern Economies: Essays of Karl Polanyi*, ed. George Dalton. Boston: Beacon Press.

———. [1957] 1971b. "The Economy as Instituted Process." Pp. 243–69 in *Trade and Market in the Early Empires*, ed. Karl Polanyi, Conrad Arensberg, and Harry Pearson. Chicago: Henry Regnery.

Polanyi, Karl, Conrad Arensberg, and Harry Pearson, eds. [1957] 1971. *Trade and Market in the Early Empires.* Chicago: Henry Regnery.

Roy, William. 1997. *Socializing Capital: The Rise of the Large Industrial Corporation in America.* Princeton: Princeton University Press.

Sachs, Jeffrey. 2000. "Notes on a New Sociology of Economic Development." Pp. 29–43 in *Culture Matters: How Values Shape Human Progress*, ed. Lawrence Harrison and Samuel Huntington. New York: Basic Books.

Schmoller, Gustav. [1884] 1902. *The Mercantile System and Its Historical Significance.* New York: Macmillan.

Schudson, Michael. 1984. *Advertising, the Uneasy Persuasion: Its Dubious Impact on American Society.* New York: Basic Books.

Schumpeter, Joseph A. 1954. *History of Economic Analysis.* London: Allen and Unwin.

Shoup, Lawrence, and William Minter. 1977. *Imperial Brain Trust: The Council on Foreign Relations and United States Foreign Policy.* New York: Monthly Review Press.

Simmel, Georg. [1907] 1978. *The Philosophy of Money.* Trans. Tom Bottomore and David Frisby. London: Routledge.

Smith, Adam. [1776] 1976. *An Inquiry into the Nature and Causes of the Wealth of Nations.* 2 vols. Oxford: Oxford University Press.

Smith, Charles. 1989. *Auctions: The Social Construction of Value.* Cambridge: Polity Press.

Solow, Robert. 1990. *The Labor Market as a Social Institution.* Cambridge, Mass.: Blackwell.

Sombart, Werner. 1902–27. *Der moderne Kapitalismus.* 3 vols. Leipzig: Duncker und Humblot.

Spence, Michael. 1974. *Market Signaling: The Informational Structure of Hiring and Related Processes.* Cambridge: Harvard University Press.

Stinchcombe, Arthur, and Bruce Carruthers. 1999. "The Social Structure of Liquidity: Flexibility, Markets, and States." *Theory and Society* 28:353–82.

Styles, John. 1993. "Manufacturing, Consumption, and Design in Eighteenth-Century England." Pp. 527–54 in *Consumption and the World of Goods*, ed. John Brewer and Roy Porter. London: Routledge.

Swedberg, Richard. 1994. "Markets as Social Structures." Pp. 255–82 in *The Handbook of Economic Sociology*, ed. Neil J. Smelser and Richard Swedberg. New York: Russell Sage Foundation; Princeton: Princeton University Press.

———. 2000. "Afterword: The Role of the Market in Max Weber's Work." *Theory and Society* 29:373–84.

———. 2003a. "The Case for an Economic Sociology of Law." *Theory and Society* 32:1–37.

———. 2003b. *Principles of Economic Sociology.* Princeton: Princeton University Press.

Thompson, Homer A., and R. E. Wycherley. 1972. *The Agora of Athens.* Athenian Agora, vol. 14. Princeton: American School of Classical Studies at Athens.

Tilly, Chris, and Charles Tilly. 1994. "Capitalist Work and Labor Markets." Pp. 283–312 in *The Handbook of Economic Sociology*, ed. Neil J. Smelser and Richard Swedberg. New York: Russell Sage Foundation; Princeton: Princeton University Press.

Toynbee, Arnold. [1884] 1969. *Toynbee's Industrial Revolution: A Reprint of Lectures on the Industrial Revolution.* New York: David and Charles.

Uzzi, Brian. 1996. "The Sources and Consequences of Embeddedness for the Economic Performance of Organizations: The Network Effect." *American Sociological Review* 61:674–98.

———. 1997. "Social Structure and Competition in Interfirm Networks: The Paradox of Embeddedness." *Administrative Science Quarterly* 42:35–67.

Uzzi, Brian, and Ryon Lancaster. 2004. "Social Embeddedness and Price Formation." *American Sociological Review* 69:319–44.

Verlinden, O. 1963. "Markets and Fairs." Pp. 119–53 in vol. 3 of *Cambridge Economic History of Europe*, ed. M. M. Postan and E. E. Rich. Cambridge: Cambridge University Press.

Veyne, Paul. 1990. *Bread and Roses.* London: Penguin.

Weber, Max. [1920] 1946. "The Protestant Sects and the Spirit of Capitalism." Pp. 302–22 in *From Max Weber*, ed. and trans. Hans Gerth and C. Wright Mills. Oxford: Oxford University Press.

———. [1904–5] 1958. *The Protestant Ethic and the Spirit of Capitalism.* Trans. Talcott Parsons. New York: Charles Scribner's Sons.

———. [1922] 1978. *Economy and Society: An Outline of Interpretive Sociology.* Ed. Guenther Roth and Claus Wittich. Trans. Ephraim Fischoff et al. 2 vols. Berkeley and Los Angeles: University of California Press.

———. [1923] 1981. *General Economic History.* New Brunswick, N.J.: Transaction Books.

———. [1898] 1990. *Grundriss zu den Vorlesungen über Allgemeine ("theoretische") Nationalökonomie.* Tübingen: J.C.B. Mohr.

———. 1999. *Max Weber Gesamtausgabe.* Pt. 1, vol. 5, *Börsenwesen. Schriften und Reden 1893–1898.* 2 half vols. Tübingen: J C.B. Mohr.

———. [1894–96] 2000. "Stock and Commodity Exchanges [*Die Börse* (1894)], Commerce on the Stock and Commodity Exchanges [*Die Börsenverkehr*]." *Theory and Society* 29:305–38, 339–71.

White, Harrison C. 1970. *Chains of Opportunity: System Models of Mobility in Organizations.* Cambridge: Harvard University Press.

———. 1981. "Where Do Markets Come From?" *American Journal of Sociology* 87:517–47.

———. 1990. "Interview: Harrison C. White." Pp. 78–95 in *Economics and Sociology*, by Richard Swedberg. Princeton: Princeton University Press.

———. 1992. *Identity and Control: A Structural Theory of Social Action.* Princeton: Princeton University Press.

———. 2001. *Markets from Networks: Socioeconomic Models of Production.* Princeton: Princeton University Press.

White, Harrison, and Robert Eccles. 1987. "Producers' Markets." Pp. 984–86 in vol. 3 of *The New Palgrave Dictionary: A Dictionary of Economic Theory and Doctrine*, ed. John Eatwell et al. London: Macmillan.

Wood, Robert. 1986. *From Marshall Plan to Debt Crisis: Foreign Aid Development Choices in the World Economy.* Berkeley and Los Angeles: University of California Press.

Wycherley, R. E. 1976. *How the Greeks Built Cities.* 2d ed. New York: W. W. Norton.

Yakubovich, Valery, and Mark Granovetter. 2001. "Electric Charges: The Social Construction of Rate Systems." University of Pennnsylvania Working Papers in Economic Sociology.

Zelizer, Viviana. 1979. *Morals and Markets: The Development of Life Insurance in the United States.* New York: Columbia University Press.

———. 1994. *The Social Meaning of Money.* New York: Basic Books.

———. 2001. "Money, Sociology of." Pp. 9991–94 in vol. 15 of *International Encyclopaedia of the Social and Behavioral Sciences*, ed. Neil J. Smelser and Paul Baltes. Amsterdam: Elsevier.

12 The Sociology of Labor Markets and Trade Unions

Wolfgang Streeck

THIS CHAPTER deals with the relationship between trade unions and labor markets. It cannot even attempt to offer a comprehensive treatment of either of the two. The first section, "Labor Markets and Trade Unions in Sociological Research and Theory," takes stock of core concepts and research traditions informing, or potentially informing, an economic sociology perspective on the subject. It is followed by a systematic discussion linking trade unionism to the interaction of supply and demand in different types of labor market, leading to a historically grounded typology of labor markets and trade unions and to an exploration of the relationship between trade unions and politics on the one hand and the economy on the other ("Labor Markets and Trade Unions: Between Economy and Society"). Next comes a stylized historical account of the coevolution of modern trade unions, labor markets, and the welfare state in different advanced industrial countries. The chapter concludes with informed speculation on the future of labor markets and trade unions in the postindustrial era ("The Rise and Decline of Trade Unions").

Inevitably the chapter trespasses on the territories of a variety of disciplines. Economic sociology has pointed out the significance for the operation of labor markets of functionally diffuse, noncontractual relations between individuals that form extended networks of communication and mutual obligation. It has also emphasized the embeddedness in such networks of the functionally specific, contractual employment relations created in labor markets. But it has conceded the formal institutions that regulate labor markets largely to economic efficiency theories (table 1). Unions as collective actors do not appear much in economic sociology either.[1] Although rooted in the same informal social structures that also underlie labor markets, they were left to political sociology and political science on the one hand and to industrial relations on the other, depending on whether they are considered in functionally diffuse political or functionally specific economic contexts.

LABOR MARKETS AND TRADE UNIONS IN SOCIOLOGICAL RESEARCH AND THEORY

The Sociology of Labor Markets

While historical sociology has explored the rise of free labor markets in the early modern period (for a summary account see Tilly and Tilly 1994, 286–91), the mainstream of recent sociological research has focused on the structured allocation of individuals to jobs of differential desirability (Berg 1981; Coleman 1991; Granovetter and Tilly 1988; Tilly and Tilly 1994). In part this seems to have been driven by political and civic concerns about equality and equal opportunity, particularly in connection with the feminization of employment and the rise of feminism and with, especially American, controversies on social and economic discrimination by race or ethnicity. Much of the current sociological literature on labor markets overlaps with the literature on social stratification and uses similar empirical techniques (Kalleberg and Sørensen 1979; Sørensen 1977). It also borders with sociological research on status assignment in large hierarchical organizations (Clegg and Dunkerley 1980; Baron and Bielby 1980).

Generally, sociological research and theory maintain that the labor market is not really a market, in the sense of a universalistic, impersonal, color- and gender-blind mechanism matching supply of, and demand for, labor.[2] Economic theory is assumed to maintain just this. It is also assumed to claim that unless price formation is interfered with, labor markets will not only clear—in the sense that they establish an equilibrium price for labor at which all who want to work are employed, and all who want to employ someone find someone willing to work for them—but that wages and access

TABLE 1. Disciplines Studying Labor Markets and Trade Unions, by Levels of Action and Types of Social Relations

	Type of Social Relation	
Level of Action	Functionally Diffuse Noncontractual	Functionally Specific Contractual
Individual action	Economic sociology	(Labor) Economics
Collective action	Political sociology, political science	Industrial relations

to employment are, or could and indeed should be, determined only by workers' marginal productivity and employers' marginal costs. Sociologists generally endeavor to show that free labor markets are impossible, and unregulated labor markets neither free nor fair. Absent corrective intervention, the social stratification generated by labor markets, or by hierarchical work organizations, is likely to be at odds with elementary requirements of social integration and political stability, if not social justice.

A central difference, then, between economists and sociologists looking at labor markets is that the former are principally concerned with efficiency—the optimal allocation of workers to jobs—whereas the latter worry, if at all, more about fairness. For economists, the condition of efficiency is satisfied if employment is affected only by those characteristics of workers that are relevant to the performance of the job in question. The result may, however, not be considered fair by sociologists if the distribution of relevant worker characteristics can be shown to be determined by factors like power, family and class, ethnic origin, and the like. On the other hand, even if sociological research can establish that employment opportunities are affected by entirely irrelevant individual properties, such as skin color for miners or bus drivers, economists can still save their concept of an efficient free market by including discrimination among the preferences ascribed to employers (Becker 1957).

More generally still, economic sociologists have argued that not only are labor markets not the sort of markets that economists believe they are, but they would not function if they were. Leading sociological work on labor markets emphasizes the essential significance for their operation of large chains, or "networks," of particularistic and per-sonal social relations, or "weak ties" (Granovetter 1973), that lie at the bottom of labor market transactions and precede, frame, constrain, and facilitate the rational strategic behavior of market participants. In other words, while recognizing that individuals seeking employment or seeking to employ others strive to maximize their utility, however widely defined, sociologists insist that they can do so only in the context of, and mediated by, social relations that require them to behave in line with rules that are social rather than economic. This is because it is only through social relations that potential employers and employees can acquire and assess information on each other and on the jobs at stake. The same applies to the indispensable establishment of trust, where transactions extend into a future that is beyond the parties' prediction or where contracts must be premised on the continuing good faith of the other party.[3]

Even though networks of social relations underlie all labor market transactions, they are not and cannot be set up for the purpose of making markets function. Rather, they are governed by a logic of interaction and social integration that presupposes a set of shared normative understandings, including at least residual acceptance of what Gouldner (1961) called a "norm of reciprocity." Self-seeking rational individualism is respected to the extent that it is normatively approved, and it is likely to be strongly normatively approved in capitalist societies where it is socially legitimate for market participants to look above all after themselves. At the same time, continuing informal relations among network participants, which are essential for the market to work, require that rational individualism not be driven beyond a point where all that an individual can reasonably assume of the other is "opportunism with guile" (Williamson 1979, 1994). In fact, actors who acquire the reputation of being nothing but opportunistic are likely to be eventually excluded from the community of those acting, and trading, in good faith. Agents that others cannot trust are not asked for information, which means that they cannot get information from others in exchange (Blau 1964), and they are unlikely to be hired if their reputation predicts constant haggling over the terms of their contract.

In sociological work on labor markets, social networks have been drawn upon to explain, not just how individuals get a job, but also why certain jobs are regarded as "appropriate" for certain groups and why some groups are over- or, for that matter, underrepresented in certain occupations.[4]

Here the logic of explanation usually involves a historical starting point, for example, a more or less accidental overrepresentation of a certain group of immigrants in the workforce of a particular industry. Over time this crystallizes in a social pattern, as workers prefer to work with their relatives and friends, personnel managers want to limit search costs and to put informal social controls among workers at the service of economic performance, and supervisors prefer workgroups to be socially homogenous to simplify communication and avoid ethnic conflict at the workplace. Once a pattern of this sort has become established, it assumes the character of an informal institution from which actors can deviate only with an effort and at a cost. Such embedding of economic behavior and "rational" economic decisions in ongoing social relationships, with their specific dynamics of suspicion and trust, uncertainty, lack of formal enforceability, informal mutual reassurance, and the like, is used to explain a wide range of phenomena, from the fact that dentists are primarily women in Russia while they are primarily men in Germany, to racial discrimination in multiethnic societies like the United States.

Access to social networks is, almost by definition, far from egalitarian. Indeed the concept of "social capital" (Bourdieu 2000) has been devised to emphasize both the high market value and the unequal distribution of informal social relations. Sociological observations on the contribution of social capital to labor market success and occupational attainment may issue in calls for political intervention, either to redistribute social capital or to neutralize its impact. Examples of such intervention are affirmative action programs or educational policies designed to disrupt existing patterns of social relations and replace them with others that are less exclusive and more universalistic. Sociologists do, of course, disagree not just about the prospects of success of social engineering of this sort, but also about its desirability.

Remarkably, although economic sociologists have insisted on the essential significance of social relations for the operation of labor markets, formal rules and institutions regulating such relations have not been at the center of sociological inquiry. Nor have corporate actors engaging in such regulation, such as trade unions. This must appear surprising, as labor law and collective bargaining obviously play a major role in the functioning of most modern labor markets. While it is true that individuals rely on informal social ties to gather information on job opportunities or on the reputation

of others as employers and employees, the rights and obligations involved in employment relationships are to a very large extent formally standardized and sanctioned by third parties, although in some countries more than in others.

Standardization of expectations and transactions through legitimate institutions cuts the information requirements of market participants and relieves them of the necessity to reinvent the wheel every time they conclude a contract. Institutional economists since John R. Commons have appreciated the importance of labor market institutions for the lowering of what are now called "transaction costs" (Williamson 1979, 1994), as well as for the flexible adjustment over time of the terms of employment contracts to changing contingencies. Mostly, however, they have explained labor market institutions and arrangements for the governance of ongoing employment relationships in efficiency-theoretical terms, that is, in terms of the interests of market participants in minimizing the costs of their transactions.[5] The sociological tradition suggests a different and, presumably, more realistic approach to institutions, one that emphasizes their normative foundation and obligatory character, as well as the fact that their evolution is governed by a variety of social forces in addition to efficiency considerations, such as the distribution of power in society or, importantly, their own past.

To develop a more historically grounded, non-functionalist and noneconomistic theory of labor market institutions, sociologists do well to start from the same informal networks of weak ties that they have identified as the social fabric supporting transactions between individual labor market participants (Granovetter 1974). Not just markets spring from networks (White 2002a) but also institutions and the corporate actors that enforce them (what Weber calls *Herrschaftsverbände*).[6] Institution building requires social networks supporting the mobilization of resources for the enforcement of specific patterns of action. Norm-enforcing organizations become legitimate institutions to the extent that they can call upon the assistance of third parties if necessary (Stinchcombe 1968). For whatever reason, the economic sociology of labor markets has been reluctant to move on to an analysis of the dynamics of institution building and institutional change inside markets.[7]

The Sociology of Trade Unions

While there is an extensive sociological literature on trade unions, it is not primarily in the context of a sociology of the economy that trade unionism became an object of sociological inquiry. Trade unions as corporate economic actors in the labor market were studied, if at all, first by economists and later by the hybrid discipline of industrial relations that was in the 1960s gradually spun off by economics when it turned increasingly formalistic. Economic debates centered on the question of whether unions were able to raise the price of labor above its equilibrium market price and, if so, what the likely consequences were for monetary stability, growth, employment, the distribution of income, and so forth. Early on the Austrian economist von Böhm-Bawerk in *Macht oder ökonomisches Gesetz* ([1914] 1968) had argued that it was impossible for unions to beat the laws of the market. Later, with the firm establishment of collective bargaining in the 1950s, economists looked at unions as would-be monopolists in the labor market and tried to account for the outcomes of their activities by developing theories of monopolistic competition (Chamberlin 1950). For Keynes and his school, unions contributed to making wages downwardly rigid, which was basically welcome as it helped stabilize demand in periods of recession. However, unions were also capable of obstructing government efforts to increase employment, deploying their organized bargaining power to absorb additional aggregate demand by raising wages for employed workers, leading to higher prices instead of expanding employment.

Largely disregarding unions as economic actors in a strict sense, sociologists considered them primarily in the context of work on social mobilization and political organization, or collective action in general, as well as on modernization, nation building, the political-institutional representation of societal cleavage structures in twentieth-century democracies, and the institutionalization and pacification of the class conflict in industrial societies. Unlike the economic sociology of labor markets, the—mostly—political sociology of trade unions was macrosociological in outlook, although in its best manifestations it combined micro- and macrosociological perspectives. Emblematic in this respect is the work of Seymour Martin Lipset, in which unions are treated as political organizations of social groups in the modern nation-state, and in particular as contributors to its democratization and transformation into the democratic welfare state of the post–World War II period.

Lipset's work on trade unions explored the roots of different forms of trade unionism, like craft and industrial unions, in the social structures of communities of workers, such as the occupational communities of skilled craftsmen or the socially secluded territorial communities of mining villages and company towns (Lipset 1960, 1983; Lipset and Marks 2000). Lipset explained how different community structures gave rise to different organizational structures of trade unions as union organizers depended, at least initially, on the networks of primary relations that organized the social lives of their constituents. But unionism was also and equally affected by the political and economic opportunity structures for trade unions, especially at the time of their first appearance. Of crucial importance in this respect were the timing of industrialization and democratization, and especially of the introduction of the general franchise; the response of state and economic elites to unionization; and the presence of religious and ethnic divides in a country's political community. Informal group structures and institutional opportunity structures, Lipset showed, interacted to account for whether unions would become radical or moderate; the extent to which they would rely on collective bargaining or on political action; what sort of welfare state they would favor; and whether their behavior in relation to employers and the state would be governed mainly by economic or by political considerations.

Central to Lipset's political sociology of trade unionism was that it analyzed the role of organized collective action in mediating between the social structures of communities of workers on the one hand and the evolution and, ideally, democratization of the modern state on the other. Lipset was not, however, primarily interested in the impact of unionization on the economy, and in fact the relationship between trade unionism and the evolution and functioning of free labor markets, unlike liberal democracy, largely remained outside his view. This was different in the work of T. H. Marshall, with its core notion of a historical sequence of institutional development from civil rights to political and social rights, the culmination of which he believed to be the post–World War II welfare state (Marshall 1964). Like Lipset, Marshall was a political sociologist interested in a macrosociological theory of the modern state, not a political economist or a sociologist concerned with the embeddedness of economic in social transactions. Fundamental to his approach, however, was the assumption of an almost dialectical tension between the free market of capitalism, including the free labor market, and the various layers of citizenship rights institutionalized in the modern state, which led him to develop a peculiar conception of trade unions as collective actors crossing the boundary between the polity and the economy and combining essential features of political and economic action.

For Marshall, the recognition of trade unionism in the process of democratization represented an intermediate step between the institutionalization of political and social rights. Unions organized to demand social rights for workers to a living wage and to dignity in the workplace, contributing to the secular progression toward effective entitlement of all members of a political community to a minimum level of subsistence. But rather than relying on political rights to democratic elections and, subsequently, on direct state intervention in the economy, unions, once they had won the right to organize, pursued their goals in the civil sphere of the marketplace by means of free and voluntary, albeit collective, contracts. Marshall believed that this should be much less threatening to capitalism than state interventionism, as it respected the logic of capitalism's core institution, the market. Collective bargaining, therefore, although it was based on collective action, Marshall conceived as rooted, not in political citizenship, but in an economic equivalent that he called "industrial citizenship," enabling workers to act collectively to gain social rights, not in the polity but in the marketplace, and not through state authority but through the elementary civil right to conclude contracts, transferred from individual workers to their organized collectivity (1964, 94).

Marshall's concept of collective bargaining as an institution inserting political action in the economy and social rights in the labor market, and of unions as political as well as economic actors transferring public citizenship into the private sphere of market and contract, contains central elements of an integrated sociological perspective on labor markets and trade unions. The same holds true for the hybrid discipline of industrial relations that grew out of economics with Dunlop's book, much inspired by Talcott Parsons, *Industrial Relations Systems* (Dunlop [1958] 1993). Originally industrial relations was above all a praxeology of how to deal with trade unions and, especially, the strike, propagated in the post–World War II period as a scientific rationale for the universal introduction of free collective bargaining as a means of domesticating the class conflict. In its more academic manifestations, industrial relations was inspired by institutional economists such as Commons (1924) and the Webbs (1911), who had been sympathet-

ic to unions, not just as political actors in the context of liberal democracy, but also as economic actors in the labor market. Relations of employment, according to Dunlop ([1958] 1993), required for their smooth operation a "web of rules" laying down rights and obligations of employer and employee. Its origin Dunlop located in interactions between employers, workers (or organized workers), and the government—the "actors" of what he called the "industrial relations system," for which Dunlop immodestly claimed the same systemic status as Parsons's polity and economy. Clearly this did not endear industrial relations as a discipline to sociologists, who at the time were still fascinated with the symmetry of fourfold tables and classifications, regardless of the overriding importance for the functioning of a modern economy that Dunlop attributed to norms and institutions. Nor did it help that Dunlop insisted that industrial relations were not identical with either politics or economics, while including elements of both, in an interesting parallel to T. H. Marshall.

The function of industrial relations, in Dunlop's view, was to generate two kinds of rules in particular: substantive rules governing the relations between employer and employee, and procedural rules determining how substantive rules were made. Substantive rules in contracts of employment laid down the terms of trade for the goods exchanged between their parties—"a good day's work" for a "good day's pay." Among other things, they stipulated how work effort was to be measured, monitored, and motivated, and valued the kind of work being paid for in comparison to other kinds of work. Partly such terms were fixed, not by the individuals immediately involved, but by the government or by collective agreement negotiated by trade unions on behalf of workers. Procedural rules regulated the process of rule making, in particular the rights and obligations of the different industrial relations actors, like the right to strike or to lock out. The general assumption was that substantive rules regulating work and employment would be more efficient and legitimate if they were made with the participation and, eventually, the agreement of workers, rather than unilaterally by employers or the state. This was modeled on the American institution of free collective bargaining, which had been a central pillar of the New Deal and was widely considered at the time as a workable solution to problems of class conflict apparently untreatable in the ideology-ridden Old World—a practice that could be empirically studied and pragmatically improved with the help of scientific theory, to be peddled to Europe and Japan as a cornerstone of democratic capitalism. That in fact collective bargaining had originated in the United Kingdom and had first been systematically analyzed as a kind of private societal rule-making under the roof of a facilitating state by authors like the Webbs and the German labor lawyer Hugo Sinzheimer ([1916] 1976) was only rarely mentioned in the predominantly American literature of the time.

As collective bargaining was being propagated worldwide in the course of post–World War II social reconstruction, different national conditions turned out to be differently receptive to its introduction, and later gave rise to differences in national industrial relations that invited comparative analysis. Originally the comparative study of industrial relations had been premised on strong assumptions on an eventual convergence of the economic and political institutions of advanced industrial countries. Most eloquently and explicitly these were expressed in the seminal book by Kerr et al., *Industrialism and Industrial Man* (1960)— a book written mostly by institutional economists who represented the state of the art of modernization theory, at least as far as labor markets and trade unions were concerned. Later, by the time of the wave of labor unrest in the late 1960s and early 1970s, the accumulated research of the discipline of industrial relations became relevant for a new generation of sociologists prompted by contemporary events to take a new look at the old themes of class and class conflict. Of course the more or less "radical" sociology of the 1970s was and remained strongly critical of the practical intentions behind industrial relations—which it understood to be to suspend the class conflict by embedding it in properly designed institutions. It also did not share industrial relations' inherent belief in universal convergence to a pacified, nonideological "industrial society" taking the place of class-divided capitalism. But institutions did become central to a sociology that in subsequent years rediscovered trade unions and labor markets, and the political economy in general, from the perspective of two central questions: the extent to which institutions, in industrial relations or in politics, could make more than a superficial difference for the functioning of a capitalist market economy, and whether national politics had a capacity to choose between different versions of industrial society or had to succumb to constraints of technology and market, forcing all countries in the end to become birds of the same— American—feather.

The 1970s saw a wave of studies on trade unions in a borderland between a sociology trying to reclaim some of the classical themes of political economy and a changing discipline of industrial relations, a field being trespassed upon by a growing number of sociologists and political scientists.[8] The rise in worker militancy and union membership after 1968 (Crouch and Pizzorno 1978), everywhere except in the United States and highly unexpected after the literature of the 1960s on an impending "withering away of the strike" (Ross and Hartmann 1960), led to new research on the causes of union growth (Visser 1990). Moreover, relating by cross-national comparison variables like union strength, in membership as well as institutional position, to macroeconomic outcomes like growth, inflation, and employment, the new literature empirically contested the view, subscribed to by most economists, that strong unions necessarily meant weak economic performance. Other studies explored, almost by necessity comparatively (Dobbin, this volume), the delicate negotiations and "political exchanges" between governments, unions, and employers—a subject that especially interested political scientists, who began to consider the degree to which unions and industrial relations were organized in a "corporatist" manner as an important property of a society's political system (see *infra*). Simultaneously, Fordism and Taylorism became concepts, not just for a particular stage in the expansion of mass markets or a specific organization of industrial work, but for the character of the totality of institutions governing labor markets and employment and organizing the capitalist economy in the postwar period, as especially in the French regulation school, which influenced many sociologists studying trade unions and industrial relations (Boyer 1986). *Ex negativo*, the two concepts figured prominently also in sociological work on Japan as a new industrial nation. In particular the writings of Ronald Dore (1986, 1987) had a major impact on the new economic sociology, with their analyses of the embeddedness of Japanese labor markets and hierarchical workplace relations in informal networks of relational contracting (see also Macauley 1963) and in a capital market regime that corresponded to and supported the specific Japanese pattern of industrial relations and employment.

Since the 1970s the sociological study of trade unions became more than ever linked to a historical-institutionalist analysis of collective employment relations (for outstanding examples see Crouch 1993 and Thelen 1991). Trade unions are today the subject of a wide variety of subdisciplines more or less close to a *sociology of the economy*. Sociologists, political scientists, and economists all discovered the politics of labor markets and employment and prominently included trade unions and industrial relations among its central actors and institutions. When class-theoretical approaches lost appeal and began to be contested by work on cross-class alliances (see *infra*), different varieties of trade unions, labor markets, and industrial relations systems came to be regarded as elements of different "models of capitalism," that is, different and competing institutional forms of a capitalist market economy with, supposedly, different comparative advantage and patterns of economic performance (Hall and Soskice 2001). Major themes of this literature are the limits and conditions of change in national systems of internally complementary economic institutions, and generally the evolution of such systems under the impact of common technological and economic challenges, in particular those related to internationalization. Once again, the core issue is convergence and divergence, and with it the general role of politics in the organization of the economy.

LABOR MARKETS AND TRADE UNIONS: BETWEEN ECONOMY AND SOCIETY

Labor markets pull together labor supply and labor demand in contractual relations of employment (for a more extended definition see Tilly and Tilly 1994, 286). Trade unions act on both labor supply and labor demand, and they undertake to regulate the relations of employment between the two. Union action in all three dimensions is constrained as well as facilitated by the social and legal order enforced by the state and interacts with the state's own interventions in the market economy (Solow 1990; see fig. 1).

The *supply* of free labor in a society—the quantity and quality of labor offered to employers at

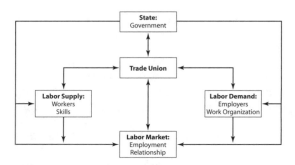

FIGURE 1.   Labor markets and trade unions in context

market price—depends on the social structure, for example, the relationship of households to the primary sector, on the distribution of income, on social norms governing preferences for income over leisure, the role of women in society, the educational system, provisions for social welfare, as well as on a wide range of other factors. Labor *demand,* in turn, is affected, among other things, by the size of product markets, available production technology, the organization of work—in particular prevailing patterns of horizontal division of labor and vertical authority at the workplace—and government economic and social policy.

The central institution of the labor market is the *employment relationship,* which in liberal societies since the end of feudal servitude is constituted by contract (Spencer [1873] 1961; Maine [1861] 1960). In a stylized account, with the progress of industrial society from early industrialization to the decades after World War II, the employment relationship as an institution has in most countries and sectors become less like a *contract of work* and more like a *contract of employment* (table 2). This corresponds to a shift from integration to separation of conception and execution, from "craft administration" (Stinchcombe 1959) of work to bureaucratic-hierarchical coordination, and from market coordination to coordination by organizational incentives inside firms (Sørensen 1994). In a contract of work, the employer pays a *price* for a

TABLE 2.   The Employment Relationship: Two Polar Types

	Contract of Work	*Contract of Employment*
Labor supply: structure of skills	Skilled: integration of conception and execution	Deskilled: separation of conception and execution
Labor demand: organization of work	Project by project craft administration	Ongoing, bureaucratic administration
Labor contract	Sale of labor, price for completed project	Sale of labor power, wage for time available

particular piece of work—a "job"—basically upon its completion. How the work is executed is left to its supplier, who essentially remains an independent subcontractor. After the work is done the relationship between the two sides ceases to exist; both are free to enter into new work relations depending on the requirements of the next job. In a contract of employment, by comparison, it is not a particular work task that is contracted for, but the availability of the worker to perform, within broad limits, any task assigned by the employer (Simon 1951). Wages are paid, not prices, and execution is separated from conception—which is in the hands of the employer and his agents. Discretion over what is done and how is transferred from worker to employer. Instead of a temporary association for the duration of a specific project, the employment relationship becomes an ongoing and, within limits, functionally diffuse organizational relationship. The person who was originally like an independent small businessman is turned into a dependent "wage earner." In Marx's terms, the sale of labor is succeeded by the sale of "labor power," placing a person's general capacity to create value at the disposal of its buyer.

The openness of the contract of employment is one of two main entry gates of sociology into the analysis of the labor market (the other being the structuration of the labor supply; see below). Not only the employment contract itself, but also its performance depends on noncontractual conditions (Durkheim [1893] 1964). Formal stipulations inevitably coexist with informal understandings, and instrumental action is and must be embedded in expressions of goodwill. Workers may shirk and employers exploit, but they also may not. Inside the organizational relationship that governs open contractual performance, skills may become idiosyncratic, making it difficult for workers to leave, while workers may become indispensable, making it difficult for employers to dismiss—both inserting particularistic social into universalistic economic relations. Trade unions act both as agents of explicit specification of contractual obligations, protecting workers from excessive demands on their labor power and making contractual performance easier to observe, and as guardians of trust in implicit and informal mutual commitments.

What has driven the transition from contracts of work to contracts of employment has been and continues to be much debated. It is clear that the transition was not universal and involved both a continuum, or spectrum, of intermediate forms and the survival of older forms in particular labor market segments, industrial sectors, and countries. Efficiency explanations emphasize the greater flexibility of contracts with unspecified, or less specified, content; their greater potential for "rationalization," that is, for reorganization of work to reduce factor inputs; and generally their better fit with the factory system and with mass production aimed at exploiting economies of scale by standardizing products and processes (Williamson, Wachter, and Harris 1975). Theories of power and exploitation, by comparison, regard the move from contracts of work to contracts of employment as the outcome of a power struggle. By "deskilling" manual work, and "degrading" work in general, employers take the management of production away from the workers, and with it the value it creates. As the latter is appropriated by employers—or allocated in part to a factory hierarchy of professional managers loyal to the employer—the rate of exploitation increases (Braverman 1974).

With the contract of employment superseding the contract of work, a voluntary relationship between two independent parties, in line with liberal concepts of freedom and self-determination, blends into a relationship of authority and control, albeit contractually based.[9] For both economists (Williamson, Wachter, and Harris 1975) and sociologists (Fox 1974), this transformation has posed an enduring puzzle. What for radical critics, many of them sociologists, was a subsumption of labor under the double despotism of market and factory (Burawoy 1983) led economists to model workers as risk-averse, that is, preferring a steady stream of income from a contract of employment to the uncertainties associated with managerial responsibilities and, in particular, with being paid out of the residual. For many economists it is this stylized "psychological" disposition that presumably makes workers prefer being controlled by others over exercising control themselves.

Labor supply and demand interact in numerous ways. Both are shaped by and affect a society's status order. For example, educational systems anticipate the structure of labor demand, and employers try to get educational institutions and policies to deliver them the labor supply they want. In addition, individuals investing in skills make bets as to what skills may be demanded in the future. But educational systems may also be expected to reproduce an existing social order or, to the contrary, change it in the name of values such as equality of opportunity or living conditions. To this extent employers must make do with the labor supply they get, and learn to accommodate it in their organization of work and the structure of authority at the workplace. For the Aix school of industrial sociology, educational systems, themselves products of long political struggles in a society over social integration and collective identity, are a major source of the "societal effect" that molds the organization of work in nationally distinctive ways (Maurice, Sorge, and Warner 1980; Maurice, Sellier, and Silvestre 1986b).

Central to sociological analyses of the labor market is the insight—sporadically rediscovered by mainstream economics (Williamson, Wachter, and Harris 1975)—that labor is a commodity with very special characteristics, and perhaps not really a commodity at all (Polanyi 1944 speaks of labor as of a "fictitious commodity"). On the surface this is indicated by its *perverse*, or *backward-bending, supply function*. Not only may the supply of labor decline as the price of labor increases, due to preferences for leisure over income in economic terms or, in sociological terms, to worker traditionalism in communities where work effort is determined by fixed needs, rather than needs expanding with growing opportunities (Marx [1867] 1984; Weber [1904] 1987). The supply of labor may also increase as wages decline, as a result of social or physical dependence of workers on a minimum level of income: if wages fall, workers cannot opt for leisure and wait for an improvement in relative prices since in between they need to pay their bills. At the bottom of this is the fact that labor as a commodity cannot be detached from the social and physical life of its seller. Another aspect of the social, personal, and physical embeddedness of labor is that its seller must be present in person while it is being used by its buyer, and indeed must actively collaborate in its use. The site of such collaboration is the firm as a social organization designed to extract labor from employed workers—which requires the workers' goodwill and cannot normally be done by despotic means alone (Burawoy 1983; Sørensen 1994). In fact in more complex production processes—or in Marxist language, in an advanced capitalist "labor process"—employers need some sort of legitimacy as wielders of authority (Bendix [1956] 1974) to mobilize normative commitment on the part of workers substituting for impracticable direct controls.[10]

Moreover, labor is not a homogenous good, and the labor of one person cannot always and easily be replaced with that of another. This gives rise to a subdivision of the labor market in more or less separate segments, forcing economists reluctantly to give up the simplifying assumption of one big market in which labor is competitively traded (Kerr 1954). In addition, as skill formation is tantamount to a process of socialization, differences in skill tend to be reflected in social identities and in social structures, that is, in divisions and relations between and within social groups. Vice versa, to the extent that differences between groups are linked to different kinds of "human capital," groups may defend their identities by monopolizing access to particular labor markets, especially if their human capital requires costly investment. Moreover, skills may be specific, or idiosyncratic, not just to social groups, but also to particular work relations and workplaces, in which case they are built up only in ongoing employment relationships. Due to their attachment to specific individuals and social relations, that is to say, the formation and utilization of skills takes place in much more particularistic and much less universalistic contexts than is captured by market models with their emphasis on impersonal competition.

This, in turn, is just another way of saying that the special characteristics of labor as a commodity give rise to inevitable *imperfections* of labor markets as markets.[11] Ultimately the perverse supply function of labor—the fact that workers cannot wait in times of declining real wages for the price of labor to recover—raises the possibility of *ruinous competition*. In addition, to the extent that the supply of labor is enmeshed in social structures and identities, and thereby difficult to convert on short order, workers may be stuck with their human capital, enabling employers to bid down their wage by threatening them with unemployment. Again, while employers can wait until workers accede to their terms, workers cannot, or not as long. The same may happen if workers have developed "idiosyncratic" skills that they can sell only to one particular employer, or group of employers; as a result they may refrain from developing such skills altogether (Williamson 1988). While the many opportunities for opportunism offered by pure labor markets to employers make such markets inefficient from an economist's viewpoint, they make them *unfair* from the perspective of workers, due to a fundamental imbalance in the power of the two parties in the labor market. In the view of classical sociology, this asymmetry makes the free labor contract free only in form and on paper and turns it into a coercive, unequal contract unless corrected by proper social institutions (Durkheim [1893] 1964).

The formation of trade unions was a historical response to the perceived unfairness of markets for labor or, in White's terms, to the gap between economic allocation in labor markets and social valuation (White 2002b). Unions close this gap by trying to shape allocation so that it conforms to valuation, mobilizing collective action out of social structures in which resides, not just information on individuals' economic utility, but also their commitment to social values. Political mobilization enables the sellers of labor to speak with one voice rather than with many, in the same way as the employer speaks with one voice. Collective action drawing on, representing, and defending the social identities and structures of the society supplying the labor, is to rectify the power imbalance inherent in fragmented competition between workers vitally dependent on employment. Unlike individual workers, labor as a corporate actor has the means to wait as long as the employer, and perhaps longer, and negotiate terms of exchange compatible with social life beyond the market and the social values that govern it.

Trade unions organize to make free labor markets fair through institutional safeguards that make them less like pure markets, especially by cartelization of the supply of labor. By limiting the reach of market relations into the social life of workers, unions contain the commodification of labor and thereby add to the imperfections of labor markets, making them less flexible by subjecting them to social regulation. At the same time, however, by suspending ruinous competition and creating institutions of contractual governance that protect workers' investment in skills, unions overcome inherent imperfections of labor markets and make them work in the first place. They can thus be seen, and have been so seen, as agents of both suspension and perfection of labor markets, of decommodification as well as commodification of labor, of fairness as well as of efficiency. This is what made them suspicious to radical socialists like Marx, and acceptable to bourgeois economists like Brentano (1871–72). The *double face* of trade unions reflects the fact that, due to the inseparable attachment of labor to social actors, labor markets and work organizations can be more than minimally efficient only to the extent that they are governed by legitimate social institutions.[12]

In sum, far from being alien to free labor markets, unions—as agents of social regulation of contractual relations of employment—have from the beginning been essential to their operation. Unions embed labor markets in social institutions and integrate them in a society's "moral economy" (Scott 1976): they make the market respect the connectedness of labor as a commodity to the physical and social life of its sellers, and ensure that the employment of labor remains compatible with the social norms and obligations to which workers are also subject. Unions promulgate social regulation of contractual relations in free labor markets to make them sufficiently predictable for participating individuals to support stable social identities and relations, and for individuals with stable identities and relations to participate in them. In this way unions try to set limits to what Polanyi (1944) calls the "satanic mill" of the market, preventing it from destroying the social fabric on which it depends for its continuing operation.

Collective action in pursuit of fairness and security protects labor from complete commodification and society from the vagaries of the market, making labor markets both socially legitimate and less than completely flexible. To make labor markets compatible with the moral economy of their members and their societies, different trade unions create different types of *market rigidities*. How much flexibility these leave, and must leave, for adjustment of firms and industries in a modern economy is a matter of debate—one that ultimately reflects the fundamental tension between the dynamism of a capitalist economy and the need for stability of social relations. Whereas economists tend to believe the best rigidities to be no rigidities, sociologists insist that there cannot be economic flexibility without social rigidity, and distinguish if at all between different sorts of more or less "flexible rigidities" (Dore 1986). Unions impose rigidities on labor markets in basically three ways: by trying to control the supply of labor, by trying to match the demand for labor to its supply, and by enforcing standardized contractual conditions on workers and employers.

Labor Supply

Unions are *cartels* of sellers of labor, exempt in all Western societies from even the strictest antitrust laws, in implicit recognition of the special characteristics of labor as a commodity. Enabling workers to speak with a collective voice, unions replace individual with collective contracts and thereby correct the imbalance of power that distorts individual bargains between workers and employers. Unions furthermore control the amount of labor employers can extract from workers, by setting and enforcing minimum wages and maximum hours. To do so, unions must be able temporarily to boycott employers by coercively cutting off their labor supply. This, too, has come to be widely accepted, even in the law of the United States, as a necessary and legitimate means to make labor markets less unfair.

Another dimension in which unions intervene in the supply of labor is *skill formation*. Here, diverse and complex bargains have emerged in different societies between organized labor on the one hand and the state and employers on the other. In some countries and industries, unions control industrial training and command a capacity to limit access to it, so as to drive up the price of skilled manual labor. In part this follows the model of the liberal professions. Elsewhere unions have to the contrary urged employers and the state to promote training, as a precondition for them to compress wage differentials; in such countries control over training is shared, with more or less union involvement. Important cross-national differences exist with respect to the role of apprenticeship in relation to public secondary and tertiary education, and to the role of unions, employers, and the state in the governance of apprenticeship (Crouch, Finegold, and Sako 1995). Differences in national systems of human capital formation are, in turn, related to differences in industrial capabilities and comparative advantage, in patterns of social stratification and social mobility, in the life courses of individuals, in political power structures, and in prevailing ideas about social justice, equality, freedom of choice, individual achievement, and so on (Maurice, Sellier, and Silvestre 1986a).

Third, unions often try to institutionalize *rules of access* to employment, based on a variety of criteria well beyond ability to do a job. Getting employers and the state to agree to limiting the pool of applicants for a particular sort of jobs, or hiring applicants only in a particular order, helps to eliminate cutthroat competition among workers. A wide variety of institutions have been invented, like hiring halls—sometimes run by the unions themselves—or the seniority principle, to introduce into otherwise chaotic or exploitative labor markets a sort of order that workers can accept as fair. Rules of access also protect workers' investment in skills where labor markets are "balkanized" (Kerr 1954) by barriers of entry that allow employers to hire only skilled workers for skilled jobs. In the literature, *occupational labor markets*, where access to employment is limited to people who certifiably belong to a particular skilled occupation, are distinguished from unskilled *general labor markets*, where access is free, and from the *internal labor markets* of large firms, where access to positions above entry-level is confined to those already em-

ployed, and where priority for employment is given to "laid-off" former employees (for various typologies see Doeringer and Piore 1971; Edwards, Reich, and Gordon 1979; Dunlop 1994; Osterman 1984; Kerr 1954). Whereas occupational labor markets protect transportable skills that are of use to more than one employer, internal labor markets protect workplace-specific skills that are built up on the job. Access rules may also be designed to protect the existence of the union as an organization if employment, in either occupational or internal labor markets, is made conditional on trade union membership (pre- or postentry closed shop). To economists, even before the final victory of neoclassical theory, institutionalized access rules in segmented labor markets represent a threat to both liberty and efficiency, even though it is sometimes grudgingly recognized that they may be a necessary condition for investment in skills, if not for a minimum of security and stability in the personal lives of workers (Kerr 1954).[13]

Fourth, unions can regulate the supply of labor by limiting working time—the locus classicus being Marx's chapter in *Capital* on the "Working Day" (Marx [1867] 1984)—and indirectly through all sorts of public policies, especially on taxation, pensions, and welfare benefits. Depending on how families are taxed, incentives for women to enter the labor market vary between countries and over time. By changing the mandatory age of retirement, governments may increase or reduce the labor supply, with unions often pressing for the latter especially in periods of high unemployment (Ebbinghaus 2001). Welfare state intervention, in the form of social assistance or unemployment benefits, creates a floor under labor markets that determines the minimum wage workers must be offered to be available for employment (the "reservation wage"). Unions' involvement in social policy, including the administration of public unemployment insurance and labor market policies, enables them to lower the economic pressure on workers to accept offers of employment that do not fit their skills or their economic needs, or that undercut current minimum standards of employed workers.

Labor Demand

Unions intervene also on the demand side of the labor market, trying to adjust demand to supply to save their members from having to adjust the supply of their labor to rapidly and erratically changing demand. Unions as political actors exert pressure, electoral and other, on governments for an economic policy that supports a high level of employment. In the period after World War II, this was to be accomplished primarily by Keynesian methods of *aggregate demand management*. Unions also sometimes support government programs to make employers hire workers that they would otherwise not have hired, to create more equal opportunities for immigrants and groups like women, disabled workers, or the long-term unemployed. At micro level, various forms of employment protection, based in law or collective agreement, are to shield workers from short-term market fluctuations and make their income more predictable. Again, due to the social closure that inevitably comes with collective organization, conflicts may arise between workers that are employed and protected, and workers seeking employment and willing to undercut existing employment conditions, even to a point where competition becomes ruinous.

Also to influence labor demand, unions intervene in the *organization of work*. In internal labor markets unions press for as many jobs as possible to be so designed that they can be filled by applicants one level lower in the hierarchy and next in the chain of promotion. By comparison, in occupational labor markets with lateral entry points, unions representing workers with transportable skills must see to it that these are matched by job descriptions. This requires that the division of labor is and remains similar in different workplaces, based on the training workers have received and the sort of labor they are therefore able to supply. In the extreme cases of Anglo-American craft unionism, this resulted in collective agreements under which skilled jobs were to be done, not just by skilled workers only, but in ways that matched the skills they had—putting sometimes severe obstacles in the way of technological and organizational progress. Conflicts over "managerial prerogative" with respect to work organization and technology tended to be particularly acrimonious in countries like Britain where occupational skills were narrow and fragmented, and where work was monitored on the basis of specific tasks and allocated to distinct "job territories" defined by "tools of the trade" (Flanders 1970). By comparison, identification of job demands on the basis of worker skills seems less inflexible where monitoring is by broad functions or procedures rather than tasks, and work is allocated on the basis of qualification instead of job territory (Marsden 1999).[14]

The Employment Relationship

Trade unions were major contributors to the transformation of employment from a spot market contract to an ongoing organizational relationship, or from a contract of work to a contract of employment. This was so especially in the post–World War II period, notwithstanding significant rearguard struggles by some unions to defend craft autonomy and by some employers to defend hiring and firing "at will." The institutionalization of the modern "wage nexus," as it eventually came to pass in all industrialized countries, albeit with significant national differences, established a sharp binary distinction between dependent employment and independent self-employment, taking the place of what had been a broad spectrum of contractual forms in between the two. It also involved recognition of a broad zone of managerial discretion in exchange for various forms of protection of workers from economic risk. This development was supported in most countries by the evolution of labor law as a subarea of contract law, spelling out special rights and obligations of the parties to an employment contract, and of the welfare state and its rules of eligibility to social insurance, for example, unemployment benefits.

Trade unions above all pressed for *standardization* of employment contracts, to protect workers from uncertainty, simplify collective regulation, decouple the economic situation of workers from that of their employing organization, and suspend as much as possible competition between workers, so as to enable them to act in solidarity. Standardization involved explicit and agreed definitions of normal effort, normal hours, and normal pay, guaranteeing employers reliable performance of predictable routine tasks at an average level of effort. Standardization was also associated with strict distinctions between work and nonwork, making work effort easy to measure for employer and employee alike, as well as for the union as the guardian of the wage-effort bargain. Generally unions tried to make explicit and formalize as many of the implicit and informal elements of the contract of employment as possible, so as to make employer demands on workers predictable and worker performance easier to measure, leaving as little space for employer judgment as possible.

All in all, unions introduced in the open employment contract elements of *status* rights for workers and status obligations for employers (Tannenbaum 1964). Status elements that in the name of "industrial justice" (Selznick 1969) entered into the individual employment contract, regardless of whether its parties would have elected them, included rights to employment protection, or at least to notice before dismissal, to unionization and workplace representation, and to individual and collective information, consultation and, in some countries, shared decision-making (Streeck 1992). To some extent, the introduction of public duties in the private employment contract had an international dimension, as it was, from as early as 1918 on, propagated worldwide by the International Labor Organization (ILO), a tripartite international organization older than the League of Nations or the United Nations.

The evolution of the open contract of dependent employment was tantamount to its infusion with institutional mechanisms of joint regulation (Dunlop [1958] 1993) of terms of exchange that can be specified *ex ante* only at heavy losses of efficiency. From the perspective of unions, joint regulation represented a necessary complement to managerial prerogative and was a precondition for fairness in unspecified contracts. (Even in the United States, nonunion settings for a long time followed the lead of the unionized sector and mimicked its regulations, if not its institutions; Jacoby 1990.) Joint regulation gave workers "voice" where "exit" would be too risky or costly in terms of other, stickier social relations. It also increased predictability, substituting for worker control over conception, and made the operation of free labor markets and open employment contracts compatible with standards of fairness, that is, with consideration of other than economic needs and values of workers.

As the unionization of labor markets and the standardization of the employment relationship proceeded, questions were asked whether socially regulated labor markets were flexible enough to adjust in time to changes in demand and technology. Some authors suspect that regulated employment in the "primary" labor market is possible only when complemented by unregulated, nonstandard, and contingent employment in a "secondary," nonunionized labor market, with "dualism" restoring the flexibility that social regulation had ended (Berger and Piore 1980). The implication is that in a market economy, reduction of economic uncertainty for some will inevitably increase uncertainty for others in weaker market or political positions, with the lines of division differing from society to society. Today, those demanding liberalization of labor markets doubt that workers, especially those with advanced human capital, are necessarily at a disadvantage in relation to employers and therefore stand to benefit from collective regulation and standardization of employment conditions. Building on theories of labor market dualism and segmentation, social protection of the employed is blamed in European welfare states for long-term unemployment and the growing gap between the employed and the unemployed. Advocates of liberalization support, together with destandardization and customization of employment conditions, a reallocation of economic risk between employers and workers, with the latter assuming more responsibility for economic outcomes, not least in the form of more contingent pay (Weitzmann 1984). By reintroducing elements of self-employment into dependent employment, this would blur the distinction between the two that was one of the hallmarks of the social order of industrial society.

A Typology of Trade Unions and Labor Markets

The first modern trade unions were formed at a time when employment was still governed mainly by contracts of work (von Beyme 1977; Katznelson and Zolberg 1986; Kendall 1975). By the middle of the nineteenth century *craft unions* had in most countries superseded the early, often anarchic protest movements of the "working poor." They organized skilled workers that were hard to distinguish from independent craftsmen, and operated much like cartels of small business firms. Craft unions often unilaterally set prices for specified jobs, rather than negotiating wages with employers. Like the guilds whose traditions they inherited, craft unions were socially and economically exclusive in that they tried to reserve market access to workers they had themselves trained. Control over training translated into control over work organization, where craft unions often succeeded in making employers organize production in ways that fitted their members' skills ("job control"). Challenged by liberal free trade policies, craft unions were eventually tolerated, especially where they remained politically indifferent or turned against socialist radicalism. In Germany under Bismarck, independent craftsmen were saved from "proletarianization" by protective legislation for small business, securing the government the unwavering support of a strong *Mittelstand*.

In early industrializing countries with liberal polities, such as Britain and the United States, craft unions managed to establish themselves in the second half of the nineteenth century as organizations of an *aristocracy of labor*. Industrialization and the advance of the factory system proceeded only slowly, and continuity with earlier guild traditions remained strong. Early extension of the franchise, in the United States even before the onset of industrialization, enabled unions to gain organizing rights by political pressure and through favorable legislation exempting them from free trade rules (Marks 1989). With ample opportunities to pursue their economic interests through collective action in the marketplace, and without first having to defeat an authoritarian state to get legal recognition, craft unions tended toward liberal politics and opposed socialist anticapitalism. Once established, they resisted bureaucratization of work organization and defended the unity of conception and execution against deskilling. In this way they delayed the advance of the modern factory and within it preserved elements of craft organization, such as the "gang system" under which employers contracted for specific jobs with a foreman who received a lump sum that he divided with his crew. As the employment relationship began to assume the form of a contract of employment, gang leaders turned into shop stewards organizing worker resistance against management and insisting on strict rules of job control to facilitate entry and exit of their members in and from different places of employment. Craft particularism also resulted in demarcation of "job territories" and gave rise to "restrictive practices" that well into the period after World War II compelled employers to adjust their technology and work organization to the skills of their workers, rather than vice versa (see Marsden 1999 on "employment systems").

In countries with established craft unions, unskilled labor became organized on a large scale only at the turn of the century, in a second wave of unionization. *General unions,* sometimes also called industrial unions, aimed at organizing all workers in a workplace or industry; in fact, given the already existing unions of the skilled, they mostly remained organizations of unskilled laborers. Since these could easily be exchanged for one another, they commanded little market power and were unable to exercise the same control over labor markets as craft unions. Typically they depended for their organization on the assistance of progressive political or religious movements, and for their operation on mass strikes and supportive political intervention. Often general unions were politically radical, like the Industrial Workers of the World (the "Wobblies"), which in the United States came closest to the anarcho-syndicalist unions of several European countries at the time. In a hostile political environment, general unions with their lack of economic clout were easy to suppress and, like the Wobblies, often became targets of violent persecution.

As the factory system spread, general unions gained in importance even in countries where there already was a union movement dominated by craft unions. In the United States, the Congress of Industrial Organizations (CIO) organized factory workers, miners, and longshoremen, sometimes against craft resistance, and grew in strength during the New Deal. Only reluctantly it was accepted by the craft-based American Federation of Labor (AFL), with which it later formed an uneasy alliance. Over time general unions in craft-dominated environments adapted elements of the modus operandi of their predecessors, resulting in job control practices—based on seniority rather than job territory—and in internal labor markets and the layoff system. In addition they undertook to strengthen the political clout of labor, to compensate for their lack of economic power. In Britain, it was mainly the general unions that were behind the foundation of the Labour Party, while the older craft unions were happy supporting the Liberals.

In late industrializing countries the advance of the factory system was faster and often proceeded under the guidance of authoritarian political regimes. They refused unions a right to organize, in the name of rapid modernization of their societies and anxious not to fall behind in international economic and military competition (Marks 1989). Guilds were abolished, and craft unions had little time to get established. Union organizing rights had to be won politically, which presupposed extension of the suffrage. Unions developed as part of a labor movement with a political and an industrial wing, the former dominating the latter at least until the achievement of democratization. As the beginnings of unionization coincided with the arrival of large factories, unions organized on a class or industrial basis, encompassing workers of all skills and trades and thereby redistributing and equalizing bargaining power between stronger and weaker sections of the workforce. Industrial unions were also often associated with political parties, of a socialist or Roman Catholic complexion. If they were fragmented, they were so by political affiliation rather than by occupation, reflecting the dominant political and social cleavages of their countries (Ebbinghaus 1995; Rokkan 1968).

Early alliances of industrial unions with political parties prefigured the various patterns of *political unionism* that emerged after democratization and laid the foundation for the evolving symbiosis of modern trade unions with the modern nation-state (Bartolini 2000; Streeck and Hassel 2003; Taylor 1989; Valenzuela 1992). Reflecting their origins as well as their heterogeneous membership that included mass workers with little economic power, industrial unions adhered to broader and more universalistic definitions of worker interest that could not be satisfied by industrial action alone. Strategically combining action in the political and industrial arenas, industrial unions were less than craft unions attached to free collective bargaining as the only mode of trade union activity. In addition they relied on favorable state intervention secured through political allies, not just for the protection of their organizations but also for a social policy that generalized social progress beyond individual occupations or the membership of trade unions.

At the workplace, industrial unions were willing to compromise with a bureaucratic factory regime, as long as they managed to circumscribe managerial prerogative by general rules in law or collective agreement. As in the political arena, where they favored social policies that benefited all citizens, industrial unions tried to equalize the pay and the employment status of workers as much as possible. Organizing across trades, they had little use for job control; and organizing industry-wide across employers, they preferred centralized collective bargaining to make the economic situation of workers as independent from that of their employer as possible. Rather than challenging the right of employers to reorganize work and introduce new technology, industrial unions defended the occupational skills of their members through involvement in industrial training and public labor market policy, and their workplace-specific skills by pressing for legal employment protection.

Political-industrial unionism, with its preferences for the standardization of employment contracts and of the relationship between skill, effort, and pay, turned out to be highly compatible with the bureaucratic-hierarchical management of "Fordist" work organizations. At the heart of what might be called the *Fordist compromise* between large mass production firms and broad-based industrial trade unions was the acceptance of *negotiated flexibility* by workers in exchange for standardization of employment and working conditions within and across firms as well as over time, insulating workers and their families from market fluctuations and giving them as much economic security as a free labor market can sustain. Unlike craft and general unions, industrial unions in Continental Europe conceded to firms high internal flexibility in the deployment of labor, as long as it was compensated by external rigidity in the form of employment security and by rights to information and consulta-

tion, and sometimes shared decision-making, enabling unions to influence employers' management of labor ("industrial democracy"; Rogers and Streeck 1995).

In countries where political democracy arrived much after industrialization, as in Japan and other Asian countries, unions organized, if at all, as *enterprise unions*. Like industrial unions, enterprise unions organize all workers in a given workplace; unlike them, their domain is confined to one employer only. Historically, enterprise unions reflect an early loss of craft independence and a capture of skilled workers in internal labor markets, at a time when unionization was still suppressed. Japanese internal labor markets are based, not on the power of unions, but on an agreement among large firms to combat the fluctuation of skilled labor by hiring at entry level only. This made it de facto impossible for workers to quit, while making dismissal for disciplinary reasons a severe sanction in the hands of employers. In the period after World War II, the bonding of workers to their employer was reinforced by a seniority wage system that pays young workers below their productivity in exchange for payment above productivity in their older years. To protect workers against employer opportunism, enterprise unions and large Japanese companies, after intense conflicts, agreed on a largely informal system of "lifetime employment." This forms the capstone of the integration of workers in the "enterprise community" of large Japanese firms, and its vigorous defense constitutes the main raison d'être of enterprise unions. Together enterprise unionism, the seniority wage system, and lifetime employment make for unique flexibility of firms in the internal deployment of labor, due to complete detachment of the organization of work from occupational skills and an unlimited possibility for managements to deploy broad general and high workplace-specific skills in optimal combination (Aoki 1988).

Enterprise unions derive their organizational security primarily from employer recognition. In Japan in the 1950s and 1960s, firms that found their unions too radical managed to replace them with more compliant "second unions." Reflecting the structure of Japanese labor markets, enterprise unions have only weak links across workplace boundaries, to political parties or union confederations. Most of the functions performed in Europe by public policy and the welfare state are in Japan internalized in the private welfare regimes of large firms, including large parts of social security and, of course, employment protection and labor market policy. Unions there-

TABLE 3. Types of Trade Unions, Labor Markets, Employment Relations, and Political Action

	Skills	*Union Structure*	*Work Organization*	*Labor Market*	*Employment*	*Union Security*	*Political Action*
Craft union	Skilled, transportable, union-controlled	Particularistic, fragmented by trade	Job control	External, occupational	Job by job	Preentry closed shop	Voluntarism, "free collective bargaining"
General union	Unskilled	Incompletely encompassing	Bureaucracy job control and seniority	Mainly external, general	At will	Postentry closed shop	Limited, due to voluntaristic tradition
Industrial union	All skills partly workplace-specific, contested control	Encompassing, "class-based"	Bureaucracy, negotiated flexibility	External-occupational and internal	Protected	Legal and political institutionalization	Political and industrial action in different combinations, tripartism
Enterprise union	All skills workplace-specific, employer-controlled	"Enterprise community"	Bureaucracy, autonomous working groups	Internal	Lifetime	"Enterprise community"	Nonpolitical

fore have little reason to get involved in the public sphere. There is also little connection between union activities at the workplace and the political activities of national confederations, which have a postwar history of extreme instability. Mostly this was due to their radical-leftist politics and the unending factional struggles to which the former gave rise, reflecting both the marginal political status of union confederations and their lack of rapport with affiliated enterprise unions.

Unions in Politics

Different types of unions rely to different degrees and in different ways on the state for their organizational survival ("union security") and for political support in regulating labor supply, labor demand, and the employment relationship (for many others see Bean 1995; table 3). Craft unions and, forced by circumstances, general unions in craft-dominated environments adhere to a *voluntaristic* mode of action based on fragmented sectional organization and free collective bargaining. Apart perhaps from political and legal guarantees of the right to organize, voluntaristic unionism favors state abstention from the regulation of labor markets and employment. Negotiated "fringe benefits" are preferred over legislated welfare entitlements, not least since the latter are available also to nonmembers. Lasting suspicion of a liberal state unlikely to offer unions more than reluctant toler-

ation makes state-free voluntary organization backed by sectional market power appear the most reliable basis for effective representation of workers. In the twentieth century, early dominance of craft unionism typically issued in adversarial, fragmented, "pluralist" patterns of industrial relations, with a tendency toward multiunionism and competitive bargaining. Adversarial industrial relations combined with a minimalist liberal welfare state (Esping-Andersen 1990) that left trade unions with strong bargaining power space to negotiate significant additional benefits for their members.

Industrial unionism, by comparison, goes together with broad and heterogeneous organization. Not beholden to a well-to-do labor aristocracy and typically aligned with progressive political parties, industrial unions tended to be receptive to egalitarian ideologies, which made them support *erga omnes* extension of collective agreements and universalistic social policies benefiting all members of the working class and, indeed, the citizenry as a whole. At the same time, regarding themselves and wanting to be regarded as representatives, not just of their members, but of all workers in their industry or society, political-industrial unions faced difficult free-rider problems. This forced them to base their organizational security in large part on legal rights[15] and political support, such as state facilitation of collective bargaining or corporatist participation in the administration of vocational training or public social security funds.

From early on, industrial unions had to define and continuously redefine a delicate balance between industrial and political action, collective bargaining and social policy, benefits for their members and welfare state provisions for citizens, and independent organizing capacities and state support. The result differed considerably between countries and over time, although generally it involved a "sharing of public spaces" between unions and the state (Crouch 1993). In Scandinavia politically undivided industrial unions remained closely linked into an equally politically unified socialist labor movement that managed to establish lasting political hegemony over its bourgeois opposition. This issued in a combination of a social-democratic, universalistic welfare state guaranteeing citizens a high "social wage," with state-free but highly centralized and economically responsible collective bargaining, which was in turn underpinned by an extensive active labor market policy. Lasting control of the labor movement over the power resources of the state enabled Swedish unions to accomplish their objectives by means of "democratic class struggle"—through elections and government policies—and without much industrial conflict (Korpi 1983).

On the European Continent, by comparison, unions were for a long time divided as the representation of the religious and political cleavages of their time of origin in their organizational structures "froze" (Ebbinghaus and Visser 2000). In addition, socialist movements split during World War I and in the interwar period. Where political divisions among unions survived, as in the countries of the Mediterranean, where late industrialization limited the opportunities for independent collective bargaining, industrial relations tended to become a vehicle of general political confrontation and contestation, with union activities often subservient to the strategies and tactics of the parties to which they were aligned. Due to conservative political dominance, the emerging welfare states of these countries also differed from the Scandinavian type in that they supported the traditional family system and were designed to preserve rather than eliminate traditional status differentials.

Conservative welfare states formed also in countries like Germany and the Netherlands, where strong Catholic influence coincided with lasting divisions among unions along religious and political lines and stood in the way of political hegemony of social democratic parties. Still, after World War II, as national economies and societies were rebuilt and religious and political cleavages attenuated, industrial relations became corporatist and cooperative. Trade unionism, just as in Sweden and, with time, in Italy, became accepted as a central pillar of the emerging "coordinated market economy" of the postwar settlement outside the Anglo-American world. In Germany, the right to free collective bargaining became enshrined in the constitution, assigning a major role in economic policymaking to unions and employer associations in spite of a basically conservative political environment.

Political-industrial unionism in its various permutations was one of the foundations of the "democratic corporatism" of the 1970s and 1980s (Wilensky 2002): a labor-inclusive political regime featuring parliamentary democracy, strong social democratic parties, centralized trade unions and employer associations, tripartite economic policymaking in a negotiated economy, and an extensive social welfare state. From the perspective of pluralist democratic theory, centralized and monopolistic interest associations, including trade unions, as they existed in a number of countries outside the Anglo-American world, appeared to be an empirical anomaly in need of explanation and justification. Gerhard Lehmbruch's work on "liberal corporatism" showed that corporatist interest representation was not only compatible with liberal democracy but, like other nonmajoritarian provisions in democratic systems, helped societies live with deeply rooted social and political cleavages (Lehmbruch 1974, 1977). Similarly, Philippe Schmitter's work on "neocorporatism" emphasized the contribution of a highly organized civil society to the governability of modern democracies (Schmitter 1974). Essentially, corporatist integration of trade unions in the political economies of the time included participation in tripartite national policymaking, also referred to as "concertation" and dealing especially with incomes policies, as well as in subnational parastate institutions of functional self-government, such as labor market policy boards or social insurance funds (for a general overview see Streeck and Kenworthy 2003). Both represented different versions of compromise between government policy and collective bargaining, and between political parties and trade unions. In retrospect, the neocorporatism of the 1970s and 1980s represented the high point of the inclusion of organized labor in the political and economic governance of the modern nation-state (Goldthorpe 1984).

Finally, in Japan enterprise unions remained nonpolitical, the ideological battles among their national federations notwithstanding, and their organizational security continued to depend on voluntary recognition by employers. In this they resembled American unions, just as the minimalist welfare state of Japan resembled the liberal welfare state of the United States. Industrial relations were, however, cooperative rather than adversarial, reflecting the community of fate between workers and employers in strictly demarcated internal labor markets. In addition, unlike Anglo-American countries Japan is a coordinated market economy that, however, differs from Continental Europe and Scandinavia in that coordination takes place largely through the state at the exclusion of unions. But as enterprise unions are inseparably linked to lifetime employment, which remains the cornerstone of social peace in Japan in the absence of a functioning external labor market and a more than minimal public welfare state, Japanese unions seem for the time being safely established in large firms even without party-political or legal backing.

As Ebbinghaus shows after careful examination of current typologies (2002a, 89), types of trade unions and industrial relations are linked to different types of welfare states ("regimes of social protection") and different models of capitalism ("regimes of production"), but only imperfectly. Cooperative industrial relations are likely to occur only in nonliberal coordinated market economies (Japan, Scandinavia, Germany, and the Netherlands), but in some such economies, like France and Italy, industrial relations are politically polarized and contested. Voluntaristic industrial relations emphasizing free collective bargaining and state abstention exist only in liberal capitalism and come together with liberal-residual welfare states (Britain, Ireland, the United States). But in one country, Japan, a liberal-residual welfare state coexists with cooperative industrial relations and a nonliberal production regime. Finally, cooperative industrial relations based on political-industrial trade unions rather than enterprise unions, while always combined with nonliberal production regimes, may exist alongside either a conservative welfare state where economic coordination takes place on a sectoral level (Germany, the Netherlands), or a universalistic welfare state where the economy is centrally coordinated (Sweden, Denmark).

Unions in the Economy

There is a broad literature on the economic effects of trade unions. Generally unionization is regarded as ambivalent for economic performance. Research and theory know positive and negative

TABLE 4.   A Schematic Presentation of the Economic Effects of Trade Unions

	Positive Effects	Negative Effects
Micro level	High trust, productivity	Low trust, rigidity
Macro level	Wage moderation, stable growth	Distributional conflict, disequilibrium

effects of union organization and action, at both micro and macro level. In some accounts the positive effects cannot be had without the negative ones, making the true effect of unionism highly contingent on economic and social circumstances (table 4).

As pointed out above, at the micro level of the firm, formalization of rights and obligations limits the flexibility of open employment contracts. At the same time, it is only through some form of regulation, joint or otherwise, that open contracts of employment are compatible with workers having trust in the employer—which in turn is a condition of informal cooperation in pursuit of higher productivity. Of course low trust may also be a *cause* of unionization, just as unionization may destroy paternalistic understandings of mutual obligations of employers and employees (Fox 1974). At macro level, collective bargaining, to the extent that its results differ from those that a free market would generate, may cause inefficient factor allocation, as evidenced in inflation, unemployment, and low growth. But a high price of labor may also force employers to increase productivity, with collective bargaining as in the Swedish model of the 1960s and 1970s operating as a "productivity whip" (Gourevitch et al. 1984). High and equal wages may also serve as a "benevolent constraint," making employers invest in skill and sophisticated quality products (Streeck 1991).

The economic literature offers two basic models to understand the economic effects of trade unions, Olson's theory of collective action (1971) and the exit-and-voice model suggested originally by Freeman and Medoff (1984). The former has been particularly attractive to sociologists and political scientists as it seems to make, not just the economic effects of trade unions, but also the substantive interests represented by them contingent on unions' organizational form. The fundamental distinction is between fragmented and encompassing organization, and the key factor is the strategic capacity of collective actors to internalize the external costs of what they do. The logic is the same at the micro as at the macro level. At the former, small unions of craft workers stand to lose more from technological change diminishing their status and diluting their skills than what would be their share in the common gain from restructuring and higher productivity. Encompassing industrial unions, by comparison, would internalize the losses suffered by the majority as a result of "restrictive practices" benefiting a small minority. Their membership, being broadly based and heterogeneous, would on average benefit from higher productivity.

Basically the same holds for the national level, where narrow unions, or interest groups in general, have an incentive to behave like "distributional coalitions" at the expense of the common good. Encompassing groups, by comparison, tend to identify with the common good out of their own self-interest (Olson 1982, 1983). For this reason they will do what they can to promote stable growth by, for example, not asking for excessive wage increases making for inefficient allocation and lost growth. While for Olson encompassing organization is only a second-best solution compared to free market allocation, his theory was much welcomed by proponents of centralized wage bargaining in a neocorporatist framework.[16] Indeed there are, or were for some time, good reasons to argue that with centralized setting of a society-wide wage norm inflation is easier to contain than with decentralized bargaining (Calmfors 1993; Calmfors and Driffill 1988; Flanagan, Soskice, and Ulman 1983; Kenworthy 1996; Newell and Symons 1987; Soskice 1990; Ulman and Flanagan 1971). Decentralized wage setting runs into the same collective action problems as interest representation by craft unions on the supply side and tends to become competitive and sectional, in the way of a prisoner's dilemma game. The advantages of centralized wage bargaining seem to prevail even in countries with an independent central bank and seemed to last well into the 1990s (Streeck and Hassel 2003).

Freeman and Medoff's general model of the economic effects of trade unions focuses on the micro level and builds on Hirschmann's distinction between "voice" and exit" as two alternative expressions of dissatisfaction. Where there are no unions, the only safe way for workers to express discontent with management is by quitting. But labor turnover is expensive as workplace-specific human capital is lost and the costs of searching for replacements are high. Freeman and Medoff show empirically that in the United States, turnover is lower in unionized firms, while productivity is higher. To them this indicates that disgruntled workers in unionized workplaces can settle their grievances by speaking through their union, and that settling such grievances increases worker satisfaction, resulting not just in lower turnover but also in better work. The model emphasizes the importance of socially accepted channels of communication for mutual trust, and thus for extended exchanges like the cooperation of workers to improving productivity. From here it is short way to what one might call an economics of cooperation (Kenworthy 1995; see also Leibenstein 1987). The drawback is that, while unionized firms in which workers have voice are more productive than nonunionized firms, they are also less profitable due to the redistributive activities in which unions also engage (Freeman and Medoff 1984). The macroeconomic consequences are likely to be conditional on a wide variety of factors.

A final model of unions' economic effects may be derived from John R. Commons's insight in his *History of Labor in the United States* (1919–35) that unions can distort market allocation of wages in line with collective norms of fairness only where they organize all firms supplying a given product market. Where this is not the case, the wage bargain comes under market pressure. So, one can add, does the union, which may be constrained to shift from a distributional and antagonistic to a cooperative stance, entering in a cross-class alliance with the employers that it organizes against those employers that are outside its jurisdiction. Such collaboration may be either protectionist or productivistic. The Japanese firm, as a competitive community of economic fate, is one example of this, and others are unions in small countries or export-dependent sectors. In sites like these, the class interests represented by unions become confounded with producer or sectoral interests shared with employers, resulting in joint pursuit of higher productivity and competitiveness. In recent years, with the economy becoming more international, this seems to have become even more widespread than in the past. Industrial cross-class alliances are similar to political cross-class alliances, for example in the creation of the welfare state, as they have recently been discovered almost everywhere by a revisionist strand of social policy research. The attempt is to show that the modern welfare state is not so much a distributive achievement of the organized working class, as a joint construction, mostly inspired by employers responding to the natural imperfections of labor markets, to make national or sectoral economies more efficient and competitive (for an outstanding recent example see Swenson 2002).

THE RISE AND DECLINE OF TRADE UNIONS

Unions emerged in conflict with economic liberalism and political authoritarianism, striving simultaneously for economic regulation and political freedom. As a result they were originally treated as conspiracies against free trade, the state, or both. But as unions established themselves as effective labor market cartels, they also became suppliers of labor to those employers willing to deal with them, and in this capacity slowly turned into "managers of industrial discontent" (Flanders 1970). Similarly, while unions represented the interests of a class often opposed to the advance of capitalism, their toleration in the course of democratization contributed to transforming liberal into organized capitalism, and was central to the institutionalization of compromise between capital and labor.

Early unions saw themselves as democratic organizations of self-help and self-government of workers independent from the feudal or bourgeois predemocratic state. Often they belonged to broader social movements that included political parties, consumer cooperatives, mutual assistance funds, educational associations, sports clubs, and the like (Ebbinghaus 1995). While unions generally resented interference of the state and the law in their internal organization and activities, they differed widely in structure and ideology. Syndicalist and anarcho-syndicalist unions, which in a number of countries remained significant well into the twentieth century, regarded themselves as constituent units of a direct democracy of producers set to replace both capitalist employers and the bureaucratic apparatus of the modern state. These traditions, which were equally opposed to capitalism and to parliamentary democracy and favored "direct action" over collective bargaining and political-electoral lobbying, culminated in the militant council movements of World War I and the revolutions following it, in the Soviet Union and elsewhere.

Integration of unions in democratic capitalism, and their recognition by governments and employers, was greatly advanced by the two world wars. Economic mobilization and the governance of the war economy required the collaboration of union leaders, which in many countries came to be co-opted into positions of quasi-public authority. In addition, enlisted soldiers had to be promised a better life in a fairer society upon their return from the battlefields, and in defeated countries traditional elites were replaced in the aftermath of war by liberal or socialist governments. Generally the end of World War I brought political democratization and, precipitated by the threat of socialist revolution, widespread acceptance of collective bargaining. But the first postwar settlement proved fragile in countries like Germany, Japan, Italy, and Spain, where unionism was soon suppressed by authoritarian regimes. Similarly, in the Soviet Union workers' councils were incorporated in the machinery of a repressive state, and unions were turned into "transmission belts" from the state to the working class. In the United States, by comparison, the New Deal extended union organizing rights, while the Swedish Social Democratic government of the 1930s and the British war cabinet of the 1940s began to develop the contours of the labor-inclusive Keynesian welfare state of the second postwar settlement.

The golden age of capitalism after 1945 saw the worldwide ascendance of a "mature" type of union (Lester 1958), centralized at the level of the national state and representing the interests of union members simultaneously through collective bargaining and political-electoral lobbying within the confines of capitalism and parliamentary democracy. This development was part of the consolidation of democratic capitalism and the nation-state in the countries under American hegemony, where legal recognition of unions and free collective bargaining, extensive social welfare provision, a sizable public sector, and politically guaranteed full employment made possible the coexistence of liberal democracy and a market economy. The normalization of unionism under "embedded liberalism" (Ruggie 1982) coincided with national regulation and standardization of the employment relationship and the social status of wage earners, which in turn corresponded to the advance of industrial mass-production. Legal and political regulation of labor markets, introduced to insulate employment and employment conditions as much as possible from economic fluctuations, reinforced union power. The economic and political role of unions appeared clearly defined and securely established in a Fordist economy generating continuing growth based on economies of scale and on steadily expanding mass consumption fueled by yearly increases in real wages; organized on a sharp categoric distinction between a majority of dependent wage earners and a minority of employers; and gradually restructuring from small companies to ever larger factory organizations using advanced mechanical technology.

The Disintegration of the Postwar Settlement

The crisis of trade unionism began with rising inflation and, in many countries, increasing worker militancy in the late 1960s and early 1970s. It proceeded in the 1980s, after the corporatist interlude in countries outside the United States, with a shift from Keynesian to monetarist economic policies, deregulation and privatization, the opening up of national markets to international competition, and generally the withdrawal of states from the kind of economic intervention that had become established in most countries between 1945 and the early 1960s. Political change was accelerated by the demise of Communism in the late 1980s, which eliminated systemic opposition to capitalism, making it less necessary for governments and employers in the West to make concessions to worker collectivism. National trajectories differ, and so do the effects of the departure from the postwar political economy on the status, the activities, and the future of trade unions.

Everywhere the 1960s and 1970s revealed a fundamental tension in the simultaneous commitment of postwar democratic capitalism to politically guaranteed full employment and an extensive welfare state on the one hand and free collective bargaining on the other. As Keynesian macroeconomic management in effect insured unions against adverse employment consequences of high wage settlements, labor market discipline eroded and inflationary pressures accumulated, giving rise to even higher wage claims especially in environments with historically high rates of economic growth. Moreover, during a wave of unofficial strikes in 1968 and 1969 it became apparent that free collective bargaining under politically guaranteed full employment potentially undermined the unions themselves, whose leaders were beginning to lose control over their members. By the early 1970s at the latest, governments throughout the OECD (Organization for Economic Cooperation and Development) world were looking for ways of restoring social discipline and economic stability.

The corporatist policies of the 1970s, which were attempted even in the United Kingdom, were to shore up the Keynesian political economy through a renewed political compact between governments, unions, and, to some extent, employers. After statutory wage and price controls had failed, governments placed their hope on voluntary agreements with union leaders, buying wage moderation in return for expanded social policies, improved organizational privileges, participation rights at the workplace, legislated employment protection, government commitments to growth-promoting macroeconomic or industrial policies, and so on. However, at the time of the second oil shock at the latest, it had become apparent that the concessions unions demanded for their cooperation in efforts to contain inflation were not only expensive but often had—long term—inflationary effects as well, not to mention the fact that union members more often than not failed to honor the commitments their leaders had made on their behalf (Streeck and Hassel 2003; Streeck and Kenworthy 2003).

The late 1970s saw a deadlock in the political economy of democratic capitalism, which manifested itself in a coincidence of high inflation, low growth, and rising unemployment. It was resolved only when the electoral success of the U.K. government under Margaret Thatcher disproved the fundamental orthodoxy of postwar liberalism: that unemployment above a low level of 3 or 4 percent not only meant sure electoral defeat of the government of the day, but was also bound to destabilize liberal democracy, just as it had done in the interwar period. Keynesianism gave way as the leading economic policy doctrine to a pervasive monetarism modeled on the policy of the independent German central bank since 1974 and of the U.S. Federal Reserve since 1979, the last year of the Carter administration. Moreover, to revitalize the capitalist political economy governments—at different paces, in different ways, and with different proximate causes—departed further from the postwar bargain by accepting and promoting a deep liberalization of national economies, including deregulation of product and factor markets, privatization of public enterprises, opening of domestic markets for foreign competition, internationalization of capital markets, retreat from sectoral industrial policies, and consolidation of public budgets. By the end of the century, Western economies were significantly more liberal than they had been at the beginning of the crisis in the 1970s, in that far more prices were now allowed to fluctuate freely and economic adjustment was sought, not through government intervention, but through flexible responses of market participants to competitive pressures.

Trade Unions in a Postindustrial Political Economy

Today trade unions in all industrialized countries are struggling to defend their postwar positions of power and influence.[17] Most unions are losing members, and organizational density is declining widely (Ebbinghaus 2002b; Ebbinghaus and Visser 2000; Visser 1992; Western 1995, 1997). In countries like the United States and the United Kingdom, hostile governments used the opportunity of economic restructuring in the 1980s to withdraw institutional supports for collective bargaining and union organizing. Elsewhere the political and institutional context remained friendlier to unions, and where this was the case, membership declined more slowly. Still, the adverse effects of changing labor markets and social structures made unions more dependent than ever for their organizing capacity on favorable institutional conditions and politically guaranteed provisions of organizational security.[18]

Patterns of postindustrial transformation, and possibly decay, of trade unions differ between world regions, nations, sectors, and even localities. Whether current differences amount to more than diverse paths to deunionization, leading to eventual disappearance of organized worker collectivism as an industrial and political force, must be considered an open question. Indications are that cross-national differences in rates of unionization have recently been rising, resulting in an increase in diversity that may, however, just be temporary. Generally, there seems to a tendency toward generational and sectoral encapsulation of trade union membership in a shrinking segment of the workforce and the economy (Ebbinghaus and Visser 2000; Ebbinghaus 2002b). Union members are growing older on average, as density among younger workers tends to be low and falling. With the decline of the two main milieus supportive of unionization, Fordist industry and the Keynesian public sector, most workers are now employed in settings where they have few contacts if any with union members. The structure of union membership in most countries resembles the employment structure of the 1970s, confining unions in a segment of the workforce that is in rapid demographic, if not economic, decline.

Union retreat from the positions and policies of the postwar settlement proceeds gradually in most countries, with unions largely living off their postwar institutional power resources. While trade unions try to adjust to the constraints and opportunities of a changing social and economic context, most governments refrain from direct attacks on their rights and organizations, as unions may still inflict considerable damage on hostile governments or, for that matter, employers. In fact many governments continue to find themselves constrained to seek accommodation with national unions, for example with respect to wage bargaining, given that high unemployment still involves electoral liabilities. Many employers also shy away from direct confrontation, in consideration of their vulnerability on more competitive product markets. Some European governments in the 1990s managed to secure union wage restraint in support of their countries' accession to European monetary union and its international stabilization regime (Regini 2000).

Especially in the 1980s, when the transition from Keynesianism to monetarism was still under way, unions and employers in a number of Continental European welfare states managed to get governments to make social insurance funds available to reduce unemployment by cutting the labor supply, awarding redundant workers early retirement or disability pensions, or placing them in labor market policy programs where they no longer counted as unemployed (Ebbinghaus 2002a). In such countries, labor supply management by means of social policy began to take the place of aggregate demand management through fiscal and monetary policy, just like the latter insuring unions against negative employment effects of labor market rigidities and overshooting wage settlements (Mares 2001). This was particularly likely where unions, usually together with employers, shared in the administration of social security and where governments had to fear electoral retaliation for cutbacks in welfare state spending.

Many of the social programs that later came to underwrite labor shedding and early exit from work had been introduced for different purposes in the Keynesian years, often as side-payments for union wage moderation. Over time they became acquired social rights. In the post-Keynesian European welfare state, voter dissatisfaction with cutbacks in social spending, especially among pensioners and people of preretirement age, became the equivalent of worker unrest in the Keynesian era, partly shifting the power base of the unions from those seeking work to those seeking retirement. State policies subsidizing a high-equality, low-activity labor market-cum–social policy regime

(Streeck 2001) are expensive and may with time unbalance public budgets. Moreover, they may give rise to distributional conflicts with taxpayers and, where social policy is funded by payroll taxes, further reduce employment by raising the non-wage labor costs of those remaining in work (Ebbinghaus 2001).

The Postindustrial Transformation of Labor Markets and Employment

Both labor supply and labor demand are changing in advanced countries, on their own and in reaction to one another. Current trends differ between countries and sectors, and exceptions from generalizations must always be admitted. Still, union control over the labor supply is weakening throughout the developed industrial world, and labor demand is more than ever in the postwar period driven by changing markets and technologies rather than by union or government intervention. Even where governments continue to defend the labor market regime inherited from the industrial era, including the position of trade unions, they seem to be unable or unwilling to make labor supply and demand fit that regime. As a result the capacity of the latter to govern employment relations is vanishing.

Labor supply in the postindustrial age is shaped by the educational revolution that began in the 1960s, which vastly increased the number of job seekers with academic training. Improved access to education also contributed to a secular rise in labor market participation of women, which in addition reflected changing social values and, later, economic pressure on households. Moreover, most countries today experience an increase in immigration, which expands their supply of unskilled labor, and welfare state reforms have lowered the reservation wage and increased the pressure especially on the low-skilled to seek employment. Overall, recent decades have seen a significant *growth* of the supply of labor to labor markets, sometimes as a result of deliberate public policies, accompanied by rising *polarization* in the human capital endowment of labor market participants.

Trends in *labor demand,* in turn, include declining mass labor markets for, mostly male, manual workers with low or intermediate skills who were the main constituency of postwar trade unions. In part this is because labor-intensive manual production can today be relocated to low-wage countries, given modern information and communication technology and low transportation costs. Employ-

ment growth has shifted to the private service sector, which employs both an underclass of, mostly immigrant, unskilled workers and an upperclass of highly specialized knowledge workers with advanced education. In both categories the share of women is high. At the same time there is in most countries stagnation and even decline in public employment, due to the end of welfare state expansion. Employment is also declining in sheltered sectors, as a result of the privatization of public services, especially but not exclusively in European countries. Private manufacturing and the public and sheltered sectors used to be union strongholds, whereas in the private service sector, unions were historically weak.

Moreover, in response to both technological change and a changed labor supply, demand for advanced workplace-unspecific formal skills is rising. Work tends to be organized in smaller, more autonomous units with lower hierarchies and less hierarchical decision-making, like work teams and small independent firms. Work units are more than before exposed to market pressures and coordinate their activities both within and across enterprise boundaries more by contractual than by hierarchical means. There also is a tendency to organize work in project groups put together at the beginning and disbanded upon the completion, of a collective task, with managerial responsibilities, for example for job assignment and cost control, largely integrated in direct production work (Cappelli et al. 1997).

Again with the necessary qualifications, interrelated changes in labor supply and demand seem to affect the operation and the institutions of *labor markets* in similar ways throughout the countries of the post–World War II settlement. Common tendencies include the following.

An increasing wage spread, with growing returns to higher education, and generally a polarization of labor markets between insiders with good market opportunities who also tend to be covered by collective bargaining and protective social policies, and mostly unskilled outsiders with little access to formal employment and little support from unions and from a welfare state designed to protect employed workers and their families (Alderson and Nielsen 2002).

A declining willingness of employers to offer long-term or lifetime employment to others than a small elite of core workers, accompanied by a decline in employment security and in prospects of internal advancement and promotion, and subsequently an increase in the significance of external as compared to internal labor markets (Abraham 1990).

More "atypical" employment, such as part-time work, fixed-term contracts in countries with strong employment protection, or employment with temporary work agencies, or casual employment (for the United States see Kalleberg, Reskin, and Hudson 2000). In a reversal of the historical trend, there also is a tendency to move from contracts of employment to contracts of work, often to evade social security taxes. Forms of atypical employment differ between countries, but their common denominator seems to be a general increase in the diversity of contractual arrangements reflecting diversity of jobs, human capital, and market conditions.

Growing informal employment due to immigration or, in European welfare states with compressed wage differentials and social security taxes that raise the price of labor, high unemployment combined with an increase in underground employment.

Generally with respect to role expectations, work ethos and allocation of economic risk, a blurring of the distinction between the status of wage earner and that of self-employed entrepreneur or professional, or between employee and employer. This is accompanied by an increase in self-employment in many countries, a growing emphasis on entrepreneurialism, even within traditional employment relationships, and a shift of the costs of training from employers. It also coincides with an increase in the share of an employee's income that depends on effort or results, of the individual or of the organization, or of both. The effect is higher variation of income over time as well as between individuals.

While these tendencies are not equally strong everywhere, and some may be at odds with others, workforces in developed industrial countries are more diverse today than they were 20 years ago; polarization of the labor supply between growing numbers of highly skilled and unskilled job seekers proceeds; the value of increasingly diversified and idiosyncratic human capital in a postindustrial "knowledge society" is still rising; labor markets have become more competitive; unemployment is high, and informal employment at the lower end of the labor market is growing. Moreover, as the costs of underwriting stable employment and a high reservation wage become excessive for cash-strapped welfare states exposed to international markets, governments are adopting policies of labor market flexibility (Boyer 1988) and "activation" rather than "decommodification" of labor, making it less possible for trade unions to rely on the welfare state for suspension of competition in labor markets, and generally for protection of workers from the fluctuations of labor and product markets.

Where the old institutions still hold, with the support of the state and legal order, less standardized types of employment beyond the categorical distinction between wage earners and self-employed employers emerge outside of them. Within work arrangements one finds a partial return of the spectrum of employment relations that was suppressed at the height of industrialism; external labor markets gain importance and become increasingly flexible, while internal labor markets become less institutionalized and more like external labor markets (Osterman 1994); and economic rewards are governed less by entitlement than by market fluctuations, less by status rights than by contingent economic results, and more by individual effort or luck than by collective regulation.

Diversity or Convergence?

At first glance, paradoxically but not dissimilarly from other spheres of social life, the present period of accelerating "globalization" may be one of growing diversity of labor markets and trade unions, compared to the decades after World War II. Diversity seems likely to increase, particularly if labor market institutions evolve along with national systems of capitalism in their search for comparative advantage resulting from specialization (Berger and Dore 1996; Crouch and Streeck 1997; Hall and Soskice 2001). There is also likely to be more internal diversity within national systems, as these will have to allow for more local or sectoral variation and flexibility (Katz and Darbishire 2000).

On the other hand, while especially in the former countries of democratic corporatism the institutional supports that unions won in the twentieth century still exist, and may yet exist for some time if only because of inertia, labor markets everywhere seem to have become less amenable to regulation by trade unions. In a nutshell, the numbers are rising of those who have enough market power to do without collective organization, as well as of those who have too little market power to be capable of it. This seems to be producing a growing gap between the position of unions in the political and legal order and their position in the economy and the labor market, resulting in a mismatch between societal institutions and local contractual constructions, or between macro- and microinstitutional arrangements. While the former still emphasize standardization, specification, and formalization, the latter may increasingly involve customized arrangements, diffuse understandings, and informal agreements. Moreover, to the extent that they concern easily replaceable workers with little human capital, they are likely to undercut the conditions that were customary in the more centrally regulated labor markets of the industrial era.

This is not to say that the labor markets of the future will be unregulated. Labor remains an imperfect commodity and continues to require rules enabling sellers of labor power to reconcile market participation and social commitments, just as open employment contracts will need formal and informal mechanisms of governance that facilitate their flexible and legitimate adjustment to changing conditions. But as the division of labor becomes ever more complex, and differences in human capital endowment and market position become more difficult for institutional intervention to override, how much and what form of regulation a worker will get may increasingly be determined by his or her market position. Private government by collective intermediaries like trade unions may be squeezed out by a liberalizing state from above and an expanding market from below, clearing the way for a new wave of commodification of labor in response to dynamically changing economic and technological conditions. To the extent that freer labor markets require new if not more rules,[19] sophisticated civil law and regulatory law—for example on equal employment opportunities—may be stepping in for the corporatist middlemen of the industrial era. Not only would this allow for more customized contracts, adapting the governance of the employment relationship to a new economic environment that puts a premium on individual initiative and investment in human capital. It also would eliminate the particularism of collective interest organizations that, in a more diverse and dynamic society, are unlikely again to be accepted as representing general interests in social progress, in favor of what seems to be increasingly regarded as a universal individual right to enter the market and compete.[20]

NOTES

I am grateful to Till Mueller-Schoell for competent research assistance, and to Britta Rehder for excellent advice when it was much needed.

1. In the subject index of the first edition of this handbook (Smelser and Swedberg 1994), one finds neither *unions* nor *trade unions* nor *labor unions.*

2. The foundational statement continues to be Granovet- ter 1992. On labor markets in economic sociology generally, see Swedberg in this volume.

3. For the treatment of markets in economic sociology—as real social relations of competition and cooperation—see Fligstein 1996; Leifer and White 1986; Swedberg 1994; and White 1981, 2002a.

4. For excellent overviews see Tilly and Tilly 1994; Granovetter 1995.

5. In other words, construing what in Durkheimian language are the "noncontractual conditions of contract" as originating in contractual agreement.

6. So does the law that shapes and is shaped by labor markets and employment relations. See Edelman and Stryker, this volume.

7. But compare the economist Clark Kerr, who writes of "institutional markets" characterized by "the substitution of institutional rules for frictions as the principal delineator of job market limits; of institutional and leadership comparisons for physical movement as the main basis for the interrelatedness of wage markets; and of policies of unions, employers, and government for the traditional action of market forces as the more significant source of wage movements. . . . Formal rules, consciously selected, supplant informal practices determined by market conditions. Nor are policies solely developed by the private governments of industry and organized labor, but also by public government," etc. (1977, 42).

8. For an entirely arbitrary sample see the contributions to Regini 1992.

9. Making the contract of employment a highly formalized case of a "relational contract" (on the concept see Macneil 1980).

10. In the language of institutional economics, this turns the labor contract into a "partial gift exchange" (Akerlof 1986), to the extent that workers contribute their labor "voluntarily." Sociology has generated a huge literature on the relationship between work organizations and trade unions that cannot be summarized in a chapter on labor markets and trade unions.

11. For an impressively radical incorporation of this fact into economic theory see Solow 1991.

12. To the extent that employers are interested in efficient labor markets and legitimate workplace authority, they may also be interested in fairness. This is the ultimate reason for the possibility of collective bargaining and of political and industrial inclusion of organized labor in a capitalist political economy.

13. To sociologists, unions promoting institutionalized labor market segmentation exhibit a double face, as agents of both equality and inequality; of social inclusion as well as social exclusion, or closure; and of universalism as well as particularism. In the political literature on trade unions, this is captured in distinctions like that between political unionism and business unionism.

14. In his book *A Theory of Employment Systems,* Marsden (1999) offers a sophisticated efficiency-theoretical analysis of work organization, i.e., of the division of labor and the structure of authority and joint regulation at the point of production. Work organization is treated as the result of an interaction between different types of work skills and labor markets, the need for both workers and employers to protect themselves against one another's opportunism, and the requirement of simple transaction rules that allow for efficient monitoring. Marsden can show that dependent on the national institutional context, this gives rise to different solutions that remain stable over time and are more or less uniformly adopted in their countries.

When the Taylorist organization of industrial work had reached its zenith in the 1970s, unions in a number of countries raised demands for new forms of work organization involving job enlargement, team working, worker involvement, direct participation, etc. To some extent this recalled past struggles over craft or bureaucratic control of the labor process. Especially in Scandinavian countries, demands for an improvement in the "quality of working life" were taken up by governments—which hoped for a shift of union policies toward nonmonetary "qualitative" objectives—and employers dissatisfied with declining productivity and product quality. In America, programs to improve the quality of working life were first put forward by management and were regarded with suspicion by unions, who were afraid of losing control over the wage-effort bargain. The movement dwindled away when rapid deindustrialization removed its cause and the return of unemployment again changed the priorities of workers, unions, and governments.

15. Ambivalent attitudes of trade unions toward the law as a repressive as well as supportive force may be reconstructed in terms of an economic sociology of law and legal practice, along the lines of the contribution of Edelman and Stryker to this volume.

16. For a cogent sociological formulation of the politics of union wage restraint see Pizzorno 1978, which emphasizes the conversion of (unrealistic) demands for redistribution into (realistic) demands for political compensations of wage moderation. On the comparative empirics of corporatist wage moderation and political exchange see Cameron 1984 and Castles 1987, for many others.

17. While in transition countries they seem to find it hard to get established in the first place (Bryant and Mokrzycki 1995).

18. The enormous literature on union density cannot be reviewed here. The research referred to above agrees that with time, institutional conditions have overall become more important determinants of unionization than the informal networks of social relations in occupational communities that seem to have dominated in the early history of trade unions. In other words, the determinants of union membership seem to have shifted from a union's "logic of membership" to its "logic of influence," i.e., the character of its relations with the state and employers. Institutional analyses have therefore superseded early econometric analyses that conceived of union membership as the result of individual decisions.

19. Paraphrasing the title of Steven Vogel's book on deregulation, *Freer Markets, More Rules* (1996).

20. This trajectory, of course, differs from that envisaged by the growing literature in the United States and Britain on a "revitalization" of trade unions as progressive-democratic popular movements (for impressive examples see Levi 2002; Voss and Sherman 2000). Unions have always attracted high expectations of intellectuals, and sometimes they have lived up to them. Intellectuals are also known for their belief in faith-healing. Today, however, it is far from clear if unions will still be able to fulfill their bread-and-butter functions in the labor market, and how. It is even less clear if the regulation of labor markets and employment can still be related to progressive politics in the centers of advanced postindustrial capitalism. Maybe the unions of the industrial age, with their combined economic and political roles, will dissolve in two separate and unrelated institutional equivalents, labor law and single-issue campaigns for social justice. If this were to happen, sociologists would at least have the concepts to account for it.

REFERENCES

Abraham, Katharine G. 1990. "Restructuring the Employment Relationship: The Growth of Market-Mediated Work Arrangements." Pp. 85–119 in *New Developments in the Labor Market: Toward a New Institutional Paradigm*, ed. Katherine G. Abraham and Robert B. McKersie. Cambridge: MIT Press.

Akerlof, George A. 1986. "Labor Contracts as Partial Gift Exchange." Pp. 66–92 in *Efficiency Wage Models of the Labor Market*, ed. George A. Akerlof and Janet L. Yellen. Cambridge: Cambridge University Press.

Alderson, Arthur S., and François Nielsen. 2002. "Globalization and the Great U-Turn: Income Inequality Trends in 16 OECD Countries." *American Journal of Sociology* 107:1244–99.

Aoki, Masahiko. 1988. *Information, Incentives, and Bargaining in the Japanese Economy.* Cambridge: Cambridge University Press.

Baron, James N., and William T. Bielby. 1980. "Bringing the Firm Back In: Stratification, Segmentation, and the Organization of Work." *American Sociological Review* 45:737–55.

Bartolini, Stefano. 2000. *The Political Mobilization of the European Left, 1860–1980.* Cambridge: Cambridge University Press.

Bean, Ron. 1994. *Comparative Industrial Relations: An Introduction to Cross-National Perspectives.* London: Routledge.

Becker, Gary S. 1957. *The Economics of Discrimination.* Chicago: University of Chicago Press.

Bendix, Reinhard. [1956] 1974. *Work and Authority in Industry: Ideologies of Management in the Course of Industrialization.* Berkeley and Los Angeles: University of California Press.

Berg, Ivar, ed. 1981. *Sociological Perspectives on Labor Market.* New York: Academic Press.

Berger, Suzanne, and Ronald Dore, eds. 1996. *National Diversity and Global Capitalism.* Ithaca, N.Y.: Cornell University Press.

Berger, Suzanne, and Michael J. Piore. 1980. *Dualism and Discontinuity in Industrial Societies.* Cambridge: Cambridge University Press.

Blau, Peter M. 1964. *Exchange and Power in Social Life.* New York: John Wiley and Sons.

Böhm-Bawerk, Eugen von. [1914] 1968. *Gesammelte Schriften.* Vol. 1, *Macht oder ökonomisches Gesetz?* Frankfurt am Main: Sauer und Auvermann. Trans. as "Control or Economic Law?" in *Shorter Classics of Böhm-Bawerk* (South Holland, Ill.: Libertarian Press, 1962), 147–99.

Bourdieu, Pierre. 2000. *Les structures sociale de l'économie.* Paris: Editions du Seuil.

Boyer, Robert. 1986. *La théorie de la régulation: Une analyse critique.* Paris: Editions La Decouverte.

———. 1988. *The Search for Labour Market Flexibility:*

The European Economies in Transition. Oxford: Clarendon Press.

Braverman, Harry. 1974. *Labor and Monopoly Capital: The Degradation of Work in the Twentieth Century.* New York: Monthly Review Press.

Brentano, Lujo. 1871–72. *Die Arbeitergilden der Gegenwart.* 2 vols. Leipzig: Duncker und Humblot.

Bryant, Chris G. A., and Edmund Mokrzycki, eds. 1995. *Democracy, Civil Society, and Pluralism in Comparative Perspective.* Warsaw: IFiS.

Burawoy, Michael. 1983. "Between the Labor Process and the State: The Changing Face of Factory Regimes under Advanced Capitalism." *American Sociological Review* 48:587–605.

Calmfors, Lars. 1993. "Centralization of Wage Bargaining and Macroeconomic Performance: A Survey." *OECD Economic Studies* 21:161–91.

Calmfors, Lars, and John Driffill. 1988. "Bargaining Structure, Corporatism, and Macroeconomic Performance." *Economic Policy* 6:14–61.

Cameron, David R. 1984. "Social Democracy, Corporatism, Labour Quiescence, and the Representation of Economic Interest in Advanced Capitalist Society." Pp. 143–78 in *Order and Conflict in Contemporary Capitalism*, ed. John H. Goldthorpe. Oxford: Clarendon Press.

Cappelli, Peter, Laurie Bassi, Harry Katz, David Knoke, Paul Osterman, and Michael Useem. 1997. *Change at Work.* Oxford: Oxford University Press.

Castles, Francis G. 1987. "Neo-corporatism and the 'Happiness Index,' or What Trade Unions Get for Their Cooperation." *European Journal of Political Research* 15:381–93.

Chamberlin, Edward H. 1950. *The Theory of Monopolistic Competition.* 6th ed. Cambridge: Cambridge University Press.

Clegg, Stewart, and David Dunkerley. 1980. *Organization, Class, and Control.* London: Routledge.

Coleman, James. 1991: "Matching Processes in the Labor Market." *Acta Sociologica* 34:3–12.

Commons, John R. 1919–35. *History of Labor in the United States.* 4 vols. New York: Macmillan.

———. 1924. *Legal Foundations of Capitalism.* New York: Macmillan.

Crouch, Colin, 1993. *Industrial Relations and European State Traditions.* Oxford: Clarendon Press.

Crouch, Colin, David Finegold, and Mari Sako. 1995. *Are Skills the Answer? The Political Economy of Skill Creation in Advanced Industrial Countries.* Oxford: Oxford University Press.

Crouch, Colin, and Alessandro Pizzorno, eds. 1978. *The Resurgence of Class Conflict in Western Europe since 1968.* London: Macmillan.

Crouch, Colin, and Wolfgang Streeck, eds. 1997. *Political Economy of Modern Capitalism: Mapping Convergence and Diversity.* London: Sage.

Doeringer, Peter B., and Michael J. Piore. 1971. *Internal Labor Markets and Manpower Analysis.* Lexington, Mass.: D. C. Heath.

Dore, Ronald. 1986. *Flexible Rigidities: Industrial Policy and Structural Adjustment in the Japanese Economy, 1970–80.* Stanford, Calif.: Stanford University Press.

———. 1987. *Taking Japan Seriously: A Confucian Perspective on Leading Economic Issues.* Stanford, Calif.: Stanford University Press.

Dunlop, John T. [1958] 1993. *Industrial Relations Systems.* Rev. ed. Cambridge: Harvard University Press.

———. 1994. "Organizations and Human Resources: Internal and External Markets." Pp. 375–400 in *Labor Economics and Industrial Relations,* ed. Clark Kerr and Paul D. Staudohar. Cambridge: Harvard University Press.

Durkheim, Émile. [1893] 1964. *The Division of Labor in Society.* Trans. George Simpson. New York: Free Press.

Ebbinghaus, Bernhard. 1995. "The Siamese Twins: Citizenship Rights, Cleavage Formation, and Party-Union Relations in Western Europe." *International Review of Social History* 40:51–89.

———. 2001. "The Political Economy of Early Retirement in Europe, Japan, and the USA." Pp. 76–101 in *Comparing Welfare Capitalism: Social Policy and Political Economy in Europe, Japan, and the USA,* ed. Bernhard Ebbinghaus and Philipp Manow. London: Routledge.

———. 2002a. "Exit from Labor: Reforming Early Retirement and Social Partnership in Europe, Japan, and the USA." Habilitation thesis, Faculty of Economics and Social Sciences, University of Cologne.

———. 2002b. "Trade Unions' Changing Role: Membership Erosion, Organisational Reform, and Social Partnership in Europe." *Industrial Relations Journal* 33:465–83.

Ebbinghaus, Bernhard, and Jelle Visser. 2000. "A Comparative Profile." Pp. 33–74 in *The Societies of Europe: Trade Unions in Western Europe since 1945,* ed. Peter Flora, Franz Kraus, and Franz Rothenbacher. London: Macmillan.

Edwards, Richard C., Michael Reich, and David M. Gordon, eds. 1979. *Labor Market Segmentation.* New York: Basic Books.

Esping-Andersen, Gøsta. 1990. *The Three Worlds of Welfare Capitalism.* Princeton: Princeton University Press.

Flanagan, Robert, David W. Soskice, and Lloyd Ulman. 1983. *Unionism, Economic Stabilization, and Incomes Policies: European Experience.* Washington, D.C.: Brookings Institution Press.

Flanders, Alan. 1970. *Management and Unions: The Theory and Reform of Industrial Relations.* London: Faber.

Fligstein, Neil. 1996. "Markets as Politics: A Political-Cultural Approach to Institutions." *American Sociological Review* 61:656–73.

Fox, Alan. 1974. *Beyond Contract: Work, Power, and Trust Relations.* London: Faber and Faber.

Freeman, Richard B., and James L. Medoff. 1984. *What Do Unions Do?* New York: Basic Books.

Goldthorpe, John H. 1984. "The End of Convergence: Corporatist and Dualist Tendencies in Modern Western Societies." Pp. 291–314 in *Order and Conflict in Contemporary Capitalism,* ed. John H. Goldthorpe. Oxford: Clarendon Press.

Gouldner, Alvin W. 1961. "The Norm of Reciprocity: A Preliminary Statement." *American Sociological Review* 25:161–79.

Gourevitch, Peter, Andrew Martin, George Ross, Stephen Bornstein, Andrei Markovits, and Christopher Allen. 1984. *Unions and Economic Crisis: Britain, West Germany, and Sweden.* London: Allen and Unwin.

Granovetter, Mark 1973. "The Strength of Weak Ties." *American Journal of Sociology* 78:1360–80.

———. 1974. *Getting a Job: A Study of Contacts and Careers.* Cambridge: Harvard University Press.

———. 1992. "The Sociological and Economic Approaches to Labor Market Analysis: A Social Structural View." Pp. 233–63 in *The Sociology of Economic Life,* ed. Mark Granovetter and Richard Swedberg. Boulder, Colo.: Westview.

———. 1995. Afterword. Pp. 139–82 in *Getting a Job.* 2d ed. Cambridge: Harvard University Press.

Granovetter, Mark, and Charles Tilly. 1988. "Inequality and Labor Processes." Pp. 175–222 in *Handbook of Sociology,* ed. Neil J. Smelser. Newbury Park, Calif.: Sage.

Hall, Peter, and David Soskice, eds. 2001: *Varieties of Capitalism: The Institutional Foundations of Comparative Advantage.* Oxford: Oxford University Press.

Jacoby, Sanford M. 1990. "Norms and Cycles: The Dynamics of Nonunion Industrial Relations in the United States, 1897–1987." Pp. 19–57 in *New Developments in the Labor Market: Toward a New Institutional Paradigm,* ed. Katherine G. Abraham and Robert B. McKersie. Cambridge: MIT Press.

Kalleberg, Arne L., Barbara F. Reskin, and Ken Hudson. 2000. "Bad Jobs in America: Standard and Nonstandard Employment Relations and Job Quality in the United States." *American Sociological Review* 65:256–78.

Kalleberg, Arne L., and Aage B. Sørensen. 1979. "The Sociology of Labor Markets." *Annual Review of Sociology* 5:351–79.

Katz, Harry C., and Owen Darbishire. 2000. *Converging Divergences: Worldwide Changes in Employment Systems.* Ithaca, N.Y.: Cornell University Press.

Katznelson, Ira, and Aristide R. Zolberg. 1986. *Working-Class Formation: Nineteenth-Century Patterns in Western Europe and the United States.* Princeton: Princeton University Press.

Kendall, Walter. 1975. *The Labor Movement in Europe.* London: Allen Lane.

Kenworthy, Lane. 1995. *In Search of National Economic Success: Balancing Competition and Cooperation.* Thousand Oaks, Calif.: Sage.

———. 1996. "Unions, Wages, and the Common Interest." *Comparative Political Studies* 28:491–524.

Kerr, Clark. 1954. "The Balkanization of Labor Markets." Pp. 94–110 in *Labor Mobility and Economic Opportunity,* by Edward W. Bakke et al. Cambridge: MIT Press.

———. 1977. "Labor Markets: Their Character and Consequences." Pp. 38–52 in *Labor Markets and Wage Determination: The Balkanization of Labor Markets and Other Essays.* Berkeley and Los Angeles: University of California Press.

Kerr, Clark, John T. Dunlop, Frederick H. Harbison, and Charles A. Myers. 1960. *Industrialism and Industrial Man: The Problems of Labor and Management in Economic Growth.* Cambridge: Harvard University Press.

Korpi, Walter. 1983. *The Democratic Class Struggle.* London: Routledge.

Lehmbruch, Gerhard. 1974. *Consociational Democracy, Class Conflict, and the New Corporatism.* Paper presented at the roundtable "Political Integration," International Political Science Association, Jerusalem, September 9–13.

———. 1977. "Liberal Corporatism and Party Government." *Comparative Political Studies* 10:91–126.

Leibenstein, Harvey. 1987. *Inside the Firm.* Cambridge: Harvard University Press.

Leifer, Eric M., and Harrison C. White. 1986. "A Structural Approach to Markets." Pp. 187–204 in *Intercorporate Relations,* ed. Mark Mizruchi and Michael Schwartz. Cambridge: Cambridge University Press.

Lester, Richard. 1958. *As Unions Mature.* Princeton: Princeton University Press.

Levi, Margret. 2002. *Organizing Power: The American Labor Movement in the Twenty-first Century.* Paper prepared for presentation at the American Political Science Association Meetings, Boston, August.

Lipset, Seymor M. 1960. "The Political Process in Trade Unions: A Theoretical Statement." Pp. 216–42 in *Labor and Trade Unionism,* ed. Walter Galenson and Seymor M. Lipset. New York: John Wiley.

———. 1983. "Radicalism or Reformism: The Sources of Working-Class Politics." *American Political Science Review* 77:1–18.

Lipset, Seymour M., and Gary Marks. 2000. *It Didn't Happen Here: Why Socialism Failed in the United States.* New York: W. W. Norton.

Macauley, Stewart. 1963. "Non-contractual Relations in Business: A Preliminary Study." *American Sociological Review* 28:55–67.

Macneil, Ian R. 1980. *The New Social Contract: An Inquiry into Modern Contractual Relations.* New Haven: Yale University Press.

Maine, Henry S. 1960. *Ancient Law: Its Connection with the Early History of Society, and Its Relations to Modern Ideas.* New York: Dutton.

Mares, Isabela. 2001. "Enterprise Reorganization and Social Insurance Reform: The Development of

Early Retirement in France and Germany." *Governance* 14:295–317.

Marks, Gary. 1989. *Unions in Politics: Britain, Germany, and the United States in the Nineteenth and Early Twentieth Centuries.* Princeton: Princeton University Press.

Marsden, David. 1999. *A Theory of Employment Systems: Micro Foundations of Societal Diversity.* Oxford: Oxford University Press.

Marshall, Thomas H. 1964. *Class, Citizenship, and Social Development.* Garden City, N.Y.: Doubleday.

Marx, Karl. [1867] 1984. *Capital.* Vol. 1. New York: International Publishers.

Maurice, Marc, François Sellier, and Jean-Jacques Silvestre. 1986a. *The Social Foundations of Industrial Power: A Comparison of France and Germany.* Cambridge: MIT Press.

———. 1986b: "The Search for a Societal Effect in the Production of Company Hierarchy: A Comparison of France and Germany." Pp. 231–70 in *Internal Labor Markets,* ed. Paul Osterman. Cambridge: MIT Press.

Maurice, Marc, Arndt Sorge, and Malcolm Warner. 1980. "Societal Differences in Organizing Manufacturing Units: A Comparison of France, West Germany, and Great Britain." *Organization Studies* 1:59–86.

Newell, Andrew, and James Symons. 1987. "Corporatism, Laissez-faire, and the Rise in Unemployment." *European Economic Review* 31:567–614.

Olson, Mancur. 1971. *The Logic of Collective Action: Public Goods and the Theory of Groups.* Cambridge: Harvard University Press.

———. 1982. *The Rise and Decline of Nations: Economic Growth, Stagflation, and Social Rigidities.* New Haven: Yale University Press.

———. 1983. "The Political Economy of Comparative Growth Rates." Pp. 7–52 in *The Political Economy of Growth,* ed. Dennis C. Mueller. New Haven: Yale University Press.

Osterman, Paul, ed. 1984. *Internal Labor Markets.* Cambridge: MIT Press.

———. 1994. "Internal Labor Markets: Theory and Change." Pp. 303–39 in *Labor Economics and Industrial Relations,* ed. Clark Kerr and Paul D. Staudohar. Cambridge: Cambridge University Press.

Pizzorno, Alessandro. 1978. "Political Exchange and Collective Identity in Industrial Conflict." Pp. 277–98 in vol. 2 of *The Resurgence of Class Conflict in Western Europe since 1968,* ed. Colin Crouch and Alessandro Pizzorno. London: Macmillan.

Polanyi, Karl. 1944. *The Great Transformation: The Political and Economic Origins of Our Time.* Boston: Beacon Press.

Regini, Marino, 2000. "Between Deregulation and Social Pacts: The Responses of European Economies to Globalization." *Politics and Society* 28:5–33.

———, ed. 1992. *The Future of Labor Movements.* London: Sage.

Rogers, Joel, and Wolfgang Streeck, eds. 1995. *Works Councils: Consultation, Representation, and Cooperation in Industrial Relations.* Chicago: University of Chicago Press.

Rokkan, Stein. 1968. "Nation-Building, Cleavage Formation, and the Structuring of Mass Politics." *Comparative Studies in Society and History* 10:173–210.

Ross, Arthur M., and Paul T. Hartmann. 1960. *Changing Patterns of Industrial Conflict.* New York: Wiley.

Ruggie, John Gerard. 1982. "International Regimes, Transactions, and Change: Embedded Liberalism in the Postwar Economic Order." *International Organization* 36:379–415.

Schmitter, Philippe C. 1974. "Still the Century of Corporatism?" *Review of Politics* 36:85–131.

Scott, James C. 1976. *The Moral Economy of the Peasant: Rebellion and Subsistence in Southeast Asia.* New Haven: Yale University Press.

Selznick, Philip. 1969. *Law, Society, and Industrial Justice.* New York: Russell Sage Foundation.

Simon, Herbert A. 1951. "A Formal Theory of the Employment Relationship." *Econometrica* 19:293–305.

Sinzheimer, Hugo. [1916] 1976. "Ein Arbeitstarifgesetz—die Idee der sozialen Selbstbestimmung im Recht." In *Arbeitsrecht und Rechtssoziologie, Gesammelte Aufsätze und Reden,* ed. Hugo Sinzheimer. Frankfurt am Main: Europäische Verlagsanstalt.

Smelser, Neil J., and Richard Swedberg, eds. 1994. *The Handbook of Economic Sociology.* New York: Russell Sage Foundation; Princeton: Princeton University Press.

Solow, Robert. 1990. "Government and the Labor Market." Pp. 275–88 in *New Developments in the Labor Market: Toward a New Institutional Paradigm,* ed. Katharine G. Abraham and Robert B. McKersie. Cambridge: MIT Press.

———. 1991. *The Labor Market as a Social Institution.* Cambridge: Basil Blackwell.

Sørensen, Aage B. 1977. "The Structure of Inequality and the Process of Attainment." *American Sociological Review* 42:965–78.

———. 1994. "Firms, Wages, and Incentives." Pp. 504–28 in *The Handbook of Economic Sociology,* ed. Neil J. Smelser and Richard Swedberg. New York: Russell Sage Foundation; Princeton: Princeton University Press.

Soskice, David. 1990. "Wage Determination: The Changing Role of Institutions in Advanced Industrialized Countries." *Oxford Review of Economic Policy* 4:36–61.

Spencer, Herbert. [1873] 1961. *The Study of Sociology.* Ann Arbor: University of Michigan Press.

Stinchcombe, Arthur L. 1959. "Bureaucratic and Craft Administration of Production." *Administrative Science Quarterly* 4:168–87.

———. 1968. *Constructing Social Theories.* New York: Harcourt.

Streeck, Wolfgang. 1991. "On the Institutional Conditions of Diversified Quality Production." Pp. 21–61 in *Beyond Keynesianism: The Socio-Economics of Production and Employment*, ed. Egon Matzner and Wolfgang Streeck. London: Edward Elgar.

———. 1992. "Revisiting Status and Contract: Pluralism, Corporatism, and Flexibility." Pp. 41–75 in *Social Institutions and Economic Performance*. London: Sage.

———. 2001. "High Equality, Low Activity: The Contribution of the Social Welfare System to the Stability of the German Collective Bargaining Regime." *Industrial and Labour Relations Review* 54:698–706.

Streeck, Wolfgang, and Anke Hassel. 2003. "Trade Unions as Political Actors." In *International Handbook of Trade Unions*, ed. John T. Addison and Claus Schnabel. London: Edward Elgar.

Streeck, Wolfgang, and Lane Kenworthy. 2003. "Theories and Practices of Neo-Corporatism." In *A Handbook of Political Sociology: States, Civil Societies, and Globalization*, ed. Thomas Janoski, Robert Alford, Alexander M. Hicks, and Margaret Schwartz. Cambridge: Cambridge University Press.

Swedberg, Richard. 1994. "Markets as Social Structures." Pp. 255–82 in *The Handbook of Economic Sociology*, ed. Neil J. Smelser and Richard Swedberg. New York: Russell Sage Foundation; Princeton: Princeton University Press.

Swenson, Peter. 2002. *Capitalists against Markets: The Making of Labor Markets and Welfare States in the United States and Sweden*. Oxford: Oxford University Press.

Tannenbaum, Frank. 1964. *The True Society: A Philosophy of Labour*. London: Jonathan Cape.

Taylor, Andrew J. 1989. *Trade Unions and Politics: A Comparative Introduction*. London: Macmillan.

Thelen, Kathleen A. 1991. *Union of Parts: Labor Politics in Postwar Germany*. Ithaca, N.Y.: Cornell University Press.

Tilly, Chris, and Charles Tilly. 1994. "Capitalist Work and Labor Markets." Pp. 283–312 in *The Handbook of Economic Sociology*, ed. Neil J. Smelser and Richard Swedberg. New York: Russell Sage Foundation; Princeton: Princeton University Press.

Ulman, Lloyd, and Robert J. Flanagan. 1971. *Wage Restraint: A Study of Incomes Policies in Western Europe*. Berkeley and Los Angeles: University of California Press.

Valenzuela, J. Samuel. 1992. "Labor Movements and Political Systems: Some Variations." Pp. 76–104 in *The Future of Labor Movements*, ed. Marino Regini. London: Sage.

Visser, Jelle. 1992. "The Strength of Union Movements in Advanced Capitalist Democracies: Social and Organizational Variations." Pp. 133–49 in *The Future of Labor Movements*, ed. Marino Regini. London: Sage.

———, ed. 1990. "In Search of Inclusive Unionism." In *Bulletin of Comparative Labor Relations*, vol. 18. Deventer: Kluwer.

Vogel, Steven K. 1996. *Freer Markets, More Rules: Regulatory Reform in Advanced Industrial Countries*. Ithaca, N.Y.: Cornell University Press.

von Beyme, Klaus. 1977. *Gewerkschaften und Arbeitsbeziehungen in kapitalistischen Ländern*. Munich: Pieper.

Voss, Kim, and Rachel Sherman. 2000. "Breaking the Iron Law of Oligarchy: Union Revitalization in the American Labor Movement." *American Journal of Sociology* 106:303–49.

Webb, Sidney, and Beatrice Webb. 1911. *Industrial Democracy*. London: Longman.

Weber, Max. [1904] 1987. *The Protestant Ethic and the Spirit of Capitalism*. Trans. Talcott Parsons. London: Unwin.

Weitzmann, Martin L. 1984. *The Share Economy: Conquering Stagflation*. Cambridge: Harvard University Press.

Western, Bruce. 1995. "A Comparative Study of Working-Class Disorganization: Union Decline in Eighteen Advanced Capitalist Countries." *American Sociological Review* 60:1979–2202.

———. 1997. *Between Class and Market: Postwar Unionization in the Capitalist Democracies*. Princeton: Princeton University Press.

White, Harrison C. 1981. "Where Do Markets Come From?" *American Journal of Sociology* 87:517–47.

———. 2002a. *Markets from Networks: Socioeconomic Models of Production*. Princeton: Princeton University Press.

———. 2002b. "Crowded Markets: Allocation with Valuation by Contexts." Typescript.

Wilensky, Harold. 2002. *Rich Democracies*. Berkeley and Los Angeles: University of California Press.

Williamson, Oliver E. 1979. "Transaction Cost Economics: The Governance of Contractual Relations." *Journal of Law and Economics* 22:233–61.

———. 1988. "Economics and Sociology of Organization." Pp. 159–85 in *Industries, Firms, and Jobs: Sociological and Economic Approaches*, ed. George Farkas and Paula England. New York: Plenum Press.

———. 1994 "Transaction Cost Economics and Organization Theory." Pp. 77–107 in *The Handbook of Economic Sociology*, ed. Neil J. Smelser and Richard Swedberg. New York: Russell Sage Foundation; Princeton: Princeton University Press.

Williamson, Oliver E., Michael L. Wachter, and Jeffrey Harris. 1975. "Understanding the Employment Relation: The Analysis of Idiosyncratic Exchange." *Bell Journal of Economics* 6:250–78.

13 Banking and Financial Markets

Linda Brewster Stearns and Mark S. Mizruchi

THE STUDY of banking and finance is assumed by many social scientists to be the purview of economists. In fact, however, there is a sociological tradition in these areas. Marx ([1894] 1967) and Weber ([1922] 1978) both wrote important works on the topic. Although financial issues received little attention from sociologists for several decades after Weber (see Smelser 1959, 358–77; Lieberson 1961 for exceptions), this neglect has been remedied significantly in recent years. Since the mid-1970s, sociologists have produced an increasing stream of research on banking and finance. Our goal in this chapter is to provide a survey and assessment of this work. Economic and sociological views on these topics have similarities and are not necessarily incompatible. In fact, we shall incorporate writings by economists at various points in our review. There are three ways, however, in which a sociological approach to banking and finance differs from conventional economic approaches. First, sociologists attempt to make explicit the ways in which power influences both economic actions and the character of economic institutions. Second, sociologists focus on the effects of social networks on economic decision making. And third, sociologists are interested in the role of culture in shaping economic behavior.[1]

Our focus in this chapter is on the relations between financial institutions and their external environments. We begin with a discussion of sociological research on banking.[2] Initially, much of this research was framed by the question, "Who controls the corporation?" We review this debate as it applies to banks and then discuss the changing role of banks in corporate financing. We then examine the changing structure of the capital market and other sources of financing, such as institutional investors, venture capital, and the stock market. We examine the regulation of capital markets and their tendency toward speculation and crisis. Given the significant cross-national variations among financial systems and the legal environments within which they operate, our focus will be primarily on the United States. We do, however, briefly address the structure of a few selected non-U.S. capital markets and the changes occurring within those markets. We conclude with an assessment of the field and some suggestions for future research.

BANKS AND CORPORATE CONTROL

Banks are the key institutions through which money is stored, created,[3] and distributed. Two types of private banks have predominated in the U.S. economy: commercial banks and savings and loan associations.[4] Prior to the 1980s, a clear division of labor existed among financial institutions in the United States (Stearns and Mizruchi 1993a). Commercial banks accepted both demand deposits (subject to check withdrawals) and time (savings) deposits and were involved primarily in short-term loans to businesses. In addition, commercial bank trust departments, along with insurance companies, were the major administrators of private pension funds. Savings and loan associations and credit unions also held both time and demand deposits and issued loans, with a focus on home mortgages. Investment banks underwrote new corporate stock and bond issues, acted as agents for the private placement of bonds, and arranged corporate mergers and acquisitions. Life insurance companies, because of the stable, long-term nature of their funds, specialized in long-term lending.

American commercial banks arose after the American Revolution as businesses began to specialize and international trade expanded (Chandler 1977, 28–31). The number of banks increased rapidly after 1790, to more than 200 by 1815. Over the next century, several key actions taken by the federal government prevented American banking from developing into the kind of centralized system found in Germany and Japan. In 1832 President Andrew Jackson refused to support a bill to recharter the Second Bank of the United States. This bank was the "first American national enterprise, coordinating the flow of money across the nation parallel to the flow of trade" (Roe 1994,

56). The National Bank Acts of 1863 and 1864 confined national banks to a single location; it was not until 1927 that these banks were allowed to establish branches within a city or town, and then only if state law permitted. When President Woodrow Wilson created the Federal Reserve System in 1913, he effectively took power away from J. P. Morgan & Co., which had become the nation's de facto central bank (Roe 1994, 40). In 1933, with passage of the Glass-Steagall Act, Congress barred commercial bank affiliates from owning and dealing in securities, thereby severing commercial banking from investment banking.

Despite a relatively decentralized banking system, there have been periods in the United States when banks were viewed as powerful. The most prominent of these periods was in the late nineteenth century, when the United States witnessed an enormous expansionary wave, coinciding with the rise of the large corporation. During this period, roughly 1880–1920, nonfinancial enterprises routinely found themselves short of cash, especially when the frequent economic downturns occurred. The depression of 1893 nearly bankrupted several major railroads in the United States. Investment bankers, especially J. P. Morgan, with privileged access to foreign as well as domestic capital, provided the capital necessary to reestablish the railroads on a sound footing. The high demand for capital together with its concentrated nature contributed to the power of financial institutions (Cochran and Miller [1942] 1961; Mizruchi 1982; Chernow 1997).

Considerable scholarly disagreement exists on the extent of bank power in the United States after 1920. Berle and Means ([1932] 1968) argued that control of the firm had passed to hired managers. Less affected by stockholder pressure (as result of widespread stock dispersal), managers were able to restrict dividends, thus increasing the amount of cash available for reinvestment. The increasing profitability created by growing market power further contributed to the availability of cash, enabling firms to finance their operations with retained earnings.

For decades, however, the only systematic study of corporations' dependence on external financing was an article by economist John Lintner (1959). Lintner found that from 1900 through 1953, nonfinancial corporations consistently met between 40 and 45 percent of their total current financial needs with external funds. In addition, although large manufacturing firms relied primarily on internal funds in the 1920s, they increasingly drew on external funding over the next 30 years, suggesting a continued dependence on financial institutions. A subsequent study by Stearns (1986) showed that although U.S. corporations obtained approximately one-third of their total funds from external sources between 1946 and 1965, they obtained almost half of their total funds from these sources between 1965 and 1980. This suggested that the power of banks fluctuated over time: relatively low during the post–World War II period, and greater between 1965 and 1980 (1986, 66–70).

Critics countered such evidence by maintaining that although corporations do borrow, their borrowing is primarily discretionary (Baran and Sweezy 1966, 15–16). Resolving this issue is a difficult task. In earlier work (Stearns and Mizruchi 1993a, 1993b; Mizruchi and Stearns 1994), we argued that if borrowing is primarily nondiscretionary, then firms with high levels of cash would tend to borrow less than firms with low levels of cash, even when the cost of capital is low. Consistent with this suggestion, we found, in a study of 22 large U.S. manufacturing firms between 1956 and 1983 (Mizruchi and Stearns 1994), that a firm's retained earnings were strongly negatively associated with its level of borrowing.[5]

Another factor that might affect firms' dependence on financial institutions is the availability of alternative forms of financing (Stearns 1986). In a study of firms' relations with investment banks, Baker (1990) showed that firms employed several different investment banks as a way to minimize their dependence on a single one. After 1980, banks began to face heightened competition from a number of sources. Corporations turned increasingly to alternative sources of financing, the most prominent of which was commercial paper (short-term notes floated by firms in the public market). By 1994 the value of outstanding commercial paper in the United States equaled that of outstanding debt to commercial banks. At the same time, the proliferation of alternative sources of savings and investment, including mutual, pension, and money market funds, led individuals to reduce their deposits in commercial banks. These developments, along with increasing competition from overseas financial institutions, suggest a significant decline between the early-1980s and the mid-1990s in the ability of U.S. commercial banks to constrain nonfinancial corporations (Davis and Mizruchi 1999). We discuss the effect of these changes in the following section.

In *The Death of the Banker* (1997) Ron Chernow describes the decline during the mid–twentieth century of the Morgan and Warburg banking dynasties. He argues that "the banker's true power in any period depends upon his relative strength compared with that of the providers and consumers of capital" (7). Changes in capital supply and demand in the early 1980s led to a decline in the power of commercial banks. However, given the historical fluctuation in the demand for capital, as well as the ever-changing conditions of capital supply, it is conceivable that banks may regain their influence over corporate decision making.

BANKING TODAY

What do today's banks do? In a recent study (Mizruchi and Stearns 2001), we gained access to the corporate banking unit of a leading multinational commercial bank. Between 1997 and 1999 we conducted semistructured interviews with 105 bankers in the bank's "global relationship banking" unit. This unit is responsible for handling the approximately 1,400 multinational corporations that the bank had targeted as its corporate customers.

The bankers whom we interviewed operate primarily as salespeople. They sell by responding to clients' requests as well as by creating demand among these clients for the bank's growing number of products. These products include not only lending (lines of credit and project finance), but also trading (derivatives and currency exchange), capital market services (syndication and securitization), and transaction services (cash management and custody).

Although many of the bankers' transactions involved loans, the bank's top management had instructed them to emphasize the bank's other product lines because they promised higher return for lower risk.[6] Because of the low interest rate spreads and the fact that the customers wanting bank loans were often among the more financially unstable, the bank preferred to make its money from fees: either the large upfront fees made in capital market services, the steady annuities earned via transaction services, or the fees accompanying high-volume trading transactions.

In *The Bankers: The Next Generation* (1997), Martin Mayer notes that since the publication of his earlier book, *The Bankers* (1974), "banking [has] changed beyond recognition" (1997, 17). "Almost nobody who has a job in a bank today works as his[7] predecessors worked as recently as twenty years ago" (19). The transformation, Mayer argues, is due primarily to changes in technology and banking regulations.

With the elimination of interest rate controls by Congress and regulators in the early 1980s, banks could exploit a variety of techniques to raise capital. These sources became increasingly important as consumer deposits became a smaller proportion of the liabilities that funded bank loans. Without this traditional source of funds, banks increasingly became "takers" rather than "makers" of interest rates. Simultaneously, the variety of funding options open to corporate borrowers increased. As a result of these trends, interest rate spreads on business loans narrowed significantly. Tight spreads in turn decreased the proportion of bank earnings obtained from business loans and encouraged banks to securitize their loan portfolios—that is, package them and sell them in the capital market.

Technology (data processing and retrieval) vastly reduced the cost of information. As Mayer notes (1997, 20), "Bankers had always thought they were being paid for their judgment, for taking risks in lending money, but in fact most of their profits had come from exploiting a rich information advantage over people who were not bankers." On the negative side, technology made it possible for nonbank corporations to compete successfully for what had been banking business. On the positive side, technology gave banks for the first time economies of both scale and scope. Credit cards, home mortgages, securities processing, foreign exchange, and derivatives trading require elaborate and hugely expensive computer installations and telecommunications expertise. Once the installations are in place, however, the next loan or transaction comes virtually free of charge. In 1994, banks invested $19 billion in technology (Mayer 1997, 26) and by 1995 banks such as Bankers Trust, Morgan Guaranty, Citicorp, and First Chicago derived more than half their operating revenues from sources other than lending (Mayer 1997, 28).

The onset of technological change, globalization, and regulatory change caused the structure of the financial services industry to implode via a dramatic increase in merger activity. Changes in state-level regulations, most notably the removal of branching restrictions, encouraged regional banks to combine to create superregionals. These superregionals then combined to create national banks. Size was seen by both the business community and government regulators as bringing with it the ability to invest in technology and to "go global." The undermining (via waivers authorized by the Federal Reserve System) and eventual repeal in 1999 of the Glass-Steagall Act encouraged mergers that blurred the boundaries between commercial banking, insurance, and investment banking. Supporters of these mergers argue that they provide cross-selling advantages and greater breadth of product lines (Wasserstein 2000, 291–98), while critics argue that such economies of scope are seldom realized (Rhoades 2000).

The 1997 merger between Dean Witter, Discover & Co., and Morgan Stanley marked the beginning of a significant shift in the nature and size of banking deals (Wasserstein 2000, 294). In response, banks began to rapidly combine, creating financial organizations of unprecedented size. In a period of less than four years, NationsBank merged with BankAmerica, Fleet with BankBoston, Banc One with First Chicago, Norwest with Wells Fargo, Firstar with U.S. Bancorp, First Union with Wachovia, Travelers with Citicorp, and Chase Manhattan (itself the result a 1995 merger between Chemical Bank and Chase Manhattan) with J. P. Morgan.

Although bank merging in the early 1990s was primarily a U.S. phenomenon, non-U.S. financial institutions, concerned about being at a competitive disadvantage, began to engage in mergers as well. In 1997, the Union Bank of Switzerland merged with Swiss Bank Corporation in preparation for the coming of the euro, and in 1998, the Deutsche Bank–Bankers Trust merger set the stage for an increase in cross-border merger activity. Japanese banks, faced with widespread instability, also began to combine in the 1990s in an effort to create more competitive and stable financial institutions.

The scope and rapidity of the changes in the banking world have far outpaced social scientists' ability to make sense of them. As a result, our prior theories of the role of banks and relations between financial and nonfinancial corporations are badly in need of revision. On one hand, the resource dependence (Pfeffer and Salancik 1978) and bank hegemony (Mintz and Schwartz 1985) theories of the 1970s and 1980s are useful in examining whether the plethora of financing options open to nonfinancial firms is associated with the declining power of banks. On the other hand, we have few systematic sociological perspectives on the overhaul that the banking industry has experienced. It will be interesting to see if the wave of megamergers that occurred during the 1990s ultimately results in a resurgence of bank power; or if, as banks shift toward service-oriented activities, they increasingly resemble accounting and law firms—losing their unique role in the business world as the key arbiter in the allocation of capital.

Commercial banks are but one of several financial intermediaries that operate in the U.S. capital market. It is to this broader financial market that we turn next.

FINANCIAL MARKETS

The capital market is the primary center of financial activity in the United States. This market consists of three groups of actors: suppliers, financial intermediaries, and users of capital. Individuals, corporations, and governments all may act as both suppliers and consumers of capital. Suppliers may provide capital directly to users or may operate through financial intermediaries. These intermediaries consist of an enormous and growing range of institutions, including Federal Reserve banks, commercial banks, insurance companies, savings and loan associations, mutual savings banks, credit unions, private pension funds, finance companies, real estate investment trusts, open-end investment mutuals, money market mutual funds, federal financial agencies and mortgage pools, and state and local employee retirement funds. These institutions distribute capital to users through investments in stocks, bonds, and loans. The interaction among suppliers, intermediaries, and users determines the supply, demand, and control over capital resources.

In 1999, approximately 92 percent of all financial assets in the U.S. capital market flowed through financial institutions. Between 1989 and 1999, the financial assets of these institutions nearly tripled. As table 1 shows, however, not all financial institutions grew at the same pace. The table suggests a continuation of the process of deconcentration within the capital market that occurred between 1979 and 1989. Most of the older, more established financial intermediaries (commercial banks, savings banks, life insurance companies, finance companies, the Federal Reserve Bank, and credit unions) lost market shares during the 1990s. The financial intermediaries that gained market shares between 1989 and 1999 handled either pension funds or mutual funds. The one exception to this trend was the growth in other financial institutions, including real estate investment trusts, security brokers and dealers, and funding corporations.[8] In 1949, pension funds, mutual funds, and other financial institutions accounted for only 4 percent of all financial assets (Stearns 1986). By 1989, their proportion had increased to over 30 percent, and in 1999 to over 50 percent.

As table 2 demonstrates, the total demand for

TABLE 1.   Financial Assets for Selected Financial Intermediaries, 1989 and 1999 (in billions of dollars)

Sector	Amount		Distribution		Change %
	1989	1999	1989	1999	1989–99
Commercial banks[a]	$3,231.1	$5,980.3	29.9%	20.6%	−9.3%
Savings banks[b]	1,516.5	1,151.4	14.1	4.0	−10.1
Life insurance companies	1,268.0	3,067.9	11.7	10.6	−1.1
Private pension funds	1,163.5	4,645.4	10.8	16.0	+5.2
State/local pension funds	727.4	2,226.8	6.7	7.7	+1.0
Mutual funds	555.1	4,538.5	5.1	15.6	+10.5
Finance companies	519.3	1,003.0	4.8	3.4	−1.4
Government lending institutions	442.4	1,720.6	4.1	5.9	+1.8
Money market mutual funds	428.1	1,578.8	4.0	5.4	+1.4
Other financial institutions[c]	434.3	2,042.2	4.0	7.0	+3.0
Federal Reserve Bank	314.7	696.9	2.9	2.4	−0.5
Credit unions	199.7	414.5	1.8	1.4	−0.4
Total	$10,800.1	$29,066.3	100.0%	100.0%	

Source: Board of Governors of the Federal Reserve System 1990, 2002.
Note: Distribution totals do not equal 100 percent due to rounding.
[a] Consists of U.S. chartered commercial banks, bank holding companies, foreign banking offices in U.S. and banks in U.S.-affiliated areas.
[b] Consists of S&L associations, mutual savings, and federal savings banks.
[c] Consists of real estate investment trusts (REITs), security brokers and dealers, and funding corporations.

capital almost tripled between 1989 and 1999. This increase occurred among all sectors of the economy. Individuals, primarily through consumer credit and home mortgages, increased their borrowing by 80.2 percent (from $4,330.7 billion to $7,804 billion). The federal government increased its demand for funds by 115 percent. And corporations borrowed more: bank loans increased by 69 percent, corporate bonds by 209 percent, and open market paper by 142 percent. The 450 percent increase in corporate securities mirrors the "bull market" of the 1990s. The increase represents an expansion in new stock issues (including initial public offerings) as well as higher stock prices in the secondary market (i.e., the resale of already issued stock). In addition to domestic sources, foreign suppliers played a role in meeting the increased demands of government and corporations. The foreign sector increased its holdings of U.S. government securities and corporate securities, bonds, and open market paper by 272 percent (from $995.7 billion in 1989 to $3,699.8 billion in 1999).

Institutional Investors

One of the most significant developments in American business during the past four decades

has been the rise of institutional investors. As the corporate equity holdings of households and personal trusts decreased from 92.5 percent in 1945 to 44.2 percent in 1998, institutional holdings increased from 1.8 percent in 1945 to 41.5 percent in 1998 (Hawley and Williams 2000). In 1985, institutional investors as a group owned 36.1 percent of the largest 25 U.S. corporations. By 1997 their share had grown to 48.7 percent. Although institutional investors encompass a number of groups, including banks and insurance companies, pension funds and mutual funds are the largest investors. In 1945 pension funds held less than 1 percent of the total equity in U.S. corporations. By 1970 pension fund holdings had increased to 9.2 percent and by 1998 to 24.8 percent. Mutual funds, the second largest institutional investor, also grew at a dramatic pace. Mutual funds held a 1.5 percent stake in total U.S. corporate equity in 1945, 5.2 percent in 1970, and 16.7 percent by 1998 (Hawley and Williams 2000).

Organizational researchers have become increasingly cognizant of the power of institutional investors to influence a variety of organizational strategies. Useem (1993, 1996) and Davis and Thompson (1994) argue that institutional shareholdings have forced large corporations to adopt a shareholder-oriented conception of corporate

TABLE 2. Total Capital Market Instruments Outstanding, 1989 and 1999 (in billions of dollars)

Instrument	Amount		Distribution		Change %
	1989	1999	1989	1999	1989–99
U.S. government securities	$3,512.4	$7,565.0	20.9%	15.2%	−5.7%
State and local securities	821.2	1,532.5	4.9	3.1	−1.8
Corporate and foreign bonds	1,502.6	4,635.8	9.0	9.3	+0.3
Corporate securities[a]	4,382.1	24,119.7	26.1	48.4	+22.3
Open market paper	579.2	1,402.4	3.5	2.8	−0.7
Bank loans	820.3	1,383.8	4.9	2.8	−2.1
Other loans	821.1	1,412.0	4.9	2.8	−2.1
Mortgages[b]	3,540.1	6,357.9	21.1	12.8	−8.3
Consumer credit	790.6	1,446.1	4.7	2.9	−1.8
Total	$16,769.6	$49,855.2	100.0%	100.0%	

Source: Board of Governors of the Federal Reserve System 1990, 2002.
Note: Distribution totals do not equal 100 percent due to rounding.
[a] Includes corporate equities and mutual fund shares.
[b] Includes home mortgages, multifamily residential mortgages, commercial mortgages, and farm mortgages.

strategy. Conglomerate acquisitions, for example, are viewed as benefiting managers rather than shareholders. Consistent with this view, Davis, Diekmann, and Tinsley (1994) found that institutional ownership had a negative effect on the rate of conglomerate acquisitions. Scholars and members of the business press have identified institutional investors as behind-the-scenes players in dislodging incumbent CEOs at economically underperforming firms such as IBM, Westinghouse, General Motors, and Sears, and promoting breakups (such as ITT and AT&T) and mergers (including Capital Cities/ABC with Walt Disney Company, and Turner Broadcasting Systems with Time Warner) when such actions are viewed as increasing shareholder value (Useem 1996; Hawley and Williams 2000).

Even arenas traditionally viewed as controlled by the board of directors, such as executive compensation, have come under the influence of institutional investors. Davis and Thompson (1994) found that between 1990 and 1992, shareholders (led by institutional investors) gained the right to vote on golden parachute pay packages, to request more detailed information on executive pay, and to seek the creation of shareholder advisory committees and consultants. Useem (1996, 244) noted that executives "have learned to appreciate that investors oppose fixed compensation, favor variable compensation, and are indifferent to amount—so long as it varies with shareholder value." As a result, companies have put more managers on contingent compensation and linked more of the contingency to expanding shareholder wealth. These findings are particularly significant when one considers the near-unanimous opposition that corporate managers initially had to such reforms.

Useem and Gottlieb (1990) found that this ownership-disciplined alignment was also responsible for changes in how top management managed. Drawing on senior management interviews and documents from six large publicly traded corporations and six small firms, Useem and Gottlieb found that managers responded to the increased pressure from institutional investors by decentralizing decision-making authority to operating business units, contracting headquarters' management and staff functions, expanding the use of performance-based compensation, and creating opportunities for internal ownership.

Contrary to the widely held belief that institutional stockholders are concerned primarily with short-term performance at the expense of long-term investment, Jarrell, Lehn, and Marr (1985) found a positive association between a firm's level of institutional ownership and its research and development expenditures. This finding gained further support from Baysinger, Kosnik, and Turk (1991), who found that a concentration of equity among institutional investors positively affected corporate R&D spending. Moreover, Chaganti and Damanpour (1991), in a study of 80 manufacturing firms in 40 industries during the mid-1980s, found that firms with high institutional shareholdings were disproportionately likely to have low debt-to-equity ratios. Although the causal ordering between ownership structure and debt was unclear, firms with high levels of institutional stockholding were less likely to be heavily indebted.

Hawley and Williams (2000) argue that the increased role of institutional investors (what they term "fiduciary capitalism") has the potential to change the nature of capitalism itself. As institutional investors increasingly become long-term and permanent holders of a wide cross-section of corporate America, they are slowly becoming concerned not only with the long-term performance of individual firms, but also with the performance of the economy as a whole. Institutional investors are also being increasingly called upon by their constituents to vote proxies in support of a broad assortment of social issues—including diversity, the environment, human rights, plant closings, and executive compensation.

Venture Capital

Another important source of corporate funding is venture capital. Venture capital (VC), in the sense of investors funding new enterprises, has existed for as long as capitalism. Since the end of World War II, it has been handled increasingly by firms, which serve as brokers between investors and midsize start-up companies.[9] The first VC firm, American Research and Development, founded in 1946, was instrumental in the development of Digital Equipment Corporation. The flow of funding into VC firms increased dramatically during the early 1980s following an amendment to the "prudent man" rule in 1979, allowing pension funds to invest in higher-risk assets (Gompers and Lerner 1999). During the 1990s approximately 40 percent of venture capital came from private and public pension funds, and an additional 15 percent came from endowments (such as universities) and foundations (Mandel 2000).

By the 1990s venture capital was the fastest-growing element of the U.S. financial system. In 1988 (the peak year during the 1980s), the amount dispersed by venture capital firms to start-ups was just over $5 billion; by 2000 this figure had grown to $91 billion.[10] The annual rate of return on venture capital between 1979 and 1999 was about 16 percent, substantially higher than other investments (Mandel 2000). By century's end, the industry consisted of several thousand professionals working at about 500 firms concentrated in California, Massachusetts, and a handful of other states (Gompers and Lerner 1999).

The use of venture capital raises a number of interesting issues involving corporate governance and control. The general strategy for VC firms is to acquire a share of the start-up's equity in exchange for the initial funds. VC firms' goal is to take public the most successful firms in their portfolios. Less successful firms are liquidated, sold to corporate acquirers, or else remain operational at a modest level of activity. Although historically only 20 to 35 percent of start-ups have been taken public, these initial public offerings (IPOs) have accounted for the bulk of VC returns (Gompers and Lerner 1999).

Given its investment in the start-up, the VC firm has a strong incentive to monitor the start-up's activities. Mandel (2000, 29–30) notes, for example, that VC firms "closely monitor the performance of the start-up and step in if necessary. Most venture investments are written with provisions that give venture capitalists either control over the board of the start-up or veto power over major operating decisions. In the extreme case, venture capitalists can replace the founder of a struggling company with an outside CEO." Despite these safeguards, many VC firms have investments in 100 or more companies, so the monitoring of individual firms can be difficult.

Economists have used agency theory to model the ways in which VC firms monitor the start-ups they finance. Gompers (1995), for example, argues that start-ups that have the highest agency costs for VC firms are those with intangible assets (which make it difficult for the VC firm to recover its investment should the start-up fail), high asset specificity (firms that require specialized knowledge are difficult to monitor), and high market-to-book values (because firms in such industries may be easily able to attract alternative investors). To test these arguments, Gompers examined a strategy widely used by VC firms: the phenomenon of "rounds," or investment at various discrete stages. VC firms use rounds as a means of continuously reevaluating the start-ups in which they invest. This approach provides significant incentives for compliance by the start-up, and thus serves as an important monitoring device. Using a random sample of 794 firms that received venture capital between January 1961 and July 1992, Gompers found that firms operating in industries with relatively few tangible assets and high R & D expenditures (characteristic of those with high asset specificity) experienced both more rounds and shorter times between the rounds, indicating that they were more closely monitored.[11]

Sociologists have also contributed to the VC literature. In an analysis of the fate of 4,064 ventures, Freeman (1999) examined the relation between the centrality of VC firms (in terms of their participation in a large number of ventures) and the probability that the venture would result in the start-up being acquired, failing, or moving to IPO status. Freeman found that VC firm centrality was positively associated with both being acquired and issuing an IPO. The first finding suggests that because of their involvement in a large number of investments, central VC firms lose patience with modestly performing firms, which renders the firms' entrepreneurs more likely to sell out when the opportunity arises. The second finding suggests that start-up firms will benefit from the advice and connections associated with having centrally located backers.

VC firms have traditionally invested in start-ups located within the same geographic region (for a study of the biotech industry see Powell et al. 2002). In recent years, these investments have started to encompass a wider geographic area. In a study of this phenomenon, Sorenson and Stuart (2001) argue that a primary reason for this expansion has been the proliferation of investment syndicates among VC firms. Because the participants in these syndicates often come from a range of areas, their evolution provides a mechanism for the erosion of geographic boundaries in the distribution of venture capital. Using a data set consisting of investments by 1,025 VC firms in 7,590 targets between 1986 and 1998, Sorenson and Stuart focused on whether the effects of geographic and industry proximity (in terms of previous investments in a particular industry) on a VC firm investing in a particular start-up are affected by the social relations among VC firms in the syndicate. The authors suggested that prior network ties among syndicate members would mitigate the negative effects of both kinds of distance. Using three indicators of network ties—the existence of prior ties between a given VC firm and others in the syndicate, the geographic distance between these tied VC firms and the start-up, and the VC firm's centrality in the syndication network—Sorenson and Stuart found support for both hypotheses. Consistent with the authors' argument, interfirm relations played a role in reducing barriers to investment across geographic regions.

Podolny (2001) used VC firms to address the distinction between what he termed "egocentric" and "altercentric" uncertainty. Egocentric uncertainty is a producer's lack of information on the market for its product, as in an automobile manufacturer that does not know how the public will respond to a new model. Altercentric uncertainty is a lack of information that consumers have about the value of a product, as in a homeowner who must select a roofer to replace the roof on her house. Podolny argues that actors that occupy "structural holes" (loosely connected personal networks; Burt 1992) will tend to move toward areas of a market that are high in egocentric uncertainty, because structural holes help reduce this uncertainty. Having high status in an industry leads to the opposite prediction, according to Podolny. Because the key advantage that status gives can only be achieved if one has a clear sense of exactly where the status will provide benefits, high-status actors gravitate toward market segments that have low egocentric uncertainty. To study this tendency, Podolny examined the rounds at which 387 VC firms made investments, on the assumption that the earlier the round, the greater the level of egocentric uncertainty. Consistent with his predictions, firms that occupied structural holes were more likely to invest in earlier rounds, while those with high status were more likely to invest in later rounds.

Interestingly, the pattern of this work resembles that of the older bank control literature. VC firms are not banks, but they are one of the primary providers of capital to start-up firms. This role gives them both the potential and the requirement to monitor, just as banks were stipulated to do in the earlier work. The VC phenomenon actually provides a much purer manifestation of the principles posited by the bank control theorists. In contrast to large nonfinancial corporations, there is no ambiguity about the extent to which start-ups require external capital: they are virtually completely dependent on it. Although the VC literature among sociologists cited previously has focused on networks, it has been sensitive to the monitoring issue as well, in fact, to a greater extent than those who have studied interfirm networks in the past.

The Stock Market

In the 1990s the U.S. stock market grew at a spectacular rate. Many analysts and laypersons justified the continuously rising stock prices as a consequence of a "new economy"—the growth of high-technology industries and improvements in productivity—and the resulting increased confidence among investors. Investors had come to accept as "truisms" the arguments of academics and finance professionals that stocks were the best long-term investment and that stock prices reflected real value. In this section we take a closer look at the efficient market theory, a view that posits that stock prices reflect the true value of firms. We pay particular attention to research findings by sociologists and organizational scholars that challenge the theory. We then address the extent to which the claims made during the 1990s paralleled those made during an earlier era—the 1920s.

Efficient Market Theory

> The concept of an efficient market is astonishingly simple and remarkably well-supported by facts. Among these facts are the rapid adjustment of security prices to public announcements of information about firms as well as the general inability of professionally managed portfolios to beat simple market indexes. Less than 30 years ago any suggestion that security investment is a fair game was generally regarded as bizarre. Today it is not only widely accepted in business schools, but it also permeates investment practice and government policy toward the security markets. (Brealey, Myers, and Marcus 2001, 362)

Efficient market theory became popular through the work of University of Chicago economist Eugene Fama and his colleagues in the late 1960s (Fama 1970). The efficient market hypothesis comes in three different forms. The weak form suggests that prices efficiently reflect all the information contained in the past series of stock prices. It is therefore impossible to earn superior returns simply by looking for patterns in stock prices. The semistrong form suggests that prices reflect all published information. This means it is impossible to make consistently superior returns simply by reading the newspaper, looking at the company's annual accounts, and other public information. For this reason, analysts can do little to help an investor earn superior returns. The strong form of the efficient market hypothesis (the one most popular in the 1990s) suggests that stock prices effectively incorporate all available information: the consequence of millions of investors competing for an edge is that virtually no source of information remains unexplored. As a result, the best an investor can do is to assume that securities are fairly priced (Brealey, Myers, and Marcus 2001, 352–54).

Since the 1980s, however, economists have uncovered several deviations from efficient market behavior. Focusing on firms, researchers found that corporate managers consistently made superior profits when they dealt in their own company's

stock (Seyhyun 1986), that small-firm stocks outperformed large-firm stocks, even on a risk-adjusted basis (Banz 1981), that firms with high ratios of book value to market value outperformed other firms (Fama and French 1992), and that there was no significant association between stock prices and expected dividend payouts (Shiller 1981, 2000). Focusing on investors, research in behavioral finance documented that prices reflected certain cognitive biases such as short-term underreaction and long-term overreaction to information (DeBondt and Thaler 1985; Jegadeesh and Titman 1993).

Sociologists, too, have examined securities markets and prices. Baker (1984), in a study of trading on the floor of the Chicago Stock Exchange, found that the size, density, and fragmentation of various communication networks affected the volatility of prices, independent of the ordinary market forces of supply and demand. Most floor trading in securities markets occurs in face-to-face interaction. Baker found that in large crowds, communication among traders was difficult. This is readily understandable in network analytic terms, in which the number of possible dyadic relations increases geometrically with the addition of each member of the network. Consequently, the density of interaction within a group will tend to be a decreasing negative function of its size. Because of the difficulty of communication, the volatility of prices was much greater in large groups than in small groups. The extent to which trading approximated a "pure" market model was thus related to the size of the group involved in trading. The smaller the group, Baker found, the more stable the prices and thus the more efficient the operation of the market. In a subsequent work, Baker and Iyer (1992) developed a mathematical model that generalized this finding. The authors showed that different network structures create different levels of information flow, which in turn affect price volatility.

Hayward and Boeker (1998) examined the determinants of analysts' ratings of securities, which in turn have been found to influence stock prices (Stickel 1992; Womack 1996). Hayward and Boeker were concerned with whether conflicts of interest between the corporate finance department and the securities analysts within the research department of an investment bank affected the latter's ratings of the bank's corporate clients' equity securities. Because the corporate finance department's primary mandate is to serve and promote its clients' financial interests, that department prefers high ratings. The job of securities analysts, on the other hand, is to provide independent and objective advice to investors about the value and merits of equity securities. The professional code of ethics within the financial community requires what analysts term a "Chinese wall"[12] to exist between the two groups. Hayward and Boeker argue that there are cracks in the wall, with the rating behavior of securities analysts reflecting the resource asymmetries and power differences between the two departments. Whereas securities analysts do not generate bank revenue directly, corporate finance departments are major contributors to bank revenues and profits. Examining over 8,000 ratings for 70 companies from five U.S. industries between 1989 and 1993, Hayward and Boeker found that securities analysts rate the securities of their bank's corporate finance clients more favorably than other analysts rating the same securities. These results indicate that the available information used in stock-purchasing decisions may be biased or inaccurate.

Zuckerman (1999) looked directly at the impact securities analysts have on stock prices through their role as "product critic." Contrary to efficient market theory, Zuckerman states that the information available to investors is often insufficient and requires decoding. The cognitive limits on information processing along with the inherent unpredictability of the economic future make stock evaluation an interpretive project. The fact that interpretations are social enterprises, carried out with an eye to how others will view the same information, complicates matters even further. Such valuation problems give rise to the need for product critics.

In the stock market, industries are the categories by which corporate equity shares are classified, and securities analysts, who specialize in particular industries, are the relevant product critics. Stocks not certified by a product critic as being a member of the critic's industry incur an "illegitimacy discount." The illegitimacy discount manifests itself in a lower stock price. Securities analysts, by addressing a firm's place within an industry, thus confer a legitimacy that in turn impacts its stock price.

Zuckerman hypothesizes that the greater the coverage mismatch (the extent to which a firm that does business in industry X is not covered by the analysts who specialize in X) experienced by a firm, the more likely the presence of an illegitimacy discount, as reflected in a lower stock price. Using sales, assets, and earnings before income tax to measure the discrepancy between the imputed value of a firm and its actual value, he found that the stock price of an American firm was discounted to the extent that the securities analysts who specialized in its industry did not cover the firm. By finding that a securities analyst's certification of a firm's membership in an industry influences its price, Zuckerman's study raises a challenge to the efficient market theory, which assumes that the relation between firm value and stock price is straightforward, and uncontaminated by social and political processes.

There are occasions in which rhetoric alone can affect a firm's stock price. Westphal and Zajac (1998) examined the effect of firms' announcements of long-term incentive plans (LTIPs) for their CEOs on the firms' stock prices. These plans are attempts to build performance contingencies into CEO compensation packages, a move most observers would expect to increase the firm's attractiveness to investors. Examining 408 large U.S. corporations from 1982 through 1992, Westphal and Zajac found that in more than 50 percent of the cases in which LTIPs were announced, they were ultimately not implemented. Among the authors' concerns were two that are especially relevant to our discussion: first, whether firms that announced but did not implement LTIPs still gained an "excess" return in their stock price (beyond their expected industry average), and second, whether firms that used the rhetoric of agency theory in making their announcements received excess returns as well. Westphal and Zajac found that regardless of whether a firm actually implemented an LTIP, the announcement of a plan resulted in excess returns to stock price, up to a period of one year after the announcement. Of equal interest, they found that regardless of whether firms actually implemented their announced LTIPs, only those that used agency theory rhetoric in their proxy statements received an excess return. These findings suggest that purely symbolic behaviors—in this case announcements of plans that are not implemented and the use of rhetoric that resonates with the views of investors—can have effects on the stock price of firms.

Speculation and Crises

> Recurrent speculative insanity and the associated financial deprivation and larger devastation are, I am persuaded, inherent in the system. Perhaps it is better that this be recognized and accepted. (Galbraith 1994, viii)

Although historians have documented cases of speculation as far back as ancient Rome during the republic of the second century B.C., speculation acquired an economic meaning only in the late eighteenth century (Chancellor 1999). Adam Smith ([1776] 1976) defined the speculator as one interested in short-term opportunities for profit. The speculator's investments were fluid, whereas those of the conventional businessperson were more or less fixed. Schumpeter (1939, 679) noted that "the difference between a speculator and an investor can be defined by the presence or absence of the intent to 'trade,' i.e., realize profits from fluctuation in security prices."

Because markets do not always work smoothly, and are frequently known to go from boom to bust, sociologists and economists have long been interested in market speculation and crisis. In his *General Economic History* ([1923] 1927), Weber discussed the great speculative crises of the eighteenth century: John Law's Mississippi scheme in France and the South Sea bubble in England (for detailed descriptions of these events see Mackay [1841] 1932). Weber treated these events as "irrational" because neither project was capable of producing the returns necessary to sustain the investment. Nevertheless, Weber termed as "rational" subsequent crises that occurred when investment in production grew faster than consumption. According to Weber, it is these types of crises to which Karl Marx referred when he predicted the downfall of capitalism.

The stock market crash of 1929 and the Great Depression that followed greatly increased economists' interest in speculation and crises. The traditional monetarist account, put forth by Friedman and Schwartz (1963), holds that the depression was the result of Federal Reserve errors in the regulation of the money supply. The traditional Keynesian explanation holds that the depression was the result of an exogenously determined decline of investment opportunities or a prior unexplained decline in consumption activity (Temin 1976). Galbraith (1994, 24) argues that "[m]arkets in our culture are a totem; [and] to them can be ascribed no inherent aberrant tendency or fault." For this reason, economists often fail to study speculation as a phenomenon sui generis. Because the market is believed to be a neutral and accurate reflection of external influences, economists prefer to locate blame outside the market rather than acknowledge that there might be any inherent and internal dynamic or error.

One of the most developed theories of speculation and crisis was presented by Kindleberger (1978). Drawing on Minsky (1972), Kindleberger suggests that a crisis usually begins with a "displacement," an exogenous shock to the macroeconomic system (1978, 15). Although the nature of this displacement varies from one speculative boom to another, it always brings new opportunities for profit. As firms and households see others making profits from speculative purchases and resales, they follow suit. Increasing speculation leads to "mania." Kindleberger uses the word *mania* to emphasize the irrationality involved in the process (1978, 17). When insiders decide to "sell out" (and thus take their profits), there ensues an uneasy period of "financial distress." As distress persists, speculators realize that the market cannot go higher and they attempt to withdraw. The race to cash in one's long-term financial assets then turns into a stampede; and panic, like speculation, feeds on itself (20).

Abolafia and Kilduff (1988) have applied Kindleberger's model to the 1980 crisis in the silver futures market. The unusually high level of inflation during 1979 led to a speculative bubble in the price of silver. For several periods during 1979, inflation actually exceeded the cost of borrowing. Following Kindleberger, Abolafia and Kilduff describe the phases of the bubble, from the mania stage, when prices increased rapidly, through the distress stage, when participants began to question whether the increase would continue indefinitely, through the panic stage, when investors began to liquidate. Unlike Kindleberger, who focused on the irrational, crowdlike behavior during crises, Abolafia and Kilduff focus on the strategic actions of buyers, sellers, bankers, and government agencies. They show that market participants both create and are affected by the environment within which trading takes place. The primary "protagonists" in this battle were the Hunt brothers, who had been buying silver since the early 1970s but who later switched to silver futures, which did not require actual delivery of the silver but merely a promise to pay at a later date. Abolafia and Kilduff show how, prodded by worried investors, the federal government stepped in to regulate the situation by tightening the money available for speculation and forcing the Hunt brothers to reduce their holdings.

Another market crisis that has received scholarly attention is the October 19, 1987, stock market crash, popularly referred to as "Black Monday," in which the Dow Jones Industrial Average fell 23 percent in a single day. In terms of efficient market theory, there was no obvious new information to justify such a sharp decline. If stock prices reflect firms' real values, as the theory suggests, then it is difficult to explain how the real values of leading U.S. corporations declined so sharply within such a brief period.

Warner and Molotch (1993) culled the *Wall Street Journal,* the *New York Times,* and the *Los Angeles Times* between October 16 and 23, 1987, to examine the media's explanation of the crash. Only two of the 261 articles located by Warner and Molotch related the market crash to investors' knowledge of declining corporate profits (a price decline in response to relevant information as suggested by efficient market theory). Instead, articles dealing with the crash fell into one or more of the following categories: (1) they examined the role of interest rates, the money supply, and the budget deficit in undermining stockholders' confidence; (2) they examined the social structure of the market, that is, how the stock market is organized through mechanisms such as government policy, investor cliques, and trading technologies; or (3) they assumed that prices were embedded in the general psychological, cultural, and social structural forces that order human affairs, that is, that traders were subject to group emotions and were influenced by others' status when making trading decisions. If, as

Warner and Molotch argue, the press both reflects and shapes popular perceptions, it is not surprising that when the Presidential Task Force on Market Mechanisms (1988) surveyed market participants' assessment of the causes of the crash, the most widely cited answer was "social factors."

The dramatic rise in the U.S. stock market in the 1990s—and the subsequent crash—has renewed interest in speculative bubbles. Most of the books and articles published in the late 1990s were written to justify and celebrate the rising market (see, for example. Dent 1998; Elias 1999; Orman 1997). A small group of authors, however, have suggested that the rise in gambling institutions and the increased frequency of actual gambling had created a culture favorable to risk taking that encouraged investing in the stock market (Chernow 1997). Others have argued that the stock market of the 1990s reflected a speculative bubble similar to that of the 1920s (Chancellor 1999; Shiller 2000). Similarities between the 1920s and the 1990s include the fact that price/earnings ratios of stocks were at historical highs in both periods (see fig. 1), the profitability of U.S. corporations was enhanced in both periods by the inability of labor to push through real wage increases, both periods witnessed the prevalence of arguments that stock provided investment returns superior to those of

Price-earnings ratio

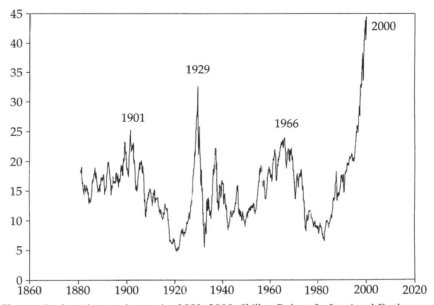

FIGURE 1. Changes in the price-earnings ratio, 1881–2000. Shiller, Robert J., Irrational Exuberance. © 2000 Robert J. Shiller, published by Princeton University Press. Reprinted by permission of Princeton University Press.

bonds, and both periods spawned claims that the United States had entered a new form of capitalism that rendered contractions a thing of the past.

The preceding suggests that speculative bubbles are recurring events with underlying patterns. Several of their causes reside in changes in economic and political institutions as well as the creation of new cultural frames. Galbraith (1994) counsels that in the aftermath of speculation excesses, the collective reality of it tends to be ignored. Although many people and institutions were involved, participants tend to attribute error, gullibility, overindulgence, or dishonesty to single individuals or corporations, rather than to the participants in general.

The collective nature of speculative bubbles raises a number of interesting sociological questions. Davis and Thompson (1994) and Fligstein (2001) have compared market behavior to social movements. Along related lines, speculative bubbles may resemble forms of collective behavior such as fads and panics. Because the state plays a central role in making and enforcing the laws that govern financial markets, what are the politics behind state actions? How are the cultural frames that trigger the process of speculative bubbles created (Collins 1981)? To what extent are the participants in these events behaving rationally? To what extent do the winners and losers fall along class or power lines? Is Galbraith correct that social scientists have failed to analyze the speculative behavior itself? If so, does this omission contribute to history repeating itself?

Merger Waves: The 1890s, 1920s, 1960s, 1980s, and 1990s

Just as speculative bubbles have occurred in different historical periods, so have merger waves. American history has witnessed five periods of heightened merger activity: the turn of the twentieth century, the 1920s, the 1960s, the 1980s, and the 1990s. Stearns and Allan (1996) have argued that the first four merger waves occurred when changes in the political and economic environment enabled once marginal actors to devise new methods to acquire firms. As these actors became increasingly successful, their innovations were mimicked throughout the business community. Stearns and Allan suggest that the 1990s wave can also be attributed to changes in the political and economic environment, but that the role of the marginal actor may have been replaced by the institutionalization of the merger market. Key components involved in the institutionalization process were the

widespread adoption of the finance conception of the firm (Fligstein 1990) and the large increase in organizations and professionals involved in merger activities in recent decades (Stearns 1995).

Stearns and Allan (1996) show that in the 1980s key antitrust enforcement positions in the Reagan administration were filled with individuals directly identified with, or openly sympathetic to, Chicago School economics. In the Chicago School approach, high market concentration is seen as having few negative consequences and mergers are viewed as generally efficiency-enhancing. In addition to a supportive state, the deconcentration of the capital market, along with the increase in foreign funds and the deregulation of savings and loan (S&L) institutions, made new sources of capital available for mergers. In 1978, foreign funds, S&Ls, and mutual funds held $103 billion, 10 percent of all corporate liabilities. By 1983, their holdings increased threefold to $302 billion, accounting for 19 percent of all corporate liabilities. Over the next six years the proportion continued to increase. In 1989, foreign funds, S&Ls, and mutual funds held $901 billion, 29 percent of all corporate liabilities. Between 1984 and 1989, these three groups thus provided the corporate sector with an additional $600 billion, a sum greater than the total capitalization of the 50 largest deals every year during the merger wave (1984–89) or the total capitalization for 50 percent of all mergers occurring during the wave.

The first actors to take advantage of these new opportunities were not the established, most powerful financial organizations, but marginal actors, challengers to the status quo. The 1980s merger movement had three sets of such challengers: a cadre of corporate raiders such as T. Boone Pickens, Ron Perelman, and the Bass brothers; the three men who engineered the leveraged buyout, Jerome Kolberg, Henry Kravis, and George Roberts (founders of the firm KKR); and most important, Michael Milken and the "second tier" investment bank for which he worked, Drexel Burnham Lambert. Although these "outsiders" came from relatively wealthy families and attended elite private universities, most were the sons or grandsons of immigrants. None worked for a Fortune 500 firm. And at a time when most CEOs were Protestants from the North, these new players were primarily Jews and/or southerners, in particular Texas- or Oklahoma-based oilmen.

Because Wall Street was viewed as a tightly controlled network unfriendly to outsiders, the insurgent actors were forced to devise novel methods for tapping the newly available capital sources. These innovations consisted of the leveraged buyout and junk bonds. A leveraged buyout occurs when a small group of investors, usually including the management, buy out a company's public shareholders by borrowing against the assets of the target company. These buyers then repay the debt either with cash from the acquired company or, more often, by selling some of the company's assets. Junk bonds are unsecured bonds whose payment of interest and repayment of principal are potentially in doubt. Because of their riskiness, their interest rates are typically higher than those of investment grade bonds. Michael Milken singlehandedly created a junk bond market. Once established, this market provided the new actors with the huge amounts of capital needed to bypass the traditional lending network. Yago (1991) has suggested that junk bonds created access to capital for small and medium-sized companies that had been previously prohibited from participating in the capital markets. In "a very real sense [this constituted] democratized capital" (9).

Sociologists and organizational theorists have paid increasing attention to the social structural and institutional influences on merger activity. Fligstein and Brantley (1992) found no association between bank interlocks and ownership and merger activity between 1969 and 1979. Contrary to this finding, however, Palmer et al. (1995) found that during the 1960s targeted firms that had interlocks with commercial and investment banks were more likely to be acquired in a friendly rather than predatory fashion. In a subsequent analysis based on the same period, Palmer and Barber (2001) found, consistent with Stearns and Allan's argument, that CEOs of relatively low social status were those most likely to pursue diversifying acquisitions.[13] Haunschild (1993), in a study of 327 large and medium-sized U.S. firms between 1981 and 1990, found that firms were more likely to engage in acquisitions if one of their top managers sat on the board of another firm that had engaged in an acquisition during the prior three years. And in a study of the 120 largest U.S. manufacturing firms from 1979, Fligstein and Markowitz (1993) found that the presence of bank officers on firms' boards increased the likelihood of a firm becoming a merger target between 1979 and 1987.

These findings on the effects of interlocks on mergers have not received unqualified support. Davis and Stout (1992), in a study of Fortune 500 firms, found no association between bank interlocks and ownership and the risk of a takeover bid between 1983 and 1990. The divergent findings on the role of financial institutions in the Fligstein and Markowitz and Davis and Stout studies may be due to sample differences or the fact that private investment banks were not included in the Davis and Stout study. Stearns and Allan (1996) show that these banks played the leading role in promoting mergers in the 1980s.

REGULATION OF CAPITAL MARKETS

One of the most controversial issues among both economists and economic sociologists is the role of state regulation of capital markets. Classical and neoclassical economists have tended to be skeptical of government regulation, but regulatory policy is a major component of economic theory, and even the most free market–oriented economists have acknowledged the need for at least a minimal level of regulation. As Joseph Stiglitz (1999, 38) has noted, "There are today few diehard free-marketeers who advocate 'free banking'—a financial sector without prudential regulation." Economic sociologists, drawing on Polanyi ([1944] 1957), have tended to view regulation as not only a necessary component of capitalist societies, but one that actually facilitates the workings of markets.

The fact that some degree of regulation of capital markets is necessary does not mean that regulation is always beneficial. In the 1980s and early 1990s, U.S. commercial banks encountered a series of difficulties, brought on by the rise of alternative sources of financing (Davis and Mizruchi 1999) and increasing competition from foreign banks (Calomiris 2000). U.S. banks found themselves increasingly shackled by state regulations that restricted branching, and by federal regulations, most notably Glass-Steagall, that placed limits on their activities (see our previous discussion). By the mid-1990s, however, most states had liberalized their branch banking laws, and Glass-Steagall was repealed in 1999. These deregulations led the way toward the creation of huge, nationwide banks that offered a range of services (Calomiris 2000, 334–38). The performance of major U.S. banks improved accordingly.

It is possible that the improved performance of U.S. banks during the 1990s was less a result of deregulation than a simple consequence of the strong overall economy. Even in cases in which it appears to be an appropriate strategy, deregulation can lead to unanticipated negative consequences. In the early 1980s, savings and loan banks in the

United States were experiencing a severe crisis because they were holding long-term low-interest mortgages at far below current interest rates (itself an artifact of regulation). In the hope of rescuing S&Ls from this predicament, Congress passed the Garn–St. Germain Act of 1982, which enabled S&Ls to diversify into other forms of investment. In their search for high returns, however, S&Ls increasingly invested in junk bonds and other high-risk instruments, which eventually led to more than 1,000 bank failures and a $200 billion taxpayer-financed bailout.

Another study that illustrates the unanticipated consequences of both regulation and deregulation is Burk's (1988) book-length treatment of attempts by the U.S. government to manage the stock market. Burk argues that the Securities and Exchange Commission was formed not simply as a direct response to the crash of 1929, as is commonly assumed, but through a snowball effect that resulted from a Senate investigation of the stock market. Public disclosure requirements were designed to limit the close-knit, insider-dominated trading that was pervasive prior to the crash. Once in place, the SEC created a very different environment for stock trading that led to a series of unanticipated consequences. "It established new confidence in the safety of stock investment, facilitated the rise of institutional stock investing, and so spurred a huge growth in market transactions and competition among market participants" (Burk 1988, 137). By the late 1960s, however, the new competition led to the undermining of the regulatory order, creating chaos in the market and resulting in the financial ruin of many firms. Between 1969 and 1970 over 100 broker-dealers went bankrupt or were forced into involuntary mergers.

Abolafia (1996) argues that too little attention has been paid to the nongovernmental systems of regulation. Trading markets (stocks, bonds, and futures) are also kept in check by informal modes of control. At the individual level, boundaries of appropriate behavior are defined by trading floor culture. Traders learn what strategies are acceptable and which ones are discouraged. Behavior is modified through such informal means as yelling at the miscreant publicly or freezing her or him out of trades. At the transactional level, self-regulatory associations have been created to restrain market behavior. Abolafia finds that these forms of control are similar to governmental regulation in that they tend to reflect the interests of the most powerful actors, create their own contradictions, and fail to prevent cycles of opportunism.

What these studies suggest is the simultaneous need for, and yet the problems created by, the regulation of markets. As Burk's study indicated, the logical outcome of unrestricted market processes was that those with more power hoarded information and took advantage of their privileges. This situation created the need for regulation. Yet attempts at regulation created an entirely new set of unanticipated problems, leading to calls for deregulation. Deregulation then led to a situation not unlike the one that created the need for the SEC in the first place. Reflecting this, Abolafia (1996) suggests that "[R]egulation will never be fine-tuned and regulator action, even in the presence of political consensus, will remain part science and part craft" (181).

One can ask whether a regulatory system with greater independence from financial community pressures would be more effective. On the other hand, the organizational literature is rife with cases in which even well-intentioned leaders become diverted by unanticipated obstacles. The sociologically significant questions for research on the regulation of financial markets involve how and by whom regulation is initiated (including the cultural context in which this takes place), the types of conflicts that arise, how are they resolved, and the consequences, both anticipated and unanticipated, of the regulation.

FINANCIAL MARKETS OUTSIDE THE UNITED STATES

The financial systems of industrialized nations vary in a number of ways. Gerschenkron (1962) and Zysman (1983) noted that historically, these financial systems could be divided into two basic types: capital market–based and credit-based. In capital market–based systems, such as the United States and the United Kingdom, security issues (stocks and bonds) have been the primary source of long-term funds, while bank lending has functioned primarily to provide short-term funds. In credit-based systems, such as France, Germany, and Japan, the stock and bond markets have not been easily accessible to private borrowers. Banks have served as the primary provider of long-term funds, often owning or voting much of the stock of important companies. Gerschenkron (1962) argued that credit-based systems were solutions to late development, while the capital market–based systems were tied to an earlier industrial transformation.

In France (historically a credit-based financial

system), most external financing of private companies has been arranged through borrowing from financial institutions rather than through the independent sale of securities. The limited importance of the securities market for corporate finance meant that firms sought external funds in the form of loans from banks. In France, the market for these loans was maintained by government intervention, since the institutions that collect short-term deposits did not always lend them to final users. Instead, these deposits flowed to specialized lending institutions, which controlled nearly a third of the funds that the financial system provided to the economy. The additional step from saver to borrower allowed the government to stand between the savings and the investment institutions and thus to influence the allocation of funds by selectively manipulating access, subsiding price, or some technique of rediscounting. In 1979, the Bank of France reported that 43 percent of all credits to the French economy were made with some kind of privilege or subsidy and that 25 percent of corporate lending was subsidized directly. These figures reflected an extensive and intimate system of ties among nonfinancial corporations, financial institutions, and the state (Zysman 1983, 112–33). Beginning in the mid-1980s, however, following a series of deregulations (including the removal of subsidized credits), the relative use of equity increased (Metais 2000). In 1985, the equity/total asset ratio for French manufacturers was 0.206 while the debt/total asset ratio was 0.736. By 1993, the equity figure had increased to 0.356 while the debt figure had declined to 0.591 (Andrés-Alonso et al. 2000).

Japan and Germany have also historically had credit-based financial systems. In both countries, corporations were dependent on banks rather than securities markets. Banks acted as the primary intermediary between savers and private companies, and external financing came primarily from bank loans. The stock market did not serve as a means of raising new funds from the household sector. Rather, in both countries, there was a high level of equity holdings between banks and firms (Franks and Mayer 1992; Gerlach 1992). In Japan, these interfirm relations, which were the outcome of repeated past transactions, often served as substitutes for price mechanisms in the distribution of funds between banks and corporations.

Japan experienced a rapid expansion during the 1980s that led eventually to a collapse during the 1990s. In the late 1980s, the use of equity financing increased precipitously, from about four million yen among all Japanese corporations in 1986, to 26 trillion yen by 1989 (Gao 2001). The relative ratio of equity to assets versus debt to assets also increased, but at a rate somewhat lower than the increase in France. In 1985, the equity/total asset ratio for Japanese manufacturers was 0.264 while the debt/total asset ratio was 0.678. By 1993, the equity figure had increased to 0.324 while the debt figure had declined to 0.634 (Andrés-Alonso et al. 2000). Although Japanese firms' use of debt therefore increased significantly during the 1990s, it did so at a much lower rate than in France. In France, the relative level of equity versus debt went from 28.0 percent in 1985 to 60.2 percent in 1993; in Japan, during the same period, the relative level of equity versus debt went from 38.9 percent to 51.1 percent. Moreover, as Gao (2001, chap. 6) notes, much of the new equity went directly into the purchase of real estate rather than toward upgrading manufacturing capability. Gao suggests that the power of Japanese banks relative to nonfinancial corporations declined during the downturn of the 1990s. Although these developments may indicate a trend in Japan away from a pure credit-based system, it would be premature to conclude that a qualitative break has occurred.[14]

Unlike France or Japan, the German government has tended to not intervene to affect the allocation of credit. Instead, banks historically were the preeminent actors in the transformation and allocation of financial resources to industry (Zysman 1983). This gave German banks power with respect to corporations because, in addition to their legal right to own substantial stock in corporations and to exercise proxy votes for other shareholders, all routes to corporate external finance, including loans, bonds, and equity, led back to the banks. The German financial system did experience changes during the 1990s. Banks began to securitize their loans (combining them into a single portfolio and selling them as a security), rather than holding them for the life of the agreement. This change, along with the growing presence of investment/pension funds as both owners and lenders, has increasingly transformed bank-firm relations from embedded (albeit asymmetric) into "arm's length" ties (Windolf 2002). As in the Japanese case, even these changes are not substantial enough as of this writing to suggest that Germany is no longer accurately described as a credit-based system. In 1985, the equity/total asset ratio for German manufacturers was 0.227 while the debt/total asset ratio was 0.538. By 1992, the equity figure had barely increased, to 0.240, while the debt figure had declined only slightly, to 0.502 (Andrés-Alonso et al. 2000).[15]

The financial system in the United Kingdom differs from France, Japan, and Germany in that like the United States, it is a capital market–based system. Most of the external financing of private companies is arranged through the sale of stocks and bonds. Similar to the United States, the securities market, once the domain of individual investors, is becoming increasingly dominated by institutions. Between 1963 and 1985, the portion of U.K. equity held by individuals dropped from 54 to 31 percent, with a corresponding increase in the proportion of institutional stockholding. These institutional investors do not make loans, however. Merchant banks arrange stock and bond offerings and commercial banks provide corporations with short-term financing. Although several markets, particularly the commercial bank market, are in effect oligopolies, power in one financial market does not necessarily translate into power in other markets. Increased competition between types of financial institutions, and between British and foreign banks, prevents businesses from having to face a single set of capital suppliers. Moreover, British firms have financed most of their expansion from savings and the sale of equity, not from credit, making them less dependent on long-term funding. As for the state, the British government does not control channels of lending. As a result, the British financial system is characterized by a lack of direct involvement between industry and financial institutions on one hand, and a lack of government involvement in the affairs of financial institutions and in the allocation of industrial credit on the other (Zysman 1983, 189–201). As we have noted, the structure of a nation's financial system differs based on whether it was an "early" or "late" developer. But Zysman argues that these systems, once in place, continue to play a major role in shaping contemporary national economies, primarily by affecting the ability of governments to develop national industrial policies.[16]

Although the classification of various industrialized nations into one of these two types was generally accepted into the early-1990s, some scholars have suggested that the differences began to become blurred as the 1990s progressed (Andrés-Alonso et al. 2000; Windolf 2002). The available data, which run through the early 1990s, indicate that there has been some movement of historical credit-based systems toward the capital market–based model. The extent of this movement remains an open question, however. The average ratio of market debt to total debt between 1985 and 1993 was 0.42 in Japan, 0.46 in Germany, and 0.48 in France on one hand, and 0.61 in Britain and 0.74 in the United States on the other. These figures suggest that we should exercise caution before assuming that the credit versus capital market distinction is no longer relevant. At the same time, the changes that have occurred, as well as the indeterminacy of trends during the last years of the twentieth century, indicate that the trajectory of these nations' financial systems deserves further attention.

THE GLOBALIZATION OF FINANCIAL MARKETS

A potentially critical issue in understanding national financial markets is the increased globalization of the capital market during the late twentieth century. There are a number of perspectives on this issue, but a central debate has occurred over the extent to which the globalization process has led to a decline in the power of individual governments to regulate their own economies. Those who make this argument tend to focus on the increased mobility of capital brought on by the deregulation of national financial markets in the wake of the collapse of the Bretton Woods agreement in the early 1970s. The ease with which capital can be moved across national borders, they suggest, has made it more difficult for governments to maintain their social safety nets (Frieden 1991; Strange 1996; Cerny 1997). The prominent role played by the International Monetary Fund and the World Bank in dictating the policies of developing countries as a condition for receiving loans is viewed as rendering already weak states even more vulnerable (see Stiglitz 2002 for a critique of IMF policies). The extent to which the globalization of trade and finance is responsible for these trends is an extremely controversial issue that is well beyond the scope of this chapter.

That globalization is real is without question. The level of cross-border economic activity increased twelvefold between 1953 and 1997, and nearly tripled as a proportion of world GDP (Fligstein 2001, 196–97). This high level of international trade is not historically unique, however (only in 1997 did it reach its level in 1914). Moreover, the process has not been a unidirectional one. U.S. banks rapidly increased their foreign operations in the 1960s and 1970s but then contracted them during the 1980s and 1990s (Mizruchi and Davis 2001). Nor does the currently high level of global economic activity by itself demonstrate that individual governments are powerless. More than 80 percent of world GDP still occurs within national borders, and despite recent increases in foreign ownership and employment, as of the mid-1990s, more than 90 percent of corporate ownership and employment in the United States, Germany, and Japan was in domestic hands (Fligstein 2001, 209). What is important for our purposes is that despite the clear significance of this issue and the considerable amount of attention it has received, we still have made little headway on resolving the debate. One possible reason is that the nature of the world financial system is such that by the time a work appears in print, conditions may have significantly changed. In the mid-1970s, for example, Japan began to liberalize its financial markets. In a sensitive historical analysis, Gao (2001) argues that this liberalization was a contributing factor to the Japanese economic crisis of the late 1990s. When the Japanese economy was experiencing rapid growth during the 1980s, few observers foresaw the severe crisis that subsequently occurred. Similarly, many observers of the United States during the recession of the early 1990s were writing about the long-run decline of the American economy. Few of them foresaw the spectacular economic boom of the late 1990s, just as few who trumpeted the U.S. economy as entering a recession-proof stage predicted the stock market collapse that began in 2000. These examples indicate why a historical perspective is so important in discussions of globalization, and financial markets in general. It is valuable, and necessary, to analyze the contemporary workings of financial phenomena. We should do so with the understanding, however, that our analyses may be proven obsolete shortly after (or even before) they appear in print.

CONCLUSION: BANKING, FINANCIAL MARKETS, AND SOCIETY

Banking and finance is now an important subarea of economic sociology. The sizable number of recent studies reported in this chapter demonstrates that sociologists can no longer be accused of ignoring these issues. Still, there is more to be done.

The banking industry changed dramatically in the last decade of the twentieth century, and these changes raise a number of important questions for economic sociologists interested in how power influences economic actions. First, what are the consequences of having fewer and larger banks involved in a greater variety of businesses? Will the increased size of individual banks and the greater concentration in the industry lead to a resurgence of bank power, or, with the shift toward service-oriented activities, will banks continue to relinquish their role as the key arbiter in the allocation of capital?

Second, we have witnessed a deconcentration of financial assets in the U.S. capital market. Because it remains a crucial resource, however, the unequal distribution of capital will always have the potential to create power differentials among social actors. The spectacular boom and bust period in the American economy at the turn of the twenty-first century offers new opportunities to study this potential. Start-up firms, for example, are virtually completely dependent on the external funding they receive from venture capitalists. As the bear market of 2001–2 made it more difficult to execute quick, highly lucrative IPOs, did venture capitalists adopt a strategy of exit, loyalty, or voice (Hirschman 1970)? What are the consequences of each of these strategies on the amount of risk taking and innovation occurring among start-up firms?

Third, the fluctuating stock market performance experienced by many firms also enables sociologists to study the power of shareholders, in particular institutional investors. Some authors have examined the power of institutional investors to influence corporate management (see Useem 1996). In the 1990s, when stock prices soared, many CEOs accepted the demands of institutional investors to tie their compensation packages to their firm's stock price. Just as salaries and perks escalated during the bull market, we would expect them to plummet in a bear market. Yet as a *New York Times* article written during the bear market of 2001–2 noted, "Companies divided into two roughly equal-size groups. The first half, which appears to believe in paying for performance, cut the pay of the top executive for the first time in years. The other half, which seems to believe simply in paying a lot, reacted to a year of recession and war often by creating the impression they had reduced pay without actually doing so" (Leonhardt 2002, 1). A systematic inquiry into the causes of such a divide is an excellent research topic for economic sociology.

Economic sociologists interested in culture might examine the role that various theories themselves play in driving economic behavior. During the 1990s bull market, efficient market theory played an important role in boosting stockholder confidence. As stock prices rose dramatically, many investors chose to stay in the market, based on the argument that stock prices reflected firms' true value. There is evidence, however, that a firm's stock price can reflect factors other than its value. As we saw earlier, Westphal and Zajac (1998) showed that in some situations a firm's rhetoric was more influential than its actual behavior in setting its stock price. And, well before the Merrill Lynch scandal made national headlines, Hayward and Boeker (1998) had shown that a security analyst's rating was in part determined by whether the firm being rated was a client of its bank's corporate finance department. Given the large numbers of individuals who have used the stock market to save for their children's education as well as their own retirement, understanding what stock prices do or do not represent becomes a vital question. Similarly, in light of the corporate scandals of the early 2000s, a better understanding of how cultural norms operate in financial markets might help us predict when ethical lapses might occur.

We mentioned previously the similarities between the 1990s and the 1920s. The 2000s began with a period of stock declines and scandals not unlike those of the 1930s. As we noted, historically, many economists preferred to locate blame outside the market rather than study speculation as a phenomenon internal to markets. Are periods of "speculative insanity" inherent in the system, as Galbraith (1994) suggests? If so, the broad perspectives within economic sociology that focus on the cultural and political embeddedness of economic phenomena and the critical role of social networks should be useful in developing a sociological account of speculative bubbles.

Finally, capitalist economies are mercurial—often changing dramatically from decade to decade. If we are to explain changes as well as recurring patterns, an important next step is to develop more theoretically driven and historically sensitive analyses. One place to start might be to inquire as to what are the motivations for banking systems to operate and under what conditions do they transform.

We want to end this chapter on an upbeat note. Economic sociologists have made important contributions to the study of banking and finance over the last decade. As the American and world economy once again enter a period of uncertainty, a sociological understanding of these topics will remain of critical importance.

NOTES

We would like to thank Walter Powell and Laurel Smith-Doerr as well as Howard Aldrich, Bruce Carruthers, Frank Dobbin, Giovanni Dosi, Mark Granovetter, and Viviana Zelizer for their comments and suggestions. We are especially indebted to Neil Smelser and Richard Swedberg for their detailed comments on an earlier draft. Finally, we thank the Russell Sage Foundation for supporting this project.

1. This chapter represents a substantial revision of the one that appeared in the first edition of the *Handbook*. We have incorporated a number of recent sociological studies of banking and finance. The sections on banks and corporate control, financial markets, institutional investors, merger waves, regulation of capital markets, and globalization of financial markets have been revised and updated. We have added new sections on banking today, venture capital, and the stock market. We deleted our previous discussion of money. See Carruthers, "The Sociology of Money and Credit," this volume.

2. See Swedberg 1989 for an earlier review of the literature on banking.

3. For discussions of money creation, see Ritter and Silber 1974 or http://www.amosweb.com/cgi-bin/cls_dsp .pl?crs=macro&fcd=lsn&lsn=19.

4. Our focus in this chapter is on private financial institutions. All industrialized societies have central banks administered by the state. These central banks serve as creditors to both private banks and the government and also play a major role in regulating the nation's money supply. See Siklos 2002 and Deane and Pringle 1999 for studies of central banks in industrial countries, and Greider 1987 and Blinder 1999 for in-depth accounts of the U.S. Federal Reserve Bank.

5. For two recent studies that deal with nonfinancial firms' dependence on banks, see Uzzi 1999 on mid-sized U.S. firms and Keister 2001 on members of Chinese business groups.

6. Among the 194 deals for which we had complete information, 27.3 percent involved loans (to be held by the bank), 22.7 percent involved capital market services, 16.5 percent involved transactional services, 16.0 percent involved securitized loans (to be sold off by the bank), and 14.4 percent involved trading. The remainder involved a combination of products.

7. Banking is in fact a relatively "feminized" industry. As Mayer notes, "Banking has a higher percentage of female officers than any other industry" (1997, 19).

8. Funding companies consist of funding subsidiaries, nonbank financial companies, and custodial accounts for reinvested collateral of securities lending operations (Board of Governors of the Federal Reserve System 2002, 73).

9. Companies too small to attract venture capital often depend on "angels" for financing (Aldrich 1999). Angels are generally former entrepreneurs who invest for a variety of reasons, ranging from an interest in mentoring new firms to making a high return on investments. In 2000 it was estimated that 50,000 companies in the United States received approximately $40 billion in angel funding (National Commission on Entrepreneurship 2002).

10. Historically, the VC industry has experienced periods of boom and bust (Gompers and Lerner 2001). In 2001 investments fell to $33 billion ("Market Perspective" 2002, 7).

11. Although the effect of industry market-to-book ratio was not significantly associated with the number or duration of rounds, Gompers argues that his hypothesis is supported because the industry market-to-book ratio is a positive predictor of the total amount of financing the start-up received. Gompers views the latter as an indicator of monitoring, suggesting that VC firms continue to invest in start-ups only because they have closely kept tabs on the firm's progress. This

view strikes us as assuming what needs to be demonstrated: that investing equals monitoring. The collapse of the dot-com industry at the turn of the twenty-first century suggests that investors may not always be aware of the potential difficulties that their start-ups face. Careful monitoring would therefore seem as likely to result in a withholding of funds as it would in a disbursement of them.

12. The Chinese wall is a metaphor used within the investment community to describe a set of internal rules and procedures that prevent one department from obtaining or providing information prejudicial to the clients of another.

13. Palmer and Barber also provided quantitative support for Stearns and Allan's assertion that marginal social status is a necessary but not sufficient condition leading corporate CEOs to pursue acquisitions. "Marginal status provides CEOs with an interest in but not the capacity to complete acquisitions. Social networks [membership in exclusive social clubs and positions on corporate boards] provide marginal members of the elite with the capacity to translate their interests into action" (Palmer and Barber 2001, 105).

14. Further evidence in support of this suggestion comes from the percentage of total debt accounted for by bank lending. In France, this figure declined from 26.3 percent in 1985 to 16.2 percent in 1993. In Japan, the percentage remained virtually unchanged during this period: 41.8 percent in 1985, 42.5 percent in 1993.

15. The percentage of total debt accounted for by bank lending in Germany remained virtually unchanged during the two periods. As in the Japanese case, the level actually increased slightly, from 29.0 percent in 1985 to 30.7 percent in 1992.

16. Scott (1987) has shown that the different forms of interfirm relations in Britain, France, and Germany can be traced to their three distinct paths of historical development: the "entrepreneurial" system in Britain, in which development was generated primarily by small, family-owned firms; the "holding" system in France, characterized by a series of interest groups centered around specific family or financial interests; and the "hegemonic" system in Germany, based on alliances of large banks and commercial firms by means of shared loan consortia, stockholding, and director interlocks.

REFERENCES

Abolafia, Mitchel Y. 1996. *Making Markets.* Cambridge: Harvard University Press.

Abolafia, Mitchel Y., and Martin Kilduff. 1988. "Enacting Market Crisis: The Social Construction of a Speculative Bubble." *Administrative Science Quarterly* 33:177–93.

Aldrich, Howard. 1999. *Organizations Evolving.* London: Sage.

Andrés-Alonso, Pablo de, Valentín Azofra-Palenzuela, Félix J. López Iturriaga, and José Miguel Rodríguez-Fernández. 2000. "The Effects of Alternative Financial System Models on Corporate Governance." Pp. 70–111 in *Strategic Challenges in European Banking,* ed. Edward P. M. Gardener and Joe Falzon. New York: St. Martin's Press.

Baker, Wayne E. 1984. "The Social Structure of a National Securities Market." *American Journal of Sociology* 89:775–811.

———. 1990. "Market Networks and Corporate Behavior." *American Journal of Sociology* 96:589–625.

Baker, Wayne E., and Ananth V. Iyer. 1992. "Information Networks and Market Behavior." *Journal of Mathematical Sociology* 16:305–32.

Banz, Rolf W. 1981. "The Relationship between Return and Market Value of Common Stocks." *Journal of Financial Economics* 9:3–18.

Baran, Paul A., and Paul M. Sweezy. 1966. *Monopoly Capital.* New York: Monthly Review Press.

Baysinger, Barry D., Rita D. Kosnik, and Thomas A. Turk. 1991. "Effects of Board and Ownership Structure on Corporate R&D Strategy." *Academy of Management Journal* 34:205–14.

Berle, Adolf A., and Gardiner C. Means. [1932] 1968. *The Modern Corporation and Private Property.* New York: Harcourt, Brace, and World.

Blinder, Alan S. 1999. *Central Banking in Theory and Practice.* Cambridge: MIT Press.

Board of Governors of the Federal Reserve System. 1990. Flow of Funds Outstanding, 1966–89. September

———. 2002. Flow of Funds Accounts, 1995–2001. March 7.

Brealey, Richard A., Stewart C. Myers, and Alan J. Marcus. 2001. *Fundamentals of Corporate Finance.* 3d ed. New York: McGraw-Hill Irwin.

Burk, James. 1988. *Values in the Marketplace.* New York: Aldine de Gruyter.

Burt, Ronald S. 1992. *Structural Holes: The Social Structure of Competition.* Cambridge: Harvard University Press.

Calomiris, Charles W. 2000. *U.S. Bank Deregulation in Historical Perspective.* Cambridge: Cambridge University Press.

Cerny, Philip G. 1997. "International Finance and the Erosion of Capitalist Diversity." Pp. 173–81 in *Political Economy of Modern Capitalism,* ed. Colin Crouch and Wolfgang Streeck. London: Sage.

Chaganti, Rajeswararao, and Fariborz Damanpour. 1991. "Institutional Ownership, Capital Structure, and Firm Performance." *Strategic Management Journal* 12:479–91.

Chancellor, Edward. 1999. *Devil Take the Hindmost: A History of Financial Speculation.* New York: Farrar, Straus and Giroux.

Chandler, Alfred D. 1977. *The Visible Hand: The Managerial Revolution in America.* Cambridge: Harvard University Press.

Chernow, Ron. 1997. *The Death of the Banker: The Decline and Fall of the Great Financial Dynasties and the Triumph of the Small Investor.* New York: Vintage.

Cochran, Thomas C., and William Miller. [1942] 1961. *The Age of Enterprise.* New York: Harper and Row.

Collins, Randall. 1981. "On the Microfoundations of Macrosociology." *American Journal of Sociology* 86:984–1014.

Davis, Gerald F., Kristina A. Diekmann, and Catherine H. Tinsley. 1994. "The Decline and Fall of the Conglomerate Firm in the 1980s: A Study in the

De-institutionalization of an Organizational Form." *American Sociological Review* 59:547–70.

Davis, Gerald F., and Mark S. Mizruchi. 1999. "The Money Center Cannot Hold: Commercial Banks in the U.S. System of Corporate Governance." *Administrative Science Quarterly* 44:215–39.

Davis, Gerald F., and Suzanne K. Stout. 1992. "Organization Theory and the Market for Corporate Control: A Dynamic Analysis of the Characteristics of Large Takeover Targets, 1980–1990." *Administrative Science Quarterly* 37:605–33.

Davis, Gerald F., and Tracy A. Thompson. 1994. "A Social Movement Perspective on Corporate Control." *Administrative Science Quarterly* 39:141–73.

Deane, Marjorie, and Robert Pringle. 1999. *The Central Banks.* New York: Viking Press.

DeBondt, Werner, and Richard H. Thaler. 1985. "Does the Stock Market Overreact?" *Journal of Finance* 40:793–805.

Dent, Harry S. 1998. *The Roaring 2000s: Building the Wealth and Lifestyle You Desire in the Greatest Boom in History.* New York: Simon and Schuster.

Elias, David. 1999. *Dow 40,000: Strategies for Profiting from the Greatest Bull Market in History.* New York: McGraw-Hill.

Fama, Eugene F. 1970. "Efficient Capital Markets: A Review of Theory and Empirical Work." *Journal of Finance* 25:383–417.

Fama, Eugene F., and Kenneth R. French. 1992. "The Cross Section of Expected Stock Returns." *Journal of Finance* 47:427–66.

Fligstein, Neil. 1990. *The Transformation of Corporate Control.* Cambridge: Harvard University Press.

———. 2001. *The Architecture of Markets.* Princeton: Princeton University Press.

Fligstein, Neil, and Peter Brantley. 1992. "Bank Control, Owner Control, or Organization Dynamics: Who Controls the Large Corporation?" *American Journal of Sociology* 98:280–307.

Fligstein, Neil, and Linda Markowitz. 1993. "Financial Reorganization of American Corporations in the 1980s." Pp. 185–206 in *Sociology and the Public Agenda,* ed. William Julius Wilson. Newbury Park, Calif.: Sage.

Franks, Julian, and Colin Mayer. 1992. "Corporate Control: A Synthesis of the International Evidence." Paper presented at the Conference on Corporate Control, San Francisco.

Freeman, John H. 1999. "Venture Capital as an Economy of Time." Pp. 460–82 in *Corporate Social Capital,* ed. Roger Th.A.J. Leenders and Shaul M. Gabbay. Boston: Kluwer Academic Publishers.

Frieden, Jeffry A. 1991. "Invested Interests: The Politics of National Economic Policies in a World of Global Finance." *International Organization* 45: 425–51.

Friedman, Milton, and Anna J. Schwartz. 1963. *A Monetary History of the United States, 1867–1960.* Princeton: National Bureau of Economic Research.

Galbraith, John Kenneth. 1994. *A Short History of Financial Euphoria.* New York: Penguin.

Gao, Bai. 2001. *Japan's Economic Dilemma: The Institutional Origins of Prosperity and Stagnation.* Cambridge: Cambridge University Press.

Gerlach, Michael L. 1992. *Alliance Capitalism: The Social Organization of Japanese Business.* Berkeley and Los Angeles: University of California Press.

Gerschenkron, Alexander. 1962. *Economic Backwardness in Historical Perspective.* Cambridge: Belknap Press of Harvard University Press.

Gompers, Paul A. 1995. "Optimal Investment, Monitoring, and the Staging of Venture Capital." *Journal of Finance* 50:1461–89.

Gompers, Paul A., and Josh Lerner. 1999. *The Venture Capital Cycle.* Cambridge: MIT Press.

———. 2001. *The Money of Invention: How Venture Capital Creates New Wealth.* Boston: Harvard Business School Press.

Greider, William. 1987. *Secrets of the Temple: How the Federal Reserve Runs the Country.* New York: Simon and Schuster.

Haunschild, Pamela R. 1993. "Interorganizational Imitation: The Impact of Interlocks on Corporate Acquisition Activity." *Administrative Science Quarterly* 38:564–92.

Hawley, James P., and Andrew T. Williams. 2000. *The Rise of Fiduciary Capitalism.* Philadelphia: University of Pennsylvania Press.

Hayward, Mathew L. A., and Warren Boeker. 1998. "Power and Conflicts of Interest in Professional Firms: Evidence from Investment Banking." *Administrative Science Quarterly* 43:1–22.

Hirschman, Albert O. 1970. *Exit, Voice, and Loyalty.* Cambridge: Harvard University Press.

Jarrell, Gregg A., Ken Lehn, and Wayne Marr. 1985. "Institutional Ownership, Tender Offers and Long-Term Investments." Working paper, Office of the Chief Economist, Securities and Exchange Commission, Washington, D.C.

Jegadeesh, Narasimhan, and Sheridan Titman. 1993. "Returns to Buying Winners and Selling Losers: Implications for Stock Market Efficiency." *Journal of Finance* 48:65–91.

Keister, Lisa A. 2001. "Exchange Structures in Transition: Lending and Trade Relations in Chinese Business Groups." *American Sociological Review* 66:336–60.

Kindleberger, Charles P. 1978. *Manias, Panics, and Crashes: A History of Financial Crises.* New York: Basic.

Leonhardt, David. 2002. "Did Pay Incentives Cut Both Ways?" *New York Times,* April 7, sec. 3, p. 1.

Lieberson, Stanley. 1961. "The Division of Labor in Banking." *American Journal of Sociology* 66: 491–96.

Lintner, John. 1959. "The Financing of Corporations." Pp. 166–201 in *The Corporation in Modern Society,* ed. Edward S. Mason. Cambridge: Harvard University Press.

Mackay, Charles. [1841] 1932. *Extraordinary Popular Delusions and the Madness of Crowds.* Boston: L. C. Page.

Mandel, Michael J. 2000. *The Coming Internet Depression.* New York: Basic Books.

"Market Perspective: Venture Capital Wanes." *New York Times,* May 5, Bu 7.

Marx, Karl. [1894] 1967. *Capital.* Vol. 3. New York: International Publishers.

Mayer, Martin. 1974. *The Bankers.* New York: Ballantine.

———. 1997. *The Bankers: The Next Generation.* New York: Truman Talley Books.

Metais, Joël. 2000. "Public Banks in France: Current Problems and Prospective Issues." Pp. 211–24 in *Strategic Challenges in European Banking,* ed. Edward P. M. Gardener and Joe Falzon. New York: Palgrave.

Minsky, Hyman. 1972. "Financial Stability Revisited: The Economics of Disaster." Pp. 95–136 in vol. 3 of *Reappraisal of the Federal Reserve Discount Mechanism,* by Board of Governors of the Federal Reserve System. Washington, D.C.: U.S. Government Printing Office.

Mintz, Beth, and Michael Schwartz. 1985. *The Power Structure of American Business.* Chicago: University of Chicago Press.

Mizruchi, Mark S. 1982. *The American Corporate Network, 1904–1974.* Beverly Hills, Calif.: Sage.

Mizruchi, Mark S., and Gerald F. Davis. 2001. "The Globalization of American Banking, 1962–1981." Paper presented at the Princeton Economic Sociology Conference, Princeton University, April.

Mizruchi, Mark S., and Linda Brewster Stearns. 1994. "A Longitudinal Study of Borrowing by Large American Corporations." *Administrative Science Quarterly* 39:118–40.

———. 2001. "Getting Deals Done: The Use of Social Networks in Bank Decision-Making." *American Sociological Review* 66:647–71.

National Commission on Entrepreneurship. 2002. *NCOE Update* No. 62, October 29.

Orman, Suze. 1997. *The Nine Steps to Financial Freedom.* New York: Crown.

Palmer, Donald A., and Brad M. Barber. 2001. "Challengers, Elites, and Owning Families: A Social Class Theory of Corporate Acquisitions in the 1960s." *Administrative Science Quarterly* 46:87–120.

Palmer, Donald A., Brad M. Barber, Xueguang Zhou, and Yasmin Soysal. 1995. "The Friendly and Predatory Acquisition of Large U.S. Corporations in the 1960s: The Other Contested Terrain." *American Sociological Review* 60:469–99.

Pfeffer, Jeffrey, and Gerald R. Salancik. 1978. *The External Control of Organizations: A Resource Dependence Perspective.* New York: Harper and Row.

Podolny, Joel M. 2001. "Networks as the Pipes and Prisms of the Market." *American Journal of Sociology* 107:33–60.

Polanyi, Karl. [1944] 1957. *The Great Transformation.* Boston: Beacon Press.

Powell, Walter W., Kenneth W. Koput, James I. Bowie, and Laurel Smith-Doerr. 2002. "The Spatial Clustering of Science and Capital: Accounting for Biotech Firm-Venture Capital Relationships." *Regional Studies* 36(3): 291–305.

Presidential Task Force on Market Mechanisms. 1988. *Report of the Presidential Task Force on Market Mechanisms.* Washington, D.C.: U.S. Government Printing Office.

Rhoades, Stephen A. 2000. "Bank Mergers and Banking Structure in the United States, 1980–98." Staff Study 174, Board of Governors of the Federal Reserve System.

Ritter, Lawrence S., and William L. Silber. 1974. *Principles of Money, Banking, and Financial Markets.* New York: Basic Books.

Roe, Mark J. 1994. *Strong Managers, Weak Owners: The Political Roots of American Corporate Finance.* Princeton: Princeton University Press.

Schumpeter, Joseph A. 1939. *Business Cycles: A Theoretical, Historical, and Statistical Analysis of the Capitalist Process.* New York: McGraw-Hill.

Scott, John. 1987. "Intercorporate Structures in Western Europe: A Comparative Historical Analysis." Pp. 208–32 in *Intercorporate Relations: The Structural Analysis of Business,* ed. Mark S. Mizruchi and Michael Schwartz. Cambridge: Cambridge University Press.

Seyhun, H. N. 1986. "Insiders: Profits, Costs of Trading, and Market Efficiency." *Journal of Financial Economics* 16:189–212.

Shiller, Robert J. 1981. "Do Stock Prices Move Too Much to Be Justified by Subsequent Movements in Dividends?" *American Economic Review* 71:421–36.

———. 2000. *Irrational Exuberance.* Princeton: Princeton University Press.

Siklos, Pierre L. 2002. *The Changing Face of Central Banking: Evolutionary Trends since World War II.* Cambridge: Cambridge University Press.

Smelser, Neil J. 1959. *Social Change in the Industrial Revolution.* Chicago: University of Chicago Press.

Smith, Adam. [1776] 1976. *An Inquiry into the Nature and Causes of the Wealth of Nations.* Oxford: Clarendon Press.

Sorenson, Olav, and Toby E. Stuart. 2001. "Syndication Networks and the Spatial Distribution of Venture Capital Investments." *American Journal of Sociology* 106:1546–88.

Stearns, Linda Brewster. 1986. "Capital Market Effects on External Control of Corporations." *Theory and Society* 15:47–75.

———. 1995. "How Markets Get Made: The Institutionalization of the U.S. Merger Market." Paper presented at the Annual Meeting of the American Sociological Association, Washington, D.C., August.

Stearns, Linda Brewster, and Kenneth D. Allan. 1996. "Institutional Environments: The Corporate Merger Wave of the 1980s." *American Sociological Review* 61:699–718.

Stearns, Linda Brewster, and Mark S. Mizruchi. 1993a. "Corporate Financing: Economic and Social Aspects." Pp. 279–307 in *Explorations in Economic Sociology,* ed. Richard Swedberg. New York: Russell Sage Foundation.

———. 1993b. "Board Composition and Corporate Financing: The Impact of Financial Institution Representation on Borrowing." *Academy of Management Journal* 36:603–18.

Stickel, Scott E. 1992. "Reputation and Performance among Security Analysts." *Journal of Finance* 47: 1811–36.

Stiglitz, Joseph E. 1999. *State versus Market.* Dhaka: University Press Limited.

———. 2002. *Globalization and Its Discontents.* New York: W. W. Norton.

Strange, Susan. 1996. *The Retreat of the State.* Cambridge: Cambridge University Press.

Swedberg, Richard. 1989. "Banks from a Sociological Perspective." Pp. 157–88 in *Sociology in the World: Essays in Honor of Ulf Himmelstrand on His 65th Birthday,* ed. Goran Ahrne et al. Uppsala: Uppsala Universitet.

Temin, Peter. 1976. *Did Monetary Forces Cause the Great Depression?* New York: W. W. Norton.

Useem, Michael. 1993. *Executive Defense: Shareholder Power and Corporate Reorganization.* Cambridge: Harvard University Press.

———. 1996. *Investor Capitalism: How Money Managers Are Changing the Face of Corporate America.* New York: Basic Books.

Useem, Michael, and Martin M. Gottlieb. 1990. "Corporate Restructuring, Ownership-Disciplined Alignment, and the Reorganization of Management." *Human Resource Management* 29:285–306.

Uzzi, Brian. 1999. "Embeddedness in the Making of Financial Capital: How Social Relations and Networks Benefit Firms Seeking Financing." *American Sociological Review* 64:481–505.

Warner, Kee, and Harvey L. Molotch. 1993. "Information in the Marketplace: Media Explanations of the '87 Crash." *Social Problems* 40:167–88.

Wasserstein, Bruce. 2000. *Big Deal: 2000 and Beyond.* New York: Warner Books.

Weber, Max. [1923] 1927. *General Economic History.* Trans. Frank H. Knight. New York: Greenberg.

———. [1922] 1978. *Economy and Society: An Outline of Interpretive Sociology.* Ed. Guenther Roth and Claus Wittich. Trans. Ephraim Fischoff et al. 2 vols. Berkeley and Los Angeles: University of California Press.

Westphal, James D., and Edward J. Zajac. 1998. "The Symbolic Management of Stockholders: Corporate Governance Reforms and Shareholder Reactions." *Administrative Science Quarterly* 43:127–53.

Windolf, Paul. 2002. *Corporate Networks in Europe and the United States.* Oxford: Oxford University Press.

Womack, Kent L. 1996. "Do Brokerage Analysts' Recommendations Have Investment Value?" *Journal of Finance* 51:137–68.

Yago, Glenn. 1991. *Junk Bonds: How High Yield Securities Restructured Corporate America.* Oxford: Oxford University Press.

Zuckerman, Ezra W. 1999. "The Categorical Imperative: Securities Analysts and the Illegitimacy Discount." *American Journal of Sociology* 104:1398–1438.

Zysman, John. 1983. *Governments, Markets, and Growth: Financial Systems and the Politics of Industrial Change.* Ithaca, N.Y.: Cornell University Press.

14 Sociology of Work and Occupations

Andrew Abbott

ECONOMIC SOCIOLOGY is said to be "[a] socio-logical perspective applied to economic phenomena" (Smelser and Swedberg 1994, n. 1). But to what extent is work an "economic phenomenon"? Of course, there are 135 million people in the American paid labor force. But in addition, nearly all American adults do housework on a regular basis, and tens of millions of them take care of children and other relatives. About half of adult Americans do some charity work in a given year, and nearly two-thirds do some home improvement. But other than the wage work, none of this immense effort appears in national labor statistics as "economic phenomena."[1] Sociologists of work have usually followed this statistical focus on paid work in the labor force, as I shall myself in most of this chapter. However, I shall begin by considering in broad outline the major problem this focus sets aside: the shifting boundaries of market work.

THE BOUNDARIES OF WORK

Marx taught us that the wage relationship is the most consequential single social relationship in modern society. Combined with kinship, it provides the wherewithal of survival to all but that tiny handful of the population dependent on direct state subsidy. And many of those subsidies derive definition and even eligibility from the wage relationship—most obviously worker's compensation and unemployment insurance, but in many places pensions and health insurance as well. But not all work is wage work. We need to reimagine non-wage forms of work—volunteer, domestic, hobby, and forced production—simply as other sectors of production, beyond the wage economy. At present, we define "sectors" only in terms of the product division of labor, and only in terms of that portion of the product division of labor that produces for the cash economy. Adopting this new image would create two cross-cutting types of sectors, allowing us to pose much more generally the question of what kinds of work are located where, when, why, how, and by whom.[2]

Thinking about this new grid of sector/product cells is important because among these "residual" cells are some massive arenas of production. For example, child day-care services are now an industry of about 44,000 taxable establishments and $8 billion (SA:771). If we directly impute the annual-payroll-per-employee figure for taxable day-care establishments ($10,167) to the 34.6 million (SA:56) family households in the United States (as if each household contained one worker doing as much child care per year as an average full-time paid day-care worker—surely a conservative estimate), we would have a $350 billion payroll, about 11 percent of the total payroll of all waged industries (SA:545). In reality, the amount should be much larger; national calculations put total unpaid household labor at a little over half of total wage income (Eisner 1989, 23–24). Students' unpaid "work" in school (valued by the opportunity cost of not working full-time in the student years, Eisner 1989, 41–42) is worth another one-sixth. Or again, the average volunteer works 3.5 hours per week (SA:396). That comes to three or four weeks of labor a year, from about half of the adult population. Although dwarfed by the figures for child care, this too is a large output, estimated to be about one-fifth of the total current labor bill of the nonprofit sector (Eisner 1989, 37, 184). Thus even in the highly marketized United States the cash economy interpenetrates with extensive and equivalent unpaid activities.

Because the situation is more extreme in less marketized economies, it is the economic anthropologists who have perforce taken the issue of market boundaries most seriously. In the classical anthropological literature, work comprised all those things involved in "getting a living" (Herskovitz 1965). To be sure, the hazy interpenetration of "economic" and "noneconomic" endures in modern societies, as the British sociological students of "means of livelihood" have shown (Gershuny 1983; Pahl 1984). But where these latter writers emphasized a move of productive work from wage employment back into the family, the economic anthropologists had more often emphasized the inseparable twining of what in the West were seen as the antipodes of work and leisure, a theme starting as early as Evans-Pritchard's work on the Nuer (1940) and epitomized in Sahlins's (1972, chap. 1) colorful labeling of the hunter-gatherer economy as "the original affluent society."

Economic anthropology was riven in the 1960s and 1970s by a controversy between formalists who wanted to apply standard economic theory worldwide and substantivists who followed Polanyi (1957), Sahlins (1972), and others in believing that primitive societies had fundamentally different economic logics. At the heart of this debate was precisely the same issue that is today central to economic sociology, the nature and degree of the separation between economic practices and other aspects of social life. The substantivists (and most of economic anthropology since) insisted on the embeddedness of productive activity in other systems of social life.[3] This concept of embeddedness was taken to the limit by Marxist anthropologists who argued for the absolute unity of production and reproduction in a "domestic community" where production and distribution unfolded through the exchange of labor, goods, and women between different age and lineage groups of men. When export capitalism arrived, it found this exchange cycle an ideal supplier of reserve labor flexibly backstopped by a domestic production sector, a pattern famously described by Meillassoux ([1975] 1981) for West African villages and later commonly delineated in new economies (e.g., Salaff 1981) and developing cities (e.g., Cabanes 2000). In this view, the "disembedding" of the market economy was merely apparent, since it required for its sustenance a correlative domestic sector to meet the labor demand peaks of good times while absorbing the excess labor in bad times. In sum, for the economic anthropologists the question of the boundaries of the market has been a central question.

The great cross-sectional differences between societies in levels and forms of marketization are of course echoed in enormous change over time within single societies. Folbre and Nelson (2000, 126) argue that as late as 1870, "40% of the entire productive labor force (paid and unpaid, male and female) was made up of full-time homemakers." By the end of the Second World War, the figure was down to about 30 percent and by 2000 to about 16 percent. Why did this happen? And why did it happen to the kinds of work that it did? So-

cial work was volunteer work in 1880, but was paid work by 1920. Friendly advice was a personal commonplace (or freely available from clergy, doctors, and other notables) in 1880, but had become a $4.2 billion psychotherapy industry a century later (Olfson and Pincus 1994).

The move of child care, food preparation, homemaking, and disinterested advice into the market sector should not blind us to the fact that perhaps as many things have moved out of the market sector as have moved in. Much of housework was in fact paid labor prior to the Second World War. When paid domestic service declined precipitously after the war, the work was left undone or demarketized. Also demarketized has been the local delivery of goods and services. Gone are milkmen, diaper services, and doctors who make house calls. Americans go to the supermarket and the doctor's office and do not get paid for transporting themselves, any more than they are paid to bring home their milk and diapers in cars whose gas they now pump for themselves. Although national-level delivery has undergone a renaissance because of catalogue and Internet orders, local delivery—230,000 workers in 1910—is gone completely. Thus, the question of what work is where in the various work sectors—wage, domestic, hobby, volunteer, forced—is not at all a residual question, but one of the central questions of economic sociology.[4]

The other great boundary of work is with leisure, now usually defined as time for self-realization. Oddly enough, many theories assume that people ultimately desire work for self-realization, whether from an instinct to workmanship (Veblen) or from an artisanal desire to produce a complete, unalienated product (Proudhon, Marx). Seidman's (1991) study of the Popular Fronts in Paris and Barcelona in the 1930s shows the dangers of this assumption, for massive resistance to work emerged under both bourgeois and worker-controlled regimes. But more important, Seidman's book points toward the tangled relation of work, workers, and organized leisure that became of central historical importance in the 1920s and 1930s. Analysis of the American case comes from Hunnicutt's (1988, 1996) studies, with their focus on the new ideology of "economic growth" and "leisure through consumption" in the period 1920–40. A central creation of this period was a consumption society—that is, a society that expected nonwork time to be filled by the purchase of enjoyment with discretionary income, rather than to be used up in what Keynes once facetiously called "psalms and sweet music."[5]

The boundary between leisure and work is hopelessly obscure. For leisure time is used not only for consumption but also for that sector of personal production called hobbies. Moreover, not only do people undertake productive activities in their leisure time, they also undertake large amounts of "leisure" activity in their work time, as Hochschild (1997) and many others have noted. This issue—which we might call the dilution of work—has been studied from many points of view: in the "work discipline" literature, in the literature on new forms of surveillance and resistance, in the old "informal relations in bureaucracy" literature, and even the literature on plant closings and their social impact. All these make it clear that for a broad variety of workers the separation of work and social life considered by many theorists to be the essential mark of modern economies is either crumbling or nonexistent.[6]

THE LEXIS STRUCTURE OF WORK

I turn now to sociological studies of work in their more usual sense of the examination of paid labor in modern societies. For perhaps three decades, the majority of sociological writing about work in the United States has circled around two topics: inequality among workers and the control and organization of work (Abbott 1993). To the general reader, the implicit message of this literature is that large social forces push small individuals around. Exogenous, "historical" things like managerial ideologies, technological development, market efficiency, legal and institutional changes, and various forms of discrimination dictate the vicissitudes of individuals who are more or less solitarily seeking "unalienated work," "satisfying careers," or "returns to education." Despite its veneer of history, this literature is quite static. Since it assumes a dominant configuration of work within which individuals' qualities have their effects, it cannot explain change either in that configuration or in the larger forces that provide the causality that flows through it.

Most of this literature is also quite unsociological. In neoclassical economics (and large portions of sociology), workers are a statistical mass, possessed individually of various qualities (gender, education, skill, and so on) that determine their wage outcomes. Even institutionalists and Marxists have sometimes been attracted to this notion of workers as an unstructured mass, a view implicit in their studies of capitalists' disciplining of random individuals into effective workers.

Because of this individualistic slant, it is about workers as an unconnected, categorized mass that we know the most. The main body of empirical writing about work in social science examines the effect of individuals' categorical properties on wages and other individual outcomes.[7] To be sure, institutionalists and Marxists—unlike neoclassicals—have been attentive to many kinds of social structures among individual workers, considering workers' agglomeration into both ephemeral social movements and more durable solidarities like unions and professions that face the firms and employers on the other side of the wage relationship. But to things like employers' associations and trade associations there are no studied equivalents on the worker side of the wage relationship, other than solidarities by gender or sometimes by ethnicity/race. Yet there might in fact be many other such solidarities in terms of individual qualities or types of individual relations to production: by educational levels, say, or by age strata, or by preferences for certain sequences of types of work within the life course. For example, we do not usually think of workers' native languages as defining social structures in production, yet the history of occupations as work more generally is littered with examples where the language spoken has strongly constrained or facilitated the distribution of workers into specific places in production.[8]

Such secondary social structures among workers seem absent even from the best theoretical work. Charles Tilly, for example, has developed a dynamic and eclectic framework that has the conspicuous virtue of insisting that we historicize studies of work.[9] But much of his historicizing comes through more detailed attention to the "larger forces" taken for granted by the synchronic empirical literature on wages and inequality. The individual worker remains curiously unhistorical.

Yet in practice not only do workers' categorical attributes define potentially important social structures within the labor force, workers' life courses provide much of the enduring historical structure of the world of work. For example, the workers retiring in the period 2000–2005 are not just an arbitrary group who happen to be retiring. On the contrary, they bring with them to the moment of the retirement decision quite specific historical baggage. Some of this baggage they can shed, like their educational level; it is not particularly consequential that they are on average considerably less educated than the currrent labor force. But some of their historical baggage is very consequential. It matters very much that about half the male workers in this retiring cohort are veterans, with a variety of special benefits available to them. It matters very much that during their early work life the union wage and benefit premium was at peak values (peak values from which then-senior union workers did very well) but that it then declined rapidly at that point in their careers when they should have been stockpiling retirement money. The resources this cohort brings to retirement are thus decisively shaped by their historical labor experience; their past is encoded into their present. Because of this encoding, these 14 million people (the retiring segment of the 55–64 cohort in the American labor force, about 55 percent of them men) provide an enormous reservoir of continuity, of process and structure, underneath the changing surfaces of the work world of the United States in the last 40 years. That continuity comprises personal memory, common social and political experiences and attitudes, common patterns of material resources, and a substantial amount of common labor force experience. It also includes "common differences," in the sense of cohort-specific distributions of differences—in education, training, aspiration, residence, language, politics, and so on. (The relative meaning of a college degree within cohort has changed enormously, to take a simple example.) Thus the continuity they provide is not merely a matter of the historical demography of labor, but also of the structural realities and possibilities that that historical demography creates.[10]

In short, we should not think of retirement in some abstract sense, even if we historicize by allowing that sense to change epochally. Every cohort will bring to retirement a varying set of things piled up by the history that they themselves have made and endured. Moreover, since retirement at any given moment involves several cohorts of potential retirees, even a period approach cannot capture the complexities that these various cohort segments bring to the totality of retirement at any given moment.

More broadly, at any given moment events and period changes are marking the experience of the various cohorts currently in the labor force. Some of these are long monotonic trends such as increasing formal education or the move of married women into the labor force. Others are more local and erratic events like fluctuations in the unemployment rate. Still others are complex structural and technological changes in the labor process. All of these mark cohorts indelibly—with characteris-

tic work trajectories, with skill and experience sets, with financial resources, with occupational and employment–specific advantage and disadvantage—and all of these marks are carried forward into the future. Note, too, that the phenomena resulting from this vast historical demographic structure include indirect effects that arise from the juxtaposition of the different cohorts and cohort segments. Such indirect effects are "structural," synchronic, in the sense that they arise in cross-sectional situations at a given time. For example, in many an occupation the wearied survivors of an oversupplied generation sit at any given time quite uncomfortably with the easy winners of an undersupplied one, as many of us who survived academic boom-and-bust over the last 30 years can attest.

All of these markings and indirect effects encoded into the labor force I shall place under the umbrella term of the *labor opportunity structure*. For they do not constitute a fixed thing, but rather a set of possibilities and constraints within which various actors must work in the present. The labor opportunity structure is the invisible historical heritage correlative with the more easily seen historical heritage of work organizations—of unions and occupations and professions on the one hand, and of firms, cartels, and industrial relations on the other. And indeed correlative as well with the lineal heritage that carries forward technology and the division of labor. We see these other continuous histories—of organized groups and of tasks—quite well. But the labor opportunity structure is mostly invisble to us.

It is essential to note that period events—the "larger forces" of most models of work—are not exogenous to this system of historical structures. They are themselves enacted as part of it. For example, employers with new technical designs or bureaucratic conceptions cannot hire specific kinds of workers if those kinds of workers do not exist. The labor opportunity structure at any given moment, that is, forces employers to respond to its constraints. While employers may make do with nonoptimal workers in the short run, in the long run they must respond. They may transform the labor process to make use of existing labor and skill supply. They may force or facilitate migration or move production to new labor markets. They may support institutions to produce particular skills. Note that all of these actions depend on still other opportunity structures: of other workers available, of technological developments to exploit, of geographical differences in labor opportunities, of institutional structures to adapt. Examples are familiar enough from the last century: European labor imports after the Second World War, the pull of women into the labor force for the "administrative revolution" (Lowe 1987), offshoring in the 1980s, and so on.

But the central fact is that there is no such thing as a "larger historical force." Actors must always act within the constraints allowed by what is encoded into the historical present that confronts them. Cohort segments and managerial revolutions and technological change must all work through the same moment of the present.[11]

In reporting the literatures on work, I hope to bring this labor opportunity structure to visibility. I begin with a review of period changes, not because I am retreating to a conception of them as exogenous, but simply as a place to begin description. I then consider first the general experience of work (wages and benefits, working conditions, satisfaction), and second the work life course, in both cases sketching changes in these experiences across periods in order to evoke the underlying cohort experiences, about which we have very little direct information. This general discussion of cohort experience then serves as a starting point for some brief comments on how—within the context of the labor opportunity structure and the other historical structures of the work world—workers have made solidarities like occupations and professions, and how they and the employers have together created an organization of work.

Many of these areas are touched in other chapters, and I cover them very briefly here: gender, labor markets, education, immigration, industrial relations. Also, I have tried throughout to draw on empirical work from outside the United States as well as within it. But my underlying argument about the importance of labor's historicality makes general comparison difficult. So, regrettably, my emphasis will perforce be on the United States.

LABOR REGIMES

Both in the United States and in Europe, a number of basic transitions define fairly clear periods in labor experience, what we might call labor regimes. In the United States, the first of these periods is the immigration era, lasting from about 1885 to the mid-1920s. In this era, the population over age 20 was from 20 to 25 percent foreign born, and immigration accounted for at least half of annual labor force expansion. The later years of this period saw (1) a fairly rapid aging of the labor

force as immigration matured, (2) the explosion of clerical work, and (3) the gradual decline of the immense casual labor force that had built the railroads and other infrastructure of American capitalism. The second period is what might best be called the transition era: the twenties with their stabilizing of employment relations, the thirties with their catastrophic unemployment, their labor conflict, and their creation of the welfare state, and the war with its many effects, from sudden deep declines in farmwork and domestic service to demand for married women in the civilian labor force. The third period comprises the glory years of postwar growth from 1945 to 1975. It began with the reabsorption of 12 million veterans into a civilian labor force of 54 million and the sudden extension of home ownership from a long-stable 45 percent of households to 60 percent in 15 short years.[12] These were years of relative labor peace (and ultimately of high union wage premiums), rapid growth of the service sector, and relatively stable employment over the individual life course. The fourth period—from 1975 to the present—is that of neoliberalism. It is a period marked by the resumption of large-scale legal and illegal immigration (actually these date from the 1960s), by legal and economic transformations that gutted the American manufacturing sector, and by a reshaping of labor and employment relations that left governments as the only major unionized workplaces and that seems to have lessened job stability and job security.[13]

Across these general periods have drifted a number of more steady processes. Two are particularly important. The first is the steady march of married women into the labor force, a march that began at least as early as the depression and that has continued steadily since. Women's age-specific labor force participation rates (LFPRs) are now within about 15 percent of the LFPRs of men of equivalent ages, which implies that this three-quarter-of-a-century transformation is nearing completion. The second major trend is the related transition of the economy toward the services. Contrary to general belief, manufacturing never dominated American employment as did agriculture and as do services. The move toward a service economy started long before the late 1970s and 1980s with their conspicuous globalization and offshoring of manufacturing. The farm sector's share of the American labor force fell steadily about 5 percent per decade from the turn of the century onward, and services broadly defined—professional workers, managers, clerical and sales workers, domestic workers, and general services—absorbed nearly all those losses after 1920. Of course, that absorption reflects the flow of married women into the labor force (and the services), but even among men, the manufacturing sector grazed 50 percent of the labor force only briefly, around 1960.

These trends of feminization and servicization are shared throughout the developed economies. But in Western Europe, the periodic structure of labor history is somewhat different. The period from the 1880s to the First World War—roughly equivalent to America's age of labor immigration—was in Europe a period of a gradual moves toward welfare capitalism combined with a steady crescendo of labor unrest. Rescued (in most cases) from that unrest by the nationalistic carnage of the First World War, the European work world spent the interwar period rebuilding its decimated labor forces. Parliamentary labor parties emerged, welfare state coverage increased. The various corporatist forces that in their extreme led to fascism transformed and strengthened many occupational organizations. Many of the French professional *ordres*, for example, got their present formation in the 1930s and under Vichy, as the German apprenticeship system did under Weimar and National Socialism (Krause 1996; Thelen and Kume 2001).

By contrast, the postwar period was Europe's great age of migrant labor, for the war destroyed so much of the working age population that country after country eventually turned to guest workers. A surprising amount of corporatism survived the wreckage of war, helping transform labor relations into the great tripartite system of government/labor/management that became the (occasional) envy of America in the 1980s. By the 1980s, however, much of Europe was facing dramatic unemployment as guest workers stayed on and swelled native labor forces now replenished from their postwar lows. Like the United States, several of the major European nations retrenched their welfare states and moved toward neoliberalism. At the same time, European labor systems retained a number of qualities absent in the United States; large part-time farm sectors that cushioned the vagaries of industrial employment, flexible production zones like southwestern Germany and northern Italy, fairly strong worker parties, and enduring, if sometimes retrenched, welfare states and corporatist politics. If we had to periodize the European case, then, the four periods would be welfare capitalism and its failure, the corporatist

recovery, the migrant recovery, and ambivalent neoliberalism.

As these periodizations make clear, most working lives in most modern economies have traversed at some point at least one major watershed of labor regime; some have crossed two. Individuals last longer than do the social structures of the work world. So it is to individuals, both by themselves and as cohort or intra- or cross-cohort structures, that we must look for the deep historicality of the world of work, a historicality that has consequences not only for them but also for the system as a whole. For example, the high unemployment rates in Europe in the 1980s (at a time of continuing immigration of foreign workers) are now understood to have derived in part from an unwillingness to take low-income, insecure jobs on the part of workers who had previously experienced the rapid rises in wages, skill, and security produced by the labor shortage in the postwar glory years. What mattered was the order of events and the encoding of that order into the minds of the existing labor supply (cf. Stalker 1994, 52).

THE INDIVIDUAL EXPERIENCE OF WORK

I shall consider the literature on the individual's work experience under two basic headings, looking first at the immediate qualities of that experience—wages, benefits, and satisfaction—and second at the life course organization of work, from labor force entry to retirement. Recall that for the present argument, these various aspects of work matter less as instantaneous or medium-run outcomes than as assets compounded over time. Wages, benefits, and satisfaction—the most studied topics in the literature—are of long-run importance only insofar as they are carried forward, encoded, into the future, by home ownership, long-running patterns of alienation, and the like. To be sure, they may also have an indirect long-run effect by providing in the short run the stimulus or foundation for collective action, a subject well studied by the new labor history and students of social movements. But in themselves, as individual outcomes, they are not historically important. Similarly, unemployment, underemployment, turnover, and so on matter not because they are the crucial descriptive contingencies of the work life course, but only insofar as they succeed in encoding themselves in ways that produce later consequences, first in the individual life course, but more important as a part of the larger labor opportunity structure.

Immediate Qualities of Work

Real GNP in the United States grew about 2 percent per annum over the late migratory and transition eras: a little slower in the 1910s and 1930s, a little faster in the 1920s. Real growth took off during the war decade and averaged close to 4 percent per annum through the glory years, but in the neoliberal age it gradually slowed, falling back to below 3 percent in the 1990s. Distributional figures tell us where this growth went. Median real household income was stagnant in the 1930s, but increased quite rapidly in the glory years—about 20 to 25 percent or more per decade. By contrast, it stagnated again in the neoliberal era, rising only 12 percent in the 30 years 1970–2000. The total income shares of the top 20 percent and top 5 percent of the income distribution tell the same story; these fell steadily to the 1970s and then rose steadily afterward. The top 5 percent share declined more, troughed later, and has not yet "recovered" as much, facts that indicate that while the upper half of the income distribution has retained nearly all of the quite considerable growth since 1970, the proceeds have been shared somewhat more widely within the top sector of that moiety.[14]

There are many complexities to these figures, both causal and demographic (migration plays an important role in the neoliberal era, for example). But the general pattern—the whipsaw of the transition years, the strong absolute growth and relative equalization in the glory years, and the slower growth and rapid inequalization in the neoliberal years—has given each passing cohort burdens and advantages to carry forward. For example, for several cohorts the income bonanza of the glory years was converted with government assistance into permanent wealth in the form of home ownership (Jackson 1985). Owner-occupied households as a percentage of all households had fallen from 48 percent in 1890 to 43 percent by 1940 (with a brief peak in the 1920s). They rose to 54 percent in 1950 and 62 percent in 1960, and then took 40 years to rise another 6 percent to 68 percent in 1999.[15]

All this means that any cohort living a substantial portion of its work life during the glory years did well financially, both absolutely and in terms of relative equalization within cohort. Moreover,

these privileges were etched in stone in various ways—through home ownership and other wealth conversion, as well as through creation and expansion of welfare programs (e.g., Medicare in 1964), that seemed just and feasible to a society flush with resources. These cohorts' future behavior—as job changers, as retirees, as workers willing to risk new occupations—reflected this encoded body of resources.

About the encoding of such other immediate qualities of work as satisfaction, we are less clear. The concept of work satisfaction as currently used (that is, as the answer to point-blank survey questions) dates from the 1930s, which brought together brand-new survey techniques and the human relations school of management with its concern for worker attitudes. It is however by no means clear what a series of such answers means over time, especially for a single individual, a fact that has led many people who think about long-run patterns of satisfaction to look at behavioral measures like turnover, strikes, and the like. Turnover was more or less constant at about four to five hires per 100 employees per month from 1920 to 1980. (We do not know much about turnover after 1982 when the Bureau of Labor Statistics gave up collecting it for want of funding.) Strikes reached major peaks in the 1930s and again in the 1950s and early 1970s, as did the percentage of workers involved in a strike. It is not clear what this means in terms of worker satisfaction. Strikes are also a measure of union strength, and the United States reached its apogee of union membership midway through the glory years. Moreover, the union premium (the relative advantage of union members over others) rose throughout that period to its peak in the 1970s (Freeman and Medoff 1984, chaps. 3, 4). So it is hard to know whether to take strikes as measures of work dissatisfaction or of worker strength.

A central difficulty with the work satisfaction concept (as with most satisfaction concepts) is that its time scale of reference is unclear. Originally conceived as a management tool, satisfaction measures are generally tied to immediate concerns in the division of labor and assume a time horizon of weeks or months. Longer duration concepts of satisfaction are quite nebulous and are generally assimilated to the equally nebulous concept of career.[16]

One important boundary between wage work and the rest of experience is the temporal arrangement and extent of work. Workdays and the workweeks fell fairly rapidly from the 12-hour day and 60-hour weeks of the late nineteenth century to the eight-hour days and 40-hour weeks enshrined in legislation in the late 1930s, whence they have not budged since, at least legally, despite some decline in practice due to sectoral shifts. In Europe the day shortened a little earlier, but 40-hour weeks generally postdate the war. (The legal week long remained at 48 hours in some European countries, although in practice most of Europe has been around 40 hours for 30 years or more. Europeans have been more willing than Americans to continue experimenting with work time.)

As for the longer rhythm of seasonality, it is surprisingly persistent in modern economies even though its roots in subsistence and part-time agriculture might have been expected to wither under advanced capitalist agriculture with its fewer workers for longer durations. In America, the seasonal farm labor force peaked in the early 1960s and has fallen off since, although seasonality remains characteristic of the immigrant labor pool from Mexico (Fritsch 1984). The small size of European nations and their enduring small-farm sectors have kept seasonality more influential there than in the United States.[17]

It is not clear whether or how temporality encodes something into the labor opportunity structure. Certainly daily and weekly experience shape time available for alternative activities decisively, and in that sense the early decline in hours created an openness in the labor opportunity structure that might have had important consequences, were the time used for moonlighting (never very widespread in America outside a narrow range of occupations) or for occupational organization and resistance. It seems, however, that the new nonwork time mostly went into leisure, which reduced its consequences for the future. Perhaps more important, however, is the demise of temporality as a political issue. Cohorts working in the immigrant and transition periods in the United States hoped for and indeed experienced a steady move toward shorter hours, while those since have not. Indeed, there are indications that work hours have grown longer for certain parts of the labor force—particularly what are called in America "salaried" workers (as opposed to "hourly" workers), who are assumed to work "whatever hours are necessary."[18] It seems most likely that the desire for declining hours was a casualty of the new consumption society with its desire for growth, possession, and consumption-based leisure. Work hours have therefore had few long-run encoded consequences.

Contingencies

Above the level of daily rewards and temporal conditions of work stands the larger logic of a work life course, through which these smaller temporal units are appended to a growing lifetime experience. This temporal trajectory of work unfolds through a characteristic set of patterns. Entry into the labor force is typically a long, gradual process through a series of part-time jobs. The majority of adults then spend about 30 to 40 years at work until retirements begin in the fifties. Throughout the main work trajectory there intervene varying contingencies: unemployment, underemployment, part-time work (voluntary or involuntary), contingent employment, removal from the labor force for parenting, and so on.

Until fairly recently, work typically ended for men not with retirement but with death; 69 percent of those over 65 were in the labor force in 1900. Spreading mandatory retirement and social support programs began in the 1930s to remove those men from work, and the period since 1950 has seen a steady further drop to the current rate of 16 percent participation for males over 65, a drop maintained since the end of mandatory retirement by financially coercive pension and social security arrangements (Kotlikoff and Wise 1989). Women over 65 have never worked in substantial numbers in the United States. Table 1 gives age-specific LFPRs for men and women throughout the twentieth century in the United States.

It is clear that the lifetime work period has been steadily compressed through the twentieth century, although in the process its edges have become quite fuzzy. The majority of the compression has come at the end of the work cycle and reflects the variety of factors conducing to retirement—increasing wealth, better health, cheap leisure, and pensions, the last often linked to retirement mandatory de jure or de facto (see Costa 1998, chap. 2). Another important determinant is the disappearance of the farm sector, which under its traditional mode of production had more uniform labor force participation over the life course than any other employment sector.

Unfortunately, there is no real literature on evolving patterns of completed careers. Early analysts of whole careers (Form and Miller 1949; Wilensky 1960, 1961) noted the characteristic career pattern of an initial part-time period, followed by a "testing" or "trial" period, and in turn followed by a more or less stable period. But we still do not know, for any large sample at any point,

TABLE 1. Age-Specific Labor Force Participation Rates (All figures in percent)

	1900	1920	1930	1940	1950	1960	1970	1980	1990	1999
					Men					
<20	66.9	52.6	41.1	34.4	35.5	35.7	56.1	60.5	55.7	52.9
20–24	93.1	91.0	89.9	88.0	75.3	79.6	83.3	85.9	84.4	81.9
25–34	96.3	97.2	97.3	95.2	88.2	90.8	96.4	95.2	94.1	93.3
35–44	96.6		97.6	94.7	92.0	93.2	96.9	95.5	94.3	92.8
45–54	95.5	93.8	96.5	92.1	89.8	93.3	94.3	91.2	90.7	88.8
55–64	90.0		90.2	83.8	81.7	83.3	83.0	72.1	67.8	67.9
>65	68.4	60.1	58.3	41.5	40.8	30.6	26.8	19.0	16.3	16.9

	1900	1920	1930	1940	1950	1960	1970	1980	1990	1999
					Women					
<20	28.2	28.4	22.8	18.7	22.2	23.9	44.0	52.9	51.6	51.0
20–24	30.8	38.1	42.4	45.1	42.7	44.9	57.7	68.9	71.3	73.2
25–34	19.9	22.4	27.8	32.9	31.7	35.3	45.0	65.5	73.5	76.4
35–44	15.6		22.6	26.9	34.9	42.6	51.1	65.5	76.4	77.2
45–54	14.7	17.1	20.4	22.1	32.8	46.7	54.4	59.9	71.2	76.7
55–64	13.2		16.1	16.4	23.4	35.0	43.0	41.3	45.2	51.5
>65	9.1	8.0	8.0	5.9	7.8	10.3	9.7	8.1	8.6	8.9

much less over time, what is the distribution of types of careers. This has been in large part for want of methodological tools.[19]

I begin with education, thought by many to be an essential resource for the labor force, and, of course, extremely highly correlated with wages and other rewards at the individual level. The large literature on education and work (see Mary Brinton's chapter in this volume) does not generally study education within the historical demographic framework followed here. We are accustomed either to think of education as a kind of period change—"the high schools expanded rapidly in the 1920s," we say, as if this meant a sudden change in education levels society-wide—or to enter education as one more variable in our equations, forgetting that over any medium-scale elapsed period education's main historical effects are uniformly colinear with age because of period changes. (Therefore our models measure only education's local, relative effects, not its more general, structural ones.) In fact, cohort education levels are set in youth and change little after age 25, at least prior to the expansion of community colleges in the 1960s. They therefore constitute one of the essential constraints imposed by the labor opportunity structure.

To see this, it suffices to think carefully about the educational level of the labor force.[20] The 1905–10 birth cohort was the first cohort to show a real leap in high school education, but they were not securely in the labor force until the late 1920s. Since median school completion rose about one year per quinquennium, the 1920–25 birth cohort was the first one to enter the labor force with half its members having completed high school, but entered the labor force only in the early war years. Viewed from the other end, the last "grade school" cohort (median education below 9.0 years, the 1900–1905 cohort) did not hit retirement (65) until around the late 1960s, well into the epoch of "postindustrial society"! The impact of college has been similarly delayed. Higher education exploded after the war with the GI Bill and increasing women's education, an explosion continued by the community college revolution of the 1960s and 1970s. We are accustomed to think of this development as revolutionizing the American workforce. But of course these students leavened the labor force only gradually, and indeed the expansion was much slower than the high school one. Forty years after the real takeoff of higher education around 1960, college completion even among whites has just reached the level of a quarter of the population over 25.

This excruciatingly slow educational upgrading of the labor force of course provided one of the great constraints on usable technology and shop floor divisions of labor in manufacturing and service production. Obvious evidence for this is the hijacking of the community colleges—which were originally planned to bring liberal education to the masses—by a business community desperate for workers trained in new skills (Brint and Karabel 1989). Nor is it surprising that by the 1980s, business was itself spending on internal training an amount commensurate with the entire higher education budget of the United States (Eurich 1985; see also the data on training in Parnes et al. 1970–75, vol. 4).

After school comes the "school-to-work transition." Recent studies of high school work make it clear that this transition is largely a myth, although we do not know for how long and for whom it has been a myth. Sample data put about half of full-time high school students in the labor force, with an average workweek, for the eleventh and twelfth graders, of about 20 hours (Mortimer and Shanahan 1994). Ninth and tenth graders work extensively in the informal economy—mowing lawns and babysitting—positions they seem to desert as soon as the law allows them to move to the formal economy. It is not clear how far back this pattern goes historically. Hollingshead (1949) seems to indicate that the working high school students in Elmtown in the early 1940s were more likely to be those of lower socioeconomic status, but overall LFPRs fell for both men and women under 20 from 1900 to about 1940, whence they rose to 1980. (The close parallel of the two sets of rates questions the usual interpretation, according to which schooling drove the early decline and the return of service men to civilian life drove the later rise.) Like most age-specific LFPRs, these have moved toward gender equality, the young men having fallen back since 1980 to 53 percent, roughly equalling the women's 51 percent.

An unknown but undoubtedly quite substantial portion of teenage work takes place in the illegal economy. Ethnographies of the drug trade make it clear that the drug industry (both in retail sales and in related work such as lookout, messenger, etc.) actually employs a substantial fraction of officially "unemployed" urban youth. We know relatively little about the total extent of this employment, which like most informal work is often episodic and part-time, and would be difficult to conceptualize and measure even if we could survey it more directly.[21]

At present, work during college seems close to universal. Even at elite colleges, few students spend four years without working during term. And the recent emergence of summer recruiting internships creates yet another link smoothing the connection of education and work (a connection infinitely smoother in Germany, for example, with its highly structured apprenticeship system). The universality of college work probably reflects the expanded coverage of education (to people who have to finance it by part-time work and debt) as much as it does a change in the college experience per se. In 1940 only about 5 percent of the population over 25 had gone to college. Over half of a cohort of eighteen-year-olds now begins college. In a way, then, we can think of education as something that has expanded into the life-period of work, rather than vice versa.[22]

The various tracks that lead into full-time employment are thus mostly gradual transitions through part-time work during schooling of various levels. The school-to-work transition—which may have been a fixture of prewar employment for some of the labor force—is now almost completely a mirage. In terms of the labor force opportunity structure, there is here no story of encoded period effects, as there is with educational level. Rather, there are some differences encoded into the labor force: educational debt for some people to carry forward but not others, employment (hoped to be) relevant to future occupation in some cases, but not in most, and so on. But the main quality of this part of the labor force is precisely that it has no memory, that it encodes next to nothing. For it is made up of workers who will spend brief periods in generic occupations that do not dictate workers' futures nor give them much—skills, debts, assets, connections, constraints—to take forward. As of 1987, for example, the median age of food counter, fountain, and related workers was 18.8. Their cumulative (all spells added together) occupational duration was 1.5 years (sampled at a moment, so the expected total duration is roughly twice that). For busboys and other food service assistants, the figures were 20.3 and 1.7, for short-order cooks, 20.9 and 2.5, for private household child-care workers, 21.9 and 2.7 (Carey 1988). These are high-turnover occupations, for young people who aim to make some money mostly for consumption although sometimes for educational expenses. Such occupations are without any real implications. From employers' point of view, the "opportunity" provided by this part of the labor force is precisely that its sense of the irrelevance of the occupation for its future gives this area of employment a spot market quality not found elsewhere.[23]

There is to be sure one drastic form of transition to work. For a very large number of American men in the middle and late twentieth century, their first full-time, regular employment was with the military. In 1950, for example, veterans were nearly 40 percent of the 20–24 male cohort of the labor force and nearly 80 percent of the 25–34 male cohort. For a huge portion of these, military service had been their first full-time work.[24] Veteran status is a central constituent of the labor opportunity structure; during the glory years, the total veteran proportion of the male labor force never went much below 40 percent. The age composition of this group changed slowly as the Second World War veterans aged, but the draft for Vietnam recreated the pattern of young veterans and pushed the total male labor force proportion of veterans to around 50 percent. Even the steady move of married women into the labor force did not offset this rise; the total veteran proportion of the labor force held constant at around 30 percent until the late 1970s.

The impact of this encoded experience was enormous. The stability of American labor regimes in the glory years was founded on the veteran-worker and indeed the veteran-boss. (The male labor force is now only about 20 percent veterans, the total labor force 12 percent veterans.) Accustomed to a large organization with a thick and often irrational command hierarchy, the veterans found themselves in quite familiar settings as civilian employees of giant organizations, under the same kinds of bosses they had had in the service. This massive memory, far more than the prescriptions of the human relations school of management, undergirded the successful move Edwards (1979) notes toward bureaucratic control in the American workplace. More recently, the disappearance of this reservoir of personal training and of this mechanism for induction into the world of large organizations has undoubtedly had major consequences for U.S. workforce control since the 1980s.

Perhaps more important, millions of young workers brought home the enlisted/officer/enemy model that any enlisted man remembers ("we hate our officers but we hate the enemy [or the Army in general] more"). Without thinking, they probably made it their model for labor relations. The surprising turn of American labor toward bread-and-butter bargaining, away from the strongly confrontational labor tactics and grand demands of the 1930s (Stepan-Norris and Zeitlin 2003) probably owes much to this transposition. No longer was it "us versus them." It was "us versus them versus THEM."[25]

A work life begun in the teens or twenties is interrupted by various contingencies. The simplest of these is job change, which most studies have defined as change of employer (rather than of occupation or occupation within employer). The distribution of job turnovers in a typical lifetime is unknown for many cohorts in the American labor force. Labor turnover occurred at extraordinary rates in the United States prior to the 1920s. The first serious figures (around 1920) put turnover (the average of accessions and departures) at about 10 per 100 employees per month in the relatively stable firms surveyed. Turnover fell to around half that level by the mid-1920s, where it remained until doubling again during the war years, then falling back to an even lower figure (around four per 100) from the 1950s until figures stopped being kept in the Reagan era. The sudden decline in turnover in the mid-1920s is undoubtedly related to the sudden ending of mass immigration in that period. The great stability since is somewhat puzzling.

Aggregate turnover figures are grossly misleading. In a definitive enterprise-based study, Brissenden and Frankel (1922) showed the now familiar (and still true) facts that unskilled workers, young workers, and female workers all turn over much faster than others and that the majority of turnover comes from rapid churning of short-stay employees in a relatively small number of slots. Over half the separating employees in their data—skilled or unskilled—had served three months or less (1922, 132). Thus the 100 percent turnover figure commonly quoted for industrial employment in the migratory period masks huge synchronic differences in employment stability. The surprise—both then and now—is not how little stability there is in the labor force, but how stability and turnover exist side-by-side. Because turnover is highly duration-dependent, the distribution of work life courses with various levels of turnovers and tenures is highly skewed.

The depression and the Second World War of course interrupted many job tenures, but it seems almost certain that typical tenures grew longer in the glory years. In a 1954 review of available work, Parnes (1954, 69) concluded that about 20 percent of the labor force was continuously employed by one employer during the 1940s, and that over a third had only one employer, but perhaps did not work continuously over the same period. These figures were higher than the Brissenden and Frank numbers on the 1910s, and later figures were higher still, as table 2 shows.

Tenures flattened (or fell) in the later glory years, a fact that is clearer if one corrects for com-

TABLE 2. Turnover Figures

	Median Current Tenure (in years)				>10 Years (in percent)			
	Male		Female		Male		Female	
	White	Black	White	Black	White	Black	White	Black
Briss/Frank 1913–4	2.9		2.4		14.9		9.4	
BLS 1951 (MLR Oct 1963)	4.0	3.1	2.3	1.7	21.4	13.2	10.7	6.5
BLS 1963 (MLR Oct 1963)	5.9	4.1	3.0	2.9	35.3	27.5	20.7	19.3
BLS 1973 (MLR Dec 1974)	4.7	4.0	2.8	3.3	30.7	23.7	17.9	18.4
BLS 1978 (MLR Dec 1979)	4.6	3.7	2.6	3.6	28.8	25.8	15.3	19.3

positional changes (chiefly the baby boom's entry to the high-turnover early work years). Although comparison can be difficult, a review of recent analyses by Neumark (2000) suggests (continuing) modest declines in job stability (turnover) and job security (involuntary turnover) in the neoliberal period. Most studies seem to indicate that this effect was stronger during the 1970s than the 1980s, but that the 1990s brought some instability and insecurity to higher status and older groups that had not known it before. Like many other labor statistics, the trends seem reversed for men and women—the former looking a little worse off, the latter perhaps a little better, the two converging. Overall, then, there is a fairly simple periodic history: a fairly decisive stabilization in the 1920s, a distinct lengthening of overall tenure by the Second World War and into the early glory years, and a slow, very gradual decline since some time in the late glory years.[26]

Turnover is not random in the life course. Hall's definitive 1982 paper rediscovered and deepened the argument of the earlier whole career literature that the early job history was filled with high-turnover jobs (on average six by age 30) and that, for a majority of the labor force in the glory years, the later career was filled with one or two long-duration jobs. At a given point (in 1978), 28 percent of the labor force was in jobs expected to last 20 years or more total and 43 percent in jobs expected to last 10 years or more total. Put another way, 40 percent of workers between 40 and 65 could expect 20 years or more on the job currently held.[27]

All of these studies sidestep the much thornier problem of occupational and skill change. In a much-cited study on a small sample in the early glory years, Wilensky (1960) showed that many workers who worked for a single employer for long periods changed occupations (jobs) very often within that employer. Indeed, it was already known that at least a third of workers change broad occupation group over a decade, much less specific occupation (Palmer 1954, 108). The problem of trajectories of change in occupation or in skills used has been difficult to investigate on an aggregate basis. (We thus have little idea whether the current vogue of "individual career growth" as an empirical practice and a human resources department ideology is really anything new.)

From a life course point of view, the main question about turnover concerns the likelihood that an individual will eventually secure one or more long-tenure employments. But our concern here is less with the life course organization of turnovers in itself than with the more dynamically important question of what that life course pattern means in terms of the encoded labor opportunity structure. Its main consequence is to increase the vulnerability of the labor force to demographic shocks. When a massive generation like the baby boom hits the narrow life course window for long tenures, there may—changes in the labor process and employment relation set aside—be fewer "long tenure" slots than can go around. For example, in 1999, 49 percent of the labor force was in the prime long-tenure years, age 35–54; in 1970, the figure had been 40.3 percent. Thus, recent cries of "declining job security" probably have compositional origins.

A more dramatic contingency is unemployment. We are fortunate to have a number of distinguished works on unemployment—of the concept (Salais, Baverez, and Reynaud 1986), of unemployment relief as a policy (Harris 1972), and even of unemployment as an experience (Keyssar 1986; Burnett 1994). As with turnover, instantaneous rates of unemployment are much better known than is its total incidence over the life course. American unemployment rates fluctuate pretty steadily with business cycles. They have reached 7 percent to 10 percent at some point in nearly every decade since 1890 and have gone below 3 percent at some point in most decades. They are highly skewed in terms of occupation (high among laborers and factory workers in the past few decades), of race (black rates are typically twice those of whites), of age (young workers, particularly those under 20, are very likely to be unemployed), and of education. The last is perhaps the most dramatic of these correlations; unemployment rates for those who have not finished high school run four or more times those of college graduates for most demographic groups in the current U.S. labor force.

From a life course point of view, the persistence and recurrence of unemployment (like turnover) in the work histories of particular individuals is an important regularity, noted by a number of European scholars (e.g., Gallie and Paugam 2000). Layte et al. (2000) use multiple and diverse evidence to show that this persistence most likely reflects individual qualities less than it does location in a disadvantaged labor market or occupational area. But unemployment seems to be broadly experienced; Paugam (2000, 92), with a sample that while not nationally representative is close to national norms in most respects, finds that nearly 30 percent of French respondents have experienced unemployment of at least three months at some point in their careers.

Unemployment episodes in the United States typically last nine weeks (median), although 10 to 15 percent last six months or more. (See Kaitz 1970 for a useful technical discussion.) The same mathematical issues arise with unemployment as with job tenure, and thus like job tenure, unemployment duration is longer than cross-sectional data make it seem, in the sense that the majority of months of unemployment that are experienced come in the guise of long-duration unemployment, just as the majority of employment years that individuals experience are in tenures longer than turnover data and current spell-length would lead one to expect (Akerlof and Main 1981). A further problem is that an unknown but substantial number of unemployment episodes are actually filled with employment in the informal economy and in domestic production of various kinds. (These tend to disappear in official statistics, because in most countries such employment would jeopardize unemployment benefits.) It is a striking fact that unemployment support regimes in Europe correlate closely with family patterns (Gallie

and Paugam 2000). Countries with extensive family dependence—and relatively strong family production—tend to have minimal unemployment benefits, relying on the family production sector to provide protection and nonmarket employment. (This is Meillassoux [1975] 1981 all over again.) Unemployment is thus a complex kind of event, tied to "sectoral" change between wage, domestic, and informal production as much as it is to the conjunctures of the wage economy. However, it is not clear what if any are the encoded implications of unemployment experience for the labor opportunity structure. By contrast, the next work life contingency—nonstandard employment relations—has fairly clear implications.

Alongside full-time, full-year (FTFY) wage/salary labor is a wide variety of alternative wage arrangements. As noted earlier, casual, high-turnover employment is both old and endemic in the American labor force. Through the immigrant and transition periods, hoboes were the core casual labor force—itinerant, young, male workers working large construction projects in the summer and labor-intensive harvests in the fall. The large-scale hobo labor force shrank during the depression and almost disappeared after the war.[28]

But while the old strongholds of casualism have drastically declined, a variety of new non-FTFY employment forms have emerged in the white-collar labor force. "Contingent employment" is work that has some formal time limit: a month, a year, up to (in the case of assistant professors) six years. (This is the French *contrat à durée determinée* [CDD].) It covers about 5 percent of the American labor force. Part-time employment, defined variously in various countries (Kalleberg 2000), usually means working less than about 80 percent of legally established full-time status, although, as I noted earlier, the actual "full-time" workweek varies widely from sector to sector. The U.S. labor force is about 20 percent part-time. Finally, alternative employment arrangements (AEAs) refer to nonstandard legal relations between employer and employee; they include independent contract relations (direct contracts for particular services with limited benefits), on-call work (work available only when the employer needs it, e.g., substitute teaching), working for a temporary agency, and subcontract employment (working for a firm that subcontracts services to other firms). AEAs involve about 8 to 10 percent of the American labor force. These various categories of course overlap in various ways.[29]

Part-time work spread steadily in the labor force

in the glory years (it was a little over 10 percent of the labor force in 1950). In part, the growth has reflected sectoral change; the service sector has more part-time jobs. It also seems to have reflected life course factors. Part-time work is concentrated among women and men outside the prime employment years. Part-time work is a little lower in the European Union than in the United Sates, although with much variation and although it has been increasing rapidly in the past decade.

Most AEAs are life-stage phenomena, from the point of view of the worker. Thus, independent contractors tend to be white males who chose the arrangement, often over 65, with lower contingency rates, higher salary and benefit rates, and longer job tenure in job than other AEAs. Independent contracting is obviously a method of gradual retirement. By contrast, contract workers are generally young men, working full-time, most often in security or technology, with high wages and fairly long tenure for AEA arrangements. A total contrast are temporary agency workers, who are more likely women (53 percent), with children (30 percent have a preschooler), young (25 percent of them under 25), working in clerical and machine operator positions (72 percent). Few (27 percent) prefer working this way, few are covered by insurance (temporary agencies and their workers are often free riding on an employed spouse's benefits), over half are contingent, and the median tenure is very brief. Finally, on-call workers are more of a sectoral or occupational phenomenon than a life course one. On-call work is very high in two traditional women's professions (teaching and nursing), as it is for men in transportation, construction, and unskilled labor.

Contingent work is far more common in Europe than in the United States; the EU rate is about 12 percent (fixed-term contracts as a percentage of all employment contracts). A detailed French study shows that temporary employment is directly related to an increase in "flexibility" (more autonomous work decisions and less hierarchical organization), but also to increasing temporal constraints, production speeds, and quality surveillance (Paugam 2000). A recent study of Japan (Gill 2001, 201) also notes a distinct rise in time-limited employees—to 7.5 percent—which couples with self-employed without employees (9 percent), family workers without contracts (5.4 percent), and day laborers (1.8 percent) to locate nearly a quarter of the Japanese labor force in various forms of nonstandard employment.

In sum, while definitions vary, forms of nonstandard employment are spreading quite rapidly in the developed world and are in most cases concentrated among women, young people, untrained workers, and retirees. These modifications of the FTFY model seem to reflect a massive change in the labor opportunity structure—the entry (in some cases reentry) into the labor force of individuals (married women, women with children, high school and college students, individuals gradualizing their retirements) who have reasons for desiring or requiring non-FTFY schedules.[30] This effect can be most easily seen for women. As table 3 shows, the female share of the labor force in the first half of the twentieth century grew at the expense of boys and very young men—the heart of the old casual labor force. The backbone of the patriarchal labor force—men in the breadwinner years—held absolutely steady at half the total jobs in the labor force through 1950 (as did older men at 10–12 percent of the labor force). As a total proportion of the labor force, the male-breadwinner age group declined—sharply but uniquely—during the glory years, recovering slightly when the baby boom fully entered it around 1990. Thus, it was the glory years that saw the major expansion of that portion of the labor force characteristically associated with non-FTFY and more casual arrangements (Hall 1982 shows that women's typical tenures were shorter than men's), and not surprisingly part-time work expanded steadily in parallel.

The long-run implication has been that after the glory years employers faced a labor force more of

TABLE 3.   Labor Force Share

	1900	1920	1930	1940	1950	1960	1970	1980	1990	1999
Percentage of LF Female	18.1	20.5	22.0	24.3	28.3	32.0	38.1	42.5	45.2	46.5
Percentage of LF Male 25–54	49.5	50.9	50.1	49.3	47.4	44.9	38.9	36.3	38.5	38.2
Percentage LF Female 25–54	8.1	10.5	12.0	14.6	18.0	20.4	22.0	26.1	29.8	33.4

which is empirically associated with non-FTFY work. Encoded into that labor force are more of the advantages and disadvantages associated with high-turnover work under unusual arrangements: increased flexibility and risk for both sides, reliance on on-the-job training, and free riding on breadwinners (parents for children, spouses for adults) for health and other benefits, for stable income, and so on. A correlative result is that the labor force is now a higher percentage of the population over 16 than ever before; the century-long increase in this figure has been steady except for momentary hesitations in 1930 for the depression and in 1965 before the maturing of the baby boom.

Few people spend their work lives in one place. Many—indeed most—geographical moves are dictated by the pushes and pulls of employment. Such labor migration can be loosely divided into internal and international. Internal labor migration we have already encountered in the casual and seasonal labor force. Migratory casual labor seems to be a life stage phenomenon, far more common among young men than any other group, but noncasual job-induced migration is extremely general in the population, probably dictating at least half of all changes of residence. International labor migration is of course one of the defining phenomena of modern labor regimes, and is particularly central to the history of the United States. The migrations up to 1924 are of definitional importance, and after a brief lull, the annual inflow has increased (from near zero) almost monotonically since 1945. During the one era when immigration doors were officially closed, the United States imported foreign labor formally under the bracero program (1942–64) in whose peak year (1956) there were 445,000 braceros (of about two million farm laborers by census estimate).[31]

From the cohort/encoding point of view adopted here, it is important to note, first, that much labor migration is temporary. The United States, for example, is estimated to have lost about one-third of those who emigrated to it between 1900 and 1980. Second, international labor migration is generally youthful. While older people do migrate, much of international labor migration is a temporary expedient of young people seeking high wages (often 10 to 50 times those of the sending country), without long-run plans. This is particularly true for illegal migration, which is estimated to be about 20 percent of the total inflow to the United States. Third, international labor migration, although common for skilled workers, is more generally a phenomenon of unskilled workers (Stalker 1994).

The central implications of migration, particularly international migration, for the labor opportunity structure lie of course in its provision of a safety valve, a reserve of workers ready to fit into places unfilled by home labor supply. This is true regionally as well as internationally, although generally employers have preferred regional relocation rather than cross-regional labor import. But the extreme transiency of much of modern international migration makes it ideal in freeing employers from local constraints.

Work careers today close with retirement, sharp or gradual. As noted earlier, workers of prior cohorts more likely left the labor force through death.[32] Retirement as a concept emerged in the 1930s, for which it was one basic strategy to reduce mass unemployment (along with part-time work and shortening the workweek). Pension-supported retirement had the triple advantage of reducing unemployment, increasing overall worker productivity (it was believed older workers were inefficient), and increasing aggregate demand by putting money into hands that would spend it. The 1950s saw the institutionalization of retirement in its modern American form and a rapid expansion of the benefits and coverage of Social Security. Welcomed by big business as an investment tool (Graebner 1980, 215ff.—funding pools that backed pensions were investment capital accounts for firms), private defined–benefit pension plans spread from 15 percent of the labor force to over 40 percent by 1960. The mass leisure sector ballooned. All this meant that retirement emerged in its modern cultural form (Grabener 1980, chap. 8), and cohorts retiring in the glory years enjoyed opportunities unimagined in their youth.

With the neoliberal transition of the 1970s, things changed. Although mandatory retirement was struck down for various reasons, the decline in the LFPR of older workers continued, driven by pension policies almost as effective as mandatory retirement itself. By the mid-1990s, however, long-term trends began to stall and reverse (Purcell 2000); pension coverage fell for men and women 55–64 and 65 and over, labor force participation rates began to climb for all age brackets over 55, and proportions of pensioners and of Social Security recipients working began to climb. After 1994, there even emerged a small move back toward full-time work among the elderly. Some of this may have reflected a hot economy, but some may also have reflected the changing provisions of Social Security and a stalling of income in the senior age brackets.[33]

From an encoding point of view, the importance of retirement lies in its guaranteeing the youth of the labor force. It stops the endless march of salaries in terms of age and employer seniority. It eradicates old distributions of education, training, and occupation. Since the employees it eliminates are generally long-tenure employees (who have preferential access to it in an age of early retirement offers) it also has a large effect on organizational memory, for good or ill. (For example, there are only a hundred or so people left in the United States with the skills to maintain the electronic switches that still handle most of the nation's long-distance phone calls.) Note that often what retirement eradicates are events long past. To take an occupational example, the baby boom drew thousands of extra people into teaching with the result that teaching (elementary and secondary especially) is today an elderly profession, from which about one-quarter of its members will disappear in the next eight years. Not only will this create an enormous present crisis, it will also induct another oversized cohort to produce another such crisis 30 years hence.

OCCUPATIONS, PROFESSIONS, AND THE ORGANIZATION OF WORK

The varying depths of life course experience at any given time, encoded into cohorts and cohort segments presently extant in the labor force, constitute the materials on which occupations are built. By "occupations" here, I mean real social things. When the census assigns people occupations, it merely locates them in a category of workers. In such an exercise occupations are just areas of tasks in a division of labor. They are not social entities with coherence and consequence.

Occupations have two other realities. Implicit in my argument so far is the first of these—the idea that occupations are particular and enduring groups of people. The various food service groups mentioned a few pages ago are not in this sense occupations. They are simply categories of work through which young people flow at a tremendous rate—what we might call "turnover occupations." So a second conception of occupations involves sustained membership by particular individuals. Yet a third way of conceiving occupations is through their institutions—associations, unions, friendly societies, licensing boards, and so on.

Research areas are sharply differentiated by their choice among these different concepts of occupa-

tion. For most quantitative analysis, occupation means the (current) task, given by the SOC (Standard Occupational Classification) codes and the triple-digit census classification. Such analysis makes strong assumptions, especially about change in the occupational system over time. The new labor history, by contrast, has begun with occupations as institutions (unions, family and employment structures, repertoires of contention), although often also amassing data on occupations as groups of people at a given moment. The professions literature—which has much more detailed individual data than does the new labor history with its working-class focus—has generally insisted on all three aspects of occupations combined, disdaining those occupations unable to connect an enduring group of people, a set of institutions, and a task area.[34]

Any serious study of occupations must begin with the question of how and when these three strands of occupation-ness can be brought together. More important, it must also understand how lineages—consistent social structures through time—can be created within each strand. How can or does a task area remain unified across time? How does a group of people maintain a position in the division of labor as they and the institutions around them age? How do occupational structures grow, develop, and die?

With respect to these questions, we know, first, a good deal about the history and current structure of task areas. For the professions we have many detailed case summaries and the general theoretical analysis of Abbott (1988). For occupations more generally we have the large literature of the new labor history and a distinguished theoretical literature on labor process. From the same sources, we know, second, much about the organizational structures of occupations themselves, particularly about unionized occupations and the professions. This was the heart of the sociology of work as it descended from Everett Hughes and has been many times reviewed. Most work about occupations is in fact about the organized structures of occupations and the actions undertaken by those structures and by current occupation members.[35]

But we know, third, next to nothing about the historical demography of occupations. Even for the well-studied professions few works track individuals through careers in any substantial numbers; virtually all studies of professions, as of internal labor markets, break careers into transitions and analyze the transitions separately. And even where they exist, little can be inferred from tenure distributions, which are largely determined by fluctuations in occupational entry.[36] The simple fact is that we do not know the number and extent of demographically coherent occupations today or for any era of the past since the rise of industrialization.[37]

If any occupations are full social entities—task, people, and organization—it is the professions and crafts. I focus here on the professions, which are larger, more powerful, and growing; the crafts are in demographic decline. A long-standing literature (e.g., Ben-David 1963) has seen the professions as a risk-averse upper-middle-class strategy for class reproduction. Current patterns of occupational choice among elite university graduates underscore this importance, also evident in the political attitudes of professionals, which are liberal on social questions and conservative on economic ones (Brint 1994).

Demographically, members of the professions remain in them longer than do members of other occupations. In part, this is because professional skills have high costs, both sunk (income forgone during training) and ongoing (debt incurred for training), and as a result individuals are reluctant to leave. At the same time, the professions have expanded considerably as a proportion of the labor force in the last century, much of that expansion coming in teaching and nursing, mass professions that together constitute nearly a third of the professional-technical sector, itself now nearly 20 percent of the labor force.

Ambitious young people choose their professions based on current educational availability (a function of professional and state policy) and current rewards (a function of the current balance of supply and demand). But this current balance of supply and demand is a function of many things. First, because of the length of professional training, demographic decisions long past are encoded into the current professional age structure, with crucial consequences for later supply. Second, the professions themselves can constrain (e.g., British lawyers) or facilitate (e.g., American lawyers) production of new professionals. The professions also generate new technologies and organizations of work that may dramatically affect professional productivity and hence demand. The state too shapes supply and demand, particularly through control of professional education, a force that of course varies with the centralization and power of the state (high in France, low in Italy, for example). State power can also have dramatic effects on professional autonomy. And for those professions—like engineering—dependent directly on commercial employ-

ment, the private sector can play important roles, partly in education, but more crucially in the size of demand and extent of autonomy.

The almost inevitable result of these various forces is a boom-and-bust cycle, which can be clearly seen in Krause's survey (1996) of four professions in five countries. Since these cycles are short relative to the professional life course, long-tenure professionals can assume that their profession's rewards and conditions of employment will change one or more times over their work lifetimes. The professions thus provide a particularly clear example of the kind of cohort-encoded labor force discussed earlier.

Organizationally, more and more American professionals have become salaried over the last 30 to 50 years. (We do not actually know how long this trend has gone on.) Moreover, the organizations in which such salaried professionals work have gotten larger and more heteronomous. And a variety of sources note the increase in new forms of accountability (on all these, see Leicht and Fennell 1997). Although the roots of these developments lie in the middle twentieth century or even earlier, the last 20 years have seen a rapid increase in them, paralleling an increasing involvement of the state and commercial sector in professional life. Overall, these changes are making American professionals more like continental ones, who have have from the beginning most often been employees or functionaries.[38]

These transformations can stand for larger transformations in the labor process throughout the labor force, since if any set of occupations can dominate their work practices, it is the professions. Transformations in the professions make a useful transition into some brief closing comments about the organization of work.

There is no space here for a serious discussion of the set of forces commonly believed to determine the division of labor on the shop floor, in the cubicle, or at the counter. The questions of work redesign, of flexibility, of worker democracy, and of the labor process more generally command independent space of their own. One important aim of this chapter, however, has been to raise the possibility that this entire literature on work organization needs to more deeply consider the labor opportunity structure as a determinant of the organization of production.[39]

We can see this determination by considering the topic of skill. The subjects of skill and technique have exercised the sociology of work from its earliest days, much of this work growing out of the satisfaction literature produced by industrial engineering. The 1950s saw a large literature on deskilling and automation, above all in France (Friedmann 1946; Touraine 1955; Naville 1963), where a mixed view was taken of the move to automated production. The downside of repetitive work and of deskilling was noticed, but automation was also thought to raise levels of skill and to create new relations betwen workers as processes became more complex and interdependent. (Similar views were urged in the United States by Blauner 1964.) The 1970s brought Braverman (1974), Burawoy (1979), and the anglophone deskilling controversy.

In these various deskilling debates (Attewell 1990 gives an excellent summary), however, the concept of skill was never treated in life course terms, but only cross-sectionally. Writers who talked of reskilling pointed to training programs and one-step transitions. But just as the concept of career was operationalized not in actual career data but in point-outcome measures, transitions, and hazard rates, no one actually has any idea how many skills a typical worker has had in a lifetime, now or for any point in the past (for ethnographic work on skills over the career, see Harper 1987, 2001).

Moreover, the present-day skill distribution is a crucial aspect of the labor opportunity structure, as we have already seen in the earlier discussion of education. But this encoded skill distribution has further structural implications. Consider the phenomenon of the occupational sorting of talent. Suppose there are some generalizable individual resources that are convertible into many different particular occupational skills. (They can be genetic or acquired—what matters is that they be generalized.) These are things like intelligence, "people skills," manual facility, and so on. Suppose also that occupations follow some kind of prestige and reward hierarchy. A simple argument predicts that workers will take their skills where they will be best rewarded. This implies that in a labor force closed to immigration, a randomly examined occupation will contain a "representative" sample of skill resources only if there are constraints that lock into particular occupations or occupational zones groups (typically, ascriptive groups) that themselves contain representative samples of skills. If all individuals are free to choose their occupations, occupations low in prestige and rewards will be systematically denuded of people with generalizable skills, since these workers will move elsewhere to get returns to their resources.

The obvious example is women, an ascriptive group within which generalizable skills take rough-ly the same distribution as they do among men. During the early years of the move of married women into the labor force, job discrimination kept women out of much of the high-rewarded labor force. As a result, the glory years labor force was full of extremely smart and well-educated secretaries, a group that largely disappeared from the labor force once the great affirmative action settlements of the 1970s made it much easier for such women to become lawyers, executives, and doctors. Could it be that one of the reasons the personal computer took off in business and professional life, indeed one of the reasons that professional workers began spending their highly paid time doing most of (what would have been seen in the 1950s as) their own secretarial work, was that there was no longer any pool of talent to do that work at the necessary quality for the wages offered? There were some personal efficiency and technological reasons for this shift, to be sure, but the necessary cause of the sheer absence of potential clerical workers of prior skill levels undoubtedly played a major role in this as in many other aspects of the reorganization of office life.

Labor force–wide, this is undoubtedly a strong effect. The opening of barriers to employment frees individuals to move their talents where they wish, with the curious result that inequality between occupations in terms of individual endowments increases; variance within becomes variance between. More generally, we can posit a kind of Say's law for occupations: at any given time, the existing division of labor can employ only those individuals who exist in the labor force at that moment. Those individuals possess a certain mix of historically encoded attributes and assets—age, skills, gender, education, wealth, and so on—on the basis of which the existing division of labor gets filled. Note that this fact places absolute constraints on the algebraic relationships between certain variables—on returns to education, for example.

This implies further that the overall parameters of the current mapping of individuals into positions are not a function of matters at the margin, as is implicit in the neoclassical way of thinking about sorting. Relations at the margin determine only instantaneous, local change. The overall nature of the occupational mapping is a function of the averages, (the marginals) which are, for the most part, deeply encoded into the demographic (broadly understood) structure of the labor force. Note that we take this argument for granted in studies of immigrant and imported labor, which we routinely explain in terms of demand for laborers of types unavailable in the current offer of the labor force. Commercial organizations unable to find what they want in the current labor force have powerful incentives to look beyond it—either geographically or socially or both.

With these few hints of the implications of a labor opportunity structure for understanding the organizational world of work I must close. I hope to have persuaded the reader that the sociology of work can be renovated by rethinking our normal strategies of analysis, which are overly reliant on a historical-forces, effects-at-the-margin, individual-outcomes model. Even the life course model, important as that is (or should be) for the sociology of work, does not go far enough. Only a general analysis of historically encoded structures—which after all include not only labor, but also technology, employment relations, occupations, firms, and so on—can really enable us to escape the ways our earlier analyses have precommitted us to certain conclusions.

The sociology of work is an old and distinguished subfield, both in the United States and in Europe. In both places it has had strong periods and weak ones. In both places it has, like the sociology of organizations in a parallel case, flirted at times with becoming a kind of of applied personnel studies for the commercial world. But its inner heritage is the radical and critical question of how exactly work is situated in human experience. The problems of the sociology of work thus present a forceful challenge to the enterprise of economic sociology. In the first instance, the question of the boundaries of work requires economic sociology to start thinking about the various "noneconomic" sectors of work and about their interrelations with wage work. In the second, economic sociology has in the concept of a labor opportunity structure a way of going beyond the structural and network/embedding insights that have been its bread and butter heretofore. A historical demography of wage labor is a preliminary to any serious account of the economy. As of the present moment, we have not even begun it.

NOTES

I would like to thank Erin York for research assistance.

1. The figures on types of work are from the *Statistical Abstract of the United States*, the 2000 issue, table 438 on p. 265 and table 637 on p. 396. All data from the *Statistical Abstract* in this chapter come from this issue, and are in the form "SA:pages" for brevity. Hence, in this case, SA 265, 367.

2. Other than this brief mention, I have omitted consideration of the various types of forced production. For an example, see Hirata 1979.

3. Polanyi's definition of market production was that it was nonembedded production. The fascination with embeddedness in economic sociology is thus a fractal return of Polanyi's view, studying embeddedness, but only within the (relatively) disembedded sector of wage production. See Abbott 2001, chap. 1.

4. Sex is another example, prostitution having seen a large decline over the past century as the young single men who were its main clientele have found free sex more available. Still another is elevator operators, of whom there were 100,000 as recently as 1950. (The Bureau of Labor Statistics reports 2,700 in 1998.) The 1950 figure is from the *Historical Statistics of the United States*, Bicentennial Edition (Washington, D.C.: GPO, 1975), 144. All subsequent citations from the *Historical Statistics* are in the form HS:page, in this case, HS:144. On family work systems, see also the chapter of Light in this volume.

5. The best conceptual overview of leisure and work remains de Grazia 1964. On consumption, see the chapter of Zelizer in this volume. The Keynes quote is Keynes [1931] 1963, 367. For want of space, I have removed here a discussion on the culture of work.

6. For the work discipline literature, see Edwards 1979. On informal relations in formal organizations, see Roethlisberger and Dickson 1939 or any other classic of the human relations school. Examples of resistance and organization against plant change include Fantasia 1988; Jermier, Knights, and Nord 1994; and Burawoy and Lukacs 1992. Also interesting in this regard is Leidner 1993.

7. For an excellent review taking this individual approach, see Mishel, Bernstein, and Schmitt 1999. James Coleman defended sociological hyperindividualization by arguing that society had become individualized and that our sociology should be apposite for its time (Coleman 1993). This argument puts the ideological cart before the empirical horse; by taking this hyperindividualized stand, social science participated in furthering the ideology of individualism. But as usual Coleman saw the issue quite clearly.

8. For language examples, see Hareven 1982; Siu 1987; and Lamphere, Stepick, and Grenier 1994. In dozens of current situations worldwide, ignorance of the local language is a crucial element of forced labor structures.

9. Granovetter and Tilly 1988; Tilly and Tilly 1994, 1998. I have not tried in this chapter to update Tilly and Tilly's chapter from the preceding edition of this handbook. I recommend it (and the book that followed) highly.

10. The "encoding" perspective adopted here differs from a life course perspective. Life course perspectives consider individual outcomes unfolding over an individual's life; social forces matter insofar as they affect this unfolding. The dependent variable is usually some general "outcome" in personal experience, important in its own right. In the status attainment and human capital perspectives, outcomes are always located at a point in time because the ultimate interest of these perspectives is deciding policy, which works at a point. In the present view, by contrast, the life course itself matters mainly because at any given time it determines important individual "asset" outcomes (things that pile up over time, positive and negative), which, along with other social states, constitute the determining forces of the present. The outcome of interest is the unfolding of the social system of work, not of individual lives, which are important only because they affect that system. And the conceptions of

causality and outcome are processual, not point-focused. On outcome concepts generally, see Abbott, forthcoming. An interesting collection of papers on work and the life course is Marshall et al. 2001.

11. The logic of how all these are tied together may make certain of them appear to be "larger," and it may be that that logic does allow some of them to govern others. But those facts should be taken as empirical possibilities, not a priori assumptions.

12. These figures give the total number of owner-occupied housing units divided by the total number of households. HS:43, 646; SA:718.

13. The percentage of Americans over 20 that are foreign born is back over 10 percent for the first time since 1950; the low came at about 6 percent around 1970 (HS:14ff.; SA:47). The average age of men in the labor force was 33 in 1900 and rose steadily till 1970 (39.9) before dipping because of the baby boom. It is currently (1999) back up to 39. Women in the labor force used to be considerably younger than men. Like the male mean, the female figure fell to 1980 (34) and has risen since (to 39). The data for the age-specific LFPRs (here and in table 1) from 1970 on are from SA:405. For 1890–1940, Sixteenth Census, Population, vol. 3, pt. 1, p. 26. For 1950, Seventeenth Census, vol. 4, Special Reports, Pt. 1B, p. 37. For 1960, Eighteenth Census, vol. 2, PC(2)6A, table 2.

14. The exact details of these series vary, but the general trends are clear. I have relied here on HS:225–26, 297, 301; SA:466. In commenting on this paper, John Muellbauer pointed out that a change in the mix of types of families may be an important factor here.

15. For home ownership figures, see HS:43, 643, 646, 713. The real bonanza for those holding mortgages came through the huge inflations of the neoliberal transition. The real value of a fixed mortgage payment fell 45 percent from 1975 to 1985 and almost 70 percent from 1965 to 1985. The slow rise of overall homeownership since 1970 conceals steady declines in age-specific home ownership rates; the rise is compositional (Myers 1999).

16. Most satisfaction studies are psychological; see, e.g., Cranny, Smith, and Stone 1992. For a more sociological example, see Freeman and Rogers 1999. Most sociological work on satisfaction assumes *ex ante* that satisfaction is a downstream, short-run variable, with no autoregression or other long-run pattern or cumulation. See the classic Parnes et al., 1970–75, 1:150ff.

17. Sources on work time include Hunnicutt 1988, 1996; Cross 1988; Thoemmes 2000.

18. The relation between the legal and actual workweek has always been loose. The legal standard exists to benchmark things like overtime and benefits. On the recent changes in work hours, see Coleman and Pencavel 1993. I unfortunately lack the space to discuss flextime and home work.

19. The scattered data on whole careers from the 1930s to the 1950s are discussed in Wilensky 1960, 553 n. 2. The whole careers tradition ended with the turns first to structural modeling of current achievement (in the 1960s) and second to hazard rate study of particular shifts (in the 1980s). The major longitudinal studies (PSID, NLS) began to produce career results in the 1980s and 1990s, but have both coverage and completion problems. Methodologically, the most likely technique for whole career data is sequence analysis (Abbott and Tsay 2000). The best general review of career studies is Rosenfeld 1992.

20. These education figures are all directly from HS:380;

SA 152, 157. I have throughout this discussion assumed that education in labor force cohorts is the same as education in adult population cohorts.

21. On drug dealing, see MacCoun and Reuter 1992 and, especially, Hagedorn 2002, who estimates that 10 percent of youth in his research areas are involved in drug sales. MacCoun and Reuter were surprised to find that most of drug workers in their sample also had legitimate employment.

22. There is little evidence that higher education produces much of a net increase in cognitive functioning once we control out selection effects; most college learning is actually maturation. The idea that increasing education means ipso facto a more highly skilled labor force is thus an egregious error. See Pascarella and Terenzini 1991 for the best general review of this topic.

23. A quick calculation based on LFPRs and Carey's figures shows that these four occupations produce about one-half of the 10 million person-years of work done by a one-year cohort as it passes through the ages from 17 to 22. Note that unlike the American labor force, the German labor force has by this age had much of its future occupational structure encoded into it through apprenticeships connected quite tightly to later occupations and employers (see the essays in Culpepper and Finegold 1999).

24. These are estimated figures, using total numbers of veterans, assuming 95 percent of them are men and that their LFPRs are the same as their age peers.' A slight deflation is probably necessary for full disability status. Note also that a surprising amount of military vocational training was used later in the civilian labor force. See Parnes et al. 1970–75, 4:43–44.

25. Like many civilian organizations, the military itself has changed in the neoliberal age into a leaner, meaner, team-based organization from which much of the old "shit-work" and stultifying bureaucracy have been outsourced. See Abbott 2002 and the sources cited therein.

26. Ten-year-plus employees still make up about 60 percent of employed men in their fifties (Jaeger and Stevens 2000). Useful references on job tenure include Akerlof and Main 1981 and Gregg and Wadsworth 1999 (on Britain, where job tenure became a major political issue in the 1990s). Interestingly, tenure distributions do not vary widely between blacks and whites (Hall 1982).

27. Hall (1982) estimates cumulative jobs over a lifetime to be about 10 for both men and women, extrapolating from data for 1968–78. High youth turnover was a truism of the early small-sample mobility literature, e.g., Davidson and Anderson 1937 and Form and Miller 1949.

28. For rewarding accounts, see Wyckoff 1898 and the unshakably classic Anderson 1923. Anderson 1940 chronicles the replacement of hoboes by temporary migrant workers in the depression.

29. Basic sources on part-time, contingent, and alternate employment are Tilly 1996; Smith 1997; Kalleberg 2000; and Carre et al. 2000.

30. The result of this (re)entry is, in most cases, that wages, benefits, working conditions, and other job qualities are lower for those in these various flexible arrangements. Much of the literature concerns whether non-FTFY work has been chosen or forced (qv. Tilly 1996), with the verdict inclining to forced, at least since 1980. The same trends have been noted in France (Paugam 2000, 76ff.). Nonetheless, the invariant and very long duration (since 1900) cross-sectional association between rates of part-time, temporary, AEA, or contingent work on the one hand and gender, young people, and so on on the other suggests that a sub-

tantial sector of the economy operates on a male-breadwinner model consciously or unconsciously or perforce.

31. On the bracero program see Goldfarb 1981, 115ff. The census calculation is my own. The classic source on the demand theory of immigration is Piore 1979. On migratory workers see, e.g., Lamphere, Stepick, and Grenier 1994 and Waldinger 1986, 1996. A general review on reasons for mobility in the glory years is Roseman 1983. For a recent econometric study (with proxies rather than actual survey responses), see Chun 1996. To save space, I have removed a section on migration in Europe.

32. For general histories of retirement in the United States, see Costa 1998 and Graebner 1980. Workers could not expect ultimately to leave the labor force by retirement rather than death until well after 1950. Calculations based on Hauser's labor force life tables (1954, 39) put the ratio of deaths to retirements at 1.3 deaths for each 1 retirement in 1947; the expected duration of retirement in 1947 was about five years. Lower death rates and earlier retirement rewrote these figures completely by the late 1970s.

33. Retirement in Europe has a slightly different history. The LFPRs of Britain, France, and Germany at age 65 have typically been from five to 20 percentage points below those in the United States in all decades since 1900 (Costa 1998, 9), probably because European nations typically adopted national pension plans two to five decades before the United States.

34. On census-type occupational classifications and their problems see Conk 1980 and Desrosières and Thévenot 1988. Examples of the new labor history are Walkowitz 1978 and Licht 1983, which exemplify its excellent prosopography. An exemplarily detailed history of a profession is Hufbauer 1982.

35. Weeden (2003) has recently shown that strategies of occupational closure make strong predictions of wage rewards, providing a serious complement to individual-level human-capital or skill accounts. But while occupational closure may have important effects, we do not in fact really know in most cases whether there is anything demographically real there to be closed. And, in the case of many unions, the closure strategies are not occupational but sectoral; Germany's great union coalitions, for example, have been industry-based. A perusal of the journals shows surprisingly little work on the structural and organizational realities of occupations in the last five years, with continuing emphasis on inequalities and on changes in the organization of work and employment. This may well be because organized or demographic occupations do not really exist, but that is an empirical proposition—as yet unevaluated for either past or present.

36. For example, extremely high tenures generally signify occupational death through nonrecruitment; barbers, farmers, and railroad conductors were the longest-tenure occupations in 1987. Unlike turnover occupations, which have a task but no enduring personnel and no organization, these are "workless occupations," occupations with personnel and in some cases organization, but no longer much of any task.

37. What occupational demography we do have (largely of unions and professions) concerns organizational leadership. For fine-grained studies of careers within structures, see the chapters of Abbott, Gaertner, Rosenbaum, and Althauser and Kalleberg in Breiger 1990, as well as Stewman 1986, which reviews some of the mathematical demography of organizations. Evans and Laumann (1983) estimated occupational retention in the professions, but their methods used age-specific, not tenure-specific decrement rates, and

so are probably untrustworthy. Rotolo and McPherson (2001) analyze occupations competing in a demographic space for members, but for them occupation members have no historical continuity. Interestingly enough, we have the same ignorance about unions; there is almost no information on turnover and tenure among rank-and-file union members.

38. For a still-relevant analysis of the future of professions and of institutionalized expertise in general, see Abbott 1991.

39. A good way into this literature is through the sources given in note 9 above. As I noted earlier, I have not summarized it here because it is well summarized elsewhere. It seemed more important to step back and view studies of work through another lens.

References

Abbott, Andrew. 1988. *The System of Professions.* Chicago: University of Chicago Press.

———. 1991. "The Future of Professions." *Research in the Sociology of Organizations* 8:17–42.

———. 1993. "The Sociology of Work and Occupations." *Annual Review of Sociology* 19:187–209.

———. 2001. *Chaos of Disciplines.* Chicago: University of Chicago Press.

———. 2002. "The Army and the Theory of Professions." Pp. 523–36 in *The Future of the Army Profession,* ed. Don M. Snider and Gayle L. Watkins. Boston: McGraw-Hill.

———. Forthcoming. "The Idea of Outcome." In *The Politics of Method in the Human Sciences,* ed. George Steinmetz. Durham, N.C.: Duke University Press.

Abbott, Andrew, and Angela Tsay. 2000. "Sequence Analysis and Optimal Matching Methods in Sociology." *Sociological Methods and Research* 29:3–33.

Akerlof, George A., and Brian G. M. Main. 1981. "An Experience-Weighted Measure of Employment and Unemployment Durations." *American Economic Review* 71:1003–11.

Anderson, Nels. 1923. *The Hobo.* Chicago: University of Chicago Press.

———. 1940. *Men on the Move.* Chicago: University of Chicago Press.

Attewell, Paul. 1990. "What Is Skill?" *Work and Occupations* 17:422–48.

Ben-David, Joseph. 1963. "Professions in the Class System of Modern Societies." *Current Sociology* 12:247–98.

Blauner, Robert. 1964. *Alienation and Freedom.* Chicago University of Chicago Press.

Braverman, Harry. 1974. *Labor and Monopoly Capitalism.* New York: Monthly Review Press.

Breiger, Ronald L. ed. 1990. *Social Mobility and Social Structure.* Cambridge: Cambridge University Press.

Brint, Steven. 1994. *In an Age of Experts.* Princeton: Princeton University Press.

Brint, Steven, and Jerome Karabel. 1989. *The Diverted Dream.* Oxford: Oxford University Press.

Brissenden, Paul F., and Emil Frankel. 1922. *Labor Turnover in Industry*. New York: Macmillan.

Burawoy, Michael. 1979. *Manufacturing Consent*. Chicago: University of Chicago Press.

Burawoy, Michael, and János Lukacs. 1992. *The Radiant Past*. Chicago: University of Chicago Press.

Burnett, John. 1994. *Idle Hands*. London: Routledge.

Cabanes, Robert. 2000. "L'anthropologie du travail au 21e siècle." *Anthropologies et sociétés* 24:79–94.

Carey, M. L. 1988. "Occupational Tenure in 1987." *Monthly Labor Review* 111(10): 3–12.

Carre, Françoise, Marianne A. Ferber, Lonnie Golden, and Steve A. Herzenberg. 2000. *Nonstandard Work*. Champaign IL: Industrial Relations Research Association.

Chun, Jinsuk. 1996. *Interregional Migration and Regional Development*. Aldershot: Avebury.

Coleman, James S. 1993. "The Rational Reconstruction of Society." *American Sociological Review* 58:1–15.

Coleman, Mary T., and John Pencavel. 1993. "Changes in Work Hours of Male Employees." *Industrial and Labor Relations Review* 46(2): 262–83.

Conk, Margo A. 1980. *The United States Census and Labor Force Change*. Ann Arbor: UMI Research Press.

Costa, Dora L. 1998. *The Evolution of Retirement*. Chicago: University of Chicago Press.

Cranny, C. J., Patricia C. Smith, and Eugene F. Stone. 1992. *Job Satisfaction*. New York: Lexington Books.

Cross, Gary. 1988. "Worktime in International Discontinuity." Pp. 155–81 in *Worktime and Industrialization*, ed. Gary Cross. Philadelphia: Temple University Press.

Culpepper, Pepper D., and David Finegold, eds. 1999. *The German Skills Machine*. New York: Berghahn Books.

Davidson, Percy E., and H. Dewey Anderson. 1937. *Occupational Mobility in an American Community*. Stanford, Calif.: Stanford University Press.

de Grazia, Sebastian. 1964. *Of Time, Work, and Leisure*. New York: Doubleday.

Desrosières, Alain, and Laurent Thévenot. 1988. *Les catégories socio-professionnelles*. Paris: Editions La Découverte.

Edwards, Richard C. 1979. *Contested Terrain*. New York: Basic.

Eisner, Robert. 1989. *The Total Incomes System of Accounts*. Chicago: University of Chicago Press.

Eurich, Nell P. 1985. *Corporate Classrooms*. Princeton: Carnegie Foundation for the Advancement of Teaching.

Evans, Mariah D., and Edward O. Laumann. 1983. "Professional Commitment." *Research in Social Stratification and Mobility* 2:3–40.

Evans-Pritchard, Edward E. 1940. *The Nuer*. Oxford: Oxford University Press.

Fantasia, Rick. 1988. *Cultures of Solidarity*. Berkeley and Los Angeles: University of California Press.

Folbre, Nancy, and Julie A. Nelson. 2000. "For Love or Money—or Both?" *Journal of Economic Perspectives* 14:123–40.

Form, William H., and Delbert C. Miller. 1949. "Occupational Career Pattern as a Sociological Instrument." *American Journal of Sociology* 54:317–29.

Freeman, Richard B., and James L. Medoff. 1984. *What Do Unions Do?* New York: Basic.

Freeman, Richard B., and Joel Rogers. 1999. *What Workers Want*. New York: Russell Sage Foundation and Ithaca, N.Y.: Cornell University Press.

Friedmann, Georges. 1946. *Problèmes humains du machinisme industriel*. Paris: Gallimard.

Frisch, C. F. 1984. "Seasonality of Farm Labor Use Patterns in the United States." Pp. 64–103 in *Seasonal Agricultural Labor Markets in the United States*, ed. Robert D. Emerson. Ames: Iowa State University Press.

Gallie, Duncan, and Serge Paugam. 2000. *Welfare Regimes and the Experience of Unemployment in Europe*. Oxford: Oxford University Press.

Gershuny, Jonathan I. 1983. *Social Innovation and the Division of Labour*. Oxford: Oxford University Press.

Gill, Tom. 2001. *Men of Uncertainty*. Albany: State University of New York Press.

Goldfarb, Ronald L. 1981. *Migrant Farm Workers*. Ames: Iowa State University Press.

Graebner, William. 1980. *A History of Retirement*. New Haven: Yale University Press.

Granovetter, Mark, and Charles Tilly. 1988. "Inequality and Labor Processes." Pp. 175–221 in *Handbook of Sociology*, ed. Neil J. Smelser. Newbury Park, Calif.: Sage.

Gregg, Paul, and Jonathan Wadsworth. 1999. *The State of Working Britain*. New York: St. Martin's.

Hagedorn, John M. 2002. "Gangs and the Informal Economy." Pp. 101–20 in *Gangs in America*, ed. C. Ronald Huff. Thousand Oaks, Calif.: Sage.

Hall, Robert E. 1982. "The Importance of Lifetime Jobs in the U. S. Economy." *American Economic Review* 72:716–24.

Hareven, Tamara K. 1982. *Family Time and Industrial Time*. Cambridge: Cambridge University Press.

Harper, Douglas. 1987. *Working Knowledge*. Chicago: University of Chicago Press.

———. 2001. *Changing Works*. Chicago: University of Chicago Press.

Harris, José. 1972. *Unemployment and Politics*. Oxford: Oxford University Press.

Hauser, Philip M. 1954. "Mobility in Labor Force Participation." Pp. 8–46 in *Labor Mobility and Economic Opportunity*, by E. Wight Bakke et al. Cambridge Mass.: Technology Press; New York: Wiley.

Herskovits, Melville J. 1965. *Economic Anthropology*. New York: W. W. Norton.

Hirata, Lucie Cheng. 1979. "Free, Indentured, Enslaved." *Signs* 5:3–29.

Hochschild, Arlie Russell. 1997. *The Time Bind*. New York: Metropolitan.

Hufbauer, Karl. 1982. *The Formation of the German Chemical Community*. Berkeley and Los Angeles: University of California Press.

Hunnicutt, Benjamin K. 1988. *Work without End*. Philadelphia: Temple University Press.

———. 1996. *Kellogg's Six-Hour Day*. Philadelphia: Temple University Press.

Hollingshead, August de Belmont. 1949. *Elmtown's Youth*. New York: Wiley.

Jackson, Kenneth T. 1985. *Crabgrass Frontier*. Oxford: Oxford University Press.

Jaeger, David A., and Ann Huff Stevens. 2000. "Is Job Stability in the United States Falling?" Pp. 31–69 in *On the Job*, ed. David Neumark. New York: Russell Sage Foundation.

Jermier, John M., David Knights, and Walter R. Nord. 1994. *Resistance and Power in Organizations*. London: Routledge.

Kaitz, H. B. 1970. "Analyzing Spells of Unemployment." *Monthly Labor Review* 93(11): 11–20.

Kalleberg, Arne L. 2000. "Nonstandard Employment Relations." *Annual Review of Sociology* 26:341–65.

Keynes, John Maynard. [1931] 1963. *Essays in Persuasion*. New York: W. W. Norton.

Keyssar, Alexander. 1986. *Out of Work*. Cambridge: Cambridge University Press.

Kotlikoff, Laurence J., and David A. Wise. 1989. *The Wage Carrot and the Pension Stick*. Kalamazoo, Mich.: W. E. Upjohn Institute.

Krause, Elliott A. 1996. *Death of the Guilds*. New Haven: Yale University Press.

Lamphere, Louise, Alex Stepick, and Guillermo Grenier, eds. 1994. *Newcomers in the Workplace*. Philadelphia: Temple University Press.

Layte, Richard, H. Levin, J. Hendrickx, and I. Bison. 2000. "Unemployment and Cumulative Disadvantage in the Labor Force." Pp. 153–74 in *Welfare Regimes and the Experience of Unemployment in Europe*, ed. Duncan Gallie and Serge Pangam. Oxford: Oxford University Press.

Leicht, K. T., and M. L. Fennel. 1997. "The Changing Organizational Context of Professional Work." *Annual Review of Sociology* 23:215–31.

Leidner, Robin. 1993. *Fast Food, Fast Talk*. Berkeley and Los Angeles: University of California Press.

Licht, Walter. 1983. *Working for the Railroad*. Princeton: Princeton University Press.

Lowe, Graham S. 1987. *Women in the Administrative Revolution*. Toronto: University of Toronto Press.

MacCoun, Robert, and Peter Reuter. 1992. "Are the Wages of Sin $30 an Hour?" *Crime and Delinquency* 38:477–91.

Marshall, Victor W., Walter R. Heinz, Helga Kruger, and Anil Verma, eds. 2001. *Restructuring Work and the Life Course*. Toronto: University of Toronto Press.

Meillassoux, Claude. [1975] 1981. *Maidens, Meal, and Money*. Cambridge: Cambridge University Press.

Mishel, Lawrence, Jared Bernstein, and John Schmitt.

1999. *The State of Working America, 1998–99*. Ithaca, N.Y.: ILR Press.

Mortimer, Jeylan T., and Michael J. Shanahan. 1994. "Adolescent Work Experience and Family Relationships." *Work and Occupations* 21:369–84.

Myers, Dowell. 1999. "Cohort Longitudinal Estimation of Housing Careers." *Housing Studies* 14:473–91.

Navile, Pierre. 1963. *Vers l'automatisme sociale?* Paris: Gallimard.

Neumark, David, ed. 2000. *On the Job*. New York: Russell Sage Foundation.

Olfson, Mark, and Harold A. Pincus. 1994. "Measuring Outpatient Mental Health Care in the United States." *Health Affairs* 13(5): 172–80.

Pahl, R. E. 1984. *Divisions of Labour*. Oxford: Blackwell.

Palmer, Gladys L. 1954. *Labor Mobility in Six Cities*. New York: Social Science Research Council.

Parnes, Herbert S. 1954. *Research on Labor Mobility*. Social Science Research Council, Bulletin No. 65. New York: SSRC.

Parnes, Herbert S., et al. 1970–75. *The Pre-retirement Years*. Vols. 1–4, 1970, 1973, 1975. Manpower Research Monograph No. 15, U.S. Department of Labor, Manpower Administration.

Pascarella, Ernest T., and Patrick T. Terenzini. 1991. *How College Affects Students*. San Francisco: Jossey-Bass.

Paugam, Serge. 2000. *Le salarié de la précarité*. Paris: Presses Universitaires Francaises.

Piore, Michael J. 1979. *Birds of Passage*. Cambridge: Cambridge University Press.

Polanyi, Karl. 1957. *The Great Transformation*. Boston: Beacon Press.

Purcell, Patrick J. 2000. "Older Workers." *Monthly Labor Review* 123(10): 19–30.

Roethlsberger, F. J., and and William J. Dickson. 1939. *Management and the Worker*. Cambridge: Harvard University Press.

Roseman, C. C. 1983. "Labor Force Migration, Non–labor Force Migration, and Non-employment Reasons for Migration." *Socio-economic Planning Sciences* 17:303–12.

Rosenfeld, Rachel A. 1992. "Job Mobility and Career Processes." *Annual Review of Sociology* 18:39–61.

Rotolo, Tom, and J. Miller McPherson. 2001. "The System of Occupations." *Social Forces* 79:1095–1130.

Sahlins, Marshall. 1972. *Stone Age Economics*. New York: Alcine de Gruyter.

Salaff, Janet W. 1981. *Working Daughters of Hong Kong*. Cambridge: Cambridge University Press.

Salais, Robert, Nicolas Baverez, and Benedicte Reynaud. 1986. *L'invention du chômage*. Paris: Presses Universitaires de France.

Seidman, Michael 1991. *Workers against Work*. Berkeley and Los Angeles: University of California Press.

Sitchter, Sharon. 1985. *Migrant Laborers*. Cambridge: Cambridge University Press.

Siu, Paul C. P. 1987. *The Chinese Laundryman*. New York: New York University Press.

Smelser, Neil J., and Richard Swedberg. 1994. "The Sociological Perspective on the Economy." Pp. 3–26 in *Handbook of Economic Sociology*, ed. Neil J. Smelser and Richard Swedberg. New York: Russell Sage Foundation; Princeton: Princeton University Press.

Smith, Vicki. 1997. "New Forms of Work Organization." *Annual Review of Sociology* 23:315–39.

Stalker, Peter. 1994. *The Work of Strangers.* Geneva: Internationl Labour Office.

Stepan-Norris, Judith, and Maurice Zeitlin. 2003. *Left Out.* Cambridge: Cambridge University Press.

Stewman, Shelby. 1986. "Demographic Models of Internal Labor Markets." *Administrative Science Quarterly* 31:212–47.

Thelen, Kathleen, and Ikuo Kume. 2001. "The Rise of Non-liberal Training Regimes." Pp. 200–227 in *The Origins of Nonliberal Capitalism*, ed. Wolfgang Streeck and Kozo Yamamura. Ithaca, N.Y.: Cornell University Press.

Thoemmes, J. 2000. *Vers la fin du temps du travail?* Paris: Presses Universitaires de France.

Tilly, Chris. 1996. *Half a Job.* Philadelphia: Temple University Press.

Tilly, Chris, and Charles Tilly. 1994. "Capitalist Work and Labor Markets." Pp. 283–312 in *Handbook of Economic Sociology*, ed. Neil J. Smelser and Richard Swedberg. New York: Russell Sage Foundation; Princeton: Princeton University Press.

———. 1998. *Work under Capitalism.* Boulder Colo.: Westview.

Touraine, A. *L'evolution du travil ouvrier aux usines Renault.* Paris: CNRS.

United States. Department of Labor. Bureau of Labor Statistics. Monthly Labor Review (MLR). Washington, D.C.: GPO.

Waldinger, Roger. 1986. *Through the Eye of the Needle.* New York: New York University Press.

———. 1996. *Still the Promised City?* Cambridge: Harvard University Press.

Walkowitz, Daniel J. 1978. *Worker City, Company Town.* Urbana: University of Illinois Press.

Weeden, Kim A. 2003. "Why Do Some Occupations Pay More Than Others?" *American Journal of Sociology* 108:55–101.

Wilensky, Harold L. 1960. "Work, Careers, and Social Integration." *International Social Science Journal* 12:543–60.

———. 1961. "Orderly Careers and Social Participation." *American Sociological Review* 26:521–39.

Wyckoff, Walter A. 1898. *The Workers.* 2 vols. New York: Scribners.

15 Culture and Consumption

Viviana Zelizer

STRANGE as it may now seem, during the 1960s many American planners argued that shopping malls could provide solutions to suburban sprawl and urban anomie. Designer and developer Victor Gruen led the chorus, building some of the country's largest and best-publicized suburban shopping centers. Moreover, he wrote eloquently about their virtues. Speaking especially of the Northland and Eastland centers his company built in the Detroit metropolitan area, Gruen crowed that they had created a new, intense kind of community:

I remember the surprised faces of my clients when we drove out to a shopping center on a Sunday and found the parking area full. The courts and malls, the lanes and promenades were filled with milling crowds dressed in their Sunday best, engaging in an activity that was believed to be long forgotten: family groups strolling leisurely, their youngsters in go-carts and dogs on the leash; relaxed and admiring the flowers and trees, sculptures and murals, fountains and ponds, and, incidentally, using the opportunity for window-shopping. To the joy of the merchants, this last resulted in strong business activity on the following weekdays. (1964, 203)

Gruen went on to boast that civic organizations, churches, hobby clubs, political rallies, art exhibitions, and theaters thrived in the new environment, even that "National minority groups arranged for special musical and folk dancing evenings" (1964, 203). Good planning, he concluded, could integrate retail activity with active social life.

A third of a century down the suburban road, political scientist turned prophet Robert Putnam offered a grimmer judgment of the shopping mall. "Rather than at the grocery store or five-and-dime on Main Street, where faces were familiar," lamented Putnam,

today's suburbanites shop in large, impersonal malls. Although malls constitute America's most distinctive contemporary public space, they are carefully designed for one primary, private purpose—to direct consumers to buy. Despite the aspirations of some developers, mall culture is not about overcoming isolation and connecting with others, but about privately surfing from store to store—in the presence of others, but not in their company. The suburban shopping experience does not consist of interaction with people embedded in a common social network. (2000, 211)

The very innovations that Gruen thought were renewing lost community, according to Putnam, actually destroyed it. Increasingly, consumption privatized and isolated Americans instead of providing occasions and means of sociability.

In a sophisticated and closely documented account, Lizabeth Cohen (2003) reports what actually went on within America's transformed consumer marketplaces. Shopping centers did offer their customers a whole range of community activities, including charity fairs, Weight Watchers meetings, and concerts. Moreover, looked at closely, shopping turns out to have often been a joint family activity; women, who were the principal shoppers, frequently took their children and their husbands along with them. Spurred by anxious merchants, however, shopping malls became much more exclusive than city streets. Legal restrictions limited the range of political activities permitted and the kinds of people who could enter the malls. Finally, the malls catered to strongly segmented populations.

When developers and store owners set out to make the shopping center a more perfect downtown, they aimed to exclude from this public space unwanted urban groups such as vagrants, prostitutes, racial minorities, and poor people. Market segmentation became the guiding principle of this mix of commercial and civic activity, as the shopping center sought perhaps contradictorily to legitimize itself as a true community center and to define that community in exclusionary socioeconomic and racial terms. (Cohen 1996, 1059)

Neither all-embracing communities nor habitats of the Lonely Crowd, shopping centers represented America as a whole: both connected and segmented, differentiated by gender, ethnicity, race, and class, mingling commercial and sociable activity, entangling consumption in the strands of meaningful social relations (see also Zukin 2003).

In principle, one might think that production, distribution, and consumption would occupy well-defined, tightly integrated, and roughly equal spaces in the work of economic sociologists. Within sociology, however, a rough division of labor has arisen: economic sociologists examine production and distribution with no more than occasional gestures toward consumption, while specialists in culture, gender, family, inequality, and other fields lavish attention on consumption almost without regard to the questions—or answers—posed by economic sociologists. Meanwhile (as the work of historian Lizabeth Cohen suggests), nonsociologists have been making major contributions to the study of consumption that have not regularly come to economic sociologists' attention.

The *Handbook*'s editors assigned me the analysis of interactions between culture and consumption, not the treatment of consumption as a whole. A full survey of consumption would require a close look at the interdependence among production, distribution, and consumption—for example, how producers promote purchase and use of newly designed goods and services. It would also entail consideration of macroeconomic interactions among prices, supply, and demand of consumer goods and services. Instead, my analysis stresses the participation of consumers in economic life. In compensation for that narrowing of its focus, it takes an exceptionally broad view of consumption.

Although this chapter concentrates on intersections of culture and consumption, the unfortunate existing division of labor between students of culture and specialists in economic processes warns precisely against the dangers of considering the two as separate spheres that only occasionally bump into each other. Reification of the boundary between culture and consumption encourages three incorrect and equally reductionist positions: (1) consumption is "really" rational maximizing behavior that acquires a carapace of culture after the fact; (2) consumption is essentially expressive behavior that does not conform at all to economic rationality; (3) consumption divides between a hard-nosed region of rational maximizing behavior and a soft-hearted region of cultural expression. In fact, all consumption (like all economic life) builds on culture in the sense of shared understandings and their representations. The secret to understanding consumption lies in careful observation of how culture, social relations, and economic processes interact.

With that aim in mind, let us take up in turn

1. Recent investigations of consumption outside of sociology
2. Sociological studies of consumption, outside the claimed territory of economic sociology
3. Consequent challenges to economic sociology

Following those three points, the chapter reviews three different sites of consumption—households, ethnic-racial communities, and retail settings—where extensive research has recently occurred, with an eye to better integration between economic sociology and empirical studies of consumption.

CONSUMPTION OUTSIDE OF SOCIOLOGY

One might have thought that consumption would preoccupy economists, since it is the point where individual lives most obviously integrate into the economy at large. Through much of the twentieth century economists did study consumption in the aggregate. Economists long collaborated with sociologists in surveys of consumer expenditures and behavior, a line of work that significantly influenced market research. Elihu Katz and Paul Lazarsfeld (1955), for example, applied the analysis of personal influence to both political and consumption behavior. Furthermore, a few economists braved the trend by giving the social determination of preferences a central place in their analysis; in a review of the topic, Juliet Schor (1998, 9) singles out Thorstein Veblen, James Duesenberry, John Kenneth Galbraith, Fred Hirsch, Tibor Scitovsky, Richard Easterlin, Amartya Sen, Clair Brown, and Robert Frank as leaders in the economic analysis of consumption (for a detailed review of consumption economics, see Frenzen, Hirsch, and Zerrillo 1994).

Nevertheless, economists have concentrated mostly on production and distribution, commonly throwing up their hands when it came to integrating change and variation in consumer preferences directly into economic analysis. As Gary Becker himself says:

The economist's normal approach to analyzing consumption and leisure choices assumes that individuals maximize utility with preferences that depend at any moment only on the goods and services they consume at that time. These preferences are assumed to be independent of both past and future consumption, and of the behavior of everyone else. This approach has proved to be a valuable simplification for addressing many economic questions, but a large number of choices in all societies depend very much on past experiences and social forces. (1996, 3–4)

Becker endogenizes preferences by retaining economics' cherished assumption of individual rational maximizing but incorporating two new aspects of human capital: *personal capital*, involving past consumption and other experiences that shape present and future preferences; and *social capital*, involving other people's past actions that shape the same preferences. Thus Becker clings to the economist's individual perspective but explicitly builds in experiential and social influences on the individual. Other economists seek to repair the conventional account of consumption by replacing abstract definitions of rational maximization with decision-making principles based on findings from psychologically sophisticated observations and experiments (see, e.g., Thaler 1991, 1999; Aversi et al. 1999). Both these "behavioral economists" and Becker-style neoclassical economists, then, sense that conventional economic accounts of consumption leave much unexplained. Similarly, psychologists in the lineage of Herbert Simon, Amos Tversky, and Daniel Kahneman have mounted influential critiques of neoclassical economics' behavioral assumptions (see, e.g., Kahneman and Tversky 1982). But they have not yet shifted the attention of most economists away from production and distribution.

Consumption has attracted much more attention outside of economics. Indeed, for the past quarter-century anthropologists, historians, cultural psychologists, marketing analysts, and cultural studies specialists have revolutionized traditional understandings of consumption. Rescuing consumption from the grip of social critics, budget experts, and marketers, scholars began asking, "Why do people want goods?" The so-called cultural turn swept away standard utilitarian and individualistic accounts of consumption as maximization. It also challenged deeply entrenched moralistic concerns about the corrupting effects of consumption by reframing the purchase and use of goods and services as meaningful practices. Similarly, students of gender countered the trivialization of consumption typical of earlier social history and social criticism. Where generations of home economists had tried to assimilate kitchen and nursery into the world of industrial efficiency, many feminists sought to identify distinctive cultural traits of woman's worlds, notably including the world of female consumption.

Specialists in gender played a crucial part in renewing consumption studies. They made a double contribution. First, they emphasized distinctions between the consumption patterns of women and men rather than taking consumption as a homogeneous expression of class or nationality. Second, they often challenged understandings of consumption as mass behavior by stressing the creativity and empowerment of female consumers. They did so by carefully investigating diverse facets of consumption's gendered practices, including interactions between saleswomen and customers in American department stores (Porter Benson 1986), middle-class women shoplifters (Abelson 1989), women's sale and use of cosmetics (Peiss 1998, 2002), immigrant housewives' expenditures (Ewen 1985), women shopping in London's West End (Rappoport 2000), Old Regime France seamstresses (Crowston 2001), and the American doll industry (Formanek-Brunell 1993). (See also Andrews and Talbot 2000; de Grazia and Furlough 1996 Horowitz and Mohun 1998; Scanlon 2000; and for male consumers Swiencicki 1999).

Meanwhile, anthropologists provided noneconomic or even antieconomic models of consumption. Marshall Sahlins's *Culture and Practical Reason* (1976) along with Mary Douglas and Baron Isherwood's *World of Goods* (1979) set the tone for the new consumption studies, boldly appropriating consumption into the domain of shared meanings. Two complementary trends occurred in anthropology, history, cultural studies, and a few corners of sociology: a shift of focus away from production and producers to consumption and consumers, as well as an increasing concentration on consumption as expressive behavior: the site of mentalities, identities, and culture.

In her contribution to a three-volume set that Craig Clunas (1999, 1497) called "a major monument in a turn toward the history of consumption and away from the history of production," Lorna Weatherill reports a characteristic study of probate inventories from late-seventeenth- and early-eighteenth-century England. Sampling from eight localities, including the London area, Weatherill reconstructs a wide range of household goods, showing variation by locality, occupation, social rank, and gender. She interprets the array of furniture, looking glasses, pictures, books, clocks, silver, and cooking utensils as expressing the special worldview of seventeenth- and eighteenth-century ordinary people. For instance, detailed inventories of cooking gear, Weatherill suggests, underline the centrality of food to daily life at that time.

More generally, Weatherill (1993, 211) declares that "material goods themselves contain implicit meanings and are therefore indicative of attitudes. Through understanding the nonmaterial attributes of goods it is possible to move to the meaning of ownership in social and other terms."

Scholars of consumption range widely, from studying economic institutions such as department stores, to analyses of commercialized leisure, taste formation, food consumption, media advertising, and household budgets (see, e.g., Miller 1981; Rosenzweig 1983; Tiersten 2001; Mintz 1996; Lears 1994; Horowitz 1985). Out of this variety of studies emerged a continuing conversation on the culture of consumption.[1]

In the 1990s, dissenting voices joined that conversation. Concerned that the "cultural turn" had gone too far, detouring its practitioners from other, crucial aspects of consumption processes, scholars urged new agendas. "Today's burgeoning cottage industry of study devoted to 'consumer culture,'" noted historians Victoria de Grazia and Lizabeth Cohen in 1999 (1), "draws its impulse . . . chiefly [from] the problem of postmodernity and the fluid social and personal identities it appears to have instated." Missing, according to de Grazia and Cohen, was the political economy of inequality and consumption, namely, its link to class relations and class power.[2] Missing as well, complained other specialists, were links between consumption and the production of goods (see, e.g., Crowston 2001; Green 1997).

In *A Consumers' Republic: The Politics of Mass Consumption in Postwar America* (2003) Lizabeth Cohen pushes forward the revised historical agenda, directly examining the political economy of American consumption in the period following the Second World War. Consumption, in her reading, is not merely expressive behavior, but a site, cause, and effect of major changes in American experience. In Cohen's view, the government-backed promotion of consumption during the 1930s as a cushion and antidote for economic crisis sowed the ground both for governmental intervention in wartime consumption and for postwar policies centered on consumption as foundation of a "consumer's republic" (for a contrary view of consumption, see Cross 2000).

Cohen's analysis demonstrates furthermore the heavy involvement of women and African-Americans in the politics of consumption. For example, Cohen reports:

Throughout the North, and less visibly in the South, the ten years between the war and the Montgomery Bus Boycott of 1955 saw an explosion in black challenges to exclusion from public accommodations, many of them sites of consumption and leisure, given that much of public life transpired in commercial venues by the postwar era. By the time of Montgomery and the lunch-counter sit-ins and boycotts of the early 1960s—usually credited with launching the modern civil rights movement through disciplined consumer action—and the passage of the federal Civil Rights Act of 1964 barring discrimination in public accommodations nationwide, politicized black consumers had already spent years agitating at the grassroots for, literally, a place at the table. That attacking segregation in public places became the focus of many local civil rights struggles after the war, particularly in the North, testified to the widespread appeal of the inclusive ideals of the Consumers' Republic. (2003, 166–67)

Thus, consumption reaches far beyond expressive behavior into the very constitution of American public politics (see also Frank 1994; Glickman 1997; Jacobs 1997).

At a smaller scale, but with no less effectiveness, anthropologist Daniel Miller has been likewise investigating the place of consumption in the constitution and maintenance of significant interpersonal relations. Miller (1987) has led the way in challenging the view of consumption as a form of subjugation and exploitation, emphasizing instead the creativity of consumers. In *A Theory of Shopping* (1998), Miller proposes a relational approach to consumption. Closely observing shopping practices of 76 households on and around Jay Road, a North London street, Miller found consumers, as he provocatively sums it up, "making love in supermarkets." Far from being "an expression of individual subjectivity and identity," shopping, Miller argues, serves as "an expression of kinship and other relationships" (35).

As Miller remarks, shopping can "best be understood as being about relationships and not about individuals" (2001, 41; see also Miller et al. 1998). Activities Miller includes are housewives selecting goods that will enhance their influence over the comportment of other household members, courting couples representing the current state of their relationship, and parents boosting the position of children within their peer groups. In a direct challenge to individualistic accounts of consumption, Miller provides evidence that sociability and purchasing of goods support each other, while isolation promotes withdrawal from consumption (1998, 34; 1995, 24).

Sociologists clearly have much to learn about consumption from scholars outside their discipline; in particular, historians and anthropologists have been proceeding quite independently to uncover the social implications and involvement of consumption behavior.

SOCIOLOGICAL STUDIES OF CONSUMPTION

Beginning with nineteenth-century concerns about the condition of the poor, from the first days of their discipline sociologists have dealt with consumption. They have, however, alternated between treatment of consumption as a process bearing heavily on the quality of life, and other interpretations of consumption as an expression of social position. Thorstein Veblen ([1899] 1953); George Simmel ([1904] 1957), Robert and Helen Lynd (1929), Theodore Caplow, Paul Lazarsfeld (1957), David Riesman (1964), and David Caplowitz (1967) wrote important works in one vein or another (for an early effort linking studies of social stratification and consumption, see Barber 1957; for a programmatic statement not much followed, see Smelser 1963, 92–98; for a recent review, see Swedberg 2003, 241–58).

In recent decades, perhaps the most influential synthesis came from sociologist Pierre Bourdieu. Bourdieu combined an ambitious theoretical program with a remarkable range of concrete studies of consumption practices, including photography ([1965] 1990) and housing markets (2000). Most notably, Bourdieu's *Distinction* (1984) introduced the ideas of cultural and social capital into the analysis of consumption. Instead of treating consumption as a straightforward reflection of class culture, Bourdieu represented occupants of different positions within fields of inequality as actively deploying their capital to enhance their own positions.

British sociologists, likewise responding to earlier class analyses, used consumption studies to examine patterns of inequality and cultural change within their own country. In these studies two currents emerged; one a post-Marxist effort to shift the focus of economic studies from production to consumption as a material experience, and the other, a more postmodern effort to treat consumption as an expression of consciousness and culture (see Campbell 1995; Slater 1997; for an attempt to link consumption, production, and distribution, see du Gay 1996).

Within North American sociology we find extensive consumption studies, but they remain remarkably fragmented, with various sociological specialists taking them up as part of other inquiries (see, e.g., Gottdiener 2000). Various dimensions of consumption have become mainly the province of specialists in family, class, gender, childhood, ethnicity, race, religion, community, the arts, and popular culture. Such talented analysts as Daniel Cook (2000), David Halle (1993), Gary Alan Fine (1996), Chandra Mukerji (1983), Michael Schudson (1984), Robert Wuthnow (1996), and Sharon Zukin (1991) have taken up topics varying from the creation of the "toddler" as a merchandising category, the purchase of art, the culture of restaurant work, circulation of mass consumer goods (pictorial prints, maps, and calicoes) in fifteenth- and sixteenth-century western Europe, to the impact of advertising, how Americans talk about their purchases, and Disney World as a "fantasy landscape." Meanwhile, George Ritzer (1996) has single-handedly initiated a somewhat separate analysis of what he calls "McDonaldization," pursuing the thesis that the spread of standardized fast food franchises creates uniform practices and understandings at a world scale (for qualifications, see Ritzer and Ovadia 2000; Ritzer 2003a, 2003b).

Thus, while there is a fair amount of consumption research in sociology, it remains segmented both within sociology and in terms of connections with consumption studies outside of sociology. For example, within the American Sociological Association, as of 2004, separate formal clusters existed for consumption, economic sociology, and the sociology of culture, drawing on vastly different constituencies and with little communication among the three (Cook 1999; see also Ritzer 2000).

Launched in 2001, the *Journal of Consumer Culture* (George Ritzer and Don Slater, editors) promised to bring together multidisciplinary European and North American work but not to bridge all other gaps. The prospectus for the new journal stressed a two-pronged program: first, the study of consumption as mediation and reproduction of culture and social structure, including that of class, second; consumer culture as a special feature of modernity and therefore a privileged prism for its examination (Ritzer and Slater 2001).

What of economic sociology itself?

HOW CONSUMPTION STUDIES CHALLENGE ECONOMIC SOCIOLOGY

Economic sociology's most prominent reader, *The Sociology of Economic Life* (2001), with 22 selections of what its two editors, Mark Granovetter and Richard Swedberg, define as "the most interesting work done in modern economic sociology" (19), barely touches on consumption. The closest instances are a famous article by Clifford Geertz (no economic sociologist) on bazaars, and an essay by Paul Hirsch on fads and fashions, which looks primarily at their production. Indeed, economic sociology grew up concentrating on production and distribution, rather than consumption.

The implicit intellectual strategy of economic sociology reinforced this emphasis. Three somewhat different approaches have characterized the field; we might call them extension, context, and alternative. They vary with respect to economics in two regards: their proximity to standard economic explanations, and their proximity to conventional economic subject matters (for elaboration of this argument see Zelizer 2001, 2002b).

Extension theorists apply relatively standard economic models to social phenomena economists themselves have not treated widely or effectively, for example household behavior, sporting competition, religious recruitment, and compliance with states. A *context* approach identifies features of social organization that work as facilitators or constraints on economic action. This position is intent on revamping economists' portrayals of individual and collective decision-making, for example by specifying conditions other than short-term gain that influence decisions. Advocates of context often speak of the "embeddedness" of economic phenomena in social processes, and often refer to interpersonal networks when they do so (see, e.g., Granovetter 1985; Granovetter and Soong 1986). Followers of this approach have focused on firms and different kinds of markets.

In the *alternative* perspective, sociologists propose competing accounts of economic transactions. Rather than expanding the economic approach or complementing it, one prominent view argues that in all areas of economic life people are creating, maintaining, symbolizing, and transforming meaningful social relations (see, e.g., Tilly and Tilly 1998; White 2002). As a result, the subject matter certainly includes firms and markets but also ranges over households, immigrant networks, informal economies, welfare transfers, or organ donations.

The first two orientations largely follow economists' own stress on production and distribution. The third deals more extensively with consumption, but without working out a consistent, comprehensive line of explanation.

A further barrier to the systematic study of consumption results from a common misunderstanding that cuts across the three different variants of economic sociology. Analysts of economic processes share a powerful view of a world split into two diametrically opposed spheres: a zone of markets and rationality, another of sentiment and meaning. In this *Hostile-Worlds* framework, production and distribution belong to the "real" economy, while consumption remains segregated into culture's expressive domain. Any contact between the two, in this view, produces contamination of one by the other: penetration of the cultural realm by the rationality of production and distribution taints its expressive and affectionate character, while the diffusion of sentiment into the world of economic rationality generates inefficiency, cronyism, and confusion.

Thus the Hostile-Worlds doctrine hinders analysis of interplay between the social relations of consumption and the processes of production and distribution. Some analysts have resolved this dualism by turning to *Nothing But* reductionist alternatives: consumption becomes nothing but a special case of economic rationality, a form of cultural expression, or an exercise of power. Thus, French sociologist Jean Baudrillard offers an extreme version of cultural reductionism:

> Consumer behavior, which appears to be focused and directed at the object and at pleasure, in fact responds to quite different objectives: the metaphoric or displaced expression of desire, and the production of a code of social values through the use of differentiating signs. That which is determinant is not the function of individual interest within a corpus of objects, but rather the specifically social functions of exchange, communication and distribution of values within a corpus of signs. (1999, 47; see also Bauman 1998, 79–85)

Neither Hostile-Worlds tropes nor Nothing-But simplifications will help us understand how consumption actually works. We need a different approach we might call Crossroads: identifying multiple forms of connections between complex social processes and their economic components.

Reaching such an intersection, we find two major forms of analysis dealing with consumption without crippling limitations. The first has a long pedigree in sociology. In the tradition of Veblen, it treats consumption as positional effort—establishment of social location, boundaries, and hierarchies through the display of goods and services. For example, Diana Crane casts a keen eye on class differences in clothing among nineteenth-century French men:

Workers behaved as if they considered some type of fashionable items, such as gloves, canes, top hats and bowlers, as inappropriate for their own use. The reluctance to use these items cannot be explained by their expense. Workers' incomes were rising throughout the period. . . . Instead, the explanation may lie in the fact that these items required a greater understanding of standards of middle-class etiquette than other items. In this sense, these sartorial signs were effective in distinguishing between those who knew the "rules" and were able to follow them and those who did not. (2000, 62)

The second approach treats consumption as relational work—the creation, maintenance, negotiation, and alteration of interpersonal connections through acquisition and use of goods and services. Thus when Elizabeth Chin (2001) worked with ten-year-old, low-income black children in New Haven, she found that the children's purchases recurrently served to affirm relations with other members of their households.

Economic sociologists have recently built social relations firmly into the analysis of connections among Australian hotel managers, negotiations among New York City apparel manufacturers, purchases of consumer durables, consumption struggles in Chilean workers' households, and rotating savings and credit associations (see Ingram and Roberts 2000; Uzzi 1997; DiMaggio and Louch 1998; Stillerman 2004; Biggart 2001. For more general treatments of culture, social relations, and consumption, see DiMaggio 1990, 1994).

Summing up that trend, Nicole Woolsey Biggart and Richard P. Castanias (2001, 491–92) enumerate five characteristics of interplay between economic transactions and social relations:

1. Social relations should not be conflated with irrationality.
2. Social relations can facilitate exchange, not only act as an impediment or friction.
3. Social relations can manage the risks associated with exchange.
4. Actors can appropriate others' social relations for their own exploitation and gain.
5. While social relations may result from exchange, social relations may be prior to economic activity and be the very reason that the transaction takes place between given parties.

This welcome trend has not gone far enough. We must probe further into the negotiation of meaning, the transformation of relations in the course of economic interaction, and the social process of valuation itself. To do so, we need a junction between research being done outside of economic sociology and the work within the field. Our agenda, however, should not be to glue everything together, but to obtain a new theory of consumption organized around meaningful, negotiated social relations. Historical evidence, ethnographic accounts, and marketing studies all can help us clarify how precisely social relations operate in consumption.

That agenda will become more concrete as we examine three major sites of consumption: households, ethnic-racial communities, and retail settings. In each case, we scrutinize consumption relations from three different angles: within the site, across the site's boundaries, and with respect with variation and change in those sites. In each case, the argument will have a negative and a positive side. Negatively, it will reject the notions that consumption is a peripheral economic process, that it resides in a separate world of sentiment, or that it consists primarily in the acquisition rather than the use of goods and services. Positively, it will show the centrality of continuously negotiated and meaningful interpersonal relations in a wide range of consumption processes. Because consumption of services often involves activation or creation of interpersonal relations by definition, the following discussion will concentrate on the less obvious side: acquisition and use of goods.

HOUSEHOLDS AS SITES OF CONSUMPTION

In the case of the household, analysts long assumed it would remain, in Christopher Lasch's (1977) terms, a "haven in a heartless world," protecting its members from the harshness of markets. Instead, we find households to be central sites of production, distribution, and consumption. Researchers have amply established, furthermore, the complex internal diversity within household units and the incessant interplay between households and extrahousehold economic activities.

Marjorie DeVault's (1991) analysis of feeding work traces the profoundly social character of households' most fundamental economic activities. The largely invisible, unpaid labor of planning, shopping, and preparing meals involves constant, often contested, negotiations of family relationships. Drawing from her interviews of a diverse set of 30 households in the Chicago area, DeVault reports women—who do most of the feeding work within households—striving to match meals with expected definitions of husband-wife or mother-child relationships. For example, appropriate meals for husbands involved enactment of deference to a man's preoccupations and responsibilities outside the household. Meals, DeVault demonstrates, involved more than nutrition or economy: they routinely symbolized appropriately gendered ties.

Food acquisition and preparation, however, inform a whole set of social relations beyond gender. DeVault provides a telling example of how Janice, a nurse living with her husband and two adult children, manages simultaneously to preserve both family cohesion and independence:

> Meals are often family events, prepared and eaten at home together. Janice or the children decide on the spur of the moment whether or not to cook, and "whoever is home sits down and eats it." Janice's shopping is what makes this kind of independence possible: "What I do is provide enough food in the house for anybody who wants to eat. And then whoever is home, makes that meal, if they want it." (1991, 63)

Each of her respondents, DeVault observes, "[t]hrough day-to-day activities . . . produces a version of 'family' in a particular local setting: adjusting, filling in, and repairing social relations to produce—quite literally—this form of household life" (1991, 91; for parallel observations on gay and lesbian households, see Carrington 1999).

To be sure, as DeVault shows, not all household relations of consumption generate harmony and collaboration. Consider another well-documented study. In his account of Philadelphia's inner-city poor African-American children Carl Nightingale (1993) reports acute rancor and conflict between parents and children in their negotiations over consumption. Parents exasperated by their kids' unreasonable and persistent demands for spending money are pitted against children disappointed by their parents' inability to provide them with material goods. Contests over how to spend limited family monies, including income tax refunds or welfare checks, Nightingale observes, severely strain household relations:

> All the kids whose families I knew well lived through similar incidents: yelling matches between Fahim and his mother on how she spent her welfare check, Theresa's disgust when she found out she was not going to get a dress because her mom's boyfriend had demanded some of the family's monthly money for crack, and Omar's decision to leave his mother's house altogether because "I hate her. She always be asking y'all [the Kids' Club] for money. That's going

to get around, and people'll be talking." Also he felt that she never had enough money for his school clothes. (1993, 159; see also Bourgois 1995)

Thus, consumption within households takes place in a context of incessant negotiation, sometimes cooperative, other times full of conflict.

As DeVault's and Nightingale's studies illustrate, negotiations over consumption within the household regularly involve the parties in economic relations that cross the household's boundaries.

Consider the purchase of a home, a household's most significant investment. In their detailed investigation of how French households acquire their homes, Pierre Bourdieu's (2000) research team observed interactions and bargaining sessions between sellers and potential buyers in home shows, recorded conversations between sellers and buyers, and interviewed salespeople, merchandisers, and builders (for changes in the Chinese housing market, see Davis 2002).

Based on those observations, Bourdieu stresses the following points:

> The purchase of a home engages interactions not only between nominal buyer and seller, but among multiple parties: other household members, friends, credit agencies, and builders.
>
> In addition to these parties, the state always plays a crucial part as guarantor, and sometimes as a direct participant in the transaction.
>
> For household members, the purchase of a home represents simultaneously a deep financial commitment, a statement concerning the household's social position, the creation of space for household activities, and a series of commitments concerning futures of the households' members. As Bourdieu summarizes: a home is a "consumer good, which, because of its high cost, represents one of the most difficult economic decisions and one of the most consequential in the entire domestic life-cycle" (2000, 33).
>
> When it comes to buyer-seller negotiations, bargaining involves elements of manipulation along with personalization.
>
> A triple negotiation takes place over the purchase of a house: identification of the suitable home, establishment of credit, and working out a story of what the house will do for the buyer.
>
> The path that led to a particular seller often passed through the buyer's friends and neighbors.

Bourdieu concludes that the housing market, while profoundly structured by established political interests, legal limitations, financial constraints, and its deep symbolic charge is, nevertheless, far from being a static, prescribed set of exchanges. Buyers and sellers' negotiations create unanticipated, often surprising outcomes. Bourdieu observes that a sale takes place

> only through a series of interactions, all of them unforeseen and aleatory—for example a couple who might have passed by, gone to another stand, or left saying they would return, actually find themselves signing a commitment. . . . Far from simply expressing the logic of the economic relation, the interaction actually creates that relation; it is always uncertain and its development is full of suspense and surprise. (2000, 210)

When Paul DiMaggio and Hugh Louch (1998) undertook their own investigation of how Americans acquired consumer durables, including homes, their findings pointed in the same direction as Bourdieu's. Analyzing a general survey of the American population, they looked closely at reports of recent major purchases.

As they examined preexisting noncommercial ties between buyers and sellers in consumer transactions involving the purchase of cars, homes, as well as legal and home repair services, DiMaggio and Louch found a remarkably high incidence of what they call within-network exchanges. Contrary to the notion of an impersonal market, a substantial number of such transactions took place not between strangers but among kin, friends, or acquaintances. Noting that this pattern applies primarily to risky one-shot transactions involving high uncertainty about quality and performance, DiMaggio and Louch conclude that consumers will be more likely to rely on such noncommercial ties when they are unsure about the outcome.

These close-up studies by DeVault, Bourdieu, DiMaggio, and Louch give us a keen sense of the importance of interpersonal ties in household consumption. They naturally provide little information, however, about larger-scale change and variation in the character of those ties. For that kind of information we must turn to another style of research. Following the trails blazed by Susan Gal and Gail Kligman (2000), Caroline Humphrey (1995), Alena Ledeneva (1998), and Katherine Verdery, Daphne Berdahl (1999) has used her sustained ethnography in Kella, an East German border village, to pursue a double comparison: between East and West Germany under separate regimes, and in East Germany before and after unification.

Among other things, Berdahl shows that interpersonal and interhousehold networks played a critical part in mutual aid under East Germany's socialist regime. Household consumption was at the very center of those exchanges. In conditions of great scarcity, as they obtained food products, clothing, and other household goods, Kella villagers depended less on available cash than on their personal connections. As one woman explained to Berdahl: "Money actually did help you: it helped maintain the connections! But the connections were most important" (1999, 120). In this informal economy, Berdahl reports "networks of friendships, acquaintances, and associates were created and maintained through gift exchange, bribes, and barter trade" (118). The type of transfer, furthermore, differed by the nature of the relationship (see Rose-Ackerman 1998 and Zelizer 1998). While gifts and barter took place among friends, kin, and acquaintances, bribes were reserved for more distant connections:

> Slipping the local grocery clerk an extra twenty marks or a western chocolate bar meant that she would probably set aside a few bananas or green peppers under the counter whenever a shipment of these or other coveted fruits and vegetables came in. A homemade wurst could guarantee being bumped to the top of the waiting list of the driving school. (Berdahl 1999, 119)

After the fall of the Wall, Berdahl suggests, consumption practices and relations were transformed. In the new market economy, as money became a greater mediator of personal relationships, informal networks lost much of their importance in providing access to consumer goods. However, consumption did not lose its importance. The character and quantity of goods and services—especially visibly expensive ones—consumed by a household, Berdahl argues, became an even greater point of distinction among households.

The very richness of Berdahl's ethnography raises the question of whether networks have actually shriveled or instead, changed in character, as seems more likely. In any case, Berdahl's close observation provides a model for the examination of variation and change in household consumption.

CONSUMPTION IN ETHNIC AND RACIAL COMMUNITIES

In history and the social sciences a great deal of attention has gone into ethnic production, especially in the form of sweatshops, labor market segregation, and the informal economy. Ethnic consumption has received somewhat less attention.

Any discussion of consumption in ethnic and racial communities, however, plays out against two general debates; one, the relative merits of assimilation versus multiculturalism, the second concerning bases of ethnic and racial inequality (for convenience the remainder of this discussion will use *ethnic communities* to signal both race and national origin). More specific debates surrounding ethnic consumption pivot on the following issues: does consumption trump ethnic solidarities by homogenizing tastes, or is consumption a means for asserting ethnic identities? Are all ethnic groups equally competent consumers, or do some ethnic populations require education? Does consumer culture oppress and exploit relatively impoverished, powerless ethnic groups, or can consumption subvert domination?

To some extent market researchers avoid these moral and political questions; they commonly seek to explain or influence the purchases by members of different demographic categories (see, e.g., Turow 1997; Schreiber 2001; Venkatesh 1995; Weiss 1988; for similar processes among gay and lesbian consumers, see Badgett 2001). In history and the social sciences, however, the discussion of consumption in ethnic communities rarely proceeds without these pressing issues in the background.

Thus, energy and imagination pour into a wide range of analyses concerning consumption in ethnic communities. As with households, this discussion will move from internal consumption practices to relations between ethnic communities and other sites, then close with change and variation among ethnic communities.

What is distinctive about ethnic communities? They have two special characteristics: first, their reinforcement through residential, labor market, and linguistic segregation and second, the frequent feeding of major segments of their population by extensive migration streams. Segregation not only sharpens the boundaries between insiders and outsiders, but also intensifies communication within the boundaries and establishes populations that share a common fate. Shared migration streams produce their own characteristic clusters of social relations, their own cultural practices, and their own lines of communication to fellow migrants elsewhere as well as to their place of origin. As Charles Tilly (1990, 84) puts it: "networks migrate; categories stay put; and networks create new categories."

All of these traits have strong implications for the culture of consumption. Let us concentrate on four salient ways in which this works within ethnic communities: first, members of the community (for example, first-generation migrants) often maintain their community's internal representation through consumption goods and practices; second, consumption marks distinctions within the ethnic community, for example young/old, male/female, rich/poor, religious/nonreligious; third, households use ethnic forms of consumption to maintain their position within the community; fourth, some members of the ethnic community—ethnic entrepreneurs—specialize in retailing ethnic merchandise representing their community.

Ewa Morawska's classic study of Eastern European immigrants and their descendants in Johnstown, Pennsylvania, shows us all four sorts of process at work. Johnstown's Slovaks, Magyars, Croatians, Serbs, Slovenes, Poles, Ukrainians, and Rusyns had members who attempted to maintain group identity and solidarity through consumption, marked their internal differences through consumption, employed ethnic involvements to meet their consumption needs, and hosted entrepreneurs who made their business the interfaces among production, distribution, and consumption. In hard times, the third process provided the means of survival. As Morawska puts it, Johnstown's ethnic communities used their connections to seek or preserve the good life:

> These options included the search, through kinship and ethnic networks, for a better job: if possible, better-skilled, as there appeared in the mills more of the mechanized tasks; if not, then more remunerative, either within the same or another Bethlehem department or with a different local manufacturer. They included, too, overtime work and moonlighting at night and during weekends. They also involved increasing the total family income by entering into the labor market all employable members of the household, keeping boarders, renting out part of a newly purchased house, reducing household expenditures through extensive reliance on home production of food from gardens and domestic animals, on women's abilities to prepare and preserve food and to sew and weave, and on men's old-country skills in carpentry, masonry, and other household repairs. (1985, 185–86)

Thus consumption did not merely reproduce, amuse, and satisfy members of Johnstown's ethnic communities. It helped them organize their social lives.

Of course, the four consumption processes often intersect. For instance, Kathy Peiss's (1998) study of the cosmetic industry in the United States provides clear indications of African-American entrepreneurship, gender distinctions within the African-American community, as well as showing the significance of the beauty culture for maintaining black solidarity. Peiss reports how, between the 1890s and 1920s, black women, along with immigrant and working-class women, pioneered the cosmetic industry. Successful African-American female entrepreneurs, such as Madam C. J. Walker and Annie Turnbo Malone. Peiss notes, "embedded the beauty trade in the daily life of black communities linked by kin, neighbors, churches, and schools" (90). Indeed, the beauty business both depended and reinforced customers' social connections:

> Word of hair growers and shampoos made by African-American women spread rapidly. Women convinced each other to try these new products, buying boxes of glossine and hair grower for relatives and friends, practicing the art of hairdressing on each other. Like many women, Elizabeth Clark placed an order with Madam Walker "not for my self" but "for a friend of mine." For these businesses, word of mouth was the finest form of advertising. (1998, 90)

The women's connections went well beyond mutual grooming. Some cosmetic entrepreneurs in fact involved themselves, their agents, and their customers in public politics. Madam Walker, for instance, not only supported her agents' participation in African-American community affairs but encouraged their political activism. Walker herself, Peiss notes, backed the politically militant National Equal Rights League and the International League of Darker Peoples. As Peiss observes: "commercial beauty culture was something much more than an isolated act of consumption or vanity. In the hands of African-American women entrepreneurs, it became an economic and aesthetic form that spoke to black women's collective experiences and aspirations" (1998, 95).

Consumption also builds connections between ethnic communities and the rest of the world. In fact, ethnic entrepreneurs often specialize in mediating between their communities and producers, distributors, or consumers outside. While doing a splendid job of portraying the internal consumption practices of Mexican immigrants in early-twentieth-century Los Angeles, George Sánchez (1993) also shows such entrepreneurs at work.

Examining the lively Mexican music industry during the 1920s, Sánchez reports ethnic middlemen's crucial role in linking promising local musicians with American recording industries (for a pioneering statement on how cultural industries operate see Hirsch 1972).

For instance, Mauricio Calderón, a noted entrepreneur and owner of the music store Repertorio Musical Mexicana,

> recruited talented musicians by advertising in the Spanish-language press, and kept an ear out for the latest musical trends among the city's performers and audiences. Not only did Calderón make money by serving as go-between between American companies and the Mexican artists, but he also held a monopoly on the area-wide distribution of these recordings through his store. (Sánchez 1993, 182)

Within the community, Calderón likewise merchandised Mexican music; for example by giving records away with purchases of a Victrola, or by playing corridas—one of the most popular musical styles—from a loudspeaker in front of his store: "a small group of men regularly stood in front of the store, listening intently and enjoying the music" (Sánchez 1993, 182).

But that was not all. Mexican-American brokers sustained a flow of musicians into Los Angeles from Mexico; they supplied music for Mexican street festivals, weddings, and other ethnic celebrations. They also exported Mexican music to Anglo festivities, as a reminder of the city's Spanish past. Pedro González, later a renowned musician, recalled playing at events sponsored by city officials and the fire department.

What is more, between the 1920s and 1930s, Spanish-language radio became a major link among entrepreneurs, Mexican immigrants, and the Anglo world. For example, Calderón and other Chicano middlemen, reports Sánchez, "profited handsomely as they negotiated with stations, paying them a flat rate during cheap broadcasting time, which they then sold to businesses advertisements" (Sánchez 1993, 183). Mexican immigrants tuned into the radio shows during early morning hours as they prepared for work, enjoying the music but also receiving crucial job information.

Behind all this cultural activity lay the work of Mexican-American entrepreneurs, who

> served as conduits between the Mexican immigrant population and the corporate world. These individuals were often the first to recognize cultural changes and spending patterns among the immigrant population. Individuals such as Mauricio Calderón and Pedro J. González were able to promote Mexican music in entirely new forms in Los Angeles because they had daily contact with ordinary members of the Los Angeles Mexican community. Although they found tangible financial rewards in their efforts, they also served

an important role in redefining Mexican culture in an American urban environment. (Sánchez 1993, 187)

Thus, ethnic entrepreneurship fed on swelling migration of Mexicans to Los Angeles, strengthening ties between Mexican and Californian cultures (for a variety of ethnic entrepreneurs and marketers, see Lamont and Molnár 2001; Nightingale 1993; Pérez Firmat 1994; Portes and Stepick 1993; Weems 1994).

Immigrant remittances similarly strengthen ties between places of origin and destination (Roberts and Morris 2003). Remittances show us, furthermore, that not all ethnic entrepreneurs stay fixed within their communities (on transnationalism see Portes 2001; Portes, Haller, and Guarnizo 2002). Sarah Mahler's (1995, 142–44) study of undocumented Salvadoran immigrants in Long Island clarifies their reliance on personal couriers for conveying goods and cash to and from their homeland. Personal couriers take their place among a variety of media for transmitting back and forth between El Salvador and Long Island: the U.S. Postal Service, Western Union–style specialized remittance organizations, and local multipurpose agencies. They carry not only money but gifts of food and clothing, including "Corn Flakes, CD players, soccer shoes . . . brand-new jeans and T-shirts" and even love notes for distant sweethearts" (Moreno 2001, B1).

Goods and services flow in both directions: Salvadoran residents supply their migrant relatives with local medicines and food: "they might bring a box stuffed with mom's grilled chicken to a lonely son or a fresh pot of mango spread to a granddaughter" (Moreno 2001, B1). Some migrants, Mahler (1995, 143) reports, "waited weeks to receive salves or pills from home instead of seeking costly medical care and prescription drugs here."

The Salvadoran remitters face a double relational problem: exchanging resources with distant family members, and establishing reliable ties with the intermediaries. The *viajeros* (couriers) establish personal relations with both senders and receivers, thus building the trustworthiness (*confianza*) of the connection. Couriers, observes Mahler (1995, 143), "seal their transactions with handshakes, not receipts." In earlier conditions of civil war, Salvadoran couriers filled in where official transactions had no power to operate.

In the Salvadoran case, senders and recipients are connected by intermediaries. In other cases, donors actually deliver money, goods, and services themselves. For example, any flight from New York City to Central America or the Caribbean—most dramatically on holidays—carries numerous migrants who are returning to their place of origin with household goods and other gifts. On their return trip, travelers usually have lighter baggage, but have stocked up on their favorite homeland products.

Peggy Levitt (2001a) describes how this transnational economy operates. In her close observation of ties between Miraflores, a Dominican Republic town, and the Boston, Massachusetts, neighborhood of Jamaica Plains where many of their relatives migrated, Levitt notes that "fashion, food, and forms of speech, as well as appliances and home decorating styles, attest to these strong connections":

> In Miraflores, villagers often dress in T-shirts emblazoned with the names of businesses in Massachusetts, although they do not know what these words or logos mean. They proudly serve their visitors coffee with Cremora and juice made from Tang. (2001a, 2)

Nonmigrant Dominicans, in turn, often provide migrants with child care, supervise their local affairs, and treat them as "royal guests" during visits. Forty-year-old Cecilia, with three siblings in Boston, "wants to give something back to her brothers and sisters, but she is exhausted when they leave" (Levitt 2001a, 90). Levitt points out that narrowly economic interchange is only part of the remittance flow; she calls attention to what she calls "social remittances," the transfer of "ideas, behaviors, identities, and social capital that flow from host-to sending-country communities" (54). Social and material remittances, however, do not constitute separate streams; in both cases people are fashioning and refashioning meaningful social relations, in some cases with consumer goods, in others with belief systems, social practices, or network connections. (On how remittance systems connect to bargaining within households, see Curran and Saguy 2001; Grasmuck and Pessar 1991.)

Collectively, remittances are consequential transfers, with large macroeconomic impact. For instance, in 1994, almost 40 percent of Miraflores's households reported that between 75 and 100 percent of their income came from remittances. Nearly 60 percent of those households reported receiving some monthly income from migrant relatives (Levitt 2001b, 200). Official estimates of national totals surely understate their true value. Nevertheless, for the Dominican Republic as a whole, the 1996 count was of $1.14 billion, while for Mexico, the official figure was $2 billion (Waller Meyers

1998; see also de la Garza and Lindsay Lowell 2002; Pew Hispanic Center 2003).

Finally, while participants and observers of remittance systems often deplore the fact that a good deal of expenditure goes into consumer display rather than productive investment, Durand, Parrado, and Massey (1996) demonstrate that in fact consumption creates large demand for both local and national producers. Even what they call "migradollars" earned by immigrants, and spent for food, drink, music, or fireworks in apparently "wasteful" local Mexican festivities, spur regional production and income. Durand, Parrado, and Massey estimate that, at the national level, the $2 billion migradollars generate $6.5 billion additional production in Mexico.

Holiday celebrations, in fact, provide an entrée to the comparative analysis of ethnic consumption. Consider this selection from the mid–nineteenth century's vast assortment of local civic holidays reported by Leigh Schmidt (1995, 33–34): New York City's republican Evacuation Day, Irish Catholics' St. Patrick's Day, Scots' St. Andrew's Day, patrician Knickerbockers' St. Nicholas's Day, New Englander's Pilgrim Day, Charlestown's Bunker Hill Day. "Ethnic particularity, eclecticism, and localism," Schmidt notes, "seemed to impede national observances at every turn" (33). Yet, by the end of the century national holiday traditions had been installed, largely propelled by the expansion of a consumerist economy and culture. Merchants, recognizing the commercial potential of holiday celebrations, displayed, promoted, and in the process nationalized both holiday observances and material symbols, such as the mass-produced greeting cards, Valentine Cupids and hearts, Santa Clauses, or chocolate Easter bunnies. "The consumer culture," Schmidt concludes, "more than folk tradition, local custom, or religious community, increasingly provided the common forms and materials for American celebrations" (297).

Yet, as with other consumer goods, people and groups, even as they shared in the increasingly nationalized, standardized, consumer-oriented celebrations, found ways to simultaneously particularize their holidays. Mary Waters (1990) has shown that contemporary Americans attach themselves to symbolic ethnicity by means of holiday celebrations, foods, and other representations of their origins. This process was already well under way a half-century ago. By the 1920s, for instance, American Jews revitalized the languishing holiday of Chanukah into what Jenna Joselit (1994, 229) calls a "functional equivalent" to Christmas, shopping for and exchanging gifts (see also Heinze 1990). Even the Christmas Club savings concept was adapted to Chanukah: "Save For Chanukah" ads by the East River Savings Institution appeared in Yiddish newspapers—although printed in Yiddish, the ads pictured a young couple standing next to a Christmas tree (Joselit 1994, 234, and personal communication). Once again, merchandisers picked up the cue, creating specialized products and connections for the Chanukah market. Toy manufacturers, for instance, produced

> Jewish-oriented novelties that ran the gamut from pinwheels and board games . . . to cookie cutters shaped like a Jewish star and oversized dreidels like the four-foot-tall "Maccabee." A creation of the Dra-Dell Corporation of Bergen, New Jersey, this object "expresses a true holiday spirit in the home . . . and is a fine addition to the Chanukah atmosphere" . . . these objects reflected the needs of a new community of Jewish consumers: children. (Joselit 1994, 80–81)

Christmas also changed. In earlier United States history, as Karal Ann Marling (2000, 256–76) points out, one of the most remarkable developments was the integration of African-Americans into public representations of Christmas. By the 1960s, however, African-Americans fashioned their own December holiday of Kwanzaa, drawing not only from Christmas, but also from African harvest festivals, Chanukah, and New Year's Eve. Elizabeth Pleck sums up the holiday's origins:

> Kwanzaa was a nationalist—specifically, black nationalist—holiday and had a specific creator [Ron (Maudana) Karenga], who designed it as a celebration of the African harvest, with the intention that American blacks, in exile from their African homeland, would continue traditions and celebrate their African heritage. (2000, 6)

Although Kwanzaa was intended to counter the commercial orientation of dominant holidays, by the early 1980s it had incorporated consumerism in its practice: the production of videos and books, Kwanzaa greeting cards and wrapping paper, cookbooks, along with Afrocentric clothes, artwork, jewelry, and music (Schmidt 1995, 300–301; Austin 1996). Recent Indian immigrants likewise construct dual holiday celebrations; one study reports Indian immigrant families celebrating Thanksgiving with turkey and stuffing combined with curries and other Indian foods (Mehta and Belk 1991, 407). Armenian families, meanwhile, serve their Thanksgiving turkey with rice pilaf, boreog, and stuffed vine leaves (Bakalian 1993, 366: see also

Gabaccia 1998; Halter 2000; Light and Gold 2000).

Clearly, across ethnic communities, culture, social relations, and consumption vary and change together in dramatic fashion.

RETAIL SETTINGS FOR CONSUMPTION

Nor does culture disappear from retail settings. On the contrary, a surprising degree of cultural work goes on within and among retail establishments—places where consumers purchase goods and services. In fact, people engage in three somewhat different types of relational activity in such settings. They acquire goods and services for other people, engage in sociable interactions with fellow customers and retail personnel, and display group memberships and differences from other people by means of their purchases.

Our earlier discussion of shopping malls, however, indicated that observers have often interpreted the expansion of retail trade as promoting commodification, thereby destroying earlier forms of meaningful social connections. Bidding up Robert Putnam, social critic Jeremy Rifkin (2000, 155), for instance, declares shopping malls' "central mission" to be "the commodification of lived experiences in the form of the purchase of goods and entertainment." Commodification, in this account, substitutes impersonal rationality for the rich, sentimental connections of earlier ages.

Yet, as we have already seen, people construct and refashion meaningful social relations across a wide variety of commercial settings. To be sure, major changes in retailing did occur from the nineteenth to the twenty-first centuries: a larger proportion of all goods and services arrive through commercial transactions, the scale and geographic concentration of retail establishments has increased, and the direct sale and delivery of goods and services to households has declined (Cowan 1983). Households, therefore, found themselves much more heavily engaged in external shopping than had once been true. At first glance, moreover, a series of innovations in retailing, for example, the one-price system, self-service, and the substitution of credit cards for local account books, seemed to replace personalized connections with impersonal routines. In fact, within the retail setting, each of these altered the terms of social interaction but without eliminating personal contact between merchant and customer. The effects of these multiple changes in retail practice, then, were never to obliterate meaningful social relations, but to alter their character and geography significantly.

Paralleling the previous discussions, this section will examine retail settings in three steps: first, relations within retail establishments, then, relations across boundaries, and, finally, change and variation.

For culturally informed social relations within retail settings, consider restaurants. In their study of food consumption outside the home in England during the 1990s, Alan Warde and Lydia Martens (2000, 108) discovered that, paradoxically, "eating out is more convivial than eating at home" (see also Illouz 1997, chap. 4). Using interviews and a survey, they found that most of their 1,001 respondents ate out with family members. Other frequent dining companions were friends and romantic partners. In fact only 2 percent reported being alone the last time they had eaten out. However, eating out did make some difference, since the effort of preparing the meal did not fall on women, as characteristically happens in households. Eating outside of the home thus provides the opportunity for a more equal exchange around the table.

What is more, eating out might even generate greater sociability than dining at home. As one respondent, Trisha, put it:

> I think it's easier, when you're sat over a meal, to talk about things. Probably if you're sat with a take-away you tend to be glued to the telly, whereas rather if you're just sat together over a meal you do tend to have a better conversation really because you haven't as many distractions and things like that, it's quite nice. You know, it's socialising involved especially with your boyfriend. (Warde and Martens 2000, 205)

Yet one might think that any sort of social interaction vanishes in the world of fast foods. After all, Edward Hopper's emblematic painting of a diner, *Nighthawks*, shows each customer and a counterman staring silently into private spaces. In the modern equivalent of the diner, the fast food palace, however, Robin Leidner (1993) observes a steady flow of social interaction between customers and serving personnel. McDonald's, of course, represents the paradigm of an impersonal, routinized consumer world. Indeed, George Ritzer (1996) has made McDonald's the central symbol of economic standardization in the world of consumption. Drawing on her fieldwork at a McDonald's franchise near Chicago, Leidner reports extensive organizational scripting of work routines, ranging from food preparation to worker-consumer interaction. The Six Steps of Window Service, for instance, closely guide workers' behavior: "(1) greet the customer, (2) take the order, (3) assemble the order, (4) present the order, (5) receive payment, and (6) thank the customer and ask for repeat business" (Leidner 1993, 68) More significantly, as Leidner shows, the rules standardized "attitudes and demeanors as well as words and actions" (73).

However, anyone who enjoys ballroom dancing, tennis, or chess knows that routinized interaction need not be impersonal. There are two fallacies to avoid: first, the notion that standardization of interpersonal relations necessarily destroys human contact; and second, the contrary view that all social interaction is intrinsically satisfying. As Leidner discovered: "despite the specificity of the script and the brevity of most encounters with customers, the service interactions were not all alike and were not necessarily devoid of personal involvement" (1993, 136). Workers enjoyed their albeit brief conversations or jokes with customers, occasionally providing some customers with extra services.

Regular customers, meanwhile, often established ongoing ties with workers. As Matthew told Leidner:

> What I like [is that] when you work window you get to know every customer that come in here every day. You get to remember their faces, you get to know what they want . . . and all they have to [do is] just show their faces, and you just grab the tray and set up everything they need, 'cause they get everything the same every day. (Leidner 1993, 141)

Personalized interactions, however, were not all cordial. Partly because of the low status of their jobs, workers were sometimes subjected to customers' "rude, sarcastic, and insulting remarks" (Leidner 1993, 132). In such cases, the interactive script broke down: the worker "might withhold smiles, risk a show of impatience or irritation with a customer, or refuse to suggest additional purchases or to encourage return business" (135; Katherine Newman [1999] reported similar interactions in New York's Harlem). Furthermore, some workers actually welcomed the protection provided by routinized interactions. The point is that whether friendly, hostile, or strictly limited, the participants were engaging in negotiated, meaningful social interactions (for discussions of conflicts between blacks and shopkeepers, see Austin 1994; Lee 2002).

The custom of thinking about retail settings as self-contained locations makes the thought of cross-cutting ties hard to manage at first. However, if we consider a retail setting to be any location in which people purchase goods and services, this immediately calls to mind, among others, supermarkets, shopping malls, department stores, country stores, video stores, garage sales, street fairs, junk shops, pawnshops, thrift shops, restaurants, coffee shops, airport shops, bookstores, newsstands, fashion outlets, automobile dealerships, art galleries, movies, theaters, and mom-and-pop stores. In all of these retail sites, relations of both consumers and merchants to such groups as neighbors, friends, households, police, protesters, looters, gangs, credit agencies, labor unions, courts, and so on, play a significant part in their operations.

Rather than focusing on the more obvious cases of department stores or supermarkets, let us take two challenging sites: pawnshops and direct-selling organizations. In both cases, we observe the intersection of an active retail setting with webs of social relations that extend far beyond that site.

The pawnshop is a remarkable device, a sort of bank that lends cash against the security of saleable objects. Pawnbrokers must develop great skills in judging other people and establishing trustworthy relations with them. With the expansion of wage labor and purchased commodities during the nineteenth century, the pawnshop became a crucial institution in working-class communities across the Western world. In the United States, Lendor Calder (1999, 43) notes, "a wide variety of people found their way into pawnshops, including salesmen and travelers with emergency needs for cash, and petty shopkeepers in need of a quick loan to pay off creditors." Commonly pawned objects ranged from items of clothing and jewelry, to musical instruments, bedding, guns, household furniture, and more exceptionally coffins, false teeth, and even automobiles (44).

Among the wide range of customers, households often balanced short-run fluctuations in their budgets by pawning or redeeming household objects. In her account of housewives' economic strategies among the London poor between 1870 and 1918, Ellen Ross reports women's extensive reliance on pawnshops to make ends meet: "COS [Charity Organisation Society] caseworkers investigating the assets of households applying for aid were invariably shown bundles of pawn tickets by the women with whom they spoke. . . . Lent, stolen, or honestly obtained pledge tickets were transferred and traded in complex patterns among groups of women" (1993, 82; see also Tebbutt 1983).

Women developed specialized bargaining skills, knowing which shops gave better value to their pledges; so much so that thieves regularly relied on women to serve as their intermediaries with pawn-brokers. While recounting his long life to Raphael Samuel during the 1970s, retired East London petty criminal, cabinetmaker, and furniture merchant Arthur Harding recalled a time before World War I:

> There was a woman in nearly every street of the East End of London who got a living taking neighbours' things to the pawn shop. The pawn-shop broker would lend her more than he would an ordinary customer on the goods because he knew that she would get 'em out again on Saturday—he trusted her. He didn't want to be lumbered up with a shop-load of stuff that wasn't going to be redeemed. He'd sooner do business with her, than a person who fetched a load of stuff in there and didn't intend to redeem 'em. (Samuel 1981, 90)

Indeed, women fashioned particularized relations with pawnbrokers' clerks. Ross reports a son describing his mother's negotiating skills:

> One went into a cubicle where the gent behind the counter usually knew his customers. "How much?" were his first words. "Ten shillings," says Mum. "Seven," said the gent behind the counter. "Oh Christ," says Mum. "Don't be like that, Sid." "All right," says Sid. "I'll make it eight bob, but don't forget it's the last time I take this lot in." (Ross 1993, 83)

Pawnshops still thrive in Western cities today. With sharpening income inequality and partial deregulation of banking, America's pawnshops, after a decline between 1930 and 1970, have multiplied since the 1980s. From a low of 4,849 in 1985, they climbed to 14,000 over the next 15 years (Manning 2000, 203). That number produced the highest per capita concentration of pawnshops in American history (Caskey 1994, 1). According to John Caskey, the customers of today's American pawnshops have low or moderate incomes, and are drawn especially from the African-American and Hispanic populations. Typical jobs include "an enlisted person in the military, a nonunion factory worker, a nurse's aid, a retail sales clerk, or a general helper in an automobile service station." Caskey reports that usually, loans cover such expenses as paying rent or a vacation, buying Christmas presents, food, alcohol, illegal drugs, lottery tickets, fixing a car, or buying gasoline (69–70). Loan customers usually lack access to credit cards and routine banking. Pawnshops thus serve as their alternative banks.

On the average, direct selling involves a somewhat more prosperous segment of the population; across the world, a wide variety of customers purchase goods not directly from stores, but from friends, neighbors, and kin who bring the goods to their home. Sometimes, rather than individual door-to-door sales, direct selling involves the creation of special social settings within homes. As Nicole Woolsey Biggart says in her classic study, direct-selling organizations counter the idea that efficiency depends on bureaucratized impersonality:

> Executives in the direct selling industry understand, just as do the leaders of many social movements, the power of preexisting social relations and networks in recruiting distributors and channeling their actions. . . . In direct selling social bonds are not an encumbrance but an instrument for soliciting and controlling a sales force and for appealing to customers. (1989, 167; see also Frenzen and Davis 1990)

Following up on Biggart's leads, British scholar Alison Clarke's (1999) analysis of Tupperware illustrates the particular intersection of retail trade with households. In the 1950s, Earl Tupper, inventor of the now emblematic airtight plastic containers, withdrew his products from retail outlets, launching the "Tupperware party" marketing strategy. Dealers went to a volunteer "hostess" home, first demonstrating, and then selling, their products to a gathering of friends and neighbors. For her efforts, the hostess received a Tupperware gift product contingent on the amount of sales. At the party, dealers recruited future hostesses, encouraging them as well to join up as commission-paid dealers. In the process, homes became intensely social retail outlets, as well as recruiting grounds for commercial operations. Tupper's marketing strategy worked. By 1997, according to Clarke, worldwide net sales were of $1.2 billion, and about 118 million people had attended a Tupperware demonstration (2).

Direct-selling organizations changed over time and varied significantly in their organizational strategies. Biggart stresses three axes of change and variation: first, the gender of salespeople, which differentiated the kinds of networks they activated; second, the degree of orientation within the organization to a single charismatic leader (e.g., Mary Kay Ash for Mary Kay cosmetics); finally, the extent of bureaucratization and differentiation, for example, the degree to which successful salespeople became full-time managers and recruiters.

Let us think of change and variation in retail settings at an international scale. Global fast food chains and electronic commerce provide two current settings in which many observers have thought that uniformity and impersonality were locked into place. Despite Leidner's demonstration of intensive social interaction within U.S. fast food outlets, a number of critics have interpreted the worldwide spread of McDonald's and other chains as the imposition of uniform impersonal forms of consumption on alien cultures. Political theorist Benjamin Barber (1995), for instance, goes so far as to portray a cosmic struggle between Jihad and McWorld, pitting the forces of religious and ethnic fragmentation against the inexorable economic homogenization of the world. Using fast food as a symbol of a much broader world conquest, Barber declares,

> Music, video, theater, books, and theme parks—the new churches of a commercial civilization in which malls are the public squares and suburbs the neighborless neighborhoods—are all constructed as image exports creating a common world taste around common logos, advertising slogans, stars, songs, brand names, jingles, and trademarks. (1995, 17)

Looked at closely, however, despite common top-down designs, fast food restaurants turn out to vary dramatically in actual social process from one locality to another. An international team of anthropologists has studied consumer behavior in McDonald's outlets across five East Asian cities. Although they certainly see an impact on local cuisine and practices, they do not observe the homogenization that many critics have feared. On the contrary, they identify a process of "localization," integrating McDonald's into different cultural settings (for various types of localization, see also Appadurai 1990; Barron 1997; Caldwell 2004; Cohen 1990; Fantasia 1995; Goody 1998; Howes 1996; Kuisel 1993; Lozada 2000; Patillo-McCoy 1999; Peiss 2002; Stephenson 1989; Warde 2000; Yan 2000). Summing up, James L. Watson says,

> East Asian consumers have quietly, and in some cases stubbornly, transformed their neighborhood McDonald's into local institutions. . . . In Beijing, Seoul, and Taipei, for instance, McDonald's restaurants are treated as leisure centers, where people can retreat from the stresses of urban life. In Hong Kong, middle school students often sit in McDonald's for hours, studying, gossiping, and picking over snacks; for them, the restaurants are the equivalent of youth clubs. (1997, 6–7)

If fast food does not stamp out local culture, what about electronic commerce? After all, at first glance electronically mediated consumption appears to reduce social interaction to its barest minimum. At any particular site, all an observer sees is a shopper and a computer interacting.

However, as in all our previous cases of culture and consumption, we find people creating, confirming, and transforming their social relations as they consume (on social relations in electronic communication, see DiMaggio et al. 2001; Miller and Slater 2000; Wellman and Haythornthwaite 2002). Take the case of Lands' End—the leading online apparel retail site. Malcolm Gladwell (1999) found customer-service representatives routinely engaged in online chats with customers. In one instance, an East Coast woman he calls Carol was trying to decide on what color to pick for an attaché case:

> Darcia [the rep] was partial to the dark olive. . . . Carol was convinced, but she wanted the case monogrammed and there were eleven monogramming styles on the Web-site page. "Can I have a personal suggestion?" she wrote. "Sure," Darcia typed back. "Who is the case for?" "A conservative psychiatrist," Carol replied. Darcia suggested block initials, in black. Carol agreed, and sent the order in herself on the Internet. "All right," Darcia said, as she ended the chat. "She feels better." The exchange had taken twenty-three minutes. (Gladwell 1999, 5–6)

"It's a mistake," concludes Gladwell, "to think that E-commerce will entirely automate the retail process. It just turns reps from order-takers into sales advisers." Indeed, Bill Bass, head of Lands' End e-commerce, told Gladwell: "One of the big fallacies when the Internet came along was that you could get these huge savings by eliminating customer-service costs . . . [but] people still have questions, and what you are getting are much higher-level questions. Like, 'Can you help me come up with a gift?' And they take longer" (Gladwell 1999, 6).

Electronic commerce does not merely present opportunities for sociability. Like other forms of consumption, it also presents problems of trust. When people purchase expensive or potentially harmful goods and services on line, they regularly seek reassurance through three social strategies that apply broadly across the whole range of consumption: by repeated interaction with the supplier; by identifying reliable suppliers through mutual ties to third parties; and by creation or consultation of monitoring agencies. All three rely on or create more trustworthy cultural knowledge, thus converting uncertainty into manageable risk.

Looking at the giant electronic emporium eBay, Peter Kollock (1999) finds that despite vast numbers of transactions and no central guarantees of quality or delivery, the default rate for trades is minimal. According to a 1997 eBay report, for instance, only 27 out of 2 million auctions that took place between May and August 1997 appeared to be fraudulent. Users prevent fraud by a series of practical procedures: first, they establish a verifiable identity for each buyer and seller; second, they post summaries of reports from previous trading partners concerning the reliability of each trader; third, groups of users create websites posting advice (including information about frequent traders) for the pursuit of trustworthy exchanges; and fourth, some participants station themselves as paid or voluntary advisers for less experienced traders. As Kollock sums up: "at least for the core users, this is not a market of atomized price-takers" (118) It is a connected web of consumers creating a distinctive set of cultural links and producing trust by recognizable social strategies.

Similar findings emerge from Laura Sartori's (2002) large Italian study of Internet users from 1998 to 2001 (on electronic commerce in Australia see Singh 1999, in England, Pahl 1999). The study as a whole included a household survey, an online questionnaire, focus groups, and in-depth interviews. Sartori sees electronic consumption as actually increasing the autonomy and effectiveness of consumers because it makes substantial amounts of confirmatory (or, for that matter, negative) evidence concerning products and traders available at very low cost. More significantly for our purposes, Sartori identifies significant variations in they ways people gather information for their purchases.

Scrutinizing online shopping, Sartori reports that persons acquiring goods and services electronically most often first entered the process with the help of others they already knew, relied on their existing networks to reduce uncertainties in their purchases, but formed new social ties electronically in the process. Thus, Sartori's respondents repeatedly emphasized the significance of kin, friends, and colleagues' opinions when shopping online. As one 33-year-old woman explained:

> I am not quite sure on what I base my decision. Surely on the advice of people at work or of friends. We often discuss it with friends. It always happens, even when I'm looking for the most stupid thing. (Sartori 2002, 139)

But respondents also regularly consulted their new virtual connections in chat, newsgroups, or discussion forums. A 25-year-old man reported:

> It's quite normal to exchange information about products or sites, or else ask advice to someone online. It's even easier to check a site directly since if one is in chat it means you are connected. Sometimes they ask me: "I'm looking for something, can you help me?" For instance it's happened with cell phones. Someone who's looking for a new cell phone and asks who knows a site. Then someone gives a name, someone else a different one, and that way the conversation begins. (Sartori 2002, 138)

However, as Sartori says, the two sources of information are not mutually exclusive; in fact, online acquaintances sometimes become friends. Sartori, therefore, makes a negative and a positive contribution to our general discussion. Negatively, her findings deny the flattening of culture by electronic media. Positively, Sartori shows us once again how creatively people adapt their social relations to different media and forms of consumption.

CONCLUSIONS

Although cultural variation plays a significant part in consumption, it is a common mistake to suppose that consumption forms a warm cultural island in a frigid economic sea. Shared understandings and their representations—the components of culture—undergird all of economic life, from e-commerce to sweatshops. Another common error portrays consumption as centering on acquisition of goods and services rather than on their uses. A much clearer understanding of consumption practices comes from recognizing how meaningful social relations pervade economic processes, including production, acquisition, and use of goods and services. Combined, the two mistakes lead to a third pervasive error: treatment of consumption as primarily expressive behavior, whether it expresses social position, local culture, or individual idiosyncrasy. Consumption, like production and distribution, actually does crucial social work, not only sustaining human lives and social institutions but also shaping interpersonal relations.

These recurrent misunderstandings of consumption directly parallel confusions about money. Scholars, social critics, and ordinary people often assume that monetizing goods, services, and social relations strips away their culturally grounded personal meanings: paid personal care, for example, necessarily lacks the intimacy and power of unpaid care. Closely observed, however, intimate social relations turn out to incorporate monetary flows quite productively over a wide range of circumstances. The confusion results from overestimating the capacity of media—money, goods, or services—to control human behavior and thereby underestimating the capacity of human beings to bend media into means of pursuing their own social lives.

Similarly, social critics frequently warn against two different versions of consumerism: first, acquisition of standardized goods and services that crush individuality, spontaneity, and local culture, and, second, a headlong rush to accumulate that leaves no time, energy, or imagination to enjoy what you already have. Some mass-produced goods do drive higher-priced, more varied, and superior goods out of markets. Some goods and services (hard drugs provide obvious examples) damage their consumers. Some people do engage in conspicuous consumption to the detriment of their welfare. But our most careful studies of consumption—inside and outside of sociology—challenge the idea that consumers in general are increasingly leading impoverished lives as a consequence of growth in consumption.

Once again, confusion stems from assuming the existence of two Hostile Worlds: a world of rationality, efficiency, and impersonality, on one side; a world of self-expression, cultural richness, and intimacy, on the other—with contact between the two worlds inevitably corrupting both of them. Nor will any of the available Nothing-Buts—nothing but economic calculation, nothing but culture, nothing but power—resolve the dilemma. We have no choice but to pave crossroads connecting continuously negotiated, meaning-drenched social relations with the whole range of economic processes.

NOTES

I have adapted a few passages from Zelizer 1999, 2001, and 2002a and 2002b. For information, research assistance, advice, and criticism, I am grateful to Fred Block, Susan Gal, Neil Smelser, Richard Swedberg, Charles Tilly, and Anna Zajacova.

1. Landmark essays in consumer culture include Appadurai 1986; Brewer and Porter 1993; Bronner 1989; Fox and Lears 1983; McKendrick, Brewer, and Plumb 1982. For an excellent bibliographic essay on the history of consumption, see Glickman 1999; for a critical review, see Agnew 2003.

2. For observations of interactions between organized politics and consumption in Great Britain, see Hilton 2002.

REFERENCES

Abelson, Elaine S. 1989. *When Ladies Go a-Thieving: Middle-Class Shoplifters in the Victorian Department Store*. Oxford: Oxford University Press.

Agnew, Jean-Cristophe. 2003. "The Give-and-Take of Consumer Culture." Pp. 11–39 in *Commodifying Everything*, ed. Susan Strasser. New York: Routledge.

Andrews, Maggie, and Mary M. Talbot, eds. 2000. *All the World and Her Husband*. London: Cassell.

Appadurai, Arjun. 1990. "Disjuncture and Difference in the Global Cultural Economy." *Public Culture* 2: 1–24.

———, ed. 1986. *The Social Life of Things*. Cambridge: Cambridge University Press.

Austin, Regina. 1994. "'A Nation of Thieves': Securing Black People's Right to Shop and to Sell in White America." *Utah Law Review* 1994:147–77.

Aversi, Roberta, Giovanni Dosi, Giorgio Fagiolo, Mara Meacci, and Claudia Olivetti. 1999. "Demand Dynamics with Socially Evolving Preferences." *Industrial and Corporate Change* 8:353–408.

———. 1996. "Kwanzaa and the Commercialization of Black Culture." University of Pennsylvania Law School, Typescript.

Badgett, M. V. Lee. 2001. *Money, Myths, and Change: The Economic Lives of Lesbians and Gay Men*. Chicago: University of Chicago Press.

Bakalian, Anny. 1993. *Armenian-Americans: From Being to Feeling Armenian*. New Brunswick, N.J.: Transaction.

Barber, Benjamin. 1995. *Jihad vs. McWorld*. New York: Times Books.

Barber, Bernard. 1957. *Social Stratification*. New York: Harcourt, Brace and World.

Barron, Hal S. 1997. *Mixed Harvest: The Second Great Transformation in the Rural North, 1870–1930*. Chapel Hill: University of North Carolina Press.

Baudrillard, Jean. 1999. "Consumer Society." Pp. 33–56 in *Consumer Society in American History: A Reader*, ed. Lawrence B. Glickman. Ithaca, N.Y.: Cornell University Press.

Bauman, Zygmunt. 1998. *Globalization: The Human Consequences*. Cambridge: Polity Press.

Becker, Gary. 1996. *Accounting for Tastes*. Cambridge: Harvard University Press.

Benson, Susan Porter. 1986. *Counter Cultures: Saleswomen, Managers, and Customers in American Department Stores, 1890–1940*. Urbana: University of Illinois Press.

Berdahl, Daphne. 1999. *Where the World Ended: Reunification and Identity in the German Borderland*. Berkeley and Los Angeles: University of California Press.

Biggart, Nicole Woolsey. 1989. *Charismatic Capitalism*. Chicago: University of Chicago Press.

———. 2001. "Banking on Each Other: The Situational Logic of Rotating Savings and Credit Associations." *Advances in Qualitative Organization Research* 3:129–53.

Biggart, Nicole Woolsey, and Richard P. Castanias. 2001. "Collateralized Social Relations: The Social in Economic Calculation." *American Journal of Economics and Sociology* 60:471–500.

Bourgois, Philippe. 1995. *In Search of Respect.* Cambridge: Cambridge University Press.

Bourdieu, Pierre. 1984. *Distinction: A Social Critique of the Judgement of Taste.* Trans. Richard Nice. Cambridge, Mass.: Harvard University Press.

———. [1965] 1990. *Photography: A Middle-Brow Art.* Cambridge: Polity Press.

———. 2000. *Les structures sociales de l'économie.* Paris: Seuil.

Brewer, John, and Roy Porter, eds. 1993. *Consumption and the World of Goods.* London: Routledge.

Bronner, Simon J., ed. 1989. *Consuming Visions: Accumulation and Display in America, 1880–1920.* New York: W. W. Norton.

Calder, Lendol. 1999. *Financing the American Dream: A Cultural History of Consumer Credit.* Princeton: Princeton University Press.

Caldwell, Melissa L. 2004. "Domesticating the French Fry! McDonald's and Consumerism in Russia." *Journal of Consumer Culture* 4:5–26.

Campbell, Colin. 1995. "The Sociology of Consumption." Pp. 96–126 in *Acknowledging Consumption*, ed. Daniel Miller. London: Routledge.

Caplowitz, David. 1967. *The Poor Pay More.* New York: Free Press.

Carrington, Christopher. 1999. *No Place Like Home: Relationships and Family Life among Lesbians and Gay Men.* Chicago: University of Chicago Press.

Caskey, John P. 1994. *Fringe Banking: Check-Cashing Outlets, Pawnshops, and the Poor.* New York: Russell Sage Foundation.

Chin, Elizabeth. 2001. *Purchasing Power: Black Kids and American Consumer Culture.* Minneapolis: University of Minnesota Press.

Clarke, Alison J. 1999. *Tupperware: The Promise of Plastic in 1950s America.* Washington, D.C.: Smithsonian Institution Press.

Clunas, Craig. 1999. "Modernity Global and Local: Consumption and the Rise of the West." *American Historical Review* 104:1497–1511.

Cohen, Lizabeth. 1990. *Making a New Deal: Industrial Workers in Chicago, 1919–1939.* Cambridge: Cambridge University Press.

———. 1996. "From Town Center to Shopping Center; The Reconfiguration of Community Marketplaces in Postwar America." *American Historical Review* 101:1050–81.

———. 2003. *A Consumers' Republic: The Politics of Mass Consumption in Postwar America.* New York: Alfred A. Knopf.

Cook, Daniel Thomas. 1999. "Consumers, Commodities, and Consumption." www.asanet.org/sections/consumers.htm. Retrieved September 2001.

———. 2000. "The Rise of 'The Toddler' as Subject and as Merchandising Category in the 1930s." Pp. 111–29 in *New Forms of Consumption*, ed. Mark Gottdiener. Lanham, Md.: Rowman and Littlefield.

Cowan, Ruth Schwartz. 1983. *More Work for Mother.* New York: Basic Books.

Crane, Diana. 2000. *Fashion and Its Social Agendas.* Chicago: University of Chicago Press.

Cross, Gary. 2000. *An All-Consuming Century: Why Commercialism Won in America.* New York: Columbia University Press.

Crowston, Clare Haru. 2001. *Fabricating Women: The Seamstresses of Old Regime France, 1675–1791.* Durham, N.C.: Duke University Press.

Curran, Sara R., and Abigail Cope Saguy. 2001. "Migration and Cultural Change: A Role for Gender and Social Networks?" *Journal for International Women's Studies* 2:54–77.

Davis, Deborah S. 2002. "When a House Becomes His Home." Pp. 231–50 in *Popular China: Unofficial Culture in a Globalizing Society.* Boulder, Colo.: Rowman and Littlefield.

de Grazia, Victoria, and Ellen Furlough, eds. 1996. *The Sex of Things: Gender and Consumption in Historical Perspective.* Berkeley and Los Angeles: University of California Press.

de Grazia, Victoria, and Lizabeth Cohen, eds. 1999. "Class and Consumption." Special issue of *International Labor and Working-Class History* 55 (spring).

de la Garza, Rodolfo O., and Briant Lindsay Lowell. 2002. *Sending Money Home: Hispanic Remittances and Community Development.* Lanham, Md.: Rowman and Littlefield.

DeVault, Marjorie L. 1991. *Feeding the Family.* Chicago: University of Chicago Press.

DiMaggio, Paul. 1990. "Cultural Aspects of Economic Action and Organization." Pp. 113–36 in *Beyond the Marketplace*, ed. Roger Friedland and A. F. Robertson. New York: Aldine.

———. 1994. "Culture and Economy." Pp. 27–57 in *The Handbook of Economic Sociology*, ed. Neil J. Smelser and Richard Swedberg. New York: Russell Sage Foundation; Princeton: Princeton University Press.

DiMaggio, Paul, Eszter Hargittai, W. Russell Neuman, and John P. Robinson. 2001. "Social Implications of the Internet." *Annual Review of Sociology* 27: 307–36.

DiMaggio, Paul, and Hugh Louch. 1998. "Socially Embedded Consumer Transactions: For What Kinds of Purchases Do People Use Networks Most?" *American Sociological Review* 63:619–37.

Douglas, Mary, and Baron Isherwood. 1979. *The World of Goods.* Cambridge: Cambridge University Press.

duGay, Paul. 1996. *Consumption and Identity at Work.* London: Sage.

Durand, Jorge, Emilio A. Parrado, and Douglas S. Massey. 1996. "Migradollars and Development: A Reconsideration of the Mexican Case." *International Migration Review* 30:423–44.

Ewen, Elizabeth. 1985. *Immigrant Women in the Land of Dollars: Life and Culture on the Lower East Side, 1890–1925.* New York: Monthly Review Press.

Fantasia, Rick. 1995. "Fast Food in France." *Theory and Society* 24:201–43.

Fine, Gary Alan. 1996. *Kitchens: The Culture of Restaurant Work*. Berkeley and Los Angeles: University of California Press.

Formanek-Brunell, Miriam. 1993. *Made to Play House: Dolls and the Commercialization of American Girlhood, 1830–1930*. New Haven: Yale University Press.

Fox, Richard Wightman, and T. J. Jackson Lears, eds. 1983. *The Culture of Consumption*. New York: Pantheon.

Frank, Dana. 1994. *Purchasing Power: Consumer Organizing, Gender, and the Seattle Labor Movement, 1919–1929*. Cambridge: Cambridge University Press.

Frenzen, Jonathan K., and Harry L. Davis. 1990. "Purchasing Behavior in Embedded Markets." *Journal of Consumer Research* 17:1–12.

Frenzen, Jonathan K., Paul M. Hirsch, and Philip C. Zerrillo. 1994. "Consumption, Preferences, and Changing Lifestyles." Pp. 403–25 in *The Handbook of Economic Sociology*, ed. Neil J. Smelser and Richard Swedberg. New York: Russell Sage Foundation; Princeton: Princeton University Press.

Gabaccia, Donna R. 1998. *We Are What We Eat: Ethnic Food and the Making of Americans*. Cambridge: Harvard University Press.

Gal, Susan, and Gail Kligman. 2000. *The Politics of Gender after Socialism*. Princeton: Princeton University Press.

Gladwell, Malcolm. 1999. "Clicks and Mortar." *New Yorker*. http://www.gladwell.com. Retrieved February 15, 2002.

Glickman, B. Lawrence. 1997. *A Living Wage: American Workers and the Making of Consumer Society*. Ithaca, N.Y.: Cornell University Press.

———, ed. 1999. *Consumer Society in American History: A Reader*. Ithaca, N.Y.: Cornell University Press.

Goody, Jack. 1998. *Food and Love: A Cultural History of East and West*. London: Verso.

Gottdiener, Mark, ed. 2000. *New Forms of Consumption*. Lanham, Md.: Rowman and Littlefield.

Granovetter, Mark. 1985. "Economic Action and Social Structure: The Problem of Embeddedness." *American Journal of Sociology* 91:481–510.

Granovetter, Mark, and Roland Soong. 1986. "Threshold Models of Interpersonal Effects in Consumer Demand." *Journal of Economic Behavior and Organization* 7:83–99.

Granovetter, Mark, and Richard Swedberg, eds. 2001. *The Sociology of Economic Life*. 2d ed. Boulder, Colo.: Westview Press.

Grasmuck, Sherri, and Patricia R. Pessar. 1991. *Between Two Islands: Dominican International Migration*. Berkeley and Los Angeles: University of California Press.

Green, Nancy L. 1997. *Ready-to-Wear and Ready-to-Work: A Century of Industry and Immigrants in Paris and New York*. Durham, N.C.: Duke University Press.

Gruen, Victor. 1964. *The Heart of Our Cities. The Urban Crisis: Diagnosis and Cure*. New York: Simon and Schuster.

Halle, David. 1993. *Inside Culture: Art and Class in the American Home*. Chicago: University of Chicago Press.

Halter, Marilyn. 2000. *Shopping for Identity: The Marketing of Ethnicity*. New York: Schocken Books.

Heinze, Andrew R. 1990. *Adapting to Abundance*. New York: Columbia University Press.

Hilton, Matthew. 2002. "The Fable of the Sheep: Or, Private Virtues, Public Vices: The Consumer Revolution of the Twentieth Century." *Past and Present* 176:222–56.

Hirsch, Paul. 1972. "Processing Fads and Fashions: An Organization-Set Analysis of Cultural Industry Systems." *American Journal of Sociology* 77:639–59.

Horowitz, Daniel. 1985. *The Morality of Spending*. Baltimore: Johns Hopkins University Press.

Horowitz, Roger, and Arwen Mohun, eds. 1998. *His and Hers: Gender, Consumption, and Technology*. Charlottesville: University Press of Virginia.

Howes, David, ed. 1996. *Cross-Cultural Consumption: Global Markets, Local Realties*. London: Routledge.

Humphrey, Caroline. 1995. "Creating a Culture of Disillusionment: Consumption in Moscow, a Chronicle of Changing Times." Pp. 43–68 in *Worlds Apart: Modernity through the Prism of the Local*, ed. Daniel Miller. London: Routledge.

Illouz, Eva. 1997. *Consuming the Romantic Utopia*. Berkeley and Los Angeles: University of California Press.

Ingram, Paul, and Peter W. Roberts. 2000. "Friendships among Competitors in the Sydney Hotel Industry." *American Journal of Sociology* 106:387–423.

Jacobs, Meg. 1997. "'How about Some Meat?': The Office of Price Administration, Consumption Politics, and State Building from the Bottom Up, 1941–1946." *Journal of American History* 84:910–41.

Joselit, Jenna Weissman. 1994. *The Wonders of America*. New York: Hill and Wang.

Kahneman, Daniel, and Amos Tversky. 1982. "The Psychology of Preferences." *Scientific American* 246: 160–73.

Katz, Elihu, and Paul F. Lazarsfeld. 1955. *Personal Influence*. New York: Free Press.

Kollock, Peter. 1999. "The Production of Trust in Online Markets." Pp. 99–123 in vol. 16 of *Advances in Group Processes*, ed. Edward J. Lawler, Michael W. Macy, Shane R. Thyne, and Henry A. Walker. Greenwich, Conn.: JAI Press.

Kuisel, Richard. 1993. *Seducing the French: The Dilemma of Americanization*. Berkeley and Los Angeles: University of California Press.

Lamont, Michèle, and Virág Molnár. 2001. "How Blacks Use Consumption to Shape Their Collective Identity: Evidence from Marketing Specialists." *Journal of Consumer Culture* 1:31–45.

Lasch, Christopher. 1977. *Haven in a Heartless World: The Family Besieged*. New York: Basic Books.

Lazarsfeld, Paul. 1957. "Sociological Reflections on Business: Consumers and Managers." Pp. 99–156 in *Social Science Research on Business: Product and Potential,* ed. Robert A. Dahl, Mason Haire, and Paul F. Lazarsfeld. New York: Columbia University Press.

Lears, Jackson. 1994. *Fables of Abundance: A Cultural History of Advertising in America.* New York: Basic Books.

Ledeneva, Alena V. 1998. *Russia's Economy of Favours: Blat, Networking, and Informal Exchange.* Cambridge: Cambridge University Press.

Lee, Jennifer. 2002. "From Civil Relations to Racial Conflict: Merchant-Customer Interactions in Urban America." *American Sociological Review* 67:77–98.

Leidner, Robin. 1993. *Fast Food, Fast Talk: Service Work and the Routinization of Everyday Life.* Berkeley and Los Angeles: University of California Press.

Levitt, Peggy. 2001a. *The Transnational Villagers.* Berkeley and Los Angeles: University of California Press.

———. 2001b. "Transnational Migration: Taking Stock and Future Directions." *Global Networks* 1:195–216.

Light, Ivan, and Steve J. Gold. 2000. *Ethnic Economies.* San Diego: Academic Press.

Lozada, Eriberto P., Jr. 2000. "Globalized Childhood? Kentucky Fried Chicken in Beijing." Pp. 114–34 in *Feeding China's Little Emperors,* ed. Jun Jing. Stanford, Calif.: Stanford University Press.

Lynd, Robert S., and Helen M. Lynd. 1929. *Middletown: A Study in American Culture.* New York: Harcourt, Brace and World.

Mahler, Sarah J. 1995. *American Dreaming: Immigrant Life on the Margins.* Princeton: Princeton University Press.

Manning, Robert D. 2000. *Credit Card Nation.* New York: Basic Books.

Marling, Karal Ann. 2000. *Merry Christmas!* Cambridge: Harvard University Press.

McKendrick, Neil, John Brewer, and J. H. Plumb. 1982. *The Birth of a Consumer Society: The Commercialization of Eighteenth-Century England.* Bloomington: Indiana University Press.

Mehta, Raj, and Russell W. Belk. 1991. "Artifacts, Identity, and Transition: Favorite Possessions of Indians and Indian Immigrants to the United States." *Journal of Consumer Research* 17:398–411.

Miller, Daniel. 1987. *Material Culture and Mass Consumption.* Oxford: Blackwell.

———. 1995. "Consumption as the Vanguard of History: A Polemic by Way of an Introduction." Pp. 1–57 in *Acknowledging Consumption,* ed. Daniel Miller. London: Routledge.

———. 1998. *A Theory of Shopping.* Ithaca, N.Y.: Cornell University Press.

———. 2001. *The Dialectics of Shopping.* Chicago: University of Chicago Press.

Miller, Daniel, Peter Jackson, Nigel Thrift, Beverley Holbrook, and Michael Rowlands. 1998. *Shopping, Place, and Identity.* London: Routledge.

Miller, Daniel, and Don Slater. 2000. *The Internet: An Ethnographic Approach.* Oxford: Berg.

Miller, Michael B. 1981. *The Bon Marché: Bourgeois Culture and the Department Store: 1869–1920.* Princeton: Princeton University Press.

Mintz, Sidney W. 1996. *Tasting Food, Tasting Freedom: Excursions into Eating, Culture, and the Past.* Boston: Beacon Press.

Morawska, Ewa. 1985. *For Bread with Butter. The Life-Worlds of East Central Europeans in Johnstown, Pennsylvania, 1890–1940.* Cambridge: Cambridge University Press.

Moreno, Sylvia. 2001. "A Courier with Connections." *Washington Post,* March 26, B1.

Mukerji, Chandra. 1983. *From Graven Images: Patterns of Modern Materialism.* New York: Columbia University Press.

Newman, Katherine S. 1999. *No Shame in My Game: The Working Poor in the Inner City.* New York: Alfred A. Knopf and Russell Sage Foundation.

Nightingale, Carl H. 1993. *On the Edge.* New York: Basic Books.

Pahl, Jan. 1999. *Invisible Money: Family Finances in the Electronic Economy.* Bristol: Policy Press.

Patillo-McCoy, Mary. 1999. *Black Picket Fences: Privilege and Peril among the Black Middle Class.* Chicago: University of Chicago Press.

Peiss, Kathy. 1998. *Hope in a Jar: The Making of America's Beauty Culture.* New York: Metropolitan Books.

———. 2002. "Educating the Eye of the Beholder—American Cosmetics Abroad." *Daedalus* 131(4): 101–9.

Pérez Firmat, Gustavo. 1994. *Life on the Hyphen: The Cuban-American Way.* Austin: University of Texas Press.

Pew Hispanic Center and the Multilateral Investment Fund. 2003. *Billions in Motion: Latino Immigrants, Remittances, and Banking.* http://www.pewhispanic.org/site/docs/pdf/billions_in_motion.pdf. Retrieved September 26, 2003.

Pleck, Elizabeth H. 2000. *Celebrating the Family: Ethnicity, Consumer Culture, and Family Rituals.* Cambridge: Harvard University Press.

Portes, Alejandro. 2001. "Introduction: The Debates and Significance of Immigrant Transnationalism." *Global Networks* 1:181–94.

Portes, Alejandro, William J. Haller, and Luis Eduardo Guarnizo. 2002. "Transnational Entrepreneurs: An Alternative Form of Immigrant Economic Adaptation." *American Sociological Review* 67:278–98.

Portes, Alejandro, and Alex Stepick. 1993. *City on the Edge: The Transformation of Miami.* Berkeley and Los Angeles: University of California Press.

Putnam, Robert D. 2000. *Bowling Alone: The Collapse and Revival of American Community.* New York: Simon and Schuster.

Rappaport, Erika Diane. 2000. *Shopping for Pleasure: Women in the Making of London's West End.* Princeton: Princeton University Press.

Riesman, David. 1964. *Abundance for What? And Other Essays.* Garden City: Doubleday.

Rifkin, Jeremy. 2000. *The Age of Access.* New York: Jeremy P. Tarcher/Putnam.

Ritzer, George. 1996. *The McDonaldization of Society.* Thousand Oaks, Calif.: Pine Forge Press.

———. 2000. "A Sub-field in Search of Discovery." *Footnotes,* February, 6.

———. 2003a. *The Globalization of Nothing.* Thousand Oaks, Calif.: Pine Forge Press.

———. 2003b. "Islands of the Living Dead. The Social Geography of McDonaldization." *American Behavioral Scientist* 47:119–36.

Ritzer, George, and Seth Ovadia. 2000. "The Process of McDonaldization Is Not Uniform, nor Are Its Settings, Consumers, or the Consumption of Its Goods and Services." Pp. 33–49 in *New Forms of Consumption,* ed. Mark Gottdiener. Lanham, Md.: Rowman and Littlefield.

Ritzer, George, and Don Slater. 2001. Editorial. *Journal of Consumer Culture* 1:5–7.

Roberts, Kenneth D., and Michael D. S. Morris. 2003. "Fortune, Risk, and Remittances: An Application of Option Theory to Participation in Village-Based Migration Networks." *International Migration Review* 37:1252–81.

Rose-Ackerman, Susan. 1998. "Bribes and Gifts." Pp. 296–328 in *Economics, Values, and Organization,* ed. Avner Ben-Ner and Louis Putterman. Cambridge: Cambridge University Press.

Rosenzweig, Roy. 1983. *"Eight Hours for What We Will": Workers and Leisure in an Industrial City, 1870–1920.* Cambridge: Cambridge University Press.

Ross, Ellen. 1993. *Love and Toil: Motherhood in Outcast London, 1870–1918.* Oxford: Oxford University Press.

Sahlins, Marshall. 1976. *Culture and Practical Reason.* Chicago: University of Chicago Press.

Samuel, Raphael. 1981. *East End Underworld. Chapters in the Life of Arthur Harding.* London: Routledge and Kegan Paul.

Sánchez, George J. 1993. *Becoming Mexican American: Ethnicity, Culture, and Identity in Chicano Los Angeles, 1900–1945.* Oxford: Oxford University Press.

Sartori, Laura. 2002. "Consumo e vita quotidiana nell'era di Internet." Ph.D. diss., Sociology and Social Research, University of Trento.

Scanlon, Jennifer, ed. 2000. *The Gender and Consumer Culture Reader.* New York: New York University Press.

Schmidt, Leigh Eric. 1995. *Consumer Rites: The Buying and Selling of American Holidays.* Princeton: Princeton University Press.

Schor, Juliet B. 1998. *The Overspent American.* New York: Basic Books.

Schreiber, Alfred L. 2001. *Multicultural Marketing.* Chicago: NTC Business Books.

Schudson, Michael. 1984. *Advertising, the Uneasy Persuasion.* New York: Basic Books.

Simmel, Georg. [1904] 1957. "Fashion." *American Journal of Sociology* 62:541–58.

Singh, Supriya. 1999. "Electronic Money: Understanding Its Use to Increase the Effectiveness of Policy." *Telecommunications Policy* 23:753–73.

Slater, Don. 1997. *Consumer Culture and Modernity.* Cambridge: Polity Press.

Smelser, Neil J. 1963. *The Sociology of Economic Life.* Englewood Cliffs, N.J.: Prentice-Hall.

Stephenson, Peter H. 1989. "Going to McDonald's in Leiden: Reflections on the Concept of Self and Society in the Netherlands." *Ethos* 17:226–47.

Stillerman, Joel. 2004. "Gender, Class, and Generational Contexts for Consumption in Contemporary Chile." *Journal of Consumer Culture* 4:51–78.

Swedberg, Richard. 2003. *Principles of Economic Sociology.* Princeton: Princeton University Press.

Swiencicki, Mark A. 1999. "Consuming Brotherhood: Men's Culture, Style, and Recreation as Consumer Culture, 1880–1930." Pp. 207–40 in *Consumer Society in American History: A Reader,* ed. Lawrence B. Glickman. Ithaca, N.Y.: Cornell University Press.

Tebbutt, Melanie. 1983. *Making Ends Meet: Pawnbroking and Working-Class Credit.* New York: St. Martin's Press.

Thaler, Richard H. 1991. *Quasi Rational Economics.* New York: Russell Sage Foundation.

———. 1999. "Mental Accounting Matters." *Journal of Behavioral Decision Making* 12:183–206.

Tiersten, Lisa. 2001. *Marianne in the Market. Envisioning Consumer Society in Fin-de-Siècle France.* Berkeley and Los Angeles: University of California Press.

Tilly, Charles. 1990. "Transplanted Networks." Pp. 79–95 in *Immigration Reconsidered. History, Sociology, and Politics,* ed. Virginia Yans-McLaughlin. Oxford: Oxford University Press.

Tilly, Chris, and Charles Tilly. 1998. *Work under Capitalism.* Boulder, Colo.: Westview.

Turow, Joseph. 1997. *Breaking Up America: Advertisers and the New Media World.* Chicago: University of Chicago Press.

Uzzi, Brian. 1997. "Social Structure and Competition in Interfirm Networks: The Paradox of Embeddedness." *Administrative Science Quarterly* 42:35–67.

Veblen, Thorstein. [1899] 1953. *The Theory of the Leisure Class.* New York: New American Library.

Venkatesh, Alladi. 1995. "Ethnoconsumerism: A New Paradigm to Study Cultural and Cross-Cultural Consumer Behavior." Pp. 26–67 in *Marketing in a Multicultural World,* ed. Janeen Arnold Costa and Gary J. Bamossy. Thousand Oaks, Calif.: Sage.

Waller Meyers, Deborah. 1998. "Migrant Remittances to Latin America: Reviewing the Literature." Working paper, Tomás Rivera Policy Institute, May.

http://www.thedialogue.org/publications/meyers .html. Retrieved February 5, 2002.

Warde, Alan. 2000. "Eating Globally: Cultural Flows and the Spread of Ethnic Restaurants." Pp. 299–316 in *The Ends of Globalization*, ed. Don Kalb, Marco van der Land, Richard Staring, Bart van Steenbergen, and Nico Wilterdink. Lanham, Md.: Rowman and Littlefield.

Warde, Alan, and Lydia Martens. 2000. *Eating Out: Social Differentiation, Consumption, and Pleasure.* Cambridge: Cambridge University Press.

Waters, Mary. 1990. *Ethnic Options.* Berkeley and Los Angeles: University of California Press.

Watson, James L., ed. 1997. *Golden Arches East: McDonald's in East Asia.* Stanford, Calif.: Stanford University Press.

Weatherill, Lorna. 1993. "The Meaning of Consumer Behavior in Late Seventeenth- and Early Eighteenth-Century England." Pp. 206–27 in *Consumption and the World of Goods*, ed. John Brewer and Roy Porter. London: Routledge.

Weems, Robert E., Jr. 1994. "The Revolution Will Be Marketed: American Corporations and Black Consumers during the 1960s." *Radical History Review* 59:94–107.

Weiss, Michael J. 1988. *The Clustering of America.* New York: Harper and Row.

Wellman, Barry, and Caroline Haythornthwaite, eds. 2002. *The Internet in Everyday Life.* Oxford: Blackwell.

White, Harrison C. 2002. *Markets from Networks. Socioeconomic Models of Production.* Princeton: Princeton University Press.

Wuthnow, Robert. 1996. *Poor Richard's Principle.* Princeton: Princeton University Press.

Yan, Yunxiang. 2000. "Of Hamburger and Social Space: Consuming McDonald's in Beijing." Pp. 201–25 in *The Consumer Revolution in Urban China*, ed. Deborah S. Davis. Berkeley and Los Angeles: University of California Press.

Zelizer, Viviana A. 1998. "How Do We Know Whether a Monetary Transaction Is a Gift, an Entitlement, or a Payment?" Pp. 329–33 in *Economics, Values, and Organization*, ed. Avner Ben-Ner and Louis Putterman. Cambridge: Cambridge University Press.

———. 1999. "Multiple Markets, Multiple Cultures." Pp. 193–212 in *Diversity and Its Discontents: Cultural Conflict and Common Ground in Contemporary American Society*, ed. Neil J. Smelser and Jeffrey Alexander. Princeton: Princeton University Press.

———. 2001. "Economic Sociology." Pp. 4128–31 in vol. 6 of *International Encyclopedia of the Social and Behavioral Sciences*, ed. Neil J. Smelser and Paul B. Baltes. Amsterdam: Elsevier.

———. 2002a. "Kids and Commerce." *Childhood* 4: 375–96.

———. 2002b. "Enter Culture." Pp. 101–25 in *The New Economic Sociology: Developments in an Emerging Field*, ed. Mauro F. Guillén, Randall Collins, Paula England, and Marshall Meyer. New York: Russell Sage Foundation.

Zukin, Sharon. 1991. *Landscapes of Power: From Detroit to Disney World.* Berkeley and Los Angeles: University of California Press.

———. 2003. *Point of Purchase: How Shopping Changed American Culture.* London: Routledge.

16 The Sociology of Money and Credit

Bruce G. Carruthers

> Who has gold has a treasure with which he gets what he wants, imposes his will on the world, and even helps souls to paradise. (Christopher Columbus)

MONEY CHARACTERIZES modern economies, but it has been of only intermittent concern to modern sociology. The uneven distribution of money across race, gender, or class has been of central interest to sociologists studying inequality. But money per se seldom preoccupies them. Money functions as the pecuniary "flip side" of market exchange: goods and services go from seller to buyer, while money goes the other way and balances the exchange. Individual transactions join into networks and circuits of exchange that engender parallel flows of money. Money accompanies commodification and the spread of markets. Under capitalism, according to social theorists ranging from Marx and Simmel to David Harvey, the cash nexus has pervaded, subverted, and otherwise transformed social relations. In short, money is an agent of social change.

Credit operates less visibly, although it too pervades market exchange. Indeed, in many economies more transactions are conducted using credit than cash. Credit involves "unbalanced" transactions, when goods and services go from seller to buyer but no money flows the other way. Instead, the seller receives a promise to repay. Credit also concerns intertemporal monetary transactions, when a lender gives money to a borrower in exchange for a promise of future repayment. Since credit involves making and accepting promises, it obviously involves trust.

Here, I describe the connections between money and credit and their roles in the governance of economic transactions and social relationships; I summarize the sociological literature on money and extend it to consider credit, a topic that sociology has mostly ignored. Money and credit have effects that go far beyond the economy, and both are affected by noneconomic factors. As institutions,

they directly link to the economy, politics, law, inequality, culture, and other areas of sociological interest. Many of the relevant issues were addressed first by Max Weber and later by Talcott Parsons. Since I intend to examine money and credit rather than Weber or Parsons on these topics, I will not summarize their arguments (Swedberg 1998; Parsons 1982). Nor shall I duplicate reviews of the sociology of money (Blomert 2001; Keister 2002), except to note that the strategy of demonstrating the embeddedness of economic institutions also extends to money (Granovetter 1985). Recent studies of money (Baker and Jimerson 1992; Carruthers and Babb 1996; Dodd 1994; Ingham 1999; Zelizer 1989, 1994, 1996) have all documented how social factors affect it.

I define money as *generalized, immediate, and transferable legitimate claims on value.* Money is important because it commands resources. It functions as a medium of exchange, and as store and measure of value. But this definition needs qualification. First, claims are general only within social communities and spheres of activity. Claims that operate in one place (cowrie shells in eighteenth-century West Africa) do not necessarily work elsewhere (twenty-first-century Evanston, Illinois). Monetary claims exercised on some things of value (shoes) do not work on others (love). Furthermore, money is not always perfectly divisible or fungible. Finally, both claims and the values to which they apply are socially constructed. What constitutes value in one society may be valueless in others. Monetary claims are conventional and depend on self-reinforcing and collective expectations (Orlean 1992): a person accepts arbitrary tokens as money because she believes that others will accept them. Money therefore raises problems of trust. Historically, sovereign governments have played a key role in the promulgation and enforcement of money claims.

Credit consists of *nongeneralized, deferred, and variably transferable legitimate claims on specific value.* The nongenerality of credit derives from its dependence on one party's obligation to another. A particular creditor has a claim over a particular debtor: Sam owes money to Esther rather than being obliged in general. Sometimes these claims can be transferred to third parties, but frequently they cannot. As credit claims become more easily transferable, however, they become more money-like. Credit involves deferred claims and so is affected by uncertainty about the future. Sovereign governments often specify the forms that credit takes, and help enforce claims, but credit has many times functioned beyond the purview of the state.

My definitions emphasize the difference between money and credit, but intermediate forms exist. As credit becomes more general, uniform, and transferable, it approximates money. No hard-and-fast distinction separates the two kinds of claims. Nor do money and credit exhaust all legitimate claims on value recognized in a particular society. Some people hold claims because of their position in a social network. For example, fathers may have claims over sons (so-called "wealth in persons").

MONEY

The use of money is highly uneven and differentiated. The perfect fungibility that modern money possesses in principle becomes in practice domesticated and restrained. Like any social object that transgresses boundaries, money is dangerous and impure in Mary Douglas's sense. The restrictions laid upon money reflect not only cultural norms about its meaning and appropriateness (Zelizer 1994), but also ordinary commercial and budgetary practices, and the fact that money flows between and within political jurisdictions. Historically, of course, money was independent of market exchange. In medieval Ireland, people used it to satisfy social obligations and remedy wrongs, not for market exchange (Gerriets 1985; Grierson 1977), and much exchange occurred without money (Spufford 1988, 17–18).

The basis for money has shifted dramatically: in the past, money involved precious commodities like silver and gold, which anchored expectations about money's acceptability. As the bullionists expressed it after the U.S. Civil War, gold possessed "intrinsic value" (Carruthers and Babb 1996). Re-

cently, however, money has become "dematerialized" and "virtual" (Evans and Schmalensee 1999, 25; Leyshon and Thrift 1997). Money is no longer tied to specie but consists of electronic accounts or pieces of paper. Thus, claims about "intrinsic worth" have lost credibility (although gold-standard advocates still exist). Furthermore, the liberalization and the integration of financial markets have been an important part of "globalization": by historical standards, international money flows are now voluminous and virtually instantaneous (Fligstein 2001, 209–13). These developments threaten the connection between money and political sovereignty.

Money and credit have clearly evolved since Marx pondered the "riddle of the money fetish," and this evolution is something economic sociologists have begun to consider. Several developments sparked debate. Economic transitions in Eastern and central Europe problematize the foundations of effective monetary and credit systems. The vitality of the informal sector in many countries, and the prevalence of nonmonetary exchange, challenge orthodox verities about the advantages of money. And continued historical and comparative scholarship has produced a wealth of new empirical findings.

Money Is What Money Does

The standard treatment of money emphasizes three functions. Money is a means of exchange, a store of value, and a unit of account (Stiglitz 1993, 880–83). Thus, money enables economies to escape the limits of barter, which depends on a "double coincidence of needs": person A has what B wants, and vice versa. Money supports multilateral exchange. By facilitating advantageous exchanges, money benefits all who participate in the monetarized economy. Functional money also has a sufficiently stable value that people will accept and hold it for future use. As a unit of account, money permits comparisons and evaluations; it measures the relative worth of commodities and services. Money commensurates alternatives and promotes rational decision-making (Espeland and Stevens 1998). Methods like cost-benefit analysis extend monetary measurement into public policy decision-making. Ideally, money reduces transaction costs and facilitates self-interested exchanges, allows people to accumulate value and make intertemporal trade-offs, and provides a common denominator with which to compare alternatives.

Functionalist discussions of money rarely examine how money came to perform these functions, whether they are equally significant, if functional alternatives exist, and whether these functions exhaust money's social significance. Money does these things, to be sure, but it is worthwhile considering its other uses. For most economists, money is so transparently advantageous that its existence seems self-explanatory (Jones 1976). Furthermore, economists and sociologists alike have overdrawn the contrast between "modern" money and "primitive" money, and embraced evolutionary arguments about the transition from one to the other (Guyer 1995, 1).

Money and Meaning

In addition to its other functions, money is a symbol that conveys information (Hart 2000, 17). In particular, by restraining and channeling the flow of money, people use it as a bearer of social meaning. Instead of interpreting restricted circulation as a sign that money has failed to perform, we should recognize that such patterns reflect the creation of meaning. Money is a way to communicate messages as well as command resources.

Zelizer (1989, 1994, 1996) documents how restrictions placed on money mark significant social boundaries (Baker and Jimerson 1992; Webley and Lea 1993). She argues against the view that modern money "dissolves" social relations by showing that social relations affect modern money. By confining money to some realms, people affirm cultural distinctions between private and public, male and female, sacred and profane. Restricting money means blocking certain transactions (Andre 1992) and creating separate spheres of exchange (Bohannan 1959; Ferguson 1992). Exchange across spheres is morally problematic, but the separation between them creates differentials of value that entrepreneurs may exploit by spanning structural holes (Barth 1967; Burt 1992). Thus, blocked exchanges and separate spheres are rarely static. This dynamism affects how cultural distinctions get articulated in terms of money, and even alters the distinctions themselves.

The differentiation of homogeneous money occurs in both "modern" and "traditional" societies. People acknowledge separate scales of value, and not just different values, by attaching prices to some objects and rejecting prices for others (so-called priceless goods). Sometimes the meanings are relatively idiosyncratic (a family heirloom), but they may be recognized by an entire community (religious artifacts, public symbols).

Contrasting monetarized from nonmonetarized is one way to elaborate meaningful differences. Another is to construct distinctions within money itself. Zelizer outlines the strategies people use to separate money into qualitatively distinct categories. Some dollars are "honest" and "clean," while others are "dirty" (Verdery 1995). Monies get earmarked by source (they derive from particular activities) or use (they fund specific expenditures). Household budgets are often structured around earmarkings that distinguish among what would otherwise be fungible monies. The classification of money reflects household rules and cultural norms about how to value household activities, and the priorities and obligations of household members. For example, people often treat bonuses, gifts, windfalls, or tips differently than regular wages. "Earned" money has a moral sobriety that unearned money frequently lacks, and hence the latter more often funds whimsical expenditures. Or family members may receive specific monies for discretionary expenses ("pocket money" "pin money"). Historically, women's wages within the family were treated differently from men's (Zelizer 1994, 27). This multiplicity makes modern money more "anthropological" (Dupre 1995).

Money may be used as much to avoid particular connotations as to signal them. Within intimate romantic relationships, men and women frame their expenditures on one another so that it is clear that neither (but especially men) is "buying" sex with money (Zelizer 2002). In contemporary United States, a man can spend large sums (dinner, flowers, etc.) in anticipation of sexual relations with the woman he is dating. And the woman who appreciates such lavish treatment may well consent to sex. But both would reject any similarity with prostitution, although the monetary value and outcome may well be identical.[1] More generally, cash connotes a social distance and anonymity that is inappropriate for certain interactions (Clark 1990, 33, 69; Prasad 1999).

Individuals and households are not the only ones making distinctions. Organizational budgets also involve earmarkings and categories. Budget items possess varying degrees of liquidity, with the most fungible resources put in the most liquid budget category (Stinchcombe 2001, 126–27). The separation of monies into different categories reflects the political commitments and priorities of organizations and their constituencies, and money budgeted into different categories can no longer be treated the same. State governments sometimes "launder" tax revenues from "unclean" sources by using them to fund "clean" activities. Money from "sin taxes" on tobacco and alcohol products supports particular ends, like public education, partly because these revenues possess a problematic political meaning that must be managed.

In general, the meaning and use of money varies with how it gets classified. Categorical distinctions introduce differences into otherwise uniform and homogeneous money. Such classifications and the meanings they engender derive from how the money flows: where it comes from, and where it goes (Carruthers and Espeland 1998).[2] In moving from place to place, money makes socially contiguous otherwise distinct activities and situations. Inconsistent and even contradictory cultural meanings become linked by money, and the resulting cultural "spillover" poses semantic challenges for those who use money. The activities that generate money vary in their social acceptability, and this colors the resulting cash flow.

In addition to functioning as medium of exchange, store of value, and unit of account, money proves also to be a surprisingly subtle vehicle for the conveyance of meaning. Money works as both an economic and a semiotic instrument, and these two modalities conflict with each other. Money functions better in the economy to the extent that it is truly uniform and fungible. But in using money to send messages, bolster status, and honor important social values, people render it less fungible. This tension rarely achieves a definitive resolution either one way or the other.

Money and Metrology

As a unit of account, money becomes a measurement instrument. The connection between money and quantity is so obvious that researchers often overlook its social aspects (but see Crump 1978). As Marx noted, money represents "values as magnitudes of the same denomination, qualitatively equal and quantitatively comparable. It thus acts as a universal measure of value" (1976, 188). With monetary valuation, qualitative differences became quantitative differences (Cooley 1913). Quantitative measurement involves attaching numbers to objects so that relations among the numbers reflect relations among the objects. Thus, if we measure object A to be 10 on some scale, and B to be 15, we can compare 10 with 15 and say something about A and B (depending on the level of measurement, since $15 \neq 10$, B is different from A; since $15 > 10$, B is more than A; since $15 -$

$10 = 5$, B is 5 units larger). Quantitative measurement connotes objectivity and precision, and this aura encompasses monetary valuation as well (Wise 1995, 1). A market price appears more "objective" than other measures of value.

Market exchange involves attaching prices to objects, and hence performing a kind of quantitative measurement (Mintz 1961). Thus, the spread of markets has expanded quantification (Porter 1995, 91), although the process is uneven and pushed by other factors as well. Crosby (1997, 31) notes the importance of religion in the quantification of time, and Alder (1995) links the invention of the metric system to nation building that sought to develop the rationality of the French economy. Hadden (1994, 114, 137, 160) argues that early modern commerce helped to develop the mathematical models applied by scientists to the natural world (see also Kaye 1998).

To have an impact, quantitative information needs a receptive audience. Scholars have marked the spread of numeracy in England and the United States (Hacking 1990; Thomas 1987; Cohen 1982), and find that merchants were usually among the most numerate. Overall levels of numeracy were affected by historical accidents like the replacement of Roman by Arabic numerals (Menninger 1969, 287–94). The mathematical skills of contemporary consumers demonstrate the situated and practical aspects of math (Lave 1988). Ferreira (1997) finds that as markets bring arithmetic into the Brazilian frontier, they confront indigenous notions of value and equivalence. Insufficiently numerate audiences are likely to "glaze over" if they face too much complex quantitative information, and rely on rules of thumb and other calculative heuristics.

Porter (1995) notes that numbers are a form of communication used for control. Quantification thus concerns both intervention and description. Numbers get deployed in the context of "mechanical objectivity:" rule-based decision-making that supersedes personal judgment and minimizes discretion. With quantitative information, decisions appear less "subjective" or "arbitrary." Such an appearance depends, of course, on the audience. Porter argues that rules that appear highly constraining to outside audiences may be known to be more flexible to insiders. In the case of accounting information, accountants are much less bound by accounting rules than outsiders believed (although recent scandals have disillusioned them). In general, however, reliance on monetary value expands the use of quantitative information, and grants to decisions an image of truth and objectivity. Monetarization exposes local transactions to more distant economic influences by inserting them into larger circuits of exchange.

Proximity to market exchange facilitates quantitative measurement. Conversely, multiple or unstandardized monies make quantitative assessments more difficult. As Woodruff points out (1999, 162), the Russian economy of the 1990s used several imperfectly convertible monies, which undercut the ability of Western consultants to value Russian firms. Furthermore, situations arise in which market exchange is unavailable to gauge value. Valuation of assets in bankruptcy court, transfer pricing within a multidivisional firm, and cost-benefit analysis of public policy all pose difficult measurement problems. Given conflicting interests and the conventional nature of accounting rules, the potential for "creative interpretation" is high. However much accountancy seems a rule-governed exercise in the measurement of economic value, it is not (Miller 1994). Accounting rules grant substantial and unavoidable flexibility to accountants, who can be remarkably creative about "massaging the numbers" (Baskin and Miranti 1997, 228, 259). Briloff (1972, 39) shows how different inventory-valuation rules (LIFO vs. FIFO) can alter profits. Depending on when firms recognize income, they can manipulate their income during a reporting period (Briloff 1972, 163). Firms often "smooth" income to make it seem more predictable (Baskin and Miranti 1997, 191). U.S. accounting rules contain fuzzy areas that were exploited during the savings and loan crisis (Calavita, Pontell, and Tillman 1997, 57), and current financial scandals (Enron, WorldCom, etc.) show how easily corporations and their auditors can manipulate accounting information.

Opacity further increases with multiple systems of accounting rules. Cost-accounting emerged in the nineteenth century to measure transactions internal to large corporations (Chandler and Daems 1979; Yates 1989, 8–9). Today business schools train students in cost, financial, managerial, and international accounting (to name just a few). Each involves different rules for producing quantitative information. Furthermore, there are competing systems of rules among capitalist countries. For instance, a transitional economy adopting Western accounting standards can choose between at least three alternatives: GAAP (generally accepted accounted principles), IAS (International Accounting Standards), and the accounting directives of the European Union.

The connection between monetary valuation and quantitative measurement gives the former an image as an objective, neutral, and precise mode of valuation. Determining monetary value involves a complex measurement process that unfolds within a set of rules. Ideally, valuation resembles the "disinterested" mechanical objectivity discussed by Porter, but in fact the rules are often too vague, incomplete, and numerous to prevent interest-driven creative interpretations. Money involves a distinctly numerical form of valuation, in sharp contrast to other modes of valuing (Anderson 1993, 10, 144–45). In this regard, modern money is a singularly reductive and one-dimensional form of valuation. Money may not have dissolved social relations, but in complex ways it has led to a proliferation of quantitative measurement.

Money and Politics

The connections between money, law, and political sovereignty are strong and old, and underscore the political uses of money. States and sovereigns promulgate money for their own purposes, and the other institutions or organizations creating money (e.g., banks) are usually subject to government oversight and accountability. Indeed, money is a public symbol of political sovereignty (Helleiner 1998; McNamara 1998, 2).

Precisely because money commands resources, it has been used for political control over regions, economies, and populations. Many parts of sub-Saharan Africa had indigenous monetary systems that colonial powers like Britain tried to supplant (Lovejoy 1974; Hogendorn and Johnson 1986, 150). Such policies integrated colonies into the colonizer's economy as suppliers of labor and raw materials, and as markets for finished goods. Colonial governments also imposed taxes payable only in cash. These fiscal obligations forced indigenous populations into the monetary economy in order to earn the money necessary to pay hut and capitation taxes (Arhin 1976; Falola 1995; Shipton 1989). Thus, taxes generated wage laborers as well as revenues.

Since prices set the market value of commodities and services, price setting is a distributional process. Prices create winners and losers by determining how much sellers receive, and buyers pay, to accomplish a transaction. Even mutually consensual exchanges can be more or less favorable to the parties involved. Given these distributional stakes, price-setting methods vary in how explicitly "political" they seem to be. The biggest difference lies between market prices and administered prices. The former appear apolitical, while the latter (whether corporate transfer prices, or prices set by central planners in a command economy) seem explicitly political. Indeed, the Soviet state had to manage the fact that how it set prices transparently burdened its citizenry (Berliner 1950). It had no "market forces" to provide political cover.

To the extent that standardized money reduces transaction costs and enhances exchange, states have a fiscal interest in its provision: more economic activity enlarges the tax base and increases revenues (Levi 1989; Spruyt 1994, 161–63). A ruler who monopolizes the supply of money also enjoys the fiscal advantages of seigniorage. Historically, complete monopolies are rare (see Martin 1977; Timberlake 1981 on nineteenth-century United States), but even when multiple monies circulate, states can use the money supply to their fiscal advantage. For example, during the U.S. Civil War, the Union government went off the gold standard and issued inconvertible paper money ("greenbacks") to meet its expenses (Bensel 1990; 14, 152, 162; Carruthers and Babb 1996, 1561–64). At that time, most paper currency was issued by private state-chartered banks (no Federal Reserve Banks existed before 1913), but the Union government still manipulated the money supply to its fiscal advantage. The National Banking Act of 1863 mandated the establishment of federally chartered banks whose notes would be backed by government bonds (Unger 1964, 15–18). To issue notes (i.e., create money), these banks had to lend to the government by purchasing its bonds. The government taxed state-chartered bank notes to encourage the incorporation of national banks (James 1978, 25). Thus, the Northern government indirectly used privately issued money to finance its deficit.

If the monetary system can increase state revenues and expenditures, it can also restrain public policy. In this regard, the choice of monetary standard has often proven fateful. Around 1870, three monetary standards existed: the gold standard (England, Brazil, Australia), the silver standard (Mexico, Asian countries, Holland, the German states), and a bimetallic standard (United States, France, Italy, Belgium). By 1880, most industrialized nations had embraced the gold standard, an arrangement that persisted until World War I. The transition to gold was contingent on war, domestic politics, trade, and network externalities (Flandreau 1996). The gold standard operated like a monetary rule: governments defined the value of their curren-

cy in terms of gold, and maintained the convertibility of their currency at that price (Bordo 1995). Trade imbalances between countries led to international flows of gold that "automatically" affected domestic money markets and interest rates in a way that redressed the trade imbalance. The main goal of central banks was to defend the national currency and maintain its convertibility (Bloomfield 1959, 23). Under the gold standard, central bank policy was *not* aimed at macroeconomic stability, economic growth, or the amelioration of unemployment. Consequently, to embrace the gold standard was to foreclose policy alternatives, including the more active and interventionist economic programs associated with Keynesianism deficit spending.[3]

Although the gold standard is no longer viable, the recent decision by European nations to form a European Monetary System meant greater harmonization of monetary policy and consequently less national autonomy. It is now much harder, if not impossible, for member nations to pursue independent macroeconomic policy (McNamara 1998). As with the gold standard, the choice of a monetary system has clear political consequences.

Most recently, monetary events in Russia illustrate the close connection between sovereignty, public policy, and money. As Woodruff (1999) argues, the authorities in transitional Russia have tried and failed to establish a monetary monopoly. Barter is common, and private monies and quasi monies circulate alongside government-issued money. A single, national currency was intended to help create an integrated Russian nation (Woodruff 1999, 5), but the central government was unable to suppress alternative monies (Woodruff 1999, 92). The other former Soviet republics issued their own currencies, as testament to their political independence, which resulted in a proliferation of currencies in the former Soviet Union (Johnson 2000, 91).

Money is a powerful but blunt political instrument. It is a building block of national markets and helps to integrate communities into a single, interdependent, whole. Money affects the fiscal interests of the state, and although it supports policy, the monetary system can also function as a constraint. Money also engages the symbolic interests of states, as a visible and ubiquitous symbol of political sovereignty.

Making Money

Although public authorities are the most important creators of money, they do not monopolize it.

There are often many kinds of money in use, not just the official currency. In some cases, the authority to create money has been delegated to private parties whose money substitutes for or supplements official money (Hurst 1973, 77). Demand deposits, for example, function as money, although because they involve a claim on an owner's checking account, they vary from owner to owner (Copeland 1981). Banks made money by issuing their own banknotes, and they also increased the money supply by making loans. Today, plastic cards provide yet another means of payment (Evans and Schmalensee 1999, 4). Some types of credit come very close to money. Hoagland (2002, 160) mentions how uneven exchanges between farmers and storekeepers in northern British Columbia were settled with the issuance of a note, by the storekeeper, to cover the balance. Depending on the storekeeper's reputation, such notes circulated locally like money and were used by third parties to settle their own transactions (see Sylla 1976).

Producing money follows a basic pattern. Most critically, "minting work" (Carruthers and Stinchcombe 1999, 366) establishes the self-fulfilling expectations that allow money to function as such. Users need to trust money, and that trust is built around their beliefs about how other users view money. These expectations depend upon the particular audience, and can be anchored in various ways. For example, money creators facing users who believed in the value of precious metal would issue coins containing the relevant metal. Only then could users expect others to accept the money. Such audiences would probably reject paper money or today's immaterial variants. Unfortunately, anchoring monetary expectations to precious metal makes money beholden to various contingencies. Rome's money supply, for example, depended on the balance of trade with extraimperial regions, the productivity of mines, conquest, and booty (Howgego 1992), and nineteenth-century economies felt the monetary effects of silver and gold discoveries (Hurst 1973, 67). Today the European Union does not worry about gold convertibility, but its supporters have been careful to make the euro look like money with respect to form and iconography. Furthermore, the EU intends to ensure that not too many euros get printed so that users will not worry about inflation.

Audiences may be strongly predisposed to support particular kinds of money, and the standards around which expectations get institutionalized can be remarkably durable. Charlemagne devised the pound, worth 20 shillings and 240 pence. This monetary unit, with its idiosyncratic divisibility, survived from the eighth century to the twentieth, and thanks to the British Empire spread around the world (Miskimin 1967). Nevertheless, beliefs about value, and the expectations they produce, are not cast in stone. Much greenback-era political rhetoric targeted the labile monetary expectations of the American public (Carruthers and Babb 1996).

Governments create money using "legal tender" status. By fiat, they can empower a particular money token so that it satisfies legal debts, public and private (Hurst 1973, 44). Thus, a creditor cannot legally enforce a debt if the debtor has repaid in legal tender (David 1986). Of course, the power to create legal tender has limits when debtors and creditors use extralegal or informal means to conduct their transactions. Furthermore, the expectations of money users may conflict with a government's wish to bestow value on fiat money. Although the Union government made greenbacks legal tender, most British suppliers refused them, insisting on payment in gold. The limits of legal tender status were reflected in the gold price of the greenback, as $100 worth of greenbacks fell from $96.60 in February 1862 to $35.09 in July 1864 (Mitchell 1908, 6).

A final issue concerns standardization. To be perfectly fungible, all monetary units must be the same, and their magnitude easy to measure. Complete standardization means that money units vary only in quantity, not quality. In earlier eras, the physical standardization of coins was the chief problem to solve. Given minting technology, money makers could produce coins within fairly well defined tolerances. But coin-shaving was always a problem as users tried surreptitiously to remove marginal amounts of metal from each coin. And issuers themselves sometimes adulterated the coinage (a strategy that led to inflation). Thus, the history of metallic money often consisted of slow but steady degradation, punctuated by recoinages in which money would be reminted.

Standardization works differently with paper money. Antebellum U.S. banknotes differed not because they conformed to different units (all were dollar denominated) but because their real value varied by issuer. A one-dollar bill issued by a solvent bank was worth more than a dollar issued by an insolvent bank. And since regulatory standards differed by state, what constituted "insolvency" also varied across jurisdictions. Gorton (1996) discusses how people managed nonstandardized money, but a better solution came with greater standardization. The National Banking Act created a more uniform currency by creating more uniform issuing banks (national banks all conformed to the same regulations, see Hurst 1973, 64; Sharkey 1959, 29). And the Federal Reserve System brought even greater uniformity to money.

Yet another mode of standardization occurs with electronic money. To make payment cards effective, promoters had to build an elaborate organizational structure to coordinate high volumes of information about issuing banks, and the credit limits and expenditures of millions of individual cardholders. This informational structure ensured that merchants could treat a Visa card issued by Citibank like a Visa issued by the First National Bank of Skokie. In order to achieve such equivalence across thousands of issuers, and millions of merchants and cardholders, card promoters had to wrestle with critical network externalities (Evans and Schmalensee 1999, 65, 149). For cardholders to hold a particular card, they had to believe that it would be accepted by many merchants. For merchants to accept a particular card, they had to believe that it would be used by many customers. Since at first there were neither cardholders nor accepting merchants, card promoters undertook a kind of "expectational bootstrapping" to create these self-fulfilling beliefs.

Money and Barter

Nonmarket exchange or special forms of valuation exclude money. But money may also simply be unavailable for ordinary exchange. In such circumstances, people use barter or credit to accomplish their exchanges. Standard economic treatments argue that money is superior to barter (Banerjee and Maskin 1996; Stiglitz 1993), and that primitive barter economies will perform better after the invention of money. Yet scholars find that money and barter coexist (Barnes and Barnes 1989; Hendley 1999; Humphrey 1985), and no simple or inevitable shift occurs from barter to money.

Economic actors sometimes use barter as a form of concealment. Money facilitates exchange, but it also facilitates the measurement of exchange by governments. The cash nexus is a convenient detection device for tax authorities, among other things. Firms wishing to avoid taxation, or which otherwise want to disguise their activities, can barter. Individuals who wish to earn untaxed income will also undertake in-kind exchanges and in effect join the informal economy (Nove 1989, 51).

Barter is common in contemporary Russia and other transitional economies (Carlin et al. 2000; Johnson 2000, 163). Some firms barter to avoid taxation, or because they or their trading partners are technically insolvent (Hendley 2001, 30; Johnson 2000, 107). Barter allows firms to evade the legal constraints that insolvency imposes (e.g., the right of creditors to seize a debtor's bank accounts). Humphrey (1985) claims out that barter works better in informationally rich environments, where the two parties know a good deal about each other.

CREDIT

No sharp line separates credit from money. Both involve legitimate claims on value and both facilitate exchange. Furthermore, both raise trust issues, albeit in different ways. Where money does not or cannot change hands, many use credit to accomplish their exchanges. Thus credit substitutes for money, and functions as the great expeditor of commerce (Inikori 1990). Historically, the money supply typically could not cover all exchanges, and so a substantial proportion of exchange occurred using credit (Anderson 1970; Balleisen 2001, 28, 44; Hoppit 1987, 133–34; Earle 1989, 115; McIntosh 1989; Nightingale 1990; Parker 1973, 9; Thorp 1991). Yet, as a topic, credit has been largely neglected by sociologists (Wiley 1967 is an exception).

Like money, credit commands resources, and so uneven access to credit has similarly important implications for social inequality (on mortgage-lending discrimination, see Yinger 1995; Ladd 1998; Munnell et al. 1996). Control over credit serves as a basis for economic and social power, and this insight has motivated a substantial literature on the power and centrality of banks within capitalist economies (Keister 2002).

Credit arises when one party lends money to another, or when one sells to another in exchange for deferred payment (trade or consumer credit). Credit involves intertemporal exchange, and most simply one party completes its side of a transaction at time 1, while the other meets its obligation at time 2. Until time 2, the second party (the debtor) is indebted to the first (the creditor). The magnitude of the debt is simply the money-value of whatever the creditor gave to the debtor at time 1.

To extend credit, the creditor must trust that debtors will repay. Unlike money, the trust problem posed by credit is very specific. For money to function, transacting parties have to trust it: they must believe that what they receive is authentic money that will retain its purchasing power over the short run. Money functions effectively when people trust money as an institution. The creators of money do a number of things to make money trustworthy, but once that trust problem gets resolved, it is resolved generally. For credit to function, however, the creditor has to trust a specific debtor at a particular point in time: will she repay in a year's time? Trust problems in credit cannot be resolved globally since they arise out of specific debtor-creditor pairings.

Heimer (2001) argues that trust involves two features: vulnerability and uncertainty. Person A is vulnerable to the actions of B, but is not sure what B will do. Can A trust B? If A lends money to B, A trusts B to repay the loan. A is vulnerable to B depending on the loan size, and because repayment occurs in the future, A cannot be certain what B will do. The effects of these information asymmetries on credit markets have been analyzed in the economics of information (Stiglitz 2000). People manage trust situations by reducing their vulnerability or their uncertainty, or both. They try to make the trustworthiness of the other person less relevant to their own interests (reduce their exposure), or they learn more about what that person will do.

Both strategies figure prominently in credit, and can be pursued individually, collectively, or institutionally (Guinnane 2001). For example, with reliable commercial law, lenders may obtain collateral for their loans, and have the right to seize assets if the borrower defaults. Attaching collateral reduces the creditor's losses, and makes the creditor less vulnerable. Creditors also acquire information before making a loan, in order to distinguish between trustworthy and untrustworthy borrowers. In gathering information, creditors focus on both the ability and willingness of the debtor to repay.

Credit is as old as money (Cohen 1992; Lopez and Raymond 1990), and although the problems of vulnerability and uncertainty have plagued creditors for millennia, the solutions vary. Credit depends upon a number of factors: the debtor, the creditor, the formal contractual and informal social relationships between them, intermediaries, third-party networks, and the commercial-legal framework. These factors sometimes covary systematically. For example, problematic contract law may force creditors to rely on other means to secure repayment. A creditor making loans in a country with an unreliable legal system typically uses informal social ties, or intermediaries, to assess and enhance the trustworthiness of the debtor.

Debtors

In deciding whether a debtor can be trusted, creditors focus on the qualities that affect the capacity and willingness of the debtor to repay. Historically, information about these features was hard to obtain, but the focus was more on willingness than capacity. Would a particular debtor repay a loan if he or she could? Did the debtor keep his or her promises? In the eighteenth and nineteenth centuries, the issue was construed almost entirely in terms of the debtor's reputation (Defoe [1726] 1987; Earling 1890; Grassby 1995, 299–300; Hilkey 1997; Hoppit 1987, 164; Prendergast 1906, 93), and character remains an important consideration for lenders' decision making (Newburgh 1991). The problem of trust had been translated into the question of personal moral fiber, and the problem for creditors was how to detect the outwards signs of good character. Assessing character inevitably mixed pop-psychology, stereotypical attribution, and outright discrimination. And given the importance of perceptions, debtors found themselves of necessity conforming to the stereotypical signals of good character (Burley 1987; Lynd and Lynd 1929, 47).

Creditors also had to worry about the capacity of the debtor. Was the debtor solvent? Would the debtor's cash flow cover the loan? Such questions were for many centuries extremely hard to answer, largely because of the absence of reliable financial information (Olegario 1998, 177). Even debtors themselves had a hard time calculating the profitability of their own operations (Carruthers and Espeland 1991). But the development of accounting standards, the imposition of regulatory and disclosure requirements, and the emergence of credit rating all made it easier for creditors to learn about debtor finances (Balleisen 2001, 146–51; Cantor and Packer 1995; Kerwer 2001; Leyshon and Thrift 1999; Madison 1974; Pixley 1999; Santiso 1999; Treacy 1998). This informational infrastructure has transformed what creditors could know about debtors.[4] As recent U.S. financial scandals have demonstrated (e.g., Enron, WorldCom, Qwest), however, no regulatory framework, expert rating apparatus, or set of accounting rules is proof against subversion and creative misinterpretation.

How debtors intend to use the loan affects their willingness and ability to repay. Since trade or consumer credit underwrites specific purchases, it is clear what the money is for. In other situations, money that generates cash flow (e.g., investing in a factory) is more likely to produce a solvent debtor than money used for consumption. Banks view firms with good business plans more favorably than those without. For individual debtors, the different meanings of money come into play and affect a debtor's sense of obligation. Someone who borrows for a frivolous purpose, like gambling, may not feel as encumbered by the debt as someone who borrowed to pay for his or her daughter's wedding.

The ability to assess a debtor's capacity and willingness to pay was affected by the shift from individuals to organizations. Consumer finance involves individuals, but business finance has been transformed by the rise of large corporations (Perrow 2002). Firms have "legal personality" (the right to own property, enter into contracts, etc.), but they do not have psychological personalities, that is, predispositions to keep promises. Thus, assessing a corporate debtor's willingness to repay is problematic, and creditors cannot simply examine a firm's "moral fiber." Lenders can, however, evaluate the personal character of top management (Standard and Poor's 2000, 19–22). The ability of creditors to assess capacity to pay has certainly been enhanced by the fact that publicly traded firms are subject to various filing and disclosure requirements. These regulations, and the information they generate, vary across jurisdictions, but they have created a considerable amount of public information (Sylla and Smith 1995). The case of sovereign debtors poses a particular set of problems for creditors, not the least of which is that enforcing loan agreements can be problematic (Eaton 1993). Despite this complication (or perhaps because of it), public borrowing has been a driving force behind the development of many financial institutions and instruments (Carruthers 1996; Weir 1989).

Creditors

Credit depends upon who extends credit and for what purpose. Some creditors must lend, but choose whom to lend to. In the colonial United States, for example, retailers had to extend credit to customers in order to make a sale (Rosen 1997, 41). Given the scarcity of money, to insist on cash would have guaranteed almost no sales at all! Customer credit remained important for mass retailers like Marshall Field's (Twyman 1954, 7, 129), and the institutionalization of installment lending was one of the great financial innovations of the con-

sumer economy (Gelpi and Julien-Labruyère 2000; Lynn 1957; Olney 1999). Today, extending credit to customers continues to play an important part in sales. Sellers try to avoid the uncreditworthy, but a firm overeager to sell may be too optimistic in evaluating the creditworthiness of potential customers.

Philanthropic lenders have a different set of goals. James (1948) discusses how English charitable endowments made loans to help the "needy" rather than to generate income. Charitable institutions were often founded to compete with other, less scrupulous lenders. In the eleventh century, monasteries and other religious houses were important sources of funds (Jordan 1993, 29, 62, 64; Little 1978, 15). The *monti di pietà* of Renaissance Italy helped to protect the poor from usurers (Parker 1973, 12). Many of the savings banks founded in nineteenth-century United States had charitable purposes (Alter, Goldin, and Rotella 1994), and similar institutions (e.g., credit cooperatives and remedial loan societies) were established in the early twentieth century (Ham and Robinson 1923). Philanthropic lenders are less concerned about earnings, and more concerned that borrowers truly deserved assistance.

Philanthropic lending is perhaps the most obvious case where noneconomic goals shape credit, but noneconomic motivations matter more generally. Muldrew (1998) argues that a "moral economy" prevailed in the local credit markets of early modern England. Credit represented an opportunity to demonstrate neighborly values, and so to privilege profit was culturally inappropriate (Davis 2000). In the same period, two rules of exchange applied in western Massachusetts. For local credit transactions, members of the community tempered their profit seeking with a communitarian sensibility that stressed cooperation and informality. For long-distance trade, people adhered to relatively formal, confrontational, and self-interested logics (Clark 1990, 27, 30–31, 35–37; see Breen 1985, 93; Konig 1979, 82, 84).

Lending also occurs for political reasons: to reward followers, build networks, or create supportive constituencies. Creditors pursing political goals do not worry about uncertainty or vulnerability in the same way. In czarist Russia, policymakers tried to establish rural credit cooperatives to help build an independent, politically conservative peasantry (Baker 1977). The attempt failed, but the goals were clearly both political and economic. According to Flam (1985), mortgage lenders used their loans in the real estate market to break the power of silk-mill workers in early-twentieth-century

New Jersey. In the postemancipation South, landlords employed credit to secure control over a nominally free black workforce. New lien laws granted landlords as creditors draconian powers over their sharecropping tenants (Woodman 1995, 39, 65, 114). Elites in the Bahamas were similarly able to use the credit system to control the workforce (Johnson 1986).[5] And Jordan observes that ecclesiastical institutions in colonial Mexico made mortgage loans to cultivate local elites (Jordan 1993, 61–62).

Formal Debtor-Creditor Relations

A loan contract between a debtor and creditor offers some reassurance that the debt will be repaid: if the debtor defaults, the creditor can use the law to secure repayment. Obviously, the effectiveness of contracts depends on a predictable legal system (Weber 1978, 1095; 1981, 276–77). Following the development of commercial law, the efficacy and the complexity of loan contracts have evolved, tracing out a gradual but never complete "formalization" of credit (Winn 1994). An eighteenth-century merchant could obtain a loan with a simple IOU, and in the 1830s the first railroads sold bonds using a three-page bond indenture (Rodgers 1965, 552–55). By the end of the nineteenth century, however, U.S. railway bond indentures were 300 pages long.

Loan contracts follow well-defined forms, some of considerable antiquity. A modern mortgage, for example, gives a lender contingent property rights over an asset of the debtor, and in the event of default the lender may activate those rights. Collateral reduces the creditor's vulnerability and bolsters the debtor's willingness to repay. In Europe, mortgage contracts go back at least to the twelfth century (Barton 1967; Berman 1982), although they differed from modern mortgages in that the lender held the collateral until the loan was repaid.[6] As mortgages evolved, the type of property securing the loan shifted from realty to personalty ("chattel mortgages"), and more recently to property that the debtor will possess in the future ("floating charges"; see Reeder 1973).[7] Another ancient contractual form was the *commenda*, a combination loan and partnership (Weber 1981). In the early Middle Ages, these funded long-distance trade and laid out the rights and obligations of the two parties (the *commendator* and *tractator*; see Pryor 1977; Udovitch 1962).[8]

Other elements of modern loan contracts address vulnerability and uncertainty, and so try to remedy the problem of trust. "Restrictive" or "protective" covenants constrain what the borrower can do in order to increase the likelihood of repayment, and they often require the provision of information to lenders. For instance, some covenants restrict the debtor's investments or total indebtedness, while others provide for financial statements, and a periodic statement of compliance (Calomiris and Ramirez 1996; Smith and Warner 1979). Other covenants restrain the fungibility of money through a kind of earmarking. These "attach strings" to the loan to ensure that money is used only for purposes approved by the lender. In addition, lenders can specify terms (loan size, duration, interest rate, etc.) to set their vulnerability in proportion to the uncertainty they face (more risk means higher interest rates).[9]

As Anglo-American legal systems have developed, credit transactions have become increasingly governed by formal contracts. In colonial New York, for example, people increasingly turned to the courts to collect debts, and so civil litigation rates increased (Rosen 1997, 83, 85). Mann (1987, 27–28) finds that in Connecticut, formal written debt instruments gradually displaced informal book debt. Of course, informal lending continued, but as the legal framework developed, debtors and creditors de-emphasized informal means for enforcing debts. Scholars observing the importance of informal relationships in contemporary Russia attribute this to the underdevelopment of the legal system (Kali 2001, 211). Even when commercial law on the books seems adequate, its implementation may leave much to be desired.

Legal evolution has also produced negotiability, a critical feature that makes debts more like money. In traditional common law, a debt could not be transferred to third parties (Carruthers 1996, 127–31; Cook 1916). Only the original creditor could enforce the claim. Thus, aside from asserting the claim, a creditor could do little with a debt. Negotiability means, however, that the original creditor can transfer the debt to a third party, and use the claim to satisfy obligations to others (Freyer 1982; Weinberg 1982). This allows a debt to function like money. Negotiability transforms the enduring relationship directly linking debtor and creditor into a much more impersonal relationship that conjoins two social roles (Mann 1987, 37).

Informal Debtor-Creditor Relations

Developed commercial laws help manage the trust problems that afflict credit, but these are a historical rarity. Much lending in the past occurred when laws were unsophisticated or unreliable, and even today considerable informal lending occurs. Social relationships between debtors and creditors can sustain rich flows of credible, detailed information and support informal sanctions or social obligations to help enforce agreements (Hoffman, Postel-Vinay, and Rosenthal 2000, 65–66; Ottati 1994; Udry 1994; Uzzi 1999). In transition economies, social ties enhance trust and trustworthiness, and so facilitate credit (Keister 2001; Treisman 1995). Social networks also influence the goals of debtors and creditors.

Extensive evidence documents the impact of social relationships on credit. Early modern merchants needed credit, whether as working or fixed capital. Sometimes they obtained trade credit by simply delaying payment to their suppliers, but otherwise merchants looked to their family or friends for money (Brettell 1999; Earle 1989, 108, 110; Grassby 1995, 84–85; Hancock 1995, 242–43). Marriage often injected new capital into the firm (Hunt 1996, 23).

For some scholars, the connection between credit and social relations illustrates a more general pattern where social relations constitute resources to achieve economic ends (e.g., Greif 1993; Landa 1994). Relationships between bankers and small business owners, for example, solve information problems (Berger and Udell 1995). By this "rational embeddedness" argument, market actors exploit their social ties. Padgett's (2001) analysis of Florentine banking at first appears to document this pattern, but he rejects instrumentalist interpretations and shows how a succession of social forms were imposed on, and constituted within, the organization of banks and banking careers. He claims that different social forms and networks brought different "logics of identity" to the operation of banks. Rather than argue that bankers rationally "exploited" their family, guild, or political connections, Padgett recognizes that these networks induced particular identities that activated the interests that market actors pursued.

Some credit institutions are built directly out of informal social relationships (Anthony 1997; Neifield 1931). Rotating credit associations use ethnicity, friendship, or some other social tie, to pool and mobilize capital. Today, they are found around the globe (Biggart 2001; Falola 1993; Light and Bonacich 1988, 243–72; Sterling 1995), commonly among groups with limited access to formal financial institutions. Similarly, the Grameen Bank and other microcredit institutions create credit by putting borrowers into groups, where they can keep each other "honest." Loans are made to indi-

viduals, but if any single person defaults, the entire group is denied credit (Pitt and Khandker 1998).

Lamoreaux's study of nineteenth-century New England banks demonstrates the importance of social networks. Bank loans were typically made to bank directors, their friends and family, or to someone with a direct tie to the bank (Lamoreaux 1994, 4, 15). "Insider lending" was widespread, and understood to be normal. Lamoreaux suggests that one advantage of "nepotistic" lending was that loans could be enforced by social as well as legal sanctions (Lamoreaux 1994, 26). Only at the end of the century did banks establish separate credit departments, charged with the task of assessing the creditworthiness of noninsider borrowers (see also Beveridge 1985; Wright 1999).

Third-Party Networks

Credit depends on the direct ties between debtor and creditor, but also on the connections they both have to third parties. Creditors sometimes deem debtors more creditworthy depending on the kinds of networks to which they belong. Relationships inducing obligations to or from debtors draw them into social networks that constrain what they do. A debtor who enjoys the support of others is more likely to be a good risk (Balleisen 2001, 73). Thus, someone with a wealthy family that can guarantee a loan will be more creditworthy. As well, a debtor whose networks induce obligations to others may also be a better risk. Married men were traditionally deemed more creditworthy than single men because their family obligations rendered them more responsible (Earling 1890, 83–84). If a debtor's third-party obligations compete with the claims of the creditor, however, then debtors will be considered less creditworthy. Creditors want to know if a debtor owes money to anyone else.

A creditor's third-party ties also matter. Creditors are often embedded in their own network of financial obligations, and so their willingness to lend is affected by their ability to borrow. Consider a retailer who borrows from suppliers and lends to customers. If suppliers pressure for repayment, the retailer will have to scale back its own credit operations. When one party tightens credit, the effects reverberate throughout the network (negotiable instruments can moderate these effects since they allow creditors to use the debts owed them to repay their own debts). Creditors may also form syndicates to share the risks involved with a particular loan.

One debtor's situation may be influenced by a creditor's other debtors. If a particular debt is part of a portfolio of loans, then whether the loan is made and how it is managed depend on the overall portfolio. Consider a modern home mortgage. In deciding whether to make a particular loan, a lender evaluates the idiosyncratic value of a home. The lender also assesses the borrower's current and future finances. This decision requires detailed information about both the borrower and the house that will secure the loan. A less informationally intensive strategy involves grouping similar mortgages into portfolios, estimating overall loan performance, default rates, and so forth, and then using them to set interest rates. Rather than assess individual loans, the lender performs actuarial calculations across a group of loans and simply builds the likelihood of default into the interest rate. Public agencies like the Federal National Mortgage Association (Fannie Mae) have helped to standardize mortgages, and made it easier to put them into homogeneous pools (Jensen 1972). The development of securitized home mortgages embodies this portfolio strategy (Carruthers and Stinchcombe 1999; Kendall 1996).

Mutual third-parties can function as intermediaries (Moulton 1920). They connect debtors with creditors, and in effect span structural holes in the credit market. They help resolve the information problems that creditors face, and sometimes provide formal or informal guarantees about borrower performance. In the nineteenth century, western farm mortgages were often originated by local mortgage companies that sold the loans to eastern investors (Brewer 1976; Snowden 1995). The local company acted as a mortgage matchmaker. In early modern France, intermediaries played a critical part in Parisian credit markets (Hoffman, Postel-Vinay, and Rosenthal 2000). The role of the notaries evolved from that of clerks transcribing loan documents to financiers linking lenders to borrowers. Notaries inserted themselves between the other two parties, undercutting direct ties between lenders and borrowers and intermediating between them (Hoffman, Postel-Vinay, and Rosenthal 2000, 114). In Burt's (1992) terminology, the notaries created a structural hole and then bridged it. Their actions increased the flow of funds across social boundaries (gender, class, and neighborhood) as debtors and creditors relied less on their own homophilous social ties.

Legal Framework

Debtors and creditors use contracts to regulate specific transactions, but these transactions are governed more generally by bankruptcy and insolvency laws. Such laws determine what happens when a debtor becomes insolvent. Each creditor has a claim on the debtor, and bankruptcy law simultaneously reconciles multiple claims within an encompassing framework. The problem is that insolvent debtors cannot meet all their obligations (Jackson 1986). The losses must be shared among the claimants, and so bankruptcy becomes a distributional process. Bankruptcy generally leads to either liquidation or reorganization (Carruthers and Halliday 1998, 35–42, 252–66). In the case of liquidation, bankruptcy law ranks creditors, recognizing that some have stronger claims than others (e.g., secured creditors enjoy higher priority than unsecured creditors). The threat of insolvency often sets off a "rush to the assets," as creditors grab what they can. Bankruptcy law forestalls the rush and provides for a systematic distribution of assets. Those with the highest priority are paid first, and claims are satisfied in order until all the assets are exhausted. The lowest-ranked claimants often receive nothing. In the case of corporate reorganization, bankruptcy law provides a venue in which to register claims and negotiate a financial and operational restructuring of the firm. Unprofitable divisions may be sold off, wages reduced, debt swapped for equity, and so on. Bankruptcy law determines the bargaining rules, shaping how much bargaining power each party enjoys in the negotiations.

Centuries ago, bankruptcy law was little more than a coercive mechanism for throwing debtors into prison (Coleman 1965). As bankruptcy laws developed, however, they distinguished between individual and corporate debtors. Individual bankruptcy usually involves a procedure in which the debtor hands her assets to a court-appointed administrator or trustee, who distributes them to the creditors. The debtor enjoys a "fresh start," with all prior debts discharged (Sullivan, Warren, and Westbrook 2000, 5, 12, 170). Sometimes, certain classes of property are exempt from the proceedings, and insolvent debtors are allowed to maintain possession. Additionally, some debts are nondischargeable. In the United States, for example, child support payments cannot be discharged by a bankrupt debtor.

Bankruptcy laws now differentiate corporate liquidations from reorganizations, and procedurally favor one over the other. People are not indifferent between the two: managers, employees, and shareholders prefer reorganizations, while secured creditors prefer liquidations. Secured creditors enjoy a high priority, and so in a liquidation they get most of their money back. Shareholders almost always receive nothing, and managers and workers simply lose their jobs. By contrast, a reorganization is like an asymmetric gamble. If successful, the firm survives, creditors are repaid, employees keep their jobs, and shareholder value grows. But if the firm fails again, the managers, workers, and shareholders all suffer, and in addition the secured creditors lose. A reorganization can benefit managers, workers, and shareholders, but it can only hurt the secured creditors. Laws vary in their emphasis on the two alternatives: "debtor friendly" laws encourage reorganizations, while "creditor friendly" laws emphasize liquidation. Legal reform can shift the balance from one to the other (Carruthers, Babb, and Halliday 2001, 105–8; Skeel 2001).

Bankruptcy law applies only in situations of financial distress, but it casts a long shadow over lending. In particular, creditors worry about their vulnerability in legal environments that are too "debtor friendly." Economists argue that creditors' rights have an important effect on investment and growth (La Porta et al. 1998; Levine 1998). Indeed, many of the reforms imposed by the IMF on Indonesia, Thailand, and South Korea after the 1997 Asian financial crisis were motivated by the conviction that foreign creditors would not invest in those countries unless bankruptcy systems were made more "creditor friendly" (Eichengreen 1999, 28, 33). Nor could these economies adequately restructure without effective laws.

Real credit processes combine these factors together: the creditor's goals, the debtor's goals, character and financial standing, formal-contractual and informal-social relationships between debtor and creditor, the third-party ties of both, and the overall legal framework. Running through all factors are the problems of vulnerability and uncertainty. Each situation involves a particular configuration, so that which factors dominate, and how they interact, varies considerably.

MONEY AND CREDIT

Money and credit facilitate market exchange and function as substitutes. Where money is absent, people turn to credit, and as credit develops, people depend less on money. Changes in the value of money directly affect credit: inflation hurts creditors and benefits debtors, while deflation has the opposite effect. Priest (2001) points out that debt litigation in colonial New England peaked during monetary crises as debtors and creditors responded to inflation or deflation.

One important parallel between money and credit concerns the role of government. Public authorities have long created and maintained money, and the state's role reflects a legitimate public interest. Even when the creation of money devolves to private actors like banks, they are almost always subject to public oversight. The involvement of the state injects politics and sovereign interests into the monetary system. Political conflict may occur over the definition of money, as in the case of postbellum America, or gold-standard countries versus silver-standard countries (Breckenridge 1995). Sovereigns sometimes devalue the currency.

Although credit is not so closely linked to sovereignty, public finance has been a driving force in the creation of credit instruments and institutions (Roseveare 1991). Furthermore, even before the rise of nation-states, credit was socially regulated. Following an Aristotelean theory of money, the medieval church prohibited usury as a sin (Kaye 1998, 79–80). This prohibition did not apply to all credit transactions (annuities were exempted), but even so lenders found ways to circumvent it (Helmholz 1986). Similar proscriptions (and circumventions) occurred in other societies (e.g., Sharma 1965), prompting Weber and others to consider more general explanations of usury (Weber 1981, 267–71; 1978, 583–89; Nelson 1969). The prohibition relaxed over time, first becoming secularized, and then proscribing interest above a certain level. Most usury laws were eventually repealed, but some still remain (Holmes 1892; Calder 1999, 114).

Governments actively shape credit, sometimes as part of an overall development strategy in which government decides which industries receive capital (e.g., South Korean "policy loans"; see Woo 1991). Their ability to dictate investment flows depends on the structure of the financial system: state intervention is easier in bank-dominated than market-dominated systems (Loriaux 1991; Zysman 1983). As part of its redistributive agrarian reforms, Nicaragua's Sandinista government directed credit to small and medium-size farmers (Jonakin and Enriquez 1999).

In most instances, public regulation of credit is less ambitious. After the Civil War, insurance companies became the biggest nonbank financial institutions. Although they mobilized large pools of capital, insurance companies were prohibited from making risky investments. New York insurance companies could not hold out-of-state mortgages (Haeger 1979; Keller 1963, 127). Few states allowed insurance companies to invest in corporate securities, a restriction that was later relaxed so they could purchase "investment grade" securities (as defined by rating agencies). Savings banks and state banks operated under similar restrictions (Van Fenstermaker 1965, 15–17, 49). Early on, the New York City Mutual Savings Bank could only buy New York State or federal government bonds, making it virtually a captive lender to the state. Gradually, these restrictions were lifted to permit investment in New York canal bonds, other state bonds, mortgages, and eventually call loans (Olmstead 1976).

Governments can also influence credit indirectly. For a mortgage to work, creditors must be able to seize the underlying real estate if the debtor defaults. Unless the creditor can take possession, the loan is effectively unsecured. In the late nineteenth century, many British investors put their money into U.S. farm mortgages. When farmers defaulted, lenders seized their land. The prospect of British ownership of American farmland offended nationalist sensibilities, and so many states restricted foreign ownership of land (Clements 1955). These discriminatory laws discouraged British investment in farm mortgages by undermining the ability of foreigners to exercise their property rights as mortgagees.[13]

A different kind of discrimination operated in federal housing policy. The underwriting, lending, and insurance standards institutionalized by the FHA (Federal Housing Administration) and HOLC (Home Owners Loan Corporation) have played a substantial role in encouraging investment in suburban, middle-class, single-family dwellings and discouraging investment in multiunit dwellings in poor urban areas (Jackson 1985; Massey and Denton 1993; Squires and O'Connor 2001). In effect, these standards deterred lending in minority neighborhoods.

Even when government does not intervene to encourage or block particular flows of credit, it may still prudentially regulate debtor-creditor exchanges. Many U.S. states passed small-loan laws to ameliorate the situation of small borrowers (Nugent 1934; Phelps 1951). The Russell Sage Foundation promoted a model small-loan law and urged passage on state legislatures (Robinson and Nugent 1935). In subsequent years, similar laws have passed at the state and federal levels to shift credit markets away from caveat emptor. Laws regulating retail installment lending had a similar political motivation (Mors 1950). Prudential measures often function to make some market actors more trustworthy and others less vulnerable.

A second parallel between money and credit concerns fungibility (the homogeneity and interchangeability of modern money). Every genuine $100 bill has the same purchasing power, and all are equally capable of satisfying a $100 debt. A person who borrows a car is supposed to return the same vehicle, but a person who borrows $100 does not have to repay the exact same bill. Money is fungible, but cars are not. Fungibility gives money the generalized purchasing power that makes it so useful, but this can also be a problem. Fungibility means that the money given to Sam by his mother to pay for a haircut can be surreptitiously diverted to purchase candy.

From Zelizer, we know that users often inscribe into fungible money a set of distinctions that render it heterogenous. Money is classified (budgetarily, normatively, or cognitively) into different categories, and these disrupt the fungibility of money. Monetary distinctions reflect larger cultural distinctions and organizational commitments. The strength of these boundaries and the vigilance with which they must be maintained (e.g., sharp distinctions between "clean" and "dirty" money, or between monies earmarked for different budget items) derive from the underlying fungibility of modern money. Modern money is not special money, so people have to make it special.

In similar fashion, creditors often try to make their loans less fungible. Through loan contracts, indenture covenants, and other legal devices they turn generalized money (which could purchase anything) into special money (which can only buy one thing). These provisions also constrain debtors to make them more likely to repay. When loans come with "strings attached," these "strings" make money less fungible. Lenders, like mothers, do not want to see fungible money diverted from its intended purpose. Although modern money is fungible, those who use money restrain, domesticate, and differentiate it so as to negate this very feature. The ongoing tension between fungibility in law and specificity in practice suggests that the development of money and credit will reach no ultimate steady state or equilibrium. Both will continue to be standardized and individualized at the same time.

A third parallel concerns trust. Both money and credit pose and resolve issues of trust. The stakes for credit are most obvious: to lend, creditors must trust that debtors will repay. The problem for creditors is always specific: will this particular debtor repay within the agreed time? Trust is not a general attitude, nor an immutable characteristic: it is always situational (Heimer and Staffen 1998, 258). But creditors rarely face this problem alone, for an elaborate system of formal institutions, professional expertise, and informal relationships has developed that provides creditors with information, simplifies the credit problem, and ameliorates creditor vulnerability. The balance between formal and informal systems varies from one context to the next. Indeed, the contrast between American and Russian credit card institutions is what makes Guseva and Rona-Tas's (2001) comparative study so interesting. Sometimes creditors depend on embedded relationships, and sometimes they use impersonal institutions. The shift from one to the other displaced and transformed trust problems but did not make them disappear.

Consider a customer who wants to buy on credit. The seller could use his personal relationship with the customer, or the customer's reputation, to decide if the customer is trustworthy enough. But suppose that the customer is a complete stranger. The seller could insist on a formal contract and consult a credit-rating agency. But recourse to formal institutions does not make the trust problem disappear. In fact, the problem has only been shifted. Instead of wondering whether to trust the debtor, the seller must decide whether to trust the law and credit-raters. And how one evaluates legal institutions and suppliers of financial information differs from how one evaluates an individual customer.

Another possibility is for the seller to insist on cash. With a COD transaction, the seller need not worry about customer creditworthiness, the reliability of the courts, or the accuracy of credit raters. Has the issue of trust disappeared? No, for now the question is whether the seller trusts money, which depends on collective, self-reinforcing beliefs about others' trust of money. Network externalities make the creation of such beliefs, and establishment of trust, a complex rhetorical and institutional process.

A final point of comparison between money and credit returns to negotiability. Money is a freely transferable claim on value. By contrast, debt claims are harder and sometimes impossible to transfer. The more negotiable and hence transferable debt is, the more it functions like money. Although this term possesses a particular legal meaning (see Holden 1955, 25), and although its evolution marks one of the more abstruse chapters in legal history, the emergence of negotiability constitutes a fundamental transformation in relations of obligation.

Consider three couples who socialize at each other's houses, trying to balance over time the number of invitations each couple extends to the others. Suppose couple A has been to couple B's house more than vice versa and so "owes" them a dinner. In addition, couple C "owes" an invitation to couple A. Two social obligations exist, from A to B, and from C to A. In American culture, these obligations are nontransferable. One cannot imagine couple A satisfying their obligation to B by giving them couple C's obligation, in other words, by arranging for C to host B. These obligations are personal and cannot be assigned to others.

In traditional common law, debts were like social obligations. As "choses in action," they were not legally transferable. The rights a creditor possessed over a particular debtor could not be given, sold, or otherwise alienated (Holden 1955, 13, 17; Johnson 1963, 20). And yet it was extremely useful to be able to satisfy obligations to one's creditors by using obligations to oneself. The incentive to transfer debts was greatest among merchants, and a kind of de facto transferability emerged first within commercial practice, then within the law merchant, and finally within the common law (Kerridge 1988, 41, 71). In England, the doctrine of negotiability was worked out and applied to financial instruments at the end of the seventeenth century (Holden 1955, 30). In the United States, further developments occurred during the nineteenth century (Banner 1998, 235–36; Horwitz 1977, 212–26), and later as states adopted a uniform Negotiable Instruments Law.

Negotiability entailed a shift away from direct, concrete relationships between specific individuals and toward abstract relationships between economic roles. With a negotiable instrument, the debtor owes whoever holds the instrument, not the person who originally loaned the money. Negotiability dislodges debts from the debtor-creditor dyads that create them, and gives them mobility. A single promissory note can satisfy multiple obligations, and as it circulates, it links transactions and traders into a network. Of course, direct relationships still matter, as Uzzi (1999) and Petersen and Rajan (1994) attest. But negotiability made credit markets more anonymous and interconnected.

A negotiable instrument acts like money except that its value depends on a particular debtor. A complex institutional apparatus can be deployed to estimate and ensure the creditworthiness of the debtor, and debts can be standardized to some extent, but the value of a particular debt eventually boils down to whether the particular debtor repays. Variably creditworthy debtors, and variable estimates of creditworthiness, introduce heterogeneity into negotiable instruments. Thus, they do not operate like uniform, standardized money. They function like special monies, not because of the imposition of earmarkings or cultural meanings, but rather because they vary with the encumbered debtor.

CONCLUSION

Knowing that social factors affect money and credit is a start, but economic sociology must now determine how and why these effects occur. Sociologists can make good analytic use of cross-national and historical variations in money and credit. The experience of transitional economies, the contrast between formal and informal economies, historical evidence from both developed and developing regions, and patterns of financial innovation in developed economies all illuminate the social dynamics of money and credit.

A number of research questions seem especially fruitful. One concerns the relationship between money, credit, and inequality. Differential access to money and credit means differential ability to command resources, and hence power differences. But many forms of money and credit exist, each associated with different kinds of inequality and producing overall effects that are not yet fully understood. This results in variable and shifting patterns of inequality rather than a monolithic domination of the disadvantaged by the advantaged. And continuous financial innovation will ensure new patterns of inequality in the future.

The importance of social relationships between debtors and creditors is a robust finding. Yet sociologists have only begun to understand this result. Why do relationships matter? Do they make creditors more trusting, debtors more trustworthy, or both? Which relationships matter most, and how does their strength affect credit? And how do relationships affect the cultural framing of transactions (whether money is a gift, investment, or show of support; see Miller 1986)? It is also important to put dyadic relationships into the context of networks. Indirect and third-party ties may have important effects in credit markets.

Although informal social relationships remain important, formal financial institutions have developed enormously. An entire apparatus produces quantitative information about creditworthiness. Credit raters now operate around the globe, and can sink corporate security prices with a single rat-ing downgrade. Credit agencies also determine whether individuals can borrow. For an industry that produces transparent information, their own activities are surprisingly opaque. Very little is known about the internal protocols and capacities of credit-raters (Stuart 2000), and we need to understand much more about the production and use of such "rationalized" information.

The relationship between formal and informal sectors seems especially complex in the case of money and credit. Sociologists have long appreciated the difference between the two, but no one has worked out the implications for credit. Most simply, formal and informal are substitutes, performing similar functions in different ways (e.g., informal credit and formal money both facilitate exchange). Or they may operate as nested constraints, in which formal arrangements set a range of possibilities within which informal factors unfold. Negotiability sanctions an entire class of legal transactions, but how people use negotiable instruments depends on other considerations. Sometimes the constraints go the other way, as when informal practices motivate change in formal procedures precisely because the two are decoupled.

Monetary innovation puts formal regulatory institutions like central banks, financial regulators, and deposit insurers into a situation of always playing catch-up. The result is not so much regulatory failure as an uneven and unstable articulation between financial markets and formal governance. The coevolution of national and international markets and institutions is well worth studying, especially given the emergence of global financial markets.

In researching money and credit, sociologists confront basic institutions of the modern economy, a major axis of power and inequality, an issue of ongoing political relevance, and a locus of meaning and signification. These topics have been a concern since the founding of sociology, but they show no signs of being exhausted.

NOTES

Thanks are due to Wendy Espeland, Ivan Light, Neil Smelser, Richard Swedberg, and members of the Economic Sociology Seminar at Northwestern for helpful comments, to Sung Kim for his research assistance, and as always thanks to the Lochinvar Society.

1. Such connotations are not universal. In contemporary Ghana people routinely acknowledge romantic relationships using money (Hart 2000, 210).

2. See also Padgett's (2001, 234–35) discussion of "translation rules."

3. Ingham outlines the politics of Britain's return to the gold standard in 1925 (Ingham 1984, 37).

4. It also institutionalized bias within the credit system. On discrimination against immigrant Jewish businesses, see Olegario 1999.

5. Debtors can also politicize credit. During the Civil War, both North and South pressured their banks to lend to the government. Such loans raised money for the state, but they also created a constituency with a financial interest in the regime's survival (Bodenhorn 2000, 231; Bensel 1990, 14, 163).

6. Simpson (1986, 141) argues that the pledging of land in England dates to the Anglo-Saxon era.

7. One form of credit used humans to collateralize loans (Lovejoy and Richardson 1999).

8. On the history of common-law debt contracts, see Baker 1979, 266–71.

9. The uniformity of terms within industries, and the variability between them, suggests that they are determined as much by social convention as by economic rationality (Fafchamps 1997; Foster 1935).

10. Similarly, social norms in rural Ireland prevented land from serving as collateral, and hence undermined rural credit cooperatives (Guinnane 1994).

REFERENCES

Alder, Ken. 1995. "A Revolution to Measure: The Political Economy of the Metric System in France." Pp. 39–71 in *The Values of Precision*, ed. M. Norton Wise. Princeton: Princeton University Press.

Alter, George, Claudia Goldin, and Elyce Rotella. 1994. "The Savings of Ordinary Americans: The Philadelphia Saving Fund Society in the Mid–Nineteenth Century." *Journal of Economic History* 54:735–67.

Anderson, B. L. 1970. "Money and the Structure of Credit in the Eighteenth Century." *Business History* 12(2): 85–101.

Anderson, Elizabeth. 1993. *Value in Ethics and Economics*, Cambridge: Harvard University Press.

Andre, Judith. 1992. "Blocked Exchanges: A Taxonomy." *Ethics* 103:29–47.

Anthony, Denise. 1997. "Micro-lending Institutions: Using Social Networks to Create Production Capabilities." *International Journal of Sociology and Social Policy* 17(7–8): 156–78.

Arhin, Kwame. 1976. "The Pressure of Cash and Its Political Consequences in Asante in the Colonial Period, 1900–1940." *Journal of African Studies* 3: 453–68.

Baker, Anita. 1977. "Community and Growth: Muddling through with Russian Credit Cooperatives." *Journal of Economic History* 37(1): 139–60.

Baker, J. H. 1979. *An Introduction to English Legal History*. 2d ed. London: Butterworths.

Baker, Wayne, and Jason Jimerson. 1992. "The Sociology of Money." *American Behavioral Scientist* 35: 678–93.

Balleisen, Edward J. 2001. *Navigating Failure: Bankruptcy and Commercial Society in Antebellum America*. Chapel Hill: University of North Carolina Press.

Banerjee, Abhijit V., and Eric S. Maskin. 1996. "A Walrasian Theory of Money and Barter." *Quarterly Journal of Economics* 111:955–1005.

Banner, Stuart. 1998. *Anglo-American Securities Regulation: Cultural and Political Roots, 1690–1860*. Cambridge: Cambridge University Press.

Barnes, R. H., and Ruth Barnes. 1989. "Barter and Money in an Indonesian Village Economy." *Man* 24:399–418.

Barth, Frederik. 1967. "Economic Spheres in Darfur." Pp. 149–89 in *Themes in Economic Anthropology*. London: Tavistock.

Barton, J. L. 1967. "The Common Law Mortgage." *Law Quarterly Review* 83:229–39.

Baskin, Jonathan Barron, and Paul J. Miranti Jr. 1997. *A History of Corporate Finance*. Cambridge: Cambridge University Press.

Bensel, Richard Franklin. 1990. *Yankee Leviathan: The Origins of Central State Authority in America, 1859–1877*. Cambridge: Cambridge University Press.

Berger, Allen N., and Gregory F. Udell. 1995. "Relationship Lending and Lines of Credit in Small Firm Finance." *Journal of Business* 68:351–81.

Berliner, Joseph. 1950. "Monetary Planning in the USSR." *American Slavic and East European Review* 9(4): 237–54.

Berman, Constance Hoffman. 1982. "Land Acquisition and the Use of the Mortgage Contract by the Cistercians of Berdoues." *Speculum* 57:250–66.

Beveridge, Andrew A. 1985. "Local Lending Practice: Borrowers in Small Northeastern Industrial City, 1832–1915." *Journal of Economic History* 45: 393–403.

Biggart, Nicole Woolsey. 2001. "Banking on Each Other: The Situational Logic of Rotating Savings and Credit Associations." *Advances in Qualitative Organization Research* 3:129–52.

Blomert, Reinhard. 2001. "Sociology of Finance: Old and New Perspectives." *Economic Sociology: European Electronic Newsletter* 2(2): 9–14.

Bloomfield, Arthur I. 1959. *Monetary Policy under the International Gold Standard: 1880–1914*. New York: Federal Reserve Bank of New York.

Bodenhorn, Howard. 2000. *A History of Banking in Antebellum America: Financial Markets and Economic Development in an Era of Nation-Building*. Cambridge: Cambridge University Press.

Bohannan, Paul. 1959. "The Impact of Money on an African Subsistence Economy." *Journal of Economic History* 19:491–503.

Bordo, Michael D. 1995. "The Gold Standard as a Rule: An Essay in Exploration." *Explorations in Economic History* 32:423–64.

Breckenridge, Keith. 1995. "'Money with Dignity': Migrants, Minelords, and the Cultural Politics of the South African Gold Standard Crisis, 1920–33." *Journal of African History* 36:271–304.

Breen, T. H. 1985. *Tobacco Culture: The Mentality of the Great Tidewater Planters on the Eve of Revolution.* Princeton: Princeton University Press.

Brettell, Caroline B. 1999. "Moral Economy or Political Economy? Property and Credit Markets in 19th Century Rural Portugal." *Journal of Historical Sociology,* 12:1–28.

Brewer, H. Peers. 1976. "Eastern Money and Western Mortgages in the 1870s." *Business History Review* 50:357–80.

Briloff, Abraham J. 1972. *Unaccountable Accounting.* New York: Harper and Row.

Burley, David. 1987. "'Good for All He Would Ask': Credit and Debt in the Transition to Industrial Capitalism—The Case of Mid–Nineteenth Century Brantford, Ontario." *Histoire Sociale—Social History* 20:79–99.

Burt, Ronald S. 1992. *Structural Holes.* Cambridge: Harvard University Press.

Calavita, Kitty, Henry N. Pontell, and Robert H. Tillman. 1997. *Big Money Crime: Fraud and Politics in the Savings and Loan Crisis.* Berkeley and Los Angeles: University of California Press.

Calder, Lendol. 1999. *Financing the American Dream: A Cultural History of Consumer Credit.* Princeton: Princeton University Press.

Calomiris, Charles W., and Carlos D. Ramirez. 1996. "The Role of Financial Relationships in the History of American Corporate Finance." *Journal of Applied Corporate Finance* 9(2): 52–73.

Cantor, Richard, and Frank Packer. 1995. "The Credit Rating Industry." *Journal of Fixed Income* 5(3): 10–34.

Carlin, Wendy, Steven Fries, Mark Schaffer, and Paul Seabright. 2000. "Barter and Non-monetary Transactions in Transition Economies: Evidence from a Cross-Country Survey." European Bank for Reconstruction and Development Working Paper No. 50, London.

Carruthers, Bruce G. 1996. *City of Capital: Politics and Markets in the English Financial Revolution.* Princeton: Princeton University Press.

Carruthers Bruce G., and Sarah Babb. 1996. "The Color of Money and the Nature of Value: Greenbacks and Gold in Postbellum America." *American Journal of Sociology* 101:1556–91.

Carruthers, Bruce G., Sarah Babb, and Terence C. Halliday. 2001. "Institutionalizing Markets, or the Market for Institutions? Central Banks, Bankruptcy Laws, and the Globalization of Financial Markets." Pp. 194–226 in *The Rise of Neoliberalism and Institutional Analysis,* ed. John L. Campbell and Ove K. Pedersen. Princeton: Princeton University Press.

Carruthers, Bruce G., and Wendy Nelson Espeland. 1991. "Accounting for Rationality: Double-Entry Bookkeeping and the Rhetoric of Economic Rationality." *American Journal of Sociology* 97:31–69.

———. 1998. "Money, Meaning, and Morality." *American Behavioral Scientist* 41:1384–1408.

Carruthers, Bruce G., and Terence C. Halliday. 1998. *Rescuing Business: The Making of Corporate Bankruptcy Law in England and the United States.* Oxford: Clarendon Press.

Carruthers, Bruce G., and Arthur L. Stinchcombe. 1999. "The Social Structure of Liquidity: Flexibility in Markets and States." *Theory and Society* 28: 353–82.

Chandler, Alfred, Jr., and Herman Daems. 1979. "Administrative Coordination, Allocation, and Monitoring." *Accounting, Organizations, and Society* 4:3–20.

Clark, Christopher. 1990. *The Roots of Rural Capitalism: Western Massachusetts, 1780–1860.* Ithaca, N.Y.: Cornell University Press.

Clements, Roger V. 1955. "British Investment and American Legislative Restrictions in the Trans-Mississippi West, 1880–1900." *Mississippi Valley Historical Review* 42:207–28.

Cohen, Edward E. 1992. *Athenian Economy and Society: A Banking Perspective.* Princeton: Princeton University Press.

Cohen, Patricia Cline. 1982. *A Calculating People: The Spread of Numeracy in Early America.* Chicago: University of Chicago Press.

Coleman, Peter J. 1965. "The Insolvent Debtor in Rhode Island, 1745–1828." *William and Mary Quarterly* 22:413–34.

Cook, Walter Wheeler. 1916. "The Alienability of Choses in Action." *Harvard Law Review* 29:816–37.

Cooley, Charles H. 1913. "The Sphere of Pecuniary Valuation." *American Journal of Sociology* 19:188–203.

Copeland, Morris A. 1981. "Bank Deposit Currency before A.D. 1700." *Research in Economic History* 6: 245–54.

Crosby, Alfred W. 1997. *The Measure of Reality: Quantification and Western Society, 1250–1600.* Cambridge: Cambridge University Press.

Crump, Thomas. 1978. "Money and Number: The Trojan Horse of Language." *Man* 13:503–18.

David, Guy. 1986. "Money in Canadian Law." *Canadian Bar Review* 65:192–223.

Davis, Natalie Zemon. 2000. *The Gift in Sixteenth-Century France.* Madison: University of Wisconsin Press.

Defoe, Daniel. [1726] 1987. *The Complete English Tradesman.* Gloucester: Alan Sutton.

Dodd, Nigel. 1994. *The Sociology of Money.* Oxford: Polity Press.

Dupre, Marie-Claude. 1995. "Raphia Monies among the Teke: Their Origin and Control." Pp. 39–52 in *Money Matters: Instability, Values and Social Payments in the Modern History of West African Communities,* ed. Jane I. Guyer. Portsmouth, N.H.: Heinemann.

Earle, Peter. 1989. *The Making of the English Middle Class.* Berkeley and Los Angeles: University of California Press.

Earling, P. R. 1890. *Whom to Trust: A Practical Treatise on Mercantile Credits.* Chicago: Rand, McNally.

Eaton, Jonathan. 1993. "Sovereign Debt: A Primer." *World Bank Economic Review* 7(2): 137–72.

Eichengreen, Barry. 1999. *Toward a New International Financial Architecture: A Practical Post-Asia Agenda*. Washington, D.C.: Institute for International Economics.

Espeland, Wendy Nelson, and Mitchell Stevens. 1998. "Commensuration as a Social Process." *Annual Review of Sociology* 24:313–43.

Evans, David, and Richard Schmalensee. 1999. *Paying with Plastic: The Digital Revolution in Buying and Borrowing*. Cambridge: MIT Press.

Fafchamps, Marcel. 1997. "Trade Credit in Zimbabwean Manufacturing." *World Development* 25:795–815.

Falola, Toyin. 1993. "My Friend the Shylock: Money-Lenders and Their Clients in South-Western Nigeria." *Journal of African History* 34:403–23.

———. 1995. "Money and Informal Credit Institutions in Colonial Western Nigeria." Pp. 162–87 in *Money Matters: Instability, Values, and Social Payments in the Modern History of West African Communities*, ed. Jane I. Guyer. Portsmouth, N.H.: Heinemann.

Ferguson, James. 1992. "The Cultural Topography of Wealthy: Commodity Paths and the Structure of Property in Rural Lesotho." *American Anthropology* 94:55–73.

Ferreira, Mariana Kawall Leal. 1997. "When 1 + 1 ≠ 2: Making Mathematics in Central Brazil." *American Ethnologist* 24:132–47.

Flam, Helena. 1985. "Democracy in Debt: Credit and Politics in Paterson, N.J., 1890–1930." *Journal of Social History* 18:439–62.

Flandreau, Marc. 1996. "The French Crime of 1873: An Essay on the Emergence of the International Gold Standard, 1870–1880." *Journal of Economic History* 56:862–97.

Fligstein, Neil. 2001. *The Architecture of Markets: An Economic Sociology of Twenty-first-Century Capitalist Markets*. Princeton: Princeton University Press.

Foster, LeBaron R. 1935. "International Credit Costs and the Consumer." *Journal of Business* 8:27–45.

Freyer, Tony. 1982. "Antebellum Commercial Law." *Kentucky Law Journal* 70:593–608.

Gelpi, Rosa-Maria, and François Julien-Labruyère. 2000. *The History of Consumer Credit: Doctrines and Practices*. Trans. Mn Liam Gavin. London: Macmillan.

Gerriets, Marilyn. 1985. "Money in Early Christian Ireland according to the Irish Laws." *Comparative Studies in Society and History* 27:323–39.

Gorton, Gary. 1996. "Reputation Formation in Early Bank Note Markets." *Journal of Political Economy* 104:346–97.

Grassby, Richard. 1995. *The Business Community of Seventeenth-Century England*. Cambridge: Cambridge University Press.

Greif, Avner. 1993. "Contract Enforceability and Economic Institutions in Early Trade: The Maghribi Traders' Coalition." *American Economic Review* 83: 525–48.

Grierson, Philip. 1977. *The Origins of Money*. London: Athlone Press.

Guinnane, Timothy W. 1994. "A Failed Institutional Transplant: Raiffeisen's Credit Cooperatives in Ireland, 1894–1914." *Explorations in Economic History* 31:38–61.

———. 2001. "Cooperatives as Information Machines: German Rural Credit Cooperatives, 1883–1914." *Journal of Economic History* 61:366–90.

Guseva, Alya, and Akos Rona-Tas. 2001. "Uncertainty, Risk, and Trust: Russian and American Credit Card Markets Compared." *American Sociological Review* 66:623–46.

Guyer, Jane I. 1995. "Introduction: The Currency Interface and Its Dynamics." Pp. 1–33 in *Money Matters: Instability, Values, and Social Payments in the Modern History of West African Communities*, ed. Jane I. Guyer. Portsmouth, N.H.: Heinemann.

Hacking, Ian. 1990. *The Taming of Chance*. Cambridge: Cambridge University Press.

Hadden, Richard W. 1994. *On the Shoulders of Merchants: Exchange and the Mathematical Conception of Nature in Early Modern Europe*. Albany: State University of New York Press.

Haeger, John Denis. 1979. "Eastern Financiers and Institutional Change: The Origins of the New York Life Insurance and Trust Company and the Ohio Life Insurance and Trust Company." *Journal of Economic History* 39:259–73.

Ham, Arthur H., and Leonard G. Robinson. 1923. *A Credit Union Primer*. New York: Russell Sage Foundation.

Hancock, David. 1995. *Citizens of the World: London Merchants and the Integration of the British Atlantic Community, 1735–1785*. Cambridge: Cambridge University Press.

Hart, Keith. 2000. *Money in an Unequal World*. New York: Texere.

Heimer, Carol A. 2001. "Solving the Problem of Trust." Pp. 40–88 in *Trust in Society*, ed. Karen S. Cook. New York: Russell Sage Foundation.

Heimer, Carol A., and Lisa R. Staffen. 1998. *For the Sake of the Children: The Social Organization of Responsibility in the Hospital and the Home*. Chicago: University of Chicago Press.

Helleiner, Eric. 1998. "Electronic Money: A Challenge to the Sovereign State?" *Journal of International Affairs* 51:387–409.

Helmholz, R. H. 1986. "Usury and the Medieval English Church Courts." *Speculum* 61:364–80.

Hendley, Kathryn. 1999. "How Russian Enterprises Cope with Payment Problems." *Post-Soviet Affairs* 15:201–34.

———. 2001. "Beyond the Tip of the Iceberg: Business Disputes in Russia." Pp. 20–55 in *Assessing the Value of Law in Transition Economies*, ed. Peter Murrell. Ann Arbor: University of Michigan Press.

Hilkey, Judy. 1997. *Character Is Capital: Success Manu-*

als and Manhood in Gilded Age America. Chapel Hill: University of North Carolina Press.

Hoagland, Edward. 2002. *Notes from the Century Before: A Journal from British Columbia.* New York: Modern Library.

Hoffman, Philip T., Gilles Postel-Vinay, and Jean-Laurent Rosenthal. 2000. *Priceless Markets: The Political Economy of Credit in Paris, 1660–1870.* Chicago: University of Chicago Press.

Hogendorn, Jan, and Marion Johnson. 1986. *The Shell Money of the Slave Trade.* Cambridge: Cambridge University Press.

Holden, J. Milnes. 1955. *The History of Negotiable Instruments in English Law.* London: Athlone Press.

Holmes, George K. 1892. "Usury in Law, in Practice, and in Psychology." *Political Science Quarterly* 7:431–67.

Hoppit, Julian. 1987. *Risk and Failure in English Business, 1700–1800.* Cambridge: Cambridge University Press.

Horwitz, Morton J. 1977. *The Transformation of American Law, 1780–1860.* Cambridge: Harvard University Press.

Howgego, Christopher. 1992. "The Supply and Use of Money in the Roman World, 200 B.C. to A.D. 300." *Journal of Roman Studies* 82:1–31.

Humphrey, Caroline. 1985. "Barter and Economic Disintegration." *Man* 20:48–72.

Hunt, Margaret R. 1996. *The Middling Sort: Commerce, Gender, and the Family in England, 1680–1780.* Berkeley and Los Angeles: University of California Press.

Hurst, James Willard. 1973. *A Legal History of Money in the United States, 1774–1970.* Lincoln: University of Nebraska Press.

Ingham, Geoffrey. 1984. *Capitalism Divided? The City and Industry in British Social Development.* New York: Schocken.

———. 1999. "Capitalism, Money, and Banking: A Critique of Recent Historical Sociology." *British Journal of Sociology* 50:76–96.

Inikori, Joseph E. 1990. "The Credit Needs of the African Trade and the Development of the Credit Economy in England." *Explorations in Economic History* 27:197–231.

Jackson, Kenneth T. 1985. *Crabgrass Frontier: The Suburbanization of the United States.* Oxford: Oxford University Press.

Jackson, Thomas H. 1986. *The Logic and Limits of Bankruptcy Law.* Cambridge: Harvard University Press.

James, Francis Godwin. 1948. "Charity Endowments as Sources of Local Credit in Seventeenth- and Eighteenth-Century England." *Journal of Economic History* 8:153–70.

James, John A. 1978. *Money and Capital Markets in Postbellum America.* Princeton: Princeton University Press.

Jensen, Raymond. 1972. "Mortgage Standardization:

History of Interaction of Economics, Consumerism, and Governmental Pressure." *Real Property, Probate, and Trust Journal* 7:397–434.

Johnson, Herbert Alan. 1963. *The Law Merchant and Negotiable Instruments in Colonial New York, 1664 to 1730.* Chicago: Loyola University Press.

Johnson, Howard. 1986. "'A Modified Form of Slavery': The Credit and Truck Systems in the Bahamas in the Nineteenth and Early Twentieth Centuries." *Comparative Studies in Society and History* 28:729–53.

Johnson, Juliet. 2000. *A Fistful of Rubles: The Rise and Fall of the Russian Banking System.* Ithaca, N.Y.: Cornell University Press.

Johnson, Marion. 1970. "The Cowrie Currencies of West Africa, Part I." *Journal of African History* 11(1): 17–49.

Jonakin, Jon, and Laura J. Enriquez. 1999. "The Nontraditional Financial Sector in Nicaragua." *Development Policy Review* 17:141–69.

Jones, Robert A. 1976. "The Origin and Development of Media Exchange." *Journal of Political Economy.* 84:757–75.

Jordan, William Chester. 1993. *Women and Credit in Pre-industrial and Developing Societies.* Philadelphia: University of Pennsylvania Press.

Kali, Raja. 2001. "Business Networks in Transition Economies: Norms, Contracts, and Legal Institutions." Pp. 211–28 in *Assessing the Value of Law in Transition Economies*, ed. Peter Murrell. Ann Arbor: University of Michigan Press.

Kaye, Joel. 1998. *Economy and Nature in the Fourteenth Century: Money, Market Exchange, and the Emergence of Scientific Thought.* Cambridge: Cambridge University Press.

Keister, Lisa A. 2001. "Exchange Structures in Transition: Lending and Trade Relations in Chinese Business Groups." *American Sociological Review* 66:336–60.

———. 2002. "Financial Markets, Money, and Banking." *Annual Review of Sociology* 28:39–61.

Keller, Morton. 1963. *The Life Insurance Enterprise, 1885–1910: A Study in the Limits of Corporate Power.* Cambridge: Harvard University Press.

Kendall, Leon T. 1996. "Securitization: A New Era in American Finance." Pp. 1–16 in *A Primer on Securitization*, ed. Leon T. Kendall and Michael J. Fishman. Cambridge: MIT Press.

Kerridge, Eric. 1988. *Trade and Banking in Early Modern England.* Manchester: Manchester University Press.

Kerwer, Dieter. 2001. "Standardising as Governance: The Case of Credit Rating Agencies." Bonn: Max-Planck-Projektgruppe Recht der Gemeinschaftsgüter.

Klink, Dennis R. 1991. "Tracing a Trace: The Identity of Money in a Legal Doctrine," *Semiotica* 83:1–31.

Konig, David Thomas. 1979. *Law and Society in Puritan Massachusetts, Essex County, 1629–1692.* Chapel Hill: University of North Carolina Press.

Ladd, Helen F. 1998. "Evidence on Discrimination in

Mortgage Lending." *Journal of Economic Perspectives* 12:41–62.

Lamoreaux, Naomi. 1994. *Insider Lending: Banks, Personal Connections, and Economic Development in New England.* Cambridge: Cambridge University Press.

Landa, Janet Tai. 1994. *Trust, Ethnicity, and Identity: Beyond the New Institutional Economics of Ethnic Trading Networks, Contract Law, and Gift-Exchange.* Ann Arbor: University of Michigan Press.

La Porta, Raphael, Florencio Lopez-de-Silanes, Andrei Shleifer, and Robert W. Vishny. 1998. "Law and Finance." *Journal of Political Economy* 106:1113–55.

Lave, Jean. 1988. *Cognition in Practice: Mind, Mathematics, and Culture in Everyday Life.* Cambridge: Cambridge University Press.

Levi, Margaret. 1989. *Of Rule and Revenue.* Berkeley and Los Angeles: University of California Press.

Levine, Ross. 1998. "The Legal Environment, Banks, and Long-Run Economic Growth." *Journal of Money, Credit, and Banking* 30:596–613.

Leyshon, Andrew, and Nigel Thrift. 1997. *Money/Space: Geographies of Monetary Transformation.* London: Routledge.

———. 1999. "Lists Come Alive: Electronic Systems of Knowledge and the Rise of Credit-Scoring in Retail Banking." *Economy and Society* 28:434–66.

Light, Ivan, and Edna Bonacich. 1988. *Immigrant Entrepreneurs: Koreans in Los Angeles, 1965–1982.* Berkeley and Los Angeles: University of California Press.

Little, Lester K. 1978. *Religious Poverty and the Profit Economy in Medieval Europe.* Ithaca, N.Y.: Cornell University Press.

Lopez, Robert S., and Irving W. Raymond. 1990. *Medieval Trade in the Mediterranean World.* New York: Columbia University Press.

Loriaux, Michael. 1991. *France after Hegemony: International Change and Financial Reform.* Ithaca, N.Y.: Cornell University Press.

Lovejoy, Paul E. 1974. "Interregional Monetary Flows in the Precolonial Trade of Nigeria." *Journal of African History* 15:563–85.

Lovejoy, Paul E., and David Richardson. 1999. "Trust, Pawnship, and Atlantic History: The Institutional Foundations of the Old Calabar Slave Trade." *American Historical Review* 104:333–55.

Lynd, Robert S., and Helen Merrell Lynd. 1929. *Middletown: A Study in Modern American Culture.* New York: Harcourt Brace.

Lynn, Robert A. 1957. "Installment Credit before 1870." *Business History Review* 31:414–24.

Madison, James H. 1974. "The Evolution of Commercial Credit Reporting Agencies in Nineteenth-Century America." *Business History Review* 48:164–86.

Mann, Bruce H. 1987. *Neighbors and Strangers: Law and Community in Early Connecticut.* Chapel Hill: University of North Carolina Press.

Martin, David. 1977. "The Changing Role of Foreign Money in the United States, 1782–1857." *Journal of Economic History* 37:1009–1027.

Marx, Karl. 1976. *Capital.* Vol. 1. New York: Vintage.

Massey, Douglas, and Nancy Denton. 1993. *American Apartheid.* Cambridge: Harvard University Press.

McIntosh, Marjorie. 1989. "Money Lending on the Periphery of London, 1300–1600." *Albion* 20:557–71.

McNamara, Kathleen R. 1998. *The Currency of Ideas: Monetary Politics in the European Union.* Ithaca, N.Y.: Cornell University Press.

Menninger, Karl. 1969. *Number Words and Number Systems: A Cultural History of Numbers.* Trans. Paul Broneer. New York: Dover.

Miller, Peter. 1994. "Accounting as Social and Institutional Practice: An Introduction." Pp. 1–39 in *Accounting as Social and Institutional Practice,* ed. Anthony Hopwood and Peter Miller. Cambridge: Cambridge University Press.

Miller, William Ian. 1986. "Gift, Sale, Payment, Raid: Case Studies in the Negotiation and Classification of Exchange in Medieval Iceland." *Speculum* 61: 18–50.

Mintz, Sydney W. 1961. "Standards of Value and Units of Measure in the Fond-des-Negres Market Place, Haiti." *Journal of the Royal Anthropological Institute of Great Britain and Ireland* 91(1): 23–38.

Miskimin, Harry A. 1967. "Two Reforms of Charlemagne? Weights and Measures in the Middle Ages." *Economic History Review* 20(1): 35–52.

Mitchell, Wesley C. *Gold, Prices, and Wages under the Greenback Standard.* Berkeley: University Press.

Mors, Wallace P. 1950. "State Regulation of Retail Instalment Financing—Progress and Problems." *Journal of Business* 23:199–218.

Moulton, H. G. 1920. "Commercial Credit or Discount Companies." *Journal of Political Economy* 28:827–39.

Muldrew, Craig. 1998. *The Economy of Obligation: The Culture of Credit and Social Relations in Early Modern England.* Houndmills: Macmillan.

Munnell, Alicia H., Geoffrey M. B. Tootell, Lynn E. Browne, and James McEneaney. 1996. "Mortgage Lending in Boston: Interpreting HMDA Data." *American Economic Review* 86:25–53.

Neifield, M. R. 1931. "Credit Unions in the United States." *Journal of Business* 4:320–45.

Nelson, Benjamin. 1969. *The Idea of Usury.* 2d ed. Chicago: University of Chicago Press.

Newburgh, Conrad. 1991. "Character Assessment in the Lending Process." *Journal of Commercial Bank Lending,* April, 34–39.

Nightingale, Pamela. 1990. "Monetary Contraction and Mercantile Credit in Later Medieval England." *Economic History Review* 43:560–75.

Nove, Alec. 1989. *An Economic History of the U.S.S.R.* 2d ed. Harmondsworth: Penguin.

Nugent, Rolf. 1934. "Small Loan Debt in the United States." *Journal of Business of the University of Chicago* 7:1–21.

Olegario, Rowena. 1998. "Credit and Business Culture: The American Experience in the Nineteenth Century." Ph.D. diss., Harvard University.

———. 1999. "'Mysterious People': Jewish Merchants,

Transparency, and Community in Mid–Nineteenth Century America." *Business History Review* 73: 161–89.

Olmstead, Alan L. 1976. *New York City Mutual Savings Banks, 1819–1861*. Chapel Hill: University of North Carolina Press.

Olney, Martha L. 1999. "Avoiding Default: The Role of Credit in the Consumption Collapse of 1930." *Quarterly Journal of Economics* 114:319–35.

Orlean, Andre. 1992. "Origin of Money." Pp. 113–43 in *Understanding Origins: Contemporary Views on the Origin of Life, Mind and Society*, ed. Francisco J. Varela and Jean-Pierre Dupuy. Dordbrecht: Kluwer Academic Publishers.

Ottati, Gabi Dei. 1994. "Trust, Interlinking Transactions, and Credit in the Industrial District." *Cambridge Journal of Economics* 18:529–46.

Padgett, John F. 2001. "Organizational Genesis, Identity, and Control: The Transformation of Banking in Renaissance Florence." Pp. 211–57 in *Networks and Markets*, ed. James E. Rauch and Alessandra Casella. New York: Russell Sage Foundation.

Parker, Geoffrey. 1973. *The Emergence of Modern Finance in Europe, 1500–1730*. London: Fontana.

Parsons, Talcott. 1982. *On Institutions and Social Evolution*. Chicago: University of Chicago Press.

Perrow, Charles. 2002. *Organizing America: Wealth, Power, and the Origins of Corporate Capitalism*. Princeton: Princeton University Press.

Petersen, Mitchell A., and Raghuram G. Rajan. 1994. "The Benefits of Lending Relationships: Evidence from Small Business Data." *Journal of Finance* 49:3–37.

Phelps, Clyde William. 1951. "The Social Control of Consumer Credit Costs: A Case Study." *Social Forces* 29:433–42.

Pitt, Mark M., and Shahidur R. Khandker. 1998. "The Impact of Group-Based Credit Programs on Poor Households in Bangladesh: Does the Gender of Participants Matter?" *Journal of Political Economy* 106:958–96.

Pixley, Jocelyn. 1999. "Impersonal Trust in Global Mediating Organizations." *Sociological Perspectives* 42: 647–71.

Porter, Theodore. 1995. *Trust in Numbers: The Pursuit of Objectivity in Science and Public Life*. Princeton: Princeton University Press.

Prasad, Monica. 1999. "The Morality of Market Exchange: Love, Money, and Contractual Justice." *Sociological Perspectives* 42:181–214.

Prendergast, William A. 1906. *Credit and Its Uses*. New York: D. Appleton.

Priest, Claire. 2001. "Currency Policies and Legal Development in Colonial New England." *Yale Law Journal* 110:1303–1405.

Pryor, John H. 1977. "The Origins of the Commenda Contract." *Speculum* 52:5–37.

Reeder, John. 1973. "Corporate Loan Financing in the Seventeenth and Eighteenth Centuries." *Anglo-American Law Review* 2:487–526.

Robinson, Louis N., and Rolf Nugent. 1935. *Regulation of the Small Loan Business*. New York: Russell Sage Foundation.

Rodgers, Churchill. 1965. "The Corporate Trust Indenture Project." *Business Lawyer* 20:551–71.

Rosen, Deborah A. 1997. *Courts and Commerce: Gender, Law, and the Market Economy in Colonial New York*. Columbus: Ohio State University Press.

Roseveare, Henry. 1991. *The Financial Revolution, 1660–1760*. London: Longman.

Santiso, Javier. 1999. "Analysts Analyzed: A Socioeconomic Approach to Financial and Emerging Markets." *International Political Science Review* 20:307–30.

Sharkey, Robert P. 1959. *Money, Class, and Party: An Economic Study of Civil War and Reconstruction*. Baltimore: Johns Hopkins University Press.

Sharma, R. S. 1965. "Usury in Early Mediaeval India (A.D. 400–1200)." *Comparative Studies in Society and History* 8:56–77.

Shipton, Parker. 1989. *Bitter Money: Cultural Economy and Some African Meanings of Forbidden Commodities*. Washington, D.C.: American Ethnological Society.

Simmel, Georg. 1991. "Money in Modern Culture." *Theory, Culture, and Society* 8:17–31.

Simpson, A. W. Brian. 1986. *A History of the Land Law*. 2d ed. Oxford: Oxford University Press.

Skeel, David A., Jr. 2001. *Debt's Dominion: A History of Bankruptcy Law in America*. Princeton: Princeton University Press.

Smith, Clifford W., Jr., and Jerold B. Warner. 1979. "On Financial Contracting: An Analysis of Bond Covenants." *Journal of Financial Economics* 7: 117–61.

Snowden, Kenneth A. 1995. "The Evolution of Interregional Mortgage Lending Channels, 1870–1940." Pp. 209–56 in *Coordination and Information: Historical Perspectives on Organization of Enterprise*, ed. Naomi R. Lamoreaux and Daniel M. G. Raff. Chicago: University of Chicago Press.

Spruyt, Hendrik. 1994. *The Sovereign State and Its Competitors*. Princeton: Princeton University Press.

Spufford, Peter. 1988. *Notes on Money and Its Use in Medieval Europe*. Cambridge: Cambridge University Press.

Squires, Gregory D., and Sally O'Connor. 2001. *Color and Money: Politics and Prospects for Community Reinvestment in Urban America*. Albany: State University of New York Press.

Standard and Poor's. 2000. *Corporate Ratings Criteria*. New York: Standard and Poor's.

Sterling, Louis. 1995. "Partners: The Social Organization of Rotating Savings and Credit Societies among Exilic Jamaicans." *Sociology* 29:653–66.

Stiglitz, Joseph E. 1993. *Economics*. New York: W. W. Norton.

———. 2000. "The Contributions of the Economics of Information of Twentieth Century Economics." *Quarterly Journal of Economics* 115:1441–77.

Stinchcombe, Arthur L. 2001. *When Formality Works:*

Authority and Abstraction in Law and Organizations. Chicago: University of Chicago Press.

Stuart, Guy. 2000. "The Production and Interpretation of Information in the Mortgage Loan Application Process." *Chicago Policy Review* 41:23–38.

Sullivan, Teresa A., Elizabeth Warren, and Jay Lawrence Westbrook. 2000. *The Fragile Middle Class: Americans in Debt.* New Haven: Yale University Press.

Swedberg, Richard. 1998. *Max Weber and the Idea of Economic Sociology.* Princeton: Princeton University Press.

Sylla, Richard. 1976. "Forgotten Men of Money: Private Bankers in Early U.S. History." *Journal of Economic History* 36:173–88.

Sylla, Richard, and George David Smith. 1995. "Information and Capital Market Regulation in Anglo-American Finance." Pp. 17–56 in *Anglo-American Financial Systems: Institutions and Markets in the Twentieth Century*, ed. Michael Bordo and Richard Sylla. Burr Ridge, Ill.: Irwin Professional Publishing.

Thomas, Keith. 1987. "Numeracy in Early Modern England." *Transactions of the Royal Historical Society*, 5th ser., 37:103–32.

Thorp, Daniel B. 1991. "Doing Business in the Backcountry: Retail Trade in Colonial Rowan County, North Carolina." *William and Mary Quarterly* 48(3): 387–408.

Timberlake, Richard H., Jr. 1981. "The Significance of Unaccounted Currencies." *Journal of Economic History* 41:853–66.

Treacy, William F. 1998. "Credit Risk Rating at Large U.S. Banks." *Federal Reserve Bulletin*, November, 898–921.

Treisman, Daniel. 1995. "The Politics of Soft Credit in Post-Soviet Russia." *Europe-Asia Studies* 47:949–76.

Twyman, Robert W. 1954. *History of Marshall Field & Co., 1852–1906.* Philadelphia: University of Pennsylvania Press.

Udovitch, Abraham L. 1962. "At the Origins of the Western *Commenda*: Islam, Israel, Byzantium?" *Speculum* 37:198–207.

Udry, Christopher. 1994. "Risk and Insurance in a Rural Credit Market: An Empirical Investigation in Northern Nigeria." *Review of Economic Studies* 61: 495–526.

Unger, Irwin. 1964. *The Greenback Era.* Princeton: Princeton University Press.

Uzzi, Brian. 1999. "Social Relations and Networks in the Making of Financial Capital." *American Sociological Review* 64:481–505.

Van Fenstermaker, J. 1965. *The Development of American Commercial Banking: 1782–1837.* Kent, Ohio: Kent State University Press.

Verdery, Katherine. 1995. "'Caritas': And the Reconceptualization of Money in Romania." *Anthropology Today* 11(1): 3–7.

Weber, Max. 1978. *Economy and Society.* Ed. Guenther Roth and Claus Wittich. Trans. Ephraim Fischoff et al. Berkeley and Los Angeles: University of California Press.

———. 1981. *General Economic History.* Trans. Frank Knight. New Brunswick, N.J.: Transaction Books.

Webley, Paul, and Stephen E. G. Lea. 1993. "The Partial Unacceptability of Money in Repayment of Neighborly Help." *Human Relations* 46(1): 65–76.

Weinberg, Harold. 1982. "Commercial Paper in Economic Theory and Legal History." *Kentucky Law Journal* 70:567–92.

Weir, David R. 1989. "Tontines, Public Finance, and Revolution in France and England, 1688–1789." *Journal of Economic History* 49:95–124.

Wiley, Norbert. 1967. "America's Unique Class Politics: The Interplay of the Labor, Credit, and Commodity Markets." *American Sociological Review* 32: 529–41.

Winn, Jane Kaufman. 1994. "Relational Practices and the Marginalization of Law: Informal Financial Practices of Small Businesses in Taiwan." *Law and Society Review* 28:193–232.

Wise, M. Norton. 1995. Introduction. Pp. 1–13 in *The Values of Precision*, ed. M. Norton Wise. Princeton: Princeton University Press.

Woo, Jung-En. 1991. *Race to the Swift: State and Finance in Korean Industrialization.* New York: Columbia University Press.

Woodman, Harold D. 1995. *New South—New Law: The Legal Foundations of Credit and Labor Relations in the Postbellum Agricultural South.* Baton Rouge: Louisiana State University Press.

Woodruff, David M. 1999. *Money Unmade: Barter and the Fate of Russian Capitalism.* Ithaca, N.Y.: Cornell University Press.

Wright, Robert E. 1999. "Banker Ownership and Lending Patterns in New York and Pennsylvania, 1781–1831." *Business History Review* 73: 40–60.

Yates, JoAnne. 1989. *Control through Communications: The Rise of System in American Management.* Baltimore: Johns Hopkins University Press.

Yinger, John. 1995. *Closed Doors, Opportunities Lost: The Continuing Costs of Housing Discrimination.* New York: Russell Sage Foundation.

Zelizer, Viviana A. 1989. "The Social Meaning of Money: Special Monies." *American Journal of Sociology* 95:342–77.

———. 1994. *The Social Meaning of Money: Pin Money, Paychecks, Poor Relief, and Other Currencies.* New York: Basic Books.

———. 1996. "Payments and Social Ties." *Sociological Forum* 11:481–95.

———. 2002. "Intimate Transactions." Pp. 274–300 in *The New Economic Sociology*, ed. Mauro F. Guillén, Randall Collins, Paula England, and Marshall Meyer. New York: Russell Sage Foundation.

Zysman, John. 1983. *Governments, Markets, and Growth.* Ithaca, N.Y.: Cornell University Press.

17 Networks and Economic Life

Laurel Smith-Doerr and Walter W. Powell

SOCIOLOGISTS AND ANTHROPOLOGISTS have long been concerned with how individuals are linked to one another and how these bonds of affiliation serve as both a lubricant for getting things done and a glue that provides order and meaning to social life. The attention to networks of association, which began in earnest in the 1970s, provided welcome texture and dynamism to portraits of social life. This work stood in stark contrast to the reigning approaches in the social sciences. In contrast to deterministic cultural (oversocialized) accounts, network analysis afforded room for human agency, and in contrast to individualist, atomized (undersocialized) approaches, networks emphasized structure and constraint (Granovetter 1985). Network studies offered a middle ground, a third way, even if no one was quite sure whether networks were a metaphor, a method, or a theory (Barnes 1979). But the sociologists and anthropologists who initially studied networks to attend to the structural aspects of society (Mitchell 1969) did not pay sustained attention to economic activity, even though some industrial sociologists (Roy 1954; Dalton 1959) had long stressed the role of informal networks as an antidote to formal organization practices and structures.

Over the past two decades, however, there has been an enormous upsurge of interest in the role of networks in the economy. This sea change has occurred in the worlds of both practice and theory. Across the social sciences, from anthropology to sociology to political science to economics, there is research on the role of networks in shaping such diverse phenomena as migration, entrepreneurship, the viability of communities, and international trade. In the world of business, an appreciation for the role of both informal and organized networks has grown markedly. The late Bennett Harrison (1994) nicely summarized this trend with his quip: "Networking among companies is now in fashion all over the world." Networks provide three broad categories of benefits: access, timeliness, and referrals (Burt 1992). Ties can facilitate access to parties that provide information or resources. Linkages that generate access in an expeditious manner afford advantage over those that lack comparable connections. Referrals offer the opportunity to bypass formal, impersonal channels. Thus, the cumulative effects of networks on economic outcomes can be considerable indeed.

Much of the literature on networks emphasizes that they are most salient in a domain between the flexibility of markets and the visible hand of organizational authority (Powell 1990). Networks provide order to disconnected parts of organizations and markets (Burt 2000). The challenge for research on networks is to explain their emergence, activation, and durability. Networks, as Mark Granovetter (1985, 491) emphasized, "penetrate irregularly and in different degrees." Thus some individuals are better placed than others, some groups are more isolated, some formal organizations have more informal cliques, and some communities have more associational life. There is wide variability in the presence of linkages across multiple levels, and in when these connections are mobilized. We know a good deal more about the effects of networks than we know about the factors that generate, sustain, and reproduce them.[1]

The empirical terrain covered in the economic sociology literature ranges widely, including the following analyses of how networks influence economic activity.

1. Networks represent informal relationships in the workplace and labor market that shape work-related outcomes. Social ties and economic exchange can be deeply interwoven, such that purposive activity becomes "entangled" with friendship, reputation, and trust.

2. Networks are formal exchanges, either in the form of asset pooling or resource provision, between two or more parties that entail ongoing interaction in order to derive value from the exchange. These more formal network relationships may be forged out of mutual need, but can also lead to interde-

pendence and repeated interactions that reduce the need for formal control.

3. Networks are a relational form of governance in which authority is broadly dispersed; such arrangements are more commonly associated with settings where both markets and environments change frequently and there is a premium on adaptability. Much of the literature has celebrated this flexibility, but it is important to recognize that this form of organizing can be found in an entrepreneurial firm, a terrorist cell, an organization with extensive use of cross-functional groups, an international company with many cross-border alliances, or an illegal drug cartel. The flexibility of networks can be tapped for good or detriment.

Studies of these diverse forms of economic activity commonly share several key assumptions. First, the analytical focus is more on the nature of the relationships than on attributes of the actors. Second, attention is directed to location within the larger context in which information and resources flow. Finally, there are increasing returns to "investments" in relationships and position, which can produce rapid mobilization, cumulative advantage, or "lock-in." Our goal in this chapter is to survey the rapidly expanding empirical literature on networks and economic life, while emphasizing the conceptual and theoretical advances that this research draws on. To serve this dual aim, we begin first with a brief overview of key analytical tools used in network research.

A CONCEPTUAL TOOLKIT

In the first edition of this handbook we argued that two branches of the network literature on economic activity—one more focused on methods, a second more concerned with governance—had developed rather separately (Powell and Smith-Doerr 1994). One branch utilized increasingly sophisticated tools to analyze networks of social actors, building on diverse theoretical perspectives, ranging from neo-Marxist to rational choice. A second literature, more united in its theoretical orientation but less so in its data and methods, employed a network metaphor to characterize a form of economic organization in which organizations have flatter job hierarchies, permeable boundaries, and numerous connections to other organizations.[2] While this division of academic labor still persists, the manner in which network ties are conceptual-

ized can provide a common language that bridges multiple lines of research.

Network analysts use concepts of location, or nodes, and the relations among these positions—termed ties, connections, or links—to argue that the pattern of relationships shapes the behavior of the occupant of a post, as well as influences others (Marsden and Friedkin 1993). As Knoke (1990, 9) tells us, "A position's power—its ability to produce intended effects on the attitudes and behaviors of other actors—emerges from its prominence in networks where valued information and scarce resources are transferred from one actor to another." Practically, a variety of images depicting the relational structure of networks provides scholars with a toolkit of concepts to draw upon in both empirical and theoretical work.

The idea of a network invokes the image of connectedness between either individuals or organizations. The work of Georg Simmel provides the classic foundation in social theory for network analysis. Simmel argued for the importance of group composition to understanding fundamental aspects of social life. For example, he contended that the differential roles of laborers and employers in the economy were explained by group size. Employers lack the sense of solidarity that workers have because of "the smaller number of employers as compared to the number of workers; the larger the number of a given kind are involved, the more readily a general concept is formed" (Simmel [1922] 1955, 176). In addition to group size, Simmel pointed out the importance of the position of an individual actor within a group. He developed the idea of *tertius gaudens*, or the third who benefits (Simmel 1950). In a triad, a third person can play off the other two against each other, benefiting from their conflict, for example, if the two are buyers and the tertius is the seller. Merton (1957) elaborated Simmel's idea in his discussion of role-set theory, positing that there may be a downside to having multiple associates calling upon an individual's different roles at the same time (think of someone who is both a parent and an employee). One strategy that a tertius can use when two others issue conflicting demands is to make that role conflict known to the other parties; thus recognition of incompatible demands may provide room for autonomy. Burt (1992) has also built on Simmel's idea of *tertius gaudens* in his discussion of how a third who connects two others who are previously unknown to each other bridges a structural hole.

The striking visual impact of network analysis

accounts for some of its popularity. As Scott (2000, 10) observes, we now have difficulty imagining that Simmel wrote of "webs of affiliation" before Moreno (1934) had devised the familiar nodes and lines of the sociogram in the 1930s. Today we have sophisticated mathematical operations coded into software (e.g., UCINET, Krack-Plot, Inflow, P-Star, Pajek) to analyze and depict features of relationships parsimoniously. While complex algorithms are necessary to analyze large-scale networks, the simple images of connection that underlie network measurement provide a key to understanding how various measures reflect substantively different configurations of social relationships. Take, for example, the contacts between a potential employee and an employer. If the employer is the friend of a friend, we can describe the relationship in terms of path length—two degrees of separation. Put colloquially, the job seeker is two handshakes away from an interview. We could also portray the relationship between a potential employee and employers in terms of the strength of their ties. Perhaps a job seeker is the best friend of one potential employer and a distant acquaintance of another. A strong tie binds the job seeker in the former relationship, while a weak tie provides the linkage to the latter. One might say the job seeker is either a handshake or a hug away from an interview. The measures of path length and tie strength can be combined to assess how many strong or weak ties separate a given individual from another in a network. These tools do not, however, explain whether an individual provided a bridge linking two disconnected networks. This example illustrates how the choice of a particular tool (or tools) facilitates predictions that can be made about network relationships.

We introduce and illustrate 11 key network concepts that we have culled from the literature. In figure 1, the dots, or nodes, represent social actors—for example, individuals, groups, or organizations. The lines in the figures represent ties, or social relationships between the actors.

The first row of figure 1 depicts the simple distinction between a group and a network. A group has some form of social boundary indicating who is in the group and who is not (illustrated by the ellipse around three dots). In contrast, a network is a set of actors, with specific types of connections to one another. For example, an industry consists of a group of companies, who may all be members of an industry trade association and listed in various industry publications. The industry affiliation

network, however, would describe alliances between firms, interlocking directorates, or supply-chain relations among buyers and sellers. While data on the relationships among group members may be more difficult to gather than membership data, they can provide insight into how the actions of one member affect another member. The second row of figure 1 shows a basic sociometric configuration, as conceived by Moreno (1934). The node in the center of the figure is the "star" of the network. Zucker, Darby, and Brewer (1998) have employed Moreno's language of network stars to analyze the scientist-entrepreneurs who combined academic and commercial science to start some of the first-generation biotechnology firms.

The idea of structural equivalence, developed by Harrison White, occurs when two actors occupy similar positions in a social system by having structurally comparable network ties (White, Boorman, and Breiger 1974; Lorrain and White 1971). The figure in the third row of figure 1 shows a simple representation of structural equivalence in networks. In the figure, the circular nodes are equivalent in that each possesses a tie to a square, a triangle, and a flattened circle. Consider two American universities, each with active ties to different corporate benefactors, student loan providers, and state governments. The universities are structurally equivalent, that is, they occupy a similar position by having the same kinds of relationships, even though their ties are not to the same organizational partners.

The idea of the strength of weak ties has become a foundational element of network research, thanks in large part to Mark Granovetter's (1973, 1974, 1995) pioneering work on the job search process. The fourth row of figure 1 represents strong and weak ties between nodes, the weaker connection demonstrated with a dashed line. One study that has looked at both kinds of relationships is Wellman and colleagues' (1996) analysis of the use of the Internet in the workplace. They found that computer-supported weak ties were more helpful than strong ones for gaining access to useful information. Similarly, in another study of a large organization, Constant, Kiesler, and Sproull (1996) found that workers with diverse online weak ties received better technical advice.

Structural holes are the natural borders in social space. The fifth row of figure 1 depicts a bridge across a structural hole in network space. The two triangular networks are not connected to each other, except through the bridging node at the

Metaphor/Measure	Relevant Authors	Visual Representation
1. Web of group affiliation, groups versus networks	Simmel [1922] 1955	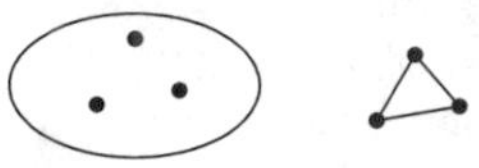
2. Sociograms, sociometric stars	Moreno 1934	
3. Structural equivalence	White, Boorman, and Breiger 1974; Burt 1992	
4. Strength of ties, weak versus strong	Granovetter 1973	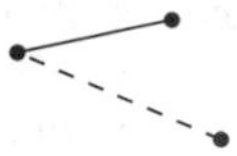
5. Bridges, structural holes, *tertius gaudens*	Burt 1992	
6. Degrees of separation, path length	Milgram 1967	
7. Interlock centrality, sphere of influence	Mizruchi 1996	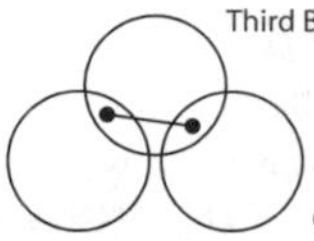 Third Board of Directors / Competitor Board 1 / Competitor Board 2
8. Local versus global network, closeness centrality	Freeman 1979	
9. Exchange, centrality versus power (A is central, but B has power because both C and D depend on B)	Bonacich 1987; Cook 1977	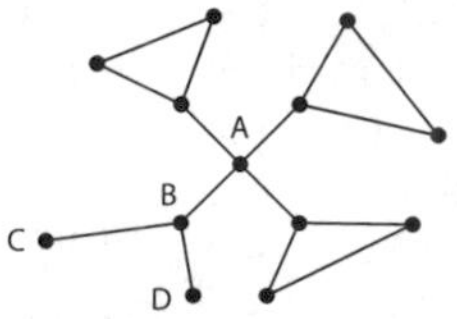 A B C D
10. Density	Barnes 1979; Marsden 1993	
11. Small-worlds	Watts and Strogatz 1998, 441	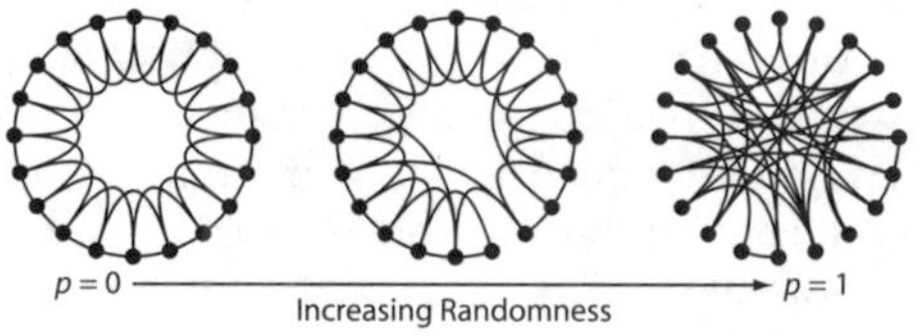 Regular / Small-World / Random / $p = 0$ — Increasing Randomness — $p = 1$

FIGURE 1. Social network conceptual toolkit. Note: Figure courtesy of *Nature*, vol. 363.

center of the figure. Managers who can create interdivisional networks in large organizations provide bridges across structural holes, combining information from disparate groups that would not otherwise communicate (Burt 1992). Research shows that managers located in such positions move more rapidly up the corporate ladder. Row 6 demonstrates the popular concept of "six degrees of separation." On the basis of his studies of the passage of correspondence among strangers, Milgram (1967) offered the provocative idea that U.S. citizens are connected by six degrees of separation or less. As the figure shows, between the node on the far left and the far right node, there are six lines, or degrees, and five other actors. Cultural industries often constitute small worlds, as new entrants rarely work with other novices, but instead affiliate with veterans. In response to the uncertainty about the audience for new films, Hollywood filmmakers often use the same artists on film after film (Faulkner and Anderson 1987). Watts and Strogatz (1998) have shown that, on average, the network of film actors is linked by fewer than four degrees of separation.

The linkages between corporate executives and business policies are often scrutinized in research on interlocking directorates (Mizruchi 1996). In the figure in row 7, the circles represent membership on corporate boards of directors. While the 1914 Clayton Act prohibits competing U.S. corporations from sharing members of their boards, companies can legally pursue interlocking directorates if each has an executive on a third board. In the 1960s, top managers joined exclusive social clubs in addition to seating outside members on their boards as a means to orchestrate acquisitions of other corporations (Palmer and Barber 2001). Here, a simple interlock between board 1 and board 2 through common membership on board 3 is illustrated.

While direct network ties frequently shape economic outcomes, research has also demonstrated that second-order ties, or the affiliations of partners, are consequential as well (Freeman 1979). The two networks depicted in the figure in row 8 demonstrate how local and global centrality differ. Consider the node in the center of the network to the left. The four connections represent direct degree centrality. If the network is expanded, as in the graph to the right, we see the centrality of this node in the overall network. In this case, centrality is weighted by the number of alters connected to the actor's partners. Shah's (2000) study of an electronics firm found that an employee's centrality in the overall network increased when the company laid off a structurally equivalent coworker. Although downsizing may have caused the individual's number of direct ties to decrease, survivors often became more central in information flows in the overall network.

Centrality, however, does not always correlate with power and influence (Bonacich 1987). Row 9 of the figure illustrates how centrality differs from power in an exchange network. In this network, lines denote a zero-sum exchange—so that if B

deals with C, it cannot deal with A. Point A is the most central in the network, but not the most powerful. Exchange theory defines power as the degree of dependency on others or a focal actor (Emerson 1962; Cook 1977). The figure shows that while A has four potential exchange partners, none is dependent solely on A. The B position occupies the most powerful location in the network because it monopolizes both C's and D's trade for a substitutable resource (Yamaguchi 1996). Haveman and Nonnemaker (2000) found that a savings and loan firm's social structural position in markets determines its pattern of competition and growth. Savings and loans with more local, single-market contact do not grow as quickly as firms with multimarket contacts. Savings and loans that compete in multiple domains tend to temper their rivalry to avoid future reprisals for cutthroat behavior. While these multimarket firms gain centrality by having more exchange partners, they also increase their dependence on rivals for mutual forbearance in markets. As Haveman and Nonnemaker show, the growth of multimarket firms eventually slows, as their various dependencies eventually constrain their expansion and result in less market power.

The figures in row 10 depict density, a measure that captures structural properties of the network as a whole rather than of an individual node (Barnes 1979; Marsden 1993). A network that is maximally connected is dense—in the figure the network of four nodes on the left has higher density than the one on the right. Biggart's (2001) analysis of rotating credit associations demonstrates that stable communities with denser social relationships provide a necessary context for successful peer group lending. The last row of the figure draws from Watts and Strogatz's (1998, 441) analyses of network topology, which show that it takes but a few small changes to tip from a random association configuration to a small world of closely connected actors. News travels quickly in small worlds, but they are also highly vulnerable to attack and perturbation; thus the removal of several highly connected hubs can destabilize an entire network (Albert, Jeong, and Barabási 2000; Barabási 2002).

This toolkit of images portraying different network configurations reveals how variation across networks can be conceptualized. These patterned differences in the shape of networks have potent effects on economic outcomes. Consider, for example, Mizruchi and Stearns's (2001) study of the effects of networks on bank decision-making. They analyze bankers' networks in terms of their tie strength and density. Bankers consult closely linked colleagues in order to feel more certain about their financial information, but this strategy does not lead to the successful closure of deals. Close ties do not result in sufficiently candid or fresh assessments of information, but rather reinforce existing opinions. Now consider a comparable study to Mizruchi and Stearns's analysis of decision-making networks, but focused on the exchange power of bankers. An assessment of how a banker utilizes colleagues for information or support to facilitate rapid promotion might find that close ties are critical for sponsorship. Thus, having a diverse intellectual toolkit affords the opportunity to understand the varied effects of different types of network configurations on economic outcomes.[3]

Progress is needed, however, in developing new tools, particularly measures that capture the kinds of information that pass through networks, as well as more macro-level measures of the cohesiveness of large networks (but see White and Harary 2001; Moody and White 2003). Measures that provide an account of network durability and experience would be useful, too. The sociology of the family, for example, has developed the study of the life course as a fruitful line of research incorporating chronology as a central feature. Studying the life course of economic relationships would allow the development of measures that capture the quality of ties, which could provide purchase across a range of organizational contexts. Longitudinal empirical studies that map regular patterns or phases in economic relationships can suggest when networks either become calcified or generate novelty, and predict the deepening or demise of ties (Powell et al. 2005). We turn now to a discussion of some of the factors that foster the development of networks.

THE FORMATION OF NETWORKS

The toolkit of network measures offers wide purchase, providing sociologists with "radiological" tools to examine the structure of social relations. Viewed from a structural perspective, networks are present in a broad range of circumstances, from markets to formal organizations. Structural analysis, however, elides the crucial questions of what factors contribute to the formation of networks, and why some networks prove beneficial and others do not. To tackle these questions, we need to explore the relationship between formal and informal organization, and develop a more general definition of networks as a form of

exchange or organization. We can then build on these ideas to explore the conditions that facilitate the formation of networks, and, in turn, analyze these networks with our array of measures.

Formal and Informal Foundations

Much of the writing in the economics and sociology of organization concerns the formal structure of authority, the incentive systems that ostensibly motivate employees, and the job ladders that employees climb throughout their careers. That there is considerable activity outside the formal channels of authority is obvious to anyone who has spent any time in organizations, but curiously there is little theory to guide us in understanding informal organization. The interplay between formal and informal structures—the chain of authority represented in the organization chart versus the soft underbelly of friendship cliques and tacit workplace norms—is not well understood.

In the much discussed Hawthorne study, Roethlisberger and Dickson (1939, 457) argued that "employees had their own rules and their own logic which, more frequently than not, were opposed to those which were imposed on them." In contrast, Burawoy (1979), in his ethnography of a piecework machine shop, argued that the myriad games and rule bending taking place on the shop floor were neither independent of, nor in opposition to, the interests of management. Research on communication networks, done in the early 1950s (Bavelas 1950; Leavitt 1951; Guetzkow and Simon 1955), suggested that hierarchical patterns inevitably emerged out of informal channels of communication. Hall (1991, 116) made a more general claim that cliques, coalitions, or other forms of informal organization "obviously begin from the established organizational order and then become variations from that order." Empirical support for Hall's claim can be found in studies like Stevenson and Bartunek's (1996), in which informal interactions among small groups of teachers in a K–12 school did not lead the groups to agree, while teachers in similar structural positions—the grades they taught—did concur on the organizational order. Krackhardt and Porter (1985) illustrate the reverse effect, showing how friendship networks influence job satisfaction and employee retention. Mintzberg (1979) offered a more dynamic view, arguing that the formal structure and informal relations are interdependent, with the formal shaping the informal, while the informal conditions what works in the formal, and may even reflect its future shape.

When the camera is directed at formal aspects of organizations, networks appear as the informal connective tissue between the formal structures. Thus, most work on intraorganizational networks focuses on informal relationships. (See Krackhardt and Brass 1994; and Raider and Krackhardt 2002 for useful reviews.) When the lens shifts to relationships among organizations, attention is directed much more at formal ties that connect organizations. (Note that there are two categories that are often neglected—formal internal networks and informal external networks.) The external linkages that connect organizations take many forms: subcontracting relationships, research consortia, strategic alliances, joint ventures, and a wide array of activities that fall under the rubric of relational contracts. Podolny and Page (1998, 59) offer a useful definition that cuts across these diverse forms of external linkage: a network form of organization is "any collection of actors that pursue repeated, enduring exchange relations with one another." These exchanges are not guided by a common central authority that can dictate the direction of the relationship or resolve disputes.

Under what circumstances are these more formal relational linkages likely to arise? What conditions promote the dominance of lateral as opposed to hierarchical relations inside organizations? And when do markets function less like the stylized spot market of isolated participants and more like a relationship of give and take, where participants exercise voice rather than exit (Hirschman 1970)? These are difficult questions, not well addressed by the literature. In an early formulation of an answer, Powell (1990, 323) observed that the origins of networks are highly contingent: "In some cases, the formation of networks anticipates the need for this particular form of exchange; in other situations, there is a slow pattern of development which ultimately justifies the form; and in other cases, networks are a response to the demand for a mode of exchange that resolves exigencies that other forms are ill-equipped to handle." A full examination of the formation question would require a chapter-length treatment of its own. Here we attend to several key factors that are most relevant to economic outcomes, including the type of work performed and the wider context in which work is carried out.

Project-Based Work

A core insight of contingency theory is that the nature of the task that needs to be executed or the problem that demands resolution has a strong effect on the form of organization (Stinchcombe 1990). Many kinds of work tend to be project-based, rather than involve the continuous production of a good or service. These temporary projects involve products that are relatively unique; hence the work process depends to a considerable degree on intuition and skill (Stinchcombe 1959; Perrow 1967). Organizations in craft-based industries have long eschewed formal organizational arrangements, opting instead for more flexible, short-term relationships. Industries such as construction (Stinchcombe 1959; Eccles 1981), book publishing (Coser, Kadushin, and Powell 1982), architecture (Blau 1984), women's clothing (Uzzi 1996), the diamond trade (Ben-Porath 1980), music (Faulkner 1983), and the film industry (Faulkner and Anderson 1987) rely, to a considerable extent, on stable and enduring personal networks based on loyalties and friendships cemented over time. In these settings, formal collaboration commonly emerges out of preexisting informal relationships. As a consequence, these forms of repeated exchange are much more than a series of bilateral relationships, but are entangled with the concerns of friendship, status, and reputation.

Information Access

Connections are also vital in high-velocity environments, but the forces fostering linkages are less driven by loyalty and association and more by a need to stay informed. In fast-paced fields, where knowledge is developing rapidly, the sources of expertise are widely dispersed, and there is uncertainty about the best approach to a problem, organizations forge connections to other parties to access relevant expertise. Access to centers of knowledge production is essential when knowledge is developing at an unprecedented pace. Moreover, much sophisticated technical knowledge is tacit in character—an indissoluble mixture of design, process, and expertise; thus it is not effectively transferred by licensing or purchase. Under conditions of uncertainty, firms seek out partners with technological complementarities. Collaboration can shorten the time it takes to bring new ideas to market, while access to a broad network of cooperative R & D provides companies with a rich portfolio of diverse information sources. Moreover, rather than simply enhancing the transfer of information between two or more parties, the relationship becomes an opportunity for novel syntheses that diverge from the stock of knowledge previously held by the individual parties (Powell, Koput, and Smith-Doerr 1996; Stuart and Podolny 1999). In such circumstances, networks can become the locus of innovation.

Organizations involved in collaborative ventures often struggle to construct a framework in which they can learn from partners without becoming unduly dependent upon them. Formal strategic alliances may lack the relational glue that project-based networks possess; hence they must rely on contractual mechanisms to curb potential opportunism. At the outset of an alliance, monitoring may be formally negotiated, with prearranged progress reports and milestone dates. Many commentators stress the fragility of such relationships (Doz and Hamel 1998); indeed there is considerable turnover in high-tech alliance partnerships (Hagedoorn 2002). But a focus on impermanence misreads both the focus of alliances and their evolving dynamics. As a rule, strategic alliances are short-term agreements designed for specific purposes—to produce a prototype, to establish a joint venture, or to enter a new market. In such settings, trust is not readily established; fear or uncertainty must be overcome before information can be shared. But once a strategic alliance is successfully pursued, further cooperation with the same partner is easier should the need arise. Moreover, participants develop reputations as either reliable or unreliable partners, sending signals that either attract or repel possible collaborators. The process is iterative—the level of cooperation increases with each agreement among common partners; at the same time, individual participants become more skilled at learning through alliances. As parties learn to rely on one another and develop reputations for effective collaboration, the amount of contractual detail that unites the parties is reduced (Lerner and Merges 1998). Various forms of monitoring are lessened, and control rights, such as an equity stake, are utilized less frequently by participants that are centrally located in an industry network (Lerner, Shane, and Tsai 2003; Robinson and Stuart 2002).

In one case, project-based networks, informal personal ties lead to repeat contracting, while in networks generated by a response to uncertainty, successful repeat contracting leads to less formal controls and a more informal basis of peer monitoring. In both circumstances, groups of collaborators become involved in multiple forms of cooperation and competition. We argue that these new patterns of affiliation, with shifting rival alliances

competing and recombining on a project-by-project basis, lead to new interpretations of the nature of competition. First, recognize how profoundly a competitive relationship is altered when two parties compete on one project, but collaborate on another. The goal of competition cannot be to vanquish your opponent lest you harm your collaborator on a different project.[4] Second, consider how the identity of the organization has changed: no longer a coherent totality, but a bundle of complex projects. Judging the likelihood of success also requires knowledge of the capabilities of a firm's partners. Finally, a reputation for successful cooperation has become a valued asset. The financial markets have learned how to evaluate the value of networks. In fields such as biotechnology and information technology, the industry business press, as well as the financial community, routinely assesses the quality of a firm's networks.

Regional Agglomeration

Perhaps the most extensive use of interorganizational linkages is found in spatially concentrated regions, sometimes referred to as industrial districts (Marshall 1920; Becattini 1978). The region dubbed the third Italy is often regarded as an exemplar of flexible, decentralized production. Networks of loosely linked, but spatially clustered, firms create a distinctive "industrial atmosphere" where the "secrets of industry are in the air" (Marshall 1920). The modus operandi of the industrial districts rests on a logic very different from that found in the vertically integrated, mass-production firm. Firms are commonly grouped in specific zones according to their products: knitwear in Modena; bicycles, motorcycles, and shoes in Bologna; food-processing machinery in Parma; and woodworking machine tools in Capri (Brusco 1982). Within the region, firms specializing in a product congregate in a specific area, serving to link industry and region closely. Work is carried out through extensive, collaborative subcontracting agreements. Only a portion of the firms market final products; the others execute operations commissioned by a group of firms that initiate production. The owners of small firms typically prefer subcontracting to expansion or integration (Lazerson 1988). Though closely related and highly cooperative, the firms remain independent.

Saxenian (1994) contends that Silicon Valley evinces many of the same characteristics as the European industrial districts. She suggests that it represents an industrial order that promotes collective learning among specialist producers of related technologies. In this decentralized system, dense social networks and open labor markets encourage entrepreneurship and the ongoing mobilization of resources. Companies compete intensely, but they simultaneously learn about changing markets and technologies through informal communications, collaborative projects, and common ties to research associations and universities.

The logic of the industrial districts is self-reinforcing. The more distinctive each firm is, the more it depends on the success of other firms' skills or products to complement its own. Repetitive contracting, embedded in local social relationships, encourages reciprocity. Monitoring is facilitated by social ties and constant contact. Indeed, trust-based governance seems easy to sustain when it is spatially clustered. Proximity, as is found in north-central Italy or Silicon Valley, seems to be both too strong and too weak an explanation for trust. Too strong in that the apparent advantages of the industrial districts seem insurmountable: How could models of production that are not as spatially concentrated generate comparable levels of trust? But too weak in that other regions that combine similar skills and advantages cannot reproduce comparable norms of reciprocity and information exchange. The simple fact of proximity among companies provides insufficient purchase on their mode of organizing. The vibrancy of the districts is not due to their geography alone, but to their social practices. To understand why districts have formed in particular locales, an analysis of the institutional infrastructure that enables economic growth is necessary.

Studies of Silicon Valley stress the unusual combination of extensive university-industry relations, initially fueled by Stanford University's Engineering School (Sturgeon 2000; Leslie 2000; Gibbons 2000), the creation and expansion of venture capital to fund start-up companies (Kenney and Florida 2000; Hellman 2000), and law firms that stressed negotiation and dispute resolution over litigation (Suchman 2000). As this region developed, professional service firms, such as consultants (McKenna 2000), accountants (Atwell 2000), and executive search firms (Friel 2000) helped sustain an ecosystem (Bahrami and Evans 2000) with highly fluid labor markets (Angel 2000) and high rates of formation and recombination of firms (Kenney and Von Burg 2000). Herrigel's (1996)

analysis of Baden-Württemberg in southwestern Germany also points to the wide availability of critical support services—excellent technical colleges and vocational training institutes, small banks willing to loan funds to local small businesses, specialized industry research programs—that encourage cooperative relations that attenuate the cutthroat aspects of competition. In the Third Italy, decentralized production also depends upon a combination of familial, legislative, political, and historical factors. The bonds of extended kinship create economic relations based on cooperation and aid the search for new employees through family and friendship networks (Lazerson 1988).

Thus, while the particular configurations of institutions may differ across regions, the common elements that give rise to the formation of districts appear to be a host of supportive intermediary organizations that promote and support risk-taking, while curbing some of the destructive aspects of intense competition by sharing risk (Kenney 2000). These supportive institutions serve as both conduits of resources and as monitoring agents that guide and structure interfirm collaboration. In such settings, competition fosters knowledge creation, while "news" circulates rapidly, as participants are connected to one another through multiple pathways. As valuable knowledge percolates through networks, participants attend to their partners with more intensity. The enhanced flow of ideas and skills then becomes an attraction, rendering the regional economy more appealing to be a part of, and more vibrant than other locales where the generation of novelty occurs less frequently (Powell 1990; Brown and Duguid 2000).

There are many other circumstances that foster networks. Smaller organizations seem to rely on external forms of support more than larger organizations, while resource-constrained firms turn to networks more readily than established, successful organizations (Baker 1990; Larson 1992). Historical contingency and founding date loom large as well. Firms established during a period when relational contracting is widely used more readily avail themselves of external linkages than do large vertically integrated firms founded during an earlier era when companies strove to be self-sufficient (Powell 2001). Table 1 summarizes key elements of the research literature on the formation of networks. We now turn from our sketch of factors that account for the origins of networks to an assessment of the performance consequences of networks.

TABLE 1. Formation of Networks

Enabling Condition	Key Ideas	Relevant Authors
Formal structure	Formal structure shapes informal coalitions.	Hall 1991; Stevenson and Bartunek 1996
Informal linkages	Informal relations serve as lubricant for economic exchange.	Larson 1992; Gulati and Garguilo 1999
Task-related contingencies	Tasks requiring coordination, sharing of information often lead to collaborative ties.	Eccles 1981; Uzzi 1996
Geographic propinquity	Regional agglomeration creates spillovers; the "secrets of industry are in the air."	Beccattini 1978; Kenney 2000
Institutional infrastructure	Historical, political, cultural context differentially affects capacity for collaboration.	Putnam 1993; Herrigel 1996; Powell 2001

THE CONSEQUENCES OF CONNECTIVITY

The consequences that accrue from one's position in a network may be positive or negative, and the goals that networks serve may be put to socially beneficial or harmful uses. Research initially focused much more on positive effects of networks, stressing their advantages over other forms of governance, such as markets or hierarchies, in terms of speed and reliability of communication. At the core of networks, however, are questions about differential access; hence the advantages that ensue from a favorable position in a network may benefit some parties while limiting others. More recently attention has focused on the ubiquity of networks and the extent to which both legal and illegal economic activity may be orchestrated through networks. The growing presence of international terrorism is a powerful reminder that cells of operatives organized as a decomposable network can create widespread destruction (Arquilla and Ronfeldt 2001).

We review the literature on the consequences of membership and position in networks, attending first to issues of performance. We then turn to distributional concerns, and assess what is known about the preferential advantages and disadvantages of networks. We conclude with a discussion of the diffusion of ideas through networks, examining both the utility of networks for accessing novel or obsolescent information and when networks "recycle" stale information.

Performance Issues

Labor market opportunities have been a rich terrain for network analysts. In a now classic study of professional men seeking work in the Boston area in the 1970s, Granovetter (1973, 1995) found that weak ties (i.e., someone with whom you are acquainted but travels in different social circles, such as a classmate from college) lead to jobs more readily than did strong ties among friends and family. Acquaintances are valuable in finding employment because they provide nonredundant information that strong ties do not. Close friends and family members have access to the same contacts and information, whereas weak ties more often supply new contacts and information. On the other hand, strong ties may be more motivated to help when one is in great need for a job. More generally, most job seekers find work through personal connections rather than formal channels (Granovetter 1995). Subsequent surveys report wide replication of Granovetter's findings. A majority of job seekers secure work through information gathered through their social network ties not only in the United States (Marsden and Campbell 1990), but also in the United Kingdom (Fevre 1989), the Netherlands (Boxman, DeGraaf, and Flap 1991), Mexico (Rogers and Kincaid 1981), and China (Bian 1997). Lin (1999) provides a comprehensive review of this growing literature.

Employing organizations also benefit from hiring through networks. Employers have a strong motivation not to hire strangers; they prefer dependable employees who have been vouched for by others. Job offers made to acquaintances of current employees are more likely to be accepted, and those hired through these channels are less likely to quit (Licht 1992; Blau and Robins 1990). Fernandez, Castilla. and Moore (2000) counted the significant economic returns that accrued to a phone center by hiring through referrals for a job with a high rate of turnover. By saving on the costs of screening applicants, the credit card phone center realized a 67 percent return rate on its investment in referral bonuses.

Besides getting a job, interpersonal networks afford individuals other career advantages. Burt (2000) argues that those who bridge unconnected groups through network ties receive more positive work evaluations, faster promotion, and greater compensation. Having a tie to a mentor with control over the fate of the organization is particularly helpful (Podolny and Baron 1997). Entrepreneurs often rely on networks to start businesses. Especially in ethnic communities, connections provide start-ups with both social and financial capital (Aldrich and Waldinger 1990).[5] Formerly wealthy Cubans who came to Miami in the 1960s with scant resources traded on their preimmigrant social ties, especially connections to bank loan officers who knew of their trustworthiness in Cuba, to obtain the financial capital to start businesses (Portes and Sensenbrenner 1993). Jewish immigrants from Eastern Europe at the turn of the nineteenth century also shared support and know-how for entrepreneurship that took them from vaudeville troupes to the creation of Hollywood movie studios (Jones 2001). Korean immigrants to Southern California in the 1970s formed rotating credit associations, pooling their limited financial capital so that each participant, in turn, had the means to start a small business (Light and Bonacich 1988). Network ties are a critical avenue through which individuals advance their careers—getting a job, a raise, or start-up capital.

At the organizational level, the performance of firms can benefit from network ties in the form of access to information and resources, more rapid product development, and enhanced innovation. Much research has suggested that close interaction among divergent organizations can produce novel recombinations of information leading to greater innovation and learning (Cohen and Levinthal 1990; Powell 1990; March 1991; McEvily and Zaheer 1999; Stuart and Podolny 1999; Ahuja 2000). For example, the biotechnology industry is rife with a wide variety of interorganizational collaborations, and the firms more centrally located in the industry networks are more scientifically capable and the first to introduce new medicines (Powell et al. 1996; Stuart, Hoang, and Hybels 1999; Baum, Calabrese, and Silverman 2000).

Interorganizational networks can also contribute to greater productivity in manufacturing, as well as facilitate the introduction of new production methods. In north-central Italy, small family-run artisanal firms generate output out of proportion to the scale of their operations. The decentralized production of knitwear permits small putting-out firms to specialize in machinery and skills that can be constantly reset after short production runs, as fashions change. Long-term relationships between manufacturers and artisanal producers have resulted in a viable strategy of making fashionable clothing at a competitive price (Lazerson 1995). Variants on this theme of rapid mobilization, such as the well-known "just in time" strategy employed by Japanese manufacturers, are also based on close, long-term ties to subcontractors. Japanese lead firms rely on extensive interaction with suppliers in lieu of haggling for the lowest bid or conflicts over faulty parts. Repeated exchange permits a manufacturer to call up a longtime subcontractor and negotiate for better terms on prices should the market change, or request replacement parts, trusting that mistakes will be corrected quickly (Dore 1983). Such give-and-take relationships enhance both speed and quality.

Connections to other organizations can also improve the likelihood of a firm's survival and ability to garner financing. Pennings and Lee (1999) demonstrate that professional service firms, such as accounting companies, with close ties to client sectors are less likely to dissolve. Pena's (2002) study of start-up firms revealed the importance of relational capital as well as intellectual capital to the survival of new ventures. In New Zealand, pastoral networks of farmers and agents led to the development of trust and successful lending to those farms that were part of the network (Ville and Fleming 2000).

Much of the literature has stressed the positive contribution of networks to economic performance. Less attention has been devoted to the ways in which networks may hinder performance or retard progress. Surely not all networks function in a similar manner; moreover, there may well be decreasing returns to connectivity. An important line of research has begun to analyze network portfolios, or the mix of different types of ties, and their relationship to performance. Uzzi (1997) found that in New York's garment industry, manufacturers with the best economic performance had networks that were neither overembedded in too many strong ties, nor underembedded in too many arm's-length contracts. A mix of strong bonds of trust with some jobbers and short-term contracts with others proved most useful. Uzzi and Gillespie (1999) also found that firms with a mix of strong and weak ties were able to obtain more advantageous terms from banks granting small-business loans. In a study of the impact of university patents, as measured by citations, Owen-Smith and Powell (2003) found that research universities lacking ties to commercial partners had less consequential patents, while universities with diverse relations with multiple partners had more high-impact patents. But when universities had very close ties to a small handful of commercial firms, they ran the risk of "capture," where their research efforts became more wedded to an applied agenda, and, consequently, their patents had less impact.

Position in a network both empowers and constrains action. A prevalence of strong ties may result in information gathering being limited to local sources. Much attention has been directed at the success of high-tech regional economies, and these technology hotbeds in the United States are often held up as models for attracting the best and brightest in the world (Florida 2002). Yet the positive effects of geographic agglomeration can be tempered when access is restricted. Sorenson and Audia (2000) report that in footwear production in the United States, spatial concentration tends to reinforce the status quo, as knowledge sharing leads to conformity. In her study of the closely knit Swiss watch industry, Glasmeier (1991) found that the densely distributed mode of production limited firms' ability to adapt new quartz technology. She argued that the decentralized network's biggest flaw was its inability to respond to the technological challenge posed by Japanese watchmakers.

Local search can result in mixed performance outcomes for individuals as well as organizations. Lee (1987) found that among employees laid off from the aerospace industry, those job searchers with low-density networks had a longer wait between jobs, but lost less income in their next position. The employees who had more dense networks were able to find jobs quickly, but on average lost significant income in changing jobs. Local search provided information that led to quick results, but meant that search for higher-paying jobs was curtailed. A similar process of fast results with a less than optimal outcome was found in the job market studied by Morris (1987) in a Welsh steel mill town. Men were hired off the books through their pub-centered, close network of strong ties. Those workers who were not part of these community networks were unable to find short-term contract work, and waited for longer periods to be hired through formal channels. The lads who were hired through the pub networks, however, had no insurance protection against accidents, being paid off the books. In this case, strong local networks resulted in more work but under more hazardous conditions.

The structure of network ties can also shape the nature of conflict in organizations. Morrill's (1995) study of corporate executives found that the emotional intensity and frequency of conflict was greater in a toy-making corporation with high informal network density because there was confusion about who held formal authority. Executives handled conflict through staged "battles" at meetings that were governed through informal norms of conflict resolution. At the more formal accounting firm that Morrill studied, senior executives settled conflicts more routinely through hierarchical fiat.

There are, obviously, trade-offs across different forms of governance. Consider the case of fish markets. The strong ties that exist in some regions between fishing boat operators and those who buy their catches result in a dampened market where the forces of supply and demand are muted, and prices are volatile for consumers. On the other hand, where markets with arm's-length contracts between buyers and sellers exist, overfishing often results (Bestor 2001; Rauch 2001). Vertical integration of the process is not the answer either, as stability in fish supply and prices is best achieved only in the frozen-fish market. Whether organized by networks, markets, or hierarchies, there are associated drawbacks—price setting, depletion of natural resources, and low quality, respectively.

Networks can also have a dark side. Dalton's (1959) classic studies of four midwestern firms in the 1950s portrayed organizations rife with cliques and rival coalitions: between staff and line and between those defending their turf and those trying to usurp it. His accounts of rivalry and revenge have parallels with studies of the organization of criminal activity. Densely knit networks are common in circumstances of danger and uncertainty. Such conditions facilitate both intense trust and bitter rivalry. Colombian drug cartels, for instance, were founded on relationships that developed between Medellín shipping partners in the gold-mining industry (Rubio 1997). The Italian Mafia is perhaps the most well known example of how networks can produce honor among thieves. Connections among mafiosi provide the protection that they sell to others. Gambetta (1993, 15) quotes a Sicilian cattle rancher who describes how he vends meat with Mafia protection: "When the butcher comes to me to buy an animal, he knows that I want to cheat him. But I know he wants to cheat me. Thus we need, say, Peppe [that is, a third party] to make us agree. And we both pay Peppe a percentage of the deal." But when Sicilians willingly pay protection, the price includes a society governed by violence rather than law.

Baker and Faulkner (1993) provide a rare analysis of how networks facilitate criminal activity among U.S. corporations. In the 1950s companies in the heavy electrical equipment industry colluded to fix prices on turbines, switchgear, and transformers. The collusive networks concealed their communication from outsiders with ingenious methods like the "phases of the moon"—a precalculated format for ensuring that the selected company had the low bid on a switchgear job. The colluders were, however, eventually caught. Baker and Faulkner showed that an executive's degree centrality predicted their fate in court. There is little benefit to holding a central network position, it turns out, when centrality means that more people can identify you to federal prosecutors.

Not all negative effects of networks are illegal; some are simply detrimental for performance. Long-term associations can lead to stagnation. When groups become too tightly knit and information passes only among a select few, networks can become competency traps. Organizations may develop routines around relationships and rules that have worked in the past, but exclude new ideas (Levitt and March 1988). Information that travels back and forth among the same participants can lead to lock-in, groupthink, and redundancy. Powell (1985, 202–7) showed how the ossification of editors' network eventually led to a decline in the quality of a publishing house's list. Grabher (1993) described how cognitive lock-in contributed to the decline of steelmaking in the tightly knit, homogeneous region of the Ruhr in Germany. Thus, the ties that bind can also become the ties that blind. Moreover, there are costs of trying to break out of strong affiliations. Portes and Sensenbrenner (1993) argue that individuals too tied into ethnic community networks can face leveling constraints. Ethnic businesspeople may be threatened with ostracism from the community if they become too economically successful.

Distributional Issues

Whether the information, relational capital, and other resources made available through network connections are beneficial or not depends largely on one's position. Within networks, ties help people get a job, start ethnic enterprises, move upward in organizations, and generally have more options. But which people or organizations garner the greatest returns? When access to the resources that aid economic performance is contingent upon selective association, there are winners and losers. Burt (1992, 2000) argues that different types of network connectivity matter for managerial careers. He finds that managers in dense networks characterized by closure wait longer to be promoted and receive smaller bonuses. In contrast, managers who serve as bridges between disconnected networks are rewarded more generously and are on the promotion fast track. These results are conditioned by race and gender, however. Both female and minority managers, as well as white male managers in structurally similar "minority" positions, are not rewarded by bridging ties in the same fashion. Burt's (1998) study of managers' networks found that women were promoted faster if they borrowed from the social capital of mentors in the organization, while men were better off building independent networks.

Female and minority managers find that they need to utilize different strategies of sponsorship, relying more on strong ties and mentors (Ibarra 1992, 1995). Typically, exclusion from dominant pathways results in less access to valued resources. But constraint has been turned into opportunity in the formation of alternative sponsorship networks by women and ethnic minorities. Discrimination against ethnic minorities can be a force that creates an "us versus them" sentiment that can generate a strong basis for trust among immigrants who invest in each other's small businesses (Portes and Sensenbrenner 1993). Portes, Haller, and Guarnizo's (2002) study of immigrant entrepreneurship shows the effects of different tie configurations for Latino businesspeople. Immigrants with mostly local ties in the United States were more likely to start domestic businesses, and less likely to start ventures that operated transnationally. Connections to their cultures of origin allowed Latinos to extend their businesses across borders. Strong local ties, however, seem to limit the scope of entrepreneurs, as well as job seekers.

When networks reinforce the perception that people can only trust those who are "one of us," access, power and resources remain concentrated (Marsden 1993). In Russia, calculating who will repay credit cards is shrouded in uncertainty, thus relatively few people have such cards (Guseva and Rona-Tas 2001). Bank managers prefer to rely on their personal networks—no distance further than friends of friends—to decide when to issue credit cards. Although Guseva and Rona-Tas find that employment in an organization with connections to the issuing bank will also provide access to credit, the Russian system creates greater stratification in credit access than the U.S. system, which is reliant on centralized and routinized credit checks. Kadushin's (1995) study of the French financial elite, which combined quantitative and qualitative data on friendship and interlock ties, shows how close-tie networks generated through common social background and educational experiences, result in an exceptionally homogeneous upper class. In France, friendship cliques account for common board membership and create a strong system of closed reproduction. In contrast, the U.S. corporate elite is rather open to new entrants, and interlocks are guided more by strategic considerations.

An important contribution of research on the distributional consequences is the insight that there is wide variability in the nature of networks and in membership in them. Common stereotypes about "old-boy" networks are tempered when faced with empirical evidence of the ubiquity of networks. The critical attributes are not simply race, class, and gender, but differential access to, and rates of formation of, networks. For example, Renzulli, Aldrich, and Moody (2000) found that having a personal network characterized mainly by kinship and other homogeneous ties was more detrimental to entrepreneurs starting a small business than being female. Smith-Doerr's (2004) research reveals that female life science Ph.D.'s employed in biotech firms—organizations enmeshed in multiple interorganizational networks—are nearly eight times more likely to move up into positions of authority than female scientists working in more hierarchically governed settings such as the academy and large pharmaceutical companies. These studies indicate that the relationship between gender inequality and networks is more complex than gender composition studies frequently imply. Often, studies of the race and gender composition of occupations assume that homosocial reproduction (bosses hiring and promoting from within their own social circles, see Kanter 1977) must be oc-

curring in organizations, without looking at the structure of individual and organizational network ties (see Smith 2002 for a review).

Diffusion

New ideas spread more rapidly through interpersonal ties than through most other kinds of communication channels, save for the mass media. The earliest studies of the diffusion of innovations through networks looked at the adoption of technological innovations. Rural sociologists found that Midwestern farmers who were more connected were the first to adopt new seed and pesticide technologies in the 1940s and 1950s (Ryan and Gross 1943; Rogers 1958). Coleman, Katz, and Menzel (1966) showed that the doctors who were first to prescribe tetracycline were those who were most central in friendship networks. Doctors isolated from friendship networks adopted much more slowly. This classic study has triggered much subsequent debate and attention. Burt (1987) and Strang and Tuma (1993) reanalyzed the original data and took issue with Coleman and colleagues' findings, pointing out that the structural equivalence of physicians—having the same kinds of ties—was a better predictor of their propensity to innovate than their direct ties. A more recent reanalysis (Van den Bulte and Lilien 2001) stresses that receptivity to advertising determined adoption. Nevertheless, in these subsequent reanalyses, position in the network structure remains key in determining access to information that lead to adoption of the new technology.

Communication networks play a critical role in the spread of models of business strategy and structure (see Davis, this volume). But the transfer of knowledge, as well as fads and fashions, is a complex process involving multiple, overlapping, yet analytically separable channels of communication. Important knowledge often flows through professional networks. Linkages of this kind have grown and become more formalized as professional and trade associations promulgate standards about appropriate professional behavior. Universities, training institutes, professional journals, and the business press also transmit information about current best practices. One key network of communication, then, is the professional or trade network. A second channel of communication is the pattern of interorganizational relations in which an organization is involved, including suppliers, key customers, members of relevant regulatory agencies, and the like. The interorganizational network is a critical source of news about administrative and technological innovations. Much of the behavior of organizations is also shaped by the activities of other organizations that are considered to be exemplars. Firms are not only embedded in an intricate network of relations with other organizations, they also attend to the actions of highly visible or prestigious organizations within their field. Early adopters of new practices are likely to be situated at the intersection of multiple networks, with links to diverse informational sources that expose them more quickly to new ideas and to critical evaluations of their merits. Research has documented that human resource management policies (Baron, Dobbin, and Jennings 1986), promotion and review procedures in law firms (Tolbert 1988) and financial reporting methods in law firms (Mezias 1990) all diffuse rapidly through interorganizational networks. Taken together, the information available through professional, resource, and status networks shapes the definition of what kinds of behavior are appropriate and sets standards that organizations seek to match.

The literature on interlocking directorates provides ample evidence that the diffusion of managerial ideas is shaped by social position. Useem (1984) showed that directors use interlocks to get information that enables them to scan their business environment. Davis (1991) found that firms were more likely to employ poison pills as a takeover defense when they shared directors with firms that were prior adopters. Davis and Greve's (1997) analysis of executive responses to hostile takeovers suggests that corporate interlocks afford more rapid diffusion of strategies than does geographic proximity. Further, information from similar corporate interlock partners seems to influence organizational behavior more than information from dissimilar partners (Haunschild and Beckman 1998). Shared boards of directors also influence the decision to change stock market listings. Rao, Davis, and Ward (2000) discovered that firms leaving the NASDAQ for the NYSE had strong prior ties to members of the New York Stock Exchange. These ties reinforced the view that a company's corporate identity did not match its NASDAQ affiliation. The opposite also obtained, companies that stayed on the NASDAQ had strong ties to core members of that exchange, and developed the perception that a NASDAQ listing matched their corporate identity.

A key feature of diffusion processes is that network position affects the social construction of identity and meaning (Strang and Soule 1998). In the development of new technologies in R & D laboratories, for example, the social networks of project members affect the interpretation of success. Smith-Doerr, Manev, and Rizova (2004) find that project managers who are more central in organizational advice networks have more flexible interpretations of the meaning of success than those less connected or central only in technical advice networks.

Recent research on diffusion processes emphasizes both the sender and receiver of signals (Strang and Tuma 1993; Strang and Soule 1998). Drawing on epidemiological research, attention has been directed to differential rates of susceptibility to external influences. For example, younger firms may be especially attentive to the opinions of other organizations, particularly if they rely on them for key resources. And the diffusion of common practices is likely to occur more rapidly in the period before standardization sets in (Swedberg 1997). We know less, however, about the circumstances under which diffusion slows, as either organizations build immunity to network-wide practices or decreasing returns to connectivity occur. Table 2 summarizes our review of the key effects of networks on performance outcomes, equality issues, and diffusion processes.

In sum, the impact of networks upon economic performance is profound, but also highly contingent upon context. No general theory has emerged that covers all situations, nor is there a single mechanism comparable to the price signal that regulates behavior. Networks are the relational structure of social and economic life. The institutional context in which network ties are formed and governed largely shapes the distribution of access to network resources. When that access is more broadly distributed and resources and information can be obtained through multiple pathways, connections can lead to entrepreneurial activities, opportunity, and learning. But when network access is restrictive and produces social closure, connections can lead to widening gaps between the haves and have-nots.

LIMITATIONS AND PROSPECTS

Any field of research that garners attention and generates a productive line of scholarship is bound to attract critics, and network analysis of the economy is no exception. We briefly sketch three of the main criticisms of network studies, as well as responses to them.

TABLE 2.   Consequences of Networks in Economic Life

Issue	Beneficial Outcomes	Relevant Authors	Detrimental or Mixed Outcomes	Relevant Authors
Economic performance	Individuals utilize networks to obtain jobs, promotions, start businesses; organizations hire with lower turnover, innovate more, produce with speed and quality, and garner financing.	Granovetter 1974; Burt 2000; Fernandez, Castilla, Moore 2000; and Powell, Koput, and Smith-Doerr 1996; Dore 1983; Baum, Calabrese, and Silverman 2000	Networks can generate local search, leading to lock-in and competency traps; collusion, price setting and fixing; small cells of multiply linked agents use networks to attack hierarchical organizations (drug cartels, terrorist networks).	Grabher 1993; Glasmeier 1991; Baker and Faulkner 1993; Arquilla and Ronfeldt 2001
Resource distribution	Exclusion from larger economy because of discrimination can lead to ethnic entrepreneurship; when entrepreneurial organizations rely on networks, women have more access than in hierarchical organizations.	Portes and Haller, this volume; Light, this volume; Aldrich, this volume; Smith-Doerr 2004	Restricted access, social closure, exclusivity, all exacerbate unequal distribution of resources.	Kanter 1977; Ibarra 1992; Kadushin 1995
Diffusion of ideas	Centrality in network leads to more rapid transmission of information and faster adoption of new technologies (be they beneficial or harmful); more effective transfer of tacit knowledge.	Davis, this volume; Rogers 1995; Strang and Soule 1998	Corporate interlocks afford elites more power to coordinate the economy; elite networks promote strategies for garnering greater influence.	Mizruchi 1996; Useem 1984; Palmer and Barber 2001

A persistent criticism of network analysis is its tendency to focus on the structure of relationships and neglect the content of ties (Goodwin and Emirbayer 1994). An overemphasis on the structure of linkages can lead to treating all ties as comparable, without regard to their content or context. Stinchcombe (1989, 1990), in his discussion of research on interlocking directorates, has voiced this criticism most forcefully:

> One has to build a dynamic and causal theory of a structure into the analysis of the links. We need to know what flows across the links, who decides on those flows in the light of what interests, and what collective or corporate action flows from the organization of links, in order to make sense of intercorporate relations. (Stinchcombe 1990, 381)

There have been several responses to concerns about the sterility of structural analyses of networks. Researchers are pursuing quantitative analyses of large data sets analyzing the duration and depth of relationships. The length of a relationship is an indirect measure of quality, but it does suggest that the parties to a relationship remain committed to one another in some fashion. Longitudinal studies of network connections capture the length of relationships and the extent to which partners share relationships with other actors at specific points in time, offering considerable insight into which participants are central in a field (Powell et al. 2005). The depth of ties can be assessed by measures of how consequential a tie is to one party in contrast to the other. A focus on differing levels or stages of investment in a relationship, and the consequences of different types of uncertainty for disparate actors, offers purchase on how the content of relationships is perceived differently by participants (Podolny 2001).

Much remains to be done to integrate quantitative and qualitative studies of networks. More process-oriented, case-based approaches provide rich accounts of why ties are created, how they are maintained, what resources flow across these linkages, and with what consequences. Two lines of research, prominent in Europe, focus more directly on the content of relationships. The markets-as-networks approach, developed largely by Swedish researchers, attends to the interdependence of companies in business markets, and analyzes how these interconnections are managed (Hägg and Johanson 1983; Håkansson 1987; Håkansson and Snehota 1989; Axelson and Easton 1992; Ford et al. 1998). The virtue of this interaction-focused approach is in showing how a relationship between two companies evolves over time, and may assume an identity of its own, independent of the characteristics and resources of the participants. The limitation of such detailed cases is that they have been, almost necessarily, limited to dyadic relationships, or to a single focal organization. More recent work, however, looks at a large production network and its frictions and interdependencies. Håkansson and Walusziewski's (2002) study of the technological changes in the pulp and paper industry, initiated by important customers and environmental groups, and the ramifications of these new more environmental-friendly techniques for forest and chemical companies and equipment companies, is one example of how an entire circuit of production and consumption can be analyzed through network lenses.

Callon (1986, 1995, 1998), Latour (1987, 1988), and others (Law and Hassard 1998) have developed an approach dubbed actor-network theory to explain when particular definitions or configurations of science and technology triumph over alternative conceptions. Actor-network theory is rather unique in including artifacts and technologies, as well as people and organizations, in its conception of network actors. In a masterful study of Pasteur's design for his sterilization process, Latour (1988) shows how Pasteur "enrolled" members of the European hygiene movement into his cause. In so doing, Pasteur gave his rivals a reason—fighting microbes—for having hospitals scrubbed and full of fresh air. Callon's (1986) study of how fishermen and scientists became allies in preserving and "domesticating" the scallops of St. Brieuc Bay provides another example of network enrollment.

The actor-network approach stresses the process of translation, in which problems are redefined, supporters mobilized, and ideas and practices transformed in the process of interpretation. Rather than treat ideas or technologies as impervious to the context in which they are imported, this approach recognizes that knowledge and artifacts are interpreted, and utilized in divergent ways in different settings. The advantages of this approach are the attention to conflict and rivalry, both with-in and across networks. Drawing on a broader science studies perspective, Knorr Cetina and Bruegger (2002) argue that network researchers have thus far utilized a rather simplistic view of knowledge. They employ a more phenomenological approach to economic sociology to analyze new, computer mediated forms of interaction in global trading markets. Knorr Cetina and Bruegger apply the actor network approach to theorize how the computers become a focal node in the structure of markets.

A second common criticism of network studies is their static character. Obviously, the charge that most network studies are cross-sectional (Burt 2000) applies primarily to North American quantitative research, and not to the markets-as-networks approach or actor-network theory, both of which look at the evolution of specific networks over time. The challenge is aimed more at scholars who are analyzing larger network structures, but do not take on the daunting task of collecting longitudinal data (McPherson, Smith-Lovin, and Cook 2001). Still, some progress has been made, both in analyzing the dynamics of dyads (Lincoln, Gerlach, and Ahmadjian 1996; Gulati and Garguilo 1999; Stuart 1998) and the evolution of entire networks. Padgett's (2001) analysis of early Renaissance Florence draws on two centuries of data to analyze the coevolution of economics, politics, and family structure. He traces four regimes of career-organization mapping: family, guild, social class, and clientage. In each transition, perturbation in one network (e.g., politics) rebounded into another (e.g., banking), triggering unanticipated cleavages in the latter network. In turn, the actors in the first network clamored to save their status and preserve the old order by reconfiguring their positions. The innovations of the Renaissance, in Padgett's analysis, were not generated by Florentine efforts to produce novelty. Just the opposite occurred; Florentines were motivated to conserve their positions, but these attempts generated waves of unanticipated changes, which took place through turbulent cross-network rewirings of careers and organizations (Padgett and Ansell 1993).

Powell and colleagues' (2005) research does not span as long a time period as Padgett's, focusing on the emergence of the field of biotechnology in the 1980s and 1990s. Still, they observe a transition as profoundly transformative in its domain as that observed by Padgett in early medieval banking. In their analysis of interorganizational collaborations among small and large firms, research universities, government institutes, and venture capitalists, they show how the roles of elite universities and smaller science-based firms assumed prominence. The growing involvement of universities in the commercialization of knowledge has altered the rules of competition among universities, remade academic careers and identities, and influenced economic growth and the fiscal health of communities where universities are located (Powell and Owen-Smith 1998; Owen-Smith 2003). One of the advantages of detailed time-series data on network evolution is the ability to show how organizational fields create tracks of career and biography sequences, and how the reproduction of networks sustains these sequences. Most social science presumes goal-oriented actors, without investigating how actors acquire these identities and goals. Longitudinal network studies can shed light on the emergence of goals and identities.

A third line of critique of network research is that such studies focus on relationships at the expense of larger concerns with politics and institutions. Boltanski and Chiapello (1999) argue that network theory is a neoliberal project, suited to a U.S. culture that stresses flexibility, impermanence, and choice. Fligstein (2001) contends that network studies are "myopic" and that consequential action occurs within political and cultural institutions. We find these comments hard to square with the multi-level nature of network analysis. A starting point of network research is recognition that individuals and organizations are engaged in several domains of exchange. Following Simmel's core insight ([1922] 1955), networks are webs of cross-cutting affiliations; they are not segregated or layered into distinct spheres of the polity, economy, or family. Thus network research is fundamentally about differential capacities for action, based on the ability to mobilize connections from different domains of economic and social life. This architectural vision, sometimes referred to as heterarchy (Stark 2001), affords insight into cross-realm influences as well as misalignments. In our view, the analysis of cross-network linkages and rewirings is central to understanding large-scale systemic transformations. Far from being divorced from the study of political institutions and culture, networks are the constitutive elements that sustain, rupture, and transform social and economic institutions.

NOTES

We are grateful to Richard Swedberg, Neil Smelser, Jason Owen-Smith, Kelley Porter, Kaisa Snellman, and the Organizations reading group at Boston University for very helpful comments on our initial drafts of the chapter.

1. There is a burgeoning literature in both physics and sociology on network topology and dynamics (Watts and Strogatz 1998, Albert and Barabási 2002; Owen-Smith et al. 2002). Thus far however, economic outcomes are not the primary focus of this work.

2. Castells (2000) provides an encyclopedic overview of this terrain in which networks become the heart of connectivity in the economy. Large organizations are internally decomposed as networks, while small and medium-sized organizations are connected through networks. These affiliations are activated in the context of projects, and reconfigure as projects are completed (Grabher 2002). At the core of these networks is the transfer, sharing, and recombination of information.

3. The above discussion and table 1 introduce only a handful of the many measures available to network researchers. See Knoke and Kuklinski 1982; Wasserman and Faust 1994; Anderson, Wasserman, and Crouch 1999; Scott 2000; and de Nooy, Mrvar, and Batagelj 2003 for more detailed surveys of the tools of network analysis.

4. Wolfgang Streeck suggested to us that this feature of network competition can give rise to claims of collusion or cartel-like behavior. To be sure, networks entail a degree of social closure and restricted access. Just how closed and restrictive, and thus anti-competitive, is an empirical question. See the chapter by Granovetter (this volume) for a discussion of how the degree of closure among business groups either retards or enhances performance.

5. See chapters in this volume by Portes and Haller, Light, and Aldrich for further elaboration on informal, ethnic, entrepreneurial networks.

REFERENCES

Ahuja, Gautam. 2000. "Collaboration Networks, Structural Holes, and Innovation: A Longitudinal Study." *Administrative Science Quarterly* 45:425–55.

Albert, Réka, and A. L. Barabási. 2002. "Statistical Mechanics of Complex Networks." *Reviews of Modern Physics* T4, 1:47–97.

Albert, Réka, H. Jeong, and A. L. Barabási. 2000. "Error and Attack Tolerance in Complex Networks." *Nature* 406:378–82.

Aldrich, Howard E., and R. Waldinger. 1990. "Ethnicity and Entrepreneurship." *Annual Review of Sociology* 16:111–35.

Anderson, Carolyn J., Stanley Wasserman, and Bradley Crouch. 1999. "A p* Primer: Logit Models for Social Networks." *Social Networks* 21:37–66.

Angel, David P. 2000. "High-Technology Agglomeration and the Labor Market: The Case of Silicon Valley." Pp. 124–40 in *Understanding Silicon Valley,* ed. Martin Kenney. Stanford, Calif.: Stanford University Press.

Arquilla, John, and David Ronfeldt, ed. 2001. *Networks and Netwars: The Future of Terror, Crime, and Militancy.* Santa Monica, Calif.: Rand.

Atwell, James D. 2000. "Guiding the Innovators: Why Accountants Are Valued." Pp. 355–69 in *The Silicon Valley Edge,* ed. Chong-Moon Lee et al. Stanford, Calif.: Stanford University Press.

Axelson, Bjorn, and Geoffrey Easton. 1992. *Industrial Networks: A New View of Reality*. London: Routledge.

Bahrami, Homa, and Stuart Evans. 2000. "Flexible Recycling and High-Technology Entrepreneurship." Pp. 165–89 in *Understanding Silicon Valley*, ed. Martin Kenney. Stanford, Calif.: Stanford University Press.

Baker, Wayne E. 1990. "Market Networks and Corporate Behavior." *American Journal of Sociology* 96: 589–625.

Baker, Wayne E., and Robert R. Faulkner. 1993. "The Social Organization of Conspiracy: Illegal Networks in the Heavy Electrical Equipment Industry." *American Sociological Review* 58:837–60.

Barabási, Albert-László. 2002. *Linked: The New Science of Networks*. Cambridge, Mass.: Perseus.

Barnes, J. A. 1979. "Network Analysis: Orienting Notion, Rigorous Technique, or Substantive Field of Study?" Pp. 403–23 in *Perspectives on Social Network Research*, ed. Paul W. Holland and Samuel Leinhardt. New York: Academic.

Baron, James P., Frank Dobbin, and P. Devereaux Jennings. 1986. "War and Peace: The Evolution of Modern Personnel Administration in U.S. Industry." *American Journal of Sociology* 92:250–83.

Baum, Joel A. C., Tony Calabrese, and Brian S. Silverman. 2000. "Don't Go It Alone: Alliance Network Composition and Startups' Performance in Canadian Biotechnology." *Strategic Management Journal* 21:267–94.

Bavelas, Alex. 1950. "Communication Patterns in Task-Oriented Groups." *Journal of the Acoustical Society of America* 22:725–30.

Becattini, Giacomo. 1978. "The Development of Light Industry in Tuscany: An Interpretation." *Economic Notes* 2(3): 107–23.

Ben-Porath, Yoram. 1980. "The F-Connection: Families, Friends, and Firms in the Organization of Exchange." *Population and Development Review* 6:1–30.

Bestor, Theodore C. 2001. "Supply-Side Sushi: Commodity, Market, and the Global City." *American Anthropologist* 102:76–95.

Bian, Yanjie. 1997. "Bringing Strong Ties Back In: Indirect Ties, Network Bridges, and Job Searches in China." *American Sociological Review* 62:366–85.

Biggart, Nicole Woolsey. 2001. "Banking on Each Other: The Situational Logic of Rotating Savings and Credit Associations." *Advances in Qualitative Organization Research* 3:129–53.

Blau, David M., and Philip K. Robins. 1990. "Job Search Outcomes for the Employed and Unemployed." *Journal of Political Economy* 98:637–55.

Blau, Judith. 1984. *Architects and Firms*. Cambridge: MIT Press.

Boltanski, Luc, and Eve Chiapello. 1999. *Le nouvel esprit du capitalisme*. Paris: Gallimard.

Bonacich, P. 1987. "Power and Centrality: A Family of Measures." *American Journal of Sociology* 92: 1170–82.

Boxman, Ed, Paul DeGraaf, and Hendrick Flap. 1991. "The Impact of Social and Human Capital on the Income Attainment of Dutch Managers." *Social Networks* 13:51–73.

Brown, John Seely, and Paul Duguid. 2000. "Mysteries of the Region: Knowledge Dynamics in Silicon Valley." Pp. 16–45 in *The Silicon Valley Edge*, ed. Chong-Moon Lee et al. Stanford, Calif.: Stanford University Press.

Brusco, Sebastiano. 1982. "The Emilian Model: Productive Decentralization and Social Integration." *Cambridge Journal of Economics* 6:167–84.

Burawoy, Michael. 1979. *Manufacturing Consent: Changes in the Labor Process under Monopoly Capitalism*. Chicago: University of Chicago Press.

Burt, Ronald S. 1987. "Social Contagion and Innovation: Cohesion versus Structural Equivalence." *American Journal of Sociology* 92:1287–1335.

———. 1992. *Structural Holes*. Cambridge: Harvard University Press.

———. 1998. "The Gender of Social Capital," *Rationality and Society* 10:5–46.

———. 2000. "The Network Structure of Social Capital." *Research in Organizational Behavior* 22:345–423.

Callon, Michel. 1986. "Some Elements of a Sociology of Translation: Domestication of the Scallops and the Fisherman of St. Brieuc Bay." Pp. 196–229 in *Power, Action, and Belief*, ed. John Law. London: Routledge.

———. 1995. "Four Models for the Dynamics of Science." Pp. 29–63 in *Handbook of Science and Technology Studies*, ed. Sheila Jasanoff, Gerald E. Markle, James C. Petersen, and Trevor Pinch. Rev. ed. Thousand Oaks, Calif.: Sage.

———, ed. 1998. *The Laws of the Market*. Malden, Mass.: Blackwell.

Castells, Manuel. 2000. *The Information Age: Economy, Society, and Culture, Vol. I: The Rise of the Network Society*. Updated ed. Oxford: Blackwell.

Cohen, Wesley, and D. Levinthal. 1990. "Absorptive Capacity: A New Perspective on Learning and Innovation." *Administrative Science Quarterly* 35: 128–52.

Coleman, James S., Elihu Katz, and Herbert Menzel. 1966. *Medical Innovation: A Diffusion Study*. New York: Bobbs-Merrill.

Constant, David, Sara Kiesler, and Lee Sproull. 1996. "The Kindness of Strangers: On the Usefulness of Weak Ties for Technical Advice." *Organization Science* 7:119–35.

Cook, Karen S. 1977. "Exchange and Power in Networks of Interorganizational Relations." *Sociological Quarterly* 18:62–82.

Coser, Lewis, Charles Kadushin, and Walter W. Powell. 1982. *Books: The Culture and Commerce of Publishing*. New York: Basic Books.

Dalton, Melville. 1959. *Men Who Manage*. New York: John Wiley and Sons.

Davis, Gerald F. 1991. "Agents without Principles? The Spread of the Poison Pill Takeover Defense through the Intercorporate Network." *Administrative Science Quarterly* 36:583–613.

Davis, Gerald F., and Henrich R. Greve. 1997. "Corporate Elite Networks and Governance Changes in the 1980s." *American Journal of Sociology* 103:1–37.

de Nooy, Wouter, Andrej Mrvar, and Vladimir Batagelj. 2003. *Exploratory Social Network Analysis with Pajek.* Cambridge: Cambridge University Press.

Dore, Ronald. 1983. "Goodwill and the Spirit of Market Capitalism." *British Journal of Sociology* 34:459–82.

Doz, Yves, and Gary Hamel. 1998. *Alliance Advantage: The Art of Creating Value through Partnering.* Boston: Harvard Business School Press.

Eccles, Robert. 1981. "The Quasifirm in the Construction Industry." *Journal of Economic Behavior and Organization* 2:335–57.

Emerson, Richard. 1962. "Power Dependence Relations." *American Sociological Review* 27:31–40.

Faulkner, Robert R. 1983. *Music on Demand.* New Brunswick, N.J.: Transaction Books.

Faulkner, Robert R., and Andy Anderson. 1987. "Short-Term Projects and Emergent Careers: Evidence from Hollywood." *American Journal of Sociology* 92:879–909.

Fernandez, Roberto M., Emilio J. Castilla, and Paul Moore. 2000. "Social Capital at Work: Networks and Employment at a Phone Center." *American Journal of Sociology* 105:1288–356.

Fevre, Ralph. 1989. "Informal Practices, Flexible Firms, and Private Labour Markets." *Sociology* 23:91–109.

Fligstein, Neil. 2001. *The Architecture of Markets.* Princeton: Princeton University Press.

Florida, Richard. 2002. *The Rise of the Creative Class.* New York: Basic Books.

Ford, David, Lars-Erik Gadde, Håkan Håkansson, Anders Lundgren, Ivan Snethota, Peter Turnbull, and David Wilson. 1998. *Managing Business Relationships.* West Sussex, U.K.: Wiley.

Freeman, Linton C. 1979. "Centrality in Social Networks: I. Conceptual Clarification." *Social Networks* 1:215–39.

Friel, Thomas J. 2000. "Shepherding the Faithful: The Influence of Executive Search Firms." Pp. 342–53 in *The Silicon Valley Edge,* ed. Chong-Moon Lee et al. Stanford, Calif.: Stanford University Press.

Gambetta, Diego. 1993. *The Sicilian Mafia: The Business of Private Protection.* Cambridge: Harvard University Press.

Gibbons, James F. 2000. "The Role of Stanford University: A Dean's Reflections." Pp. 200–217 in *The Silicon Valley Edge,* ed. Chong-Moon Lee et al. Stanford, Calif.: Stanford University Press.

Glasmeier, Amy. 1991. "Technological Discontinuities and Flexible Production: The Case of Switzerland and the World Watch Industry." *Research Policy* 20:469–85.

Goodwin, Jeff, and Mustafa Emirbayer. 1994. "Network Analysis, Culture, and the Problem of Agency." *American Journal of Sociology* 99:1411–54.

Grabher, Gernot. 1993. "The Weakness of Strong Ties: The Lock-in of Regional Development in the Ruhr Area." Pp. 255–77 in *The Embedded Firm,* ed. Gernot Grabher. London: Routledge.

———. 2002. "Cool Projects, Boring Institutions: Temporary Collaboration in Social Context." *Regional Studies* 36(3): 205–14.

Granovetter, Mark. 1973. "The Strength of Weak Ties." *American Journal of Sociology* 78:1360–80.

———. 1974. *Getting a Job.* Cambridge: Harvard University Press.

———. 1985. "Economic Action, Social Structure, and Embeddedness." *American Journal of Sociology* 91: 481–510.

———. 1995. *Getting a Job: A Study of Contacts and Careers.* 2d ed. Chicago: University of Chicago Press.

Guetzkow, Harold, and Herbert Simon. 1955. "The Impact of Certain Communication Networks upon Organization and Performance in Task-Oriented Groups." *Management Science* 1:233–50.

Gulati, Ranjay, and Martin Gargiulo. 1999. "Where Do Interorganizational Networks Come From?" *American Journal of Sociology* 104:1439–93.

Guseva, Alya, and Akos Rona-Tas. 2001. "Uncertainty, Risk, and Trust: Russian and American Credit Card Markets Compared." *American Sociological Review* 66:623–46.

Hagedoorn, John. 2002. "Inter-firm R&D Partnerships: An Overview of Major Trends and Patterns since 1960." *Research Policy* 31:477–92.

Hägg, Ingemund, and Jan Johanson. 1983. *Firms in Networks: A New View of Competitive Power.* Stockholm: Business and Social Research Institute.

Håkansson, Håkan, ed. 1987. *Industrial Technological Development: A Network Approach.* London: Croom Helm.

Håkansson, Håkan, and Ivan Snehota. 1989. "No Business Is an Island: The Network Concept of Business Strategy." *Scandinavian Journal of Management* 5:187–200.

Håkansson, Håkan, and Alexandra Walusziewski. 2002. *Managing Technological Development: IKEA, the Environment, and Technology.* London: Routledge.

Hall, Richard H. 1991. *Organizations.* 5th ed. Englewood Cliffs, N.J.: Prentice-Hall.

Harrison, Bennett. 1994. *Lean and Mean: The Changing Landscape of Corporate Power in an Age of Flexibility.* New York: Basic Books.

Haunschild, Pamela R., and Christine M. Beckman. 1998. "When Do Interlocks Matter? Alternate Sources of Information and Interlock Influence." *Administrative Science Quarterly* 43:815–44.

Haveman, Heather A., and Lynn Nonnemaker. 2000. "Competition in Multiple Geographic Markets: The Impact on Growth and Market Entry." *Administrative Science Quarterly* 45:232–67.

Hellman, Thomas F. 2000. "Venture Capitalists: The Coaches of Silicon Valley." Pp. 276–94 in *The Sili-*

con Valley Edge, ed. Chong-Moon Lee et al. Stanford, Calif.: Stanford University Press.

Herrigel, Gary. 1996. *Industrial Constructions: The Sources of German Industrial Power.* Cambridge: Cambridge University Press.

Hirschman, Albert. 1970. *Exit, Voice, and Loyalty.* Cambridge: Harvard University Press.

Ibarra, Herminia. 1992. "Homophily and Differential Returns: Sex Differences in Network Structure and Access in an Advertising Firm." *Administrative Science Quarterly* 37:442–47.

———. 1995. "Race, Opportunity, and Diversity of Social Circles in Managerial Networks." *Academy of Management Journal* 38:673–703.

Jones, Candace. 2001. "Coevolution of Entrepreneurial Careers, Institutional Rules, and Competitive Dynamics in American Film, 1895–1920." *Organization Studies* 6:911–44.

Kadushin, Charles. 1995. "Friendship among the French Financial Elite." *American Sociological Review* 60: 202–21.

Kanter, Rosabeth Moss. 1977. *Men and Women of the Corporation.* New York: Basic Books.

Kenney, Martin, ed. 2000. *Understanding Silicon Valley: The Anatomy of an Entrepreneurial Region.* Stanford, Calif.: Stanford University Press.

Kenney, Martin, and Richard Florida. 2000. "Venture Capital in Silicon Valley: Fueling New Firm Formation." Pp. 98–123 in *Understanding Silicon Valley,* ed. Martin Kenney. Stanford, Calif.: Stanford University Press.

Kenney, Martin, and Urs Von Burg. 2000. "Institutions and Economies: Creating Silicon Valley." Pp. 218–40 in *Understanding Silicon Valley,* ed. Martin Kenney. Stanford, Calif.: Stanford University Press.

Knoke, David. 1990. *Political Networks: The Structural Perspective.* Cambridge: Cambridge University Press.

Knoke, David, and James H. Kuklinski. 1982. *Network Analysis.* Beverly Hills, Calif.: Sage.

Knorr Cetina, Karin, and Urs Bruegger. 2002. "Global Microstructures: The Virtual Societies of Financial Markets." *American Journal of Sociology* 107:905–50.

Krackhardt, David, and Daniel J. Brass. 1994. "Intraorganizational Networks." Pp. 207–29 in *Advances in Social Network Analysis,* ed. Stanley Wasserman and Joseph Galaskiewicz. Thousand Oaks, Calif.: Sage.

Krackhardt, David, and L. W. Porter. 1985. "When Friends Leave: A Structural Analysis of the Relationship between Turnover and Stayers' Attitudes." *Administrative Science Quarterly* 30:242–61.

Larson, Andrea. 1992. "Network Dyads in Entrepreneurial Settings: A Study of the Governance of Exchange Processes." *Administrative Science Quarterly* 37:76–104.

Latour, Bruno. 1987. *Science in Action.* Cambridge: Harvard University Press.

———. 1988. *The Pasteurization of France.* Cambridge: Harvard University Press.

Law, John, and John Hassard. 1998. *Actor Network Theory and After.* Malden, Mass.: Blackwell.

Lazerson, Mark H. 1988. "Organizational Growth of Small Firms." *American Sociological Review* 53: 330–42.

———. 1995. "A New Phoenix? Modern Putting-Out in the Modena Knitwear Industry." *Administrative Science Quarterly* 40:34–59.

Leavitt, Harold J. 1951. "Some Effects of Certain Communication Patterns on Group Performance." *Journal of Abnormal and Social Psychology* 46:38–50.

Lee, R. M. 1987. "Looking for Work." Pp. 109–26 in *Redundancy and Recession in South Wales,* ed. C. C. Harris et al. Oxford: Basil Blackwell.

Lerner, Josh, and R. Merges. 1998. "The Control of Technology Alliances: An Empirical Analysis of the Biotechnology Industry." *Journal of Industrial Economics* 46:125–56.

Lerner, Josh, Hilary Shane, and Alexander Tsai. 2003. "Do Equity Financing Cycles Matter? Evidence from Biotechnology Alliances." *Journal of Financial Economics* 67:411–46.

Leslie, Stuart W. 2000. "The Biggest Angel of Them All: The Military and the Making of Silicon Valley." Pp. 48–67 in *Understanding Silicon Valley,* ed. Martin Kenney. Stanford, Calif.: Stanford University Press.

Levitt, Barbara, and James G. March. 1988. "Organizational Learning." *Annual Review of Sociology* 14: 319–40.

Licht, Walter. 1992. *Getting Work: Philadelphia, 1840–1950.* Cambridge: Harvard University Press.

Light, Ivan, and Edna Bonacich. 1988. *Immigrant Entrepreneurs: Koreans in Los Angeles, 1965–1982.* Berkeley and Los Angeles: University of California Press.

Lin, Nan. 1999. "Social Networks and Status Attainment." *Annual Review of Sociology* 25:467–87.

Lincoln, James, Michael Gerlach, and Christina Ahmadjian. 1996. "Keiretsu Networks and Corporate Performance in Japan." *American Sociological Review* 61:67–88.

Lorrain, F., and Harrison C. White. 1971. "The Structural Equivalence of Individuals in Social Networks." *Journal of Mathematical Sociology* 1:49–80.

March, James G. 1991. "Exploration and Exploitation in Organizational Learning." *Organization Science* 2: 71–87.

Marsden, Peter V. 1993. "The Reliability of Network Density and Composition Measures." *Social Networks* 15:399–421.

Marsden, Peter V., and Karen Campbell. 1990. "Recruitment and Selection Processes: The Organization Side of Job Searches." Pp. 59–79 in *Social Mobility and Social Structure,* ed. Ronald L. Breiger. Cambridge: Cambridge University Press.

Marsden, Peter V., and Noah Friedkin. 1993. "Network Studies of Social Influence." *Sociological Methods and Research* 22:127–51.

Marshall, Alfred. 1920. *Industry and Trade.* London: Macmillan.

McEvily, William J., and Akbar Zaheer. 1999. "Bridging Ties: A Source of Firm Heterogeneity in Competitive Capabilities." *Strategic Management Journal* 20:1133–56.

McKenna, Regis. 2000. "Free Advice: Consulting the Silicon Valley Way." Pp. 370–79 in *The Silicon Valley Edge*, ed. Chong-Moon Lee et al. Stanford, Calif.: Stanford University Press.

McPherson, J. Miller, Lynn Smith-Lovin, and James Cook. 2001. "Birds of a Feather: Homophily in Social Networks." *Annual Review of Sociology* 27: 415–44.

Merton, Robert K. 1957. *Social Theory and Social Structure.* New York: Free Press.

Mezias, Stephen J. 1990. "An Institutional Model of Organized Practice: Financial Reporting at the Fortune 200." *Administrative Science Quarterly* 35: 431–57.

Milgram, Stanley. 1967. "The Small World Problem." *Psychology Today* 2:60–67.

Mintzberg, Henry. 1979. *The Structuring of Organizations.* Englewood, N.J.: Prentice Hall.

Mitchell, J. Clyde. 1969. "The Concept and Use of Social Networks." In *Social Networks in Urban Situations,* ed. J. Clyde Mitchell. Manchester: Manchester University Press.

Mizruchi, Mark S. 1996. "What Do Interlocks Do? An Analysis, Critique, and Assessment of Research on Interlocking Directorates." *Annual Review of Sociology* 22:271–98.

Mizruchi, Mark S., and Linda B. Stearns. 2001. "Getting Deals Done: The Use of Social Networks in Bank Decision-Making." *American Sociological Review* 66:647–71.

Moody, James, and Douglas R. White. 2003. "Social Cohesion and Embeddedness: A Hierarchical Conception of Social Groups." *American Sociological Review* 68:103–27.

Moreno, Jacob L. 1934. *Who Shall Survive?* Washington, D.C.: Nervous and Mental Diseases Publishing.

Morrill, Calvin. 1995. *The Executive Way: Conflict Management in Corporations.* Chicago: University of Chicago Press.

Morris, Lydia D. 1987. "The Household and the Labour Market." Pp. 127–40 in *Redundancy and Recession in South Wales*, ed. C. C. Harris et al. Oxford: Basil Blackwell.

Owen-Smith, Jason. 2003. "From Separate Systems to a Hybrid Order: Accumulative Advantage across Public and Private Science." *Research Policy* 32:1081–1104.

Owen-Smith, Jason, and Walter W. Powell. 2003. "The Expanding Role of University Patenting in the Life Sciences: Assessing the Importance of Experience and Connectivity." *Research Policy* 32:1695–1711.

Owen-Smith, Jason, M. Riccaboni, F. Pammolli, and Walter W. Powell. 2002. "A Comparison of U.S. and European University-Industry Relations in the Life Sciences." *Management Science* 48(1): 24–43.

Padgett, John F. 2001. "Organizational Genesis, Identity, and Control: The Transformation of Banking in Renaissance Florence." Pp. 211–57 in *Markets and Networks*, ed. James E. Rauch and Alessandra Casella. New York: Russell Sage Foundation.

Padgett, John F., and Christopher Ansell. 1993. "Robust Action and the Rise of the Medici, 1400–34." *American Journal of Sociology* 98:1259–319.

Palmer, Donald, and Brad M. Barber. 2001. "Challengers, Elites, and Owning Families: A Social Class Theory of Corporate Acquisitions in the 1960s." *Administrative Science Quarterly* 46:87–120.

Pena, Inaki. 2002. "Intellectual Capital and Business Start-up Success." *Journal of Intellectual Capital* 6: 469–78.

Pennings, Johannes M., and Kyungmook Lee. 1999. "Social Capital of Organizations: Conceptualization, Level of Analysis, and Performance Implications." Pp. 43–67 in *Corporate Social Capital and Liability*, ed. Roger Leenders and Shaul M. Gabbay. Boston: Kluwer.

Perrow, Charles. 1967. "A Framework for the Comparative Analysis of Organizations." *American Sociological Review* 32:194–208.

Podolny, Joel M. 2001. "Networks as the Pipes and Prisms of the Market." *American Journal of Sociology* 107:33–60.

Podolny, Joel M., and James N. Baron. 1997. "Resources and Relationships: Social Networks and Mobility in the Workplace." *American Sociological Review* 62:673–93.

Podolny, Joel M., and Karen L. Page. 1998. "Network Forms of Organization." *Annual Review of Sociology* 24:57–76.

Portes, Alejandro, William J. Haller, and Luis Eduardo Guarnizo. 2002. "Transnational Entrepreneurs: An Alternative Form of Immigrant Economic Adaptation." *American Sociological Review* 67:278–98.

Portes, Alejandro, and Julia Sensenbrenner. 1993. "Embeddedness and Immigration: Notes on the Social Determinants of Economic Action." *American Journal of Sociology* 98:1320–50.

Powell, Walter W. 1985. *Getting into Print: The Decision-Making Process in Scholarly Publishing.* Chicago: University of Chicago Press.

———. 1990. "Neither Market Nor Hierarchy: Network Forms of Organization." Pp. 295–336 in vol. 12 of *Research in Organizational Behavior*, ed. L. L. Cummings and B. Shaw. Greenwich, Conn.: JAI Press.

———. 2001. "The Capitalist Firm in the Twenty-first Century: Emerging Patterns in Western Enterprise." Pp. 33–68 in *The Twenty-first-Century Firm: Changing Economic Organization in International Perspective,* ed. Paul DiMaggio. Princeton: Princeton University Press.

Powell, Walter W., Kenneth W. Koput, and Laurel Smith-Doerr. 1996. "Interorganizational Collaboration and the Locus of Innovation: Networks of

Learning in Biotechnology." *Administrative Science Quarterly* 41:116–45.

Powell, Walter W., and Jason Owen-Smith. 1998. "Commercialism in Universities: Life Sciences Research and Its Linkage with Industry." *Journal of Policy Analysis and Management* 17(2): 253–77.

Powell, Walter W., and Laurel Smith-Doerr. 1994. "Networks and Economic Life." Pp. 368–402 in *Handbook of Economic Sociology*, ed. Neil J. Smelser and Richard Swedberg. New York: Russell Sage Foundation; Princeton: Princeton University Press.

Powell, Walter W., Douglas White, Kenneth W. Koput, and Jason Owen-Smith. 2005. "Network Dynamics and Field Evolution: The Growth of Interorganizational Collaboration in the Life Sciences." *American Journal of Sociology*, forthcoming.

Putnam, Robert D. 1993. *Making Democracy Work: Civic Traditions in Modern Italy*. Princeton: Princeton University Press.

Raider, Holly, and David Krackhardt. 2002. "Intraorganizational Networks." Pp. 58–74 in *Companion to Organizations*, ed. Joel A. C. Baum. Malden, Mass.: Blackwell.

Rao, Hayagreeva, Gerald F. Davis, and Andrew Ward. 2000. "Embeddedness, Social Identity, and Mobility: Why Firms Leave the NASDAQ and Join the New York Stock Exchange." *Administrative Science Quarterly* 45:268–92.

Rauch, James E. 2001. "Business and Social Networks in International Trade." *Journal of Economic Literature* 39:1137–76.

Renzulli, Linda A., Howard Aldrich, and James Moody. 2000. "Family Matters: Gender, Networks, and Entrepreneurial Outcomes." *Social Forces* 79:523–46.

Robinson, David, and Toby E. Stuart. 2002. "Just How Incomplete Are Incomplete Contracts?" Working paper, Graduate School of Business, Columbia University.

Roethslisberger, Fritz J., and William J. Dickson. 1939. *Management and the Worker*. Cambridge: Harvard University Press.

Rogers, Everett M. 1958. "Categorizing the Adopters of Agricultural Practices." *Rural Sociology* 23:346–54.

———. 1995. *Diffusion of Innovations*. 4th ed. New York: Free Press.

Rogers, Everett M., and Lawrence Kincaid. 1981. *Communication Networks: Toward a New Paradigm for Research*. New York: Free Press.

Roy, Donald. 1954. "Efficiency and 'the Fix'": Informal Intergroup Relations in a Piecework Machine Shop." *American Journal of Sociology* 60:255–67.

Rubio, Mauricio. 1997. "Perverse Social Capital—Some Evidence from Colombia." *Journal of Economic Issues* 31:805–16.

Ryan, Bryce, and Neal C. Gross. 1943. "The Diffusion of Hybrid Seed Corn in Two Iowa Communities." *Rural Sociology* 23:15–24.

Saxenian, AnnaLee. 1994. *Regional Advantage: Culture and Competition in Silicon Valley and Route 128*. Cambridge: Harvard University Press.

Scott, John. 2000. *Network Analysis: A Handbook*. 2d ed. London: Sage.

Shah, Priti Pradhan. 2000. "Network Destruction: The Structural Implications of Downsizing." *Academy of Management Journal* 43:101–13.

Simmel, Georg. 1950. *The Sociology of Georg Simmel*. Trans. Kurt H. Wolff. New York: Free Press.

———. [1922] 1955. *Conflict and the Web of Group Affiliations*. Trans. Richard Bendix. New York: Free Press.

Smith, Ryan A. 2002. "Race, Gender, and Authority in the Workplace: Theory and Research." *Annual Review of Sociology* 28:509–42.

Smith-Doerr, Laurel. 2004. "Flexibility and Fairness: Effects of the Network Form of Organization on Gender Equality in Life Science Careers." *Sociological Perspectives* 47:25–54.

Smith-Doerr, Laurel, Ivan Manev, and Polly S. Rizova. 2004. "The Meaning of Success: Network Position and the Social Construction of Project Outcomes in an R&D Lab." *Journal of Engineering and Technology Management* 21:51–81.

Sorenson, Olav, and Pino G. Audia. 2000. "The Social Structure of Entrepreneurial Activity: Geographic Concentration of Footwear Production in the United States, 1940–1989." *American Journal of Sociology* 106:424–62.

Stark, David. 2001. "Ambiguous Assets for Uncertain Environments: Heterarchy in Postsocialist Firms." Pp. 69–104 in *The Twenty-first Century Firm*. Princeton: Princeton University Press.

Stevenson, William B., and Jean M. Bartunek. 1996. "Power, Interaction, Position, and the Generation of Cultural Agreement in Organizations." *Human Relations* 49:75–104.

Stinchcombe, Arthur L. 1959. "Bureaucratic and Craft Administration of Production." *Administrative Science Quarterly* 4:194–208.

———. 1989. "An Outsider's View of Network Analyses of Power." Pp. 119–33 in *Networks of Power*, ed. Robert Perucci and Harry R. Potter. New York: Aldine.

———. 1990. "Weak Structural Data (Review of Mizruchi and Schwartz)." *Contemporary Sociology* 19:380–82.

Strang, David, and Sarah A. Soule. 1998. "Diffusion in Organizations and Social Movements: From Hybrid Corn to Poison Pills." *Annual Review of Sociology* 24:265–90.

Strang, David, and Nancy B. Tuma. 1993. "Spatial and Temporal Heterogeneity in Diffusion." *American Journal of Sociology* 99:614–39.

Stuart, Toby E. 1998. "Network Positions and Propensities to Collaborate: An Investigation of Strategic Alliance Formation in a High-Technology Industry." *Administrative Science Quarterly* 43:668–98.

Stuart, Toby E., Ha Hoang, and Ralph Hybels. 1999.

"Interorganizational Endorsements and the Performance of Entrepreneurial Ventures." *Administrative Science Quarterly* 44:315–49.

Stuart, Toby E., and Joel M. Podolny. 1999. "Positional Consequences of Strategic Alliances in the Semiconductor Industry." Pp. 161–82 in vol. 16 of *Research in the Sociology of Organizations*, ed. Steven Andrews and David Knoke. Greenwich, Conn.: JAI Press.

Sturgeon, Timothy J. 2000. "How Silicon Valley Came to Be." Pp. 15–47 in *Understanding Silicon Valley*, ed. Martin Kenney. Stanford, Calif.: Stanford University Press.

Suchman, Mark. 2000. "Dealmakers and Counselors: Law Firms as Intermediaries in the Development of Silicon Valley." Pp. 71–97 in *Understanding Silicon Valley*, ed. Martin Kenney. Stanford, Calif.: Stanford University Press.

Swedberg, Richard. 1997. "New Economic Sociology: What Has Been Accomplished, What Is Ahead?" *Acta Sociologica* 40:161–82.

Tolbert, Pamela S. 1988. "Institutional Sources of Organizational Culture in Major Law Firms." Pp. 101–13 in *Institutional Patterns and Organizations*, ed. Lynne G. Zucker. Cambridge, Mass.: Ballinger.

Useem, Michael. 1984. *The Inner Circle: Large Corporations and the Rise of Business Political Activity.* Oxford: Oxford University Press.

Uzzi, Brian. 1996. "The Sources and Consequences of Embeddedness for the Economic Performance of Organizations: The Network Effect." *American Sociological Review* 61:674–98.

———. 1997. "Social Structure and Competition in Interfirm Networks: The Paradox of Embeddedness." *Administrative Science Quarterly* 42:35–67.

Uzzi, Brian, and James J. Gillespie. 1999. "Corporate Social Capital and the Cost of Financial Capital: An Embeddedness Approach." Pp. 446–59 in *Corporate Social Capital and Liability*, ed. Roger Th. A. J. Leenders and Shaul M. Gabbay. Boston: Kluwer.

Van den Bulte, Christophe, and Gary L. Lilien. 2001. "Medical Innovation Revisited: Social Contagion versus Marketing Effort." *American Journal of Sociology* 106:1409–35.

Ville, Simon, and Grant Fleming. 2000. "The Nature and Structure of Trade-Financial Networks: Evidence from the New Zealand Pastoral Sector." *Business History* 42:41–58.

Wasserman, Stanley, and Katherine Faust. 1994. *Social Network Analysis: Methods and Applications.* Cambridge: Cambridge University Press.

Watts, Duncan J., and S. H. Strogatz. 1998. "Collective Dynamics of Small-World Networks." *Nature* 363: 202–4.

Wellman, Barry, Janet Salaff, Dimitrina Dimitrova, Laura Garton, Milena Gulia, and Caroline Haythornthwaite. 1996. "Computer Networks as Social Networks: Collaborative Work, Telework, and Virtual Community." *Annual Review of Sociology* 22:213–38.

White, Douglas R., and Frank Harary. 2001. "The Cohesiveness of Blocks in Social Networks: Node Connectivity and Conditional Density." *Sociological Methodology* 31(1): 305–59.

White, Harrison C., Scott A. Boorman, and Ronald L. Breiger. 1974. "Social Structure from Multiple Networks. I. Blockmodels of Roles and Positions." *American Journal of Sociology* 81:730–80.

Yamaguchi, Kazuo. 1996. "Power in Networks of Substitutable and Complementary Exchange Relations: A Rational Choice Model and Analysis of Power Centralization." *American Sociological Review* 61: 308–22.

Zucker, Lynne G., Michael R. Darby, and Marilyn B. Brewer. 1998. "Intellectual Human Capital and the Birth of U.S. Biotechnology Enterprises." *American Economic Review* 88:290–306.

18 The Informal Economy

Alejandro Portes and William Haller

THE SET OF ACTIVITIES that comprise the informal economy is vast and offers a unique instance of how social forces affect the organization of economic transactions. We describe in the following sections the history of the concept, its changing definitions, and the attempts made to measure it empirically. However, our main aim in this chapter is to highlight the paradoxical character of informal economic activity and the way in which social structures decisively affect its onset and development.

The phenomenon of the informal economy is both deceivingly simple and extraordinarily complex, trivial in its everyday manifestations and capable of subverting the economic and political order of nations. We encounter it in our daily life in such simple activities as buying a cheap watch or a book from a street vendor, arranging for a handyman to do repair work at our home for cash, or hiring an immigrant woman to care for the children and clean the house while we are away. Such apparently trivial encounters may be dismissed as unworthy of attention until we realize that, in the aggregate, they cumulate into the billions of dollars of unreported income and that the humble vendor or cleaning woman represents the end point of complex subcontracting, labor recruitment, and labor transportation chains.

We do not commonly realize that the clothing we wear, the restaurant meals we eat, and even the laptop computer we regularly use may have something to do with the informal economy. In fact they do, and the intricate ways in which informal labor and goods enter into production and distribution chains underlie both the lower cost of the final products and their ready availability. To take the mystery away from these assertions, we will simply mention the facts underlying them: (*a*) The garment industry that produces the clothing items we buy and use is commonly anchored, at the other end of the production chain, by unregulated or poorly regulated sweatshops and home workers sewing, stitching, and packing for a piece rate and with no social benefits (Fernández-Kelly and Garcia 1989; Gereffi 1999); (*b*)

the "back of the house" staff that does much of the cleaning and food preparation in many restaurants is composed of immigrants, frequently recently arrived and undocumented, who are paid in cash and are not covered by labor contracts (Chavez 1988); (*c*) the computer industry that produces our laptops is known for subcontracting assembly of circuit boards and other components to small, often unregulated shops and even home workers; these subcontractors are paid a piece rate in an updated version of the "putting out" system. Lozano, who studied these practices in Silicon Valley, concludes that

> the computer industry requires a reliable supply of basic components that can be delivered quickly. Many small and medium-sized firms compete effectively as subcontract vendors with operations overseas. One of my respondents works for such a subcontractor out of her garage, putting together the most labor intensive portion of an assembly. . . . Rush jobs, custom work, confidential projects—managers describe them as rare events. . . . But when all these rare events are aggregated, we find that every day another "entrepreneur" . . . joins the ranks of the self-employed. (1989, 54, 59)

The examples could be multiplied. However, our purpose is not to describe the vast range of informal enterprises covered in the literature, but to explore how these activities interact with existing social structures and the policies and enforcement practices of national states. It is in these interactions that the paradoxical character of the informal economy emerges clearly and where its lessons for both economic and sociological theories of market behavior are shown most compellingly. After examining alternative definitions and measurement approaches, we focus on these dynamics centered on four paradoxes: the social underpinnings of the informal economy; its ambiguous relationships with state regulation; its elusiveness; and its functionality for the economic and political institutions that it supposedly undermines.[1]

DEFINITIONS

Origins of the Concept

The concept of informal economy was born in the Third World, out of a series of studies on urban labor markets in Africa. Keith Hart, the economic anthropologist who coined the term, saw it as a way of giving expression to "the gap between my experience there and anything my English education had taught me before" (1990, 158). In his view, the empirical observations about popular entrepreneurship in Accra and other African capitals were at odds with received wisdom from "the western discourse on economic development" (1990, 158).

In his report to the International Labour Office (ILO), Hart postulated a dualist model of income opportunities of the urban labor force, based largely on the distinction between wage employment and self-employment. The concept of informality was applied to the self-employed. Hart emphasized the notable dynamics and diversity of these activities that, in his view, went well beyond "shoeshine boys and sellers of matches" (1973, 68). This dynamic characterization of the informal sector was subsequently lost as the concept became institutionalized within the ILO bureaucracy, which essentially redefined informality as synonymous with poverty. The informal economy was taken to refer to an "urban way of doing things" characterized by (1) low entry barriers in terms of skill, capital, and organization; (2) family ownership of enterprises; (3) small scale of operation; (4) labor-intensive production with outdated technology; and (5) unregulated and competitive markets (Sethuraman 1981; Klein and Tokman 1988).

Additional characteristics derived from this definition included low levels of productivity and a low capacity for accumulation (Tokman 1982). In later publications of the ILO's Regional Employment Programme for Latin America (PREALC), employment in the informal sector was consistently termed *underemployment* and assumed to affect workers who could not gain entry into the modern economy (PREALC 1985; Garcia 1991; Klein and Tokman 1988). This characterization of informality as an excluded sector in less developed economies has been enshrined in numerous ILO, PREALC, and World Bank studies of urban poverty and labor markets (Sethuraman 1981; Gerry 1978; Perez-Sainz 1992).

This negative characterization of the informal sector has been challenged by other students of the subject who see it in the opposite light. From this alternative stance, informal activities are a sign of the popular entrepreneurial dynamism, described by Hart (1990, 158) as "people taking back in their own hands some of the economic power that centralized agents sought to deny them." The Peruvian economist Hernando de Soto reformulated Hart's original theme and gave it renewed impulse. In *The Other Path* (1989), de Soto defines informality as the popular response to the rigid "mercantilist" states dominant in Peru and other Latin American countries that survive by granting the privilege of legal participation in the economy to a small elite. Hence, unlike its portrayal by ILO and PREALC as a survival mechanism in response to insufficient modern job creation, informal enterprise represents the irruption of real market forces in an economy straitjacketed by state regulation (Portes and Schauffler 1993).

Contemporary Definitions

The strong normative component attached to these competing analyses of the informal sector in the Third World is not entirely absent in the industrialized countries, but research there has attempted to arrive at a more precise and less tendentious definition. There appears to be growing consensus among researchers in the advanced world that the proper scope of the term *informal sector* encompasses "those actions of economic agents that fail to adhere to the established institutional rules or are denied their protection" (Feige 1990, 990). Or, alternatively, it includes "all income-earning activities that are not regulated by the state in social environments where similar activities are regulated" (Castells and Portes 1989, 12). These definitions do not advance an a priori judgment of whether such activities are good or bad, leaving the matter to empirical investigation. In this sense, they seem heuristically superior to those used in the Third World, which anticipate from the start the conclusions to be reached. However, even neutral definitions are hampered by the very breadth of the subject matter they try to encompass. Writing from the perspective of the new institutional economics, Feige proposes a useful taxonomy as a way of specifying the relevant universe further. His classification is based on the institutional rules that go unobserved by a particular economic activity. Under the umbrella term *underground economy,* he distinguishes four subforms:

1. The *illegal* economy encompasses the production and distribution of legally prohibited goods and

services. This includes such activities as drug trafficking, prostitution, and illegal gambling.

2. The *unreported* economy consists of actions that "circumvent or evade established fiscal rules as codified in the tax code" (Feige 1990, 991). The amount of income that should be reported to the tax authorities but is not represents a summary measure of this form.

3. The *unrecorded* economy encompasses activities that circumvent reporting requirements of government statistical agencies. Its summary measure is the amount of income that should be recorded in national accounting systems but is not.

4. The *informal* economy comprises economic actions that bypass the costs of, and are excluded from the protection of, laws and administrative rules covering "property relationships, commercial licensing, labor contracts, torts, financial credit, and social security systems" (Feige 1990, 992).

Of course, there is much overlap between these various forms since activities termed informal are also, for the most part, unrecorded and unreported. The most important conceptual distinction is that between informal and illegal activities, since each possesses distinct characteristics that set them apart from the other. Sociologists recognize that "legal" and "criminal," like "normal" and "abnormal," are socially defined categories subject to change. However, illegal enterprise involves the production and commercialization of goods that are defined in a particular place and time as illicit, while informal enterprise deals, for the most part, with licit goods.

Castells and Portes (1989) clarified this distinction in the diagram reproduced as figure 1. The basic difference between formal and informal does not hinge on the character of the final product, but on the manner in which it is produced and exchanged. Thus, articles of clothing, restaurant food, or computer circuit boards—all perfectly licit goods—may have their origins in legally regulated production arrangements or in those that bypass official rules. By explicitly distinguishing these three categories—formal, informal, and illegal activities—we can explore their mutual relationships systematically, a task that becomes difficult when illegal and informal are confused. Blanes Jimenez (1989), for example, analyzed the pervasive effects of the Bolivian drug economy on that country's formal and informal sectors. Similar interrelationships were studied in the former Soviet Union and its Eastern European satellites by Stark (1989) and Grossman (1989).

I. Definitions:

+ = Licit
− = Illicit

Process of Production and Distribution	*Final Product*	*Economic Type*
+	+	Formal
−	+	Informal
−	−	Criminal

II. Relationships:

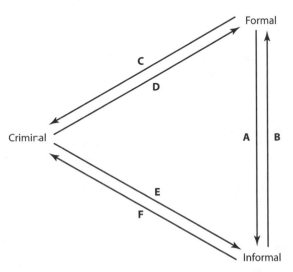

FIGURE 1. Types of economic activities and their interrelationships. A. State interference, competition from large firms, sources of capital and technology. B. Cheaper consumer goods and industrial inputs, flexible reserves of labor. C. State interference and disruption, supplies of certain controlled goods. D. Corruption, "gatekeeper's rents" for selected state officials. E. Capital, demand for goods, new income-earning opportunities. F. Cheaper goods, flexible reserves of labor. Source Castells and Portes 1989, 14.

A Functional Typology

These studies plus a number of others have given rise to a functional classification of informal activities according to their goals. Such activities—always defined as those taking place outside the pale of state regulation—may aim, first, at the survival of the individual or household through direct subsistence production or through simple sale of goods and services in the market. Second, they may be oriented toward increasing managerial flexibility and decreasing labor costs of formal sector firms through off-the-books hiring and subcontracting of informal entrepreneurs. Third, they may be organized for capital accumulation by small firms through mobilization of their solidary relationships, greater flexibility, and lower costs. These three types are labeled informal economies of respectively *survival, dependent exploitation,* and *growth* (Portes, Castells, and Benton 1989). The self-construction of shelter and the proliferation of street vending in cities of the Third World are commonly cited as examples of the first type (Roberts 1989a; Cross 1998). The relationships between underground immigrant subcontractors, jobbers, and large firms in the U.S. apparel industry provide an example of the second (Waldinger 1986; Sassen 1989; Schoepfle and Perez-Lopez 1992). The highly successful networks of artisan microproducers in central Italy represent an instance of the third (Sabel 1986, 1989; Capecchi 1989).

In practice, the three types are not mutually exclusive, either in terms of their coexistence in the same urban settings or in the intentions of participants. Thus, the same work that represents survival for an informal laborer may be appropriated as flexibility by the formal firm that hires him or her. Similarly, informal subcontractors linked in subordinate relations with larger firms may amass sufficient capital and cooperative ties to launch themselves into an autonomous path of growth. The three types are distinguished less by the motivation of actors than by the successively more complex levels of social organization that they require. Hence, while survival strategies of informal vendors in Third World cities are by no means simple, they are in a plane different altogether from the complex coordination required by an entire community of producers to achieve sustained growth (Benton 1989; Sabel 1994; Brusco 1982).

A final definition of informality, pioneered by Gershuny, Pahl, and other British sociologists, links the concept with the self-provisioning of goods and services by households in developed economies (Gershuny 1978, 1985; Pahl 1980; Pahl and Wallace 1985). Such activities as home repair or vegetable gardening represent direct subsistence production, except that they are not carried out by impoverished actors, but by middle-income households seeking to maximize the efficient allocation of time. Self-provisioning represents a kind of activity different from those labeled informal since it neither contravenes state regulation nor involves active market participation. Indeed, the principal aim of self-provisioning is to withdraw certain areas of household consumption from dependence on marketed goods and services. This set of activities studied by English researchers falls, more properly, under the category of direct subsistence production.

THE SOCIAL DYNAMICS OF INFORMALITY

The Paradox of Embeddedness

Because of the absence of state regulation, informal transactions are commonly portrayed as the play of pure market forces. Indeed, celebratory accounts of the informal economy often define it as the irruption of the "true market" in an otherwise straitjacketed economy stifled by state regulation (de Soto 1989). Based on his African experience, Hart (1990, 158) called it the "untamed market" and declared that such liberating practices are becoming global in scope. On the eve of Communism's demise in Eastern Europe, a number of analysts argued that the free market forces unleashed by the informal or "second" economy in these countries were a key solvent that undermined the political legitimacy of state socialism and would lead to its ultimate implosion (Grossman 1989; Borocz 1989; Gabor 1988; Rev 1986).

The substantive problem is, however, that the absence of state regulation in informal exchange opens the door for violations of normative expectations and widespread fraud. The question arises: In the absence of supervisory agents, who is to control unscrupulous producers, purveyors of adulterated goods, and defaulters on loans? Isolated arm's-length transactions may still occur among strangers, such as the quick sale of a contraband good, but the activities that require greater resources and a longer time perspective are subject to every kind of uncertainty and peril. The problem manifests itself even at the level of short-term face-to-face transactions. The immigrant laborers who are commonly seen standing on street corners waiting for work in New York, Miami, Los Angeles, and other cities exemplify the dilemma (Stepick 1989; Millman 1992; Cornelius 1998). They are commonly picked up by contractors who hire them for days or even weeks only to defraud them at the end by paying them lower wages than originally promised. In the absence of a contract and a secure legal status in the country, how are these immigrants to seek redress?

It is worth noticing the significant difference in this respect between practices defined as illegal or as informal. Illegal enterprise that provides illicit goods or services on a recurrent basis is always accompanied by some means of enforcing agreements, usually by force. This is the role played by the pimp in prostitution, the bouncer in underground night spots, and the professional enforcer in Sicilian crime families (Gambetta 1993). Here the illegal economy is closer to the formal in the sense that both possess established systems of redress and enforcement, be they through the police and the courts or through specialized enforcement personnel. In contrast, many of the practices defined as informal are devoid of such protection. The garment subcontractor who delivers one hundred shirts to an informal middleman on the promise of future payment is entirely at the mercy of that promise. Similarly, the immigrant worker who is hired informally by a labor contractor has no means of enforcing his claim to the stipulated wage.

The first paradox of the informal economy is that the more it approaches the model of the "true market," the more it is dependent on social ties for its effective functioning. The dynamics that Granovetter (1985, 1993) labeled "the problem of embeddedness" are nowhere clearer than in transactions where the only recourse against malfeasance is mutual trust by virtue of common membership in some overarching social structure. Trust in informal exchanges is generated both by shared identities and feelings and by the expectation that fraudulent actions will be penalized by the exclusion of the violator from key social networks and from future transactions. To the extent that economic resources flow through such transactions, the socially enforced penalty of exclusion can become more threatening, and hence effective, than other types of sanctions.

The Central Italian Informal Economy

Examples of this paradox abound in the literature. The famed Italian industrial district in the central region of Emilia-Romagna is composed of small, highly dynamic firms many of which started as informal enterprises and continue to use informally produced inputs and labor. According to Capecchi, relationships of *complicity* rather than of exploitation or pure competition characterize the daily interactions between employers and workers and among owners of firms. Small enterprises in textiles, ceramics, metallurgy, and others seek to respond quickly to market demand, specializing in particular market niches, cooperating with each other in meeting sudden surges in demand, and resisting outside manipulations to undercut prices. Workers are hired informally, but are paid reliably

and are treated as apprentices who eventually may be able to set up their own firms:

> [M]any small firms concentrated on performing certain manufacturing operations or on producing certain manufacturing operations or on producing certain parts of the machine. . . . Thus a subsystem of enterprises gradually evolved in which there was no leading firm. The factory that produced the final good did not necessarily constitute the center of the system because its role was often only that of assembling various parts produced by other firms. (Capecchi 1989, 200–201)

This system of egalitarian flexible specialization, explicitly opposed to the regulatory dictates emanating from the central government in Rome, is anchored in tightly bound community networks identified by a common political culture. Emilia-Romagna is the core of the Italian "red belt" that witnessed militant organized opposition to the Fascist regime and, subsequently, to the designs of Christian Democratic governments to industrialize the nation on the basis of mass-producing companies concentrated in Turin and other northern Italian cities. Instead, the Communist regional government of Emilia-Romagna encouraged and sponsored skilled workers and artisans to develop their own firms as an alternative to deskilling and mass migration north. The successful small firms thus created were not isolated instances, but became embedded in an overarching normative framework. This framework promoted solidarity grounded on a common history and political outlook and ostracized those behaving as "true" market competitors. Such a normative structure allowed the industrial system *as a whole* to compete effectively in export markets (Brusco 1982; Sabel 1986, 1994).

Williamson (1975, 1994) has emphasized the counterpoint between hierarchies and markets as alternative forms of conducting business and maximizing efficiency. As is well known, hierarchical transactions are those conducted under the command structure of the firm; market exchange involves arm's-length contact between impersonal profit maximizers. The operation of the informal economy is characterized by the general *absence* of both of these forms of exchange and their substitution by socially monitored transactions. Lacking any hierarchical system or any legal means to sanction contractual irregularities, the success of informal enterprise is predicated entirely on this third form of regulation. Powell (1990, 317) labels it the *network form* of economic organization and describes its operation as involving "scant separation of formal business roles and personal roles. One's standing in one arena often determines one's place in the other. As a result, there is little need for hierarchical oversight, because the desire for continued participation successfully discourages opportunism."

Informality under Socialist Regimes

By definition, informal economic activities bypass existing laws and the regulatory agencies of the state. It follows that the more pervasive the enforcement of state rules and the greater the penalties for violation, the more socially embedded informal transactions must be. This is so because their success in highly repressive situations depends not only on preventing malfeasance by partners but on avoiding detection by the authorities. Secrecy in these situations demands a high level of mutual trust, and the only way trust can be created is through the existence of tight social networks.

The operation of the Jewish informal economy in the former Soviet Republic of Georgia represents a good example of this situation. The system centered on the clandestine production and distribution of consumer goods. Production took place in state-owned factories and with state-provided raw materials in direct violation of official rules. Heavy prison sentences awaited those caught. Despite this threat, the system flourished and functioned smoothly for years (Lomnitz 1988, 51). It required securing low official production targets and a high wastage allowance to accommodate clandestine production. Bookkeeping was systematically altered. Production lines, for example, were declared "in maintenance" at times of peak unofficial production. Substandard parts and inputs were used to fulfill the official quota in order to increase the supply of parts going into clandestine goods.

Georgian Jews could sustain this complex informal system only through the operation of strong networks cemented on a common culture and historical experience. Altman (1983, 4–6), who studied the system, observed, "Trust is a fundamental requirement in the operation of the second economy. . . . A man's word has to be his bond." In case of trouble with the authorities, such as police raids and infiltration by state agents, the network bailed out threatened members and obliterated incriminating evidence (Lomnitz 1988, 52). The high level of mutual trust required to overcome totalitarian repression was reinforced by periodic rites of

solidarity that included lavish feasts in which other network members were entertained, often at great expense (Altman 1983).

High levels of state repression and external threat clearly strengthen solidarity bonds among those involved in informal activities. Bounded solidarity among network members—symbolized and strengthened by the rites just described—represents an added element supporting clandestine transactions and preventing breaches of secrecy (Lomnitz 1988). Nevertheless, it is not a spontaneous feeling of solidarity, but the enforcement capacity of the community that constitutes the ultimate guarantee against violations.

Recent reports from Cuba—the last formally socialist regime in the west—confirm these observations. Despite the threat of heavy fines and prison terms and the omnipresence of the state, the Cuban informal economy has flourished, comprising, according to a recent estimate, up to 40 percent of the national domestic product in 2000 (Roque 2002; Henken 2002). There are clandestine factories making and repairing motors for water pumps and refrigerators, manufacturing soft drinks and beer, and producing cigars for export. Home construction and, especially, home repairs are increasingly informalized. In all instances, inputs for production, construction, and repairs come from thefts of state property.

While short-term transactions involving black market goods do not require any particular social bond, entire clandestine factories and marketing enterprises are invariably undergirded by family and other ties between implicated state personnel, middlemen or *bisneros* (from "businessman"), and final consumers. As in Soviet Georgia, those bonds are indispensable for generating enforceable trust, which, in turn, makes possible extensive and sustained informal enterprise:

> Legally, it is impossible to own a small enterprise in Cuba. Yet there is a great variety of clandestine enterprises with a notable capacity of innovation and accumulation. . . . When one enters the exclusive zone of Maramar in Havana, vendors call in a low voice "microwave," "air conditioner," "bedroom set," "parabolic antenna" . . . a great variety of products forbidden to Cubans. Where do they get them? Without doubt from state supplies, but there are also clandestine networks departing from the special export processing zones. Here we find everything: theft, corruption, speculation, delivery of products by foreign firms to their Cuban workers for sale in the black markets. (Roque 2002, 10–11)

THE ROLE OF THE STATE

The Paradox of State Control

As an example of what he calls the "predatory state" in the Third World, Evans (1989) describes the case of Zaire. Under the long regime of Mobutu Sese Seko, the Zairian state degenerated into a collection of fiefdoms—offices freely bought and sold—that thrived on the collection of "gatekeepers' rents" from firms and from the population at large. The situation is one in which state officials squeeze resources from civil society "without any more regard for the welfare of the citizenry than a predator has for the welfare of its prey" (Evans 1989, 582). Evans notes that this is an extreme example, buttressing the critique by public choice theorists about the nefarious consequence of state interference in the economy. For public choice advocates, all states sooner or later become predatory (Buchanan, Tollison, and Tullock 1980).

The logical corollary of this position, and more broadly that advanced by neoutilitarian theorists, is the complete removal of state interference from the market as inimical to its development. This position finds an enthusiastic Third World echo in the critique of the mercantilist state advanced by de Soto and his followers. There is, however, another perspective from which the behavior of rapacious state officials may be described. More than predators, these officials can be defined as de facto employees of outside entrepreneurs who hire their services in order to obtain privileged access to scarce government resources—be they contracts or the nonobservance of regulations. The more state officials are willing to bend the rules for a price, the more the situation approaches that of a free market in which goods and services—in this case those purveyed by the state—are sold to the highest bidder (Moya-Pons 1992).

This marketization of the state does not represent the triumph of the informal economy so much as the elimination of the distinction between the two sectors. Where the state does not regulate anything because it is at the mercy of market forces, there is no formal economy. Hence, the formal/informal distinction loses meaning since all economic activities approach the character of those labeled informal. This triumph of the "invisible hand" does not lead to capitalist development, as would be anticipated from public choice theory and from de Soto's critique of the mercantilist state; the opposite is actually the case. In the absence of a stable legal framework and credible enforcement of contracts, long-term productive investment becomes impossible. Under these conditions, entrepreneurship consists of the opportunistic appropriation of rents through purchase of state privileges rather than of any long-term planning for profit. Since there is no outside arbiter of market competition, the rules become uncertain, frustrating systematic capitalist planning and the development of a modern bourgeoisie.

Man's natural propensity to "truck, barter, and exchange one thing for another," the Smithian dictum so dear to neoclassical theorists, does not in fact furnish a basis for economic development on a national scale. Someone must stand outside the competitive fray, making sure that property rules are enforced and contracts observed. Otherwise no grounds exist for predictable exchange among a myriad of anonymous actors, as it occurs in real markets. More than 40 years ago, Polanyi ([1944] 1957) argued that "natural propensities" did not create markets. Instead, "the road to the free market was opened and kept open by an enormous increase in continuous, centrally organized, and controlled interventionism" (140).

It is the intervention of the state in economic life that creates a "formal space" of predictable and enforceable transactions where modern capitalism can flourish. There is, however, a flip side to this situation well captured by Richard Adams's (1975, 69) epigram that "the more we organize society, the more resistant it becomes to our ability to organize it." A naive evolutionary view of the informal economy would depict it as dominant during an early era of weak regulation, while gradually becoming marginal and even insignificant as all facets of economic activity fall under state control. In fact, largely the opposite is the case. Since informal activities are defined precisely by their bypassing and escaping such controls, it follows that the greater the scope and reach of attempted state regulations, the more varied the opportunities to bypass them.

Lomnitz (1988, 54) states the point succinctly: "Order creates disorder. The formal economy creates its own informality." *The paradox of state control is that official efforts to obliterate unregulated activities through the proliferation of rules and controls often expand the very conditions that give rise to these activities.* The point is graphically portrayed in figure 2. Under conditions of limited state control, most economic activity is self-regulated but not informal since it does not contravene any official rule. As rules expand, opportunities to bypass them increase concomitantly until, at the limit, the

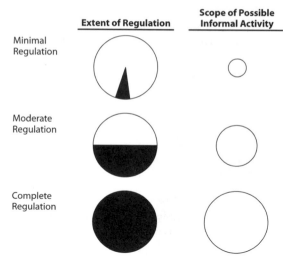

Extent of Regulation   **Scope of Possible Informal Activity**

Minimal Regulation

Moderate Regulation

Complete Regulation

FIGURE 2.   The paradox of state control: regulation and the informal economy

entire economy is subject to the possibility of rule violation for profit. To illustrate the point with a case familiar to most readers, tax havens and tax-avoiding schemes would not exist if there were no taxation system. The more intrusive the latter, the greater the incentive and the broader the opportunities to seek redress through concealment and through various transfer ploys (Ghersi 1997; Leonard 1998).

State Capacities and Intent

The complex relationship between the state and the informal economy does not end here, however. Figure 2 makes clear that state regulation can create informality or, put differently, that the informal economy would not exist without a universe of formal, controlled activities. Yet empirical evidence indicates that the scope of the informal economy varies greatly among states with comparable formal regulations and, within nation-states, among different regions and localities. For example, the economies of northern European nations are highly regulated, but this has not produced a parallel bourgeoning informal sector, as could be predicted from figure 2 (Reenoy 1984; Dallago 1990; Leonard 1998). Similarly, rising unemployment in the old industrial cities of the U.S. Northeast did not lead to a massive informal economy organized by members of the old displaced working class. While these workers commonly engaged in casual income-earning and self-provisioning activities, the construction of complex chains of informal industrial subcontracting was beyond their

reach. In the United States, these chains remained confined, for the most part, to immigrant enclaves (Waldinger 1985, 1986; Sassen 1989; Guarnizo 1994; Zhou 1992).

In the light of this and other evidence, Adams's and Lomnitz's hypothesis, summarized in figure 2, can be reformulated as predicting that the expansion of state regulation enhances the *opportunities* for engaging in irregular activities, but does not determine their actual size or form. The actual implementation of these opportunities depends on two other factors: (*a*) the state's regulatory capacity; and (*b*) the social structure and cultural resources of the population subject to these regulations. It is obvious that the capacity of official agencies to enforce the rules that they promulgate affects the extent to which informal opportunities can be implemented and the forms that they can take. It is less obvious that state strength is, in principle, independent of the set of rules that it seeks to enforce. Put differently, states with comparable regulatory capacities may assign to themselves very different "loads" of attempted control of private economic activity. The point is presented in figure 3, which distinguishes among several ideal-typical situations.

States with little enforcement capacity may be conscious of that fact and leave civil society to its own devices. This leads to a "frontier" economy where observance of commitments and regulation of economic exchanges depend on private force or traditional normative structures. Alternatively, a weak state may seek to transform this frontier economy into a more law-abiding one by promulgating a limited set of rules. This would lead naturally to a partition between an "enclave" of formal capitalism and legal enforcement of contracts and a largely self-regulated economy on the outside. This situation is typical of many Third World nations, where the formal enclave is usually limited to the capital city and its environs (Macharia 1997; Perez-Sainz 1992).

Zaire under Mobutu (as described by Evans) or the Peruvian mercantilist state (as portrayed by de Soto) can be regarded as instances of a third situation where extensive paper regulations of the economy coexist with an inept and weak state. This is the situation that favors the rise of a predatory pattern in which only a small elite benefits from state protection and resources, either controlling directly by manipulating the application of rules to the exclusion of others, or controlling indirectly, through bribed officials (Cross 1998; Bromley 1994).

State Strength	Regulatory Intent		
	Minimal	Limited	Total
Weak	The "Frontier" State	The "Enclave" State	The "Mercantilist" State
Strong	The Liberal State	The Social Democratic Welfare State	The Totalitarian State

FIGURE 3.   State regulatory power and the extent of regulation

Strong states oscillate, in turn, between a circumspect approach to regulation of the private economy and an attempt to supplant or control its every aspect. The first type represents the laissez-faire state so dear to liberal theorists: markets operate with limited, but reliable, supervision, and the state orients its considerable resources toward other pursuits. The opposite extreme devolves into totalitarianism, as exemplified by the nations of the defunct Soviet bloc. In these situations, the state seeks to subsume civil society, provoking both widespread resistance to the rules and multiple opportunities for their violation. In between are those governments that seek an activist, but partial regulatory role for the sake of a more equitable distribution of wealth. The welfare states of Western Europe fall into this last type (Western 1998).

The Role of Civil Society

Variations in the scope of official regulations and states' differential capacity to police them interact with the characteristics of the population subject to these rules. It stands to reason that societies vary in their receptivity or resistance to official regulation and in their ability to organize underground forms of enterprise. The same variation exists among groups and communities within a specific nation-state. A population that is socialized into regular waged employment as the normal form of work, that channels demands through unions and other formal associations, and that weathers economic downturns through state-provided welfare and unemployment benefits is unlikely to organize an underground economy and is far more inclined to denounce those who engage in such activities (Roberts 1989b).

This is the case in Germany, which offers the most generous unemployment benefits in Western

Europe, but has also legislated tough sentences for those engaging in off-the-books economic activities while receiving those benefits (Leonard 1998). The policy is reported to receive strong support from public opinion, which regards such "side" employment as free riding on law-abiding and tax-paying citizens. The British working class during the period of Thatcherist economic adjustment in the 1980s offers a parallel example. Despite double-digit rates of unemployment, declining wages, and widespread dissatisfaction with state policies, widespread informalization failed to emerge in Britain. Instead, those displaced from full-time formal work turned to part-time legal employment and to self-provisioning (Standing 1989).

In his study of 730 working-class and middle-class households in the island of Sheppey, Pahl found, for example, that 55 percent engaged in self-provisioning for a variety of goods and services but only 4 percent performed the same tasks for informal wages outside the home (Pahl and Wallace 1985, 212–13). Roberts (1989b, 1991) argues that a large informal economy failed to materialize in Britain despite increasingly precarious employment conditions because of the individualistic character of the welfare system, which fragments community solidarity, and to a working-class tradition that supports state control of the economy. In this context, independent efforts at informal entrepreneurship are more likely to be denounced as violations of the law than supported by neighbors and fellow workers.

At the opposite end, networked communities accustomed to relying on their own devices for survival and suspicious of official intervention are more likely to view the organization of informal enterprise as a normal part of life and involvement in the underground economy as a justifiable form of resistance. Such communities are capable of sustaining regular economic transactions in "frontier" situations where little official regulation exists (see fig. 2). This is the case of stateless or nearly stateless nations where tribal and clan solidarities occupy the place of official regulation. Somalia, a stateless country with a functioning private economy, offers a case in point (Lacey 2002). Such a self-reliant community confronts state efforts to expand and strengthen the formal sector with an awesome adversary: no matter how strong the state apparatus is, a densely networked civil society is capable of derailing and resisting official authority at every turn. The Emilian story of resistance to the dictates of the central Italian state offers another example, in an altogether different context, of the potential effects of such networks (Capecchi 1989).

It is thus necessary to supplement the typology of state regulation in figure 3 with one that incorporates the characteristics of the population subject to it. This modified ideal typology is presented in figure 4. The resulting sixfold classification highlights the point that an individualistic, atomized society "works" well only in tandem with states able to enforce limited regulation of market activity and to respond effectively to economic downturns through universalistic welfare programs. The advanced democracies of Western Europe approximate this type. In the limiting case of little state control over an atomized population, the situation would revert to a Hobbesian generalized war. At the opposite extreme of complete atomization coupled with a powerful state, we would have the basis for totalitarianism, as society lies defenseless before official power. The Soviet Union in the heyday of Stalinism approximated this type (Nove 1969; Grossman 1989).

It is difficult, however, to identify empirical instances of either extreme type because, in the absence of effective state regulation that meets basic needs of the population, the latter tends to self-organize on the basis of whatever grounds for social solidarity and normative enforcement can be found. In "frontier" situations, Hobbesian wars are commonly prevented by the emergence of unofficial hierarchies grounded on tradition and able to enforce minimum order. In the totalitarian case, the initially unchecked government power becomes increasingly contested by sectors of civil society that find grounds for solidarity and ways to bypass the omnipresent rules. The end stage of this confrontation commonly features a state economy weakened, in multiple ways, by its inability to stamp out popular initiatives, while simultaneously dependent on them. This is what happened in the former Soviet Union and its East European satellites, where the "second" economy undermined and eventually replaced the state as the true pivot of economic activity (Rev 1986; Treml 1985; Stark 1989). The current situation in Cuba, as described by local independent economists, seems to be approaching this point (Perez Roque 2002).

A logical corollary of this analysis is that the high point of formal regulation of the economy and ability to neutralize recalcitrant sectors is achieved in the midrange of limited oversight of private enterprise by a competent state apparatus. Attempts to go beyond this limit inevitably trigger resistance, reducing the very scope of control that pro-

Character of Civil Society	Extent of Regulation		
	Minimal	Limited	Total
Atomized (Individualistic)	Hobbesian War	Universalistic Enforcement of Rules (Western Democracies)	Stalinist Planning
Networked	Social Enforcement Structures	Competing Legal/Social Enforcement Structures	Widespread Anti-Statist Resistance

FIGURE 4.   Civil society and state regulation of the economy

liferating rules seek to achieve. Figure 5 highlights the complementary point that densely networked communities are more difficult to subdue at any level of state regulation. This helps explain why organized informal subcontracting and other forms of informal enterprise in Western democracies are commonly rooted in tightly knit ethnic enclaves (Sassen 1989; Zhou 1992; Zhou and Bankston 1995). It also explains why the most effective challenges to Soviet totalitarianism were mounted by groups who, like the Georgian Jews, could rely on solidary networks and a cultural basis for norm enforcement.

To summarize, the basic paradox of state control is that increased official regulation of economic activity does not necessarily reduce the informal economy, but may expand it by creating opportunities for profitable violation of the rules. However, the extent to which these opportunities are implemented varies with the scope of attempted official control, the effectiveness of the state apparatus, and the countervailing power of society to resist or bypass official rules. A corollary of this conclusion is that efforts by strong states to stamp out all

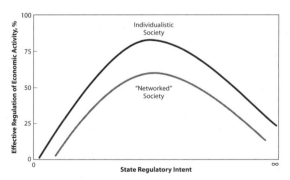

FIGURE 5.   State regulatory power and the extent of regulation

traces of nonregulated economic activity seldom succeed, as they consistently activate latent sources of solidarity among the population, leading to consequences opposite to those intended.

MEASURING THE UNMEASURABLE

The Labor Market Approach

By definition, informal activities violate the law, and thus participants seek to conceal them. This makes it impossible to arrive at precise and reliable estimates of the extent of these activities or the number of people involved. The capacity of society to confront the state is nowhere clearer than in its ability to mislead taxmen, inspectors, and statisticians as to what is really taking place on the ground. This capacity gives rise to a third paradox that we will examine later in this section.

In the absence of precise measures of the informal economy, a variety of approximations have been devised. They fall into four main categories: (*a*) the labor market approach; (*b*) the small-firm approach; (*c*) the household consumption approach; (*d*) the macroeconomic discrepancy approach. Labor market approximations estimate the percentage of the total or economically active population (EAP) that works informally on the basis of specific employment categories identified in censuses or nationally representative surveys. The assumption is that certain categories of people are more prone to conceal all or some of their income-earning activities from taxing and recording authorities. The self-employed are foremost among these groups.

Presumably, as Molefsky points out (1981, 25), "the self-employed have greater opportunities to hide income and participate in the underground economy than other workers." Indeed, a study by the U.S. Internal Revenue Service, cited by this author, found that 47 percent of workers classified as independent contractors did not report any of their earnings for tax purposes (Molefsky 1981, 25). A similar rationale has led the International Labour Office (ILO) and its regional affiliates, such as the Regional Employment Program for Latin America (PREALC) to categorize the self-employed, minus professionals and technicians, as part of the informal sector.

A second suspect category is the unemployed because of the possibility that they may be working "on the side" while receiving benefits. This rationale is not plausible in Third World countries where unemployment benefits are nonexistent, but it is quite applicable in advanced countries. For the United States, economist Peter Gutmann stated flatly that "the U.S. unemployment rate, on which so much government policy depends, is substantially overstated" (1979, 22). He went on to estimate that the overcount of the unemployed was approximately 1.5 percent or approximately one million workers in 1980. In Gutmann's view, reinforced by later authors, about one in five of the officially unemployed is really a disguised informal worker or entrepreneur (Leonard 1998).

In a field study in Cleveland, MacDonald (1994) found that working while claiming benefits was "a way of life" among the poor, justified as a necessary strategy to make ends meet. Informal employment was provided by subcontractors who paid low wages for work that was often irregular. A similar pattern has been uncovered in a number of European countries. In Italy, the national statistical agency, ISTAT, estimated an irregular labor force in the construction industry numbering half a million workers in the early 1990s. These workers combine spells of unemployment, funded by state benefits, with periods of formal or informal employment. A common pattern is for construction firms to hire workers on the books for the minimum number of weeks legally required for benefits and then to dismiss them and rehire them informally through subcontractors. Similar findings have been reported in Greece and in Northern Ireland (Mingione 1990; Leonard 1994, 1998).

A fourth category is the occupationally inactive. The rationale is that those not working and not looking for work are more likely to engage in underground income-earning activities, at least on a part-time basis. Gutmann used the recorded decline in male labor force participation between 1951 and 1976 and again between 1970 and 1990 to hypothesize that many of these dropouts had actually moved to the underground economy (Gutmann 1978; Greenfield 1993). This hypothesis is open to challenge on a number of counts, including the fact that the largest and only significant declines took place among male workers aged 55 or older. Clearly, other factors such as ill health, disability, or retirement can play a major role in accounting for these figures. In other age categories, male labor force participation rates fluctuated erratically while, among females, they increased consistently and sizably for all age groups, except the oldest (Greenfield 1993, 80–81). These inconsistencies have led to the dismissal of labor force nonparticipation as a reliable indicator of informality.

TABLE 1.   Estimates of the Informal Economy Based on Selected Employment Categories, 1980–98

Country[a]	Year	Employment Category			
		Workers in Micro-enterprises[b] %	Own Account Workers[c]	Domestic Servants	Total %[d]
Argentina	1980	10.1	32.2	3.9	46.2
	1998	15.7	19.6	4.8	40.1
Brazil	1980	10.7	19.3	7.5	37.5
	1997	9.7	25.8	8.6	44.1
Costa Rica	1981	10.0	16.7	5.5	32.2
	1998	10.6	15.4	4.8	30.8
Mexico	1984	e	24.7	2.6	e
	1998	14.9	20.5	4.1	39.5
Panama	1979	e	17.3	6.1	e
	1998	6.4	18.2	6.6	31.2
Uruguay	1981	8.8	17.7	7.5	34.0
	1998	10.6	19.9	7.2	37.7
Venezuela	1981	20.2	18.0	6.1	44.3
	1994	9.2	27.4	4.0	40.6
United States	1980	4.0	4.5	0.9	9.4
	2000	3.6	4.0	0.5	8.1
California	1980	4.0	4.5	0.8	9.3
	2000	3.3	4.3	1.0	8.6
Florida	1980	4.5	4.5	0.6	9.6
	2000	4.0	3.5	0.5	8.0
New York	1980	3.9	2.5	0.9	7.3
	2000	4.0	2.9	0.7	7.6

Source: Economic Commission for Latin America and the Caribbean (ECLAC) 2000, tables 6, 11; U.S. Bureau of the Census 1980, 2000a; 2000b.

[a] For all Latin American countries estimates are available only for the urban economically active population.

[b] As percent of the civilian economically active population aged 15 to 64.

[c] Salaried and unpaid family workers in firms employing less than 5 workers.

[d] Self-employed individuals minus professionals and technicians.

[e] No data available for this category of workers.

The ILO adds other occupational categories to the informal sector based primarily on data from less developed countries but with applications to wealthier nations as well. Domestic servants and unpaid family workers are thus classified as informal. So are workers in microenterprises that employ up to five workers on the rationale that these enterprises are either off the books or, if registered, commonly fail to observe legal rules in their hiring practices (Perez-Sainz 1992; Klein and Tokman 2000). Based on these employment categories, as recorded in national household surveys, UN agencies can provide estimates of the informal labor force for most countries. Table 1 presents these estimates for selected Latin American countries and their evolution during the last two decades ending in 2000. For comparative purposes, figures for the United States and for three major states are also presented.

The 1980s and 1990s are generally regarded as a period of severe economic adjustment in Latin America following the regional debt-induced crisis in the wake of the Mexican default of 1982 (Klein and Tokman 2000; Portes 1997). Despite major economic policy changes during this period, the proportion of the economically active population (EAP) estimated to be informally employed barely budged. The figure fluctuated between 30 and 45 percent of the EAP across countries, and changes during these years were small and did not follow a consistent pattern. The corresponding figures for the United States are much lower, representing less than 10 percent of the adult civilian population. Even this small proportion declined marginally during the last decades. To see if there were significant regional variations in these estimates, we examined the series for California, Florida, and New York—states where rising informal activities associated with mass immigration have been reported (Sassen 1989; Lozano 1989). As shown in table 1, the state-level series follow closely the national pattern and provide no evidence of a significant rise in informal employment anywhere.[2] According to these figures, informal employment represents a phenomenon of limited significance in the United States involving less than one decile of its labor force.

The Small-Firm and Household Consumption Approaches

A second, related method is based on the evolution of the number and proportion of "very small enterprises" (VSEs) as an indicator of change in informal activities. VSEs are defined as those employing fewer than 10 workers. This approach has been applied in the United States in lieu of labor market data. The assumption is that, in advanced countries, most activities defined as informal occur in smaller enterprises because of their lesser visibility, greater flexibility, and greater opportunities to escape state controls. Larger firms are assumed to be more vulnerable to state regulation and more risk-averse to potential penalties. Hence, they are less likely to engage in informal activities directly, although they can subcontract work to smaller firms that do (Portes and Sassen 1987; Sassen and Smith 1992).

The idea for this approach came from interviews with officials of the Wage and Hour Division of the U.S. Department of Labor, the agency charged with enforcing minimum wage, overtime, and other protective codes for American workers. The interviews indicated widespread violations of the labor codes among garment, electronics, and construction subcontractors as well as in all kinds of personal and household services, especially in large metropolitan areas. Most of the enterprises involved were small, employing fewer than 10 workers (Fernández-Kelly and Garcia 1989; Sassen and Smith 1992). A separate study by the General Accounting Office identified the restaurant, apparel, and meat-processing industries—all sectors where small firms predominate—as having the greatest incidence of "sweatshop practices." Included in this category were failure to keep records of wages and work hours, wages below the legal minimum or without overtime pay, employment of minors, fire hazards, and other unsafe work conditions (General Accounting Office 1989).

As an indicator of the extent of informality, the evolution of VSEs is subject to two contrary biases. First, not all small firms engage in informal practices, which leads to an overestimate; second, fully informal VSEs escape all government record-keeping, which leads to underestimation. The extent to which these biases neutralize each other is not known. In this situation, the statistical series are best interpreted as a rough estimate of the evolution of the informal sector on the basis of those recorded firms that most closely approximate it.

Table 2 presents the proportion of VSEs and their employees in the country as a whole during the period 1965–99. Also included is the propor-

TABLE 2. Number of Units and Employment in Very Small Establishments (VSEs) in the United States, 1965–99

	United States		California			Florida			New York		
Year	Firms (%)	Employees (%)	Firms (%)	Employees (%)	San Diego County Firms (%)	Firms (%)	Employees (%)	Dade County Firms (%)	Firms (%)	Employees (%)	Queens County Firms (%)
1965	76.0	14.1	75.1	14.7	76.9	75.2	17.4	70.8	75.2	13.1	77.0
	(3.5)	(47.7)	(0.34)	(4.5)	(0.12)	(1.3)			(0.38)	(5.4)	
1970	70.6	11.9	71.0	12.4	71.2	70.5	14.1	66.7	71.8	11.2	74.8
1975	77.2	16.3	77.0	17.0	78.4	77.8	20.0	77.1	78.9	15.5	80.2
1980	74.1	15.2	73.5	15.2	74.9	75.7	18.7	74.4	76.5	14.8	78.5
1985	75.9	15.8	75.3	15.2	76.2	77.7	18.7	78.6	77.9	14.8	79.7
1990	74.2	15.0	73.4	14.4	73.6	76.6	18.0	78.4	76.9	14.5	79.7
1995	74.3	14.7	74.1	14.6	74.9	77.3	17.1	79.3	77.6	14.8	81.0
1999	73.6	14.0	72.9	13.5	72.9	77.3	15.5	79.6	77.1	14.6	80.6
	(7.1)	(110.7)	(0.78)	(12.3)	(0.07)	(0.42)	(5.9)	(0.07)	(0.49)	(7.1)	(0.04)

Source: U.S. Bureau of the Census, 1965–2000.

Note: VSEs are defined as establishments employing fewer than 10 workers. Figures in parentheses are absolute numbers, in millions.

tion of these units and their employees in the states of New York, Florida, and California and of establishments in the counties of Queens, New York; Dade, Florida; and San Diego, California. As mentioned previously, these are the sites of recent studies that describe the growth of informal activities primarily associated with a rapid rise in immigration. Number of employees broken down by size and class of establishment is not available for counties in the census data.

About three-fourths of U.S. establishments counted by the census were VSEs in 1965, and they absorbed approximately one-seventh of the economically active population. By 1985, the figures were almost exactly the same, although the variations along the way are instructive. Between 1965 and 1970, there was a 6 percent decline in the proportion of VSEs and a 2 percent drop in the proportion of the labor force employed by them. The reversal of this trend between 1970 and 1975 is an artifact of the small size-class of establishment reported by the census—from fewer than eight to fewer than 10 employees. Thereafter and until 1980, there was again a gradual decline, but, in that year, the trend reversed once more with the proportion of VSEs in 1985 reaching the same level as in 1965. After 1985, there has been a new slow decline in the relative number of VSEs and the proportion of the labor force employed by them.

State figures follow a similar pattern except that, by 1985, VSEs were more common in Florida and New York than in the country as a whole. Thereafter, the figures declined in California, where the relative number of VSEs dropped below the national average by 1989, while in Florida and New York it remained significantly above. The three county series show a similar evolution, but, in each instance, the proportion of VSEs was larger than in the respective state in 1985 and in the cases of Dade (Miami) and Queens (New York) much higher than the national average. Thereafter, the county and state figures converged for California, while Queens County and Dade County continued to report consistently larger proportions of VSEs than their respective states and the nation. This result is in line with ethnographic studies that report a high incidence of small firms and informal activities in these urban areas (Sassen 1989; Stepick 1989; Guarnizo, Sanchez, and Roach 1999). Contrary to the labor market approach, we do find significant regional variations in the presence of the firms most closely associated with the informal economy.

The third approach, the household consumption method, is based on the recognition that direct survey measures of informal employment are difficult to obtain in developed countries. For this reason, James Smith and his associates (Smith 1987; McCrohan, Smith, and Adams 1991) developed an ingenious method based on the consumption of informally provided goods and services by American households. The studies were based on national probability surveys conducted by the Survey Research Center of the University of Michigan in 1981, 1985, and 1986. Informal activity was defined as market transactions that should be recorded or taxed but were not. Respondents were asked to report the amounts spent over the preceding year on goods and services acquired off the books or on the side. On the basis of these results, the authors estimated that U.S. households spent a maximum of $72.4 billion in informal purchases, representing 14.6 percent of all expenditures (formal and informal) in 1985. The study also reported that fully 83 percent of all American households made use of at least one type of informal supplier. Home repairs and improvements topped the list in terms of dollars spent followed by food purchases, child care, other personal and domestic services, and auto repairs (McCrohan, Smith, and Adams 1991, 37).

This method has the merit of relying on direct and statistically representative survey measures and hence yielding an authoritative estimate of household consumption. As an indicator of the scope of informality in the national economy, it suffers the fatal flaw of neglecting informally produced inputs for larger firms and irregular labor practices within them. In other words, the entire universe of informal subcontracting in the apparel, electronics, furniture, construction, and many other industries as well as off-the-books employment by formal enterprises is precluded by a measurement approach focused exclusively on final household consumption. This method shares with the VSEs approach the key assumption that informality is found predominantly in the smallest economic units. However, in both cases, there is considerable slippage between what actually happens and what the numbers can tell us.

Macroeconomic Estimates

The fourth strategy, the macroeconomic discrepancy method, attempts to measure the magnitude of the total underground economy as a proportion of the gross national product (GNP). This method is based on the existence of at least two different but comparable measures of some aspect of a national economy. Discrepancies between these measurements are then attributed to underground activities. For example, gaps in the income and expenditure side of national accounts can be used to estimate the size of unreported income to the extent that individuals can be assumed to be less likely to misrepresent their expenditures than to misrepresent their incomes (Feige 1990). These methods have been more popular in the advanced countries, where government record-keeping and national accounts are better developed and where the probability of obtaining valid reports on individual participation in underground activities through survey questions is low. The more elaborate of these estimating methods, based on the ratio of currency in circulation to demand deposits, was pioneered by Gutmann (1977, 1979) and subsequently modified by Feige (1979) and Tanzi (1980, 1983). Their "currency ratio" approach is based on the assumption that informal transactions are conducted mostly in cash in order to avoid detection by fiscal authorities.

The approach consists of arriving at an estimate of the currency in circulation required by the operation of legal activities and subtracting this figure from the actual monetary mass. The difference, multiplied by the velocity of money, provides an estimate of the magnitude of the underground economy. The ratio of that figure to the observed GNP then gives the proportion of the national economy represented by subterranean activities. The method depends on the identification of a base period in which the underground economy was assumed to be insignificant. The ratio of currency in circulation to the reference figures (demand deposits for Gutmann; GNP for Feige; M2 for Tanzi) is established for this period and then extrapolated to the present. The difference between this estimate and the actual ratio provides the basis for calculating the magnitude of underground activities. Using this approach, Feige (1990, 997) reported that the U.S. underground economy as a proportion of total reported adjusted gross income (AGI) rose from 0 in 1940 (the base year) to 20 percent in 1945, declined subsequently to about 6 percent in 1960, increased rapidly to reach 24 percent in 1983, and then declined again to about 18 percent in 1986. Despite the differences in measurement procedures, this evolution corresponds fairly well, during the period 1965–89, with that based on the relative number of VSEs, reported in table 2.

More recently, Feige (1997) noted that earlier calculations had been grossly distorted by the failure to take into account currency that left the United States to serve as a deposit of value or a means of exchange in other countries. According to his calculations, up to 80 percent of U.S. currency is unaccounted for, and much of it is held abroad. After a series of complex calculations, Feige concludes that unreported income in the United States was approximately $700 billion in 1991 and not the over $1 trillion estimated with unadjusted models. Even after this adjustment, the size of the unreported economy reached again 25 percent of reported AGI in 1990–91 (Feige 1997, 201).

Macroeconomic methods for estimating the size of the underground economy through unreported income have been increasingly used by economists in other countries. In Canada, for example, various researchers utilizing these methods arrived at figures ranging from 2.8 percent of GDP in 1981 (reported by Statistics Canada) to 14.1 percent (reported by Mirus using Tanzi's approach). Ten years later, Gutmann's method, as applied by Karoleff, Mirus, and Smith (1993), yielded an estimate of 21.6 percent of GDP, but the figure from Statistics Canada remained at 2.7 percent (Smith 1997, table 3).

The macroeconomic procedures have serious weaknesses that have been noted by a number of analysts (Feige 1990; Portes and Sassen 1987). First, the assumption that informal transactions take place mostly in cash is questionable in settings where bank checks and other instruments can be used with little fear of detection by the authorities. Second, the assumption that informal activities did not exist in some arbitrarily designated period is also subject to question. Third, and most important, these estimates do not differentiate between illegal and informal activities. As seen above, informal activities involve goods and services that are otherwise licit, but whose production or distribution bypasses official channels. Hence, the huge estimates of the subterranean economy sometimes reached through these methods can be due to the presence of a large criminal underground whose operation and character are quite different from those of the informal economy proper.

Finally, estimates based on these macroeconomic methods vary widely according to the assumptions and figures employed. Porter and Bayer (1984) replicated the methods used by Gutmann, Feige, and Tanzi to obtain estimates of the absolute and relative size of the U.S. underground economy between 1950 and 1980. Their results

TABLE 3.   Estimates of the U.S. Underground Economy according to Macroeconomic Discrepancy Methods

Year	Guttmann		Tanzi		Feige	
	Billions $	*% of GNP*	*Billions $*	*% of GNP*	*Billions $*	*% of GNP*
1950	15.9	5.6	14.5	5.1	27.6	9.6
1955	14.7	3.7	12.8	3.2	1.7	0.4
1960	17.3	3.4	20.7	4.1	−3.4	−0.7
1965	31.6	4.6	26.3	3.8	9.6	1.4
1970	62.4	6.3	45.6	4.6	101.0	10.2
1975	150.8	9.7	77.0	5.0	467.3	30.2
1979	317.8	13.1	130.7	5.4	628.4	26.0
1980	372.8	14.2	159.9	6.1	1,095.6	41.6

Source: Porter and Bayer 1984, 178.

are reproduced in table 3. The three sets of estimates vary widely. In 1980, for example, Gutmann's method (as applied by Porter and Bayer) yielded an estimate of the underground economy of 14 percent of the GNP; Tanzi's approach reduced the figure to 6 percent, while Feige's method increased it to 42 percent. Similar discrepancies are found in estimates for other countries such as Canada, Great Britain (Burton 1997), Germany (Enste and Schneider 1998), and Mexico (CEESP 1987).

The Measurement Paradox

The limitations of all existing methods of measurement stem from the nature of the phenomenon they attempt to gauge, which is elusive by definition. However, the extent to which informal activities are concealed is not uniform. There are levels of concealment depending on the character of state regulation and the effectiveness of its enforcement. In settings where the informal economy is widespread and semiopen, as in many Third World countries and several Eastern European nations, it is possible to arrive at reliable estimates of its size on the basis of direct surveys. Lax enforcement and the generalized character of these activities make informal owners and workers less apprehensive about answering questions about their work. In Latin America several surveys have produced acceptable estimates of the size of the labor force employed by the informal sector in several metropolitan areas (Carbonetto, Hoyle, and Tueros 1985; Lanzetta de Pardo and Murillo Castano 1989; Roberts 1992).

When state regulation is both highly effective and extensive, as in many industrialized countries, the situation changes. In these instances, informal activities are better concealed and, as we have seen,

generally embedded in tighter social networks. Hence, no matter how well organized the official record-keeping apparatus is, it is likely to miss a significant amount of informal activity. In the United States, for instance, analysts have long discounted the possibility of measuring the informal or underground economy through direct survey questions and hence are forced to rely on the approximate methods described earlier. Despite the progressive weakening of the Wage and Hour Division and other enforcement agencies since the Reagan administration in the 1980s, informal workers and entrepreneurs are still reluctant to talk about their work (Fernández-Kelly and Garcia 1989). The measurement alternatives, from household consumption patterns to macroeconomic discrepancy ratios, have yielded estimates too feeble to guide either theory or policy.

The third paradox of the informal economy is that the more credible the state enforcement apparatus is, the more likely its record-keeping mechanisms will miss the actual extent of the informal economy and, hence, the feebler the basis for developing policies to address it. If Feige's estimates are taken at face value, an entire quarter of all economic activity in the United States took place outside the pale of state regulation in the early 1990s. Since the government knows little about the character and scope of these practices, it proceeds as if, in effect, they did not exist. The assumption can lead to serious policy consequences:

To the extent that national accounting systems are based on data sources primarily collected from the formal sector, a large and growing informal economy will play havoc with perceptions of development based on official statistics, and consequently with policy decisions based exclusively on information provided by official sources. (Feige 1990, 993)

This statement must be qualified, however, by the previous discussion concerning the extent of state enforcement and the character of the civil society subject to it. As shown in figures 4 and 5, the informal economy is likely to be weakest when limited regulation of economic activity by a competent state apparatus is coupled with a population accustomed to regular waged employment and to legal avenues for demand-making and redress of grievances. In these situations, working "on the side" or "off the books" is likely to meet with disapproval, leading to a situation in which society itself, and not only the state, becomes an enforcer of legal rules. Informal enterprise in these contexts is limited to fringe sectors, and the bulk of the "unreported economy" is probably accounted for by criminal, not informal, activities.

At the other extreme, the capacity of civil society to resist complete absorption by an authoritarian state is nowhere clearer than in its withdrawal of information from state record-keeping agencies. The best example of the third paradox is provided by the now-defunct Eastern European command economies. There, state policies aimed at controlling every aspect of economic activity required vast amounts of information in order to function properly. However, the same policies gave rise to a vast underground economy whose existence depended precisely on escaping official detection. The result was that the information on which state managers had to rely became progressively illusory and the subsequent policies unrealistic (Burawoy and Lukács 1985; Stark 1989; Rev 1986). Firms and state agencies in the "first" economy became trapped in a make-believe world, feeding each other's misperceptions and operating at an ever-growing distance from the real world. The outcome is well known.

CONCLUSION: THE CHANGING BOUNDARIES OF INFORMALITY

Reprise

In this chapter, we have reviewed various definitions of the informal economy, distinguished it from criminal and underground activities, and explored some of its peculiar characteristics. From the definition of the phenomenon used in the analysis, it is clear that the elements composing the informal sector vary across countries and over time. The relationship between the state and civil society defines the character of informality, and this relationship is in constant flux. The changing geometry of formal/informal economic activities follows the contours delineated by past history and the nature of state authority. There is thus no great mystery in the diversity of formal-informal interactions reported in the literature. Every concrete situation has in common the existence of economic practices that violate or bypass state regulation, but what these are varies according to state-society relations. Hence, what is informal and persecuted in one setting may be perfectly legal in another; the same activity may shift its location across the formal-informal divide over time. Lastly, the very notion of informality may become irrelevant in cases where the state abdicates its regulatory role.

The informal economy may be characterized as a constructed response by civil society to unwanted state interference. The universal character of the phenomenon reflects the considerable capacity of resistance in most societies to the exercise of state power. An activity can be made illegal without disappearing; entire economic sectors may be legislated out of existence yet still flourish underground. The universality of the informal economy is confirmed by a burgeoning research literature that describes its characteristics and consequences in settings as diverse as Canada, California, the Netherlands, Mexico, Jordan, and South Africa (Smith 1997; Lozano 1989; Lomnitz 1977, 1988; Doan 1992; McKeever 1998).

This literature also illustrates the diverse functionality of informal activities for the actors involved. While a good portion of this literature, coming from economics, views the phenomenon as tax evasion (Spiro 1997), detailed field studies take a more nuanced view. It is obvious that informal enterprise is "functional" for those so employed in terms of providing a minimum means of survival. It is equally obvious that the formal firms that subcontract production and marketing to informal entrepreneurs or who hire workers off the books benefit from the higher flexibility and lower costs thus obtained. It is less evident, however, that the informal economy can also have positive consequences for the very actor whose existence and logic it challenges.

A Final Paradox

The fourth paradox of the informal economy is that it commonly yields a series of positive effects for the state, the very institution charged with its suppression. This paradox also adopts different forms depending on national context. In less developed countries, where protective labor legislation often runs way ahead of the capacity of the formal economy to provide full employment, informal enterprise has a double function. First, it employs and provides incomes to a large segment of the population that otherwise would be deprived on any means of subsistence. The "cushion" provided by the informal economy can make all the difference between relative tranquility and political upheavals in these nations (Meagher 1995; Cheng and Gereffi 1994; Diaz 1993).

Second, the goods and services provided by informal producers lower the costs of consumption for formal workers and the costs of production and distribution for formal firms, thus contributing to their viability (Portes and Walton 1981). The low wages received by formal sector employees in Third World nations are partially compensated for by the greater acquisitive power of these wages through informally produced goods and services. In turn, large firms can compensate for costly tax and labor codes by restricting the size of their formally employed labor force and subcontracting the rest to informal entrepreneurs. Through these mechanisms, the informal economy contributes to the political stability and economic viability of poorer nations. These realities help explain why informal activities are commonly tolerated by many governments, in contradiction to their law-enforcement duties (Cross 2000; Kempe 1993; Birbeck 1978).

In the advanced countries, the cushioning function of informality is also present, especially in relation to marginal segments of the population. When for political or economic reasons, unemployment and other state-provided benefits are meager, recipients compensate by finding additional sources of income, commonly through informal employment. This gives rise to the situation reported by Mac-Donald (1994) in Cincinnati, where combining welfare with off-the-books casual jobs becomes a "way of life" for minority workers in the inner city. While such arrangements are regularly condemned by the media and by government officials, conveniently forgotten is the fact that these casual jobs make possible the perpetuation of a low-cost social welfare system bearing little relation to the actual cost of living (Uehara 1990; Fernández-Kelly 1995; Edin and Lein 1997).

Informality can also provide a protective environment for fledgling, but innovative, forms of entrepreneurship. The Italian case again offers the best example. Though the government in Rome took a dim view of what was taking place in Emilia Romagna, the informal networks of cooperation and solidarity among Emilian artisans eventually gave rise to a system of flexible specialization that became a world model (Capecchi 1989). This is not the sole example of this "incubator" function, as the experiences of Silicon Valley firms, started in owners' garages and basements, attest (Lozano 1989). For fledgling but viable entrepreneurial ventures, the informal economy can operate as a protective environment sparing them from burdensome and costly regulations that can prematurely sink them or compromise their growth. As firms mature, they enter the formal economy, contributing to its growth. This is what happened in central Italy, in Silicon Valley, and elsewhere.

The various functions of the informal economy may help explain why governments in both advanced and less developed countries often adopt an ambiguous attitude toward these activities, tolerating their existence at least on a temporary basis. Too much tolerance would compromise the credibility of the rule of law and the willingness of formal firms and taxpayers to continue shouldering their obligations. On the other hand, too repressive a stance would do away with the "cushion" provided by informal activities or, what is worse, drive them further underground, depriving authorities of any information or control on them. The systematic withdrawal of information from government agents has proven by far the most effective tool in the hands of civil society to resist authoritarian rule.

The complex relationships between the state and the informal economy and the multiple forms adopted by the latter rule out an approach to this phenomenon based on a simple tax-evasion perspective. The analytic stance to study these phenomena must be as nuanced and flexible as they have proven to be, combining the use of aggregate statistics and large surveys with careful firsthand investigation. Only in this manner can we approach with some success the elusive world of informality and learn from its complex character.

NOTES

This is a revised version of a chapter published in first edition of the *Handbook of Economic Sociology.* We are indebted to Miguel Angel Centeno, Patricia Fernández-Kelly, Viviana Zelizer, and Saskia Sassen for ideas and comments on the earlier version. The chapter is our sole responsibility.

1. The first version of this chapter, published in the first edition of this *Handbook,* discussed the first three paradoxes, but omitted the fourth. We examine it in the concluding section. The analysis of the second paradox has also been substantially modified from its earlier treatment, which we

now feel was incomplete. The review of various estimation approaches to measure the informal economy in the United States and other countries has been expanded, with new figures provided.

2. Figures presented in table 3 are not strictly comparable because the series for Latin America are limited to urban areas. The bias introduced by this limitation is conservative since it reduces the magnitude of the observed differences between the United States and Latin America. The reason is that the proportion of the rural labor force employed informally is higher than in urban areas in all countries of the region.

REFERENCES

Adams, Richard N. 1975. "Harnessing Technological Development." Pp. 37–68 in *Rethinking Modernization: Anthropological Perspectives*, ed. John J. Poggie and Robert N. Lynch. Westport, Conn.: Greenwood Press.

Altman, Jonathan. 1983. "A Reconstruction Using Anthropological Methods of the Second Economy of Soviet Georgia." Ph.D. diss., Middlesex Polytechnic Institute.

Benton, Lauren A. 1989. "Industrial Subcontracting and the Informal Sector: The Politics of Restructuring in the Madrid Electronics Industry." Pp. 228–44 in *The Informal Economy: Studies in Advanced and Less Developed Countries*, ed. Alejandro Portes, Manuel Castells, and Lauren A. Benton. Baltimore: Johns Hopkins University Press.

Birbeck, Chris. 1978. "Garbage, Industry, and the 'Vultures' of Cali, Colombia." Pp. 161–83 in *Casual Work and Poverty in Third World Cities*, ed. Ray Bromley and Chris Gerry. New York: John Wiley.

Blanes Jimenez, Jose. 1989. "Cocaine, Informality, and the Urban Economy in La Paz, Bolivia." Pp. 135–49 in *The Informal Economy: Studies in Advanced and Less Developed Countries*, ed. Alejandro Portes, Manuel Castells, and Lauren A. Benton. Baltimore: Johns Hopkins University Press.

Borocz, Jozsef. 1989. "Mapping the Class Structures of State Socialism in East-Central Europe." *Research in Social Stratification and Mobility* 8:279–309.

Bromley, Ray. 1994. "Informality, de Soto Style: From Concept to Policy." Pp. 131–51 in *Contrapunto: The Informal Sector Debate in Latin America*, ed. Cathy A. Rakowski. Albany: State University of New York Press.

Brusco, Sebastiano. 1982. "The Emilian Model: Productive Decentralization and Social Integration." *Cambridge Journal of Economics* 6(2): 167–84.

Buchanan, James M., Robert D. Tollison, and Gordon Tullock. 1980. *Toward a Theory of the Rent-Seeking Society*. College Station: Texas A&M University Press.

Burawoy, Michael, and Janos Lukács. 1985. "Mythologies of Work: A Comparison of Firms in State Socialism and Advanced Capitalism." *American Sociological Review* 50:723–37.

Burton, John. 1997. "The Underground Economy in Britain." Pp. 209–15 in *The Underground Economy: Global Evidence of Its Size and Impact*, ed. Owen Lippert and Michael Walker. Vancouver: Fraser Institute.

Capecchi, Vittorio. 1989. "The Informal Economy and the Development of Flexible Specialization." Pp. 189–215 in *The Informal Economy: Studies in Advanced and Less Developed Countries*, ed. Alejandro Portes, Manuel Castells, and Lauren A. Benton. Baltimore: Johns Hopkins University Press.

Carbonetto, Daniel, Jenny Hoyle, and Mario Tueros. 1985. *Sector Informal en Lima Metropolitana*. Research Progress Report. Lima: CEDEP.

Castells, Manuel, and Alejandro Portes. 1989. "World Underneath: The Origins, Dynamics, and Effects of the Informal Economy." Pp. 11–37 in *The Informal Economy: Studies in Advanced and Less Developed Countries*, ed. Alejandro Portes, Manuel Castells, and Lauren A. Benton. Baltimore: Johns Hopkins University Press.

Centro de Estudios Económicos del Sector Privado (CEESP). 1987. *La Economía Subterranea en Mexico*. Mexico City: Editorial Diana.

Chavez Leo R. 1988. "Settlers and Sojourners: The Case of Mexicans in the United States." *Human Organization* 47:95–108.

Cheng, Lu-lin, and Gary Gereffi. 1994. "The Informal Economy in East Asian Development." *International Journal of Urban and Regional Research* 18:194–219.

Cornelius, Wayne A. 1998. "The Structural Embeddedness of Demand for Mexican Immigrant Labor: New Evidence from California." Pp. 115–55 in *Crossings: Mexican Immigration in Interdisciplinary Perspective*, ed. Marcelo Suárez-Orozco. Cambridge: Center for Latin American Studies, Harvard University.

Cross, John C. 1998. *Informal Politics: Street Vendors and the State in Mexico City*. Stanford, Calif.: Stanford University Press.

Dallago, Bruno. 1990. *The Irregular Economy: The Underground Economy and the Black Labor Market*. Aldershot, U.K.: Dartmouth.

de Soto, Hernando. 1989. *The Other Path*. New York: Harper and Row.

Diaz, Alvaro. 1993. "Restructuring and the New Working Classes in Chile: Trends in Waged Employment and Informality." Working Paper No. DP47, United Nations Research Institute for Social Development, October.

Doan, Rebecca. 1992. "Class Differentiation and the Informal Sector in Amman, Jordan." *International Journal of Middle East Studies* 24 (February): 27–38.

Economic Commission for Latin America and the Caribbean (ECLAC). 2000. *Social Panorama of Latin America, 1999–2000*. Annual report. Santiago de Chile: ECLAC.

Edin, Kathryn, and Laura Lein. 1997. "Work, Welfare, and Single Mothers' Economic Survival Strategies." *American Sociological Review* 62:253–66.

Enste, Dominik, and Friedrich Schneider. 1998. "Increasing Shadow Economies All Over the World—Fiction or Reality?" Discussion Paper No. 26, Institute for the Study of Labor, Bonn, Germany.

Evans, Peter B. 1989. "Predatory, Developmental, and Other Apparatuses: A Comparative Political Economy Perspective on the Third World State." *Sociological Forum* 4:561–87.

Feige, Edgar L. 1979. "How Big Is the Irregular Economy?" *Challenge* 22:5–13.

———. 1990. "Defining and Estimating Underground and Informal Economies: The New Institutional Economics Approach." *World Development* 18:989–1002.

———. 1997. "Revised Estimates of the Underground Economy: Implications of U.S. Currency Held Abroad." Pp. 151–208 in *The Underground Economy: Global Evidence of Its Size and Impact*, ed. Owen Lippert and Michael Walker. Vancouver: Fraser Institute.

Fernández-Kelly, M. Patricia. 1995. "Social and Cultural Capital in the Urban Ghetto: Implications for the Economic Sociology of Immigration." Pp. 213–47 in *The Economic Sociology of Immigration: Essays in Network, Ethnicity, and Entrepreneurship*, ed. Alejandro Portes. New York: Russell Sage Foundation.

Fernández-Kelly, M. Patricia, and Anna M. Garcia. 1989. "Informalization at the Core: Hispanic Women, Homework, and the Advanced Capitalist State." Pp. 247–64 in *The Informal Economy: Studies in Advanced and Less Developed Countries*, ed. Alejandro Portes, Manuel Castells, and Lauren A. Benton. Baltimore: Johns Hopkins University Press.

Gabor, Istvan R. 1988. "Second Economy and Socialism: The Hungarian Experience." Pp. 339–60 in *The Underground Economies*, ed. Edgar L. Feige. Cambridge: Cambridge University Press.

Gambetta, Diego. 1993. *The Sicilian Mafia: The Business of Private Protection*. Cambridge: Harvard University Press.

Garcia, Norberto. 1991. *Restructuración, Ahorro, y Mercado de Trabajo*. Santiago de Chile: PREALC.

General Accounting Office. 1989. "Sweatshops in the United States: Opinions on Their Extent and Possible Enforcement Options." Briefing Report HRD-89-101 BR.

Gereffi, Gary. 1999. "International Trade and Industrial Upgrading in the Apparel Commodity Chain." *Journal of International Economics* 48:37–70.

Gerry, Chris. 1978. "Petty Production and Capitalist Production in Dakar: The Crisis of the Self-Employed." *World Development* 6:1187–98.

Gershuny, Jonathan I. 1978. *After Industrial Society: The Emerging Self-Service Economy*. London: Macmillan.

———. 1985. "Economic Development and Change in the Mode of Provision of Services." Pp. 128–64 in *Beyond Employment: Household, Gender, and Subsistence*, ed. Nanneke Redclift and Enzo Mingione. Oxford: Basil Blackwell.

Ghersi, Enrique. 1997. "The Growing Importance of Informality." Pp. 223–37 in *The Underground Economy: Global Evidence of Its Size and Impact*, ed. Owen Lippert and Michael Walker. Vancouver: Fraser Institute.

Granovetter, Mark. 1985. "Economic Action and Social Structure: The Problem of Embeddedness." *American Journal of Sociology* 91:481–510.

———. 1993. "The Nature of Economic Relationships." Pp. 3–41 in *Explorations in Economic Sociology*, ed. Richard Swedberg. New York: Russell Sage Foundation.

Greenfield, Harry. 1993. *Invisible, Outlawed, and Untaxed: America's Underground Economy*. Westport, Conn.: Praeger.

Grossman, Gregory. 1989. "Informal Personal Incomes and Outlays of the Soviet Urban Population." Pp. 150–72 in *The Informal Economy: Studies in Advanced and Less Developed Countries*, ed. Alejandro Portes, Manuel Castells, and Lauren A. Benton. Baltimore: Johns Hopkins University Press.

Guarnizo, Luis. 1994. "Los 'Dominican Yorkers': The Making of a Binational Society." *Annals of the American Academy of Political and Social Science* 533:70–86.

Guarnizo, Luis, Arturo I. Sanchez, and Elizabeth M. Roach. 1999. "Mistrust, Fragmented Solidarity, and Transnational Migration: Colombians in New York and Los Angeles." *Ethnic and Racial Studies* 22 (March): 367–96.

Gutmann, Peter M. 1977. "The Subterranean Economy." *Financial Analysts Journal* 33(6): 27–34.

———. 1978. "Are the Unemployed Unemployed?" *Financial Analysts Journal* 34(5): 26–29.

———. 1979. "Statistical Illusions, Mistaken Policies." *Challenge* 22:14–17.

Hart, Keith. 1973. "Informal Income Opportunities and Urban Employment in Ghana." *Journal of Modern African Studies* 11:61–89.

———. 1990. "The Idea of the Economy: Six Modern Dissenters." Pp. 137–60 in *Beyond the Marketplace: Rethinking Economy and Society*, ed. Roger Friedland and A. F. Robertson. New York: Aldine de Gruyter.

Henken, Ted. A. 2002. "Condemned to Informality: Cuba's Experiment with Self-Employment during the Special Period." Ph.D. diss., Department of Sociology, Tulane University.

Karoleff, Vladimir, Rold Mirus, and Roger S. Smith. 1993. "Canada's Underground Economy Revisited: Update and Critique." Paper presented at the 49th Congress of the International Institute of Public Finance, Berlin, August.

Kempe, Ronald Hope. 1993. "Growth and Impact of the Subterranean Economy in the Third World." *Futures* 1:864–76.

Klein, Emilio, and Victor E. Tokman. 1988. "Sector Informal: Una Forma de Utilizar el Trabajo como Consecuencia de la Manera de Producir y No Viceversa." *Estudios Sociologicos* 6(16): 205–12.

———. 2000. "La Estratificación Social bajo Tension en la Era de la Globalización." *Revista de la CEPAL 72* (December): 7–30.

Lacey, Marc. 2002. "To Fuel the Mideast's Grills, Somalia Smolders." *New York Times,* July 25, A4.

Lanzetta de Pardo, Monica, and Gabriel Murillo Castano. 1989. "The Articulation of Formal and Informal Sectors in the Economy of Bogota, Colombia." Pp. 95–110 in *The Informal Economy: Studies in Advanced and Less Developed Countries,* ed. Alejandro Portes, Manuel Castells, and Lauren A. Benton. Baltimore: Johns Hopkins University Press.

Leonard, Madeleine. 1994. *The Informal Economy in Belfast.* Aldershot, Ireland: Avebury.

———. 1998. *Invisible Work, Invisible Workers: The Informal Economy in Europe and the U.S.* London: Macmillan.

Lomnitz, Larissa. 1977. *Networks and Marginality: Life in a Mexican Shantytown.* New York: Academic Press.

———. 1988. "Informal Exchange Networks in Formal Systems: A Theoretical Model." *American Anthropologist* 90:42–55.

Lozano, Beverly. 1989. *The Invisible Work Force: Transforming American Business with Outside and Home-Based Workers.* New York: Free Press.

MacDonald, R. 1994. "Fiddly Jobs, Undeclared Working, and the Something for Nothing Society." *Work, Employment, and Society* 8:507–30.

Makaria, Kinuthia. 1997. *Social and Political Dynamics of the Informal Economy in African Cities.* Lanham, Md.: University Press of America.

McCrohan, Kevin, James D. Smith, and Terry K. Adams. 1991. "Consumer Purchases in Informal Markets: Estimates for the 1980s, Prospects for the 1990s." *Journal of Retailing* 67:22–50.

McKeever, Matthew. 1998. "Reproduced Inequality: Participation and Success in the South African Informal Economy." *Social Forces* 76:1209–41.

Meagher, Kate. 1995. "Crisis, Informalization, and the Urban Informal Sector in Sub-Saharan Africa." *Development and Change* 26 (April): 259–84.

Millman, Joel. 1992. "New Mex City." *New York 7:* 37–42.

Mingione, Enzo. 1990. "The Case of Greece." Pp. 23–58 in *Underground Economy and Irregular Forms of Employment, Final Report,* ed. P. Barthelemy, Migueliz, E. Mingione, R. Pahl, and A. Wenig. Luxembourg: Commission of the European Communities.

Molefsky, Barry. 1981. "American's Underground Economy." Report No. 81-181E, Congressional Research Service, Library of Congress, Washington, D.C.

Moya-Pons, Frank. 1992. *Empresarios en Conflicto.* Santo Domingo: Fondo Para el Avance de las Ciencias Sociales.

Nove, Alec. 1969. *An Economic History of the USSR.* London: Allen Lane, Penguin Press.

Pahl, Raymond E. 1980. "Employment, Work, and the Domestic Division of Labor." *International Journal of Urban and Regional Research* 4:1–20.

Pahl Raymond E., and Claire Wallace. 1985. "Household Work Strategies in Economic Recession." Pp. 189–227 in *Beyond Employment: Household, Gender, and Subsistence,* ed. Nanneke Redclift and Enzo Mingione. Oxford: Basil Blackwell.

Perez Roque, Martha Beatriz. 2002. "Economía Informal en Cuba." Report commissioned by the Center for Migration and Development, Princeton University, May.

Perez-Sainz, Juan Pablo. 1992. *Informalidad Urbana en America Latina: Enfoques, Problematicas e Interrogantes.* Caracas: Editorial Nueva Sociedad.

Polanyi, Karl. [1944] 1957. *The Great Transformation.* Boston: Beacon Press.

Porter, Richard D., and Amanda S. Bayer. 1984. "A Monetary Perspective on Underground Economic Activity in the United States." *Federal Reserve Bulletin* 70:177–89.

Portes, Alejandro. 1997. "Neoliberalism and the Sociology of Development: Emerging Trends and Unanticipated Facts." *Population and Development Review* 23 (June): 229–59.

Portes, Alejandro, Manuel Castells, and Lauren A. Benton. 1989. "The Policy Implications of Informality." Pp. 298–311 in *The Informal Economy: Studies in Advanced and Less Developed Countries,* ed. Alejandro Portes, Manuel Castells, and Lauren A. Benton. Baltimore: Johns Hopkins University Press.

Portes, Alejandro, and Saskia Sassen. 1987. "Making It Underground: Comparative Materials on the Informal Sector in Western Market Economies." *American Journal of Sociology* 93:30–61.

Portes, Alejandro, and Richard Schauffler. 1993. "Competing Perspectives on the Latin American Informal Sector." *Population and Development Review* 19: 33–60.

Portes, Alejandro, and Julia Sensenbrenner. 1993. "Embeddedness and Immigration: Notes on the Social Determinants of Economic Action." *American Journal of Sociology* 98:1320–50.

Portes, Alejandro, and John Walton. 1981. *Labor, Class, and the International System.* New York: Academic Press.

Powell, Walter W. 1990. "The Transformation of Organizational Forms: How Useful Is Organization Theory in Accounting for Social Change?" Pp. 301–29 in *Beyond the Marketplace: Rethinking Economy and Society,* ed. Roger Friedland and A. F. Robertson. New York: Aldine de Gruyter.

Programa Regional de Empleo para America Latina (FREALC). 1985. *Más Allá de la Crisis.* Santiago de Chile: PREALC.

Reenoy, Piet H. 1984. "Twilight Economy: A Survey of the Informal Economy in the Netherlands." Research Report, Faculty of Economic Sciences, University of Amsterdam.

Rev, Ivan. 1986. "The Advantages of Being Atomized."

Working paper, Institute for Advanced Study, Princeton University.

Roberts, Bryan R. 1989a. "Employment Structure, Life Cycle, and Life Chances: Formal and Informal Sectors in Guadalajara." Pp. 41–59 in *The Informal Economy: Studies in Advanced and Less Developed Countries*, ed. Alejandro Portes, Manuel Castells, and Lauren A. Benton. Baltimore: Johns Hopkins University Press.

———. 1989b. "The Other Working Class: Uncommitted Labor in Britain, Spain, and Mexico." Pp. 352–72 in *Cross-National Research in Sociology*, ed. Melvin L. Kohn. Newbury Park, Calif.: Sage.

———. 1991. "Household Coping Strategies and Urban Poverty in a Comparative Perspective." Pp. 135–68 in *Urban Life in Transition*, ed. M. Gottdiener and Chris G. Pickvance. Newbury Park, Calif.: Sage.

Sabel, Charles. 1986. "Changing Modes of Economic Efficiency and Their Implications for Industrialization in the Third World." Pp. 27–55 in *Development, Democracy, and the Art of Trespassing: Essays in Honor of Albert O. Hirschman*, ed. Alejandro Foxley, Michael S. McPherson, and Guillermo O'Donnell. Notre Dame, Ind.: Notre Dame University Press.

———. 1989. "Flexible Specialization and the Re-emergence of Regional Economies." Pp. 28–29 in *Reversing Industrial Decline? Industrial Structure and Policy in Britain and Her Competitors*, ed. Paul Hirst and Jonathan Zeitlin. New York: Berg.

———. 1994. "Learning by Monitoring: The Institutions of Economic Development." Pp. 137–65 in *The Handbook of Economic Sociology*, ed. Neil J. Smelser and Richard Swedberg. New York: Russell Sage Foundation; Princeton: Princeton University Press.

Sassen, Saskia. 1989. "New York City's Informal Economy." Pp. 60–77 in *The Informal Economy: Studies in Advanced and Less Developed Countries*, ed. Alejandro Portes, Manuel Castells, and Lauren A. Benton. Baltimore: Johns Hopkins University Press.

Sassen, Saskia, and Robert C. Smith. 1992. "Post-industrial Growth and Economic Reorganization: Their Impact on Immigrant Employment." Pp. 35–69 in *US-Mexico Relations: Labor Market Interdependence*, ed. Jorge A. Bustamante, Clark W. Reynolds, and Raúl A. Hinojosa Ojeda. Stanford, Calif.: Stanford University Press.

Schoepfle, Gregory K., and Jorge F. Perez-Lopez. 1992. "The Underground Economy in the United States." Occasional Paper Series on the Informal Sector No. 2. Bureau of International Labor Affairs, U.S. Department of Labor.

Sethuraman, S. V. 1981. *The Urban Informal Sector in Developing Countries*. Geneva: International Labour Office.

Smith, James D. 1987. "Measuring the Informal Economy." *Annals of the American Academy of Political and Social Science* 493:83–99.

Smith, Philip M. 1997. "Assessing the Size of the Underground Economy: The Statistics Canada Perspective." Pp. 11–36 in *The Underground Economy: Global Evidence of Its Size and Impact*, ed. Owen Lippert and Michael Walker. Vancouver: Fraser Institute.

Spiro, Peter S. 1997. "Taxes, Deficits, and the Underground Economy." Pp. 37–52 in *The Underground Economy: Global Evidence of Its Size and Impact*, ed. Owen Lippert and Michael Walker. Vancouver: Fraser Institute.

Standing, Guy. 1989. "The 'British Experiment': Structural Adjustment or Accelerated Decline?" Pp. 279–97 in *The Informal Economy: Studies in Advanced and Less Developed Economies*, ed. Alejandro Portes, Manuel Castells, and Lauren Benton. Baltimore: Johns Hopkins University Press.

Stark, David. 1989. "Bending the Bars of the Iron Cage: Bureaucratization and Informalization in Capitalism and Socialism." *Sociological Forum* 4:637–64.

Stepick, Alex. 1989. "Miami's Two Informal Sectors." Pp. 111–34 in *The Informal Economy: Studies in Advanced and Less Developed Countries*, ed. Alejandro Portes, Manuel Castells, and Lauren A. Benton. Baltimore: Johns Hopkins University Press.

Tanzi, Vito. 1980. *The Underground Economy in the United States and Abroad*. Lexington, Mass.: D. C. Heath.

———. 1983. "The Underground Economy in the United States: Annual Estimates, 1930–80." *International Monetary Fund Staff Papers* 30:283–305.

Tokman, Victor. 1982. "Unequal Development and the Absorption of Labour: Latin America, 1950–1980." *CEPAL Review* 17:121–33.

Treml, Vladimir. 1985. "Purchases of Food from Private Sources in Soviet Urban Areas." Berkeley-Duke Occasional Papers on the Second Economy No. 3, September.

U.S. Bureau of the Census. 1965–2000. *County Business Patterns*. Washington, D.C.: U.S. Government Printing Office.

———. 1980. *Current Population Surveys*. Washington, D.C.: U.S. Government Printing Office.

———. 2000a. *Current Population Surveys*. Washington, D.C.: U.S. Government Printing Office.

———. 2000b. *Statistical Abstract of the United States*. 120th ed. Washington, D.C.: U.S. Government Printing Office.

Uehara, Edwina. 1990. "Dual Exchange Theory, Social Networks, and Informal Social Support." *American Journal of Sociology* 96:521–57.

Waldinger, Roger. 1985. "Immigration and Industrial Change in the New York City Apparel Industry." Pp. 323–49 in *Hispanics in the U.S. Economy*, ed. George J. Borjas and Marta Tienda. New York: Academic Press.

————. 1986. *Through the Eye of the Needle: Immigrants and Enterprise in New York's Garment Trade*. New York: New York University Press.

Western, Bruce. 1998. "Institutions and the Labor Market." Pp. 224–43 in *The New Institutionalism in Sociology*, ed. Mary C. Brinton and Victor Nee. New York: Russell Sage Foundation.

Williamson, Oliver. 1975. *Markets and Hierarchies*. New York: Free Press.

————. 1994. "Transaction Cost Economics and Organization Theory." Pp. 77–107 in *The Handbook of Economic Sociology*, ed. Neil J. Smelser and Richard Swedberg. New York: Russell Sage Foundation; Princeton: Princeton University Press.

Zhou, Min. 1992. *New York's Chinatown: The Socioeconomic Potential of an Urban Enclave*. Philadelphia: Temple University Press.

Zhou, Min, and Carl L. Bankston. 1995. "Entrepreneurship." Pp. 511–28 in *Asian American Almanac*, ed. I. Natividad. Columbus, Ohio: Gale Research.

Part II

The Economic Core: Economic Systems, Institutions, and Behavior

Section C: The Sociology of
Firms, Organizations,
and Industries

19 Business Groups and Social Organization

Mark Granovetter

INTRODUCTION: THE PROBLEM OF "BUSINESS GROUPS"

"Business groups" are sets of legally separate firms bound together in persistent formal and/or informal ways. The level of binding is intermediate between, and should be contrasted to, two extremes that are not business groups: sets of firms linked merely by short-term strategic alliances, and those legally consolidated into a single entity. Because business groups dominate the economies of many emerging and developed countries, they are worth considerable attention.[1]

Understanding business groups is a special case of a central problem of modern sociology: what determines the scope of relationships in which individuals and larger social units engage. Microsociology has much to say about this, but typically considers individuals in groups that lack formal structures, persistent identity, and written rules of interaction that may be codified by laws regulating and requiring involvement with political authorities.

Organization theory, developed specifically to address the issues that such formal structures imply, confined its analysis to single units until the 1960s, when theorists first objected to analyzing organizations without reference to their environments. Among the environments then scrutinized for impact were those constituted by consumers, government, the general public, and especially other organizations. Subsequently, analysts drew on population ecology and treated organizations as competitors for resources in niches that could not bear unlimited occupancy (see Hannan and Freeman 1989). But organization theorists were slower to see organizations as forming larger social entities, networks of cooperating units. The spectacular success during the 1980s of Japan and South Korea, however, forced attention to the fact that the identity of individual firms in these countries was less significant than, and subordinated to, that of larger groups of organizations with which

they were connected. The new interest in the *chaebol* of Korea and the *keiretsu* of Japan raised to prominence the importance of "business groups" in modern capitalist economies. But such groups hardly originated in this period; instead, the economies of many countries had been dominated by such well-defined collections of firms for decades and in some cases a century or more.

That theory was slow to address this reality should not surprise. In economics, there was little sustained attention even to the question of why such an entity as a "firm" should exist at all until Ronald Coase wrote his pathbreaking 1937 paper "The Nature of the Firm." It was clear to Coase, and indeed to any casual observer, that isolated individuals hardly mattered in the production of goods and services compared to individuals organized into social units called "firms." Yet the classical economic theory of production treated firms as no more than individual actors. Our recognition here of the central role of business groups in relation to firms elevates Coase's insight on the relation of firms to individuals to a higher level of analysis.[2]

My treatment of business groups in this chapter is more inclusive than some valuable recent accounts that limit their focus to "diversified business groups," which comprise firms in a wide variety of industries "under the general guidance of a single entrepreneur" (Guillén 2001, 60; cf. Ghemawat and Khanna 1998, 35). Confining our attention to these would exclude important cases such as Japan, Taiwan, and others, where diversification and coordination among group firms are variable and often limited. But my definition is not endlessly inclusive: because it specifies that the formal and informal ways in which a collection of firms is bound together must be "persistent," networks of firms with shifting ties, and without clearly persistent subsets, should not be considered "business groups." Thus, sets of firms in industrial districts, connected to one another by a dense network of ties, may or may not be classed as groups, depending on whether clearly identifiable cliques of firms persist over time.

My definitional requirement that group firms be legally independent is useful but arbitrary. Some multidivisional firms are technically legally integrated, yet individual division managers may be more autonomous than those in business groups whose firms are legally separate. Despite legal separation, one or more central individuals, often a family, may own a controlling interest in every group firm, directly, or indirectly through holding companies and pyramids, thus making component firms' legal independence virtually meaningless. Adding to confusion, the term *conglomerate* is used loosely in the literature for both kinds of collections of units, and at times interchangeably with *business group*.

A reasonable operational criterion for distinguishing which conglomerates should not be treated as business groups is suggested by Harry Strachan: exclude cases where a "common parent owns the subsidiaries but generally few operational or personal ties exist among the sister subsidiaries . . . [since] within business groups . . . there are generally personal and operational ties among all the firms" (1976, 20). Most American conglomerates fit the first description, as component companies are acquired and divested mainly on financial grounds. Such a set is likely to be reshuffled as financial outcomes dictate, rather than stable and closely related over time, rotating personnel back and forth, and sharing resources, brand names, and a single identity. I therefore do not treat conglomerates like Tyco or Berkshire Hathaway as business groups.

But some cases still resist easy classification by this criterion. Some conglomerates are mixtures of divisions and subsidiaries,[3] such as General Electric. Companies previously organized as multidivisional firms may reorganize their divisions as subsidiaries for financial reasons, such as tax advantage (see Prechel 2000). Such "families" of firms may continue to operate in many ways as they did when the subsidiaries were divisions, to the extent this is not forbidden by law. And there are groups of firms controlled by American families that look substantially like business groups in other countries, but whose public profile is very low. For example, the Pritzker family of Chicago (see Weber and Woellert 2001; Kilman, Brinkley, and Bulkeley

2002) controls a variety of interests, including the Marmon group—more than 60 legally separate companies tied together, as indicated on the group's web site (www.marmon.com): "While the member companies operate independently, a small professional organization in Chicago, Illinois—The Marmon Group, Inc.—manages and invests the member companies' financial resources and advises them on accounting, tax, finance, legal, regulatory, real estate and other matters." There are many such family-dominated groups and multisubsidiary firms in the United States (see the Dun and Bradstreet directory *America's Corporate Families*), and what is most striking is their absence from public or scholarly discussion, perhaps because of the dominant image of American companies as individual enterprises. In this absence, it is hard to form a clear impression of their overall role in the American economy (but see Bethel and Liebeskind 1998, 50 for some limited data on the prevalence of large U.S. firms that have domestic subsidiaries).

Because of these definitional ambiguities, there are collections of firms whose status as business groups is arguable. Ultimately we would want a more refined way to classify collections of firms that are linked to one another than whether or not they should be called "business groups," and such a classification should consider several dimensions of how firms in such collections relate to one another. Nevertheless, for many purposes it is reasonably clear whether a set of firms is a business group as defined here, and it is useful to develop arguments about such groups; therefore in the remainder of this chapter I abstract away from the ambiguities.

Because component firms are legally separate, business groups can be invisible. This is one reason they were largely ignored in theories of economic organization until recent years.[4] Countries vary dramatically in the extent to which groups have name recognition, but it is very rare for the groups to have clear legal status. (One exception is Chile; see Khanna and Palepu 1999a, 272n.) Chung points out that corporate law worldwide is highly focused on the idea of the corporation as an autonomous unit, and rarely recognizes the reality of complex network relationships within groups of corporations. This focus makes regulation of groups difficult, ad hoc, and often ineffectual (Chung 2000, chap. 5; Maman 2003; also see Teubner 1990; Antunes 1994; Dine 2000).

Inhabiting a legal limbo does not reduce business groups' economic clout. To give just a few examples, at the end of the 1980s, the top 20 groups in India accounted for more than two-thirds of private sector industrial assets (Ghemawat and Khanna 1998, 42); the top 100 groups in Taiwan produced 45 percent of the 1996 GNP (Chung 2001, 722); and by the mid-1990s, "business groups had already come to dominate the Chinese economy" (Keister 2000, 9), despite not having existed until the 1980s. Collin (1998, 726) reports that the two largest groups in Sweden controlled corporations that in 1995 represented about 52 percent of the Stockholm stock exchange's capitalization. And the 10 largest national private groups in Mexico include 127 of the country's 500 biggest companies (Garrido 1994, 166).

WHY BUSINESS GROUPS? EXPLAINING THE ORGANIZATIONAL FORM

I ask first why firms adopt the organizational form of the business group rather than some other form, and what explains the many variations in the way business groups are constructed. In subsequent sections I inquire as to the efficiency and consequences of the business group form, and then consider the future of business groups in the modern economy.

The Emergence of Business Groups: General Arguments

Some general discussions of business groups suggest that actors may choose from among a variety of organizational forms in order to get goods and services produced. Thus we might consider the business group an organizational form "competing" with the forms of separate individual firms, multinational enterprises, and state-owned firms, as in Guillén (2001). What the balance of such forms might be in a given situation has been addressed by organizational ecology (Ruef 2000), transaction cost economics (Williamson 1985), and the "new sociological institutionalism" (e.g., Scott 1995). As Ruef notes, however, despite "considerable theoretical interest in form emergence, these major organizational paradigms have yet to produce a generalizable explanatory model" (2000, 659). This is in part because the requirements for such a model are daunting: the emergence of forms "is best understood in the context of a concrete system of interrelationships between organizational suppliers, consumers, regulators and intermediaries operating in an institutional arena" (Ruef 2000, 660). Ruef develops such an analysis

with rich data for American health care organizations No such comprehensive analysis is in view for generalized business organization forms, and it is unclear whether the data for such an analysis could be acquired, or even clearly defined. This high standard of analysis, however, is useful to keep in mind as we assess the validity of what *has* been argued.

I classify arguments about the emergence of organizational forms according to the level of analysis emphasized. Some focus on the rational action of individuals or organizations trying to produce the best results. In the case of business groups, what such theories look like should depend on whether a group emerges out of a single firm that acquires or spins off multiple related and subordinate firms, or coalesces from a set of previously independent firms without a clear central firm that organizes the group. These two ways that groups can emerge are ends of a continuum, but it is convenient to think of them as separate ideal types. In the latter case, typical of some Latin American groups (see, e.g., Strachan 1976), one would need to consider what benefits individual firms derive from alliance. But virtually all recent literature confines itself to the special case where groups emerge from the diversification activity of a single firm.

Standard economics and organization theory long ignored why firms grow, including diversification. This silence was broken by Penrose's influential 1959 work, which conceptualized the firm as a "collection of physical and human resources" that needed to be managed to extract maximum benefit, and originated what has come to be known as the "resource-based" view of the firm. Growth, she argued, results from rational effort to exploit underutilized resources. Penrose broached a theme that became common in later discussions of the evolution of firms and their structure, that unrelated diversification is unlikely to persist over long periods because it does not make optimum use of the firm's existing resources. No firm, she suggests, can "acquire every likely firm in sight . . . ; it must choose . . . those enterprises which seem most likely to complement or supplement its existing activities" (1995, 129); and while there are conglomerate firms whose acquisitions do not focus on any particular field, they are unlikely to be profitable or even survive over long periods. "Sooner or later such 'firms' either break up or settle down to the exploitation of selected fields. The force responsible is that of competition" (1995, 131).[5]

Bethel and Liebeskind (1998) consider why diversified firms might choose to operate as "corporate groups," making some lines of business legally separate subsidiaries rather than divisions. Their argument goes beyond Penrose's emphasis on competition, to the importance of corporate law, including a desire for "reduction or avoidance of the costs of product liability and other types of tort liability" (1998, 50), tax advantages (cf. also Prechel 2000 and Chung 2000, chap. 5), and the ability of large shareholders to leverage their control through pyramids. They add to these a stylized model in which under certain well-defined circumstances, corporate groups "can economize on transaction costs, relative to a simple corporation" (1998, 50) by resolving conflicts of interest between fixed and residual claimants to a firm's profits.

Economists working in an evolutionary tradition considered broader aspects of firms' environments than competition and the legal system. Teece et al., for example, assessed how a variety of factors in firms' environments affects the likelihood of survival for unrelated diversification (1994; see also Lowe, Boerner, and Teece 2001). They suggest that with low path dependency, slow learning, and weak selection, conglomerates with few intracorporate transactions may persist, but that as selection tightens, "such as during recessions, we expect that the most egregious examples of this form will get weeded out. Conglomerates are thus a transitional form" (24). On the other hand, in situations of rapid learning, colliding technological trajectories, and tight selection, network firms may arise, in which firms become "enveloped in a dense skein of intercorporate relationships involving partial equity holdings and joint ventures," and such network firms may persist (24). Guillén (2001) focuses on the impact of government economic policies on organizational form. In particular, he argues that diversified business groups have an advantage and can effectively profit in circumstances where government policy is asymmetric between whether it allows outward and inward flows of capital and goods to and from its country. In his view, organizational form is determined by strategic actors whose possibilities are shaped by a nation's institutional traditions and constraints, insofar as these determine policies on finance and trade.

All of these arguments posit firms rationally trying to maximize economic results, and focus in a bottom-up way on strategic actors coping with their particular environment. The environment appears as a constraining background factor, rather than a major focus of analysis. A different argument, made since the beginning of serious discussion of business groups, is that groups result from the need to compensate for market failures. This gives more emphasis to the level of entire economic systems, and less to that of strategic actors. Leff suggested, for example, that the "group pattern of industrial organization is readily understood as a microeconomic response to well-known conditions of market failure in the less developed countries" (1978, 666), especially imperfect markets in capital and intermediate products. Khanna and Rivkin (2001) broaden this account by arguing that groups may fill a number of "voids left by the missing institutions that normally underpin the efficient functioning of product, capital and labor markets" (46–47), such as labor market intermediaries, business schools, well-functioning judicial institutions, venture capitalists, financial analysts, mutual funds, and a vigorous financial press (cf. Khanna and Palepu 1999a). Groups fill these voids, they argue, because it is profitable to do so, and that the effort is sustained so long as it is beneficial for the overall economy.

One troublesome finding in relation to these assertions is that it is very variable, as I detail below, whether groups and group firms are indeed more profitable than other organizational forms. Khanna and Rivkin address this variation by suggesting that inability to profit from group membership indicates "poorly developed selection environments, where weak organizational forms are not weeded out" (2001, 47). This comment, however, must raise the question of whether functionalist explanations for the persistence of the business group form are falsifiable. There are two issues in the logic of such an argument. The first is how one might show that an organizational form such as the business group arises as a "response" to market failure. This ostensibly historical statement may in fact result from telling an "adaptive story" (Gould and Lewontin 1979) about what environmental problems business groups solve. But it could be that groups do not emerge to solve problems, but rather because of special skills and abilities of entrepreneurs, families, and alliances to mobilize resources. The visible groups at any moment are those that survived, in part because they developed capabilities superior to nongroup firms. It is then tempting to interpret this in cross-section as a response to some imputed market "failures." Without detailed historical evidence that groups were a response to such failure, this imputation is problematic.

A second issue is how to validate the implicit assumption that there exists an ideal state in which individual firms would not *need* to affiliate with one another because the missing institutional functions that groups serve would be managed by intermediaries that emerge from the market. Having arisen from market processes, these would be as efficient as possible. Thus, once economies reach this ideal state, the need for business groups disappears and they will disintegrate. (See, e.g., Khanna and Palepu 1999b, 126.) To be persuasive, such an argument would require detailed institutional analysis comparing the costs and effectiveness of economic functions performed inside versus outside of business groups. The idea that product, labor, and capital market intermediation can be performed at lower cost outside groups assumes that market discipline forces nongroup intermediaries to operate at minimum cost. In fact, however, this is highly problematic even in advanced economies. Such institutions as business schools, the financial press, venture capital, and mutual funds operate in highly constrained environments, and are supported and shaped by a wide variety of institutional forces many of which are not subject to market discipline, and which may impose their own costs on the economy as externalities difficult to bring into account. On the other hand, the same functions when performed within business groups are themselves under pressure for efficient operation from the market competition groups impose on one another. Therefore it is by no means self-evident without detailed study of particular cases that the evolution of market institutions should undercut the value added by groups. I address this question in more detail below under the topics of the success and future of business groups.

Finally, Feenstra and Hamilton (forthcoming) consider all these accounts only partially persuasive, because they slight analysis of the particular economic tasks firms are trying to execute, and how these change over time. Focusing especially on manufacturing, they suggest that a crucial question is how upstream-downstream relations among firms that involve intermediate goods can best be managed. They suggest that different institutional and structural features of nations, combined with changes in global demand, may create conditions in which business groups dominate some sectors of the economy, but in quite different ways across countries.

These widely varying accounts of how the business group form originates result in part from the actual enormous variations among business groups around the world. To treat this variation as representing a single "organizational form" may be misleading and a source of theoretical confusion.

Thus, a more feasible task in our present state of knowledge might be to make arguments that try to account for these variations. Before doing so, I pause to outline the main dimensions of variation.

Variations in the Form of Business Groups

Business groups vary along six dimensions:[6]

1. Source of solidarity. Many business groups have some sense of identity based on common social bonds among component firms and their personnel, often involving association with a single family. Though mid-twentieth-century modernization theory argued that economic development required the detachment of family and kinship from business, detailed empirical analysis such as that of La Porta, Lopez-de-Silanes, and Shleifer 1999 shows that families still control most firms around the world, including those in the advanced economies.[7] Both family-run groups and others may achieve solidarity in part because key members derive from the same ethnic, religious, or regional origin.

2. Extent of "moral economy." Groups may but need not be coherent social systems in which participants have a strong sense of moral obligation to other members and a well-defined conception of what is proper behavior. Such conceptions are almost invariably accompanied by a strong sense of group identity, which confers a normative and extraeconomic meaning on economic action.

3. Structure of ownership. Groups vary from those that are essentially owned by a single family—very common, though this ownership may be masked by indirect control through holding companies and pyramids—to those composed of independent firms that have allied with one another. These latter alliances are enduring, rather than strategic, and at times involve substantial crossshareholding among component firms.

4. Structure of authority. Groups vary from those quite loosely coordinated, with no real central authority, such as some large Japanese *keiretsu* (see Gerlach 1992), to those ruled with an iron hand by a single group chairman, typical of Korean *chaebol*, especially in the 1960s and 1970s. Centralized ownership may be the vehicle for centralized control, but the correlation is far from perfect.[8] For example, Chang's sophisticated network analysis shows that in Korea, strong central control is supported by patterns of shareholding that concentrate ownership in a single family, across large numbers of group firms (1999); but a similar analysis by Chung (2004) for Taiwan,

shows that while shareholding is similarly structured, control is more loosely coordinated, and a "set of core leaders . . . occupy duplicate leadership positions in various group firms" (Chung 2000, 76).

I note that nearly all of the extant literature on business groups assumes the special case of highly centralized ownership and authority.

5. The role of financial institutions. Since the provision of capital to group firms is a central issue everywhere, many but not all business groups include among their member firms one or more banks or nonbank financial institutions (such as insurance companies). There is great variation in the power position of such financial firms within and beyond the groups. In some groups, they dominate to such an extent that analysts refer to them as "financial groups" (e.g., Kurgan–Van Hentenryk 1997), and may even pose a serious competitor to the state for national sovereignty (see Makler and Ness 2002, especially 7–8). In others, they are clearly subordinate to the head office, and perhaps to the state as well (cf. the cases of China, Keister 2000, 88, 97; and of Korea from the 1960s to the 1990s, Kim 1997). Johnson notes that although Russian groups are known as "financial-industrial groups" (FIGs), the main banks in some of them were clearly subordinate to industrial firms with which they allied (2000; chap. 5). In many family-run groups, the situation may not be much different from early-nineteenth-century New England, where banks were not independent actors, but rather the "financial arms of the extended kinship groups that dominated the economy" (Lamoreaux 1986, 659; see also Lamoreaux 1994).

6. Relation of groups to the state. Business groups' autonomy in relation to the state runs the gamut. Some groups evolve largely independent from government sponsorship and at times in clear opposition to political elites and mandates (cf. Camp 1989 for Mexico). In other cases, groups are assembled by the state from state-owned firms (Keister 2000 for China and Johnson 2000, 159, for Russia) or by leading political actors who use the state apparatus for their own business purposes (Indonesia under Suharto, see Robison 1986; or Nicaragua under Somoza, see Strachan 1976). Where groups are independent, the state may still dominate them, as in 1960s and 1970s Korea. But as Kim (1997) notes, the more effective states are in creating successful business groups, the more likely are the groups to become independent power centers that ultimately resist state control, and become at least coequal actors.

National Institutions, Isomorphism, and Business Group Form

The theories of business group origins reviewed previously (in "The Emergence of Business Groups: General Arguments"), which stress bottom-up rational action of a single founder, may have difficulty illuminating the dimensions I have listed, beyond those of ownership and authority. Top-down interpretations of groups as responses to market failures suggest that groups' distribution across these dimensions should derive from the set of institutions missing in their countries. Poorly developed capital markets should lead to a dominant focus on finance and capital allocation. Lack of education and training for managers should prompt groups to internalize educational functions and put substantial energy into developing employee skills. A nation's institutions would then impact business group form insofar as they determined which economic functions markets cannot fulfill.

This implies that some organizational form always arises to handle essential tasks that markets fail to manage. Though we may doubt such inevitability, the argument does help us identify which functions business groups have economic incentives to tackle, which is important to know. This does little, however, to explain the axes of solidarity, the nature of ownership and authority, the existence of normative consensus, or the group's relation to the state.

Many scholars argue that to understand these requires careful attention to legal, political, and normative structures that make some business forms far more plausible and likely than others. This argument doubts that all organizational forms will eventually be driven by market competition toward some common model that optimizes returns to firms and owners by solving "agency" problems. Dobbin refers to "industrial logics" that vary by country and derive principally from their political systems (1994). In their study of the auto industry, Biggart and Guillén propose that each country has a prevailing "institutional logic," and that business practices that diverge from it will not be easily comprehensible to the relevant actors (1999, 726). Whitley refers to national "business systems" that vary in the "degree and mode of authoritative coordination of economic activities, and in the organization of, and interconnections between, owners, managers, experts and other employees" (1999, 33). Hollingsworth and Boyer speak of "social systems of production"—the way a country's economic institutions combine with its politics and with "customs and traditions as well as norms, moral principles, rules, laws and recipes for action" (1997, 2).

Such theorists argue that institutions have more causal force than individuals' strategic action. Thus, Hollingsworth and Boyer comment that whereas the "neoclassical paradigm assumes that individuals are sovereign, we argue that individual action is influenced by the hold that institutions have on decision making" (1997, 3). Hall and Soskice occupy a middle ground by acknowledging the importance of "varieties of capitalism," but arguing that institutions do not fully determine the contours of the economy; rather there are multiple equilibria in which the strategic action of actors and firms can make a major difference. Though game-theoretic in spirit, their argument acknowledges that what "leads the actors to a specific equilibrium is a set of shared understandings about what other actors are likely to do, often rooted in a sense of what it is appropriate to do in such circumstances. . . . [This is] an entry point in the analysis for history and culture" (2001, 13).[9]

Hall and Soskice argue that national economies fall broadly into two categories: liberal market economies (LMEs) and coordinated market economies (CMEs). In the former (e.g., the United States), coordination and agency problems are resolved through markets, and such economies "usually lack the close-knit corporate networks capable of providing investors with inside information about the progress of companies that allows them to supply finance less dependent on quarterly balance sheets and publicly available information" (2001, 29). In CMEs, companies are more likely to have access to finance that does not depend on such current data. This "patient capital" allows firms to retain skilled workers in downturns and make long-term investments. Investors assess performance through "network monitoring": dense networks across firms based in part on extensive cross-holdings. This argument implies that business groups will be less prevalent in LMEs than in CMEs, which the empirical data support.

I now focus more closely on institutional elements that affect the capacity and likelihood for corporate actors to coordinate with one another in ways that might favor the emergence of business groups. High on any such list would be "company" or "corporate" law that prescribes the bounds of permissible collaboration and regulates owner-

ship concentration. Collaboration and common ownership are conceptually separate, but empirically related. Independent firms may collaborate without common ownership. But one typical reason why they do collaborate is that individuals, families, or financial institutions hold substantial ownership in the separate companies and coordinate the firms' activities in an attempt to improve their own financial or social situations.

If corporate law strongly shapes organizational form, what shapes corporate law? Law and economics scholars usually argue that it evolves so as to resolve economic problems and maximize overall wealth (cf. Posner 1998). Agency theory proposes that the role of corporate law is to establish governance of corporations in such a way as to align managers' incentives with those of owners. In this view, market forces help shape corporate law so that managers are disciplined and discouraged from seeking their own advancement at the expense of shareholders. This implies that some statutes are superior to others and that as countries advance, they will increasingly adopt similar legislation.

This view dates especially from the 1980s, when the phrase *corporate governance* first came into vogue (Blair 2001). It is widely accepted in law and economics, debated within more general economics, and greeted with some skepticism outside these circles. One general line of argument that leads in a different direction is the "new institutionalism" in the sociological theory of organizations (e.g., DiMaggio and Powell 1983; Powell and DiMaggio 1991), which proposes that "structural change in organizations seems less and less driven by competition or by the need for efficiency. Instead . . . forms of organizational change occur as the result of processes that make organizations more similar without necessarily making them more efficient" (DiMaggio and Powell 1983, 147). One such source is what they call "coercive isomorphism," including the state and its laws.

Consistent with this view is Roe's influential argument (1994) that corporate law varies by country in ways that primarily reflect political processes. Arguing that law about the economy derives from noneconomic sources tilts against convergence assumptions. In theory, idealized markets operate the same everywhere, so that if law were endogenous to market process, any well-functioning market would eventually produce the same efficient legal structures. But if law about the economy is shaped by politics, this is far less plausible, requiring the assumption that political structures will also converge everywhere—a proposal sometimes made (e.g., Fukuyama 1992), but belied by the events of recent years.

Though not directly addressing the issue of business groups, Roe inquires why the shareholding of American firms is more dispersed than in most other major economies. I note that this dispersed shareholding is inconsistent with the form of business groups, typically characterized by highly centralized shareholding or by extensive cross-holdings among group firms, or by both. Roe notes that while American firms typically coordinate through merger, such as vertical integration, there is an alternative: institutions like banks or mutual funds could hold big blocks of stock in firms as well as in their customers and suppliers, and these firms could then remain separate and be coordinated by the large shareholders. Instead of one firm being a division of the other, "each would be partially owned by an overlapping group of financial institutions. Neither would be a controlled subsidiary, but there would be connections, information, exchange, and . . . a mediator to settle . . . disputes" (1994, 14).

But Roe asserts that American politics deliberately fragmented ownership. It "preferred Berle-Means corporations [i.e., with strong managers and weak owners] to the alternative of concentrated institutional ownership, which it precluded" (1994, 22). The reason is not economic, but political and ideological: Since the founding of the republic, American public opinion has mistrusted large private accumulations of power. Moreover, relevant legislation was more readily passed in a federal political system that allowed localized interests more leverage in Congress than would be available in a more centralized system. Sanders (1986) makes a similar point in her account of how regional rivalries in the late nineteenth century produced antitrust legislation (see also Fligstein 1990). Correspondingly, managers threatened by takeovers in the 1980s—the "discipline" that agency theory recommends—persuaded legislatures in most states to enact antitakeover legislation, supported by labor and the general public, which resented the costs of corporate disruptions to their careers and communities (Roe 1994, chap. 10; see also Davis and Thompson 1994). Roe concludes that firms in "nations that have tolerated large pools of private economic power evolved differently than did firms in nations that have repeatedly fragmented financial institutions, their portfolios, and their ability to network blocks of stock. The firm is not isolated. . . . it operates not just in an economic environment but in a political environment as well" (1994, 285–86).

Chung (2000) points out that although legislation is important in determining organizational form, it is important to carefully examine the feedback from organizations to legislation. Taiwanese company law established important tax advantages for the business group form, which helps explain its initial establishment. Further legislation was the result of a continuous struggle among different political and economic interests, and was deeply influenced by business interests themselves once the business group form was dominant (Chung 2000, chaps. 2, 5; 2001). In countries where the form of business groups was not originally strongly affected by legislation, its maintenance is subsequently facilitated by revisions in corporate law and regulatory procedures on which the groups themselves actively lobby (as is well documented for Korea; see Kim 1997; Chang 2003). The case of Germany from the 1980s on illustrates that complex controversies that work themselves out through court decisions can produce a body of de facto administrative law (here called *Konzernrecht*) that is not easily traced in any deterministic way to national institutions, but may still open the way for strategic actors to use the new rules, as suggested by Hall and Soskice (2001). In particular, German industry participants created a new form called the "management holding," closely resembling a business group, in which a parent company confines itself to strategy and finance, and owns operational subsidiaries that are legally separate. Part of the reason for this was for the parent firm to avoid legal liability for mistakes of the subsidiary firms, given the doctrines of responsibility that had evolved in German law. This form spread rapidly, in part through imitation, and has been credited with reviving the fortunes of major German industries such as machine tools (Griffin 1997, chap. 5; Herrigel 1999).

There are situations where the coercive aspect of isomorphism is even more palpable than that of legislation, as when the leaders of South Korean *chaebol* were all arrested shortly after General Park Chung Hee's 1961 coup, and released only on condition of cooperating with the general's plan to revitalize the Korean economy. This plan focused the lion's share of resources on a few large business groups, and led to growth that astounded the world in the 1960s and 1970s (see, e.g., Jones and Sakong 1980). Even the details of how *chaebol* would invest were determined by state policy. Expansion by debt rather than profit maximization followed from negative real interest rates and the likelihood of bailouts in case of failure. And the high debt-to-equity ratio made it especially easy for families to control a large number of firms with relatively small outlay of capital. Diversification was sensible since state-mandated target sectors changed rapidly enough to make it imprudent not to have a finger in every pie (Chang 1999). (Note that although this account is standard, Feenstra and Hamilton [forthcoming], strongly dispute the centrality of the Korean state in producing business group [*chaebol*] domination of the economy, asserting that this outcome resulted from a combination of national institutions and global patterns of product demand, and would have occurred even in the absence of strong state action, albeit at a slower pace.)

In Japan, from the 1930s on, the business groups known as *zaibatsu* were forced by the state to adopt more centralized governance, and non-*zaibatsu* firms were pushed in this direction as well, to serve increasing military needs (Lincoln and Gerlach 2002, chap. 6). Thus, the dense web of connections that Allied occupation forces sought to break up after the Second World War, often attributed to Japanese cultural sources, were in part the product of government fiat.

Even when political forces do not explicitly prescribe an organizational form, they may bear indirect responsibility for it. Highly centralized political structures, such as that of General Park in Korea, Juan Perón in Argentina, or August Pinochet in Chile, create a situation in which the central political figure prefers to deal only with a few leading businessmen. Even if it is not technically required, business groups then find it expedient to become highly centralized themselves so as to be able to negotiate effectively with the corresponding centralized interlocutors in the state.

DiMaggio and Powell (1983, 152) argued that norms and ideas held by influential social groups may impact organizational form. Their main example was professionals, whose networks "span organizations and across which new models diffuse rapidly" (1983, 152). A different type of pressure toward uniformity in organizational form is what I would call *cross-institutional isomorphism*, in which business organizations take on a form similar to that of nonbusiness institutions with which they are involved. Chang (1999) argues, for example, that Korean family structure is distinctive even within Asia, and that the form of the *chaebol* derives clearly from the norms and traditions that surround families. Biggart (1991) suggests that

the Korean feudal tradition impacts the conduct of business groups. Feenstra and Hamilton (forthcoming) stress the long Korean tradition of primogeniture in inheritance, and patrimonialism in politics, in which systems of control over slaves, tenants, and other political dependents were organized as extensions of family authority. This made an economy organized through large firms centrally controlled by a single family a path of least cultural resistance. Makler (2001, 5664) makes a similar argument for Brazil, in discussing the relation of the central government to leading regional families and their banks.

Very general sets of cultural ideas and preferences can also cross over to impact the form of economic institutions, especially through political action. One example already discussed is Roe's assertion of the centrality to American political life of pervasive suspicion of large private accumulations of power. Another has to do with the way governments in developing countries deal with multinational corporations (MNCs). As Guillén (2001) and others have argued, what goods and investment capital governments allow MNCs to import makes a difference in what space is available for business groups, and whether those groups are autonomous or work closely with large foreign firms and investors. Such government decisions are affected by the attitude of important interest groups in the economy. Guillén notes, for example, that Spanish labor has been positive on globalization and multinationals since the 1960s, thus allowing governments to bring MNCs in as partners—which, he argues, combined with export orientation, has made it difficult for business groups to persist (2001, 147–54); Argentine labor, by contrast, has been persistently anti-MNC, which has often affected government policy and at times led to dominance of the economy by business groups (2001, 133–40).

Feelings of national pride that result from political history may strongly impact policy. When General Park drafted *chaebol* leaders into his 1961 scheme for economic development, it would have been theoretically plausible for him to partner instead with multinational corporations that already had the capital and know-how that had to be painstakingly assembled by the *chaebol*. But as E.M. Kim notes, given Korean political sensitivities after a half-century of Japanese colonial domination, it would have been "politically suicidal" for even a military strong man to bring in large foreign investors in such a dominant position (1997, 119).

The ideology of political elites may influence

their economic policies, which in turn facilitate or block the formation of business groups. Comparing South Korea and Israel, Maman notes that in both cases, during the 1960s and 1970s, state elites enacted policies that were either directly (as in Korea) or indirectly (as in Israel) friendly to group formation, because they "held a developmental ideology, did not count on market forces for economic development, and had a desire to greater economic and military self-sufficiency" (2002, 738). But quite opposite ideologies, such as neoliberalism among elites, may also create fertile conditions for group formation. Thus, Garrido reports that privatization, carried out by the substantial sale of state industrial assets in Mexico in the late 1980s and early 1990s, ended up as a "great act of business re-engineering guided by the State, whose strategy was aimed at strengthening the big national private groups as actors in the new economic model, by transferring to them its share of economic power" (1994, 167). Goldstein and Schneider (forthcoming) similarly observe that state-directed privatization presented unparalleled opportunities for business interests to expand or create entirely new conglomerate groups in Brazil, Chile, Argentina, and Mexico, among others (cf. also Makler 2000).

Finally, we should not underestimate the impact of cross-national mimetic isomorphism. Once models are well known, they may lead to imitation. Korean *chaebol* mimicked Japanese business group forms in the 1950s because the *zaibatsu* were still familiar from the period of Japanese colonial domination; later, in the 1980s, Japanese multinationals invested large amounts in Korea, and Korean firms had to reorganize to match their own functions with those in corresponding Japanese companies (Kim 1997, 84–89). Imitation can be quite self-conscious; thus, Keister reports that reformers in China "studied the *keiretsu* and the *chaebol* for many years and, in the mid-1980s, began building a Chinese version of these conglomerates" (2000, 9). Aside from imitating success, reformers also were attracted by the prestige of creating forms that looked like these well-known models (Keister 2000, 74–75). Similarly, Johnson indicates that in supporting FIGs (financial-industrial groups) during the 1990s, the Russian government invoked the "example of South Korean and Japanese conglomerates" (2000, 161). And imitation may result from conceptions of business organization carried by migrants across national borders. Thus, many of the early Israeli entrepreneurs and managers who constructed groups were from Germany

and central or eastern Europe, where the "German model of capitalism, including organizing business in the form of *konzernen* [conglomerate business groups] was dominant before the rise of Communism" (Maman 2002, 740).

FACTORS AFFECTING BUSINESS GROUP PERFORMANCE

One main reason to analyze organizational forms is to understand their consequences. Thus it is worth asking whether the business group form is successful and efficient compared to alternate ways of organizing the economy. In this section, I first summarize some findings on business group performance, and then discuss two important determinants of such performance: the extent of common identity among firms in a business group, and the network overlap between business groups and other institutional sectors.

Performance: Innovation and Profitability in Business Groups

Among the many possible measures of how well business groups perform, I select two of great importance: the ability of business groups to create innovations, and the extent of groups' profitability. In both cases, one must compare the performance of groups to that of stand-alone firms.

Regarding innovation, there are few studies that directly compare groups to firms, but an interesting clue is provided by the distinction drawn by Hall and Soskice between "incremental" and "radical" innovation. By "incremental" they mean "continuous but small-scale improvements to existing product lines and production processes," and by "radical," "substantial shifts in product lines, the development of entirely new goods, or major changes to the production process" (2001, 38–39).

They do not analyze the relative strength of organizational forms in these different types of innovation, but instead broadly generalize that economies characterized largely by market coordination ("liberal market economies") are weak in incremental but strong in radical innovation, with the opposite being true for economies where nonmarket coordination is strong ("coordinated market economies"). The logic is that in the latter case, employment is secure and close interfirm collaboration "encourages clients and suppliers to suggest incremental improvements to products or production processes" (Hall and Soskice 2001, 39). The dense network of intercorporate linkages is associated with a system of corporate governance that insulates firms against hostile takeovers, and thus reduces sensitivity to immediate profits. This encourages "corporate strategies based on product differentiation rather than intense product competition," and a "reputation for risk-taking or cutthroat competition is rarely an asset in such networks" (40). By contrast, in liberal market economies, the stress on current profits implicit in the market for corporate control reduces employment security and thus discourages employees from cooperating in attempts to innovate. Instead, they cultivate their own career and general skills above loyalty to company; moreover, contract and antitrust law discourages collaboration between firms on incremental innovation. However, the fluid labor market and the ability of firms "seeking access to new or radically different technologies to do so by acquiring other companies with relative ease" encourage radical innovation (2001, 40).

Though couched at the level of entire national economies, all these considerations map easily onto the distinction between business groups and stand-alone firms, and imply that groups will excel at incremental innovation but separate firms at radical innovation. A similar argument seems implicit in the work of Amsden and Hikino (1994), who propose that one great advantage of diversified business groups in emerging economies late in the twentieth century was their superior ability to execute technology transfer from more industrially advanced nations. Though they do not distinguish between incremental and radical innovation, the kind of transfer they discuss seems to be incremental, as it does not involve creating entirely new products or diverging dramatically from existing ones.

If high technology innovation counts as "radical," it does appear that this has emerged mainly from liberal market economies, such as that of the United States, with other more coordinated market economies specializing in incremental improvements to the new models. It also seems clear, however, that even if a liberal market economy is a necessary condition for radical innovation, it is not sufficient, as such innovation rarely occurs. Saxenian's well-known arguments about divergences between regions in the United States in their capacity for radical innovation suggest that even within a "liberal market economy" with stand-alone firms, some sectors or regions may not produce the relevant conditions (Saxenian 1994). And this sug-

gests that it may be hazardous to extrapolate from arguments about the innovative potential of organizational forms to that of entire economies, because countries may vary widely internally in the distribution of forms and even of types of coordination (cf. Locke 1995 on Italy; Herrigel 1996 on Germany; and the rapidly growing literature on the mixed economy of China).

Further insight may come from an argument on a different plane from those on entire economies, but which may point to a similar conclusion: David Stark's emphasis on the importance for dramatic innovation of a diverse population of firms whose networks can be easily shifted and recombined, in industries where it is important to avoid adaptation at the expense of adaptability (2001, 72–74). If this is correct, then the stable identity of the firms that compose a business group, which is part of the way I have defined such groups, may hinder innovations that require firms to rapidly shift the composition of interfirm alliances from which they derive technological insight.

Profitability has been studied more systematically than innovation. Khanna and Rivkin (2001) analyzed 14 emerging economies where groups are significant: Argentina, Brazil, Chile, India, Indonesia, Israel, Mexico, Peru, the Philippines, South Africa, Korea, Taiwan, Thailand, and Turkey. They found that business group "affiliates perform better than nonaffiliates in six countries and worse than nonaffiliates in three, with no difference in profitability levels in the remaining five countries" (2001, 46). Though consultants often advise governments to rein in the diversification of business groups in favor of greater focus, they report that in 11 of the 14 countries there is no evidence of a diversification discount, and "if anything, there is often evidence of a diversification premium" (2001, 47). Thus they suggest that "owners and managers of business groups should be wary of strategy advice from advisors whose knowledge base originates in advanced economies" (47).[10]

Profitability varies across nations because groups have sources of both performance strength *and* weakness in their structures, and which dominates often depends on circumstances outside their control, including government policy, political change, international financial markets, and noneconomic social institutions. For Korea, Chang (2003, chap. 3) notes that the extensive group-level sharing of resources, such as brands, technology, and personnel, and also group-level organizational structure help firms learn from one another's experience and enhance profitability. But these synergies can be eroded in several ways. First, as more affiliates become listed companies, minority shareholders object to resource flow out of their company with no immediate return. (Major shareholders do not object since they are typically composed of the family that controls other companies in the group.) Perhaps more significant, especially in the crisis of the late 1990s, the "value creation that occurred at the individual [group firm] level through resource sharing was often totally wasted in some other part of the group due to ill-conceived strategies or to cross-subsidization of poorly performing affiliates" (2003, 107). The same centralized structures that led to useful synergies between affiliates increasingly became a liability from the 1980s on, due to bad decisions. The problem arose because once the state backed off of bailouts and strong control of strategy, the groups did not have a functioning governance system to perform due diligence on major decisions (Chang 2003, chap. 3).

This should remind us that groups are more than the sum of their firms. Because they are internally socially structured, it is misleading to measure average profitability of firms within a group, as each may play a different role and thus achieve correspondingly different financial results. Chang, for example, referring to the fact that single families typically dominate even the largest of the Korean *chaebol*, calls these organizations "privately owned social structures." His blockmodel analysis of 1989 equity ownership ties among firms within the top 49 groups shows that group firms are arranged in a "nested hierarchy": that is, there is asymmetry in sending and receiving equity ties across blocks (1999, 136–40).[11] Portfolio management is "targeted at maintaining family control rather than the returns they can expect from the investment" (1999, 148). If profit maximization were the goal, we would expect to see higher ROA (return on assets) for firms higher up in the structural hierarchy, but in fact the opposite is the case. Those firms are not free to invest for highest yield, but instead must play their network role and invest in appropriate chaebol subsidiaries. Thus, the higher a firm is in the network of directed ties, the greater its opportunity cost. This means that other things equal, ROA is negatively correlated with position in the hierarchy (1999, 149). On the other hand, when growth is the dependent variable, a measure of "control efficiency" that "captures the degree of control amplification through crossholdings" does have predictive value across groups (169–79).

Thus, a focus on family control may compete with short-term profit maximization. Even in the absence of a controlling family, individual firms' profit maximization may be subordinated to group welfare when group identity is strong. Japan presents a striking example. It has long perplexed analysts that companies affiliated with the six largest intermarket (i.e., cross-industry) *keiretsu* are less profitable and show lower rates of sales growth than unaffiliated firms. Lincoln and Gerlach (2002, chap. 5) reproduce this common finding in their analysis of Japan's 200 largest manufacturing firms. But they point out that this is misleading, since the typical OLS (ordinary least squares) specification of the outcome does not take a firm's own past performance into account in assessing the impact of *keiretsu* membership They stress especially whether a firm has been in serious trouble, not merely experiencing stagnant earnings, but actually losing money, which harms a firm's reputation and that of its main bank and close partners. Going into the red is more likely than weak performance to provoke a rescue response from other group members. Using such measures, they find that group membership has quite a different impact on different firms: it helps weak firms, hurts strong ones, and leaves middling performers alone.

Economists often interpret mutual assistance and bailouts within Japanese groups as a rational insurance scheme, in which strong performers pay a "premium" by helping weak firms, so that they will receive help in case of future problems. But since there is little evidence that firms think about bailouts in this way, or indeed that strong firms ever collect on such insurance "investments," this seems more an expression of faith in rational action than a falsifiable argument. Lincoln and Gerlach suggest instead that strong firms could not take advantage of weaker group members because they would be sanctioned by other group firms for "deviating from the norms of the community by extracting rents from business partners" (2002, 5–25). They go on to say that the rational mutual insurance argument assumes a "degree of individual self-interest seeking unconstrained by social commitments and normative rules that is scarce in Japan. The network structures within which Japanese economic action is embedded allow corporations limited degrees of freedom to chart their own course, to freely pick and choose alliances . . . on the basis of unilateral calculations of advantage" (2002, 5–75).

Thus, in both Korea and Japan, it is misleading to measure the average performance of group firms because the social structure of the group makes it inappropriate to consider an individual firm's performance without accounting for the role it plays in relation to other group firms. The extent to which a firm's performance is closely tied to that of others in the group rather than being decoupled in ways that justify separate analysis depends significantly on the strength of overall group identity. Such identity is a factor in determining behavior and performance that is difficult if not impossible to explain from a purely economic viewpoint.

Sources of Business Group Identity

Family domination of groups provides one common source of identity. We have no detailed catalogue of family involvement that would allow us to classify business groups worldwide as to which are family dominated. But the results of La Porta, Lopez-de-Silanes, and Shleifer (1999) on large and medium-sized publicly traded firms in the 27 richest countries—where most analysts previously would have been especially skeptical that family control of large and medium-sized firms persisted—are intriguing. They find that only a couple of countries—especially the United States and the United Kingdom—have many widely held firms, and where, more typically, there is controlling ownership, it is "surprising that by far the dominant form . . . is not that by banks or other corporations, but rather by families" (1999, 496). Their results

> leave us with a very different picture . . . than that suggested by Berle and Means. Widely held firms appear to be relatively uncommon. . . . In contrast, family control is very common. Families often have control rights over firms significantly in excess of their cash flow rights, particularly through pyramids, and typically manage the firms they control. . . . Family control appears to be . . . typically unchallenged by other equity holders. (1999, 502, 505)

Since firms in poorer and less developed economies are quite likely to be even more family-dominated than in the richer ones in this study, it is not hard to conclude that families dominate most firms worldwide. Extending our chain of circumstantial inference, it would follow that the typical business group would also be family dominated. Where detailed studies are available, this is clearly the case, as for Korea, India, Chile, and others. It was also true in Japan until the occupation forces removed *zaibatsu* families from control of their groups, in an (as it happened, fruitless) attempt to break up business groups and implement a more Americanized market system. Khanna and

Palepu's study of Chilean and Indian groups indicates that most groups in the two countries are "strongly affiliated with a single family" (1999a, 279) and that only one of the 18 groups in their two-country sample has no family affiliation (280n). They comment that it makes sense for families to "invest" in group identity because the family "creates a system of social norms that reduces intragroup transaction costs by encouraging information dissemination among group firms, reducing the possibility of contractual disputes, and providing a low-cost mechanism for dispute resolution" (1999a, 280). While this is unexceptionable, it distracts from the interesting and key question of how families are able to achieve and maintain control over long periods, which is by no means automatic.

In fact, the extent to which this can be managed is extremely variable. Within nations, some families do this much better than others. Families are not always a fount of dispassionate, rational behavior. Consider cases such as the Hyundai group, once Korea's largest *chaebol*, which rapidly disintegrated after the death of founder Chung Ju Yung in 2001, because his six living sons could not restrain the feuds kept within bounds during their father's lifetime (cf., e.g., Kirk 2001). And not just family disputes, but also the perils of demography may threaten persistent family control. Lindgren (2002) shows that for the Swedish Wallenberg family, which dominates Sweden's largest business group, over the course of the twentieth century, there were a number of points when the principle of passing control down through the male line very nearly came undone, due to lack of a suitable heir.

Entire countries may have kinship structures and contexts that make it hard for families to manage large business empires. For example, the Kenyan businessmen studied by Marris and Somerset "seldom find a way to assimilate kinship successfully within a hierarchy of managerial authority," which puts them at a massive disadvantage in relation to Asian, especially Indian businesses, which are built along kinship lines (1971, 35). This results in part because the Asians, "as a minority excluded from agriculture by colonial policy, could bring much stronger sanctions to bear in their business relationships. A man who cheated his family or caste could be ostracized from commercial employment and had few other sources of livelihood to turn to" (1971, 45). In this early period of Kenyan development, however, business was a peripheral activity for Africans, and relatives who did not perform competently or honestly could not be easily controlled by others in the family since they could return to farming with little trouble. Similarly, overseas Chinese in Southeast Asia typically are far more efficient than native populations in creating kin-based business groups, for reasons that may have to do with differences in the kinship system between China and other Southeast Asian cultures (see Granovetter 1995b for a more detailed argument), as well as their limited options outside of business in these countries.

The sense of identity that families bring to business groups may be amplified by additional sources of solidarity. Business groups in India, for example, are typically led by ethnically homogeneous individuals. The Tata group, long among the top few, has historically been closely associated with the small Parsee minority, and the large Birla group with the Marwaris.[12] India provides mind-boggling caste/ethnic/religious group variation as raw material for constructing business group solidarities. But even countries that are more ethnically homogeneous, such as Korea, allow for extrafamilial solidarities through recruitment of compatriots from the same college, high school, and home region, as is common in the *chaebol*.

Operational practices in business groups may also contribute to a sense of group identity. Frequent rotation of personnel across group affiliates reduces managers' identification with any individual firm and increases it with the group as a whole. One consequence is that the more intragroup mobility managers experience, the more homogeneous they become in their view and practices. This facilitates resource sharing, but may reduce resistance when the leading family proposes disastrous business decisions (cf. S. Chang 2003, chap. 3, for the Korean case). We may contrast this with some multidivisional firms in which managers have strong divisional identities from long tenures, so that central managers must take their views into account for overall planning in order to achieve good outcomes (as in the case of General Motors, analyzed by Freeland 2001). In Japan, firms in a group that are members of the Presidents' Council (*shacho-kai*) have a much stronger sense of themselves as group members than other firms, from their frequent meetings. They constitute a "self-conscious clique of firms whose reciprocal commitments stem from long association and strong collective identity." Indeed, such companies are "automatically eligible for bailouts or other adjustments to raise or lower profitability. Noncouncil firms are subject to such adjustments only if they have extensive dealings with the group" (Lincoln and Gerlach 2002, 5–45, 46).

Generally speaking, other things equal, the older

a business group, the stronger its internal identity. The reasons for this may include all those discussed earlier, as well as others that are harder to pin down, but relate to the accretion of tradition. Thus in their finding about how Japanese groups offer assistance to their own troubled affiliates, Lincoln and Gerlach note that of the six major postwar intermarket groups, such intervention is more likely among the groups with longer histories than among the newer city bank–centered groups that emerged only after the war. And where interventions do occur in the newer groups, they appear to be economically targeted, compared to companies from much older groups like Sumitomo and Mitsubishi, which are "all around busybodies" and intervene even if they are not the main lender or stockholder in a company (2002, 5–44), which would entail more clear economic incentives.

Network Overlap between Business Groups and Other Institutional Sectors

The argument thus far about how efficient business groups are has focused on their own internal functioning. But how well economic actors succeed in their endeavors often depends on how much their networks overlap with those in other institutional sectors. The simplest example of this has already been broached: the extensive overlap of business with kinship systems around the world. The goals of families can conflict with profit maximization for the groups and firms they dominate. At times the clash is entirely financial, as when families shift resources around business groups at the expense of minority shareholders in order to enrich themselves. Such families are still maximizing profits. But families often want more than wealth from their business activities: they also want to enhance their social status. For example, Ghemawat and Khanna note that in India, "as in many other Asian societies, there seems to be a stigma associated with restructuring" (1998, 55). The Tata family, long the dominant force in India's leading business group, enjoys exalted social status based in part on its reputation as an enlightened employer. Thus, when Tata Steel felt compelled in 1999 to lay off 35,000 workers, the "sackings so offended Tata Culture that the company agreed to pay the workers' salaries until the age of 60" (Ellis 2002).[13]

Or, for Japan, Takeda notes that *zaibatsu* shareholders between the two world wars

did not demand a high dividend rate. . . . Family members were neither allowed to sell their own equity nor to become independent from the family business. The ultimate obligation of family members was to take their family business which had been inherited from their parents' generation, to develop it and pass it on to their children's generation. . . . in Mitsui's case [then and now one of the largest groups] in order to avoid the loss of family assets and to keep the reputation of the family business, the Family Constitution . . . prescribed to the family members to avoid extravagance. (1999, 94)

From a purely economic viewpoint, such tendencies are frictions that derail economic rationality. But a clearer understanding of how business groups function requires a broader view. Especially since families dominate business groups in most countries, our analytical understanding of how they operate has to consider in a single framework their economic as well as their noneconomic goals. In the case of *zaibatsu* families, or the Tatas in India (and their group, the Parsees), one would like to know, for example, where they stand in the overall social status structure of their country, and how their economic and noneconomic goals intersect. Such an analysis would be useful for most of the leading business groups, but would require a kind of sociological-cum-economic analysis that is rarely attempted. Each discipline follows its comparative advantage and stresses especially the set of motives that its theories illuminate. The absence of a unified social science that allows economic and noneconomic motives to be understood jointly, as they operate in real actors, makes it especially difficult for us to comprehend the development of business group strategy.

The extent to which families and business groups are involved in politics is also important but relatively neglected. While virtually all analysts agree that regulation of groups by the state strongly shapes their structures and strategies, state and business are often treated as separate actors. Yet few doubt that the way business and the state influence one another is mediated by the personal networks that link the two sectors. Evans coined the term *embedded autonomy* to describe the characteristics requisite for a state to influence the economy positively—meaning a professionalized bureaucracy largely autonomous from business but with social ties linking to business leaders that are the channels through which influence may be exercised (Evans 1995).

But the network overlap between the state and business has not been studied in careful detail. There are some tantalizing clues. For Japan, Taira and Wada (1987) described a "todai-yakkai-zaikai complex"—the overlapping networks of graduates of leading universities, leading families, and top executives—and how these ties facilitate contacts among government and business leaders, who are quite accustomed to interacting in nonbusiness spheres. They go so far as to say that the resulting networks "render the formal structural distinction of government and business almost meaningless in Japan" (1987, 264). It is in part because of this dense network that government can regulate with a relatively light hand and yet have an impact beyond what could be expected from visible formal mandates. This disjunction between the formal and the informal is one reason why there is so much controversy over how powerful the Japanese regulatory system is—one's conclusion depends on whether one focuses on formal actions or actual outcomes. A well-known practice that reinforces network overlap is the colorfully named *amakudari*—"descent from heaven"—the movement of retired government officials to positions in industry from which they activate their social networks in the state bureaucracy to help coordinate state-business interactions. Though *amakudari* is a widely understood pattern, no detailed study of it and the webs it creates across sectors has yet been accomplished.[14]

Where governments or influential political organizations themselves own or run business groups, we can expect to see this affect their views on regulation. Chung reports that the Kuomintang (KMT)—the party of Chiang Kai-shek, which dominated Taiwan in single-party rule from 1949 to the democratization of the 1980s—was also itself a major business interest, controlling 168 corporations in 1996. He refers to it as a "*de facto* business group" that, if ranked among the top 100 groups in Taiwan in 1998 would be twenty-fourth. In part because the party depended heavily on these businesses to support its political campaign, it actively supported limits on government regulation (Chung 2000, chap. 5).

A pioneering attempt to measure the overlap among business, politics, and kinship is Zeitlin and Ratcliff's 1988 study of Chile in the 1960s, which develops the idea of a "kinecon," a "complex social unit in which economic interests and kinship bonds are inextricably intertwined"—a set of "primary, secondary and other relatives among the officers, directors, and principal shareowners, whose combined individual and indirect (institutional) shareholdings constitute the dominant proprietary interest in the corporation" (55). Carefully tracing kinship ties at an unprecedented level of detail, they show that families not only control most of the major corporations through complex pyramids, but that supposed divisions among industrial and agrarian landowning classes are bridged by a dense web of kinship ties, and that leading members of these families are prominent in the state apparatus as well (1988, chap. 5).

Korea is another case where kinship ties between business and the state have attracted considerable attention. It is also a case that illustrates how changes in network overlap can affect economic outcomes. As Kim (1997) points out, during the administration of Syngman Rhee (1948–60), the overlap was very direct: many members of Rhee's Liberal Party were founders, owners, or large stockholders of the *chaebol* (1997, 113). In this classic "rent-seeking" situation, the state became the captive of special interests, and heavily subsidized them, in part possible because of the large infusions of foreign aid from the West following the Korean War. The military coup of General Park Chung Hee in 1961 completely changed this situation. The class and family backgrounds of the new regime were quite different from those of previous elites, and many, including Park himself, were from peasant families. E.M. Kim comments that this new "distance allowed the state to be autonomous from the interests of the landed and industrial classes" (1997, 112). Park's dramatic gesture of arresting major *chaebol* presidents for corruption just 12 days after the coup was facilitated by the little-noticed fact that these business leaders were not well organized to resist—few "formal organizations among businesses existed at the time" (1997, 118). It would be interesting to speculate why the business class was fragmented in this period, and whether this had to do with regional or other rivalries that divided leaders. This new social autonomy of the state from business allowed it to adopt firm policies and demand strong economic performance from the business groups.

But as the economy grew and the state apparatus became more institutionalized, we should perhaps not be surprised to learn that the "number of marriages between the offspring of state officials and business leaders increased leading to blurred class distinction between the two groups" (Kim 1997, 173). The Korean popular press took a special interest in such alliances, with particular attention to the marriage in 1992 of the president's daughter to the son of the chairman of a major *chaebol*, one of many such cross-sector marriages noted by Darlin (1992). Indeed, Cumings (1997, 329) estimates that in the 1990s, about one-third of fathers-in-law of *chaebol* owners were high-ranking government officials. This was one among several factors that reduced the independent power of the state vis-à-vis the *chaebol* in the 1980s (Kim 1997, chap. 6).

The problem in analyses of business-political network overlap, however, is that—especially in relatively small countries like South Korea and Chile—it is hard to know what the null hypothesis is for how many prominent people should be related to one another—the baseline against which we should be impressed by the number of parents, children, spouses, aunts, uncles, and cousins who are represented in the ownership and control of major corporations and linkages to the state. Moreover, showing that many leading co-owners are related to one another or to political figures, or are themselves in politics, does not in itself prove that action has been either coordinated or effective. Guillén notes, for example, that business groups "have loomed large in Argentine politics. . . . Cabinet ministers and other top political appointees have frequently been recruited among the managerial ranks of the largest groups. . . . The Argentine business groups, though, have not always succeeded in influencing policymaking in their favor" (2001, 83).

Thus, we have only scratched the surface of research on this important topic of network overlap among institutional sectors. In the early twenty-first century, when methods for analyzing and visualizing social networks have achieved remarkable advances, in tandem with dramatic increases in computing power on our desktops, the possibility of collecting and mapping data on network overlap in a sophisticated way is real for the first time. Such an effort must be accompanied, however, by better conceptualization and measurement of the consequences of the network patterns we find, including measures of how well different organizational forms achieve their diverse goals.

ANACHRONISM OR AVATAR? THE FUTURE OF BUSINESS GROUPS

One's view of where the organizational form of business groups comes from, and how successful it is, will strongly affect judgment about whether groups are an anachronism that arises for lack of a better and more efficient form of organization—such as that provided by a "well-functioning" market, or an avatar of modern organizational forms, which have developed new ways to mobilize resources across disparate social sectors so as to focus on unprecedented new and complex tasks (cf. White 1992; Burt 1992; Granovetter 2002). During the 1970s and 1980s, when the economies of Japan and Korea were considerably more robust and successful than those of the West, the business press, and leading academics (e.g., Vogel 1979), argued that patterns of complex cooperation found in these systems could profitably supplant the (imagined to be) more common Western pattern of widely held autonomous firms that answered only to shareholding owners. When the economic situations reversed in the 1990s, most opinions swung to the other extreme, accounting in part for the often disastrous advice offered to countries emerging from state socialism. In 2003, after several years of weak economic growth and swirling scandals in the United States, previously thought the strongest fortress of shareholder value and accounting transparency, this view is harder to support; thus, no single model now commands universal attention or approval.

Progress requires recognizing that to assess organizational forms from their most recent results is not viable as a theoretical stance nor as a long-term strategy. It makes more sense to look closely at how business groups have responded to changes in the economies they inhabit, and at how we understand their capacities and the way they change over time.

The view that business groups arise in response to missing institutions implies that if those institutions should emerge, groups will lose their competitive advantage and selection pressures will fragment and dissolve them in favor of individual firms. Thus, Khanna and Palepu urge governments not to try dismantling business groups, but rather to build up market institutions. "The dismantling of business groups will, we believe, follow naturally once those institutions are in place" (1999b, 126). Similarly, Chang suggests that because the Korean "chaebols are creatures of market imperfections and government intervention . . . as these forces diminish, chaebols will decline in the long run" (2003, 238).

But as Keynes remarked, "in the long run we are all dead."[15] In the short to medium run, which we are constrained to inhabit, the picture is murkier. Chang himself goes on to note that *chaebol* and "business groups in other countries will not . . . disband overnight. It takes time to build institutions and for the effects of competition to be felt" (2003, 239). Consider Khanna and Palepu's study of how business groups in Chile and India responded to major policy shocks brought on by privatization and deregulation. Despite the shocks, the large groups in both countries did not reduce

their activities or narrow their focus. Instead, and belying the "traditional view that liberalization is likely to reduce the role of the largest and the most diversified business groups in the economy," they strengthened their internal structures and processes in ways that "will enable them to increase their role as intermediaries in domestic product, labor and capital markets, and in international markets for capital and technology," and furthermore, "their actions are associated with performance improvements" (1999a, 274) and with an increase of group identity. Khanna and Palepu attribute this outcome to the fact that deregulation alone does not build institutions, so that when the government exits functions it had previously performed, and new institutional intermediaries do not immediately arise, the groups see opportunities to increase their own intermediation.

There is in fact considerable evidence that since the mid–twentieth century, business groups have typically defied predictions of their imminent demise, surviving both conscious attempts by political authorities to break them up and the impact of financial crises. In Japan, American occupation forces meant to dissolve the powerful *zaibatsu* complexes—family-owned business groups that dominated much of Japan's industrial production through the Second World War. By banning the holding companies through which families exercised control, purging families of any role in their former business empires, and directly dissolving the largest *zaibatsu* groups, they imagined that they could engineer a competitive economy made up of many small firms (Hirschmeier and Yui 1981, chap. 4). But despite having been beheaded and dissolved, three and perhaps four of the largest groups reassembled themselves in the postwar period and resumed a position of economic dominance. Planners had dramatically underestimated the extent to which the dense web of ties connecting firms within these groups, and the resulting sense of group identity and patterns of customary cooperation, could persist and regenerate even without direction from family owners.

For Chile, Khanna and Rivkin (2000) note that the stock market returns of companies within groups covary more than equity interlocks alone can explain, which suggests that investors assume that nonequity ties, including kinship, link such firms. They note that this matters a great deal in countries like Korea or South Africa where governments attempt to dismantle groups by unbundling formal ownership ties. They suggest that these ties are just the tip of the iceberg, and that governments may have to sever many bonds other than direct equity interlocks in order to break up established groups. Indeed, many of the bonds that appear to be at least somewhat relevant can hardly be legislated. . . . It may require a substantial and sustained effort to replace directors, eliminate owner overlap, install new managers, and alter personal relations. (2000, 35)

In Southeast Asia, economic crisis has severely tested the business group form. The currency shocks of 1997 severely disrupted many Asian economies, and in some of the most seriously affected countries, such as Korea, the International Monetary Fund demanded strong reforms as a condition for bailout loans. The Korean government enacted many of these, aiming to weaken the large groups, reduce their scope, and narrow their focus. They also meant to increase transparency in intragroup transactions, and to ban transactions that had previously supported risky investments, such as mutual loan guarantees among group companies, and excessive cross-holdings (see the excellent account in S. Chang 2003). As a result of the crisis, half of the 30 largest groups in 1997 were reduced in size or liquidated.

But in 2003, what is most remarkable is this story's surprise ending. The Korean economy has substantially recovered and is enjoying economic growth, at a level unimaginable in the darkest hours of the 1997 crisis. Yet this new growth has occurred despite the failure of most reform efforts. Though, as noted, many *chaebol* failed (which would not have been permitted during the period of strong state support in the 1960s and 1970s), the failures were among groups already weak and severely overextended; by contrast, in four of the five largest groups, the number of member firms has actually increased. Thus, E.M. Kim and D. Chang note that "it is difficult to conclude that the corporate restructuring measures succeeded in reducing the influence of the largest *chaebol* in the South Korean economy, which was arguably one of the not-so-hidden agendas of the corporate sector restructuring" (2002, 32).

D. Chang argues that one reason the reforms failed is that they treated the *chaebol* as if they were collections of individual firms; but in fact they responded to the crisis as network units. Repeating the blockmodel analysis he had done for ownership ties in 1989 for 1998 data, Chang found that the hierarchical organization of ties within *chaebol* remained solid; because they wanted to retain control of their *chaebol*, families did not redeploy their investments to more profitable locations. But the

nested hierarchy of the earlier period was refined by the most successful groups, in such a way as to increase the leverage available from relatively small holdings; and the more successful *chaebol* are especially those that did so. Chang (2000) refers to this as a "network survival strategy."

In Japan the economy was under pressure for a longer period. The stunning growth of the 1980s ended in 1991, leading most commentators to call the 1980s a "bubble." Japan then entered an economic downturn that persists to the present time. Lincoln and Gerlach carried out a blockmodel analysis of the 259 largest firms in the Japanese economy as of 1980, without making any prior assumptions about *keiretsu* membership, to see if the data reduction reproduced what are usually considered *keiretsu* groupings. In the most comprehensive such analysis ever attempted, they considered four types of interfirm ties: lending, trade, shareholding, and director dispatch. The business press has generally asserted that in the economic crisis of the 1990s, Japanese firms have been jettisoning the excess baggage of *keiretsu* ties and obligations, in order to move toward a more efficient free market economy. But the Lincoln-Gerlach analysis shows something quite different: it was in fact during the 1980s bubble that group ties frayed substantially. During the 1990s, the three groups that had emerged anew after the Second World War (Sanwa, DKB, and Fuyo) did not regain their earlier cohesion, and showed some decline. To some extent we can see these three groups merging into one, so there would now be four major intermarket groups (Lincoln and Gerlach 2002, 6–20). But the older groups with strong *zaibatsu* roots, Mitsui, Mitsubishi, and Sumitomo, clearly strengthened during this crisis period. Lincoln and Gerlach suggest what they call a "countercyclical change": network forms expand and contract inversely with business conditions. During a boom period, the mutual support that group firms offer one another is relatively less important, as the rising tide lifts all boats. During a crisis, groups that can manage to do so return to their group identities for the vital support that flows from them (Lincoln and Gerlach 2002, chap. 3).

It is likely no accident that in both Korea and Japan, the groups that were most resilient were the oldest ones with the strongest sense of group identity. The oldest Korean groups, Samsung and LG, seem especially stable. And in India, the Tata group, with nineteenth-century roots, shows few signs of breakup despite the fragility of some newer business houses. The ties of sentiment and identity that infuse such groups both lower transaction costs across group firms and produce noneconomic motivations among participants for the groups' success. For this reason, we might imagine that countries in economic crisis where groups are of quite recent origin—as in the formerly state socialist countries of Russia and eastern europe—might see groups dissolve much more readily than countries where groups and their families and other participants have long history and tradition to draw upon.

Thus, the argument that emerging market institutions will make groups unnecessary in the long run must confront their apparent resilience in the face of crisis and direct frontal attack by governments. This is not to say that groups might never become superfluous and fade away. What we need, however, to understand this more clearly, is a better-developed theoretical argument about the origins of institutions that mediate between individuals and larger economic structures in the capital, product, labor, and other markets. If business groups already profit from intermediation and add value to their economies by doing so, it seems likely that they will resist attempts to build new mediating institutions that would undercut their functions, and that this resistance may succeed.

New institutional intermediaries that replace business group activity do not emerge magically or instantaneously from free market interactions, but rather in a political context. They must be built by institutional entrepreneurs who have the ability to mobilize resources. In countries that business groups already dominate, the financial and political space for such entrepreneurs to operate in outside of groups is significantly narrowed. Without strong pressures from external, global-level actors such as the International Monetary Fund, it is not clear from what sector or with what resources local actors could manage this feat. To persuade supporters that this would be a good use of resources, such entrepreneurs would need to demonstrate that the new institutions would be profitable and also improve economic and social outcomes for large segments of the population. Such demonstration is most likely to occur in a political arena, including new legislation that might be fiercely contested (cf. Chung 2000, chap. 5 for the case of Taiwan). Resulting compromises are quite likely to preserve important functions that business groups already serve. Predictions for any given country about the future of its business groups therefore should depend heavily on the balance of political forces among major stakeholders in the economy, includ-

ing not only business, but also consumers, labor, and the state bureaucracy. Strategic actors in all sectors will draw on economic resources, but also on social networks and reservoirs of identity and sentiment, in staking their claims. As in so many social science conundrums, progress in understanding the future of organizational forms depends on our ability to develop a more unified social science with better arguments that privilege neither the political, the economic, nor the social aspects of action, but instead seek to understand how all these intersect in real actors and institutions.

NOTES

For their immensely helpful comments on earlier drafts, I am grateful to Neil Smelser, Richard Swedberg, Chi-nien Chung, Giovanni Dosi, Neil Fligstein, Gary Hamilton, Harry Makler, Daniel Maman, Kiyoteru Tsutsui, Valery Yakubovich, and Harrison White.

1. The present chapter complements rather than replaces my 1994 *Handbook* chapter "Business Groups," so the reader may also want to consult the earlier version. At the time of the first edition, the topic was little discussed. But it has since risen to considerable prominence, and here I attempt to bring some order to the recent outpouring of literature.

2. For further discussion of Coase's arguments and how they relate to business groups, see Granovetter 1995a.

3. A "subsidiary" is a corporation whose stock is majority owned by another, "parent" corporation.

4. The history, causes, and scope of this invisibility are discussed in Granovetter 1995a, 97–100.

5. But see Penrose's discussion of "combines," collections of firms acquired by a single entrepreneur and loosely integrated under a holding company ([1959] 1995, 186–89). This form fits her general discussion only with difficulty, and she discusses it in a section entitled "Empire-Building and Merger," as an example of the effect of "abnormally expansive behavior" (186). She recognizes that such firms may persist and even become profitable and dominant, noting that the activities of such an entrepreneur are "closer to those of the 'financier' than to those of the 'industrialist' and that creates special difficulties for the unambiguous definition of the industrial firm" (189).

6. These are the same six that I discussed in greater detail in Granovetter 1994, 461–70.

7. There is no way of determining from the LaPorta et al. data what proportion of family-dominated firms fall within business groups, but it is clearly substantial or dominant in many countries.

8. See related comments in Granovetter 1994, 464–66, 470.

9. Note that both Hollingsworth and Boyer (1997) and Hall and Soskice (2001) make these comments in introducing edited volumes in which many other authors then develop specific analyses within the general framework they propose.

10. For a much more detailed account of the advantages of group firms in India see Khanna and Palepu 2000.

11. As is typical in sociometric analysis, asymmetry is used as a measure of hierarchy. In this case, a firm or block that

sends equity ties to another but receives none back is considered higher, as the equity tie reflects ownership and possibly control.

To simplify exposition, I refer to "blocks" in Chang's analysis. Because he uses a role-equivalence algorithm to reduce the data, he refers instead to "role-sets." See Chang 1999, 115n, and the detailed discussion in Wasserman and Faust 1994, chaps. 10–12.

12. See Timberg 1978 for a useful discussion of how complex the "Marwari" category is.

13. More detail on the House of Tata can be found in Khanna, Palepu, and Wu 1998.

14. But see the promising leads in Taira and Wada 1987, 285–88.

15. This famous quip comes from chapter 3 of his *Tract on Monetary Reform* (1924), where he argues that the "long run is a misleading guide to current affairs. In the long run we are all dead. Economists set themselves too easy, too useless a task if in tempestuous seasons they can only tell us that when the storm is long past the ocean is flat again."

References

Amsden, Alice, and Takashi Hikino. 1994. "Project Execution Capability, Organizational Know-how and Corporate Growth in Late Industrialization." *Industrial and Corporate Change* 3(1): 111–47.

Antunes, Jose. 1994. *Liability of Corporate Groups: Autonomy and Control in Parent-Subsidiary Relationships in U.S., German, and EU Law—an International and Comparative Perspective.* Boston: Kluwer Law and Taxation Publishers.

Bethel, Jennifer, and Julia Liebeskind. 1998. "Diversification and the Legal Organization of the Firm." *Organization Science* 9(1): 49–67.

Biggart, Nicole Woolsey. 1991. "Institutionalized Patrimonialism in Korean Business." Pp. 113–33 in *Business Institutions*, vol. 12 of *Comparative Social Research*, ed. Craig Calhoun. Greenwich, Conn.: JAI Press.

Biggart, Nicole Woolsey, and Mauro Guillén. 1999. "Developing Difference: Social Organization and the Rise of the Auto Industries of South Korea, Taiwan, Spain, and Argentina." *American Sociological Review* 64:722–47.

Blair, Margaret M. 2001. "Corporate Governance." Pp. 2797–2803 in *International Encyclopedia of the Social and Behavioral Sciences*, ed. Neil J. Smelser and Paul B. Baltes. Amsterdam: Elsevier.

Burt, Ronald. 1992. *Structural Holes.* Cambridge: Harvard University Press.

Camp, Roderic A. 1989. *Entrepreneurs and Politics in Twentieth-Century Mexico.* Oxford: Oxford University Press.

Chang, Dukjin. 1999. "Privately Owned Social Structures: Institutionalization-Network Contingency in the Korean Chaebol." Ph.D. diss., Department of Sociology, University of Chicago.

———. 2000. "Financial Crisis and Network Response: Changes in the Ownership Structure of the Korean Chaebol since 1997." Working Paper, Ewha Women's University, Seoul, Korea.

Chang, Sea-Jin. 2003. *The Rise and Fall of Chaebols: Financial Crisis and Transformation of Korean Business Groups.* Cambridge: Cambridge University Press.

Chung, Chi-nien. 2000. "Markets, Culture, and Institutions: The Formation and Transformation of Business Groups in Taiwan, 1960s–1990s." Ph.D. diss., Department of Sociology, Stanford University.

———. 2001. "Markets, Culture, and Institutions: The Emergence of Large Business Groups in Taiwan, 1950s–1970s." *Journal of Management Studies* 38: 719–45.

———. 2004. "Institutional Transition and Cultural Inheritance: Network Ownership and Corporate Control of Business Groups in Taiwan, 1970s–1990s." *International Sociology* 19:25–50.

Coase, Ronald. 1937. "The Nature of the Firm." *Economica*, n.s. 4:386–405.

Collin, Sven-Olof. 1998. "Why Are These Islands of Conscious Power Found in the Ocean of Ownership? Institutional and Governance Hypotheses Explaining the Existence of Business Groups in Sweden." *Journal of Management Studies* 35:719–46.

Cumings, Bruce. 1997. *Korea's Place in the Sun: A Modern History.* New York: W. W. Norton.

Darlin, Damon. 1992. "South Korea Contract Award Spotlights Marriage of the Nation's Political and Business Families." *Wall Street Journal*, Eastern Edition, August 21, A4.

Davis, Gerald, and T. Thompson. 1994. "A Social Movement Perspective on Corporate Control." *Administrative Science Quarterly* 39:141–73.

DiMaggio, Paul, and Walter W. Powell. 1983. "The Iron Cage Revisited: Institutional Isomorphism and Collective Rationality in Organizational Fields." *American Sociological Review* 48:147–60.

Dine, Janet. 2000. *The Governance of Corporate Groups.* Cambridge: Cambridge University Press.

Dobbin, Frank. 1994. *Forging Industrial Policy.* Princeton: Princeton University Press.

Ellis, Eric. 2002. "Tata Steels Itself for Change." *Fortune*, April 29.

Evans, Peter. 1995. *Embedded Autonomy.* Princeton: Princeton University Press.

Feenstra, Robert, and Gary Hamilton. Forthcoming. *Emergent Economies, Divergent Paths: Organization and Transformation in the Economies of South Korea and Taiwan.* Cambridge: Cambridge University Press.

Fligstein, Neil. 1990. *The Transformation of Corporate Control.* Cambridge: Harvard University Press.

Freeland, Robert. 2001. *The Struggle for Control of the Modern Corporation.* Cambridge: Cambridge University Press.

Fukuyama, Francis. 1992. *The End of History and the Last Man.* New York: Free Press.

Garrido, Celso. 1994. "National Private Groups in Mexico, 1987–1993." *CEPAL Review* 53 (August): 159–75.

Gerlach, Michael. 1992. *The Alliance Structure of Japanese Business.* Berkeley and Los Angeles: University of California Press.

Ghemawat, Pankaj, and Tarun Khanna. 1998. "The Nature of Diversified Business Groups: A Research Design and Two Case Studies." *Journal of Industrial Economics* 46(1): 35–61.

Goldstein, Andrea, and Ben Ross Schneider. Forthcoming. "Big Business in Brazil: States and Markets in the Corporate Reorganization of the 1990s." In *Brazil and South Korea: Economic Crisis and Restructuring*, ed. E. Amann and H. J. Chang. Washington, D.C.: Brookings Institution Press.

Gould, Stephen, and Richard Lewontin. 1979. "The Spandrels of San Marco and the Panglossian Paradigm: A Critique of the Adaptationist Programme." *Proceedings of the Royal Society of London* B205: 581–98.

Granovetter, Mark. 1994. "Business Groups." Pp. 453–74 in *The Handbook of Economic Sociology*, ed. Neil J. Smelser and Richard Swedberg. New York: Russell Sage Foundation. Princeton: Princeton University Press.

———. 1995a. "Coase Revisited: Business Groups in the Modern Economy." *Industrial and Corporate Change* 4(1): 93–130.

———. 1995b. "The Economic Sociology of Firms and Entrepreneurs." Pp. 128–65 in *The Economic Sociology of Immigration: Essays in Networks, Ethnicity, and Entrepreneurship*, ed. Alejandro Portes. New York: Russell Sage Foundation.

———. 2002. "A Theoretical Agenda for Economic Sociology." Pp. 35–59 in *The New Economic Sociology: Developments in an Emerging Field*, ed. Mauro F. Guillén, Randall Collins, Paula England, and Marshall Meyer. New York: Russell Sage Foundation.

Griffin, John. 1997. "The Politics of Ownership and the Transformation of Corporate Governance in Germany, 1973–1995." Ph.D. diss., Department of Political Science, Massachusetts Institute of Technology.

Guillén, Mauro. 2001. *The Limits of Convergence: Globalization and Organizational Change in Argentina, South Korea, and Spain.* Princeton: Princeton University Press.

Hall, Peter, and David Soskice. 2001. *Varieties of Capitalism: The Institutional Foundations of Comparative Advantage.* Oxford: Oxford University Press.

Hannan, Michael, and John Freeman. 1989. *Organizational Ecology.* Cambridge: Harvard University Press.

Herrigel, Gary. 1996. *Industrial Constructions: The Sources of German Industrial Power.* Cambridge: Cambridge University Press.

———. 1999. "Governance of Small and Medium Sized Firms Manufacturing in Germany." *Entreprises et histoire* 21 (June): 59–69.

Hirschmeier, Johannes, and Tsunehiko Yui. 1981. *The Development of Japanese Business: 1600–1980.* 2d ed. London: George Allen and Unwin.

Hollingsworth, J. R., and Robert Boyer. 1997. *Contemporary Capitalism: The Embeddedness of Institutions.* Cambridge: Cambridge University Press.

Johnson, Juliet. 2000. *A Fistful of Rubles.* Ithaca, N.Y.: Cornell University Press.

Jones, Leroy P., and Il Sakong. 1980. *Government, Business, and Entrepreneurship in Economic Development: The Korean Case.* Cambridge: Harvard University Press.

Keister, Lisa. 2000. *Chinese Business Groups: The Structure and Impact of Interfirm Relations during Economic Development.* Oxford: Oxford University Press.

Khanna, Tarun, and Krishna Palepu. 1999a. "Policy Shocks, Market Intermediaries, and Corporate Strategy: The Evolution of Business Groups in Chile and India." *Journal of Economics and Management Strategy* 8(2): 271–310.

———. 1999b. "The Right Way to Restructure Conglomerates in Emerging Markets." *Harvard Business Review,* July–August, 125–34.

———. 2000. "Is Group Affiliation Profitable in Emerging Markets? An Analysis of Diversified Indian Business Groups." *Journal of Finance* 54:867–91.

Khanna, Tarun, Krishna Palepu, and Danielle Wu. 1998. "House of Tata, 1995: The Next Generation (A)." Harvard Business School Case 9-798-037.

Khanna, Tarun, and Jan Rivkin. 2000. "Ties That Bind Business Groups: Evidence from an Emerging Economy." Working paper, Harvard Business School.

———. 2001. "Estimating the Performance Effects of Business Groups in Emerging Markets." *Strategic Management Journal* 22:45–74.

Kilman, Scott, Christina Brinkley, and William Bulkeley. 2002. "An Empire on the Brink: If Pritzker Family's Infighting Breaks Up Its Conglomerate, Proceeds Would Be Immense." *Wall Street Journal,* December 12.

Kim, Eun Mee. 1997. *Big Business, Strong State: Collusion and Conflict in South Korean Development, 1960–1990.* Albany: State University of New York Press.

Kim, Eun Mee, and Dukjin Chang. 2002. "State-Business Relations: Managing Corporate Sector Restructuring." Working paper, Ewha Women's University, Seoul, Korea.

Kirk, Don. 2001. "As Korean Heirs Feud, an Empire is Withering." *New York Times,* April 26.

Kurgan–Van Hentenryk, Ginette. 1997. "Structure and Strategy of Belgian Business Groups (1920–1990)." Pp. 88–106 in *Beyond the Firm: Business Groups in International and Historical Perspective*, ed. Takao Shiba and Masahiro Shimotani. Oxford: Oxford University Press.

La Porta, Rafael, Florencio Lopez-de-Silanes, and Andrei Shleifer. 1999. "Corporate Ownership around the World." *Journal of Finance* 54:471–16.

Lamoreaux, Naomi. 1986. "Banks, Kinship, and Economic Development: The New England Case." *Journal of Economic History* 46:647–67.

———. 1994. *Insider Lending: Banks, Personal Connec-*

tions, and Economic Development in Industrial New England. Cambridge: Cambridge University Press.

Leff, Nathaniel. 1978. "Industrial Organization and Entrepreneurship in the Developing Countries: The Economic Groups." *Economic Development and Cultural Change* 26:661–75.

Lincoln, James, and Michael Gerlach. 2002. *Japan's Network Economy: Structure, Persistence, and Change*. Draft manuscript. Forthcoming, 2004, Cambridge University Press.

Lindgren, Hakan. 2002. "Succession Strategies in a Large Family Business Group: The Case of the Swedish Wallenberg Family." Paper prepared for the Sixth European Business History Association Annual Congress, Helsinki.

Locke, Richard. 1995. *Remaking the Italian Economy*. Ithaca, N.Y.: Cornell University Press.

Lowe, R. A., C. S. Boerner, and D. J. Teece. 2001. "Diversification and Economies of Scale." Pp. 3797–3801 in *International Encyclopedia of the Social and Behavioral Sciences*, ed. Neil J. Smelser and Paul B. Baltes. Amsterdam: Elsevier.

Makler, Harry M. 2000. "Bank Transformation and Privatization in Brazil." *Quarterly Review of Economics and Finance* 40:45–69.

———. 2001. "Financial Institutions in Economic Development." Pp. 5661–65 in *International Encyclopedia of the Social and Behavioral Sciences*, ed. Neil J. Smelser and Paul B. Baltes. Amsterdam: Elsevier.

Makler, Harry M., and Walter Ness. 2002. "How Financial Intermediation Challenges National Sovereignty in Emerging Markets." *Quarterly Review of Economics and Finance* 183:1–25.

Maman, Daniel. 2002. "The Emergence of Business Groups: Israel and South Korea Compared." *Organization Studies* 23:737–58.

———. 2003. "The Interplay between Global and Local: The New Israeli Corporate Law." Department of Sociology, Hebrew University.

Marris, Peter, and Anthony Somerset. 1971. *The African Businessman: A Study of Entrepreneurship and Development in Kenya*. London: Routledge and Kegan Paul.

Penrose, Edith. [1959] 1995. *The Theory of the Growth of the Firm*. Oxford: Oxford University Press.

Posner, Richard. 1998. *Economic Analysis of Law*. 5th ed. New York: Aspen Law and Business.

Powell, Walter W., and Paul DiMaggio, eds. 1991. *The New Institutionalism in Organizational Analysis*. Chicago: University of Chicago Press.

Prechel, Harland. 2000. *Big Business and the State*. Albany, N.Y.: SUNY Press.

Robison, Richard. 1986. *Indonesia: The Rise of Capital*. Sydney: Allen and Unwin.

Roe, Mark. 1994. *Strong Managers, Weak Owners: The Political Roots of American Corporate Finance*. Princeton: Princeton University Press.

Ruef, Martin. 2000. "The Emergence of Organizational Forms: A Community Ecology Approach." *American Journal of Sociology* 106:658–714.

Sanders, Elizabeth. 1986. "Industrial Concentration, Sectional Competition, and Antitrust Politics in America: 1880–1980." Pp. 142–213 in vol. 1 of *Studies in American Political Development*, ed. Karen Oren and Stephen Skowronek. New Haven: Yale University Press.

Saxenian, AnnaLee. 1994. *Regional Advantage*. Cambridge: Harvard University Press.

Scott, W. Richard. 1995. *Institutions and Organizations*. Thousand Oaks, Calif.: Sage.

Stark, David. 2001. "Ambiguous Assets for Uncertain Environments." Pp. 69–104 in *The Twenty-First Century Firm*, ed. Paul DiMaggio. Princeton: Princeton University Press.

Strachan, Harry. 1976. *Family and Other Business Groups in Economic Development: The Case of Nicaragua*. New York: Praeger.

Taira, Koji, and T. Wada. 1987. "Business-Government Relations in Modern Japan: A Todai-Yakkai-Zaikai Complex?" Pp. 264–97 in *Intercorporate Relations: The Structural Analysis of Business*, ed. Mark Mizruchi and Michael Schwartz. Cambridge: Cambridge University Press.

Takeda, Haruhito. 1999. "Corporate Governance of Zaibatsu during the Interwar Period." *Entreprises et histoire* 21 (June): 90–99.

Teece, David, Richard Rumelt, Giovanni Dosi, and Sidney Winter. 1994. "Understanding Corporate Coherence: Theory and Evidence." *Journal of Economic Behavior and Organization* 23:1–30.

Teubner, Gunther. 1990. "Unitas Multiplex: Corporate Governance in Group Enterprises." Pp. 67–104 in *Regulating Corporate Groups in Europe*, ed. David Sugarman and Gunther Teubner. Baden-Baden: Nomos.

Timberg, Thomas. 1978. *The Marwaris: From Traders to Industrialists*. New Delhi: Vikas.

Vogel, Ezra. 1979. *Japan as Number One: Lessons for America*. Cambridge: Harvard University Press.

Weber, Joseph, and Lorraine Woellert. 2001. "An Empire Trembles: Can a New Generation of Pritzkers Halt the Slide in the Family's Fortunes?" *Business Week*, September 10, 92–96.

White, Harrison C. 1992. *Identity and Control: A Structural Theory of Social Action*. Princeton: Princeton University Press.

Whitley, Richard. 1999. *Divergent Capitalisms: The Social Structuring and Change of Business Systems*. Oxford: Oxford University Press.

Williamson, Oliver. 1985. *The Economic Institutions of Capitalism*. New York: Free Press.

Zeitlin, Maurice, and Richard Ratcliff. 1988. *Landlords and Capitalists: The Dominant Class of Chile*. Princeton: Princeton University Press.

20 Entrepreneurship

Howard E. Aldrich

SOCIOLOGISTS have made major contributions toward understanding the conditions under which new organizations are created, as well as proposing which social locations are most likely to spawn their creators. Beginning with Weber's (1930) analysis of ascetic Protestantism's contributions to the entrepreneurial spirit, sociologists have offered cultural- and societal-level interpretations of entrepreneurial phenomena. Over the past several decades, with the emergence of entrepreneurship as an academic field, sociological analyses of entrepreneurship have become multifaceted. Today, sociologists conduct multilevel investigations, ranging from the personal networks of individual entrepreneurs to an entire society's transition from socialism to capitalism.

Sociological concern for entrepreneurship can be linked with at least three broad themes in recent theory and research. First, entrepreneurs can both reproduce and challenge the existing social order. Stinchcombe (1965) argued that people construct organizations that are culturally embedded and historically specific, reflecting societal conditions at a particular historical conjuncture. Thus, in societies characterized by tendencies toward social inequality in the distribution of income, wealth, political power, and other valued resources, we might expect to see such inequality reproduced within the founding process of new economic organizations.[1]

Second, entrepreneurship ensures the reproduction of existing organizational populations and lays a foundation for the creation of new populations. Organizational ecologists have mainly focused on dynamics within existing populations, noting that most founding attempts reproduce existing organizational forms and comprise incremental rather than novel additions to the organizational landscape (Carroll and Hannan 2000). By contrast, evolutionary theorists have focused on the generation of new populations, analyzing the conditions under which new forms of organizations carve out niches for themselves (Aldrich and Fiol 1994). Whether a new business simply copies an existing form or strikes off into novel territory depends upon the extent to which its founding members possesses diverse outlooks and skills, as well as on the sociopolitical context in which it is created.

Third, entrepreneurship affects levels of stratification and inequality in a society by shaping the life chances of founders and their employees. Organizational foundings and disbandings generate a great deal of employment volatility through job creation and destruction. For example, between 1992 and 1996, about 48 million jobs were created or destroyed in the United States through firms' foundings, disbandings, and mergers and acquisitions. Of the 11.2 million *net* new jobs, about 70 percent were created by new organizations (Birch 1997). Figures from other industrialized nations are similar. For example, in Japan, between 1996 and 1999 about 40 million jobs were created or destroyed (Kodera 2002). At any given time, we observe only a surviving fraction of a much larger pool of start-ups begun but abandoned by nascent entrepreneurs (Katz and Gartner 1988). Failure to appreciate the level of turnover and turbulence in business populations has blinded social scientists to the organizational fermentation simmering just below the surface in modern capitalist societies.

Sociologists, of course, are not the only scholars interested in entrepreneurs and entrepreneurship. Economists, beginning with Schumpeter, have offered their own analyses, and psychologists, historians, anthropologists, political scientists, and others have had a keen interest in entrepreneurship. For example, political scientists have used the label *entrepreneur* as a term for individuals who change the direction and flow of politics (Schneider and Teske 1992). Anthropologists studying the economic adaptation of immigrants to their host society have viewed "entrepreneurship" as a response to blocked opportunities (Wong 1998). Entrepreneurial concepts and explanatory principles have thus found their way into entrepreneurship research by scholars in many disciplines.

Plan of This Chapter

I begin by reviewing the growth of entrepreneurship as an academic field, noting its heterogeneous interdisciplinary nature, and its struggle for legitimacy in the academic world.[2] I then examine what authors appear to mean when they use the term *entrepreneur*, beginning with the classic contribution of Joseph A. Schumpeter. I note that at least four different perspectives are involved in disputes over the definition of *entrepreneur* and *entrepreneurship*.[3] Of the many definitions, the one I have found most useful is of entrepreneurship as the creation of new organizations, and I will label the people who create organizations as entrepreneurs. Relying on this definition, I have chosen several issues to review.

I review research on the process of founding a business, focusing on entrepreneurs and firms as units of analysis. I assess research concerning nascent entrepreneurs, social networks and opportunities, founding teams, and the financial resources raised by start-ups. Then I turn to the population level of analysis, focusing first on the contributions of organizational ecology and then on research and theorizing concerning the growth of new industries. I conclude with issues that might interest us in the future. For additional reviews and information on these issues, readers should consult several recent review articles, anthologies, and edited collections (Sexton and Landstrom 2000; Shane 2002; Swedberg 2000b; Thornton 1999).[4]

THE GROWTH OF ENTREPRENEURSHIP AS AN ACADEMIC FIELD

Enthusiastic advocates proposed a new field of entrepreneurship studies in the early 1970s. Since then, it has attracted a heterogeneous group of researchers and practice-oriented academics, generating a great deal of vitality in the resulting debates, but also raising questions in some circles about its academic legitimacy.[5] Considering all published articles and books, sociologists have been minor players in the field's evolution, except for those trained in organization theory who have taken up positions in business school departments of management and strategy. Nonetheless, entrepreneurship scholars today use many concepts first developed by sociologists, leading to a growing sociological presence within entrepreneurship studies.

A Brief History

As Abbott (1993, 187–88) observed, understanding an academic field requires we situate it "historically and disciplinarily." Entrepreneurship, as a field of study, has faced numerous barriers to its acceptance, as Cooper (2003) noted. Just as "industrial sociology" gradually moved into the applied setting of business schools after World War II (Abbott 1993), so too did the study of entrepreneurship. Within business schools, the study of entrepreneurship arose from the practice-oriented field of small-business studies. Although a few courses on entrepreneurship were offered as early as 1947 at the Harvard Business School and in 1953 at New York University, the courses focused on small-business management rather than entrepreneurship theory. A conference on entrepreneurship held at Purdue University in 1970 seemed to catalyze interest among entrepreneurship scholars in pursuing collective action. Following that conference, a small group began lobbying the Academy of Management and succeeded in creating an entrepreneurship interest group. It took them until 1987, however, to achieve full status as a division of the academy. Many other conferences were held throughout the 1970s, and attempts were made to create professional associations of entrepreneurship scholars.[6] Most of them did not succeed, in part because researchers identified more strongly with their academic disciplines than with the field of entrepreneurship studies.

Lack of scholarly publishing venues constituted another major hurdle for entrepreneurship research. No major journals for entrepreneurship existed until the 1980s, and the one potentially prestigious outlet, a journal begun at Harvard in 1949 called *Explorations in Entrepreneurial History*, later changed its name to *Explorations in Economic History*. With little disciplinary interest in entrepreneurship research, and no major journals focused on the subject, few scholars from prestigious universities with international reputations were attracted to the field. Research questions were not usually theoretically based, study designs were often weak, and publications consisted primarily of case studies and problem-focused analyses. As Swedberg (2000a) implied, discipline-based scholars, particularly economists, often wrote on the topic of entrepreneurship, or described research findings with implications for entrepreneurship, but did not identify with the field of entrepreneurial studies.

In their continuing struggle to earn greater academic legitimacy, numerous professional associations and universities have created journals specializing in entrepreneurship. The *American Journal of Small Business*, started in 1975, changed its name to *Entrepreneurship Theory and Practice* in 1988. In 1985, Ian MacMillan started the *Journal of Business Venturing*, which has remained the most respected of all the entrepreneurship journals. Four other specialized journals have been created since 1988: *Family Business Review*, *Small-Business Economics*, *Small Business Strategy*, and *Entrepreneurship and Regional Development*. In addition, entrepreneurship scholars in finance, working with commercial publishers, have created several finance-oriented journals, such as *Venture Capital*.

Another major development in the institutionalization of entrepreneurship as an academic field began with the initiation of entrepreneurship conferences. Babson College initiated its annual Entrepreneurship Research Conference in 1981, and since then, that conference has served as the intellectual heart of entrepreneurship research for business school researchers. Discipline-based scholars, however, have been notable by their absence, and very few sociologists have participated. Another attempt to create an intellectual touchstone for the emerging field was the organization of "state of the art conferences" to produce handbooks and readers on entrepreneurship. A small group of chaired professors led that effort, with the first event held in 1980. As of 2002, various teams of editors had produced six volumes of edited papers (e.g., Sexton, Kent, and Vesper 1982; Sexton and Smilor 1986).

The Field Today

As the proliferation of conferences and journals in entrepreneurship studies indicates, interest in entrepreneurship as an academic field accelerated in the 1980s. Growth was spurred in part by political interest in Birch's (1979) work on new and small firms' role in the job generation process and subsequent debate over his interpretation (Davis, Haltiwanger, and Schuh 1996; Harrison 1994). Birch's work attracted the attention of politicians around the world, and he was called upon to consult with presidents and prime ministers in North America, Europe, and Asia.[7] A booming economy, explosive growth in the stock market, and dot-com mania heightened popular and academic interest in entrepreneurship in the 1990s. In table 1, I present some indicators of the field's contemporary popular and academic state (Katz 2003).

Books and magazines published for practitioners constituted a lucrative market for publishers throughout the 1990s. Although many of them did not survive the stock market crash of April 2000, 17 periodicals oriented toward entrepreneurship were still being published as of August 2002. My search of Amazon.com turned up over 7,000 books that have *entrepreneurship* as one of their keywords, and 49 books had *start-up* in the title. For a time, entrepreneurs enjoyed iconic status in America, with well-known entrepreneurs such as Bill Gates, Larry Ellison, and Steve Jobs featured on the cover of popular magazines and newspapers. A similar phenomenon occurred in Europe. For example, a cover story in the Swedish paper *Aftonbladet* featured a photo of black-clad Jonas Birgersson, twenty-something founder of the dot-com compa-

TABLE 1.   Indicators of the Institutionalization of Entrepreneurship in 2002

As a popular field	
Periodicals published for practitioners	17
Books on Amazon.com with *entrepreneurship* as a keyword	7,120
Books with *start-up* in the title	49
As an academic field	
Entrepreneurship centers in North America	93
Colleges with majors in entrepreneurship or small business	223
Endowed professorships in entrepreneurship	271
Average endowment of professorships created in 1998–99	$2.16 million
Entrepreneurship journals published for academics	48
Annual research reviews published	3
Books in the Library of Congress, in any language, on entrepreneurs or entrepreneurship	1,853

ny Framfab, alongside Bill Gates and Bill Clinton (Rönn 2000). Accounting fraud and financial manipulations somewhat dimmed the luster of entrepreneurship after the summer of 2002, and popular articles began to appear, complaining of the egomania and arrogance of founders and CEOs (Walker 2002).

Enthusiastic academic interest is apparent in the indicators shown in table 1. The number of centers devoted to entrepreneurship grew to 93 in 2002, with many funded by entrepreneurial families. The number of endowed chairs in entrepreneurship grew so quickly in the 1990s that many were left empty for several years, and others only filled when scholars were recruited from other fields.[8] Entrepreneurship researchers can now choose from many publication outlets, including 48 English-language journals and a number of annual review series. Commercial as well as academic publishers, such as Stanford University Press, have begun edited series on entrepreneurship topics (Schoonhoven and Romanelli 2001). Several foundations fund university chairs in entrepreneurship, as well as academic research, such as the Coleman and the Ewing Marion Kauffmann Foundations.

Relatively few sociologists have been directly involved in the field's growth. One indication of a discipline's interest in the subject area can be found in the frequency with which the term *entrepreneur* appears in the text of journal articles. Using JSTOR, I found 1,055 articles published between 1980 and 2002 in 46 business journals that used the term *entrepreneur* at least once.[9] For the 13 major sociology journals covered by JSTOR, there were 168 articles using the term. For the three senior journals—the *American Sociological Review*, the *American Journal of Sociology*, and *Social Forces*—there were 96 mentions, but a closer look revealed only 27 percent actually dealt with the phenomenon of business creation.

As an academic field, entrepreneurship is now firmly entrenched in the undergraduate and MBA curricula of most American business schools, although not at the doctoral level. Only two business schools have doctoral programs specifically dedicated to entrepreneurship, but dozens of others allow students to specialize in the field. With regard to tenure and promotion decisions, however, committees routinely downgrade entrepreneurship articles not published in the leading disciplinary journals. Adjunct and part-time faculty teach many, if not most, entrepreneurship courses. Within sociology, many scholars interested in organization and management issues have moved to business schools, rather than sociology departments. Many of them study the creation of new businesses, but typically from an ecological or institutional perspective, rather than from the perspective of classic entrepreneurship theory.

SCHUMPETER, SOCIOLOGY, AND USES OF THE TERM *ENTREPRENEUR*

Examining how scholars actually use the term reveals a great deal about their theoretical assumptions and conceptual biases. I began with the earliest coherent statement by a scholar with sociological aspirations: Joseph Schumpeter (1883–1950). Although he was trained as an economist, he also wrote as a social theorist (Schumpeter 1942). Schumpeter's major statements concerning entrepreneurship appeared in two places. The first was in chapter 2 of his book on economic development (Schumpeter 1912), and the second was in a chapter he prepared in 1928 for an economics handbook (Schumpeter 2003). His chapter on entrepreneurship in the economic development book has become widely known, but his fully developed statement, in the handbook, has not, probably because it was not published in English until very recently. Swedberg (2000a) referred to it in his summary of Schumpeter's contributions, and Becker and Knudsen (2003) have now translated it into English and written a commentary on it. Subsequent work on entrepreneurship has borrowed a great deal from Schumpeter, but the field has also forgotten much of what he proposed. Here I note a few central points.

First, in the first edition of his chapter on entrepreneurship for his theory book, Schumpeter (1912) had proposed a rather heroic conception of entrepreneurs and their activities. He posited that some people had a capacity for being entrepreneurial, and others simply did not. He attributed almost superhuman powers of leadership to entrepreneurs. Conversely, by the time of his handbook chapter, he focused his attention more strongly on the entrepreneurial function, and not the person carrying it out. In 1912, he had noted that entrepreneurship involved the creation of a "new combination" of already existing materials and forces, but in his handbook chapter he focused on the *activities* carried out by entrepreneurs, rather than their *personal characteristics*. As Becker and Knudsen (2003) implied, this depersonalized conception made entrepreneurship a much more contingent activity. Entrepreneurship scholars rediscovered this conception in the 1980s (Gartner 1988).

Second, Schumpeter argued that entrepreneurship must be placed in its social and historical context. Swedberg noted that, according to Schumpeter, "No one is an entrepreneur forever, only when he or she is actually doing the innovative activity" (Swedberg 2000a, 18). Schumpeter also pointed to several types of entrepreneurial behaviors, including introducing new goods and production methods, opening new markets, and obtaining new sources of raw materials. In this depersonalized view, the collective activity of many people acting within a particular historical epoch is the key, not the actions of particular individuals.

Third, Becker and Knudsen (2003) argued that Schumpeter flirted with Darwinian ideas of selection in his handbook chapter. The evolutionary principle of selection is implicit in his rejection of theories of economic stages that were prevalent in economic theorizing of his time, especially in historicist accounts of economic development. He emphasized competitive struggle and the fundamental persistence of core features of economic organization, even as economies were continually undergoing change. Unfortunately, although he turned toward more sociological thinking in the 1940s, he never followed up on these thoughts in his published work. We can only speculate what the future of entrepreneurial studies might have been, had he developed into a full-fledged evolutionary theorist. A tantalizing hint of this possibility has turned up in a recently discovered essay, heretofore unpublished, in which Schumpeter favorably reviewed the work of both Darwin and Mendel (Schumpeter 1932).

Schumpeter Sidelined?

Today, few academic researchers studying entrepreneurship refer to Schumpeter, and fewer still actually use his ideas to study the creation of new enterprises. To illustrate the extent to which authors credit Schumpeter's ideas in their work, I used JSTOR to examine the joint occurrence of the words *Schumpeter* and *entrepreneur* in several groups of journals. Table 2 shows the results.

First, over the period from 1980 to 2002, 134 articles in 46 business journals jointly mentioned *Schumpeter* and *entrepreneur*. All together, 1,055 articles mentioned *entrepreneur* at least once, with the majority in economics journals. Second, within the five top organization theory journals, there were 274 mentions of *entrepreneur*, but only 14 percent involved co-occurrences of the two terms. More than half of the articles concerned "entrepreneurial management," rather than the creation of new economic entities. Only nine of the papers actually dealt with the creation of new firms. Third, within the top three sociology journals, Schumpeter was mentioned in 72 articles in a wide variety of contexts. *Entrepreneur*, by itself, was mentioned 94 times. Only 10 percent of these involved the joint occurrence of *Schumpeter* and *entrepreneur*. Of these, only two were about new firms. By contrast, over this same period in the same journals, Max Weber was jointly mentioned with the term *entrepreneur* 29 times, although again only two mentions concerned new firms.

TABLE 2.   Schumpeter Sidelined? Uses of His Work from 1980 to 2002

All business journals covered by JSTOR (*N* = 46)
  Number of articles jointly mentioning *Schumpeter* and *entrepreneur*: 134
    Number in economics journals: 97
    Number in all other journals: 37

Five top organization theory journals covered by JSTOR (*Administrative Science Quarterly, Academy of Management Review, Academy of Management Journal, Strategic Management Journal, Organization Science*)
  Number of articles directly mentioning *Schumpeter* and *entrepreneur*: 37
    Number on start-ups, new firms, and foundings: 9
    Number on *entrepreneurial management*: 20
    Number other uses: 8

Three top sociology journals covered by JSTOR (*American Sociological Review, American Journal of Sociology, Social Forces*)
  Number of articles mentioning *Schumpeter*: 72
    Number mentioning *Schumpeter* and *entrepreneur*: 9
    Number on start-ups, new firms, and foundings: 2

Neither authors writing for organization theory journals nor those writing for sociology journals about entrepreneurs make much use of Schumpeter's work. Even when Schumpeter is mentioned in an article that also mentions entrepreneurs, it is more likely to be about "entrepreneurial management" than it is about new firms. Perhaps this is because his concepts have become part of a taken-for-granted understanding in the field, at least among sociologists and economists. For example, in a recent article explicitly examining the dynamics of new industry emergence, Schumpeter's name was never mentioned, even though the phrase "creative destruction" was used (Louçã and Mendonça 2002). Alternatively, perhaps Schumpeter's revised conception of entrepreneurship still focused too strongly on individuals' actions, from the viewpoint of sociologists.

Disputes over the Definition of Entrepreneurship

Entrepreneur and *entrepreneurship* constitute still somewhat contested terms, especially outside of the community of scholars who regularly publish in entrepreneurship journals (Gartner 1985). Debates over the meaning of the terms became a regular feature of conference presentations and journal articles in the 1970s, as the field struggled for academic legitimacy. Some of the debates reflected the field's attempt to distinguish the field of "entrepreneurship" from the field of "small business studies," which had been the traditional home of people studying business start-ups. The debate also reflected disciplinary disputes over units and levels of analysis, time frame, methods, and theoretical perspective, as Gartner (2001) noted in his comprehensive review. Articles offering conceptual schemes, taxonomies, and typologies to define *entrepreneur* appeared regularly after the Babson College entrepreneurship conferences began in the 1980s and additional entrepreneurship journals were founded.

Four competing perspectives highlight the themes in this debate, as shown in table 3. First, some scholars argued that high-capitalization and high-growth businesses were the proper focus of entrepreneurship studies. They distinguished such businesses from so-called lifestyle or traditional businesses, which were seen as founded by people who were content with low growth and low returns to their enterprises (Carland et al. 1984). Second, based on their reading of Schumpeter, others argued that entrepreneurship was about innovative activity and the process by which innovations led to new products and new markets. For example, business strategy authors often use the term *entrepreneurial* in referring to managers and executives who take innovative action in established firms, associating it with *corporate venturing*, *intrapreneurship*, and similar neologisms. Kanter (1983, 395) noted, "On the association of innovation with internal entrepreneurs, it is common among experts on R&D . . . to use the term 'entrepreneur' to describe the people behind an innovation, those who pick up an idea and drive it toward support and use within an organization." In a later book, Kanter (1989, 313–19) repeated this argument, writing of "entrepreneurial careers"

TABLE 3.   Competing Interpretations of the Term *Entrepreneur*

Interpretation	Problems Posed
High growth and high capitalization	Selection bias: growth is an outcome; high capitalization does not guarantee high growth, e.g. Carland et al. 1984
Innovation and innovativeness	Selection bias: difficult to classify acts as innovative a priori; does not distinguish field of entrepreneurship from general field of business management, e.g. Schumpeter 1912; Kanter 1983
Opportunity recognition	Turns entrepreneurship into a problem within cognitive psychology, e.g. Shane and Venkataraman 2000
Creation of new organizations	Difficult to determine when new social entities emerge: focus on boundaries, intentions, exchange, and resources, e.g. Katz and Gartner 1988

that involve being innovative with well-established companies. She also noted, however, that the ideal-typical entrepreneur was still someone who started his or her own business as an autonomous entity.

Third, following Kirzner (1997), some scholars argued that "opportunity recognition" was at the heart of entrepreneurship and entrepreneurial activities. From this perspective, the amount of initial resources was not an issue, but rather the ability of some individuals to detect potentially valuable opportunities that others overlooked. This view accords with the outlook of investors and business strategy theorists, who often talk of the importance of future considerations, such as prospective market size, in funding ventures. Stevenson and Gumpert (1985), for example, defined entrepreneurship as the pursuit of opportunities without regard to resources controlled. Shane and Venkataraman (2000, 220) published a manifesto for entrepreneurship researchers, arguing that "Although recognition of entrepreneurial opportunities is a subjective process, the opportunities themselves are objective phenomena that are not known to all parties at all times."

Some economists have been concerned with the seemingly irrational nature of some entrepreneurs' perceptions of opportunities and subsequent decisions to enter self-employment, given the poor returns to their human capital obtained by most self-employed people. Research on investment behavior (Thaler 1994), as well as data on the true economic returns to self-employment and business ownership, raises questions about simple economic models of entrepreneurship. People seem to disregard cost-benefit calculations when they become entrepreneurs. In contrast, sociologists have been more concerned with the social context in which entry occurs and the mobility opportunities presented by such entry.[10]

Fourth, some entrepreneurship researchers urged their colleagues to focus on what it was that entrepreneurs were trying to do, which is to found a new organization. For example, in his review of the literature on the alleged traits of entrepreneurs, Gartner (1988) argued that entrepreneurship should be studied by focusing on the behaviors and activities of people trying to create businesses, rather than on their psychological states and personality characteristics. In her review of the sociological literature on entrepreneurship, Thornton (1999, 20) adopted a similar position: "I define entrepreneurship as the creation of new organizations . . . which occurs as a context-dependent, so-

cial and economic process." From this perspective, entrepreneurs are people who create new social entities. This view fits the conventional use of the term *entrepreneur*, referring to those who take the risk of founding an organization, regardless of its size.

Problems with several of these perspectives became apparent as entrepreneurial studies evolved from mostly policy-oriented writing and case studies toward a more empirically oriented research field. First, confining studies of entrepreneurship and entrepreneurial ventures to high-growth companies introduces a strong selection bias into research. Growth is an *outcome* of an uncertain process, and research has shown that it is difficult to predict which firms will grow (Aldrich 1999, 168–69). For example, PC Connection began with $8,000 in a small town in rural New Hampshire in 1982, and despite its humble beginnings, grew to sales of about $300 million by 1995 (Chura 1995). Regardless of their intentions, many innovative and opportunity seeking entrepreneurs create short-lived ventures. Even highly capitalized firms run into problems they cannot overcome, as the Internet dot-com bust in 2000 demonstrated. Similarly, in spite of their best efforts, venture capital firms have done poorly at picking high-growth firms from among their clients (Gorman and Sahlman 1989). Understanding which activities lead to successful start-up and growth, in varying environments, requires that researchers cast as wide a net as possible, beginning with even very modest and unlikely start-up efforts.

Second, using degree of innovativeness as a criterion for picking entrepreneurs and entrepreneurial ventures to study also introduces selection bias into research. Innovation is typically a classification of activities as new to a particular set of users and a particular environment, and is thus relative to existing conditions (Rogers 1995). A priori, it is difficult to classify which acts are innovative and which are not, until they have been introduced and others' reactions gauged. Moreover, as the above quote from Kanter illustrates, using "innovativeness" as the criterion for picking individuals and firms to study would seem to rule out entrepreneurship as a specialized field of study. The literature on innovation and management is huge, and covering that literature would take us into the territory of occupations and careers, as well as business strategy.[11]

Third, as with the concept of "innovation," the "opportunity recognition" perspective is potentially applicable to many endeavors. It does not distinguish the study of entrepreneurship from other fields, until we add the qualification that the opportunities in question should lead to the formation of new businesses. In practice, opportunity recognition scholars work with the implicit assumption that the domain of potential opportunities studied includes those that could lead to business start-ups (Fiet 2002). The opportunity recognition approach seems to give priority to psychology as the discipline best suited to study the cognitive capabilities enabling individuals to recognize potential opportunities.

Fourth, treating entrepreneurship as the creation of new organizations requires that investigators identify when new social entities begin. As goal-directed, boundary-maintaining activity systems, organizations become new social entities that have a taken-for-granted presence in a society (Aldrich 1999). Katz and Gartner (1988) noted that the boundary between preorganization and organization is ambiguous, and suggested four criteria for identifying when an organization comes into existence: intentionality, perhaps as reflected in stated goals; mobilization of necessary resources; coalescence of boundaries, such as through formal registration and naming of the entity; and the exchange of resources with outsiders.

Over the past decade, several teams of researchers have used this scheme to study the emergence of new organizations, with the largest being the Panel Study of Entrepreneurial Dynamics, or PSED. The PSED is a nationally representative sample of 830 people in the process of starting a business, called nascent entrepreneurs, and a comparison sample of 431 nonentrepreneurs. It includes three waves of data, begun in 1999.[12] Their investigations show that researchers must accept some degree of imprecision and ambiguity in deciding when entrepreneurs have truly "created" an organization. Working within this perspective, researchers do not sharply delimit the concepts of "self-employment" from "creating an organization," or make someone's status as an entrepreneur dependent on whether he or she employs others. Sociologically, an "organization" exists to the extent that a socially recognized bounded entity exists that is engaged in exchanges with its environment.[13] In their chapter "The Informal Economy" in this *Handbook*, Portes and Haller have followed a similarly inclusive strategy.

In the remainder of this chapter, I focus on the study of entrepreneurship as the creation of new organizations, and I will label the people who create organizations as "entrepreneurs," in keeping

with the way sociological research on entrepreneurship is characteristically framed. Entrepreneurship researchers often draw on several perspectives in framing their research problems, and therefore all four views of the field have a following. Disputes still occasionally occur, but mainly among people new to the field. Practicing researchers now simply go about their business and assume that their audience will understand their intended meaning.

EMERGENCE: THE PROCESS OF ORGANIZATIONAL FOUNDING

Over the past several decades, researchers have turned their attention to the process by which new businesses emerge. By studying the founding process, rather than established firms, investigators have shed light on the social contexts that spawn entrepreneurs. I turn now to a closer examination of these findings. Key points are summarized in table 4.

Nascent Entrepreneurs

The concept of nascent entrepreneur captures the flavor of a chaotic and disorderly business-founding process. A nascent entrepreneur is defined as someone who initiates serious activities that are intended to culminate in a viable business start-up (Reynolds and White 1997). Operationally, people are called nascent entrepreneurs if they are currently giving "serious thought to the new business" and are also engaged in at least one of many possible entrepreneurial activities. For example, they may have looked for facilities or equipment, or written a business plan. In Reynolds and White's research (1997), the median number of start-up activities reported was 7.0, and the average was 6.7.

Three characteristics of these activities show the complexity of the business-founding process. First, many different combinations of activities have been uncovered, and the activities do not form a scale of any kind (Carter, Gartner, and Reynolds 1996). Second, the activities occur in many different orders, and nascent entrepreneurs follow no fixed sequence of activities. Third, follow-up studies have found a lengthy gestation period before intensive activities begin. For example, a follow-up study of a Wisconsin sample found that, on the average, about 15 months elapsed between the time people began to give "serious thought" to a business and

TABLE 4.   Research on Emergence: Definitions and Some Empirical Generalizations

Nascent entrepreneur: definition	Person who initiates serious activities intended to culminate in a business start-up
Previous work experience and its effect on entrepreneurs	Generates opportunities Provides relevant experience Creates transferable knowledge
Social networks	Diverse networks create favorable social locations for entrepreneurship Brokers can bridge structural holes for entrepreneurs
Founding team composition	High level of homophily by sex, ethnicity, and occupation
Financial resources	Most firms begin small, without outside funds Venture capital funding and IPOs are rare events

their first attempt to actually construct a business (Reynolds and White 1997). The range was considerable—some actually engaged in behaviors before giving serious thought to the business, and some waited years before acting, a result confirmed in the PSED (Carter et al. 2002).

Using the criterion of two or more activities, 3.9 percent of adults were classified as nascent entrepreneurs in a nationally representative sample of the United States in 1993 (Reynolds and White 1997). About half of the nascent entrepreneurs made the transition to an operating business, with the average founder taking a little less than a year to achieve fledgling status. Another nationally representative study, conducted in 1997, arrived at comparable estimates, after allowing for slight differences in definitions (Dennis 1997). A study conducted in 1999–2000, at the height of the Internet boom, reported that slightly over 6 percent of the adult population were nascent entrepreneurs (Reynolds 1999). Extrapolating from these results, millions of adults participate each year in entrepreneurial behavior in the United States. Perhaps as many as 7 million people take part in such activities, involving as many as 3.3 million start-up attempts.

Entrepreneurship and the Life Course

Most entrepreneurs are in their late 30s or early 40s when they make their first founding attempt. By that point, they have accumulated enough work experience to believe that they can recognize potential business opportunities. A few have also accumulated considerable financial resources, although lack of resources does not appear to deter people. Where they have worked, however, does make a difference. Nascent entrepreneurs often capitalize on knowledge gained and contacts made in their previous jobs. However, relying on previous experiences also constrains their search for opportunities and limits the scope of the strategies they consider (Boeker 1988; Freeman 1983; Romanelli 1989). Labor market theories of human capital stress the investment employees have made in their firm- and industry-specific knowledge (Becker 1993). Nascent entrepreneurs only realize the full value of such investments if they capitalize on them by pursuing similar activities, because such knowledge may be less useful in other contexts.

Previous work experience affects potential founders in three ways. First, ideas about opportunities emerge from existing networks of ties within organizations and with outsiders. Certain work settings provide their incumbents with many opportunities to generate foundings (Romanelli 1989). For example, founders of innovative new high-technology ventures in Silicon Valley who were formerly employed in well-connected firms were more successful at raising outside funding than other founders (Burton, Sorenson, and Beckman 2002). Second, owners tend to set up businesses in product or service lines similar to those in which they previously worked, serving a number of the same customers (Cooper 1986). For example, in his study of Swedish entrepreneurs, Johannisson (1988) found that over half of the recently founded firms were supplying their former employer or their former employer's customers. Third, workers in occupational subcommunities develop practices, values, vocabularies, and identities that they can transfer to other contexts (Van Maanen and Barley 1984). For example, former police officers often found detective and home security agencies.

Social Networks and Opportunities

Some social locations provide substantial entrepreneurial advantages to their incumbents (Aldrich and Zimmer 1986; Thornton and Flynn 2003). Not all members of a society are in positions where they can readily respond to organizing opportunities. Various individuals and groups are either blocked from favorable locations or lack connections that would enable them to exploit such locations. Regardless of their personal networking abilities, nascent entrepreneurs who occupy impoverished social locations may find themselves cut off from emerging opportunities and essential resources.

Portes, Haller, and Guarnizo (2002) noted that a new form of entrepreneurship, "transnational," has arisen because some immigrants engage in economic activities that straddle national borders. As Saxenian (2001) pointed out, ethnic immigrants in the United States today are found not only in their traditional niche of small shopkeepers, but also in Silicon Valley, as high-technology entrepreneurs. Her study of highly skilled scientists and engineers from India and China showed that they built "long-distance social and economic network connections to their home countries that further enhanced entrepreneurial opportunities within Silicon Valley" (Saxenian 2001, 69).

In the search for entrepreneurial opportunities, people need access to information and other resources. Multiple diverse contacts are important, regardless of their strength (Burt 1992). Diversity is enhanced by ties to persons of differing social locations and characteristics, along a variety of dimensions, such as sex, age, occupation, industry, and ethnicity. Such contacts increase access to a wider circle of information about potential markets, new business locations, innovations, sources of capital, and potential investors.

Diversity can be increased if nascent entrepreneurs move through a wide range of sectors. Social ties can become *bridges* between sectors where a nascent entrepreneur currently has no direct ties. Diversity also depends on the number of structural holes in a nascent entrepreneur's network. *Structural holes* exist when persons linked to entrepreneurs are not themselves connected to one another (White, Boorman, and Breiger 1976). For example, a nascent entrepreneur may have direct ties to a banker and an accountant, neither of whom knows the other.

From a strategic viewpoint, a network made up of homogenous ties is of limited value to a nascent entrepreneur (Granovetter 1974). In homogeneous networks, information known to one person rapidly diffuses to others, who interpret it in similar ways. Ties to more than one person with similar characteristics or in similar social locations are *redundant* and thus of questionable value in providing new information. For this reason, Burt (1992) argued that the strength of ties is less important than whether they are nonredundant with other ties. However, strong ties may be very important when entrepreneurs put together their founding teams.

From a structural point of view, positions well connected to others but not constrained by them are the most advantageous for nascent entrepreneurs (Burt 1992). Well-organized sectors and those dominated by a few powerful actors pose the most severe constraints on entrepreneurial action. Few nascent entrepreneurs are powerful enough to create structural holes in the social landscape, which requires breaking up organized coalitions and reducing their power. Nonetheless, nascent entrepreneurs who recognize their situation can take steps to improve their network position (Aldrich, Elam, and Reese 1996; Lazerson and Lorenzoni 1996). Successful entrepreneurs are not necessarily those who create holes, but rather those who know how to use the holes they find.

Nascent entrepreneurs not already in advantageous locations, or not directly tied to others who can assist them, are not completely blocked. They may have no direct ties to the people or resources they need, but they can establish indirect connections via brokers. In social network terms, brokers are people who facilitate links between persons who are not directly connected. Studies of the job search process have found that people obtain better jobs by using high-status intermediaries in their search (Lin, Ensel, and Vaughn 1981; Marsden and Hurlbert 1988). High-status people—with more social resources, power, or prestige than others—can play important roles in linking nascent entrepreneurs to resources and opportunities (Renzulli and Aldrich 2002). They can screen contacts for nascent entrepreneurs and get information to them in timely fashion. For example, venture capitalists often play broker roles because they bring together technical experts, management consultants, and financial planners to supplement an entrepreneur's limited knowledge and experience (Steier and Greenwood 1995).

Founding Team Composition

About half of all efforts to found a new business involve teams of two or more people, with the rest being solo efforts (Reynolds and White 1997; Ruef, Aldrich, and Carter 2003). In a few knowledge-intensive industries, founding teams of four or five persons are common. For example, in the semiconductor industry, founding team size has ranged from one to seven people, with an average of three persons involved (Eisenhardt and Schoonhoven 1990). Cooper's (1986) review of 10 studies of high-technology start-ups showed that the median percentage of founders with two or more full-time partners was 70 percent. Teach, Tarpley, and Schwartz (1986) obtained similar results in their study of microcomputer software firms. In France, Mustar (1998, 221) found that solo entrepreneurs started very few of the high-tech firms in biotechnology, artificial intelligence, and information technology.[14]

Using a nationally representative sample of organizational founding teams, Ruef, Aldrich, and Carter (2003) tested for the operation of five mechanisms affecting the composition of entrepreneurial groups. They found especially strong support for one mechanism that influences group composition: homophily with respect to both ascriptive and achieved characteristics. Men and women were both disproportionately likely to form same-sex teams, compared to their underlying distribution in the population of nascent entrepreneurs. They also found a pronounced tendency for coethnics to join together, rather than forming teams across ethnic lines, and also for occupational homophily. They found mixed support for two other mechanisms—network and ecological constraint. The network constraint imposed by strong ties, such as romantic relationships and family ties, was quite pronounced, but weak ties, measured by whether people were acquainted through business relations, were not important. They suggested that ecological constraint contributes to the disproportionate isolation of numerical minorities, such as women and blue-collar workers, in the population of entrepreneurs.

Financial Resources

Most founders begin their new ventures without much capital. Every five years, the Bureau of the Census conducts a special survey to ascertain the amount of original capital owners needed to start or acquire their businesses (Bureau of the Census 1997).[15] In results from the 1992 survey, two points stand out. First, the majority of owners required less than $5,000 to start their businesses— 54 percent of the nonminority men and 64 percent of the women (118). Minority owners started with even less. Second, only a small percentage required more than $100,000: about 5 percent of the men and 4 percent of the women. Less than half of 1 percent of either group required a million dollars or more. (In absolute terms, around 51,000 men and 24,000 women required that amount.) Even among the nonminority men whose firms had one million dollars or more in sales at the time of the survey, only 23.5 percent had begun with more than one million dollars or more in capitalization. Studies in Germany have found higher capitalization requirements, perhaps because of tighter government rules and regulations (Albach 1983).

Founders in some sectors, of course, require a great deal of capital. For example, the high-technology firms in Silicon Valley identified by the Stanford Project on Emerging Companies (SPEC) found that the average firm required about $2.5 million in start-up funds (Burton 1995). The 172 firms in the SPEC sample were founded no earlier than 1984 and had 10 employees or more by 1994. Investments in them ranged from $10,000 to $30,000,000. As fast-growth firms in the high-technology sector, they represent an extreme position in capital requirements.[16]

Informal Sources of Capital

Most businesses start small because of the terms on which resources are available to them. Founders are often unsure of the market for what they offer and thus must begin with an exploratory probing of the market. Owners generally do not borrow capital to start their businesses, either because they do not need it or because of the unacceptable terms that outsiders offer. The 1992 Characteristics of Business Owners survey found that 68 percent of the nonminority men and 72 percent of the women owned businesses either did not need or did not borrow any capital at start-up (Bureau of the Census 1997).

Rather than borrowing, nascent entrepreneurs normally draw upon their own savings and personal assets in constructing their organizations. Few have accumulated sufficient resources to give themselves a cushion in their early days. Although some economists have argued that liquidity constraints—lack of funds—inhibit people from attempting to start businesses, research does not support that argument. Dunn and Holz-Eakin (1996), in a nationally representative longitudinal survey study, found that level of personal assets did not predict which respondents would enter self-employment. Kim, Aldrich, and Keister (2003), using data from the Panel Study of Entrepreneurial Dynamics, found that personal net wealth was not associated with being a nascent entrepreneur.

Very few founders receive any capital from their parents or other family members. Even when parental wealth is potentially available, it does not seem to make a difference in which people actually try to start businesses (Aldrich, Renzulli, and Langton 1998). Few women or non-minority men obtain funding from their families, according to the CBO (Bureau of the Census 1997, 134): about 5 percent of the women and men borrowed from family members. Friends also played a minor role. Building up debt on a personal credit card was just as likely as borrowing from friends.

Business angels are affluent individuals who invest in business start-ups. They have amassed their wealth through inheritance, savings, or the sale of a business. Many became wealthy when a firm they founded or worked for was sold through an initial public offering (IPO) or was acquired by a larger firm. Rather than investing their wealth in the stock market or with investment firms, they look for opportunities to invest directly in new ventures. They not only help fund a new business but also provide expert advice and assistance to nascent entrepreneurs during the founding process. Business angels base their financing decisions on intuition and personal relationships with others involved, using their personal networks and brokers to find investment opportunities.

Observers have estimated that wealthy individuals provide the funding for many more start-ups than banks or venture capital firms. Business angels prefer investing in early stage ventures because they seek active involvement in the business and accept lower rates of return on their investments than venture capitalists. For example, in the United Kingdom, van Osnabrugge (1998) estimated that business angels had invested almost four times as much capital in early stage entrepreneurial firms as venture capitalists. Because business angels invest small amounts in each firm, van Osnabrugge calculated that they probably had invested in as many as 30 to 40 times more new businesses than venture capitalists.

Formal Sources of Capital

Banks and other lending institutions are reluctant to lend money to start-ups, except on terms that many nascent entrepreneurs find oppressive. Banks base their loan policies on their loss experience with previous loans in the same class, and thus their managers realize the high risks involved in start-ups (De Meza and Southey 1996). Because of the high failure rates of start-ups, bankers demand extensive collateral and high interest rates from borrowers. Unlike most business angels, bankers conduct extensive due diligence on nascent entrepreneurs, involving background checks on the founders and a thorough assessment of the venture's financial prospects.

Banks face the classic problems identified by transaction cost economics and agency theory: moral hazard and adverse selection (Eisenhardt 1989). Borrowers pose a moral hazard to banks because they have strong incentives to conceal their shortcomings and overstate their competencies. The problem of adverse selection for lenders arises because the applicant pool for bank loans tends to contain the weaker ventures. New ventures strong enough to obtain financial commitments from private sources do not need bank funding and so do not apply for loans. Bank managers have difficulty evaluating the abilities of nascent entrepreneurs, who have every motive to hide their deficiencies and trumpet their strengths. Banks must therefore offer terms to cover applicants who will, on the average, not do very well.

Venture capitalists show little interest in small new firms, except for a small number who specialize in seed capital (Gifford 1997). Start-ups have no track record on which to raise equity from public offerings, and until they build a record, they must rely on other funding sources. Studies show that formal sources are just not very important in explaining founding rates, even for technology-based organizations (Hart and Denison 1987).[17] Venture capital firms have had no discernible effect on the overall start-up rate in the United States: between 1982 and 1997, they never funded more than 2,800 companies a year (Richtel 1998). Investments increased in the late 1990s, but fell again after April 2001. The amount of venture capital invested in young firms has fluctuated wildly over the past few decades. Total venture capital investments rose from less than $5 billion in the early 1990s to $107 billion in 2000, but then dropped back to $41.7 billion in 2001 (PricewaterhouseCoopers 2003). Through the third quarter of 2002, venture capital investment had fallen to $17 billion. For more information on the venture capital industry, see the chapter by Stearns and Mizruchi in this *Handbook*.

Founders have two external routes for realizing the wealth represented by the successful growth of their firms. First, founders of high-growth firms can take their firms public, through an IPO. Second, they can sell out to a larger firm. Both exit options are relatively rare, compared to the start-up rate. The frequency of cashing out through taking firms public has been rather low. In 1997, there were 537 IPOs, but their number fell steadily over the next 5 years, and in 2001, only 88 firms had an IPO. An IPO is not a guarantee of longevity. Of the 3,186 firms that went public in the 1980s and had their company listed on a stock exchange, only 58 percent were still listed by the end of 1989 (Welbourne and Andrews 1996).

The other route to realizing substantial wealth involves being acquired by a larger firm, but that exit has also been difficult to achieve. Founders who pursue that dream face long odds. For example, between 1983 and 1992, the number of announced acquisitions of privately owned companies only averaged a little over 1,000 per year (Merrill Lynch 1994). Instead of being acquired by a larger firm, most businesses whose owners wish to exit are sold to other owners, often through a business broker. Business brokers specialize in finding buyers for firms whose owners wish to realize the value of their business, retire, or enter another line of work.

Dominating all other statistics on new organizations is one inescapable fact: the bulk of new ventures begin small. If they need funding, they obtain it from their own savings, rather than outside sources. Using their own funds allows them to remain autonomous. However, they also start smaller and are thus more vulnerable to competitive pressures than organizations with outside funding. Initial endowments are critical to organizational survival, and thus organizations that begin with few resources face a high risk of early disbanding (Baum and Oliver 1996; Fichman and Levinthal 1991). In contrast, well-funded founders gain an advantage that carries them through the difficult early months and years of a founding (Levinthal 1991). For example, Brüderl and Preisendörfer (1998) found that the likelihood of disbanding among businesses was strongly affected by their initial size.

Issues Raised by Research on Emergence

Of the many issues raised in the literature on emergence, two are of particular interest to sociologists: why women not only own a disproportionately small share of all businesses but also why they are less likely to become nascent entrepreneurs, and the extent to which cultural capital seems to make a difference in which entrepreneurs mobilize the resources they need.

Gender

Studies in Wisconsin and in a nationwide sample showed that, in 1993, women were about 60 percent as likely as men to be nascent entrepreneurs (Reynolds and White 1997). The PSED 1999–2000 nationally representative study found that men were slightly more than twice as likely to become nascent entrepreneurs as women (Kim, Aldrich, and Keister 2003). Women's businesses still tend to be smaller and concentrated in the retail and service sectors (Baker, Aldrich, and Liou 1997; Brush 1992). Founding rates for women-owned businesses in western Europe are also substantially lower than the rates for men-owned businesses (ENSR 1993). Observing similarly low rates of entrepreneurship among women in Israel, a team of investigators attributed the low rates of business ownership to women's restricted access to government and business contacts, limiting their abilities to "obtain information and resources necessary for business creation and growth" (Lerner, Brush, and Hisrich 1997, 320).

The historical underrepresentation of women in ownership is clearly linked to their exclusion from men's business discussion networks (Carter 1994). If women do not occupy key posts in banks, investment firms, and other financially significant positions, then men are unlikely to encounter them in daily business relations (Rytina and Morgan 1982). The female labor force participation rate in the United States, defined as the percentage of women over 16 who are employed or looking for work, began to increase in the late 1940s, and now stands at about 60 percent, compared to about 75 percent for men. In the past, a lower participation rate plus occupational sex segregation kept women out of many high-paying jobs (Rosenfeld 1992). As employment opportunities improved for women over the past several decades, women have founded businesses at a much higher rate than in earlier generations, raising the likelihood that men's business discussion networks will change. Women's share of sole proprietorships, for example, grew from less than 5 percent in 1970 to over 33 percent in the mid-1990s (Department of Commerce 1996).

Men's inclusion of mostly other men in their networks reflects the societal distribution of power and ownership positions, as well as the tendency of people of the same sex to choose others like themselves (Kanter 1977; McPherson, Smith-Lovin, and Cook 2001). For example, research in the 1980s and 1990s in the United States, Canada, Italy, Northern Ireland, Japan, Sweden, and Norway found that men business owners almost never included women in their strong tie circles (Aldrich, Reese, and Dubini 1989; Aldrich and Sakano 1998). Such gender homogeneity within men's strong-tie circles creates a substantial barrier to the free flow of information to women (Renzulli, Aldrich, and Moody 2000). However, women's strong-tie networks usually contain quite a few men, and thus there are points of gender overlap. Nonetheless, a sizable gender gap remains in start-up rates in most developed nations, and the gap is not accounted for by income, wealth, or standard demographic and human capital factors (Kim, Aldrich, and Keister 2003). Exploring why this gap exists requires comparative cross-national research.

Cultural Capital

The rhetoric of "leadership" and "charisma" in the classical entrepreneurship literature implied a more hierarchical structure to fledgling organizations than they actually possess. It also underemphasized the socially constructed nature of emergent organizations (Calàs 1993). In the founding process, founders' intentions interact with those of others in the situation, especially those contributing resources, such as other founders, family, friends, and potential employees. Given the small size and precarious status of fledgling organizations, few founders can afford unilateral actions. Although they must occasionally pursue strategic actions that split their opponents and prevent them from cooperating (Burt 1992), they more often seek ways of eliciting cooperation.

Jóhannesson (2002) argued that an entrepreneur's ability to obtain the cooperation of others depends, in part, on his or her cultural capital. Bourdieu (1986) wrote that cultural capital is enriched through investments made by families in children, and by individuals themselves. Cultural capital enhances entrepreneurs' skills in framing issues and communicating goals to others in a way that draws them into a project. Jóhannesson described an Icelandic entrepreneur who, through education and training, gained skill as a storyteller and communicator and was seen by others as a dependable figure. Such cultural capital is valuable to nascent entrepreneurs because they need strategies for encouraging other people's beliefs in their competence and trustworthiness, such as through issue framing.

Issue framing can enable entrepreneurs to create new schemata with powerful psychological effects (Gartner, Bird, and Starr 1992).[18] For example, in describing leaders' relations with their followers, Czarniawska-Joerges (1989, 7) noted a leader's "capacity to offer a convincing interpretation of reality, an attractive vision of the possible future, and a prescription on how to reach that vision." Founders who can behave as if the activity were a reality—producing and directing great theater, as it were—may convince others of the tangible reality of the new activity. Skillful founders can use strong ties and network brokers to certify their reliability and reputation, as well as drawing on their own social skills for securing cooperation based on interpersonal relations (Baron 1998).

POPULATIONS AS UNITS OF ANALYSIS IN THE STUDY OF ENTREPRENEURSHIP

Organizational ecology has made two related contributions to research on entrepreneurship. First, rather than focusing on individual entrepreneurs and organizations, ecologists study organizations as members of populations. Second, rather than examining single events, ecologists study rates of events within organizational populations. They posit that populations change because of differential founding and mortality rates, not because organizations live forever by adapting to each change as it occurs. For example, Haveman and Rao (1997, 1646) showed that the primary engine of organizational evolution in the early thrift industry in California was the founding of new thrift organizations and the "death of old ones (selection)—not the restructuring of existing organizations (adaptation)."

The founding of new organizations thus constitutes a critical event for organizational ecologists (Baum and Singh 1994). By replacing disbanding organizations, and organizations that exit from a population through mergers, acquisitions, and other routes, foundings preserve a population's viability and enable it to grow. Instead of focusing on the traits of entrepreneurs, which deflect attention away from the volatile nature of organizational populations, ecologists "emphasize contextual causes that produce variations in organizational founding and failure rates over time by influencing opportunity structures that confront potential organizational founders and resource constraints that face existing organizations" (Baum and Amburgey 2002, 305).

Density Dependence and Founding Rates

Density dependence refers to the dependence of founding and disbanding rates on the size of the population itself. Hannan (1986) developed a model in which the size of an organizational population reflects two underlying processes: legitimation and competition. Increasing organizational density at the beginning of a new organizational form raises cognitive and sociopolitical legitimacy, facilitating an increase in foundings. Later, at higher levels of density, factors inhibiting foundings become dominant, heightening competition for resources. Considered jointly, these two processes create a nonmonotonic, inverse-U-shaped pattern between organizational density and founding rates. Many studies have confirmed such a pattern (Carroll and Hannan 2000). However, as Carroll and Hannan (2000, 228) noted, "the theory of density-dependent legitimation and competition has not escaped criticism."

In addition to Hannan's argument regarding growing legitimacy as an explanation for density's effects, several alternative interpretations have been proposed. First, legitimacy might be an issue mainly for new populations, not established ones. Second, density might actually be a proxy for the effects of other forces, in addition to the processes of legitimation. Processes associated with rising density include the growth of organizational knowledge and opportunities for nascent entrepreneurs to learn effective routines and competencies, and the growth of extensive social networks. Ecologists are well aware of criticisms of the model. Regardless of which interpretations ultimately withstand criticism, the fundamental empirical generalization linking density and founding rates is robust across various populations, industries, and nations (Carroll and Hannan 2000, 228–32).

Resource Partitioning and Foundings

Ecologists make a distinction between specialist and generalist organizational forms, based on the width of the niche occupied by organizations. Organizations sacrifice a degree of competitive edge when they spread their fitness over a broad rather than a narrow niche. Specialists concentrate their fitness in a narrow band, whereas generalists spread their fitness over a wider range of their environments. Generalists' broad appeal to multiple market segments potentially leaves open many small, specialized niches, depending upon a market's level of concentration. In concentrated markets, generalists and specialists compete for the same resources, giving an edge to the generalists. As concentration increases, generalists engage in fierce competition for the center of the market, whereas specialists exploit peripheral niches and avoid direct competition with generalists, thus creating a condition of resource partitioning.

The high disbanding rate of generalist organizations in concentrated markets releases resources that nascent entrepreneurs can acquire. Because most new organizations are specialists when founded, resource availability increases the founding rate of specialists. For example, in the American wine industry between 1941 and 1990, Swaminathan (1995) found strong evidence that increasing concentration raised the founding rate of specialists. The pattern was also found in a study of small specialty brewers in the United States, as specialty brewery foundings and microbrewery foundings increased with concentration in the brewing industry (Carroll and Swaminathan 2000). Carroll and Swaminathan (2000, 721–22) noted that prediction has also been confirmed for foundings of newspapers, telephone companies, banks, and nine other industries.

The conceptual and methodological tools provided by ecologists have led many researchers to reframe classical issues in entrepreneurship, such as the importance of spatial location and geographic clustering. For example, Sorenson and Audia (2000, 426) argued that "dense local concentrations of structurally equivalent organizations increase the pool of potential entrepreneurs in a region, thereby increasing founding rates." Their analysis was explicitly formulated in terms of founding rates, rather than the traits of founders, and their statistical model took account of local and nonlocal organizational density. Similarly, in his study of Tokyo banking from 1894 to 1936, Greve (2002, 871) showed that "the attractiveness of areas to organizations depends largely on how early the local density becomes high enough to spur local legitimation processes." Thus, by focusing on the population level of analysis and studying founding rates, rather than individual entrepreneurs, population ecology has deepened our understanding of the contextual factors affecting entrepreneurship.

ENTREPRENEURSHIP AND THE CREATION OF NEW INDUSTRIES

Although Schumpeter raised the possibility that entrepreneurs could use their resources to create entirely new industries, for many years entrepreneurship researchers did not distinguish between new firms in established versus emerging industries. By contrast, industrial economists expressed great interest in new industries, focusing on the role that technological innovation and market demands played in the growth of business populations (Klepper and Graddy 1990). Indeed, Louçà and Mendonça (2002) explicitly rejected Chandler's "continuity hypothesis," which claimed that some large firms enjoyed uninterrupted dominance of core industries throughout the twentieth century. Instead, they argued that their findings were consistent with "a pattern of dramatic changes in the dominant techno-economic paradigm, opening windows of opportunity for diversification and for the entry of new firms with the emergence of new sectors" (818).

Although not often thought of as an entrepreneurship researcher, Stinchcombe (1965) offered a comprehensive sociological approach to the study of entrepreneurship that was unparalleled in its scope and number of testable propositions. Ideas from his work are still finding their way into the sociological study of organizations, and in particular, into studies of organizational creation and new organizational forms. For example, Stinchcombe coined the phrase *liability of newness* to refer to the difficult early days facing young organizations.[19]

Organizations Are Imprinted by Social Structure

One of Stinchcombe's major contributions to entrepreneurial studies was his observation that "organizational forms and types have a history" (1965, 153) and that the historical period within which organizations are founded sometimes makes a lasting impact on forms. Certain forms, once established, remain viable with their original form intact for a considerable length of time, whereas others change rapidly (Aldrich 1979, 197–218). The changing role of the state, the development of a market-oriented economy, and other forces affecting the distribution of resources account for the major waves of differing organizational forms. Within a given historical epoch, Stinchcombe argued that three factors are especially useful in explaining the emergence of new forms: technological innovations and social structural support for new technical developments, entrepreneurs' access to power and wealth, and the changing structure of labor markets.

Stinchcombe (1965, 168) summarized his analysis by noting, "Organizations which are founded at a particular time must construct their social systems with the social resources available." Nascent entrepreneurs, especially those adopting a new form, must overcome many obstacles to survival as they seek a niche for their businesses. Workforce characteristics, such as levels of skill and literacy, affect the type of control and communications structures that new firms can adopt. Market characteristics, such as barriers to entry and the level of concentration in an industry, also affect new firms' viability by making access to required resources more difficult. Legal constraints, whether governmentally or privately enforced, severely limit entry or restrict it only to those businesses complying with the practices of existing organizations (Suchman, Steward, and Westfall 2001).

Institutional Factors Affecting New Industries

Stinchcombe's ideas concerning new industries were given renewed vitality within sociology by organizational ecology's emphasis on the population level of analysis. Interest in the genesis of new populations in the 1980s (Hannan and Freeman 1986) generated a model that synthesized neoinstitutional and ecological concepts. Drawing upon Parsons's (1956) insight that access to resources by organizations depends upon their societal legitimacy, Meyer and Rowan (1977, 345) argued that the "building blocks for organizations come to be littered around the societal landscape; it takes only a little entrepreneurial energy to assemble them into a structure. And because these building blocks are considered proper, adequate, rational, and necessary, organizations must incorporate them to avoid illegitimacy." Table 5 summarizes the main points in this section.

Although he agreed that organizations depend upon social legitimacy, Hannan implicitly disagreed with the claim that organization building required little entrepreneurial energy. Instead, with his students (Hannan and Carroll 1992; Ranger-Moore, Banaszak-Holl, and Hannan 1991), he argued that population growth depended upon achieving cognitive and sociopolitical political legitimacy, requiring a considerable expenditure of effort.[20] Building on these notions, and incorporating concepts from the neoinstitutional school in sociology, Aldrich and Fiol (1994) and others have theorized about the conditions facing entrepreneurs who create the first firms within a nascent industry, using a multilevel evolutionary model.

TABLE 5. Entrepreneurship and New Industries

Stinchcombe's contribution	Organizations are imprinted by social structure—reflect societal conditions at a particular historical conjuncture
Institutional factors affecting new industries	Learning: development of new knowledge Cognitive legitimacy: acceptance of a new venture as a taken-for-granted feature of the environment Sociopolitical legitimacy: acceptance by key stakeholders of a new venture as appropriate and right (moral and regulatory acceptance)
Levels of action	Organizational Collective: population and community

Learning and Legitimacy as Problems

Two problems confront nascent entrepreneurs in new industries, the first involving learning and the second involving legitimacy. First, entrepreneurs must discover or create effective routines and competencies under conditions of ignorance and uncertainty. Second, new organizations must establish ties with an environment that might not understand or acknowledge their existence. Entrepreneurs who design, copy, or stumble onto strategies to deal with these problems, at the individual and collective levels, increase their chances of surviving selection pressures.

With regard to learning, some of the knowledge used in new populations exists in the form of scientific laws and regularities that can be discovered by organizational experimentation. For example, in technology-based industries, applied research and development activities focus on turning basic scientific knowledge into commercial products or services (Murmann and Tushman 2001). Other knowledge must be enacted through an arbitrary but creative recombination of existing knowledge. For example, fads and fashions in cultural industries—music, theater, the arts, and so forth—spring from new ways of looking at existing knowledge. Beneficial knowledge may even exist already in the form of well-understood and legitimated models that can simply be copied.

With regard to legitimacy, Aldrich and Fiol (1994), building on Hannan and Carroll (1992), suggested a two-part typology of cognitive and sociopolitical legitimacy. *Cognitive legitimacy* refers to the acceptance of a new kind of venture as a taken-for-granted feature of the environment. The highest form of cognitive legitimacy exists when a new product, process, or service is accepted as part of the sociocultural and organizational landscape. When an activity becomes so familiar and well known that people take it for granted, new entrants to an industry are likely to copy an existing organizational form, rather than experiment with a new one.

Sociopolitical legitimacy refers to the acceptance by key stakeholders, the public, key opinion leaders, and government officials of a new venture as appropriate and right. It has two components: *moral acceptance*, referring to conformity with cultural norms and values, and *regulatory acceptance*, referring to conformity with governmental rules and regulations. Indicators of conformity to moral norms and values include the absence of attacks by religious and civic leaders on the new form, and heightened public prestige of its leaders. Indicators of conformity to governmental rules and regulations include laws passed to oversee an industry, and the granting of government subsidies.

Aldrich and Fiol (1994) argued that the process of learning and building legitimacy begins at the organizational level and ultimately involves three other levels of analysis: within populations, between populations, and the entire community of populations. Founders can pursue strategies individually, but very little will be accomplished without collaboration with other founders. As I review each of the two major legitimacy problems and how entrepreneurs respond, I examine actions at each of the four levels.

Learning and Cognitive Legitimacy

Cognitive issues, involving the lack of organizational knowledge and low levels of legitimacy, rather than sociopolitical issues, constitute the immediate dilemma facing founders of entirely new activities. The fundamental rules of organizing are widely diffused in all societies, and thus nascent entrepreneurs start by taking such culturally defined building blocks for granted. If founders of ventures in new populations were simply trying to reproduce the most common forms in familiar populations, they would find knowledge widely available. However, given their origins in new and untested organizational knowledge, pioneering new ventures face critical problems of cognitive legitimacy. Without clear guidelines for assessing performance in an emerging industry, a new venture's stakeholders have difficulty weighing risk/reward trade-offs.

Entrepreneurs can take advantage of the inherent ambiguity in interpreting new behaviors by skillfully framing and editing their behaviors and intentions vis-à-vis the trusting parties, as I noted earlier in discussing entrepreneurs' cultural capital. Pettigrew (1979, 574) argued that entrepreneurs not only create the rational and tangible aspects of organizations, but also "symbols, ideologies, languages, beliefs, rituals, and myths, aspects of the more cultural and expressive components of organizational life." Founders can emphasize those aspects of their ventures and their own backgrounds that evoke identities that others will understand as risk-oriented but responsible. Biggart (1989) noted that people in direct-selling organizations take on new identities as "entrepreneurs" and "independent business owners" that enhance their sense of self-worth and give them occupational prestige in their communities.

Some problems regarding learning and systematizing new knowledge generate attempts at collective action by entrepreneurs. Under the right circumstances, founders can imitate other entrepreneurs who have developed effective routines and competencies (Miner and Haunschild 1995). Convergence on a dominant design then eases the way for new entrants. Movement toward convergence is facilitated if entrepreneurs obtain collective agreement on standards and designs so that the population becomes a taken-for-granted reality by its constituents. A substantial literature in industrial economics and business strategy has examined the conditions under which dominant designs emerge within new industries (Dosi 1988; Teece 1986).

Learning and legitimacy are both facilitated by population-level collective action. Cognitive legitimacy is more likely if a critical mass of founders discovers a way to unite and build a reputation of their new industry as a visible and taken-for-granted entrant into the larger community. Business interest associations and political action groups that organize across industry boundaries facilitate population-level learning and cognitive legitimacy. Initial collaborations between organizations usually begin informally, in networks of interfirm relations, but later they develop into more formalized strategic alliances, consortia, and trade associations (Powell 1990).

Sociopolitical Legitimacy

Entrepreneurs in new populations also face the problem of sociopolitical legitimacy. Founders must find ways of adapting to existing norms and laws or changing them. In the process, they may have to fend off attacks from religious and civic leaders, and find ways of raising the public image of the population. Through strategic social action, entrepreneurs attempt to construct new meanings that may eventually alter community norms and values and lead to new rules and regulations.

In their communities, new organizational forms that are firmly embedded in local networks of trust begin with a reservoir of moral legitimacy. For example, in the early twentieth century, the emerging population of credit unions in the United States benefited from network ties among early members that diffused information to potential new members (Barron 1995, 148–49). A related form, mutual savings and loan associations, began as "friendly societies" in Pennsylvania, in the 1830s (Haveman and Rao 1997). Founded on networks of interpersonal trust, they drew their members from local ethnic neighborhoods and were staffed by officials drawn from the membership. With the goal of enabling members to build their own homes, their structures were simple and officials' actions easily monitored.

At the organizational level, few founders face serious moral legitimacy issues in established capitalist societies, because entrepreneurs have a presumptive right to create new ventures. Nonetheless, new organizational forms occasionally provoke public resentment or even condemnation.[21] For example, the life insurance industry in America was initially condemned as a vulgar commercialization of the sacredness of life (Zelizer 1978). The first newspaper editor in the United States was jailed (Delacroix and Carroll 1983), and many forms of interbusiness alliances were ruled illegal in the nineteenth century (Staber and Aldrich 1983). In the past several decades in the United States, the toxic waste disposal industry, the nuclear power industry, biotechnology, on-line pornography, and family-planning clinics have been attacked as immoral and a threat to certain cherished values.

Cross-national differences in cultural norms and values mean that some activities are morally suspect in one society but not another. For example, the emerging biotechnology industry in Germany has faced more severe sociopolitical legitimacy problems than its American counterpart. In the 1990s, the German public opposed biotechnology so vigorously that German companies had to go abroad, to the United States or Japan, to test their products. In addition to federal regulatory barriers, local elected officials in Germany were hostile to biotechnology laboratories in their communities. Environmentalists, such as the politically powerful Green movement, spearheaded public opposition to genetic technology research and production.

By themselves, individual founders can do little to overcome the moral deficiencies attributed to them. Collective action constitutes the foundation of sociopolitical strategies for population-level action, typically involving the formation of other types of organizations. Gaining moral legitimacy for a new population involves altering or fitting into existing norms and values, something individual organizations lack the resources to accomplish. Similarly, winning legal and regulatory acceptance generally requires campaign contributions, political action committees, lobbying, and other costly activities beyond the reach of individual organizations. Thus, interorganizational action has the greatest impact on sociopolitical issues early in a new industry's growth. Collective action through trade associations, industry councils, and other groups allows a population to speak with one voice.

Sociological analysis of the genesis of new populations has thus placed the study of entrepreneurship in the context of other research on culture and social structure, invigorating the sociology of entrepreneurship and showing its relevance to other important issues in social research. Analysts are using a multilevel model to understand strategic social actions for generating and sustaining new organizational knowledge and legitimacy. Stinchcombe's initial insights into the precarious conditions confronting new organizations stand out when analysts examine entirely new populations of organizations. By emphasizing the collective action problems posed for entrepreneurs in new populations, the approach I have reviewed gets away from the classical approach, which viewed entrepreneurs as heroic and isolated individuals.

PROMISING QUESTIONS FOR FURTHER RESEARCH ON ENTREPRENEURSHIP

Among the many new lines of inquiry begun by entrepreneurship scholars, I will mention a few interesting possibilities: why do most start-ups simply reproduce existing organizational forms, why does the start-up rate vary so widely across industrialized societies, and to what extent does the start-up process reproduce existing patterns of social and economic inequality?

First, although the popular press portrays the typical entrepreneur as someone like Bill Gates of Microsoft, in fact the overwhelming majority of entrepreneurs start small "reproducer" organizations. Reproducer organizations are defined as those organizations started in an established industry that are only minimally, if at all, different from existing organizations in the population. Compared to the number of reproducer firms, the number of entrepreneurs creating innovative new firms that could potentially open up new niches or even entirely new industries is very small. What forces channel new ventures in that direction of reproducing existing organizational forms? An institutional explanation points to the extent to which knowledge of organizations as a social form is deeply embedded in the cultures of industrial societies, leading nascent entrepreneurs to take for granted certain fundamental rules of organizing. The institutional-ecological synthesis concerning the growth of new industries emphasizes legitimacy deficits as the crucial barrier facing new forms. Opportunity recognition theorists point to cognitive failures, whereas those inclined toward technological explanations emphasize the failure of laws designed to protect intellectual property rights and a consequent failure to invest in research and development (Rogers 1986). Few investigators have studied the genesis of new industries, however, and so the power of the alternative explanations has not yet been tested.

Second, organizations are the dominant, taken-for-granted tools of collective action in industrialized societies. As products of particular cultural and social structural conditions, strategies of collective action differ across societies, as do rates of business founding. Including individuals who are trying to start a new firm or who own or manage an active business less than 42 months old, the rate of total entrepreneurial activity varies from less than 5 percent in Belgium to approximately 18 percent in Mexico (Reynolds et al. 2001). Across the 29 countries included in the Global Entrepreneurship Monitor (GEM) Report, 16 European nations plus Israel form a rather homogeneous group, with substantial differences between them and three Latin American countries. Sociological analyses could shed light on the social structural and institutional sources of such cross-national variations in rates.

For example, because the GEM project used a standardized method for collecting information across nations, it can be used to investigate associations between personal wealth accumulation and levels of entrepreneurial activity, such as the informal financial capital provided by business angels. Treated as a proportion of the population aged 18 and older, the prevalence rate of informal investors ranged from less than 1 percent in Brazil to slightly over 6 percent in New Zealand. When aggregated across all 29 countries in the study, the level of funding provided by informal investors amounted to about 1.1 percent of the countries' combined gross domestic products. In all the countries studied, informal investors accounted for more funding of business start-ups and growing businesses than did professional venture capital firms. What structural and institutional factors enable individuals to accumulate enough wealth to become business angels, and to what extent do social networks affect in whom they invest?

Third, entrepreneurship can have a major impact on social and economic inequality in societies. For entrepreneurs, creating a new business contains the potential for upward social mobility (Bates 1997; Nee and Sanders 1985). Many business owners employ family members in their business ventures, and some pass on the wealth gained from them to their families, either during their lives or as part of an inheritance (Keister and Moller 2000). Entrepreneurs who successfully accumulate financial assets can invest in their children's human capital, and they may be able to expand their children's social capital and occupational opportunities (Nee and Sanders 1996). For employees, organizational foundings and disbandings can disrupt careers and destroy accumulated savings, or create opportunities for advancement and facilitate the acquisition of additional human capital (Carroll and Mosakowski 1987; Haveman and Cohen 1994). Social relations established in workplaces or through other commercial contacts may shape people's choices of with whom to affiliate as they consider joining a new business team.

CONCLUSION

Entrepreneurship has become institutionalized as an academic field, as indicated by the growing number of journals, conferences, endowed chairs, institutes, and centers. During the boom days of the 1990s, resources poured into business schools in support of entrepreneurial initiatives, increasing the number of scholars interested in research on entrepreneurship. The volume of research thus emanating from business schools substantially eclipsed that from sociology departments, although sociologists have made their presence felt in organizational behavior and strategy departments of business schools. More important than the numbers of sociologists working in entrepreneurship has been the impact of sociological ways of thinking about entrepreneurial issues.

I have reviewed a few significant sociological contributions to entrepreneurship research, especially Stinchcombe's (1965) pioneering essay on the social structural and institutional conditions favoring organizational foundings. Organizational sociology's growing emphasis on organizations as units of analysis, rather than on the behavior inside organizations, has spurred interest in the issue of organizational emergence. Organizational ecology's focus on populations, rather than single organizations, has sparked interest in founding rates and the conditions under which such rates grow or decline. Advances in the sampling of rare populations have led to several national studies, such as the panel study on entrepreneur dynamics (PSED), that have allowed researchers to track entrepreneurial emergence, rather than just entrepreneurial successes.

I noted earlier that new organizations could both reproduce and challenge the existing social order, and that specific historical conditions affects the kinds of organizations people construct. Within the United States, the composition of entrepreneurial founding teams is strongly conditioned by the level of societal sex, ethnic, and occupational homophily. If emerging businesses benefit from strong, in-group-based ties among their members, then homophily should have a positive effect on survival. If, however, such ties reduce a team's ability to respond to unforeseen or radically changing circumstances, then homophily may be a handicap.

In either case, the new business's fate rests on the larger social context in which it is embedded. Sociological analysis of entrepreneurship has many such lessons to teach us.

Notes

Thanks to Andy Abbott, Amy Davis, Bill Gartner, Stephen Lippmann, Linda Renzulli, Martin Ruef, Neil Smelser, Richard Swedberg, and Pat Thornton.

1. Stinchcombe's essay covered economic and noneconomic organizations. In this chapter, I will focus on economic organizations only: businesses, trade associations, consortia, and other primarily economically oriented organizations.

2. In another paper, I have reviewed similarities and differences in North American and European approaches to the study of entrepreneurship (Aldrich 2000). I noted four similarities: on both continents, research on entrepreneurship and research on organizations have developed in partial isolation from one another, resulting in entrepreneurship researchers duplicating some of the same disputes that earlier characterized organization theory; a strong normative and prescriptive orientation underlies research; entrepreneurship research has historically focused more on description than on hypothesis testing, although signs of change are apparent; and researchers have focused mainly on established organizations, rather than the founding process. I also noted three differences: scholars on the two continents differ in the extent to which they build their models on the assumption that their findings are universal as opposed to nation-specific, and in the extent to which researchers rely on qualitative fieldwork methods, as opposed to other designs, and there is a sizable difference in the level of government and foundation support for entrepreneurship research between North America and Europe.

3. In reviewing the history of entrepreneurship scholarship, I have been mindful of two extremes in historical studies of science (Knudsen 2003). On the one hand, the "internalist" tradition stresses the evolution of ideas themselves, treating them as cultural products in their own right (Collingwood 1956). On the other hand, the "externalist" tradition stresses the role of social relations and group dynamics in sustaining and perpetuating ideas (Bloor 1976). My implicit argument is that community dynamics have probably triumphed over ideas in the evolution of the field.

4. In the first edition of this *Handbook*, Alberto Martinelli (1994) covered slightly different ground, and interested readers might want to consult his chapter. He reviewed the classic interpretations of entrepreneurship, and then discussed major theories of entrepreneurship, focusing on questions such as whether entrepreneurs possess distinctive social and psychological traits, what cultural and structural conditions produce them, and how entrepreneurs actually behave. He covered entrepreneurial management, which I do not consider in this chapter. He also examined "the business class" as a collective actor, a topic covered by Mark Granovetter in his chapter for this edition.

5. For example, when entrepreneurship faculty come up for tenure in business schools, senior faculty with strong disciplinary roots often question why entrepreneurship scholars have not published in the leading journals of a specific social science discipline.

6. Several business school faculty at Ohio State University organized an effort in 2002 to found an Academy of Entrepreneurship Scholars.

7. Birch's consulting firm, Cognetics, Inc., is based in Boston and produces policy-oriented accounts of regional differences in entrepreneurship and business growth rates that are closely followed in the business press. Birch himself, in recent years, has become deeply interested in building world-class sailboats.

8. Highly ranked business schools have found few entrepreneurship scholars to their liking, and so they have asked well-trained researchers in other fields, such as marketing and business strategy, to retool and become "entrepreneurship" professors.

9. JSTOR is an electronic database of leading academic journals including established journals in anthropology, economics, general science, history, literature, philosophy, political science, and sociology. These journals are almost entirely in English. I use information from JSTOR to illustrate my argument at several points. Not all journals are covered through 2002 in JSTOR, e.g., coverage of the *American Sociological Review* ends in 1996. However, the number of journal-years covered is sufficiently broad for my purposes, as I am not testing hypotheses but instead seeking to illustrate important trends.

10. For example, Hamilton (2000) showed that, on average, self-employed persons would have been better off economically as employees, and a more comprehensive study extended his results (Moskowitz and Vissing-Jorgensen 2002). Cognitive heuristics and decision biases clearly play a role in decisions to start firms (Dosi and Lovallo 1997).

11. Rogers's (1995) massive review of the innovation literature should give pause to anyone contemplating equating "entrepreneurial" with "innovativeness."

12. Further details are available on the Institute for Social Research website at http://projects.isr.umich.edu/psed.

13. For example, regardless of its size, technology, or growth rate, PC Connection was an organization in 1982, when it landed its first contract and was included in various credit-reporting agencies' databases (Chura 1995). Or, as a famous cartoon in the *New Yorker* magazine put it more prosaically, "On the Internet, no one knows you're a dog."

14. In the Stanford Project on Emerging Companies (SPEC), researchers deliberately chose a sample of 73 young high-technology firms in Silicon Valley so as to limit possible "sources of variation in founders' models" (Burton 2001, 15). Even within the restrictive conditions of Silicon Valley, where a few dominant organizing models prevailed, founding models still varied by the founders' strategic focus and a founding team's characteristics, such as their level of industry experience.

15. The information is only for surviving firms, and excludes start-ups that disbanded before they could be surveyed. Thus, it undoubtedly overestimates the amount of capital with which businesses begin.

16. The extreme difference between capitalization requirements for Silicon Valley high-technology start-ups and the typical start-up in the United States illustrates the dilemma facing entrepreneurship researchers. For much of the past decade, researchers mesmerized by high-tech fast-growth start-ups focused on venture capitalists and initial public offerings, which constituted a tiny fraction of all start-ups. They ignored the much bigger story that was unfolding, concerning an increase in "normal" start-ups by people who were investing little or none of their own funds.

17. For an exception, see Delacroix and Solt 1988.

18. Issue frames are important not only because of their psychological consequences, but also because of their value as legitimating and motivating symbols. Perceptions and evaluations of risk are highly subjective. The framing of an issue, rather than its actual content, often determines whether people see it as a foolish risk, especially in the absence of objective standards (Tversky and Kahneman 1981).

19. Between 1965 and 2002, the specific phrase *liability of newness* appeared in 114 articles published in the business journals. Organizational ecologists have made particularly heavy use of that concept. Ecologists now agree that much of what appears to be a negative-duration dependence of age on survival actually results from substantial heterogeneity across start-ups. Start-ups differ widely in their capitalization, business model, organizational form, and other characteristics relevant to survival. In the first few years, much of this diversity is weeded out by selection forces (Carroll and Hannan 2000, 3–4).

20. Subsequently, Carroll and Hannan (2000) have emphasized cognitive over sociopolitical legitimacy, for theoretical and methodological reasons.

21. Populations that succeed in creating a strong organization to represent their interests may use their position to block the way for alternative organizational forms. Populations that not only solicit favorable treatment from the state but also cloak themselves in moral legitimacy are especially blessed. For example, funeral home owners in the United States enjoyed great success for many years in controlling state regulation of the industry (Torres 1988). Locally owned homes controlled most state boards regulating the industry by playing on the twin themes of local control of business and respect for the sacredness of their practices. They successfully blocked alternatives to their services, such as chain-owned funeral homes.

REFERENCES

Abbott, Andrew. 1993. "The Sociology of Work and Occupations." Pp. 187–209 in *Annual Review of Sociology*, ed. Judith Blake and John Hagen. Palo Alto, Calif.: Annual Reviews.

Albach, Horst. 1983. *Zur Versorgung der Deutschen Wirtschaft mit Risikokapital*. Bonn: Institut für Mittelstandsforschung.

Aldrich, Howard E. 1979. *Organizations and Environments*. Englewood Cliffs, N.J.: Prentice-Hall.

———. 1999. *Organizations Evolving*. London: Sage.

———. 2000. "Learning Together: National Differences in Entrepreneurship Research." Pp. 5–25 in *The Blackwell Handbook of Entrepreneurship*, ed. Donald L. Sexton and Hans Landstrom. Oxford: Blackwell.

Aldrich, Howard E., Amanda Brickman Elam, and Pat Ray Reese. 1996. "Strong Ties, Weak Ties, and Strangers: Do Women Business Owners Differ from Men in Their Use of Networking to Obtain Assistance?" Pp. 1–25 in *Entrepreneurship in a Global Context*, ed. Sue Birley and Ian MacMillan. London: Routledge.

Aldrich, Howard E., and Marlene C. Fiol. 1994. "Fools Rush In? The Institutional Context of Industry Creation." *Academy of Management Review* 19: 645–70.

Aldrich, Howard E., Pat Ray Reese, and Paola Dubini. 1989. "Women on the Verge of a Breakthrough? Networking among Entrepreneurs in the United States and Italy." *Journal of Entrepreneurship and Regional Development* 1:339–56.

Aldrich, Howard E., Linda Renzulli, and Nancy Langton. 1998. "Passing on Privilege: Resources Provided by Self-Employed Parents to Their Self-Employed Children." Pp. 291–318 in *Research in Social Stratification and Mobility*, ed. Kevin Leicht. Greenwich, Conn.: JAI.

Aldrich, Howard E., and Tomoaki Sakano. 1998. "Unbroken Ties: How the Personal Networks of Japanese Business Owners Compare to Those in Other Nations." Pp. 32–52 in *Networks and Markets: Pacific Rim Investigations*, ed. Mark Fruin. Oxford: Oxford University Press.

Aldrich, Howard E., and Catherine Zimmer. 1986. "Entrepreneurship through Social Networks." Pp. 3–23 in *The Art and Science of Entrepreneurship*, ed. Donald L. Sexton and Raymond W. Smilor. Cambridge, Mass.: Ballinger.

Baker, Ted, Howard E. Aldrich, and Nina Liou. 1997. "Invisible Entrepreneurs: The Neglect of Women Business Owners by Mass Media and Scholarly Journals in the United States." *Entrepreneurship and Regional Development* 9:221–38.

Baron, Robert A. 1998. "Cognitive Mechanisms in Entrepreneurship: Why and When Entrepreneurs Think Differently Than Other People." *Journal of Business Venturing* 13:275–94.

Barron, David N. 1995. "Credit Unions." Pp. 137–62 in *Organizations in Industry: Strategy, Structure, and Selection*, ed. Glenn R. Carroll and Michael T. Hannan. Oxford: Oxford University Press.

Bates, Timothy. 1997. *Race, Self-Employment, and Upward Mobility: An Illusive American Dream*. Baltimore: Johns Hopkins University Press.

Baum, Joel A. C., and Terry L. Amburgey. 2002. "Organizational Ecology." Pp. 305–26 in *Companion to Organizations*, ed. Joel A. C. Baum. Oxford: Blackwell.

Baum, Joel A. C., and Christine Oliver. 1996. "Toward an Institutional Ecology of Organizational Founding." *Academy of Management Journal* 39:1378–1427.

Baum, Joel A. C., and Jitendra V. Singh. 1994. "Organizational Hierarchies and Evolutionary Processes." Pp. 3–20 in *Evolutionary Dynamics of Organizations*, ed. Joel A. C. Baum and Jitendra V. Singh. Oxford: Oxford University Press.

Becker, Gary S. 1993. *Human Capital*. Chicago: University of Chicago Press.

Becker, Markus C., and Thorbjørn Knudsen. 2003. "The Entrepreneur at a Crucial Juncture in Schumpeter's Work: Schumpeter's 1928 Handbook Entry. 'Entrepreneur.'" Pp. 199–234 in *Advances in Aus-*

trian Economics, ed. Roger Koppl, J. Birner, and P. Kirruld-Klitgaard. Amsterdam: Elsevier.

Biggart, Nicole Woolsey. 1989. *Charismatic Capitalism: Direct Selling Organizations in America.* Chicago: University of Chicago Press.

Birch, David L. 1979. *The Job Generation Process.* Cambridge: MIT Program on Neighborhood and Regional Change.

———. 1997. *Small Business Research Summary.* RS Number 183. Washington, D.C.: United States Small Business Administration.

Bloor, David. 1976. *Knowledge and Social Inquiry* London: Routledge and Kegan Paul.

Boeker, Warren. 1988. "Organizational Origins: Entrepreneurial and Environmental Imprinting at the Time of Founding." Pp. 33–51 in *Ecological Models of Organization*, ed. Glenn. R. Carroll. Cambridge, Mass.: Ballinger.

Bourdieu, Pierre. 1986. "The Forms of Capital." Pp. 241–58 in *Handbook of Theory and Research for the Sociology of Education*, ed. J. G. Richardson. Westport, Conn.: Greenwood Press.

Brüderl, Josef, and Peter Preisendörfer. 1998. "Network Support and the Success of Newly Founded Businesses." *Small Business Economics* 10:213–25.

Brush, Candida G. 1992. "Research on Women Business Owners: Past Trends, a New Perspective, and Future Directions." *Entrepreneurship Theory and Practice* 16:5–30.

Bureau of the Census. 1997. *Characteristics of Business Owners, 1992 Economic Census.* Washington, D.C.: U.S. Department of Commerce.

Burt, Ronald S. 1992. *Structural Holes: The Social Structure of Competition.* Cambridge: Harvard University Press.

Burton, M. Diane. 1995. "The Emergence and Evolution of Employment Systems in High Technology Firms." Ph.D. diss., Department of Sociology," Stanford University.

———. 2001. "The Company They Keep: Founders' Models for Organizing New Firms." Pp. 13–39 in *The Entrepreneurship Dynamic*, ed. Claudia Bird Schoonhoven and Elaine Romanelli. Stanford, Calif.: Stanford University Press.

Burton, M. Diane, Jesper Sorenson, and Christine Beckman. 2002. "Coming from Good Stock: Career Histories and New Venture Formation." Pp. 229–62 in *Social Structure and Organizations Revisited*, ed. Michael Lounsbury and Marc Ventresca. Amsterdam: JAI/Elsevier.

Calàs, Marta. 1993. "Deconstructing. 'Charismatic Leadership': Re-reading Weber from the Darker Side." *Leadership Quarterly* 4:305–28.

Carland, James W., Frank Hoy, W. R. Boulton, and Jo Ann C. Carland 1984. "Differentiating Entrepreneurs from Small Business Owners: A Conceptualization." *Academy of Management Review* 9: 354–59.

Carroll, Glenn R., and Michael T. Hannan. 2000. *The Demography of Corporations and Industries.* Princeton: Princeton University Press.

Carroll, Glenn R., and Elaine Mosakowski. 1987. "The Career Dynamics of Self-Employment." *Administrative Science Quarterly* 32:570–89.

Carroll, Glenn R., and Anand Swaminathan. 2000. "Why the Microbrewery Movement? Organizational Dynamics of Resource Partitioning in the U.S. Brewing Industry." *American Journal of Sociology* 106:715–62.

Carter, Nancy. 1994. "Reducing Barriers between Genders: Differences in New Firm Startups." Paper presented at the Academy of Management Meetings, Dallas.

Carter, Nancy M., William B. Gartner, and Paul D. Reynolds. 1996. "Exploring Start-Up Sequences." *Journal of Business Venturing* 11:151–66.

Carter, Nancy M., William B. Gartner, Kelly G. Shaver, and Elizabeth J. Gatewood. 2002. "The Career Reasons of Nascent Entrepreneurs." *Journal of Business Venturing* 17:1–28.

Chura, Hillary. 1995. "Computer Software Visionary Makes Millions." *Raleigh News and Observer*, September 17, F4.

Collingwood, Robin G. 1956. *The Idea of History.* Oxford: Oxford University Press.

Cooper, Arnold C. 1986. "Entrepreneurship and High Technology." Pp. 153–68 in *The Art and Science of Entrepreneurship*, ed. Donald L. Sexton and Raymond W. Smilor. Cambridge, Mass.: Ballinger.

———. 2003. "Entrepreneurship: The Past, the Present, the Future." Forthcoming in *Handbook of Entrepreneurship: Research: An Interdisciplinary Survey and Introduction*, ed. Zoltan J. Acs and David B. Audretsch. Boston: Kluwer.

Czarniawska-Joerges, Barbara. 1989. *Economic Decline and Organizational Control.* New York: Praeger.

Davis, Steven J., John C. Haltiwanger, and Scott Schuh. 1996. *Job Creation and Destruction.* Cambridge: MIT Press.

De Meza, David, and Clive Southey. 1996. "The Borrower's Curse: Optimism, Finance, and Entrepreneurship." *Economic Journal* 106:375–86.

Delacroix, Jacques, and Glenn R. Carroll. 1983. "Organizational Foundings: An Ecological Study of the Newspaper Industries of Argentina and Ireland." *Administrative Science Quarterly* 28:274–91.

Delacroix, Jacques, and Michael E. Solt. 1988. "Niche Formation and Foundings in the California Wine Industry, 1941–1984." Pp. 53–70 in *Ecological Models of Organization*, ed. Glenn R. Carroll. Cambridge, Mass.: Ballinger.

Dennis, William J., Jr. 1997. "More Than You Think: An Inclusive Estimate of Business Entries." *Journal of Business Venturing* 12:175–96.

Department of Commerce. 1996. *Economic Census: Survey of Women-Owned Businesses.* Washington, D.C.: U.S. Government Printing Office.

Dosi, Giovanni. 1988. "Sources, Procedures, and Microeconomic Effects of Innovation." *Journal of Economic Literature* 26:1120–71.

Dosi, Giovanni, and D. Lovallo. 1997. "Rational Entrepreneurs or Optimistic Martyrs? Some Considerations on Technological Regimes, Corporate Entries, and the Evolutionary Role of Decision Biases." Pp. 236–63 in *Technological Innovation: Oversights and Foresights*, ed. Raghu Garud, P. R. Nayyar, and Zur Shapira. Cambridge: Cambridge University Press.

Dunn, Thomas, and Douglas Holtz-Eakin 1996. "Financial Capital, Human Capital, and the Transition to Self-Employment: Evidence from Intergenerational Links." Working Paper No. 5622, National Bureau of Economic Research.

Eisenhardt, Kathleen M. 1989. "Agency Theory: An Assessment and Review." *Academy of Management Review* 14:57–74.

Eisenhardt, Kathleen M., and Claudia Bird Schoonhoven. 1990. "Organizational Growth: Linking Founding Team, Strategy, Environment, and Growth among U.S. Semiconductor Ventures, 1978–1988." *Administrative Science Quarterly* 35:504–29.

European Network for SME Research (ENSR). 1993. *The European Observatory for SMEs: First Annual Report.* Zoetermeer, The Netherlands: European Observatory for SME Research and EIM Small Business Research and Consultancy.

Fichman, Mark, and Daniel A. Levinthal. 1991. "Honeymoons and the Liability of Adolescence: A New Perspective on Duration Dependence in Social and Organizational Relationships." *Academy of Management Review* 16:442–68.

Fiet, James O. 2002. *The Systematic Search for Entrepreneurial Discoveries.* Westport, Conn.: Quorum Books.

Freeman, John Henry. 1983. "Entrepreneurs as Organizational Products: Semiconductor Firms and Venture Capital Firms." Pp. 33–52 in *Advances in the Study of Entrepreneurship, Innovation, and Economic Growth*, ed. Gary D. Libecap. Vol. 1. Greenwich, Conn.: JAI Press.

Gartner, William B. 1985. "A Conceptual Framework for Describing the Phenomenon of New Venture Creation." *Academy of Management Review* 10: 696–706.

———. 1988. "'Who Is an Entrepreneur?' Is the Wrong Question." *American Journal of Small Business* 12: 11–32.

———. 2001. "Is There an Elephant in Entrepreneurship? Blind Assumptions in Theory Development." *Entrepreneurship Theory and Practice* 25:27–39.

Gartner, William B., Barbara Bird, and Jennifer Starr. 1992. "Act as If: Differentiating Entrepreneurial from Organizational Behavior." *Entrepreneurship: Theory and Practice* 16:13–32.

Gifford, Sharon. 1997. "Limited Attention and the Role of the Venture Capitalist." *Journal of Business Venturing* 12:459–82.

Gorman, Michael, and William A. Sahlman. 1989.

"What Do Venture Capitalists Do?" *Journal of Business Venturing* 4:231–48.

Granovetter, Mark. 1974. *Getting a Job: A Study of Contacts and Careers.* Cambridge: Harvard University Press.

Greve, Henrich R. 2002. "An Ecological Theory of Spatial Evolution: Local Density Dependence in Tokyo Banking, 1894–1936." *Social Forces* 80: 847–79.

Hamilton, Barton H. 2000. "Does Entrepreneurship Pay Off? An Empirical Analysis of the Returns to Self-Employment." *Journal of Political Economy* 108:604–31.

Hannan, Michael T. 1986. "Competitive and Institutional Processes in Organizational Ecology." Technical Report 86-13. Department of Sociology, Cornell University.

Hannan, Michael T., and Glenn R. Carroll. 1992. *Dynamics of Organizational Populations: Density, Legitimation, and Competition.* Oxford: Oxford University Press.

Hannan, Michael T., and John Henry Freeman. 1986. "Where Do Organizational Forms Come From?" *Sociological Forum* 1:50–72.

Harrison, Bennett. 1994. *Big Firms, Small Firms, Network Firms.* New York: Basic Books.

Hart, Stuart, and Daniel R. Denison. 1987. "Creating New Technology-Based Organizations: A System Dynamics Model." *Policy Studies Review* 6:512–28.

Haveman, Heather A., and Lisa E. Cohen. 1994. "The Ecological Dynamics of Careers: The Impact of Organizational Founding, Dissolution, and Merger on Job Mobility." *American Journal of Sociology* 100: 104–52.

Haveman, Heather A., and Hayagreeva Rao. 1997. "Structuring a Theory of Moral Sentiments: Institutional and Organizational Coevolution in the Early Thrift Industry." *American Journal of Sociology* 102:1606–51.

Jóhannesson, Gunnar Thor. 2002. "Entrepreneurs as 'Social Capitalists'—Tourism, Entrepreneurship, and Social Capital." Paper presented at the conference "Mobility, Culture, and Tourism," Höfn í Hornafirði, Iceland.

Johannisson, Bengt. 1988. "Business Formation: A Network Approach." *Scandinavian Journal of Management* 3:83–99.

Kanter, Rosabeth Moss. 1977. *Men and Women of the Corporation.* New York: Basic Books.

———. 1983. *The Change Masters: Innovations for Productivity in the American Corporation.* New York: Simon and Schuster.

———. 1989. *When Giants Learn to Dance: Mastering the Challenge of Strategy, Management, and Careers in the 1990s.* New York: Simon and Schuster.

Katz, Jerome. 2003. "Entrepreneurship Education on the Web." http://eweb.slu.edu/Default.htm. February 4.

Katz, Jerome A., and William B. Gartner. 1988. "Properties of Emerging Organizations." *Academy of Management Review* 13:429–41.

Keister, Lisa A., and Stephanie Moller. 2000. "Wealth Inequality in the United States." Pp. 63–81 in *Annual Review of Sociology*, ed. Karen Cook and John Hagan. Palo Alto, Calif.: Annual Reviews.

Kim, Phillip H., Howard E. Aldrich, and Lisa A. Keister 2003. "Does Wealth Matter? The Impact of Financial and Human Capital on Becoming a Nascent Entrepreneur." Paper presented at the Academy of Management Annual Meetings, Seattle.

Kirzner, Israel M. 1997. "Entrepreneurial Discovery and the Competitive Market Process: An Austrian Approach." *Journal of Economic Literature* 35:60–85.

Klepper, Steven, and Elizabeth Graddy. 1990. "The Evolution of New Industries and the Determinants of Market Structure." *Rand Journal of Economics* 21:27–44.

Knudsen, Thorbjørn. 2003. "A Neo-Darwinian Model of Science." Pp. 79–119 in *The Evolution of Scientific Knowledge*, ed. Hans S. Jensen, Lykke M. Richter, and Morten T. Vendelø. Cheltenham, U.K.: Edward Elgar.

Kodera, Shingo. 2002. "Job Creation and Destruction Among SMEs." Pp. 173–89 in *White Paper on Small and Medium Enterprises in Japan: The Age of the Local Entrepreneur—Birth, Growth, and Revitalization of the National Economy*, ed. Takehiko Yasuda. Tokyo: Small and Medium Enterprise Agency, Ministry of Economy, Trade, and Industry.

Lazerson, Mark H., and Gianni Lorenzoni 1996. *The Networks That Feed Industrial Districts: A Return to the Italian Source*. Bologna: University of Bologna, Faculty of Economics.

Lerner, Miri, Candida Brush, and Robert Hisrich. 1997. "Israeli Women Entrepreneurs: An Examination of Factors Affecting Performance." *Journal of Business Venturing* 12:315–39.

Levinthal, Daniel. 1991. "Organizational Adaptation and Environmental Selection—Interrelated Processes of Change." *Organization Science* 2:140–45.

Lin, Nan, Walter M. Ensel, and John C. Vaughn. 1981. "Social Resources and Strength of Ties: Structural Factors in Occupational Status Attainment." *American Sociological Review* 46:393–405.

Louçã, Francisco, and Sandro Mendonça. 2002. "Steady Change: The 200 Largest US Manufacturing Firms throughout the 20th Century." *Industrial and Corporate Change* 11:817–45.

Marsden, Peter V., and Jeanne S. Hurlbert. 1988. "Social Resources and Mobility Outcomes: A Replication and Extension." *Social Forces* 66:1038–59.

Martinelli, Alberto. 1994. "Entrepreneurship and Management." Pp. 476–503 in *The Handbook of Economic Sociology*, ed. Neil J. Smelser and Richard Swedberg. New York: Russell Sage Foundation; Princeton: Princeton University Press.

McPherson, J. Miler, Lynn Smith-Lovin, and James M. Cook. 2001. "Birds of a Feather: Homophily in So-cial Networks." Pp. 415–44 in *Annual Review of Sociology*, ed. Karen Cook and John Hagan. Palo Alto, Calif.: Annual Reviews.

Merrill Lynch. 1994. *Mergerstat Review*. Schaumburg, Ill.: Merrill Lynch Business Brokerage and Valuation.

Meyer, John W., and Brian Rowan. 1977. "Institutionalized Organizations: Formal Structure as Myth and Ceremony." *American Journal of Sociology* 82: 340–63.

Miner, Anne S., and Pamela R. Haunschild. 1995. "Population Level Learning." Pp. 115–66 in *Research in Organizational Behavior*, ed. Barry M. Staw and Larry L. Cummings. Greenwich, Conn.: JAI Press.

Moskowitz, Tobias J., and Annette Vissing-Jorgensen. 2002. "The Returns to Entrepreneurial Investment: A Private Equity Premium Puzzle?" NBER Working Paper No. 8876.

Murmann, Johann Peter, and Michael L. Tushman. 2001. "From the Technology Cycle to the Entrepreneurship Dynamic: The Social Context of Entrepreneurial Innovation." Pp. 178–203 in *The Entrepreneurship Dynamic*, ed. Claudia Bird Schoonhoven and Elaine Romanelli. Stanford, Calif.: Stanford University Press.

Mustar, Philippe. 1998. "Partnerships, Configurations, and Dynamics in the Creation and Development of SMEs by Researchers." *Industry and Higher Education* 12:217–21.

Nee, Victor, and Jimy M. Sanders. 1985. "The Road to Parity: Determinants of the Socioeconomic Achievements of Asian Americans." *Ethnic and Racial Studies* 8:75–93.

———. 1996. "Immigrant Self-Employment: The Family as Social Capital and the Value of Human Capital." *American Sociological Review* 61:231–48.

Parsons, Talcott. 1956. "Suggestions for a Sociological Approach to the Theory of Organization, I and II." *Administrative Science Quarterly* 1:63–85, 225–39.

Pettigrew, Andrew. 1979. "On Studying Organizational Culture." *Administrative Science Quarterly* 24: 570–81.

Portes, Alejandro, William J. Haller, and Luis Eduardo Guarnizo. 2002. "Transnational Entrepreneurs: An Alternative Form of Immigrant Adaption." *American Sociological Review* 67:278–98.

Powell, Walter W. 1990. "Neither Market nor Hierarchy: Network Forms of Organization." Pp. 295–336 in *Research in Organizational Behavior*, ed. Barry M. Staw and Larry L. Cummings. Greenwich, Conn.: JAI Press.

PricewaterhouseCoopers. 2003. "National Venture Capital Survey." National Venture Capital Association. www.nvca.org. January 24.

Ranger-Moore, James, Jane Banaszak-Holl, and Michael T. Hannan. 1991. "Density-Dependent Dynamics in Regulated Industries: Founding Rates of Banks and Life Insurance Companies." *Administrative Science Quarterly* 36:36–65.

Renzulli, Linda A., and Howard E. Aldrich 2002.

"Friends in High (and Low) Places: Small Business Owners' Access to Resources." Paper presented at the Southern Sociological Society Meetings, Baltimore.

Renzulli, Linda, Howard E. Aldrich, and James Moody. 2000. "Family Matters: Consequences of Personal Networks for Business Startup and Survival." *Social Forces* 79:523–46.

Reynolds, Paul D. 1999. "National Panel Study of U.S. Business Start-Ups: First Annual Overview." http://projects.isr.umich.edu/psed/History.htm. August 15.

Reynolds, Paul D., S. Michael Camp, William D. Bygrave, Erkko Autio, and Michael Hay 2001. *Global Entrepreneurship Monitor: 2001 Executive Report.* Kansas City, Mo.: Kauffman Center for Entrepreneurial Leadership.

Reynolds, Paul D., and Sammis B. White. 1997. *The Entrepreneurial Process: Economic Growth, Men, Women, and Minorities.* Westport, Conn.: Quorum Books.

Richtel, Matt. 1998. "Venture Capital Is Alive, and Plentiful." *New York Times*, April 6, C3.

Rogers, Everett M. 1986. "The Role of the Research University in the Spin-Off of High-Technology Companies." *Technovation* 4:169–81.

———. 1995. *Diffusion of Innovations.* New York: Free Press.

Romanelli, Elaine. 1989. "Organization Birth and Population Variety: A Community Perspective on Origins." Pp. 211–46 in *Research in Organizational Behavior*, ed. Barry M. Staw and Larry L. Cummings. Greenwich, Conn.: JAI Press.

Rönn, Cina. 2000. "Jonas Birgersson på toppmöte med Clinton och Gates." Aftonbladet.http://www.aftonbladet.se/nyheter/0001/27/jonas.html. August 6.

Rosenfeld, Rachel A. 1992. "Job Mobility and Career Processes." Pp. 39–61 in *Annual Review of Sociology*, ed. Judith Blake and John Hagan. Palo Alto, Calif.: Annual Reviews.

Ruef, Martin, Howard E. Aldrich, and Nancy M. Carter. 2003. "The Structure of Organizational Founding Teams: Homophily, Strong Ties, and Isolation among U.S. Entrepreneurs." *American Sociological Review* 68:195–222.

Rytina, Steve, and David Morgan. 1982. "The Arithmetic of Social Relations: The Interplay of Category and Network." *American Journal of Sociology* 88:88–113.

Saxenian, Annalee. 2001. "The Role of Immigrant Entrepreneurs in New Venture Creation." Pp. 68–108 in *The Entrepreneurship Dynamic*, ed. Claudia Bird Schoonhoven and Elaine Romanelli. Stanford, Calif.: Stanford University Press.

Schneider, Mark, and Paul Teske. 1992. "Towards a Theory of the Political Entrepreneur." *American Political Science Review* 86:737–47.

Schoonhoven, Claudia Bird, and Elaine Romanelli, eds.

2001. *The Entrepreneurship Dynamic: Origins of Entrepreneurship and the Evolution of Industries.* Stanford, Calif.: Stanford University Press.

Schumpeter, Joseph. 1912. *The Theory of Economic Development.* Cambridge: Harvard University Press.

———. 1932. "Entwicklung" ('Development'). Trans. Markus C. Becker and Thorbjørn Knudsen. http://www.schumpeter.info/Edition-Evolution.htm. February 11.

———. 1942. *Socialism, Capitalism, and Democracy.* New York: Harper.

———. 2003. "Entrepreneur." Trans. Markus C. Becker and Thorbjørn Knudsen. Pp. 235–66 in *Advances in Austrian Economics*, ed. R. Koppl, J. Birner, and P. Kirruld-Klitgaard. Amsterdam, The Netherlands: Elsevier.

Sexton, Donald L., Calvin A. Kent, and Karl H. Vesper, eds. 1982. *Encyclopedia of Entrepreneurship.* Englewood Cliffs, NJ: Prentice-Hall.

Sexton, Donald L., and Hans Landstrom, eds. 2000. *The Blackwell Handbook of Entrepreneurship.* Oxford: Blackwell.

Sexton, Donald L., and Raymond W. Smilor, eds. 1986. *The Art and Science of Entrepreneurship.* Cambridge, Mass.: Ballinger.

Shane, Scott, ed. 2002. *The Foundations of Entrepreneurship.* Cheltenham, U.K.: Edward Elgar.

Shane, Scott, and S. Venkataraman. 2000. "The Promise of Entrepreneurship as a Field of Research." *Academy of Management Review* 25:217–26.

Sorenson, Olav, and Pino G. Audia. 2000. "The Social Structure of Entrepreneurial Activity: Geograhic Concentration of Footwear Production in the United States, 1940–1989." *American Journal of Sociology* 106:424–62.

Staber, Udo H., and Howard E. Aldrich. 1983. "Trade Association Stability and Public Policy." Pp. 163–78 in *Organization Theory and Public Policy*, ed. Richard Hall and Robert Quinn. Beverly Hills, Calif.: Sage.

Steier, Lloyd, and Royston Greenwood. 1995. "Venture Capitalist Relationships in the Deal Structuring and Post-investment Stages of New Firm Creation." *Journal of Management Studies* 32:337–57.

Stevenson, Howard H., and David E. Gumpert. 1985. "The Heart of Entrepreneurship." *Harvard Business Review* 63:85–94.

Stinchcombe, Arthur L. 1965. "Social Structure and Organizations." Pp. 142–93 in *Handbook of Organizations*, ed. James G. March. Chicago: Rand McNally.

Suchman, Mark C., Daniel J. Steward, and Clifford A. Westfall. 2001. "The Legal Environment of Entrepreneurship: Observations on the Legitimation of Venture Finance in Silicon Valley." Pp. 349–82 in *The Entrepreneurship Dynamic*, ed. Claudia Bird Schoonhoven and Elaine Romanelli. Stanford, Calif.: Stanford University Press.

Swaminathan, Anand. 1995. "The Proliferation of Specialist Organizations in the American Wine Industry, 1941–1990." *Administrative Science Quarterly* 40:653–80.

Swedberg, Richard. 2000a. "The Social Science View of Entrepreneurship: Introduction and Practical Applications." Pp. 7–44 in *Entrepreneurship: The Social Science View*, ed. Richard Swedberg. Oxford: Oxford University Press.

———, ed. 2000b. *Entrepreneurship: The Social Science View*. Oxford: Oxford University Press.

Teach, Richard D., Fred A. Tarpley, and Robert G. Schwartz. 1986. "Software Venture Teams." Pp. 546–62 in *Frontiers of Entrepreneurship Research*, ed. Ron Ronstadt. Wellesley, Mass.: Babson College.

Teece, David J. 1986. "Profiting from Technological Innovation: Implications for Integration, Collaboration, Licensing and Public Policy." *Research Policy* 15:285–305.

Thaler, Richard H. 1994. *The Winner's Curse: Paradoxes and Anomalies of Economic Life*. Princeton: Princeton University Press.

Thornton, Patricia H. 1999. "The Sociology of Entrepreneurship." Pp. 19–46 in *Annual Review of Sociology*, ed. Karen S. Cook and John Hagan. Palo Alto, Calif.: Annual Reviews.

Thornton, Patricia H., and Katherine Flynn. 2003. "Entrepreneurship, Networks, and Geographies." Pp. 401–33 in *Handbook of Entrepreneurship Research: An Interdisciplinary Survey and Introduction*, ed. Zoltan J. Acs and David B. Audretsch. Boston: Kluwer.

Torres, David L. 1988. "Professionalism, Variation, and Organizational Survival." *American Sociological Review* 53:380–94.

Tversky, Amos, and Daniel Kahneman. 1981. "The Framing of Decisions and the Psychology of Choice." *Science* 211:453–58.

Van Maanen, John, and Stephen Barley. 1984. "Occupational Communities: Culture and Control in Organizations." Pp. 287–365 in vol. 6 of *Research in Organizational Behavior*, ed. Barry M. Staw and Larry L. Cummings. Greenwich, Conn.: JAI Press.

Van Osnabrugge, Mark. 1998. *Comparison of Business Angels and Venture Capitalists: Financiers of Entrepreneurial Firms*. London: British Venture Capital Association.

Walker, Rob. 2002. "Egomania? We Can Rebuild It." *Wired*, July, 30–32.

Weber, Max. 1930. *The Protestant Ethic and the Spirit of Capitalism*. Trans. Talcott Parsons. New York: Scribner.

Welbourne, Theresa M., and Alice O. Andrews. 1996. "Predicting the Performance of Initial Public Offerings: Should Human Resource Management Be in the Equation?" *Academy of Management Journal* 39:891–919.

White, Harrison C., Scott A. Boorman, and Ronald L. Breiger. 1976. "Social Structure from Multiple Networks I." *American Journal of Sociology* 81:730–80.

Wong, Bernard. 1998. *Ethnicity and Entrepreneurship: The New Chinese Immigrants in the San Francisco Bay Area*. Boston: Allyn and Bacon.

Zelizer, Vivian A. 1978. "Human Values and the Market: The Case of Life Insurance and Death in Nineteenth-Century America." *American Journal of Sociology* 84:591–610.

21 Firms and Environments

Gerald F. Davis

FROM ITS ORIGIN as a distinct domain in the 1950s through the late 1980s, organization theory focused primarily on elaborating and testing theories about organizations as discrete social units. In the foundational text for modern organization theory, March and Simon (1958, 4) defined organizations as "assemblages of interacting human beings [that are] the largest [groups] in our society that have anything resembling a central coordinative system. . . . [This] marks off the individual organization as a sociological unit comparable in significance to the individual organism in biology." In this high-modernist conception,[1] organizations were goal-oriented, boundary-maintaining systems that *contained* their members (Aldrich 1999, 2). Organizations were born, they grew, and sometimes they died. Populations of them, distinguished by their common morphology, waxed and waned at different times, as new industries arose and old ones died out. Moreover, in some places (notably the United States) organizations had expanded their domains to encapsulate ever more of the lives of their constituents. "[T]he appearance of large organizations in the United States makes organizations the key phenomenon of our time, and thus politics, social class, economics, technology, religion, the family, and even social psychology take on the character of dependent variables. . . . organizations are the key to society because *large organizations have absorbed society*. They have vacuumed up a good part of what we have always thought of as society, and made organizations, once a part of society, into a surrogate of society" (Perrow 1991, 725–26). Explaining organizational dynamics was thus tantamount to explaining contemporary social structure.

Theories about organizations proliferated into a set of distinct paradigms that highlighted different aspects of organizations: what shaped their internal structures, where they placed their boundaries, how they gained and used power, how they responded to external assessments, why they were born and died. In his masterful 1967 synthesis *Organizations in Action*, James D. Thompson argued that organization structure and action are largely the result of efforts to balance off the need for rational planning with the requirements imposed by an unpredictable outside world, for instance by sealing off a technical core from the external environment. Subsequent theorists elaborated on themes raised by Thompson. Much of the environmental uncertainty an organization faces comes from the fact that its exchange relations with other organizations create power and dependence relations; thus, resource dependence theorists asked, "What tactics and structures are used to reduce or co-opt the power of outside actors on which the organization is dependent?" (Pfeffer and Salancik 1978). Transaction cost theorists highlighted the factors that make relations with particular buyers and suppliers particularly valuable for the creation of products and services. The animating question of this approach was, "Where do organizations place their boundaries, that is, which activities are done inside the firm, and which are left to outsiders?"—also known as the make-or-buy problem (Williamson 1975).

Organizational ecologists argued that many of the processes that organizations use to create stability thereby make them rigid and unreactive to significant change. Thus, to address the question, "Why are there so many kinds of organizations?" ecologists focused not on (relatively rare) changes in structure but the births and deaths of organizations with particular structures (Hannan and Freeman 1977). New institutional theorists asserted that in many domains organization structures reflected pressures to conform to the expectations of outside evaluators, such as government agencies and professional bodies. These structures, moreover, were often decoupled from the actual work that went on in the technical core. From this perspective, the most compelling question was, "What processes generate the spread of conformity and standardization in organizational practices and structures?" (Meyer and Rowan 1977; DiMaggio and Powell 1983). And in financial economics, an entirely separate approach evolved to explain the survival and proliferation of large public corporations by examining the institutional mechanisms that make possible the separation of ownership and control (Jensen and Meckling 1976).

For several years, research in organization theory followed the path of normal science laid out by these paradigms (see Davis and Powell 1992 for an extensive review). Students of transaction costs studied make-or-buy decisions across various industries, documenting that firms often brought specialized suppliers in-house but purchased unspecialized inputs on the open market. Resource dependence scholars found that the structure of interorganizational ties, such as shared directors across industries, often mapped onto power/dependence relations. Ecologists found regularities in the patterns of organizational birth and death in industry after industry. Institutionalists documented contagion in managerial practices in both public and private sectors.

Yet the normal science approach to theory development and testing has been largely abandoned in empirical work in organization theory since the late 1980s. Thompson's core question—"How can organizations be structured to achieve rationality in an uncertain world?"—has given way to a newer set of questions: What organizational processes underlay the shape of China's transition from state socialism? Why do industrial districts thrive in some locations and not others? How do previously protected sectors, such as health care and education, adjust to the advent of market pressures? How does law influence the structure and operations of corporations around the world, and how do business elites get the law they want? This chapter focuses on these and other questions, drawing in particular on sociologically oriented organizational research published since 1990. I find that organization theories have not been abandoned; rather, they are used as essentially a toolkit of mechanisms from which middle-range explanations can be constructed in the service of problem-driven research.

Why has organization theory changed from a paradigmatic endeavor to a problem-driven one? A little archaeology of knowledge suggests an answer. It is somewhat remarkable that a single four-year period saw the major foundational statements of transaction cost economics (Williamson 1975), the agency theory of the firm (Jensen and Meckling 1976), organizational ecology (Hannan and Freeman 1977), the new institutional theory of organizations (Meyer and Rowan 1977), and resource dependence theory (Pfeffer and Salancik

1978). Drawing on a common pool of social mechanisms, each of these approaches staked out a niche in an ecology of assumptions, often defining itself in terms of its contrasts to the others. Transaction cost reasoning emphasized that pressure from product markets drove decision makers in organizations to adapt cost-minimizing structures from among the (cognitively) available options; to fail to do so was to be slated for extinction at the hands of lower-cost rivals. Resource dependence argued that there was much adaptation, but in contrast to transaction cost thinking it was aimed at reducing dependency even if this came at the expense of profitability; selection was not seriously contemplated.

Ecologists countered both approaches by arguing that adaptation was rare and often fatal, and (like transaction cost analysis) highlighted competition and selection as dominant influences on the demography of the organizational landscape. Institutionalists saw adaptation as routine, but often merely a facade; organizations often persisted for long periods *in spite of* strategies and structures adapted for the sake of outside evaluators, or simply because they were widespread. And agency theorists argued that one particular type of outside evaluator—financial markets—had a predominant influence over how public corporations were organized and how they evolved within their institutional surround.

These approaches largely covered the mosaic of possibilities for distinct theories of organizations. They differed in what they saw as the most important thing to be explained about organizations, but—like chefs shopping for fresh ingredients at a small market—generally drew from the same set of mechanisms for constructing explanations: imitation, diffusion through networks, prevalence-based legitimation, selection, and so on (see Hedstrom and Swedberg 1998).

But while the niche space for new theories of organization may have been filled by 1980, the objects of explanation themselves changed. To a great extent, the major paradigms reflected the stylized facts of their location and era, the corporate economy of the United States in the mid-1970s. Firms had increased in size and scope over the prior decades, and it appeared that this would continue indefinitely, as corporate assets grew concentrated in the hands of a relative handful of firms. At the same time, corporate ownership had grown increasingly dispersed among atomized shareholders, leaving corporate managers the undisputed masters of their domain (Useem 1984). These managers were free to pursue the types of strategies described in resource dependence theory, growing and diversifying their firms to increase their power (Fligstein 1990). Bureaucratic processes associated with growth had rendered these large firms relatively inert, as emphasized by ecologists: "Corporate America's sluggish response to oil crises, Japanese competition, and other changes had much to do with its conglomerate tangles of the 1960s" ("Mad Mergers" 1992, 18).

The trends of increasing corporate size, scope, integration, and ownership dispersion prevalent when the major organizational paradigms were created ended fairly abruptly during the 1980s, as the institutional structure of the U.S. economy underwent a substantial shift. More than one-quarter of the largest manufacturers in 1980 received takeover bids in the subsequent decade, frequently resulting in the firm's being split into its component parts, thereby leaving the typical corporation far more industrially focused in 1990 than it was in 1980 (Davis, Diekmann, and Tinsley 1994). White (2001, 24) found that "Aggregate concentration in the U.S.—the fraction of private-sector economic activity accounted for by the largest X companies in the U.S.—declined during the 1980s, and declined further in the early 1990s and then increased by the late 1990s only to the levels of the late 1980s or early 1990s. Overall, aggregate concentration . . . has declined since the early 1980s, despite the substantial merger wave of the 1980s and the far greater merger wave of the 1990s." The few hundred behemoths in the right tail of the size distribution were hardly representative of the 4.3 million corporations in the United States in 1994, and nearly 40 percent of employees worked for firms with fewer than 100 employees (Aldrich 1999, 10–11). The disaggregation of diversified giants into focused components has been accompanied by a proliferation of network forms of production reconnecting the parts, partly reflected in the vast increase in the number of corporate alliances during the 1980s and 1990s (Gulati 1995). At the same time, corporate ownership passed from the hands of individual investors to money managers acting on their behalf: pension funds and mutual funds greatly increased their share of corporate ownership and with it their ability to influence how their portfolio firms were structured and run. By 2001, the parent of the Fidelity mutual funds alone owned 10 percent or more of nearly one in 10 large U.S. corporations (Davis and Yoo 2002).

The image of organizations as basic units of social structure analogous to individual organisms was increasingly belied by boundary-breaching forms of production (Piore and Sabel 1984). In many contexts—particularly in high-technology and cultural production industries—seeking to distinguish separate organizations was like trying to separate out distinct lumps in a bowl of oatmeal. Unlike the production of Model T cars, the production of movies, skyscrapers, jets, and women's better wear was accomplished by shifting congeries of persons, firms, roles, and brands (or other identities). Boundaries around industries similarly became difficult to locate, as deregulation and new technologies encouraged permeability. Telecommunications, information technology, computers, software, and media blurred into an amorphous metaindustry; insurance, commercial banking, and investment banking morphed into "financial services." New industries drew on models and personnel from old while engaging in distinctly new forms of activity (e.g., in biotech and web design). And even determining whether a company was engaged in "manufacturing" or "service" proved increasingly difficult: manufacturers attentive to labor costs increasingly contracted out the actual production of branded goods from PCs (e.g., Hewlett-Packard) to hot dogs (Sara Lee) in favor of the higher value-added activities of design and marketing; industrial conglomerate GE came to derive most of its profits from financial services as it grew into the largest lender and leaser in the United States. The postindustrial economy glimpsed in the 1970s had reached a mature stage.

The blurring of boundaries at the organizational and industry levels was mirrored at the national level, as global trade achieved a level lost since the First World War and international financial flows reached $1.5 trillion per day. The spread of capital accompanied the spread of neoliberal ideology and a particular financial-market-based theory of national economic development. The number of nations with stock exchanges nearly doubled after 1980, and portfolio investment flooded these markets during the 1990s, creating pressures for indigenous companies seeking capital to adopt the structures favored by institutional investors in the United States and Europe. Determining the nationality of a corporation became as problematic as determining its industry. For example, in 2001 Tommy Hilfiger Corporation was headquartered in Hong Kong, incorporated in the British Virgin Islands, listed on the New York Stock Exchange, owned primarily by international institutional investors, held its annual meeting in Barbados, sourced production to manufacturers in Mexico and Asia, licensed its name to producers globally, and retailed its "classic American clothing" in Europe and North America. Enron had over 3,500 separately incorporated subsidiaries, many in offshore tax havens such as the Cayman Islands, seemingly designed to baffle investors and outside analysts. Locating the boundaries, industry, or nationality for such organizations, typologizing their structures, or even defining dates of birth had become considerable challenges.

Finally, research outside North America demonstrated just how idiosyncratic the large U.S. corporations that were the object of the 1970s-vintage organization theory were. In spite of the convincing theoretical rationale for the efficiency benefits of the large, vertically integrated firm (e.g., Chandler 1977), industrial districts consisting of shifting sets of small specialist firms persisted and thrived as functional alternatives to the "one big firm" (Piore and Sabel 1984). Around the world, sovereign and autonomous organizations appeared rare, while long-standing networks and business groups were both common and influential—to understand a given large corporation in most industrial nations required knowing its group membership (Granovetter 1994). Even the very idea of a "firm" as a basic unit turned out to be quite problematic in some East Asian contexts (Biggart 1992). And when large corporations did exist, they nearly always had a dominant outside owner—either a family or a governmental entity (Davis and Useem 2002). In short, sociological theories about firms and environments increasingly described a world of large, vertically integrated, relatively autonomous corporations that no longer existed.

From some perspectives, this could be seen as a paradigm failure. The notion of cumulative research on organizations would seem like a vain endeavor in this context. Organization theorists failed to construct a model scientific community with boundary control and supporting institutions, with the notable exception of organizational ecologists (Pfeffer 1993). Studies were rarely susceptible to the sort of metaanalysis common in lab-based studies in psychology, and topics flowed more from events in the world than from the internal development of theory. Aldrich (2001, 118–19) points out the problems with such outcome-driven explanations, where researchers begin with endings and work their way backwards to an account for why it happened—like Kipling's just-so stories.

Yet studies continued to be published at a pro-lific pace. Researchers have largely abandoned the paradigm-driven "normal science" approach in favor of phenomenon-driven work. The community of scholars has come to look more like Greenwich Village than the normal-science Brasilia. "Making sense of transitions" has become both a driver and a focus of research, as many of the papers reviewed here attest. In a sense, Perrow was right when he argued that organizations had become the independent variable to explain politics, social class, economics, technology, religion, and other social outcomes. He was right, however, not because organizations have "absorbed" society, but because organizational *mechanisms* often produce societal outcomes of interest.

Consider how social stratification occurs. Federal legislation creates a particular definition of nondiscriminatory employment practices, and thus influences the career prospects of nonwhite workers, because of the diffusion process by which firms establish a formal personnel function (Sutton et al. 1994). Japanese firms abandon the traditional practice of lifetime employment in waves, restructuring the mobility system of the nation, because they are less likely to be singled out for opprobrium when "everybody else is doing it" (Ahmadjian and Robinson 2001). Deregulation of financial services influences the careers of individuals through the vital rates of organizations (Haveman and Cohen 1994). In each case, organizational processes of the sort described in older organizational theories are the cogs and wheels of larger explanations: diffusion through networks mediates between governmental policy and the career trajectories of nonwhite minorities; social learning and mimesis translate economic pressures into the loss of traditional institutions for employment security; organizational births and deaths following regulatory shifts drive the job changes of financial managers.

In addition to breaking out of the normal science mold, contemporary research on firms and environments is distinguished by two other features. First, the preferred unit of analysis is often implicitly or explicitly the *field* rather than the organization. Bourdieu defines a field as "A space in which a game takes place, a field of objective relations between individuals or institutions who are competing for the same stake," and later as "a network, or a configuration, of objective relations between positions" (Bourdieu and Wacquant 1992, 97). Fields have rules or logics, patterns of relations, and actors that may be human, organizational, or "other." The point of studying fields rather than (populations of) organizations is that one does not presume the relevant actors (organizations, industries, persons) occupying positions in advance. In health care, for instance, the composition of the field in the United States changed from relatively straightforward just after World War II (community hospitals and physicians in private practice, who were usually members of the American Medical Association) to Byzantine by the 1990s (hospitals, freestanding clinics, HMOs, health "networks," partnerships, and dozens of specialized professional associations, among others; Scott et al. 2000). Hollywood films, once made by vertically integrated studios, came to be created by shifting networks of persons with particular roles (actors, directors) and organizations performing narrowed tasks (Baker and Faulkner 1991). By examining the field over time without presuming that it will be populated by organizations, analysts gain a more subtle and accurate understanding.

Second, there was increasing recognition that findings about business organizations are intrinsically tied to particular places and times. That is, the naive scientism that underlay the notion of a "general theory of organizations" largely gave way to an approach emphasizing context and periodization (see Aldrich 1999, chap. 8). Studies using identical sampling frames and variables turned up divergent results. For example, an animating question in agency theory is, "Why do corporations get taken over through hostile bids?" In the 1960s, the answer was, "Because they had low stock market valuations and their boards were not well-connected" (Palmer et al. 1995). In the 1980s, the answer was, "Because they had low stock market valuations brought about by over-diversification"; their boards' social connections had no impact (Davis, Diekmann, and Tinsley 1994). And in the 1990s, it was, "Because they operated in industries where deregulation prompted consolidation among rivals" (such as defense); neither market valuation, connections, nor industrial diversification made takeover more likely (Davis and Robbins, forthcoming).

Because of inherent limitations of space and comprehensiveness, this chapter takes a relatively circumscribed view of the contemporary economic sociology of organizations. I focus here specifically on recent (primarily since 1990) sociological research on firms and environments. Excellent reviews that trace the study of organizations over extended periods are readily available (e.g., Scott 2003; Aldrich 1999). For a review of paradigm-based research on organizations through 1990, see Davis and Powell 1992. There are, of course, vast expanses of research on firms and environments in the fields of corporate strategy, economics, finance, accounting, law, and elsewhere, each with their own paradigms and problematics. My aim here is to focus on the works likely to be of greatest interest to those that would accept the label *economic sociologist*.

The chapter has three parts. The first section examines issues of strategy, structure, and performance: Why do organizations adopt the strategies and structures they do? How do insiders and outsiders assess their performance? The work here reflects traditions following from the behavioral theory of the firm (Cyert and March 1963), Stinchcombe's (1965) analysis of the impact of social structure on organizational founding, persistence, and mortality, and Thompson's (1967) analysis of the sources of structure. The second section examines fields, states, and institutions. While some of the motivating questions arise out of the new institutionalism (particularly DiMaggio and Powell 1983; and Fligstein 1990), subsequent work has not been particularly bound by these antecedents. Finally, the third section discusses research on network forms and network dynamics, an area drawing on both network methodology and research on elites (e.g., Mills 1956).

STRATEGY, STRUCTURE, AND FIRM PERFORMANCE

The Sociological Approach to Corporate Strategy

Research on corporate strategy has traditionally sought to answer the question, "Why do some firms perform better than others?" The general answer has three parts: some industries have structures that lend themselves more readily to monopolies than others; managers of firms can implement strategies that make their firm more monopoly-like, such as through their choice of industry segment; and firms can adopt organization designs in discriminating ways to fit their industry and strategy (Thompson 1967). The traditional approach to research in this area is to examine the performance consequences of different industries, different strategies, and different structures, and to study the process by which firms move toward performance-enhancing combinations of strategy and structure. Organizational sociologists have long since lost interest in this plain-vanilla approach (so much the worse for organizational sociology, according to Donaldson [1995]) and instead have focused on the *antecedents* of strategy and structure rather than their performance *consequences*. Why do firms choose the strategies and structures that they do? What counts as performance? Addressing these questions has generated a sociological approach to strategy and structure, emphasizing the effects of public policy, cognitive models, and social processes over the influence of industry structure per se.

Choices of Strategy and Structure

Effects of Public Policy and Founding Conditions

Since Stinchcombe (1965) published his analysis of social structure and organizations, organization theorists have found evidence for the ongoing influence on strategy and structure of the prevailing social conditions at the time an organization was founded. In particular, state policies influence decisions about whether to open or close a business, what markets are entered or avoided, what structures and employment practices firms adopt, and how firms compete. State policies favoring cartels increased founding rates of Massachusetts railroads, while antitrust policies depressed them (Dobbin and Dowd 1997). State-level regulations mediated U.S. federal energy policy, thus generating cross-state variation in the creation of independent power producers (Russo 2001). Conversely, business failure rates varied across the states in the 1970s and early 1980s according to state fiscal and labor policies and the power of local labor organizations (Grant 1995). (Aldrich, this volume, reviews research on birth rates.)

State policy itself reflects the broader national culture: Dobbin (1994) accounts for variation among the industrial policies that characterize France, the United States, and the United Kingdom by arguing that cultural paradigms for generating political order were transferred to the project of generating order in the economic realm. This is why the United States has decentralized industries organized around the idea of natural selection, whereas France traditionally had a more centrally ordered system dominated by state-owned firms. He finds that once this pattern was set for railroads—the first modern, national industry—the basic template was adopted across later industrial contexts. Once in place, national paradigms influence the subsequent reception and implementation of organizational innovations. Casper and Hancke (1999) found that the introduction of standardized systems of quality management had divergent impacts in the French and German auto industries: ISO 9000 reinforced a Taylorist hierarchical system in

France but supported the autonomy of skilled craftspeople in Germany. Rademakers (1998) found that producers in the Indonesian *jamu* (herbal medicine) industry, some of which are owned by ethnic Chinese families and some by ethnic Indonesians, followed characteristic Chinese family business patterns adapted to the indigenous economic institutions. Moreover, firms with owners of both types also maintained paternalistic relations with buyers and suppliers, reflecting a characteristically Javanese form of household relationship that entails both obedience and obligation. And Biggart and Guillén (1999) find enduring differences in the structure and developmental paths of the auto industries in Argentina, South Korea, Spain, and Taiwan that trace back to culturally specific patterns of family ownership. Small family firms thrive in Spain and Taiwan, and both produce auto components, whereas Korean *chaebol* conglomerates mass-produce branded autos for export, suggesting that initial conditions critically influence possible paths of national economic development and industrial organization.

The American approach to antitrust had a predominant influence on the form that U.S. corporate capitalism came to have. In a sweeping study of the evolution of large U.S. firms in the first eight decades of the twentieth century, Fligstein (1990) found that changes in antitrust policy reverberated across the economy by their influence on how firms created strategies and structures. Firms choose strategies in large part to stabilize their environments and achieve greater certainty, an echo of Thompson's (1967) argument. Yet stability for firms often means oligopoly or monopoly for consumers. Thus, the federal government has at different points enacted policies that ruled out some strategies in wide use (e.g., merger among large competitors), an exogenous shock that prompted firms to experiment with alternatives. When an innovator happens on a strategy that achieves stability and growth, other firms emulate it—often prompting yet another regulatory response, which in turn leads to another round of innovation. Horizontal integration (acquiring competitors) was succeeded by vertical integration (acquiring suppliers and distribution channels), which was succeeded by product-related diversification (acquiring firms that made related products), which was succeeded by conglomeration (acquiring firms in unrelated industries, creating the "portfolio firm").

While Fligstein's account takes the American federal government as a relatively exogenous force that intermittently drops in to constrain the strategies available to firms, Perrow (2002) provides a prehistory of how states shaped economic activity before there were large businesses on any significant scale. Like Dobbin, Perrow sees railroads as the first large-scale national industry and as the prototype for subsequent genres of regulation, but attributes the form of regulation that emerged in the United States less to national culture and more to the actions of powerful elites shaping the exercise of state power. The relatively weak national state and relatively stronger state and local governments (compared to Western Europe) opened up avenues for corruption that were exploited by wealthy elites to build vast, privately controlled business organizations. By the time the Progressive movement arose to limit the power of big business through a strengthened national state at the turn of the twentieth century, big business had already taken hold and laid the tracks for subsequent corporate evolution. (The theme of elite influence on law and the state is taken up in more detail in a subsequent section.)

In the postwar period, Western European corporations followed a trajectory broadly similar to the United States in terms of strategies and structures while maintaining characteristic national patterns of ownership and corporate governance. According to Mayer and Whittington (1999, 951), "Regardless of country, by the early 1990s, the typical large industrial firm in Western Europe was diversified and divisionalized. France, Germany and the United Kingdom now all follow the Harvard model discovered two or three decades ago by Chandler (1962) and Rumelt (1974) in the United States," which represented a substantial shift from the early 1960s. Davies, Rondi, and Sembenell (2001) further find that with the greater economic integration of the European Union since the mid-1980s, European manufacturers rapidly become more multinational, while their industrial diversification declined slightly.

At the organizational level, strategies that come to dominate a field benefit individuals with backgrounds in particular functional areas of the corporation, who become solutions to organizational problems through the toolkit that their "conception of control" provides. Leaders with a manufacturing background predominate in a field where vertical integration is the dominant strategy; those with a marketing background are advantaged when related diversification is popular; and finance executives gain favor when conglomeration is per-

ceived as the route to organizational success (Fligstein 1990). Dobbin and Dowd (2000) amend this account by pointing to the role of powerful extraindustry actors in shaping the types of corporate strategies adopted by Massachusetts railroads in response to antitrust: after cartels were banned by an 1897 Supreme Court decision, financiers with strong vested interests promoted the adoption of a model of consolidation to replace the forbidden strategy of cartelization. Moreover, choices made by a firm's leader at its founding have ongoing influences both on the firm's employment practices (Baron, Hannan, and Burton 1999) and in how the firms respond to policy changes. U.S. banks, for instance, responded differently to enforcement of the Community Redevelopment Act depending on the strategy they had in place at the outset (Fox-Wolfgramm, Boal, and Hunt 1998). Surprisingly, sometimes even epochal shifts at the level of the state do not substantially alter the trajectories set by firms early on: domestically owned Hungarian enterprises looked much the same before and after the collapse of state socialism in terms of their products and organizational structures (Whitley and Czaban 1998).

In addition to their direct influence on the strategies pursued by corporate executives, changes in state policy can create second-order effects by loosing other forces. During the 1980s, U.S. policy eliminated most barriers to hostile takeovers, enabling "raiders" to buy conglomerates with the intention of splitting them up and selling the parts to their industry rivals (Davis, Diekmann, and Tinsley 1994). Thus, in contrast to prior antitrust policies that encouraged the voluntary adoption of some strategies (e.g., conglomeration) by eliminating preferred alternatives, policy in the 1980s had its effect by making it profitable for outsiders to reverse the strategies of incumbents (Stearns and Allen 1996). State influence is not limited to domestic businesses: in a fascinating study of the influence of alcohol prohibition laws on beer makers, Wade, Swaminathan, and Saxon (1998) find that state-level prohibition enhanced both the founding and survival rates of breweries in neighboring states (up to a point), suggesting that citizens of "dry" states crossed the border to neighboring states to drink, to the benefit of local brewers.

Performance Assessment

Other than changes in state policy, why do firms change course? A robust basic model comes out of the behavioral theory of the firm (Cyert and March

1963): decision makers in firms assess the firm's performance relative to an *aspiration level,* which is in turn a function of the firm's own prior performance and the performance of its peers or competitors. Firms search for alternatives to the extent that performance fails to meet aspirations. Thus, among airlines, good past performance generated organizational inertia, while operating in diverse markets discouraged it (Miller and Chen 1994). In contrast, when radio broadcasters fell short of aspiration levels, they were more likely to undertake risky changes, such as altering their formats (Greve 1998). Further, the effects of change on subsequent performance varied according to what precipitated the change. Broadcasters that performed poorly prior to changing format were likely to do better after the change—above and beyond the expected regression to the mean—while better performers were actually likely to do *worse* after changing formats (Greve 1999). There is also evidence that aspiration levels, like structures, reflect the preferences of founders: whether or not a venture is closed in the face of poor performance depends on thresholds set by its entrepreneur-owner (Gimeno et al. 1997).

If firms—like people—assess their performance relative to their peers, then how do they know who their peers are? In a study of the Scottish knitwear industry, Porac et al. (1995) examined this question by mapping the cognitive models of industry participants. As one might expect from White's (1981) discussion of industry boundaries, who counts as a rival depends on who is observable and whether they share certain attributes—location, styles of product, size, and so on. Although Scottish knit goods may compete with products from Italy and China on store shelves, perceived rivals were those closer at hand. Choice of peers also depends on the audience, according to another study (Porac, Wade, and Pollock 1999): when a change in U.S. policy required firms to publish comparisons of their performance with that of a set of peers to provide a context for executive compensation, firms were given discretion over their choice of peer group. Of course the choices were strategic, with industries being defined broadly when the firm had performed poorly or its primary industry had done well, and narrowly otherwise. Alternatively, industry niches in knowledge-based industries such as semiconductors can be defined by the technological arena laid out by patents—firms can be arrayed in a conceptual space created by patent "neighborhoods"

linked by cocitations (Podolny, Stuart, and Hannan 1996).

Social Influences on the Adoption of Strategies and Structures

The influence of "peers" and other alters is not limited to a firm's assessment of its performance, but extends to basic choices of structure and strategy, such as entry into new markets. Semiconductor firms that recruited experienced managers from their rivals were subsequently more likely to enter into similar product markets as the executives' old employers (Boeker 1997). In both the computer and branded foods industries, ties of top executives *within* their industry pushed toward conformity to industry norms, while ties *outside* the industry facilitated deviance (Geletkanycz and Hambrick 1997). Similarly, firms that listed shares on Nasdaq were more likely to react to the defections of their interlock partners to the New York Stock Exchange by also defecting to the extent that they were well connected to NYSE firms, while ties to other Nasdaq firms encouraged Nasdaq firms to stay (Rao, Davis, and Ward 2000).

Social influences travel through multiple channels, by both direct contact and observation at a distance. Shared directors, for instance, influenced large firms' propensities to make acquisitions in the late 1980s (Haunschild 1993) and adopt the multidivisional structure in the mid-1960s (Palmer, Jennings, and Zhou 1993). The choice of Japanese auto suppliers to establish their first plant in the United States or Canada in the 1980s was conditioned on location decisions of (actual or potential) buyers and by suppliers (Martin, Swaminathan, and Mitchell 1998). And Japanese multinationals chose the location of new overseas plants in part based on the paths blazed by other Japanese multinationals before them (Henisz and Delios 2001). Conversely, the decision to relocate a plant *out* of a company's home in New York state looked different to "core" and peripheral firms: core firms could migrate for cost savings, while peripheral firms were held back by social and other ties to their particular locale (Romo and Schwartz 1995).

Firms learn about the appropriateness of certain strategies by observing competitors as well as by direct contact with alters. Both organizational characteristics such as size, and observing others enter a market (especially successful others) influenced the likelihood that savings and loan organizations (S&Ls) in California expanded into new markets traditionally served by commercial banks, such as nonresidential mortgages and mortgage-backed securities (Haveman 1993). Contact across multiple markets (that is, operating branches in many of the same counties as one's rivals) also influenced the strategic choices of S&Ls (Haveman and Nonnemaker 2000). Similarly, nursing home chains in Ontario chose the locations of acquisition targets based on their own prior experiences and by imitating the choices of competitors (Baum, Li, and Usher 2000). In an uncertain world, choices of strategy and structure turn out to be decisively shaped by firms' social environment—the choices made by buyers, suppliers, rivals, and peers.

Audience Effects

In the behavioral theory of the firm, organizations assessed their performance relative to peers and their own prior performance. But as Thompson (1967, chap. 7) pointed out, organizations are often assessed by *external* constituencies using different and sometimes incompatible yardsticks, and organizations are most alert to the criteria emphasized by the most visible and powerful stakeholders. In the United States, financial markets achieved the position of "most powerful stakeholders" during the 1980s, and a vibrant literature grew around analyzing how the criterion of "shareholder value" came to influence how corporations were run. The capacity of audiences to impose standards changes with political and institutional conditions: prior to regulatory changes sought by institutional investors, shareholders of U.S. corporations were forbidden from engaging in collective action involving more than four owners, which (given the dispersion of shareholdings) significantly reduced their power with respect to management (Davis and Thompson 1994). Firms that failed to live up to the standards of financial investors were frequently undervalued (Zuckerman 1999), taken over (Davis and Stout 1992), or subject to visible pressures from institutional investors and analysts (Useem 1996). The responses of firms followed the well-worn paths suggested by prior work on organizations: compliance and decoupling. Firms operating in diverse industries spun off parts when those parts did not fit the market's conception of the firm (Zuckerman 2000). When investors attempted to change how they were run, firms set up "investor relations" offices with little operational influence (Rao and Sivamakur 1999). And managers adopted tokens of compliance, such as announcing stock buyback plans that markets favored (but often without actually implementing them; Westphal and Zajac 2001) or justifying their compensation plans in terms of shareholder value (Zajac and Westphal 1995). The ensuing scandal of corporate governance suggests that the Potemkin village approach may not be a sufficient way to run a corporation, however. (See Davis and Useem 2002 for an extensive review of work in this area.)

FIELDS, STATES, AND INSTITUTIONAL CHANGE

The Concept of Field

The advent of the new institutionalism in the study of organizations pushed toward a recognition of the "field" as an appropriate unit of analysis for making sense of organizational and societal processes. DiMaggio and Powell (1983, 148) defined an organizational field as "those organizations that, in the aggregate, constitute a recognized area of institutional life: key suppliers, resource and product consumers, regulatory agencies, and other organizations that produce similar services or products." But subsequent work highlighted the fact that a field need not be composed exclusively of organizations, and that it is best to remain agnostic about the types of actors comprising it rather than assuming a field will be like an urn filled with balls called organizations (e.g., Scott et al. 2000 on the health care sector). Rather, following Bourdieu, it is useful to see a field as a place for a game characterized by objective relations among actors, which may be persons, organizations, or other institutions. In Hollywood, for instance, some of the most important actors are, in fact, actors and not firms (Baker and Faulkner 1991).

The study of fields gained a substantial infusion of order with Scott's 1995 book *Institutions and Organizations*. Two significant contributions of this book were its parsing of the construct of *institution* and its framework for studying multilevel institutional change processes. "Institutions consist of cognitive, normative, and regulative structures and activities that provide stability and meaning of social behavior. Institutions are transported by various carriers—culture, structures, and routines—and they operate at multiple levels of jurisdiction" (Scott 1995, 33). Thus, institutions have three "pillars": a regulative pillar focused on formal and informal rules that constrain and regularize behavior; a normative pillar focused on values and norms that prescribe and evaluate action; and a cognitive pillar focused on common frames of meaning and interpretation that define situations in which action is taken. Legitimacy is then defined as alignment with one of the institutional pillars. The multilevel framework conceives institutional layers in which actors are embedded in governance structures (organizations and fields), which are in turn embedded in societal institutions that provide models and menus for action. "Societal institutions provide a context within which more specific institutional fields and forms exist, shaping them as both agent and environment. Organizational fields operate at intermediate levels, providing institutional structures within which specific organizations operate. And organizations provide institutional contexts within which particular actors are located and take action" (Scott 1995, 141). Institutional change in this approach can be top-down or bottom-up, and studies of field transitions typically highlight one form or another.

Origins and Transitions of Fields

Where Do Fields Come From?

Fields rarely emerge without precedent but are created when technological or financial shifts create pressures for existing arrangements. Thus, the answer to the question "Where do fields come from?" is "Other fields." Health care experienced a transformative shift in the post–World War II era, in a story well told by Scott and colleagues (2000). For decades, the field was characterized by professional dominance, with physicians and their guild (the American Medical Association) effectively governing entry, training, and work conditions for the practice of medicine and resisting the encroachment of organizations beyond the nonprofit community hospital. It is not obvious on the face of it why the field of "health care" should or should not include barbers and manicurists, cosmetic surgeons, chiropractors, psychiatrists, midwives, drug and alcohol abuse treatment counselors, acupuncturists, or other professionals oriented toward human well-being. Under the era of professional dominance, however, boundary control by the AMA ensured a particular strict definition of "health care provider." The rise of medical specialties and specialist organizations to rival the AMA after World War II and the expansion of medical education set the stage for fragmentation. The creation of Medicare (federal health insurance for the elderly) and Medicaid (state insurance for the poor), and the emergence of a large number of regulatory bodies, created governmental counterweights to the AMA, and a number of new types of organizations proliferated alongside traditional community hospitals after 1965, such as home health agencies and renal

disease centers. Finally, during the early 1980s deregulation and formalized cost-benefit analysis by insurers and others created opportunities for novel for-profit business, and the HMO—combining the functions of insurance and provision of health care services—came to be the predominant type, displacing non-profit community hospitals and freestanding physicians. Both the configuration of the field and the types of actors predominating in it underwent a dramatic transformation.

The emergence of fields often involves institutional mimicry or pilferage, in which templates for organized action in one domain are transferred and adapted to a new one. This is particularly useful in fields in which legitimacy cannot be taken for granted. Clemens (1993) describes this process for women's movements at the turn of the twentieth century, drawing on the notion of organizational repertoires in institutional theory to make sense of social movement organizations. Similarly, consumer watchdog organizations drew on culturally prevalent organizational forms to legitimate their activity in what was at the time an entirely new field (Rao 1998). Mimicry also shapes collective-level institutions. Ingram and Inman (1996) document the construction of competing institutional umbrellas by groups of rival hotels on the U.S. and Canadian sides of Niagara Falls, and argue that the creation of these institutions by competing firms was actually helped by the existence of a rival field across the border. Once created, organizations in a field and their institutional surround evolve together, as suggested by Fligstein's (1990) study of federal antitrust policy and the prevalence of organizational forms. Haveman and Rao (1997) argue for a similar coevolutionary story in examining the early savings and loan industry in California. Different types of S&Ls embodied different "theories of moral sentiments": early members of the industry were oriented toward cultivating virtues of prudence, discipline, and citizenship via home ownership, but how this was accomplished varied by organizational type (or "plan"). Haveman and Rao link the changing theories embodied in the different plans to demographic and political shifts in the state. They find that shifts in the predominant "theory of thrift" were manifested in the deaths of S&Ls carrying the old theory and the births of S&Ls carrying the new theory, thus transforming the demographic profile of thrifts in the state.

Markets, Legitimacy, and Change in Fields

Across a range of research domains, studies of fields find that market pressures are often the root of the most significant field-level change. To quote the old political economist, "All that is solid melts into air, all that is sacred is profaned." From a scholarly perspective, the classic liberal arts college is one of the most sacred places, and the business school perhaps the most profane. Yet when the baby boom generation in the United States exited its college years, liberal arts colleges were faced with a smaller group of "education consumers" who preferred more practical education. A few colleges, particularly the high-status selective schools in the East, held firm to their ancient identity, but the vast majority of colleges ended up offering professional and vocational training—particular a business curriculum—while those that failed to change to meet consumer demands were likely to fail (Kraatz and Zajac 1996). Similarly, rural hospitals facing competitive pressures such as those described in the previous section often adapted by changing forms radically, into nursing homes, drug treatment facilities, or outpatient clinics (D'Aunno, Succi, and Alexander 2000). Even ideologically driven organizations such as kibbutzim in Israel, organized around socialist-Zionist principles that forbade the hiring of outside labor, nonetheless succumbed in the face of pressures from banks and markets (Simons and Ingram 1997). Organizations turn out not to be as inert as we previously thought, and the constraints imposed by legitimacy concerns may not always be binding.

There appears to be a common dynamic to how markets trump legitimacy (cf. Schumpeter 1934). Stearns and Allen (1996) find that merger waves in the United States during the twentieth century followed a similar trajectory in which marginal players find an innovative but often illegitimate means of making money, which is then emulated by core players who thus bring legitimacy to the practice. During the 1960s, for example, acquirers were often of marginal status with respect to the dominant corporate elite of the time (Palmer and Barber 2001), while firms with well-connected managers were less likely to be targets than their disconnected peers (Palmer et al. 1995). By the 1980s, takeovers were allowed and even encouraged by federal policy, and well-connected firms were both the acquirers and the targets (Davis and Stout 1992; Haunschild 1993).

Once a practice proves profitable, whole fields can change their shape through the entry of newcomers and the restructuring of incumbents. Moreover, appropriate practice becomes codified in a new logic of appropriateness, reflected in both rhetoric and practice. The appropriate way to run a large corporation changed from the "portfolio model" of the 1970s, which supported unrelated diversification, to a "core competence" model of the 1980s, which promoted operating in a single focused industry (Davis, Diekmann, and Tinsley 1994). When college publishers were primarily privately owned family businesses, they followed an "editorial logic" in which publishing was a profession built on personal ties between authors and editors, while after conglomerates began acquiring publishers in the 1970s and turning them into profit centers, they became mere businesses following a "market logic"; these logics were reflected in the process by which top executives were replaced during the two periods (Thornton and Ocasio 1999).

While the advent of markets may act as a solvent for legitimacy, the absence of markets can have a similar effect. As part of the transition from state socialism, Russia and the Czech Republic implemented plans of mass privatization intended to allocate shares in state-owned enterprises to the public. The theory was that having publicly traded companies would be an apt step in the path toward advanced industrial capitalism. But because the financial markets on which shares might trade lacked sufficient institutional infrastructure, the allocation of ownership rights ended up being channeled largely through illegal or politically motivated means (Kogut and Spicer 2002). In other words, markets may trump legitimacy, but politics trumps markets.

It is important to note that those running large enterprises around the world are not simply dupes of prevailing logics, and that they can be quite cagey when carrying out actions likely to be perceived as illegitimate. The institution of lifetime employment among core firms in Japan had become quite entrenched by the 1990s, supported by years of growth in which implicit guarantees of long-term employment were readily honored by growing firms. A lengthy economic slump undermined the economic rationale for lifetime employment and made it costly to sustain. Yet firms that shrunk their employment rolls were exposed to opprobrium in the press and tarnished reputations among potential employees. Firms responded by following a "safety in numbers" approach, abandoning lifetime employment en masse so that specific firms were less likely to be sanctioned individually (Ahmadjian and Robinson 2001).

How Changes Become Settlements

Once a field has been restructured, either due to state actions or market pressures, the next step is for a new set of practices to become a settlement—the way things are done around here. For the movie industry, the rise of the blockbuster in the early 1970s prompted a change in the organization of the field, and in particular in the configuration of the roles of producer, director, and screenwriter. Prior to 1972, firms with a combination of a full-time producer and a combined director-screenwriter had poor financial performance. But 1972's *The Godfather,* which used this configuration, became the first blockbuster, and other filmmakers imitated this combination, which (after 1972) provided on average the best financial performance (Baker and Faulkner 1991). Thus, this combination became legitimate, widely imitated, and successful in Hollywood.

In addition to the appearance of successful models, settlements require a framework to make them comprehensible and to provide a basis for shared understandings, such as norms of exchange. Mary Douglas (1986) argues that analogies provide a robust basis for making conventions seem "natural" by providing a comprehensible parallel for social arrangements. The early radio industry, with signals sent out over invisible airwaves, provided a puzzle for governments seeking a basis for regulation. Was it most like a public utility such as the post office, or a "magazine of the air"? Eventually, radio came to be seen as analogous to public waterways, providing a transferable set of understandings for the appropriate role of governments and private parties (Leblebici et al. 1991). Field-level organizations can also facilitate certain solutions by making them visible and legitimate. Nearly all colleges and universities had recycling programs in place by the early 1990s, but while most simply added recycling to the responsibilities of an existing maintenance department, others created a new position for a full-time recycling coordinator, often staffed by an activist. These latter tended to be the schools with stronger ties to the Student Environmental Action Coalition, a national social movement organization that advocated the professional staffing model (Lounsbury 2001).

Once an order has been established, a number of processes can make the order self-reproducing (Stinchcombe 1968; White 1981). Podolny (1993, 1994) finds that investment banks tend to affiliate with others of similar status when doing deals and that their status position both enables and constrains the types of business they can do. High-status investment banks, paradoxically, have cost advantages: they do not need to advertise as much, they do not need to devote as much effort to con-

vincing buyers of their claims, they can acquire capital more cheaply, and they can pay their employees less. Why, then, do the high-status banks not grow to dominate the market? Because their status (and associated cost advantages) would be compromised by doing the kinds of business low-status banks do. (This is the same reason Nordstrom's does not sell bologna at its food counter, as Jim Baron once put it.) Thus, status constrains the kinds of business banks can do and the kinds of other banks they can consort with, generating a self-sustaining status order (Podolny 1993, 1994).

States and Organizational Fields

Firms as Interpreters and Shapers of Law

One of the most important contributions of organizational sociology in the past decade has been work unpacking the impact of law on the structure and practices of the corporate sector. (See the chapter by Edelman and Stryker, this volume.) One might ingenuously expect that governments create laws with particular mandates for firms, and firms obediently follow them. But in practice laws are often quite ambiguous, and what counts as compliance is ill-specified. Moreover, managers typically seek to minimize encroachment on their prerogatives. Response to new laws thus entails organizations experimenting with alternative forms of compliance that, once they prove sufficient, spread throughout the field and become institutionalized (Edelman 1992). After the enactment of the Civil Rights Act of 1964, private employers with 15 or more employees were prohibited from discriminating on the basis of race, sex, religion, or national origin—a significant incursion into the employment practices of firms, but with no bright line test for compliance. Some employers responded by establishing "equal employment opportunity policies" and "affirmative action offices" as visible tokens of compliance; once these proved adequate, they diffused widely among employers, even as legal pressures for EEO waned during the 1980s (Edelman 1992). They had become part of the standard package for what employers did. Moreover, the impact of EEO legislation extended to employment practices associated with internal labor markets—particularly formal job descriptions, performance evaluations, and salary classifications—which rapidly spread through associations of personnel professionals after the Civil Rights Act (Dobbin et al. 1993).

Two things happen to seal these solutions in place. First, courts may validate particular structures and practices generated by experimenting organizations, recognizing them as sufficient for compliance and thus institutionalizing them (Edelman, Uggen, and Erlanger 1999). Second, the origins of certain employment practices as grudging responses to legal mandates are often lost, and a new Whiggish history emerges among business managers in which the practices were the spontaneous and economically sensible creation of the businesses themselves (Dobbin and Sutton 1998).

Moreover, once these new structures were in place, they had more far-reaching consequences. The establishment of personnel, benefits, and EEO offices created constituencies within firms for the promotion of policies advocated by their professional networks (Sutton et al. 1994; Sutton and Dobbin 1996). Firms with benefits offices were more likely to create formal maternity leave policies, consistent with the types of policies advocated in their professional journals (Kelly and Dobbin 1999). Thus, although firms may create formal structures with the intention of decoupling them from the "real" operations of the organization, these structures have the effect of linking firms to professional communities attuned to changes in federal policy and establishing a class of professionals that in turn promotes further organizational changes.

Firms as Sources of Law

Fields of firms connected by professional networks generate responses to laws and regulations once these are enacted, but they are also actively engaged in shaping law in the first place. A perennial debate in political sociology concerns whether business elites are unified by a common class interest that they are able to press on state actors (the elite theory view) or whether what divides them is even greater, creating a powerful-but-fractious business class (the pluralist view). Mizruchi (1992) argued that this question is best framed not as a dichotomy but as a variable: *under what conditions* are business executives able to act in a unified fashion when seeking to influence state policy? Drawing on resource dependence and network approaches, he documents that the extent to which businesses contributed money to the same portfolio of political candidates, or sent representatives to testify before Congress on the same side of issues, was contingent on the extent to which the businesses were well connected generally and tied to the same financial institutions in particular: "The number of ties that firms shared with the same financial institutions . . . was the most consistently significant predictor of similar political behavior

across different measures of the variable" (Mizruchi 1992, 243). Well-organized business elites were particularly influential up until the early part of the Reagan administration (roughly 1981), but business unity at the national level seemed to break down after that (Akard 1992). Ironically, although Reagan was clearly the preferred presidential candidate of business executives, his lenient policies with respect to takeovers rendered these executives more susceptible to unemployment than they had been in decades (Davis and Stout 1992). Thwarted at the federal level, however, business executives did manage to get protective laws passed by nearly all U.S. state legislatures, and the better organized they were (i.e., the more densely their corporate boards were connected within a state), the faster the legislature was to pass the laws that they wanted (Vogus and Davis, forthcoming).

Changes in Field Composition: Diffusion and Institutionalization

One of the most persistent findings in organizational research in the 1990s has been that corporate managers are followers of fads and fashions when it comes to strategies and structures. Business cycles set a context for which types of management approaches are advocated by fad entrepreneurs: a caring, employee-centered approach when unemployment is low, and a more efficiency-oriented approach when unemployment is high (Abrahamson and Fairchild 1999). Once a practice is coded as a solution to an organizational problem (e.g., scientific management as a solution to inefficient work practices; corporate culture as a solution to unmotivated workers), it often diffuses through a network-based process. Diffusion offers a very general mechanism for organizational change at the aggregate level, conditioned by the characteristics of fields (e.g., the network structure of the field, the perceived legitimacy of the practice, the ease of observability of adoption, and so on; see Rogers 1995).

Interorganizational contagion processes have been documented across a wide range of contexts, including why denominations began to ordain women (Chaves 1996); why coal miners in the French Third Republic went on strike (Conell and Cohn 1995); why firms adopted poison pill takeover defenses and golden parachutes in the 1980s (Davis and Greve 1997); why corporations in Minneapolis–St. Paul gave to certain charities (Galaskiewicz and Burt 1991); why radio stations adopted (Greve 1995) and abandoned (Greve 1996) programming formats; and why U.S. firms made acquisitions (Haunschild 1993), paid the prices they did (Haunschild 1994), and retained particular investment banks when they made acquisitions (Haunschild and Miner 1997). Across these varied situations, diffusion among organizations follows a set of regularities familiar from the more general diffusion of innovation literature, with the difference being that organizational innovations are often difficult to undo. When the multidivisional form spreads from firm to firm through shared directors (Palmer, Jennings, and Zhou 1993), the aggregate result is that it is normal and expected that corporations will have a multidivisional structure.

Consequences of Diffusion

Although diffusion has been widely studied, its consequences have been much less examined. The standard diffusion study treats the innovation as a dichotomy: an actor either does or does not adopt, say, a golden parachute. But most innovations in organizations are more like a continuum: there are casual symbolic adopters, fanatical converts, and everything in between. Total Quality Management (TQM), for instance, was a wildly popular business trend during the 1990s, and most large firms would report that they had "adopted" quality. But TQM consists of a large number of linked practices, from statistical process control to particular compensation policies, and firms varied widely in how and to what extent they adopted TQM. An excellent study of hospitals found that the organizations implemented a different portfolio of TQM practices depending on whether they were early adopters (typically adopting to gain in efficiency) or later adopters (often adopting in order to appear legitimate to outside stakeholders; Westphal, Gulati, and Shortell 1997). This is an area of research with great potential that has yet to be plumbed.

NETWORKS IN AND AROUND ORGANIZATIONS

Network forms of production within and among organizations gained great prominence during the late 1980s and 1990s, and parallel methodological advances meant that network analysis gained a substantial foothold in the study of firms and environments. Indeed, there was some ambiguity as the term *network organization* came to take on a number of divergent meanings. Baker (1992, 398) defined a network organization as "a social network that is *integrated* across formal boundaries. Interpersonal ties are formed without respect to formal

groups or categories." That is, the relevant nodes in the network were persons within an organization, and the criterion was met if formal boundaries (of departments, for instance) were not a constraint on the formation of work-related ties. In contrast, Miles and Snow (1992, 53) defined network organizations as "clusters of firms or specialist units coordinated by market mechanisms instead of chains of command." Nodes in this case were firms, and ties were alliances or long-term exchange relations (governed by implicit or explicit contracts) among firms. Given the focus of this chapter, we will lean toward the latter definition and examine interfirm ties: interlocks (ties created through shared directors on the corporation's board), alliances, investment ties, and ties through common ownership by a third party. Levels of analysis run from the firm (or firmlike network) to the dyad to the business group to the overall network structure of the economy. (See Smith-Doerr and Powell, this volume, for a more extensive discussion of interorganizational networks.)

Network Forms of Organization

The dichotomy between "make" and "buy" that defined the transaction cost agenda began to break down with Granovetter's (1985) theoretical critique, Piore and Sabel's (1984) revival of the study of industrial districts, and Powell's (1990) delineation of the range of alternative relational types between these two poles. (See Williamson's chapter in the previous edition of this *Handbook* for his response.) The language of networks, and the analytical tools provided by social network analysis, proved to be an apt way to describe production processes outside of vertically integrated firms. The study of industrial districts, largely dormant in Anglo-American circles since Alfred Marshall, became a growth industry thanks to new tools and concepts from network analysis. Becattini (1990, 39) defined an industrial district as "a socio-territorial entity which is characterized by the active presence of both a community of people and a population of firms in one naturally and historically bounded area." Defined in this way, industrial districts turned out to be quite common, and they were often more effective producers than vertically integrated firms. Network forms of production long thought extinct were found, on further examination, to be thriving. Lazerson (1995) found that the Modena knitwear industry maintained an updated version of the "putting-out" system that had predated the modern factory. Moreover, this system of household microfirms was economically quite sustainable when placed in a supportive institutional environment, in contrast to the usual expectations of transaction cost analysts.

Once network forms were identified, the next step was to typologize them and track their performance: as with traditional organizational designs, some network forms work better than others for some purposes. Paniccia (1998) argued that much of the recent enthusiasm for industrial districts came from the fact that a handful of case studies of successful instances, such as Silicon Valley and certain northern Italian districts, had inappropriately been taken to be typical, and thus prototypes of a superior model of production. But a 40-year comparison of 24 small and medium-sized enterprise districts in Italy showed that few of them matched the ideal type industrial district; they did not always have superior performance; and social ties among participants did not rule out deceit, opportunism, or free riding. Paniccia's (1998) study shows that industrial districts are not a panacea. Other researchers have also worked toward coming up with typologies and performance comparisons across network systems. Thus, network forms of mental health services vary in their effectiveness in terms of client outcomes (Provan and Milward 1995), and interfirm networks in the U.S. wood products–manufacturing industry faced multiple hurdles to demonstrate their legitimacy (Human and Provan 2000). Sturgeon (2002) coined the term *modular production network* to describe the evolving system in the electronics industry in which lead firms design, market, and service end products under their own name, while contracting out production to globally dispersed "box stuffers" with the capacity to mass-produce a wide range of electronics products (such as computers and cell phones) with relatively low labor costs. And Windeler and Sydow (2001) find that the industrial organization of television production in Germany has followed a similar path as the U.S. film industry, in which vertically integrated studios morphed into a virtual Hollywood industrial district. By the same token, television programs in Germany are now made by relatively short-term networks organized by producers and comprised of independent directors, authors, actors, and freelance crew members recruited for specific projects.

Formation and Dissolution of Network Ties

Studies of ties among dyads are analogous to ecological studies of foundings and mortality, and draw on similar methodological tools. Rather than the births and deaths of *organizations,* however, network researchers study the births and deaths of *relationships* between firms.

Formation of Ties

Interfirm alliances increased enormously in prevalence after the 1970s, and they have now become an accepted part of doing business around the globe. Findings at the firm level on the propensity of pairs to form dyads paralleled analogous social psychological research on persons: firms were more likely to form alliances with other firms they had allied with before than with "strangers" (Gulati 1995), and pairs of firms were more likely to ally when they had a third partner in common (Gulati and Gargiulo 1999); thus, network structures have an endogenous dynamic that shapes the structure of the larger overall network. Networks beget other networks across a variety of tie types in biotechnology, reflecting the industry's base on knowledge and innovation rather than production (Powell, Koput, and Smith-Doerr 1996). Semiconductor firms with widely cited patents, and those in segments with high rates of patents, were more prone to forming alliances than firms with few or poorly cited patents (Stuart 1998). At a dyadic level, ties involving high-growth firms show the prospects for using mechanisms of social control, as opposed to contractual control (Larson 1992). Finally, interfirm ties (such as alliances and shared directors) are sensibly considered as one path among many for firms to achieve certain ends; thus, if interlocks are a monitoring or information device, then it makes sense that firms that have alternative channels for such information or monitoring (e.g., membership by their managers in the same elite social clubs) would form ties for different reasons than firms without access to these functional substitutes (Kono et al. 1998).

Dissolution of Ties

While much work has been done in recent years on why firms create ties, far less work has examined why these ties lapse. Levinthal and Fichman (1988) found that firms had an initial "honeymoon period" with their auditor, in which they were unlikely to switch to another accounting firm, but that there was a rapid rise subsequently in the risk of dissolution, followed by a steady decline—similar to the so-called seven-year itch in marriages, but on a faster scale. Baker, Faulkner, and Fisher (1998) examined the ties between firms and their advertising agencies, finding that the propensity of clients to fire ad agencies also followed an inverse-U curve, but peaking much later (at 11 years). Personal ties from client to agency tended to protect the relationship, as did the status and centrality of the agency and the size of the client. And Palmer (1983) studied the reconstitution of interlock ties "accidentally" broken when a director serving on two boards died or retired, concluding that their rare reconstitution argued against such ties serving a significant corporate function. The causes of the dissolution of ties is another underresearched domain that deserves further work.

Impact of Ties on Firm Performance and Action

Performance

Networks can have two types of effects on firm performance. The first follows from the standard definition of social capital as "The ability of actors to secure benefits by virtue of membership in social networks or other social structures" (Portes 1998, 2). Network ties are conduits for resources. But networks can be "prisms" as well as "pipes," with connections having their effect through the status they confer (Podolny 2001). The best-developed account of networks as "pipes" is Burt's (1992) theory of structural holes. Structural holes are gaps in social structure; an actor has a network rich in structural holes to the extent that his or her contacts belong to network clusters that are disconnected from each other—this disconnection is the "hole." This form of social capital provides opportunities to use financial and human capital productively by giving advantages in access (receiving valuable information and knowing who can use it), timing (being apprised of information before competitors get it), and referrals (getting one's name mentioned at the right time in the right places). Summarizing Burt (1992), a network rich in structural holes has contacts established in the right places where useful information is likely to be aired, providing a reliable flow of information to and from these places, thus creating power to broker transactions among disconnected clusters. Although the theory has a great deal of support at the individual level (see Burt 2000 for a summary), support has been more mixed at the firm level. Burt (1992, chap. 3) finds that margins are higher in industries characterized by structural holes (roughly the extent to which a producer's industry is concentrated and its buyers and suppliers are dispersed). But Ahuja (2000) finds that ties increase firms' rates of innovation (as indicated by patents) in the international chemical industry, but does

not find such effects for structural holes—if anything, they had a negative impact. The translation from industry-level to firm-level effects is rather subtle, and suitable firm-level data turn out to be rather difficult to come by.

A major exception to this is the work of Brian Uzzi on the New York garment industry. The dominant union for garment workers has historically kept track of firm-level transactions for compliance purposes, allowing Uzzi to map out the exchange network at the level of the firm rather than the industry. Both social and economic networks are rife in this industry, as buyers and suppliers are often family members, neighbors, or long-term exchange partners. Uzzi's results suggest that there is an optimal level of embeddedness (i.e., a firm's portfolio of relations among buyers and suppliers): having a large number of arm's-length ties is hazardous for a firm's survival prospects, but so is overreliance on a single customer. Rather, the best case is a combination of embedded ties (large-volume exchanges, perhaps underlain by social connections) and arm's-length transactions to hedge one's bets (Uzzi 1996, 1997).

Ties among businesses can also act as a signal of quality to third parties, above and beyond their influence on exchanges. Particularly under conditions of uncertainty, when evaluation of "true" quality is difficult *ex ante*, outside evaluators often rely on a firm's affiliations to assess its status (Podolny 1993). Endorsements through affiliations with high-status actors have documented benefits in investment banking (Podolny 1993), wine making (Benjamin and Podolny 1999), and biotechnology (Stuart, Hoang, and Hybels 1999). Importantly, the effect of high-status affiliations is not merely perceptual, as it affects firms' cost structures and choices about product quality, as well as their ability to woo investors. In a postindustrial economy, perceived facts are real in their economic consequences.

Diffusion and Social Influence

Diffusion through networks is one of the best-studied topics in the sociology of organizations of the past 15 years (see Hedstrom and Swedberg 1998 on this and other mechanisms). Strang and Soule (1998) provide an excellent review of diffusion in social movements and organizations. Focusing specifically on network effects, researchers have found that U.S. corporations were more likely to adopt the highly controversial poison pill takeover defense when they shared directors with prior adopters—experienced directors could explain the costs and benefits and potential political fallout from adoption (Davis 1991). Their opinions were particularly impactful when the other firms on whose boards they served were similar to the potential adopter (e.g., similar industry or size). Firms were also likely to adopt contentious golden parachute contracts when other firms headquartered in the same locale had previously done so and thus legitimated it according to the local standard (Davis and Greve 1997). Ties to prior adopters made firms more prone to adopting the multidivisional form in the 1960s (Palmer, Jennings, and Zhou 1993), and well-connected corporate leaders made more acquisitions during the 1960s than their disconnected colleagues (Palmer and Barber 2001). Firms listed on the Nasdaq stock market in the mid-1980s were more likely to relist on the New York Stock Exchange when the firms they were tied to through shared directors had done so, but the strength of this effect depended on ties to Nasdaq versus NYSE firms (Rao, Davis, and Ward 2000). Serving on the board of an acquirer prompted firm executives of large firms to make acquisitions themselves (Haunschild 1993), particularly when the prior acquirer was similar to the potential acquirer. This effect is most likely due to informational rather than purely normative influences, as access to alternative information sources (such as when the CEO is a member of a business association with other large firms) generally reduced the impact of board ties (Haunschild and Beckman 1998). Having a banker on the board increased borrowing by firms from the mid-1950s to the early 1980s (Mizruchi and Stearns 1994; see the chapter by Stearns and Mizruchi in this volume for further discussion of the causes and consequences of firm-bank ties). And corporate ties to philanthropic leaders influenced the magnitude of charitable giving in the Twin Cities in the late 1970s and the late 1980s (Galaskiewicz 1997). Across a broad range of board-level decisions, it is evident that the social networks in which directors are embedded have strong influence on corporate actions.

Business Groups as Networks

The 1990s saw a much greater attention to business groups around the world. As Granovetter pointed out in the prior edition of this handbook, business groups are the norm in most industrial economies. These may take the form of family-based ownership groups or simply a set of affiliated companies. Unlike the types of networks described in the U.S. case, however, such groups are often quite exclusive in their ties, with member firms avoiding exchange with firms that are members of competing groups. Japan has two types of business group. Vertical networks are organized hierarchically around banks, while horizontal networks of cross-shareholding, interlocking directorates, and preferential exchange link large, established firms into relatively homophilous groups (Lincoln, Gerlach, and Takahashi 1992; Gerlach 1992). *Keiretsu* membership is consequential for performance, but the effects are quite complex: *keiretsu* members have lower performance on average, but over time the impact of group membership is in effect to speed regression to the mean, as low performers that are group members improve more rapidly than nonmembers, while high performers decline more rapidly than nonmembers (Lincoln, Gerlach, and Ahmadjian 1996).

Based on the evident success of the Japanese model and its Korean adaptation for rapid economic development (see Evans 1995), China has consciously emulated the business group model since the early 1980s. Unlike the case of Japan, however, group membership still had a positive performance benefit during the late 1980s, particularly in nonhierarchical groups (Keister 1998). The impact of within-group ties became even more important over time, according to data from the 1990s, and firm managers continued to express a preference for exchange with fellow group members (those they had done business with before) even when "cheaper" alternatives were available (Keister 2001).

The differences in performance among business groups between Japan and China may reflect their stage of economic development, as a frequently observed tendency is for groups to break down over time. Chilean business networks partially unraveled after the national push for privatization and the increasing prevalence of exchange-traded firms (Khanna and Palepu 2000). Kock and Guillén (2001) argue that this may represent a predictable trajectory, as entrepreneurs in the early stages of economic growth in late-developing nations can reap the greatest rewards as network builders connecting foreign technologies to local markets. This networking skill is broadly applicable across industries, and thus such entrepreneurs tend to build diversified business groups that are profitable early on but that eventually become unwieldy. Thus, diversified business groups tied by ownership links may predominate in early stages of economic development but disperse at later stages. Even such unraveling still leaves certain network properties in place, however. Networks among German corporations formed by having a major owner in common continued to form a "small world" (in which companies are clustered in network "neighborhoods" but still connected by short paths to most other firms) during the mid-1990s, even after substantial changes in patterns of bank ownership and corporate governance. Firms connected by short common-ownership paths were also more likely to merge than firms connected by long paths (Kogut and Walker 2001). Ironically, and in precise contrast to Germany, U.S. corporate ownership became vastly more concentrated during the 1990s due to the growth and consolidation of a handful of financial service firms, and at decade's end 60 percent of large corporations were tied into a single network component based on common owners (Davis and Yoo 2003).

Aggregate Structures of Networks

The aggregate structure of an economy, like that of an organization or an industrial district, can be represented in network terms. In building their theory of financial hegemony, Mintz and Schwartz (1985) documented the overlaps between financial flows and ties among boards of directors, finding that financial institutions—particularly money center commercial banks—persistently held the most central positions. While this situation held for decades in the United States, it began to change in the 1980s as credit-worthy corporate borrowers increasingly moved toward market-based sources of financing; this in turn was reflected in the declining centrality of commercial banks in the overall intercorporate network (Davis and Mizruchi 1999). Yet in spite of major aggregate changes in banking, corporate governance, and the nature of the economy in the United States, corporate elites continued to be connected to each other through very few "degrees of separation," and the diameter of the corporate network remained quite stable in spite of the hollowing out of its core (Davis, Yoo, and Baker 2003). The German corporate ownership network proved similarly resilient in the face of globalization (Kogut and Walker 2001), indicating that a little bit of structure goes a long way in social networks (Watts 1999). As methodological tools, computing power, and cross-national data become more readily available, we may look forward to seeing more work of this sort with both historical and cross-national comparisons.

Networks in Economic Transitions

A taste of this future style of work appeared in a handful of excellent research articles documenting changes in firms and environments in the transition from socialism. Stark (1996) argued that firms responded to the new types of uncertainty arising in transition in Hungary by diversifying their assets and blurring their boundaries. Guthrie (1997) similarly found that Chinese firms in Shanghai responded to economic instability and administrative instability caused by reform by diversifying into fast-growth ventures in the service sector. Nee (1992) argued that China's transition should not be conceived as a linear process leading to a standard form of capitalism, but pointed to a lengthy, path-dependent, coevolutionary process in which collectives and state-owned firms would morph into hybrid forms ranging from nonmarketized firms to marketized firms to private firms. And Boisot and Child (1996) extend this notion to argue that China is developing a distinct form of "network capitalism" that is institutionally different from prior forms of capitalism. Network-based analyses of economic transitions should be one of the most fruitful areas of future work, applicable to a wide range of research topics at the industry and economy-wide level.

CONCLUSION

The years since 1990 have been an eventful period for the study of business organizations, marked by vast economic and political transitions. European economic integration, the breakdown of state socialism in Eastern Europe, China's transition to a hybrid form of capitalism, and the apotheosis of "shareholder value" in the corporate sector of the United States have all altered the face of national capitalisms. Financial markets spread and grew around the world, along with a neoliberal ideology about the proper route to economic growth. Transnational corporations elaborated production chains that spanned the globe, while new indigenous industries took root. Underlying the shifts in forms of finance and production were advances in information and communication technologies that substantially expanded the range of possible organizational structures and repertoires. While the hype around the "new economy" was undoubtedly overdone, there was also real and fundamental change in the world of organizations.

These changes were reflected in the research reviewed in this chapter. In the late 1980s, it was straightforward to write a survey of firms and environments organized around discrete organizational theories (Davis and Powell 1992). This is no longer true. Economic transitions posed challenges for theories rooted in the experience of American corporations of the 1960s and 1970s. Economic activity in the world was no longer adequately captured by the old paradigms, which contemplated a world of states containing bounded organizations that in turn contained members. One might view this situation as a failure to build a research program on organizations qua organizations—yet organizational research proliferated. Rather, the work surveyed here displays an eclectic approach to theory rather than the prosecution of a fixed theoretical agenda.

In some sense, this makes the sociology of organizations more consistent with general trends in sociology as a discipline. Indeed, many researchers that would have been labeled organizational theorists now refer to themselves as economic sociologists. In practice, this has meant that the characteristic kinds of problems studied are not limited to those that flowed naturally from theories of organization, such as, "When should a firm make or buy an input?" or, "How does age affect organizational death rates?" Rather, researchers took on topics of broader sociological significance that could not be answered from within a particular organizational paradigm: How does national culture influence the shape of organizational fields? How do networks among corporations shape their response to legal changes? What happens when markets intrude on formerly "noneconomic" realms of organizational life? It was problems in the world more than problems of theory that drove most of the research described here.

The value of problem-driven research, of course, depends on what the "problem" is. Critics have argued that since its migration from social science departments to business schools, the study of organizations has been increasingly captured by business definitions of worthy problems (e.g., Stern and Barley 1996). Mayer Zald writes, "Organizational studies could be a powerful applied discipline if the scientific base of the field was strong. Since it is not, organizational studies follows the ratings, responding not only to academic fads, but to the whims and foibles of academic hucksters and the problem definitions of corporate executives" (1993, 514). But problem-driven research need not be mere hucksterism or current events: consider *The Eighteenth Brumaire of Louis Bonaparte* or *The Protestant Ethic and the Spirit of Capitalism.* The tension is perhaps between aspirations to grand theory, on the one hand, and to making sense of the intersection of biography and history in social structure on the other (Mills 1959). In times of social change, social research might do better in the middle range. One could try to unite the diverse threads of organization theory with an overarching framework: Aldrich (1999) suggests that evolutionary theorizing can subsume much of the field, and makes a heroic effort to bring a vast amount of work under a big tent organized around variation, selection, and retention. But as Gould (1997, 50) writes, "If we want a biological metaphor for cultural change, we should probably invoke infection rather than evolution." To the extent that organizational change is cultural change, then perhaps we should use a broader set of tools.

Eclecticism in problem-driven work can easily devolve into dilettantism. Yet many of the studies we have considered provide a model of how to use organization theory as a toolkit to be drawn on for elements of explanation. A pragmatic approach uses theory to answer questions better, rather than as dogma. Thus, when explaining widespread change in the mix of organizations, voluntary change in response to student preferences provides an explanation for why liberal arts colleges turned into trade schools (Kraatz and Zajac 1996); organizational births and deaths in the face of political and demographic shifts accounts for changing forms of S&Ls in California (Haveman and Rao 1997); and legal changes enabling hostile bust-up takeovers, followed by changed growth norms, led to the decline of the conglomerate in the United States (Davis, Diekmann, and Tinsley 1994). Mass adaptation, births and deaths, and coercive change are all bits of "sometimes-true theory" that can be drawn on to make sense of events in the world. If the next two decades are like the last two, we can expect to see still more theoretical eclecticism in the economic sociology of organizations in response to social change in the broader world.

NOTES

I thank Chris Marquis, Mark Mizruchi, Woody Powell, Neil Smelser, Richard Swedberg, and Mayer Zald for their comments. I am especially indebted to Howard Aldrich for his extensive dissection of prior drafts and for his constructive disagreements with my Whiggish interpretations.

1. James Scott describes the ideology of "high modernism" in his book *Seeing Like a State* (1997). The core idea is that clearly bounded and centrally administered territorial states could improve the human condition using scientific principles of rational bureaucratic control.

REFERENCES

Abrahamson, Eric, and Gregory Fairchild. 1999. "Management Fashion: Lifecycles, Triggers, and Collective Learning Processes." *Administrative Science Quarterly* 44:708–40.

Ahmadjian, Christina L., and Patricia Robinson. 2001. "Safety in Numbers: Downsizing and the Deinstitutionalization of Permanent Employment in Japan." *Administrative Science Quarterly* 46:622–54.

Ahuja, Gautam. 2000. "Collaboration Networks, Structural Holes, and Innovation: A Longitudinal Study." *Administrative Science Quarterly* 45:425–55.

Akard, Patrick J. 1992. "Corporate Mobilization and Political Power: The Transformation of U.S. Economic Policy in the 1970s." *American Sociological Review* 57:597–615.

Aldrich, Howard E. 1999. *Organizations Evolving.* Thousand Oaks, Calif.: Sage.

———. 2001. "Who Wants to Be an Evolutionary Theorist?" *Journal of Management Inquiry* 10:115–27.

Baker, Wayne E. 1992. "The Network Organization in Theory and Practice." Pp. 397–429 in *Networks and Organizations: Structure, Form, and Action*, ed. Nitin Nohria and Robert G. Eccles. Boston: Harvard Business School Press.

Baker, Wayne E., and Robert R. Faulkner. 1991. "Role as Resource in the Hollywood Film Industry." *American Journal of Sociology* 97:279–309.

Baker, Wayne E., Robert R. Faulkner, and Gene A. Fisher. 1998. "Hazards of the Market: The Continuity and Dissolution of Interorganizational Market Relationships." *American Sociological Review* 63:147–77.

Baron, James N., Michael T. Hannan, and M. Diane Burton. 1999. "Building the Iron Cage: Determinants of Managerial Intensity in the Early Years of Organizations." *American Sociological Review* 64:527–47.

Baum, Joel A. C., Stan Xiao Li, and John M. Usher. 2000. "Making the Next Move: How Experiential and Vicarious Learning Shape the Locations of Chains' Acquisition." *Administrative Science Quarterly* 45:766–801.

Becattini, Giacomo. 1990. "The Marshallian Industrial District as a Socio-economic Notion." Pp. 37–51 in *Industrial Districts and Inter-Firm Co-operation in Italy*, ed. Frank Pyke, Giacomo Becattini, and Werger Sengenberger. Geneva: International Institute for Labor Studies.

Benjamin, Beth A., and Joel M. Podolny. 1999. "Status, Quality, and Social Order in the California Wine Industry." *Administrative Science Quarterly* 44:563–89.

Biggart, Nicole Woolsey. 1992. "The Western Bias of Neoclassical Economics: On the Limits of a Firm-Based Theory to Explain Business Networks." Pp. 471–90 in *Networks and Organizations: Structure, Form, and Action*, ed. Nitin Nohria and Robert G. Eccles. Boston: Harvard Business School Press.

Biggart, Nicole Woolsey, and Mauro F. Guillén. 1999. "Developing Difference: Social Organization and the Rise of the Auto Industries of South Korea, Taiwan, Spain, and Argentina." *American Sociological Review* 64:722–47.

Boeker, Warren. 1997. "Executive Migration and Strategic Change: The Effect of Top Manager Movement on Product-Market Entry." *Administrative Science Quarterly* 42:213–36.

Boisot, Max, and John Child. 1996. "From Fiefs to Clans and Network Capitalism: Explaining China's Emerging Economic Order." *Administrative Science Quarterly* 41:600–628.

Bourdieu, Pierre, and Loïc J. D. Wacquant. 1992. *An Invitation to Reflexive Sociology.* Chicago: University of Chicago Press.

Burt, Ronald S. 1992. *Structural Holes: The Social Structure of Competition.* Cambridge: Harvard University Press.

———. 2000. "The Network Structure of Social Capital." *Research in Organization Behavior* 22:345–423.

Casper, Steven, and Bob Hancke. 1999. "Global Quality Norms within National Production Regimes: ISO 9000 Standards in the French and German Car Industries." *Organization Studies* 20:961–85.

Chandler, Alfred D. 1977. *The Visible Hand: The Managerial Revolution in America.* Cambridge: Harvard University Press.

Chaves, Mark. 1996. "Ordaining Women: The Diffusion of an Organizational Innovation." *American Journal of Sociology* 101:840–73.

Clemens, Elisabeth S. 1993. "Organizational Repertoires and Institutional Change: Women's Groups and the Transformation of U.S. Politics, 1890–1920." *American Journal of Sociology* 98:755–98.

Conell, Carol, and Samuel Cohn. 1995. "Learning from Other People's Actions: Environmental Variation and Diffusion in French Coal Mining Strikes, 1890–1935." *American Journal of Sociology* 101:366–403.

Cyert, Richard M., and James G. March. 1963. *A Behavioral Theory of the Firm.* Englewood Cliffs, N.J.: Prentice-Hall.

D'Aunno, Thomas, Melissa Succi, and Jeffrey A. Alexander. 2000. "The Role of Institutional and Market Forces in Divergent Organizational Change." *Administrative Science Quarterly* 45:679–703.

Davies, Stephen, Laura Rondi, and Alessandro Sembenell. 2001. "European Integration and the Changing Structure of EU Manufacturing, 1987–1993." *Industrial and Corporate Change* 10:37–75.

Davis, Gerald F. 1991. "Agents without Principles? The Spread of the Poison Pill through the Intercorporate Network." *Administrative Science Quarterly* 36:583–613.

Davis, Gerald F., Kristina A. Diekmann, and Catherine H. Tinsley. 1994. "The Decline and Fall of the Conglomerate Firm in the 1980s: The Deinstitutionalization of an Organizational Form." *American Sociological Review* 59:547–70.

Davis, Gerald F., and Henrich R. Greve. 1997. "Corporate Elite Networks and Governance Changes in the 1980s." *American Journal of Sociology* 103:1–37.

Davis, Gerald F., and Mark S. Mizruchi. 1999. "The Money Center Cannot Hold: Commercial Banks in the U.S. System of Corporate Governance." *Administrative Science Quarterly* 44:215–39.

Davis, Gerald F., and Walter W. Powell. 1992. "Organization-Environment Relations." Pp. 315–75 in vol. 3 of *Handbook of Industrial and Organizational Psychology*, ed. Marvin D. Dunnette and Leaetta M. Hough. 2d ed. Palo Alto, Calif.: Consulting Psychologists Press.

Davis, Gerald F., and Gregory E. Robbins. Forthcoming. "The Fate of the Conglomerate Firm in the United States." In *How Institutions Change*, ed. Walter W. Powell and Daniel L. Jones. Chicago: University of Chicago Press.

Davis, Gerald F., and Suzanne K. Stout. 1992. "Organization Theory and the Market for Corporate Control: A Dynamic Analysis of the Characteristics of Large Takeover Targets, 1980–1990." *Administrative Science Quarterly* 37:605–33.

Davis, Gerald F., and Tracy A. Thompson. 1994. "A Social Movement Perspective on Corporate Control." *Administrative Science Quarterly* 39:141–73.

Davis, Gerald F., and Michael Useem. 2002. "Top Management, Company Directors, and Corporate Control." Pp. 233–59 in *Handbook of Strategy and Management*, ed. Andrew Pettigrew, Howard Thomas, and Richard Whittington. London: Sage.

Davis, Gerald F., and Mina Yoo. 2003. "Le monde toujours plus petit des grandes entreprises americaines: Participationes communes et liens dans les conseils d'administration (1990–2001)." *Gerer et comprende* 74:51–62.

Davis, Gerald F., Mina Yoo, and Wayne E. Baker. 2003. "The Small World of the American Corporate Elite, 1982–2001." *Strategic Organization* 1:301–26.

DiMaggio, Paul J., and Walter W. Powell. 1983. "The Iron Cage Revisited: Institutional Isomorphism and Collective Rationality in Organizational Fields." *American Sociological Review* 48:147–60.

Dobbin, Frank. 1994. *Forging Industrial Policy: The United States, Britain, and France in the Railway Age*. Cambridge: Cambridge University Press.

Dobbin, Frank, and Timothy J. Dowd. 1997. "How Policy Shapes Competition: Early Railroad Foundings in Massachusetts." *Administrative Science Quarterly* 42:501–29.

———. 2000. "The Market That Antitrust Built: Public Policy, Private Coercion, and Railroad Acquisition, 1825 to 1922." *American Sociological Review* 65: 631–57.

Dobbin, Frank, and Frank R. Sutton. 1998. "The Strength of a Weak State: The Rights Revolution and the Rise of Human Resources Management Divisions." *American Journal of Sociology* 104:441–76.

Dobbin, Frank, John R. Sutton, John W. Meyer, and W. Richard Scott. 1993. "Equal Opportunity Law and the Construction of Internal Labor Markets." *American Journal of Sociology* 99:396–427.

Donaldson, Lex. 1995. *American Anti-management Theories of Organization: A Critique of Paradigm Proliferation*. Cambridge: Cambridge University Press.

Douglas, Mary. 1986. *How Institutions Think*. Syracuse, N.Y.: Syracuse University Press.

Edelman, Lauren B. 1992. "Legal Ambiguity and Symbolic Structures: Organizational Mediation of Civil Rights Law." *American Journal of Sociology* 97: 1531–76.

Edelman, Lauren B., Christopher Uggen, and Howard S. Erlanger. 1999. "The Endogeneity of Legal Regulation: Grievance Procedures as Rational Myth." *American Journal of Sociology* 105:406–54.

Evans, Peter. 1995. *Embedded Autonomy: States and Industrial Transformation*. Princeton: Princeton University Press.

Fligstein, Neil. 1990. *The Transformation of Corporate Control*. Cambridge: Harvard University Press.

Fox-Wolfgramm, Susan J., Kimberly B. Boal, and James G. Hunt. 1998. "Organizational Adaptation to Institutional Change: A Comparative Study of First-Order Change in Prospector and Defender Banks." *Administrative Science Quarterly* 43:87–126.

Galaskiewicz, Joseph. 1997. "An Urban Grants Economy Revisited: Corporate Charitable Contributions in the Twin Cities, 1979–81, 1987–89." *Administrative Science Quarterly* 42:445–71.

Galaskiewicz, Joseph, and Ronald S. Burt. 1991. "Interorganization Contagion in Corporate Philanthropy." *Administrative Science Quarterly* 36:88–105.

Geletkanycz, Marta A., and Donald C. Hambrick. 1997. "The External Ties of Top Executives: Implications for Strategic Choice and Performance." *Administrative Science Quarterly* 42:654–81.

Gerlach, Michael L. 1992. "The Japanese Corporate Network: A Blockmodel Analysis." *Administrative Science Quarterly* 37:105–39.

Gimeno, Javier, Timothy B. Folta, Arnold C. Cooper, and Carolyn Y. Woo. 1997. "Survival of the Fittest? Entrepreneurial Human Capital and the Persistence of Underperforming Firms." *Administrative Science Quarterly* 42:750–83.

Gould, Steven J. 1997. "Evolution: The Pleasures of Pluralism." *New York Review of Books*, June 26, 47–52.

Granovetter, Mark. 1985. "Economic Action and Social

Structure: The Problem of Embeddedness." *American Journal of Sociology* 91:481–510.

———. 1994. "Business Groups." Pp. 453–75 in *Handbook of Economic Sociology*, ed. Neil J. Smelser and Richard Swedberg. New York: Russell Sage Foundation; Princeton: Princeton University Press.

Grant, Don Sherman. 1995. "The Political Economy of Business Failures across the American States, 1970–1985: The Impact of Reagan's New Federalism." *American Sociological Review* 60:851–73.

Greve, Henrich R. 1995. "Jumping Ship: The Diffusion of Strategy Abandonment." *Administrative Science Quarterly* 40:444–73.

———. 1996. "Patterns of Competition: The Diffusion of a Market Position in Radio Broadcasting." *Administrative Science Quarterly* 41:29–60.

———. 1998. "Performance, Aspirations, and Risky Organizational Change." *Administrative Science Quarterly* 43:58–86.

———. 1999. "The Effect of Core Change on Performance: Inertia and Regression toward the Mean." *Administrative Science Quarterly* 44:590–614.

Gulati, Ranjay. 1995. "Social Structure and Alliance Formation Patterns: A Longitudinal Analysis." *Administrative Science Quarterly* 40:619–52.

Gulati, Ranjay, and Martin Gargiulo. 1999. "Where Do Interorganizational Networks Come From?" *American Journal of Sociology* 104:1439–93.

Guthrie, Douglas. 1997. "Between Markets and Politics: Organizational Responses to Reform in China." *American Journal of Sociology* 102:1258–1304.

Hannan, Michael T., and John Freeman. 1977. "The Population Ecology of Organizations." *American Journal of Sociology* 82:929–64.

Haunschild, Pamela R. 1993. "Interorganizational Imitation: The Impact of Interlocks on Corporate Acquisition Activity." *Administrative Science Quarterly* 38:564–92.

———. 1994. "How Much Is That Company Worth? Interorganizational Relationships, Uncertainty, and Acquisition Premiums." *Administrative Science Quarterly* 39:391–411.

Haunschild, Pamela R., and Christine M. Beckman. 1998. "When Do Interlocks Matter? Alternate Sources of Information and Interlock Influence." *Administrative Science Quarterly* 43:815–44.

Haunschild, Pamela R., and Anne S. Miner. 1997. "Modes of Interorganizational Imitation: The Effects of Outcome Salience and Uncertainty." *Administrative Science Quarterly* 42:472–500.

Haveman, Heather A. 1993. "Follow the Leader: Mimetic Isomorphism and Entry into New Markets." *Administrative Science Quarterly* 38:593–627.

Haveman, Heather A., and Lisa E. Cohen. 1994. "The Ecological Dynamics of Careers: The Impact of Organizational Founding, Dissolution, and Merger on Job Mobility." *American Journal of Sociology* 100: 104–52.

Haveman, Heather A., and Lynn Nonnemaker. 2000. "Competition in Multiple Geographic Markets: The Impact on Growth and Market Entry." *Administrative Science Quarterly* 45:232–67.

Haveman, Heather A., and Hayagreeva Rao. 1997. "Structuring a Theory of Moral Sentiments: Institutional and Organizational Coevolution in the Early Thrift Industry." *American Journal of Sociology* 102:1606–51.

Hedstrom, Peter, and Richard Swedberg. 1998. *Social Mechanisms: An Analytical Approach to Social Theory*. Cambridge: Cambridge University Press.

Henisz, Witold J., and Andrew Delios. 2001. "Uncertainty, Imitation, and Plant Location: Japanese Multinational Corporations, 1990–1996." *Administrative Science Quarterly* 46:443–75.

Human, Sherrie E., and Keith G. Provan. 2000. "Legitimacy Building in the Evolution of Small Firm Multilateral Networks: A Comparative Study of Success and Demise." *Administrative Science Quarterly* 45: 327–65.

Ingram, Paul, and Crist Inman. 1996. "Institutions, Intergroup Competition, and the Evolution of Hotel Populations around Niagara Falls." *Administrative Science Quarterly* 41:629–58.

Jensen, Michael C., and William H. Meckling. 1976. "Theory of the Firm: Managerial Behavior, Agency Cost, and Ownership Structure." *Journal of Financial Economics* 3:305–60.

Keister, Lisa A. 1998. "Engineering Growth: Business Group Structure and Firm Performance in China's Transition Economy." *American Journal of Sociology* 104:404–40.

——— 2001. "Exchange Structures in Transition: Lending and Trade Relations in Chinese Business Groups." *American Sociological Review* 66:336–60.

Kelly, Erin, and Frank Dobbin. 1999. "Civil Rights Law at Work: Sex Discrimination and the Rise of Maternity Leave Policies." *American Journal of Sociology* 105:455–92.

Khanna, Tarun, and Krishna Palepu. 2000. "The Future of Business Groups in Emerging Markets: Long-Run Evidence from Chile." *Academy of Management Journal* 43:268–85.

Kock, Carl J., and Mauro F. Guillén. 2001. "Strategy and Structure in Developing Countries: Business Groups as an Evolutionary Response to Opportunities for Unrelated Diversification." *Industrial and Corporate Change* 10:77–113.

Kogut, Bruce, and Andrew Spicer. 2002. "Capital Market Development and Mass Privatization Are Logical Contradictions: Lessons from Russia and the Czech Republic." *Industrial and Corporate Change* 11:1–37.

Kogut, Bruce, and Gordon Walker. 2001. "The Small World of Germany and the Durability of National Networks." *American Sociological Review* 66:317–335.

Kono, Clifford, Donald Palmer, Roger Friedland, and Matthew Zafonte. 1998. "Lost in Space: The Ge-

500   *Davis*

ography of Corporate Interlocking Directorates." *American Journal of Sociology* 103:863–911.

Kraatz, Matthew S., and Edward J. Zajac. 1996. "Exploring the Limits of the New Institutionalism: The Causes and Consequences of Illegitimate Organizational Change." *American Sociological Review* 61: 812–36.

Larson, Andrea. 1992. "Network Dyads in Entrepreneurial Settings: A Study of the Governance of Exchange Relationships." *Administrative Science Quarterly* 37:76–104.

Lazerson, Mark. 1995. "A New Phoenix? Modern Putting-out in the Modena Knitwear Industry." *Administrative Science Quarterly* 40:34–59.

Leblebici, Huseyin, Gerald R. Salancik, Anne Copay, and Tom King. 1991. "Institutional Change and the Transformation of Interorganizational Fields: An Organizational History of the U.S. Radio Broadcasting Industry." *Administrative Science Quarterly* 36:333–63.

Levinthal, Daniel A., and Mark Fichman. 1988. "Dynamics of Interorganizational Attachments: Auditor-Client Relationships." *Administrative Science Quarterly* 33:345–69.

Lincoln, James R., Michael L. Gerlach, and Christina L. Ahmadjian. 1996. "Keiretsu Networks and Corporate Performance in Japan." *American Sociological Review* 61:67–88.

Lincoln, James R., Michael L. Gerlach, and Peggy Takahashi. 1992. "Keiretsu Networks in the Japanese Economy: A Dyad Analysis of Intercorporate Ties." *American Sociological Review* 57:561–85.

Lounsbury, Michael. 2001. "Institutional Sources of Practice Variation: Staffing College and University Recycling Programs." *Administrative Science Quarterly* 46:29–56.

"Mad Mergers in Europe." 1992. *Economist*, February 1, 18–19.

March, James G., and Herbert A. Simon. 1958. *Organizations*. New York: Wiley.

Martin, Xavier, Anand Swaminathan, and Will Mitchell. 1998. "Organizational Evolution in the Interorganizational Environment: Incentives and Constraints on International Expansion Strategy." *Administrative Science Quarterly* 43:566–601.

Mayer, Michael C. J. and Richard Whittington. 1999. "Strategy, Structure and 'Systemness': National Institutions and Corporate Change in France, Germany and the UK, 1950–1993." *Organization Studies* 20:933–59.

Meyer, John W., and Brian Rowan. 1977. "Institutionalized Organizations: Formal Structure as Myth and Ceremony." *American Journal of Sociology* 83:41–62.

Miles, Raymond E., and Charles C. Snow. 1992. "Causes of Failure in Network Organizations." *California Management Review* 34(4): 53–72.

Miller, Danny, and Ming-Jer Chen. 1994. "Sources and Consequences of Competitive Inertia: A Study of the U.S. Airline Industry." *Administrative Science Quarterly* 39:1–23.

Mills, C. Wright. 1956. *The Power Elite*. Oxford: Oxford University Press.

———. 1959. *The Sociological Imagination*. Oxford: Oxford University Press.

Mintz, Beth, and Michael Schwartz. 1985. *The Power Structure of American Business*. Chicago: University of Chicago Press.

Mizruchi, Mark S. 1992. *The Structure of Corporate Political Action: Interfirm Relations and Their Consequences*. Cambridge: Harvard University Press.

Mizruchi, Mark S., and Linda Brewster Stearns. 1994. "A Longitudinal Study of Borrowing by Large American Corporations." *Administrative Science Quarterly* 39:118–40.

Nee, Victor. 1992. "Organizational Dynamics of Market Transition: Hybrid Forms, Property Rights, and Mixed Economy in China." *Administrative Science Quarterly* 37:1–27.

Palmer, Donald A. 1983. "Broken Ties: Interlocking Directorates and Intercorporate Coordination." *Administrative Science Quarterly* 28:40–55.

Palmer, Donald, and Brad M. Barber. 2001. "Challengers, Elites, and Owning Families: A Social Class Theory of Corporate Acquisitions in the 1960s." *Administrative Science Quarterly* 46:87–120.

Palmer, Donald, Brad M. Barber, Xueguang Zhou, and Yasemin Soysal. 1995. "The Friendly and Predatory Acquisition of Large U.S. Corporations in the 1960s: The Other Contested Terrain." *American Sociological Review* 60:469–99.

Palmer, Donald A., P. Devereaux Jennings, and Xueguang Zhou. 1993. "Late Adoption of the Multidivisional Form by Large U.S. Corporations: Institutional, Political, and Economic Accounts." *Administrative Science Quarterly* 38:100–131.

Paniccia, Ivana. 1998. "One, a Hundred, Thousands of Industrial Districts: Organizational Variety in Local Networks of Small and Medium-Sized Enterprises." *Organization Studies* 19:667–99.

Perrow, Charles. 1991. "A Society of Organizations." *Theory and Society* 20:725–62.

———. 2002. *Organizing America: Wealth, Power, and the Origins of Corporate Capitalism*. Princeton: Princeton University Press.

Pfeffer, Jeffrey. 1993. "Barriers to the Advance of Organizational Science: Paradigm Development as a Dependent Variable." *Academy of Management Review* 18:599–620.

Pfeffer, Jeffrey, and Gerald R. Salancik. 1978. *The External Control of Organizations: A Resource Dependence Perspective*. New York: Harper and Row.

Piore, Michael J., and Charles F. Sabel. 1984. *The Second Industrial Divide*. New York: Basic Books.

Podolny, Joel M. 1993. "A Status-Based Model of Market Competition." *American Journal of Sociology* 98:829–72.

———. 1994. "Market Uncertainty and the Social Character of Economic Exchange." *Administrative Science Quarterly* 39:458–83.

———. 2001. "Networks as the Pipes and Prisms of the Market." *American Journal of Sociology* 107:33–60.

Podolny, Joel M., Toby E. Stuart, and Michael T. Hannan. 1996. "Networks, Knowledge, and Niches: Competition in the Worldwide Semiconductor Industry, 1984–1991." *American Journal of Sociology* 102:659–89.

Porac, Joseph F., Howard Thomas, Fiona Wilson, Douglas Paton, and Alaina Kanfer. 1995. "Rivalry and the Industry Model of Scottish Knitwear Producers." *Administrative Science Quarterly* 40:203–27.

Porac, Joseph F., James B. Wade, and Timothy G. Pollock. 1999. "Industry Categories and the Politics of the Comparable Firm in CEO Compensation." *Administrative Science Quarterly* 44:112–44.

Portes, Alejandro. 1998. "Social Capital: Its Origins and Applications in Modern Sociology." *Annual Review of Sociology* 24:1–24.

Powell, Walter W. 1990. "Neither Market nor Hierarchy: Network Forms of Organization." *Research in Organization Behavior* 12:295–336.

Powell, Walter W., Kenneth W. Koput, and Laurel Smith-Doerr. 1996. "Interorganizational Collaboration and the Locus of Innovation: Networks of Learning in Biotechnology." *Administrative Science Quarterly* 41:116–45.

Provan, Keith G., and H. Brinton Milward. 1995. "A Preliminary Theory of Interorganizational Network Effectiveness: A Comparative Study of Four Community Mental Health Systems." *Administrative Science Quarterly* 40:1–33.

Rademakers, Martijn F. L. 1998. "Market Organization in Indonesia: Javanese and Chinese Family Business in the Jamu Industry." *Organization Studies* 19:1005–27.

Rao, Hayagreeva. 1998. "Caveat Emptor: The Construction of Nonprofit Consumer Watchdog Organizations." *American Journal of Sociology* 103:912–61.

Rao, Hayagreeva, Gerald F. Davis, and Andrew Ward. 2000. "Embeddedness, Social Identity, and Mobility: Why Firms Leave the NASDAQ and Join the New York Stock Exchange." *Administrative Science Quarterly* 45:268–92.

Rao, Hayagreeva, and Kumar Sivakumar. 1999. "Institutional Sources of Boundary-Spanning Structures: The Establishment of Investor Relations Departments in the Fortune 500 Industrials." *Organization Science* 10:27–42.

Rogers, Everett M. 1995. *Diffusion of Innovations.* 4th ed. New York: Free Press.

Romo, Frank P., and Michael Schwartz. 1995. "The Structural Embeddedness of Business Decisions: The Migration of Manufacturing Plants in New York State, 1960 to 1985." *American Sociological Review* 60:874–907.

Russo, Michael V. 2001. "Institutions, Exchange Relations, and the Emergence of New Fields: Regulatory

Policies and Independent Power Producing in America, 1978–1992." *Administrative Science Quarterly* 46:57–86.

Schumpeter, Joseph A. 1934. *The Theory of Economic Development.* Cambridge: Harvard University Press.

Scott, James C. 1997. *Seeing Like a State: How Certain Schemes to Improve the Human Condition Have Failed.* New Haven: Yale University Press.

Scott, W. Richard. 1995. *Institutions and Organizations.* Thousand Oaks, Calif.: Sage.

———. 2003. *Organizations: Rational, Natural, and Open Systems.* 5th ed. Upper Saddle River, N.J.: Prentice Hall.

Scott, W. Richard, Martin Ruef, Peter J. Mendel, and Carol A. Caronna. 2000. *Institutional Change and Healthcare Organizations.* Chicago: University of Chicago Press.

Simons, Tal, and Paul Ingram. 1997. "Organization and Ideology: Kibbutzim and Hired Labor, 1951–1965." *Administrative Science Quarterly* 42:784–813.

Stark, David. 1996. "Recombinant Property in East European Capitalism." *American Journal of Sociology* 101:993–1027.

Stearns, Linda Brewster, and Kenneth D. Allan. 1996. "Economic Behavior in Institutional Environments: The Corporate Merger Wave of the 1980s." *American Sociological Review* 61:699–718.

Stern, Robert N., and Stephen R. Barley. 1996. "Organizations and Social Systems: Organization Theory's Neglected Mandate." *Administrative Science Quarterly* 41:146–62.

Stinchcombe, Arthur L. 1965. "Social Structure and Organizations." Pp. 142–93 in *Handbook of Organizations,* ed. James G. March. Chicago: Rand McNally.

———. 1968. *Constructing Social Theories.* Chicago: University of Chicago Press.

Strang, David, and Sarah A. Soule. 1998. "Diffusion in Organizations and Social Movements: From Hybrid Corn to Poison Pills." *Annual Review of Sociology* 24:265–90.

Stuart, Toby E. 1998. "Network Positions and Propensities to Collaborate: An Investigation of Strategic Alliance Formation in a High-Technology Industry." *Administrative Science Quarterly* 43:668–98.

Stuart, Toby E., Ha Hoang, and Ralph C. Hybels. 1999. "Interorganizational Endorsements and the Performance of Entrepreneurial Ventures." *Administrative Science Quarterly* 44:315–49.

Sturgeon, Timothy J. 2002. "Modular Production Networks: A New American Model of Industrial Organization." *Industrial and Corporate Change* 11:451–96.

Sutton, John R., and Frank Dobbin. 1996. "The Two Faces of Governance: Responses to Legal Uncertainty in U.S. Firms, 1955 to 1985." *American Sociological Review* 61:794–811.

Sutton, John R., Frank Dobbin, John W. Meyer, and W. Richard Scott. 1994. "The Legalization of the

Workplace." *American Journal of Sociology* 99: 944–71.

Thompson, James D. 1967. *Organizations in Action.* New York: McGraw-Hill.

Thornton, Patricia H., and William Ocasio. 1999. "Institutional Logics and the Historical Contingency of Power in Organizations: Executive Succession in the Higher Education Publishing Industry, 1958–1990." *American Journal of Sociology* 105:801–43.

Useem, Michael. 1984. *The Inner Circle.* Oxford: Oxford University Press.

———. 1996. *Investor Capitalism: How Money Managers Are Changing the Face of Corporate America.* New York: Basic Books.

Uzzi, Brian. 1996. "The Sources and Consequences of Embeddedness for the Economic Performance of Organizations: The Network Effect." *American Sociological Review* 61:674–98.

———. 1997. "Social Structure and Competition in Interfirm Networks: The Paradox of Embeddedness." *Administrative Science Quarterly* 42:35–67.

Vogus, Timothy J., and Gerald F. Davis. Forthcoming. "Elite Mobilizations for Antitakeover Legislation, 1982–1990." In *Social Movements and Organization Theory,* ed. Gerald F. Davis, Doug McAdam, W. Richard Scott, and Mayer N. Zald. Cambridge: Cambridge University Press.

Wade, James B., Anand Swaminathan, and Michael Scott Saxon. 1998. "Normative and Resource Flow Consequences of Local Regulations in the American Brewing Industry, 1845–1918." *Administrative Science Quarterly* 43:905–35.

Watts, Duncan J. 1999. "Networks, Dynamics, and the Small-World Phenomenon." *American Journal of Sociology* 105:493–527.

Westphal, James D., Ranjay Gulati, and Stephen M. Shortell. 1997. "Customization or Conformity? An Institutional and Network Perspective on the Content and Consequences of TQM Adoption." *Administrative Science Quarterly* 42:366–94.

Westphal, James D., and Edward J. Zajac. 2001. "Decoupling Policy from Practice: The Case of Stock Repurchase Programs." *Administrative Science Quarterly* 46:202–28.

White, Harrison C. 1981. "Where Do Markets Come From?" *American Journal of Sociology* 87:514–47.

White, Lawrence J. 2001. "What's Been Happening to Aggregate Concentration in the United States? (And Should We Care?)." Department of Economics, New York University.

Whitley, Richard, and Laszlo Czaban. 1998. "Institutional Transformation and Enterprise Change in an Emergent Capitalist Economy: The Case of Hungary." *Organization Studies* 19:259–80.

Williamson, Oliver E. 1975. *Markets and Hierarchies: Analysis and Antitrust Implications.* New York: Free Press.

Windeler, Arnold, and Jorg Sydow. 2001. "Project Networks and Changing Industry Practices: Collaborative Content Production in the German Television Industry." *Organization Studies* 22: 1035–60.

Zajac, Edward J., and James D. Westphal. 1995. "Accounting for the Explanations of CEO Compensation: Substance and Symbolism." *Administrative Science Quarterly* 40:283–308.

Zald, Mayer N. 1993. "Organization Studies as a Scientific and Humanistic Enterprise: Toward a Reconceptualization of the Foundations of the Field." *Organization Science* 4:513–28.

Zuckerman, Ezra W. 1999. "The Categorical Imperative: Securities Analysts and the Illegitimacy Discount." *American Journal of Sociology* 104:1398–1438.

———. 2000. "Focusing the Corporate Product: Securities Analysts and De-diversification." *Administrative Science Quarterly* 45:591–619.

Part III

Intersections of the Economy

22 The State and the Economy

Fred Block and Peter Evans

RECENT WORK in economic sociology and related fields has challenged the familiar terms for analyzing the relationship between state and economy that have dominated much of the social science literature since Adam Smith ([1776] 1976).[1] Contemporary scholarship rejects the assumption, traditionally shared by both advocates and critics of market allocation, that state and market are distinct and opposing modes of organizing economic activity (Block 1994; Evans 1995; Fligstein 2001). In this chapter, we intend to extend and develop this alternative perspective and also demonstrate its value in recasting established debates. We will make our case by focusing on three specific substantive arenas—developing and transitional societies, advanced industrial welfare states, and supranational economic governance.

Our perspective can be briefly summarized in three general propositions. First, state and economy are not analytically autonomous realms but are mutually constituting spheres of activity. Second, both states and economies are embedded in societies that have specific institutional structures, and this embeddedness plays a critical role in both economic and political outcomes. Third, this embedding is dynamic; it is often reshaped by institutional innovations that reshape the ways that states and economies intersect. In the next part of the chapter, we will explain these propositions and then introduce the substantive sections to follow.

A DIFFERENT CONCEPTUAL FRAMEWORK

For too long, debates on the relationship between economy and state have centered on a single question—how large or small a role should the state play in the economy? Implicit in that question is the dubious assumption that the state and economy are separate analytic spheres that can function autonomously. Against this assumption, we insist that the state and the economy should be seen as mutually constituting spheres of activity—neither of which can function without the other (see also Migdal 2001). One side of this mutual dependence is not controversial; states obviously depend on the economy for the flows of revenue that finance state activity (Tilly 1990). This dependence helps explain why purely predatory forms of government rule are relatively rare; even the greediest rulers tend to learn that without placing limits on their predation, production will contract because people need some assurance that they will be able to retain some of the fruits of their labors (Levi 1988).

The reciprocal case for mutual dependence is more contested. The economy's dependence on the state tends to be flatly denied by free market theorists who argue that market economies function best with minimal government "interference" (Friedman and Friedman 1980; Hayek [1944] 1976). Economic sociologists have challenged this claim by arguing that even the most market-oriented economies depend on legal and political structures.[2] Weber ([1922] 1978) argued that the unique form of "rational capitalism" that became dominant in Western Europe depended heavily on the effectiveness of laws of property and contract designed to ensure that profits were generated primarily through productive activity rather than through parasitical extractions (see Swedberg 1998). This lesson was recently relearned when the application of "shock therapy" to facilitate a rapid transition to capitalism in Russia produced not rational capitalism, but an explosion of criminality because the legal and political structures were too weak to channel entrepreneurial activity into productive channels (Woodruff 1999; King 2003).

Karl Polanyi ([1944] 2001) deepened Weber's argument by showing that market economies rely on three critical inputs that cannot be supplied through market activity alone. He used the term *fictitious commodity* to characterize land, labor, and money because economic theorists must pretend that these items were produced for sale on the market in the same way as other goods (Block 2001). However, labor is simply the activity of human beings, land is nature divided into parcels, and the money that circulates in national economies almost always relies on the "full faith and credit" of one or another government. In all of these cases, the necessary activity of regulating the supply of these fictitious commodities falls to government and encompasses different initiatives. Regulating the supply of money, for example, includes the creation of a viable currency, the activity of central bankers, and oversight over banks and other financial institutions that shape the supply of credit. Adjusting the supply of labor includes policies that influence the in-migration and out-migration of people, education and technology policies, and social welfare policies designed to provide resources to households and individuals without sufficient employment income. Finally, managing the supply of land encompasses environmental planning, transportation policies, farm policies, and other land use planning. To be sure, there is no assurance that government will manage these fictitious commodities wisely; the point is rather that there is no clear alternative to government action.

The idea of the mutual constitution of state and economy is often expressed in the shorthand that economies are embedded within social and political structures. Our intention here is to deepen the embeddedness argument by clarifying *in what* the economy is actually embedded. Our argument is that market economies are embedded within a *civil society* that is both structured by, and in turn helps to structure, the state.[3]

Civil society, in our view, encompasses both the variety of nongovernmental associational activities from trade associations and fraternal organizations to trade unions, protest movements, political parties, and the "public sphere" in which citizens form their political preferences (Ehrenberg 1999; Habermas 1989; Keane 1988, 1998). There is considerable variation across societies both in the density of associational life and in the particular ways in which civil societies are structured (Putnam 1993, 2000). But civil societies are deeply penetrated by law and other governmental practices; both the structures and the responsibilities of trade unions or trade associations are significantly shaped by legal rules and institutionalized patterns of interaction with government officials. Yet, ideally, civil societies retain sufficient autonomy from the state to place significant limits and constraints on the exercise of governmental authority. As many theorists have insisted, the viability of democratic institutions rests ultimately on the capacity for political mobilization by citizens in civil society (Ehrenberg 1999; Keane 1988).

The substance of civil society is the activity of real human beings with associational ties forged out of kinship, neighborhood, ethnicity, religion, class, and other identities. These individuals are simultaneously economic actors and political actors. In both realms, they rely on normative understandings that are ultimately grounded in the interactional order. Norms of reciprocity, for example, facilitate both economic exchanges and political transactions in which citizens provide votes and politicians promise to pursue policies that meet their needs. A dense civil society that encompasses both associational ties and normative understandings plays a central role in the effective functioning of both economy and state (Evans 1997b).

At the same time, our view rejects the idea that strengthening civil society and producing more "social capital" is sufficient to solve society's problems (Smith and Kulynych 2002). We see the dynamism of civil society as a necessary but not sufficient condition for solving economic and political problems. For one thing, new policy ideas and proposals have to be created, disseminated, and legitimated. While this is more likely to occur in a society with a vigorous public sphere, there is nothing automatic about the process. Entrenched ideas can effectively preempt the policy space and preclude the development of new ideas. Moreover, economic or political elites often resist changing existing practices even in the face of considerable pressures from civil society. Hence, strategies that simply strengthen civil society can fall far short of meaningful social changes.

The triangular approach helps to overcome modes of thinking that attribute developmental successes or failures within particular societies to the operation of a single principle—for example, the scope given to market forces or the degree of state strength. It suggests instead that both developmental successes and failures should be understood in terms of the synergy or lack of synergy among civil society, economy, and the state. It implies multiple institutional routes to a successful economy and to effective governance (Block 1990). This approach also makes sense of the research findings of the growing body of literature that has analyzed the "varieties of capitalism"—the systematic variations in institutional practices among different contemporary market-oriented societies (Crouch and Streeck 1997; Hall and Soskice 2001b; Hollingsworth and Boyer 1997; Kitschelt et al. 1999; Orrù, Biggart, and Hamilton 1997). That these societies differ in labor relations, in the organization of the financial system, in the structure of corporations, and in systems for generating innovations is not the result of a purely economic or a purely statist logic; the differences are the result of the complex historical interplay among state, economy, and civil society.

There is no guarantee that such interplay will move automatically from one well-functioning "variety of capitalism" to another. Societies can suffer extended periods of institutional crisis in which any new initiatives are blocked by stalemate of competing social forces, and they can also experiment with policy directions that are ultimately abandoned because they lead nowhere (Polanyi [1944] 2001). There can be both positive and negative consequences of any specific form of embeddedness. The specific ways in which the economy is embedded in civil society and the specific institutional connections between civil society and the state can produce both dysfunctional and functional outcomes. It would also be misleading to portray embeddedness as static; something akin to the heavy hand of tradition limiting the options available to individuals. To be sure, the concept is intended to highlight the fact that individual economic action is always structured by certain understandings and institutional arrangements. But these understandings and arrangements are dynamic in market societies; there are considerable incentives for innovations and for the construction of new institutions to change the way that economic action is embedded.

Polanyi ([1944] 2001) sought to characterize this dynamism by arguing that market societies are continually being reshaped by two conflicting movements—the first is the movement for laissez-faire—to expand the scope of markets and the second is the movement for social protection to limit the scope of market forces. The movement for laissez-faire often demands the expansion and enforcement of the property rights of wealth holders, while the opposing movement frequently centers on securing social rights. Polanyi suggests that both of these movements operate through institutional innovations. The New Poor Law in England in 1834 was a triumph of the movement for laissez-faire; it sought to institutionalize a "free labor market" by eliminating outdoor relief and establishing the poorhouse as the only alternative to paid employment (Block and Somers 2003). Polanyi's critical insight was that even those who insist that all they want is to allow markets to work depend upon state power and institutional structures to achieve their ends. Shortly after the New Poor Law, the other movement passed the Factory Acts

that placed limits on the length of the working day and established a system of factory inspectors. In short, both movements changed the way that labor markets were embedded, and both altered the interface between civil society and the state.

Polanyi's double-movement framework is open to a variety of criticisms. It probably overstates the strength of the movement for laissez-faire within some of the non-Anglo-Saxon "varieties of capitalism," and the idea of expanding the scope of the market is problematic because all market arrangements require certain restrictions on who is allowed to do business and what can be bought or sold.[4] Nevertheless, Polanyi's formulation is still extremely useful in conveying that there are several different dynamics at play to change the ways that economic activities are embedded.

The key point is that embeddedness changes through institutional innovations. Sometimes this occurs largely on the terrain of civil society; through the creation of new associations or institutions intended to organize or coordinate economic activity (Fligstein 1990). But even in these cases, if the new forms are to endure, they have to be supported and legitimated by the state. Other times, the initiative comes through the state or by way of cooperation between actors in the state and actors in civil society (Evans 1995). But all of these innovations tend to reconfigure the state-economy relationship. Rather than seeing economic success as rooted in a particular configuration of states and markets, we emphasize the importance of this capacity for institutional reconfiguration to explain why some societies have been more successful than others in solving their political-economic problems (Evans 1995, 1997b; Sabel 1994).

In sum, our perspective offers a way to escape the familiar and often sterile debate between adherents of the "free market" on the one side and advocates of strengthening government regulation and public provision on the other. It directs attention instead to the qualitative issues of how and for what ends markets and states should be combined and what structures and practices in civil society will sustain a productive synergy of states and markets.

Three Substantive Areas

Our three propositions are of obvious relevance to the case of developing and transitional economies. The great success stories, including the extraordinary gains made by developmental states in East Asia—particularly Japan, South Korea, and Taiwan—cannot be explained either by "reliance on free markets" or "state-sponsored accumulation" (Evans 1995; Wade 1990). The developmental state must itself be understood as an institutional innovation whose success is explained by the intricate relationships connecting state, economy, and civil society. But recently, development and transition scholars have increasingly focused on the more numerous cases of failure, since over the last 25 years, many countries have experienced disappointing growth rates and significant reductions in the provision of essential public goods. But here as well, the most promising prospects for improvement center on institutional innovations that engage civil society in the reconstruction of economic governance.

The contemporary dilemmas of advanced industrial societies demand a similar kind of analysis. Here, the argument has centered on the welfare state with market liberals insisting that the overdeveloped systems of public provision in Western Europe have caused the slower growth and higher unemployment rates experienced by much of Europe as compared to the United States over the past 20 years. On the other side, defenders of the welfare state have insisted that generous public provision has been a critical part of a "Rhenish" variety of capitalism that has produced higher standards of living than the American model (Albert 1993). Yet at the current moment, the debate has reached an impasse. On the one side, a growing body of empirical work has failed to substantiate the claim that European economic performance has suffered because of generous welfare state provision (Huber and Stephens 2001; Lindert 2004; Swank 2002; Wilensky 2002; see also Huber and Stephens in this volume). On the other, it is also obvious that some of the most generous European welfare states have been and will be forced to retrench because current benefits levels are simply unsustainable (Huber and Stephens 2001). Our perspective focuses attention not on the quantitative issue of welfare state expansion or contraction, but on institutional innovations that modify the forms of public provision as societies struggle to redefine the goals of the welfare state.

Finally, at the global level of analysis, the necessity of institutional innovation is increasingly obvious, as is the importance of analyzing the novel linkages among state, civil societies, and economies that shape the possibilities for effective global economic governance. The East Asian economic crisis of 1997–98 offered a glimpse of the fragility of current forms of supranational economic governance and exposed the potential for failures of catastrophic proportions (Soros 2002; Stiglitz 2002). Moreover, we think these dangers are intensified by a current of opinion that espouses a contemporary variant of "market utopianism"— the belief that global market self-regulation can be the basis for a viable world economy. Avoiding a return to "depression economics" (Krugman 1999) depends on the ability of states and civil societies to shape new forms of global governance. While one can speak of a global civil society only as an emergent tendency, the bifurcation between the World Economic Forum and the World Social Forum—implied in their names—suggests the diversity of social forces that are attentive to these issues. Both of these organizations—in very different ways—represent efforts to escape market utopianism and construct new forms of governance. By definition, all of these efforts to construct global governance regimes are efforts at institutional innovation. But they come into direct conflict with the logic of global neoliberalism that imposes a kind of "institutional monocropping" that severely constrains the possibilities for innovation both within and across societies.

DEVELOPING AND TRANSITIONAL SOCIETIES

Development transforms political, economic, and social structures, creating new bases for productivity, ideally enabling people to "lead lives they have reason to value" (Sen 1999).[5] Defined in this way, "development" is the archetypal problem for theories of state and economy. That development is first and foremost about institutional transformation rather than simply growth or the accumulation of capital is now accepted canon (cf. Rodrik et al. 2002; Evans 2002). Douglass North's (1981) pioneering analysis of development among the original industrializers exemplifies the "institutional turn." In North's view of the expansion of markets, the state's role in the provision of norms and laws defining and protecting property rights is central. By emphasizing the importance of informal social norms in fostering (or impeding) development, he also makes it clear that markets cannot be disembedded from society.

Like North, Polanyi and Gerschenkron exemplify an institutional perspective on the dynamics of development in the European context. For Polanyi ([1944] 2001, 146), "The road to the free market [in England] was opened and kept open by an enormous increase in continuous, centrally organized and controlled interventionism." In short, the construction of the "free market" was an institutional innovation that required the active involvement of the state. Gerschenkron (1962) extended the argument, showing that English institutional innovations were insufficient for "late developers" such as Germany and Russia. Lacking individual capitalists able to assume risks at the scale required by modern technology, these countries depended on the state not just to construct markets but to serve as investment banker and to bear entrepreneurial risks.

In the period after World War II, even the rich nations of the North appeared to recognize that additional institutional innovation would be required to spread development to the South. Development became an ideologically explicit "project" (see McMichael 2000) because the nations of Asia, Africa, and Latin America faced substantial obstacles. The competitive gap between their economies and those of the industrialized North was larger than the one that European latecomers had faced. Their politically dominant local elites were wedded to agrarian structures that preserved privilege at the expense of productivity, and there was no reason to expect that more entrepreneurial elites would emerge "naturally."

If manufacturing was going to take its place along side agriculture, local manufacturers needed public investments in energy production and transportation and protection from rich country imports. Private investors also faced a collective action problem. Investment in manufacturing would make more sense if other local entrepreneurs were making complementary investments that would provide needed inputs; otherwise, investment seemed quixotic. Albert Hirschman (1958) provided an elegant vision of the sort of institutional innovation that could shift prevailing social perceptions of economic opportunity. For Hirschman (1958, 35), eliciting entrepreneurship in the simple sense of "the perception of investment opportunities and transformation into actual investments" was the key problem. The state could help induce private capitalists to play their role not only by supplying infrastructure but by building confidence among individual entrepreneurs that their initiatives were part of a general, mutually reinforcing set of investment decisions.

"Hirschmanian" institutional strategies worked during the fifties and sixties, for "third world" countries as different as India and Brazil, stimulating the emergence of local industrial elites and resulting in impressive rates of economic growth. Nonetheless, by the end of the 1970s, development strategies in Africa, Latin America, and South Asia were faltering. Despite impressive industrialization (Arrighi, Silver, and Brewer 2003), imports grew faster than exports, creating balance of payments problems. At the same time, state expenditures outran revenues, creating fiscal problems and massive external debt. Industrial transformation was clearly insufficient to give most of the citizens of the South the full possibility of "leading lives they had reason to value."

One of the reasons that the "development project" of the fifties and sixties failed to deliver was that its success required benign, capable state policymakers able to disentangle collective goals from the particular interests of elite private actors. Once the development project began to falter, this premise was quickly questioned. The ties that bound state actors to local elites and civil society appeared to be a perverse "antimarket" form of embeddedness rather than a means of generating entrepreneurship. State policies protecting local entrepreneurs from foreign competition led industrialists to focus on the unproductive quest for political favor rather than on competitiveness (Krueger 1974). At the same time, the development project was characterized as victimizing those who lacked strong connections to the state—most dramatically the peasantry (Bates 1981). At the extreme, predatory states like Mobutu's Zaire were aggregations of self-interested elites grabbing society's surplus for their own benefit without providing the collective goods necessary for growth or social protection.

There was much merit to the critique, but the simplistic policy conclusion that some drew from it—that a return to laissez-faire was the solution—was clearly wrong. As the first generation of "development projects" were falling into disarray, new models of institutional innovation, equally removed from the utopian notion of disembedded markets, were appearing elsewhere. Following Japan's footsteps, Korea, Taiwan, and Singapore were dramatically shifting their position in the world economic hierarchy, challenging Northern industrial supremacy with growth rates six times those of the Industrial Revolution. Even more impressive, the new model went beyond accumulation. Public investments propelled rapid rises in education levels and improvements in public health.

This new set of "developmental states" also involved tight connections between economy, state, and certain segments of civil society, but, as before, success required institutional innovation. While these innovations unquestionably depended on a unique confluence of local cultural and social structural features inserted into a particular geopolitical context, analytical features of broad relevance could also be extracted. Starting with Johnson's (1982) analysis of Japan, a massive literature, extending from institutionally oriented political economy (see, for example, Akyüz 1999; Amsden 1989; Chang 1994; Wade 1990) to mainstream development economics (see Meier and Rauch 2000, chap. 9) and the international policy community (see World Bank 1997), generated a surprising degree of consensus as to what made the model work.

The "East Asian miracles" engaged intensively with global markets while connecting state and civil society in the form of "embedded autonomy," the paradoxical ability to maintain autonomy from private elites while simultaneously developing close ties to them (Evans 1995). As in the earlier developmental project, state investment in essential modern infrastructure was combined with subsidies and selective protection against external competition. The big difference, as Amsden (1989) emphasizes, was the ability of the state to make its support contingent on local elites creating internationally competitive industrial capacity.

The possibility of being connected to, but still independent of, private economic elites depended in turn on the presence of capable, coherent state bureaucracies built on meritocratic recruitment and public service careers offering long-term rewards commensurate with those available in the private sector. These basic state characteristics predict more rapid economic growth, not just in East Asia, but across a broad range of developing countries (Evans and Rauch 1999).

None of this is to say that East Asia had discovered a formula that ensured a productive, dynamic relationship among economy, state, and civil society. As the financial crises of 1997–98 revealed, these developmental states can no more afford to rest on their institutional laurels than their predecessors could. To be sure, gains from the institutional innovations embodied in the "embedded autonomy" model still persist. Korea, Singapore, and Taiwan still continue to outperform all but a few countries in the global South (or, for that matter, in the North). What these East Asian cases offer is a double lesson. On the one hand, they show the magnitude of the gains that can flow from finding more effective ways of connecting state, economy, and civil society. At the same time, they make it clear that, unless the triangular relationship is periodically reinvented, even the most successful developmental performance will deterio-

rate over time. The challenge for analysts is trying to identify the next set of innovations, as, for example, in O'Riain's (2004) work on the "developmental network state."

"Transitional" Cases

Turning from developing to transitional countries, one might expect a very different set of findings and conclusions. Whereas relative insulation from global markets was one of the primary defining features of the state socialist countries that are now called "transitional," the states and social structures of the global South are the product of centuries of integration into the capitalist world economy. The extent to which the experience of transitional countries reinforces conclusions drawn from the developing cases is, therefore, striking.

Russia, one of the two most important "transitional" cases, demonstrates the pitfalls of trying to implant markets without thinking carefully about how they will connect with existing states and social structures. Terrified that the Soviet party-state would somehow survive, Russian "reformers" and their Western patrons tried to impose the formalities of Western market rules as quickly and thoroughly as possible. The results did not just disappoint from the point of view of preserving social protection. They also failed to deliver productivity-enhancing economic transformation and produced perverse effects in terms of effective legal norms and social order (cf. King 2002; King and Szelényi, this volume).

China and Vietnam supply contrasting cases suggesting that constructing innovative institutional hybrids based on local social structures makes for a more effective transition. Increased participation in global markets and internal shifts to market economies have been combined with caution in opening up capital markets, stubborn preservation of prior state structures, and efforts to avoid the complete erosion of socialist civil society. The result is a distinctly hybrid triangular relationship that has produced (after some hiatus in the case of Vietnam) rapid rates of growth.

China and Vietnam show that market disciplines and incentives can be a source of new dynamism in systems that had been dominated by an overbearing state apparatus. But it is critical that the old state apparatus continue to supply enough discipline over market actors to prevent the emergence of a Mafia-style, predatory capitalism as in Russia. Nee (2000, 64) emphasizes the "crucial role of the state in establishing a market economy" in the

Chinese case. Indeed, one could argue that these two Asian transitional successes represent a variation on the earlier success of the capitalist "Asian tigers," which were also examples of adding increased engagement with international markets to previously overbearing state apparatuses, while firmly preserving the state's role.[6]

The comparison of the world's two largest countries—China and India—underlines the extent to which developing and transitional countries yield common lessons. In both cases, size and relatively robust (if not agile) state apparatuses have allowed partial adaptation to global market liberalism and improved their economic performance as a result. At the same time, these countries have escaped, at least up to now, the fate of "would-be overconformers" such as Argentina among the developing countries and Russia among the transitional ones.

China and India are certainly not models that are easily copied or that are without pitfalls. The success of China's new romance with markets has depended in part on having inherited the advantages of a very egalitarian income distribution and exceptional provision—relative to its income level—of collective goods. How long the fruits of this inheritance will persist is unclear. Growing disparities between urban and rural areas and between the southeast coast and the interior of the country cannot help but create equally serious social tensions. Combined with the diminishing legitimacy of the ruling party and the normative confusion introduced by trying to maintain "capitalist Leninism," the sustainability of China's current trajectory cannot be assumed. The case of India is similar. Prior to the current move toward market liberalism, the cumbersome and confusing, but surprisingly effective, carapace of India's secular democracy managed to sustain political stability for half a century. The anxieties, uncertainties, and increased inequality inherent in the risky and less protective contemporary relations between state and economy may be as much of a threat to India's political system as increasing social disparities are to China's. Certainly, the dramatic recent examples of communal violence and the increasingly sectarian tone of political debate in India suggest that further reinvention must be on the agenda.

The Politics of Institutional Innovation

If developmental success requires continual reinvention of the triangular relationship connecting state, economy, and civil society, it is both an insti-

tutional problem and a political problem. Despite the fact that democracy is one of the central pillars of current global ideology, current models of economic governance in the global South do not lend themselves to building more effective connections between civil society and the state. The political model being purveyed globally combines the assumption that global markets are the best source of political discipline for profligate states with the oddly "statist" assumption that external "statelike" institutions of global governance, rooted in the societies and power structures of the industrial North, will be the most effective agents of institutional change in the countries of the South.

The results have been efforts to impose "cookie cutter" versions of advanced country institutions. This "institutional monocropping" (Evans 2002) ignores the basic logic of embeddedness. It does produce occasional "honeymoons" during which the enthusiasm of rich-country investors generates a brief spurt of financial flows, but there is little evidence that this works as a strategy of growth, to say nothing of a strategy of development. Again, Argentina offers a particularly dramatic case. Neither the economic discipline imposed by a complete opening to competition from foreign goods and investors, nor the "credible commitment" by the state to maintain the value of the currency, sufficed to convince private local or global elites to make investments that would expand local productive activities.

What is the alternative? Since we have already seen that the developmental state is a political tool of diminishing effectiveness, is there a possibility that civil society could bolster the inadequate disciplinary capacity of markets and states? More specifically, is the idea of some kind of bottom-up "democratic discipline" a utopian prospect? Despite the rhetorical hegemony of electoral democracy, the state of democratic institutions at the national level is discouraging. Since policy autonomy is limited, electoral success hardly guarantees success in forging new policies or in reconfiguring the triangular relation of state, economy, and civil society. Growing popular disengagement from the electoral process is a natural result. If one believes that the solutions are "more market," this political disengagement is not a problem. In fact, market liberals are suspicious that democratic politics will lead to populist pandering that diverts resources to unproductive welfare expenditures or outright corruption. If, however, we start from the assumption that engagement with civil society is central to both the effective functioning of the state and to developmental success (cf. Migdal, Kohli, and Shue 1994; Evans 1997b), then the anemic character of contemporary democracy is a real problem.

Yet there are some promising experiments at the local level. At least two disparate cases, the state of Kerala in India and the city of Porto Alegre in Brazil, have gained attention for successfully implanting deliberative democratic institutions. These institutions in turn have worked effectively to discipline state elites, reducing corruption and increasing the effectiveness of service delivery (see Heller 2001; Fung and Wright 2003; Baiocchi 2003). Unfortunately, there is no evidence that these innovations can be extended to have analogous effects on private elites, and it is not clear how they might be "scaled-up" to provide more general solutions to the "discipline" problem. Nonetheless, they remain hopeful exemplars in a panorama where institutional imagination seems to have atrophied. It would, indeed, be ironic if, in an era of globalization, the local ended up being the locus of needed institutional innovation.

Overall, developing and transitional cases underline the proposition that taking embeddedness seriously means rejecting simple "high modernist" formulas for the organization of states and markets (Scott 1998). The disappointing results of the current wave of institutional monocropping suggests that formulaic impositions on the global South are likely to undermine already precarious levels of social protection without producing any compensating acceleration of growth rates. In contrast, there are numerous examples in which innovative institutional changes at the national level in the global South have restructured the relationship of state, economy, and civil society in ways that have accelerated development. Early post–World War II "developmental states" worked for a time. East Asian developmental states worked better and longer. The odd hybrid capitalism of China and Vietnam has also produced impressive results. None of these institutional forms is a lasting solution. They must all be seen as temporary platforms on which to construct the next set of innovations.

This vision of institutional innovation raises an obvious question. Does it apply only to the global South and transitional countries, or is it a general frame? Our contention is that it applies equally well to the advanced industrial North, even though societal goals are defined less in terms of "development" and more in terms of preserving and expanding the quality of life associated with the "welfare state."

WELFARE STATES

In developed societies, debates over the welfare state closely parallel arguments over the optimal development strategy for developing and transitional societies. On the one side, market liberals insist that state provision of welfare interferes with the effective functioning of markets (McKenzie and Lee 1991; Friedman 1999). On the other, proponents of welfare state development generally focus on the negative social and political outcomes when societies depend on market processes alone to allocate income (Kuttner 1996; Piven and Cloward 1997). But for more than a century of this debate, both critics and advocates of welfare state provision have shared the underlying premise that states and markets are analytically separate realms each with its own autonomous logic. In the 1970s, this shared dualism produced some convergence in the arguments of market liberals and left-wing defenders of the welfare state. Market theorists argued that an "excess of democracy" had led politicians to expand welfare state spending beyond sustainable levels requiring significant cutbacks to restore the economy's health (Bacon and Eltis 1976; OECD 1977). Analysts on the left argued that the conflicting logics of legitimation and accumulation had produced an unsustainable expansion in public provision that necessitated either severe retrenchment or a definitive break with the logic of capitalism (Habermas 1975; O'Connor 1973).

But these formulations produced wildly inaccurate predictions. Western European nations have long spent far more than the United States on welfare state provision, and there have been few signs that the gap is narrowing (Huber and Stephens 2001). For a while, it was possible for analysts to argue that the Europeans were using a variety of protectionist measures to insulate their economies from the efficiency-reducing consequences of high welfare state spending. But during the 1980s and 1990s, processes of "globalization" eroded some of Europe's key protectionist measures. In theory, as investors within Europe were freed from controls that restricted their ability to send capital abroad and as trade barriers were reduced, those nations with large and expensive welfare commitments would start paying a more visible price for their inefficient choices. Facing floods of imported goods from more dynamic economies and steady outflows of investment capital in search of higher rates of return, these societies would be forced to reign in welfare spending to increase economic efficiency (Scharpf [1991] was a pioneer in anticipating the strains that globalization would place on European welfare states). However, a series of studies has found that the very large gaps in welfare spending between the United States and Western Europe persisted into the second half of the 1990s (Huber and Stephens 2001; Wilensky 2002). One study designed to test the specific impact of globalization concludes that "the preceding analysis offers little evidence for the conventional view that rises in capital mobility are systematically related to retrenchments, rollbacks and neoliberal structuring of the contemporary welfare state" (Swank 2002, 117). Furthermore, there is little support for the claim that welfare state generosity depresses rates of economic growth (Lindert 2004).

These findings highlight the need for an analysis of welfare state spending that begins not from a state-economy dualism, but from the recognition that state and economy are mutually constituting. In such a view, welfare state spending is not treated simply as a cost that is imposed on the economy, but as a key input into core economic processes (Block 1987a). Recent work in the "varieties of capitalism" literature has begun to fill out this argument. Germany and Sweden are examples of societies that have focused their manufacturing economies on diversified quality production (DQP)—sophisticated products that require high levels of employee skill and commitment. It follows that high levels of welfare state spending for pensions, for unemployment, and for training and retraining programs are a critical ingredient in the labor-management cooperation that is necessary for DQP (Esteven-Abe, Iversen, and Soskice 2001; Hall and Soskice 2001a; Soskice 1999; Streeck 1992, 1997). These cases stand in stark contrast to less generous welfare states, such as the United States and the United Kingdom, where DQP plays a far less important economic role. But even in the less generous welfare states, public provision plays a critical role in the effective functioning of the economy. For example, outlays on public old-age pensions can be understood as a form of productive investment because reducing economic insecurity for the elderly has positive consequences for prime age workers. It simultaneously reduces the economic burden of caring for their aging parents and provides a palpable feeling of security about their own futures. Both of these effects probably help sustain higher levels of cooperation between employees and management (Block 1990, 82–85).

But if welfare states provide key economic inputs, then the welfare state conversation should not be restricted—as it often has been—to the richest developed societies. One would expect to find strong pressures for expanded public provision in developing societies, and this is, in fact, the case. Successful late industrializers such as Taiwan and South Korea have been expanding their welfare states, albeit not always following European or North American models (Aspalter 2001; Tang 2000). And there is a growing debate about how poorer developing nations can do more to stabilize income among the poorest population groups, as it has become more apparent that this income instability is itself an obstacle to development (Lustig 2001). The irony is that the "stabilization" policies imposed on developing nations by the World Bank and the International Monetary Fund are responsible for some of the greatest income shocks experienced by households in the developing world (Lustig 2001). As we will touch on later, this is another important reason why the current structures of global governance are now the subject of fierce contestation.

Explaining Welfare State Development

Moving beyond the dualist analysis of welfare states also requires rethinking the conditions under which welfare states developed. Both critics and defenders of the welfare state often invoke a class power explanation in which welfare state provision is seen as a victory of the organized working-class movement—either directly when carried out by social democratic parties or indirectly, when implemented by parties struggling to contain the influence of working-class movements (Korpi 1983). Telling this history without recognizing the central role of working-class movements would be deeply mistaken (Hicks 1999), but recent work has begun to complicate the story considerably. One complexity is to recognize that while the initiative for welfare state development has usually come from working-class movements or political leaders, business interests—both directly and indirectly—have often played active roles in shaping the particular institutional forms of welfare state provision (Mares 2001; Swenson 1997, 2002). Another complexity is to recognize the ongoing processes of adjustment and adaptation through which successive political administrations modify the design and organization of particular welfare state programs.

Often this works through party alternation; when the party that had been in opposition comes into power, it might repeal some elements of its opponent's welfare state initiatives and retain others—producing over time a kind of evolutionary selection mechanism (Glyn 2001; Pierson 1996).

Both of these complexities are consistent with placing civil society at the center of the analysis of welfare states. It is not one group—labor—but the array of different groups in civil society—including labor, business, and other interest groups—that has produced varying arrays of public provision in different societies. But it is also in the public sphere that societies make judgments about which welfare state programs are working, which require redesign or repeal, and which are the best ways to finance welfare provision. It is probably through such debates within the public sphere, for example, that most European societies have opted to fund their expensive welfare states in ways that do not place a heavy tax burden on business interests. But it has also been through ongoing consultations among peak organizations of business and labor that business groups have come to understand some of the productive consequences of welfare state programs. Hence, it is within a particular civil society that diverse groups come to perceive their own particular interests. The consequences can be intense social polarization over welfare state spending as well as effective and durable class compromises.

Welfare state institutions are also a paradigmatic case of the dynamic process by which the boundary between civil society and the state is constantly being renegotiated. For example, a common type of unemployment insurance—the Ghent system—that gives responsibility for the administration of funds to trade unions has been an important element in achieving high rates of union density in certain countries (Swenson 2002). More generally, specific welfare state programs often help to construct political constituencies that then serve as major defenders of the same programs in electoral contests. At the same time, welfare state programs—from the earliest public health initiative in Western Europe—can also be seen as part of the process by which states seek to influence and control the behavior of citizens (Foucault 1977; Scott 1998). Most recently, theorists of the "new paternalism" have recycled a very old theme—the desirability of states structuring assistance in ways that would wean recipients away from bad habits such as sexual promiscuity and lack of work discipline (Mead 1986; Block and Somers 2003). In short, virtually every new welfare state program produces new institutional connections between state and civil society.

Recognizing the economic functions of welfare state spending and the embeddedness of welfare regimes within civil societies makes it seem highly unlikely that Western Europe will soon shift to the U.S. model of far more limited welfare state spending. However, it is also a mistake to ignore the significant indicators of stress within contemporary welfare states. Some of these stresses have already been addressed through incremental retrenchment efforts designed to contain costs, particularly for pension programs. In other countries, particularly Germany, strains on the pension system are already serious, and major reforms will be necessary to put the system of old-age pensions on a sustainable basis (Hinrichs 2001; Huber and Stephens, this volume). But beyond these immediate economic pressures, there lie deeper problems. The European welfare states were consolidated in the 1940s, 1950s, and 1960s when the industrial working class was still growing and married women were working primarily in the home at domestic tasks. When these trends were reversed in the decades that followed, the tension between the existing forms of the welfare state and social needs increased (Block 1990; Esping-Andersen 1999). Three of these tensions are particularly important. First, the "industrial" welfare state started from a basic homogenization of social life; programs were based on the idea that people move through the life course in basically similar patterns. Postindustrial developments, however, tend to produce a pluralization of social life (Offe 1996) with greater unevenness in work careers and increasingly complex patterns of family life. Second, the contraction of industrial jobs combined with obstacles to the growth of the service sector have led to substantially higher unemployment rates in much of Europe and the expansion of marginal and temporary employment. This has created new dangers of a marginalized population—often young—at risk for social exclusion (Esping-Andersen 1999; Rosanvallon 2000). Third, even some of the most advanced European welfare states have been slow to develop the range of services and supports needed to support the movement of women into paid labor. Esping-Andersen (1999) has argued that this neglect has been a factor in declining European birth rates that will ultimately place more strain on welfare state financing.[7]

These changes have also weakened some of the established normative supports for the welfare state. The pluralization of both work trajectories and forms of family life has undermined the appeal of universal programs that provide a single set of benefits to all recipients. While some view these strains as indicators of the impending death of the European welfare state, they can also be seen as challenges that will produce a renewal of welfare state policies.

Possibilities for Institutional Innovation

While our argument here is necessarily tentative and speculative, we want to suggest that the last years of the twentieth century and the early years of the twenty-first century might ultimately be recognized as beginning a major new epoch in welfare state history.[8] This new epoch is suggested through the emergence of new normative foundations for welfare state spending, the appearance of new policies, and a process of institutional innovation. To be sure, this remains a terrain of struggle; some of the innovations and new ideas have been embraced both by market liberals who are hostile to the welfare state and by theorists and politicians who favor one or another "third way" between market liberalism and social democracy (Giddens 1994, 2000). Hence, the situation continues to be in flux; these innovations could foreshadow a renewal of the welfare state as well as a deeper crisis.

One of the new normative justifications is an emphasis on "social inclusion." The concept focuses attention on those individuals and households whose lack of access to key resources makes it difficult to function as full members of society. Since a just society must pursue policies to facilitate social inclusion, the key policy issue becomes how to distribute resources to minimize social exclusion. This rhetoric has made inroads even in the United States; in his 2000 presidential campaign, George W. Bush made extensive use of the Children's Defense Fund's slogan—"Leave no child behind" to convey his message of "compassionate conservatism."[9]

Another new normative justification has emerged out of feminist concerns with the "ethic of care" (Tronto 1993). The argument is that the quality of care of dependent populations such as children, the elderly, and the infirm is a crucial social indicator. With the shrinking of the traditional housewife role, societies experience a growing "care deficit" (Hochschild 1997). Since neither the market nor bureaucracies are reliable mechanisms to produce quality care, new arrangements are necessary to reduce this deficit (Jenson and Sineau 2001; Meyer 2000).

These normative arguments are being widely debated, and they have generated new policy initiatives that could prefigure welfare state renewal. On the issue of social exclusion, France has transformed its system of family allowances that had its origins in right-wing and Catholic doctrines. Some of the child allowance funding is now used to finance a guaranteed minimum income program designed to combat social exclusion among the youthful unemployed (Levy 1999). This is part of a more general move toward substituting income-tested benefits that place far less strain on government budgets than universal benefits. Advocates of income-testing programs argue that they can redistribute income without producing the stigma or degradation that was historically associated with means-tested programs. This logic of income testing is further developed in benefit programs that are integrated into the tax systems such as the Earned Income Tax Credit in the United States or the Canadian Old Age Security and Child Tax Benefits (Myles and Pierson 1997). These are variants of the negative income tax where recipients who fall below a certain income level receive a government transfer—a negative tax payment.

Some analysts have followed this idea to its logical conclusion and have argued that the future of the welfare state lies in the provision of an Unconditional Basic Income (UBI) to all citizens (Standing 2002; Suplicy 2002; Van Parijs 1992). By providing everyone with a subsistence income, governments would eliminate the need for a wide variety of specific insurance programs designed to protect individuals and households from such contingencies as unemployment, family dissolution, and disability. While UBI is still extremely controversial, the debates around it have produced new visions of how the welfare state might evolve.

On the care issue, the focus of new policies is on developing debureaucratized forms of service delivery (Block 1987b, 29–33; see also Rothstein 1996) either by creating new and more decentralized public agencies or by using state funds to encourage the expansion of nongovernmental organizations. These latter initiatives are distinct from the privatization schemes advocated by market liberals who want to extract the government from responsibility for providing services. The difference lies in the recognition that continuous government budgetary commitments will be necessary to assure quality care for those with only limited incomes.

One of the most interesting of the initiatives has been the development of the "social economy" in the province of Quebec over the past 15 years

(Levesque and Ninacs 2000; Mendell 2002; on community development initiatives in the United States, see Simon 2001). This is a broad effort to strengthen economic development through new institutions including social funds that support investment by cooperatives, nonprofits, and small businesses. Most relevant to the current discussion is that activists have mobilized in support of service delivery through employee cooperatives and other nonprofit agencies in a period of intense budgetary pressures on the provincial government. As a result, child care and home health assistance are increasingly being provided through new forms of collaboration between the public sector and networks of newly created employee cooperatives. From these kinds of examples, one can extrapolate a vision of the welfare state based on a new division of labor between government and a revitalized civil society (Castells and Himanen 2002; Unger 1998; Archibugi 2000).

To be sure, in the first years of the twenty-first century, these possible signs of welfare state renewal have not been the main focus of media or scholarly attention. The big story—almost everywhere—continues to focus on the powerful economic pressures to limit welfare state expenditures and a growing public disillusionment with the ability of politics and government to make significant changes. But if our emphases on the productiveness of welfare state spending and the long-term capacity of civil societies to produce institutional innovations are even partly correct, then it is important to take seriously scenarios of welfare state renewal—as unlikely as they may seem in the short term.

SUPRANATIONAL INSTITUTIONS AND GLOBAL GOVERNANCE

In the contemporary "post-Westphalian" world, analysis of the interaction of state and economy can no longer be confined to the level of the nation-state. Nor can the analysis of the associational structures of civil society be confined to the national level. Just as markets must be analyzed at both global and national levels, governance is now embodied in "statelike" institutions, not just at the national (and subnational) levels, but at the supranational level as well. Likewise, the social groups and organizations that make "civil society" a political actor operate transnationally as well as nationally. A multilevel perspective on state and economy complicates the analysis, but contemporary dilemmas cannot be comprehended without such a perspective.

The multilevel dynamics of state and economy play themselves out in different ways in different regions of the world. In the South, global markets and global governance looked like institutional impositions controlled by others long before cross-border ties were described as "globalization." The states of the North have a different relation to the global political economy. In addition to their economic and political-military power as individual states, they exercise a disproportionate share of control over global governance institutions. The intricate ties binding Northern state apparatuses to the private elites that run global corporations further accentuate the different ways in which North and South confront the multilevel dynamics of the global economy.[10]

Despite the complexity and variation, the themes that have been central to our analysis of both rich and poor countries reemerge again in a multilevel analysis as useful general lenses of the triangular relation among state, economy, and civil society. It is sometimes argued that national markets are always embedded, but that global markets really are beyond institutional control. But this is a mischaracterization; the emergence of global markets has been fundamentally dependent on the creation of an impressive array of new global governance institutions. Markets do not just "spring up" at the transnational level any more than they did at the national level. They depend on an intricate array of political and legal innovations. To be sure, global governance institutions are even more likely than national ones to be biased and inadequate, and even more difficult to connect to civil society in ways that are effective.

The dilemmas of the Polanyian "double movement" play themselves out most dramatically at the global level (cf. Silver and Arrighi 2003), as do the dynamics of institutional innovation. Possibilities for institutional innovation depend on interaction among local, national, and global levels. The process of construction of new global institutions exemplifies (for better or worse) the process of institutional innovation. In their current form, the most powerful of the global institutions are an increasingly important impediment to institutional innovation at the national level. At the same time, renovated global governance institutions could be a potentially powerful stimulant to institutional innovation at other levels. It is hardly surprising that global governance institutions have become targets of transnational mobilization by such a variety of civil society groups (Evans 2000; Khagram, Riker, and Sikkink 2002).

Nation-States and Global Governance

A multilevel analysis should still start with the nation-state. Far from being "irrelevant" or "eclipsed," state institutions at the national level continue to play a key role in the operation of global markets, even as those same institutions are being transformed by the global markets that they helped create. While the global market liberal regime may inadvertently end up fatally weakening the nation-state, this is not its political agenda (cf. Sassen 1998). Constructing markets and securing the property rights of global corporate actors still requires enhancing certain kinds of governance capacity at the national as well as at the global level.

The dependence of global corporations on their home states (Wade 1996) ranges from the most general tasks, like protecting the value of the currencies in which their major assets are held, to concrete mercantilist tasks like extracting legal concessions from other countries in which these corporations invest. The key assets of these corporations are often intangible,[11] which increases their need for state support in securing returns from their property (Arrow 1962). Even a powerful home state apparatus is not likely to suffice; willing and able state apparatuses in those countries where they market their goods are also necessary (Evans 1997a).

Nor is there any logical reason to expect that opening markets to international competition will reduce the necessity for domestic regulation. As his pithy title—*Freer Markets, More Rules*—indicates, Steven Vogel's (1996) analysis of the consequences of increased openness in advanced industrial countries suggests the opposite. Vogel shows that the process of increasing the exposure of national industries such as telecommunications and banking to greater international competition actually involves more elaborate rules that ultimately are enforced by national regulatory institutions.

The crucial role of state capacity at the national level is perhaps clearest in the preeminent globalized economic arena—finance. One of the lessons of the Asian financial crisis was how great a danger inadequately regulated domestic financial markets could pose for international investors. Korea, for example, prompted by both the desire to conform to prevailing global norms and the increasingly international orientation of its own local elites, relinquished controls over international financial flows

before constructing appropriate mechanisms for regulating national financial markets, with catastrophic results. Analysts of global financial markets, such as Barry Eichengreen (1998, 8), drew the obvious conclusion from the East Asian financial crisis "as in other forms of financial regulation, it is smart to err in the direction of caution—to be absolutely sure that the necessary preconditions are in place before opening the capital account."

Even if the national regulatory capacities on which the survival of global markets depends are successfully preserved, national capacities to offer social and environmental protections and collective goods such as health and education could still be destroyed. For private elites and, even more, for their political allies managing the apparatus of the nation-state, the supposed power of global markets is the perfect excuse. Confronted with demands for social protection, taxing the returns on capital, or preserving basic workplace rights, politicians and state officials can say, with absolute sincerity, "My hands are tied by global market liberalism."

It is hardly surprising that contemporary global governance institutions "tie the hands" of national political actors trying to respond to demands for social protection while facilitating the ability of those same national political actors to service the needs of transnational corporate actors. Corporate elites, powerful actors in civil society as well as in markets, were effectively shaping the construction of global governance institutions while other groups, trade unions for example, were still fully occupied by battles at the national level. Yet the current relationship between global governance and civil society should not be taken as foreordained and unchangeable.

Global Governance Institutions

Immediately after World War II, it seemed that the construction of global public institutions would mean an extension of the democratic, social rights state that was being reconstructed in Europe and prevailed in an attenuated form in the United States. The United Nations "system" of international organizations with its initial emphasis on universal human rights was the most conspicuous example, but there was also a significant attempt to incorporate social rights into global economic governance as well.

The Havana Charter, approved in 1948 by 53 nations from both North and South to set up an "International Trade Organization," captured the prevailing views toward global economic governance. Rather than simply a device for removing barriers to the flow of goods and capital, the ITO would have had a real governance role. For example, a preparatory paper by eventual Nobel laureate Jan Timbergen made the argument that access to markets should be contingent on effective social protection:

> The community of countries adhering to a full-employment policy should have the right to restrict their imports from those other countries that have not followed an adequate employment policy. In order to avoid . . . deliberate nationalist trade restrictions, its supervision should be placed in the hands of an international agency, perhaps the International Trade Organization. (Quoted in Levinson 2002, 22)

While this kind of vision was never represented organizationally in the system of global economic governance, it did become embodied diffusely in the post–World War II international system that Ruggie (1982) called "embedded liberalism," helping to create the almost 25-year-long "golden age of capitalism."

The ITO was stillborn primarily because of opposition from the American corporate elite. The surviving institutions of global economic governance were the "Bretton Woods twins"—the World Bank (International Bank for Reconstruction and Development) and the International Monetary Fund. "The Bank" and the "The Fund" were intended in principle to provide collective goods: grants and low-cost loans for public infrastructure and development projects in the case of the Bank and assistance to counterbalance the volatility of global fluctuations in currency values in the case of the Fund. The price of U.S. (and other rich-country) support for this provision of collective goods was, however, a set of thoroughly undemocratic rules for the governance of the two organizations themselves (Evans and Finnemore 2001).

Over time, the roles of the Bank and the Fund have shifted to focus on lending and the enforcement of "conditionality" in the global South rather than reconstruction and exchange rate stability among the countries of the industrialized North. The Fund especially has come to look more and more like an apparatus for protecting the financial assets of Northern creditors and administering the enforcement of their preferred economic policies, rather than providing the countries of the South with insulation from the volatility (and occasional irrationality) of global financial markets. Consequently, the undemocratic character of their governance has become more oppressive. If the

Bretton Woods twins have long appeared coercively intrusive from the point of view of the South, the World Trade Organization and multilateral agreements like the WTO and North American Free Trade Agreement are beginning to look the same way in the North. Barenberg and Evans (2002, 28) summarize the impact of NAFTA's Chapter 11 on U.S. governance as follows:

> [T]he substantive rules of the NAFTA model embody to an astonishing degree the "restorationist" program . . . to bring back the pre–New Deal economic constitution under which property holders' common-law rights are strictly protected against regulation in the name of public welfare—a constitution designed originally to block the advent of the modern regulatory state and, today, to roll back the regulatory state.

The central issue is whether the current focus on market access and global protection of property rights will continue to dominate the agendas of global governance institutions. Even more grimly, the current weaknesses of these institutions raise the specter of a failure of global governance in which volatile global markets generate the kind of chaos and devastation that partially destroyed the global economy in the first half of the twentieth century. But is it possible that the trajectory of governance at the global level could be pushed to replicate the trajectory of governance at the level of the nation-state, as it occurred in the industrialized countries from the nineteenth to the mid–twentieth century, complementing protection of property rights with protection of social rights? In our perspective, the answer depends on the triangular relation connecting states, markets, and civil society, and most importantly on the kind of agency that civil society is able to exercise.

Countervailing Tendencies

Given the forcefulness of the current movement back to a nineteenth-century priority on expanding markets and protecting property rights, it would be puzzling if there were no evidence of a Polanyian "double movement" today. While global social movements do not yet have the power and momentum that enabled social movements in nineteenth and twentieth centuries to reshape the character of the state at the national level, they are persistent and proliferating. Likewise, just as the early-nineteenth-century nation-state contained the germ of a more democratic construction of economic policy, so the early-twenty-first-century institutions of global economic governance contain possibilities for democratic control.

The original elements of post–World War II global governance, however beleaguered they may be, have not evaporated. Hampered by lack of power and resources, the various organizations that comprise the UN system nonetheless continue to serve as organizational focal points for normative change and the organization of transnational civil society. Whether it is facilitating the enthusiasm for environmental change in Rio in 1992, or helping to generate a "normative cascade" (Finnemore and Sikkink 1998) around issues of women's rights through a series of global women's conferences, the UN system continues to serve as a catalyst for normative change.

Even with respect to the core organizations of global economic governance, the picture is not quite as bleak as it at first appears. Despite the undemocratic character of the Bank, the Fund, and (in practice) the WTO, they may still be a significant improvement over the traditional "anarchy" of the interstate system, especially as the United States, unconstrained by rival superpowers, slips into a "might makes right" mode of global dominance. For the weak, institutionalization (even biased institutionalization) is generally an improvement over individual confrontations with the strong. For Costa Rica, being able to take its disputes to a WTO arbitration panel, however small its chances of winning, is still likely to be an improvement on having to confront the United States behind closed doors in bilateral negotiations.

This point becomes even more interesting when one examines the internal governance at the Bank, the Fund, and the WTO. The executive board, which is the Fund's working governance body, usually makes decisions by consensus, and consensus must include the 11 (out of 24) executive directors who represent the countries of the South. So far the South has been unable to muster the political will to overcome the obviously formidable collective action problems necessary to take advantage of this structure, but the possibility remains. At the same time, the Bank has shown itself vulnerable to pressure from NGOs and social movements, shifting its positions on environmental issues and the importance of building in "participation" of those who are affected by projects (see Fox and Brown 1998; Keck and Sikkink 1998; Narayan 1994). In the WTO, the formal rules give each member state an equal vote. The fact that decisions are made in practice by "consensus" allows an informal oligarchy of rich countries (led by the United States) to shape agendas and outcomes, but the countries of the South have occasionally managed to overcome their daunting collective action problems to block the rich country oligarchy or force compromise (e.g., in the selection of the current director-general, in Seattle in 1999, and in Doha in 2001).

These possibilities for "democratization" should not be exaggerated. They would lead, at best, toward a "Westphalian democracy," empowering the representatives of national elites, not communities or individuals. To move beyond Westphalian democracy, a broader range of actors must gain access to global governance institutions. But this is precisely what a broad segment of the multistranded, transnational "global justice movement" is trying to do (cf. Khagram, Riker, and Sikkink 2002). Creative new organizational forms like ATTAC (Association for the Taxation of Financial Transactions for the Aid of Citizens) (see Ancelovici 2002) have helped redefine the relationship between "civil society" and "globalization." Old organizational forms like trade unions are trying to reinvent themselves as transnational alliances (Anner 2002). Groups whose interests in redefining the way the economy works grow out of the efforts to overturn "micro" level injustices find themselves embedded in transnational networks (Keck and Sikkink 1998; Thayer 2000).

The basic challenge facing the current "multilevel" system of economic governance can be simply restated. Can it succeed in delivering globally what the nation-state succeeded in delivering in the industrial North during the mid-twentieth-century "golden age of capitalism," namely complementing property rights with a wide range of social rights, thereby combining economic growth with general improvements in welfare? Success will depend on a complementary combination of astute exploitation of the opportunities for "Westphalian" democratization already contained within existing global institutions and effective political action on the part of oppositional social movements at both global and national levels. Most of all, success will depend on multiple forms of institutional innovation: reconstructing existing global governance institutions, inventing new organizational vehicles for transnational mobilization, and finding better ways to stimulate "norm cascades."

Conclusion

State and economy are not analytically separable spheres that can function autonomously from each other. Consequently, centering debate around the question, "Which is better, more state or more market?" is a theoretically sterile approach. We gain both analytic leverage and the capacity to conceptualize effective politics and policies by reframing the discussion around the insight that institutional structures are required both to contain and to expand markets and that these structures are built through the interaction of state and civil society.

Our approach began with the insight that market economies, even the most ideologically laissez-faire market economies, remain always embedded in *civil society*, a concrete set of social relationships, cultural understandings, and institutional and organizational forms that shape the possibilities for economic action. Civil society is structured by state institutions, including legal rules and the organizational practices of government, but civil societies also shape state action and state structures. We then traced the triangular relationship among state, economy, and civil society in three very different contexts: the developing and transitional societies of the global South, the welfare states of the rich countries of the global North, and the multilevel relationships that constitute the contemporary global political economy. In each of these contexts, moving beyond the question of "more state or more market" has helped us to clarify the insights of recent scholarship and shed light on central policy debates.

The current literature on developing and transitional countries shows that trying to generate sustained growth on the basis of externally imposed systems of economic incentives produces disappointing results. At the same time, "more state" is no panacea. Development has always required active involvement of the state, but the states have also been deeply implicated in decay and stagnation. Success depends, not on finding some magical balance between market and state, but on constructing institutions that enable the productive interaction of state structures, market actors, and civil society. Developmental "success stories" in different regions and time periods have been built on institutional innovations that reconstruct relations between state and civil society. From Gerschenkron's analysis of nineteenth-century European latecomers to twenty-first-century hybrids like China and Vietnam, successful innovations embed market rules in civil society and deploy the legal and organizational capacities of the state in ways that build the potential for economic and social transformation.

This perspective has implications for two key substantive debates over development strategy.

First, it suggests that seeing the divide in development strategies in terms of "accumulation versus social protection" is as misguided as seeing it as "states versus markets." A single-minded focus on what are supposedly "accumulation-oriented" policies will be self-defeating if it undermines the way in which markets are embedded in civil society or the ability of the state to supply the legal and institutional framework that both markets and civil society require. Indeed, this was the problem in dramatic neoliberal failures like Russia and Argentina. Despite being seen by the citizenry as "legitimate" in the sense of being the only "reasonable" alternative, even as they move to the brink of failure, market liberal strategies still do not work because the ability of markets to produce development is intrinsically dependent on being connected to civil society and state structures.

Second, this perspective makes it possible to reframe the "democracy and capitalist development" debate. Older views in which democracy (even defined narrowly as the selection of political elites) is suspected of "antiaccumulation" populist pandering are too jaundiced. A more indeterminate view, such as that offered by Przeworski and his collaborators (2000), fits better. To be sure, democratic politics may fail to facilitate interaction between states and civil society consistent with effective markets, and authoritarian regimes may sometimes succeed in developing systematic, economically effective, ties to civil society. Nonetheless, democratic institutions that enable civil society to connect effectively to the administrative apparatus of the state are more likely to produce development than arbitrary rule by elites with highly selective and idiosyncratic connections to the rest of society. The economic impact of political regimes must be judged by the ways in which they mold the structure of the triangular relationship among state, economy, and civil society.

When our analysis turns from developing and transitional countries to the rich, Northern welfare states at the other pole of the contemporary global political economy, the analytical lessons are surprisingly parallel. Once again, "how much state versus how much market" is not the question. Likewise, it is a mistake to frame the debate in terms of "trade-offs" between welfare provision and economic growth. The claim that the development of welfare institutions necessarily undercuts growth lacks empirical support. On the other hand, the necessity for institutional innovations to sustain both growth and welfare outcomes is as clear in rich countries as in poor ones.

Our review of the literature suggests that welfare spending must be recognized as a key input into the effective functioning of national economies, and that conflicts and debates within civil societies—including the mobilization of labor and business—play a central role in adjusting and readjusting the ways that welfare state programs are financed and organized. We also recognize that in the current period, the European welfare states are undergoing increasing strain both as a result of budgetary pressures and a mismatch between some of the historic beneficiaries of welfare spending and current social needs. But rather than imagine large-scale welfare state retrenchment and convergence on the Anglo-American model of much less generous welfare spending, we suggested a number of indicators of potential reconstruction of advanced welfare states. One direction for this reconstruction would build on the Quebecois "social economy" with public sector subsidies for the provision of "caring" services through employee cooperatives nurtured and supported within civil society.

Examining the multilevel complexities of the global political economy further vindicates our emphasis on analyzing states and economies as mutually constitutive. The past 60 years have witnessed the construction of statelike governance institutions aimed at trying to manage an increasingly integrated global economy. Here, as well, we have seen that both efforts to expand the scope of markets globally and initiatives to place limits and restraints on global market forces require the construction of global institutions. Not surprisingly, the specific forms in which supranational governance is embodied are the target of increasing mobilization within an emergent global civil society that extends from the corporate citadels of the World Economic Forum to the popular insurgencies of the World Social Forum.

Looking at the supranational level makes it clear that institutional innovations at different levels are interdependent in a variety of ways. Arguments that globalization has eclipsed the nation-state notwithstanding, national politics, and especially the politics of the world's only remaining superpower, are a powerful impediment to institutional innovations at the global level. Just as in national societies, the exertion of raw political power can produce political stalemates that prevent institutional renovation at the global level. At the same time, the relationship between global and national political institutions is partially symbiotic. Global governance institutions depend on the complementary capacities of national governments, and a host of global organizations, public and private, have sprung up to aid the regulatory efforts of nation-states. What is worrisome, however, is that the "rules of the game" currently enforced by global governance institutions can represent a powerful constraint against institutional innovations at the national level, with a particularly powerful impact on the poor countries of the South, as in the case of what we have called "institutional monocropping."

Interdependencies among different levels of governance imply potential for a virtuous cycle of multilevel institutional innovation as well. Changes in global governance could open up space for institutional innovations at the national level that could accelerate development in poor countries and encourage new welfare state initiatives in rich ones. Innovations at the national level that deepen democracy and economic vitality would, in turn, expand the local roots of transnational constituencies working toward further institutional renewal at the global level, allowing the cycle to repeat itself.

Virtuous circles of institutional innovation are possibilities, not predictions. Nonetheless, for the first time in human history, the basic institutional arrangements that govern global society are the subject of debates that include participants from every corner of the globe and every social status. The existence of this debate is, in itself, a source of hope that the future will hold more fruitful forms for the triangular linkage of state, economy, and civil society.

NOTES

We would like to thank the editors, Antonio Barros de Castro, and Frank Dobbin for their comments on an earlier draft and Sarah Staveteig for her impeccable research assistance. The order of the authors' names is alphabetical.

1. This essay builds on and seeks to go beyond the analysis in Fred Block, "The Roles of the State in the Economy," that appeared in the first edition of *The Handbook of Economic Sociology*. Readers are directed to that discussion for a more extensive critique of conventional perspectives on the state and the economy.

2. Even in economics, some recent work on the role of the state in defining property rights has become more respectful toward the state's economic functions. See, particularly, Barzel 2002.

3. In developing this argument, we have been influenced by the formulations of Burawoy 2003. We are also following Zukin and DiMaggio (1990) in conceptualizing embeddedness as having multiple dimensions—it is simultaneously social, legal, political, and cognitive. See also Krippner 2001 for a valuable critique of the use of the embeddedness concept.

4. Most regulatory initiatives simultaneously eliminate some market opportunities and create new ones. For exam-

ple, social insurance schemes simultaneously reduce the labor market participation by those eligible for assistance—what Esping-Andersen (1990) has termed "decommodification" of labor, but they simultaneously create marketing opportunities for those who can now sell more to those with benefit income.

5. This section draws substantially on Evans 2001.

6. The contrast between the agonies of Russia and transitional success stories in Hungary, Poland, and the Czech Republic reinforces the proposition that locally constructed hybridity produces better results than institutional monocropping (cf. Stark and Bruszt 1998).

7. The strains come from smaller cohorts entering the workforce needed to finance the retirement of larger cohorts. These strains could be offset by higher rates of immigration, but increased immigration creates other political tensions.

8. For a contrasting argument for the existence of a new epoch, see Rosanvallon 2000.

9. As the U.S. example suggests, increased discussion of social inclusion hardly means that problems of social exclusion are being effectively ameliorated.

10. Even among the different regions of the North the dynamics are different. As Fligstein and Mérand (2002) note, supranational governance and transnational markets look more like "Europeanization" than "globalization" when viewed from Europe.

11. E.g., ideas or images, whether logical structures of bits like Windows or the formula for Coca-Cola, or cultural representations like Mickey Mouse and "Air" Jordan.

REFERENCES

Akyüz, Yilmaz, ed. 1999. *East Asian Development: New Perspectives.* London: Frank Cass.

Albert, Michel. 1993. *Capitalism vs. Capitalism.* Trans. Paul Haviland. New York: Four Walls Eight Windows.

Amsden, Alice. 1989. *Asia's Next Giant: South Korea and Late Industrialization.* Oxford: Oxford University Press.

Ancelovici, Marcos. 2002. "Organizing against Globalization: The Case of ATTAC in France." *Politics and Society* 30(3): 427–63.

Anner, Mark, 2002. "Between Economic Nationalism and Transnational Solidarity: Labor Responses to Internationalization and Industrial Restructuring in the Americas." Paper presented at Annual Meeting of the American Political Science Association.

Archibugi, Franco. 2000. *The Associative Economy: Insights beyond the Welfare State and into Post-capitalism.* Hampshire: Macmillan.

Arrighi, Giovanni, Beverly Silver, and Benjamin Brewer. 2003. "Industrial Convergence and the Persistence of the North-South Divide." *Studies in Comparative International Development* 38(1): 3–31.

Arrow, Kenneth. 1962. "Economic Welfare and the Allocation of Resources for Invention." Pp. 609–25 in *The Rate and Invention of Inventive Activity: Economic and Social Factors,* ed. NBER. Princeton: Princeton University Press.

Aspalter, Christian. 2001. *Conservative Welfare State Systems in East Asia.* Westport, Conn.: Praeger.

Bacon, Robert, and Walter Eltis. 1976. *Britain's Economic Problem: Too Few Producers.* London: Macmillan.

Baiocchi, Gianpaolo. 2003. "Participation, Activism, and Politics: The Porto Alegre Experiment and Deliberative Democratic Theory." Pp. 47–84 in *Deepening Democracy: Institutional Innovations in Empowered Participatory Governance,* ed. Archon Fung and Erik Olin Wright. London: Verso.

Barenberg, Mark, and Peter Evans. 2002. "The FTAA's Impact on Democratic Governance." Paper presented at conference "FTAA and Beyond: For Integration in the Americas." Punta del Este, Uruguay, December 15–16.

Barzel, Yoram. 2002. *A Theory of the State: Economic Rights, Legal Rights, and the Scope for the State.* Cambridge: Cambridge University Press.

Bates, Robert H. 1981. *Markets and States in Tropical Africa: The Political Basis of Agricultural Policies.* Berkeley and Los Angeles: University of California Press.

Block, Fred. 1987a. "Rethinking the Political Economy of the Welfare State." Pp. 109–60 in *The Mean Season: The Attack on the Welfare State,* ed. Fred Block, Richard A. Cloward, Barbara Ehrenreich, and Frances Fox Piven. New York: Pantheon.

———. 1987b. *Revising State Theory.* Philadelphia: Temple University Press.

———. 1990. *Postindustrial Possibilities.* Berkeley and Los Angeles: University of California Press.

———. 1994. "The Roles of the State in the Economy." Pp. 691–710 in *The Handbook of Economic Sociology,* ed. Neil J. Smelser and Richard Swedberg. New York: Russell Sage Foundation; Princeton: Princeton University Press.

———. 2001. Introduction. Pp. xviii–xxxviii in *The Great Transformation,* by Karl Polanyi. Boston: Beacon Press.

Block, Fred, and Margaret Somers. 2003. "In the Shadow of Speenhamland: Social Policy and the Old Poor Law." *Politics and Society* 31(2):283–323.

Burawoy, Michael. 2003. "For a Sociological Marxism: The Complementary Convergence of Antonio Gramsci and Karl Polanyi." *Politics and Society* 31(2): 193–261.

Castells, Manuel, and Pekka Himanen. 2002. *The Information Society and the Welfare State: The Finnish Model.* Oxford: Oxford University Press.

Chang, Ha-Joon. 1994. *The Political Economy of Industrial Policy.* London: Macmillan.

Chang, Ha-Joon, and Peter Evans. 2000. "The Role of Institutions in Economic Change." Paper presented at conference "The Other Canon and Economic Development," Oslo, Norway.

Crouch, Colin, and Wolfgang Streeck, eds. 1997. *Political Economy of Modern Capitalism: Mapping Convergence and Diversity.* Thousand Oaks, Calif.: Sage.

Ehrenberg, John. 1999. *Civil Society: The Critical History of an Idea.* New York: New York University Press.

Eichengreen, Barry. 1998. "Capital Controls: Capital Idea or Capital Folly?" Available at http://emlab .berkeley.edu/users/eichengr/policy.html.

Esping-Andersen, Gosta. 1990. *The Three Worlds of Welfare Capitalism.* Princeton: Princeton University Press.

———. 1999. *Social Foundations of Postindustrial Economies.* Oxford: Oxford University Press.

Estevez-Abe, Margarita, Torber Iversen, and David Soskice. 2001. "Social Protection and the Formation of Skills: A Reinterpretation of the Welfare State." Pp. 145–83 in *Varieties of Capitalism: The Institutional Foundations of Comparative Advantage,* ed. Peter A. Hall and David Soskice. Oxford: Oxford University Press.

Evans, Peter. 1995. *Embedded Autonomy: States and Industrial Transformation.* Princeton: Princeton University Press.

———. 1997a. "The Eclipse of the State? Reflections on Stateness in an Era of Globalization." *World Politics* 50:62–87.

———. 2000. "Fighting Marginalization with Transnational Networks: Counter-hegemonic Globalization." *Contemporary Sociology* 29(1): 230–41.

———. 2001. "Development and the State." Pp. 3557–60 in *International Encyclopedia of the Social and Behavioral Sciences,* ed. Neil J. Smelser and Paul B. Baltes. Amsterdam: Elsevier.

———. 2002. "Beyond 'Institutional Monocropping': Institutions, Capabilities, and Deliberative Development." Typescript.

———, ed. 1997b. *State-Society Synergy: Government Action and Social Capital in Development.* Berkeley and Los Angeles: University of California Press.

Evans, Peter, and Martha Finnemore. 2001. "Organizational Reform and the Expansion of the South's Voice at the Fund." Paper prepared for the G-24 Technical Group Meeting, Washington, D.C., April 17–18.

Evans, Peter, and James Rauch. 1999. "Bureaucracy and Growth: A Cross-National Analysis of the Effects of 'Weberian' State Structures on Economic Growth." *American Sociological Review* 64:748–65.

Finnemore, Martha. and Kathryn Sikkink. 1998. "International Norm Dynamics and Political Change." *International Organization* 52:887–917.

Fligstein, Neil. 1990. *The Transformation of Corporate Control.* Cambridge: Harvard University Press.

———. 2001. *The Architecture of Markets: An Economic Sociology of Twenty-first-Century Capitalist Societies.* Princeton: Princeton University Press.

Fligstein, Neil, and Frédéric Mérand. 2002. "Globalization or Europeanization: Changes in the European Economy, 1980–2000." *Acta Sociologica* 45:7–22.

Foucault, Michel. 1977. *Discipline and Punish: The Birth of the Prison.* Trans. Alan Sheridan. New York: Pantheon.

Fox, Jonathan, and David L. Brown, eds. 1998. *The Struggle for Accountability: The World Bank, NGOs, and Grassroots Movements.* Cambridge: MIT Press.

Friedman, Milton, and Rose Friedman. 1980. *Free to Choose: A Personal Statement.* New York: Harcourt Brace Jovanovich.

Friedman, Thomas L. 1999. *The Lexus and the Olive Tree: Understanding Globalization.* New York: Farrar, Straus and Giroux.

Fung, Archon, and Erik Wright, eds. 2003. *Deepening Democracy: Institutional Innovations in Empowered Participatory Governance.* London: Verso.

Gerschenkron, Alexander. 1962. *Economic Backwardness in Historical Perspective.* Cambridge: Harvard University Press.

Giddens, Anthony. 1994. *Beyond Left and Right: The Future of Radical Politics.* Stanford, Calif.: Stanford University Press.

———. 2000. *The Third Way and Its Critics.* Cambridge: Polity Press.

Glyn, Andrew, ed. 2001. *Social Democracy in Neoliberal Times: The Left and Economic Policy since 1980.* New York: Oxford University Press.

Habermas, Jürgen. 1975. *Legitimation Crisis.* Translated by Thomas McCarthy. Boston: Beacon Press.

———. 1989. *The Structural Transformation of the Public Sphere: An Inquiry into a Category of Bourgeois Society.* Trans. Thomas Burger. Cambridge: MIT Press.

Hall, Peter A. and David Soskice. 2001a. "An Introduction to Varieties of Capitalism." Pp. 1–70 in *Varieties of Capitalism,* ed. Peter A. Hall and David Soskice. Oxford: Oxford University Press.

———, eds. 2001b. *Varieties of Capitalism: The Institutional Foundations of Comparative Advantage.* Oxford: Oxford University Press.

Hayek, Friedrich A. [1944] 1976. *The Road to Serfdom.* Chicago: University of Chicago Press.

Heller, Patrick. 2001. "Moving the State: The Politics of Democratic Decentralization in Kerala, South Africa, and Porto Alegre." *Politics and Society* 29(1): 131–63.

Hicks, Alexander. 1999. *Social Democracy and Welfare Capitalism: A Century of Income Security Politics.* Ithaca, N.Y.: Cornell University Press.

Hinrichs, Karl. 2001. "Elephants on the Move: Patterns of Public Pension Reform in OECD Countries." Pp. 77–102 in *Welfare State Futures,* ed. Stephan Liebfried. Cambridge: Cambridge University Press.

Hirschman, Albert. 1958. *The Strategy of Economic Development.* New Haven: Yale University Press.

Hochschild, Arlie Russell. 1997. *The Time Bind: When Work Becomes Home and Home Becomes Work.* New York: Henry Holt.

Hodgson, Geoff. 1988. *Economics and Institutions.* Cambridge: Polity Press.

Hollingsworth, J Rogers, and Robert Boyer, eds. 1997. *Contemporary Capitalism: The Embeddedness of Institutions.* Cambridge: Cambridge University Press.

Howell, David R. 2002. "Increasing Earnings Inequality and Unemployment in Developed Countries: Markets, Institutions, and the Unified Theory." *Politics and Society* 30(2): 193–244.

Huber, Evelyne, and John D. Stephens. 2001. *Development and Crisis of the Welfare State: Parties and Policies in Global Markets.* Chicago: University of Chicago Press.

Jenson, Jane, and Mariette Sineau. 2001. *Who Cares? Women's Work, Childcare, and Welfare State Redesign.* Toronto: University of Toronto Press.

Johnson, Chalmers. 1982. *MITI and the Japanese Miracle: The Growth of Industrial Policy, 1925–1975.* Stanford, Calif.: Stanford University Press.

Keane, John. 1988. *Democracy and Civil Society.* London: Verso.

———. 1998. *Civil Society: Old Images, New Visions.* Stanford, Calif.: Stanford University Press.

Keck, Margaret, and Kathryn Sikkink. 1998. *Activists beyond Borders.* Ithaca, N.Y.: Cornell University Press.

Khagram, Sanjeev, James V. Riker, and Kathryn Sikkink, eds. 2002. *Restructuring World Politics: Transnational Social Movements, Networks, and Norms.* Minneapolis: University of Minnesota Press.

King, Lawrence. 2002. "The Emperor Exposed: Neoliberal Theory and De-modernization in Postcommunist Society." Typescript. December 6.

———. 2003. "Shock Privatization: The Effects of Rapid Large-Scale Privatization on Enterprise Restructuring." *Politics and Society* 31(1): 3–30.

Kitschelt, Herbert, Peter Lange, Gary Marks, and John Stephens, eds. 1999. *Continuity and Change in Contemporary Capitalism.* Cambridge: Cambridge University Press.

Korpi, Walter. 1983. *The Democratic Class Struggle.* London: Routledge.

Krippner, Greta. 2001. "The Elusive Market: Embeddedness and the Paradigm of Economic Sociology." *Theory and Society* 30:775–810.

Krueger, Anne O. 1974. "The Political Economy of the Rent-Seeking Society." *American Economic Review* 64:291–303.

Krugman, Paul. 1999. *The Return of Depression Economics.* New York: W. W. Norton.

Kuttner, Robert. 1996. *Everything for Sale.* New York: Knopf.

Levesque, Benoit, and William A. Ninacs. 2000. "The Social Economy in Canada: The Quebec Experience." Pp. 112–29 in *Social Economy: International Debates and Perspectives,* ed. Eric Shragge and Jean-Marc Fontan. Montreal: Black Rose.

Levi, Margaret. 1988. *Of Rule and Revenue.* Berkeley and Los Angeles: University of California Press.

Levinson, Mark. 2002. "Trading Places: Globalization from the Bottom Up." *New Labor Forum* 11:20–28.

Levy, Jonah. 1999. "Vice into Virtue? Progressive Politics and Welfare Reform in Continental Europe." *Politics and Society* 27(2): 239–73.

Lindert, Peter H. 2004. *Growing Public: Social Spending and Economic Growth since the Eighteenth Century.* Vol. 1. Cambridge: Cambridge University Press.

Lustig, Nora. 2001. Introduction. Pp. 1–20 in *Shielding the Poor: Social Protection in the Developing World,* ed. Nora Lustig. Washington, D.C.: Brookings Institution and Inter-American Development Bank.

Mares, Isabela. 2001. "Firms and the Welfare State: When, Why, and How Does Social Policy Matter to Employers?" Pp. 213–46 in *Varieties of Capitalism,* ed. Peter A. Hall and David Soskice. Oxford: Oxford University Press.

McKenzie, Richard, and Dwight Lee. 1991. *Quicksilver Capital: How the Rapid Movement of Wealth Has Changed the World.* New York: Free Press.

McMichael, Philip. 2000. *Development and Social Change: A Global Perspective.* 2d ed. Thousand Oaks, Calif.: Pine Forge Press.

Mead, Lawrence. 1986. *Beyond Entitlement: The Social Obligations of Citizenship.* New York: Free Press.

Meier, Gerald, and James Rauch. 2000. *Leading Issues in Economic Development.* 7th ed. Oxford: Oxford University Press.

Mendell, Marguerite. 2002. "The Social Economy in Quebec: Discourses and Strategy." Pp. 319–43 in *Critical Political Studies: Debates and Dialogues from the Left,* ed. Abigail B. Bakan and Eleanor Macdonald. Montreal: McGill-Queen's University Press.

Meyer, Madonna Harrington. 2000. *Care Work: Gender, Labor, and the Welfare State.* London: Routledge.

Migdal, Joel. 2001. *State in Society: Studying How States and Societies Transform and Constitute One Another.* Cambridge: Cambridge University Press.

Migdal, Joel, Atul Kohli, and Vivienne Shue, eds. 1994. *State Power and Social Forces: Domination and Transformation.* Cambridge: Cambridge University Press.

Myles, John, and Paul Pierson. 1997. "Friedman's Revenge: The Reform of Liberal Welfare States in Canada and the United States." *Politics and Society* 25(4): 443–72.

Narayan, Deepa. 1994. *The Contribution of People's Participation: Evidence from 121 Rural Water Supply Projects.* Washington, D.C.: World Bank.

Nee, Victor. 2000. "The Role of the State in Making a Market Economy." *Journal of Institutional and Theoretical Economics* 156(1): 64–88.

North, Douglass C. 1981. *Structure and Change in Economic History.* New York: W. W. Norton.

———. 1990. *Institutions, Institutional Change, and Economic Performance.* Cambridge: Cambridge University Press.

O'Connor, James. 1973. *The Fiscal Crisis of the State.* New York: St. Martin's.

O'Riain, Seán. 2004. *The Politics of High Tech Growth: Developmental Network States in the Global Economy.* Cambridge: Cambridge University Press.

Offe, Claus. 1996. *Modernity and the State: East, West.* Cambridge: MIT Press.

Organization for Economic Cooperation and Development (OECD). 1977. *Towards Full Employment and Price Stability.* Paris: OECD.

Orrù, Marco, Nicole Woolsey Biggart, and Gary Hamilton. 1997. *The Economic Organization of East Asian Capitalism.* Thousand Oaks, Calif.: Sage.

Pierson, Paul. 1996. "The New Politics of the Welfare State." *World Politics* 48:143–79.

———, ed. 2001. *The New Politics of the Welfare State.* Oxford: Oxford University Press.

Piven, Frances Fox, and Richard A. Cloward. 1997. *The Breaking of the American Social Compact.* New York: New Press.

Polanyi, Karl. [1944] 2001. *The Great Transformation: The Political and Economic Origins of Our Times.* Boston: Beacon Press.

Przeworski, Adam, Michael E. Alvarez, Jose Antonio Cheibub, and Fernando Limongi. 2000. *Democracy and Development: Political Institutions and Well-Being in the World, 1950–1990.* Cambridge: Cambridge University Press.

Putnam, Robert. 1993. *Making Democracy Work: Civic Traditions in Modern Italy.* Princeton: Princeton University Press.

———. 2000. *Bowling Alone: The Collapse and Revival of American Community.* New York: Simon and Schuster.

Rodrik, Dani, Arvind Subramanian, and Francesco Trebbi. 2002. "Institutions Rule: The Primacy of Institutions over Geography and Integration in Economic Development." NBER Working Paper No. W9305.

Rosanvallon, Pierre. 2000. *The New Social Question: Rethinking the Welfare State.* Princeton: Princeton University Press.

Rothstein, Bo. 1996. *The Social Democratic State: The Swedish Model and the Bureaucratic Problem of Social Reforms.* Pittsburgh: University of Pittsburgh Press.

Ruggie, John. 1982. "International Regimes, Transactions, and Change: Embedded Liberalism in the Postwar Economic Order." *International Organization* 36(2): 379–415.

Sabel, Charles. 1994. "Learning by Monitoring: The Institutions of Economic Development." Pp. 137–65 in *The Handbook of Economic Sociology,* ed. Neil J. Smelser and Richard Swedberg. New York: Russell Sage Foundtion; Princeton: Princeton University Press.

Sainsbury, Diane. 1999. "Gender, Policy Regimes, and Politics." Pp. 245–75 in *Gender and Welfare State Regimes,* ed. Diane Sainsbury. Oxford: Oxford University Press.

Sassen, Saskia. 1998. *Globalization and Its Discontents: Essays on the New Mobility of People and Money.* New York: New Press.

Scharpf, Fritz. 1991. *Crisis and Choice in European Social Democracy.* Ithaca, N.Y.: Cornell University Press.

Scharpf, Fritz, and Vivien A. Schmidt, eds. 2000. *Wel-*

fare and Work in the Open Economy. 2 vols. Oxford: Oxford University Press.

Scott, James C. 1998. *Seeing Like a State: How Certain Schemes to Improve the Human Condition Have Failed.* New Haven: Yale University Press.

Sen, Amartya. 1999. *Development as Freedom.* New York: Alfred A. Knopf.

Silver, Beverly, and Giovanni Arrighi. 2003. "Polanyi's 'Double Movement': The Belle Époques of British and U.S. Hegemony Compared." *Politics and Society* 31(2): 325–55.

Simon, William H. 2001. *The Community Economic Development Movement: Law, Business, and the New Social Policy.* Durham, N.C.: Duke University Press.

Smith, Adam. [1776] 1976. *The Wealth of Nations.* Chicago: University of Chicago Press.

Smith, Stephen Samuel, and Jessica Kulynych. 2002. "It May Be Social, but Why Is It Capital? The Social Construction of Social Capital and the Politics of Language." *Politics and Society* 30(1): 149–86.

Soros, George. 2002. *On Globalization.* New York: Public Affairs Press.

Soskice, David. 1999. "Divergent Production Regimes: Coordinated and Uncoordinated Market Economies in the 1980s and 1990s." Pp. 101–34 in *Continuity and Change in Contemporary Capitalism,* ed. H. Kitschelt et al. Cambridge: Cambridge University Press.

Standing, Guy. 2002. *Beyond the New Paternalism: Basic Security as Equality.* London: Verso.

Stark, David, and Laszlo Bruszt. 1998. *Postsocialist Pathways: Transforming Politics and Property in East Central Europe.* Cambridge: Cambridge University Press.

Stiglitz, Joseph. 2002. *Globalization and Its Discontents.* New York: W. W. Norton.

Streeck, Wolfgang. 1992. "Productive Constraints: On the Insitutional Conditions of Diversified Quality Production." Pp. 1–40 in *Social Institutions and Economic Performance: Studies of Industrial Relations in Advanced Capitalist Economies,* ed. Wolfgang Streeck. London: Sage.

———. 1997. "German Capitalism: Does it Exist? Can it Survive?" Pp. 33–54 in *Political Economy of Modern Capitalism: Mapping Convergence and Diversity* ed. Colin Crouch and Wolfgang Streeck. Thousand Oaks, Calif.: Sage.

Suplicy, Eduardo Matarazzo. 2002. *Renda de cidadania: A saída é pela porta.* São Paulo: Cortez Editora Editora Fundação Perseu Abramo.

Swank, Duane. 2002. *Global Capital, Political Institutions, and Policy Change in Developed Welfare States.* Cambridge: Cambridge University Press.

Swedberg, Richard. 1998. *Max Weber and the Idea of Economic Sociology.* Princeton: Princeton University Press.

Swenson, Peter. 1997. "Arranged Alliance: Business Interests in the New Deal." *Politics and Society* 25(1): 66–116.

————. 2002. *Capitalists against Markets: The Making of Labor Markets and Welfare States in the United States and Sweden.* Oxford: Oxford University Press.

Tang, Kwong-Jeung. 2000. *Social Welfare Development in East Asia.* Hampshire: Palgrave.

Tendler, Judith. 1997. *Good Government in the Tropics.* Baltimore: Johns Hopkins University Press.

Thayer, Millie. 2000. "Traveling Feminisms: From Embodied Women to Gendered Citizenship." Pp. 203–33 in *Global Ethnography: Forces, Connections and Imagination in a Postmodern World*, ed. Michael Burawoy. Berkeley and Los Angeles: University of California Press.

Tilly, Charles. 1990. *Coercion, Capital, and European States, A.D. 990–1992.* Oxford: Blackwell.

Trigilia, Carlo. 2002. *Economic Sociology: State, Market, and Society in Modern Capitalism.* Oxford: Blackwell.

Tronto, Joan. 1993. *Moral Boundaries: A Political Argument for an Ethic of Care.* London: Routledge.

Unger, Roberto Mangabeira. 1998. *Democracy Realized: The Progressive Alternative.* London: Verso.

Van Parijs, Philippe, ed. 1992. *Arguing for Basic Income.* London: Verso.

Vogel, Steven K. 1996. *Freer Markets, More Rules: Regulatory Reform in Advanced Industrial Countries.* Ithaca, N.Y.: Cornell University Press.

Wade, Robert. 1990. *Governing the Market: Economic Theory and the Role of Government in Taiwan's Industrialization.* Princeton: Princeton University Press.

————. 1996. "Globalization and Its Limits: Reports of the Death of the National Economy Are Greatly Exaggerated." Pp. 60–88 in *National Diversity and Global Capitalism*, ed. Suzanne Berger and Ronald Dore. Ithaca, N.Y.: Cornell University Press.

Weber, Max. [1922] 1978. *Economy and Society: An Outline of Interpretative Sociology.* Ed. Guenther Roth and Claus Wittich. Trans. Ephraim Fischoff et al. 2 vols. Berkeley and Los Angeles: University of California Press.

Wilensky, Harold. 2002. *Rich Democracies: Political Economy, Public Policy, and Performance.* Berkeley and Los Angeles: University of California Press.

Woodruff, David. 1999. *Money Unmade: Barter and the Fate of Russian Capitalism.* Ithaca, N.Y.: Cornell University Press.

World Bank (IBRD). 1997. *World Development Report: The State in a Changing World.* Oxford: Oxford University Press.

Zukin, Sharon, and Paul DiMaggio. 1990. Introduction. Pp. 1–36 in *Structures of Capital: The Social Organization of the Economy*, ed. Sharon Zukin and Paul DiMaggio. Cambridge: Cambridge University Press.

23 A Sociological Approach to Law and the Economy

Lauren B. Edelman and Robin Stryker

IRONICALLY, law is "all over," yet marginal in economic sociology. Despite law's centrality to classical sociological understandings of the economy (see Smelser and Swedberg, this volume), law is not often a sustained object of inquiry in its own right for "new" economic sociologists. In addition, there has been scant attention to systematizing and critically examining the way economic sociologists have treated law or law's role in sociological explanations for economic behavior and institutions. We agree with Swedberg (2002, 2) that there is need to develop a "general sociological analysis of the role that law plays in economic life."

We work toward this goal by combining ideas in economic sociology with sociological perspectives more directly addressing connections among law, politics, and culture. We develop a conceptual framework for examining interrelationships between law and the economy. so that an "economic sociology of law" becomes an integral part of a more general economic sociology. This in turn will enable economic sociologists to capture more fully the social character and situatedness of economic action, and thus to offer a compelling alternative to economists' accounts.

Our key premise is that both law and the economy are deeply embedded in social action and organization and linked through political and institutional mechanisms. Both sets of mechanisms underscore the centrality of power. In addition, because legal and economic concepts, rules and routines, and institutions are mutually or reciprocally constructed and reconstructed over time *through* political and institutional mechanisms, it does not make sense to treat law as only an "independent" variable or only a "dependent" variable with respect to the economy. Rather, an economic sociology of law should theorize and research how law, politics, and culture—and their interplay—shape the nature of, and causal relationships among, "economic variables" and "legal variables" themselves.

The theoretical framework we suggest is less an "economic sociology of law" (Swedberg 2002) than it is a *sociology of law and the economy*. Whereas the former term would suggest that we were using existing *economic sociology* perspectives to explain the role of law in society, the latter term implies theorizing and empirically investigating the *multiple social mechanisms or processes* through which legal and economic action and institutions become part of an *interconnected causal dynamic.*

Our sociological model stands in stark contrast to the current dominant paradigm for understanding the relation of law to the economy: post-Coasean "law and economics" (Mercuro 1989; Cooter and Ulen 2000; Posner 1987, 1998). An offshoot of neoclassical economics, post-Coasean law and economics assumes that individuals are rational actors who seek to maximize their preferences. Law and economics scholarship generally treats preferences as fixed and as exogenous; the social (and indeed, legal) origins of preferences are outside the economic model.[1]

In virtually all economic accounts, moreover, the individual is the fundamental unit of economic behavior. Aggregate constructs such as "society" are dismissed in favor of understandings of aggregation as no more than the sum of the individual parts. The interaction of rational individuals, each maximizing his or her own self-interest, tends toward an "equilibrium" or steady state that will not change in the absence of outside forces. Markets tend toward the steady state of "efficiency," an equilibrium state that maximizes the preferences of the participating actors.[2] A "market" is the aggregate result of individuals maximizing their preferences; there is nothing "social" or "cultural" or "political" about markets.

From a law and economics perspective, government regulation is unnecessary and counterproductive in perfectly competitive markets, but it is justified by various market failures. These include monopoly, information asymmetries together with strategic behavior, "free-rider problems" (where a good is available to the public without cost so that there is little incentive for private support), and "externalities" (or costs incurred by parties not directly involved). In these cases, the market "fails" to provide efficient outcomes, and regulation may be used as a remedy for market inefficiencies.

Law and economics scholarship offers a theoretically informed set of principles for identifying how law can promote efficiency in policy arenas ranging from the economic realm (e.g., property and antitrust law) to areas generally thought to be outside economics (e.g., criminal law). The seminal principle underlying the field is the Coase theorem, which states that "when parties are free to bargain costlessly they will succeed in reaching efficient outcomes regardless of the initial allocations of legal rights" (Donahue 1988, 906). But law and economics scholars recognize (as did Coase) that bargaining almost always involves "transaction costs"; parties to a dispute, for example, incur costs when they hire lawyers or consultants, when they travel to negotiation sites or miss work, or when they must expend resources to discover information.

Employing the notion of transaction costs, law and economics scholars analyze how, and under what circumstances, legal rules can be used to restore allocative efficiency where transaction costs produce inefficient outcomes. Normative law and economics offers advice to policymakers on what types of legal rules are efficient under various circumstances, whereas positive law and economics seeks to explain common-law trends in terms of efficiency principles. The "new institutional economics" uses similar principles to show how transaction costs can explain the relative efficiency of markets and bureaucratic governance (Williamson 1975, 1979).

Law and economics scholarship is important for our purposes primarily because it attends to the relationship between legal and economic orders. In contrast, sociological thinking about law tends to theorize the relation of law to social structure, norms, and culture, de-emphasizing connections between law and the economy. From a sociological perspective, a major problem with post-Coasean law and economics is that its search for parsimonious models renders irrelevant the social, political, and legal construction of efficiency. The questions of how law and culture shape individual preferences and constrain individual "choice" are "outside the box" for most law and economists.[3] Yet these questions must be central for a sociology of law and the economy, which seeks to elucidate causes and consequences of the unequal resource distributions across social strata. To the extent that culture or politics shapes individuals' economic expectations or visions of justice, preferences must be understood as *endogenous*—determined *within* the analytic model of law and the economy rather than outside of it. Sociological studies of inequality suggest, for example, that extant wage patterns lead women to expect lower wages than do men for the same work, that workplace stratification and work-family concerns condition women to "prefer" lower-status and lower-paid jobs, and that the prevalence of racial discrimination and poverty can make it difficult for minorities to imagine (and therefore to "prefer") the same housing or credit or contract terms that whites might prefer (see, e.g., Schultz 1990). In short, preferences are a product of social background, cultural expectations, and experience. Political actions, public policy, legal rights, and social norms affect experience and thus preferences, as politics, culture, and law both produce and limit realms of active, economic choice.

By treating individual preferences as exogenous and their collective maximization as resource-efficient, law and economics tends to treat efficiency as a *neutral* (and hence, fair) criterion. As law and economics scholarship increasingly permeates the judiciary and the legal academy, ideas about justice are progressively infused with this logic of efficiency. But by bracketing out the question of the social construction of preferences, law and economics' concepts of efficiency tend to favor the status quo. A sociology of law and the economy offers an important corrective to law and economics, by identifying conditions under which maximizing individual preferences perpetuates the very injustices that legal rights seek to restructure.

By introducing the legal and cultural construction of preferences and the social embeddedness of economic action, a sociology of law and the economy will necessarily be less elegant than post-Coasean law and economics. Many questions about the law's value and impact that have clear answers through economic analyses will have murky answers or no definitive answer when addressed through a sociological lens. But what is lost in parsimony will be gained in accuracy because life—even economic life—is complex.

While our model of a sociology of law and the economy differs markedly from post-Coasean law and economics, it draws inspiration and important orienting principles from classical sociological theory, especially Weber, and from early-twentieth-century institutional economics (sometimes called Progressive Era law and economics—see, e.g., Hovencamp 1990).[4] In addition, our model draws on extant work in economic sociology, and research in political economy, political sociology, sociology of law, and legal history. Putting concepts and insights of these approaches together, we can highlight and correct underdeveloped aspects of new economic sociology. We also sketch a research agenda for examining the social mechanisms linking legal and economic behavior and institutions.

To present our sociological model of law and the economy, we first discuss the nature of law. In contrast to the notion of law as formally enacted edicts that characterize both economic sociology and scholarship in law and economics, we argue that law should be understood as a broad set of norms, customs, schema, and symbols. These include, but are not restricted to, formal rules. We further argue that, given this broader conception of law, the appropriate unit of analysis is the "legal field," or the social realm surrounding legal institutions. Second, we suggest that law and the economy be understood as overlapping social fields that are mutually constituted through two processes: institutional meaning-making processes and political power-mobilization processes (Edelman 1964; Stryker 1980; Edelman 1992; Stryker 1994). Third, we draw on Edelman and Suchman's (1997) typology of legal environments both to provide a systematic review of extant research on the intersection of law and the economy and to further elucidate how institutional and political processes link law and the economy. We conclude by providing a summary of our theoretical model and discussing its implications for future research both in economic sociology and in law and economics. Because of space limitations, we confine our discussion to the role of law in the development and dynamics of capitalist political economies. We encourage readers intrigued by our conceptual framework to treat Stryker (2003) as a companion piece, especially in its extended concrete examples of cultural and political processes through which labor and employment statutes, executive orders, regulations, and court decisions have shaped the U.S. economy.

THE NATURE OF LAW

Economic sociologists tend to equate law with formal rules (particularly statutes) promulgated by state actors, including legislatures and courts. They generally portray legal rules as among determinants of economic growth and development, and also of the reach, organization, institutional logic (including models of competition and conceptions of control), and even the existence of markets (Flig-

steir. 1990, 2001; Fligstein and Stone Sweet 2002; Dotbin 1994; Dobbin and Dowd 2000; Evans 1995; Evans and Rauch 1999; Carruthers, Babb, and Halliday 2001; Spicer 2002; Schneiberg 2002).

Law is relevant to the economy primarily because it facilitates and promotes particular kinds of economic interactions and organization, and because it provides an incentive structure in which firms' rational strategizing occurs. By altering perceived costs and benefits of taking one route over another, law can help favor development of some economic strategies while eliminating others (Fligstein 1990, 2001). For example, law specifies property rights; facilitates commerce (guiding economic exchange through contract doctrine as well as banking, finance, and credit laws); stipulates standards for trade and competition (through various regulatory regimes and antitrust law); and protects consumers, employees, and others (through employment, product, environment, and health and safety laws). In addition, a political economy organized according to the "rule of law" provides the stability and predictability needed for a full-blown capitalist economy.

The vision of law in extant economic sociology captures and elaborates some of the key themes emphasized by classical sociologists such as Durkheim and especially Weber, when they theorized the relationship between legal change and economic modernity (see Stryker 2003 for details). But because extant economic sociology associates law with state-promulgated formal rules and because law is generally treated as an exogenous, determinative, and coercive force, economic sociologists miss the full power of law to "make a world" (White 1985).

We suggest that a sociology of law and the economy must adopt a more sociological conception of law—one that goes beyond law as public edict to recognize the cultural and political elements of law. Just as economic sociologists theorize markets as embedded within a broader social and political realm (Smelser and Swedberg, this volume), we suggest that law should be understood as intricately interwoven with social forces. We draw on the sociology of law to propose some basic, empirically grounded assumptions about the nature of law.

Law as Legality

The sociology of law rejects the legal formalism (or the focus solely on formal codes and judicial decisions) that tends to be found in traditional jurisprudence and much contemporary legal scholarship. Instead, sociologists of law emphasize a much broader idea of law, including not just codified rules but also social behaviors that mobilize and enact law and ritual and the symbolic (or meaning-making) elements of law. In addition, sociologists of law emphasize the ambiguous boundaries between formal rules and social norms, the role of social context in fixing law's form and impact, and the interplay between legal language and broader cultural language and ways of thinking. Thus reconceptualized, law includes *both* state-promulgated formal rules and law-related ideas, ideals, principles, and rituals that permeate society.

Law is not just formalized doctrine; it is *legality* (cf. Ewick and Silbey 1998; Selznick 1969). The idea of legality suggests that formal legal "rules on the books," for example, statutes, directives, executive orders, and judicial opinions, are important, but cannot be understood fully apart from their social context. Two key elements of that social context are the *law in action*, which refers to the behavior of law, legal actors, and legal institutions; and *legal consciousness*, which refers to how law is experienced and understood by individuals in and through their legal experiences.

Research on law in action suggests that a narrow focus on formal law misses a great deal. The vast majority of legal action takes place far from the courtroom and with only the most tangential (if any) reference to formal law. Much economic exchange occurs in the absence of formal contracts, and few disputes that arise within contractual relationships are resolved by courts, or even with the involvement of lawyers (Macaulay 1963; Lempert and Sanders 1986). Local norms matter more than does formal law in guiding grievants toward solutions (Ellickson 1986, Engel 1998; Merry 1979).

In fact, only a miniscule proportion of persons who believe that they have been wronged take any legal action. Most resort instead to informal non-legal methods of dispute resolution such as self-help, gossip, violence, or other forms of retribution, third-party conciliation by ministers or other nonlegal personnel, consultation with government agencies, or (as is most often the case) doing nothing (Mnookin and Kornhauser 1979; Erlanger, Chambliss, and Melli 1997; Bumiller 1987, 1988; Miller and Sarat 1980; Saks 1992). In many cases, persons who have legal rights do not even recognize that they have suffered a legal injury (Felstiner, Abel, and Sarat 1980).

Conversely, judges, lawyers, magistrates, clerks, cops, mediators, and other legal system actors play a role in bringing society into the law. They act as gatekeepers and filters, using their discretion and invoking their biases and misconceptions in ways

that greatly influence how and when law matters (Friedman 1975, 1984; Frohmann 1997; Resnik 1982; Adamany and Grossman 1983; Gibson 1981; Heinz and Laumann 1977; Sarat and Felstiner 1995; Nelson 1988; Suchman and Cahill 1996; Harcourt 2001).

Research on legal consciousness focuses on the symbolic elements of law, and on the meaning of law to individuals (Sarat 1990; Silbey 2001; Ewick and Silbey 1998; Kostiner 2003; Nielsen 2000; Sarat 1990; Engel 1998; Merry 1986; Levine and Mellema 2001). This work emphasizes the multiple (and sometimes contradictory) meanings of law. The formal legal ideal of an autonomous and just (in Weber's terms "formal rational") legal order coexists in legal consciousness with alternative visions of law. People can simultaneously see the law (as well as lawyers and legal institutions) as just and as oppressive, as a tool to be used and as a formidable enemy (Sarat 1990; Ewick and Silbey 1998). How people envision the law in turn affects whether and how people mobilize legal tools at their disposal (Fuller, Edelman, and Matusik 2000).

Legal consciousness is important not just as a set of rules but as a cultural resource. Not withstanding the definition of law and rights by legislatures, or their interpretation by courts, the language of law and legal rights operates as a general cultural resource and does significant cognitive work. Law helps to define moral boundaries and is, in turn, often the terrain on which moral boundaries are contested (Gusfield 1966). The symbolism of law, moreover, helps to constitute social discourse. To characterize a demand as a "right" rather than as a "need" tends to confer legitimacy on the demand and to define the claimant as a rights-bearer. To articulate a grievance as a violation of law frames not only the claim but the debate that takes place around that claim (Silbey and Sarat 1989; Milner 1989; Minow 1987; McCann 1998).

Following work in the sociology of law, then, we suggest that a sociology of law and the economy understand law as legality. The notion of law as legality provides a richer toolkit for conceptualizing both how legal schemas shape economic schemas (including ideas of rationality and efficiency), values and interests, behavior and institutions, and conversely, how law is responsive to all these aspects of the economy.

The Legal Field as Unit of Analysis

Drawing on our understanding of law as legality, we suggest that the appropriate unit of analysis for the study of law is the *legal field*. Centered on legal institutions and actors, legal fields also include the much broader set of legal ideals and norms, rituals and symbols, social behaviors that mobilize and enact the law, and patterns of social thought related to legal ideals (Bourdieu 1987; Edelman, Fuller, and Mara-Drita 2001; Edelman 2002). Professional understandings of law, managerial rhetoric about law, symbolic representations of law, and negotiations in the shadow of law are important elements of legal fields.

The idea of the legal field is analogous—and complementary to—new institutionalist ideas about economic (or organizational) fields. As elaborated in neoinstitutional organization theory, economic fields include producers of particular products or services, in interaction with their key suppliers, consumers, and state regulators (DiMaggio and Powell 1983; Powell and DiMaggio 1991; Fligstein 2001). Economic fields are centered on economic actors and organizations, but they also include prevailing ideas about efficiency and rationality, ideas about the value of work and workers, prevalent technologies, and scientific knowledge (Stryker 2003).

By focusing on legal and economic fields as the primary units of analysis, our sociology of law and the economy can portray the social embeddedness of both law and markets. Further, this conceptualization allows us to focus our analysis on the intersection of legal and economic fields as the key site for reciprocal construction and reconstruction of legal and economic actors, institutions, and consciousness.

The intersection of legal and economic fields provides rich terrain for cross-fertilization. It is in this social space that legal procedures, norms, and concepts work together to shape economic actors and institutions, and that economic structures, norms, and rituals shape the law. Just as law shapes the economy, the everyday conflicts of the workplace—and organizational solutions to those conflicts—are raw materials that legislators, regulators, and judges use to construct the law. Formal law, including statutes and judicial decisions, depends on what conflicts are brought into the public arena and how those conflicts are framed.

A POLITICAL-INSTITUTIONAL PERSPECTIVE ON THE INTERSECTION OF LAW AND THE ECONOMY

Building on the broad conception of law as legality that we presented in the previous section, we now turn to our sociological framework for understanding law and the economy. We suggest that two distinct but interrelated social processes are at work in linking law and the economy: *institutional* processes that involve the production and widespread acceptance of particular constructions of law and compliance, and *political* processes that help to shape which constructions of law are produced and become institutionalized and who benefits from those constructions. We discuss these processes (and review the literature that supports them) in this section.[5]

We will show that institutional and political processes operate to embed markets deeply within legal frameworks and to infuse law with economic logic so that the development of legal and economic fields are linked. Through institutional and political processes, law shapes all things economic, including understandings of rationality, efficiency, and even what constitutes an economic actor. Conversely, law and legal institutions are constituted and reconstituted by economic institutions and actors.

Our perspective suggests that both market rationality and law are "socially constructed" or given meaning through social interaction. In contrast to post-Coasean law and economics, which treats preferences as exogenous, we suggest that preferences are shaped not just by formal legal policy but by the law in action and legal consciousness that defines that policy. And in contrast to economic sociology, which treats law as exogenous, our perspective will show how the meaning and enactment of law take form within economic fields.

Institutional Processes of Social Change

Neoinstitutional organization theory highlights an evolutionary vision of change, in which models of rationality are socially constructed, diffused, and "institutionalized" over time within organizational fields (Meyer and Rowan 1977; DiMaggio and Powell 1983; Meyer and Scott 1983; Powell and DiMaggio 1991).[6] Within these fields, organizations tend to incorporate institutionalized models less because of strategic, cost-benefit calculations and more because certain actions, forms, or rituals come to be understood as proper and natural.

Different versions of neoinstitutional theory emphasize different mechanisms by which institutionalized models spread throughout organizational fields. DiMaggio and Powell (1983) identify three mechanisms of institutionalization: mimetic isomorphism (organizations imitate the apparently rational structures of other organizations); normative isomorphism (professionals advocate particular structures); and coercive isomorphism (rules, usually issued by the state, mandate particular structures). Suchman and Edelman (1996) distinguish cognitive institutional models (in which organizations incorporate structures because they are so taken-for-granted as to appear natural, proper, and rational) from normative institutional models (in which organizations more actively seek to respond to cultural norms) and behavioral institutional models (which are agnostic as to the causal mechanism but focus on the diffusion of models).

Institutional processes have proved quite useful to explain the legalization of organizational life over time (Edelman 1990, 1992; Sutton et al. 1994; Dobbin and Sutton 1998; Edelman and Petterson 1999; Edelman, Uggen, and Erlanger 1999; Heimer 1999). In her research on compliance with equal employment law, Edelman (1990, 1992) argues that organizations are highly responsive to their *legal environments* or the law-related aspects of organizational fields. Legal environments include formal law and its associated sanctions; informal practices and norms regarding the use, nonuse, and circumvention of law; ideas about the meaning of law and compliance with law, and the broad set of principles, ideas, rituals, and norms that may evolve out of law (Edelman and Suchman 1997; Cahill 2001). Organizations most vulnerable to public scrutiny respond early to change in their legal environments by elaborating formal structures to mimic elements of the public legal order, such as formal due process mechanisms that mimic courts, special compliance offices that mimic administrative agencies, and rules that mimic legislation. Over time, these structures become institutionalized symbols of compliance, and other organizations become increasingly likely to adopt them (Edelman 1992).

Friedland and Alford (1991) provided the key insight that fields are imbued with "institutional logics." While logics become institutionalized in one field, they may flow into and influence other fields. This insight may be extended to show the interplay between legal and economic fields. As laws and legal principles are constructed, interpreted, and institutionalized by economic actors (managers, employers, compliance officers, legal counsel), the law tends both to influence ideas of rationality and to become infused by managerial and capitalist logic. Edelman and her colleagues (Edelman, Uggen, and Erlanger 1999; Edelman, Fuller, and Mara-Drita 2001; Edelman 2002), for example, suggest that over time, managerial logic

and strategies of compliance, such as the construction of employee due process grievance procedures within the firm, tend to receive the formal imprimatur of law. This, in turn, reaffirms the legitimacy of such managerial ideas and effectively changes the meaning and requirements of formal law.

Two lines of work, one in sociology of law, the other in political sociology, extend the notion of institutional logics by suggesting that new ideas form at the intersection of fields with differing logics (Edelman 2002; Edelman, Uggen, and Erlanger 1999; Clemens and Cook 1999; Stryker 2000a, 2002). Specifically elaborating the idea of overlap between legal and organizational fields, Edelman argues that law is *endogenous*, or constructed within the social fields that it seeks to regulate. In this view, legal ideas and forms of compliance are constructed and institutionalized within organizational fields. But because the logics of organizational and legal fields overlap, courts tend to accept—sometimes unwittingly—institutionalized ideas of legality that developed within organizational fields. Change in legal institutions, then, is part of an interrelated, continuous *social change system* in which law's content, mobilization, and reach are simultaneously products and sources of economic behavior.

Consistent with ideas of law as legality and symbols, legal power resides not only in the overt exercise of law but also in the form of cultural hegemony—in subtle understandings of rights, responsibilities, and rational action. Beliefs and practices that are highly institutionalized are a very potent form of power, acquiring mythical status as rational or proper or fair, with the result that they go unchallenged and become nonissues. For example, it is widely thought to be rational and fair for employers to pay employees "market wages," or the wage that an employee could (at least in theory) receive from other employers. Employees, employers, and even courts commonly accept this rationale without recognizing that institutionalized ideas about paying employees their "market value" may systematically disadvantage female or minority workers (Nelson and Bridges 1999; England 1993; Edelman 2002).

Political Processes of Social Change

Whereas neoinstitutional theories emphasize concepts of institution and institutionalization that imply cognitive and normative taken-for-grantedness as a primary mechanism of change and stabilization in legal fields, political theories emphasize overt conflict and contestation (see Stryker 2000a, 2002). Political approaches view legal change less as a result of nonconflictual diffusion of ideas, norms, and ideals and more as a result of diverse types of manifest conflict over and involving legal schema.

Following Weber, economic sociologists generally have a "power-oriented concept of economic action" (Swedberg and Granovetter 1992, 8). Likewise, explicitly political approaches to market structuration are prominent in economic sociology (Fligstein 2001). In parallel fashion, albeit in somewhat different ways, both sociologists of law and political sociologists draw on Marx and Weber to suggest that law is linked to the economy through processes involving both overt resource mobilization and the exercise of covert power.

The general tenets of Marx's historical materialism relegate "bourgeois" law—along with the rest of the democratic state—to reflecting and reinforcing the domination of capital. But Marx's (1967) analysis of the nineteenth-century Factory Acts in *Capital* evidences a more nuanced appreciation for law as an object of class conflict. In that work, Marx argues that the Factory Acts, which limited the length of the working day in Britain, were an outgrowth of sustained working-class organization and struggle.

Sociologists of law tend to emphasize the role of law as ideological superstructure (Stone 1985). Sociologists of law point out that formal-rational law differs from overt politics in that it depends for its legitimacy on the liberal legal notion that its rule application is *apolitical*. Legal liberalism maintains that, although legal disputes are a form of institutionalized conflict, legal principles applied to resolve them are generally and universally applicable, and autonomous from partisan political interests, social classes, formal politics, or other aspects of society (Sarat 1998). In contrast, neo-Marxist work in the sociology of law suggests that the liberal legal ideal is, in fact, a hegemonic ideology masking political-economic power while simultaneously legitimating that power. Neo-Marxist scholars suggest that both form and content of the law consistently favor interests of the dominant class or dominant elites, even while celebrating ideals such as equal protection and due process for all (Balbus 1977; Genovese 1976; Spitzer 1983; Collins 1982; Stone 1985; Chambliss 1964; Klare 1998; Freeman 1990).

Sociolegal scholarship on rights is similarly skeptical about the justice- and equality-enhancing impact of rights. Scheingold (1974) identifies the "myth of rights" inherent in liberal legal ideology, suggesting that rights are valuable only to the extent that they are politically mobilized (cf. McCann 1994; Rosenberg 1991). Critical legal scholars point to the instability and political manipulability of rights (Tushnet 1984; Aron 1989). Feminist legal scholars suggest that rights embody male norms and therefore tend to harm women (Olsen 1984; MacKinnon 1989). And critical race scholars appreciate the ideological aspects of rights, but contend that rights may be socially empowering for minorities even when they are hard to mobilize in court (Williams 1991; Minow 1987).

Scholars focusing on law in action analyze legal institutions as arenas for resource mobilization and conflict. In a classic essay, Marc Galanter (1974) suggests that the structure of adversary litigation gives substantial advantages to parties that have greater organizational and economic resources. Numerous studies since then have documented a variety of advantages for "haves" over "have-nots" in civil litigation (Bumiller 1988; Yeager 1990; Nielsen 2000; Yngvesson 1988; Albiston 1999; Edelman and Suchman 1999).

While much sociology of law emphasizes the inherent tendency of law to favor the power elite, political sociologists emphasize the contests and power struggles themselves. Building on Weber's (1978) definition of power as the capacity to realize one's will even against resistance in overt conflict, political sociologists suggest that both the form and content of law are actively constructed and mobilized as power-resources. Stryker (2000a, 2003), for example, portrays law as both a resource for and a result of political conflict; she invokes a broad definition of politics as the mobilization and countermobilization of resources in interest-based, value-based, and cognitively based conflicts, whether these are played out in the formal political sphere or elsewhere. Pedriana and Stryker (1997) show, however, that law's resource value does not flow automatically from formal statutes. Because its resource value at any given time results from a prior politics of law interpretation and enforcement, law is a "moving target" (Pedriana and Stryker, 2004).

Law is mobilized not just by dominant classes and class segments, but also by subordinate classes and class segments, diverse race, gender, ethnic, or religious groups, myriad non-class-based social movements and groups, and diverse professional and technical experts, to help enhance economic well-being, income and wealth, social status and prestige, self-esteem and dignity, and authority, autonomy, and power (Sabatier 1975; Lempert and Sanders 1986, Yeager 1990; Stryker 1994; Saguy 2003). A standard assumption is that law is limited in its capacity for restraining market logic and economic power (Stryker 1989; Yeager 1990).[7] However, under some conditions, law can also serve as a force for enhancing equality and justice in capitalist political economies (Sabatier 1975; Pedriana and Stryker 1997, 2004; Stryker 2003).

Political sociology, then, reiterates the theme in critical sociology of law that legal power operates covertly, by creating political "nonissues" as well as issues (see Lukes 1974). Law as politics involves stabilizing and transforming both concrete legal rules and broader visions of legality. Like current writings in the sociology of law, current research in political sociology emphasizes that visions of a neutral, apolitical legally legitimate capitalism, contain conflict in institutionalized forms, and channel it away from revolutionary rupture toward reform. Paradoxically then, when "have-nots" succeed in mobilizing legal discourse and procedures for concrete social, political, or economic gains, they help validate the idea of law as autonomous from economic elites. In turn, this helps elites prevent more radical redistributions of economic wealth and power.

The political mobilization and countermobilization of law are also evident in historical accounts. For example, Tomlins (1985, 1993) and Forbath (1991a, 1991b) show that changing concepts of property and criminal conspiracy in common law and changes in statutory antitrust law shaped the interests and strategies, cognitions, values and collective identity of the American labor movement. Legal power both overt and covert is involved in their accounts of why the American labor movement abandoned class-based radical politics and legislative reform for "economic voluntarism" and business unionism. For example, in fighting court injunctions against labor collective action, union leaders mobilized "recessive, radical strains and possibilities" in the rhetoric of private rights that pervaded constitutional law (Forbath 1991a, 135). At the same time, union leaders reinforced the economic and legal power of this constitutional rights discourse, "ratify[ing] many of industry's asymmetries of power" (Forbath 1991a, 135). In comparative view, legal differences, including an absence of judicial review and divergent legal procedures and substantive law even in common-law Britain (otherwise more similar to the United States than were the code law nations of Continental Europe) helped ensure enduring differences

of ideology and of collective identity, as well as of strategy and structure, between labor movements in the United States and Europe (Rogers 1990; Forbath 1991b; Voss 1993).

Historical and comparative scholarship on labor movements highlights the complexity inherent in law's political nature. Because overt mobilization of law on behalf of subordinate economic actors occurs within a broader political-economic environment in which formal-legal discourse and legal culture reinforce the ideological hegemony of capital, law is a resource for equality and justice, but only within limits leaving private ownership, market logic, and the economic power asymmetries between capital and labor intact (Stryker 2003).[8]

In sum, just as political approaches in economic sociology conceptualize economic action as conflictual and political (Fligstein 2001), we suggest that likewise, law is conflictual, political, and deeply implicated in the stabilization and transformation of power, *including* economic power and control (Stryker 2003). The financial, technical, and organizational resources accompanying economic power *do* provide economic "haves" with systematic advantages in "realizing their will" in formally egalitarian legal processes. But because legal principles operate as resources in complex and contradictory ways, law in capitalist political economies also provides openings for "have-nots."

An Institutional and Political Approach

To understand the interplay of law and the economy in today's globalized, multilevel, and highly institutionally differentiated political economy, we combine the ideas of institutionalization and of politics in legal fields. Following Stryker (2000a, 2002, 2003), we suggest that neoinstitutional theories of organization be modified to emphasize *both* institutional conditions under which taken-for-grantedness is likely to prevail *and* institutional conditions in which taken-for-grantedness is likely to be fragile, such that latent conflicts of meaning, values, and interests evolve into manifest conflicts.

Clearly, both institutional and political forces help to forge the intersection of law and the economy. Institutional processes may lead to widespread acceptance of certain forms of corporate compliance and constructions of legal rules affecting industries and organizations. But political contestation and power are critical factors in determining *which* legal principles and structures, forms of compliance, and constructions of rules come to dominate the economic world. To understand the interplay of law and the economy in today's differentiated and globalized political economy thus requires us to combine the ideas of institutionalization and of politics in legal fields. We must analyze how legal and economic ideas and ideals, norms and values, interests and power, behavior and institutions are mutually endogenous. To analyze endogeneity, we should examine the role of conflict and contestation—as well as their circumscription and limitation—in particular historical contexts.

THE INTERSECTION OF LAW AND THE ECONOMY

In this section, we review the extant theoretical and empirical work in light of the political-institutional framework on law and the economy that we outlined in the previous section. We draw on the extant literature to further elucidate how institutional meaning-attribution and political power-mobilization processes combine, so that legality shapes almost every aspect of economic life, and economic actors and institutions shape legality. No one piece of research explicitly examines all aspects of how law and the economy interrelate through the political and institutional processes we have specified. However, our political-institutional framework helps us systematize contributions and clarify gaps in the empirical research.

Our framework presumes that legal constructs, principles, and institutions shape the organizational forms and identities of economic actors, and they shape central elements of capitalist economic fields, such as valuation, exchange, and strategies of competition and cooperation. They do so both because legal constructs and institutions are incorporated into the logic and assumptions of economic activity, and because they serve as—or to help construct—cultural resources that economic actors can mobilize. In turn, as legal actors reframe economic conflicts in legal language so that they can adjudicate them, law necessarily incorporates some of the assumptions, language, and institutional logic of economic fields. Just as a capitalist economy is endogenous to law, law is endogenous to the economy. Law is shaped within economic fields by the very actors whose interactions the law seeks to constitute, facilitate, and regulate. Although framed in terms of recent developments in organizational and political sociology and the sociology of law, our framework is quite consistent with Max Weber's (1978) vision of how the rationalization of law—itself achieved through power struggles

among social groups—facilitated, promoted, legitimated, and reinforced economic rationalization.

We draw on Edelman and Suchman's (1997) typology of legal environments to show how extant research fits into our political-institutional framework and to help identify areas for future research. Edelman and Suchman suggest that legal environments operate as *facilitative* tools allowing organizations to structure their relations with competitors, customers, and suppliers; as *regulatory* edicts actively imposing societal authority on various aspects of economic life; and as *constitutive* constructs subtly influencing ideas about efficient organizational form and structure. In each of these forms, legal environments operate as portals through which legality constructs and is constructed by the economy.

Facilitative, regulatory, and constitutive legal environments should be understood as ideal types analytically distinguishing among diverse ways in which law matters to actors in economic fields. While we organize the literature in terms of these types, it is important to note that research often implicitly addresses two or all three of these types as well as the linkage between them. Far from representing intellectual sloppiness, the insight that each type of legal environment is likely to shape the others through a combination of institutional and political processes (so that any concrete empirical situation involves more than one of the types) is an essential feature of our theoretical framework.

The Facilitative Legal Environment

The *facilitative legal environment* includes passive procedural vehicles and forums that organizations may mobilize to resolve disputes, to structure their relations with other organizations, to govern their employees, to influence the behavior of regulatory agencies, and to gather information. When the facilitative environment is mobilized, it becomes implicated in overt political processes, as economic actors draw on legal constructs, procedures, and techniques as resources in the production, distribution, exchange, and consumption of goods and services, and to enhance their competitive position. At the same time, institutional processes play a role in the attribution of meaning to, and diffusion of, facilitative legal environments.

The role of the facilitative legal environment can be seen in Weber's (1978) comparative studies of law and the rise of capitalism. Weber showed that such legal tools as agency, negotiability, and the idea of the juristic or legal person facilitated development of capitalist economic action and institutions that had a very high degree of predictability, calculability, and systematization. For example, agency is the idea that one person (an agent) represents another (the principal) with the other's consent. Negotiable instruments include checks, banknotes, and other representations of unconditional promises to pay. Without these ideas and tools, commerce would be more difficult and less predictable. Without the idea of the legal person, a complex business organization could not be a legitimate party to a contract, because it would not be possible to know the standing of a business firm or its parts (see Trevino 1996 for an especially accessible discussion of Weber's ideas).

Further development and empirical instantiation of Weber's arguments may be found in contemporary work emphasizing the enabling aspects of corporation law (Sklar 1988; Roy 1990; Hurst 1970, 1982). Hurst (1970) highlights the key role of limited liability in promoting shareholder investment and economic growth in the early history of the United States, when commercial banks and business loans were not available to entrepreneurs. Differences in legal schema pertaining to the status of land (with the United States accepting land as a fully fledged tradable commodity) helped set divergent paths for U.S. and British economic development (Hurst 1982). Fligstein (2001) and Waarden (2002) emphasize law's role in stabilizing markets by reducing uncertainty, coordinating competition, and facilitating economic survival and growth. Fligstein (1990), and Carruthers, Babb, and Halliday (2001) highlight the role of law as a tool for additional economic resource acquisition or for managing debt.

Horowitz (1977) argues that in the pre–Civil War period, courts and judges adopted a new, "instrumental" view of the common law. In contrast to their eighteenth-century counterparts, who interpreted common-law rules with reference to fairness among private litigants, nineteenth-century judges interpreted these rules according to a different standard: how a given decision would affect American commerce. This fundamental shift made common law a powerful force for American economic development. Far from merely responding to "new or special economic or technological pressure," innovative reconceptualization of the role of common law often preceded economic innovation (Horowitz 1977, 3).

Sklar (1988) provides an account of the reciprocal relationship between specific legal and economic changes in the late-nineteenth- and early twentieth-century United States. Sklar (1988) highlights the many contradictions and inconsistencies in legal doctrine, noting for example, that from 1897 to about 1911–14, changes in property law established both legal and intellectual grounds for the corporate reorganization of property, while antitrust law still worked to inhibit this very same economic reorganization.

A key tool in the management of competition and conflict, the facilitative legal environment also comes into play in businesses' use of civil litigation (Cheit 1991; Galanter and Rogers 1991) and in the concomitant rise in the number and status of both in-house counsel and independent corporate law firms (Galanter and Rogers 1991). The increase in litigation itself results in increased insurance use (Cheit 1991); elevated bankruptcy rates (Delaney 1989); and less willingness to undertake high-risk innovation (Cheit 1991).

Organizations also engage the facilitative environment when they seek legal constraints on the market or the regulation of competitive industries. Industries use law strategically to secure direct government subsidies and rules that limit entry into the industry, that hinder competitors or otherwise provide an advantage against competitors, and that allow the management of competition (Stigler 1971; Gable 1953; Pfeffer 1974; Zhou 1993). Industries and organizations also seek favorable rule-making outcomes from administrative agencies (Posner 1974; Clune 1983; Hawkins 1984; Blumrosen 1993).

Often, alignments between industries and regulators come about over time through meaning-attribution and power-mobilization processes of law enforcement that we outlined previously. In the case of property insurance, for example, rate regulation was enacted over industry opposition but produced institutions and political settlement that protected insurance companies and agents from price competition (Schneiberg 1999; Schneiberg and Bartley 2001). In an important article on enforcing environmental laws, Sabatier (1975) emphasized that monitoring and active political mobilization by citizens' groups help counteract ordinary technical, financial, and access advantages of powerful firms and industries.

While our discussion so far has focused on formal legal procedures, the facilitative legal environment also provides an arena in which institutionalized norms and rituals develop around legal processes, often becoming more influential than formal law itself. Macaulay's (1963) seminal study of contract disputes showed that businessmen preferred to handle exchange relationships informally and to resolve disputes according to the norms of the business community rather than through lawsuits. Business culture is central to Macaulay's analysis, but businessmen themselves see informal dispute resolution as more efficient than litigation.

More recent work shows a rise in the use of alternative dispute resolution techniques such as mediation and arbitration to handle interbusiness disputes (Lande 1998; Morrill 1995) as well as a dramatic rise in the use of internal grievance procedures and various informal dispute resolution techniques for handling intraorganizational conflict (Edelman et al. 1993; Edelman and Cahill 1998; Edelman, Uggen, and Erlanger 1999; Edelman and Suchman 1999). Other work focuses on differences in disputing norms across organizations (Cahill 2001) and nations (Gibson and Caldiera 1996; Kagan and Axelrad 2000; Kagan 2001; Cahill 2001). This work suggests that when negotiation occurs in the "shadow of the law" (Mnookin and Kornhauser 1979), bargaining forms and outcomes are determined by a combination of expectations about what would happen if the dispute were negotiated in court and by institutionalized norms about economic behavior that depend on history, culture, and power (Commons 1924; Lempert and Sanders 1986).

In sum, the literature on the facilitative environment reveals both institutional and political processes at work. While the facilitative environment provides an arena in which certain types of transactions, relationships, and governance structures come to be taken-for-granted forms of economic exchange, it is also an arena of political struggle and the reproduction of power (Dezalay and Garth 1996). Legal procedures that facilitate economic activity for some actors often constrain the economic activity of other actors. Legal constraints on certain types of economic relationships render some industries more powerful than others, enhance the power and prestige of some professions, and alter the balance of power between labor and management. For example, the same legal principles in U.S. property and contract law that facilitated large-scale industrial organization and growth simultaneously constrained unionization and working-class collective action (Commons 1924; Tomlins 1993; Forbath 1991a).

Thus, facilitative legal environments provide a venue for the institutionalization of forms of economic exchange, association, and competition and for the reproduction of economic inequality and power. Our political-institutional perspective on law and the economy suggests that questions of *what the law facilitates* and *for whom* should be important guides to empirical research.

The Regulatory Legal Environment

The *regulatory legal environment* consists of substantive rules that impose societal authority on various aspects of organizational life. Antitrust, health and safety, environmental, and labor and employment statutes and directives all regulate organizations. Enforcement agencies such as the U.S. Environmental Protection Agency, National Labor Relations Board, and Equal Employment Opportunity Commission issue myriad administrative regulations, standards, and adjudicative rulings and guidelines, and courts issue substantive decisions articulating common-law principles and interpreting constitutions, treaties, statutes, directives, and administrative regulations. The regulatory environment also includes informal norms that have lawlike functions, for example, norms about diversity or consistent treatment of employees.

Both institutional and political processes operate in the regulatory context. Economic actors incorporate and respond to the normative ideals of their regulatory environments, just as legal actors incorporate and respond to the normative ideals that evolve in economic fields. Meanwhile, regulatory environments are sites for overt contestation over normative rules, as well as for mobilizing these rules as resources.

The politics of mobilization and countermobilization are particular salient in the context of regulation (see Stryker 2000b; Kagan and Axelrad 2000). Regulatory "capture" is said to occur when organizational power leads regulators to overlook or even to facilitate legally questionable practices of regulated organizations (Blumrosen 1965, 1993; Wirt 1970; Ackerman et al. 1974; Conklin 1977; Diver 1980; Clune 1983; Vaughan 1983; Hawkins 1984; but see Levine 1981; Horwitz 1986; Luchansky and Gerber 1993). Industry exercises significant power over regulators because of cash flow to political candidates who then appoint regulators and also because public agencies tend to rely on industry for expertise, information, and personnel to staff their agencies (Bardach 1989; Breyer 1982; Makkai and Braithwaite 1992; Yeager 1990).

Political processes are also evident in research showing how the consistent mobilization of social movement pressures on behalf of economically disadvantaged groups can help combat regulatory capture (Sabatier 1975; Pedriana and Stryker 1997, 2004). Stryker (1989) and Pedriana and Stryker (2004) showed that, in contexts of relentless social movement pressures from below, the National Labor Relations Board, the Equal Employment Opportunity Commission, and ultimately the Supreme Court interpreted and applied new statutory principles of labor or employment law in ways that, at least for a time, expanded employment and other workplace benefits for labor, minorities, and women. Capture is less likely when regulatory agencies actively organize the information acquisition and monitoring capacities of citizen groups (Sabatier 1975), when the federal government intervenes on behalf of women and minorities (Burstein 1991), and when employees can mobilize cultural resources to influence management (Scully and Segal 2002).

Research highlighting political processes emphasizes that legal rules may produce unintended economic results (see, e.g., Sklar 1988; Roe 1994; Fligstein 2001). For example, Dobbin and Dowd (2000) show how a Supreme Court decision unexpectedly upholding central provisions of the Interstate Commerce and Sherman Acts set off a chain of interest-based adaptation that had profound, though not readily predictable, results. The Court ruling made collusion among competitors illegal without mandating an alternative, so the Court undermined cartels without providing a business replacement. A politics of mobilization and countermobilization of alternative business competition principles ensued, and finance capitalists prevailed, giving them disproportionate influence on subsequent economic development.

Institutional approaches to the regulatory environment suggest that regulation also affects economic fields through more subtle institutional processes that do *not* hinge on such overt conflict. Because much law regulating organizations is ambiguous, the meaning of compliance tends to be collectively constructed by organizations over time. Organizations respond to ambiguous legal norms by creating "symbolic structures" such as affirmative action offices or discrimination grievance procedures that visibly demonstrate a commitment to legal ideals. Over time, those structures tend to acquire an institutionalized status as "rational" forms of compliance (Edelman 1992). The regulatory environment takes form gradually through organizational mimicry, the diffusion of professional norms, and the normative influence of state rules. In general, private organizations that are closer to the public sector—either through administrative or contractual linkages—tend to incorporate institutionalized ideas earlier than organizations further from the public sector (Edelman 1990, 1992; Sutton et al. 1994; Dobbin et al. 1993; Dobbin and Sutton 1998; Edelman, Uggen, and Erlanger 1999; Heimer 1999; Kelly and Dobbin 1998).

Although institutional processes lead to a diffusion of legalized symbolic structures, those structures may become vehicles for the transformation of legal ideals. Professionals who manage legal requirements and handle law-related complaints tend to recast legal norms in ways that infuse law with managerial logic (Edelman, Erlanger, and Lande 1993; Edelman, Abraham, and Erlanger 1992; Edelman, Fuller, and Mara-Drita 2001). Furthermore, as these "managerialized" understandings of law become widely accepted, they appear increasingly rational and gain legitimacy in the eyes of judges and juries. Courts tend to reconceptualize law in a way that subtly incorporates organizationally constructed forms of compliance, rendering the law "endogenous" to organizational fields (Edelman, Uggen, and Erlanger 1999; Edelman 2002).

There is debate within the literature about whether organizations experience their regulatory environment primarily as a set of externally imposed constraints altering their cost-benefit calculi, or as a set of normative ideals and institutionalized models of compliance. Economists, including law and economics scholars, generally favor the first approach, while sociologists of law generally favor the second. Economic and political sociologists are divided.

Work by economists investigating the impact of civil rights law on the employment of women and minorities suggests that regional and historical differences in laws and their enforcement promoted region- and time-specific incentive structures for employment by race and gender (Donahue and Heckman 1991; Smith and Welch 1984; Leonard 1984, 1986). Scholars who view organizations primarily as rational actors in their response to law suggest that organizations will calculate the relative value of compliance and noncompliance and alter their behavior accordingly (Diver 1980; Paternoster and Simpson 1996; Braithewaite and Makkai 1991; Genn 1993).

However, sanctions associated with noncompliance often are insufficient to deter illegal behavior because the risk of legal judgments or administrative fines often seems minimal compared to market-related risks such as product failure. That is, legal sanctions usually are too small and slow to affect rational organizational planning (Stone 1975; Jowell 1975). Moreover, decentralization tends to obscure the locus of negligence in organizations and to foster interdepartmental competition that subordinates legal compliance to market performance.

In short, rational choice deterrence models give a misleading picture of compliance. This does not, however, negate the idea of economic interest-based adaptation to regulatory environments. Rather, as we have tried to show, perceived strategic adaptations are socially constructed through the very institutional and political processes that we previously have outlined. For example, Edelman, Uggen, and Erlanger (1999) show that when personnel professionals began to advocate internal due process grievance procedures as devices to insulate organizations from external lawsuits, these procedures did not, in fact, decrease external lawsuits. Yet, over time, courts acknowledged and incorporated these procedures as evidence of compliance, so that what had been entirely "rational myth" began to confer economic cost savings.

In addition to Dobbin and Dowd's (2000) research showing how late-nineteenth-century constitutional law helped promote new models of business competition, mid-twentieth-century changes in antitrust legislation and—even earlier—in Justice Department enforcement strategies promoted new concepts of business control (Fligstein 1990). In general, antitrust laws in the United States and Europe shaped firms and markets in both intended and unintended ways (Jacoby 1985; Roy 1990; Fligstein 2001). Much scholarship documents the impact of labor law on unionization and strikes and analyzes cross-national variation in regulatory regimes (Rubin, Griffin, and Wallace 1983; Isaac and Griffin 1989; Ebbinghaus and Visser 1999; McCammon 1990; Kagan and Axelrad 2000). Streeck (this volume) shows that laws involving pension provision and financing, unemployment insurance, and social assistance have affected employment, wages, and unionization. Deregulation of capital flows appears to intensify the relationship between methods of social security financing and unemployment rates (Scharpf and Schmidt 2000). Stryker and Eliason (2003) suggest that cross-national variation in laws pertaining to day-care provision and labor market flexibility contributes to variation in female labor force participation across Europe.

The empirical patterns detailed by all these authors are consistent with an assumption that economic actors' perceptions of their interests, and the costs and benefits of alternative lines of action,

do play some role in law-economy connections. However, because economic sociologists ordinarily view law as exogenous to economic fields, there has been little recognition of how what is perceived to be economically and legally strategic is *mutually constituted* through interrelated institutional and political processes. Fligstein's *The Architecture of Markets* (2001, 84) exemplifies the view of law as exogenous:

> The transformation of existing markets results from exogenous forces: invasion, economic crisis or political intervention by states. . . . I propose an exogenous theory of market transformation that views the basic cause of changes in market structure as resulting from forces outside the control of producers, due to shifts in demand, invasion by other firms, or actions of the state [including law].[9]

In sum, research on the regulatory environment shows that both overt political processes and more subtle institutional processes shape the form and impact of regulation on the economy and infuse economic interests into the law. Extant work on institutional processes has focused on the United States. Thus, it is important that economic sociologists researching other parts of the world examine empirically how institutional processes interact with the political processes that have—to date—been emphasized in research on regulation in Europe (e.g., Weiler 1990; Majone 1994; Vogel 1996).

Similarly, in contrast to the portrait of law as exogenous that is found in much economic sociology, some recent research suggests that regulation often follows and reflects business practices and institutions that were themselves responses to the regulatory environment. Thus, researchers would do well to abandon models of law as exogenous influence in favor of an explicitly dynamic view that examines the reciprocal reshaping of legal and economic actors and institutions. Fligstein's research with Stone Sweet (2002) on the interrelated dynamics of law and markets in the European Community is exemplary in this regard, although it focuses almost exclusively on political mechanisms of institutionalization. The authors show that contests between the European Court of Justice and national legal regimes affected trade patterns, which in turn spurred more litigation. More litigation both further expanded cross-border trade and promoted EC-level legislation and lobbying, which then increased trade still further. Another excellent example of an endogenous approach to regulation is Schneiberg's (forthcoming) nuanced analysis of how state policies and market failures altered political alignments and institutional arrangements in the American property insurance industry, allowing new groups to mobilize legal resources to reshape policy and markets.

Future research should treat the endogeneity of law and the relative role of political and institutional processes as empirical questions. It is likely that under certain conditions, law acts as an exogenous shock and under other conditions is simultaneously constitutive of and constituted by economic forces within intersecting legal and economic fields. It is also likely that in some situations law operates primarily as a set of incentives and disincentives and in others as a set of normative ideals.

The Constitutive Legal Environment

The *constitutive legal environment* consists of concepts, definitional categories, labels, and ideas that play a subtle and often invisible role in how economic actors, including but not restricted to organizations, come into existence, organize their activities and relationships, and arrange their governance. Rather than providing procedural tools or substantive rules—as do facilitative and regulatory legal environments—the constitutive legal environment provides cognitive possibilities and values that influence the structure, form, and strategies of organizations.

For example, law generates understandings of what is and is not a corporation, of who is and who is not an employee, and of what constitutes a binding agreement between employer and employee or between organizations. Similarly, law helps define "economic" categories of competition, cooperation, and exchange, as well as such fundamental constructs as economic fairness, efficiency, rationality, and value. Legal labels such as *corporate person, employee, union, property, mutual fund, security,* and *bankruptcy* help to define which interactions and activities are legitimate and which are not. Further, many conceptual dichotomies that are central to the economy, such as employer/employee, public/private, procedure/substance, capital/labor, labor market/domestic labor, exempt/nonexempt, full time/part time, and permanent/contingent, derive meaning and impact in part from the constitutive legal environment. Similarly, the constitutive environment confers meaning on labor-market related concepts such as "labor pool," "applicant," "qualified," and "merit."

Legal categorizations define opportunities and limits for economic actors to take formal-political roles, defining rules of the game for fund-raising and lobbying. Similarly, legal constructs such as "standing to sue," "limited liability," "corporate veil," "sovereign immunity," and "federal question" define which economic disputes may be resolved within the legal system and which are outside the purview of law.

The constitutive legal environment is also a key factor in legitimating and institutionalizing various organizational institutions, so that organizational routines for hiring, firing, and promotion, or practices and policies regarding leave, dress, language, or accent appear natural and normal. Constitutive legal environments, moreover, shape abstract economic thinking about the nature of markets, of capitalism, and of how economy and polity are distinct, differentiated realms (cf. Krippner 2001). For example, Majone (1994) points out that a key impact of the European Court of Justice and the recent creation of "American-style" regulatory agencies to police newly privatized industries in Europe was that, for the first time, the concept of regulation had a meaning in Europe similar to its meaning in the United States.

The constitutive legal environment, then, is the arena of meaning-making with regard to both law and the economy. Consistent with our political-institutional framework, material manifestations of normative and cognitive frames are socially constructed through *both* institutional processes and political processes. A number of studies that have already been discussed in connection with the facilitative and regulatory legal environments also address the constitutive environment.

Among such research are studies on employee governance structures and logics (e.g., Edelman 1992; Sutton et al. 1994), conceptions of control and models of competition in firms, markets, and economic fields (Roy 1990; Fligstein 1990, 2001; Dobbin and Dowd 2000), and the collective identity and behavior of the U.S. labor movement (Forbath 1991a; Tomlins 1985, 1993). Also included are studies of such new organizational forms and actors in the economy as corporations and their boards of directors (Commons 1924; Hurst 1970, 1982), multinationals and conglomerates (Fligstein 2001), investment funds and capital markets in post-Communist Russia (Spicer 2002), financial markets in the United States (Roe 1994), cooperative and mutual organizational forms in the United States (Schneiberg 2002), and trading areas and monetary unions (Majone 1994; Fligstein and Mara-Drita 1996; Scharpf 1999; Fligstein and Stone Sweet 2002). Some of these studies emphasize the causal significance of institutional processes (e.g., Edelman 1990, 1992; Edelman, Uggen, and Erlanger 1999; Dobbin and Sutton 1998; Sutton et al. 1994); others of these studies emphasize the causal significance of political processes (e.g., Fligstein 1990, 2001; Fligstein and Mara-Drita 1996; Fligstein and Stone Sweet 2002; Spicer 2002; Schneiberg 2002; Dobbin and Dowd 2000; Scharpf 1999).

Research on the constitutive legal environment also has addressed ways in which contract law delineates symbols and rituals for forming binding agreements (Suchman 1995); how property law shapes ideas about organizations' control over resources and ideas (Campbell and Lindberg 1990); and how bankruptcy law affects organizations' priorities with respect to their various stakeholders (Delaney 1989). Other studies show that law generates particular organizational features, such as affirmative action policies (Edelman and Petterson 1999) or the "poison pill" takeover defense (Powell 1993; Davis 1991). Yet other research suggests that law codifies ground rules for entire organizational forms. For example, law helped to construct the modern limited-liability corporation (Coleman 1974, 1990; Seavoy 1982; Roy 1990; Creighton 1990; Klein and Majewski 1992) and to shape the boundaries between, and forms of, private firms, public agencies, collective enterprises, and nonprofit organizations (Nee 1992; Hansmann 1996; Campbell and Lindberg 1990).

There is much empirical research showing that the rise of the regulatory state and cross-national differences in its form and content are bound up with the creation of new occupational categories in the economy. Edelman (1992), Edelman, Uggen, and Erlanger (1999) and Edelman, Fuller, and Mara-Drita (2001) show that the post-1964 American regulatory state gave rise to the professional roles of diversity trainer and affirmative action officer. Similarly, Jacoby (1985), Sutton et al. (1994), Dobbin and Sutton (1998), and Baron, Dobbin, and Jennings (1986), highlight how legal changes both before and especially after World War II influenced growth of the personnel profession in the United States. Stryker (1994) emphasizes how "technocratization" of law in regulatory states created new occupational roles, such as the professional expert witness, for scientists. Halliday (1987) shows that changing capacities of the American state influenced the collective identity of the American legal profession over time. Finally, Rueschemeyer (1986) highlights differences in state structures in the United States, Germany, Britain, and Japan that resulted in cross-national variation in these countries' legal professions.

At the most fundamental level, the constitutive legal environment profoundly shapes social norms about human agency, responsibility, and accountability (Lempert and Sanders 1986). Likewise, it shapes concepts of economic rationality and efficiency, offering basic logics that seep into the culture and infrastructure of social interaction within organizations. In a now classic article, Meyer and Rowan (1977) emphasized that both modern organizations and modern law embrace a logic of legal rationality, or the importance of general and distinctively legal rules. Legal rationality is not entirely the product of formal law; formal-legal and organizational actors interact in ways that reinforce the logic of legal rationality in both law and the economy, generating lawlike ideas of industrial citizenship (Selznick 1969) and fairness (Edelman 1990).

As we discussed in prior sections, research by Edelman and her colleagues (e.g., Edelman 1992; Edelman, Uggen, and Erlanger 1999) elucidates institutional mechanisms through which constitutive legal environments work. Edelman (Edelman, Uggen, and Erlanger 1999; Edelman, Fuller, and Mara-Drita, 2001) describe reciprocal meaning-attribution processes through which economic and formal-legal actors interact to make their world. Managers and professionals in organizations construct the meaning of compliance, and courts incorporate these interpretations into the meaning of formal law. In all this research, endogeneity of law works by infusing into the law evolving ideas of justice, legality, and rationality in the economic realm.

Edelman, Uggen, and Erlanger (1999) show that ideas about good-faith efforts at compliance and rational organizational governance that were devised by organizations in response to the overt politics of the civil rights movement and attendant civil rights legislation in the 1960s were uncritically accepted as rational and just by courts in the 1980s. And Edelman, Fuller, and Mara-Drita (2001) show that ideas about civil rights were transformed in the context of managerial rhetoric about diversity. Similarly, courts tend to accept ideas about "rational" economic behavior that originate in economic fields, thus legitimating organizational practices such as word-of-mouth hiring, accent and language requirements, dress codes, internal labor market procedures, and market-based pay rates (Edelman 2002; Edelman, Uggen, and Erlanger 1999; Nelson and Bridges 1999).

Research on the constitutive environment, then,

suggests that because of the overlap between economic and legal fields, ideas about the rationality of economic institutions that develop within economic fields flow easily into legal fields. Thus when employers cite the "efficiency" of particular practices, courts tend to accept that logic as legitimate and to overlook the role of these practices in perpetuating disadvantage for groups that the law views as requiring extra protection. For example, word-of-mouth hiring often severely disadvantages racial minorities (Kirschenman and Neckerman 1991), historical race and gender stereotypes are perpetuated through apparently neutral internal labor market job categorizations (Baron 1991), and internal grievance procedures may legitimate discriminatory practices (Edelman, Erlanger, and Lande 1993).

While much of the work of the constitutive environment occurs through subtle institutional processes, overt politics also play a role as organizations and lawyers seek to construct their legal environments through litigation and lobbying—often devising new conceptual categories or manipulating legal symbols for political advantage (Powell 1993; Suchman 1995). For example, employers successfully defended Title VII discrimination claims based on comparable worth principles, by mobilizing taken-for-granted market logics to argue against their own responsibility and legal liability (England 1993). Similarly, employers successfully mobilized such logics in equal pay litigation, diminishing the resource value of equal pay legislation for American women (Nelson and Bridges 1999). Yeager (1990) shows that taken-for-granted notions of the worthiness of private business activity led regulators to treat environmental crime as less deserving of moral disapprobation than street crime, and thus to weaken environmental enforcement.

In short, political and institutional processes operate in tandem to produce meanings that are shared across legal and economic fields.[10] Research on the constitutive environment highlights "the limits of law." While court adjudication is a realm for overt resource mobilization, as is the contestation and negotiation between regulatory agencies and regulated parties, taken-for-granted assumptions shape how these conflicts are framed and may limit the impact of regulation. More generally, research suggests that the constitutive legal environment plays a critical role in shaping facilitative and regulatory legal environments. The cross-fertilization of ideas at the intersection of legal and economic fields provides fodder for new ways of employing law in economic transactions and new ways of responding to or circumventing regulation.

Further research on the constitutive environment should explore the interplay between overt political contestation of meanings and more covert institutional diffusion of meanings. It may be that we should expect an overt politics of law to dominate in periods of economic or political crisis, while institutional processes dominate during periods of more routine response to law. At the same time, both theoretical and empirical work show that overt politics are not banished in "more routine" settings, but rather contained within substantive and procedural limits (Stryker 1994, 1996).

Research should also examine cross-national differences in the meanings attributed to legal constructs. Legal concepts may be expressed in superficially similar language, yet have a long history of diverse meanings across contexts. For example, the meaning of *employment* in Britain simply denotes an occupation undertaken for remuneration and subordinate to an employer. It does not imply any rights of protection whereas the French *emploi* (employment) does invoke norms of protection (Clarke, Gijsel, and Janssen 2000).

Conclusion

The framework that we have developed in this chapter offers a sociological approach to the interplay of law and the economy. It builds on classical social theory—in particular the work of Max Weber—and on the broader notion of law as legality that is central to the sociology of law. The central tenet of our approach is the endogeneity of both law and the economy: legality derives meaning from and sustains economic structures, action, and power, while economic structures, action, and power draw on and reconstitute legality. The reciprocal construction and reconstruction of law and the economy occurs at the intersection of legal and economic fields, which are social realms that are centered upon legal and economic institutions, respectively. We identify two processes that promote this endogeneity: institutional processes that involve taken-for-granted meanings, and political contests and power struggles that involve overt conflict. The two are interrelated in multiple ways: for example, institutionalized rituals and taken-for-granted routines shape interests and coalitions and help to define the boundaries of disputes; actors mobilize institutionalized rituals and models as symbolic resources for political struggles; political shifts may disrupt institutionalized patterns and allow new institutional processes to arise. The interaction of institutional and political processes helps to explain both stability and change in legal and economic fields.

To review extant knowledge about the interplay of law and the economy, we used Edelman and Suchman's (1997) typology of legal environments. The three facets of legal environments that we discussed represent different aspects of intersection between legal and economic fields and further illuminate how legality and market logics may be mutually constitutive through institutional and political processes.

The facilitative legal environment is the realm of procedure. Here law provides a set of tools, norms, and routines that shapes the form of economic action. And conversely, economic strategies and political interests shape the range of legal tools that are available and conventions about how and under what conditions these tools are used. The facilitative legal environment is simultaneously a set of institutionalized conventions that shape the use of law and a set of resources that may be mobilized in power struggles over market share, occupational boundaries, the use of technology, conditions of labor, and many other elements of economic life.

The regulatory legal environment is the realm of normative social control. Here law operates both as a set of incentives and disincentives and as a set of normative ideals that shape the behavior of firms. In contrast to accounts that see regulation as an exogenous force to which organizations respond, our model suggests that the norms embodied by the regulatory environment are responsive to the everyday problems and institutionalized rituals of economic life and that they are often the subject of battles between industries, labor and management, and other economic constituencies. Political lobbying, regulatory capture, structural networks, and social movements render the regulatory legal environment as much the product as the producer of economic life.

The constitutive legal environment is the realm of meaning-making, symbols, and culture. Institutional processes within the constitutive legal environment powerfully bind the logics of legal and economic fields as legal language and constructs shape the form and basis of capitalism and capitalist logics shape legal conceptions of fairness, efficiency, rationality, and business necessity. But political processes are also operative as opposing forces contest the meaning of law and justice.

In all three types of legal environments, we emphasized both the overt and covert exercise of power. We showed how the interplay of these two forms of power contributed to the complex and sometimes contradictory nature of the role that law plays in overlapping legal and economic fields. Capitalist political economies are characterized both by opportunities for enhanced justice and by the "limits of law." The openings that law provides to increase the well-being of disadvantaged economic actors are circumscribed in ways that keep fundamental asymmetries of economic power intact.

While the three facets of legal environments are presented as analytically distinct ideal types, any empirical situation (say, firms responding to antitrust law or unions responding to labor law) is likely to involve multiple facets at once. More important, the three types of legal environments affect each other through interrelated institutional and political processes. Changes in the constitutive legal environment affect the legal tools available through the facilitative environment and the meaning of rules in the regulatory environment, and the reverse is true as well. Regulation is itself a facilitative tool in some contexts as industries seek to control competition through rate regulation or tariffs or antitrust maneuvers. And the facilitative environment shapes the constitutive and regulatory environments, as the creative use of legal procedures often generates new symbols, meanings, norms, principles, and substantive rules.

The political-institutional model we propose has significant implications for economic sociology. First and foremost, our model suggests that the insights of economic sociology on the social embeddedness of markets must be extended to law. While law may operate under some circumstances as an exogenous shock to economic fields, law and legality are more often both produced by and a product of economic constructions. Most obviously, economic actors lobby and litigate for particular legal rules and administrative interpretations of rules. Somewhat less obviously, judicial constructions of law necessarily reflect conceptions of rationality, efficiency, fairness, and compliance that are tested, contested, institutionalized, and sometimes fractured within economic fields. Lawyers, judges, personnel professionals, employers, and employees act as conduits of institutionalized ideas and as contestants in political battles to shape the meaning of law in overlapping legal and economic fields. It is therefore critical that economic sociology treat law not as a force outside of the socially embedded economy but rather as a force within, and a product of, that economy. Ordinarily, legal and economic fields will be mutually endogenous, through a reciprocal, causal dynamic that is, at once, institutional and political.

Our model also stands as a sociological alternative to law and economics scholarship. We incorporate the notion from economic sociology that markets should be understood not as the interaction of individual preference-maximizing rational actors but rather as social fields in which ideas about rationality are collectively defined and institutionalized. But by also incorporating a broader notion of law as legality manifested in institutionalized social fields overlapping with economic fields, we challenge the idea that "economic rationality" can be understood apart from its law-related social construction.

Law both incorporates and reinforces economic understandings of rational action, and of the preferences that economic models usually treat as exogenous. Rather than providing a context within which actors make "rational choices," law tends to reify ideas of rationality that predominate in economic fields. To the extent that institutionalized ideas in economic fields bolster the power of capitalists over workers or support organizational practices that discriminate against minorities and women, law tends to legitimate those power relations. Extraordinary conditions, such as economic crises and depressions, and massive crises of political legitimacy coupled with sustained social movement pressure from below, loosen the taken-for-grantedness of prior economic routines. This creates somewhat larger openings for the disadvantaged to influence institutionalization in intersecting legal and economic fields. Short of such extraordinary conditions, law in capitalist political economies tends to legitimate and reify the status and power hierarchies that are played out in economic life.

NOTES

1. Preferences, moreover, are often understood as "revealed" through an individual's choices. Thus the actions that individuals take are assumed to reveal their preferences irrespective of social constraints that may shape individual actions, rendering the revealed preference theory tautological (Gould 1992). Choices that appear to deviate from rationality, moreover, tend to be explained as involving the maximization of a different dimension or are attributed to lack of information.

2. Economists define *Pareto efficiency* as the condition where no person can be made better (according to his own preferences) without another person being made worse off. A variant, *Kaldor-Hicks efficiency*, holds that some persons could be made better off if they would at least in theory be willing to compensate those who are made worse off (Cooter and Ulen 2000).

3. Recently, some law and economics scholars have begun to elaborate neoclassical economic theory to posit endogenous preferences (Dau-Schmidt 1990; Sunstein 1993). Although these accounts come considerably closer to recognizing the social embeddedness of economic action, they generally recognize the role of law but not of culture in shaping preferences, and they retain the assumption of preference-maximizing rational actors.

4. Building on the Progressive Era tradition, Rose-Ackerman's (1988, 343) "reformist law and economics" takes issue with dominant strands of contemporary law and economics. While operating within the basic paradigm of economic theory and retaining methodological individualism, Rose-Ackerman does not presume the primacy of existing property rights distributions or the superiority of common law to legislation.

5. There are multiple strands of institutional theory in sociology, and each conceptualizes institutions and institutional processes somewhat differently (see Scott 2003; Stryker 2003). Those who emphasize how state institutions shape the relationship between politics and policies sometimes call themselves political or historical institutionalists. Neoinstitutionalists of organization have been criticized for insufficiently attending to political conflicts, but some have emphasized such conflicts (see Powell and DiMaggio 1991; Stryker 2000a). To enhance the analytic clarity and utility of our framework, we provide particular conceptualizations of "institutional" and "political" processes, highlighting the two as *distinct* social (and causal) mechanisms. However, because broader traditions labeled institutional and political intersect, some of the literature we cite can be appropriated fairly by either or both traditions.

6. Prior to the 1970s, most work in organization theory focused on organizations as the key unit of analysis and conceptualized organizations as rational and goal-oriented. Consistent with much thinking in economics, scholars sought to understand how organizations could most efficiently respond to their technological needs, hire and manage labor, and manage competition (Blau and Scott 1962; Thompson 1967; Pfeffer and Salancik 1978; see Scott 2003 for a review).

7. Debating issues such as the "relative autonomy of the state," neo-Marxist political sociology in the 1960s and 1970s provided a foundational set of concepts and social mechanisms to specify possibilities and limits of progressive social reform in democratic capitalism (e.g., Miliband 1969; Poulantzas 1973; Offe 1975; Therborn 1978; Block 1987). Causal mechanisms often were divided into those considered "instrumental" and those considered "structural." The former operated through overt resource mobilization, whereas the latter operated covertly, including through capital's ideological hegemony. Structural mechanisms also depended on the fact that capitalist states were excluded from private economic production, but depended on capital accumulation in the private economy for their capacity and legitimacy in governing.

8. For a more complete summary of this argument, including extended elaboration of examples, see Stryker 2003. The legal history literature makes much the same points about the constitutive power of law as do sociologists of law who emphasize law as legality.

9. Fligstein (2001) recognizes that law as a dependent variable varies according to the balance of power among diverse political-economic actors. But his 2001 book does not

recognize that legal and economic forms, norms, and fields are intricately intertwined in an endogenous system.

10. Interestingly, post-Coasean law and economics scholarship implicitly incorporates elements of the constitutive environment without appreciating its full implications. For example, law and economics scholars note that law may affect the relative appeal of "constituting" market contracts as opposed to hierarchical organization through its impact on bargaining costs or "transaction costs" (Williamson 1975, 1981, 1985, 1991; Posner 1972; Masten 1990). Likewise, law in many ways constitutes the market and the economy by establishing property rights and other rules that affect the power balance among economic actors (Campbell and Lindberg 1990). Yet law and economics scholars do not recognize the *social construction* of economic rationality and of economic efficiency. The social construction of efficiency is a clear implication of our explicit development of the ideas of the constitutive legal environment and the mutual endogeneity of law and the economy.

REFERENCES

Ackerman, Bruce A., Susan Rose Ackerman, James W. Sawyer Jr., and Dale W. Henderson. 1974. *The Uncertain Search for Environmental Quality*. New York: Free Press.

Adamany, David, and Joel B. Grossman. 1983. "Support for the Supreme Court as a National Policymaker." *Law and Policy Quarterly* 5:405–37.

Albiston, Catherine. 1999. "The Rule of Law and the Litigation Process: The Paradox of Losing by Winning." *Law and Society Review* 33:869–910.

Aron, Nan. 1989. *Liberty and Justice for All: Public Interest Law in the 1980s and Beyond*. Boulder, Colo.: Westview Press.

Balbus, Isaac. 1977. "Commodity Form and Legal Form: An Essay on the 'Relative Autonomy' of the Law." *Law and Society Review* 11:571–88.

Bardach, Eugene. 1989. "Social Regulation as a Generic Policy Instrument." Pp. 197–230 in *Beyond Privatization: The Tools of Government Action*, ed. Lester M. Salamon. Washington, D.C.: Urban Institute Press.

Baron, James M. 1991. "Organizational Evidence of Ascription in Labor Markets." Pp. 113–43 in *New Approaches to Economic and Social Analyses of Discrimination*, ed. Richard R. Cornwall and Phanindra V. Wunnava. Westport, Conn.: Praeger.

Baron, James M., Frank R. Dobbin, and P. Devereaux Jennings. 1986. "War and Peace: The Evolution of Modern Personnel Administration in U.S. Industry." *American Journal of Sociology* 92:350–83.

Blau, Peter M., and W Richard Scott. 1962. *Formal Organizations: A Comparative Approach*. San Francisco: Chandler.

Block, Fred. 1987. *Revising State Theory: Essays in Politics and Post-Industrialism*. Philadelphia: Temple University Press.

Blumrosen, Alfred W. 1965. "Anti-discrimination Laws in Action in New Jersey: A Law-Sociology Study." *Rutgers Law Review* 19:187–287.

———. 1993. *Modern Law: The Law Transmission System and Equal Employment Opportunity*. Madison: University of Wisconsin Press.

Bourdieu, Pierre. 1987. "The Force of Law: Toward a Sociology of the Juridical Field." *Hastings Law Journal* 38:814–53.

Braithwaite, John, and T. Makkai. 1991. "Testing an Expected Utility Model of Corporate Deterrence." *Law and Society Review* 25:7–40.

Breyer, Stephen. 1982. *Regulation and Its Reform*. Cambridge: Harvard University Press.

Bumiller, Kristin 1987. "Victims in the Shadow of the Law: A Critique of the Model of Legal Protection." *Signs* 12:421–34.

———. 1988. *The Civil Rights Society: The Social Construction of Victims*. Baltimore: John Hopkins University Press.

Burstein, Paul. 1991. "Legal Mobilization as a Social Movement Tactic: The Struggle for Equal Employment Opportunity." *American Journal of Sociology* 96:1201–25.

Cahill, Mia. 2001. *The Social Construction of Sexual Harassment Law: The Role of the National, Organizational, and Individual Context*. Burlington, Vt.: Ashgate/Dartmouth.

Campbell, John L., and Leon Lindberg. 1990. "Property Rights and the Organization of Economic Activity by the State." *American Sociological Review* 55:634–47.

Carruthers, Bruce G., Sarah Babb, and Terence C. Halliday. 2001. "Institutionalizing Markets, or the Market for Institutions? Central Banks, Bankruptcy Laws, and the Globalization of Financial Markets." In *The Rise of Neoliberalism and Institutional Analysis*, ed. John L. Campbell and Ove K. Pederson. Princeton: Princeton University Press.

Chambliss, William J. 1964. "A Sociological Analysis of the Law of Vagrancy." *Social Problems* 12:67–77.

Cheit, Ross E. 1991. "Corporate Ambulance Chasers: The Charmed Life of Business Litigation." *Studies in Law, Politics, and Society* 11:119–40.

Clarke, Linda, Peter de Gijsel, and Jörn Janssen. 2000. "Wage Relations and European Wage Policy." Pp. 3–10 in *The Dynamics of Wage Relations in the New Europe*, ed. Linda Clarke, Peter de Gijsel, and Jörn Janssen. Boston: Kluwer Academic.

Clemens, Elisabeth S., and James M. Cook. 1999. "Politics and Institutionalism: Explaining Durability and Change." *Annual Review of Sociology* 25:441–66.

Clune, William H. 1983. "A Political Model of Implementation and the Implications of the Model for Public Policy, Research, and the Changing Role of Lawyers." *Iowa Law Review* 69:47–125.

Coleman, James S. 1974. *Power and the Structure of Society*. New York: W. W. Norton.

———. 1990. *Foundations of Social Theory*. Cambridge: Belknap Press of Harvard University.

Collins, Hugh. 1982. *Marxism and Law*. Oxford: Clarendon Press.

Commons, John R. 1924. *The Legal Foundations of Capitalism*. Madison: University of Wisconsin Press.

Conklin, J. E. 1977. *Illegal but Not Criminal: Business Crime in America*. Englewood Cliffs, N.J.: Prentice-Hall.

Cooter, Robert, and Thomas Ulen. 2000. *Law and Economics*. Reading, Mass.: Addison-Wesley.

Creighton, Andrew. 1990. *The Emergence of Incorporation as a Legal Form for Organizations*. Ph.D. diss., Department of Sociology, Stanford University.

Dau-Schmidt, Kenneth G. 1990. "An Economic Analysis of the Criminal Law as a Preference Shaping Policy." *Duke Law Journal* 1990:1–38.

Davis, Gerald F. 1991. "Agents without Principles? The Spread of the Poison Pill through Intercorporate Networks." *Administrative Science Quarterly* 36:583–613.

Delaney, Kevin J. 1989. "Power, Intercorporate Networks, and 'Strategic Bankruptcy.'" *Law and Society Review* 23:643–66.

Dezalay, Yves, and Bryant G. Garth. 1996. *Dealing in Virtue: International Commercial Arbitration and the Construction of a Transnational Legal Order*. Chicago: University of Chicago Press.

DiMaggio, Paul, and Walter W. Powell. 1983. "The Iron Cage Revisited: Institutional Isomorphism and Collective Rationality in Organizational Fields." *American Sociological Review* 48:147–60.

Diver, Colin. 1980. "A Theory of Regulatory Enforcement." *Public Policy* 28:257–99.

Dobbin, Frank. 1994. *Forging Industrial Policy: The United States, Britain, and France in the Railway Age*. Cambridge: Cambridge University Press.

Dobbin, Frank, and Timothy Dowd. 2000. "The Market That Antitrust Built: Public Policy, Private Coercion, and Railroad Acquisitions, 1825–1922." *American Sociological Review* 65:635–57.

Dobbin, Frank, and John R. Sutton. 1998. "The Strength of a Weak State: The Rights Revolution and the Rise of Human Resource Management Divisions." *American Journal of Sociology* 104:441–76.

Dobbin, Frank, John R. Sutton, John W. Meyer, and W. Richard Scott. 1993. "Equal Employment Opportunity Law and the Construction of Internal Labor Markets." *American Journal of Sociology* 99:396–427.

Donahue, John J., III. 1988. "Law and Economics: The Road Not Taken." *Law and Society Review* 22:902–26.

Donahue, John J., and James Heckman. 1991. "Continuous vs. Episodic Change: The Impact of Civil Rights Policy on the Economic Status of Blacks." *Journal of Economic Literature* 29:1603–43.

Ebbinghaus, Bernard, and Jelle Visser. 1999. "When Institutions Matter: Union Growth and Decline in Western Europe, 1950–1995." *European Sociological Review* 15:135–58.

Edelman, Lauren B. 1990. "Legal Environments and Organizational Governance. The Expansion of Due Process in the Workplace." *American Journal of Sociology* 95:1401–40.

———. 1992. "Legal Ambiguity and Symbolic Structures: Organizational Mediation of Civil Rights Law." *American Journal of Sociology* 97:1531–76.

———. 2002. "Legality and the Endogeneity of Law." In *Legality and Community: On the Intellectual Legacy of Philip Selznick*, ed. Robert Kagan, Martin Krygier, and Kenneth Winston. Lanham, Md.: Rowman and Littlefield.

Edelman, Lauren B., Steven E. Abraham, and Howard S. Erlanger. 1992. "Professional Construction of the Legal Environment: The Inflated Threat of Wrongful Discharge Doctrine." *Law and Society Review* 26:47–83.

Edelman, Lauren B., and Mia Cahill. 1998. "How Law Matters in Disputing and Dispute Processing; or, the Contingency of Legal Matter in Alternative Dispute Resolution." In *How Does Law Matter?* ed. Bryant G. Garth and Austin Sarat. Evanston, Ill.: Northwestern University Press.

Edelman, Lauren B., Howard S. Erlanger, and John Lande. 1993. "Internal Dispute Resolution: The Transformation of Civil Rights in the Workplace." *Law and Society Review* 27:497–534.

Edelman, Lauren B., Sally Riggs Fuller, and Iona Mara-Drita. 2001. "Diversity Rhetoric and the Managerialization of Law." *American Journal of Sociology* 106:1589–1641.

Edelman, Lauren B., and Stephen Petterson. 1999. "Symbols and Substance in Organizational Response to Civil Rights Law." *Research in Social Stratification and Mobility* 17:107–35.

Edelman, Lauren B., and Mark C. Suchman. 1997. "The Legal Environments of Organizations." *Annual Review of Sociology* 23:479–515.

———. 1999. "When the 'Haves' Hold Court: The Internationalization of Law in Organizational Fields." *Law and Society Review* 33:941–92.

Edelman, Lauren B., Christopher Uggen, and Howard Erlanger. 1999. "The Endogeneity of Legal Regulation: Grievance Procedures as Rational Myth." *American Journal of Sociology* 105:406–54.

Edelman, Murray. 1964. *The Symbolic Uses of Politics*. Urbana: University of Illinois Press.

Ellickson, Robert C. 1986. *Order without Law: How Neighbors Settle Disputes*. Cambridge: Harvard University Press.

Engel, David. 1998. "How Does Law Matter in the Constitution of Legal Consciousness?" Pp. 109–44 in *How Does Law Matter?* ed. Bryant G. Garth and Austin Sarat. Evanston, Ill.: Northwestern University Press.

England, Paula. 1993. *Comparable Worth: Theories and Evidence*. New York: Aldine de Gruyter.

Erlanger, Howard S., Elizabeth Chambliss, and Marygold S. Melli. 1997. "Participation and Flexibility in

Informal Processes: Cautions from the Divorce Context." *Law and Society Review* 21:585–604.

Evans, Peter. 1995. *Embedded Autonomy: States and Industrial Transformation*. Princeton: Princeton University Press.

Evans, Peter, and James Rauch. 1999. "Bureaucracy and Growth: A Cross-National Analysis of the Effects of 'Weberian' State Structures on Economic Growth." *American Sociological Review* 64:748–65.

Ewick, Patricia, and Susan S. Silbey. 1998. *The Common Place of Law: Stories from Everyday Life*. Chicago: University of Chicago Press.

Felstiner, William, Rick Abel, and Austin Sarat. 1980. "Naming, Blaming, and Claiming." *Law and Society Review* 15:631–54.

Fligstein, Neil. 1990. *The Transformation of Corporate Control*. Cambridge: Harvard University Press.

———. 2001. *The Architecture of Markets: The Economic Sociology of Twenty-first-Century Capitalist Societies*. Princeton: Princeton University Press.

Fligstein, Neil, and Iona Mara-Drita. 1996. "How to Make a Market: Reflections on the Attempt to Create a Single Market in the European Union." *American Journal of Sociology* 102:1–33.

Fligstein, Neil, and Alec Stone Sweet. 2002. "Constructing Politics and Markets: An Institutionalist Account of European Integration." *American Journal of Sociology* 107:1206–43.

Forbath, William. 1991a. *Law and the Shaping of the American Labor Movement*. Cambridge: Harvard University Press.

———. 1991b. "Courts, Constitutions, and Labor Politics in England and America: A Study of the Constitutive Power of Law." *Law and Social Inquiry* 16:1–34.

Freeman, Alan. 1990. "Anti-discrimination Law: The View from 1989." *Tulane Law Review* 64:1407–41.

Friedland, Roger, and Robert Alford. 1991. "Bringing Society Back In: Practices and Institutional Contradictions." Pp. 232–63 in *The New Institutionalism in Organizational Analysis,* ed. Walter W. Powell and Paul J. DiMaggio. Chicago: University of Chicago Press.

Friedman, Lawrence. 1975. *The Legal System: A Social Science Perspective*. New York: Russell Sage Foundation.

———. 1984. *American Law: An Introduction*. New York: W. W. Norton.

Frohmann, Lisa. 1997. "Convictability and Discordant Locales: Reproducing Race, Class, and Gender Ideologies in Prosecutorial Decision-Making." *Law and Society Review* 31:531–56.

Fuller, Sally Riggs, Lauren B. Edelman, and Sharon Matusik. 2000. "Legal Readings: Employee Interpretation and Enactment of Civil Rights Law." *Academy of Management Review* 25:200–216.

Gable, Richard. 1953. "NAM: Influential Lobby or Kiss of Death?" *Journal of Politics*. 15:254–73.

Galanter, Marc. 1974. "Why the Haves Come Out Ahead: Speculation on the Limits of Legal Change." *Law and Society Review* 8:95–160.

Galanter, Marc, and Joel Rogers. 1991. "A Transformation of American Business Disputing? Some Preliminary Observations." Working paper, Institute for Legal Studies, Madison, Wis.

Genn, Hazel. 1993. "Business Responses to the Regulation of Health and Safety in England." *Law and Policy* 15:219–33.

Genovese, Eugene. 1976. *Roll, Jordan, Roll*. New York: Pantheon.

Gibson, James L. 1981. "The Role Concept in Judicial Research." *Law and Policy Quarterly* 3:291–311.

Gibson, James L., and Gregory A. Calderia. 1996. "The Legal Cultures of Europe." *Law and Society Review* 30:55–85.

Gould, Mark. 1992. "Law and Sociology: Some Consequences for the Law of Employment Discrimination Deriving from the Sociological Reconstruction of Economic Theory." *Cardozo Law Review* 13:1517–78.

Gusfield, Joseph R. 1996. *Contested Meanings: Construction of Alcohol Problems*. Madison: University of Wisconsin Press.

Halliday, Terence C. 1987. *Beyond Monopoly: Lawyers, State Crises, and Professional Empowerment*. Chicago: University of Chicago Press.

Hansmann, H. 1996. *The Ownership of Enterprise*. Cambridge: Belknap Press of Harvard University Press.

Harcourt, Bernard E. 2001. *Illusion of Order: The False Promise of Broken Windows Policing*. Cambridge: Harvard University Press.

Hawkins, Keith. 1984. *Environment and Enforcement: Regulation and the Social Definition of Pollution*. Oxford: Clarendon Press.

Heimer, Carol. 1999. "Competing Institutions: Law, Medicine, and Family in Neonatal Intensive Care." *Law and Society Review* 33:17–67.

Heinz, John P., and Edward O. Laumann. 1977. *Chicago Lawyers: The Social Structure of the Bar*. New York: Russell Sage Foundation.

Horowitz, Morton J., 1977. *The Transformation of American Law, 1780–1860*. Cambridge: Harvard University Press.

Horwitz, Robert B. 1986. "Understanding Deregulation." *Theory and Society* 15:139–74.

Hovencamp, Herbert. 1990. "The First Great Law and Economics Movement." *Stanford Law Review* 42:993–1058.

Hurst, James Willard. 1970. *The Legitimacy of the Business Corporation in the Law of the United States, 1870–1970*. Charlottesville: University of Virginia Press.

———. 1982. *Law and Markets in United States History: Different Modes of Bargaining among Interests*. Madison: University of Wisconsin Press.

Isaac, Larry, and Larry J. Griffin. 1989. "Ahistoricism in Time-Series Analysis of Historical Process: Critique, Redirection, and Illustrations from US Labor History." *American Sociological Review* 54:873–90.

Jacoby, Sanford. 1985. *Employing Bureaucracy: Man-*

agers, Unions, and the Transformation of Work in Industry, 1900–1945. New York: Columbia University Press.

Jowell, Jeffrey L. 1975. *Law and Bureaucracy: Administrative Discretion and the Limits of Legal Action.* Port Washington, N.Y.: Kennikat.

Kagan, Robert. 2001. *Adversarial Legalism: The American Way of Law.* Cambridge: Harvard University Press.

Kagan, Robert, and Lee Axelrad. 2000. *Regulatory Encounters: Multinational Corporations and American Adversarial Legalism.* Berkeley and Los Angeles: University of California Press.

Kelly, Erin, and Frank R. Dobbin. 1998. "How Affirmative Action Became Diversity Management." *American Behavioral Scientist* 41:960–84.

Kirschenman, Joleen, and Kathryn M. Neckerman. 1991. "We'd Love to Hire Them but . . . : The Meaning of Race to Employers." Pp. 203–32 in *The Urban Underclass,* ed. Christopher Jencks and Paul Peterson. Washington, D.C.: Brookings Institution Press.

Klare, Karl E. 1998. "Critical Theory and Labor Relations Law." Pp. 539–68 in *The Politics of Law,* ed. David Kairys. New York: Basic Books.

Klein Daniel B., and John Majewski. 1992. "Economy, Community, and Law: The Turnpike Movement in New York, 1797–1845." *Law and Society Review* 26:469–512.

Kostiner, Idit. 2003. "Evaluating Legality: Toward a Cultural Approach to the Study of Law and Social Change." *Law and Society Review* 37:323–68.

Krippner, Greta. 2001. "The Elusive Market: Embeddedness and the Paradigm of Economic Sociology." *Theory and Society* 30:775–810.

Lande, John. 1998. "The Diffusion of a Process Pluralist Ideology of Disputing: Factors Affecting Opinions of Business Lawyers and Executives." Ph.D. diss., University of Wisconsin, Madison.

Lempert, Richard, and Joseph Sanders. 1986. *An Invitation to Law and Social Science: Desert, Disputes, and Distribution.* London: Longman.

Leonard, Jonathan S. 1984. "Antidiscrimination or Reverse Discrimination: The Impact of Changing Demographics, Title VII, and Affirmative Action Productivity." *Journal of Human Resources* 19:145–74.

———. 1986. "The Effectiveness of Equal Employment Law and Affirmative Action Regulation." *Research in Labor Economics* 8:319–50.

Levine, Kay, and Virginia Mellema. 2001. "Strategizing the Street: How Law Matters in the Lives of Women in the Street-Level Drug Economy." *Law and Social Inquiry* 26:169–207.

Levine, M. 1981. "Revision Revised? Airline Deregulation and the Public Interest." *Law and Contemporary Problems* 44:179–95.

Luchansky B., and J. Gerber. 1993. "Constructing State Economy: The Federal Trade Commission and the

Celler-Kefauver Act." *Sociological Perspectives* 36: 217–40.

Lukes, Steven. 1974. *Power: A Radical View.* London: Macmillan.

Macaulay, Stewart. 1963. "Non-contractual Relations in Business: A Preliminary Study." *American Sociological Review* 28:55–67.

MacKinnon, Catherine. 1989. *Toward a Feminist Theory of the State.* Cambridge: Harvard University Press.

Majone, Giandomenico. 1994. "The Rise of the Regulatory State in Europe." *West European Politics* 17: 77–101.

Makkai, T., and John Braithewaite. 1992. "In and Out of the Revolving Door: Making Sense of Regulatory Capture." *Journal of Public Policy* 12:61–78.

Marx, Karl. 1967. *Capital: A Critique of Political Economy.* Vol. 1. New York: International Publishers.

Masten, S. E. 1991. "A Legal Basis for the Firm." Pp. 196–212 in *The Nature of the Firm: Origins, Evolution, and Development,* ed. Oliver E. Williamson and Sidney G. Winter. New York: Oxford University Press.

McCammon, Holly J. 1990. "Legal Limits on Labor Militancy: US Labor Law and the Right to Strike." *Social Problems* 37:206–29.

McCann, Michael. 1994. *Rights at Work: Pay Equity Reform and the Politics of Legal Mobilization.* Chicago: University of Chicago Press.

McCann, Michael. 1998. "How Does Law Matter for Social Movements?" Pp. 76–108 in *How Does Law Matter?* ed. Bryant G. Garth and Austin Sarat. Evanston, Ill.: Northwestern University Press.

Mercuro, N., ed. 1989. *Law and Economics.* Boston: Kluwer Academic.

Merry, Sally Engle. 1979. "Going to Court: Strategies of Dispute Management in an American Urban Neighborhood." *Law and Society Review* 13:891–925.

———. 1986. "Everyday Understandings of the Law in Working Class America." *American Ethnologist* 13: 253–70.

Meyer, John W., and Brian Rowan. 1977. "Institutionalized Organizations: Formal Structure as Myth and Ceremony." *American Journal of Sociology* 83: 340–63.

Meyer, John. W., and W. Richard Scott. 1983. *Organizational Environments: Ritual and Rationality.* Beverly Hills, Calif.: Sage.

Miliband, Ralph. 1969. *The State in Capitalist Society.* New York: Basic Books.

Miller, Richard E., and Austin Sarat. 1980. "Grievances, Claims, and Disputes: Assessing the Adversary Culture." *Law and Society Review* 15:525–65.

Milner, Neal. 1989. "The Denigration of Rights and the Persistence of Rights Talk: A Cultural Portrait." *Law and Social Inquiry* 14:765–87.

Minow, Martha. 1987. "Interpreting Rights: An Essay for Robert Cover." *Yale Law Journal* 96:1860–1915.

Mnookin, Robert, and Lewis Kornhauser. 1979. "Bargaining in the Shadow of the Law: The Case of Divorce." *Yale Law Journal* 88:950–97.

Morrill, Calvin. 1995. *The Executive Way: Conflict Management in Corporations.* Chicago: University of Chicago Press.

Nee, Victor. 1992. "Organizational Dynamics of Market Transition: Hybrid Forms, Property Rights, and Mixed Economy in China." *Administrative Science Quarterly* 37:1–27.

Nelson Robert L. 1988. *Partners with Power: Social Transformation of the Large Law Firm.* Berkeley and Los Angeles: University of California Press.

Nelson, Robert L., and William Bridges. 1999. *Legalizing Gender Inequality: Courts, Markets, and Unequal Pay for Women.* Cambridge: Cambridge University Press.

Nielsen, Laura Beth. 2000. "Situating Legal Consciousness: Experiences and Attitudes of Ordinary Citizens about Law and Street Harassment." *Law and Society Review* 34:1055–90.

Offe, Claus. 1975. "The Theory of the Capitalist State and the Problem of Policy Formation." Pp. 125–44 in *Stress and Contradiction in Modern Capitalism,* ed. Leon N. Lindberg, Robert Alford, Colin Crouch and Claus Offe. Lexington, Mass.: Lexington Books.

Olsen, Frances. 1984. "Statutory Rape: A Feminist Critique of Rights Analysis." *Texas Law Review* 63: 397–432.

Paternoster, Raymond, and Sally Simpson. 1997. "Sanction Threats and Appeals to Morality: Testing a Rational Choice Model of Corporate Crime." *Law and Society Review* 30:549–83.

Pedriana, Nicholas, and Robin Stryker. 1997. "Political Culture Wars, 1960s Style: Equal Opportunity–Affirmative Action Law and the Philadelphia Plan." *American Journal of Sociology* 103:633–91.

———. 2004. "The Strength of a Weak Agency: Early Enforcement of Title VII of the Civil Rights Act of 1964 and the Expansion of State Capacity." *American Journal of Sociology* 110, forthcoming.

Pfeffer, Jeffrey. 1974. "Administrative Regulation and Licensing: Social Problem or Solution?" *Social Problems* 21:468–79.

Pfeffer, Jeffrey, and Gerald R. Salancik. 1978. *The External Control of Organizations: A Resource Dependence Perspective.* New York: Harper and Row.

Posner, Richard. 1972. *Economic Analysis of Law.* Boston: Little, Brown.

———. 1974. "Theories of Economic Regulation." *Bell Journal of Economic and Management Science* 5: 335–58.

———. 1987. "The Law and Economics Movement." *American Economic Review* 77:1–13.

———. 1998. *Economic Analysis of Law.* 5th ed. New York: Aspen Law and Business.

Poulantzas, Nicos. 1973. *Political Power and Social Classes.* London: New Left Books.

Powell, Michael J. 1993. "Professional Innovation: Corporate Lawyers and Private Lawmaking." *Law and Social Inquiry* 18:423–52.

Powell Walter. W., and Paul DiMaggio, eds. 1991. *The New Institutionalism in Organizational Analysis.* Chicago: University of Chicago Press.

Resnik, Judith. 1982. *Managerial Judges.* Santa Monica, Calif.: Rand.

Roe, Mark. 1994. *Strong Managers, Weak Owners: The Political Roots of American Corporate Finance.* Princeton: Princeton University Press.

Rogers, Joel. 1990. "Divide and Conquer: Further Reflections on the Distinctive Character of American Labor Laws." *Wisconsin Law Review* 1990:1–147.

Rose-Ackerman, Susan. 1988. "Progressive Law and Economics and the New Administrative Law." *Yale Law Journal* 98:341–68.

Rosenberg, Gerald N. 1991. *The Hollow Hope: Can Courts Bring About Social Change?* Chicago: University of Chicago Press.

Roy, William. 1990. "Functional and Historical Logics in Explaining the Rise of the American Industrial Corporation." *Comparative Social Research.* 12:19–44.

Rubin, Beth A., Larry J. Griffin, and Michael E. Wallace. 1983. "Provided Only That Their Voice Was Strong: Insurgency and Organization of American Labor from NRA to Taft-Hartley." *Work and Occupations* 10:325–47.

Rueschemeyer, Dietrich. 1986. "Comparing Legal Professions Cross-Nationally: From a Professions-Centered to a State-Centered Approach." *American Bar Foundation Research Journal* 1986:415–46.

Sabatier, Paul. 1975. "Social Movements and Regulatory Agencies: Toward a More Adequate—and Less Pessimistic—Theory of 'Clientele Capture.'" *Policy Sciences* 6:301–42.

Saguy, Abigail C. 2003. *Is This Sexual Harassment?* Berkeley and Los Angeles: University of California Press.

Saks, Michael J. 1992. "Do We Really Know Anything about the Behavior of the Tort Litigation System—and Why Not?" *University of Pennsylvania Law Review* 104:1147–84.

Sarat, Austin. 1990. "The Law Is All Over: Power, Resistance, and the Legal Consciousness of the Welfare Poor." *Yale Journal of Law and the Humanities* 2:343–79.

———. 1998. "Going to Court: Access, Autonomy, and the Contradictions of Liberal Legality." Pp. 97–114 in *The Politics of Law: A Progressive Critique,* ed. David Kairys. New York: Basic Books.

Sarat, Austin, and William Felstiner. 1995. *Divorce Lawyers and Their Clients: Power and Meaning in the Legal Process.* Oxford: Oxford University Press.

Scharpf, Fritz. 1999. *Governing in Europe: Effective and Democratic?* Oxford: Oxford University Press.

Scharpf, Fritz, and Susanne Schmidt, eds. 2000. *Welfare and Work in the Open Economy.* Vol. 1, *From Vulnerability to Competition.* Oxford: Oxford University Press.

Scheingold, Stuart. 1974. *The Politics of Rights.* New Haven Yale University Press.

Schneiberg, Marc. 1999. "Political and Institutional Conditions for Governance by Association: Private Order and Private Controls in American Fire Insurance." *Politics and Society* 27:67–103.

———. 2002. "Organizational Heterogeneity and the Production of New Forms: Politics, Social Movements, and Mutual Companies in American Fire Insurance, 1900–1930." *Research in the Sociology of Organizations* 19:39–89.

Schneiberg, Marc, and T. Bartley. 2001. "Regulating American Industries: Markets, Politics, and the Institutional Determinants of Fire Insurance Regulation." *American Journal of Sociology* 107:101–46.

Schultz, Vicki. 1990. "Telling Stories about Women and Work: Judicial Interpretations of Sex Segregation in the Workplace in Title VII Cases Raising the Lack of Interest Argument." *Harvard Law Review* 103:1750–1843.

Scott, W. Richard. 2003. *Organizations: Rational, Natural, and Open Systems.* Englewood Cliffs, N.J.: Prentice Hall.

Scully, Maureen, and Amy Segal. 2002. "Passion with an Umbrella: Grassroots Activists in the Workplace." *Research in the Sociology of Organizations* 19:127–70.

Seavoy, Ronald. 1982. *The Origins of the American Business Corporation, 1784–1855: Broadening the Concept of Public Service during Industrialization.* Westport, Conn.: Greenwood Press.

Selznick, Philip. 1969. *Law, Society, and Industrial Justice.* New York: Russell Sage Foundation.

Silbey, Susan S. 2001. "Legal Culture and Consciousness." Pp. 8623–29 in *International Encyclopedia of the Social and Behavioral Sciences,* ed. Neil J. Smelser and Paul B. Baltes. Amsterdam: Elsevier.

Silbey, Susan S., and Austin Sarat. 1989. "Dispute Processing in Law and Legal Scholarship: From Institutional Critique to the Reconstruction of the Juridical Subject." *Denver University Law Review* 66:437–98.

Sklar, Martin J. 1988. *The Corporate Reconstruction of American Capitalism, 1890–1916: The Market, the Law, and Politics:* Cambridge: Cambridge University Press.

Smith, James, and Finis Welch. 1984. "Affirmative Action and Labor Markets." *Journal of Labor Economics* 2:269–301.

Spicer, Andrew. 2002. "Political Revolution and New Organizational Forms: The Emergence and Transformation of Investment Funds in Post-Communist Russia." *Research in the Sociology of Organizations* 19:91–126.

Spitzer, Stephen. 1983. "Marxist Perspectives in the Sociology of Law." *Annual Review of Sociology* 9:103–24.

Stigler, George. 1971. "The Theory of Economic Regulation." *Bell Journal of Economic and Management Science* 2:3–21.

Stone, Alan. 1985. "The Place of Law in the Marxian Structure-Superstructure Archetype." *Law and Society Review* 19:39–67.

Stone, Christopher D. 1975. *Where the Law Ends: The Social Control of Corporate Behavior.* New York: Harper and Row.

Stryker, Robin. 1989. "Limits on Technocratization of the Law: The Elimination of the National Labor Relations Board's Division of Economic Research, 1935–40." *American Sociological Review* 54:341–58.

———. 1994. "Rules, Resources, and Legitimacy Processes: Some Implications for Social Conflict, Order, and Change." *American Journal of Sociology* 99:847–910.

———. 1996. "Beyond History vs. Theory: Strategic Narrative and Sociological Explanation." *Sociological Methods and Research* 24:306–54.

———. 2000a. "Legitimacy Processes as Institutional Politics: Implications for Theory and Research in the Sociology of Organizations." *Research in the Sociology of Organizations* 17:179–223.

———. 2000b. "Government Regulation." Pp. 1089–1111 in vol. 2 of *Encyclopedia of Sociology,* ed. Edgar F. Borgatta and Rhonda J. V. Montgomery. 2d ed. New York: Macmillan.

———. 2002. "A Political Approach to Organizations and Institutions." *Sociology of Organizations* 19:171–93.

———. 2003. "Mind the Gap: Law, Institutional Analysis, and Socio-Economics." *Socio-economic Review* 1:335–68.

Stryker, Robin, and Scott Eliason. 2003. "The Welfare State, Gendered Labor Markets, and Political Orientations in France, Belgium, Germany, Italy, Denmark, and Britain, 1977–1994." Robert Schuman Center No. RSC 2003120, European University Institute, Florence.

Stryker, Sheldon. 1980. *Symbolic Interaction: A Social Structural Version:* Menlo Park, Calif.: Benjamin-Cummings.

Suchman, Mark. 1995. "Localism and Globalism in Institutional Analysis: The Emergence of Contractual Norms in Venture Finance." Pp. 39–63 in *The Institutional Construction of Organizations: International and Longitudinal Studies,* ed. W. Richard Scott and Søren Christensen. Thousand Oaks, Calif.: Sage.

Suchman, Mark, and Mia Cahill. 1996. "The Hired Gun as Facilitator: Lawyers and the Suppression of Business Disputes in Silicon Valley." *Law and Social Inquiry* 21:679–712.

Suchman, Mark C., and Lauren Edelman. 1996. "Legal-Rational Myths: The New Institutionalism and the Law and Society Tradition." *Law and Social Inquiry* 21:903–41.

Sunstein, Cass R. 1993. "Endogenous Preferences, Environmental Law." *Journal of Legal Studies* 22:217–54.

Sutton, John R., Frank Dobbin, John W. Meyer, and W. Richard Scott. 1994. "Legalization of the Workplace." *American Journal of Sociology* 99:994–71.

Swedberg, Richard. 2002. "The Case for an Economic Sociology of Law." Paper presented at Princeton Economic Sociology Conference, February 22–23, Princeton, N.J.

Swedberg, Richard, and Mark Granovetter, eds. 1992. *The Sociology of Economic Life.* Boulder, Colo.: Westview Press.

Therborn, Goran. 1978. *What Does the Ruling Class Do When It Rules?* New York: Schocken.

Thompson, James D. 1967. *Organizations in Action: Social Science Bases of Administrative Theory.* McGraw-Hill.

Tomlins, Christopher. 1985. *The State and the Unions: Labor Relations, Law, and the Organized Labor Movement in America, 1880–1960.* Cambridge: Cambridge University Press.

———. 1993. *Law, Labor, and Ideology in the Early American Republic.* Cambridge: Cambridge University Press.

Trevino, A. Javier. 1996. *The Sociology of Law: Classical and Contemporary Perspectives.* New York: St. Martins.

Tushnet, Mark. 1984. "An Essay on Rights." *Texas Law Review* 62:1363–1403.

Vaughan, Diane. 1983. *Controlling Unlawful Organizational Behavior: Social Structure and Corporate Misconduct.* Chicago: University of Chicago Press.

Vogel, Steven K. 1996. *Freer Markets, More Rules: Regulatory Reform in Advanced Industrial Countries.* Ithaca, N.Y.: Cornell University Press.

Voss, Kimberly 1993. *The Making of American Exceptionalism: The Knights of Labor and Class Formation in the Nineteenth Century.* Ithaca, N.Y.: Cornell University Press.

Waarden, Frans van. 2002. "Market Institutions as Communicating Vessels: Change between Economic Coordination Principles as a Consequence of Deregulation Policies." Pp. 171–212 in *Advancing Socio-Economics: An Institutionalist Perspective,* ed. J. Rogers Hollingsworth, Karl H. Müller, and Ellen Jane Hollingsworth. Lanham, Md.: Rowman and Littlefield.

Weber, Max. 1978. *Economy and Society: An Outline of Interpretive Sociology.* Ed. Guenther Roth and Claus Wittich. Trans. Ephraim Fischoff et al. Berkeley and Los Angeles: University of California Press.

Weiler, Joseph H. H. 1990. "The Transformation of Europe." *Yale Law Review* 100:2403–83.

White, James Boyd. 1985. *The Legal Imagination.* Chicago: University of Chicago Press.

Williams, Patricia J. 1991. *The Alchemy of Race and Rights.* Cambridge: Harvard University Press.

Williamson, Oliver E. 1975. *Markets and Hierarchies: Analysis and Antitrust Implications.* New York: Free Press.

———. 1979. "Transaction Cost Economics: The Governance of Contractual Relations." *Journal of Law and Economics* 22:233–61.

———. 1981. "The Economics of Organization: The Transactions Cost Approach." *American Journal of Sociology* 87:548–77.

———. 1985. *The Economic Institutions of Capitalism.* New York: Free Press.

———. 1991. "Comparative Economic Organization: The Analysis of Discrete Structural Alternatives." *Administrative Science Quarterly* 36:269–96.

Wirt, Frederick. 1970. *The Politics of Southern Equality: Law and Social Change in a Mississippi County.* Chicago: Aldine.

Yeager, Peter C. 1990. *The Limits of Law: The Public Regulation of Private Pollution.* Cambridge: Cambridge University Press.

Yngvesson, Barbara. 1988. "Making Law at the Doorway: The Clerk, the Court, and the Construction of Community in a New England Town." *Law and Society Review* 22:409–48.

Zhou, X. 1993. "Occupational Power, State Capacities, and the Diffusion of Licensing in American States, 1890–1950." *American Sociological Review* 58:536–52.

24 Welfare States and the Economy

Evelyne Huber and John D. Stephens

THE LITERATURE on welfare states or, more modestly, systems of social protection, has expanded rapidly over the past few decades. Since the publication of the first edition of this handbook, major progress has been made in three research areas: the relationship between welfare states and production regimes, gendered determinants and outcomes of welfare state regimes, and the distributive outcomes of welfare states. Esping-Andersen ended his chapter in the first edition with a call for an embedded approach to the study of welfare states, for a relational analysis of the welfare state–economy nexus. Two developments have contributed to the advancement of such an approach: progress in research on production regimes in advanced industrial societies, and the dramatic impact of economic transformations on the systems of social protection in former Communist countries and in Latin America. Progress in research on the gender dimension of the welfare state–economy nexus has been spurred by changes in demographic structures, particularly falling fertility rates and the decline of the traditional male breadwinner family that had been at the center of many welfare state programs. Finally, progress in research on distributive outcomes has been heavily driven by the greater availability of reliable and comparable data and new statistical techniques, specifically the Luxembourg Income Study and techniques for the analysis of unbalanced panel data.

Of course, the progress made in the 1990s was possible because researchers could build on knowledge accumulated by previous studies of welfare states, spanning a quarter-century. These earlier studies had taken the form of quantitative analyses on the one hand and case studies or comparative analyses of a small number of cases on the other hand. The former had begun with a focus on the determinants of welfare state expenditures (Wilensky 1975; Stephens 1979; Korpi 1983) and gradually added measures of specific benefits and public employment (Myles 1984; Pampel and Williamson 1989). The latter progressed from comparing welfare states in two or three countries or individual welfare state programs in a larger number of countries to studying configurations of programs or welfare state regimes in the universe of advanced industrial democracies (Esping-Andersen 1990).

THEORIES OF WELFARE STATE FORMATION AND RETRENCHMENT

Theories of welfare state formation can be grouped into three categories, according to the emphasis they put on clusters of causal variables: the *logic of industrialism*, *state-centric*, and *political class struggle* approaches.[1] The authors proposing the logic of industrialism approach argued that industrialization and urbanization broke up traditional systems of social protection through the family and local communities and required the state to take on the responsibility for the welfare of industrial workers. At the same time, the growing affluence resulting from advances in industrialization made resources available to the state to perform these functions. Thus, both the growth and cross-national differences in welfare state effort could be explained by industrialization and its demographic and social organizational consequences (Wilensky 1975; Pampel and Williamson 1989). A related influential point of view held that economic openness caused vulnerability of workers to external shocks and thus led governments to build extensive systems of social protection (Cameron 1978). Since small countries generally had a higher degree of economic openness, welfare states grew particularly generous there (Katzenstein 1985).

The state-centric approach is internally quite diverse, with some authors focusing on the initiatives of state bureaucrats who were assumed to have a high degree of autonomy (Heclo 1974), and others on state capacity, state structure, and policy legacies (Skocpol 1988; Weir, Orloff, and Skocpol 1988; Immergut 1992; Orloff 1993a; Amenta 1998; Maioni 1998). In this perspective, cross-national differences in the development of comprehensive welfare state programs are a result of differential state capacity, the degree of power dispersion and the consequent availability of veto points, and the structure of welfare state programs set at their origin, before the period of expansion.

The political class struggle approach—also known as *power resources approach* (Korpi 1980, 1983)— is based on the premise that state policy is heavily shaped by the distribution of power in civil society and in government. The balance of power between organized labor and left-wing parties on the one hand, and capital and center and right-wing parties on the other hand accounts for the extent of government correction of market outcomes through the welfare state (Stephens 1979; Castles 1982; Hicks and Swank 1984; Myles 1984; Esping-Andersen 1985, 1990; Korpi 1989). The focus on incumbency produced early on the insight that Christian democracy is also associated with generous welfare states but with a less progressive profile than welfare states built under left or social democratic auspices (Stephens 1979; Wilensky 1981).

There is some theoretical overlap among these perspectives. The political class struggle perspective emphasizes density and centralization of labor organization, and centralization of collective bargaining, along with strength of prolabor parties as indicators of left or labor power. Density and centralization of labor organization, or labor strength, is also seen as a cause of corporatism, that is, institutionalized tripartite consultation between capital, labor, and the government on essential policy issues (Stephens 1979; Western 1991). Corporatism, then, has been treated as an institutional variable that, once established, becomes a cause of welfare state expansion in its own right (Hicks 1999; Swank 2002; Wilensky 2002). Since these dimensions of left/labor power are so closely related, it is impossible to adjudicate the competing theoretical claims on statistical grounds. Comparative historical evidence indicates that incumbency of left parties is crucial for welfare state development (Huber and Stephens 2001a).

Quantitative studies have found that variables emphasized in all three theoretical schools are statistically significant predictors of welfare state effort (Huber, Ragin, and Stephens 1993; Hicks 1999; Swank 2002). Demographic variables matter because, at any given level of entitlements, a larger number of old people or the unemployed drives up expenditures. Level of GDP per capita, as a measure of economic development, tends not to explain much variation in welfare state effort among advanced industrial democracies, but if the comparison encompasses developing countries, then its importance increases. The provision of multiple veto points in the constitutional structure, that is, dispersion of power through presidentialism, strong bicameralism, federalism, and popular referenda, is one of the most consistent and important obstacles to expansion of welfare state effort (Huber and Stephens 2001a). Finally, the strength of organized labor and length of incumbency of left-wing or Christian democratic parties is associated in a highly consistent and significant manner with various dimensions of welfare state effort.

Focusing on dimensions of welfare state effort, or on social rights directly, rather than simply on aggregate welfare state spending, was the key to Esping-Andersen's (1990) seminal contribution of the concept of welfare state regimes. He built on other, in part common, efforts to measure social rights and explain their determinants (Myles 1984; Korpi 1989), and he identified different dimensions or characteristics of the way in which welfare states provide social rights. He argued that these dimensions or characteristics were linked in systematic patterns and clustered around three types, a social democratic or institutional type, a conservative or "corporativistic" type, and a liberal or residual type. With some modifications, specifically the renaming of the conservative as Christian democratic type and the addition of a fourth wage earner welfare state regime (Castles and Mitchell 1993) and sometimes a fifth southern European regime (Leibfried 1992; Ferrera 1996), this typology has shaped most subsequent research.

Social democratic welfare state regimes are characterized by universalism in coverage and in the nature of benefits, by rights to a large array of benefits based on citizenship or (more recently) residence, and by public provision of a large array of services. Christian democratic welfare states are characterized by universalism in coverage but (at least historically) with different benefits under different programs, by rights to benefits based on employment categories, and by public financing of privately provided services. Liberal welfare states are characterized by partial or residual coverage with different benefits, by rights to most benefits based on need and thus means testing, and by the scarcity of publicly provided or financed social services. These regime types correspond to value commitments and particular views on the desirable relationship between state, market, community, and family. The social democratic type reflects the values of solidarity and equality, and the view that the state is charged with counteracting market forces to realize these values. The Christian democratic type reflects the Catholic doctrine of harmony and subsidiarity, where the state is charged with keeping people out of poverty but not changing the social order, and with performing only the functions that are not performed well by the family or civil society (van Kersbergen 1995). The liberal type reflects the values of individual responsibility and efficiency, and the view that the state should primarily rely on market forces and work with these forces to prevent destitution and provide essential social services. The groups of countries corresponding to the three regime types are the Nordic countries, the continental European countries, and the Anglo-American countries, respectively. In reality, of course, several countries have somewhat mixed welfare state characteristics, reflecting the influence of different political forces involved in their formation.

The main theoretical contribution from a feminist perspective was to draw attention to the fact that these welfare state typologies were essentially built on the assumption of standard citizens, with low, average, or high earnings, and that this assumption fit predominantly males. Gender did not figure as a dimension in the original conceptualization of welfare state regimes, and it was obviously crucial to understanding gender-specific impacts of these regimes (Orloff 1993b). A number of studies have investigated the extent to which regime types are useful in explaining systematic differences in outcomes for women (Lewis 1992; Hobson 1994; Orloff 1997; Sainsbury 1999), and though there is no real consensus, considerable evidence supports the usefulness of the regime approach. Numerous studies have also investigated the role of women's mobilization and pressures for welfare state expansion, or what Hernes (1987) called women-friendly policies (Jenson and Mahon 1993; Lewis 1994; Hill and Tigges 1995; Stetson and Mazur 1995; Hobson and Lindholm 1997; Bergquist 1998; O'Connor, Orloff, and Shaver 1999). Most of their findings are compatible with a power resources approach, but power based on gender mobilization, not on class. Generally, progress in policies promoting gender equity was the result of women organizing inside and outside of political parties, in independent women's movements, and of fostering a commitment to the goal of gender equity within incumbent left-wing parties.

Whether the traditional theories of welfare state formation are also useful for an analysis of the period of welfare state retrenchment or defense, which began in the 1980s, is a contested issue. Pierson (1994, 1996) has argued for a "new politics of the welfare state," and indeed quantitative studies have shown that the magnitude of partisan effects decreased greatly (Stephens, Huber, and Ray 1999). In the context of slower economic growth than in the first three decades after World War II, higher unemployment, comprehensive and mature welfare state programs and consequent high expenditures, both the Left and the Right have been constrained in their reform efforts. The Right has been constrained in efforts to cut welfare state entitlements significantly, because the entitlements that affect large numbers of people are widely popular. The Left has been constrained in efforts to expand entitlements because raising taxes has not been popular and deficit financing out of the question. Still, in qualitative studies differences between governments of different color remain visible; right-wing governments have been more likely to push an agenda of welfare state austerity and tax cuts, whereas left-wing governments have been more intent on protecting entitlements (Huber and Stephens 2001a). Demographic and state structure variables have remained important as well, but have tended to work in the opposite direction from the one during the period of welfare state expansion. Whereas multiple veto points had slowed down expansion, now they have slowed down retrenchment (Bonoli and Mach 2000). Whereas episodes of high unemployment had given the impetus for improvements in unemployment insurance, now sustained levels of higher unemployment have given the impetus for cuts in entitlements.

Among the developing areas of the world, Latin America has seen the strongest thrust toward welfare state development. By 1980 the most advanced countries had systems of social protection that could be called welfare states.[2] The volume of literature on the formation of welfare states in Latin America is small, and a theoretical debate is largely absent. A number of studies describe the evolution of systems of social protection, but they tend to focus on economic and organizational aspects and neglect to ask why systems were formed in a certain way (Mesa-Lago 1978, 1989; Raczynski 1994). The picture that emerges from these studies is one of highly fragmented and often inegalitarian systems, where entitlements were based on the insurance principle and differed greatly between occupational categories. The main programs were old-age and disability pensions and health care insurance, and in some countries family allowances. These systems resembled the Christian democratic type characteristic of continental Europe, but were much less generous and more inegalitarian and restricted in coverage. Coverage depended on employment in the formal sector, and the rural and informal sectors were very large in most of these countries, with the result that in the vast majority of countries less than 60 percent of the population had coverage as of 1980.

Most studies of social policy formation emphasize preemptive, or paternalistic, action on the part of the state to incorporate the most important occupational groups and gain their political support (Mesa-Lago 1978; Malloy 1979; Spalding 1978). Another perspective emphasizes diffusion of models of social insurance from more advanced countries via international organizations, particularly the International Labor Office (ILO) (Collier and Messik 1975). However, there was clearly differential adoption of these models, and this variation needs to be explained. Even under authoritarian rule, the strength and political importance of pressure groups mattered, and thus to understand the expansion of social protection to a large part of the population, the mobilization capacity of organized labor and its importance as a support base of governments have to be taken into account (Dion 2002). Coverage expanded most during periods of strong growth of import substitution industrialization (ISI) behind high tariff walls and with strong government intervention in capital markets to support industrialization. These were periods of growth of the industrial labor force and often also of labor movements. Labor organization and mobilization is most likely to grow under democratic regimes, specifically in the presence of strong reformist parties, and under authoritarian leaders who deliberately promote labor organization.[3] Indeed, of the five Latin American countries (not counting Cuba) with most extensive coverage of social security, that is, above 60 percent of the population as of 1980, three had the longest democratic experiences and comparatively strong reformist parties (Uruguay, Chile, Costa Rica), and two had historical episodes of leaders attempting to build organized labor into a power base (Perón in Argentina, Vargas in Brazil). Compared to Europe, then, the much lower size and generosity of Latin American systems of social protection can be attributed to a combination of lower levels of industrialization, the scarcity of democratic periods, and the weaker position of reformist parties and organized labor.[4]

Theoretical accounts of retrenchment of systems of social protection in Latin America, which has been much more dramatic than in advanced industrial democracies, have emphasized the debt crisis and consequent economic transformations as common causes. They have explained differences between countries in the extent and nature of social policy reforms with the extent of liberalization of markets for goods and capital, power concentration in the hands of the executive versus fragmentation of political institutions and power, the influence of international financial institutions (IFIs), specifically the International Monetary Fund, the World Bank, and the Inter-American Development Bank, the financial pressures on the established systems, policy legacies, and the balance of power between proponents (large capital interests, technocrats, executives) and opponents (organized labor, pensioners, the political Left) of reforms, with emphasis on these different factors varying by author (Weyland 2002; Huber 1996, forthcoming; Kay 1998; Madrid 2002; Dion 2002).

A final theoretical perspective to be considered is the economic one. This literature does not really address theoretical questions of the causes of welfare state formation and of cross-national differences in welfare state design. The classical liberal and neoliberal perspectives take a normative position, that market allocation should not be distorted by state intervention, and they claim that there is a fundamental trade-off between equity and efficiency (Okun 1975). In particular, they argue that state intervention and redistribution distort incentives and thus efficiency of resource allocation (Lindbeck 1994). Less dogmatic economists distinguish between the goals of welfare states, which they attribute to the realm of politics or norms, and the means by which these goals are to be achieved, which they regard as a technical question and the proper field of study for economics (Barr 1998). There is considerable research on the effects, as disincentives to work, of generous social safety nets in the case of sickness and unemployment, but the findings are often ambiguous and weak (Atkinson and Mogensen 1993; Atkinson and Mickelwright 1991).

WELFARE STATES, PRODUCTION REGIMES, AND GLOBALIZATION

As we have mentioned, by the early 1990s, a number of authors had noted that there was strong affinity and perhaps a causal relationship between corporatism, often indexed by the degree of bargaining centralization, and welfare state generosity. Esping-Andersen (1990) and Kolberg and Esping-Andersen (1992) drew attention to other links between labor market arrangements and welfare state types: high levels of public social service employment and of female labor force participation in the social democratic welfare states, high levels of private service employment in liberal welfare states, low levels of service employment and female employment in Christian democratic welfare states, and high levels of early retirement in Christian democratic welfare states. In the course of the 1990s, a new line of thinking, the varieties of capitalism approach, emerged that stressed other dimensions of variation among advanced capitalist economies (e.g., Soskice 1990, 1999; Albert 1991, Hollingsworth, Schmitter, and Streek 1994; Hollingsworth and Boyer 1997).

The most influential typology has been that of Soskice (1999; Hall and Soskice 2001). Soskice shifts from the focus on unions and union confederations characteristic of the corporatism literature to a focus on employers and firms and their capacity to coordinate their actions. In his view, employer organization takes three distinctive forms: coordination at the industry or subindustry level in Germany and in most northern European economies (industry-coordinated market economies; CMEs); coordination among groups of companies across industries in Japan and Korea (group coordinated market economies); or absence of coordination in the deregulated systems of the Anglo-American countries (liberal market economies; LMEs). In coordinated economies, employers are able to organize collectively in training their labor force, sharing technology, providing export marketing services and advice for R & D and for product innovation, setting product standards, and bargaining with employees. The capacity for collective action on the part of employers shapes stable patterns of economic governance encompassing a country's financial system, its vocational training, and its system of industrial relations. In liberal market economies, in contrast to both types of coordinated economy, training for lower-level workers is not undertaken by private business and is generally ineffective. Bank-industry ties are weak, and industries have to rely on competitive markets to raise capital.

It is obvious that theses types of production regimes are associated with Esping-Andersen's types of welfare state regimes. Moreover, it is arguable that there is at least a "mutually enabling fit" between the welfare state and production regimes types (Huber and Stephens 2001a, chap. 4): Specifically, wage levels and benefit levels have to fit, and labor market and social policies have to be in accord such as not to create perverse incentives. In addition, the type of production for the world market has to fit with the qualification of the labor force and with wage and benefit levels. In CMEs, business-labor-government coordination in R & D, training, and wage setting makes it possible to engage in high-quality production and thus to sustain high wages and a high social wage.

Recent work suggests an even tighter fit between welfare state and production regimes. Iversen and Soskice (2001) argue that the industry- and firm-specific nature of many of the skills acquired in vocational education systems characteristic of CMEs results in higher support for social spending as workers with these skills are vulnerable to longer spells of unemployment and to loss of income if forced to move between jobs with different skill requirements (also see Estevez-Abe, Iversen, and Soskice 2001). In their view, employers as well as workers have an interest in such social spending because it insures that workers will in fact invest in acquisition of the specific skills that the employers require. Swenson (2002) also argues that the varying interests of cross-class coalitions of employers and workers account for differences in social policy. He argues that in Sweden employers and workers both supported the expansion of social insurance because social insurance removes private employer benefits from wage competition.

This recent work would appear to sharply conflict with power resources theory, which is widely perceived by comparative welfare states specialists (e.g., see Orloff 1993b; Myles and Quadagno 2002) to be the currently dominant explanation of welfare state development. This is a dispute that is unlikely to be resolved by statistical analysis because of the strong intercorrelations between the potential causal factors. The centralization of employer confederations, the centralization of union confederations, union density, long-term patterns of partisan government, the extent of vocational education, and various measures of welfare state effort are moderately to strongly correlated to each other, and the multiple correlations of two or three of these indicators with another of them are invariably extremely high.

The resolution of this debate will have to await the kind of careful comparative historical work that has been done on the development of the welfare state but that has not been done on the development of production regimes. Thelen's (2004) work on the development of vocational training in Germany, Britain, Japan, and the United States is probably indicative of the kind of answers such analyses will reveal. For example, she finds that the German employers initially introduced the system with the intention of dividing the nascent working-class movement, but that over the course of the past hundred-odd years the system has been progressively transformed by shifting coalitions of labor market and political forces.[5] The functional fit one observes by taking a single cut in time is, she argues, quite misleading. It is our hunch that the early organization of employers will figure as an important factor in the development of coordinated market economies, as employer organization as of 1914 identifies post–World War II CMEs quite well (Crouch 1993, 112; also see Hicks 1999, chap. 5). In dialectical fashion, employer organization seems to have stimulated union organization and centralization, which in turn increased the political strength of the Left at a later period of time (Stephens 1979; Kjellberg 1983). In the postwar period, left party power facilitated union organization and vice versa (Western 1997; Wallerstein 1989), and these two factors in turn propelled welfare state expansion. This kind of causal account squares much better with the historical record of consistent right-wing (the parties representing employer interests) opposition to tax increases for welfare state financing than accounts stressing employer-worker coalitions in support of the welfare state.

It is important not to exaggerate the fit between welfare state and production regime. Above all, CMEs are equally compatible with social democratic or Christian democratic welfare states, and these two welfare state types have distinctive characteristics that have a major impact on their future viability. As we have noted in passing above, the social democratic welfare states are characterized by very high levels of public health, education, and welfare (HEW) employment. This high level of public HEW employment is both a result and cause of the high levels of women's labor force participation. The growth of women's labor force participation beginning in the 1960s stimulated demands by women for the expansion of day care and other social services that, along with social democratic governance, helped fuel the growth of public social service sector employment. These public social service jobs were filled very disproportionately by women, so this in turn stimulated a further expansion of women's labor force participation. The continental Christian democratic welfare states followed a quite different trajectory. Foreign labor was imported in large numbers, arguably due to a combination of Christian democratic emphasis on the traditional male breadwinner family and weaker union influence on labor recruitment policies. Moreover, in these countries, union contracts cover a large proportion of the labor force, which prevented a rapid expansion of a low-wage service sector, a source of employment for women in liberal welfare states (Esping-Andersen 1990). As a result, women's labor force participation was the lowest in the continental Christian democratic welfare states, of the three welfare state types.

A related difference between social democratic and Christian democratic welfare states is the much greater emphasis on active labor market measures as a response to unemployment in the social democratic welfare states. By contrast, as mentioned above, the Christian democratic welfare states have tended to resort to labor supply reduction measures, such as early retirement and easy access to disability pensions, in response to rising unemployment after 1973. Together these policy differences have resulted in much higher levels of labor force participation of both men and women in social democratic welfare states.

Australia and New Zealand are generally classified as liberal market economies and liberal welfare states in the varieties of capitalism and welfare state literatures, which is a correct characterization of the contemporary political economies of these countries. However, prior to the reform process initiated in the early eighties, these countries had distinctive systems of social protection, as Castles (1985) has argued. In the nineteenth century, these countries' economies were dominated by exports from the pastoral sector, later to be supplemented by mineral exports in the Australian case. The industrial sector developed behind high tariff barriers; thus these political economies were ISI economies similar to Latin America. In the early twentieth century, the labor movements of these countries, which were very powerful by international standards, secured systems of compulsory arbitration that delivered high "male breadwinner" wages and later benefits such as sick pay, which in other advanced capitalist countries were delivered by the welfare states. Thus, these two countries resembled Latin America, as formal sector urban workers received comparatively high wages and benefits due to protective tariffs, with the important difference that the informal sector was quite small compared to Latin America.

Production regimes in Latin America were characterized by extensive state intervention in all areas of economic life up to the 1980s. As a result of the depression, governments in the more advanced

Latin American countries had become convinced that they needed to promote domestic industrialization. They did so through high protective tariffs, subsidized credit from state development banks, preferential allocation of foreign exchange, and other kinds of incentives. Of course, ISI required significant imports of capital goods and other industrial inputs, which were financed by raw material exports. There were differences in the timing of ISI and in the extent of state involvement, but virtually all countries followed this model by the late 1960s. The social security systems for disability and old-age pensions and for health care developed in tandem with ISI, as governments also became heavily involved in regulating labor relations and saw social security as a tool to foster labor compliance. Financing depended heavily on employer contributions, which were tolerable because they could be passed on to consumers in these highly protected markets. However, only in Uruguay did the percentage of the labor force in industry surpass 30 percent by 1980; in seven more countries the percentage was between 20 and 30 percent, and in the rest even lower (World Bank 1982). Since most of agriculture and the entire large informal part of the service sector were without coverage, this is a good gauge of the restricted reach of social protection.

In the last two decades, almost all advanced welfare states have experienced at least some retrenchment, reversing the trend of the previous three decades, which was one of unprecedented welfare state growth in all of these countries. Many journalists and political observers and some academics, particularly economists, have attributed this retrenchment to "globalization," the increasing economic openness of the national economies and integration of the world economy. In this view, the emergence of a single global market and global competition has reduced the political latitude for action of national states and imposed neoliberal policies on all governments. Proponents contend that as markets for goods, capital, and, more recently, labor have become more open, all countries have been exposed to more competition, and the liabilities of state economic intervention and deviation from market-oriented "best practices" have become more apparent because these raise the cost of production. As capital markets have become more open and capital controls increasingly unworkable, capital in these countries moves elsewhere in search of lower production costs. Thus, governments must respond and reduce state intervention to stem the outflow of capital. There is

also a social democratic version of the globalization thesis, essentially an extension of the argument on the structural dependence of the state on capital. In this view, the opening of international capital markets beginning in the 1970s and accelerating in the 1980s and 1990s greatly increased the power of capital to do "regime shopping" and thus to force national states to retreat from effective interventionist policies and generous, egalitarian welfare state policies.

There is very little empirical evidence to support the neoliberal version of the globalization thesis (Garrett 1998; Swank 2002). The generous welfare states of northern Europe were developed in economies that were always very open to trade and very dependent on exports. Thus, for example, in the midnineties, at the very moment when the German and Swedish governments were cutting welfare state benefits, albeit modestly, the German and Swedish export sectors were turning in outstanding performances. The absence of any relationship between exposed sector employment performance and the level of taxes and social security contributions also argues against the thesis that generous welfare states makes export industries uncompetitive (Scharpf 2000, 78).

On the other hand, there is some evidence in favor of the social democratic version of the globalization thesis. To identify the causes of retrenchment, we draw on case studies of 12 countries (Huber and Stephens 2001a, chap. 7; Stephens, Huber, and Ray 1999) as well as studies of additional countries in Scharpf and Schmidt 2000, thus covering all but a few of the advanced industrial democracies. These country studies indicate two different dynamics: ideologically driven cuts, which occurred in only a few cases, and unemployment-driven cuts, which were pervasive. The question then becomes, what caused the increases in unemployment?[6] As Glyn (1995) points out, it was not the low level of job creation, since employment growth after 1973 was as rapid as before. Rather, rising labor force participation due to the entry of women into the labor force is one proximate cause of the increase in unemployment. As mentioned previously, the inability of the Christian democratic welfare states to absorb this increase either through an expansion of low-wage private service employment as in the liberal welfare states or through the expansion of public services as in the social democratic welfare states is one reason why the unemployment problem in these countries has been particularly severe. The other proximate cause is the lower levels of growth in the post-

1973 period. This in turn can be linked in part to lower levels of investment, which in turn can be linked in part to lower levels of savings, to lower levels of profit, and to higher interest rates.

It is on this point that we find some support for the social democratic globalization thesis on the negative impact of financial market deregulation. Real interest rates increased from 1.4 percent in the sixties to 5.6 percent in the early nineties (OECD 1995, 108). The deregulation of international and domestic financial markets is partly responsible for this increase in interest rates.[7] As a result of the elimination of controls on capital flows between countries, governments cannot control both the interest rate and exchange rate. If a government decides to pursue a stable exchange rate, it must accept the interest rate that is determined by international financial markets. As a result of decontrol of domestic financial markets (which was in many cases stimulated by international financial deregulation), government's ability to privilege business investors over other borrowers also became more limited. Countries that relied on financial control to target business investment were particularly hard hit as businesses moved from a situation in which real interest rates offered to them via government subsidies, tax concessions, and regulations were actually negative to a situation in which they had to pay the rates set by international markets. External financial decontrol also limits a government's ability to employ fiscal stimulation as a tool, as fiscal deficits are considered risky by financial markets and either require a risk premium on interest rates or put downward pressure on foreign exchange reserves. Thus, at least a portion of the increase in unemployment can be linked to globalization in the form of deregulated capital markets.

There were only a few cases of large-scale ideologically driven cuts. The most dramatic were Thatcher in Britain, the National (conservative) government in New Zealand, and the Reagan administration in the United States. In the case of the Reagan administration the cuts were focused on cash and in-kind benefits to the poor, a small but highly vulnerable minority, while Social Security was preserved by a large increase in the contributions. In any case, the United States cannot have been said to have made a "system shift" if only because it already had the least generous welfare state of any advanced industrial democracy. Only in Britain and New Zealand could one speak of an actual system shift from welfare state regimes that used to provide basic income security to welfare

state regimes that are essentially residualist, relying heavily on means testing. We argue that the exceptional nature of these two cases can be traced to their political systems, which concentrate power (unicameral or very weakly bicameral parliamentary governments in unitary political systems) and make it possible to rule without a majority of popular support (single-member districts and plurality elections that allow parties with a minority of votes to enjoy large parliamentary majorities). Thus, in both cases, the conservative governments were able to pass legislation that was deeply unpopular.

In contrast to welfare states in advanced industrial societies, globalization had a dramatic impact on systems of social protection in Latin America. Globalization was a major contributor to the debt crisis that spurred a transformation of the economies, a process largely guided by the international financial institutions, and economic transformation in turn required reforms of the traditional social security systems. The ISI model began to run into balance-of-payments problems in the 1950s. It was given a new lease on life in the 1970s because of the easy availability of cheap loans on the expanding international capital markets. However, these markets imposed rapidly rising interest rates in the early 1980s, at the same time as commodity prices fell. When the big international banks reacted to solvency problems of some major debtors with a complete stop of new lending, Latin America was plunged into the debt crisis (Dornbusch 1989). This crisis gave great leverage to the IFIs and the American Treasury, and these institutions pushed for a radical liberalization of the Latin American economies. They were influential not only through their imposition of conditionality on debt renegotiations (Stallings and Kaufman 1989; Kahler 1989), but also because of another aspect of globalization, the spread of educational circuits that brought talented Latin Americans to graduate schools in economics in the United States, where they absorbed the hegemonic neoliberal view of the world. Many of the leading government officials shared such backgrounds with officials in the IFIs, and many had worked for some time in the IFIs as well. This facilitated the formation of networks involving technocrats in the IFIS and national governments, where reform ideas were discussed over long periods of time and the neoliberal solutions were advocated (Teichman 2001).

At first governments and IFIs were preoccupied with economic stabilization and structural adjustment, but by the late 1980s, when the costs of the crisis and the austerity and adjustment measures became clear, they developed an acute concern with the political sustainability of reforms and thus "adjustment with a human face." The economic austerity programs entailed devaluation, reduction of public expenditures, wage freezes, and restrictive monetary policies. Together with the structural adjustment policies, they fundamentally transformed the Latin American production regimes. The main points of the structural adjustment agenda were liberalization of markets for goods and capital, privatization of state enterprises, and deregulation of all kinds of economic activity. On average, the countries in the region pushed ahead rapidly with trade liberalization and financial liberalization; less in privatization, and mixed in general deregulation. The average tariff rate was lowered from 49 percent in the mid-1980s to 11 percent in 1999, and nontariff restrictions were reduced from covering 38 percent of imports in the prereform period to 6 percent of imports in the mid-1990s (Lora 2001). Though these tariff levels remain higher than in advanced industrial countries, the lowering had a dramatic impact on many Latin American economies, particularly where it was done in a very short period of time. Many enterprises went bankrupt, which meant that many formal sector jobs were lost. Liberalization of capital markets stimulated significant inflows of capital in the early 1990s, but also rendered the economies vulnerable to rapid changes in investor confidence and thus renewed balance-of-payments crises.

Social expenditures had decreased as part of the austerity programs. Unemployment had increased greatly due to austerity-induced recession and liberalization of imports. The combination of high inflation and high unemployment had played havoc with the financial base of the social security systems, and employers rebelled against high social security contributions in the new open economic environment.[8] The reforms pushed by the IFIs included privatization of the pension systems and large parts of the health care systems, decentralization of social services, and targeting of public expenditures on the poor, particularly through demand-driven social emergency funds. The degree to which countries followed these prescriptions, though, varied greatly, more so than in the economic reforms proper.

Chile implemented these reforms earlier and to a greater extent than any other country under the military dictatorship. Power was highly concentrated in the hands of Pinochet, and opposition was dealt with ruthlessly. The neoliberal project was attractive to the military not only for economic but also for political reasons, because it would atomize civil society and remove the state as a target for collective action (Garretón 1989). In addition to slashing tariffs and financial regulation and privatizing a large number of state-controlled enterprises, the government fully privatized the pension system and transformed a large part of the public into a private health insurance and delivery system. The reduced public expenditures were targeted on preventive and nutritional programs and a temporary employment program for the poor (Raczynski 1994). In the wake of the high economic growth rates—and thus high rates of return on the individual private pension accounts—achieved in Chile from the mid-1980s to the mid-1990s, the Chilean model became the poster child for neoliberals and was held up as a model to emulate for other Latin American countries.

No other country carried out reforms quite as rapidly and comprehensively as Chile. Argentina under Menem moved very rapidly on economic reforms and on a plan to privatize social security, but opposition was strong enough to force concessions on keeping a public basic tier and leaving a large part of the health insurance system under the control of the unions. Altogether, nine Latin American countries have implemented and a tenth has legislated full or partial privatization of their pension system. In five cases, privatization was total and the public system was closed down; in five cases it was partial and the private system remained a supplementary or a parallel option (Muller 2002). Reforms in health care have been more heterogeneous, though in general the private sector has expanded its role, sometimes by design and sometimes by default as a result of serious underfunding of the public system. In the 1980s, there was virtually no investment in public health care facilities, and wages for public health care professionals declined precipitously. In the 1990s, most countries raised their social expenditures, so that they increased from 10.4 percent of GDP to 13.1 percent (CEPAL 2002), slightly above the level of 1980. Growth in the various categories of social expenditure, that is, education, health care and nutrition, social security, and housing and sanitation was roughly similar, with social security continuing to absorb the bulk of social expenditure, at 4.8 percent of GDP in 1998–99, followed by education with 3.9 percent and health care and nutrition with 2.9 percent (CEPAL 2002, 26). Clearly, these levels of expenditure remain far below what would be needed for a concerted and successful attack on poverty and improvement of the human capital base.

In order to raise expenditures significantly, tax collection systems would need to be improved. Latin America as a whole is clearly undertaxed, with an average tax burden of 14 percent of GDP in the first half of the 1990s, compared to 17 percent of GDP in a group of East and Southeast Asian countries (IADB 1996, 128). Tax reform has been part of structural adjustment, but it has emphasized lowering marginal tax rates for individuals and corporations and raising the value-added tax. Tax collection rates are still very poor. Direct taxes amount to about 25 percent of tax revenue only, and of this amount some 60–80 percent come from corporate tax payments, while only 10–15 percent come from private individuals (CEPAL 1998, 72). Interestingly, the situation in the English-speaking Caribbean is very different, with an average tax burden in the first half of the 1990s of 27–28 percent of GDP, essentially double the rate of Latin America, and direct taxation accounting for 40 percent of tax revenue (CEPAL 1998, 66–72). This contrast suggests that the fundamental reasons for the poor tax collection performance in Latin America are political, rather than related to low levels of economic development and technological capacity.

DEMOGRAPHY, GENDER, AND WELFARE STATES

In contrast to the dominant view in the political debate that paints globalization as an inexorable force undermining the bases of the welfare state everywhere, the strongest current in the academic debate squares with our arguments about the limited impact of globalization on welfare states in advanced industrial societies. Instead, this current identifies domestic pressures, specifically changing demographics and changes in lifestyles and labor markets, as major factors that demand adaptation of welfare state structures now and will do so even more urgently in the future (Esping-Andersen 1999; essays in Pierson 2001). The most obvious of these pressures is the growing share of the aged in the population. The growth in life expectancy has meant a higher share of pensioners and thus greater financial pressures on the pension and the health care systems. In the social democratic and the liberal welfare states, increasing female labor force participation counterbalanced the growth of the aged population and actually improved the ratio between the economically active and the total dependent population, old and young, from 1960 to 1989. In the Christian democratic welfare states,

however, where female labor force participation has remained lower, this ratio has remained at a significantly lower level (Huber and Stephens 2001a, 238–39). As mentioned above, in Christian democratic welfare states the growing unemployment pressures in the 1980s and 1990s were in part handled through early retirement and generous disability pensions, which in combination with the low female labor force participation led to a real and perceived crisis of inactivity.

The real crisis for Christian democratic welfare states, though, is ahead. Whereas in 1960 the average fertility rate in Western Europe stood at 2.6, by the 1990s it had fallen to 1.5; in Italy and Spain it had fallen to 1.3 and in Germany to 1.4, in contrast to Sweden with 2.1 (Esping-Andersen 1999, 68). The social democratic welfare states provide a significant array of family services and thus make it possible for women to combine paid work with raising a family. Liberal welfare states do not provide these services, but their unregulated labor markets have generated a considerable private market for day care, though with a lower end of questionable quality. Christian democratic welfare states do not provide these services, and their comparatively high floor of wages and payroll taxes prevent the emergence of a significant private market in family services, which essentially forces women to choose family or career. The response of an increasing number of women has been to opt for a career. The societal-level consequences are falling fertility rates and future dependency ratios with possibly disastrous implications for welfare states. Allowing higher rates of immigration, for which there is great external demand, would be a solution to this problem, but the strength of internal anti-immigrant sentiment makes this a politically highly controversial solution.

Rising female labor force participation and rising divorce rates have also contributed to a greater share of single parent households. Single parent households, in turn, are more likely to be poor than households with both parents, thus putting greater demands on the welfare state. This situation calls for a change in the organization of welfare state programs, away from the traditional male breadwinner model whose dependents are protected through his employment-based entitlements, to a structure of entitlements for individuals based on citizenship or residency and their responsibilities. Still other developments have rendered welfare state structures designed in the 1960s and 1970s and based on the assumption of a typical male industrial worker with lifelong employment and a wife and children obsolete. The shift from employment growth in manufacturing to services has brought more frequent interruptions in jobs and the need for additional training, that is, a greater likelihood of interruption of gainful employment. In this situation, job-based entitlements both for workers and their dependents are not an effective safety net (Esping-Andersen et al. 2002). What these pressures call for is adaptation of welfare state designs, not retrenchment per se. However, given the macroeconomic context, these adaptations can be at best cost neutral. The adaptations have the greatest potential to sustain generous welfare states if they are aimed at improving the human capital base and raising overall activity levels.

In Latin America the domestic pressures are somewhat different. In the more advanced countries, an aging population has increased pressures on the pension systems and on curative health care. In many cases, these pressures were dealt with by adjusting the retirement age upward from 60, or even lower, to 62 or 65, and by restricting pension entitlements based on length of service. The proportion of female-headed households varies greatly between countries and across social classes, being higher among the lower classes and in the Caribbean, where it ranged mostly between 30 percent and 40 percent in the period 1985–97 (CEPAL 1997). In the more advanced countries, it has not changed much since 1980, ranging from 17 percent to 25 percent (CEPAL 1997). Lack of data prevents a more systematic historical view, but the anthropological literature suggests that female-headed households have a long tradition among the lower classes and particularly in the Caribbean. Given that these heads of households typically work in the informal sector, they and their children have long been excluded from employment-based pension and health care entitlements.

The problems of restricted coverage of systems of social protection in Latin America have been aggravated by the economic transformations discussed above. Thus, the challenge for these systems remains a widening of coverage and an introduction of unemployment insurance. The key change needed is also a transition from entitlements for a breadwinner and dependents based on employment to entitlements for individuals based on citizenship and responsibilities for dependents. Given the macroeconomic situation of these countries, the level of benefits obviously has to be very basic. However, as we will argue below, such basic benefits are essential for a strengthening of the human capital base and thus economic development.

OUTCOMES OF WELFARE STATES FOR HUMAN WELFARE

There are several ways to look at the outcomes of welfare states with regard to human welfare. Arguably the most fundamental outcome is poverty reduction. Whereas advocates of social democratic, Christian democratic, and liberal welfare state regimes disagree on other goals, particularly the goal of reducing inequality, they do agree on the goal of reducing poverty—at least among the "deserving poor" who because of adverse circumstances cannot keep themselves out of poverty (Goodin et al. 1999). Thus, the question is which welfare state regime performs best on this indicator. A second relevant outcome is reduction of inequality. As Esping-Andersen pointed out in his contribution to the last edition of this handbook, there is a lot of conceptual confusion with regard to equality and equity as orienting principles of welfare state construction. Only social democrats embrace the principle of equality outright, but advocates of all political persuasions use the concept of equity to legitimize welfare state programs with very different distributional implications. A third important outcome concerns gender equity, another contested concept. Proponents of shared and equal gender roles advocate equity in the sense of welfare state structures that facilitate the combination of career and family for both men and women. Proponents of separate gender roles advocate equity in the sense of welfare state structures that recognize and reward women's responsibility for care of family members and entitle women to benefits of their own on this basis, rather than treating them as dependents of their husbands.

Due to the availability of Luxembourg Income Study (LIS) data, it is possible to look at before-tax-and-transfer income of individuals and households and after-tax-and-transfer income separately. It is also possible to look at specific age and gender categories. Finally, there are by now several waves of LIS data, which make it possible to go beyond the traditional cross-sectional research designs and use a design with unbalanced pooled cross-sections and time series. Researchers have found that the overall amount of welfare state spending is a good predictor of poverty reduction (Kenworthy 1999; Smeeding, Rainwater, and Burtless 2000). As table 1

TABLE 1. Pre- and Post-tax-and-transfer Poverty Rates among the Working-Age Population (advanced industrial democracies)

	Year of LIS Survey	Pre-tax-and-transfer Poverty	Post-tax-and-transfer Poverty
Social democratic welfare states			
Sweden	1995	21.8	4.0
Norway	1995	15.6	4.3
Denmark	1992	19.0	4.4
Finland	1995	17.6	3.6
Mean		18.5	4.1
Christian democratic welfare states			
Austria	1987	n.a.	4.8
Belgium	1992	15.4	3.8
Netherlands	1994	18.2	6.8
Germany	1994	14.7	7.6
France	1994	23.6	7.8
Italy	1995	25.4	16.2
Switzerland	1992	13.2	11.0
Mean		18.4	8.3
Liberal welfare states			
Canada	1994	19.4	11.2
Ireland	1987	26.7	13.4
United Kingdom	1979	24.8	11.9
United States	1997	18.1	15.5
Mean		22.3	13.0
"Wage earner" welfare states			
Australia	1994	19.3	9.4
Grand Mean		19.5	8.7

Source: Luxembourg Income Study, authors' own calculations.
Note: Cell entries are percentage of the population aged 25–59 with income less than 50 percent of the median.

demonstrates, poverty levels are highest and poverty reduction is lowest in liberal welfare states, where spending is lowest. This is so despite the fact that many programs are means tested and thus directed at the poor. These means-tested programs are simply not generous enough to combat poverty effectively. Poverty levels are lowest and poverty reduction highest in social democratic welfare states, even when pensioners are excluded from the calculations (Moller et al. 2003). Excluding pensioners is important because in countries with comprehensive and generous public pension systems large percentages of pensioners have no other income and thus are poor according to before-tax-and-transfer income (Mäkkinen 1999). The Christian democratic welfare states are between the other two types; most of them start with higher poverty levels than social democratic welfare states, comparable to poverty levels in liberal welfare states, but they reduce poverty more effectively than liberal welfare states and thus end up with lower poverty levels, though still higher than in social democratic welfare states.[9] Since Christian democratic welfare states spend similar overall amounts to social democratic welfare states, their lower effectiveness in reducing poverty stems from a less progressive structure of the tax and transfer system than in social democratic welfare states.

The difference in the distributive profile of the Christian democratic and social democratic welfare states is largely governed by the differential commitment of their political promoters to the goal of redistribution and equality. Social democratic commitments have historically been shaped by their deep anchoring in labor movements, whereas Christian democratic commitments reflect their cross-class social base, held together by religious appeals (van Kersbergen 1995). The former have promoted values of equality, the latter of harmony and conciliation of interests. Long-term incumbency of these political forces has indeed resulted in welfare states with a distinctively different structure. Countries with social democratic welfare states start out with a more equal income distribution than countries with Christian democratic welfare states, and the difference increases after taxes and transfers are taken into account.[10] The tax and transfer systems of social democratic welfare states redistribute income to a greater extent than those of Christian democratic welfare states and thus reduce the Gini index of income inequality to a greater extent (Bradley et al. 2003). If social services were included in the measurements, the difference would be even more pronounced. Social democratic welfare states provide a wider array of free or subsidized services, entitlement to which is based on citizenship or residence and thus universally available. By analyzing data for the working age population only, these recent studies based on LIS data have conclusively refuted the critique that welfare states are at best redistributive across the life-cycle but not across income classes. By demonstrating the importance of social democratic incumbency, they have also provided strong support for the power resources theoretical tradition (Bradley et al. 2003).

Countries with liberal welfare states start out and end up with the highest levels of income inequality, as their welfare states are too small to effect much redistribution, despite the widespread use of targeting of benefits. On the face of it, the heavy reliance on earnings-related benefits in Christian democratic welfare states would lead one to expect less redistribution on average there than in liberal welfare states. Korpi and Palme (1998) call this the paradox of redistribution. The paradox can be explained with the fact that the generous public schemes in Christian democratic welfare states crowd out private alternatives, which are invariably even more inegalitarian than earnings-related public schemes (Kangas and Palme 1993).

Given the different notions of gender equity, many analysts prefer the concept of "women-friendly" policies (Hernes 1987), which accommodates policies from support for mother's employment to pension credits for child rearing. Interestingly, looking at individual policies separately, there is often no clear clustering according to welfare state regimes. In particular, the Christian democratic welfare states are very heterogeneous with regard to services and transfers that affect women differently from men (Sainsbury 1999). However, if one looks at the big picture, such as a number of policies summarized by one index of support for mother's employment (Gornick, Meyers, and Ross 1998), or actual outcomes like the proportion of

single mothers in poverty (Huber et al. 2001), one does find a consistent pattern. The social democratic welfare states as a group perform best, with Norway being a laggard; the liberal welfare states perform worst; the Christian democratic welfare states are in the middle, with France and Belgium coming close to the social democratic model in their support for mothers' employment (Gornick, Meyers, and Ross 1998). In women's labor market participation and women's share of total earnings, again the social democratic regimes perform best, with Norway lagging a bit, but here the Christian democratic welfare state regimes are at the bottom and the liberal regimes in the middle (Sainsbury 1999). In the level of poverty among single mothers, a good indicator of the crucial gender equity dimension of women's capacity to form autonomous households (Orloff 1993b), social democratic welfare state regimes effect the greatest reduction from pre- to post-tax-and-transfer poverty and thus produce roughly three times lower poverty levels than Christian democratic welfare states and five times lower levels than liberal welfare state regimes (Huber et al. 2001). What is behind these findings is support for equality of gender roles and thus women's integration into the labor market in social democratic parties, support for separate gender roles and women's responsibility for family care combined with a commitment to keeping women and children out of poverty in Christian democratic parties, and little support for welfare state services and transfers in secular center and right-wing parties.

Critics of the welfare state might argue that its achievements in reducing poverty and inequality do little more than repair the damage done to pre-tax-and-transfer poverty by generous income support systems that serve as work disincentives. We have already pointed to the weak and inconsistent results of research on work disincentives (Atkinson and Mogensen 1993). Here we can add the evidence from the LIS-based studies on pre-tax-and-transfer household income. Countries with social democratic welfare state regimes have the lowest pre-tax-and-transfer levels of poverty and inequality among the working age population and poverty among single mothers. The difference between countries with Christian democratic and with liberal welfare state regimes is less clear, as the Christian democratic category is quite heterogeneous, but the former perform somewhat better on average on inequality and single mothers in poverty, and are about comparable on poverty among the working age population (Moller et al.

2003; Bradley et al. 2003; Huber et al. 2001). In other words, there is no evidence that generous welfare states are associated with higher levels of pre-tax-and-transfer poverty and inequality. Moreover, a direct statistical test of the effect of welfare state generosity on pre-tax-and-transfer inequality showed no such effect (Bradley et al. 2003). We will take up the question of a possible indirect effect via unemployment below.

For Latin America, the literature on welfare state outcomes is again rather scarce. The poor quality of data is a major obstacle; there simply are no reliable data on social expenditures for the pre-1980 period, and even for the past two decades the comparability of the data is poor (Cominetti 1994). Moreover, reliable and comparable data on poverty levels are a rather scarce commodity, not to speak of income distribution. This should not be surprising, if we keep in mind that the LIS data, which are the first truly comparable data for advanced industrial democracies, have only been collected over the past three decades and are only available for one time point for some of them. Latin American case studies for the pre-1980 period suggest that the pension part of social security systems was highly inegalitarian because of the highly unequal benefits received by different occupational groups, the restricted coverage of pension systems, and the fact that the uninsured paid part of the cost through general taxes and through higher prices resulting from employers passing on the cost of their social security contributions to consumers (Borzutzky 1983, 98–113; Mesa-Lago 1989, 130). The health care part of social security tended to be more progressive, and the most progressive kinds of social expenditures were public health expenditures.

For the 1990s, CEPAL (2002) comes to a largely similar assessment: Social security expenditures, which continue to absorb the largest part of social expenditures, have a less redistributive impact than expenditures on primary and secondary education and on health and nutrition, because they provide relatively greater benefits to middle- and upper-income groups. In a study of eight countries, CEPAL found that on average lower-income strata receive transfers and free or subsidized services, including social security, equivalent to 43 percent of total household income, compared to 13 percent and 7 percent for the fourth and fifth income quintiles. Nevertheless, in some of these countries the actual amount of the transfers to the richest stratum was twice as much as that going to the poorest stratum (CEPAL 2002, 28). If social secu-

rity is excluded, households in the lowest quintile, with 4.8 percent of total before-tax-and-transfer income, receive 28 percent of total social expenditure, whereas the highest quintile, with 51 percent of pre-tax-and-transfer income, receives 12 percent of total expenditure (CEPAL 2002, 27).

After having reduced social expenditures significantly in the 1980s, most countries raised them again in the 1990s in both absolute terms and as a percentage of GDP. On average, social expenditure rose from 10.4 percent of GDP in 1990 to 13.1 percent in 1999 (CEPAL 2002, 23). This increase, however, even combined with economic growth, was not nearly sufficient to lower poverty effectively and undo the damage done in the 1980s. Poverty did decrease from 48.3 percent of the population in 1990 to 43.8 percent in 1999, but this figure remained above the 40.5 percent of the population who had been poor in 1980. In absolute terms, the number of poor people increased by 11 million in the 1990s (CEPAL 2002, 14–15). Progress in reducing inequality was nil; Latin America remains the region with the most unequal income distribution. Inequality had increased in most countries in the 1980s, and in some countries it continued to increase in the 1990s. It is worth pointing out here that the two countries that performed clearly best in protecting the lowest levels of inequality were Uruguay and Costa Rica (CEPAL 2002, 18). These two countries spent the highest percentage of GDP on social expenditures, along with Argentina and Brazil, but in contrast to Argentina and Brazil, they had built up more solidaristic social security systems and health care systems, with larger coverage, before the 1980s, and then reformed them only slowly and cautiously.

GROWTH AND EMPLOYMENT OUTCOMES OF WELFARE STATE REGIMES

The impact of the welfare state on growth and employment is contested terrain both politically and academically. Indeed, it would be no exaggeration to say that this is the central issue separating the Left and the Right in advanced industrial democracies, with the Right contending that increasing social spending (and taxes) retards economic growth and employment growth and thus results in welfare losses, while the Left argues that increasing spending does not affect growth and employment and may even have positive effects on them. Neoclassical economists argue that intervening in markets will create inefficiency and lower economic performance; there is a "big trade-off" between "equality and efficiency" (Okun 1975; also see Bacon and Eltis 1976; Lindbeck 1981). Even new growth theorists who argue that economic institutions and government policies can theoretically have a positive effect on growth are generally hostile to high taxation and social welfare spending. For instance, new growth theorists hypothesize that inequality retards growth because "in an unequal society, with many poor agents relative to the average, the majority will then vote for high taxation, which . . . will discourage investment and therefore growth" (Alesina and Perotti 1997, 27).

Welfare state detractors point to negative work incentives created by high taxes that reduce the return on additional hours of work, and generous benefit levels that discourage from seeking work or returning to work. High taxes also crowd out productive investment, in their view. Supporters of generous welfare states counter that spending on health and education, active labor market policy, and policies that enable combining work and family, such as parental leave and day care, improve human capital and increase labor supply. It can also be argued that skill levels at the bottom are in part a direct product of welfare state redistribution, as average skill levels at the fifth, twenty-fifth, and fiftieth percentile of the skill level as measured by the OECD/HRDC (1997) literacy study are very highly negatively correlated with post-tax-and-transfer inequality and not very highly correlated with public educational expenditure, public and private educational expenditure, or secondary school completion rates (Huber and Stephens 2001b). As to the microincentives question, Atkinson and Mogensen's (1993) comprehensive survey of research on Denmark, Sweden, Germany, and Britain on the impact of taxes and social policy on work incentives finds some evidence for both sides in this debate but notes that in most cases the effects were quite small.

Given the centrality of the debate on welfare state generosity and economic growth to contemporary politics, it is surprising that there is not a rich quantitative literature and that, as Saunders (1986) points out, the few early studies were plagued by underspecification, in part because of the small number of cases in the cross-sectional designs in these studies. Castles and Dowrick's (1990) pooled time series analysis of growth over four time periods from 1950 to 1985 stands out as the single most comprehensive attempt to test the hypothesis that welfare spending has a negative (positive) effect on medium-term growth (also see Korpi 1985).[11] Their results "rule virtually out of

court any interpretation that argues for a statistically significant negative relationship between the level of government revenues or the components of government expenditure and medium-term growth" (200–201). On the other hand, they do find some support for a positive relationship between transfers and growth, but it is weak.

Castles and Dowrick's study was published the same year as Esping-Andersen's study and does not reflect the shift in the welfare state literature from the study of variations in welfare state generosity to the study of welfare state regimes. However, the literature on social democratic corporatism and growth is highly relevant here because of the previously mentioned high correlation between corporatism and the welfare state and production regime types. The seminal Lange and Garrett (1985) piece spawned a series of articles (Garrett and Lange 1986; Jackman 1987, 1989; Hicks 1988; Hicks and Patterson 1989; Alvarez, Garrett, and Lange 1991; Beck et al. 1993; Grier 1997; Garrett 1998; also see Schmidt 1983; Cameron 1984; Wilensky 2002), culminating in Scruggs's (2001) contribution, which summarizes, improves on, and updates the previous contributions to this debate. Scruggs improves on previous contributions by using the Summers and Heston (1991) measure of per capita growth measured at purchasing power parities and by including variables measuring alternative causes of growth, such as initial level of economic development (Hicks 1988; Barro and Lee 1994), firm-level cooperation (Hicks and Kenworthy 1998), and consensual democratic institutions (Crepaz 1996). He confirms the central hypothesis of Lange and Garrett (1985) that strong and centralized union confederations combined with left government yield better growth than the inconsistent regimes of left government and no corporatism or corporatism and right government. However, he contests the implication that most of the social democratic corporatism advocates draw, that social democratic corporatism performs better than the other consistent regime, liberal market capitalism (no corporatism and right government). He finds that social democratic corporatist regimes performed no better than the liberal market capitalist regimes in the 1974–84 period and worse in the 1985–95 period.

How does one reconcile Scruggs's findings with those of Castles and Dowrick? One might conclude that social democratic corporatism and generous welfare states have become an economic liability in the post-1985 era of globalization. However, it is likely that Scruggs's results for

1985–95 are heavily driven by the economic crises in Finland and Sweden. The very strong economic performance of these two economies in the late 1990s and early 2000s indicates that economic mismanagement and cyclical features and not institutional arrangements were responsible for these crises. OECD data for 1995–2002 indicate that one could not replicate the finding for this period. It is our conclusion that there is no evidence that one of the welfare state and production regimes performs better than the others with regard to economic growth. This is also the conclusion of Hall and Soskice (2001, 21). They argue that the differential institutional structures of CMEs and LMEs result in comparative institutional advantages in producing different products: "the institutional frameworks of liberal market economies provide companies with better capacities for radical innovation, while those of coordinated market economies provide superior capacities for incremental innovation" (41). They contend that globalization should sharpen these differences, resulting in further divergence rather than the convergence predicted by neoliberals.

With regard to unemployment, the social democratic corporatism literature usually but not invariably (e.g., see Beck et al. 1993) showed a positive effect of corporatism on unemployment. The shift to an analysis by regime type and a focus on employment rather than unemployment yields a much clearer picture (e.g., see Esping-Andersen 1990, 1999; Scharpf 2000; Huber and Stephens 2001a). The shift to a focus on the total level of employment, usually measured as the employed population as a percentage of those aged 15 to 64, was motivated by the fact that many Christian democratic welfare states had resorted to placing able-bodied workers below retirement age in early pension schemes or disability schemes in order to reduce unemployment, thus hiding the true unemployment level. Because of its policies facilitating combining work and family, the related high level of public sector employment, and active labor market policies, the social democratic regime clearly outperformed the other two regimes in overall employment levels. The high levels of wage dispersion characteristic of liberal welfare states have facilitated the development of a large low-wage private service sector in these countries, resulting in employment levels higher than the Christian democratic welfare states but lower than the social democratic welfare states. The OECD figures for unemployment in 2001 show a similar pattern, with the social democratic welfare states (5.4 per-

cent) and liberal welfare states (5.5 percent) performing better than the Christian democratic welfare states (6.8 percent).

Our positive assessment of the employment performance of the social democratic welfare states is at variance with the evaluation of the OECD Jobs Study, which touts the liberal model as the one best way and recommends that European countries increase wage dispersion, roll back welfare state benefits, especially for the unemployed, reduce employment protection, and cut taxes to facilitate the expansion of low-wage employment. Our view is supported by Bradley's (2001) comprehensive test of the OECD diagnosis. In a pooled time series analysis with employment levels as the dependent variable, Bradley finds that wage dispersion, welfare state generosity, and employment protection laws are not related to employment levels. Total taxes, active labor market policies, high short-term unemployment benefits, and bargaining centralization are positively related to employment levels, while payroll taxes and high long-term unemployment benefits are negatively related to employment levels. This fits very well with our outline of the performance of the regime types (also see Scharpf 2000), as these positive features are all characteristics of social democratic welfare states, while the negative features are characteristics of Christian democratic welfare states.

ADVANCES IN WELFARE STATE RESEARCH AND FUTURE DIRECTIONS

To summarize our discussion of progress in welfare state research, we can begin by pointing out that in terms of theoretical approaches, recent studies of welfare state formation tend to be synthetic. The main emphasis is on power distributions, but institutional factors are treated as essential explanatory factors as well. Considerations of power distribution include not only labor movements in the form of unions and left parties, but also political parties based on religious appeals with their own distinctive welfare state project. Moreover, gender is added to class and religion as a possible basis for organization and political mobilization in support of specific welfare state programs. Comparative research on gender mobilization is hampered by data problems, though. Whereas there are by now excellent data on unionization, there are only very spotty, survey-based data on membership in women's groups, or on female membership in political parties.

A further theoretical advance is the use of welfare state regimes as essential analytical category. The conceptualization of regimes is based on constellations of social rights, or welfare state entitlements, given by the structure of the respective welfare states. Empirically, there has been considerable progress in measuring social rights (Korpi 1989; Esping-Andersen 1990), but these measurements are mainly tapping rights to transfers. Given the importance of social services and the great differences in the extent to which welfare states take responsibility for financing or delivering them, progress in developing good measures of rights to free or subsidized social services will be an essential contribution to welfare state research. They will also help us better to understand the gender-specific impact of different welfare state regimes.

Connecting welfare state regimes in a systematic way with production regimes has been another step forward in welfare state research. This connection is best seen as a mutually supportive or enabling one, not as a necessary correspondence. Indeed, it is important to emphasize that welfare state regimes can be adapted to changes in production regimes while protecting their essential features. The closest link between production and welfare state regimes is in the countries with reliance on high tariff protection and state intervention in other areas to promote ISI. There, a turn away from this production regime made certain features of the welfare state regime unviable.

There has been considerable research on the impact of globalization on welfare state regimes. This research has found few if any direct effects on welfare state regimes in advanced industrial societies, but it has found some indirect effects via higher levels of unemployment, particularly in coordinated market economies where globalization deprived governments of some policy tools they had used to stimulate investment and employment. Qualitative research has added to this a shift in power relations in favor of capital and thus greater ability to pressure governments and labor movements for concessions on tax financing of welfare state provisions. Nevertheless, the general picture is one of remarkable resilience of welfare state regimes in advanced industrial societies. There have been cutbacks almost everywhere, and some of considerable magnitude, but one could really only talk of regime shifts in two cases, Britain and New Zealand. In contrast, the impact of globalization on countries with ISI production regimes, Australia and New Zealand and the Latin America countries, was

quite dramatic. They had to restructure their systems of social protection, and in most cases this restructuration was governed by a neoliberal blueprint pushed by the international financial institutions. But even in these cases, the examples of Australia, Uruguay, and Costa Rica demonstrate that it is possible to adapt in a way that preserves more generous and solidaristic welfare state regimes than the neoliberal model prescribes. Comparative research on cases of countries that have been undergoing a transition from ISI to more open economies is scarce and is badly needed to elucidate the determinants of modes of adaptation that preserve or construct effective systems of social protection.

Notwithstanding the general picture of resilience of welfare state regimes in advanced industrial societies in the face of globalization, research has identified serious pressures from other sources that have the potential to escalate in the future. The most serious of these pressures are demographic, specifically the increase in life expectancy and consequent growth of the elderly proportion of the population. In countries with Christian democratic welfare states, particularly in southern Europe, this problem is aggravated by declining fertility rates. Research is needed to identify solutions to this dilemma, that is, paths toward increasing female labor force participation rates while simultaneously facilitating the combination of paid work with family care obligations. Other pressures on established welfare state models, such as labor markets with more frequent interruptions of careers and changing household structures, are not as dramatic but still call for research on creative adaptations of income support programs.

Given these pressures and the reliance by Christian democratic welfare state regimes on reduction of labor supply to deal with unemployment, there is considerable convergence toward the view that this regime type is the one confronting the most serious challenges. The turnaround in the Nordic countries after the crisis of the early 1990s, combined with overall low dependency ratios, suggests that the social democratic welfare state regime is a sustainable model. The liberal welfare state regime also appears sustainable, though it entails serious social costs in terms of high poverty and inequality. It is the Christian democratic welfare state regime, with its low overall labor force participation rate, unfavorable demographic trends, and great reliance on payroll taxes for welfare state financing that is in danger of becoming unsustainable. How to restructure that system and how to make the solutions politically palatable is a major research area for the near future.

A further area of major progress in welfare state research concerns outcomes for human welfare. The availability of comparable data over time for advanced industrial democracies has made it possible to demonstrate the differential effectiveness of welfare state regimes in reducing poverty and inequality. All three of them reduce both poverty and inequality, but social democratic welfare state regimes achieve consistently the best results and the liberal welfare state regimes the worst, with Christian democratic welfare state regimes in the middle. The difference between the social democratic and the Christian democratic welfare state regimes lies in the progressive structure of the tax and transfer systems; the difference between the Christian democratic and the liberal welfare state regimes lies in overall generosity. The liberal welfare states simply do not devote enough resources to combating poverty to achieve the same results as the Christian democratic welfare state regimes, regimes that are similarly oriented toward poverty reduction only and not toward reduction of inequality per se. Low spending on their systems of social protection, of course, constrained by low tax burdens, is what keeps the great majority of Latin American countries from combating poverty effectively.

In the literature on welfare states and growth and employment, we noted a surprising scarcity of tests of the growth relationship. The most comprehensive of the studies that have been done did not find any negative effects of government revenue or components of government expenditure on medium-term economic growth. Nor did researchers find any conclusive evidence that a particular combination of welfare state and production regimes performed better than another in economic growth. However, with regard to employment there is evidence that social democratic welfare state regimes and labor market policies performed better than both liberal and Christian democratic welfare state regimes. Moreover, the social democratic are the most redistributive welfare state regimes, and lower levels of inequality are closely associated with higher skill levels at the lower end of the skills distribution. This reinforces the overall assessment that the social democratic welfare state regimes do not only have the best consequences for human welfare in terms of poverty and inequality but are also economically sustainable because of their investment in human capital and in labor mobilization.

Notes

1. For a recent review of political theories of the welfare state see Myles and Quadagno 2002.

2. In Asia, Japan belongs to the set of advanced industrial countries, but lagged behind in welfare state development. A large part of the social safety net was based on employment in large corporations, which included some 25–30 percent of the workforce, and on redistribution of benefits through the family. Despite the establishment of national pension and health insurance programs in the 1960s and a push for welfare state expansion in the 1970s, public social expenditures remained low compared to those of other advanced industrial societies. In the East Asian newly industrialized countries, serious efforts to establish national welfare state programs began only in the 1970s (Korea) or in the 1980s (Taiwan) (Goodman and Peng 1996; Pempel 2002). In other East Asian countries, public welfare state efforts came similarly late and remained low (Haggard and Kaufman 2002).

3. We choose the term "reformist" to include all left-of-center parties, ranging from mildly social democratic to radical left.

4. Haggard and Kaufman (2002) emphasize primarily regime type and secondarily strength of left-of-center parties, but discount strength of labor movements in their analysis of welfare state expansion in Latin America.

5. For a general exposition of the analytical strategy she pursues, see Thelen (2003).

6. The following few paragraphs summarize our arguments in Huber and Stephens (2001a, chap. 7).

7. Another part of the reason is competition from non-OECD countries for investment funds (Rowthorn 1995) and the world wide debt buildup in the wake of the two oil shocks.

8. Kaufman and Segura-Ubiergo (2001), in a pooled cross-section and time series analysis of changes in social expenditure in Latin America, found a statistically significant negative effect of trade opening; in other words, the faster a country opened its economy, the more likely it was to lower social expenditure.

9. Pre-tax-and-transfer poverty levels are largely a result of labor market variables, specifically the size of industrial employment and the level of unemployment (Moller et al. 2003).

10. The differences in before tax and transfer inequality are accounted for by levels of unemployment, proportion of single mother families, and union density (Bradley et al. 2003).

11. The hypothesis is properly tested on medium term growth which eliminates business cycle effects. Friedland and Sanders (1985) find little support for the neo-liberal view even on short term growth.

References

Albert, Michel. 1991. *Capitalisme contre capitalisme.* Paris: Seuil.

Alesina, Alberto, and Roberto Perotti. 1997. "The Politics of Growth: A Survey." Pp. 11–49 in *Government and Growth*, ed. Villy Bergström. Oxford: Clarendon Press.

Alvarez, R. Michael, Geoffrey Garrett, and Peter Lange. 1991. "Government Partisanship, Labor Organization, and Macro-economic Performance." *American Political Science Review* 85:539–56.

Amenta, Edwin. 1998. *Bold Relief: Institutional Politics and the Origins of Modern American Social Policy.* Princeton: Princeton University Press.

Atkinson, A. B., and J. Mickelwright. 1991. "Unemployment Compensation and Labour Market Transitions: A Critical Review." *Journal of Economic Literature* 29:1679–727.

Atkinson, A. B., and Gunnar Viby Mogensen. 1993. *Welfare and Work Incentives: A North European Perspective.* Oxford: Clarendon Press.

Bacon, Robert W., and Walter A. Eltis. 1976. *Britain's Economic Problem: Too Few Producers?* London: Macmillan.

Barr, Nicholas. 1998. *The Economics of the Welfare State.* 3d ed. Stanford, Calif.: Stanford University Press.

Barro, Robert, and Jong-Wha Lee. 1994. "Sources of Economic Growth." *Carnegie-Rochester Series on Public Policy* 40:1–46.

Beck, Nathaniel, Jonathan Katz, Michael Alvarez, Geoffrey Garrett, and Peter Lange. 1993. "Government Partisanship, Labor Organization, and Macroeconomic Performance: A Corrigendum." *American Political Science Review* 87:645–48.

Bergqvist, Christina. 1998. "Still a Woman-Friendly Welfare State? The Case of Parental Leave and Child Care Policies in Sweden." Paper presented to the Eleventh International Conference of Europeanists, Baltimore, February 26–March 1.

Bonoli, Giuliano, and André Mach. 2000. "Switzerland: Adjustment Politics with Institutional Constraints." Pp. 131–72 in *Diverse Responses to Common Challenges*, vol. 2 of *Welfare and Work in the Open Economy*, ed. Fritz Scharpf and Vivien A. Schmidt. Oxford: Oxford University Press.

Borzutzky, Silvia. 1983. "Chilean Politics and Social Security Policies." Ph.D. diss., Department of Political Science, University of Pittsburgh.

Bradley, David. 2001. "The Political Economy of Employment Performance: Testing the Deregulation Thesis." Ph.D. diss., Department of Political Science, University of North Carolina at Chapel Hill.

Bradley, David, Evelyne Huber, Stephanie Moller, François Nielsen, and John Stephens. 2003. "Distribution and Redistribution in Post-industrial Democracies." *World Politics.* 55:193–228.

Cameron, David. 1978. "The Expansion of the Public Economy." *American Political Science Review* 72:1243–61.

———. 1984. "Social Democracy, Corporatism, Labour Quiescence, and Representation of Economic Interest in Advanced Capitalist Society." Pp. 143–78 in *Order and Conflict in Contemporary Capitalism: Studies in the Political Economy of Western European Nations*, ed. John Goldthorpe. Oxford: Clarendon Press.

Castles, Francis G. 1985. *The Working Class and Welfare.* Sydney: Allen and Unwin.

———, ed. 1982. *The Impact of Parties.* Beverly Hills, Calif.: Sage.

Castles, Francis G., and Steve Dowrick. 1990. "The Impact of Government Spending Levels on Medium-Term Economic Growth in the OECD, 1960–85." *Journal of Theoretical Politics* 2(2): 173–204.

Castles, Francis G., and Deborah Mitchell. 1993. "Three Worlds of Welfare Capitalism or Four?" In *Families of Nations: Public Policy in Western Democracies*, ed. Francis G. Castles. Brookfield, Vt.: Dartmouth.

Collier, David, and Richard E. Messick. 1975. "Prerequisites versus Diffusion: Testing Alternative Explanations of Social Security Adoption." *American Political Science Review* 69:1299–315.

Cominetti, Rossella. 1994. *El Gasto Social en América Latina: Un Examen Cuantitativo y Cualitativo.* Santiago: Naciones Unidas, CEPAL.

Comision Económica para América Latina (CEPAL). 1993. *Social Panorama of Latin America.* Santiago: CEPAL.

———. 1998. *The Fiscal Covenant: Strengths, Weaknesses, Challenges.* Santiago: CEPAL.

———. 2002. *Social Panorama of Latin America, 2000–2001.* Santiago: CEPAL.

Crepaz, Markus. 1996. "Consensus versus Majoritarian Democracy: Political Institutions and the Impact on Macroeconomic Performance and Industrial Disputes." *Comparative Political Studies* 29(1): 4–26.

Crouch, Colin. 1993. *Industrial Relations and European State Traditions.* Oxford: Clarendon Press.

Dion, Michelle. 2002. "The Progress of Revolution? Mexico's Welfare Regime in Comparative and Historical Perspective." Ph.D. diss., Department of Political Science, University of North Carolina at Chapel Hill.

Dornbusch, Rudiger. 1989. "The Latin American Debt Problem: Anatomy and Solutions." Pp. 7–22 in *Debt and Democracy in Latin America*, ed. Barbara Stallings and Robert Kaufman. Boulder, Colo.: Westview Press.

Esping-Andersen, Gøsta. 1985. *Politics against Markets.* Princeton: Princeton University Press.

———. 1990. *The Three Worlds of Welfare Capitalism.* Princeton: Princeton University Press.

———. 1999. *Social Foundations of Postindustrial Economies.* Oxford: Oxford University Press.

Esping-Andersen, Gøsta, Duncan Gallie, Anton Hemerijck, and John Myles. 2002. *Why We Need a New Welfare State.* Oxford: Oxford University Press.

Estevez-Abe, Margarita, Torben Iversen, and David Soskice. 2001. "Social Protection and the Formation of Skills: A Reinterpretation of the Welfare State." Pp. 145–83 in *Varieties of Capitalism*, ed. Peter A. Hall and David Soskice. Oxford: Oxford University Press.

Ferrera, Maurizio. 1996. "Il modello Sud-Europeo di welfare state." *Rivista Italiana di Scienza Politica* 1:67–101.

Friedland, Roger, and Jimy Sanders. 1985. "The Public Economy and Economic Growth in Western Market Economies." *American Sociological Review* 50: 421–37.

Garretón, Manuel Antonio. 1989. "Popular Mobilization and the Military Regime in Chile: The Complexities of the Invisible Transition." Pp. 259–77 in *Power and Popular Protest: Latin American Social Movements*, ed. Susan Eckstein. Berkeley and Los Angeles: University of California Press.

Garrett, Geoffrey. 1998. *Partisan Politics in the Global Economy*. Cambridge: Cambridge University Press.

Garrett, Geoffrey, and Peter Lange. 1986. "Performance in a Hostile World: Domestic and International Determinants of Economic Growth in the Advanced Capitalist Democracies, 1974–1982." *World Politics* 38:517–45.

Glyn, Andrew. 1995. "The Assessment: Unemployment and Inequality." *Oxford Review of Economic Policy* 11:1–25.

Goodin, Robert E., Bruce Headey, Ruud Muffels, and Henk-Jan Dirven. 1999. *The Real Worlds of Welfare Capitalism*. Cambridge: Cambridge University Press.

Goodman, Roger, and Ito Peng. 1996. "The East Asian Welfare States: Peripatetic Learning, Adaptive Change, and Nation-Building." Pp. 192–224 in *Welfare States in Transition: National Adaptations in Global Economies*, ed. Gøsta Esping-Andersen. London: Sage.

Gornick, Janet, Marcia K. Meyers, and Katherin E. Ross. 1998. "Public Policies and the Employment of Mothers: A Cross-National Study." *Social Science Quarterly* 79:35–54.

Grier, Kevin B. 1997. "Governments, Unions, and Economic Growth." Pp. 149–82 in *Government and Growth*, ed. Villy Bergström. Oxford: Clarendon Press.

Haggard, Stephan, and Robert Kaufman. 2002. "The Expansion of Welfare Commitments in Latin America and East Asia: 1950–1980." Paper prepared for the Annual Meeting of the American Political Science Association, Boston, August 25–30.

Hall, Peter A., and David Soskice. 2001. *Varieties of Capitalism: The Institutional Foundations of Comparative Advantage*. Oxford: Oxford University Press.

Heclo, Hugh. 1974. *Modern Social Politics in Britain and Sweden*. New Haven: Yale University Press.

Hernes, Helga Maria. 1987. *Welfare State and Woman Power: Essays in State Feminism*. Oslo: Norwegian University Press.

Hicks, Alexander. 1988. "Social Democratic Corporatism and Economic Growth." *Journal of Politics* 50:677–704.

———. 1999. *Social Democracy and Welfare Capitalism: A Century of Income Security Policies*. Ithaca, N.Y.: Cornell University Press.

Hicks, Alexander, and Lane Kenworthy. 1998. "Cooperation and Political Economic Performance in Afflu-

ent Democratic Capitalism." *American Journal of Sociology* 103:1631–72.

Hicks, Alexander, and William Patterson. 1989. "On the Robustness of the Left Corporatist Model of Economic Growth." *Journal of Politics* 51:662–75.

Hicks, Alexander, and Duane Swank. 1984. "On the Political Economy of Welfare Expansion: A Comparative Analysis of 18 Advanced Capitalist Economies, 1960–1971." *Comparative Political Studies* 17:81–118.

Hill, Dana Carol Davis, and Lean M. Tigges. 1995. "Gendering the Welfare State: A Cross-National Study of Women's Public Pension Quality." *Gender and Society* 9:99–119.

Hobson, Barbara. 1994. "Welfare Policy Regimes, Solo Mothers, and the Logics of Gender." In *Gendering Welfare States*, ed. Diane Sainsbury. London: Sage.

Hobson, Barbara, and Marika Lindholm. 1997. "Collective Identities, Women's Power Resources, and the Construction of Citizenship Rights in Welfare States." *Theory and Society* 26:475–508.

Hollingsworth, J. Rogers, and Robert Boyer, eds. 1997. *Contemporary Capitalism: The Embeddedness of Institutions*. Cambridge: Cambridge University Press.

Hollingsworth, Rogers, Philippe Schmitter, and Wolfgang Streeck, eds. 1994. *Governing Capitalist Economies*. Oxford: Oxford University Press.

Huber, Evelyne. 1996. "Options for Social Policy in Latin America: Neoliberal versus Social Democratic Models." Pp. 141–91 in *Welfare States in Transition: National Adaptations in Global Economies*, ed. Gøsta Esping-Andersen. London: Sage.

———. Forthcoming. "Globalization and Social Policy Development in Latin America." In *Politics Matters: Globalization and Social Welfare Policy in Cross-Regional Comparison*, ed. Miguel Glatzer and Dietrich Rueschemeyer.

Huber, Evelyne, Charles Ragin, and John D. Stephens. 1993. "Social Democracy, Christian Democracy, Constitutional Structure, and the Welfare State." *American Journal of Sociology* 99:711–49.

Huber, Evelyne, and John Stevens. 2001a. *Development and Crisis of the Welfare State: Parties and Policies in Global Markets*. Chicago: University of Chicago Press.

———. 2001b. "Globalization, Competitiveness, and the Social Democratic Model." *Social Policy and Society* 1(1): 47–57.

Huber, Evelyne, John D. Stephens, David Bradley, Stephanie Moller, and Francois Nielsen. 2001. "The Welfare State and Gender Equality." Luxembourg Income Study Working Paper No. 279, September.

Immergut, Ellen. 1992. *The Political Construction of Interests: National Health Insurance Politics in Switzerland, France, and Sweden, 1930–1970*. Cambridge: Cambridge University Press.

Inter-American Development Bank (IADB). 1996. *Economic and Social Progress in Latin America: 1996 Report*. Washington, D.C.: IADB.

Iversen, Torben, and David Soskice. 2001. "An Asset

Theory of Social Policy Preference." *American Political Science Review* 95:875–910.

Jackman, Robert. 1987. "The Politics of Economic Growth in Industrial Democracies, 1974–1980: Leftist Strength or North Sea Oil?" *Journal of Politics* 49:202–12.

———. 1989. "The Politics of Economic Growth: Once Again." *Journal of Politics* 51:646–61.

Jenson, Jane, and Rianne Mahon. 1993. "Representing Solidarity: Class, Gender, and the Crisis in Social-Democratic Sweden." *New Left Review* 201:76–100.

Kahler, Miles. 1989. "International Financial Institutions and the Politics of Adjustment." Pp. 139–59 in *Fragile Coalitions: The Politics of Economic Adjustment*, ed. Joan M. Nelson. Washington, D.C.: Overseas Development Council.

Kangas, Olli, and Joakim Palme. 1993. "Statism Eroded? Labor-Market Benefits and Challenges to the Scandinavian Welfare States." Pp. 3–24 in *Welfare Trends in the Scandinavian Countries*, ed. Erik Jørgen Hansen, Robert Erikson, Stein Ringen, and Hannu Uusitalo. Armonk, N.Y.: M. E. Sharpe.

Katzenstein, Peter. 1985. *Small States in World Markets: Industrial Policy in Europe*. Ithaca, N.Y.: Cornell University Press.

Kaufman, Robert R., and Alex Segura-Ubiergo. 2001. "Globalization, Domestic Politics, and Social Spending in Latin America." *World Politics* 53:553–88.

Kay, Stephen. 1998. "Politics and Social Security Reform in the Southern Cone and Brazil." Ph.D. diss., Department of Political Science, University of California, Los Angeles.

Kenworthy, Lane. 1999. "Do Social-Welfare Policies Reduce Poverty? A Cross-National Assessment." *Social Forces* 77:1119–39.

Kjellberg, Anders. 1983. *Facklip Organisering I Tolv Länder*. Stockholm: Arkiv.

Kolberg, Jon Eivind, and Gøsta Esping-Andersen. 1992. "Welfare States and Employment Regimes." Pp. 3–36 in *The Study of Welfare State Regimes*, ed. Jon Eivind Kolberg. Armonk, N.Y.: M. E. Sharpe.

Korpi, Walter. 1980. "Approaches to the Study of Poverty in the United States: Critical Notes from a European Perspective." Swedish Institute for Social Research Working Paper No. 64, Stockholm.

———. 1983. *The Democratic Class Struggle*. London: Routledge and Kegan Paul.

———. 1985. "Economic Growth and the Welfare State: Leaky Bucket or Irrigation System." *European Sociological Review* 1:97–118.

———. 1989. "Power, Politics, and State Autonomy in the Development of Social Citizenship: Social Rights during Sickness in Eighteen OECD Countries since 1930." *American Sociological Review* 54:309–29.

Korpi, Walter, and Joakim Palme. 1998. "The Strategy of Equality and the Paradox of Redistribution." *American Sociological Review* 63:661–87.

Lange, Peter, and Geoffrey Garrett. 1985. "The Politics of Growth: Strategic Interaction and Economic Performance in the Advanced Industrial Democracies, 1974–80." *Journal of Politics* 47:792–827.

Leibfried, Stephan. 1992. "Towards a European Welfare State: On Integrating Poverty Regimes in the European Community." Pp. 245–80 in *Social Policy in a Changing Europe*, ed. Z. Ferge and J. E. Kolberg. Frankfurt am Main: Campus Verlag.

Lewis, Jane. 1992. "Gender and the Development of Welfare Regimes." *Journal of European Social Policy* 2:159–73.

———. 1994. "Gender, the Family, and Women's Agency in the Building of 'Welfare States': The British Case." *Social History* 19:37–55.

Lindbeck, Assar. 1981. "Work Disincentives in the Welfare State." Institute for International Economic Studies, University of Stockholm, Reprint Series No. 176.

———. 1994. "The Welfare State and the Employment Problem." *American Economic Review* 71–75.

Lora, Eduardo. 2001. "Structural Reforms in Latin America: What Has Been Reformed and How to Measure It." Inter-American Development Bank, Research Department, Working Paper No. 466, December.

Madrid, Raúl L. 2002. "The Politics and Economics of Pension Privatization in Latin America." *Latin American Research Review* 37(2): 159–82.

Maioni, Antonia. 1998. *Parting at the Crossroads: The Emergence of Health Insurance in the United States and Canada*. Princeton: Princeton University Press.

Mäkinen, Tiina. 1999. "Contradictory Findings? The Connection between Structural Factors, Income Transfers, and Poverty in OECD Countries." *International Social Security Review* 52:3–24.

Malloy, James M. 1979. *The Politics of Social Security in Brazil*. Pittsburgh: University of Pittsburgh Press.

Mesa-Lago, Carmelo. 1978. *Social Security in Latin America: Pressure Groups, Stratification, and Inequality*. Pittsburgh: University of Pittsburgh Press.

———. 1989. *Ascent to Bankruptcy: Financing Social Security in Latin America*. Pittsburgh: University of Pittsburgh Press.

Moller, Stephanie, David Bradley, Evelyne Huber, François Nielsen, and John D. Stephens. 2003. "Determinants of Relative Poverty in Advanced Capitalist Democracies." *American Sociological Review* 68:22–51.

Muller, Katharina. 2002. "Privatising Old-Age Security: Latin America and Eastern Europe Compared." Research report, Institute for Transformation Studies, Frankfurt am Main, March.

Myles, John. 1984. *Old Age and the Welfare State*. Boston: Little, Brown.

Myles, John, and Jill Quadagno. 2002. "Political Theories of the Welfare State." *Social Science Review*, March, 34–57.

O'Connor, Julia S., Ann Shola Orloff, and Sheila Shaver. 1999. *States, Markets, Families: Gender, Liberalism, and Social Policy in Australia, Canada, Great Britain, and the United States.* Cambridge: Cambridge University Press.

Okun, Arthur. 1975. *Equality and Efficiency, the Big Tradeoff.* Washington, D.C.: Brookings Institution.

Organization for Economic Cooperation and Development (OECD). 1995. *Historical Statistics, 1960–1993.* Paris: OECD.

Organization for Economic Cooperation and Development and Human Resources (OECD and HRDC). 1997. *Literacy Skills for the Knowledge Society: Further Results from the International Adult Literacy Survey.* Paris: OECD; HRDC.

Orloff, Ann. 1993a. *The Poltics of Pensions: A Comparative Analysis of Britain, Canada, and the United States, 1880–1940.* Madison: University of Wisconsin Press.

———. 1993b. "Gender and the Social Rights of Citizenship: The Comparative Analysis of Gender Relations and Welfare States." *American Sociological Review* 58:303–28.

———. 1997. "Motherhood, Work, and Welfare in the United Sates, Britain, Canada, and Australia." Paper presented at the conference "Welfare States at the Crossroads," Sigtuna, Sweden, January.

Pampel, Fred, and John Williamson. 1989. *Age, Class, Politics, and the Welfare State.* Cambridge: Cambridge University Press.

Pempel, T. J. 2002. "Labor Exclusion and Privatized Welfare: Two Keys to Asian Capitalist Development." Pp. 277–300 in *Models of Capitalism: Lessons for Latin America,* ed. Evelyne Huber. College Park: Pennsylvania State University Press.

Pierson, Paul. 1994. *Dismantling the Welfare State?* Cambridge: Cambridge University Press.

———. 1996. "The New Politics of the Welfare State." *World Politics* 48:143–79.

———, ed. 2001. *The New Politics of the Welfare State.* Oxford: Oxford University Press.

Raczynski, Dagmar 1994. "Social Policies in Chile: Origin, Transformations, and Perspectives." Democracy and Social Policy Series, Working Paper No. 4, Kellogg Institute, University of Notre Dame.

Rowthorn, Robert. 1995. "Capital Formation and Unemployment." *Oxford Review of Economic Policy* 11: 29–39.

Sainsbury, Diane, ed. 1999. *Gender and Welfare State Regimes.* Oxford: Oxford University Press.

Saunders, Peter. 1986. "What Can We Learn from International Comparisons of Public Sector Size and Economic Performance." *European Sociological Review* 2(1): 52–50.

Scharpf, Fritz W. 2000. "Economic Changes, Vulnerabilities, and Institutional Capabilities." In *From Vulnerability to Competitiveness,* vol. 1 of *Welfare and Work in the Open Economy,* ed. Fritz W. Scharpf and Vivien A. Schmidt. Oxford: Oxford University Press.

Scharpf, Fritz W., and Vivien A. Schmidt, eds. 2000. *Welfare and Work in the Open Economy.* 2 vols. Oxford: Oxford University Press.

Schmidt, Manfred G. 1983. "The Welfare State and the Economy in Periods of Economic Crisis: A Comparative Study of Twenty-three OECD Nations." *European Journal of Political Research* 11:1–26.

Scruggs, Lyle. 2001. "The Politics of Growth Revisited." *Journal of Politics* 63(1): 120–40.

Skocpol, Theda. 1988. "The Limits of the New Deal System and the Roots of Contemporary Welfare Dilemmas." Pp. 293–312 in *The Politics of Social Policy in the United States,* ed. Margaret Wier, Ann Shola Orloff, and Theda Skocpol. Princeton: Princeton University Press.

Smeeding, Timothy M., Lee Rainwater, and Gary Burtless. 2000. "United States Poverty in Cross-National Context." Luxembourg Income Study Working Paper No. 244.

Soskice, David. 1990. "Wage Determination: The Changing Role of Institutions in Advanced Industrial Countries." *Oxford Review of Economic Policy* 6 36–61.

———. 1999. "Divergent Production Regimes: Coordinated and Uncoordinated Market Economies in the 1980s and 1990s." Pp. 101–34 in *Continuity and Change in Contemporary Capitalism,* ed. Herbert Kitschelt, Peter Lange, Gary Marks, and John D. Stephens. Cambridge: Cambridge University Press.

Spalding, Rose J. 1978. "Social Security Policy Making: The Formation and Evolution of the Mexican Social Security Institute." Ph.D. diss., University of North Carolina at Chapel Hill.

Stallings, Barbara, and Robert Kaufman, eds. 1989. *Debt and Democracy in Latin America.* Boulder, Colo.: Westview Press.

Stephens, John. D. 1979. *The Transition from Capitalism to Socialism.* London: Macmillan.

Stephens, John D., Evelyne Huber, and Leonard Ray. 1999. "The Welfare State in Hard Times." Pp. 164–93 in *Continuity and Change in Contemporary Capitalism,* ed. Herbert Kitschelt, Peter Lange, Gary Marks, and John D. Stephens. New York: Cambridge University Press.

Stetson, Dorothy McBride, and Amy G. Mazur, eds. 1995. *Comparative State Feminism.* Thousand Oaks, Calif.: Sage.

Summers, Robert, and Alan Heston. 1991. "The Penn World Tables (Mark 5): An Expanded Set of International Comparisons." *Quarterly Journal of Economics* 106:327–68.

Swank, Duane. 2002. *Global Capital, Political Institutions, and Policy Change in Developed Welfare States.* Cambridge: Cambridge University Press.

Swenson, Peter. 2002. *Capitalists against Markets: The Making of Labor Markets and Welfare States in the*

United States and Sweden. Oxford: Oxford University Press.

Teichman, Judith A. 2001. *The Politics of Freeing Markets in Latin America.* Chapel Hill: University of North Carolina Press.

Thelen, Kathleen. 2003. "How Institutions Evolve: Insights from Comparative Historical Analysis." Pp. 20–40 in *Comparative Historical Analysis in the Social Sciences,* ed. James Mahoney and Dietrich Rueschemeyer. Cambridge: Cambridge University Press.

———. 2004. *How Institutions Evolve: The Political Economy of Skills in Germany, Britain, the United States, and Japan.* Cambridge: Cambridge University Press.

van Kersbergen, Kees. 1995. *Social Capitalism.* London: Routledge.

Wallerstein, Michael. 1989. "Union Organization in Advanced Industrial Democracies." *American Political Science Review* 83:481–501.

Weir, Margaret, Ann Shola Orloff, and Theda Skocpol. 1988. "Introduction: Understanding American Social Politics." Pp. 1–37 in *The Politics of Social Policy in the United States,* ed. Margaret Weir, Ann

Shola Orloff, and Theda Skocpol. Princeton: Princeton University Press.

Western, Bruce. 1991. "A Comparative Study of Corporatist Development." *American Sociological Review* 56:283–94.

———. 1997. *Between Class and Market: Postwar Unionization in the Capitalist Democracies.* Princeton: Princeton University Press.

Weyland. Kurt. 2002. *The Politics of Market Reform in Fragile Democracies: Argentina, Brazil, Peru, and Venezuela.* Princeton: Princeton University Press.

Wilensky, Harold. 1975. *The Welfare State and Equality.* Berkeley and Los Angeles: University of California Press.

———. 1981. "Leftism, Catholicism, and Democratic Corporatism." Pp. 314–78 in *The Development of the Welfare State in Europe and America,* ed. Peter Flora and Arnold Heidenheimer. New Brunswick, N.J.: Transaction Press.

———. 2002. *Rich Democracies: Political Economy and Performance.* Berkeley and Los Angeles: University of California Press.

World Bank. 1982. *World Development Report, 1982.* Oxford: Oxford University Press; World Bank.

25 Education and the Economy

Mary C. Brinton

IT HAS NOW BEEN over 25 years since Bowles and Gintis published their classic *Schooling in Capitalist America* (1976). In proposing that the relationship between education and the capitalist economy is best understood through the lens of Marxist analysis, the book engendered a series of far-reaching commentaries and debates. While Bowles and Gintis's conception of a "correspondence principle" that links social relationships in schools to social relationships in the capitalist workplace may not have been fully embraced by any but the most ardent Marxists, their analysis nevertheless demonstrated the fundamental importance of understanding the relationship between schools and workplaces—between education and the economy. Most importantly, their work raised crucial questions about how the intersection of the educational system and employer behaviors affects the reproduction of social class inequalities.

Contemporary economic sociologists might take note, for research on the education-economy interface has not played a prominent role in the reinvigorated American economic sociology of the past 15 years. It is not immediately clear why this should be the case, but a number of reasons may be at work. As other chapters in this volume (e.g., Zelizer; England and Folbre) note, the new economic sociology has focused heavily on studies of private for-profit enterprise, especially in the financial sector of advanced industrial economies. Educational institutions do not easily fall under this rubric. Moreover, two groups of sociologists whose work bears strongly on issues concerning the education-economy link—educational sociologists and social stratification researchers—are rarely identified (or self-identified) as economic sociologists. Whether this is due more to the organization of the sociological discipline in the United States across an abundance of substantive specialties or to differences in scholars' intellectual proclivities across the areas of education, inequality, and economy, this chapter will argue that the richness of the questions raised by the education-economy interface merit their inclusion in the collective research agenda of American economic sociology. Moreover, along with Morris and Western (1999), I will argue that if sociologists do not take up the intellectual challenges of analyzing how the institutions of capitalist economies are related to labor market inequalities among social groups, we may soon cede this terrain to economists and to political scientists.

We can conceptualize two principal intersections between education and the economy: the reciprocal effects between economic change and the expansion of schooling, especially at the level of secondary education (the macro-level intersection), and the translation of individuals' education into outcomes in the labor market (the intersection of education and the economy at the micro level). There are of course many other areas that fall under the rubric of "education and the economy," including the politics of public education spending, the ways that educational systems develop in response to national politics and to international educational models, the role of education in enhancing not just individuals' human capital but also their cultural and social capital, and many additional areas that are generally considered part of the sociology of education subfield itself. Rather than attempting broad coverage of the varied themes that could be considered to fall under the umbrella of "education and the economy," this chapter will focus on a particular conceptualization of the education-economy link. This choice is based on the fact that many single themes receive chapter-length treatment in the *Handbook of the Sociology of Education*, a very useful resource, and that in the first edition of the *Handbook of Economic Sociology*, Rubinson and Browne focused mainly on the macro-level connection between the economy and education, reviewing the main theories and bodies of empirical evidence on the effect of education on economic growth and conversely, the effect of the economy on educational expansion (1994). The present chapter will follow this by turning to the micro-level intersection—the way that individuals' education is rewarded in the labor market—and will do so in a comparative-institutional context.

While education and stratification researchers in sociology have devoted intensive efforts to documenting inequalities among social groups in educational attainment and in the labor market rewards to that attainment, much less attention has been directed to the social-institutional underpinnings of inequality patterns—those features of educational systems and of labor markets that structure inequality among social groups. In the case of gender inequality, for example, this is partly a natural result of American stratification researchers' predominant emphasis on the United States rather than on comparisons among postindustrial societies.[1] The concentration on one national case renders consideration of the institutions underlying patterns of inequality quite difficult, as many such institutions are in effect "held constant" (see also Allmendinger 1989; Blau and Kahn 1996b; Kalleberg 1988; Müller and Shavit 1998). Yet the study of institutions—their origins, their stasis or transformation, and their effects on individual lives—is an important motivating force behind much of the sociological enterprise, especially economic sociology.

The present chapter is divided into two parts. The first half reviews recent comparative work in the social sciences (not restricted to sociology) that bears on how the educational and economic institutions of capitalism affect patterns of inequality. I attempt to provide an overview of the varied theoretical attempts by sociologists, political scientists, and economists to link inequality patterns to the institutional variation across capitalist economies. As will be discussed, these attempts typically focus *either* on the structure of the educational system *or* on specific labor market institutions (e.g., collective bargaining arrangements, unionization, or types of labor markets). These foci differ according to academic discipline and to disciplinary subfield, resulting in a sometimes confusing mélange of research articles and books.

In the second half of the chapter I suggest a conceptualization of the education-economy interface based on the institutional arrangements in the educational and the economic spheres that are responsible for two processes: (1) individuals' human capital or skill development, and (2) the recruitment of individuals into jobs. I then explore the possible relationship between different types of education-economy regimes and the degree of inequality across social groups, drawing upon empirical work from the social sciences—particularly sociology and labor economics.

In proposing that economic sociologists study

how the linkage between the educational system and the workplace affects individuals, I locate human capital development and recruitment processes in the larger context of the institutions of advanced capitalism. While modern nation-states designate the formal educational system as the main locus of human capital development, education takes place in other sites as well, especially the workplace. Human capital development can thus be problematized as involving a division of labor between the educational and economic spheres (schools and firms).[2] The division of labor for human capital development becomes institutionalized in every society, and the pattern of this institutionalization generates implications for patterns of inequality.

Given that labor recruitment processes also take place within the context of existing educational and economic institutions, they too may differ in important ways across capitalist economies. The analysis of recruitment processes involves looking at how individuals are recruited into their first full-time job after (or during) completion of education as well as how individuals are recruited from one job (or from the state of unemployment) into another; that is, we need to consider mechanisms operating in the school-work transition and those operating in moves of individuals across employers or firms. In societies with very loosely coupled schools and firms, these processes may be similar to each other. Societies with close school-work linkages, on the other hand, will have mechanisms of moving youth into jobs that may be significantly different from the mechanisms governing interfirm mobility at later career stages. What are the implications of both sets of mechanisms for patterns of inequality? An ever-growing comparative literature on the school-work transition in industrial societies has provided rich descriptive information on variation in the institutions undergirding school-work processes (Shavit and Müller 1998; Rosenbaum and Kariya 1989; Ryan 2001), but the possible implications for inequality patterns remain largely unexplored.

Given the scope of the questions raised in considering how the structure of educational and economic systems affects inequality patterns via the mechanisms of skill development and labor recruitment, I further limit the scope of this chapter in two ways.

First, I focus primarily on how training and human capital development are institutionally embedded and only secondarily on how recruitment processes are similarly embedded. Granovetter's landmark work on job search in the United States has spawned a rich sociological literature on job-search and recruitment processes. That literature is too large to consider here; moreover, only a portion of it is relevant to the present purpose of thinking through how recruitment processes are institutionally embedded.[3]

Second, I restrict the discussion of inequality to two types: the wage gap by skill/education and by gender. Both are empirically important and both vary considerably across capitalist economies with varied institutional configurations in education and the economy. American sociologists have on the one hand largely ceded the study of the skill/education wage gap to their neighbors in other social science disciplines (especially labor economics) and on the other hand have focused a great deal of attention on the gender wage gap, albeit mainly within the United States. There is a big opening for economic sociologists' expertise in institutional analysis to inform the *comparative* study of both types of inequality.

In arguing that economic sociologists turn their attention to the institutional patterning of the education-economy interface and its relationship to inequality, I end up following not so much the lead of Marx (via Bowles and Gintis) but rather Weber, as I wish to make the case that we are well equipped to approach the subject using two tools of the Weberian approach: comparative institutional analysis and ideal types (see Hamilton's chapter in the first edition of this handbook, 1994; also see Dobbin, chapter 2 in the present handbook). In the second half of the chapter I use three ideal-typical cases—the United States, Germany, and Japan—to explore how the education-economy interface structures training and human capital development and thereby affects inequality across social groups. These capitalist societies differ very considerably in the division of responsibility between the formal educational system and firms in individuals' skill development and placement into specific jobs. As such, they demonstrate that capitalist societies have specific institutional arrangements that are intimately related to the historical path of development in state-education-economy relationships. The origins of these institutional variations, as well as their implications for inequality, are important and neglected subjects for analysis by economic sociologists.

THE EDUCATION-ECONOMY INTERFACE: COMPARATIVE ANALYSES

Scholarship on the institutional context governing human capital development as well as inequality is widely scattered across the disciplines of sociology, political science, and economics, and

cross-references are unusually sparse. This first half of the chapter reviews key pieces in each field.

Sociological Perspectives

Within economic sociology, Fligstein has recently argued for the importance of understanding the emergence of distinct employment systems—defined as the rules that structure careers—in different capitalist economies (2001).[4] Employment systems specify the nature of the relationship between workers and employers and how control over training, compensation systems, and other aspects of employment is shared among different parties. Fligstein uses the United States, Japan, France, and Germany to illustrate variants of the three ideal-typical employment systems he identifies: professionalism, managerialism, and vocationalism.

While skill development and recruitment are a part of what Fligstein discusses under the rubric of employment systems, they are not his central focus, nor is inequality. Rather, his principal concern is to conceptualize an employment system and to explore how variance in employment systems is produced by the interaction among groups vying for control over the rules of employment. These groups include employers, workers, the state, professionals and their associations, and educators.

Fligstein's exploration of how the educational system and the organization of the firm in advanced capitalist economies interact to produce distinctive types of employment trajectories for individuals is similar to Baron and Bielby's now-classic call to "bring the firms back in" (1980) in terms of reorienting us to the study of institutions and organizations. Morris and Western also argue for such a reorientation in their analysis of research on widening wage inequalities in the United States (1999). They note American sociologists' preoccupation with the *allocation* of positions rather than with the *structure* of positions and with the institutions that create and maintain that structure (see also chap. 12 by Streeck in the current handbook). This theme is echoed in various places in the stratification literature, such as in the study of job mobility. More than a decade ago Rosenfeld suggested, "What we need is not a proliferation of 'structural' variables to include in models of job shifts, but a better understanding of the dimensions and mechanisms that define 'opportunity structures'" (1992, 57). This is representative of many sociologists' call for greater attention to the mechanisms underlying stratification and inequality.

Although individuals move between the worlds of education and work, some repeatedly across the first half of their life cycle, when American stratification researchers pay attention to institutions, they tend to divide into those who specialize in the study of educational institutions and those who specialize on workplace institutions and labor markets.[5] This segmentation between scholars interested in education and scholars interested in employment is of course not an absolute one. Studies of intragenerational mobility have paid considerable attention to how features of the educational system structure career mobility; see for example the comparative studies of Blossfeld (1987), DiPrete et al. (1997), Haller et al. (1985), and König and Müller (1986). But in general the sociology of education literature and the labor markets literature have moved forward without a great deal of theoretical cross-fertilization regarding the *mechanisms* producing stratification. Moreover, the educational stratification literature has been dominated by American sociologists' abiding interest in intergenerational status or class mobility, while the labor markets literature has been driven largely by the focus on cross-sectional wage inequalities between individuals of varying ascriptive characteristics (especially race and gender). In short, separate and voluminous stratification literatures have developed side by side, with each focusing on a different set of institutions and a different dependent variable or way of measuring labor market outcomes. And while each literature has at times approached the issue of how institutional variation across capitalist economies arose and what its implications are for the structure of positions (in the educational system or in the labor market), both literatures have ultimately paid much more attention to *who* is selected into different positions, as Morris and Western (1999) and Streeck (in this volume) have noted.

Sociology of Education

Educational sociologists have generally considered occupational attainment to be the principal dimension of social stratification in advanced capitalist societies (Kerckhoff 2001). The effects of educational attainment on individual labor market outcomes have thus largely been studied in terms of occupational status attainment. The most ambitious comparative research agendas linking educational institutions to inequality outcomes are those represented by Allmendinger (1989), Kerckhoff (1995, 2000, 2001), and Shavit and Müller (1998). All have emphasized the considerable variation in educational systems across advanced industrial societies and the likely implications of this for individuals' labor market outcomes. In Allmendinger's words, "Educational opportunities, and the specific structures of educational systems, are as consequential for mobility in labor markets as are the attributes of the individuals who make careers in those markets." She continues, "I attempt to show that educational *systems* define occupational opportunities for individuals at entry into the labor market, and that these systems have long-term implications for how people are matched to jobs" (1989, 232).

Three dimensions of educational systems that have been particularly emphasized by sociologists of education are standardization, stratification, and vocational specificity (Kerckhoff 2000, 2001). Standardization refers to the degree of centralized decision-making over programs and curricular content, and stratification refers to the degree of students' separation into different kinds of educational programs (as opposed to following a unified comprehensive curriculum throughout their schooling). Vocational specificity signifies the degree to which educational systems offer training geared to particular occupations.

Both Allmendinger and Kerckhoff followed a strategy of examining variation in educational systems in the United States and several European societies, and generating hypotheses about how this variation contributed to labor market outcomes (measured as labor force participation and as occupational status). Ishida's three-country (United States, Japan, Great Britain) study of intergenerational mobility considered the effects of education and family background on first and subsequent occupational status (1993), paying close attention to the institutional differences in educational systems. His study was unusual in its inclusion of current income as an additional labor market outcome. Shavit and Müller's study of the transition from school to work in 13 countries represents the broadest comparative-institutional analysis to date on how educational qualifications affect occupational attainment (1998). In collaboration with several research teams, they studied the effect of educational attainment on the occupational prestige of individuals' first jobs and on individuals' probability of entering the labor force in skilled versus unskilled jobs in the 13 national settings. As Müller and Shavit note at the outset, "Countries differ in the way they organize education and channel each new generation through their diverse educational systems. Countries also differ in labour-market institutions." They stress in particular their concern with "varying institutional characteristics of educational systems and their effects on occupational outcomes" (1998, v). This passage represents nicely the *theoretical* accord paid by educational sociologists to variation in both educational and labor market institutions, and their subsequent *empirical* concentration on the first source of institutional variation—the effects of educational institutions—on individual-level outcomes.

All of the institutionally oriented educational sociologists discussed so far pay considerable homage to Maurice, Sellier, and Silvestre's *The Social Foundations of Industrial Power: A Comparison of France and Germany* (1986) as a landmark comparative study. Maurice, Sellier, and Silvestre develop a theoretical framework for the study of the links between educational qualifications and labor-market outcomes, based on how employers use workers' qualifications in the firm. Their attempt in many ways presages the "varieties of capitalism" literature in political science that I will discuss shortly. They use the contrasting cases of France and Germany to show that countries utilize different methods of developing workers' skills, and argue that this is based on the way that the educational system and the workplace work together. After making point-by-point comparisons in workplace organization, inequality between white-collar and blue-collar workers, skill training, and labor-management relations, they move to a more abstract level of analysis and argue that the relationships among these categories of analysis should congeal into "broader, permanent social trends" (1986, 155–56). In a wonderful turn of phrase, they refer to differences between France and Germany in "the logic that governs the social determination of qualification" (1986, 166). In France the "organizational domain" is central, whereas in Germany it is the "qualification or professional domain" that is crucial in determining worker mobility and rewards. As will be explored in greater depth in the three cases (United States, Germany, and Japan) utilized illustratively in the second half of this chapter, some countries have an education-economy interface that gives pride of place to standardized vocational qualifications acquired in school and in school-firm partnerships (Germany), whereas others follow a model in which the majority of workers enter the labor force with highly general educational credentials (U.S. and Japan) and firms independently assume the responsibility of providing training to workers (Japan and, to a lesser extent, the United States).

While not the central theme of their empirical work, wage inequality between workers was also examined by Maurice, Sellier, and Silvestre. They found that wage determination principles differ significantly in France and Germany, in ways that correspond to the importance of organizational affiliation versus qualifications:

> the importance attached in Germany to professional autonomy within fairly uniform strata of the work force (and to controlling worker movements within the organization) tends to make constant expansion of the job spectrum (and thus constant increase in the ratio of highest to lowest wages . . .) less inevitable than it is in France. By contrast the fact that the stability of the French system results from worker mobility within the firm tends to widen the gap between the highest and lowest wages. (1986, 171)

Their empirical analysis demonstrates that wage inequalities among industrial workers are greater in France than in Germany no matter how workers are categorized by the analyst—skilled versus unskilled, nonmanual versus manual, office versus production, supervisory versus nonsupervisory.

In their concluding chapter Maurice, Sellier, and Silvestre return to their broad comparative aim of showing the interdependencies among institutions that structure the employment relationship, arguing that the differences they observe in France and Germany "form a pattern that can be related to fundamental features of advanced capitalist societies and economies. Making this relation explicit is the fundamental goal of comparative social analysis" (1986, 195).[6] In sum, the comparative work of Maurice and his colleagues, based on extensive fieldwork and surveys in two very different capitalist economies, was a significant departure from research that looked at only one side of the education-economy interface—either the effect of the educational system on individual worker outcomes, or the rewards attached to education under different labor market structures.

Since Maurice, Sellier, and Silvestre's classic study, American educational sociologists' research on comparative educational systems and individual labor market outcomes has produced a significant body of information about the contours of institutional variation in education across advanced industrial societies, especially those in Europe and North America. The broad conclusions of the literature include a set of generalizations about how standardization, stratification, and vocational specificity affect the occupational status of individuals or their prospects for intergenerational status mobility (see Müller and Shavit 1998 for a review). But educational sociologists have not necessarily taken up the gauntlet thrown down by the classic France-Germany comparison to develop an *integrated theory* of how educational systems and employment systems are linked, and how this linkage affects inequality patterns. As Kerckhoff stressed throughout his body of comparative-institutional work on social mobility, the institutional arrangements of education and work are interrelated, and together they organize stratification processes; as Maurice et al. showed, this applies not only to the attainment of occupational status and social mobility but also to *wage differences* among groups of workers, the point taken up in the second half of this chapter.

Labor Market Segmentation

The sociological literature on labor market inequality has developed orthogonally to the literature on the structure of educational systems and inequality. This is ironic given the shared emphasis of the two literatures on institutions and structure. Labor market theorists in economics and sociology developed a structuralist critique of the neoclassical paradigm in the late 1970s and 1980s that emphasized the segmentation of the labor market. Doeringer and Piore's work on internal labor markets (1971) is usually referred to as the early harbinger of these studies, which proceeded in sociology along two lines: theoretical attempts to develop a labor market typology that could capture the relevant differentiation among labor markets, and empirical attempts to link the structure of labor markets to the wages of individuals, especially by race and gender. It is not necessary to attempt to summarize here these two voluminous literatures, as excellent summaries exist elsewhere (see, for example, Althauser 1989; Rosenfeld 1992). Instead I will note some of the characteristics of the sociological labor markets literature that have perhaps made it less informative than it might be for our understanding of the relationships between the education-economy interface and patterns of inequality.

First, education in the form of on-the-job training played an important role both in Doeringer and Piore's work and in many of the subsequent attempts to construct labor market typologies, with firm-specific training being an important identifying characteristic of the prototypical firm-internal labor market. But the relationship between the organization of training systems in firms to national educational systems was rarely mentioned; as in the sociology of education literature, the education-economy link was undertheorized. This may be partly attributable to the fact that the labor market segmentation literature mainly grew up in the American context and did not proceed to develop in a fundamentally comparative direction. There was, therefore, no natural theoretical possibility for conceptualizing the relationship between skill development in firms and in the educational system.

Second, when labor market segmentation theory *was* applied to other countries, it tended to be just that: the application of a labor market typology derived in the American context to another national case. These one-country studies by and large focused on a subset of the issues American researchers had investigated in the United States: the extent to which a given form of labor market segmentation characterized an economy, and how it affected the mobility of workers across jobs. For example, Blossfeld and Mayer (1988) looked at labor market segmentation in Germany and concluded that barriers to mobility across sectors are more structured by the importance of qualifications than by firm size and firm-internal versus external recruitment practices. (This nicely parallels Maurice, Sellier, and Silvestre's more qualitative analysis.) Similarly, many scholars have commented that the segmentation of labor markets in Japan represents a quintessential "dualism" (between the large-firm or primary sector and the small-firm, secondary sector); within the large-firm sector, Japanese firm-internal labor markets constitute virtually a textbook version of internal labor markets (Brown et al. 1997; Kalleberg and Lincoln 1988; Sakamoto and Chen 1993; Spilerman and Ishida 1996).

The labor market literature, then, is nearly silent on the issue of how labor market structuration is related to patterns of inequality across capitalist economies. Moreover, as Morris and Western note, neither labor market sociologists nor other stratification researchers have picked up on the empirical importance of the greatly widened wage gap by skill/education in the United States versus other countries in the past two decades. A result is that some important theoretical opportunities have been forgone. Sociologists have made surprisingly few attempts to make generalizations about how the nature of the wage determination process, as embodied in labor market structures, affects either the gender wage gap or the education wage gap. On the gender wage gap, most stratification researchers would likely agree with a statement such as, "Economies that have many firms with internal labor markets tend to exhibit high gender inequality." But oddly, it is virtually impossible to find such statements in the literature.[7] In their study of the gender wage gap in four countries, Rosenfeld and Kalleberg remarked that "systematic cross-national statistical analyses of the earnings gap are rare" (1990, 70). Unfortunately, this statement is still surprisingly accurate, even though most sociologists would agree with the conclusion reached even earlier by Treiman and Roos and cited by Rosenfeld and Kalleberg: income determination processes seem to indicate "deeply entrenched institutional arrangements that limit women's opportunities and achievements" (Rosenfeld and Kalleberg 1990, 70).

Why have stratification researchers neglected the "big picture" of labor market structures' effect on the gender wage gap? Part of the answer lies undoubtedly in the fact that micro-level data on wage determination are hard to come by for many countries. But as I discuss below, this has not deterred labor economists from producing comparative research on the wage gap by gender as well as by education. Labor economics at the beginning of the twenty-first century boasted a much larger comparative literature than social stratification research on the role of institutions in exacerbating or compressing wage gaps. Many of these analyses have been carried out with aggregate data, so perhaps sociologists' preoccupation with individual-level data partly explains the collective reticence. Another reason may be the preoccupation of gender stratification researchers since the 1980s with occupational sex segregation and its contribution to the gender wage gap. This preoccupation may be misplaced in comparative studies of gender inequality, as occupational sex segregation is not necessarily predictive of cross-national variation in the gender earnings gap (Brinton 1993; Brinton and Ngo 1993; see also OECD 2002, table 2.17; and Rosenfeld and Kalleberg 1990). Focusing instead on the gender wage gap and on the institutional arrangements that appear to widen it—such as internal labor markets—may be a much more fruitful strategy.[8]

Sociological labor market researchers' neglect to study the institutional determinants of the skill gap in wages in industrial societies is also rather remarkable given the empirical importance of this gap and the dubious distinction of the United States in exhibiting wide wage differentials compared to all of its industrial counterparts save the United Kingdom. As with gender inequality, a major issue here is the set of choices American researchers have made vis-à-vis dependent variables: just as sociology of education researchers have concentrated on occupational status and intergen-

erational mobility, labor market researchers have concentrated on mobility across sectoral boundaries. The latter have largely conducted research in the context of one economy at a time.

Political scientists and economists have produced bodies of research on the relationship between capitalist institutions and inequality that are highly relevant for economic sociologists interested in the education-economy link. I turn first to the political science literature, with which many economic sociologists may be less familiar than the labor economics literature.

The Welfare State and "Varieties of Capitalism"

As reviewed by Huber and Stephens in chapter 24 of this handbook, Esping-Andersen conceptualized three ideal-typical welfare regimes in his seminal 1990 volume *The Three Worlds of Welfare Capitalism*—the social democratic, conservative, and liberal—based on the types and sources of social protection provided to citizens (Esping-Andersen 1990). His typology spawned a very extensive literature, some of which looks at the distributive implications of different welfare-state regimes. Gender inequality is one such distributive implication (Gornick, Meyers, and Ross 1998; Orloff 1993), as is the poverty rate (see Huber and Stephens, especially their table 1, in this volume). Save a few related efforts such as Chang's development of a typology of "occupational sex segregation regimes" (2000), the mainstream social stratification and labor markets literature in sociology continues to show almost no relationship to the burgeoning welfare-state literature in political science and sociology. But the recent "varieties of capitalism" scholarship, located in the welfare state tradition in political science, is particularly relevant to theorizing how the education-economy interface affects stratification outcomes.

Proponents of the varieties of capitalism approach share the concern of other welfare state theorists with how the provision of social protection (e.g. employment, unemployment, and wage protection) varies across advanced industrial democracies. Their main focus is on production regimes and their complementarity with social policies (Estevez-Abe, Iversen, and Soskice 2001; Hall and Soskice 2001; Hollingsworth and Boyer 1997). Production regimes are conceptualized as the institutional configurations that lead to an economy's particular set of product strategies for the international market. An important part of such strategies is the development and maintenance of labor force skills. For instance, economies that develop high-quality products for niche markets require workers that are highly skilled in specific industries. Alternatively, economies that specialize in mass-produced goods require a labor force with basic literacy but fewer industry- or firm-specific skills. In recognizing such distinctions, varieties of capitalism scholars bring employers' interests in workers' skill formation and protection into the picture in a more central way than does the welfare-state literature. This theoretical turn toward the middle range (organizational and employer interests) is strikingly similar to what Fligstein does in his analysis of employment systems.

In work that is particularly relevant for stratification researchers and economic sociologists interested in the education-economy link, Estevez-Abe, Iversen, and Soskice (2001) seek to demonstrate the complementarity between systems of social protection and skill development regimes on the one hand, and the resulting implications for wage inequality on the other. Their argument is that different systems of social protection affect individuals' (employers' as well as workers') incentives to invest in particular types of skills. They identify three types of skill-formation regimes, and these correspond respectively to Fligstein's professional, managerial, and vocational models of employment systems: regimes that emphasize general skills, firm-specific skills, or industry-specific skills. Unlike Fligstein, Estevez-Abe, Iversen, and Soskice's goal is not to explain the origins of these regimes or systems. Rather, their aim is to explore the implications of these regimes for wage inequality across social groups. As they state, "Some skill equilibria—sustained by different systems of social protection—produce more inequalities based on the academic background of workers, while others produce more inequalities based on gender" (2001, 147). Categorizing skills as general, industry-specific, or firm-specific, Estevez-Abe argues that skill regimes that concentrate on firm-specific skills are the most disadvantageous to women (2002). This is because women have less incentive to invest in these skills if they anticipate breaks in employment due to family responsibilities, and employers likewise have less incentive to invest in women than in men, as the latter can be assumed to have more continuous work histories. This argument effectively moves in the direction of comparative inquiry into the relationship between skill-formation regimes and gender inequality.

Labor Economics

Finally, a quite orthogonal literature that speaks to the education-economy interface and its impli-

cations for inequality is in labor economics. A standard complaint in much of the economic sociology literature is that American economists do not pay sufficient attention to institutional contexts. For the case of comparative gender inequality, this is a point well taken. Like sociologists, labor economists have devoted many more pages to gender inequality in the United States than to the standing of the United States relative to other industrial countries (but see the recent landmark comparative work of Blau and Kahn 1996a, 1996b, 2002). Pride of place is usually given to individual earnings equations and especially to the role of women's differential human capital across countries in contributing to the gender gap in earnings. Because analyses of the gender wage gap must necessarily pay attention to the relative educational composition of the male and female labor force and the relative propensities for some groups of women to exhibit discontinuous work histories, attention has also been paid to labor market policies that make it easier or harder for women to combine family and work life. The indirect effect of wage-setting institutions on the gender wage gap has also been given considerable attention (Blau and Kahn 1996b). But how training is orchestrated between schools and firms has not surfaced as a central institutional factor in economists' analyses of gender wage inequality.

In their analysis of the recent increase in earnings inequality by skill level, however, leading American labor economists have devoted considerable attention to labor market institutions in the past 15 years. Wage inequality between high- and low-skilled workers increased sharply in two industrial democracies in the 1980s: the United States and the United Kingdom. These two stood apart from other OECD economies, which showed varying education-wage trajectories (Blau and Kahn 1996a, 2002; Card and DiNardo 2002; Freeman and Katz 1995; Gottschalk and Joyce 1998; Gottschalk and Smeeding 1997; Juhn, Murphy, and Pierce 1993; Katz and Autor 1999). Labor economists have devoted considerable research effort to documenting the cross-country trends and to exploring the reasons why the returns to education increased so dramatically in the United States and United Kingdom. Under the direction of Richard Freeman, the National Bureau of Economic Research (NBER) initiated a Comparative Labor Markets series that has produced a number of edited volumes examining the contours of wage inequality across advanced industrial economies. NBER-affiliated economists produce such a steady stream of papers on wage inequality that it is hard to keep up with their collective output. While these studies are predictably impressive in quantitative sophistication, they are also impressive in their comparative breadth. Even more striking from a sociological viewpoint, many of the papers pay considerable attention to labor market institutions and policy.[9]

The labor economics literature has produced broad agreement over the facts of increased wage inequality by skill level, as well as a dominant orthodoxy about some of the major causes. Chief among these are two: (1) in the United States and the United Kingdom, the demand for skilled labor in the past two decades outpaced the increase in supply, thereby pushing up skilled wages; and (2) the wage-compression effect of wage-setting institutions in continental European countries played a key role in forestalling large increases in the skill gap in pay in those countries. The latter explanation is an institutional one, centered on how variance in wage-setting institutions across advanced industrial economies affects wage dispersion across less- and more-skilled workers. The labor economics literature thus shares with the political science literature an emphasis on the importance of wage-setting institutions in exacerbating or dampening wage inequality. Labor economists focus heavily on the fact that the U.S. labor force has a low unionization rate relative to most other industrial countries and that collective bargaining in the United States is decentralized. Local unions play a greater role than broader wage-setting institutions in the United States, and there is a prevalence of single-firm agreements (Blau and Kahn 2002; Freeman 1994).[10] For these reasons, labor economists are in broad agreement that the United States represents an extreme in terms of the absence of coordinated labor market institutions and regulation.

Nevertheless, there seems to be general agreement among labor economists that changes in the relative supply of skills and the wage-compression effects of labor market institutions in many European countries do not fully explain the variation in wage inequality trends across countries. A third explanation involves the effect of technology adoption on the demand for highly skilled workers.[11] The role of technology in explaining international comparisons has been a subject of intense debate (Autor, Katz, and Krueger 1998; Bound and Johnson 1992; Card and DiNardo 2002; Juhn, Murphy, and Pierce 1993; Krueger 1993; Murphy and Welch 1993). DiPrete and McManus (1996) offer an excellent critique of labor economists' strong focus on the effects of technology on wages. More importantly, they point out that when the

economic literature turns to institutional explanations the emphasis is rather single-mindedly on unions and wage-setting institutions.

From the viewpoint of this chapter, there are two additional theoretically intriguing institutional possibilities in the labor economics literature. The first concerns the interaction between technology adoption and a country's existing skill bias. Acemoglu (2002) argues that the relative demand for skilled labor (irrespective of supply) simply did not increase as much in continental Europe as in the United States. He develops a theoretical framework wherein changes in employers' relative skill demands depend partly on the perceived substitutability of skilled and unskilled labor. In most continental European economies, employers pay higher wages to unskilled workers than they would in the absence of labor market institutions that raise the "floor" (minimum wage). Given that employers are already paying relatively high wages to their unskilled workers, they have an incentive to increase the productivity of these workers. "Put differently, the labor market institutions that push the wages of these workers up make their employers *the residual claimant* of the increase in productivity due to technology adoption, encouraging the adoption of technologies complementary to unskilled workers in Europe" (2002, 7–8). Because of this, there may have been a smaller increase in the demand for skilled workers in Europe than in the United States in the past two decades.[12]

Acemoglu's theoretical framework is intriguing in that he posits an interaction between technology adoption and the existing relative wages in the economy; employers' use of technology is at least in part endogenously driven by the socially and politically determined wage structure. In contrast to the argument in some of the labor economics literature that a compressed wage structure reduces employer investments in human capital, Acemoglu and Pischke suggest that such a wage structure may instead *encourage* employers to provide general training to workers, including the less skilled. They write, "we expect that European and Japanese labor market institutions may increase one of the components of investment in human capital, firm-sponsored general training, and possibly even contribute to total human capital accumulation" (1999, 542). I return to this comparative prediction in the second half of the chapter.

A fourth explanation for how some countries were able to maintain fairly low wage inequality throughout the 1980s and early 1990s involves the use of training strategies (Freeman and Katz 1995). This appears to be the most underexplored of the institutional explanations in the labor economics literature, far surpassed by the focus on wage-setting institutions. At the end of their review of comparative wage inequality trends in the mid-1990s, Freeman and Katz note the following:

> Germany and Japan appeared fairly successful through much of the 1980s in maintaining the earnings and employment of non-college-educated workers. German institutions constrain wage setting, *but they also offer apprenticeships and further training opportunities that try to make supply consistent with wage policies.* The Japanese have succeeded with basic education and much informal firm-based training. . . . international differences in recent labor market experiences strongly suggest that policies to buffer the earnings of the less educated by institutional wage setting work best *when accompanied by institutions that augment those workers' skills as well.* (1995, 20–21; emphasis added)

The suggestion that training policies may augment wage-setting institutions' compression of the skill wage gap is connected with the varieties of capitalism literature that discuss skill formation regimes. It does not appear that these two groups of scholars—labor economists versus political scientists developing the varieties of capitalism approach—are engaged in sustained dialogue with each other, but from the viewpoint of economic sociologists there is an interesting synergy here. It is also worth noting that these two sets of scholars are highly sensitive to the range of institutional alternatives in contemporary capitalism. This is of course a central assumption in economic sociology.[13] But as I have argued, it has not necessarily been an assumption shared by stratification researchers in sociology, especially those working in the status-attainment tradition and concentrating on intergenerational mobility.

This part of the chapter has reviewed literature in four areas—two subdisciplines of sociology (sociology of education and sociology of labor markets), political science, and labor economics—to identify the dominant conceptualizations of institutions as they relate to inequality patterns. While a few scholars have attempted to conceptualize the education-economy link as it bears on inequality, these attempts have been scattered and there has been little cross-fertilization on the theoretical front, especially across disciplinary boundaries. The dominant mode has been for researchers to choose features of *either* the educational system or the economy and theorize about the implications for inequality. Each subfield or discipline has also privileged certain outcomes or dependent variables over others. Table 1 summarizes the institutions that each discipline or subdiscipline emphasizes and the inequality outcomes to which it pays the greatest attention.[14]

In the remainder of the chapter I explore a formulation of the education-economy link that can be termed an economy's *human capital development system,* and I suggest that it may have potential explanatory power for inequality patterns. I do not mean to argue that this is a panacea for the cacophony of partial conceptualizations of the education-economy interface. But I do argue that economic sociologists have a comparative advantage (to make an unfortunate pun) in doing comparative-institutional analysis of how societies organize *in tandem* their educational systems and labor markets. Among the fields surveyed in this chapter, the ones that come closest to doing this are labor economics and the varieties of capitalism approach in

TABLE 1. Analysis of Institutions and Inequality, by Discipline

Discipline or Subdisciplinary group	Institutions Used as Independent Variables	Dependent Variables
Sociology of education researchers	Characteristics of educational systems	Occupational status; skilled vs. unskilled work; intergenerational social mobility
Labor market sociologists	Types of labor markets	Wage inequality by race and gender; job mobility; occupational sex segregation
Welfare-state and "varieties of capitalism" researchers	Wage-setting institutions; "production regimes" and "skill development regimes"	Distribution of income inequality; gender wage inequality
Labor economists	Wage-setting institutions; unions	Distribution of income inequality; gender wage inequality

political science. But both underemphasize the importance of how the educational system operates in conjunction with workplace training systems; they concentrate instead on training in the workplace.

To demonstrate some of the cross-national variance that exists in the configuration of institutions governing human capital development, I use the cases of the United States, Germany, and Japan. The institutional configurations in these countries were produced by very different historical circumstances surrounding the development of the "modern" educational system and employment relations during industrialization. I suggest that the resulting human capital development systems have implications for cross-national variation in the education (skill) wage gap and the gender wage gap. This approach takes variation in the institutional arrangements of capitalism as a natural outcome of different historical trajectories initiated in the course of industrialization.

I restrict the ensuing theoretical and empirical exploration to two types of inequality: (1) the education wage gap,[15] and (2) the gender wage gap.[15] To reiterate briefly why these and not others: First, I have shown that the dependent variables used in the analysis of inequality vary tremendously across disciplines. These disciplinary interests can be bridged by a focus on how different educational attainments as well as gender translate into wages in comparative settings. Second, skill/education and gender inequality show considerable variation across national cases that vary institutionally (in their education-economy linkages), making exploration of the possible relationship to institutional configurations an important one. Third, both the education wage gap and the gender wage gap changed substantially in magnitude—and in opposite directions—in the United States during the last few decades of the twentieth century. Wage differentials by education widened markedly in the late-twentieth-century United States, whereas the gender wage gap changed in the opposite direction, narrowing more since 1980 than in any other period in the century. Particularly in the case of the education wage gap, the United States (along with Great Britain) represents an important deviation from the trajectory of change in other OECD countries.

HUMAN CAPITAL DEVELOPMENT SYSTEMS AND INEQUALITY

The United States, Germany, and Japan demonstrate radically different systems for educating,

training, and recruiting workers. This is due to the very different types of education-economy interfaces that developed historically and have persisted in the three countries. Following terminology I developed in earlier work on gender stratification (1988, 1993), I suggest that it makes sense to think of countries exhibiting different *human capital development systems*. These systems are defined by how the division of labor for human capital development is shared across institutions. This division of labor may have implications for the degree of gender inequality in an economy because it affects who is responsible for human capital development decisions and how the timing of these decisions is distributed across the life cycle. For the purposes of this chapter, the most important characteristics of a human capital development system are the relative role played by employers versus schools, and the way that recruitment into work is structured. The human capital development systems epitomized by the United States, Germany, and Japan demonstrate varied implications for gender wage inequality and for the education wage gap as well.

Table 2 presents the three ideal-typical institutional arrangements governing skill development that are represented by the United States, Germany, and Japan; alongside these are the resultant dominant forms of human capital in each economy. As developed by Becker, human capital theory distinguishes between general and specific skills (1993). The worker invests in and reaps the return from general skills, which are portable across employers. Worker's specific skills, on the other hand, are also invested in by the employer and are particularly useful to him or her. I suggest that the United States, Germany, and Japan represent a continuum in terms of employer involvement in skill development. The United States shows considerable variation across employers in terms of the degree to which they train their own workers; German employers invest in worker training through their participation in apprenticeship programs that have a high level of standardization through occupational certification; and Japanese employers invest individually in worker skills and use compensation rules that highly reward length of tenure. The German case therefore represents a concentration on a type of skill that is occupation-specific rather than general or firm-specific. The returns to occupational skills are shared more collectively across employers than is the case with firm-specific skills, as occupational certification standards confer a degree of interfirm portability. Firm-specific skills, represented by the Japanese case, are the

TABLE 2.   Comparative Human Capital Development Systems and Inequality

Country	Dominant Site of Human Capital Development	Dominant Form of Human Capital	Effect on Education Wage Gap	Effect on Gender Wage Gap
United States	School	General	Positive (widening)	Negative (narrowing)
Germany	School plus firm	General plus occupation-specific	Negative (narrowing)	Positive (widening), through occupational sex segregation
Japan	School plus firm	General plus firm-specific	Negative (narrowing)	Positive (widening), through firm-internal labor markets

least portable among general, occupational, and firm-specific skills.

It can be hypothesized that human capital development systems that involve employers as central actors in human capital investment decisions will tend to produce contradictory effects on educational wage inequality and gender wage inequality. Employer-directed training (as in Japan and Germany) will tend to *narrow* the wage differential between high- and low-skilled workers compared to the differential produced under human capital development systems where workers receive most of their training in the educational system (the United States). Conversely, employer-directed training will tend to *widen* the wage differential between men and women compared to what it would be in a system where educational credentials have greater importance than employer-based training. This is because a human capital development system in which employers are important actors will have a wage determination process that tends to disadvantage women and recruitment patterns that also tend to distinguish between male and female applicants either through selection into internal labor markets (Japan) or through sex-stereotyping in occupational training (Germany). Based on this, we would predict that the United States, Germany, and Japan are on a continuum in terms of the edu-

cation wage gap, with the United States an extreme case of a large education or skill differential and Germany and Japan as cases that have much smaller wage differentials based on skill. In contrast, Japan will be the outlier in demonstrating severe gender wage inequality, with Germany and the United States exhibiting less. These predictions are included in table 2.

Table 3 shows the concomitant recruitment patterns that go along with the dominant type of skill development in each economy. The lack of employer involvement in training is connected in the United States to a highly unstructured recruitment process, with personal connections being the most common job search method.[17] I postulate that the absence of systematic recruitment processes, particularly from school to work, is highly disadvantageous to less-educated workers and contributes to the discrepancy in wages between those workers and their highly educated counterparts. The gender effects are neutral to the extent that women are in networks that facilitate their job search (Petersen, Saporta, and Seidel 2000).

The United States: General Human Capital

The United States stands out in its marked lack of a systematic approach to workforce training. As

TABLE 3.   Recruitment Mechanisms and Inequality

Country	Dominant Recruitment Mechanisms	Effect on Education Wage Gap	Effect on Gender Wage Gap
United States	Personal networks	Positive (widening)	Neutral
Germany	School-firm partnerships (through apprenticeships)	Negative (narrowing)	Positive (widening)
Japan	School-firm implicit recruitment contracts	Negative (narrowing)	Positive (widening)

stated starkly by Crouch, Finegold, and Sako, "The most obvious characteristic of skill creation in the USA is the absence of any generalizable system. . . . Indeed, the very concept of the improvement of workforce skills as a national project is difficult to envisage in the USA, where it is not clear that there can be national projects for what are essentially seen as matters for individual persons and individual companies, with possibly some contribution from local or state governments" (1999, 205).

The main locus of human capital development in the United States is the school, and the majority of American students receive general as opposed to vocationally specific training through the high school level. The United States made an early commitment to mass secondary education and, to a considerable degree, higher education as well. It led the rest of the world in the extension of secondary school education to "ordinary citizens" in the first half of the twentieth century, in contrast to most European countries, where secondary education was reserved for those who would continue on to college (Goldin and Katz 2001). Between 1900 and 1960 the rate of high school enrollment in the United States increased from just over 10 percent to nearly 90 percent, and the graduation rate increased from about 7 percent to 70 percent (Goldin 1999).

Analysts of American educational expansion have emphasized its "demand-driven" character (Walters 2000). Educational consumers in the United States could influence the supply of schooling in part because there were thousands of fiscally independent school districts that could make their own decisions about school funding, in contrast to the centralized fiscal situation in many European countries (Goldin and Katz 2001). The extension of the vote was also very important, as it gave citizens the ability to pressure the state to provide educational opportunities (Walters 2000).[18]

Compared to Germany and Japan, American employers' role in shaping how schools interfaced with the economy was minor and continues to be so. Unlike the situation in Germany, where collective bodies establish the guidelines for occupational skills, employer associations in the United States have historically been weak and have not assumed the role of helping to organize training and certification programs or set skill requirements for different jobs (Freeman 1994; Kerckhoff and Bell 1998). Geographical mobility, extensive employment opportunities for apprentices, and relatively weak unions have all been cited as reasons why apprenticeship training did not flourish in the United States (Lynch 1993).

The imparting of general skills at the secondary school level in the United States carries over to four-year bachelor's programs (Mortimer and Krüger 2000). American youth who pursue postbaccalaureate professional degrees enter the labor market with a much greater degree of occupation-specific preparation than their counterparts who leave school at the university or secondary level, but this currently accounts for less than 8 percent of the population of 30–34-year-olds (National Center for Education Statistics 2002).[19]

In sum, human capital development in the United States is marked by the development of general skills through high school and to a great extent through postsecondary institutions, and occupational (professional) development for the small minority of students who go on to postgraduate education in professional schools. A relatively undifferentiated curriculum leaves American employers with few signals to rely upon when they hire new graduates, save the quantity of education (number of years) a student has received and the presumed "quality" of that education, indexed especially in the case of university by the academic rank of the school (see for example Frank 1998).[20]

Given the emphasis on general skill acquisition and the American meritocratic ideology that anyone can go to college if he or she tries, vocational education courses have consistently been viewed as "second best" in American high schools. Shavit and Müller have pointed out that academic discussions of vocational education in the United States have rarely considered its possible role in keeping some high school or postsecondary graduates from ending up in the lowest-paying jobs; instead, debate has centered on the tracking function played by vocational education (Shavit and Müller 2000). Opponents of vocational education argue that lower-class students are overrepresented and that it therefore reinforces the intergenerational transmission of status, diverting these youth from postsecondary education and higher occupational attainment. But this begs the question of how vocational education graduates do in the labor market relative to their counterparts who do *not* proceed on to postsecondary education, namely those who complete secondary school and enter the labor market or those who drop out of school (Bishop 1989; Rosenbaum 1996).

Recent attempts to compare American high school and postsecondary graduates who have specific vocational training to their counterparts with a general high school diploma, an associates' degree, or a bachelors' degree provide evidence that some types of vocational education are indeed valuable in the U.S. labor market, at least in graduates' early careers. Arum and Hout show that there are early positive occupational status and wage returns to those vocational high school programs in the United States with fairly specific content (1998). Females who follow a business or commercial curriculum in high school garner higher initial wages and status than their counterparts who enter the labor market with a general high school education. Likewise, some vocational programs lead to a first job with higher occupational status for both men and women than the general high school track. These results lead Arum and Hout to conclude that despite the importance of higher education in the United States for entry into white-collar jobs, "A differentiated vocational high-school curriculum, however, affects occupational outcomes for those that have not been singled out as the most likely candidates for the mental labours of the upper white-collar stratum. . . . To the extent that this curriculum specializes in areas that are valued by employers, these programmes provide an alternative route to higher wages" (1998, 507–8).[21] These findings are complemented by Kerckhoff and Bell's research on the value of specific credentials obtained in postsecondary education (1996).

Employer-Provided Training in the United States

Once American students leave school, through what means do they receive further training? A substantial proportion of youth cycle in and out of the labor force and school during the first 10 years of their worklife, thereby seeking additional skills from formal educational institutions even after they have entered their first full-time job (Arum and Hout 1998). Systematic evidence on the incidence of employer-based training in the United States is sparse (Knoke and Kalleberg 1994), but OECD estimates indicate that formal workplace training is considerably less prevalent in the United States than in Japan and a number of European countries. In their work on this issue, Acemoglu and Pischke cite OECD figures indicating that formal employer-provided training is provided to 72 percent of young workers in Germany and 67 percent of new hires in Japan, whereas 10 percent of U.S. workers receive formal training over the course of their first seven years in the labor market (Acemoglu and Pischke 1999, 542).[22] Lynch also points out that most employer-provided formal

training in the United States is given to college graduates, especially those employed in the finance, insurance, and real estate industries. The recipients of employer-based training are concentrated in professional, technical, and managerial jobs (Lynch 1992a, 1992b). American employers are sometimes criticized for investing little in either the recruitment or training of non–college graduates in particular, and very few large American corporations hire new high school graduates into jobs with career potential (Rosenbaum 2001).

Implications for the Education Wage Gap

How might the institutional division of labor for human capital development in the United States be related to the large wage gap between low- and high-skilled workers? The United States began the 1980s with a larger skill wage gap than most industrial countries. Freeman and Katz (1995) report a figure of 1.23 for the log of the ratio of wages received by workers in the top decile versus those in the bottom decile (the 90-10 ratio), compared to figures of just 0.78 in Germany and 0.95 in Japan. In the ensuing decade the United States and United Kingdom experienced the greatest increases in wage inequality, with the U.S. figure rising to 1.40 by 1990. Meanwhile, Germany experienced no noticeable change in wage differentials, and the wage gap in Japan increased only slightly.

Are these patterns linked to institutional arrangements, particularly the division of labor between schools and workplaces for human capital development and the presence or absence of school-work mechanisms, especially for the less educated (high school graduates)? The most marked aspect of the skill wage gap in the United States is that it is particularly large at the *bottom* of the wage distribution; the 50-10 wage gap (ratio of workers' wages in the fiftieth percentile of the distribution relative to workers in the tenth percentile) is nearly twice as large as in other countries, whereas the 90-50 gap is only slightly larger in the United States. Blau and Kahn calculate that about 40 percent of the difference in the 50-10 differential between the United States and other countries is attributable to productivity-related worker characteristics (Blau and Kahn 2002). This is *before* international differences in wage-setting institutions are taken into consideration.

This raises the question of whether institutional explanations of the education wage gap across countries should rest so heavily on wage compression via institutionalized wage-setting, the overriding explanation offered by political scientists and labor economists. In a recent comparison of the wage distribution in Germany and the United States, Freeman and Schettkat (2000) ask whether low-skilled workers are paid higher relative wages in Germany because they benefit from institutionalized wage-setting policies that raise the minimum wage level or because they are more skilled. This in essence is a contest between two competing explanations for the lower wage gap in Germany: wage compression or skill compression. They find that German workers do exhibit less variation in skill levels and that this supplements wage-setting institutions in the explanation of the concentration in the earnings distribution.[23] This supports my assertion here that it is important to consider not just wage-bargaining institutions, but also how the skill development system affects the wage distribution across workers. Estevez-Abe, Iversen, and Soskice (2001) provide an illuminating counterpoint in their demonstration that almost 70 percent of the variation in earnings inequality across 17 OECD countries can be explained by the form of countries' wage-bargaining and skill systems taken together.

It seems clear that the absence of a national system of occupational training in the United States or of a systematic way of matching new graduates with employers poses the greatest disadvantage to the least educated. American youth are on their own in developing and demonstrating occupational proclivities in their early jobs, and this experience results in labor market "floundering" for considerable numbers of youth during their early twenties. The disorderliness of the United States school-work transition has set off a lively debate in sociology and economics as to whether early full-time but transitory job experiences are a waste of time or, on the other hand, contribute to long-term human capital development and an upward earnings trajectory; a similar debate surrounds the issue of youth working part-time while in school (Gardecki and Neumark 1997; Mortimer and Krüger 2000; Neumark 1998; Ruhm 1995). Some who criticize the absence of a systematic school-work transition in the United States also claim that it results in an overall loss in aggregate human capital, as workers in their early twenties who could be receiving systematic training are instead wandering around in the labor market trying to find their place (Hamilton 1990).

The lack of regularized communication between businesses and high schools in the United States is also important because it means that employers do not directly communicate to students what types of skills are required on the job. A considerable body of evidence suggests that American employers do not base their hiring decisions on students' performance in school (Bishop 1989; Rosenbaum 2001; Rosenbaum and Kariya 1991). In an extensive school-work research agenda, Rosenbaum in particular has argued that this makes it very difficult for American high school students to see the connection between school performance and their future worklife (Rosenbaum 1990, 1996, 2001; Rosenbaum and Kariya 1989).

In sum, the large wage gap by education in the United States seems highly consistent with the features of the American human capital development system: an emphasis in the educational system on general skill development for all, a corresponding employer emphasis on quantity of education (in the absence of signals by which to differentiate applicants' occupational proclivities), a comparatively low rate of employer-based training (especially for less-skilled workers), and a disorderly school-work trajectory with no institutionalized job-matching mechanisms for less-skilled workers.

Implications for the Gender Wage Gap

The implications of the type of human capital development system exhibited by the United States may be quite different for gender wage inequality than for education wage inequality. Given that so much human capital investment is based on individual initiative, that training is non–occupationally specific, and that the educational system is structured in such a way that individuals can leave the workforce and return for advanced schooling or professional degrees, Americans arguably face a relatively flexible institutional environment. When the site of human capital development is instead primarily the school-employer nexus, as in the German occupational training system, or the firm, as in the Japanese firm-based training system, pre-existing gender inequalities may be more easily reproduced. The mechanisms are different in the case of occupational skill-based systems (Germany) versus firm-specific skill-based systems (Japan), but the implications for gender inequality may be quite similar.

As with the education wage gap, one can choose either to analyze the static cross-country differentials in the gender wage gap or the trajectory of change over time. In static terms, the United States does not exhibit one of the lowest gender wage gaps among industrial nations (Blau and Kahn 1996b, 2002). Blau and Kahn (1996b) argue that the lower gender wage gaps in a number of European countries are associated with compressed wage structures. This suggests a positive relationship between the gender wage gap and the skill wage gap, which is opposite to the prediction I suggested earlier. Their logic is based on the fact that women tend to be disproportionately concentrated in low-paying jobs; raising the wage floor therefore should especially benefit women. While this is theoretically appealing, it does not necessarily hold across countries. When adjustments are made for the effect of wage structure, the gender wage gap does decline in the United States and the United Kingdom, the two countries with the most unequal wage distribution across skill levels. But it *increases* in a number of other countries including the Netherlands and Austria, and remains nearly the same in Germany (OECD 2002).[24]

It is important to note that Blau and Kahn focus on the presence of collective bargaining agreements as the institutional reason for a compressed wage structure; these raise wages at the bottom of the distribution for union workers and sometimes extend to nonunion workers as well. But as I have discussed in this chapter, a human capital development system that is more oriented to imparting skills to less-educated workers may be another institutional mechanism influencing lower wage inequality. Therefore, it is worth exploring how the *sources* of wage compression affect gender inequality.

If one source of this compression is employer-organized training, this may exacerbate rather than lessen gender wage inequality. There are two principal mechanisms through which this may occur: vocational training that tends to reproduce existing occupational sex-stereotyping (the German case), and firm-specific training that employers tend to reserve for men, in the expectation that women have less continuous work histories and less commitment to the firm (the Japanese case). In the latter instance, female workers may experience considerable discouragement as they observe that more on-the-job training is given to men, and this may prompt married women to exit the labor force in higher numbers than they would otherwise (Ogasawara 1998).[25] Even in the United States, where rates of employer-provided formal training are much lower than in Japan, women are significantly less likely to receive such training or to participate in apprenticeships. When they are provided company-based training, the duration is considerably shorter than the training periods for men (Altonji and Spletzer 1992; Barron, Black, and Loewenstein 1987; Lynch 1993).

In terms of the cross-sectional gender wage gap,

the distinction among the United States, Germany, and Japan is clearest between the first two countries and Japan. The female-male median weekly earnings ratio for full-time workers in Japan in the late 1990s was just 63.6 percent; the comparable figures in the United States and Germany were 76.3 percent and 75.5 percent respectively (Blau and Kahn 2002).

The issue of selectivity into the labor force is of course very substantial in the case of women, and has important implications for the wage gap. There is not enough space to discuss this here, but it bears noting that American women demonstrate very different work patterns by marital and childbearing status than women in Germany and Japan. The proportion of women who exit the labor force at the time of childbirth is lowest in the United States (16 percent), compared to 25 percent in Germany (OECD 2002) and an astounding 75 percent in Japan, a figure that has not changed in the past two decades (Japan Institute of Labour 2003). An additional 21 percent of working women in Germany reduce their working hours upon the birth of a child, compared to 10 percent of American working women (OECD 2002). Overall, German and Japanese working women are much more likely to participate in the labor force part-time than American women. Nineteen percent of American female labor force participants are part-time workers, compared to 34 percent of German women and 39 percent of Japanese women (OECD 2002, table 2.1).

But the most striking feature of the gender pay gap in the United States is that it declined dramatically in the past 20 years after having been relatively stable for most of the twentieth century. This decline outpaced that in other OECD countries by a wide margin. The United States showed a percentage change of 22 between 1979 and 1998, compared to a figure of 8 percent for Japan and 5 percent for Germany over the same period (Blau and Kahn 2002).

Blau and Kahn argue that the narrowed U.S. gap indicates that American women have been "swimming upstream" against the simultaneous widening of the wage gap by skill over the same period (1997). In a decomposition of the narrowed gender wage gap in the 1980s, they show that increases in full-time labor force experience and changes in occupational affiliation accounted for about three-quarters of the increase in women's relative wages, followed by a small boost from women's increased educational attainment. They argue that it is fortunate that women did experience increases in human capital and changes in their occupational locations, as the rewards to skill were increasing at the same time and women would have been increasingly left behind had they not been able to make these gains (1997, forthcoming).

Although American women's years of education did not increase dramatically during this period, their chosen fields of study demonstrated significant change. Gender segregation in field of study at college dropped dramatically between 1965 and 1985 and continued to decline in the late 1980s. There was also a decline in segregation by field for master's degrees in the 1980s (Jacobs 1995). Women's participation in professional degree programs such as law, business, and medicine also increased substantially, affording them credentials that were largely portable across employers.

American women's wage gains since 1970 coincided with the first major decline in occupational sex segregation in the twentieth century (England and Folbre, chapter 27 in this handbook; Jacobs 1989). The fact that changes in occupational affiliation and workforce experience account for so much of the narrowed gender pay gap may be related to women's increased entry into previously male-dominated majors and into professional schools. In this regard it is well worth considering how the shape of the human capital development system in the United States and the permeability of the boundaries of training systems (generally located in the educational system) may have sped women's wage progress. In short, women in particular may benefit from systems that in principle allow people to return to school to obtain educational credentials—particularly professional degrees—that employers value, in contrast to systems where there are strong age barriers to training. As I show below, Japan provides a strong contrast to the United States. Japanese universities have traditionally had age barriers to entry. Moreover, there has been no institutional equivalent to American law schools, and attempts to create business schools in Japan have met with mixed success.

Human Capital Development in Germany: General and Occupationally Specific

Germany and the "modified apprenticeship countries" (Austria, Denmark, Germany, Luxembourg, and Switzerland) represent a radical departure from the tendency of the American educational system to produce individuals with high levels of general human capital and little occupation-specific capital. Following four years of primary school, students are tracked into lower secondary school (*Hauptschule*), middle secondary school (*Realschule*), or upper secondary school (*Gymnasium*). All of these constitute general studies, but students who continue their education after *Hauptschule* or *Realschule* participate in Germany's famed "dual system" that combines part-time vocational school and apprenticeship with an employer (Blossfeld 1993; Mortimer and Krüger 2000; Witte and Kalleberg 1995). The certificates awarded upon completion of vocational training correspond to about 400 officially recognized occupations, the majority of which require apprenticeship experience.

In an international comparison of the types of training youth receive, Crouch, Finegold, and Sako (1999) report that nearly 80 percent of German secondary school students compared to just over 25 percent of Japanese students were enrolled in vocational or technical education rather than general education. (It is not possible to calculate an exactly comparable figure for the United States, since many students take a few vocational courses in the process of obtaining their general high school diploma.) Of the 80 percent in Germany, more than two-thirds of students were in the dual system and the remainder participated in school-based vocational training. Not surprisingly, Germany ranked first in providing qualifications to 18-year-olds and the United States and Japan ranked at the bottom. (A distinct minority of Japanese students choose the vocational high school track.) Conversely, the United States and Japan ranked first and third respectively in the proportions of 18-year-olds who had access to general as opposed to vocational higher education, and Germany ranked twelfth out of the 14 countries in the study.

The German dual system stems from a very different history of employer involvement in education than in either the United States or Japan. Thelen and Kume provide a comparative view of how training systems developed in Germany and Japan (1999). In the early industrial period, the German government instituted policies that allowed the highly organized and progressive artisanal sector to coordinate skill formation and certification. Unions later joined to maintain the quality rather than the supply of skills, unlike in Britain. The result was a collective solution to the problem of training skilled laborers. Individual employers benefited from providing apprenticeships and paying low wages during the training period, and since workers' skills were occupationally rather than firm-specific, employers also benefited from being able to hire experienced workers from other firms.

The contrast is great between the American system of general (and, for a minority of youth, professional) human capital development and the German system that combines general and occupation-specific human capital development for a majority of youth. Although German firms provide training, it is unusual for workers to go beyond the occupational level for which formal education qualifies them (Mortimer and Krüger 2000). Moreover, the high level of standardization in apprenticeship programs and the existence of national certification for occupational skills means that employers recognize the credentials workers have obtained while working as apprentices for other firms (Witte and Kalleberg 1995). Credentials are, in short, portable.

Consistent with Maurice, Sellier, and Silvestre's argument about "qualification space" in Germany, Blossfeld and Mayer found in their research on job mobility that only 16 percent of all job transitions "are mediated through the institutional structure of an internal labor market" (1988, 138). Hannan, Schömann, and Blossfeld (1990) found German labor markets to correspond poorly to sociological labor market theorists' textbook version of a privileged primary sector characterized by internal labor markets where workers experience wage growth versus a secondary sector characterized by wage stagnation. As they reported, "Male and female workers in sectors that can reasonably be characterized as having internal labor markets did not experience higher than average wage growth within jobs. This challenges the core assumption of theories of labor market segmentation. . . . There are many important differences in employment relations between the FRG [Federal Republic of Germany] and the U.S. over the period studied. Perhaps theories of labor market segmentation have implicitly assumed structures that are unique to the U.S. and that do not hold in other industrialized, capitalist economies" (1990, 709–10). Moreover, Hannan and colleagues found no statistically significant relation between men's and women's first-job earnings and either firm size or job skill level.

The school-work transition for the approximately 70 percent of youth who do apprenticeships is also markedly different from the transition to work for American non–college graduates. In contrast to the radical disconnect American youth often perceive between what happens in school and in one's later worklife, German youth are purportedly motivated to achieve in school in order to enter a de-

sirable apprenticeship (Lynch 1993; Mortimer and Krüger 2000).

Implications for the Education Wage Gap

Wage differentials by level of education in Germany are consistently reported to be much lower than in the United States. The difference is especially marked in the lower half of the income distribution; the 50-10 wage differential in Germany is less than half that in the United States (Blau and Kahn 1996a). In a comparison of the wage determination process in 13 European countries, the wage penalty for completing less than upper secondary education was low in Germany relative to other countries (OECD 2002).

In terms of change across time in the skill wage gap, Hannan et al. found that the relative advantage of higher education for first-job earnings declined sharply for both men and women between cohorts who entered the labor market between 1950 and 1975 (1990). Acemoglu (2002) and Freeman and Katz (1995) also report that in contrast to the United States, the wage gap by skill remained relatively stable in Germany over the past 15 years.

Implications for the Gender Wage Gap

The traditional sociological focus on occupations rather than wages, contrary to labor economics, has led researchers to describe the German employment relations system in occupational closure terms. The institution of apprenticeship sets up entry barriers to occupations, whereas promotion into skilled positions in the United States is based more on general educational credentials and on work experience in a specific enterprise (Haller et al. 1985). It is intriguing to surmise that occupational closure may have contradictory effects on the skill wage gap and the gender wage gap, helping to maintain a relatively low gap in the former case and a wider one in the latter. As discussed in the preceding section on the United States, the gender wage gap is no smaller in Germany than the United States, and the rate of labor force participation among married women is considerably lower in Germany, demonstrating less overall labor force attachment on the part of women. The "occupational space" of Germany, operating through the mechanism of occupational closure, may lead to the maintenance of a sizable wage gap through occupational sex segregation. I will discuss below the radical difference between this mechanism and those in the human capital environment of Japan, where the male-female wage gap is even larger.

Witte and Kalleberg report extreme sex segregation in the most common 16 apprenticeship fields in Germany (1995). In five of the 16 areas, women comprised over 70 percent of all apprentices, and in another seven areas, women comprised less than 10 percent. This presages a relatively high degree of occupational sex segregation in the labor force (Anker 1998; Blossfeld 1987; Witte and Kalleberg 1995). Similarly, Hannan, Schömann, and Blossfeld suggest that occupational sex segregation seems to account for more of the difference in German men's and women's wages than differences in the amount of education per se; women's concentration in the professional service sector (including health and education) in particular disadvantages them in wage terms (1990). As mentioned earlier, they found virtually no support for the idea that firm-internal labor markets are crucial for wage determination in Germany and that women's exclusion from such markets is a mechanism contributing to the gender wage gap. In contrast to the United States, there is little evidence that occupational sex segregation has declined in recent years in Germany (OECD 2002).

Human Capital Development in Japan: General and Firm-Specific

Japan has a markedly different type of human capital development system than either the United States or Germany, and a radically different institutional configuration governing the school-work transition as well. If Germany represents the quintessential "occupational space," then Japan on the other hand represents the quintessential "organizational space."[26] Japanese high school and university graduates typically construct their goals not in terms of the occupation in which they wish to be employed but in terms of the company for which they wish to work. The fixation on workplace rather than occupation arose out of historical circumstances that gave pride of place to the firm rather than to the occupation as a central determinant of workers' identity as well as work rewards. Central to this phenomenon is the way that Japanese employers shaped the wage determination process during industrialization; this privileged job tenure is an important basis for compensation. The strategies of Japanese employers were related to the qualifications of labor supplied by the nascent national educational system and to the role of the state in shaping employer-employee relations.

Research on the origins of the Japanese employment system is extensive. Following Abegglen's assertion that the postwar Japanese employment system could be traced to "traditional" employment practices of the nineteenth century (1958), the origins of the system during and after the World War I period became an object of debate in the 1960s and 1970s among Japanese scholars and foreign specialists on Japanese economy and society. The debate was polarized between scholars who, following Abegglen, argued for the historical-cultural roots of Japanese manufacturing firms' stress on "lifetime employment," seniority wages, and a pseudofamilial work atmosphere, and those scholars who claimed that the origins of the Japanese employment system could be traced almost entirely to reasons of economic efficiency (cf. Taira 1962; Sumiya 1966). Cole (1971) summarized these viewpoints nicely, situating the development of the permanent employment system in the context of employers' skillful deployment of traditional cultural symbols in their attempt to bind skilled workers to the firm. He draws attention to the full constellation of social actors involved in the creation of the employment system and to the historically based power relations among them, stressing the centrality of employers in the fashioning of what was to become the prototypical Japanese employment relationship.

Cole's early article viewed Japan through a comparative lens with Germany, and this has been followed in more recent work by Thelen and Kume on the historical origins of training systems. They characterize skill formation regimes based on "solidarism" among employers versus "segmentalism,"[27] and point out that "the very different interaction between the state, artisans, industry, and labor pushed Japan towards a 'segmentalist' rather than 'solidaristic' approach to skill formation" (1999, 51) Literacy rates in Japan at the beginning of the twentieth century were very high by international standards, but the technical skills needed in the country's emerging heavy industries were not well represented in the human capital stock of artisans. Unlike Germany, the Japanese government of the late nineteenth century chose not to encourage the modernization of the artisan sector through means such as the standardization of apprenticeships. Facing a shortage of skilled labor, employers in the early twentieth century of necessity were in the position of having to train new recruits and then attempt to keep them from being bid away by competing firms. This spurred the development of training and compensation systems that were the early seeds of Japan's so-called "permanent employment system." As Crawcour notes:

> With unskilled labor and the raw material for skilled labor—that is to say, school and college leavers—in abundant supply, the strategy of employing only young unskilled workers and internalizing training within the firm could produce a situation in which the supply of skilled labor could be controlled by the employment and training policies of the firm itself. The evolution of the main features of the Japanese employment system—wages related to length of service, lifetime employment, welfare based on employment and suppression of organized labor except for purposes of harmony within the firm as a community—can be understood largely as the process by which employers sought to bring this situation about. . . . The key innovation was a system of wages under which payments were related to length of service to the firm rather than to skill. (1978, 233–34)

Japanese firms' competition for workers and their collective strategies to dampen such competition are a good example of the "search-induced monopsony" analyzed by Acemoglu and Pischke (1999): In an environment where it is costly for a worker to change employers, the firm has a degree of monopsony power and can capture part of the output from the worker's higher productivity. The costs workers face in trying to change employers are the risk of unemployment and the risk that they will not experience a wage increase by moving to a new employer. In these situations (especially when exit rates from unemployment are low), there may be more firm-sponsored formal training programs. While Acemoglu and Pischke's analysis does not refer to historical examples, it is an apt characterization of the evolution of the interwoven institutions in prewar Japan that later came to be known as the distinctive Japanese employment system.

In the aftermath of World War II the impetus for Japanese firms to extend implicit promises of stable employment to workers came more strongly from workers themselves. Employment stability was a major demand of postwar labor unions, and internal labor markets became the normative employment model for firms large enough to develop them. On-the-job training is prevalent in Japanese firms. Consistent with Acemoglu and Pischke's analytical framework linking employer-provided training to workers' risks of not being able to become re-employed once they enter unemployment, the monthly exit rate from unemployment in Japan is half that in the United States (22 vs. 48 percent; Acemoglu and Pischke 1999).

Japanese employers' pattern of recruiting workers with general human capital directly from school has continued throughout the postindustrial period in surprisingly robust form. The Japanese educational system prior to World War II was relatively stratified and bore a greater resemblance to European systems than to the American. Compulsory education ran for six years, after which students were separated into tracks; only a small minority of students eventually attended university. The post–World War II reforms undertaken by the U.S. occupation simplified the system along the "6-3-3" American model, making six years of primary education and three years of junior high school compulsory for all students (Rohlen 1983). This system has remained in place for the past 50 years, although secondary schooling has nearly assumed the status of de facto compulsory education, with more than 90 percent of Japanese students completing it (a rate that exceeds that of the United States).

Significant stratification occurs at two points in Japanese students' careers: during ninth grade and during the senior year in high school. Ninth-grade students take practice high school entrance exams and receive intensive in-school counseling regarding which high school in their district to apply to (LeTendre 1996). Public high schools, attended by the majority of students, are finely ranked according to the minimum admissible score on regional standardized tests given to ninth graders. Students who do not score highly on practice exams end up in one of the lowest-ranked general high schools in their school district (Brinton 1998). A vocational education alternative also exists for students who are unlikely to make it into a highly ranked high school—every prefecture has several public vocational high schools, most of which offer either industrial or commercial training.[28] The second sorting point in Japanese students' educational trajectories occurs at the completion of high school. A minority of graduates enter the labor force; most aim instead for some form of postsecondary education. Chief among the latter are four-year universities and two-year junior colleges.[29] A third alternative, *senmon gakkô* (specialized two-year training schools), saw considerable growth in the past 20 years and has become a popular postsecondary alternative for those students who want further education but cannot pass the entrance exam for a reasonably prestigious university or junior college (Slater 2002). The content of the vocational training offered by *senmon gakkô* is not regulated by the government, and its utility is highly variable across schools.

The Japanese educational system bears considerable surface similarity to the American. Both countries have an educational system with a 6-3-3 structure, a societal norm of high school attendance, a preponderance of students who graduate from high school with general rather than occupationally specific human capital, and a relatively high proportion of students who receive postsecondary education (between 50 and 60 percent in each country), again of a highly general rather than vocationally specific nature. Compared to the German and American educational systems, Japan stands closer to the German in terms of instructional standardization, in-between the German and American in terms of the degree to which students are stratified across curricula as they move through the system, and much more similar to the American in terms of the lack of vocational specificity in education.

But despite considerable surface similarity between the American and Japanese educational systems, the interface between the educational system and the workplace is very different in Japan in two ways: (1) the institutionalized nature of the school-work transition process, (2) the extent to which educational training continues in the workplace, as implemented by individual employers. These, I argue, have significant ramifications for the skill wage gap and the gender wage gap.

Implications for the Education Wage Gap

Unlike the United States and similar to Germany, the Japanese transition from school to work is a very discrete process.[30] The orderly sequencing from full-time education to full-time labor force participation has undergone change along with the turbulence of the Japanese economy since the early 1990s, and it is possible that the diversification of early life course transitions will evidence itself in Japanese data on very recent cohorts. But this would break from the strong normative sequencing apparent in the experiences of prior cohorts.[31]

University graduates move into work organizations through networks that are more university-based and less personalistic than in the United States. The linkages between prestigious Japanese universities and large firms bear some resemblance to those between professional schools and firms in the United States, such as the recruiting relationships between prestigious business and law schools and high-profile firms (Brinton and Kariya 1998). At the high school level, schools and employers are linked together not through apprenticeship arrangements as in the German case but rather through the legal encouragement of recruitment relationships resembling implicit contracts (Brinton 2000; Rosenbaum and Kariya 1989). Japanese high school graduates' entry into the labor market is effected largely through employers' direct contact with the schools from which they wish to recruit, followed by schools' recommendation of one student per job opening. Prior to the onset of serious economic recession in 1992, the system of matching high school graduates to jobs appears to have resulted in little of the labor market "floundering" experienced by many high school graduates in the United States (Genda and Kurosawa 2001; Rosenbaum and Kariya 1989; Ryan 2001).

Japanese high school graduates fortunate enough to have attended a high school with many employer contacts are likely to be able to enter a company that puts them on a track parallel to university graduates (viz. white-collar workers) in terms of the provision of on-the-job training, seniority wages, and job security (Dore and Sako 1998). If German labor markets correspond poorly to the specifications of segmented labor market theory as developed in the United States, Japan corresponds very well. Wages are closely related to firm size and to progression through firm-internal labor markets in large firms (Brown et al. 1997; Kalleberg and Lincoln 1988; Spilerman and Ishida 1996). Occupational category is a poor predictor of both workers' self-identification and their market rewards. In studying earnings inequality in American and Japanese manufacturing firms, Kalleberg and Lincoln stated starkly, "We have clear and consistent evidence that attributes of jobs play a greater role in the determination of earnings in our American than in our Japanese sample" (1988, S142).

Firm-internal labor markets and the so-called permanent employment system developed first in heavy industries, and from the beginning involved male manufacturing workers. The later development of firm-based unions meant that full-time blue- and white-collar employees negotiated wage increases together. Koike has aptly described the similarity of age-earnings trajectories between male white-collar and blue-collar workers in Japan as "the white-collarization of blue-collar workers" in large firms, and has demonstrated the similarity between the age-wage profile for male blue-collar workers in such firms in Japan and white-collar workers in a number of European countries (Koike 1994; Koike and Inoki 1990). The education or skill wage gap is considerably smaller in Japan than in the United States (Brown et al. 1997; Freeman and Katz 1995; Ishida 1993; Katz and Ravenga 1989; Koike 1994; Nakata and Mosk 1987; Spilerman and Ishida 1996). Furthermore, the gap between high school graduates' lifetime earnings and those of university graduates *declined* in the 1960–80 period and rose very slightly in the 1980s (Nakata and Mosk 1987), while the gap in the United States rose sharply.

Implications for the Gender Wage Gap

Japan exhibits perhaps the clearest case of how compensation systems rooted in firm-internal labor markets disadvantage women. I have written extensively on this elsewhere (1993, 2001) and so will only briefly summarize the arguments here.

In comparisons of wage determination across countries, researchers have consistently found that a high premium is attached to job tenure in Japan (Brown et al. 1997; Hashimoto and Raisian 1985; Kalleberg and Lincoln 1988; Spilerman and Ishida 1996). Cross-sectional data on male employees' average length of stay in a firm verify that Japanese men tend to exhibit longer spells with one employer than men in Germany or the United States. The respective figures are 11.3, 9.7, and 7.4. years. Likewise, the proportion of male employees who have spent less than one year in their current firm is over three times as high in the United States (26 percent) as in Japan (7.6 percent). The corresponding figure in Germany stands in between, at 16.1 percent (Crouch, Finegold, and Sako 1999).

Japanese employers' investment in on-the-job training and their commitment to seniority wages is heavily skewed toward male workers. Women are as likely as men to enter large firms upon graduation, but they are much less likely to receive on-the-job training (Brinton 1989, 1991, 1993). Across the life cycle, Japanese women are much more likely than men to move into the classic "secondary" small-firm sector of the economy (Brinton 1989; Brinton, Ngo, and Shibuya 1991). Employers' practice of prodding women to quit the firm upon marriage, often with the enticement of a "retirement payment," has been formally illegal since the enactment of an Equal Opportunity Employment Law in 1986. But the practice persists. This reinforces a vicious cycle wherein employers assume that women have low work commitment and accordingly place them in dead-end jobs outside of internal labor markets. When many women subsequently exit these dead-end jobs upon marriage or childbirth, employers' self-fulfilling prophecy is realized. Large companies' creation of a dual-

track system for women in the late 1980s, consisting of the conventional dead-end track and a management track, has largely backfired since the Japanese economy went into recession in the early 1990s: many young women choose the dead-end track in hopes of increasing their chances to get hired at all. The Japan Institute of Labour recently reported that just 2 percent of all management positions in large firms are held by women (Ministry of Health, Labour, and Welfare 2001).

In sum, Japan represents a dramatic counterpoint to the United States in its human capital development system and inequality patterns. General human capital development through educational institutions is heavily complemented by on-the-job training for those workers in whom employers choose to invest. The recipients of on-the-job training and internal labor market placement are not nearly as differentiated by skill level as in the United States, and have entered the workplace through a process that is highly coordinated between schools and firms. The beneficiaries of this human capital development system are strongly differentiated by gender rather than prior education or skill level. Men are heavily privileged because employers perceive that they can more safely assume that men's length of service (and hence the employers' own returns to productivity-enhancing skill investments) will be substantial. The result of this form of human capital development system is a narrow skill wage gap and a wide gender wage gap.

CONCLUSION: THE COMPARATIVE-INSTITUTIONAL ANALYSIS OF EDUCATION-ECONOMY LINKAGES AND ECONOMIC INEQUALITY

In this chapter I have argued for the idea that economic sociologists could profitably set as one of their research agendas the theoretical articulation of how education-economy linkages structure and reproduce patterns of inequality across postindustrial societies. I have conceptualized two education-economy linkages as theoretically fruitful to examine: the division of labor between schools and firms for individuals' human capital development, and the recruitment mechanisms structuring individuals' movement out of school and into the workplace as well as those structuring movement across jobs. Economic sociologists have based much of their claim to originality on the careful analysis of how institutional arrangements form the context within which individual economic behaviors take place. Given these strengths, the extension of economic sociological inquiry into the study of comparative inequality regimes based on varied education-economy linkages would seem very promising.

Much of the theoretical and empirical work to date on the relationship between institutional arrangements and inequality patterns across industrial societies has been done outside of sociology. The neighboring disciplines of political science and labor economics have focused considerable attention on cross-national variation in wage compression across skill boundaries. In closing I would suggest that economic sociologists can profitably draw on the extensive empirical work by labor economists and the theoretical exploration of wage-setting arrangements by both labor economists and proponents of the varieties of capitalism approach. Building upon the theoretical formulations of educational and stratification researchers, economic sociologists can fashion a comparative research agenda designed to further specify how skill and gender wage gaps are influenced by the varied institutional arrangements of capitalism. Many of these institutional arrangements stand precisely at the intersection of education and the economy.

NOTES

I am grateful to Mary Mosley for her general assistance in the preparation of the first draft of this chapter, and to Carolyn Wong for bibliographical help.

1. For exceptions in sociology, see Chang 2000; Rosenfeld and Kalleberg 1990; and Wright, Baxter, and Birkelund 1995.

2. See Brinton 1988, 1993 for a related discussion, relevant to gender inequality.

3. See Brinton and Kariya 1998 for a consideration of the social embeddedness of recruitment processes.

4. Also see Dobbin's chapter 2 in this handbook for a review of comparative-historical studies of management systems and industrial relations.

5. This is reified in the organization of sections in the American Sociological Association. The Education and the Organizations, Occupations, and Work sections are both relatively large in terms of membership and oddly, there is no Social Stratification section in the ASA that would bridge the spheres of education and work. The recent creation of a section on Labor and Labor Movements has drawn together scholars interested in labor politics and processes.

6. What then is the causal connection between the system of wage determination and the structure of the educational system? Müller and Shavit suggest that Maurice and colleagues' work shows that employers adapt their training and recruitment policies to the educational system. I would modify this by suggesting that the direction of the relationship may be historically contingent, dependent on the relative timing in any particular country of the development of the educational system on the one hand and employers' recruitment and training strategies on the other.

7. DiPrete and Soule (1988) found that women were less likely than men to be promoted from lower- to upper-tier jobs in the U.S. federal bureaucracy; several other studies looked at men's and women's promotions in internal labor markets in specific firms. Spilerman and Ishida (1996) excluded women from their study of career advancement in a large Japanese financial firm. Only 1 percent of managerial employees were women, whereas all of the clerical workers were female; there was no mobility between the clerical and managerial ranks.

8. See Brinton 1988, 1993, 2001 for a development of this line of argumentation.

9. Witness Freeman's statement in the introductory chapter of his *Working under Different Rules:* "In Economics I, the invisible hand of market forces sets wages, prices, and quantities, aided perhaps by a Wizard of Oz 'auctioneer' who calibrates prices and wages until all markets clear. In real labor markets, however, matters are more complicated and interesting. Every country has its own labor market institutions—unions, management, organizations, government agencies—and rules that help determine outcomes" (1994, 14–15).

10. But there is also sensitivity in the literature to the fact that strong unions and centralized wage-bargaining do not necessarily go hand in hand, making it necessary to consider them separately.

11. Increased international trade, varying across countries, has also been investigated as a source of differential change in the demand for skilled workers. See reviews in Acemoglu 2002 and in Katz and Autor 1999.

12. Acemoglu further points out that under this scenario, job creation would be less desirable and unemployment would increase across skill levels, and that this is consistent with European trends and with the contrast between the United States and continental Europe.

13. As Dobbin notes in his chapter in this handbook, an important issue for economic sociologists is to explain the diversity of economic systems that operate effectively. He notes, "The question of what kinds of economic behavior patterns are actually extinguished by their inefficiency is an important one, but it is remarkable how many different behavior patterns are not extinguished, or have not yet been" (Dobbin, xx).

14. Both political scientists and economists also consider poverty rates cross-nationally. This is beyond the scope of this chapter as I have formulated it. A considerable amount of empirical research has been done using the Luxembourg Income Study, although there are some important exceptions (such as Japan) in the coverage of the data sets (see Gottschalk and Smeeding 1997).

15. Issues of ethnic inequality are also embedded in analysis of the first type of inequality to the extent that significant educational differences persist across ethnic groups.

16. I originally intended to include social class reproduction as a third type of inequality that may be linked to national institutional variation in the education-economy linkage. However, the literature on social class reproduction is vast and involves a number of issues that go beyond the boundaries of a chapter on education and the economy. Of particular importance for intergenerational class inheritance, of course, is the issue of who gets educated. This is logically prior to the issue of how different amounts of education translate into labor market returns and how this process may differ by ascriptive characteristics (gender and ethnicity). It is this latter issue that I focus on here—how the translation of education into labor market rewards for different groups may depend in part on the institutional arrangements governing human capital development and recruitment.

17. As initiated by Granovetter's classic study (1995), the job search literature has consistently documented the important role played by social ties in American workers' job searches. More recent literature specifically on the school-work transition reiterates the finding that social ties are important at this stage as well, given the lack of formal institutions structuring the school-work process in the United States (Rosenbaum et al. 1990; Rosenbaum 2001).

18. It may be no accident that human capital theory, with its highly individualistic conception of how skill development takes place, had its birthplace in the United States. The lack of organized apprenticeship programs or systematic employer investments in training means that a great deal of human capital development occurs before individuals enter the workplace on a full-time basis. This leaves much decision-making control over human capital investments squarely in the hands of youth and their families. The degree of status transmission across generations is high in the United States; contrary to the implications of Turner's classic depiction of the United States as a "contest mobility" regime (1960), American intergenerational class inheritance is as high as in many other advanced industrial economies (Ishida 1993).

19. At the professional level, of course, professional associations have played a major role in the construction of certification standards (Abbott 1988).

20. At the secondary education level, Kirschenman and Neckerman show that many Chicago employers use the high school name or even the fact that the job applicant graduated from one of the city's public high schools as an indication that he or she is unqualified (1991).

21. In stating this, they suggest that there is a way in which vocational programs in secondary schools and non-university postsecondary educational institutions may *reduce* intergenerational status reproduction, as the students in these programs are disproportionately from disadvantaged backgrounds but reap the benefits of employer-valued educational training. This area will undoubtedly continue to be one of heated debate within the sociology of education.

22. Loewenstein and Spletzer report a higher figure for the proportion of new workers who receive informal training by U.S. employers (1999), but Acemoglu and Pischke (1999) note that even the higher figure is still only about one-half the figure for formal training by German and Japanese employers.

23. The widely cited *International Adult Literacy Survey* found American workers to be more concentrated in the extremes of the verbal and quantitative skill distributions than German workers, who were bunched in the middle (National Center for Education Statistics and Statistics Canada 1995; see also Freeman and Schettkat 2000). Unfortunately Japan was not included in the study. As is well known, international comparisons of students' performance in mathematics and science consistently rank Japan at or near the top of the distribution (National Center for Education Statistics 2002). It is principally the variance in the distribution with which we are concerned here; studies have reported low variance in the Japanese scores.

24. This is based on OECD statistics published in 2002. Blau and Kahn (1996b) report the same results for Germany and Austria; the Netherlands is not in their sample.

25. The Korean labor market bears some resemblance to the Japanese, although firm-internal labor markets are less widespread. Notably, Japan and Korea are the only two OECD countries where the labor force participation rates of married women with tertiary education are similar to or

lower than those of women with less education (Brinton 2001).

26. Japan frequently falls out of comparative research for a number of reasons. One is certainly the language barrier, which is formidable. A second reason is that micro-level data are extremely hard to obtain in Japan (see Brinton 2003, for a review of the reasons). A third is that Japan has not participated in a number of the collaborative efforts to obtain comparable data sets across countries; the Luxembourg Income Study is a case in point.

27. They cite an unpublished piece by Peter Swenson as the source of this terminology ("Employers Unite: Labor Market Control and the Welfare State in Sweden and the U.S.," 1996).

28. A smaller number of vocational high schools specialize in training for agriculture, fisheries, home economics, and nursing.

29. Both expanded their enrollments exponentially in the post–World War II period, with junior college becoming almost entirely a female track and remaining so.

30. While a sizable proportion of each year's entering cohort at the nation's most prestigious universities are students who "sat out" for a year in order to retake the university entrance exam in order to gain admission to their top-choice school (Ono 1999), these students are not ones who, as in the United States, took a year off to experience the world of work and to think over their future occupational choices. Rather, they are primarily male students who wish to enter prestigious universities, nearly always with the purpose of gaining the credential necessary to subsequently enter one of Japan's large firms offering the promise of stable employment.

31. To date the Social Stratification and Mobility Survey, conducted every 10 years in Japan since 1955, has always collected work history information that begins after completion of formal schooling. Unlike the United States, data analysis problems based on individuals' subsequent return to schooling and reentry to the labor force have been so trivial as to occasion little debate over whether to reword the survey questions.

REFERENCES

Abbott, Andrew. 1988. *The System of Professions: An Essay on the Division of Expert Labor.* Chicago: University of Chicago Press.

Abegglen, James C. 1958. *The Japanese Factory: Aspects of Its Social Organization.* Glencoe, Ill.: Free Press.

Acemoglu, Daron. 2002. "Cross-Country Inequality Trends." NBER Working Paper No. 8832.

Acemoglu, Daron, and Jorn-Steffen Pischke. 1999. "The Structure of Wages and Investment in General Training." *Journal of Political Economy* 107:539–72.

Allmendinger, Jutta. 1989. "Educational Systems and Labor Market Outcomes." *European Sociological Review* 5(3): 231–50.

Althauser, Robert P. 1989. "Internal Labor Markets." *Annual Review of Sociology* 15:143–61.

Altonji, Joseph, and James Spletzer. 1992. "Worker Characteristics, Job Characteristics, and the Receipt of On-the-Job Training." *Industrial and Labor Relations Review* 45:58–79.

Anker, Richard. 1998. *Gender and Jobs: Sex Segregation of Occupations in the World*. Geneva: International Labour Office.

Arum, Richard, and Michael Hout. 1998. "The Early Returns: The Transition from School to Work in the United States." Pp. 130–46 in *From School to Work: A Comparative Study of Educational Qualifications and Occupational Destinations*, ed. Yossi Shavit and Walter Müller. Oxford: Clarendon Press.

Autor, David, Lawrence F. Katz, and Alan B. Krueger. 1998. "Computing Inequality: Have Computers Changed the Labor Market?" *Quarterly Journal of Economics* 113:1169–213.

Baron, James N., and William T. Bielby. 1980. "Bringing the Firms Back In: Stratification, Segmentation, and the Organization of Work." *American Sociological Review* 45:737–65.

Barron, John M., Dan Black, Dan, and Mark Loewenstein. 1987. "Employer Size: The Implications for Search, Training, Capital Investment, Starting Wages, and Wage Growth." *Journal of Labor Economics* 5:76–89.

Becker, Gary S. 1993. *Human Capital*. Chicago: University of Chicago Press.

Bishop, John H. 1989. "Why the Apathy in American High Schools?" *Educational Researcher* 18:6–13.

Blau, Francine D., and Lawrence M. Kahn. 1996a. "International Differences in Male Wage Inequality: Institutions versus Market Forces." *Journal of Political Economy* 104:791–837.

———. 1996b. "Wage Structure and Gender Earnings Differentials: An International Comparison." *Economica* 63:S29–S62.

———. 1997. "Swimming Upstream: Trends in the Gender Wage Differential in the 1980s." *Journal of Labor Economics* 15(1): 1–42.

———. 2002. *At Home and Abroad: U.S. Labor Market Performance in International Perspective*. New York: Russell Sage Foundation.

———. Forthcoming. "The Gender Pay Gap: Going, Going . . . but Not Gone." In *The Declining Significance of Gender? Essays on Gender Inequality in the U.S.*, ed. David Grusky, Francine D. Blau, and Mary C. Brinton. New York: Russell Sage Foundation.

Blossfeld, Hans-Peter. 1987. "Labor-Market Entry and the Sexual Segregation of Careers in the Federal Republic of Germany." *American Journal of Sociology* 93:89–118.

———. 1993. Changes in Educational Opportunities in the Federal Republic of Germany: A Longitudinal Study of Cohorts Born between 1916 and 1965." Pp. 51–74 in *Persistent Inequality: Changing Educational Attainment in Thirteen Countries*, ed. Yossi Shavit and Hans-Peter Blossfeld. Boulder, Colo.: Westview.

Blossfeld, Hans-Peter, and Karl Ulrich Mayer. 1988. "Labor Market Segmentation in the Federal Republic of Germany: An Empirical Study of Segmentation Theories from a Life Course Perspective." *European Sociological Review* 4(2): 123–40.

Bound, John, and George Johnson. 1992. "Changes in the Structure of Wages in the 1980s: An Evaluation of Alternative Explanations." *American Economic Review* 82:371–92.

Bowles, Samuel, and Herbert Gintis. 1976. *Schooling in Capitalist America: Educational Reform and the Contradictions of Economic Life*. New York: Basic Books.

Brinton, Mary C. 1988. "The Social-Institutional Bases of Gender Stratification: Japan as an Illustrative Case." *American Journal of Sociology* 94:300–334.

———. 1989. "Gender Stratification in Contemporary Urban Japan." *American Sociological Review* 54: 542–57.

———. 1991. "Sex Differences in On-the-Job Training and Job Rotation in Japanese Firms." *Research in Social Stratification and Mobility* 10:3–25.

———. 1993. *Women and the Economic Miracle: Gender and Work in Postwar Japan*. Berkeley and Los Angeles: University of California Press.

———. 1998. "From High School to Work: Lessons for the United States?" *Social Service Review*, December, 442–51.

———. 2000. "Social Capital in the Japanese Youth Labor Market: Labor Market Policy, Schools, and Norms." *Policy Sciences* 33:289–306.

———. 2001. "Married Women's Labor in East Asian Economies." Pp. 1–37 in *Women's Working Lives in East Asia*, ed. Mary C. Brinton. Stanford, Calif.: Stanford University Press.

———. 2003. "Fact-Rich, Data-Poor: Japan as Sociologists' Heaven and Hell." Pp. 87–110 in *Doing Fieldwork in Japan*, ed. Theodore C. Bestor, Patricia Steinhoff, and Victoria Lyon Bestor. Honolulu: University of Hawaii Press.

Brinton, Mary C., and Takehiko Kariya. 1998. "Institutional Embeddedness in Japanese Labor Markets." Pp. 181–207 in *The New Institutionalism in Sociology*, ed. Mary C. Brinton and Victor Nee. New York: Russell Sage Foundation.

Brinton, Mary C., and Hang-Yue Ngo. 1993. "Age and Sex in the Occupational Structure: A United States–Japan Comparison." *Sociological Forum* 8:93–111.

Brinton, Mary C., Hang-Yue Ngo, and Kumiko Shibuya. 1991. "Gendered Mobility Patterns in Industrial Economies: The Case of Japan." *Social Science Quarterly* 72:807–16.

Brown, Clair, Yoshifumi Nakata, Michael Reich, and Lloyd Ulman. 1997. *Work and Pay in the United States and Japan*. Oxford: Oxford University Press.

Card, David, and John E. DiNardo. 2002. "Skill Biased Technological Change and Rising Wage Inequality: Some Problems and Puzzles." NBER Working Paper No. 8769.

Chang, Mariko Lin. 2000. "The Evolution of Sex Segregation Regimes." *American Journal of Sociology* 105:1658–701.

Cole, Robert E. 1971. "The Theory of Institutionaliza-tion: Permanent Employment and Tradition in Japan." *Economic Development and Cultural Change* 20(1): 47–70.

Crawcour, Sydney. 1978. "The Japanese Employment System." *Journal of Japanese Studies* 4(2): 225–45.

Crouch, Colin, David Finegold, and Mari Sako. 1999. *Are Skills the Answer? The Political Economy of Skill Creation in Advanced Industrial Countries.* Oxford: Oxford University Press.

Crouch, Colin, and Wolfgang Streeck, eds. 1997. *The Political Economy of Modern Capitalism.* London: Sage.

DiPrete, Thomas A., Paul M. de Graaf, Ruud Luijkx, Michael Tahlin, and Hans-Peter Blossfeld. 1997. "Collectivist versus Individualist Mobility Regimes? Structural Change and Job Mobility in Four Coun-tries." *American Journal of Sociology* 103:318–58.

DiPrete, Thomas A., and Patricia McManus. 1996. "In-stitutions, Technical Change, and Diverging Life Chances: Earnings Mobility in the United States and Germany." *American Journal of Sociology* 102: 34–79.

DiPrete, Thomas A., and Whitman T. Soule. 1988. "Gender and Promotion in Segmented Job Ladder Systems." *American Sociological Review* 53:26–40.

Doeringer, Peter B., and Michael J. Piore. 1971. *Inter-nal Labor Markets and Manpower Analysis.* Lexing-ton, Mass.: Heath.

Dore, Ronald P., and Mari Sako. 1998. *How the Japanese Learn to Work.* London: Routledge.

Esping-Andersen, Gøsta. 1990. *The Three Worlds of Wel-fare Capitalism.* Princeton: Princeton University Press.

Estevez-Abe, Margarita. 2002. "Gendering the Varieties of Capitalism: Gender Bias in Skills and Social Po-licies." Department of Government, Harvard University.

Estevez-Abe, Margarita, Torben Iversen, and David Soskice. 2001. "Social Protection and the Forma-tion of Skills: A Reinterpretation of the Welfare State." Pp. 145–83 in *Varieties of Capitalism: The Institutional Foundations of Comparative Advan-tage,* ed. Peter A. Hall and David Soskice. Oxford: Oxford University Press.

Fligstein, Neil. 2001. *The Architecture of Markets: An Economic Sociology of Twenty-first-Century Capital-ist Societies.* Princeton: Princeton University Press.

Frank, Robert H. 1998. "Winner-Take-All Labor Markets and Wage Discrimination." Pp. 208–23 in *The New Institutionalism in Sociology,* ed. Mary C. Brinton and Victor Nee. New York: Russell Sage Foundation.

Freeman, Richard B., ed. 1994. *Working under Differ-ent Rules.* New York: Russell Sage Foundation.

Freeman, Richard B., and Lawrence F. Katz. 1995. *Dif-ferences and Changes in Wage Structure.* Chicago: University of Chicago Press.

Freeman, Richard B., and Ronald Schettkat. 2000. "Skill Compression, Wage Differentials, and Employ-ment: Germany vs. the U.S." NBER Working Paper No. 7610.

Gamoran, Adam. 1996. "Educational Stratification and Individual Careers." Pp. 59–74 in *Generating So-cial Stratification: Toward a New Research Agenda,* ed. Alan C. Kerckhoff. Boulder, Colo.: Westview Press.

Gardecki, Rosella, and David Neumark. 1997. "Order from Chaos? The Effects of Early Labor Market Ex-periences on Adult Labor Market Outcomes." NBER Working Paper No. 5899.

Genda, Yuji, and Masako Kurosawa. 2001. "Transition from School to Work in Japan." *Journal of the Jap-anese and International Economies* 15:465–88.

Goldin, Claudia. 1999. "Egalitarianism and the Returns to Education during the Great Transformation of American Education." *Journal of Political Economy* 107(6): S65–S94.

Goldin, Claudia, and Lawrence F. Katz. 2001. "The Legacy of U.S. Educational Leadership: Notes on Distribution and Economic Growth in the Twenti-eth Century." *American Economic Review* 91(2): 18–23.

Gornick, Janet C., Marcia K. Meyers, and Katherine E. Ross. 1998. "Public Policies and the Employment of Mothers: A Cross-National Study." *Social Science Quarterly* 79(1): 35–54.

Gottschalk, Peter, and Mary Joyce. 1998. "Cross-National Differences in the Rise in Earnings In-equality: Market and Institutional Factors." *Review of Economics and Statistics* 80:489–502.

Gottschalk, Peter, and Timothy M. Smeeding. 1997. "Cross-National Comparisons of Earnings and In-come Inequality." *Journal of Economic Literature* 35:633–87.

Granovetter, Mark. 1995. *Getting a Job: A Study of Con-tacts and Careers.* 2d ed. Chicago: University of Chicago Press.

Hall, Peter A., and David Soskice. 2001. *Varieties of Capitalism: The Institutional Foundations of Com-parative Advantage.* Oxford: Oxford University Press.

Haller, Max, Wolfgang Konig, Peter Krause, and Karin Kurz. 1985. "Patterns of Career Mobility and Structural Positions in Advanced Capitalist Soci-eties: A Comparison of Men in Austria, France, and the United States." *American Sociological Review* 50:579–603.

Hamilton, Gary G. 1994. "Civilizations and the Organi-zation of Economies." Pp. 183–205 in *The Hand-book of Economic Sociology,* ed. Neil J. Smelser and Richard Swedberg. New York: Russell Sage Foun-dation; Princeton: Princeton University Press.

Hamilton, Stephen F. 1990. *Apprenticeship for Adult-hood: Preparing Youth for the Future.* New York: Free Press.

Hannan, Michael T., Klaus Schömann, and Hans-Peter Blossfeld. 1990. "Sex and Sector Differences in the Dynamics of Wage Growth in the Federal Republic of Germany." *American Sociological Review* 55: 694–713.

Hashimoto, Masanori, and John Raisian. 1985. "Em-ployment Tenure and Earnings Profiles in Japan and the United States." *American Economic Review* 75: 721–35.

Hollingsworth, J. Rogers, and Robert Boyer. 1997. *Contemporary Capitalism: The Embeddedness of Institutions*. Cambridge: Cambridge University Press.

Ishida, Hiroshi. 1993. *Social Mobility in Contemporary Japan*. Stanford, Calif: Stanford University Press.

Jacobs, Jerry A. 1989. *Revolving Doors: Sex Segregation and Women's Careers*. Stanford, Calif: Stanford University Press.

———. 1995. "Gender and Academic Specialties: Trends among Recipients of College Degrees in the 1980s." *Sociology of Education* 68(2): 81–98.

Japan Institute of Labour. 2002. *Japanese Working Life Profile*. Tokyo: Japan Institute of Labour.

———. 2003. *Japan Labor Bulletin*, January.

Juhn, Chinhui, Kevin M. Murphy, and Brooks Pierce. 1993. "Wage Inequality and the Rise in Returns to Skill." *Journal of Political Economy* 101:410–42.

Kalleberg, Arne L. 1988. "Comparative Perspectives on Work Structures and Inequality." *Annual Review of Sociology* 14:203–25.

Kalleberg, Arne L., and James R. Lincoln. 1988. "The Structure of Earnings Inequality in the United States and Japan." *American Journal of Sociology* 94:S121–53.

Katz, Lawrence F., and David Autor. 1999. "Changes in the Wage Structure and Earnings Inequality." Pp. 1463–555 in vol. 3 of *Handbook of Labor Economics*, ed. Orley Ashenfelter and Richard Layard. Amsterdam: North-Holland.

Katz, Lawrence F., and Ana L. Ravenga. 1989. "Changes in the Structure of Wages: The United States versus Japan." *Journal of the Japanese and International Economies* 3:522–53.

Kerckhoff, Alan C. 1995. "Institutional Arrangements and Stratification Processes in Industrial Societies." *Annual Review of Sociology* 15:323–47.

———. 2000. "Transition from School to Work in Comparative Perspective." Pp. 453–74 in *Handbook of the Sociology of Education*, ed. Maureen T. Hallinan. New York: Kluwer Academic Press.

———. 2001. "Education and Social Stratification Processes in Comparative Perspective." *Sociology of Education*, extra issue, 3–18.

Kerckhoff, Alan C., and Lorraine Bell. 1998. "Hidden Capital: Vocational Credentials and Attainment in the United States." *Sociology of Education* 71(2): 152–74.

Kirschenman, Joleen, and Kathryn Neckerman. 1991. 'We'd Love to Hire Them, but . . .': The Meaning of Race for Employers." Pp. 203–32 in *The Urban Underclass*, ed. Christopher Jencks and Paul E. Peterson. Washington, D.C.: Brookings Institution.

Knoke, David, and Arne L. Kalleberg. 1994. "Job Training in U.S. Organizations." *American Sociological Review* 59:537–46.

Koike, Koike. 1994. *The Economics of Work in Japan*. Tokyo: LTCB International Library Foundation.

Koike, Koike, and Takenori Inoki. 1990. *Skill Formation in Japan and Southeast Asia*. Tokyo: University of Tokyo Press.

König, W., and Walter Müller. 1986. "Educational Systems and Labour Markets as Determinants of Work-life Mobility in France and West Germany: A Comparison of Men's Career Mobility, 1965–1970." *European Sociological Review* 2(2): 73–96.

Krueger, Alan B. 1993. "How Computers Have Changed the Wage Structure: Evidence from Micro-data, 1984–1989." *Quarterly Journal of Economics* 108(1): 33–60.

LeTendre, Gerald K. 1996. "Constructed Aspirations: Decision-Making Processes in Japanese Educational Selection." *Sociology of Education* 69:193–216.

Loewenstein, Mark A., and James R. Spletzer. 1999. "General and Specific Training: Evidence and Implications." *Journal of Human Resources* 34:710–33.

Lynch, Lisa M. 1992a. "Differential Effects of Post-school Training on Early Career Mobility." NBER Working Paper No. 4034.

———. 1992b. "Private-Sector Training and the Earnings of Young Workers." *American Economic Review* 82:299–312.

———. 1993. "The Economics of Youth Training in the United States." *Economic Journal* 103:1292–302.

Maurice Marc, François Sellier, and Jen-Jacques Silvestre. 1986. *The Social Foundations of Industrial Power*. Cambridge: MIT Press.

Ministry of Health, Labour, and Welfare. 2001. *Basic Survey on the Employment of Women*. Tokyo: Management and Coordination Agency.

Morris, Martina, and Bruce Western. 1999. "Inequality in Earnings at the Close of the Twentieth Century." *Annual Review of Sociology* 25:623–57.

Mortimer, Jeylan T., Carolyn Harley, and Pamela J. Aronson. "How Do Prior Experiences in the Workplace Set the Stage for Transitions to Adulthood?" Pp. 131–59 in *Transitions to Adulthood in a Changing Economy: No Work, No Family, No Future?* ed. Ann C. Crouter, Alan Booth, and Michael J. Shanahan. Westport, Conn.: Praeger.

Mortimer, Jeylan T., and Helga Krüger. 2000. "Pathways from School to Work in Germany and the United States." Pp. 475–97 in *Handbook of the Sociology of Education*, ed. Maureen T. Hallinan. New York: Kluwer Academic Press.

Müller, Walter, and Yossi Shavit. 1998. "The Institutional Embeddedness of the Stratification Process: A Comparative Study of Qualifications and Occupations in Thirteen Countries." Pp. 1–48 in *From School to Work: A Comparative Study of Educational Qualifications and Occupational Destinations*, ed. Yossi Shavit and Walter Müller. Oxford: Oxford University Press.

Murphy, Kevin M., and Finis Welch. 1993. "Occupational Change and the Demand for Skill, 1940–1980." *American Economic Review* Papers and Proceedings, 83(2): 122–26.

Nakata, Yoshi-fumi, and Carl Mosk. 1987. "The Demand for College Education in Postwar Japan." *Journal of Human Resources* 22:377–404.

National Center for Education Statistics. 2002. *The Condition of Education, 2002. Washington, D.C.: U.S. Department of Education.

Neumark, David. 1998. "Youth Labor Markets in the U.S.: Shopping Around vs. Staying Put. NBER Working Paper No. 6581.

Ogasawara, Yuko. 1998. *Office Ladies and Salaried Men: Power, Gender, and Work in Japanese Companies.* Berkeley and Los Angeles: University of California Press.

Ono, Hiroshi. 1999. "For What It's Worth: The Value of College Education in Japan." Department of Sociology, University of Chicago.

Organization for Economic Cooperation and Development (OECD). 2002. *OECD Employment Outlook.* Paris: OECD.

Organization for Economic Cooperation and Development (OECD), Statistics Canada. 1995. *Literacy, Economy, and Society.* Paris: OECD; Ottawa: Statistics Canada.

Orloff, Ann Shola. 1993. "Gender and the Social Rights of Citizenship: The Comparative Analysis of State Policies and Gender Relations." *American Sociological Review* 53:303–28.

Petersen, Trond, Ishak Saporta, and Marc-David L. Seidel. 2000. "Offering a Job: Meritocracy and Social Networks." *American Journal of Sociology* 106:763–816.

Rohlen, Thomas P. 1983. *Japan's High Schools.* Berkeley and Los Angeles: University of California Press.

Rosenbaum, James E. 1989. "What If Good Jobs Depended on Good Grades?" *American Educator* 13 (winter): 10-43.

———. 1996. "Policy Uses of Research on the High School–Work Transition." *Sociology of Education,* extra issue, 102–22.

———. 2001. *Beyond College for All.* New York: Russell Sage Foundation.

Rosenbaum, James E., and Takehiko Kariya. 1989. "From High School to Work: Market and Institutional Mechanisms in Japan." *American Journal of Sociology* 94:1334–65.

———. 1991. "Do School Achievements Affect the Early Jobs of High School Graduates in the United States and Japan?" *Sociology of Education* 64:78–95.

Rosenbaum, James E., Takehiko Kariya, Rick Settersten, and Tony Maier. 1990. "Market and Network Theories of the Transition from High School to Work: Their Application to Industrialized Societies." *Annual Review of Sociology* 16:263–99.

Rosenfeld, Rachel A. 1992. "Job Mobility and Career Processes." *Annual Review of Sociology* 18:39–61.

Rosenfeld, Rachel A., and Arne L. Kalleberg. 1990. "A Cross-National Comparison of the Gender Gap in Income." *American Journal of Sociology* 96:69–106.

Rubinson, Richard, and Irene Browne. 1994. "Education and the Economy." Pp. 581–99 in *The Handbook of Economic Sociology,* ed. Neil J. Smelser and

Richard Swedberg. New York: Russell Sage Foundation; Princeton: Princeton University Press.

Ruhm, Christopher J. 1995. "Is High School Employment Consumption or Investment?" NBER Working Paper No. 5030.

Ryan, Paul. 2001. "The School-to-Work Transition: A Cross-National Perspective." *Journal of Economic Literature* 39(1): 34–92.

Sakamoto, Arthur, and Meichu D. Chen. 1993. "Earnings Inequality and Segmentation by Firm Size in Japan and the United States." *Research in Social Stratification and Mobility* 12:185–211.

Shavit, Yossi, and Walter Müller. 2000. "Vocational Secondary Education, Tracking, and Social Stratification." Pp. 197–224 in *Handbook of the Sociology of Education,* ed. Maureen T. Hallinan. New York: Kluwer Academic.

———, eds. 1998. *From School to Work: A Comparative Study of Educational Qualifications and Occupational Destinations.* Oxford: Clarendon Press.

Slater, D. 2002. "Classculture: Pedagogy and Politics at a Japanese Working-Class High School in Tokyo." Department of Anthropology, University of Chicago.

Spilerman, Seymour, and Hiroshi Ishida. 1996. "Stratification and Attainment in a Large Japanese Firm." Pp. 317–42 in *Generating Social Stratification: Toward a New Research Agenda,* ed. Alan C. Kerckhoff. Boulder, Colo.: Westview.

Sumiya, Mikio. 1966. "The Development of Japanese Labour-Relations." *Developing Economies* 4:499–515.

Swenson, Peter. 1996. "Employers Unite: Labor Market Control and the Welfare State in Sweden and the U.S." Typescript.

Taira, K. 1962. "Characteristics of Japanese Labor Markets." *Economic Development and Cultural Change* 10:150–69.

Thelen, Kathleen, and Ikuo Kume. 1999. "The Rise of Nonmarket Training Regimes: Germany and Japan Compared." *Journal of Japanese Studies* 25(1): 33–64.

Turner, Ralph H. 1960. "Sponsored and Contest Mobility and the School System." *American Sociological Review* 25:855–67.

Walters, P. B. 2000. "School Expansion, School Reform, and the Limits of Growth." Pp. 241–61 in *Handbook of the Sociology of Education,* ed. Maureen T. Hallinan. New York: Kluwer Academic Press.

Witte, James C., and Arne L. Kalleberg. 1995. "Matching Training and Jobs: The Fit between Vocational Education and Employment in the German Labour Market." *European Sociological Review* 11(3): 293–317.

Wright, Erik Olin, Janeen Baxter, and Gunn Elisabeth Birkelund. 1995. "The Gender Gap in Workplace Authority: A Cross-National Study." *American Sociological Review* 60:407–35.

26 New Directions in the Study of Religion and Economic Life

Robert Wuthnow

A GENERATION AGO, studies of the relationships between religion and economic life were often framed within a view of modern society that emphasized institutional differentiation and secularization. As a result, studies of economic behavior seldom paid attention to religion, and studies of religion seldom dealt with economic activities (Beckford 1985). In recent years, more borrowing across subdisciplinary lines is evident. Studies of religion incorporate insights from economic sociology about economic preferences, markets, and organizational structure, while research in economic sociology sometimes draws on ideas about ritual and ceremony, symbolism, testimonials, ethnic and religious communities, and sacralization. Beyond these mutual influences, there has been a more important shift in thinking about the nature of religion itself. The new directions resulting from this shift converge in significant ways with current thinking in economic sociology (Swedberg 1991).[1]

Theories of modernization suggested that religion would become increasingly differentiated from other institutions, including the political and economic spheres. These theories also argued that religion was becoming privatized, leaving behavior that truly mattered in the larger society free of religious influences. These arguments, as well as increasing specialization within the social sciences themselves, often made it possible to ignore the role of religion. Even on topics in which religious considerations might have been evident, such as immigration (Portes 1998; Portes and Rumbaut 1990), lower-income African American neighborhoods (Wilson 1980), and trust (Coleman 1990), these considerations were often neglected.

Mutual influences between studies of religion and economic sociology have grown in response to the neoinstitutional approach to organizations (Powell and DiMaggio 1991) and emphasis on the social embeddedness of economic transactions (Granovetter 1990). These influences are evident in such work as Chaves's (1997) study of organizational innovation among religious denominations in decisions concerning the ordination of women, Becker's (1999) study of conflict in congregations, and Finke and Stark's (1992) study of denominational growth and decline. In economic sociology and related subdisciplines, some interest in religion or concepts from scholarship on religion is evident in discussions of the ceremonial aspects of formal organizations (Meyer and Rowan 1991), trust (Fukuyama 1995; Seligman 1997), and social capital (Putnam 2000). Some convergence between studies of religion and economic sociology can be seen in Etzioni's (1988) and Selznick's (1994) treatments of the moral dimensions of economic life. Other studies have examined the economic aspects of religious organizations themselves, especially finances and fund-raising (Ronsvale and Ronsvale 1996; Hoge 1996; and Vallet and Zech 1995), and some attention has been paid to the commercialization of religion (Moore 1994).

There has, however, been a more general reorientation of scholarship on religion, including studies that bear directly on economic life. This reorientation works within the framework of questions raised by the founding figures in sociology, especially questions about the conditions under which religion and economic life bear affinities with each other or conflict with each other. Long-standing questions about religion accommodating to economic conditions or serving as modes of resistance also remain. Recent work has not so much abandoned these questions as responded to earlier answers that posed additional problems. New directions in the study of religion and economic life emphasize culture, social practices, agency, constructedness, and embeddedness in many of the same ways that economic sociology does (DiMaggio 1994). Rather than being regarded as a separate institution or as a set of ideas, religion is viewed as "lived religion" (Hall 1997) or as "practice" (McDannell 2001). It therefore has economic dimensions and is part of the fabric of communities, social relationships, power arrangements, and policy deliberations in which economic behavior is embedded.

THE CLASSICAL LEGACY

Understanding the recent shifts in orientation is best done in comparison with emphases evident in classical work and studies following in those traditions. The relationships between religion and economic life were emphasized especially by Karl Marx and Max Weber, and to a considerable degree by Émile Durkheim. Their contributions have been examined on many occasions and have been increasingly regarded as open-ended, complex, and multivalent (Calhoun 1996; O'Toole 2001). A brief review will thus be helpful (see also Wuthnow 1994b; Fenn 2001; O'Toole 2001; and Giddens 1975).

Although Marx and Engels ([1846] 1947, 1967) wrote extensively about religion, their work on this topic is scattered and for this reason is best understood within the framework of their larger contributions to the study of capitalism. In their view religion is a form of ideology or consciousness that composes part of the societal superstructure that is in turn shaped by the mode of production and relations of production that form the societal infrastructure. In causal language, religion is thus a dependent variable the shape and content of which are determined by a set of economic conditions. There are of course ways in which religion and other forms of ideology act back upon economic conditions (such as reinforcing passivity or encouraging dissent), but these relations are not as powerful within the larger Marxian understanding of society as the internal dynamics of capitalism itself. Thus, Marx and Engels argue that the shift from agrarian to industrialized societies under capitalism is accompanied by a split between the bourgeoisie who own the means of production and the proletariat who provide labor but do not participate fully in the fruits of their labor because profits are appropriated by the bourgeoisie. Religion reflects this division between bourgeoisie and proletariat. For the bourgeoisie, religion provides legitimation for its power and privilege by emphasizing individualism and the just rewards of entrepreneurialism. For the proletariat, religion becomes in Marx and Engels's famous phrase an "opium of the masses," masking the true source of their oppression through beliefs about the divine nature of inequality and anticipation of rewards in the life to come.

Weber's most important contribution to thinking about religion and economic life is his discussion of the role played by the Protestant ethic in the rise of rational bourgeois capitalism. For Weber, capitalism was encouraged by a wide range of developments, including technological advances that made industrialization possible, separation of business from households, and rational methods of bookkeeping. These, however, were in his view insufficient to explain the rise of capitalism because people still required motivation to save, plan, and work hard in worldly pursuits. The Protestant ethic provided such motivation, Weber claimed. It did so inadvertently by teaching that only God's foreordained "elect" would receive eternal salvation, but emphasizing that God's inscrutability made it impossible for the elect to be certain of salvation. Faced with such uncertainty, Puritans argued that hard work, service, sobriety, and moral discipline were ways of obeying God and that the material success deriving from this kind of behavior could be taken as a sign of God's favor. In subsequent work, Weber compared the world's major religious traditions, showing that each sought to provide a cosmological framework in which life ultimately made sense. All such traditions ran into the problem of evil or theodicy (how a good God or supreme being could permit evil) and thus developed explanations for evil that implied modes of possible salvation. Protestantism and other forms of what Weber termed inner-worldly asceticism were conducive to rational economic behavior, while other religions diverted attention more to mysticism or otherworldly expectations.

Durkheim's *Elementary Forms of the Religious Life* ([1915] 1995) was not as directly concerned with the relationships between religion and economic life as the work of Marx or Weber. But the *Elementary Forms* can be viewed as the culmination of Durkheim's long quest to understand the changing bases of social solidarity under conditions of industrialization. In his early work on the division of labor in society, Durkheim described a shift from what he termed mechanical solidarity, based on homogeneity, to organic solidarity, based on heterogeneity. In complex societies, economic development required an increasing division of labor or occupational specialization that in turn required people to interact because of economic interdependence. Durkheim was concerned, however, that economic exchange alone could not provide a sufficient basis for social cohesion. For this reason, he considered ways of supplementing economic transactions, including occupational and professional organizations, public education, and representative government. He eventually settled on religion as an important way of reinforcing social cohesion because of its capacity for symbolically representing the whole collectivity (the gods, he argued, reflected the collectivity), drawing people together in rituals, and reinforcing social classification schemes demarcating the sacred and the profane. Durkheim nevertheless envisioned religion becoming increasingly focused around what he called the cult of the individual as societies became more economically differentiated.

Marx's discussion of the formative influences of bourgeoisie and proletariat class relations on religion, along with some of Weber's remarks about status groups serving as carriers for religious ideologies, resulted in a long line of scholarship focusing on the relationships between social class and religion (Estus and Overington 1970). Scholars theorized that social class influenced religion in at least two ways. First, social class affected people psychologically, encouraging those with fewer economic opportunities to look more fervently toward the spiritual realm as a kind of substitute for material achievement, and perhaps encouraging the economically privileged to abandon religion altogether. Second, social class exposed people to different subcultures and provided their religious organizations with different amounts of economic wherewithal. For instance, working-class people might join or form sectarian organizations whose patterns of worship required little in the way of professional clergy or elaborate buildings and whose codes of conduct encouraged simple living that might result in upward social mobility.

Weber's work on the relationship of Protestantism to the rise of capitalism generated at least three distinct lines of investigation. First, historians and sociologists have examined more closely the specific linkages between religion and economic behavior in early modern Europe with the aim of seeing whether or not other factors could better account for the rise of capitalism and whether other aspects of Protestant teaching should be emphasized. Second, scholars have compared the economic achievements of Protestants and Catholics to see whether Weber's arguments still hold or have been superseded. And third, scholars have sought to apply Weber's arguments to other cases, such as the Middle Ages or early modern Japan, or to related topics, such as law and political protest.

Durkheim's contributions have resulted in fewer studies concerned specifically with religion and economic life but have generated scholarship on related topics. For example, studies of so-called mass society considered the expansion of commercial markets and the mass media and suggested that Durkheim might be right about religion becoming focused more on the individual. Other studies have combined insights from Durkheim and Tocqueville to suggest that market expansion necessarily increases self-interest that in turn needs to be checked by the kinds of associations and religious rituals that interested Durkheim.

As scholarship became more abundant in these various areas of investigation, observations started to be made about the relationships between religion and economic life that ran counter to classical assumptions or that could not easily be addressed within these earlier frameworks. Investigations of the relationships between social class and religion, for instance, suggested that working-class people were neither as alienated nor as passive as previous arguments had suggested. It became evident, too, that certain kinds of religion, such as fundamentalism, did not fit expected patterns. Fundamentalists were often middle-class people whose adherence to religious orthodoxy could not be explained in terms of economic marginalization. Studies also suggested that resistance to economic injustice was not limited to large-scale political insurrections. Researchers began to question whether some forms of religion might actually be empowering the economically disadvantaged (Scott 1977; Ranajit and Scott 1999). Thinking also began to focus more on passive or quiet resistance of the kind that might take place among women's groups in religious organizations (Higginbotham 1993) or through civic training programs (Verba, Schlozman, and Brady 1995). More broadly, this reorientation in thinking about resistance may have been furthered by the collapse of the Soviet Union, which may have caused some scholars to assume that resistance to oppression created by capitalism would have to come from the inside, as it were, rather than from a completely different form of economy organized around socialism or communism. It was more likely reinforced by the rise of so-called Western Marxism or cultural Marxism (Anderson 1976), which focused more attention on the ways in which power and possibilities for resisting power were built into language, discourse, and social interaction.

Scholarship rooted in Weber's work on Protestantism and capitalism also started to turn in new directions. Research focusing on elective affinities between religious beliefs and certain economic conditions, or on internalized motives connecting the two, gave way to studies that sought to pin down more concretely the social settings in which such affinities and motives might take root. For instance, Zaret (1985) examined how Protestant teachings shifted to put more emphasis on this-worldly achievements, showing that the power relationships among front-line parish clergy, lay parishioners, and higher religious officials needed to be considered. Similarly, Gorski (1993) examined Dutch Calvinist conventicles, showing that Calvinist discipline was not simply a function of beliefs but was enacted and enforced in the small-group meetings of which these conventicles were composed. Scholars also turned Weberian questions about the process of rationalization in new directions. For instance, Dobbin (1994) examined how different ideas of rationality were constructed in European policy debates, and Biernacki (1995) combined Weberian and Durkheimian insights to suggest that industrial firms developed rituals that became encoded in the uses of space and time to reinforce certain understandings of rationality.

The Durkheimian legacy was rich with insights about symbolism, ritual, culture, and classification. Consequently, research following this tradition shifted increasingly toward examining specific settings in which rituals and beliefs sacralized social arrangements and toward paying greater attention to Durkheim's idea of religious experience as a kind of social sensory system (Nielsen 1999, 2001). Douglas (1966) and Foucault (1977), among others, showed that the human body and rituals pertaining to it (including eating and dress) dramatized certain regularities in the economic and political system. Douglas (1986) also examined formal organizations, applying insights from studies of religion and ritual to suggest that these organizations "think" in the sense of making some assumptions more plausible than others. Durkheim's interest in community encouraged other scholars to look more closely at the symbolic boundaries defining race and ethnicity, at public discourse that may undermine a sense of community (Bellah et al. 1985), at the dramatization of collective memory, and at public rituals.

Broader attempts to generalize about modernization also raised questions about the relationships between religion and economic conditions. Modernization theory suggested that economic relations would increasingly become the same everywhere, governed by universal considerations of rationality and market exchange. Yet studies of the spread of these modernizing tendencies suggested that they came about through imitative processes that sometimes consisted of ritualistic performance and display, like religious behavior, rather than being driven by economic principles. Other studies suggested that ethnic and religious communities channeled modernizing processes in different directions and were sometimes powerful, if ambivalent, forces of resistance to these processes. Muslim banking practices (Saeed 1996), Jewish and Muslim antimodernizing movements in the Middle East (Heilman 1992; Euben 1999), and Pentecostal movements in Latin America (Garrard-Burnett and Stoll 1993) served as examples. Phrases such as "selective modernization" and "controlled acculturation" (Antoun 2001) pointed to the importance of looking more closely at local contexts and at processes of resistance and negotiation.

NEW APPROACHES AND ASSUMPTIONS

The scholarly emphases that have emerged over roughly the past two decades contrast sharply with the concepts and assumptions set forth by the classical theorists and in much of the work that followed directly in this lineage. These contrasts are summarized in table 1. The recent work has not developed in specific opposition to the earlier work. It is better understood as a variety of efforts, largely through empirical investigations, to work out some of the questions that the earlier work left unanswered, while remaining indebted to that work for the ways it had framed many of these questions. For instance, recent studies have grappled with the fact that religion seems not to have diminished in importance to the extent that the earlier writers assumed, but these studies have still been interested in how religion is influenced by such processes as urbanization and societal complexity. The recent work has also been influenced by dissatisfaction with the positivist assumptions that guided some of the earlier work and has been less interested in defining and defending disciplinary boundaries. Studies of religion have been particularly eclectic, as the examples discussed in this chapter will illustrate. They represent contributions by scholars in a variety of disciplines and programs, including sociology, anthropology, religious studies, history, and American studies.

Scope of Inquiry

Studies produced by the classical theorists and by scholars following them (which I will refer to simply as old) contrast with more recent (new) approaches in the degree to which they emphasize

TABLE 1. Comparison of Old and New Perspectives

	Old	New
Scope of inquiry	Acontextual, macroscopic, causal generalizations	Contextual, microscopic, acausal interaction
Object of study	Patterns, classification schemes, taxonomies	Processes, contingencies
Explanatory emphasis	Structure, constraint	Agency, empowerment
Locus of power	Ascribed or given, systems of stratification	Negotiated, resistance
View of culture	Values, beliefs, ideas, teachings	Discourse, social practices, production, enactment
Institutional logics	Differentiated, formal, reified, gendered	Transgressive, constructed
Religion	Declining importance, secularization	Continuing presence
Economic action	Rationalized models and markets, autonomous preferences	Socially embedded
Preferred methods	Quantitative, comparative-historical	Qualitative, ethnographic

contextualizing their conclusions. The earlier work privileged the search for acontextual patterns that could be viewed as generalizations or even laws about human society. While this was more true for some of the classical theorists than others (Marx, say, more than Weber), their work was generally concerned with large social phenomena and developments covering considerable territory and time (such as capitalism or the West). Subsequent work often focused more narrowly on, say, a single organization or community, but was oriented toward establishing generalizations (for instance, about religious sects or about social mobility). Recent studies have been less optimistic about finding useful generalizations. These investigations are more likely to emphasize the distinctive characteristics of specific cases or events. While they do not abandon interest in generalizations, they often emphasize contingencies or cases that run counter to previous generalizations.

Object of Study

The old lines of investigation paid a great deal of attention to patterns, causal relationships, typologies, and taxonomies. Broad distinctions became common: traditional versus modern, rational versus nonrational, sacred versus profane, to name a few. The new approaches focus more on processes. Processes are concerned with near-term change rather than long-term developments; they emphasize doing, making, assembling, planning, mobilizing, and creating. The search for patterns went hand in hand with the idea that broad acontextual generalizations could be found. Once scholars became less convinced about finding such generalizations, their interest turned toward describing processes. Patterns deal more with the lay of the land, so to speak, while processes are concerned with what people do and say. The old view might be typified by Marx's description of differences between proletariat and bourgeoisie; the new, by a study that examined how working-class people come together, perhaps through a religious network, to form an opposition movement.

Explanatory Emphasis

While studies continue to emphasize the interaction between social structure and human agency, there has been a notable tilt away from the former and toward the latter. The earlier work was interested in showing how people are constrained by the social structures surrounding them. Studies of working-class churches, for instance, would have emphasized how beliefs and practices were dictated by the stratification system. The newer studies have been interested in seeing departures from such determining factors. They have been more likely to emphasize individuals' and groups' capacity to make decisions and mobilize despite the constraints with which they are faced. A focus on agency is illustrated in studies of religious movements, cultural production, and managerial practice. Whereas structure implies unwitting acceptance, agency suggests that structures supply resources and that actors create strategies.

Locus of Power

In the older view, power was generally built into the system, as it were. It was ascribed by the system of social relationships and by institutions, such as the state, that held formal authority. Power differentials in gender relations or class relations were taken for granted as being relatively fixed, even though they were acknowledged to be exploitative or unjust. Studies of revolutions, collective behavior, and social movements played an important role in shifting attention to possibilities for challenging ascribed power arrangements. Recent work has gone a step further. It has emphasized the role of culture, language, and personal interaction in maintaining power; thus, by localizing power, it has also been able to suggest that power can be negotiated. Resistance has become a topic of increasing interest. Resistance involves constructing new myths, neutralizing the legitimacy of dominant ideas, and subverting the power of dominant groups.

View of Culture

The older view emphasized beliefs and values, ideas, doctrines, and formal teachings. Culture included religion and religious teachings reflected economic conditions, as Marx and to some extent Durkheim argued, or became internalized as motives for action that influenced economic behavior, as Weber emphasized. In the older view, culture was often conceived of as a schema of means and ends, or norms and values capable of guiding goal-oriented behavior. The newer view stresses discourse, cultural toolkits, the symbolic resources through which people make sense of their lives, the dynamic interaction among producers and consumers of culture, and such cultural objects as texts, rituals, and public performances. Many of these emphases are captured in the concept of social practices. Practices are strings of behavior woven together around habits and rules and embedded in traditions and social settings that reinforce their meaningfulness (Turner 1994; MacIntyre 1984). Economic action is harder to separate from culture in the newer view. Advertising, for example, is both cultural and economic; sermons are

cultural but may also be part of the fund-raising campaigns of religious organizations.

Institutional Logics

Institutions were regarded in the older view as formal systems of norms and values that became increasingly differentiated in modern societies. Religion was differentiated from the economy, and thus one could examine relationships between the two. Scholars assumed that the distinguishing features of religion and the economy were inherent in the nature of action within each system. They also wrote inadvertently in ways that differentiated the two; for example, describing economic behavior in masculine terms as rational and public; religious faith in feminine terms as irrational and private. The newer view downplays predefined boundaries separating institutions. While agreeing that there may be different logics in different institutions, it suggests that these logics are socially and culturally constructed. It also emphasizes the transgressive nature of social action: logics from one institution may penetrate another institution (not simply become isomorphic with them through impersonal processes). For example, market logics may be seen in religious settings, and religious rituals may be orchestrated in ways that sacralize economic space.

Religion

The earlier view emphasized secularization as the key to understanding religion's relationship to the economy. Modern economies were thought to function increasingly in terms of secular considerations and thus to marginalize the values espoused by religious people. Studies of religion were concerned with its decline, while studies of economic life were able to ignore religion. The newer view emphasizes the continuing presence of religion in societies characterized by very different kinds of economic relationships. Religion varies and changes qualitatively, but remains a powerful force that must be considered in studying economic behavior. Religion is also understood to be more than a set of ideas and organizations devoted exclusively to otherworldly concerns; religion is a complex of practices that is intertwined with everyday life (and thus with work and consumption), and these practices have economic dimensions and implications (such as spiritual practices that result in heavily funded health and counseling programs).

Economic Action

The economic sphere in the older view was composed of rationalized systems of exchange and thus was understandable in terms of formalized relationships among entrepreneurs and workers, markets, and consumer preferences. The older view held that the economic sphere became increasingly differentiated from other activities, and this autonomy necessitated treating it as if it operated according to its own laws. The newer view emphasizes the social embeddedness of economic action. Exchange takes place among people who interact in noneconomic as well as economic ways. It involves trust and requires that people make sense of their behavior.

Preferred Method

The search for broad generalizations in the older view led scholars to engage in metaempirical theoretical speculation and to privilege comparative and historical research. Increasingly, scholars also relied on advanced statistical analysis of quantitative data in hopes of establishing generalizations. While continuing to make use of comparative, historical, and quantitative data, the newer studies have made greater use of ethnographic research and indepth interviews. Scholars consider qualitative data valuable for understanding the processes, meanings, and complex relationships that may not be illuminated by quantitative data.

While these broad shifts in orientation can be seen in a number of studies, they are not universal. Recent contributions to understanding religion and economic life are seldom framed as studies specifically or exclusively about the relationships between religion and economic behavior. Instead, we must look to a variety of studies to see how scholars currently understand the complex, intertwined social practices that have both religious and economic dimensions. We can see how these practices are being examined by considering recent scholarship in the following areas: ethnoreligious communities, fundamentalism, faith-based organizations, religion and markets, working life, and policy domains.

ETHNORELIGIOUS COMMUNITIES

I will define ethnoreligious communities as subpopulations of larger societies that are bounded by ethnic traditions and distinctive religious customs. Ethnoreligious communities have been interesting sites for research because of questions about their persistence and functioning in relation to immigration and assimilation. Studies of such communities generally recognize that the religious and ethnic practices through which people seek and maintain

identities have implications for the conduct of economic life.

One of the more influential studies of an ethnoreligious community is Robert Orsi's (1985) *Madonna of 115th Street*, an ethnographic history of Italian Harlem from 1880 to 1950. During this period, Italian Harlem underwent dramatic economic and social change, initially as a result of rapid immigration and population growth and later in response to a sagging economy, changing labor market, and new opportunities for employment and housing in the suburbs of New York City. Orsi contends that the social identity of Italian Harlem and the solidarity of its social networks remained remarkably stable despite these dramatic changes. To explain why, he examines the rituals and symbolic practices of the community. Most important of these is the festa that is held every year on July 16. The festa is an all-day event at Our Lady of Mount Carmel on 115th Street that draws the entire community together. Women prepare food and prepare their homes for overnight guests days in advance. After a solemn high mass, the great Mount Carmel parade begins, with thousands of marchers, several bands, and numerous brightly decorated floats and banners. The community then spends the evening in the streets, at the church, and in homes, consuming ethnic food, listening to music, dancing, and socializing.

The festa makes public and emotionally reinforces both the solidarity that holds the community together and the internal demarcations that give it identity. The parade winds through the various neighborhoods and precincts of which Italian Harlem is composed, symbolically tying them together as it progresses. The marchers themselves are organized in groups that reflect the community's ranks and social division: prominent members of the community, such as physicians and lawyers, toward the front; lower-income people and penitents, some walking barefoot, at the rear; priests separated from laypeople; men and boys walking separately from women and girls. The gendered division of labor is further exemplified in the cooking and family rituals, while family loyalty is often demonstrated by the presence of adult children who have moved to the suburbs.

Underlying the festa is what Orsi calls the *domus*, which he says "*is* the religion of Italian Americans" (77). A domus-centered society attaches fundamental loyalty to the family and with it, the domestic space in which the family lives, the gendered work rules that govern that space, and the extended network of kin relations that link home and community. Loyalty to the domus involves eating together, which in turn prohibits transgression of family schedules by work or entertainment. It involves defining money as "family money," rather than individual money, which means that working members of the household contribute to a common pool and that "pin money" (Zelizer 1994) is to be spent on household purchases rather than for personal pleasure. Children are taught to respect their parents and to believe that such respect is a distinctive trait of Italian Americans. Blood ties are considered sacred, and one of the worst forms of punishment is expulsion from the domus. Individual households are linked through complex kin and godparentage (*comari* and *compari*) relationships.

But the domus system necessarily experienced strains as the community underwent economic and social change. First-generation immigrants often expressed fear that the entire social order was in danger of collapse and thus sought to impose a kind of "authoritarian purity" (108) to prevent this from happening. Offspring felt suffocated by unrelenting demands for family loyalty and self-sacrifice. Anger welled up and rivalries developed between competing families and conceptions of status. Dating and marriage became contested issues between generations. Youth gangs developed among young men, and opportunities for freedom, education, and careers for young women were severely restricted.

These strains were not simply resolved, not by the festa and not by people silently slipping away from the community (although many did). The religious and family practices of which the domus was composed instead provided resources with which resistance could be waged. Women especially gained power in this way, seizing control of many of the church's functions, drawing lines that circumscribed the influence of (male) clergy, and demanding allegiance from husbands and sons in the name of ethnic principles. The Madonna symbolized the special authority of women, but also served as an occasion for prayer, expressing anger, seeking forgiveness, and securing comfort. In commemorating the Madonna, the festa provided both a brief respite from the usual burdens and a figure that commended continuing self-sacrifice.

The Madonna of 115th Street was written as a contribution to American religious history, rather than economic sociology, but is rich with implications for the latter. Shades of Marxian concerns about oppression, resistance, and false consciousness are evident, as are Durkheimian themes of ritual solidarity, moral community, and division of labor, and Orsi's discussion of the domus is reminiscent of Weber's treatment of substantive rationality. The analysis is similar to that of historical and anthropological studies of village life. It demonstrates that economic relations are embedded in deeply valued social relationships. In the case of Italian Harlem, demands for a more highly educated, professional, and occupationally specialized labor force eventually did much to undermine the stability of the community, as did changing patterns of racial and ethnic housing. Yet the strength of community ties was also evident in the number of Italian Americans who stayed in the neighborhood, passed up opportunities to take higher-paying jobs elsewhere, and continued to interact regularly with neighbors and relatives. The study does not opt for one-sided answers to questions about resistance and accommodation, but suggests that both happened and that their simultaneity accounts for some of the power of the festa. The study also illustrates the shift away from separating religion from economic life, emphasizing the intermingling of the two in popular religion and the domus. It conceives of religion, not as an internalized set of beliefs and values guiding individual actors, but as social practices that unfold in everyday life and on ritual occasions (Orsi 1997).

Marie Griffith's *God's Daughters* (1997) illustrates how the kind of analysis evident in Orsi's study can be extended beyond a geographically defined community. Griffith's book examines a social movement composed of evangelical and Pentecostal women in the United States known as Women's Aglow. Founded in the early 1970s, the Women's Aglow Fellowship coincided with the women's liberation movement and over the next two decades developed in concert with women's inclusion in the paid labor force to become the largest interdenominational women's mission organization in the United States. Women's Aglow espoused a conservative theological orientation that encouraged submissiveness within the home among women and discouraged their participation in the labor force. Yet its members adapted to changing economic circumstances and, Griffith argues, found ways to resist the strict rules and codes of the movement itself. How was this possible?

Like Orsi, Griffith emphasizes the role of ritual and the religious practices accompanying it. The central ritual for Women's Aglow members was the collective prayer service that took place during weekly meetings of local chapters, many of which ranged from 10 to 20 members. Through praying about their concerns, hearing others pray, telling their personal stories, and studying biblical examples, the women learned a model of "healing and transformation" (17) that empowered them. The stories they told and heard became templates for their own self-identity. Consequently, they came to believe that they could change and often did change. They stood up to abusive husbands, tried harder to be good mothers, went back to school, took jobs, switched churches, and made friends. The prayer groups provided a safe, supportive space in which to imagine being different and the stories furthered the process of imagination.

Griffith's study does not suggest that prayer groups necessarily lead to upward socioeconomic mobility. In many cases, "transformation" meant adjusting emotionally to a bad situation, rather than deciding to escape that situation. Her study, however, illustrates one way in which people in groups may create ideas that reinforce new self-concepts that in turn open new possibilities for economic behavior. It suggests that economic and religious ideas may not be understandable in terms of inherent affinities. Instead, religious convictions become the occasion for social interaction that results in unanticipated consequences. Her study strongly asserts the importance of agency, not simply as a form of willed behavior, but as a manifestation of personal resources (especially a strong self-concept) that become mobilized in religious settings.

Whereas Orsi and Griffith include economic behavior as only one of many social aspects of the groups they studied, Prema Kurien's *Kaleidoscopic Ethnicity* (2002) is more directly concerned with the relationships between religion and economic behavior. Kurien examined differences in temporary migration patterns to Persian Gulf countries, remittance use, and migration-induced social change by comparing three communities in the Indian province of Kerala: Mappila Muslims, Ezhava Hindus, and Syrian Christians. Kurien's comparison of these ethnoreligious communities was prompted by discovering in early phases of her fieldwork that patterns of migration and their effects on sending communities could not be understood in terms of the degree of traditionalism or modernization in these communities. Instead, she found that ethnic and religious differences channeled behavior in significantly different ways. The Muslim village had a high degree of group solidarity and

family structure that was patrilineal, patrilocal, and patriarchal. With high fertility rates and low education levels among women, coupled with strong religious sentiments among both men and women, nearly all the migrants to the Middle East from the village were men, many of whom went with the help of relatives, illegally, or under the guise of making religious pilgrimages. Their remittances flowed to a wide circle of people in the village, were used for religious purposes, and resulted in caste cleavages being eroded. The Hindu village had lower group solidarity, more competition and conflict among groups in the village, matrilocal households, smaller families, and greater equality between men and women. Migrants from the village were predominately male, and they paid professional agents to find them jobs. Their remittances supported elaborate religious rituals involving gift giving among a relatively small circle of family and friends all of which altered members' position in the caste system but did not fundamentally change the system. The Christian community was more individualistic, had nuclear families that were patrilocal, but also had more egalitarian gender relationships, which included later marriages and more younger women in white-collar occupations. Migrants from the Christian community were recruited directly by Middle Eastern companies and included men and women in approximately equal numbers. Remittances were largely retained by the nuclear family and used for savings or dowries; the effect of this pattern was to reinforce the existing caste system.

Kurien's study clearly suggests the importance of taking account of the social relationships in which economic behavior is embedded. She rejects arguments that reduce religion to a set of worldviews or that simply point to everything being connected to everything else. In trying to sort out what matters in her three case studies, she emphasizes that religious and ethnic traditions were longstanding customs that deeply influenced the social structure of each village. These influences were especially evident in defining group boundaries and the status distinctions accompanying these boundaries. Kin networks and gender differences proved to be especially important in understanding the further effects of migration. These networks and differences were relatively stable, but were also reinforced by religious festivals that, in turn, determined to some extent how money would be spent and how honor or shame would be bestowed. Refracted through these social relationships, the patterns of who migrated, how they found employment, what they did with their earnings, and how these earnings subsequently influenced social statuses differed dramatically from village to village (see also Kearney 1986).

FUNDAMENTALISM

Studies of fundamentalism are at first glance an odd place to look for interesting relationships between religion and economic life; yet several considerations have made them attractive: fundamentalism appears to violate assumptions about the decline of religion in modern societies, it may provide opportunities to examine the effects of economic disprivilege on religious beliefs, it may somehow constitute a form of resistance to modern secular society, and it may at least be organized in relatively well-bounded communities that make it attractive as a location for ethnographic research. While earlier studies posited a rather straightforward relationship between economic disadvantage and attraction to fundamentalism as a form of otherworldly solace, research conducted more recently has emphasized more complex relationships.

Nancy Ammerman's *Bible Believers* (1987) was one of a number of studies of fundamentalism conducted in the 1980s as a result of interest sparked by the rise to political prominence of the Reverend Jerry Falwell's Moral Majority movement and a more general reawakening of political activity among American fundamentalists and evangelicals. Ammerman rejected arguments by Hunter (1983) and others who viewed fundamentalism as a belief system embraced by people who remained outside the mainstream of modern economic and cultural influences. She suggested that twentieth-century fundamentalism was more aptly characterized as a religion composed of people who actively rejected these modern influences. Through ethnographic research, she examined how fundamentalist beliefs and practices played off exposure to modernity. The people she studied held regular jobs, usually in lower-middle-class occupations, interacted regularly with nonfundamentalists, and sent their children to public schools. Yet they maintained an alternative "plausibility structure" (Berger 1966) that helped them reject the values and lifestyles of their neighbors and coworkers. This plausibility structure consisted of a clearly articulated set of religious beliefs oriented around the literal truth of the Bible, extensive interaction with other members of their congregation, and high regard for their pastor, who served as a strong authority fig-

ure. In return, they acquired a sense of ultimate meaning in life that exceeded the gratifications they received from their work. Ammerman observed that the group imposed strict gender distinctions on members, calling on women to be submissive and perform nearly all household work, yet (like Griffith) she discovered that the church was also a source of empowerment for these women, particularly through church work and prayer circles that gave them opportunities to redefine themselves.

Ammerman's study provides an interesting look at what it may take for people to develop and maintain alternative values from those associated with the market economy. Fundamentalists at the church she studied did this partially and on a piecemeal basis. Unlike members of communes who may retreat from the larger economy by developing their own means of livelihood and pooling assets, Ammerman's fundamentalists remained involved in the larger economy. They nevertheless contributed amply of time and money to the church, and sometimes made decisions that lowered their children's chances for upward mobility.

The contribution of studies such as Ammerman's is partly to demonstrate that traditional religion and modern economic behavior relate in more complex ways than earlier scholarship may have recognized. Lynn Davidman's *Tradition in a Rootless World* (1991) offers a further contribution of this kind. Davidman conducted participant observation and in-depth interviews among two communities of Jewish women who had chosen to become Orthodox. Nearly all the women were from middle- or upper-middle-class backgrounds, had earned college educations or graduate degrees, and in many cases had already begun successful careers in professional-level jobs. Yet they became discontent, dropped out of these careers or career paths, took lower-paying or menial jobs, and became intensely devoted to Orthodox practices. Davidman was interested in learning what had caused them to drop out and how they made sense of their decision to do so.

She found that dropping out was usually the result of a personal or family crisis, such as a divorce or separation, a romantic relationship ending, an illness, or a death in the family. These crises precipitated deeper questions about meaning in life, which the women said could not be addressed satisfactorily through ordinary careers or consumer behavior. Religion offered them a sense of focus and a source of comfort they had been unable to find elsewhere. Davidman suggests that it was the interaction with other women and feeling of rootedness in a tradition that mattered most, rather than religious beliefs (many were unsure of God's existence). The women nevertheless had to undergo a process of resocialization to become comfortable with their new identities. This process, Davidman says, consisted of focusing increasing attention on private life, substituting religious involvement and more traditional roles as mothers and wives for the earlier family relationships that had gone awry. Interestingly, then, dropping out of mainstream economic life worked better at reconstructing their private lives than it did at providing an alternative way of being engaged in public life.

While Ammerman and Davidman add complexity to previous understandings of the tensions between fundamentalism and economic activities by emphasizing the role of gender, a different approach to these tensions is evident in Susan Harding's *Book of Jerry Falwell* (2000). Harding conducted ethnographic research at Falwell's Thomas Road Baptist Church in Lynchburg, Virginia, in the early 1980s and then turned to examining the wider fundamentalist movement through its sermons, television programs, books, and other publications. Her research pays closer attention to the content and rhetorical style of these materials than most other studies of fundamentalism do (see also Witten 1993). She concludes that there is power in the words themselves, and not just in the social processes involved in fundamentalist communities. She shows, for example, how an interview with a fundamentalist pastor who used the occasion for proselytization drew her in, established a verbal relationship between herself and the pastor's story of himself, and then supplied language that she discovered herself using later to describe her own emotions. Harding emphasizes two ways in which fundamentalist discourse bears on economic behavior. One is a tight, internally consistent set of stories that provides an alternative explanation for world events, including the trajectory of history. Thus, it becomes possible for fundamentalists to believe that history is moving toward final judgment at the hands of God, rather than only experiencing a series of business cycles, and to view an urban setting like New York City as a place of evil rather than evidence of progress. The other is to incorporate advanced thinking about economics and technology into their own ministries. Through an examination of television ministries, for instance, she shows how makeup, camera angles, and styles of speech effectively mimic those of secular television programs while offering a different message.

The significance of studies such as this for broader inquiries in economic sociology lies in at least three areas. First, fundamentalists (and evangelicals, who are somewhat closer in beliefs and lifestyles to those of other Americans) make up a large minority of the American population (not to mention in other parts of the world), which means that studies of general economic patterns may need to take these communities into account. Second, the tensions and processes of resistance and accommodation identified in studies of fundamentalism may be similar to those in other settings, such as communes, ethnic groups, families, or even occupational groups (such as some helping professions) in which relationships with broader market structures are negotiated. And third, these studies suggest some of the ways in which socialization and resocialization occurs—which may resemble processes in high-involvement work settings, such as hospitals, military units, fire companies, and graduate programs.

FAITH-BASED ORGANIZATIONS

The study of faith-based organizations has been motivated by concerns quite different from studies of fundamentalism. Whereas fundamentalist congregations may have only an implicit connection with economic behavior, faith-based organizations bear directly and explicitly on such behavior. Faith-based organizations in the United States are broadly of two kinds: those that engage in service activities and those that focus on community organizing.

The discussion of faith-based service organizations has been prompted by shifts in public policy, particularly the Charitable Choice provision included in welfare reform legislation in 1996 and Bush administration efforts to expand faith-based initiatives in 2001. While much of this discussion lies outside the present chapter and has been considered elsewhere (Cadge and Wuthnow 2003; Wuthnow 2004), several studies have examined faith-based organizations in ways that contribute to new understandings of the relationships between religion and economic life.

Jerome Baggett's (2001) study of Habitat for Humanity situates this religiously initiated nonprofit service organization within a larger discussion of the voluntary sector, which he (following others) contrasts with the for-profit or market sector and the governmental sector. Noting that both Weber and Tocqueville mention the importance of religious teachings about charity to the historic formation of this sector, Badgett argues that religious parachurch organizations make up an important and growing part of the voluntary sector. Why this is the case and what accounts for the success of some organizations, such as Habitat for Humanity, is the question Baggett seeks to answer. He rejects functionalist economistic theories (Weisbrod 1988) that attribute the existence of nonprofit organizations simply to their ability to fulfill economic goals not suited to for-profit organizations. He instead emphasizes Habitat's religious vision, which gave it legitimacy among church leaders who supported it and helped recruit volunteers; its critique of government and the market, which gives it a distinct niche to fill; and its three-tier organizational structure, which imitates businesses and government agencies. More than these, though, he argues that Habitat succeeds by providing tangible ways in which both volunteers and recipients feel empowered. This sense of empowerment also comes about symbolically because volunteers and recipients feel they have extended themselves in bridging class boundaries. Baggett suggests, however, that Habitat is subject to constant pressures from the marketplace: "The market reaches into this institution when the organizational decisions that were freely made at its founding are constrained toward greater commercialization, and when professionalization curtails . . . grassroots participation" (178).

Diane Winston's (1999) study of the Salvation Army tackles questions similar to those of Baggett, but moves further from conventional treatments of the market and its tensions with religious organizations. Tracing the Army's history from its arrival in New York in 1880 through the 1950s, when it was poised to emerge as the nation's largest faith-based nonprofit service organization, Winston argues that the Army's success runs counter to earlier scholars' assumptions about the incompatibility of religion with urban commercial society. The Army succeeded, she suggests, by developing new practices that were suited to this environment: street revivals and open air meetings that took advantage of New York's high population density, its network of soup kitchens and rescue homes for indigent immigrants, fund-raising kettles and bell ringers stationed near department stores, brass bands and colorful garb that attracted journalists, and programs that imitated theater productions. In the process, the Army did not simply become secular, but "sought to saturate the secular with the sacred" (4). It did so by deliberately transgressing boundaries previously separating commercial life from religion. Salvationist parades became flamboyant incursions into commercial territory, women dressed in military uniforms jarred Gilded Age sensibilities, and minstrel shows and vaudeville with religious themes blurred boundaries between piety and entertainment.

As a contribution to economic sociology, Winston's study is most provocative in its emphasis on the ways in which inventive social practices rearrange social categories. A religious organization like the Salvation Army, she contends, should not be regarded simply as a dependent variable that was more influenced by commercial culture than the reverse. Rather, she wants us to see that social change comes about through effective leadership (agency) that not only mobilizes resources but also uses these resources to challenge preconceived ideas about the arrangement of social life. In the case of the Salvation Army, this challenge came about not so much through talk as through performance. Public events, clothing, buildings, and even food became ways of enacting new meanings and relationships. Urban religion was born, and in the process the commercial arena also gained a kind of sanctity it had not known before. Winston's study is thus an example of how recent work that focuses on social practices rather than ideas and beliefs blurs the boundaries between religion and economic activity.

Studies of faith-based community organizing pose a different set of questions that focus more squarely on ways in which religion comes into opposition with economic arrangements. Following the Alinsky model of community organizing developed in the 1950s and 1960s, faith-based community organizing in the United States has enlisted between one and two million volunteers in recent decades. Through regional networks of churches, volunteers undergo training to work with labor unions, stage protest demonstrations, and engage in political action aimed at achieving economic justice for the poor. While studies of these organizations are usually framed in terms of religion and politics (Hart 2001) or religion and race (Wood 2002), they also raise interesting questions about religion and economic behavior.

Mark Warren's (2001) study of the Industrial Areas Foundation Texas Network argues that faith-based community organizing is a potentially important way of opposing economic exploitation in contemporary society. The problem, Warren suggests, is that economic inequality not only dries up economic resources in low-income communities but also reduces the likelihood that low-income families will have social networks and community organizations through which to mobilize their political interests. He finds that in Texas, churches remain one of the few community organizations in low-income communities. Churches' ideology favors helping the poor, and church structures sometimes span racial and social class lines. Yet churches often focus only on personal piety rather than political mobilization. IAF leadership and training played a key role in helping these churches mobilize.

Paul Lichterman (2005) also tackles the question of how religious groups move from focusing on personal piety to taking a more active role in their communities and thus opposing economic inequality. Through an examination of two interfaith coalitions in Wisconsin, he suggests that being interested in helping the needy is not enough. Religious groups that engage in service and advocacy can do so with little sense of what Lichterman calls social membership; that is, participating as a group with other groups on behalf of some larger collectivity. Moving to this level of social awareness, he suggests, depends less on organization or doctrine and more on interactive processes that transform individuals and group identities.

Warren and Lichterman contribute to our understanding of economic sociology by reminding us that religion interacts with economic life through *political* means. In their studies, churches occupy a private or nonpolitical space in most cases, and church members function as isolated individuals—patterns consistent with views of how economic modernization marginalizes religion. Taking a more active stance in opposition to economic inequality and injustice, therefore, requires churches to develop a political voice. Doing so is likely to require outside expertise, training, and leadership, overcoming what Warren refers to as utopian preferences for participatory democracy, and moving toward Lichterman's idea of social membership.

RELIGION AND MARKETS

A variety of studies have focused in new ways on the intersection between religion and markets. Recognizing that markets are a form of economic organization that spills into other realms of life, the authors of these studies have emphasized how religion adapts to these influences. Some studies extend current thinking about markets by suggesting that not-for-profit enterprises like religious organizations compete for customers much like for-profit firms do, and thus develop forms that resemble markets. Other studies take up the idea of market niches and show that niches develop not only through market competition but through the symbolic strategies of religious organizations and through contingent rearrangements of economic and political factors. Yet another line of investigation has examined the marketization of religious practices themselves.

One strand of research has drawn loosely on the idea of market competition to explain the persistence of religion in the United States and relative growth or decline among particular religious groups. This research emphasizes the fact that the United States is characterized by religious pluralism and suggests that pluralism results in a kind of competitive market, similar to markets in the economic sphere, which encourages entrepreneurship and leads to overall religious vitality (Warner 1993). In *The Churching of America, 1776–1990*, Roger Finke and Rodney Stark (1992) examine the rising proportion of Americans who claimed church membership during the nineteenth century and compare the relatively high rates of growth during this period among Baptists and Methodists with lower growth among Episcopalians and Presbyterians. They also examine various other Protestant sects and Catholics and discuss the decline of mainline Protestant denominations in the last third of the twentieth century. Their key analytic device is what they call religious economies. In the United States, they argue, religion is unregulated (unlike in European countries where state churches limit free expression of religion), and thus the relative size of denominations is a function of the choices of individuals. That being the case, religion can be viewed as a kind of market in which religious organizations compete for members. More specifically, the face of religious firms is a function of their organizational structures, their sales representatives, their products, and their marketing techniques. Thus, the relatively high growth rates of Baptists and Methodists in the nineteenth century can be understood as a function of a less restrictive denominational polity, a more aggressive strategy of evangelization and church planting, and a theology that provided people with more persuasive reasons to join (see also Stark and Finke 2000).

A similar argument has been put forth by Iannaccone (1994) in an examination of growth and decline among Protestant denominations in the 1970s and 1980s. He finds that members of "extremist sects" are more likely than members of mainline denominations to devote more time and money to their churches, socialize more with fellow church members, and be less involved in secular organizations. He argues that these findings can be explained by an application of rational choice theory that emphasizes the value of doctrinal and behavioral strictness for discouraging members from being free riders.

Critics (Chaves 1995; Chaves and Cann 1992) argue that hypotheses drawn from rational choice theory are sometimes difficult to disprove or that its applications are limited to a relatively narrow range of religious activities (such as denominational choice). Economic sociologists also stress that differences in independent variables (such as "strictness") still have to be explained and usually require paying attention to cultural factors and institutional arrangements. A study that illustrates the value of bringing in considerations of this kind is Christian Smith's *American Evangelicalism* (1998). Like Iannaccone, Smith is interested in accounting for the growth and high levels of religious commitment among conservative Protestants. But through a national survey and in-depth interviews, Smith shows that strictness provides an inadequate explanation. Self-identified evangelicals are more active than self-identified fundamentalists, despite not being as strict, and these evangelicals are scattered among a number of different denominations. Drawing on Fischer's (1975) concept of subcultures, Smith suggests that self-identified evangelicals have developed an identity as an embattled subculture. They maintain this identity through beliefs and activities that pit themselves against worldliness in the wider culture and against what they perceive as relativism in liberal churches. Within this subculture, they are actually quite diverse and in many ways similar to other Americans, but public pronouncements and a few hot-button issues (such as abortion) maintain their symbolic separation from the wider culture. This subculture, Smith suggests, defines a niche for them in the larger religious market that encourages participation and growth. Smith's study, therefore, illustrates how religious leaders actively create and maintain a market niche for themselves and their followers, rather than being governed by market forces that only bear on the choices of isolated individuals.

Another adaptation of niche theory is illustrated by my study of the comparative success or failure of social movements associated with the Protestant Reformation, Enlightenment, and rise of socialism in Western Europe between the sixteenth and early twentieth centuries (Wuthnow 1989). In this study, economic conditions emerged as important factors in the growth of religious and other ideological movements, but not straightforwardly through market expansion or industrialization. Instead, economic conditions influenced the relative position of status groups, and this influence created space for movements that capitalized on the changing circumstances. I developed arguments about the ways in which niches emerge for social movements by piecing together ideas about the population ecology and institutional environments of organizations with ideas about state building and the political economy of world systems. I suggested that shifts in the configuration of economic resources lead to changes in institutional arrangements, especially conflicts and stalemates between rising and decline elites. Under these conditions, a social space emerges in which social movements can develop. Once a space of this kind emerges, multiple social movements usually occur, which can be analyzed in terms of a three-phase process of production, selection, and institutionalization. The economic environment does not dictate which movements are successful, but movement leaders do attempt to articulate appeals that make sense of changing economic conditions. New ideas are produced by these social movements, not as simple reflections of social conditions but as creative constructions of social horizons, discursive fields that set the parameters for (often polarized) public debates, and figural actors or textualized versions of movement leaders, heroes, and martyrs. Through comparisons of the economic, social, political, religious, and intellectual histories of European countries and regions during the three periods under consideration, I was able to show how the political economy of niche formation helped to account for variations in the rise of the Reformation, Enlightenment, and socialist movements.

Another set of studies has examined the relationships between recent changes in the *quality* of American religion and developments in markets and related activities, such as consumerism. Drawing on Leers (1981), Berger (1963, 1999), and others, this research suggests that insights about markets may be useful for understanding the ways in which people regard their religious commitments and put them into practice. Some of this work emphasizes the fluidity and apparent shallowness of religious commitments, contrasting these commitments with ones of an earlier era that supposedly demonstrated more stability and a more unified sense of self or character (Hunter 2001). These depictions associate superficiality with broader cultural changes brought about by mass-marketed goods and advertising. They sometimes also link religious superficiality to self-interest and an emphasis on personal feelings, which are said to be reinforced by market capitalism (Bellah et al. 1985). Some researchers, however, argue that religion has merely adapted to the commercial culture, changing form but not necessarily being weakened or strengthened in the process (Schmidt 1995).

In *Spiritual Marketplace* (1999), Wade Clark Roof attempts to make sense of a wide variety of late-twentieth-century religious developments by viewing them as if they had taken place, as it were, in a giant supermarket. Building on previous work that described a "new voluntarism" (Roof and McKinney 1987) in American religion and a "generation of seekers" (Roof 1993), Roof emphasizes that choice, religious switching, and eclecticism became more common than in the past among people who came of age in the 1960s. Unlike Iannaccone, he is less interested in explaining the particular denominational choices people make (recognizing that these are only some of the ways in which choice affects religion) and more interested in understanding the phenomenon of the spiritual marketplace itself. He suggests that the spiritual marketplace can be understood in terms of the social world, producers, the audience, and cultural objects. Globalization, which brings non-Western religions to Americans' attention, is an example of a change in the social world. In examining producers, he emphasizes authors, publishing houses, bookstores, and television, all of which have emerged alongside more conventional sources of religious information. The audience, he says, is characterized by self-reflexivity, by which he means awareness of having to make choices, and by anxieties from living in a world of abundant choices. Cultural products that appeal to this kind of consumer include ones that appeal to personal spirituality rather than organized religion, that mix spirituality with health and therapy, and that offer new understandings of gender, sexuality, or ethnicity. Roof suggests that the spiritual marketplace is redrawing the map of American religion, for instance, separating those with more dogmatic or traditional beliefs from self-styled spiritual seekers. He also associates the new contours of spirituality with possible consequences for the economic sphere, such as people feeling dissatisfied with work and money or taking longer to decide on meaningful careers.

Examining some of these same aspects of the spiritual marketplace, my research on American religion has sought to understand changes in the economic sphere in conjunction with changes in other social institutions and then to examine the effects of these changes on religion and spirituality. In *The Restructuring of American Religion* (1988), I extended an earlier argument about the relationship between transitions in international economic arrangements and social movements (Wuthnow 1987) to examine ways in which shifts from an industrial to a service economy, uncertainties about the rules governing international trade, educational upgrading, realignments among elites, and accompanying opportunities for moral experimentation destabilized adherence to traditional denominational and ethnic communities and resulted in new schisms that cut across many of these communities. While this work treated economic factors largely as causal variables, it sought to move away from arguments about direct influences of modernization or commercialization to ones emphasizing social uncertainties brought about by a kind of shifting of gears in economic arrangements. In *After Heaven* (1998a), I turned from public religion to questions about personal spirituality, arguing that a spirituality of dwelling that had become prominent during the 1950s as a result of the Cold War and an emphasis on homes and child rearing was gradually replaced by a spirituality of seeking that drew inspiration from the affluence, social mobility, and social movements of the late 1960s and 1970s, and that remained strong despite political movements in the 1980s that tried to impose moral discipline. In a related work (Wuthnow 1998b) I examined changes in family arrangements, economic organization, politics, and communities, suggesting that expanding markets and technological changes in the capacity to exchange information had resulted in porous institutions that permitted goods, people, and information to flow across institutional boundaries with greater frequency and ease; under these conditions, religious loyalties also became more fluid. These arguments emphasized how economic conditions influence religious practices, but tried to suggest that this influence was mediated by families, neighborhoods, the mass media, social movements, and religious organizations.

While studies of the relationships between religion and markets have been a rich area of investigation, it is clear that scholars disagree on which aspects of markets to emphasize and how exactly to demonstrate their effects on religious behavior. Most studies, however, appear to take for granted that causal influences flow more obviously from economic arrangements to religion than the reverse. That being the case, studies nevertheless dismiss straightforward or one-to-one correspondences between economic conditions and religion, arguing instead that religious movements, entrepreneurs, political agencies, and individuals all play an active role in constructing religious meanings.

WORKING LIFE

Changes in working conditions and the labor force, such as the rise of a professional-managerial class, longer working hours, expansion of the service economy and nonprofit sector, and inclusion of women in the paid labor force, have prompted a number of studies that attempt to relate religion to these changes. As studies of fundamentalists suggest, some of this research has been concerned especially with apparent conflicts between traditional religion and women's inclusion in the labor force. Other research has examined the effects of religious commitment on decisions about the balance between work and family life or on work satisfaction and attitudes toward money. Much of this research draws inspiration from classical theory, such as Weber's discussion of Protestant teachings about vocation and divine calling, or considers churches and synagogues as places where values are shaped. However, some of the new assumptions about religion that I discussed earlier are also evident in this literature.

In a U.S. study of the relationships among moral understandings, religion, work, and money (Wuthnow 1994a, 1996), I suggested that it might be helpful to move past economic explanations that attribute work to workers' desire for money and thus to view work differently from a simple form of utility maximization. I argued that evidence from a wide variety of studies indicates that people do not work only for money but work in order to give what I termed a legitimate account of themselves—to friends and family, coworkers, and themselves. Through in-depth interviews I showed that people do have readily available accounts of why they work, why they work where they do, and what they like and dislike about their work. These accounts connected people's work with their sense of self-identity. However, they were also heavily influenced by the workplace itself, leading people to adopt what I called a "workplace self" that was often disconnected from other values and other aspects of their selves. For instance, people in large

corporations sometimes spoke of their workplaces as if they were "mom and pop" or family stores and emphasized the "ladder" they were climbing instead of how their work might be furthering the good of society or their own fulfillment. Similarly, people constructed accounts about their money and their purchases, but these accounts were more private than the accounts people gave about their work; indeed, there was a noticeable taboo against talking about money. In the absence of public discussions about money, people tended to construct their accounts largely from advertisements that encouraged them to do comparison shopping rather than think about relationships between goods and larger values. I also examined historical changes in the ways people talked about work and money, similarities and differences between working-class and middle-class Americans and between new immigrants and native-born Americans, and suggested how a small minority of Americans have tried to reintegrate their thinking about work with broader considerations from religion, art, literature, and politics. The study suggested that places of employment and economic ways of framing discussions of money do have a powerful influence in people's lives, but sought to show that these influences come about through cultural practices that mask the degree of choice people actually have. In short, people feel that they are exercising choice but fail to see how the range of choices they consider is limited.

Michele Lamont's (2000) study of working men in the United States and France is also concerned with the ways in which people come to understand their work and themselves. The black and white working men she interviewed in the suburbs of New York and Paris were keenly aware that they were employed in low-status occupations. Thus, Lamont was interested in how these men were able to diminish the importance of people in higher-status occupations and make claims about their own worth. She found that black and white workers alike emphasized hard work, personal integrity, and traditional morality as ways of compensating for low socioeconomic status. Religious belief and involvement was especially important in reinforcing their claims about adherence to traditional morality. Being part of a church, for instance, provided these men with talking points to use in arguing that they really were more moral than others who presumably did not attend church. Black workers were more likely than white workers to draw on religious language and within this language to emphasize religious scripts about caring and family loyalty rather than individual morality.

Lamont's study points to the importance in economic sociology of considering the status differentials involved in all economic transactions and to examine how people may neutralize or minimize these differentials. Work is embedded in the larger set of activities and scripts through which people acquire feelings of self-worth. People may emphasize the money they earn as an indication of worth or the cultural tastes that this money supports (as she found in a previous study of professional men; Lamont 1992). Status claims may also emphasize the sheer fact of working hard and doing hard work or activities that may be only peripherally associated with their work, such as hobbies or religion. These sources of self-worth are not matters strictly of private assessment but are part of the social worlds in which people live. They create what Lamont calls a "world in moral order" (17)—a sense that the world is structured or ordered in ways that place a person on the side of good rather than evil.

Research has also contributed to understandings of the conditions under which people may opt out of work oriented toward maximizing economic interests in favor of altruistic pursuits. In *The Heart of Altruism* (1996), Kristen Monroe investigates the outlooks of people during World War II who risked their lives to rescue potential victims of the Holocaust. She argues that psychobiological and economistic explanations that account for such heroic acts in terms of self-interest are unconvincing. She shows instead that rescuers had through family experiences, education, and other socializing experiences developed an overriding sense of common humanity. Thus, they were unable to pass opportunities to rescue humans whose lives were in danger. In *Acts of Compassion* (1991), I examined the seeming contradiction between the United States being a culture driven by economic self-interest and expressive individualism (Bellah et al. 1985) and its high and apparently rising levels of voluntary caring for the needy. Through in-depth interviews and a national survey, I showed that individualists and caregivers were often the same people, rather than two competing segments of the population. The in-depth interviews revealed that people reconcile these two sides of themselves by developing heteroglossic stories about their motives for being altruistic. Heteroglossia permits them to have multiple motives and to register self-interest while also denying it. Nonprofit organizations also help to reconcile altruism with individualism by circumscribing the roles caregivers are expected to play. In *Learning to Care* (1995), I

further examined the process by which people may decide to enter caregiving careers. Through a national study of teenagers, I discovered that community service programs create opportunities for young people to move past idealistic understandings of caring that were common in their families and to develop role-specific views of caring that relate both to their self-identity and their familial values. These community service projects train young people in the kinds of role expectations they will need as they enter careers, but encourage them to channel these expectations toward caregiving careers. Rebecca Allahyari, in *Visions of Charity* (2000), presents a similar idea through her ethnographic study of adult volunteers in service organizations. She demonstrates that volunteers construct moral selves that link their emotions with moral rhetoric that in turn redefines their sense of self-worth.

Research on working lives underscores what economic sociology has also asserted about work and money, namely, that their meanings are worthy of examination (Zelizer 1994). These meanings may be reduced to economic preferences for purposes of modeling economic behavior. But if we wish to achieve a more complete understanding of human life, we need to take into consideration the meaning-making capacity of our species. People construct accounts of their work and money. These accounts are often shaped by the workplace and marketplace in ways that reinforce commitment and derail people from thinking about other pursuits. However, some studies also point to the ways in which behavior that cannot easily be understood in terms of economic calculation, such as altruism, is chosen and regarded as legitimate.

POLICY DOMAINS

Apart from the personal pursuits that characterize individuals in their religious congregations or at work, religion and economic life frequently come together in debates about public policy. Examples include discussions of debt relief for economically disadvantaged countries, which have been put forward by religious organizations, movements nurtured in religious settings that sought to overcome racial discrimination and promote equal economic opportunities, and efforts to halt wars or human rights violations that were deemed by religious groups to be worthwhile even though they may have contradicted arguments rooted in economic self-interest. Although the relationships between religion and economic policy occur at a different level of social organization, studies suggest that some of the same thinking about religious practices and cultural constructions applies.

An important example of work bringing religion together with policy concerns is Melani McAlister's (2001) study of American attitudes toward the Middle East during the last half of the twentieth century. McAlister argues that U.S. policies toward the Middle East were shaped by U.S. oil interests *and* perceptions of the Middle East as a holy land. Her study is thus concerned with pivotal episodes in which these two sources of American attitudes—the economic and the religious—came together. She examines "biblical epics," such as *Ben Hur*, *Quo Vadis*, *The Ten Commandments*, and other films, in the 1950s; the Middle East in African American cultural politics during the era of the civil rights movement; the oil crisis of the 1970s; U.S. relationships with Israel in the 1970s; the Iranian revolution and its aftermath in the 1980s; and the Gulf War and its aftermath in the 1990s. She analyzes a wide variety of materials, including films, popular magazines, newspaper articles, television news, museum exhibits, religious fiction, and sermons. She concludes that U.S. imperial power in the Middle East has been refracted through new lenses that have permitted Americans to make sense of their interests in the Middle East, to see continuity with long-standing images of the region, and to adjust these images to fit new understandings of themselves.

McAlister's study is situated explicitly in relation to Edward Said's (1979) influential treatise on Orientalism, which in turn serves as a link to Max Weber and modernization theory in sociology. Said argued that a long tradition of European and American scholarship, which developed in the eighteenth and nineteenth centuries and ranged from literature and history to the social sciences, depicted the world in a way that privileged and legitimated economic and geopolitical power. In these depictions, the world was divided in two unequal halves, Occident and Orient. One was economically developed, superior; the other, underdeveloped, subordinate; both were described monolithically, and the two stood in a symbiotic relationship, the identity of each depending on the other. Weber's characterization of Western religion as more rational and more conducive to modernization than Eastern religions is an example of the kind of work Said criticized. McAlister identifies two problems with Said's analysis that in her view render it unsatisfactory for understanding American percep-

tions of the Middle East in the postcolonial period. First, his argument that East and West were each viewed as homogeneous entities does not fit Americans' actual and perceived emphasis on internal diversity. Second, his argument that the West has consistently been depicted in masculine terms while the East has been described in feminine terms needs to be reconsidered in light of shifting understandings of gender in the United States.

McAlister shows that American attitudes toward the Middle East adjusted and became more complex during the second half of the twentieth century in conjunction with changing understandings of race, gender, and religion. During the civil rights movement, for example, African American leaders drew on biblical themes of exodus that envisioned continuity with the Holy Land as paradise and symbol of freedom, while growing numbers of African American Muslims sought to distance themselves from oppressive Christianity by identifying with the Muslim Middle East. In the 1970s, the popularity of the Treasures of Tutankhamun exhibit prompted new discussions of the Middle East that, taking place in the aftermath of the 1973 oil embargo, reinforced a rhetoric of imperial stewardship over resources in the Middle East. Racial themes continued in new discussions of whether the ancient Egyptians were black or white. During the same period, American support for Israel came to be understood within a new framework. Israel became "*less* a symbol of religious and cultural affiliation for Americans (as it had been in many ways in the years immediately following the Holocaust and the founding of the state) and more an emblem for a conservative argument about the legacies of Vietnam. In that logic, Israel, unlike the United States, seemed to many to be a nation that was not afraid to fight—and win" (42).

Themes of adaptation and reinterpretation also figure prominently in McAlister's analysis of the Iranian hostage crisis and the Gulf War. In the former, a language of threat and containment developed around an emerging interest in antiterrorism and was accentuated by a reversal of Said's masculine-feminine dichotomy in which American hostages and their families were portrayed with images of domesticity and femininity to construct an "aggrieved space" distinguished by suffering. Portrayals of the Gulf War incorporated America's new sense of its own racial and ethnic diversity by creating images of "military multiculturalism" that depicted the armed forces as a microcosm of the larger society. McAlister anticipates some of the consternation that emerged after the September 11, 2001, attacks on New York and Washington by suggesting that the Gulf War understandings of multiculturalism worked by presenting the Middle East as an outsider and thus excluding consideration of the presence of Arab Americans and other Muslims in the United States.

McAlister integrates these various case studies by borrowing Michael Shapiro's (1994) concept of moral geographies. Each of the various themes that emerges in her analysis constitutes a moral geography or set of "cultural and political practices that work together to mark not only states but also regions, cultural groupings, and ethnic or racial territories" (McAlister 2001, 4). Highlighting these moral geographies is a way of disclosing the silent ethical assertions that guide thinking about a part of the world. In this conception, understandings of the Middle East are not simply frameworks or arguments, but practices that embody public discussion, images, emotion, and behavior. Such practices are often internally contradictory, McAlister says, but on the whole they provide an important cultural underpinning for U.S. national expansion in the Middle East.

The contribution of McAlister's work to economic sociology lies in showing that a foreign policy, such as U.S. policy toward the Middle East, is guided not only by straightforward economic interests, but by an embedding of these interests in cultural frameworks that often carry religious connotations. While her argument might be interpreted simply as one of religion legitimating economic interests, the real contribution of her work is to show how strands of economic and religious reasoning are actually woven together. Her model provides an answer to questions about why economic interests are so robust, even in the face of changing cultural understandings and criticism. Imperial power is not easily diagnosed or criticized because of its capacity to surround itself with these complex threads of meaning. Resistance rooted in new understandings of racial and gender identity was absorbed into American attitudes toward the Middle East, criticizing earlier notions of American power, but at the same time transforming the United States into a postcolonial power intent on defending its interests. Her work suggests the importance of examining pivotal moments in which public debate emerged around policy issues and of focusing not only on specific policies themselves but on the collateral images from film, religion, and other sources that frame attitudes toward policies. Understanding these pivotal events requires

paying attention to the producers of culture, such as filmmakers and religious leaders, and looking at interaction among these producers, rather than focusing only on a single source, such as religion or film.

John Evans (2002) illustrates a different approach to the relationships between religion and economic policies in his study of bioethics. Although human genetic engineering (HGE) may be less obviously a matter of economic policy than U.S. relations to the Middle East, the technology underlying HGE and its implications for business are indications of its relevance. Evans observes that in the 1960s theologians were among the first to raise ethical questions about HGE and did so in reference to broad considerations about human nature. Between the early 1960s and mid 1990s, though, public debates about HGE policy came increasingly to be dominated by professional bioethicists who focused on more practical issues, such as feasibility, cost, risk reduction, and byproducts. The shift can, in one sense, be viewed as a straightforward process of rationalization (including secularization) of the kind Weber described (from a consideration of ends to a focus on adjusting ends to fit means). Evans argues, however, that this shift from what he terms substantive rationality to formal rationality did not come about automatically. Rather, it occurred through a series of discussions that resulted in increasing intervention by government agencies. Between the late 1950s and early 1970s, theologians and scientists mostly debated the issue in substantive terms having to do with broad arguments about ends. During the late 1970s and early 1980s, scientists advocated the creation of government advisory commissions. These commissions asked for a formally rational type of argumentation that, in turn, resulted in the emergence of a new profession called bioethics. As professional bioethicists came increasingly into the picture, they challenged arguments about broad human ends as being too vague, but gradually institutionalized their own conceptions of ends, which included beneficence and autonomy. With growing interest in HGE within the research community, autonomy increasingly replaced beneficence.

Evans's study, then, falls squarely within the Weberian tradition of asking questions about potential conflict and accommodation between religious values and economic interests. More so than McAlister's, his argument focuses on explaining a series of specific policy outcomes (decisions to authorize stem cell research, for example). His study illustrates the importance, as economic sociologists also urge, of situating economic decisions in institutional contexts. When economic decisions become matters of public debate, government is likely to be invited to arbitrate, but its intervention may alter both the terms of debate and the set of participants who are invited to the table. Other studies that point to similar conclusions (although not necessarily with reference to religion) include Steensland's (2002) investigation of moral claims in debates about public welfare policy during the Nixon and Carter administrations, Espeland's (1998) study of water policies in the Southwest, and Moody and Thévenot's (2000) discussion of environmental policies in California and France.

FUTURE DIRECTIONS

The institutionalization of economic sociology as a subdiscipline appears to have (perhaps ironically) been accompanied by a wider variety of scholarship that does not claim this label but contributes in its own way toward greater understanding of economic behavior, including the role of religion in this behavior. Future work will probably be guided to some extent by two opposing tendencies: an elevation of disciplinary walls aimed at defining what counts as economic sociology and what does not, and growth in scholarship that draws eclectically from a variety of disciplines and subdisciplines.

I have tried to suggest that recent studies of religion and economic life stand loosely in the tradition defined by Marx, Weber, Durkheim, and other earlier contributors to the social sciences. But scholarly inquiries develop both by tracing lineage to earlier work and by rejecting that work (Zald 1995). Some of the present diversity is a reflection of the fact that scholars have disagreed about the importance of various interpretations of the classics from virtually the start. I do not propose, therefore, that the studies discussed here represent anything like a new paradigm. Rather, there are certain common tendencies in some of this work and, at the same time, serious points of disagreement.

The common tendencies include paying close attention to what can broadly be considered culture, now conceived less as mental or internalized ideas and values and more as enacted practices of ideological and ritual production, discourse, and symbolization. Economic behavior is understood to be guided less by internalized preferences and more by active interpretation and negotiation that takes place within fields of symbolic messages and

imagery. The common tendencies also include focusing on interactive processes involving economic resources, interest groups, power arrangements, media, gender roles, and religious institutions, rather than assuming that the relationships between economic conditions and religious behavior can be understood in terms of the social psychology of individual actors (Swidler and Arditi 1994). The points of disagreement concern which of these various factors to emphasize, whether rational choice models are helpful or unhelpful, and how much to think about religion's relative autonomy from economic conditions or its dependence on these conditions.

One conclusion that can scarcely be ignored is that much of the recent work seems to have abandoned claiming to being scientific. Particularities replace the quest for universals and description takes precedence over causal analysis. This makes it difficult to say whether or not the recent work represents progress or not. But it is equally clear that recent scholarship continues to be a rigorous search for verifiable evidence and that it is organized around central questions that bear the marks of earlier studies. In this sense, recent studies contribute to our understanding of religion and economic life by filling in gaps, addressing puzzling empirical regularities, and illustrating the complexity of human behavior.

We should not minimize the importance of studies emphasizing the messiness of economic transactions and preferences. Economics has advanced by bracketing much of this messiness in order to discover aspects of social interaction that can be understood in terms of simple models. Economic sociology reminds us that these models are simplifications of real life. Studies of religion cannot be interpreted as showing that economic life is rational while religious belief is irrational. Rather, these studies show that both religious and economic practices depend on assumptions that in turn are influenced by the communities in which people live and the circumstances in which they work.

Having established that social life is messy, scholars now face the more difficult task of reimposing some order on that messiness. Thus far, the quest for such reordering has taken place within the context of multiple analytic languages and competing perspectives. This will probably continue. But there may also be a desire among the next generation of scholars for greater closure and consensus. Paying closer attention to frequently used concepts, such as markets, rationality, and resistance, and emphasizing the influences of power, gender relationships, inequality, and the cultural construction of meaning, may be fruitful first steps.

The greatest empirical challenge will be pushing research beyond relatively accessible sites to those that have been more shielded from public view. Churches are relatively accessible, for instance, whereas corporate boardrooms are less so. Interviews can ask individuals about religion's influences on their private lives, but it is more difficult to learn how the lending policies of major banks may be influenced by noneconomic criteria such as religious or moral values. Studies of remittances appear especially promising; yet it will be hard for researchers to gain access to informal economies that may govern remittances through ethnic or religious loyalties.

One final observation is that economic sociology and sociology of religion have often been guided by scholars' desire to establish their subdisciplines as legitimate enterprises. This desire has led to a certain amount of understandable and useful disciplinary posturing. What has remained evident, though, are some of the normative concerns that animated the earliest work in these fields—concerns about inequality, injustice, power, resistance, representation, meaning, and fulfillment, to name a few. If these concerns continue, then future scholarship will stand proudly in the lineage initiated by the founders of our field.

NOTE

1. In the chapter I wrote for the first edition of this handbook (Wuthnow 1994b), I focused on the contributions of classical economics and of the Weberian, Marxian, and Durkheimian traditions to the discussion of religion and economic life and discussed theoretical elaborations of those traditions, chiefly with respect to questions of religion and ethical restraint, theories of action, the relationships between means and ends, rationality, the calling and work, stewardship and money, and the poor and economic justice; the present chapter is completely new and reflects both the substantial research that has been devoted to the relationships between religion and economic life in the past few years and my own rethinking about the dominant orientation of this research.

REFERENCES

Allahyari, Rebecca Anne. 2000. *Visions of Charity: Volunteer Workers and Moral Community.* Berkeley and Los Angeles: University of California Press.

Ammerman, Nancy Tatom. 1987. *Bible Believers: Fundamentalists in the Modern World.* New Brunswick, N.J.: Rutgers University Press.

Anderson, Perry. 1976. *Considerations on Western Marxism.* London: NLB.

Antoun, Richard T. 2001. *Understanding Fundamentalism: Christian, Islamic, and Jewish Movements.* Walnut Creek, Calif.: AltaMira.

Baggett, Jerome P. 2001. *Habitat for Humanity: Building Private Homes, Building Public Religion.* Philadelphia: Temple University Press.

Becker, Penny Edgell. 1999. *Congregations in Conflict: Cultural Models of Local Religious Life.* Cambridge: Cambridge University Press.

Beckford, James A. 1985. "The Insulation and Isolation of the Sociology of Religion." *Sociological Analysis* 46:347–54.

Bellah, Robert N., Richard Madsen, William M. Sullivan, Ann Swidler, and Steven M. Tipton. 1985. *Habits of the Heart: Individualism and Commitment in American Life.* Berkeley and Los Angeles: University of California Press.

Berger, Peter L. 1963. "A Market Model for the Analysis of Ecumenicity." *Social Research* 30:77.

———. 1966. *The Sacred Canopy: Elements of a Sociological Theory of Religion.* New York: Doubleday.

———. 1999. "The Desecularization of the World: A Global Overview." Pp. 1–18 in *The Desecularization of the World: Resurgent Religion and World Politics,* ed. Peter L. Berger. Grand Rapids, Mich.: Eerdmans.

Biernacki, Richard. 1995. *The Fabrication of Labor: Germany and Britain, 1640–1914.* Berkeley and Los Angeles: University of California Press.

Cadge, Wendy, and Robert Wuthnow. 2003. "Religion and the Nonprofit Sector." Pp. 444–66 in *The Nonprofit Sector: A Research Handbook,* ed. Richard Steinberg and Walter Powell. 2d ed. New Haven: Yale University Press.

Calhoun, Craig. 1996. "Whole Classics? Which Readings? Interpretation and Cultural Difference in the Canonization of Sociological Theory." Pp. 70–96 in *Social Theory and Sociology,* ed. S. P. Turner. Oxford: Blackwell.

Chaves, Mark. 1995. "On the Rational Choice Approach to Religion." *Journal for the Scientific Study of Religion* 34:98–104.

———. 1997. *Ordaining Women: Culture and Conflict in Religious Organizations.* Cambridge: Harvard University Press.

Chaves, Mark, and David E. Cann. 1992. "Regulation, Pluralism, and Religious Market Structure: Explaining Religion's Vitality." *Rationality and Society* 4: 272–90.

Coleman, James A. 1990. *Foundations of Social Theory.* Cambridge: Harvard University Press.

Davidman, Lynn. 1991. *Tradition in a Rootless World: Women Turn to Orthodox Judaism.* Berkeley and Los Angeles: University of California Press.

DiMaggio, Paul J. 1994. "Culture and Economy." Pp. 27–57 in *The Handbook of Economic Sociology,* ed. Neil J. Smelser and Richard Swedberg. New York:

Russell Sage Foundation; Princeton: Princeton University Press.

Dobbin, Frank. 1994. *Forging Industrial Policy: The United States, Britain, and France in the Railway Age*. Cambridge: Cambridge University Press.

Douglas, Mary. 1966. *Purity and Danger: An Analysis of Concepts of Pollution and Taboo*. London: Penguin.

———. 1986. *How Institutions Think*. Syracuse: Syracuse University Press.

Durkheim, Émile. [1915] 1995. *Elementary Forms of the Religious Life*. Trans. by Karen Fields. New York: Free Press.

Espeland, Wendy Nelson. 1998. *The Struggle for Water: Politics, Rationality, and Identity in the American Southwest*. Chicago: University of Chicago Press.

Estus, Charles W., and Michael A. Overington. 1970. "The Meaning and End of Religiosity." *American Journal of Sociology* 75:760–78.

Etzioni, Amitai. 1988. *The Moral Dimension: Toward a New Economics*. New York: Free Press.

Euben, Roxanne. 1999. *Enemy in the Mirror: Islamic Fundamentalism and the Limits of Modern Rationalism*. Princeton: Princeton University Press.

Evans, John H. 2002. *Playing God? Human Genetic Engineering and the Rationalization of Public Bioethical Debate, 1959–1995*. Chicago: University of Chicago Press.

Fenn, Richard K., ed. 2001. *The Blackwell Companion to Sociology of Religion*. Oxford: Blackwell.

Finke, Roger, and Rodney Stark. 1992. *The Churching of America, 1776–1990: Winners and Losers in Our Religious Economy*. New Brunswick, N.J.: Rutgers University Press.

Fischer, Claude. 1975. "Toward a Subcultural Theory of Urbanism." *American Journal of Sociology* 80: 1319–41.

Foucault, Michel. 1977. *Discipline and Punish: The Birth of the Prison*. Trans. Alan Sheridan. New York: Random House.

Fukuyama, Francis. 1995. *Trust: The Social Virtues and the Creation of Prosperity*. New York: Free Press.

Garrard-Burnett, Virginia, and David Stoll, eds. 1993. *Rethinking Protestantism in Latin America*. Philadelphia: Temple University Press.

Giddens, Anthony. 1975. *The Class Structure of Advanced Societies*. New York: Harper.

Gorski, Philip S. 1993. "The Protestant Ethic Revisited: Disciplinary Revolution and State Formation in Holland and Prussia." *American Journal of Sociology* 99:265–316.

Granovetter, Mark. 1990. "The Old and the New Economic Sociology: A History and an Agenda." Pp. 89–112 in *Beyond the Marketplace: Rethinking Economy and Society*, ed. Roger Friedland and A. Robertson. New York: Aldine.

Griffith, R. Marie. 1997. *God's Daughters: Evangelical Women and the Power of Submission*. Berkeley and Los Angeles: University of California Press.

Hall, David D., ed. 1997. *Lived Religion in America: Toward a History of Practice*. Princeton: Princeton University Press.

Harding, Susan Friend. 2000. *The Book of Jerry Falwell: Fundamentalist Language and Politics*. Princeton: Princeton University Press.

Hart, Stephen. 2001. *Cultural Dilemmas of Progressive Politics: Styles of Engagement among Grassroots Activists*. Chicago: University of Chicago Press.

Heilman, Samuel. 1992. *Defenders of the Faith: Inside Ultra-Orthodox Jewry*. New York: Schocken Books.

Higginbotham, Evelyn Brooks. 1993. *Righteous Discontent: The Women's Movement in the Black Baptist Church, 1880–1920*. Cambridge: Harvard University Press.

Hoge, Dean R. 1996. *Money Matters: Personal Giving in American Churches*. Louisville: Westminster John Knox.

Hunter, James Davison. 1983. *American Evangelicalism: Conservative Religion and the Quandary of Modernity*. New Brunswick, N.J.: Rutgers University Press.

———. 2001. *The Death of Character: On the Moral Education of America's Children*. New York: Basic Books.

Iannaccone, Laurence R. 1994. "Why Strict Churches Are Strong." *American Journal of Sociology* 99: 1180–211.

Kearney, Michael. 1986. "From the Invisible Hand to Visible Feet: Anthropological Studies of Migration and Development." *Annual Reviews of Anthropology* 15:331–61.

Kurien, Prema. 2002. *Kaleidoscopic Ethnicity: International Migration and the Reconstruction of Community Identities in India*. New Brunswick, N.J.: Rutgers University Press.

Lamont, Michèle. 1992. *Money, Morals, and Manners: The Culture of the French and the American Upper-Middle Class*. Chicago: University of Chicago Press.

———. 2000. *The Dignity of Working Men: Morality and the Boundaries of Race, Class, and Imagination*. Cambridge: Harvard University Press.

Lears, T. Jackson. 1981. *No Place of Grace: Antimodernism and the Transformation of American Culture, 1880–1920*. New York: Pantheon.

Lichterman, Paul. 2005. *Elusive Togetherness: Religion in the Quest for Civic Renewal*. Princeton: Princeton University Press.

MacIntyre, Alasdair. 1984. *After Virtue: A Study in Moral Theory*. 2d ed. Notre Dame: University of Notre Dame Press.

Marx, Karl, and Friedrich Engels. [1846] 1947. *The German Ideology*. New York: International Publishers.

———. 1967. *The Communist Manifesto*. London: Penguin.

McAlister, Melani. 2001. *Epic Encounters: Culture, Media, and U.S. Interests in the Middle East, 1945–2000*. Berkeley and Los Angeles: University of California Press.

McDannell, Colleen, ed. 2001. *The Practice of Religions*

in the United States. 2 vols. Princeton: Princeton University Press.

Meyer, John W., and Brian Rowan. 1991. "Institutionalized Organizations: Formal Structure as Myth and Ceremony." Pp. 41–62 in *The New Institutionalism in Organizational Analysis*, ed. Walter W. Powell and Paul J. DiMaggio. Chicago: University of Chicago Press

Monroe, Kristen Renwick. 1996. *The Heart of Altruism: Perceptions of a Common Humanity*. Princeton: Princeton University Press.

Moody, Michael and Laurent Thévenot. 2000. "Comparing Models of Strategy, Interests, and the Public Good in French and American Environmental Disputes." Pp. 273–306 in *Rethinking Comparative Cultural Sociology: Repertoires of Evaluation in France and the United States*, ed. Michèle Lamont and Laurent Thévenot. Cambridge: Cambridge University Press.

Moore, R. Laurence. 1994. *Selling God: American Religion in the Marketplace of Culture*. Oxford: Oxford University Press.

Nielsen, Donald A. 1999. *Three Faces of God: Society, Religion, and the Categories of Totality in the Philosophy of Émile Durkheim*. Albany: State University of New York Press.

———. 2001. "Transformations of Society and the Sacred in Durkheim's Religious Sociology." Pp. 120–32 in *The Blackwell Companion to Sociology of Religion*, ed. Richard K. Fenn. Oxford: Blackwell.

Orsi, Robert Anthony. 1985. *The Madonna of 115th Street: Faith and Community in Italian Harlem, 1880–1950*. New Haven: Yale University Press.

———. 1997. "Everyday Miracles: The Study of Lived Religion." Pp. 3–21 in *Lived Religion in America: Toward a History of Practice*. Princeton: Princeton University Press.

O'Toole, Roger. 2001. "Classics in the Sociology of Religion: An Ambiguous Legacy." Pp. 133–60 in *The Blackwell Companion to Sociology of Religion*, ed. Richard K. Fenn. Oxford: Blackwell.

Portes, Alejandro, ed. 1998. *The Economic Sociology of Immigration: Essays on Networks, Ethnicity, and Entrepreneurship*. New York: Russell Sage Foundation.

Portes, Alejandro, and Ruben G. Rumbaut. 1990. *Immigrant America: A Portrait*. Berkeley and Los Angeles: University of California Press.

Powell, Walter W., and Paul J. DiMaggio, eds. 1991. *The New Institutionalism in Organizational Analysis*. Chicago: University of Chicago Press.

Putnam, Robert D. 2000. *Bowling Alone: The Collapse and Revival of American Community*. New York: Simon and Schuster.

Ranajit, Guha, and James C. Scott. 1999. *Elementary Aspects of Peasant Insurgency in Colonial India*. Durham, N.C.: Duke University Press.

Ronsvale, John, and Sylvia Ronsvale. 1996. *Behind the Stained Glass Windows: Money Dynamics in the Church*. Grand Rapids, Mich.: Baker.

Roof, Wade Clark. 1993. *A Generation of Seekers: The Spiritual Journeys of the Baby Boom Generation*. San Francisco: Harper Collins.

———. 1999. *Spiritual Marketplace: Baby Boomers and the Remaking of American Religion*. Princeton: Princeton University Press.

Roof, Wade Clark, and William McKinney. 1987. *American Mainline Religion: Its Changing Shape and Future*. New Brunswick, N.J.: Rutgers University Press.

Saeed, Abdullah. 1996. *Islamic Banking and Interest: A Study of the Prohibition of Riba and Its Contemporary Interpretation*. Leiden: E. J. Brill.

Said, Edward. 1979. *Orientalism*. New York: Vintage.

Schmidt, Leigh Eric. 1995. *Consumer Rites: The Buying and Selling of American Holidays*. Princeton: Princeton University Press.

Scott, James C. 1977. *Moral Economy of the Peasant: Rebellion and Subsistence in Southeast Asia*. New Haven: Yale University Press.

Seligman, Adam B. 1997. *The Problem of Trust*. Princeton: Princeton University Press.

Selznick, Philip. 1994. *The Moral Commonwealth: Social Theory and the Promise of Community*. Berkeley and Los Angeles: University of California Press.

Shapiro, Michael. 1994. "Moral Geographies and the Ethics of Post-sovereignty." *Public Culture* 3:41–70.

Smith, Christian. 1998. *American Evangelicalism: Embattled and Thriving*. Chicago: University of Chicago Press.

Stark, Rodney, and Roger Finke. 2000. *Acts of Faith: Explaining the Human Side of Religion*. Berkeley and Los Angeles: University of California Press.

Steensland, Brian. 2002. "The Failed Welfare Revolution: Policy, Culture, and the Struggle for Guaranteed Income in the U.S., 1964–1980." Ph.D. diss., Princeton University.

Swedberg, Richard. 1991. "Major Traditions of Economic Sociology." *Annual Review of Sociology* 17:251–76.

Swidler, Ann, and Jorge Arditi. 1994. "The New Sociology of Knowledge." *Annual Review of Sociology* 20: 305–29.

Turner, Stephen. 1994. *The Social Theory of Practices: Tradition, Tacit Knowledge, and Presuppositions*. Chicago: University of Chicago Press.

Vallet, Ronald E., and Charles E. Zech. 1995. *The Mainline Church's Funding Crisis: Issues and Possibilities*. Grand Rapids, Mich.: Eerdmans.

Verba, Sidney, Kay Lehman Schlozman, and Henry E. Brady. 1995. *Voice and Equality: Civic Voluntarism in American Politics*. Cambridge: Harvard University Press.

Warner, R. Stephen. 1993. "Work in Progress toward a New Paradigm for the Sociological Study of Religion in the U.S." *American Journal of Sociology* 98:1044–93.

Warren, Mark R. 2001. *Dry Bones Rattling: Community Building to Revitalize American Democracy*. Princeton: Princeton University Press.

Weber, Max. [1922] 1993. *The Protestant Ethic and the Spirit of Capitalism*. Trans. by Talcott Parsons. New York: Scribners.

Weisbrod, Burton A. 1988. *The Nonprofit Economy*. Cambridge: Harvard University Press.

Wilson, William Julius. 1980. *The Declining Significance of Race: Blacks and Changing American Institutions*. 2d ed. Chicago: University of Chicago Press.

Winston, Diane. 1999. *Red-Hot and Righteous: The Urban Religion of the Salvation Army*. Cambridge: Harvard University Press.

Witten, Marsha G. 1993. *All Is Forgiven: The Secular Message in American Protestantism*. Princeton: Princeton University Press.

Wood, Richard L. 2002. *Faith in Action: Religion, Race, and Democratic Organizing in America*. Chicago: University of Chicago Press.

Wuthnow, Robert. 1987. *Meaning and Moral Order: Explorations in Cultural Analysis*. Berkeley and Los Angeles: University of California Press.

———. 1988. *The Restructuring of American Religion: Society and Faith since World War II*. Princeton: Princeton University Press.

———. 1989. *Communities of Discourse: Ideology and Social Structure in the Reformation, the Enlightenment, and European Socialism*. Cambridge: Harvard University Press.

———. 1991. *Acts of Compassion: Caring for Others and Helping Ourselves*. Princeton: Princeton University Press.

———. 1994a. *God and Mammon in America*. New York: Free Press.

———. 1994b. "Religion and Economic Life." Pp. 620–46 in *The Handbook of Economic Sociology*, ed. Neil J. Smelser and Richard Swedberg. New York: Russell Sage Foundation; Princeton: Princeton University Press.

———. 1995. *Learning to Care: Elementary Kindness in an Age of Indifference*. Oxford: Oxford University Press.

———. 1996. *Poor Richard's Principle: Recovering the American Dream through the Moral Dimension of Work, Business, and Money*. Princeton: Princeton University Press.

———. 1998a. *After Heaven: Spirituality in America since the 1950s*. Berkeley and Los Angeles: University of California Press.

———. 1998b. *Loose Connections: Joining Together in America's Fragmented Communities*. Cambridge: Harvard University Press.

———. 2004. *Saving America? Faith-Based Services and the Future of Civil Society*. Princeton: Princeton University Press.

Zald, Mayer N. 1995. "Progress and Cumulation in the Human Sciences after the Fall." *Sociological Forum* 10:455–79.

Zaret, David. 1985. *The Heavenly Contract: Ideology and Organization in Pre-Revolutionary Puritanism*. Chicago: University of Chicago Press.

Zelizer, Viviana A. 1994. *The Social Meaning of Money*. New York: Basic Books.

27 Gender and Economic Sociology

Paula England and Nancy Folbre

THIS CHAPTER concerns the role of gender in the economy, how the conceptual tools of economic sociology help us understand gender in the economy, and how gender studies provide a lens from which to reconsider the boundaries and claims of economic sociology. We start with a discussion of what topics economic sociology covers, arguing that subtle gender bias may have caused us to focus on formal organizations and exclude household behavior and much of even the paid care sector from economic sociology. If we take a broader view of the "economy," it includes households, the organizations in which people work for pay and from which they purchase goods and services, and the markets in which any of these are embedded. We then discuss the conceptual toolkit usually associated with economic sociology: (1) social networks, (2) culture, norms, and institutions, and (3) critiques of neoclassical economics. We appreciate these tools, but express disappointment that economic sociologists have not taken a more integrative view. We prefer to integrate what is valuable from the rational choice perspective of economists' analysis of market phenomena with considerations of networks and institutions, rather than rejecting the economic view whole cloth. We are equally disappointed that economists have taken so little interest in sociologists' insights. We apply our integrative view of economic sociology to explaining gender differentiation and inequality in paid employment and the household. We consider occupational sex segregation and the sex gap in pay. In the household, we consider couples' division of labor, power dynamics, and exits from marriages. We also consider the "care sector" that cross-cuts the family, paid employment, and the state. We focus on employment and household activities because most gender patterns are rooted in these two venues; most of us spend most of our time on the job and at home.

GENDER AND THE SUBJECT MATTER OF ECONOMIC SOCIOLOGY

What is the subject matter of economic sociology? For the most part the boundaries of economic sociology have been set de facto rather than with programmatic statements. De facto, the post-1980 iteration of the subfield has come largely from sociologists studying formal organizations, mostly in the private sector. These sociologists, such as Granovetter (1985), Burt (1982), White (1981), and Powell and DiMaggio (1991), have disagreed with both the orthodox economic theory of the firm and the newer "neoclassical institutionalism." The latter includes the transaction cost economics of Oliver Williamson (1985) and theories of implicit contracts and efficiency wages (discussed in England 1992, chap. 2). The longer tradition of economic sociology, described in Smelser and Swedberg's (1994) introduction to the earlier edition of this handbook, also de facto took "the economy" to be largely the activities of owners, managers, and workers of businesses as they hire workers, carry out their jobs, produce goods and services, and sell them to other businesses or consumers. This is made more explicit by Fligstein (2002), who says that economic sociology is about market behavior. These topical boundaries are quite consistent with how economists have traditionally defined the arena they study (although they have included consumer behavior more than economic sociologists typically have).

This topical delineation of the field of economic sociology has not gone unchallenged. Indeed, Milkman and Townsley's chapter on "Gender and the Economy"[1] in the previous (1994) edition of this handbook begins this way:

Economic life is organized around gender in all known human societies. Despite this fact, conventional economic analysis [by which the authors refer to writings of economists] characteristically excludes women and their activities from serious research and inquiry. . . . The challenge is to integrate the insights of the new gender-centered scholarship into the broader sociological critique [of economic views] emphasizing the social and cultural embeddedness of economic categories that is now being developed. . . . Although cultural and social constructions of gender, as well as psychological processes, sexual dynamics, and social re-production [by which the authors refer to the rearing and socialization of children] more broadly, are critical to broader economic processes, they have been ignored or treated as epiphenomenal in conventional economic analysis. When they are considered at all, these "noneconomic" practices and processes are often constructed as "intersecting" or as lying "adjacent" to the economy proper. (600)

Milkman and Townsley subsequently remark,

Economic sociology as a field has yet to be truly sensitized to the gender dimension of economic life. The recent flurry of attention to the Polanyian concept of embeddedness, which has striking gender implications, has yet to persuade most sociologists of the economy to seriously integrate gender concerns into their analyses. Gender-centered research, although plentiful, remains essentially ghettoized and ignored by the mainstream. (614)

Zelizer (2002) argues that economic sociology and economics still have a narrow view, and suggests that gender bias may produce the exclusion of the household from the boundaries of economic sociology.

We argue here for a broader view of economic sociology. In the introduction to the previous edition of this handbook, Smelser and Swedberg (1994) argue for a broad definition of the field: "the application of the frames of reference, variables, and explanatory models of sociology to that complex of activities concerned with the production, distribution, exchange, and consumption of scarce goods and services" (3). Clearly that definition would include production in the household—the making of meals, cleaning of houses, and delivering by parents of child care and educational services to children. The fact that these are usually services rather than goods is no reason not to include them, since an increasing proportion of the paid economy is services. The broader definition would include the large distributive flows of resources (money and time) that pass between spouses, extended family members living apart, adult children and their parents, and parents and chil-

dren. Yet these matters were little discussed in the previous edition of the handbook except in the chapter on gender mentioned above. The chapters in the book were largely about what goes on in firms or the markets in which firms participate, except in a final section titled "Intersections of the Economy," where the relationship of "the economy" and education, gender, religion, leisure, the state, and the environment were considered. Even Portes's (1994) entry on the informal economy excluded housework and child rearing in the home from both the formal and informal economy. This was presumably due to his definition of the informal economy as activity outside established institutional rules. (No norms are broken when women take care of their families at home.) Thus, de facto, what is relevant to business seems to be relevant to economic sociology.

Contestation of what "the economy" or "economics" is comes from within economics as well. Feminist economist Julie Nelson (1993) begins an essay entitled "The Study of Choice or the Study of Provisioning? Gender and the Definition of Economics," in the influential anthology *Beyond Economic Man* (Ferber and Nelson 1993), this way:

So what is economics? . . . Does economics include any study having to do with the creation and distribution of the "necessaries and conveniences of life," as Adam Smith said in 1776? Or is it about goods and services only to the extent that they enter into a process of exchange? Or is the core of economics to be found in mathematical models of individual choice, which sometimes leads to hypothetical exchange? There is no doubt that while room exists around the fringes for other sorts of studies, the last definition of economics is the one that is currently dominant in the most highly regarded research and in the core of graduate study.

Nelson's complaint is about limiting the conceptual apparatus as severely as neoclassical economists do, a complaint shared by most economic sociologists. However, she points out that, because economics has been defined around a paradigm of rational choice with highly deductive formal models, economists, when deciding to define the field by topic or by whether this choice-theoretic model can be applied, generally opt for the latter. Perhaps this is why the "new home economics" of Gary Becker (1991) and others has gained a respectable place within economics. (See England and Budig 1998 for an overview.) One sense in which Becker is a good feminist is that he recognizes women's work in the household as work, as "production," even as part of the economy, despite the relatively narrow set of conceptual tools that he applies. Unfortunately, de facto, economic sociology has even narrower topical boundaries than economics!

We redress the narrow topical boundaries of economic sociology by including discussion of the household, and by considering employment-family linkages. We also discuss how gender structures the more traditionally defined economy. In our concluding remarks we consider what it would mean to the rest of economic sociology to be informed by the knowledge gained in the systematic study of gender.

THE CONCEPTUAL TOOLKIT OF ECONOMIC SOCIOLOGY

In broad brushstrokes, we see three major conceptual tools in economic sociology as practiced today.

1. *Social networks* (or social capital). Economic actors are embedded in concrete social networks. These network relations affect the information they have, the norms to which they become committed, and the persons to whom they feel loyalty and obligation. To the extent that one's network position and connections are exogenous to one's economic behavior, networks have a causal effect on economic outcomes (Granovetter 1985, 2002; Coleman 1988; White 1981, 2002; Powell and Smith-Doerr 1996; Burt 2002; for applications to gender, see Smith-Lovin and McPherson 1993; Ibarra and Smith-Lovin 1997; Ibarra 2001).

2. *Culture, social norms, and institutions.* We use the terms *culture* and *social norms* interchangeably here. By culture, we simply mean ideas derived from the social environment (whether the whole society or a subgroup of which one is a part). These may be conscious or subconscious (tacit), they may be logically consistent or inconsistent, and they may take the form of values (what we ought to do), beliefs about the world, or strategies of action that are taken for granted. Anthropologists and sociologists see these ideas as important determinants of economic behavior (Zelizer 2002; DiMaggio 1994; Swidler 1985). When culture takes the form of tacit or explicit prescriptions of practices, it involves social norms. Sometimes culture or norms are ossified into "institutions" with the weight of the law or organizational rules behind them (Powell and DiMaggio 1991; Edelman 1992; North 1991). Sometimes sociologists use the word *insti-*

tution to denote this greater ossification into law or formal rules, as well as the greater biting power behind rules on which states and organizations base punishments or rewards. Other times the word *institution* is used to refer to parts of culture or norms—taken-for-granted assumptions that prescribe certain practices or make them seem like the only option.[2]

3. *Self-interested rational choice* is also a key part of life in families and paid work. The rational choice theoretical perspective has been expunged to an excessive degree from economic sociology in an overreaction to the hegemony of neoclassical economics. Rational choice theory is gaining adherents in most social science disciplines. When amended by a recognition of bounded rationality, endogenous preferences, and the role of emotions, it provides one useful lens on behavior. (For integrative uses of the theory, see Frank 2000; England and Farkas 1986; Folbre 1994b; England and Folbre 2003; Hodgson 1994).

Below we apply these tools to explaining gendered patterns in the economy, construed broadly. A limitation of our review is its focus largely on the contemporary period, and on literature on the United States.

OCCUPATIONAL SEX SEGREGATION

As women have entered paid employment, most have gone into predominantly female occupations (Reskin and Roos 1990; Reskin 1993). (For international comparisons, see Anker 1998.) The labor market has been extensively sex segregated, with men predominating in upper management, the most prestigious professions, blue-collar crafts, certain kinds of manufacturing work, transportation, and constructions. Women have numerically dominated professions such as nursing, teaching, and librarianship. Nonprofessional but white-collar occupations of clerical and (noncommission) retail sales work have been largely done by women, as have manufacturing jobs in nondurable-goods industries (e.g. electronics, garments), and domestic work and child care. After small decreases earlier in the century, occupational sex segregation in the United States began to decline seriously after 1970 (Jacobs 1989; Reskin and Roos 1990).

Table 1 shows the trend in segregation from 1970 to 2000. The statistic used to measure segregation is the index of dissimilarity, *D*, which, roughly speaking, tells us what percentage of men or women would have to change occupations in

TABLE 1. Trends in Occupational Sex Segregation in the United States Measured by the Weighted and Size-Standardized Index of Dissimilarity

Year	Index of Dissimilarity	Size-Standardized Index of Dissimilarity
1970[a]	68	68
1980	60	60
1990	56	60
2000	52	58

Source: Jacobs 1989, 2001, 2003. Underlying data from U.S. Census of Population, except 1990 and 2000, which are from Current Population Survey.

Note: Some caution should be applied in interpreting the change from 1980 to 1990 since the index tends to produce values a few points higher when calculated on the CPS, with its smaller n in each occupation, than on the census.

[a] Uses 1980 occupational classification.

order for the proportion of male and female in each occupation to match that of employed people as a whole.[3] For example, if employed persons are 45 percent female, then *D* would be 0 only if every occupation were 45 percent female; deviations from this figure in either direction push *D* up. If occupations were entirely segregated, *D* would be 100. *D* is calculated such that it is self-weighting; occupations employing more people count more than smaller ones. This is appropriate if we want to know how segregated the job experience of the average person is. Using detailed Census Bureau occupational categories, table 1 shows continuous declines in *D*, such that in 1970 more than two-thirds of men or women would have had to change occupations, but by 2000, just over half would have to change occupations to achieve integration. More integration has occurred in managerial and professional white-collar areas than in other jobs (Jacobs 2003). The size-standardized index, which weights all occupations equally, paints a different picture after 1980 (it is identical to *D* in showing decline from 68 to 60 from 1970 to 1980). After 1980, decline in the size-standardized index is trivial. The two series together tell us that the reduction in *D* since 1980 has arisen entirely because of disproportionate growth in occupations that were already more integrated (or more decline in the size of more segregated occupations). On net, individual occupations have not integrated since 1980.

Debates about what causes and perpetuates segregation often hinge on how much is explained on the supply versus the demand side of labor markets. Demand-side explanations are of two types: either (1) that employers engage in discrimination

in the sense of (conscious or unconscious) disparate treatment of similarly qualified men and women in hiring and placement, or (2) that they use criteria for selection that have an unintended but disparate impact by sex. As the courts have interpreted Title VII of the Civil Rights Act of 1964, the major federal legislation dealing with hiring discrimination by race or sex, using a screening device (e.g., a given score on a test, an educational credential, or experience requirement) resulting in a disparate impact by race or sex is illegal if employers cannot show that the screening device leads to hiring workers better qualified for the job. However, if employers can show that the screening device generally yields workers that do the job better, there is no legal discrimination despite the adverse effects on women. (This is referred to as the business necessity defense.) Both of these demand-side factors, both differential treatment and the use of criteria with disparate impacts, undoubtedly contribute to segregation (Reskin and Roos 1990; Reskin 1998), although it seems quite likely that disparate treatment discrimination has diminished in the last three decades due to cultural shifts and some enforcement of antidiscrimination law (Edelman 1992). It is less clear that policies having a disparate impact have shifted, but it is also unclear if courts would find many of them discriminatory under current legal precedents. There is also evidence for supply-side contributions to segregation, different occupational aspirations and choices of men and women, as we will see below. As important as putting the issue this way—discrimination versus worker choice—is in lawsuits where the issue is whether employers are guilty of discrimination and will have to change their ways and compensate victims, we think it equally important analytically to consider how each of the three major perspectives of economic sociology sheds light on segregation.

Networks

A key claim of Smith-Lovin and McPherson's (1993) version of network theory is that informal networks tend toward homophily in socially salient characteristics. Homophily by gender in early ties to playmates leads boys and girls to move into sex-differentiated network locations early in life. These network connections encourage later network ties to be sex differentiated. These sex-differentiated network locations, both affecting and affected by women's child-rearing responsibilities, push women into more kin-related and men into more occupationally relevant networks. Even when job information is exchanged in female networks, it is likely to be about female-typical courses, majors, interests, and occupations. In a strong version of the structuralist network view, gender differences in dispositions are not deeply internalized in early life, but rather, men and women's behavior is a situational response to their current set of network ties. That is, while behavior may be guided by individuals' preferences or information, these factors come from networks, and thus can change quickly if networks change.

How much of this network view of segregation is supported by evidence? What has been documented is the strongly gender-segregated nature of children's play groups, and the fact that later networks are less strongly but still somewhat sex segregated, and that this is more true of young parents. Women's networks have a higher proportion of kin in them. Women belong to fewer and smaller voluntary organizations. A number of these network differences disappear under controls for employment, occupation, and other social locational variables, suggesting that these social locations affect networks (or vice versa). When women find jobs through male contacts, the jobs are more likely to be of high status. (See Smith-Lovin and McPherson 1993 for citations on these empirical points.)

But largely because of lack of ideal network data, the propositions about causal links between networks and segregated occupations have received little testing. Burt (2002) provides some evidence from corporate data that strong, multiplex ties (for example, those involving friendship as well as business discussion) benefit professional or managerial women more than "weak" ties, whereas the opposite is true for men. He interprets this result to mean that low-status individuals (women) need strong ties to get past the suspicion of their incompetence or untrustworthiness. (See Ibarra 2001 for discussion.)

There is evidence about the segregative effects of employers' use of workers' networks as a hiring strategy. Reskin and McBrier (2000) use a national sample of organizations to show that, net of controls for the composition of the labor supply, open recruitment methods are associated with women holding a greater share of management jobs, while recruitment through informal networks increases men's share. Formalizing personnel practices also reduces men's share, presumably because it lessens ascription in hiring or job assignments. Hiring by networks is an example of a practice by employers that may be undertaken simply to save time and money, rather than because of a discriminatory animus, but which may have an important disparate impact by sex.

Culture, Social Norms, Institutions

Cultural arguments about segregation usually take the form of "socialization" arguments. The simplest version is that the process of cultural transmission creates different preferences, interests, and aspirations in males and females. These differences then lead to training for, and applying for, different jobs. There is some evidence in favor of this pattern; males and females aspire to very different jobs from very early ages and choose different courses of study in school, although differences have diminished (Marini and Brinton 1984; Marini and Fan 1997). Early occupational aspirations have a (weak) effect on the sex composition of the occupation attained (Okamoto and England 1999). It is unclear from this evidence whether preferences consistent with broader cultural norms are internalized deeply or whether they respond flexibly to changes in individuals' social networks or structural positions. Jacobs (1989, 1999, 2001) has argued that early socialization is clearly not the whole story, pointing to the instability of many individuals' job aspirations and choices as they move through the life cycle. That is, correlations between the sex composition of the job aspired to or held at two points in time, while positive, are surprisingly small. Jacobs argues that, given this instability, some social forces must keep pushing women back into female, and male back into male, spheres; early socialization is insufficiently strong.

Jacobs's (1989) view, minimizing the role of socialization, has been the popular view among sociologists of gender. (For others taking this view, see Epstein 1988; Aries 1996; Ridgeway and Smith-Lovin 1999; Reskin and Roos 1990; Bielby and Bielby 2002.) Why have socialization or cultural views been so unpopular among sociologists of gender? In part it is a fear that socialization seems to "blame the victim" and can be used against attempts to get employers to stop discriminating. (It seems to be saying that women want what they get.) These fears have practical merit, but have little to say about the accuracy of the view. Theoretical turf wars between psychologists and sociological social psychologists, or between network theorists reacting against Parsons's emphasis on internalized norms may also have contributed. These reactions too are somewhat extrascientific. However, social psychologists' research on what they call "fundamental attribution error," referring to the tendency of people to explain behavior by characteristics of the person rather than the situation, even when the latter is the operative cause (Aries 1996, 19–20, 193), does provide one scientific reason to think that, without constant reminders the other way, most people revert to explanations that exaggerate the role of internalized preferences and skills while forgetting about the shaping role of social pressures and other constraints and incentives in the context in which the individual operates.

But we should not throw out the baby (culture and socialization) with the bathwater (views that emphasize internalized states to the exclusion of immediate social context). Browne and England (1997) argued that, in fact, virtually every theory explicitly or implicitly assumes some preference or belief to be internalized and "carried on the person" across situations. This, of course, does not necessarily imply complete unchangeability across situations. Take, for example, the application of ethnomethodology to gender, the "doing gender" framework. Its proponents claim to eschew deep internalization, and emphasize that gender is something we actively do, not something socialized in once and for all (West and Zimmerman 1987; West and Fenstermaker 1993). In this view, women wear women's clothes, care for their families, and choose womanly jobs not so much because they believe in the "rightness" of the choices, or out of fear of reprisals (as would be emphasized in a rational choice view of norms), but because, if they do not, their actions will simply not make any sense to others. That each of us is held accountable is an external constraint, but the norms people are holding each other accountable for *are* assumed to be internalized. They are not preferences for one's own behavior, but beliefs about what self and others are expected to do to make sense. Thus this view does assume that something is internalized. Moreover, most of the evidence offered for the "doing gender" view seems to us to be equally consistent with a notion of internalized (though not entirely unchangeable) values or practices.

Beliefs consistent with gender-related cultural norms affect the behavior of decision makers who control hiring as well as workers selecting jobs. Norms about the appropriate sex for jobs may contribute powerfully to segregation. For example, consider the possibility that employers believe that it is important that child care workers be women (for example, they fear that any men who would want to do such work are sexually predatory). Or

they may assume that men are better at construction work and thus prefer men for these jobs. Or some employers may think that it is simply unseemly to have women negotiating contracts at out-of-town hotels. Such beliefs would undoubtedly affect hiring in these jobs. These are all examples of culture affecting segregation. In addition, workers may hold such gendered beliefs. This may lead to some degree of harassment of women in men's jobs. (One might think that it would also lead to harassment of men in women's jobs, but Williams's [1995] and Budig's [2002] work shows that men get paid more than women and rise to the top in "women's jobs.") Informal interview evidence of discrimination and harassment abounds (Reskin and Roos 1990), although we really have embarrassingly little direct evidence of what portion of segregation this explains, how this has changed, or whether norms or some more money-related motive of employers animates their segregative actions.

Institutional rules, formal and informal, used in hiring may be a demand-side factor in segregation. The hiring and placement criteria that have a disparate impact by sex are good examples of institutional rules that perpetuate segregation; as discussed above, they are sometimes legal and sometimes not (Burstein and Pitchford 1990; Williams and Segal 2003). Reskin (2002) calls the use of screening criteria that have a disparate impact "structural discrimination," whether or not they are relevant to productivity on average (i.e., whether or not our legal system would consider them illegal discrimination). The fact that screening criteria for many jobs were developed when few women were employed makes it likely that they may be harder for women to meet. Indeed, Acker (1990) has argued that most expectations developed around an assumption of a male worker who had a woman at home taking care of domestic matters. In that sense, she argues that occupations and organizations are "gendered" in constitutive assumptions. Some feminist legal scholars make a similar argument, labeling demands that make it more difficult for those with parenting responsibilities to succeed as forms of discrimination (Williams 2001; Williams and Segal 2003).

In sum, we have less evidence than we would want to adjudicate the role of culture. There is a long tradition of survey questions on gender-role attitude and occupational aspiration, so we know a good deal about the aspirations that individuals hold. But how much these reflect broader cultural norms that affect occupational choices is not well understood.

Rational Choice Explanations

Economists have attempted to explain occupational outcomes with human capital theory. While human capital models of earnings focus on years of education, this has never been the emphasis in explaining gender inequality, since, in the United States, men and women obtain similar amounts of education (although the male distribution has a higher variance). Indeed, in recent cohorts, a higher proportion of women than men has gone to and graduated from college in the United States and most of Europe (Eurostat 2002; DiPrete and Buchmann 2003). In the case of gender, human capital theorists have tried to explain why men and women getting the same amount of education would choose different fields. At first glance, it is hard to imagine any money-related motive that would lead women to choose "female" occupations, since they pay less. Polachek (1981, 1984) argued, however, that women may be optimizing *lifetime* earnings. He argued that differences in men's and women's initial plans for continuity of employment will lead to different job choices. Since more women than men plan breaks for homemaking, they may choose jobs that have low depreciation of human capital during years away from the job, and thus a lower drop in wage when one returns from a stint of home time. Polachek provided evidence for this thesis using broad occupational categories, but subsequent research using more detailed categories has not found higher wage drops for time out of employment in traditionally male than female jobs (England 1982, 1984). A related argument, derived from human capital theory, is that jobs offering formal or informal on-the-job training will, ceteris paribus, have lower starting wages (i.e., employers charge employees for some of their training costs) but steeper wage trajectories with seniority. If this is true, those who plan to drop out of employment for child rearing would be more likely to choose jobs with higher starting wages but less steep wage trajectories since doing so would optimize income if they planned to drop out soon. But if this is what is generating segregation, we should find higher starting wages in female jobs (net of educational requirements). In fact, however, starting wages are lower in predominantly female jobs, net of other factors (England, Reid, and Kilbourne 1996).

Economists do not emphasize discrimination because neoclassical theory implies that discrimination should erode in competitive markets. Indeed, they believe the employer pays a price for discrimination. The idea is that if one group of employers will not hire women assembly line workers, for example, then women will have to offer themselves at a lower wage to be hired (which they might do if their other alternatives are even lower). In this case, it is the employers who *will* hire women who benefit from the lower wages. This disadvantages the discriminators in product or capital markets. As discriminators come to hold less market share, maybe even go out of business, the remaining nondiscriminators can no longer can get away with paying women a lower wage when the discriminators are gone. This is seen as a long-term process, and there is little evidence for whether it actually occurs (See discussions of this economic argument in England 1992, chap. 2; and Sunstein 1991.)

There are two types of segregation-encouraging actions of employers that neoclassical economists have considered. The first is policies that have a disparate impact by sex but get more productive workers. They would not see such policies as discrimination at all, since they define discrimination in terms of treating equally productive workers differently (contra Reskin 2002).

The second demand-side view accepted in the "new information economics" is statistical discrimination Suppose that recognizable groups (by race, sex, or language) differ in average productivity, and that net of the kinds of human capital that employers can cheaply screen, such as education and experience, women are less productive, on average. (Some versions of the theory focus on group differences in variances rather than means. See England 1992, chap. 2 for discussion.) The idea is that it is expensive to measure individual productivity before hire, so employers use averages formed by informal or formal data-gathering to make predictions about individuals. They might then treat men more favorably. In economists' thinking, this differential treatment would create roughly the degree of pay gap between men and women that is commensurate with the average productivity gap. However, individuals atypical for their sex will have job assignments or pay out of whack with their capabilities (Aigner and Cain 1977). Economists are less sure that this type of discrimination will erode in competitive markets, as it may be profit-maximizing for employers, absent legal enforcement against it. Again, we have little clear evidence of how much of the discrimination observed is of this sort. (See Bielby and Baron 1986 for one socio-logical attempt to sort out this issue.)

THE SEX GAP IN PAY: THE PAY FOR "WOMEN'S WORK"

Trends in pay among full-time year-round work-ers are shown in table 2. Segregation started declin-ing in the 1970s and the pay gap began to decline in the 1980s. The ratio of (median) women's to men's pay hovered around 0.60 for decades preceding 1980. Then within a decade it rose rapidly from 0.60 to 0.72. However, in the 1990s the ratio moved only from 0.72 to 0.73. Here, as with segregation, there is some indication that progress is stalling out.

In a proximate sense, the sex gap in pay is explained largely by two factors, women's child-rearing responsibilities, which creates an experi-ence gap, and the segregation of women into lower-paying jobs. The best studies examining the role of the experience gap use panel data that follow the same people for many years and thus afford good measures of their employment history. Using such data from the Panel Study of Income Dynamics, Wellington (1994) found that experience, seniori-ty, and related measures of labor supply explained 37 percent of the sex gap in pay in 1976 (similar to what Corcoran and Duncan reported in 1979). These same factors explained a slightly larger pro-portion (42 percent) of the smaller pay gap that existed in 1985, suggesting some diminution of differential treatment discrimination. Women's em-ployment has become more continuous (Goldin 1990), and this accounts for some of the decrease in the sex gap in pay (Smith and Ward 1984; O'Neill and Polachek 1993; Wellington 1993).

Most economists explain these findings using human capital theory. Their assumption is that work experience entails learning and thus increased productivity, and it is the increased productivity that explains the higher pay. In fact, even when economists relax assumptions that pay tracks pro-ductivity over time, they invoke efficiency explana-tions of pay systems that reward experience. For ex-ample, they argue that paying less during training and more than productivity later in the career mo-tivates workers to stay long enough to repay train-ing, but their overpayment later in the life cycle may motivate employers to try to get rid of older workers, sometimes through golden parachute of-fers (Lazear 1990). One could also interpret re-turns to experience from an institutional model,

TABLE 2.   Trends in the Ratio of U.S. Women's to Men's Median Annual Earnings for Full-Time Year-Round Workers, 1960–2000

Year	Ratio
1960	0.61
1965	0.60
1970	0.59
1975	0.59
1980	0.60
1985	0.65
1990	0.72
1995	0.71
2000	0.73

Source: Institute for Women's Policy Research website, 2001. Underlying data from Current Population Surveys.

however; paying by seniority and experience is a re-flection of a value premise that has been institu-tionalized in organizations and endures irrespective of whether it relates to productivity. We have little evidence on which interpretation is more accurate.

Sex differences in experience result from the as-signment of child rearing in the home to women. While biology undoubtedly affects this (women birth and breast-feed), norms also have a powerful role. Sex-segregated networks may encourage wom-en's domestic and men's employment interests as well. Once a couple starts a gender-specialized pat-tern, small initial differences encourage later dif-ference based on incentives for family income max-imization (Becker 1991). Here too we really know little about the relative contribution of these fac-tors. It is clear that early socialization is not the *whole* story; if it were, it would be hard to under-stand how fast women's employment and deseg-regation increased in the 1970s among women brought up in the traditional 1950s.

Whatever the causes of segregation, it is linked to the pay gap because predominantly female jobs pay less, on average, than predominantly male jobs. If we get detailed enough job categories, rel-atively little of the pay gap is within jobs (Petersen and Morgan 1995), although the within-job dif-ferentials are probably largest in the highest-paying fields. But why do women's jobs pay less? It is mys-terious at first glance because women's jobs cover the full range of educational requirements, and re-quire about as much cognitive skill as men's, on average; women are not concentrated in menial jobs. Part of the reason for the higher pay of pre-dominantly male jobs is that more of them involve authority over coworkers (England 1992; Wright,

Baxter, and Gunn 1995). In addition, women's occupations are concentrated in lower-paying (particularly service sector) industries and firms, and in the public sector (England 1992; Johnson and Solon 1986; Tam 1997; MacPherson and Hirsch 1995). Even within broad industry groupings, women are concentrated in lower-paying firms (Carrington and Troske 1993; Groshen 1991).

Two explanations for the lower pay of occupations with a high percentage of female workers are favored by economists using rational choice principles. The first is "compensating differentials." The idea is that the full pay of a job consists of both pecuniary (wage) and nonpecuniary compensation, the latter being the (dis)utility experienced from doing the work itself. Jobs with more comfortable, less hazardous working conditions can be filled with lower wages, ceteris paribus. The idea is that perhaps women care more about nonpecuniary rewards (such as avoiding physical danger, or having mother-friendly work conditions) than men, while men focus more on maximizing earnings. Most attempts to test this view have failed to find that it explains much of the lower pay of women's jobs (Jacobs and Steinberg 1990; England 1992; Kilbourne et al. 1994; Glass 1990; Glass and Camarigg 1992). The idea seems on first glance consistent with the finding that mothers earn less than nonmothers, even after controlling for part-time work status, experience, and seniority (Waldfogel 1997, 1998; Lundberg and Rose 2000; Budig and England 2001). But neither Glass (1990) nor Glass and Camarigg (1992) found women's jobs to have more mother-friendly characteristics. Similarly, Budig and England (2001) could not find any job characteristics except part-time status that reduced the motherhood wage penalty much.

A second economic explanation for the lower pay in female jobs is crowding. Bergmann (1974, 1986) argues that women's jobs pay less because they are "crowded." In this view, women seeking to enter male occupations face sex discrimination in hiring, leading to a supply of applicants for traditionally female jobs that is larger than it would be in the absence of hiring discrimination, as women denied entrance to male jobs crowd the female jobs. This "excess" supply lowers wages in female jobs. While this account is plausible, it is very difficult to test directly.

Evidence that female jobs pay less than comparably skilled male jobs is also consistent with the devaluation thesis, a sociological cultural-institutional argument. The devaluation thesis explains the lower pay in women's jobs by the sort of wage disparity at issue in the debate about comparable worth, against which U.S. law provides little protection. The claim is that jobs filled mostly by women pay less than they would if the same jobs were filled mostly by men (Steinberg 2001). At first glance, this is easy to confuse with the more familiar kind of discrimination that occurs when an employer does not provide equal pay for equal work, so that men and women in the same job with the same seniority performing the same work equally well are not paid the same. This would be a violation of the 1963 Equal Pay Act, as well as of Title VII of the Civil Rights Act. Comparable worth involves a distinct issue because it refers to comparisons between the pay in different jobs, jobs that differ in that they entail at least some distinct tasks. The allegation of discrimination is based on the claim that the difference between the pay of the two jobs results from gender bias in wage setting rather than from other factors about the jobs.

The evidence for the devaluation view is the finding that the sex composition of an occupation or job exerts a net effect on its wage level. Such effects of sex composition, net of the factors discussed above, have led some researchers to conclude that employers set lower wages (relative to job demands) when jobs are filled largely by women. One type of study takes the U.S. Census's detailed occupational categories as units of analysis, and researchers use national data to assess the effect on wages of different percentages of female workers, after controlling for education and skill requirements. Studies generally find that both men and women earn less when in a more "female" occupation (England et al. 1988; England 1992; Parcel 1989; England, Thompson, and Aman 2001). (Filer 1989 failed to find this penalty.) Other studies use individuals or person-years (with person-fixed effects) as units and occupational or job sex composition as contextual variables. Such studies find a net negative effect on both men's and women's wages of the percentage female in their occupation (Johnson and Solon 1986; Sorensen 1994; England et al. 1988; Kilbourne et al. 1994; Tomaskovic-Devey 1993; MacPherson and Hirsch 1995). (See Tam 1997, 2000; and England, Hermsen, and Cotter 2000 for debate.) Studies of a single employer also generally find that female jobs pay less, relative to male jobs, than would be expected based on measures of job skill and demands (Steinberg et al. 1986; Acker 1989; Orazem and Mattila 1989; Baron and Newman 1989; Nelson and Bridges 1999).

The mechanism adduced for these effects by sociologists is generally cultural and institutional. Cultural ideas deprecate work done by women, and cultural beliefs lead to cognitive errors in which decision makers underestimate the contribution of female jobs to organizational goals, including the goal of increasing profits through increasing productivity. Once wage scales are set up, the disparities are perpetuated by organizational inertia in the form of using past wages within the organization to set present wages, or the use of market surveys of wages in other firms to set jobs' pay levels. That is, wage scales get "institutionalized." But, while the evidence of the penalty for working in female jobs is quite strong, there is really no direct evidence on the mechanism producing it. Economists think it impossible for such disparities to stand if there were not hiring barriers. In their view, unless women were kept out of male jobs, they would not stay in underpaid female jobs. If they did, it would be "revealed preference" evidence that women must want the jobs more than they want the extra income, in which case economists see it as a case of compensating differentials.

One example of the devaluation of women's work is the devaluation of care work—such as child care, teaching, health care service provision, counseling, and so forth (Cancian and Oliker 2000; Folbre and Nelson 2000). Care work pays less than other work requiring the same amount of skill, effort, and risk (England and Folbre 1999; England, Budig, and Folbre 2002). One cultural explanation of the devaluation of care sees it as part of the more general devaluation of women's work; cultural schema see women's care as the air we breathe—priceless, but invisible, to be taken for granted, thus not really valued. Although gendered devaluation is undoubtedly one cause of the low pay of care work (relative to its skill demands), there must be other explanations as well because analyses show care work to be paid even less than other female jobs (net of education and so forth) (England, Budig, and Folbre 2002). Moreover, while most organizations have both male and female jobs, care work is often in organizations where care is the entire mission of the organization. Thus, the opportunity of employers to pay noncare workers more than care workers doing similarly skilled work in the same organization is limited. Accordingly, to get the whole story we must look for explanations of the "care penalty" other than devaluation.

Care work is often motivated at least in part by real care, an intrinsic or altruistic motivation. We certainly hope for this when we choose a caregiver for a child, parent, or ourselves. Economists tend to assume that the wage "penalty" is not really a penalty but a balancing of the pecuniary rewards with the intrinsic rewards (as in the doctrine of compensating differentials discussed above).

Another possible explanation for the low pay of care work is that it is difficult to get all the indirect beneficiaries of care work to pay care providers, because care work creates positive externalities or public goods (England and Folbre 1999, 2000, 2003). In rational choice theory, "public goods" are defined (in part) in terms of the practical impossibility of keeping those who do not pay from receiving benefits from the good. This is called *nonexcludability*. Some jobs pay well because they involve providing a valuable good or service to someone who will be kept from getting the fruits of the work if s/he does not pay. Nonpayers are "excludable." Caring labor deviates from this ideal type of "excludability" in that there is no way for the care provider to collect from many of the beneficiaries via market processes. Care providers contribute to the development of human capabilities that are of value not only to the client, but to all those who interact with him or her. How could the teacher collect from the future employer or spouse of the student who later benefits from her labors? The work of caring is unusual in the extent to which benefits are spread beyond direct recipients of the service. This diffusion makes it easy for others to free ride, enjoying the benefits of care without paying the costs, making the work pay less than it would without this feature (England, Thompson, and Aman 2001; England and Folbre 1999).

Care work may also pay badly because the "customers" that most need it often cannot afford to pay much. Children, the sick, the disabled, and the elderly are cases in point. Unless a third party, typically a family member, the state, or a nonprofit, subsidizes the caring labor, it will be badly paid, unpaid, or go undone. The fate of those who need care as well as of those who do the work is affected by the affluence of third parties as well as their altruism toward caregivers and recipients.

The low pay of care work may also be because the quality of care services is especially difficult to measure. Information problems loom large. Sometimes, the person receiving the service (e.g., children, the elderly with impaired capacities) is not competent to judge its quality. Employers of care workers can sometimes monitor physical abuse and technical incompetence. But more subtle emotional aspects of care, such as warmth, nurturance, reassurance, and the sense of "being cared for" are very difficult to monitor. Furthermore, care skills have a significant person-specific component. Third-party payers of education and health care (insurance or the state) often limit the ability to shop around, so even if consumers can monitor quality, they may not be able to use the information. Given the fact that the quality of care is hard to assess, we might ask why care workers are not among those who generally receive an "efficiency wage." In such models (discussed without reference to care work in Akerlof 1982; Stiglitz 1987; Bulow and Summers 1986; England 1992, chap. 2), higher wage costs can be counterbalanced by higher effort, which in turn leads to higher output per worker. The idea is that paying above market-clearing wages may elicit effort more cost-effectively than surveillance. One reason this may not operate for care work is that the efficiency-wage strategy hinges on the assumption that average output per worker can be measured, even if individual effort cannot. As for quality, consumers will pay more if they can be sure their product is of higher quality. In the case of care services, however, "outputs" as well as "inputs" are difficult to measure (though it is important not to exaggerate the point and say that no assessments of quality can be made). Given these issues, it seems that care work is unlikely to pay well without government funding—whether subsidizing private sector wages or making care workers well-paid government employees. Where we see the gender bias of culture entering is in the collective willingness to do this with the military, but not with care work, despite the fact that each provides a public good. In fact, this is a special case of a more general theme emphasized by scholars writing on gender and the welfare state: that the construction of what makes a citizen with rights to governmental assistance is based on a male model that valorizes paid work or military service. Thus, for example, old-age pensions are based on having been a breadwinner or soldier and go mostly to men (or women based on their marital tie to such men). In most nations, but particularly in the United States, these are more generous than payments to single mothers who are raising their children at home—raising children does not confer the same rights and privileges as breadwinning or being a soldier. This same bias may limit the services such as child care governments are willing to provide, as well as how much they are willing to pay the largely female care workers who provide such services. While the same gender biases are present in most modern systems, public support for child rearing is much more generous in Europe than the United States, and more generous in Nordic than in other European countries. (On gender and social welfare programs, which are largely beyond our scope here, see O'Connor, Orloff, and Shaver 1999; Sainsbury 2000; Folbre 1994b).

THE GENDER DIVISION OF LABOR, POWER, AND EXIT IN COUPLES

Families meet their material and emotional needs through employment that earns money to buy things for the household, through household work (providing meals and a serviceable and pleasant house), and through care work that tends and socializes children and provides physical and emotional care for all family members. If we divide this set of needs into two parts, household work and employment, the task is to explain the gender "segregation" or division of labor in these two areas. We also consider how the division of labor affects or is affected by power relations within couples.

Rising women's employment is ubiquitous in modern nations (Van der Lippe and Van Dijk 2001). Economists attribute the increase to rising wages that increased the opportunity cost of being a homemaker (Bergmann 1986). Another factor is the disproportionate employment growth in the service occupations that had always hired mostly women (Oppenheimer 1970). That latter explanation presumes norms about the appropriate gender for specific jobs, and perhaps gendered networks bringing women in, echoing our earlier discussions of segregation. Sociologists often talk about women's increased employment as if it were motivated by the increased need for two paychecks—that is, by a decline in men's real wages. It is true that, adjusted for inflation, men's wages in the United States are lower today than they were in the early 1970s (Bernhardt et al. 2001), and at any one time women with higher-earning husbands are more likely to be employed, *net of their own earning power.* But a woman's own earning power has always affected employment as well. Women with higher education are more likely to be employed than less educated women, despite the fact that they are more likely to be married and tend to be married to men with higher earnings (Juhn and Murphy 1997). Thus, for any given woman, these two factors tend to cut against each other. Cohen and Bianchi (1999) have shown that, over time, the effect of husbands' income has decreased and

TABLE 3. Change between 1978 and 1998 in Indicators of Involvement in Paid Work for All Women and Married Women with Children under Six

	1978	*1998*	*% Change*
Percentage employed the week previous to survey			
All women	56	71	27
Wives with child under six	38	58	53
Percentage employed full-time the week previous to survey			
All women	38	51	34
Wives with child under six	21	35	67
Annual hours of paid work the previous year			
All women	1002	1415	41
Wives with child under six	583	1094	88

Source: Adapted and calculated from Casper and Bianchi 2002, table 10.1, p. 290. Underlying data are from U.S. Government Current Population Surveys.

the effect of women's own education has increased. This is inconsistent with the notion that declining male wages are the main reason for women's increased employment. Overall, the evidence is more consistent with a view in which economic incentives increased women's employment, and once a large share of wives were employed, the increased living standards their paychecks afford made other couples want two incomes to "keep up with the Joneses." The latter is an example of how social norms and network processes may affect employment behavior.

Table 3 shows trends in women's employment. In 1978, 56 percent of U.S. women were employed for pay; by 1998 this figure was up to 71 percent. The proportion of women working full time (at least 35 hours/week) was 38 percent in 1978, moving to 51 percent in 1998. Wives with children under six were less likely to be employed and often worked part time. However, in percentage terms, they showed larger increases, moving from 38 percent to 58 percent employed, and from 21 percent to 35 percent employed full time. If we look at annual hours of paid employment, which reflects both weeks per year and hours per week, table 3 shows a 41 percent increase for all women and an 88 percent increase for wives with children under six.

What about change in household work, and total work when paid and unpaid is combined? Table 4 contains computations from two data sets containing time diary information from probability samples of Americans, the first in 1965 and the second in 1998 (Bianchi, Robinson, and Sayer

2001; see also Bianchi et al. 2000). Respondents are asked to recount what they did every period of the previous day. For each time segment, they list their primary activity, and whether they were doing a second activity simultaneously (e.g., one might be cooking dinner while watching television or cleaning while watching a child). Using the primary activities, table 4 shows that in 1965, sex differentiation was extreme. Men averaged 46 hours per week in market work, while women averaged only 15 (because most women were not employed). Women did 41 hours per week of unpaid work, while men did only 11. If we total paid and market work, despite their strong gender division of labor, women and men worked a similar number of hours in total. In fact, men worked one hour more per week.

By 1998 things had changed substantially. Women had doubled their hours of market work from an average of 15 to 30 hours per week. They had reduced their household work across the period by about 12 hours. This reflects declining fertility, the increase in employment, and the use of child care during job hours. But since the increase in employment was more than the decrease in unpaid work, women's total work hours had increased by three hours! Men increased their unpaid work by a substantial seven hours, but their increase was less than women's decrease in housework, or than women's increase in paid work. Men also decreased their market work by eight hours. Other data suggest that this reduction is not due to a reduction of hours for the typical employed man (which Jacobs and Gerson 1998 show to have

TABLE 4. Average Hours per Week Spent in Unpaid and Market Work by U.S. Men and Women in 1965 and 1998

	Unpaid Work			Market Work			Total Work (Unpaid + Market)		
	1965	*1998*	*Increase*	*1965*	*1998*	*Increase*	*1965*	*1998*	*Increase*
Women	41	29	−12	15	30	15	56	59	3
Men	11	18	7	46	38	8	57	56	−1
Difference (women − men)	30	11	−19	−31	−8	23	−1	3	4

Source: Adapted and computed from Sayer 2001, tables 6.2 and 6.3.

Notes: Nonmarket work includes housework, child care, and shopping. Market work includes time in paid employment and travel to work. Respondents were aged 18–65 in both surveys.

been fairly constant for men in recent decades), but rather due to an increased proportion of men out of the labor force as more men stay in school longer, retire earlier, or are discouraged workers at the bottom of the class structure who stop trying to find jobs eventually. Overall, men reduced their average workload an hour. One net effect of all these changes was that the total workweek, including paid and unpaid work, was three hours longer for women than men by 1998, whereas it had been one hour shorter in 1965. A 1989 book by Arlie Hochschild had the evocative title *The Second Shift*. The imagery was that things have changed from men having one job for pay and women one job at home to men working one but women working two shifts (one at work and one at home). Table 4 shows that this is an exaggeration, since the average woman still works fewer hours in the market than men, and men have picked up some household work. But the metaphor captured something correct in diagnosing a trend toward women's total work burden increasing relative to men's. Changes were not symmetrical.

How do we explain the gender division of labor between market and household work? The network perspective emphasizes how kin-centered networks might encourage women to feel more responsibility for household work. Of course, it is also likely that kin-centered networks are a consequence of the cultural construction of women as responsible for child care. Most of the literature on household work has centered on debating among three other perspectives, two of which come from the rational choice camp, and one of which is about culture, including the social forces to "do gender."

Among economists, the dominant view is that of Gary Becker (1991), who emphasizes that household decisions are made rationally with an eye to ef-

ficiency in production for the entire family. Becker ignores conflicts of interest between husbands and wives. Rather, he assumes considerable altruism in the family and a single family utility function. Family members cooperate to produce utility for all. This is done in part through purchasing goods and services with earnings from market work, and in part through household production. Becker argues that specialization is efficient in the family just as it is in the factory. In his view, men generally do more market and women more household work because women are better at child rearing. He attributes this largely to biology (e.g., women's advantage in breast-feeding) and the efficiency of having women do household tasks easily combined with child rearing. (Becker hints at a role for socialization, but even here assumes that parents would not gender-differentiate socialization unless it was training children for what they are biologically destined to be more efficient in.) When couples specialize on this basis early in the marriage, this generates differences in experience-based human capital and earnings, which creates an even greater incentive for male specialization in market work later in the life cycle. Becker acknowledges, but does not emphasize, that discrimination in labor markets may also create an economic incentive for couples' specialization. While the efficiency perspective predicts a gender-based division of labor, it also predicts differences between couples in the degree of this specialization. The higher one partner's potential wage rate, the greater the gain to the family of that partner doing market work, and thus the more market work and less household work s/he will do. Thus, as womens' wage relative to that of their husbands' increases, their hours of market work should go up and their hours of household work should go down to allow allocating more time to market work. A similar prediction comes from the "time availability" perspective of some sociologists, arguing that decisions about hours of market work affect how much time is left for household work (for reviews see Shelton 1992). Thus, the efficiency perspective predicts that each spouse's wage will negatively affect his or her household work, whether wage and housework are measured absolutely and or relative to the other partner. (For reviews and critique of Becker's view, see England and Budig 1998; Pollak 2003.)

Bargaining/exchange models are a second rational choice view. They explicitly take into account differences in bargaining power between spouses, assume that most people would prefer to do less housework, and use information on earnings or other resources to predict power and thereby freedom from doing housework. The general idea is that money talks; a partner with higher earnings is more likely to get his or her way in a disagreement, not only on the issue of who is doing the housework. If these models are correct, then they imply that, whatever the efficiency advantages of a traditional gender division of labor, it clearly disadvantages women in decision-making power, and more generally in the distribution of resources, material and otherwise, in marriage. This is a possibility Becker ignores. From a feminist point of view, it is important to have a theory that does not obscure this disadvantage to women of traditional arrangements.

From within economics, this bargaining view has been developed in recent decades with formal game-theoretic models of the family (Manser and Brown 1980; McElroy and Horney 1981; McElroy 1990; Chiappori 1992; Lundberg and Pollak 1993, 1996). Many of these models were not developed as part of a program of gender scholarship but lead to some of the same insights developed in less formal but more substantive terms by gender scholars (England and Farkas 1986, chap. 3; Sen 1990; England and Kilbourne 1990; Folbre 1994b, 1997; Agarwal 1997; Kabeer 2001; Katz 1997; England 2000a, 2000b). Both groups characterize their conclusions as inconsistent with Becker.

Why might bringing money or other resources into the household give one power? Economists' bargaining models (drawing from game theory) use the concept of "threat points" (Lundberg and Pollak 1996). "Divorce threat point" (also called "external threat point") models emphasize that bargaining within marriage is conducted in the shadow of the possibility of divorce. An individual's threat point is what s/he has to fall back on if the marriage dissolves. This is influenced by one's own earnings, position in the market for a new partner, life skills, and preferences that affect one's enjoyment of being single. Utility outside marriage is also influenced by how much gender discrimination there is in the labor market, the amount of child support payments the state makes absent parents pay and how strongly this payment is enforced, as well as state payments to single individuals or parents. McElroy (1990) calls these factors "extrahousehold environmental parameters," while Folbre (1997) calls them "gender-specific environmental parameters."

Consider a couple, A and B. The better off A would be if the marriage dissolved, the better the deal B needs to provide to A to make it worthwhile for A to stay in the marriage. Individuals make concessions to their partners to keep their marriages intact if they would be worse off without the spouse than in the marriage even after having made the necessary concessions. Even within the range where both are better off within than outside the marriage, the two spouses' relative threat points are seen to affect in whose interest the "deal" is struck, according to the Nash bargaining model. If both spouses act this way, it follows that the better A's alternatives outside (relative to inside) the marriage, or the worse B's outside alternatives, the better a bargain A (and worse B) can strike in the marriage. Resources that one could withdraw from one's partner or retain for oneself if the marriage dissolved are those that increase bargaining power.

Lundberg and Pollak (1993, 1996) also discuss "internal threat point models." Here the issue is what one spouse can withhold from the other without leaving the marriage, and what that leaves the other to fall back on within the marriage. In such models, money that comes into the household through partner A gives A power because s/he could possibly fail to share some or all of the income, even without divorce or separation. Here too, earnings should lead to some power, because they are a resource one shares or could withhold. But in this model the relevance of earnings to bargaining power does not hinge on their portability if one leaves the relationship as it does in the divorce threat model.

The threat point models discussed above resonate theoretically with derivations from sociological exchange theory. (For an overview of exchange theory see Molm and Cook 1995; Cook 1987. For applications to marital power, see Heer 1963; Scanzoni 1979; England and Farkas 1986; Molm and Cook 1995, 220.) The power-dependence tradition of exchange theory states that if A is more dependent on B, A will give more and receive less in the exchange. In this tradition, A is seen as more independent, or less dependent, to the extent that s/he has access to more resources, including from potential exchange partners other than B. The reasoning in exchange theory about why dependence lowers one's rewards has a similar logic to that of either internal or external threat point models. A can make a more credible threat to stop exchanging with B if A has other exchange partners from whom s/he can get (more) resources in trade for what s/he has to offer. Exchange theory says this will increase what B gives A in exchange. Exchange theory is general enough that it encompasses the logic of both internal and external threat point models.

Resources not only allow one to get one's way in a relationship, but they allow one to leave the relationship if desired. Thus, the exchange or bargaining perspective implies that spouses with more resources are likely either to negotiate a good deal for themselves in the relationship or to leave. This view has distinct predictions about who is likely to initiate divorce. Since earnings are an example of a resource shared with a spouse within marriage but portable out of the marriage if it ends, the prediction is that men's earnings increase men's bargaining power within marriage as well as men's propensity to initiate divorce if unhappy, and women's earnings will increase women's power in marriage as well as their propensity to initiate divorce if unhappy. The effect of women's employment on initiating divorce has been called the "women's independence" effect (Ruggles 1997; Schoen et al. 2002), and is seen by many as part of the explanation for increases in divorce throughout the century.

There is some evidence to support the bargaining view of marriage. Recent studies show that where women have more access to and control over economic resources (relative to men), more is spent on children (Thomas 1990; Alderman et al. 1995; Lundberg, Pollak, and Wales 1997). Research on divorce has been mixed in its support for the notion that the same things encouraging a stronger bargaining position also allow exit. Divorce has been found more likely when men's earnings are lower (Hoffman and Duncan 1995; South and Lloyd 1995) or declining (Weiss and Willis 1997). Findings on the effects of women's earnings are less consistent. Some studies find that women's earnings are positively related to divorce (Heckert, Nowak, and Snyder 1998; Hiedemann,

Suhomlinova, and O'Rand 1998; Moore and Waite 1981; Ono 1998; Ross and Sawhill 1975; Spitze and South 1985), especially when men's earnings are lower (Heckert, Nowak, and Snyder 1998; Ono 1998), but others find no effect of women's earnings (Greenstein 1995; Hoffman and Duncan 1995; Mott and Moore 1979; Sayer and Bianchi 2000; South and Lloyd 1995; Tzeng and Mare 1995), and a few suggest that women's earnings, like men's, stabilize marriage (Hoffman and Duncan 1995; and for changes in earnings, Weiss and Willis 1997). While the century-long increase in both divorce and women's employment seems consistent with the exchange/bargaining view, the fact that divorce has not increased since 1980 despite ongoing increases in women's real earnings seems inconsistent with the view.

How do bargaining models apply to predicting housework? They reach the same conclusion as the efficiency view that relative wages will affect relative contributions to housework, but deploy an entirely different logic. The idea is that the partner with higher earning power is able to bargain to do less household work, and through this to do less total work (paid and unpaid) and to have more leisure. Whereas in a Beckerian world, the family has a single utility function and cooperates to allocate each partner's time efficiently in the service of this unitary utility function, in a bargaining world, partners are not entirely altruistic, and where they have a conflict of interest, resources affect whose interests prevail. Thus, if you earn more, you can get your partner to do the housework you do not like doing, while you enjoy leisure, and this is true even if the two of you work the same hours of market work. To see the difference between the logic of the efficiency and bargaining views, consider a couple in which each partner already works 40 hours of market work per week. They are deciding how each partner will spend the next few hours, in market work, household work, or leisure. In the efficiency view, the person with the higher wage is less likely to spend the next few hours in *either* housework or leisure because the opportunity cost (i.e., the gain foregone) of using the hours in leisure or housework is greater. (At least this is true if we hold constant productivity in household work and taste for leisure.) Thus, in Becker's view, one's wage rate reduces one's housework *through* its effect on the optimal hours of market work. There is nothing in the Beckerian view to dictate that the partners with the higher wage will get more *leisure* from their freedom from household work. Indeed, they are likely to take less leisure, because from the point of view of the couple's single utility function, "purchasing" leisure for the higher-wage partner is more expensive than for the lower-wage partner. Now consider this same couple, with each partner having each worked 40 hours of market work this week, deciding how to spend the next few hours in the world described by bargaining theory. Let us assume that most people would prefer to have more leisure and do less housework. If bringing money into the household increases one's bargaining power, then the partner with higher earnings will do less housework *and* get more leisure in the next few hours. This will be true even in couples with equal hours of market work, or, more generally, it should hold net of hours of market work. Several sociological studies have found effects of relative earnings on the division of housework (Ross 1987; Presser 1994; Brines 1994; Greenstein 2000; Bittman et al. 2003; Evertsson 2004). Some do not control adequately for the number of hours of market work done by both spouses, and thus could be indicative of either bargaining or specialization. Using Australian and U.S. data, Bittman et al. 2003 control for market hours and find women do less when they have higher relative earnings, at least in the range between equal earnings and men providing most of the earnings.

The more "gendered" perspective in this literature is an argument about cultural norms or "doing gender"; gender often trumps, even when bargaining or efficiency perspectives would predict otherwise. Consistent with this expectation, women do more and men less household work than can be explained by either an efficiency or bargaining perspective, and these perspectives explain only a small share of the variance in *which* men and women do more (Berk 1985; Shelton 1992). Some studies (reviewed in Greensteen 2000) find that traditional gender beliefs lead men to do more and women to do less household work. As discussed above, women have reduced household work much more than men have increased it. But child care is still largely women's responsibility. Despite egalitarian trends in attitudes, Americans and Australians have moved more strongly toward believing in women's equal rights to jobs and pay than in believing that children are not hurt by women's employment (Badgett, Davidson, and Folbre 2002; Bittman and Pixley 1997). This suggests a special resistance to having men replace women in parenting. Studies predicting men's and women's hours of household work separately find a much higher proportion of variance explained for women than men,

irrespective of what variables are put in the model (e.g., Brines 1994; Greenstein 2000). Where studies do find factors that affect men's housework, these often do not fit either efficiency or bargaining perspectives. For example, Hochschild (1989) found that among couples where women earned more than men, women nonetheless did the majority of household work. Brines (1994) and Greenstein (2000) found that men's hours of housework are increased by the share of income provided by women up to the point where women contribute equally, as bargaining or efficiency theories would predict, but beyond this, men reduce their housework contributions as women's share of income provision increases. The "doing gender" interpretation is that women's employment is now acceptable, but men are supposed to be the *main* breadwinners, and not to earn less than their wives. The more men are in this situation, unable to display male gender, Brines argues that they are unwilling to do housework or their wives disinclined to push them to do what would "feminize" them even more. However, Gupta (1999) and Bittman et al. (2003) replicated Brines and show that removing 3–4 percent of men who are most economically dependent makes the curvilinearity of the effect of relative income disappear; thus this appears to happen only among extremely low income men. In general, in the United States, the shape of distributions seems consistent with bargaining theory, but there is a large residual of women's excess housework not explained. In Australia, however, in the range between equal income provision and women providing all the income, women's housework actually increases (Bittman et al. 2003). Evertsson (2004) finds this for the United States as well.

CONCLUSION

The three major perspectives of economic sociology emphasize (1) networks, (2) rational choice, and (3) cultural (social) norms, sometimes embedded in institutions. Each is useful for understanding gender. Indeed, often empirical patterns are consistent with at least two of the perspectives. For example, returns to experience, which disadvantage women because of their time in child rearing, may be instituted by employers because experienced workers are more productive, or because turnover is expensive, especially where employers invest in training, as economists say. Or this may be an institutionalized norm having a disparate impact against women despite no link to productivity. Or take statistical discrimination: it may be engaged in to get better workers, despite its illegality and unfairness to those members of groups with lower average qualifications on unobservables who, as individuals, are high outliers in their group. This is the rational choice story. But patterns of ethnic or gender segregation might also be explained by beliefs in gender differences that have the sign right but exaggerate the magnitude, or by worker network recruitment, or by entirely erroneous racist or sexist cultural beliefs. All are consistent with finding an effect of ascriptive characteristics net of observable qualifications. Sorting out the explanatory power of these three perspectives is a formidable challenge in research on gender and other topics. In the case of networks, a major impediment is lack of adequate data sets that include network measures that are longitudinal (to allow better causal modeling). In the case of culture, the challenge is to measure values or beliefs independent of the behaviors they are to explain. Often rational choice explanations that feature material interests are more testable with existing data; here the impediment is less a lack of data than the tendency of economists to take their paradigm so for granted that they are not interested in testing predictions against competing claims from perspectives outside the rational choice paradigm.

What lessons does the study of gender have for the rest of economic sociology? Often scholars studying women's spheres of activity find many ways that standard assumptions and tools do not fit well. Looking closely at these may illuminate places where models are in tension with reality on other topics as well, but the lack of fit is not quite so obvious on more conventional topics. Let us close with two examples.

Women typically do the work of care, whether it is paid or unpaid. The emerging study of care work shows it to fit many standard assumptions badly, and to challenge many dichotomies. The work seems to produce externalities and public goods, and even economists admit that such factors "muck up" their usual assumptions that markets achieve efficiency. The work is often done for a mix of pecuniary and intrinsic motives; and the intrinsic motive in question, altruism, is at odds with the usual "selfishness" assumption of actors in markets. Care workers develop emotional connections with the consumers of their services. These intrinsic motives make it hard to predict how they will negotiate self-interestedly for wages, but sometimes they do. Our reaction to such self-interested negotiation is

sometimes that it violates norms that some things should be done only "for love." But, while all these things may be more true of care work, the quintessential "women's work," than of other work, are they not partly true of most work? Don't many kinds of work produce positive or negative externalities? Don't many jobs attract workers with the appropriate intrinsic motives, and develop those motives as "endogenous tastes" as the work is done? Are not workers in many jobs often connected emotionally to coworkers and clients or customers? Thus, the ways that care work challenges the economic model may apply more broadly (Folbre and Nelson 2000; England and Folbre 2003). Economic sociologists who position themselves "contra economics" will probably applaud this conclusion. But is it not true of economic sociology as well as of neoclassical economics that scholars tend to exclude from study—as "not economic"—precisely those areas of human activity where love, emotional connection, altruism, and norm-based commitment are involved? Economic sociologists talk a lot about networks and institutions, but they too have shied away from considerations of emotional commitments and connections.[4]

The study of gender takes us into realms such as the family where emotional ties and norm-based commitments are taken for granted (though not always observed). If we take seriously the admonition of gender scholars to acknowledge that the household is part of the economy, then the following question emerges: What determines which spheres of human activity are characterized by long-term commitments and which are more characterized by each party self-interestedly treating others as in textbook market or exchange models? Economists have a strong tendency, even when they become "institutionalists," to answer that norms and institutions evolve because they are efficient. Indeed, Becker has argued that it is efficient to have altruism govern the family economy and self-interest govern the market economy. Economic sociologists, focusing on markets, have rightly seen it a ridiculous claim that efficiency always reigns. We agree, but think economic sociologists should not simply ignore questions about efficiency. Moreover, because they ignore the household, economic sociologists seldom give much thought to whether it is equally ridiculous to think that altruism reigns in the family. If we avoid dichotomizing views, it leads to two deep and important questions that we challenge future generations of economists and economic sociologists to consider, across boundaries of families and formal organizations: What mix of commitment and marketlike incentives produces efficient outcomes? What are the distributional effects of these two principles in various contexts?

NOTES

1. The reader will benefit by consulting the Milkman and Townsley (1994) chapter, which includes more historical material than this chapter. We focus on empirical studies of gender in labor markets and families from the last 20 years of study by American sociologists and economics, and on debates between sociologists' and economists' perspectives on these topics.

2. Some critics of this chapter have urged us to be clearer about the distinctions between culture, norms, and institutions. But consideration of their advice has convinced us that sociologists do not use these terms consistently. What one calls culture, another calls norms, and yet another calls institutions. Some believe internalized preferences should be called norms, while others reserve the term *norms* for standards involving sanctions. Some reserve the term *institution* for explicit official rules that allocate punishments and rewards, while others use the term to include taken-for-granted assumptions about how things should be done.

3. More precisely, *D* is a ratio in which the numerator is the proportion of women (men) who would have to change occupations from the current distribution in order to integrate occupations, and the denominator is the number of moves women (or men) would have to make to integrate occupations if, instead of the current distribution, occupations were maximally segregated such that all occupations were entirely of one sex or the other. Occupations are considered to be integrated when women's (men's) proportion of each occupation is the same as women's (men's) proportion of the labor force as a whole.

4. We ourselves have been accused of being overly economistic in our exclusion of discussions of sexuality and emotion in this paper, and we acknowledge the merit of the critique while begging lack of space.

REFERENCES

Acker, Joan. 1989. *Doing Comparable Worth: Gender, Class, and Pay Equity.* Philadelphia: Temple University Press.

———. 1990. "Hierarchies, Jobs, Bodies: A Theory of Gendered Organizations." *Gender and Society* 4: 139–58.

Agarwal, Bina. 1997. "'Bargaining' and Gender Relations: Within and beyond the Household." *Feminist Economics* 3:1–50.

Aigner, Dennis J., and Glen G. Cain. 1977. "Statistical Theories of Discrimination in Labor Markets." *Industrial and Labor Relations Review* 30:175–87.

Akerlof, George A. 1982. "Labor Contracts as Partial Gift Exchange." *Quarterly Journal of Economics* 47: 543–69.

Alderman, Harold, Pierre-André Chiappori, Lawrence Haddad, John Hoddinott, and Ravi Kanbur. 1995.

"Unitary versus Collective Models of the Household: Is It Time to Shift the Burden of Proof?" *World Bank Research Observer* 10:1–19.

Anker, Richard. 1998. *Gender and Jobs: Sex Segregation of Occupation in the World.* Geneva: International Labour Office.

Aries, Elizabeth. 1996. *Men and Women in Interaction: Reconsidering the Differences.* Oxford: Oxford University Press.

Badgett, Lee, Pamela Davidson, and Nancy Folbre. 2002. "Breadwinner Dad, Homemaker Mom: An Interdisciplinary Analysis of Changing Gender Norms in the United States, 1977–1998." Department of Economics, University of Massachusetts, Amherst.

Baron, James N., and Andrew E. Newman. 1989. "Pay the Man: Effects of Demographic Composition on Prescribed Wage Rates in the California Civil Service." Pp. 107–30 in *Pay Equity: Empirical Inquiries*, ed. Robert T. Michael, Heidi I. Hartmann, and Brigid O'Farrell. Washington, D.C.: National Academy Press.

Becker, Gary. 1991. *A Treatise on the Family.* Enlarged Ed. Cambridge: Harvard University Press.

Bergmann, Barbara. 1974. "Occupational Segregation, Wages, and Profits When Employers Discriminate by Race or Sex." *Eastern Economic Journal* 1:103–10.

———. 1986. *The Economic Emergence of Women.* New York: Basic Books.

Berk, Sarah Fenstermaker. 1985. *The Gender Factory: The Apportionment of Work in American Households.* New York: Plenum.

Bernhardt, Annette, Martina Morris, Mark S. Handcock, and Marc A. Scott. 2001. *Divergent Paths: Economic Mobility in the New American Labor Market.* New York: Russell Sage Foundation.

Bianchi, Suzanne M., Melissa A. Milkie, Liana C. Sayer, and John P. Robinson. 2000. "Is Anyone Doing the Housework? Trends in the Gender Division of Household Labor." *Social Forces* 79:191–228.

Bianchi, Suzanne M., John P. Robinson, and Liana C. Sayer. 2001. *Family Interaction, Social Capital, and Trends in Time Use Study Project Report.* College Park: Survey Research Center, University of Maryland.

Bielby, William, and James Baron. 1986. "Men and Women at Work—Sex Segregation and Statistical Discrimination." *American Journal of Sociology* 91: 759–99.

Bielby, William, and Denise Bielby. 2002. "Telling Stories about Gender and Effort: Social Science Narratives about Who Works Hard for the Money." Pp. 193–217 in *The New Economic Sociology: Developments in an Emerging Field*, ed. Mauro Guillén, Randall Collins, Paula England, and Marshall Meyer. New York: Russell Sage Foundation.

Bittman, Michael, Paula England, Liana Sayer, Nancy Folbre, and George Matheson. 2003. "When Does Gender Trump Money: Bargaining and Time in

Household Work." *American Journal of Sociology.* 109:186–214.

Bittman, Michael, and Jocelyn Pixley. 1997. *The Double Life of the Family.* St. Leonards: Allen and Unwin.

Brines, Julie. 1994. "Economic Dependency, Gender, and the Division of Labor at Home." *American Journal of Sociology* 100:652–88.

Browne, Irene, and Paula England. 1997. "Oppression from Within and Without in Sociological Theories: An Application to Gender." *Current Perspectives in Social Theory* 17:77–104.

Budig, Michelle J. 2002. "Male Advantage and the Gender Composition of Jobs: Who Rides the Glass Escalator?" *Social Problems* 49:258–77.

Budig, Michelle J., and Paula England. 2001. "The Wage Penalty for Motherhood." *American Sociological Review* 66:204–25.

Bulow, Jeremy I., and Lawrence H. Summers. 1986. "A Theory of Dual Labor Markets with Application to Industrial Policy, Discrimination, and Keynesian Unemployment." *Journal of Labor Economics* 4: 376–414.

Burstein, Paul, and Susan Pitchford. 1990. "Social-Scientific and Legal Challenges to Education and Test Requirements in Employment." *Social Problems* 37:243–257.

Burt, Ronald. 1982. *Toward a Structural Theory of Action: Network Models of Social Structure.* New York: Academic Press.

———. 2002. "The Social Capital of Structural Holes." Pp. 148–90 in *The New Economic Sociology: Developments in an Emerging Field,* ed. Mauro Guillén, Randall Collins, Paula England, and Marshall Meyer. New York: Russell Sage Foundation.

Cancian, Francesca, and Stacy J. Oliker. 2000. *Caring and Gender.* Thousand Oaks, Calif.: Pine Forge Press.

Carrington, William J., and Kenneth R. Troske. 1993. "Gender Segregation in Small Firms." *Journal of Human Resources* 30:503–33.

Casper, Lynne M., and Suzanne M. Bianchi. 2002. *Continuity and Change in the American Family.* Thousand Oaks, Calif.: Sage.

Cherlin, Andrew J. 1992. *Marriage, Divorce, Remarriage.* Cambridge: Harvard University Press.

Chiappori, Pierre-André. 1992. "Collective Labor Supply and Welfare." *Journal of Political Economy* 100: 437–67.

Cohen, Philip N., and Suzanne M. Bianchi. 1999. "Marriage, Children, and Women's Employment: What Do We Know?" *Monthly Labor Review* 122:22–31.

Coleman, James. 1988. "Social Capital in the Creation of Human Capital." *American Journal of Sociology* 84:S95–S120.

Cook, Karen S., ed. 1987. *Social Exchange Theory.* Newbury Park, Calif.: Sage.

Corcoran, Mary, and Greg J. Duncan. 1979. "Work History, Labor Force Attachment, and Earnings Differences between Races and Sexes." *Journal of Human Resources* 14:3–20.

DiMaggio, Paul. 1994. "Culture and Economy." Pp. 27–57 in *The Handbook of Economic Sociology,* ed. Neil J. Smelser and Richard Swedberg. New York: Russell Sage Foundation; Princeton: Princeton University Press.

DiPrete, Thomas, and Claudia Buchmann. 2003. "Gender-Specific Trends in the Value of Education and the Emerging Gender Gap in College Completion." Paper presented at the meeting of Research Committee 28 of the International Sociological Association, New York University, August.

Edelman, Lauren. 1992. "Legal Ambiguity and Symbolic Structures: Organizational Mediation of Civil Rights Law." *American Journal of Sociology* 97: 1531–76.

England, Paula. 1982. "The Failure of Human Capital Theory to Explain Occupational Sex Segregation." *Journal of Human Resources* 18:358–70.

———. 1984. "Wage Appreciation and Depreciation: A Test of Neoclassical Economic Explanations of Occupational Sex Segregation." *Social Forces* 62: 726–49.

———. 1992. *Comparable Worth: Theories and Evidence.* New York: Aldine de Gruyter.

———. 2000a. "Conceptualizing Women's Empowerment in Countries of the North." Pp. 15–36 in *Women's Empowerment and Demographic Processes: Moving Beyond Cairo,* ed. Harriet B. Presser and Gita Sen. Oxford: Oxford University Press.

———. 2000b. "Marriage, the Costs of Children, and Gender Inequality." Pp. 320–42 in *The Ties That Bind: Perspectives on Marriage and Cohabitation,* ed. Linda J. Waite. New York: Aldine de Gruyter.

England, Paula, and Michelle Budig. 1998. "Gary Becker on the Family: His Genius, Impact, and Blind Spots." In *Required Reading: Sociology's Most Influential Books,* ed. Dan Clawson. Amherst: University of Massachusetts Press.

England, Paula, Michelle Budig, and Nancy Folbre. 2002. "The Wages of Virtue: The Relative Pay of Care Work." *Social Problems* 49:455–73.

England, Paula, and George Farkas. 1986. *Households, Employment, and Gender: A Social, Economic, and Demographic View.* New York: Aldine.

England, Paula, George Farkas, Barbara Stanek Kilbourne, and Thomas Dou. 1988. "Explaining Occupational Sex Segregation and Wages: Findings from a Model with Fixed Effects." *American Sociological Review* 53:544–58.

England, Paula, and Nancy Folbre. 1999. "The Cost of Caring." *Annals of the American Academy of Political and Social Science* 561:39–51.

———. 2000. "Reconceptualizing Human Capital." Pp. 126–28 in *The Management of Durable Relations,* ed. Werner Raub and Jeroen Weesie. Amsterdam: Thela Thesis Publishers.

———. 2002. "Care, Inequality, and Policy." Pp. 133–44 in *Child Care and Inequality: Re-thinking Carework for Children and Youth,* ed. Francesca

Cancian, Demie Kurz, Andrew S. London, Rebecca Reviere, and Mary Tuominen. New York: Routledge.

———. 2003. "Contracting for Care." Pp. 61–80 in *Beyond Economic Man: Feminist Theory and Economics Today*, ed. Marianne A. Ferber and Julie A. Nelson. Chicago: University of Chicago Press.

England, Paula, Joan M. Hermsen, and David A. Cotter. 2000. "The Devaluation of Women's Work: A Comment on Tam." *American Journal of Sociology* 105:1741–51.

England, Paula, and Barbara Kilbourne. 1990. "Markets, Marriage, and Other Mates: The Problem of Power." Pp. 163–88 in *Beyond the Marketplace: Rethinking Economy and Society*, ed. Roger Friedland and Sandy Robertson. New York: Aldine de Gruyter.

England, Paula, Lori L. Reid, and Barbara Stanek Kilbourne. 1996. "The Effect of the Sex Composition of Jobs on Starting Wages in an Organization: Findings from the NLSY." *Demography* 33:511–21.

England, Paula, Jennifer Thompson, and Carolyn Aman. 2001. "The Sex Gap in Pay and Comparable Worth: An Update." Pp. 551–56 in *Sourcebook on Labor Markets: Evolving Structures and Processes*, ed. Ivar Berg and Arne Kalleberg. New York: Plenum.

Epstein, Cynthia Fuchs. 1988. *Deceptive Distinctions: Sex, Gender, and the Social Order*. New Haven: Yale University Press.

Eurostat. 2002. *The Life of Women and Men in Europe: A Statistical Portrait*. Luxembourg: Eurostat.

Evertsson, Marie. 2004. *Facets of Gender: Analyses of the Family and the Labour Market*. Stockholm: Swedish Institute for Social Research.

Ferber, Marianne A., and Julie A. Nelson, eds. 1993. *Beyond Economic Man: Feminist Theory and Economics*. Chicago: University of Chicago Press.

Filer, Randall K. 1989. "Occupational Segregation, Compensating Differentials, and Comparable Worth." Pp. 153–70 in *Pay Equity: Empirical Inquiries*, ed. Robert T. Michael, Heidi I. Hartmann, and Brigid O'Farrell. Washington, D.C.: National Academy Press.

Fligstein, Neil. 2002. "Agreements, Disagreements, and Opportunities in the 'New Sociology of Markets.'" Pp. 61–78 in *The New Economic Sociology: Developments in an Emerging Field*, ed. Mauro Guillén, Randall Collins, Paula England, and Marshall Meyer. New York: Russell Sage Foundation.

Folbre, Nancy. 1994a. "Children as Public Goods." *American Economic Review* 84(2): 86–90.

———. 1994b. *Who Pays for the Kids? Gender and the Structures of Constraint*. London: Routledge.

———. 1997. "Gender Coalitions: Extrafamily Influences on Intrafamily Inequality." Pp. 263–74 in *Intrahousehold Resource Allocation in Developing Countries: Models, Methods, and Policy*, ed. Lawrence Haddad, John Hoddinott, and Harold Alderman. Baltimore: Johns Hopkins University Press.

Folbre, Nancy, and Julie A. Nelson. 2000. "For Love or Money—or Both?" *Journal of Economic Perspectives* 14:123–40.

Frank, Robert. 2000. *Microeconomics and Behavior*. 4th ed. New York: McGraw-Hill.

Glass, Jennifer. 1990. "The Impact of Occupational Segregation on Working Conditions." *Social Forces* 68: 779–96.

Glass, Jennifer, and Valerie Camarigg. 1992. "Gender, Parenthood, and Job-Family Compatibility." *American Journal of Sociology* 98:131–51.

Goldin, Claudia. 1990. *Understanding the Gender Gap: An Economic History of American Women*. Oxford: Oxford University Press.

Granovetter, Mark. 1985. "Economic Action and Social Structure: The Problem of Embeddedness." *American Journal of Sociology* 91:481–510.

———. 2002. "A Theoretical Agenda for Economic Sociology." Pp. 35–60 in *The New Economic Sociology: Developments in an Emerging Field*, ed. Mauro Guillén, Randall Collins, Paula England, and Marshall Meyer. New York: Russell Sage Foundation.

Greenstein, Theodore N. 1995. "Gender Ideology, Marital Disruption, and the Employment of Married Women." *Journal of Marriage and the Family* 57: 31–42.

———. 2000. "Economic Dependence, Gender, and the Division of Labor in the Home: A Replication and Extension." *Journal of Marriage and the Family* 62:322–35.

Groshen, Erica L. 1991. "The Structure of the Female/Male Wage Differential." *Journal of Human Resources* 26:457–72.

Gupta, Sanjiv. 1999. "Gender Display? A Reassessment of the Relationship between Men's Economic Dependence and Their Housework Hours." Paper presented at the Annual Meeting of the American Sociological Association, Chicago.

Heckert, D. Alex, Thomas C. Nowak, and Kay A. Snyder. 1998. "The Impact of Husbands' and Wives' Relative Earnings on Marital Disruption." *Journal of Marriage and the Family* 60:690–703.

Heer, David. 1963. "The Measurement and Bases of Family Power: An Overview." *Marriage and Family Living* 25:133–39.

Hiedemann, Bridget, Olga Suhomlinova, and Angela M. O'Rand. 1998. "Economic Independence, Economic Status, and Empty Nest in Midlife Marital Disruption." *Journal of Marriage and the Family* 60:219–31.

Hochschild, Arlie Russell. 1989. *The Second Shift: Working Parents and the Revolution at Home*. New York: Viking.

Hodgson, Geoffrey M. 1994. "The Return of Institutional Economics." Pp. 58–76 in *The Handbook of Economic Sociology*, ed. Neil J. Smelser and Richard Swedberg. Princeton: Princeton University Press.

Hoffman, Saul D., and Greg J. Duncan. 1995. "The Effect of Incomes, Wages, and AFDC Benefits on

Marital Disruption." *Journal of Human Resources* 30:19–41.

Ibarra, Herminia. 2001. "Social Networks and Gender." Pp. 14384–88 in vol. 21 of *International Encyclopedia of the Social and Behavioral Sciences*, ed. Neil J. Smelser and Paul B. Baltes. Amsterdam: Elsevier.

Ibarra, Herminia, and Lynn Smith-Lovin. 1997. "New Directions in Social Network Research on Gender and Careers." Pp. 359–84 in *Creating Tomorrow's Organization*, ed. Cary L. Cooper and Susan E. Jackson. New York: John Wiley and Sons.

Institute for Women's Policy Research. 1996. *The Wage Gap: Women's and Men's Earnings.* Washington, D.C.: Institute for Women's Policy Research.

Jacobs, Jerry A. 1989. *Revolving Doors: Sex Segregation and Women's Careers.* Stanford, Calif.: Stanford University Press.

———. 1999. "Sex Segregation of Occupations: Prospects for the Twenty-first Century." Pp. 125–141 in *Handbook of Gender in Organizations*, ed. Gary Powell. Thousand Oaks, Calif.: Sage.

———. 2001. "Evolving Patterns of Sex Segregation." Pp. 535–50 in *Sourcebook of Labor Markets: Evolving Structures and Processes*, ed. Ivar Berg and Arne L. Kalleberg. New York: Kluwer Academic, Plenum Publishers.

———. 2003. "Detours on the Road to Equality: Women, Work, and Higher Education." *Contexts* 2:32–41.

Jacobs, Jerry A., and Kathleen Gerson. 1998. "Who Are the Overworked Americans?" *Review of Social Economy* 56:442–59.

Jacobs, Jerry A., and Ronnie Steinberg. 1990. "Compensating Differentials and the Male-Female Wage Gap: Evidence from the New York State Comparable Worth Study." *Social Forces* 69:439–68.

Johnson, George, and Gary Solon. 1986. "Estimates of the Direct Effects of Comparable Worth Policy." *American Economic Review* 76:1117–25

Juhn, Chinhui, and Kevin M. Murphy. 1997. "Wage Inequality and Family Labor Supply." *Journal of Labor Economics* 15:72–97.

Kabeer, Naila. 2001. "Family Bargaining." Pp. 5314–19 in vol. 8 of *International Encyclopedia of the Social and Behavioral Sciences*, ed. Neil J. Smelser and Paul B. Baltes. Amsterdam: Elsevier.

Katz, Elizabeth. 1997. "The Intra-household Economics of Voice and Exit." *Feminist Economics* 3(3): 25–46.

Kilbourne, Barbara S., Paula England, George Farkas, Kurt Beron, and Dorothea Weir. 1994. "Returns to Skill, Compensating Differentials, and Gender Bias: Effects of Occupational Characteristics on the Wages of White Women and Men." *American Journal of Sociology* 100:689–719.

Lazear, Edward. 1990. "Pensions and Deferred Benefits as Strategic Compensation." Pp. 109–26 in *The Economics of Human Resource Management*, ed. Daniel J. B. Mitchell and Mahmood A. Zaidi. Oxford: Blackwell.

Lundberg, Shelly, and Robert A. Pollak. 1993. "Separate Spheres Bargaining and the Marriage Market." *Journal of Political Economy* 101:988–1010.

———. 1996. "Bargaining and Distribution in Marriage." *Journal of Economic Perspectives* 10:139–58.

Lundberg, Shelly, Robert A. Pollak, and Terence J. Wales. 1997. "Do Husbands and Wives Pool Their Resources? Evidence from the U.K. Child Benefit." *Journal of Human Resources* 32:463–80.

Lundberg, Shelly, and Elaina Rose. 2000. "Parenthood and the Earnings of Married Men and Women." *Labour Economics* 7:689–710.

MacPherson, David A., and Barry T. Hirsch. 1995. "Wages and Gender Composition: Why Do Women's Jobs Pay Less?" *Journal of Labor Economics* 13: 426–71.

Manser, Marilyn, and Murray Brown. 1980. "Marriage and Household Decision-Making: A Bargaining Analysis." *International Economic Review* 21:31–44.

Marini, Margaret Mooney, and Mary C. Brinton. 1984. "Sex Typing in Occupational Socialization." Pp. 192–232 in *Sex Segregation in the Workplace: Trends, Explanations, Remedies*, ed. Barbara F. Reskin. Washington, D.C.: National Academy Press.

Marini, Margaret Mooney, and Pi-Ling Fan. 1997. "The Gender Gap in Earnings at Career Entry." *American Sociological Review* 62:588–604.

McElroy, Marjorie B. 1990. "The Empirical Content of Nash-Bargained Household Behavior." *Journal of Human Resources* 25:559–83.

McElroy, Marjorie B., and Mary Jean Horney. 1981. "Nash Bargained Household Decisions." *International Economic Review* 22:333–49.

Milkman, Ruth, and Eleanor Townsley. 1994. "Gender and the Economy." Pp. 600–619 in *The Handbook of Economic Sociology*, ed. Neil J. Smelser and Richard Swedberg. New York: Russell Sage Foundation; Princeton: Princeton University Press.

Molm, Linda, and Karen Cook. 1995. "Social Exchange and Exchange Networks." Pp. 209–35 in *Sociological Perspectives on Social Psychology*, ed. Karen Cook, Gary Fine, and James House. Needham Heights, Mass.: Allyn and Bacon.

Moore Kristin A., and Linda J. Waite. 1981. "Marital Dissolution, Early Motherhood, and Early Marriage." *Social Forces* 60:20–40.

Mott, Frank L., and Sylvia F. Moore. 1979. "The Causes of Marital Disruption among Young American Women: An Interdisciplinary Perspective." *Journal of Marriage and the Family* 41:355–65.

Nelson, Julie A. 1993. "The Study of Choice or the Study of Provisioning? Gender and the Definition of Economics." Pp. 23–36 in *Beyond Economic Man: Feminist Theory and Economics*, ed. Marianne A. Ferber and Julie A. Nelson. Chicago: University of Chicago Press.

Nelson, Robert, and William Bridges. 1999. *Legalizing Gender Inequality.* Cambridge: Cambridge University Press.

North, Douglass C. 1991. "Institutions." *Journal of Economic Perspectives* 5:97–112.

O'Connor, Julia, Ann Shola Orloff, and Sheila Shaver. 1999. *States, Families, Markets: Gender, Liberalism, and Social Policy in Australia, Canada, Great Britain, and the United States.* Cambridge: Cambridge University Press.

Okamoto, Dina, and Paula England. 1999. "Is There a Supply Side to Occupational Sex Segregation?" *Sociological Perspectives* 42:557–82.

O'Neill, June, and Solomon Polachek. 1993. "Why the Gender Gap in Wages Narrowed in the 1980s." *Journal of Labor Economics* 11:205–28.

Ono, Hiromi. 1998. "Husbands' and Wives' Resources and Marital Dissolution." *Journal of Marriage and the Family* 60:674–89.

Oppenheimer, Valerie. 1970. *The Female Labor Force in the United States.* Berkeley: University of California Institute of International Studies.

Orazem, P. F., and P. Mattila. 1989. "Comparable Worth and the Structure of Earnings: The Iowa Case." Pp. 179–99 in *Pay Equity: Empirical Inquiries,* ed. Robert T. Michael, Heidi I. Hartmann, and Brigid O'Farrell. Washington, D.C.: National Academy Press.

Parcel, Toby L. 1989. "Comparable Worth, Occupational Labor Markets, and Occupational Earnings: Results from the 1980 Census." Pp. 134–52 in *Pay Equity: Empirical Inquiries,* ed. Robert T. Michael, Heidi I. Hartmann, and Brigid O'Farrell. Washington, D.C.: National Academy Press.

Petersen, Trond, and Laurie A. Morgan. 1995. "Separate and Unequal: Occupation, Establishment, Sex Segregation, and the Gender Wage Gap." *American Journal of Sociology* 101:329–65.

Polachek, Solomon. 1981. "Occupational Self Selection: A Human Capital Approach to Sex Differences in Occupation Structure." *Review of Economics and Statistics* 58:60–69.

———. 1984. "Women in the Economy: Perspectives on Gender Inequality." Pp. 34–53 in *Comparable Worth: Issue for the 80's: A Consultation of the U.S. Commission on Civil Rights.* Washington, D.C.: U.S. Commission on Civil Rights.

Pollak, Robert A. 2003. "Gary Becker's Contributions to Family and Household Economics." *Journal of Household Economics* 1:111–41.

Portes, Alejandro. 1994. "The Informal Economy and Its Paradoxes." Pp. 426–52 in *The Handbook of Economic Sociology,* ed. Neil J. Smelser and Richard Swedberg. New York: Russell Sage Foundation; Princeton: Princeton University Press.

Powell, Walter W., and Paul J. DiMaggio, eds. 1991. *The New Institutionalism in Organizational Analysis.* Chicago: University of Chicago Press.

Powell, Walter W., and Laurel Smith-Doerr. 1996. "Networks and Economic Life." Pp. 368–402 in *The Handbook of Economic Sociology,* ed. Neil J. Smelser and Richard Swedberg. New York: Russell Sage Foundation; Princeton: Princeton University Press.

Presser, Harriet B. 1994. "Employment Schedules among Dual-Earner Spouses and the Division of Labor by Gender." *American Sociological Review* 59:348–69.

Reskin, Barbara F. 1993. "Sex Segregation in the Workplace." *Annual Review of Sociology* 19:241–70.

———. 1998. *The Realities of Affirmative Action in Employment.* Washington, D.C.: American Sociological Association.

———. 2002. "Rethinking Employment Discrimination and Its Remedies." Pp. 218–44 in *The New Economic Sociology: Developments in an Emerging Field,* ed. Mauro Guillén, Randall Collins, Paula England, and Marshall Meyer. New York: Russell Sage Foundation.

Reskin, Barbara F., and Debra Branch McBrier. 2000. "Why Not Ascription? Organizations Employment of Male and Female Managers." *American Sociological Review* 65:210–33.

Reskin, Barbara F., and Patricia Roos. 1990. *Job Queues, Gender Queues.* Philadelphia: Temple University Press.

Ridgeway, Cecilia L., and Lynn Smith-Lovin. 1999. "The Gender System and Interaction." *Annual Review of Sociology* 25:191–216.

Ross, Catherine E. 1987. "The Division of Labor at Home." *Social Forces* 65:816–33.

Ross, Heather L., and Isabel Sawhill. 1975. "Marital Instability." Pp. 35–66 in *Time of Transition: The Growth of Families Headed by Women.* Washington, D.C.: Urban Institute.

Ruggles, Steven. 1997. "The Rise of Divorce and Separation in the United States, 1880–1990." *Demography* 34:455–66.

Sainsbury, Diane. 2000. *Gender and Welfare State Regimes.* Oxford: Oxford University Press.

Sayer, Liana C. 2001. "Time Use, Gender, and Inequalty: Differences in Men's and Women's Market, Nonmarket, and Leisure Time." Ph.D. diss., Department of Sociology, University of Maryland.

Sayer, Liana C., and Suzanne M. Bianchi. 2000. "Women's Economic Independence and the Probability of Divorce: A Review and Reexamination." *Journal of Family Issues* 21:906–43.

Scanzoni, John. 1979. "A Historical Perspective on Husband-Wife Bargaining Power and Marital Dissolution." Pp. 10–36 in *Divorce and Separation,* ed. George Levinger and Oliver C. Moles. New York: Basic Books.

Schoen, Robert, Nan Marie Astone, Kendra Rothert, Nicola J. Standish, and Young J. Kim. 2002. "Women's Employment, Marital Happiness, and Divorce." *Social Forces* 81:643–62.

Sen, Amatya K. 1990. "Gender and Co-operative Conflicts." Pp. 123–49 in *Persistent Inequalities: Women and World Development,* ed. Irene Tinker. Oxford: Oxford University Press.

Shelton, Beth Anne. 1992. *Women, Men, and Time: Gender Differences in Paid Work, Housework, and Leisure.* New York: Greenwood Press.

Smelser, Neil J., and Richard Swedberg. 1994. "The Sociological Perspective on the Economy." Pp. 3–26 in *The Handbook of Economic Sociology*, ed. Neil J. Smelser and Richard Swedberg. New York: Russell Sage Foundation; Princeton: Princeton University Press.

Smelser, Neil J., and Richard Swedberg, eds. *The Handbook of Economic Sociology*. New York: Russell Sage Foundation; Princeton: Princeton University Press.

Smith, James P., and Michael P. Ward. 1984. *Women's Wages and Work in the Twentieth Century*. Santa Monica, Calif.: Rand Corporation.

Smith-Lovin, Lynn, and J. Miller McPherson. 1993. "You Are Who You Know: A Network Approach to Gender." Pp. 223–51 in *Theory on Gender/Feminism on Theory*, ed. Paula England. Hawthorne, N.Y.: Aldine de Gruyter.

Sorensen, Elaine. 1994. *Comparable Worth*. Princeton: Princeton University Press.

South Scott J., and Kim Marie Lloyd. 1995. "Spousal Alternatives and Marital Dissolution." *American Sociological Review* 60:21–35.

Spitze, Glenna D., and Scott J. South. 1985. "Women's Employment, Time Expenditure, and Divorce." *Journal of Family Issues* 6:307–29.

Steinberg, Ronnie. 2001. "Comparable Worth in Gender Studies." Pp. 2293–97 in vol. 4 of *International Encyclopedia of the Social and Behavioral Sciences*, ed. Neil J. Smelser and Paul B. Baltes. Amsterdam: Elsevier.

Steinberg, Ronnie, Lois Haignere, Carol Possin, Cynthia H. Chertos, and Donald Trieman. 1986. *The New York State Pay Equity Study: A Research Report*. Albany: Center for Women in Government, SUNY Press.

Stiglitz, Joseph E. 1987. "The Causes and Consequences of the Dependence of Quality on Price." *Journal of Economic Literature* 25:1–48.

Sunstein, Cass. 1991. "Why Markets Don't Stop Discrimination." *Social Philosophy and Policy* 8:22–37.

Swidler, Ann. 1985. "Culture in Action: Symbols and Strategies." *American Sociological Review* 51:273–86.

Tam, Tony. 1997. "Sex Segregation and Occupational Gender Inequality in the United States: Devaluation or Specialized Training?" *American Journal of Sociology* 102:1652–92.

———. 2000. "Occupational Wage Inequality and Devaluation: A Cautionary Tale of Measurement Error." *American Journal of Sociology* 105:1752–60.

Thomas, Duncan. 1990. "Intra-household Resource Allocation: An Inferential Approach." *Journal of Human Resources* 25:635–64.

Tomaskovic-Devey, Donald. 1993. *Gender and Racial Inequality at Work: The Sources and Consequences of Job Segregation*. Ithaca, N.Y.: ILR Press.

Tzeng, Jessie M., and Robert D. Mare. 1995. "Labor Market and Socioeconomic Effects on Marital Stability." *Social Science Research* 24:329–51.

Van der Lippe, Tanja, and Liset Van Dijk, eds. 2001.

Women's Employment in a Comparative Perspective. New York: Aldine de Gruyter.

Waerness, Kari. 1987. "On the Rationality of Caring." Pp. 207–34 in *Women and the State*, ed. Ann Showstack Sassoon. London: Hutchinson.

Waldfogel, Jane. 1997. "The Effect of Children on Women's Wages." *American Sociological Review* 62:209–17.

———. 1998. "Understanding the 'Family Gap' in Pay for Women with Children." *Journal of Economic Perspectives* 12:137–56.

Weiss, Yoram, and Robert Willis. 1997. "Match Quality, New Information, and Marital Dissolution." *Journal of Labor Economics* 15:S293–S329.

Wellington, Allison J. 1993. "Changes in the Male-Female Wage Gap, 1976–1985." *Journal of Human Resources* 28:383–411.

———. 1994. "Accounting for the Male/Female Wage Gap among Whites: 1976 and 1985." *American Sociological Review* 59:839–84.

West, Candace, and Sarah Fenstermaker. 1993. "Power, Inequality, and the Accomplishment of Gender: An Ethnomethodological View." Pp. 151–74 in *Theory on Gender/Feminism on Theory*, ed. Paula England. New York: Aldine de Gruyter.

West, Candace, and Don H. Zimmerman. 1987. "Doing Gender." *Gender and Society* 1:125–51.

White, Harrison C. 1981. "Where Do Markets Come From?" *American Journal of Sociology* 87:514–47.

———. 2002. "Markets and Firms: Notes toward the Future of Economic Sociology." Pp. 129–47 in *The New Economic Sociology: Developments in an Emerging Field*, ed. Mauro Guillén, Randall Collins, Paula England, and Marshall Meyer. New York: Russell Sage Foundation.

Williams, Christine L. 1995. *Still a Man's World: Men Who Do Women's Work*. Berkeley and Los Angeles: University of California Press.

Williams, Joan. 2001. *Unbending Gender: Why Family and Work Conflict and What to Do About It*. Oxford: Oxford University Press.

Williams, Joan, and Nancy Segal. 2003. "Beyond the Maternal Wall: Relief for Family Caregivers Who Are Discriminated Against on the Job." *Harvard Women's Law Journal* 26:77–162.

Williamson, Oliver E. 1985. *The Economic Institutions of Capitalism: Firms, Markets, Relational Contracting*. New York: Free Press.

Wright, Erik Olin, and Janeen Baxter, with Elisabeth Birkelund Gunn. 1995. "The Gender Gap in Workplace Authority: A Cross-National Study." *American Sociological Review* 60:407–35.

Zelizer, Viviana. 2002. "Enter Culture." Pp. 101–28 in *The New Economic Sociology: Developments in an Emerging Field*, ed. Mauro Guillén, Randall Collins, Paula England, and Marshall Meyer. New York: Russell Sage Foundation.

28 The Ethnic Economy

Ivan Light

MAX WEBER ([1927] 1981, sec. 6C) briefly addressed the sociology of "alien traders" in comparative economic development. He thus founded what later became known as middleman minority theory (Bonacich 1973). Middleman minorities specialize in trade and commerce in which they have centuries of historical experience. From this experience they have evolved special expertise in commercial entrepreneurship. Examples include the Jews of Europe, Armenians, Gypsies, overseas Chinese, Sikhs in East Africa, the Hausa of Nigeria, and Marwaris and Parsees in India.[1] This substantial literature, reviewed in the first edition of this *Handbook*, generally proposes a three-cornered conflict in which colonial elites covertly support alien merchants because of their profitability, but abandon them to outrages and murder when merchant-customer conflicts bubble over into rioting and mayhem. On these sanguinary occasions, the deluded masses vent their economic frustration upon alien merchants. Rather than blaming the economic system, the real source of their frustration, natives blame the merchants who mediate their access to goods. Middleman minority theory is a scapegoat theory. Simple as is the underlying theoretical idea, middleman minority theory has enormously clarified the commonalties that underlie some of the ugliest hatreds in human history, rendering them amenable to sociological analysis. Recently Chirot and Reid (1997; also Schmidt 2000, 354–55) have extended and continued this tradition with their comparison of Jews in Europe and Chinese in Southeast Asia, both of them classic mercantile minorities, and both subject to violent and enduring hatreds as a result. Similarly, Min (1996; and also Yoon 1997, 174–228) drew successfully upon middleman minority theory to explain anti-Korean agitation and rioting in New York City and Los Angeles in the 1990s. Returning to the classic three-cornered model, Min depicted immigrant Korean merchants as "caught in the middle" in a racial conflict of blacks and whites.[2]

The ethnic economy literature descends from middleman minority theory, a subject it continues to include. However, ethnic economy literature now more broadly addresses the economic independence of immigrants and ethnic minorities in general, not just of middleman minorities (Light and Bonacich 1991, xii–xiii).[3] This expansion releases the subject from narrow concentration upon historical trading minorities, and opens discussion of the entire range of immigrant and ethnic minority strategies for economic self-help and self-defense. Economic independence represents a ubiquitous self-defense of immigrants and ethnic minorities who confront exclusion or disadvantage in labor markets. Ethnic economies permit immigrants and ethnic minorities to reduce disadvantage and exclusion, negotiating the terms of their participation in the general labor market from a position of greater strength. Unable to find work in the general labor market, or unwilling to accept the work that the general labor market offers, or just reluctant to mix with foreigners, immigrants and ethnic minorities have the option of employment or self-employment in the ethnic economy of their group. Although ethnic and immigrant groups differ in how much they avail themselves of this defense (Logan and Alba 1999, 179; Light and Gold 2000, 34; Collins 2003), none lacks an ethnic economy.[4]

The first *Handbook of Economic Sociology* defined an ethnic economy as "the ethnic self-employed and employers, their unpaid family workers, and their co-ethnic employees" (Light and Karageorgis 1994, 648).[5] A decade later, this definition of ethnic economy has become the *ethnic ownership economy*, itself only a coequal *component* of an ethnic economy, not the whole of it. As currently understood, an *ethnic economy* consists of two sectors: the ethnic-controlled economy and the ethnic ownership economy.[6] An *ethnic ownership economy* is still defined by business ownership.[7] In contrast, an *ethnic-controlled economy* requires ethnic control, not ownership. Ethnic-controlled economies exist where and to the extent that coethnic *employees* "exert significant and enduring" market power over the workplace, usually because of their numbers, clustering, and organization, but also, where appropriate, because of external political or economic power (Light and Gold 2000, 23). An ethnic-dominated craft union is a fine example. Unions influence the hiring and pay policies of businesses they do not own, exerting their influence for the benefit of members. When a union sets the pay scale, or even influences the pay scale, it usurps authority ostensibly monopolized by owners. Although control defines the boundary of the concept, control is uncommon; *influence* is common. Immigrants rely upon social networks for job access to the mainstream; networks breed clustering, and clustering breeds influence (Sanders, Nee, and Sernau 2002, 306).[8] Even when industries or trades are saturated, ethnic influence raises depressed wages and secures privileged hiring access to coethnics (Model 1997, 454; Rogerson 1999). Job capture arises when ethnic minority or immigrant employees are able to tilt the odds of employment in their trade, industry, or workplace in favor of coethnics (D. Kim 1999). *Absolute job capture* occurs when, thanks to coethnic control, only coethnics are hired. Much more commonly, *relative job capture* occurs when, thanks to various constraints, employers hire coethnics appreciably above levels normally expected in a meritocratic marketplace. Originating in the political realm, government affirmative action policies promote relative job capture, thus strengthening ethnic-controlled economies in trades, industries, and workplaces.

The new distinction between ethnic ownership economy and ethnic-controlled economy parallels the classic distinction between ownership and control of corporations. Just as, for many purposes, it makes little difference that stockholders own the corporations that managements control, so it sometimes makes little difference who owns enterprises if and to the extent that coethnic employees *control* them (Waldinger 1995). Indeed, control is better than ownership insofar as employees thereby obtain some benefits of ownership (setting pay scales, making hiring decisions) without the financial risks of ownership. As the directors of Enron, WorldCom, and Global Crossing taught us, managers can enrich themselves at the expense of owners. Blue-collar ethnic minority and immigrant employees also materially benefit at the expense of the owners when they can influence pay scales or hiring. Ethnonationalism is not a necessary cause of ethnic clustering in occupations, nor of ethnic control expressed in ethnocentric hiring policies. After all, if hiring is restricted to friends, relatives, and neighbors of current employees, which is the usual product of ethnic control, the unintended result will be relative job capture by the predominant ethnic group just because friends, relatives, and neighbors are normally coethnics. Additionally, a control base in a trade or industry supports and promotes the self-employment of coethnics, who usually originated as employees in the same industry (Mata and Pendakur 1999, 397).

Both the ethnic ownership economy and the ethnic-controlled economy have formal, informal, and illegal subsectors (Tienda and Raijman 2000, 292–96; Perberdy and Rogerson 2003). These sectors are conceptually different (Quassoli 1999, 225). The formal sector consists of firms that pay taxes and enjoy official enumeration. If coethnic employees control these firms without owning them, the employees work in the formal subsector of the ethnic-controlled economy. If coethnics own these firms, then both the owners and their coethnic employees work in the formal subsector of the ethnic ownership economy, still the heartland of the existing literature. The informal sector (see the chapter on this topic by Portes and Haller, this volume) contains firms that, producing legal commodities, produce them without paying taxes or obtaining licenses (Bourgeois 1995). The key issue is the *existence* of firms in the informal economy rather than, as Neef (2002) supposes, the inability of governments to regulate those firms. If the existence of informal sectors is not recognized, analysis will be restricted to the formal sector, a grave distortion. Wilson (1996; also Rifkin 1996) falls into this error. Tracking adverse employment trends in the general labor market, Wilson declared that African Americans' work had just "disappeared,"[9] ignoring their work in the informal economy. Unless they analyze the ethnic economy in relationship to the general labor market, tracking movements back and forth across the border, as did Nee, Sanders, and Sernau (1994; also Yoon 1997, 133), labor market analysts misunderstand labor.

Firms are the basic units of the informal economy as well as of the formal economy. An unemployed warehouseman who starts a business has moved his economic activity from the category of labor to that of capital. In point of fact, the rate of immigrant self-employment is higher in the informal sector than in the formal sector, and both rates increase drastically when multiple job-holding is considered.[10] When immigrants and ethnic minorities own firms in the informal sector, the informal subsector houses that portion of their ethnic own-

TABLE 1.   Ethnic Economy: Sectors and Subsectors

Sector	Ethnic Ownership Economy			Ethnic-Controlled Economy		
Subsector	Formal (1)	Informal (2)	Illegal (3)	Formal (4)	Informal (5)	Illegal (6)

Examples
1. Owners of dry-cleaning retail store, their unpaid family workers, and their coethnic employees
2. Owners of unlicensed garment factory, their unpaid family workers, and their coethnic employees
3. Owners of bookmaking business, their unpaid family workers, and their coethnic employees
4. Coethnic employees who control the dry-cleaning business that employs them
5. Coethnic employees who control off-the-books garment factory in which they work
6. Coethnic employees who control the illegal lottery that employs them

ership economy. When coethnic employees control informal firms without actually owning them, then the informal firm lies in the *ethnic-controlled economy*.[11] The illegal subsector consists of firms that manufacture or distribute proscribed commodities to willing buyers, especially drugs, gambling, and prostitution, but also bogus immigration documents, pornography, and pirated videos.[12] As before, coethnic ownership of illegal firms falls into the ethnic ownership economy, whereas coethnic employee control falls into the ethnic-controlled economy (table 1).[13]

All coethnics working in either the ethnic ownership economy *or* the ethnic-controlled economy belong to the ethnic economy of their group.[14] The size of ethnic economies vis-à-vis the employment mainstream varies historically and among ethnocultural groups (Shrover 2001; Light 1972). Among some groups, most coethnics find employment in the ethnic economy; among others, few do (Boyd 2000, 2001a). Nonetheless, the absolute and relative sizes of ethnic economies are of great importance to the economic prospects of immigrants and ethnic minorities. As matters stand, however, only the ethnic ownership economies of the formal subsector can be estimated from official data sources. Ethnic-controlled economies and ethnic ownership economies in the informal subsector and the illegal subsector are inaccessible from official sources, and must be estimated from social science research. Accordingly, just improving and debating the adequacy of size estimates is a continuing methodological concern of research in ethnic economies (Sik 1998, 5–8, 59–68; Cross 1998, 9–10).

As one result, researchers have developed quantitative methods that permit them to estimate the size of ethnic economies from public data sources (Hum 1997; Logan and Alba 1999; Logan et al. 2000; Wilson, 2003). These methodologies permit analysts to estimate the size of ethnic econo-

mies of a multiplicity of ethnoracial groups in multiple locations, whereas previous methodology relied upon case studies of one group in a single location. Still the most accurate method, one-group, one-place studies do not yield the broad generalizations scholars often want. Estimates indicate that ethnic economies are surprisingly large. Ethnic economies employed one-quarter of immigrants in Germany in 1992 (Guerrero 2000, 117). Reviewing the American literature, Light and Gold (2000, 34) found that just the formal subsector's ethnic ownership economies contained 11 percent of the labor force of all foreign-born persons in 1990.[15] Constituent groups had grossly different self-employment rates. Among Hispanics, the percentage was 9.9 percent; among African Americans, 5.6 percent; among Asians, 19.2 percent; and among Koreans more than 50 percent. Light and Gold (2000, 52) estimated that 10 percent of the average American ethnic group's workers found employment in the informal sector of the ethnic ownership economy; using somewhat different definitions, Wilson (2003) reported that 14 percent of the American labor force worked in ethnic niches, but 31 percent of non-European ethnic groups did so.[16] Specific groups fall above and below this average, which also varies from city to city and country to country (Langlois and Razin 1995, 587). In the most comprehensive and serious effort to measure informal sector self-employment using a case study, Tienda and Raijman found that 38 percent of Mexican immigrant households in Chicago worked in the informal economy.[17]

A large and even historical literature attempts to measure the size of ethnic niches, which are now usually defined as industrial or occupational clusters of coethnics in excess of 150 percent of their expected number (Boyd 2001b, 89; Logan and Alba 1999; Wilson 2003).[18] Since clustering implies control, measures of ethnic niches crudely estimate the extent of ethnic-controlled economies in the formal subsector.[19] Clustering varies widely from group to group, city to city, and decade to decade. Its causes are not always the same (Talwar 2001, 121). Among African Americans, the public sector represents the main ethnic niche (Boyd 1993). About 20 percent of the average ethnoracial group works in ethnic-controlled economies (Light and Gold 2000, 52). Adding this 20 percent to the 20 percent who worked in the ethnic ownership economy's formal or informal subsectors, plus 1 percent estimated to work in the illegal economy, exclusive of incarcerated persons, Light and Gold (2000, 52) estimated that 41 percent of the American labor force worked in ethnic economies.[20]

SINGLE AND DOUBLE DISADVANTAGE

Immigrant and ethnic minority workers often turn to self-employment because of disadvantage (Martiniello and Jamin 2000, 63; Raes 2000, 34; Tienda and Raijman 2000, 300; Di Natale et al. 1999; Phizaclea and Ram 1996). Other circumstances being equal, disadvantage increases self-employment in the informal as well as in the formal sector (Bean and Spener 1999, 14).[21] Racial, ethnic, and religious discrimination is a major cause of disadvantage, but lack of language skill and unaccredited human capital are as important. Disadvantage is not a simple concept. Current thinking distinguishes labor market disadvantage from resource disadvantage. Both affect ethnic economies, but they do so independently. *Labor market disadvantage* occurs when workers cannot obtain wage or salary employment that reaches the prevailing market return on their productivity (Light and Rosenstein 1995, 153–55). The most extreme labor market disadvantage is long-term unemployment, which one expects to last forever. All forms of labor market disadvantage give employees an unusually powerful incentive to undertake self-employment. In extreme cases, self-employment offers the only possible income for employees who have given up all hope of ever finding a wage job; in less extreme cases, disadvantaged employees hope that self-employment might improve their economic or social situation.

Groups experience *resource disadvantage* when, as a result of some current or past historical experience, such as slavery or peonage, members enter the labor market with fewer resources than others. Resources include all attributes that improve the productivity of employees, notably human capital,

but also a positive work ethic, good health, contact networks, self-esteem, and so on. Even if resource-disadvantaged employees earn the expected wage, their wages will be low because they are unproductive. In this case, they experience only one disadvantage, resource disadvantage. Their problem is low resources, not lower than expected pay given their low productivity. They are singly disadvantaged. However, when labor force disadvantage and resource disadvantage combine, both affecting the same group, those doubly disadvantaged are low-wage, low-productivity employees. Because subject to discrimination and unproductive, the doubly disadvantaged lack the resources to support self-employment in the formal sector. As a result, their multiple disadvantages impel them into the ethnic economy's informal sector, where slender resources suffice. In the informal sector, they generally earn little. On the other hand, when immigrants or ethnic minorities have strong resources of human, social, cultural, and financial capital, and when they sustain only labor force disadvantage, the disadvantaged immigrants and ethnic minorities have resources that empower their self-employment. They need not tolerate abuse in the general labor market; hence, self-employment offers them some right of economic appeal against the judgment of the labor market.

This *resource constraint version* of disadvantage theory explains anomalies that arise from the highly unequal rates of self-employment among disadvantaged ethnonational and ethnoreligious groups (Light and Gold 2000, 34; Fairlie and Meyer 1996). Since this debate has raged for a century, its resolution represents progress.[22] The basic conundrum has been to explain unequal rates of self-employment among the disadvantaged. If disadvantage causes self-employment, why do disadvantaged blacks, Mexicans, and Central Americans display low self-employment rates, whereas disadvantaged Asians display high self-employment rates? (Yoon 1997, 37; see Light and Gold 2000, 34, 66, 208–9). In response, resource constraint theory proposes that doubly disadvantaged groups have the expected motive to undertake self-employment, but they *lack essential resources*. As a result, their self-employment develops in the informal sector rather than in the formal sector (Conley 1999, 21; Duneier 1999).[23] Conversely, well-educated immigrants have the resources to undertake self-employment in the formal sector when disadvantaged in the labor market.

Admittedly, when successful in the informal sector, immigrant and ethnic minority firms occasionally upgrade into the formal sector (Raijman and Tienda 1999; Robert and Bukodi 2000, 151). In these cases, business owners who were initially doubly disadvantaged obtained new resources through informal sector self-employment. These *acquired resources* (money, contacts, experience) then fuel the transition from informal to formal sector business ownership. This upgrade epitomizes the American Dream of rags-to-riches (Wyllie 1954). True, if the frequency of life history transitions from informal to formal sector were high, we would find no association between ethnoracial origins and informal or formal sector entrepreneurship. Starting in the informal sector would not reduce anyone's likelihood of winding up in the formal sector. Since very powerful associations do exist, with the doubly disadvantaged entrepreneurs occupying the informal sector while the labor market disadvantaged occupy the formal sector, we conclude that double disadvantage is infrequently overcome by entrepreneurial success in the ethnic economy's informal sector.

This conclusion does not justify dismissing the American Dream as fiction. After all, the transition from informal sector business ownership to formal sector business ownership (and also from the illegal sector to the formal sector), although infrequently accomplished, is accomplished *frequently enough* to impact the social structure of immigrant and ethnic minority communities. First, doubly disadvantaged adults past the school-leaving age have no way to access the middle class other than entrepreneurship. For poorly educated adults, business ownership in the informal and illegal sectors of the ethnic economy permits more lifetime mobility into the middle class than do all other avenues of mobility together.[24] Second, doubly disadvantaged adults substitute street wisdom for formal education. The informal economy rewards this form of human capital. Third, business owners provide the stratum from which immigrant and ethnic minorities have always recruited political and social leadership (Bodnar 1985, 117–42; Guerrero 2000, 117). For these structural reasons, organized crime and petty entrepreneurship still create what Daniel Bell (1960, 115–36) once called a "queer ladder of social mobility."

INCOME AND WEALTH

How lucrative is ethnic self-employment? This subject continues to attract interest in the United States—but not in Europe (Barrett, Jones, and McEvoy 1996). Cultural influences are probably at work. In the United States, the debate reawakens the nation's historic preoccupation with self-made men (Wyllie 1954), a cultural legacy that Europe does not share.[25] Rags-to-riches enters the ethnic economy debate because of the claim, initially made by Portes and Bach (1985) and subsequently by Portes and Zhou (1996; 1998, table 2) that the formal subsector of the ethnic enclave economy generated higher education-adjusted earnings than did the wage-earning mainstream. If so, the more coethnics became self-employed, the higher would be the average income of their group. Moreover, to the extent that ethnic enclave economies actually enjoy an earnings advantage, ethnic economies would impede assimilation, which is driven by surrender of ethnicity in exchange for higher earnings (Werbner 2001, 677; Bankston and Zhou 1996, 39). That is, if people earned more in ethnic economies, then ethnic economies would be more economically advantageous than integration into the mainstream, the terminus ad quem of assimilation theory. The recent development of ethnic suburbs in North American cities, where the unassimilated enjoy home ownership, awakens the same debate (Logan, Alba, and Zhang 2002, 300, 320).

For the most part, research since 1994 has continued to compare the education-adjusted earnings of coethnics in ethnic enclave economies *and* ethnic ownership economies with those in the employment mainstream (Spener and Bean 1999). New results reach the same inconclusive results reviewed in the preceding *Handbook*. These results sometimes show the self-employed earning more than equally qualified coethnic wage earners and sometimes show them lagging. There is variation by ethnic group, by gender, by industry, and by locality (Li 1994; Devine 1994; Light and Roach 1996; Yoon 1997, 136; Logan and Alba 1999, 192).[26] The share of self-employed professionals also tends to drive up average earnings of the self-employed in general (Bradley 2003). In an important methodological contribution, Portes and Zhou (1996) showed that specification of earnings equations affected the results obtained. When outliers were suppressed or incomes entered in relative, rather than absolute form, analysts minimized the economic advantageousness of self-employment, and vice versa. The safest overall conclusion is that in many important and significant cases the self-employed report more income than comparably educated coethnic wage earners of the mainstream economy. On the other hand, the education-adjusted earnings advantage of self-employment is not invariant. The self-employed earn less than comparably educated wage earners as often as they earn more. To this extent the ideal of economic integration retains plausibility. On average, across all ethnic groups in all locations, the self-employed and their coethnic equivalents in the mainstream's wage and salary sector probably earn *about the same* annual education-adjusted incomes. The trouble is, a mean glosses over particular groups in particular localities; yet these localities are precisely the source whence flow the real empirical consequences of interest.

Attacks on ethnic ownership have been more successful when they focused on the claim, initially made by Portes and his associates, that not only the self-employed but even their coethnic employees earned higher education-adjusted incomes than did their coethnic equivalents in mainstream wage and salary employment. Small business firms tend overwhelmingly to hire coethnics (Romney 1999). Research has found that coethnic employees of ethnic business firms occasionally earn as much as their equivalents in the mainstream, as they did in Portes's Miami data. However, that result does not generally obtain. On the contrary, coethnic employees within ethnic ownership economies generally earn lower education-adjusted incomes than do coethnic equivalents in the mainstream economy. On average, the ethnic ownership economy's coethnic employees earn about 80 percent of what their coethnic equivalents earn in the mainstream.[27]

Recent attention to wealth rather than to income raises new questions about the economic advantages of business ownership.[28] In general, the self-employed have 10 to 14 times more wealth than do employees. This wealth accumulates as the owners' equity share of their business. As owners increase their equity share, the owners' *wealth grows* even when their income does not. When they sell their business, the owners will finally tap this wealth. Even if business owners receive the same income as do coethnic employees in the mainstream, the owners' real economic welfare might be superior because of their superior wealth. However, their real advantage is smaller than this estimate indicates because of employees' pension benefits. If owners sell their business to fund their retirement, then their business assets must be evaluated against employees' pension rights. Owners have wealth stored in the business; employees have pensions. In fact, however, in terms of household gross assets, employees' pension benefits were only half the size of business assets in 1995, suggesting

that the wealth advantage of the self-employed more than compensated the pension benefits of employees (Keister 2000, 69, 123).

EXPLOITATION AND GENDER

About two-thirds of personnel in ethnic ownership economies are owners or unpaid family members, not employees. Therefore, the welfare of employees is of less general importance than the welfare of the self-employed and their family members. Moreover, even lower than prevailing wages in ethnic ownership economies do not justify the charge of labor exploitation frequently leveled against ethnic business owners (Gold 1994, 217; Loucky et al. 1994; Gilbertson 1995, 668; Wong 1998, 74; Hillmann 1999, 269; Timm 2000, 374). In its Marxist sense, exploitation depends upon the ratio of wages to profits.[29] In the Marxist sense, exploitation cannot occur where there is no profit. The profit of a business does not include the owner's labor charge (Barrett, Jones, and McEvoy 1996, 788). Small ethnic minority and immigrant businesses are usually unprofitable.[30] After taking out return on invested capital, Bates (1997, 249) found that when owners were college graduates, Asian American business owners earned $6.00 per hour of labor in their business; African American owners earned $6.41 an hour. Owners without college education earned only $3.00 per hour of their own labor.[31] These earnings approximate the current minimum wage. Even when small firms are profitable, they are often the least profitable firms in their industry. In the garment-manufacturing industry of Los Angeles, where virtually all contractors are foreign born (Light, Bernard, and Kim 1999; Light and Ojeda 2001), Bonacich and Appelbaum (2000, 2) showed that the top of the food chain, garment retailers and manufacturers, obtained more than half of the industry's gross revenues. Contractors received 15 percent, and production workers divided just 6 percent of the industry's gross. If exploitation exists in the garment industry, immigrant contractors are not the principal beneficiaries.

Unprofitable firms cannot exploit their coethnic employees no matter how poorly their employees are paid![32] All too often, the low wages of ethnic economy employees are a condition of their employment in that their employer's firm only exists because it pays low wages. Ethnic economies soak up the unemployment the mainstream leaves. The same considerations apply to the alleged exploitation of unpaid family workers, especially the wives of owners.[33] Embodying social capital, families normally enjoy internal relationships of trust, solidarity, and moral community that greatly facilitate concerted economic action (Sanders and Nee 1996, 237). Nonetheless, it is widely maintained (Hiebert 2003; Struder 2001) that husbands gain more from family firms than do wives or children. Husbands and fathers may gain economically at the expense of wives and children if they compel them to work in the family firm even when they have better earning chances elsewhere or if the fathers and husbands usurp the income. Should this happen, it would not amount to exploitation in the Marxist sense. Moreover, there is no convincing evidence that either of these conditions obtains very often. First, apropos wives, the only evidence offered observes that marriage increases men's self-employment rates.[34] From this fact, authors infer that ethnic minority and immigrant patriarchs appropriate the unpaid labor of children and wives in order to operate a business that benefits the patriarch more than the others (Struder 2001). However, except for African Americans, both men and women have higher self-employment rates when married or even previously married than when single (Devine 1994, table 4; Sanders and Nee 1996, 240). Marriage increases women's self-employment rates more than men's.[35] Marriage does not uniquely benefit the entrepreneurship of men. Indeed, self-employed women work more hours weekly than do women who co-own business firms with their husbands.[36] As for children, if they had been exploited, they should complain when they reach adulthood, but they do not. On the contrary, when adult children are asked about their experience as unpaid child labor in their parents' family business, they acknowledge long hours of unpaid toil. However, perceiving this toil as a condition of the firm's survival, the adult children do not call it exploitation. They say that helping out "was the least we could do" to repay their parents' self-sacrifice and hard work (Song 1999, 76).

The exceptional African American case is instructive. Unlike other ethnoracial groups, marriage does not increase African American self-employment, male or female. However, African American self-employment rates are low, and their nuclear families small and unstable. Arguably, small and unstable African American families do not provide a base for self-employment. If so, one might infer that ethnic self-employment requires patriarchs who can subordinate their wife and children, but African American men cannot accomplish this sub-ordination (Green and Pryde 1997, 74–75). In this case, the low self-employment rates of African Americans would reflect the relative weakness of patriarchy in that population.[37] Alternatively, one might propose that the African Americans' lack of family-centric social capital disarms the advantages that family firms normally enjoy, rendering married African Americans no more effective entrepreneurs than single ones (Sanders and Nee 1996). This judgment implies that marriage partners cannot trust one another, nor can they control their children. The social penalty is lack of the usual family resources for self-employment; hence, poverty. Although these explanations appear antagonistic, and neither can be accepted right now, both reduce to the failure of normative integration in African American families: patriarchy does not work, but no other norms have arisen to integrate families, thus salvaging their social capital for the family firm.

Owners exploit workers, not co-owners. Therefore, when wives are co-owners with husbands of "mom and pop" businesses, Pop cannot *exploit* Mom, although he can *cheat* her. Such cases are not uncommon.[38] If husband co-owners coerce wife co-owners into working as co-owners in the family firm, even when wives have superior wage-earning opportunities elsewhere, the problem is ultimately a patriarchal culture that legitimates or even requires feminine sacrifices rather than a structural characteristic of the family firm as such. If co-owning wives cannot obtain their share of the business income, even when they have equal legal right to it, the legal structure is not the source of female subordination. Even when husbands are sole owners of ethnic firms, rather than co-owners with wives, husband-owners cannot *exploit* their unpaid wives or children in the absence of profit. More likely, a husband-owner's struggling firm exists only because he has access to unpaid family labor (Hillmann 2000, 429). Similar arguments apply to immigrant women who work for lower-than-prevailing wages in ethnic economies. In many cases, immigrant husbands restrict their wives to ethnic economy jobs in the belief that these jobs fall within the moral compass of the traditional community. Therefore, jobs in the ethnic economy are decent, safe, and conservative of religio-ethnic values. Under these circumstances, immigrant women earn less than they otherwise could, but it is their *husband* who compels them to stay in a low-wage environment. In general, when they seek work, women rely on interpersonal ties more than do men (Sanders, Nee, and Sernau 2002, 306–7). Finally, immigrant and ethnic minority women often prefer to work in ethnic economy jobs. Immigrant women commonly report that noneconomic advantages of ethnic economies outweigh the low wages they receive in them.[39] They like the proximity of their job to their home, the native language work environment, and the coethnic networks that form in the workplace. The right to mind one's children at work is more commonly available in the ethnic economy than in the general labor market.

SAVING AND CREDIT

Although banks deliver service effectively to the mainstream, they have long failed to deliver savings and credit outside the mainstream (see the article by Stearns and Mizruchi, this volume). Banks neglect and have always neglected low-income customers, small business, inner cities, slums, immigrants, and nonwhites (Uzzi 1999, 495; Tseng and Zhou 2001, 245). Since ethnic ownership economies locate in exactly these niches, ethnic ownership economies operate in credit-starved environments. This neglectful coincidence constrains the entrepreneurship of the resource disadvantaged, causing their ethnic economies to grow more slowly than they otherwise would have, thereby driving up unemployment rates (Immergluck and Mullen 1998, 1). Hoping to rectify this situation, the U.S. Congress passed the Community Reinvestment Act in 1977. CRA requires banks to report to bank regulators the number of loans they have made in poor neighborhoods (Squires 1994, 67–71). Despite the CRA, the financial situation of American inner cities has worsened in the last two decades. When, following Reagan-era deregulation (1980–88), banks reduced their service presence in American inner cities, the already inadequate level of financial service in these areas deteriorated even further, and is now worse than it was before deregulation (Squires and O'Conner 1997). Banks closed branches in inner cities, which were already underserved. In the wake of the departing bank branches, check-cashing outlets and pawn shops have proliferated.[40] Excluding racketeer-sponsored lotteries (Light 1977), check-cashing outlets and pawnshops are now the financial agencies most available to inner-city residents (Hudson 1997). Check-cashing outlets charge customers 3 percent of face value just to cash a paycheck or a welfare check. Neither pawnshops nor check-cashing outlets offer savings accounts. Therefore, in inner cities, financial management is more expensive and less convenient than elsewhere, reminding us that the poor still "pay more" (Caplovitz 1963).

The banking industry denies responsibility for this wretched state of affairs. In its view, cost constraints doom the poor, slums, and immigrants to inferior banking service. The bankers' case rests on four arguments. First, small loans are unprofitable. It costs banks as much to issue a loan of $1,000 as to issue a loan of $100,000, but their earnings are only one-hundredth as large. Second, unemployed, immigrant, ethnic minority, and low-income borrowers are rarely creditworthy (see the chapter by Carruthers, this volume). To be creditworthy, borrowers require steady jobs, assets to pledge, and a personal history of repaying prior loans. Distressed borrowers typically lack one or more of these prerequisites. Third, banks are not charities. They have obligations to stockholders, depositors, and regulators such that they cannot lend money to individuals unlikely to repay. Fourth, banks have every institutional reason to lend wherever a profit is likely, and major banks actually own many check-cashing outlets, proof of their devotion to inner-city neighborhoods. For these reasons, the banking industry declares itself not responsible for the inferior service it offers the poor, immigrants, small business, and ethnic minorities.

This plausible rebuttal has not, however, stopped the movement for banking reform. A series of studies, initiated by sociologists, has found evidence that credit markets were segregated by race such that ethnic minorities received less conventional funding than whites net of creditworthiness (Immergluck and Mullen 1998; Immergluck 1999; Light and Gold 2000, 217). These results confirm the independent contribution of social discrimination to loan denials, weakening the bankers' defense, but they do not demolish the defense. Taken together, strictly economic and cost-relevant factors, such as creditworthiness, have proven more important than race in determining loan policies. If creditworthiness is already the main determinant of lending, and the additional contribution of race is minor, then the elimination of racially motivated denials will have a minor impact upon lending. Of course, this consideration does not derail the movement for banking reform, which has plausible grounds for expecting that institutional and legal changes in the banking industry will inject more capital into low-income and minority neighborhoods. There is every legal and practical reason to drive racial discrimination out of banking.

Nonetheless, the current debate about banking reform returns the ethnic economy literature to its starting point (Light 1972, chaps. 2, 3): the reliance of ethnic ownership economies upon internal financing. Banks have never financed small business in the past, nor offered adequate savings facilities to the needy, and there is scant likelihood that banking reform will compel them to do so in the future. Under the circumstances, immigrant and ethnic minorities still must have or must build internal resources for saving and lending. Without such resources, the growth of ethnic ownership economies will be stunted.[41] Family and friends provide 70 to 80 percent of small business start-up loans in ethnic minority and immigrant communities (Bond and Townsend 1996; Yoo 1999, chap. 6). Beyond family and friends, ethnic minority and immigrant communities turn to the rotating savings and credit association. The locus classicus of ethnic financial resource is the rotating savings and credit association (ROSCA), whose supportive role in Asian American ethnic economies before World War II drew initial attention to the ethnic economy (Light 1972, 27–44). ROSCA is the generic name for a popular financial system found in many countries of Asia, Latin America, and Africa. Members of a ROSCA, usually numbering 10 to 30, come together monthly or weekly to make a contribution to a common fund, which is lent in turn to each member until all members have received the fund (Sterling 1995). At that point, the club is disbanded, and a new one formed, usually with substantial continuity of membership. Early recipients of ROSCA funds are borrowers, who may pay interest to the fund; later recipients are savers, who may receive interest (Light and Gold 2000, 218–21).

ROSCAs are not a historical relic (Ardener 1995, 2). That once-popular belief has been discarded.[42] On the contrary, ROSCAs are thriving in the Third World and in immigrant communities within developed countries. West Indian, Hispanic, and Asian immigrant groups in Britain and in the United States and abroad continue to utilize ROSCAs now as in the past (Light, Im, and Deng 1990; Johnson 1995; Sterling 1995; Srinivasan 1995).[43] In some cases, ROSCAs convey large sums of money, even millions of dollars; in most cases, ROSCAs convey ten thousand dollars or less. Business owners are overrepresented in ROSCAs, but they are by no means the only members. Although most celebrated for their role in debt financing of business start-ups (Bates 1997, 122), the very task banks reject, ROSCAs also reduce business owners' cash flow problems and stimulate consumer saving. Most participants in ROSCAs are savers, not business owners (D. Kim 1999). As immigration has increased, American courts have regulated ROSCAs in response to complaints (Cao 1999). As an unfortunate result, ROSCAs now face legal barriers put in place by uninformed judges who confuse ROSCAs with illegal lotteries. ROSCA participants successfully lend money to people in their circle, including those who are not also family or personal friends. Lacking equivalent social capital, bankers cannot do the same. Therefore, ROSCAs have a structural advantage, and can service *communities* where banks see only *markets*.[44] The dependence of ROSCAs upon social capital is extreme, solidly documented, and well understood (Biggart 2001). Indeed, modern reference to social capital's economic utility (but not the words *social capital*) first appeared in the ethnic economy literature, which discussed ROSCAs in precisely this connection (Light 1972, chap. 2). A common mistake is to suppose that ROSCAs only require social capital to function. In fact, ROSCAs cannot be utilized by groups (such as Europeans) that lack cultural familiarity with this institution. ROSCAs require cultural capital as well as social capital. Billionaires of social capital, the Amish in Pennsylvania believe in lending money to coreligionists, and abundantly do so.[45] But, lacking a cultural tradition of rotating credit associations, the Amish do not disperse loans through ROSCAs.

Microcredit agencies have proliferated in the Third World since 1980, and are now developing in the United States, where limited evidence suggests some success in opening microbusiness opportunities to the disadvantaged.[46] Invented in Bangladesh by Mohammed Yunus (1999), founder of the Grameen Bank, microcredit agencies offer credit to impoverished people who not only lack knowledge of ROSCAs, but even lack social capital. In this sense, microcredit is more versatile than ROSCAs. Microcredit agencies organize impoverished people, mostly women, into "solidarity groups" of five. Borrowers lack jobs, human capital, and collateral.[47] Borrowers receive small loans, which they are required to invest in a microbusiness such as chair caning. Loans are not made for consumption. Proceeds of the microbusiness repay the loans. When each borrower has repaid her loan, plus interest, then all her solidarity group members may receive another, larger loan in a second loan cycle. If even one member does not repay, then none may receive a larger loan (Servon 1998, 125). In this way, the microcredit agency first creates social capital in solidarity groups, then exploits it to assure repayment. Mother of all microcredit agencies, the Grameen

Bank of Bangladesh reports repayment rates of 98 percent or higher from impoverished borrowers. Interest paid by the borrowers supports the bank, creating in microcredit a self-sustaining institution that turns beggars into business owners.

NORTH AMERICAN CRITICS OF INTERACTIONISM

The first edition of this *Handbook* declared interactionism a "dominant movement of thought" in ethnic economy literature. Although this conclusion is still true, research has importantly changed interactionism since the first edition. *Interactionism* taught that immigrant and ethnic minority business depend upon the fit between what groups can supply and locales demand (Razin and Langlois 1996, 705). Interactionism predicts, for example, that Chinese will operate more restaurants in New York, whose non-Chinese inhabitants like Chinese food, than in Akron, where Chinese food is less popular. The older textbook view had claimed that self-employment depended upon the supply side as well as upon the demand side (Light and Rosenstein 1995, 73).[48] However, interactionism went beyond that older view, explaining not only that supply and demand both contributed to self-employment, but also the exact manner in which they contributed (Waldinger, Aldrich, and Ward 1990, 33) The older textbook view did not afford this refinement. Finally, interactionism critiqued what was widely perceived as overemphasis in the literature upon cultural causality to the neglect of opportunity conditions (Kloosterman and Rath 2003).

However, the honeymoon over, interactionism encountered empirical and conceptual criticism in the last decade. The first criticism was methodological. In order to demonstrate that interaction of supply and demand explains self-employment, interaction theory requires data that permit simultaneous variation on the demand side and on the supply side. The empirical literature then available actually offered very few research designs that met this methodological requirement (Light and Rosenstein 1995, 75–79). The prevailing research design, exploring one group in one locality, did not allow the bilateral variation necessary to prove interactionism. Interactionism lacked supporting evidence. A second objection was substantive. When finally tested against research designs that did permit simultaneous variation on the supply side and on the demand side, interactionism failed. Interactionism expects the local interaction of supply and demand to explain all the intergroup, interlocality

variation in self-employment rates. That is, the local self-employment rate of any ethnoracial group should be obtained from the self-employment rates of various metropolitan areas interacted with group characteristics. If so, the main effects of demand and supply should have no direct influence on self-employment rates net of the interactions.

When this test was applied to a data set consisting of four ethnoracial categories in 272 metropolitan areas of the United States, the main effects overpowered the interaction effects (Light and Rosenstein 1995, 140). That is, the direct effects of demand and supply, especially supply, explained more intermetropolitan variation in self-employment rates and ranks than did the interaction terms. The authors distinguished specific and general resources. Specific resources were monopolized by specific groups as, for example, Chinese monopolize the skills required in cooking Chinese food. General resources are common to all groups, so they are not monopolized by any. Literacy, numeracy, and business acumen are general ethnic resources. Money is a general class resource. This conceptual distinction modified interactionist theory, which had wrongly assumed that all ethnic resources were specific. However, direct effects of group characteristics suggested the existence of general ethnic resources that did not narrowly link groups to this or that local opportunity structure, as interactionists had expected, but tended instead to promote group self-employment in any and all localities. Groups with high self-employment rates in one locality tended to have them in all (Light and Rosenstein 1995, table 3.8; Razin and Langlois 1996, 708). Incompatible with interactionism, this result is compatible with middleman minority theory, according to which their generalized or ethnic business acumen permits middleman minorities to prosper in any demand environment.[49] Nonetheless, distinguishing general and specific resources salvages interactionism by explaining why supply/demand interactions based on generalized resources show up statistically as main effects, not interactions.

EUROPEAN CRITICISM OF INTERACTIONISM

A third and quite different criticism of interaction theory came from European researchers. In the last two decades, European societies have witnessed the growth of ethnic minority and immigrant self-employment, which now equals or, in some cases, surpasses the self-employment rate among native-born white citizens (Kloosterman and Rath 2003; Razin and Scheinberg 2001, 272; Barrett, Jones, and McEvoy 2001, 244; Echikson 2000; Farina 2000, 19; Martiniello and Jamin 2000, 48–63; Mung 1994; Hillmann 1999, 271–73; Barrett, Jones, and McEvoy 1996, 783; Beltran 2000; Kloosterman, van der Leun, and Rath 1999, 253; Pairault 1995).[50] To interpret this change, European scholars turned initially to American models; but American models did not always fit European conditions (Engelen 2001; Kloosterman 2000).[51] Compelled to cast about for alternative explanations, Dutch researchers contributed an important theoretical corrective to interactionist theory (Kloosterman, van der Leun, and Rath 1999; Rath 2002a).[52] Dutch researchers had watched ethnic economies develop in societies whose regulatory regimes were more obtrusive than in the United States (Boissevain 1997, 313).[53] As a result, the Dutch researchers noticed regulatory issues that had escaped American researchers whose vision included government assistance to small business, but not government regulation of small business (Min and Bozorgmehr 2003).[54] European societies are strong state, weak market societies, just the opposite of the United States.[55] Political regulation of ethnic ownership economies is much more apparent in Europe than in the United States (Kloosterman 2000).[56] Public regulation affects immigrant and ethnic minority entrepreneurship in three basic ways. First, public regulation influences the number and characteristics of immigrants as well as their legal right to self-employment. European societies do not offer fast-track entrepreneur visas as do the United States, Canada, and Australia (Tseng 2000a; Froschauer 2001; Marger 2002).[57] They have not, until very recently, offered fast-track visas to high-technology employees, who often become entrepreneurs. As a result, European societies have arguably not attracted so rich a mixture of entrepreneurial resources as have the United States, Canada, and Australia. Moreover, unlike the United States, Canada, and Australia, immigrants to many European societies do not immediately enjoy immediate legal access to self-employment (Mung and Lacroix 2003; Haberfellner 2003). Usually self-employment is permitted only to immigrants who have lived in a European country for four to six years, if even then.[58] Ethnic economies took longer to develop in Europe because immigrants had to live in Europe longer before legally qualified to start businesses. Second, public regulation influences the legal requirements that govern access to self-employment. European states

require the self-employed to undertake formal apprenticeships, to pass examinations of vocational proficiency, to satisfy authorities that their projected enterprise is in the public interest, and, once in business, to undergo detailed regulation of labor standards, wages and hours, social security payments, and product quality. Third, European welfare states treat the unemployed more generously than does the American neoliberal state. Unemployment benefits are higher in Europe, benefit eligibility broader, and benefit receipt extended in time. Therefore, unemployed immigrants in Europe do not face the same incentives for self-employment that immigrants in America confront (Freeman and Oegelman 2000, 118–22).

That said, just as in the United States, Canada, and Australia, immigrants in Europe increasingly conclude that self-employment offers the best long-term solution to their economic disadvantage and cultural marginality. Therefore, since regulatory regimes ration access to self-employment, hopeful immigrant entrepreneurs struggle for the legal right to undertake self-employment, and, once self-employed, struggle against regulation. In most cases immigrant entrepreneurs seek freedom from regulation, but also, it must be acknowledged, where regulation serves their interest, they demand regulation (Ram et al. 2002; Freeman and Oegelman 2000).[59] The immigrants' struggle with regulators does not require mass political activity. Rather, immigrant entrepreneurs in Europe just ignore rules, regulations, and laws, and then try to escape punishment (Kloosterman, van der Leun, and Rath 1999, 258).[60] Thus, some immigrants not legally authorized to undertake self-employment do it anyway. These entrepreneurs build ethnic ownership economies in the informal sector. Immigrants who fail vocational proficiency tests practice their trades anyway. Required to use expensive ingredients, immigrant bakers clandestinely substitute cheap ingredients. Required to pay social security contributions, immigrant entrepreneurs keep fraudulent books. Needless to say, the immigrant entrepreneurs of Europe are not malevolent; rather, the combination of straitened resources, labor market disadvantage, and market competition compels them to subvert laws and regulations in order to make an adequate living or even just to survive.[61]

Jan Rath (2002a) and colleagues undertook a coordinated international study of comparative industrial regulation in the garment industry. This study coordinated research on the garment industry in Paris, London, the West Midlands, Amsterdam, New York, Miami, and Los Angeles. In each of these metropolitan areas, immigrant entrepreneurs controlled the garment-manufacturing industry in which immigrant workers provided the labor supply. The survival of the garment industry depended everywhere upon massive evasion of laws regulating hours of labor, wages, sanitary conditions, industrial homework, taxation, health care, and social contributions. In each of these cities, garment factory owners did not pay employees for all the hours they worked, nor did they maintain legally required sanitary and safety conditions in their plants. The immigrant entrepreneurs also imposed illegal homework, evaded income taxation, and did not make legally mandated social security contributions.[62] Although frequently subject to journalistic exposes, garment sweatshops rarely attracted serious intervention by authorities, who tolerated industrial lawlessness. Bribery was sometimes involved, but a policy of toleration was probably more important. To keep the immigrants' jobs in town, police and politicians tolerated garment manufacturers' violations of industrial regulations. They considered toleration a liberal and proimmigrant policy.

Amsterdam provides the decisive case (Raes et al. 2002). Probably because the Netherlands is among the most corporatist of Europe's corporatist economies, Amsterdam authorities finally enforced the industrial code that governed garment manufacturing. Amsterdam's police raided garment factories and seized their books. Police fined and shut down entrepreneurs who were out of compliance with law. Within three years, law enforcement had closed 90 percent of Amsterdam's garment factories (Rekers and van Kempen 2000, 66). Many garment firms relocated to Poland, where cheaper labor and lower labor standards provided a haven. Nonetheless, back in Amsterdam, strict law enforcement had stripped the city's immigrant entrepreneurs of their garment-manufacturing firms and their immigrant employees of their low-wage jobs. Therefore, successful law enforcement left Amsterdam with additional unemployed immigrants, leaving open the possibility that strict enforcement of industrial regulations had not been in the city's economic interest, much less the immigrants'.

Since unreconstructed interactionism had ignored regulation, the Dutch research on international garment factories called attention to an important gap in theory. The Dutch concept of *mixed embeddedness* welds interactionist theory to an opportunity structure that now has a regulatory component as well as a demand side (Klooster-

man, van der Leun, and Rath 1999, 257; Rath 2002a). Reconstructed interactionism holds that ethnic economies depend upon the fit between what groups can supply and are *permitted* to supply, not between consumer demand and what groups *can* supply. Bringing the state into the process, this revised interactionist formulation corrects the economism of Waldinger, Aldrich, and Ward (1990) without demolishing interactionism as such. In comparison, the American critique strengthens cultural causality against interactionism's challenge. However, even the American critique is technically compatible with interactionism inasmuch as resources still interact with demand to determine outcomes.[63] As a result, one may conclude that, a decade later, interactionism still rules the ethnic economy literature, but it is a more sophisticated interactionism that now includes regulation as well as generalized ethnic resources.

GLOBALIZATION

Looking now forward to new frontiers of research, an already substantial and still growing body of research addresses ethnic business in the context of globalization, a master trend of the last two decades and presumably of the next as well. Arguably, globalization moves the interactionist context to a higher level, now asking about the fit between ethnic economies and a *global* opportunity structure with local nodes. Answers are emerging. Globalization encourages ethnic minority and immigrant business in several ways (Collins 1998, 1:26). On the demand side, globalization everywhere expands consumers' taste repertoires, encouraging ethnic businesses that supply culturally exotic and specialized products and services (Collins et al. 1995, 101; Bhachu 2003, 142). Promoting the interdependence of economies, globalization increases the advantageousness of the biculturalism and bilingualism that immigrant entrepreneurs typically enjoy (Light 2001; Collins 1998, 2:399). Globalization also increases the income share of the more affluent, thus creating effective demand for cosmopolitan goods that ethnics and immigrants provide. Growing consumer acceptance of, and effective demand for, foreign products strengthens ethnic minority and immigrant business. The popularity of the Turkish *donar kebab* in Germany offers one illustration; the popularity of Chinese acupuncture offers a second. German consumers now eat Turkish food and consult Chinese doctors where, a generation ago, they did neither (Wilpert

2003; Hillmann and Rudolph 1997; Rudolph and Hillman 1998; Gabaccia 1998, 120). In turn, enhanced and irrepressible consumer demand for ethnic goods and services has compelled regulatory regimes to modify laws that formerly hobbled ethnic business. European financial circles increasingly recognize the economic attraction of internal tourism to ethnic communities (Tait 2001; Rath 2002b). In California, the "Doctor of Oriental Medicine" license authorizes Asian doctors to practice medicine, a profession that once lawfully excluded non-Western medical traditions from any market access (Hui, Yu, and Zylowska, 2002). The promotion of tourism in ethnic and immigrant neighborhoods has also compelled European authorities to rethink regulations governing housing of foreign populations.

On the supply side, four changes are already strengthening ethnic ownership economies, and are likely to continue to do so in the next decade. First, microcredit is now a policy tool (Anthony 1997; Yunus 1999). Now a favorite instrument of governments, microcredit programs cost-effectively turn the unemployed into business owners. Microcredit agencies have already expanded ethnic minority business ownership in the United States, especially among the most disadvantaged (Painter and Tang 2001). Microcredit agencies reach disadvantaged persons otherwise least able to access business development assistance. Second, high-technology immigrants and entrepreneurship visa programs inject foreign-born workers who have resources to start businesses in the formal sector. In 1990, one-quarter of Silicon Valley entrepreneurs were foreign born (Saxenian 2000a, 2000b; Shin 2000). Their number included the founders of Yahoo and Hotmail. In hope of attracting highly skilled workers, Britain and Germany have introduced visas comparable to the American H1B visa.[64] Third, immigration is increasingly transnational. Transnsationalism creates electronically coordinated ethnic diasporas that produce many times more entrepreneurs per thousand immigrants than did past migrations (Portes, Haller, and Guarnizo, 2002, 285). Transnational immigrant entrepreneurs promote and expand American and Canadian merchandise exports, but do not increase imports (Light 2001).[65] Transnational entrepreneurs also build bigger businesses than do nontransnational immigrants. Fourth, global development, promotion, and distribution of real property in major cities has greatly increased ethnic business in localities. International capital follows ethnic social networks into localities when seeking overseas real estate investments (Light 2002; Tseng 1994, 2000b). Immigrant real property developers serve as point men for international banks (Tseng and Zhou 2001).

Of these trends, microcredit, transnationalism, export promotion, high-technology immigrants, entrepreneurship visas, and international real estate development, all are aspects of globalization (Wong 1997). Because of globalization, what were formerly local ethnic economies are increasingly integrated into global production and distribution chains (Portes, Haller, and Guarnizo 2002; Pecoud 2000, 442). Once the ethnic mom-and-pop store on the corner sold local products to non-coethnics. Now the immigrant-owned store often peddles goods that passed along a global supply chain of coethnics before finally coming to rest on its shelves (Chan and Ong 1995, 527). Many of these goods are not culturally marked (Tseng 1995; Zhou 1996, 1998; Leung 2002). Thus, international networks of Chinese and South Asians manufacture, transport, and distribute computer software and hardware. These international business networks are ethnic in composition, but there is nothing ethnic about their products.[66] In this key industry, Silicon Valley's immigrant entrepreneurs exploit social capital that connects them with Asia. Similarly, Chinese and Korean banks inject capital into American real estate markets in support of immigrant property developers, whose competitive advantage importantly resides in their exclusive access to Asian venture capital and overseas marketing capabilities. In the past, like other minority business, African American real estate developers operated only at the local level (Walker 1998, 196–200). Now, a local ethnic or immigrant realtor's storefront office is often a terminus in a global network that connects storefront and diaspora (Li 1998; Teixeira 1997; Tseng 1997). An ethnic diaspora is a small business analog to a transnational corporation. Just like the corporation, a diaspora's ethnic network operates branch offices in many countries, and can shift production or distribution among the many lands in which it operates. In English-speaking countries, which are unusually monolingual, bilingual and bicultural immigrant businesses support exports whose marketing depends on foreign language skills and cultural knowledge (Gould 1994; Wong 1998, 85–95; Light 2001). The growth of international commerce has also created opportunities for bicultural immigrants to find employment in marketing departments of transnational corporations.

Political backlash might damage ethnic economies in the next decade. In 2000–2001, immigrant-owned Chinese business came briefly under McCarthyite attack in the United States on grounds of national security (Piller 2002).[67] In Europe, political attacks on immigration and on terrorists have intensified suspicion of immigrant business. However, even if political backlash against immigrants should intensify, as seems likely, then blocked opportunities for employment and mobility would encourage more ethnic business as foreign-born workers turn to self-employment in desperation. Indeed, the gathering political backlash against immigration has already strengthened the immigrant-smuggling business, which depends upon closed borders for its livelihood. Immigrant smuggling is an illegal and globalized ethnic business (Kyle and Koslowski 2001). Immigrant smugglers help their customers illegally to enter exclusive countries and to stay in them illegally once there (Barnes 2000). Smugglers operate through international ethnic networks that connect the smugglers with one another as well as with potential customers in their homeland or in their diaspora (International Organization for Migration 2002). Immigrant smugglers obtain coethnic customers exclusively via network referrals, a recruitment process that inescapably builds ethnicity into the smuggling business (Chin 1999, 36).[68] Smugglers collect a fee from customers, whom they transport illegally (Witkin 1997). Since their business requires the smugglers to move customers along a series of temporary stops toward their target, the smugglers require international networks that enjoy strong social capital. This requirement strengthens the ethnic homogeneity of the smuggling networks. As the smuggling industry has matured, it has increased its capacity, moving more people than ever, and refining its methods in response to strengthened law enforcement. Most importantly, industrial maturation of the smuggling industry has permitted lower prices for consumers, rendering it cheaper than ever to buy illegal access to a host society (Orrenius 1998, 12–14). Even the provision of forged and stolen immigration documents has become an ethnic business, simultaneously supporting the smugglers, and promoting illegal immigration. Finally, international prostitution, sex tourism, and narcotic drug rings also operate as ethnic businesses because they must rely upon ethnic social capital for security

(Salt and Stein 1997; Chin 1999, 35; Staring 2000; Friman 2001).

CONTROVERSIES AND CRITICISMS

More than most areas of social science, ethnic economy research has awakened passionate debate, some of it ideological. It was not just that ethnic economy research treated entrepreneurship as "causally significant" in Wilken's (1979, 4–6) sense, thus bringing ethnic economy research into collision with both Marxists and neoclassical economists, who dispute and dismiss the independent importance of entrepreneurship.[69] Ethnic economy research also made early and extensive use of the concepts of social capital and cultural capital. Indeed, the now voluminous literature of ethnic economies still offers the most abundant empirical documentation of these concepts of any area in social science. Therefore, scientific resistance to these concepts appropriately targeted the ethnic economy literature, which is useless if these concepts are useless. Recognizing only human and financial capital, conservative economists flatly refused to recognize any economic role for cultural or social capital (Bates 1997, 21).[70] However, this ultraconservative position is impossible to sustain now (Pecoud 2000, 455). First, human capital is often but not invariably associated with increased probability of self-employment (Le 2000), a result incompatible with the conservatives' reduction of self-employment to human capital. Second, although the contribution of culture to self-employment can be minimized, given the weight of evidence, it simply cannot be excluded (Silverman 1999a; Teixeira 1998; Der-Martirosian 1996; Kraybill and Nolt 1995; Metcalf, Modood, and Virdee 1997; Mavratsas 1995). Third, neoclassical economists now generally try to build social capital and cultural capital into their models rather than to deny their existence (Lentz and Laband 1990; Glasser 2001; Ghatak and Guinnane 1999; Collins 1998, 1:80; Rauch 2001). Indeed, Watson, Keasey, and Becker (2000; also Morris 2001) persuasively restate the case for ethnic economies from a business school perspective whose standard vocabulary expands to encompass ethnic resources very well.

Given the legacy of Max Weber, social scientists rarely disputed the existence of social capital and cultural capital. Among social scientists, other criticisms have been central. One view claims that ethnic economy research essentializes and reifies culture as unchangeable timeless endowments (Timm 2000, 364). There is some truth to this complaint. In order to observe cultural change, any subject needs historical studies. Ethnic economy research has been overwhelmingly short-term and cross-sectional.[71] Reliance upon this methodology has tended to obscure cultural change. However, the solution is more historical studies. Another criticism complains that ethnic economy research wrongly describes as ethnicity what is really just a census or government category. Certainly there is a problem here too, but research into internal ethnicity has explored the existence of ethnic economies within ethnic economies (Halter 1995; Light et al. 1994), sensitizing researchers to the error of ascribing real characteristics to census categories. Thus, talk of Asian business in North America overlooks the multiplicity of Asian groups (Chinese, Korean, Filipino, Vietnamese, Cambodian) as well as the internal distinctions within nationality groups: Chinese from Hong Kong are independent of Chinese from Taiwan. The solution would be multilocal field studies that respect real ethnic boundaries; the methodological problem is the ready availability of census data that does not respect ethnic boundaries, but is cheap and quantifiable.

However, the major argument has always revolved around resources. Do immigrant and ethnic minorities really have resources, or are they powerless? In Belgium what Pang (2003) identifies as the "paradigm of minorization" denies altogether that immigrants or ethnic minorities have resources, can exert agency, or can achieve upward mobility. Minorities are helpless. This widely held view, called political correctness in the United States (Cummings 2001; Bhachu 2003), can be dismissed because incompatible with abundant research results that prove the contrary. A much more sophisticated and continuing debate concerns how much emphasis to place upon social capital and cultural capital (Levenstein 1995; Min and Bozorgmehr 2000; Hiebert 2000; Rath and Kloosterman 2000; Vermeulen 2001). The persistent distinction between class and ethnic resources (both of which include social and cultural capital) continues to focus this debate, the subtlety of which has immeasurably increased since the first edition of this *Handbook* appeared.[72] Instead of arguing whether ethnic or class resources do everything, as was once the practice, current researchers posit a balance of ethnic and class resources that tilts in one direction or another in response to changing circumstances (Pessar 2000, 390; Wright and Ellis 2000; Kaplan 1997; Razin and Scheinberg 2001;

Friman 2001, 330; Collins 2003). Thus, long-term critics of the cultural approach Barrett, Jones, and McEvoy (2003) now concede that ethnic resources are useful "up to a point" but insist that passage beyond that point requires class resources. Again, Marger (2001) proposes that immigrants who have abundant human capital will rely on it; only those lacking human capital turn to ethnic social capital. Again, class resources promote breakout, the escape into mass markets, but ethnic resources are essential to start-up (Drori and Lerner 2002; Walton-Roberts and Hiebert 1997; Jones, Barrett, and McEvoy 2000, 43; Engelen 2001; Peters 1999, 180). In terms of social capital, strong ties are essential for borrowing money, but weak ties maximize information retrieval (Bager and Razaei 2000, table 4.4; Yoo 2000; Flap, Kumcu, and Bulder 2000, 154). The examples illustrate the subtle, second-generation research issues now under discussion. Strong ties and start-ups depend upon ethnic background, but information retrieval and breakout require class resources. A mixture of class and ethnic resources may be the best overall endowment, but, of course, neither start-up nor breakout is an *overall process*. Both happen at discrete moments in time—so it matters which resources are available when.

Ironically, the very success of ethnic economy research has created a new and telling scientific criticism. When mainstream capitalism was conceptualized as individualized actors operating at arm's length, which was still the orthodoxy until the mid-1990s, ethnic economies were treated like primitive survivals in which culture, norms, solidarity, networks, and trust still mattered (Flap, Kumcu, and Bulder 2000). The ethnic economy literature then demonstrated the surprising advantages that accrued to ethnic and immigrant groups as a result of these very atavisms (Levitt 1995, 128–33). This empirical demonstration was and still remains the empirical stock in trade of the ethnic economy literature, which has always insisted that trust and solidarity are essential resources of entrepreneurship. Times have changed, and younger scholars never understood that this view was once heretical. Now the concept of social capital has been exported to business schools (Woolcock 1998, 2001; Sorenson and Audia 2000), whose professors declare that *all entrepreneurs*, not just immigrant entrepreneurs, rely on social networks (Johannisson 2000; Burt 2000). Hence, the formerly sharp boundary between the ethnic economy, where social capital mattered, and the mainstream economy, where it did not, has blurred. "What distinguishes ethnic entrepreneurship from other forms of entrepreneurship?" is a question ever more frequently encountered (Bond and Townsend 1996, 24; Ram and Smallbone 2002, 243; Rath 2000, 5; Barrett, Jones, and McEvoy 1996, 804; Pecoud 2000, 456). For these reasons, the paucity of research comparing immigrant groups with nonimmigrants has become a bigger and more embarrassing limitation now than when Aldrich, Cater, Jones, and McEvoy (1981) first detected the problem.

Economic sociology needs to learn whether, to what extent, and how the ethnic or immigrant entrepreneurs differ from nonimmigrant entrepreneurs; happily, something useful can already be said about that subject. First, all ethnoracial and ethnonational groups utilize networks in business, native as well as immigrant, but all users do not deploy identical social networks (Ram 1996; Drakopoulou and Patra 2002). We are increasingly discussing kinds of social network, not simply the existence of social networks. Intergroup differences in network form and extent now represent a research frontier. Second, immigrants "tend to differ in the bundle of resources (human, financial, social, and cultural capital) at their disposal when compared to their indigenous counterparts" (Kloosterman and Rath 2001, 191). Mapping and measuring intergroup differences in modal resource packages will be essential in the next decade, but we know already that differences exist. Third, in pluralistic, multiethnic societies, nonimmigrant entrepreneurs and immigrant/ethnic minority entrepreneurs operate out of social networks with minimal overlap. Bonding social capital is ubiquitous within the blocs; bridging capital is scarce. This structure results in a sense of social separation in the economic realm.[73] Finally, ethnic entrepreneurs and mainstream entrepreneurs often have different cultural norms.[74] Thus, native-born white Americans disapprove of mixing family and business. However, immigrant Hindustanis celebrate this practice (Vermeulen 2001, 38). Again, the role of women in business varies greatly among cultural groups. British Moslems restrict women's business; British Hindus expand it (Metcalf, Modood, and Virdee 1997). For all these reasons, the ethnic economy exists now as a distinct sphere of business activity even though nonimmigrant entrepreneurs also have norms and make use of social networks. The examination of points of divergence and similarity between mainstream and ethnic networks, norms, and structures will be a central research focus in the next decade.

Now turning to the ideological side of the debate, left-wing critics accuse ethnic economy research of promoting a political agenda of cryptocapitalism; right-wing critics complain that the masses are incapable of entrepreneurship (Panayiotopoulos 1997; Bates 1997). Never tired of waiting for the revolution, left critics want ethnic capitalism replaced before it has exhausted its utility. However much detested by left-wing intellectuals, immigrant-owned business is overwhelmingly popular among immigrants.[75] Proclaiming the economic incompetence of the masses, right-wing critics return to the great man theory of entrepreneurship. Only these great entrepreneurs will save the incompetent masses, who should forego independent economic action on their own account. In the middle of the debate, a centrist, policy-oriented criticism complains that ethnic economy research offers politicians the option of promoting minority self-employment instead of combating racism. For this reason, Barrett, Jones, and McEvoy (1996, 803) caution against "the customary uncritical acceptance of entrepreneurship as a prescriptive remedy, a kind of policy Prozac for those disadvantaged by racism." Here critics address ways in which laissez-faire ideologues could abuse scientific results to frame obnoxious social policies, implying that research should be discontinued in order to prevent this possibility. However, if so, why stop with ethnic business? Why not preemptively discontinue any scientific research that politicians might abuse? This remedy amounts to the suppression of research, as all research results can be abused by someone.

The rest of the ideological criticism is simply misguided. Ethnic economy research does not equate "success" with entrepreneurship, as Werbner (1999) complains. On the contrary, the findings of ethnic economy research, reviewed at length above, have undermined the simplistic equation of success with self-employment that many social scientists thoughtlessly imbibed from Anglo-American culture (including, in this respect, African American culture; Woodard 1998. Ethnic economy research does not oppose ethnic or immigrant integration, acculturation, and assimilation into the mainstream just because ethnic business owners often do oppose them (Silverman 1999a, 1999b). However objectionable ethnic business owners may be, and they have few fans in social science, they will not go away if scholars ignore them. Attacks on the morality of ethnic economies leave the realm of social science altogether (Bonacich 1993).[76] Even if the moral complaints were fully justified, which they are not, moral denunciation is not social science. Finally, one might ask why the world would be improved if only white, native-born citizens owned business enterprises, which would be the case except for ethnic economies.

NOTES

The author thanks the Hansewissenschaftskolleg for support that made time available to complete this review.

1. See the special issue of the *Asian and Pacific Migration Journal* (vol. 10, 2001) "The Chinese Ethnic Economy." This issue offers a tour de force on overseas Chinese business.

2. On this subject, see also Light, Har-Chvi, and Kan 1994; Light and Rosenstein 1995, 195–201; Yeung 1999; K. Kim 1999; Lee 2000, 2002).

3. Broader than Hillman's (2000, 419) definition because it includes ethnic minorities, but otherwise identical: "Alles was von Ausländern als Selbstständigkeit betrieben wird."

4. "Thus even after controlling for group differences in individual variables typically used to estimate earnings equations, there are enormous differences in self-employment rates across ethnic/racial groups in the United States" (Fairlie and Meyer 1996, 771).

5. This review of literature assumes that readers have familiarity with the 1994 review.

6. One must differentiate an ethnic ownership economy from an ethnic enclave economy. The terms are not synonyms, although they are often carelessly treated as if they were. An ethnic enclave economy is an ethnic ownership economy that is geographically clustered around a high-density residential core (Light et al. 1994; Werbner 2001). Ethnic enclave economies are a special case of an ethnic ownership economy. Of hundreds of ethnic ownership economies, only 14 were also ethnic enclave economies (Logan, Alba, and McNulty 1994).

7. The definition of business ownership is more complicated than it seems. The U.S. Census offers two tests: declared self-employment, and self-employment income. Members of the first group say they are self-employed; the second group has obtained income from self-employment. The overlap between these two categories is only 60 percent (Light and Rosenstein 1995, 44). Many persons are self-employed in addition to wage employment (Li 2001).

8. True, clustering also saturates labor markets, thus driving down wages. However, at that point it becomes the task of employee organization to raise wages (cf. Catanzarite and Aguilera 2002, 101).

9. At one point, Wilson (1996, 74) acknowledges that work did not really disappear because many jobless are "nonetheless involved in informal kinds of work." He makes no effort to follow up this observation.

10. "The pervasiveness of self-employment is appreciably greater if multiple job holding is considered" (Tienda and Raijman 2000, 300).

11. The firm's owners and their coethnic employees would fall into another group's ethnic ownership economy. The same firm could appear in group A's ethnic-controlled economy and group B's ethnic ownership economy.

12. An older terminology calls this sector *organized crime*. For research in this area, see Passas 1995.

13. This taxonomy classifies all the possible cases, thus putting boundaries around the concept of ethnic economy, but categories 5 and 6 are empirically less common than the others. Stepick (1998, 48) documents wage labor in the informal economy of Miami.

14. In principle, majority ethnic groups have ethnic economies, but the existing empirical literature ignores this case. Since the existing empirical literature addresses only immigrant and minority ethnic groups, this restriction governs this review of literature too.

15. "46 percent of all employees in Australia were employed in small enterprises. If we add to this figure the unpaid family workers, the employers and self-employed business owners-managers, then just under two-thirds (63 percent) of the total Australian workforce are part of the small business sector. This is a little over the median for all seven countries" (Collins et al. 1995, 112).

16. Sik (1998, 77) estimates that 11 percent of aggregate household expenditures entered the informal economy of Hungary in 1997.

17. "To work in the informal market is the prevalent mode of economic incorporation for immigrants in Portugal" (Baganha 2000, 99).

18. An extreme but illustrative case: immigrants from India own half the motels in the United States, and, of these owners, 70 percent bear the family name Patel. See Varadarajan 1999.

19. "Ethnic niches emerge when a group is able to colonize a particular sector of employment in such a way that members have privileged access to new job openings, while restricting that of outsiders" (Portes 1998, 13).

20. Fairlie (1999, 8) concludes that about 2.4 percent of young Americans sold narcotics at least once in 1980. Another 13 percent sold hashish.

21. "Haitians become full-time informal sector entrepreneurs usually when they have no choice, when they lose or cannot obtain wage-labor employment. These activities are survival strategies that provide an income close to the poverty threshold" (Stepick 1998, 45).

22. "The most thoughtful criticism [of self-help doctrine] came from Lester F. Ward, a liberal sociologist. Writing for the *Forum* in 1886, when the worship of success was at its peak, Ward called attention to the fact that self-help advisers completely ignored the operation of the social factors in the achievement of success" (Wyllie 1954, 142).

23. If this were not true, then one could not explain why the great disadvantages of African Americans, which Oliver and Shapiro (1998, 45) plead, created less-than-average self-employment in the formal sector while creating more-than-average self-employment in the informal sector.

24. Doubly disadvantaged adults lack educational credentials, so the relevant comparison is with comparable adults who have passed the school-leaving age.

25. Asked to explain their business success, entrepreneurs usually attribute it to superior morality on their part (Wyllie 1954, 65; Chan and Chiang 1994, viii; Woodard 1998).

26. On gender, see Hillmann 1999; Dallalfar 1994.

27. Most ethnic economy employees obtain jobs and therewith income that they would not have obtained had they relied only upon the mainstream labor market. Employment at low wages is better than unemployment, the mainstream's offer. In that sense, the ethnic economy is an economic resource for its employees even though its wages are below those of the mainstream.

28. The same is true of poverty, which is much worse in the absence of social capital. "A family's ability to borrow $500 had as much [reduction] effect on hardship as multiplying its current income by a factor of three" (Mayer and Jencks 1988, 108–9).

29. Marx defined the exploitation ratio as $P/(P + W)$ where P is profit and W is wages.

30. But Asian immigrant entrepreneurs in Britain express more satisfaction with income and profits than do white British entrepreneurs (Barrett, Jones, and McEvoy 1996, 797).

31. They earned average incomes because they worked more hours per year than employees.

32. Paying the same low wages, but earning profits, the fast food industry *does* exploit its teenage workers (Schlosser 2002, 73).

33. "The exploitation of female kinship labour is even considered by some authors to be a building stone for the development of the entrepreneurship of ethnic minorities in Britain" (Hillmann 1999, 269).

34. "In point of fact, successful moneymakers were married men more often than not. Almost 97 percent of the millionaires of the nineteenth century were married, and 94 percent of those of the twentieth century. In each of these eras, wealthy men ranked well above the average for adult males in the matter of taking vows" (Wyllie 1954, 31).

35. But marriage increases women's self-employment rate 4.5-fold, whereas it increases men's self-employment rate only 2.6-fold.

36. A Spanish study found that, in terms of total hours worked weekly, including household labor, women codirectors of family businesses worked about 10 percent more than women family workers or self-employed women (Actis, Pareda, and de Prada 2001, 630–32).

37. "By drawing on their internal solidarity and common self-interests, immigrant families utilize fungible social capital that enhances the probability of achieving business-ownership" (Sanders and Nee 1996, 236–37).

38. In rural Bangladesh, even when women receive the business loans, their male relatives often obtain control over them (Goetz and Gupta 1996).

39. "Immigrant Chinese women with little English and few job skills often find working in Chinatown a better option despite low wages. . . . In Chinatown, jobs are easier to find, working hours are more flexible, employers are more tolerant to children's presence, and private child-care . . is more accessible and affordable. At work women are able to socialize with other coethnic women" (Zhou 2001b, 149).

40. John R. Wilke, "Back-Door Loans: Some Banks' Money Flows into Poor Areas—and Causes Anguish," *Wall Street Journal*, October 21, 1991, A1; Caskey 1994, 93; Sassen 1997; James F. Peltz, "Rights Group Finds Mortgage Lending Bias," *Los Angeles Times*, December 24, 1997, D1.

41. "My key substantive conclusion is that social structure stratifies market outcomes by influencing both who gets credit and what that credit costs" (Uzzi 1999, 502).

42. "[A]s we progress in our understanding of the sociology of the economy, we will find a surprisingly large role for the supposedly archaic categories of ethnicity and kinship; the idea that these are superseded in the economy of the modern world by efficient and impersonal institutions is a wishful vestige of Enlightenment idealism that careful analysis does not sustain" (Granovetter 1995, 157).

43. "Within the family name associations, there were once informal credit clubs called 'hui' that operated on a voluntary basis. . . . This kind of informal credit arrangement is no longer practiced by the family name associations for it is rather risky and is not enforceable by law. Credit unions and banks are now the institutions new immigrants use for loans. One association, the Lee Family Association, has its own credit union for members" (Wong 1998, 22–23).

44. The Arabic Hawala system, also utilizing social capital, has become the vehicle by which Islamicist terrorists transmit funds internationally (Godefroy 2002).

45. "The church encourages members to make mutual aid their first priority. Successful business owners are expected to extend low-interest loans to fellow members. Most make funds equally available to prospective farmers and beginning entrepreneurs" (Kraybill and Nolt 1995, 156). See also Solely, Ainlay, and Siemens 1995.

46. In a major study, 72 percent of poor microentrepreneurs experienced income gains in the five years after start-up. Fifty-three percent of poor entrepreneurs had household gains large enough to move them out of poverty. See Clark and Kays 1999, vii.

47. "At Women's Initiative, intangible assets such as trustworthiness, integrity, and dedication substitute for the hard assets such as collateral that determine creditworthiness in banks" (Servon 1998, 122).

48. Smelser (1976, 126) writes that "like all markets, the market for entrepreneurial services has a demand and a supply side."

49. Razin and Langlois (1996, 708) report similar results in Canada: "Our data clearly show that country of birth, combined with ethnicity, is a major factor influencing the propensity to become self employed, whereas the metropolitan area has a secondary influence."

50. Europeans have their own measurement problems. European statistics do not make it possible to distinguish immigrants from foreign nationals temporarily sojourning abroad (Leung 2002, 279).

51. "The United States is unique in its willingness to admit vast numbers of unskilled settlers, legal and illegal, and acquiesce in the development of an extensive system of low-end subcontracting" (Freeman and Oegelman 2000, 117).

52. The venerable theory of ethnic succession also fell. Criticizing Waldinger's (1996) succession model of ethnic business, Rath (2003; 2000, 10) observed that Europe, unlike North America, had no prior waves of immigrants whose occupational or industrial egress could suck lower-ranking newcomers into their vacated niches. Looking back into the nineteenth century, Shrover (2001, 295–96) even finds that historical niches vacated by immigrants in the Netherlands simply disappeared when the immigrants left them because there was no replacement labor available.

53. North American literature did observe and comment on entrepreneurs' rule-breaking in the informal sector of the ethnic economy. See Duneier 1999.

54. "Much of the American literature on immigrant and ethnic entrepreneurship takes regulation for granted, assuming that regulation is not relevant in liberal welfare states such as the United States" (Rath 2002a, 17).

55. In order to avoid too gross an international generalization, it is better to follow Freeman and Oegelman (2000, 118), who divided European societies into three tiers, each defined by the extent of integration into national policy-making. In the top tier are the Netherlands, Austria, Sweden, and Norway; in the middle tier are Germany, Denmark, Belgium, Switzerland, and Finland; in the lowest tier, most similar to the United States is Great Britain.

56. But regulation is not absent in the United States either: "in New York, a person found vending without a license will lose her or his wares as well as face substantial fines and court fees" (Austin 1994, 2129).

57. The United States' E-5 visa allows foreigners investing at least $500,000 and creating or preserving 10 U.S. jobs to receive immigrant visas. Several consulting firms were established in the 1990s to help foreigners to receive green cards

by putting up only $100,000 of their own money and borrowing the rest. The INS in 1998 declared that such investments do not qualify a foreigner for an immigrant visa, and stopped issuing investor visas unless applicants put the full $500,000 at risk. *Migration News* 9, no. 3 (2002).

58. For example, in Germany, "the right to self-employment for foreigners from outside of the EU depends upon the nature of their residence permit." It takes eight years of legal residency to obtain the *Aufenthaltsberechtigung*, which eliminates all legal restrictions on self-employment—except one must still consult the Chamber of Commerce and Industry, which will decide whether one's proposed venture "is considered harmful or not to the overall economy." If the Chamber approves, one still has to obtain approval from the *Handwerksrolle*, which requires proof of occupational competence (Wilpert 2003).

59. Unable to obtain a dentistry license in California, Armando began clandestinely to treat patients in his home, which carries no external identification as a dental clinic. "Armando's patients are almost all Mexican immigrants who cannot afford to go to a regular dental clinic" (Zlolniski 1994, 2329).

60. For an empirical study of small business compliance with minimum wage legislation in Britain, see Ram et al. 2001.

61. Risk taking and innovation have long defined entrepreneurship. Why should successful law violation not be understood as a form of risk taking an innovation? Strictly from a business point of view, cheating the state and the public can be an efficient business strategy, as Enron and WorldCom have recently reminded the world. Disadvantaged entrepreneurs have an added incentive to violate laws at the risk of imprisonment as well as financial loss. For example, if they can evade taxes and escape punishment, entrepreneurs obtain a business advantage over competitors who paid. Similarly, if they can dump industrial wastes in vacant lots and avoid punishment, entrepreneurs obtain advantage over competitors who, complying with regulation, pay for haulage and sanitary disposal of industrial wastes. When they cannot escape regulation, entrepreneurs can negotiate their compliance with enforcement agents, possibly obtaining for themselves individually, or for their entire class, privileges that, strictly speaking, the law does not permit.

62. "Despite the whole body of employment, health and safety regulations, illegal practices are still common at some of Britain's small clothing enterprises. Poor working conditions are a feature of many firms in the West Midlands clothing industry, and the West Midlands Low Pay Unit found clothing firms operating from 'Disused factories, old warehouses, back street rooms above shops and people's front rooms.' People are working in cramped conditions, with inadequate lighting, ventilation and sanitation facilities. Health and safety aspects were unsatisfactory, there were no emergency fire procedures and the exit doors were blocked" (Ram, Jerraud, and Husband 2001, 82).

63. But some resources are general, and thus capable of promoting enterprise in any opportunity environment.

64. "A global immigration market whose nation states competed with each other to attract potential business immigrants emerged in the 1980s" (Tseng 1999, 49). Visit Germany's recruitment website in English: www.arbeitsamt.de/zav/services/greencard/starte.html.

65. "Immigrants strengthen U.S. international finance and trade relationships with their home countries or regions. These are often nations with which the United States has had little commerce and in which cultural values and business practices differ greatly from those in the United States" (Franklin, Romine, and Zwanzig 1998, 182).

66. "Of all the 128 people interviewed in the three surveys, there was none for whom their ethnicity was completely irrelevant to their economic activities" (Lever-Tracy, Ip, and Tracy 1999, 101).

67. In the United States, political attacks on Chinese business are increasing. "In the wake of allegations that the Chinese may have stolen nuclear secrets from U.S. labs, China's critics in Washington have called for stepped-up scrutiny of the ethnic Chinese business and scientific community and tougher controls on U.S. high-tech exports. The trigger for these efforts was a report on Chinese espionage earlier this year by Rep. Christopher Cox (R-Newport Beach), alleging that as many as 3,000 Chinese state-owned firms operating in the U.S. might be engaging in covert activities" (Iritani 1999, n.p.).

68. Smugglers "naturally gravitated to their ancestral province of Fujian where they speak the same dialects and often have relatives. Thus it was only natural for Taiwanese smugglers to gravitate to Fuzhou and its environs to establish contacts and recruit clients" (Zhang and Gaylord 1996, 5).

69. "Viewing entrepreneurship as automatic, the Neoclassical and Marxian perspectives also reduce entrepreneurial decision making to the level of a trivial endeavor. It is implicitly assumed that all entrepreneurs operate the same way, regardless of the entrepreneurial role, the industry, sector, economic activity, organizational size, level of development, or the nation, region and locality where the entrepreneurial action is undertaken. This supposition is further reinforced in the Neoclassical construct by optimization assumptions that require perfect knowledge of the context, and ignore individual tolerance in overcoming difficulties, and differences in individual satisfaction with the outcomes obtained" (Suarez-Villa 1989, 13).

70. See also the debate between Timothy Bates and Salome Raheim in *Journal of Developmental Entrepreneurship* 1 (1996): 1–29.

71. Exceptions include Light 1972; Levenstein 1995; Walker 1998; and Robert Boyd's many publications.

72. On the distinction between ethnic and class resources, see Light and Gold 2000, 83–130.

73. Pieterse (2003) is right about the tendency of ethnic economy literature to stress bonding over bridging social capital, but he overlooks the huge disparity in frequency of these two forms of social capital and the unavoidable competitive implication of this disparity.

74. The Amish believe one should lend money to a family member who is starting a business; Americans think business and family should be kept separate. Cf. Kraybill and Knolt 1995; Lee 2000.

75. Eighty-two percent of immigrants in Italy supported "enterprise building as a way to put the immigrants' intellectual and professional skills to good use" (Di Natale et al. 1999, 134).

76. "By putting moral and political debates aside, they are in fact adopting a moral standpoint that is implicit rather than explicit" (Pecoud 2000, 445).

REFERENCES

Actis, Walter, Carlos Pareda, and Miguel Angel de Prada, et al. 2001. *Mujer, Inmigracion y Trabajo*. Madrid: Ministerio de Trabajo y Asuntos Sociales.

Aldrich, Howard, J. C. Cater, Trevor Jones, and David McEvoy. 1981. "Business Development and Self-Segregation: Asian Enterprise in Three British Cities." Pp. 170–90 in *Ethnic Segregation in Cities*, ed. Ceri Peach, Vaughn Robinson, and Susan Smith. London: Croom Helm.

Anthony, Denise Lynne. 1997. "Investing in Trust: Building Cooperation and Social Capital in Micro-credit Borrowing Groups." Ph.D. diss., University of Connecticut.

Ardener, Shirley. 1995. "Women Making Money Go Round: ROSCAs Revisited." Pp. 1–19 in *Money-Go-Rounds: The Importance of Rotating Savings and Credit Associations for Women*, ed. Shirley Ardener and Sandra Burman. Oxford: Oxford University Press.

Austin, Regina. 1994. "An Honest Living: Street Vendors, Municipal Regulation, and the Black Public Sphere." *Yale Law Journal* 103:2119–31.

Baganha, Maria Ioannis. 2000. "The Economic Incorporation of Immigrants in the Portuguese Informal Economy." Pp. 93–124 in *Southern Europe*, vol. 2 of *Towards Emerging Ethnic Classes in Europe?* ed. Eliseo Aja et al. Weinheim, Germany: Freudenberg Stiftung.

Bager, Torben, and Shahamak Rezaei. 2000. "Immigrant Businesses in Denmark: Captured in Marginal Business Fields?" Paper presented at the Eleventh Conference on Small Business Research, Aahus, Denmark, June 18–20.

Bankston, Carl L., and Min Zhou. 1996. "Go Fish: The Louisiana Vietnamese and Ethnic Entrepreneurship in an Extractive Industry." *National Journal of Sociology* 10:37–55.

Barnes, Edward. 2000. "Two Faced Woman." *Time*, July 31, 46–50.

Barrett, Giles A., Trevor P. Jones, and David McEvoy. 1996. "Ethnic Minority Business: Theoretical Discourse in Britain and North America." *Urban Studies* 33:783–809.

———. 2001. "Socio-economic and Policy Dimensions of the Mixed Embeddedness of Ethnic Minority Business in Britain." *Journal of Ethnic and Migration Studies* 27:241–58.

———. 2003. "United Kingdom: Severely Constrained Entrepreneurialism." Pp. 101–22 in *Immigrant Entrepreneurs: Venturing Abroad in the Age of Globalization*, ed. Robert Kloosterman and Jan Rath. Oxford: Berg.

Bates, Timothy. 1997. *Race, Self-Employment, and Upward Mobility*. Baltimore: Johns Hopkins University Press.

Bean, Frank D., with David Spener. 1999. "Self-Employment Concentration and Earnings among Mexican Immigrants in the United States." *Social Forces* 77:1021–47.

Bell, Daniel. 1960. *The End of Ideology*. Glencoe, Ill.: Free Press.

Beltran, Joaquin. 2000. "Empresa Familiar: Trabajo, Redes Sociales y Familia en el Collectivo Chino." *Ofrim* 6:29–154.

Bhachu, Parminder. 2003. "Designing Diasporic Markets: Asian Fashion Entrepreneurs in London." Pp. 139–58 in *Re-orienting Fashion: The Globalization of Asian Dress*, ed. Sandra Niessen, Ann Marie Leshkowich, and Carla Jones. Oxford: Berg.

Biggart, Nicole Woolsey. 2001. "Banking on Each Other: The Situational Logic of Rotating Savings and Credit Associations." *Advances in Qualitative Organization Research* 3:129–53.

Bodnar, John. 1985. *The Transplanted*. Bloomington: Indiana University Press.

Boissevain, Jeremy. 1997. "Small European Entrepreneurs." Pp. 301–23 in *Small Business Entrepreneurs in Asia and Europe*, ed. Mario Rutten and Carol Upadhya. New Delhi: Sage.

Bonacich, Edna. 1973. "A Theory of Middleman Minorities." *American Sociological Review* 38:583–94.

———. 1993. "The Other Side of Ethnic Entrepreneurship." *International Migration Review* 27:686–92.

Bonacich, Edna, and Richard P. Appelbaum. 2000. *Behind the Label: Inequality in the Los Angeles Apparel Industry*. Berkeley and Los Angeles: University of California Press.

Bond, Philip, and Robert Townsend. 1996. "Formal and Informal Financing in a Chicago Ethnic Neighborhood." *Economic Perspectives* 10:3–28.

Bourgeois, Phillippe. 1995. *In Search of Respect: Selling Crack in El Barrio*. Cambridge: Harvard University Press.

Boyd, Robert L. 1993. "Differences in the Earnings of Black Workers in the Private and Public Sectors." *Social Science Journal* 30:133–42.

———. 2000. "Race, Labor Market Disadvantage, and Survivalist Entrepreneurship: Black Women in the Urban North during the Great Depression." *Sociological Forum* 15:647–70.

———. 2001a. "Black Enterprise in the Retail Trade during the Early Twentieth Century." *Sociological Focus* 34:241–50.

———. 2001b. "Ethnicity, Niches, and Retail Enterprise in Northern Cities, 1900." *Sociological Perspectives* 44:89–110.

———. 2002. "Ethnic Competition for an Occupational Niche: The Case of Black and Italian Barbers in Northern U.S. Cities during the Late Nineteenth Century." *Sociological Focus* 35:247–66.

Bradley, Don E. Forthcoming. "A Second Look at Self-Employment and the Earnings of Immigrants." *International Migration Review*.

Burt, Robert S. 2000. "The Network Structure of Social Capital." *Research in Organizational Behavior* 22:345–423.

Cao, Lan. 1999. "Looking at Communities and Markets." *Notre Dame Law Review* 74:841–924.

Caplovitz, David. 1963. *The Poor Pay More*. Glencoe, Ill.: Free Press.

Caskey, John. 1994. *Fringe Banking*. New York: Russell Sage Foundation.

Catanzarite, Lisa, and Michael Bernabe Aguilera. 2002. "Working with Coethnics: Earnings Penalties for Latino Immigrants at Latino Jobsites." *Social Problems* 49:101–27.

Chan, Kwok Bun, and Claire Chiang. 1994. *The Making of Chinese Entrepreneurs*. Singapore: National University of Singapore.

Chan, Kwok Bun, and Jin Hui Ong. 1995. "The Many Faces of Immigrant Entrepreneurship." Pp. 523–26 in *Cambridge Survey of World Migration*, ed. Robin Cohen. Cambridge: Cambridge University Press.

Chin, Ko-Lin. 1999. *Smuggled Chinese*. Philadelphia: Temple University Press.

Chirot, Daniel, and Anthony Reid, eds. 1997. *Essential Outsiders*. Seattle: University of Washington Press.

Clark, Peggy, and Amy Kays. 1999. *Microenterprise and the Poor*. Washington, D.C.: Aspen Institute.

Collins, Jock. 1998. "Cosmopolitan Capitalism: Ethnicity, Gender and Australian Entrepreneurs." 2 vols. Ph.D. diss., University of Wollongong.

———. 2003. "Australia: Cosmopolitan Capitalists Down Under." Pp. 61–78 in *Immigrant Entrepreneurs: Venturing Abroad in the Age of Globalization*, ed. Robert Kloosterman and Jan Rath. Oxford: Berg.

Collins, Jock, Katherine Gibson, Caroline Alcorso, Stephen Castles, and David Tait. 1995. *A Shop Full of Dreams: Ethnic Small Business in Australia*. Leichhardt: Pluto Press.

Conley, Dalton. 1999. *Being Black, Living in the Red*. Berkeley and Los Angeles: University of California Press.

Cross, John C. 1998. *Informal Politics: Street Vendors and the State in Mexico City*. Stanford, Calif.: Stanford University Press.

Cummings, Michael S. 2001. *Beyond Political Correctness: Social Transformation in the United States*. Boulder, Colo.: Lynne Rienner.

Dallalfar, Arlene. 1994. "Iranian Women as Immigrant Entrepreneurs." *Gender and Society* 8:541–61.

Der-Martirosian, Claudia. 1996. "Economic Embeddedness and Social Capital of Immigrants: Iranians in Los Angeles." Ph.D. diss., University of California, Los Angeles.

Devine, Theresa J. 1994. "Characteristics of Self-Employed Women in the United States." *Monthly Labor Review* 117:20–34.

Di Natale, Rosanna, et al. 1999. "Migration, Intelligence, and Enterprise in the Age of Globalization." Project IC/0487/E2/I/M of the European Social Fund and Italian Ministry for Employment and Social Security, Rome.

Drakopoulou, Sarah, and Eleni Patra. 2002. "National Differences in Entrepreneurial Networking." *Entrepreneurship and Regional Development* 14:117–34.

Drori, Israel, and Miri Lerner. 2002. "The Dynamics of Limited Breaking Out: The Case of the Arab Man-ufacturing Businesses in Israel." *Entrepreneurship and Regional Development* 14:135–54.

Duneier, Mitchell. 1999. *Sidewalk*. New York: Farrah, Straus and Giroux.

Echikson, William. 2000. "Europe's Immigrant Entrepreneurs Are Creating Thriving Businesses—and Thousands of Jobs." *Businessweek Online*, February 28.

Engelen, Ewald. 2001. "'Breaking In' and 'Breaking Out': A Weberian Approach to Entrepreneurial Opportunities." *Journal of Ethnic and Migration Studies* 27:203–23.

Fairlie, Robert W. 1999. "Drugs and Legitimate Self-Employment." Department of Economics, University of California, Santa Cruz.

Fairlie, Robert W., and Bruce D. Meyer. 1996. "Ethnic and Racial Self-Employment Differences and Possible Explanations." *Journal of Human Resources* 31: 757–93.

Farina, Patrizia. 2000. "Housing Segregation and Ethnic Economies in Large Cities." Pp. 18–20 in *Southern Europe*, vol. 2 of *Towards Emerging Ethnic Classes in Europe?* ed. Eliseo Aja et al. Weinheim, Germany: Freudenberg Stiftung.

Flap, Henk, Adem Kumcu, and Bert Bulder. 2000. "The Social Capital of Ethnic Entrepreneurs and Their Business Success." Pp. 142–61 in *Immigrant Businesses: The Economic, Political, and Social Environment*," ed. Jan Rath. London: Macmillan.

Franklin, J. James, Jeff A. Romine, and Peter E. Zwanzig. 1998. "The Effects of Immigration on Urban Communities." *Cityscape* 3:171–92.

Freeman, Gary P., and Nedim Oegelman. 2000. "State Regulatory Regimes and Immigrants' Informal Economic Activity." Pp. 107–23 in *Immigrant Businesses: The Economic, Political, and Social Environment*," ed. Jan Rath. London: Macmillan.

Friman, H. Richard. 2001. "Informal Economies, Immigrant Entrepreneurship, and Drug Crime in Japan." *Journal of Ethnic and Migration Studies* 27:313–33.

Froschauer, Karl. 2001. "East Asian and European Entrepreneur Immigrants in British Columbia, Canada: Post-migration Conduct and Pre-migration Context." *Journal of Ethnic and Migration Studies* 27:225–40.

Gabaccia, Donna R. 1998. *We Are What We Eat*. Cambridge: Harvard University Press.

Ghatak, Maitreesh, and Timothy W. Guinnane. 1999. "The Economics of Lending with Joint Liability: Theory and Practice." *Journal of Development Economics* 60:195–228.

Gilbertson, Greta A. 1995. "Women's Labor and Enclave Employment: The Case of Dominican and Colombian Women in New York City." *International Migration Review* 29:657–70.

Glasser, Edward L. 2001. "The Formation of Social Capital." *Isuma: Canadian Journal of Policy Research* 2:34–40.

Godefroy, Thierry. 2002. "Systemes informels de transfert de fonds: Trois example vus de France." Colloque, Paper presented at the conference "Economie de bazar dans les metropoles euromediterraneennes," Lames, MMSH, Aix-en-Provence, May 29–31.

Goetz, Anne Marie, and Rina Sen Gupta. 1996. "Who Takes the Credit? Gender, Power, and Control over Loan Use in Rural Credit Programs in Bangladesh." *World Development* 24:45–63.

Gold, Steven. 1994. "Chinese-Vietnamese Entrepreneurs in California." Pp. 196–228 in *The New Asian Immigration in Los Angeles and Global Restructuring*, ed. Paul Ong, Edna Bonacich, and Lucie Cheng. Philadelphia: Temple University Press.

Gould, David M. 1994. "Immigrant Links to the Home Country: Empirical Implications for U.S. Bilateral Trade Flows." *Review of Economics and Statistics* 76: 302–16.

Granovetter, Mark. 1995. "The Economic Sociology of Firms and Entrepreneurs." Pp. 128–65 in *The Economic Sociology of Immigration: Essays on Networks, Ethnicity, and Entrepreneurship*, ed. Alejandro Portes. New York: Russell Sage Foundation.

Green, Shelley, and Paul Pryde. 1997. *Black Entrepreneurship in America*. New Brunswick, N.J.: Transaction.

Guerrero, Teresa Jurado. 2000. "Towards an Emerging Ethnic Class in Germany?" Pp. 81–128 in *Western Europe*, vol. 3 of *Towards Emerging Ethnic Classes in Europe?* ed. Angela Hayes et al. Weinheim, Germany: Freudenberg Stiftung.

Haberfellner, Regina. 2003. "Austria: Still a Highly Regulated Economy." Pp. 213–32 in *Immigrant Entrepreneurs: Venturing Abroad in the Age of Globalization*, ed. Robert Kloosterman and Jan Rath. Oxford: Berg.

Halter, Marilyn. 1995. "Ethnicity and the Entrepreneur: Self-Employment among Former Soviet Jewish Refugees." Pp. 43–58 in *New Migrants in the Marketplace*, ed. Marilyn Halter. Amherst: University of Massachusetts Press.

Hiebert, Daniel. 2000. "Economic Associations of Immigrant Self-Employment in Canada." *International Journal of Entrepreneurial Behaviour and Research* 8(1–2): 93–112.

———. 2003. "Canada: A False Consensus." Pp. 39–60 in *Immigrant Entrepreneurs: Venturing Abroad in the Age of Globalization*, ed. Robert Kloosterman and Jan Rath. Oxford: Berg.

Hillmann, Felicitas. 1999. "A Look at the Hidden Side: Turkish Women in Berlin's Ethnic Labour Market." *International Journal of Urban and Regional Research* 23:267–82.

———. 2000. "Ethnisierung oder Internationalisierung?" *Prokla* 120:415–32.

Hillmann, Felicitas, and Hedwig Rudolph. 1997. "Redistributing the Cake? Ethnicisation Processes in the Berlin Food Sector." Discussion Paper FS97-101, Wissenschaftszentrum Berlin für Zozialforschung.

Hudson, Michael. 1997. "Fringe Banks that Exploit the Poor." Pp. 46–52 in *Real World Banking*, ed. Mark Breslow, Jim Campen, Ellen Frank, John Miller, and Abby Scher. 3d ed. Somerville, Mass.: Dollars and Sense.

Hui, Ka-Kit, Jun-liang Yu, and Lidia Zylowska. 2002. "The Progress of Chinese Medicine in the United States of America." Pp. 345–76 in *The Way Forward for Chinese Medicine*, ed. Kelvin Chan and Henry Lee. London: Taylor and Francis.

Hum, Terry. 1997. "The Economics of Ethnic Solidarity: Immigrant Ethnic Economies and Labor Market Segmentation in Los Angeles." Ph.D. diss., University of California, Los Angeles.

Immergluck, Daniel. 1999. "Intrametropolitan Patterns of Small-Business Lending." *Urban Affairs* 34: 787–804.

Immergluck, Daniel, and Erin Mullen. 1998. *Getting Down to Business*. Chicago: Woodstock Institute.

International Organization for Migration. 2002. *Irregular Migration and Smuggling of Migrants from Armenia*. Yerevan: International Organization for Migration.

Iritani, Evelyn. 1999. "In Silicon Valley, China's Brightest Draw Suspicion." *Los Angeles Times*, October 18.

Johannisson, Bengt. 2000. "Networking and Entrepreneurial Growth." Pp. 368–86 in *The Blackwell Handbook of Entrepreneurship*, ed. Donald L. Sexton and Hans Landström. Oxford: Blackwell.

Johnson, Violet. 1995. "Culture, Economic Stability, and Entrepreneurship: The Case of British West Indians in Boston." In *New Migrants in the Marketplace*, ed. Marilyn Halter. Amherst: University of Massachusetts Press.

Jones, Trevor, Giles Barrett, and David McEvoy. 2000. "Market Potential as a Decisive Influence on the Performance of Ethnic Minority Business." Pp. 37–53 in *Immigrant Businesses: The Economic, Political, and Social Environment*," ed. Jan Rath. London: Macmillan.

Kaplan, David. 1997. "The Creation of an Ethnic Economy: Indochinese Business Expansion in Saint Paul." *Economic Geography* 73:214–33.

Keister, Lisa A. 2000. *Wealth in America*. Cambridge: Cambridge University Press.

Kim, Dae Young. 1999. "Beyond Coethnic Solidarity: Mexican and Ecuadorean Employment in Korean-Owned Businesses in New York City." *Racial and Ethnic Studies* 22:583–607.

Kim, Kwang Chung, ed. 1999. *Koreans in the Hood: Conflict with African Americans*. Baltimore: Johns Hopkins University Press.

Kloosterman, Robert. 2000. "Immigrant Entrepreneurship and the Institutional Context: A Theoretical Exploration." Pp. 90–106 in *Immigrant Businesses: The Economic, Political, and Social Environment*," ed. Jan Rath. London: Macmillan.

Kloosterman, Robert, and Jan Rath. 2001. "Immigrant Entrepreneurs in Advanced Economies: Mixed Embeddedness Further Explored." *Journal of Ethnic and Migration Studies* 27:189–201.

——. 2003. "Introduction." In *Immigrant Entrepreneurs: Venturing Abroad in the Age of Globalization*, ed. Robert Kloosterman and Jan Rath. Oxford: Berg.

Kloosterman, Robert, Joanne van der Leun, and Jan Rath. 1999. "Mixed Embeddedness: (In)formal Economic Activities and Immigrant Businesses in the Netherlands." *International Journal of Urban and Regional Research* 23:252–66.

Kraybill, Donald B., and Steven M. Nolt. 1995. *Amish Enterprise: From Plows to Profits*. Baltimore: Johns Hopkins University Press.

Kyle, David, and Rey Koslowski, eds. 2001. *Global Human Smuggling*. Baltimore: Johns Hopkins University Press.

Langlois, André, and Eran Razin. 1995. "Self-Employment among French-Canadians: The Role of the Regional Milieu." *Ethnic and Racial Studies* 18:581–604.

Le, Ahn T. 2000. "The Determinants of Immigrant Self-Employment in Australia." *International Migration Review* 34:183–214.

Lee, Jennifer. 1998. "Cultural Brokers: Race-Based Hiring in Inner-City Neighborhoods." *American Behavioral Scientist* 41:927–37.

——. 2000. "Immigrant and African American Competition: Jewish, Korean, and African American Entrepreneurs." Pp. 322–44 in *Immigration Research for a New Century*, ed. Nancy Foner, Ruben G. Rumbaut, and Steven J. Gold. New York: Russell Sage Foundation.

——. 2002. "From Civil Relations to Racial Conflict: Merchant-Customer Interactions in Urban America." *American Sociological Review* 67:77–98.

Lentz, Bernard, and David Laband. 1990. "Entrepreneurial Success and Occupational Inheritance among Proprietors." *Canadian Journal of Economics* 23:563–79.

Leung, Maggi W. H. 2002. "Get IT Going: New Ethnic Chinese Business: The Case of Taiwanese-Owned Computer Firms in Hamburg." *Journal of Ethnic and Migration Studies* 27:277–94.

Levenstein, Margaret. 1995. "African American entrepreneurship: The View from the 1910 Census." *Business and Economic History* 24:106–22.

Lever-Tracy, Constance, David Ip, and Noel Tracy. 1999. "Old Ties Abroad, New Friends at Home: Networks of Australian Chinese Entrepreneurs." Pp. 97–116 in *Asian Migration: Pacific Rim Dynamics*, ed. Yen-Fen Tseng, Chilla Bulbeck, Lan-Hung Nora Chiang, and Jung-Chung Hsu. Taipei: National Taiwan University.

Levitt, Peggy. 1995. "The Social Basis for Latino Small Businesses." Pp. 120–40 in *New Migrants in the Marketplace*, ed. Marilyn Halter. Amherst: University of Massachusetts Press.

Li, Peter S. 1994. "Self-Employment and Its Economic Return for Visible Minorities in Canada." Pp. 181–

99 in *Discrimination in Employment*, vol. 2 of *New Approaches to Employee Management*, ed. D. M. Saunders. Stanford, Calif.: JAI Press.

——. 2001. "Immigrants' Propensity to Self-Employment: Evidence from Canada." *International Migration Review* 35:1106–28.

Li, Wei. 1998. "Anatomy of a New Ethnic Settlement: The Chinese *Ethnoburb* in Los Angeles." *Urban Studies* 35:479–501.

Light, Ivan. 1972. *Ethnic Enterprise in America*. Berkeley and Los Angeles: University of California Press.

——. 1977. "Numbers Gambling among Blacks: A Financial Institution." *American Sociological Review* 42:892–904.

——. 2001. "Globalization, Transnationalism, and Trade." *Asian and Pacific Migration Journal* 10:53–79.

——. 2002. "Immigrant Place Entrepreneurs in Los Angeles, 1970–1999." *International Journal of Urban and Regional Research* 26(2): 215–28.

Light, Ivan, Richard B. Bernard, and Rebecca Kim. 1999. "Immigrant Incorporation in the Garment Industry of Los Angeles." *International Migration Review* 33:5–25.

Light, Ivan, and Edna Bonacich. 1991. *Immigrant Entrepreneurs*. Berkeley and Los Angeles: University of California Press.

Light, Ivan, and Steven Gold. 2000. *Ethnic Economies*. San Diego: Academic Press.

Light, Ivan, Hadas Har-Chvi, and Kenneth Kan. 1994. "Black/Korean Conflict in Los Angeles." Pp. 72–87 in *Managing Divided Cities*, ed. Seamus Dunn. London: Keele University.

Light, Ivan, and Stavros N. Karageorgis. 1994. "The Ethnic Economy." Pp. 647–71 in *The Handbook of Economic Sociology*, ed. Neil J. Smelser and Richard Swedberg. New York: Russell Sage Foundation; Princeton: Princeton University Press.

Light, Ivan, Jung Kwuon Im, and Zhong Deng. 1990. "Korean Rotating Credit Associations in Los Angeles." *Amerasia* 16:35–54.

Light, Ivan, and Victoria D. Ojeda. 2002. "Los Angeles: Wearing Out Their Welcome." Pp. 151–68 in *Unravelling the Rag Trade*, ed. Jan Rath. Oxford: Berg.

Light, Ivan, and Elizabeth Roach. 1996. "Self-Employment: Mobility Ladder or Economic Lifeboat?" Pp. 193–214 in *Ethnic Los Angeles*, ed. Roger Waldinger and Mehdi Bozorgmehr. New York: Russell Sage Foundation.

Light, Ivan, and Carolyn Rosenstein. 1995. *Race, Ethnicity, and Entrepreneurship in Urban America*. Hawthorne, N.Y.: Aldine de Gruyter.

Light, Ivan, George Sabagh, Mehdi Bozorgmehr, and Claudia Der-Martirosian. 1994. "Beyond the Ethnic Economy." *Social Problems* 41:601–16.

Logan, John R., and Richard D. Alba. 1999. "Minority Niches and Immigrant Enclaves in New York and Los Angeles: Trends and Impacts." Pp. 172–93 in *Immigration and Opportunity*, ed. Frank D. Bean and Stephanie Bell-Rose. New York: Russell Sage Foundation.

Logan, John R., Richard D. Alba, Michael Dill, and Min Zhou. 2000. "Ethnic Segmentation in the American Metropolis: Increasing Divergence in Economic Incorporation, 1980–1990." *International Migration Review* 34:98–132.

Logan, John R., Richard D. Alba, and Thomas L. McNulty. 1994. "Ethnic Economies in Metropolitan Regions: Miami and Beyond." *Social Forces* 72:691–724.

Logan, John R., Richard D. Alba, and Wenquan Zhang. 2002. "Immigrant Enclaves and Ethnic Communities in New York and Los Angeles." *American Sociological Review* 67:299–322.

Loucky, James, Maria Soldatenko, Gregory Scott, and Edna Bonacich. 1994. "Immigrant Enterprise and Labor in the Los Angeles Garment Industry." Pp. 345–61 in *Global Production*, ed. Edna Bonacich, Lucie Cheng, Norma Chinchilla, Norma Hamilton, and Paul Ong. Philadelphia: Temple University Press.

Marger, Martin N. 2001. "The Use of Social and Human Capital among Canadian Business Immigrants." *Journal of Ethnic and Migration Studies* 27:439–53.

———. 2002. "Attacting Immigrant Entrepreneurs: The Canadian and American Experiences." Paper presented at the Fifteenth World Congress of Sociology, Brisbane, July 11.

Martiniello, Marco, and Jérôme Jamin. 2000. "Towards an Emerging Ethnic Class in Belgium?" Pp. 11–80 in *Western Europe*, vol. 3 of *Towards Emerging Ethnic Classes in Europe?* ed. Angela Haynes et al. Weinheim, Germany: Freudenberg Stiftung.

Massey, Douglas S., and Emilio Parrado. 1998. "International Migration and Business Formation in Mexico." *Social Science Quarterly* 79:1–20.

Mata, Fernando, and Ravi Pendakur. 1999. "Immigration, Labor Force Integration, and the Pursuit of Self-Employment." *International Migration Review* 33:378–402.

Mavratsas, Caesar. 1995. "Greek-American Economic Culture: The Intensification of Economic Life and a Parallel Process of Puritanization." Pp. 97–119 in *New Migrants in the Marketplace*, ed. Marilyn Halter. Amherst: University of Massachusetts Press.

Mayer, Susan E., and Christopher Jencks. 1988. "Poverty and the Distribution of Material Hardship." *Journal of Human Resources* 24:88–113.

Metcalf, Hilary, Tariq Modood, and Satnam Virdee. 1997. *Asian Self-Employment in Britain*. London: Policy Studies Institute.

Min, Pyong Gap. 1996. *Caught in the Middle: Korean Merchants in America's Multiethnic Cities*. Berkeley and Los Angeles: University of California Press.

Min, Pyong Gap, and Mehdi Bozorgmehr. 2000. "Immigrant Entrepreneurship and Business Patterns: A Comparison of Koreans and Iranians in Los Angeles." *International Migration Review* 34:707–38.

———. 2003. "United States: The Entrepreneurial Cut-

ting Edge." Pp. 17–38 in *Immigrant Entrepreneurs: Venturing Abroad in the Age of Globalization*, ed. Robert Kloosterman and Jan Rath. Oxford: Berg.

Model, Suzanne. 1997. "Ethnic Economy and Industry in Mid–Twentieth Century Gotham." *Social Problems* 44:445–63.

Morris, Michael. 2001. "The Critical Role of Resources." *Journal of Developmental Entrepreneurship* 6:5–7.

Mung, Emmanuel Ma. 1994. "L'entreprenariat ethnique en France." *Sociologie du travail* 2:185–209.

Mung, Emmanuel Ma, and Thomas Lacroix. 2003. "France: The Narrow Path." Pp. 173–94 in *Immigrant Entrepreneurs: Venturing Abroad in the Age of Globalization*, ed. Robert Kloosterman and Jan Rath. Oxford: Berg.

Nee, Victor, Jimy Sanders, and Scott Sernau. 1994. "Job Transitions in an Immigrant Metropolis: Ethnic Boundaries and the Mixed Economy." *American Sociological Review* 59:849–72.

Neef, Rainer. 2002. "Aspects of the Informal Economy in a Transforming Country: The Case of Romania." *International Journal of Urban and Regional Research* 26:299–322.

Oliver, Melvin, and Thomas M. Shapiro. 1997. *Black Wealth/White Wealth*. London: Routledge.

Orrenius, Pia. 1998. "The Role of Income Shocks and Family Network in Migration and Migrant Self-Selection: The Case of the Return Migrants from Mexico: 1965–1994." Ph.D. diss., University of California, Los Angeles.

Painter, Gary, and Shui-Yan Tang. 2001. "The Microcredit Challenge: A Survey of Programs in California." *Journal of Developmental Entrepreneurship* 6:1–16.

Pairault, Thierry. 1995. *L'integration silencieuse: La petite entreprise chinoise en France*. Paris: L'Harmattan.

Panayiotopoulos, Prodromos. 1997. "Small Enterprise Development—'Making It Work' and 'Making Sense.'" *Brainstorm*, January, 4–9.

Pang, Ching Lin. 2003. "Belgium: From Proletarians to Proteans." Pp. 195–212 in *Immigrant Entrepreneurs: Venturing Abroad in the Age of Globalization*, ed. Robert Kloosterman and Jan Rath. Oxford: Berg.

Passas, Nikos, ed. 1995. *Organized Crime*. Aldershot: Dartmouth.

Peberdy, Sally, and Christian M. Rogerson. 2003. "South Africa: Creating New Spaces?" Pp. 79–100 in *Immigrant Entrepreneurs: Venturing Abroad in the Age of Globalization*, ed. Robert Kloosterman and Jan Rath. Oxford: Berg.

Pécoud, Antoine. 2000. "Thinking and Rethinking Ethnic Economies." *Diaspora* 9:439–61.

Pessar, Patricia R. 1995. "The Elusive Enclave: Ethnicity, Class, and Nationality among Latino Entrepreneurs in Greater Washington, D.C." *Human Organization* 54:383–92.

Peters, Nonja Ivonne. 1999. "Trading Places: Greek,

Italian, Dutch, and Vietnamese Enterprise in Western Australia." Ph.D. diss., University of Western Australia.

Phizaclea, Annie, and Monder Ram. 1996. "Being Your Own Boss: Ethnic Minority Entrepreneurs in Comparative Perspective." *Work, Employment, and Society* 19:319–39.

Pieterse, Jan Nederveen. 2003. "Social Capital and Migration." *Ethnicities* 3:29–58.

Piller, Charles. 2002. "U.S. to Curb Computer Access by Foreigners." *Los Angeles Times*, March 7.

Portes, Alejandro. 1998. "Social Capital: Its Origins and Applications in Modern Society." *Annual Review of Sociology* 24:1–24.

Portes, Alejandro, and Robert Bach. 1985. *Latin Journey*. Berkeley and Los Angeles: University of California Press.

Portes, Alejandro, William J. Haller, and Luis Eduardo Guarnizo. 2002. "Transnational Entrepreneurs: An Alternative Form of Immigrant Economic Adaptation." *American Sociological Review* 67:278–98.

Portes, Alejandro, and Min Zhou. 1996. "Self-Employment and the Earnings of Immigrants." *American Sociological Review* 61:219–30.

———. 1998. "Entrepreneurship and Economic Progress in the 1990s: A Comparative Analysis of Immigrants and African Americans." Pp. 143–71 in *Immigration and Opportunity*, ed. Frank D. Bean and Stephanie Bell-Rose. New York: Russell Sage Foundation.

Quassoli, Fabio. 1999. "Migrants in the Italian Underground Economy." *International Journal of Urban and Regional Research* 23:212–31.

Raes, Stephan. 2000. "Regionalisation in a Globalising World: The Emergence of Clothing Sweatshops in the European Union." Pp. 20–36 in *Immigrant Businesses: The Economic, Political, and Social Environment*, ed. Jan Rath. London: Macmillan.

Raes, Stephan, Jan Rath, Marja Dreef, Adem Kumcu, Flavia Reil, and Aslan Zorlu. 2002. "Amsterdam: Stitched Up." Pp. 89–112 in *Unravelling the Rag Trade: Immigrant Entrepreneurs in Seven World Cities*, ed. Jan Rath. Oxford: Berg.

Raijman, Rebecca, and Marta Tienda. 1999. "Immigrants' Socioeconomic Progress Post-1965: Forging Mobility or Survival?" Pp. 239–55 in *The Handbook of International Migration: The American Experience*, ed. Charles Hirschman, Philip Kasinitz, and Josh DeWind. New York: Russell Sage Foundation.

Ram, Monder. 1996. "African-Caribbeans in Business." *New Community* 22:67–84.

Ram, Monder, Paul Edwards, Mark Gilman, and James Arrowsmith. 2001. "The Dynamics of Informality: Employment Relations in Small Firms and the Effects of Regulatory Change." *Work, Employment, and Society* 15:845–61.

Ram, Monder, Bob Jerrard, and Joy Husband. 2001. "West Midlands: Still Managing to Survive." Pp.

73–88 in *Unravelling the Rag Trade: Immigrant Entrepreneurship in Seven World Cities*, ed. Jan Rath. Oxford: Berg.

Ram, Monder, Trevor Jones, Tahir Abbas, and Balihir Sanghera. 2002. "Ethnic Minority Enterprise in Its Urban Context: South Asian Restaurants in Birmingham." *International Journal of Urban and Regional Research* 26:24–40.

Ram, Monder, and David Smallbone. 2002. "Ethnic Minority Business Policy in the Era of the Small Business Service." *Environment and Planning C: Government and Policy* 20:235–49.

Rath, Jan. 2000. "Introduction: Immigrant Businesses and Their Economic, Politico-Institutional, and Social Environment." Pp. 1–19 in *Immigrant Businesses: The Economic, Political, and Social Environment*, ed. Jan Rath. London: Macmillan.

———. 2002a. " Needle Games: Mixed Embeddedness of Immigrant Entrepreneurs." Pp. 1–28 in *Unraveling the Rag Trade: Immigrant Entrepreneurship in Seven World Cities*, ed. Jan Rath. Oxford: Berg.

———. 2002b. "Immigrants and the Tourist Industry." Paper presented at the Fifteenth World Congress of Sociology, Brisbane, July 10.

———. 2003. " 'Do Immigrant Entrepreneurs Play the Game of Ethnic Musical Chairs? A Critique of Waldinger's Model of Immigrant Incorporation." Pp. 141–60 in *West Europe Immigration and Immigrant Policy in the New Century*, ed. Anthony M. Messina. Westport, Conn.: Praeger.

Rath, Jan, and Robert Kloosterman. 2000. "A Critical Review of Research on Immigrant Entrepreneurship." *International Migration Review* 34:657–82.

Rauch, James E. 2001. "Black Ties Only? Ethnic Business Networks, Intermediaries, and African American Retail Entrepreneurship." Pp. 270–309 in *Networks and Markets*, ed. James E. Rauch and Alessandra Casella. New York: Russell Sage Foundation.

Razin, Eran, and Andre Langlois. 1996. "Metropolitan Characteristics and Entrepreneurship among Immigrants and Ethnic Groups in Canada." *International Migration Review* 30:703–27.

Razin, Eran, and Dan Scheinberg. 2001. "Immigrant Entrepreneurs from the Former USSR in Israel: Not the Traditional Enclave Economy." *Journal of Ethnic and Migration Studies* 27:259–76.

Rekers, Ans, and Ronald van Kempen. 2000. "Location Matters: Ethnic Entrepreneurs and the Spatial Context." Pp. 54–69 in *Immigrant Businesses: The Economic, Political, and Social Environment*," ed. Jan Rath. London: Macmillan.

Rifkin, Jeremy. 1996. *The End of Work*. New York: G. P. Putnam's Sons.

Robert, Peter, and Erzsebet Bukodi. 2000. "Who Are the Entrepreneurs and Where Do They Come From? Transition to Self-Employment before, under, and after Communism in Hungary." *International Review of Sociology* 10:147–71.

Rogerson, C. M. 1999. "International Migrants in the

South African Construction Industry: The Case of Johannesburg." *Africa Insight* 29:40–51.

Romney, Lee. 1999. "Minority-Owned Firms Tend to Hire within Own Ethnic Group." *Los Angeles Times*, September 18, C1.

Rudolph, Hedwig, and Felicitas Hillman. 1998. "How Turkish Is the Donar Kebab? Turks in Berlin's Food Sector." *Scottish Geographical Magazine* 114:138–47.

Salt, John, and Jeremy Stein. 1997. "Migration as a Business: The Case of Trafficking." *International Migration* 35:467–90.

Sanders, Jimy, and Victor Nee. 1996. "Immigrant Self-Employment: The Family as Social Capital and the Value of Human Capital." *American Sociological Review* 61:231–49.

Sanders, Jimy, Victor Nee, and Scott Sernau. 2002. "Asian Immigrants' Reliance on Social Ties in a Multiethnic Labor Market." *Social Forces* 81:281–314.

Sassen, Saskia. 1997. "The Informal Economy: Between New Developments and Old Regulations." *Yale Law Review* 103:2289–304.

Saxenian, AnneLee. 2000a. "Silicon Valley's New Immigrant Entrepreneurs." Paper presented at the Center for Comparative Immigration Studies of the University of California, San Diego, May 12.

———. 2000b. "Networks of Immigrant Entrepreneurs." Pp. 248–68 in *The Silicon Valley Edge: A Habitat for Innovation and Entrepreneurship*, ed. Chong-Moon Lee, William F. Miller, Marguerite Gong Hancock, and Henry S. Rowen. Stanford, Calif.: Stanford University Press.

Schlosser, Eric. 2002. *Fast Food Nation*. London: Penguin.

Schmidt, Dorothea. 2000. "Unternehmertum und Ethnizitaet: Ein seltsames Paar." *Prokla* 120:353–362.

Servon, Lisa J. 1998. "Credit and Social Capital: The Community Development Potential of US Micro-enterprise Programs." *Housing Policy Debate* 9:115–49.

Shin, Dong-Ho. 2000. "Structures, Strengths, and Beneficiaries of Entrepreneurial Networks: Korean-American High Technology Firms in Silicon Valley." *Journal of Korean Small Business Studies* 22:289–312.

Shrover, Marlou. 2001. "Immigrant Business and Niche Formation in Historical Perspective: The Netherlands in the Nineteenth Century." *Journal of Ethnic and Migration Studies* 27:295–311.

Sik, Endre. 1998. *Hidden Economy in Hungary*. Budapest: Hungarian Central Statistical Office.

Silverman, Robert Mark. 1999a. "Ethnic Solidarity and Black Business." *American Journal of Economics and Sociology* 58:829–41.

———. 1999b. "Black Business, Group Resources, and the Economic Detour." *Journal of Black Studies* 30:232–58.

Smelser, Neil J. 1976. *The Sociology of Economic Life*. 2d ed. Englewood Cliffs, N.J.: Prentice-Hall.

Solely, Calvin, Stephen C. Ainlay, and Robert Siemens.

1995. *Mennonite Entrepreneurs*. Baltimore: Johns Hopkins University Press.

Song, Miri. 1999. *Helping Out: Children's Labor in Ethnic Businesses*. Philadelphia: Temple University Press.

Sorenson, Olav, and Pino G. Audia. 2000. "The Social Structure of Entrepreneurial Activity: Geographic Concentration of Footwear Production in the United States, 1940–1989." *American Journal of Sociology* 106:424–62.

Spener, David, and Frank D. Bean. 1999. "Self-Employment Concentration and Earnings among Mexican Immigrants in the United States." *Social Forces* 77:1021–48.

Squires, Gregory D. 1994. *Capital and Communities in Black and White: The Intersections of Race, Class, and Uneven Development*. Albany: State University of New York Press.

Squires, Gregory D., and Sally O'Conner. 1997. "Fringe Banking in Milwaukee: The Rise of Check-Cashing Businesses and the Emergence of a Two-Tiered Banking System." Paper presented at the Annual Meeting of the American Sociological Association, Toronto, August 11.

Srinivasan, Shaila. 1995. "ROSCAs among South Asians in Oxford." Pp. 199–208 in *Money-Go-Rounds: The Importance of Rotating Savings and Credit Associations for Women*, ed. Shirley Ardener and Sandra Burman. Oxford: Oxford University Press.

Staring, Richard. 2000. "International Migration, Undocumented Immigrants, and Immigrant Entrepreneurship." Pp. 182–98 in *Immigrant Businesses: The Economic, Political, and Social Environment*, ed. Jan Rath. London: Macmillan.

Stepick, Alex. 1998. *Pride against Prejudice: Haitians in the United States*. Boston: Allyn and Bacon.

Sterling, Louis. 1995. "Partners: The Social Organization of Rotating Savings and Credit Associations among Exilic Jamaicans." *Sociology* 29:653–66.

Struder, Inge R. 2001. "Migrant Self-Employment in a European Global City: The Importance of Gendered Power Relations and Performances of Belonging for Turkish Women in London." Paper presented at the Annual Conference of the Association of American Geographers, February.

Suarez-Villa, Luis. 1989. *The Evolution of Regional Economies*. New York: Praeger.

Tait, Simon. 2001. "Opening up Time for Chinatown." *Financial Times* (London), May 20, 3.

Talwar, Jennifer Parker. 2001. "Contradictory Assumptions in the Minimum-Wage Workplace." *Journal of Contemporary Ethnography* 30:92–127.

Teixeira, Carlos. 1997. "The Role of Ethnic Real Estate Agents in the Residential Relocation Process: A Case Study of Portugese Homebuyers in Suburban Toronto." *Urban Geography* 18:497–520.

———. 1998. "Cultural Resources and Ethnic Entrepreneurship: A Case Study of the Portuguese Real Estate Industry in Toronto." *Canadian Geographer* 42:267–81.

Tienda, Marta, and Rebecca Raijman. 2000. "Immigrants' Income Packaging and Invisible Labor Force Activity." *Social Science Quarterly* 81:291–310.

Timm, Elisabeth. 2000. "Kritik der ethnischen Oekonomie." *Prokla* 120:363–76.

Tseng, Yen-Fen. 1994. "Chinese Ethnic Economy: San Gabriel Valley, Los Angeles County." *Journal of Urban Affairs* 16:169–89.

———. 1995. "Beyond 'Little Taipei': The Development of Taiwanese Immigrant Businesses in Los Angeles." *International Migration Review* 29:33–58.

———. 1997. "Immigration Industry: Immigration Consulting Firms in the Process of Taiwanese Business Immigration." *Asian and Pacific Migration Journal* 6:275–94.

———. 1999. "The Mobility of People and Capital: Divergent Patterns of Taiwanese Capital-Linked Migration." Pp. 49–68 in *Asian Migration: Pacific Rim Dynamics*, ed. Yen-Fen Tseng, Chilla Bulbeck, Lan-Hung Nora Chiang, and Jung-Chung Hsu. Taipei: National Taiwan University.

———. 2000a. "The Mobility of Entrepreneurs and Capital: Taiwanese Capital-Linked Migration." *International Migration* 38:143–68.

———. 2000b. "Immigrant Firms and Transnational Embeddedness: Chinese Entrepreneurs in Los Angeles." Pp. 263–82 in *Embeddedness and Corporate Change in a Global Economy*, ed. Rueyling Tseng and Brian Uzzi. New York: Peter Lang.

Tseng, Yen-Fen, and Yu Zhou. 2001. "Immigrant Economy in a Pacific Rim Context: Chinese Business in Los Angeles." Pp. 239–51 in *The Chinese Triangle of Mainland-Taiwan–Hong Kong: Comparative Institutional Analyses*, ed. Alvin So, Nan Lin, and Dudley Poston. Westport, Conn.: Greenwood.

Uzzi, Brian. 1999. "Embeddedness in the Making of Financial Capital: How Social Relations and Networks Benefit from Seeking Financing." *American Sociological Review* 64:481–505.

Varadarajan, Tunku. 1999. "A Patel Motel Cartel?" *New York Times Magazine*, July 4, 36–39.

Vermeulen, Hans. 2001. *Culture and Inequality: Immigrant Cultures and Social Mobility in Long-Term Perspective*. Amsterdam: Institute for Migration and Ethnic Studies.

Waldinger, Roger. 1995. "The Other Side of Embeddedness: A Case-Study of the Interplay of Economy and Ethnicity." *Ethnic and Racial Studies* 18:555–80.

———. 1996. *Still the Promised City? African Americans and New Immigrants in Postindustrial New York*. Cambridge: Harvard University Press.

Waldinger, Roger, Howard Aldrich, and Robin Ward. 1990. "Opportunities, Group Characteristics, and Strategies." Pp. 13–48 in *Ethnic Entrepreneurs*, ed. Roger Waldinger, Howard Aldrich, and Robin Ward. Newbury Park, Calif.: Sage.

Walker, Juliet E. K. 1998. *The History of Black Business in America*. New York: Twayne.

Walton-Roberts, Margaret, and Daniel Hiebert. 1997. "Immigration, Entrepreneurship, and the Family: Indo-Canadian Enterprise in the Construction of Greater Vancouver." *Canadian Journal of Regional Science* 20:119–40.

Watson, Robert, Kevin Keasey, and Mae Becker. 2000. "Small Firm Financial Contracting and Immigrant Entrepreneurship." Pp. 70–89 in *Immigrant Businesses: The Economic, Political, and Social Environment*, ed. Jan Rath. London: Macmillan.

Weber, Max. [1927] 1981. *The General Economic History*. Trans. Frank Knight. New Brunswick, N.J.: Transaction.

Werbner, Pnina. 1999. "What Color Success? Distorting Values in Studies of Ethnic Entrepreneurship." *Sociological Review* 47:548–79.

———. 2001. "Metaphors of Spatiality and Networks in the Plural City: A Critique of the Ethnic Enclave Economy Debate." *Sociology* 35:671–93.

Wilken, Paul H. 1979. *Entrepreneurship*. Norwood, N.J.: Ablex.

Wilpert, Czarina. 2003. "Germany: From Workers to Entrepreneurs." Chap. 12 in *Immigrant Entrepreneurship: Venturing Abroad in the Age of Globalization*, ed. Robert Kloosterman and Jan Rath. Oxford: Berg.

Wilson, Franklin D. 2003. "Ethnic Niching and Metropolitan Labor Markets." *Social Science Research* 32:429–466.

Wilson, William Julius. 1996. *When Work Disappears*. New York: Alfred Knopf.

Witkin, Gordon. 1997. "One Way, $28,000: Why Smuggling Aliens into America is a Booming Business." *U.S. News and World Report*, April 14, 39–42.

Wong, Bernard. 1998. *Ethnicity and Entrepreneurship: The New Chinese Immigrants in the San Francisco Bay Area*. Boston: Allyn and Bacon.

Wong, Lloyd W. 1997. "Globalization and Transnational Migration: A Study of Recent Chinese Capitalist Migration from the Asian Pacific to Canada." *International Sociology* 12:329–51.

Woodard, Michael D. 1998. *Black Entrepreneurs in America*. New Brunswick, N.J.: Rutgers University Press.

Woolcock, Michael. 1998. "Social Capital and Economic Development: Toward a Theoretical Synthesis and Policy Framework." *Theory and Society* 27:151–208.

———. 2001. "The Place of Social Capital in Understanding Social and Economic Outcomes." *Isuma: Canadian Journal of Policy Research* 2:11–17.

Wright, Richard, and Mark Ellis. 2000. "The Ethnic and Gender Division of Labor Compared among Immigrants to Los Angeles." *International Journal of Urban and Regional Research* 24:583–600.

Wyllie, Irwin G. 1954. *The Self-Made Man in America*. New York: Free Press.

Yeung, Henry Wai-Chung. 1999. "The Internationalization of Ethnic Chinese Business Firms from Southeast Asia: Strategies, Processes, and Competitive Advantage." *International Journal of Urban and Regional Research* 23:103–27.

Yoo, Jin-Kyung. 1999. *Korean Immigrant Entrepreneurs.* New York: Garland.

———. 2000. "Utilization of Social Networks for Immigrant Entrepreneurship: A Case Study of Korean Immigrants in the Atlanta Area." *International Review of Sociology* 10:347–63.

Yoon, In-Jin. 1997. *On My Own: Korean Businesses and Race Relations in America.* Chicago: University of Chicago Press.

Yunus, Muhammed, with Alan Jolis. 1999. *Banker to the Poor.* London: Aurum Press.

Zhang, Sheldon, and Mark S. Gaylord. 1996. "Bound for the Golden Mountain: The Social Organization of Chinese Alien Smuggling." *Crime, Law, and Social Change* 25:1–16.

Zhou, Min. 2001. "Assimilation the Ethnic Way: Lessons from the Asian American Experience." Pp. 139–53 in *Reinventing the Melting Pot*, ed. Tamar Jacoby. New York: Basic.

Zhou, Yu. 1996. "Inter-firm Linkages, Ethnic Networks, and Territorial Agglomeration: Chinese Computer Firms in Los Angeles." *Papers in Regional Science* 75:265–91.

———. 1998. "Beyond Ethnic Enclaves: Location Strategies of Chinese Producer Firms in Los Angeles." *Economic Geography* 74:228–51.

Zlolniski, Christian. 1994. "The Informal Economy in an Advanced Industrialized Society: Mexican Immigrant Labor in Silicon Valley." *Yale Law Journal* 103:2305–35.

29 Technology and the Economy

Giovanni Dosi, Luigi Orsenigo, and Mauro Sylos Labini

IN THIS CHAPTER we address general properties of technological change and its coevoluntionary patterns with the economic and social contexts in which it occurs.

Of course it would be a futile enterprise to attempt to survey in a single chapter all the facets of the relationships between the "modern Prometheus" (as David Landes puts it) of technological innovation, on the one hand, and economic development, on the other. Rather, we confine ourselves to aspects of such relationships with straightforward bearings on the *social embeddedness*—to use Granovetter's (1985) fortunate expression—of the process of generation of "useful knowledge" and its economic exploitation.

We undertake such an exercise from an evolutionary economics perspective: diverse discussions of such a broadly defined research program may be found in Nelson and Winter (1982), Hodgson (1993), Metcalfe (1998), Dosi and Winter (2002), Nelson and Winter (2002), and Coriat and Dosi (1998). For our purposes here, let us just emphasize the overlap between "evolutionary" and a few "socioeconomic" interpretations of the fabrics and changes of both technological knowledge and economic structures. In brief, they all share microfoundations grounded on heterogeneous agents, multiple manifestations of "bounded rationality" diverse learning patterns, and diverse behavioral regularities (much more on that in Dosi, Marengo, and Fagiolo 1996). At the same time, social embeddedness entails also the long-lasting influences of socioeconomic factors upon the rates and directions of accumulation of technological knowledge.

In this respect intricate puzzles concern "what ultimately determines what": for example, is resource accumulation what primarily fosters the exploration of novel innovative opportunities, or, conversely, does innovation drive capital accumulation? Do new technological opportunities emerge mainly from some extraeconomic domain ("pure science"), or are they primarily driven by economic incentives? Or are they crucially molded by social interests and politics? Should one assume

that the institutions—however defined—supporting technical change are sufficiently adaptive to adjust to whatever economic inducement emerges from market interactions; or, conversely, are they inertial enough to shape the rates and directions of innovation and diffusion?

A first issue that we shall address in the following concerns the identification of possible invariances in the patterns of technological search and knowledge accumulation, together with discrete differences across sectors and industries.

Relatedly, second, a general question regards what one may call the *degrees of plasticity* of technological changes vis-à-vis economic and social drivers as distinct from the inner momentum that technology-specific opportunities happen to provide. Pushing it to caricatural extremes, what are the constraints to what "money can buy"? And, conversely, are there hard boundaries imposed by natural law to what social dynamics may "negotiate"?

In any case, third, we shall argue that the revealed economic impact of technological innovation crucially depends upon some sorts of *combinatorics*, entailing "matching"/"mismatching" patterns between (*a*) the opportunities and constraints offered in any given period by the major available technologies; (*b*) the structures and behaviors of business firms; and (*c*) the characteristics of broader institutions governing, for example, markets in labor, finance, and product.

Our discussion will begin with a brief overview of some fundamental "stylized facts," that is, relatively robust historical regularities at different levels of observation—from the very micro to broad societal ones—that motivate interest in the relationships between technological and economic change and also highlight some interpretative puzzles. Next, we will offer our interpretation of the structure and dynamics of technological knowledge and tackle a few related debates, including those impinging on the degrees of embodiment of technological knowledge within business organization; the role of "information" as distinct from "knowledge" *stricto sensu*; and the importance of incentives such as appropriability, on the one hand, and various other social processes, on the other, in driving the rates and directions of technological innovation. The last part of the chapter addresses more explicitly "macro" issues regarding some conjectural properties of the mentioned "combinatorics" between technology, economic structure, and institutions.

References in the following to arcane debates among economists of different breeds will be kept to a minimum, with the inevitable downside of a bias toward the specific authors' interpretative perspective. But fruitful interactions with economic sociology may be enhanced.

SOME STYLIZED FACTS ON TECHNOLOGY AND ECONOMIC DYNAMICS

Let us begin by presenting some broad historical regularities concerning technological change, the patterns of economic organization, and economic growth.

Technical Change, Economic Growth, and International Trade

Since the Industrial Revolution a highly skewed international distribution of innovative activities has emerged, starting from rather homogeneous conditions in Europe, China, and the Arab world (Cipolla 1965).

Table 1 provides a highly impressionistic but revealing picture of the international distribution of innovations from 1750. Although there is probably Anglo-American bias in the data, a similar pattern is revealed by long-term patenting activities (see Dosi, Pavitt, and Soete 1990):[1] Innovation appears to be highly concentrated in a small group of industrialized countries (see also table 2 on patenting). The club of major innovators has been quite

small over the whole period of around two centuries and half with both restricted entry (with Japan as the only major entrant in the twentieth century) and a secular pace of change in relative rankings.

At the same time, since the Industrial Revolution one observes the explosion of diverging income patterns, starting from quite similar preindustrial per capita levels. Bairoch (1981, 5) presents estimates showing that before the Industrial Revolution the income gap between the poorest and the richest countries was certainly smaller than the ratio 1 to 2 and probably on the order of only 1 to 1.5. Conversely, the dominant tendency after the Industrial Revolution is one with fast increasing differentiation among countries and overall divergence (see Bairoch 1981, 7–8, for evidence). Even in the post–World War II period, commonly regarded as an era of growing uniformity, the hypothesis of global convergence (that is, convergence of the whole population of countries toward increasingly similar income levels) does not find support from the evidence (DeLong 1988; Easterly et al. 1992; Verspagen 1991; Soete and Verspagen 1993; Durlauf and Johnson 1992; Quah 1996; Pritchett 1997). Rather, one finds some—although not overwhelming—evidence of local convergence, that is, within subsets of countries grouped according to some initial characteristics such as income levels (Durlauf and Johnson 1992) or geographical locations. Still, across-groups differences in growth appear to be striking high.

A delicate but crucial issue concerns the relation between patterns of technical change and patterns of economic growth. Of course, technological learning involves many more elements than simply inventive discovery and patenting: equally important activities are imitation, reverse engineering, adoption of capital-embodied innovations, learning by doing, and learning by using (Freeman 1982; Dosi 1988; Pavitt 1999). Moreover, tech-

TABLE 1.   Major Inventions, Discoveries, and Innovations by Country (percentage of total)

	Total	Britain	France	Germany	United States	Others
1750–75	30	46.7	16.7	3.3	10.0	23.3
1776–1800	68	42.6	32.4	5.9	13.2	5.9
1801–25	95	44.2	22.1	10.5	12.6	10.5
1826–50	129	28.7	22.5	17.8	22.5	8.5
1851–75	163	17.8	20.9	23.9	25.2	12.3
1876–1900	204	14.2	17.2	19.1	37.7	11.8
1901–25	139	13.7	9.4	15.1	52.5	9.4
1926–50	113	11.5	0.9	12.4	61.9	13.3

Source: Dosi, Pavitt, and Soete 1990.

TABLE 2.   Patents Granted in the United States by Country of Origin, 1883–1999 (as a percentage of all foreign patenting)

	1883	1900	1929	1958	1973	1986	1990	1995	1999
Australia	1,11	2,33	1,96	0,6	0,92	1,14	1,01	1,00	1,02
Austria	2,62	3,36	2,47	1,12	1,02	1,09	0,91	0,74	0,69
Belgium	1,59	1,35	1,3	1,14	1,23	0,74	0,73	0,87	0,93
Canada	19,94	10,54	10,25	7,99	6,2	4,01	4,33	4,61	4,64
Denmark	0,56	0,46	0,71	0,74	0,7	0,56	0,37	0,44	0,70
France	14,22	9,79	9,76	10,36	9,38	7,22	6,67	6,18	5,49
Germany	18,67	30,72	32,36	25,6	24,25	20,8	17,72	14,45	13,42
Italy	0,24	0,92	1,19	3,02	3,39	3,05	2,93	2,36	2,14
Japan	0,16	0,03	1,4	1,93	22,1	40,35	45,43	47,64	44,70
Netherlands	0,24	0,75	1,57	5,71	3,03	2,2	2,23	1,75	1,79
Norway	0,32	0,49	0,71	0,61	0,42	0,25	0,26	0,28	0,32
Sweden	0,95	1,32	3,19	4,64	3,4	2,7	1,79	1,76	2,01
Switzerland	1,75	2,27	4,46	8,8	5,79	3,7	2,99	2,31	1,84
United Kingdom	34,55	30,52	22,23	23,45	12,56	7,37	6,49	5,42	5,13
Eastern Europe[a]	0,40	1,49	1,62	0,55	2,53	1,13	0,35	0,26	0,29
NICs	0,4	1,12	1,03	1,31	1,36	1,5	3,19	7,33	12,09
Others	3,28	2,54	3,07	2,43	1,72	2,19	2,61	2,59	2,79

Sources: Elaboration on Dosi, Pavitt, and Soete 1990 and National Science Board 2000.

[a] Including Russia.

nological change often goes together with organizational innovation. Still, it is important to notice the existence of significant links between innovative activities (measured in a rather narrow sense, i.e., in terms of patenting and R & D activities) and GDP per capita (for the time being we shall avoid any detailed argument on the direction of causality).

As discussed in Dosi, Freeman, and Fabiani 1994, evidence concerning OECD countries appears to suggest that the relationship between innovative activities and levels of GDP has become closer over time, and is highly significant after World War II. Moreover, innovative dynamism, expressed by the growth of patenting by foreign firms and individuals in the United States, always appears positively correlated with per capita GDP growth. The link is particularly robust between 1913 and 1970. (Conversely a sign that the regime of international growth might have changed in the 1970s is that in this period the relation gets weaker and loses statistical significance.)

In general, at least since World War II, the rates of growth of GDP appear to depend on (*a*) domestic innovative activities, (*b*) the rates of investment in capital equipment, and (*c*) international technological diffusion (Fagerberg 1988; DeLong and Summers 1991; Meliciani 2001).

In turn, capability of innovating and quickly adopting new technologies are strongly correlated with successful trade performance (Dosi, Pavitt, and Soete 1990).

Moreover, although technological diffusion is taking place at a rather high rate, at least among OECD countries, important specificities in "national systems of innovation" persist related to the characteristics of the scientific and technical infrastructure, local user-producer relationships, and other institutional and policy features of each country (Lundvall 1988, 1992; Nelson 1993; Archibugi, Howells, and Michie 1999).

Firms, Industrial Structures, and Dynamics

In contemporary economies, business firms are a fundamental locus of technological accumulation. This is revealed also by the (high and growing) shares of the total domestic research and development they undertake (see figure 1 on U.S. evidence). However, the directions and the rates at which they learn vary considerably, depending on the sectors in which they operate and, relatedly, on the technologies they access (Pavitt 1984; Levin, Cohen, and Mowery 1985; Dosi 1988; Freeman 1994; Freeman and Soete 1997).

In any case, neither the secularly growing importance of innovative research internalized within firms, nor the more recent ability of the latter to utilize "artificial" exploration and design technologies—from CAD to simulation models—has eliminated the intrinsic uncertainty associated with the innovation process. Trials and errors, unpredictable failures, and unexpected successes contin-

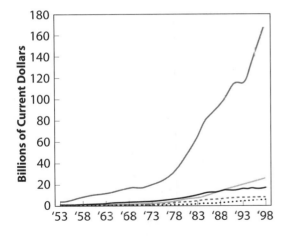

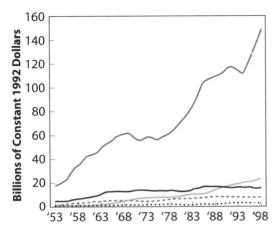

———— Industry

———— Federal Government

———— Universities and Colleges

- - - - FFRDCs

·········· Nonprofit Organizations

FIGURE 1.   National R & D performance, by type of performer, 1953–1998. Source: National Science Board 2000.

ue to be a general feature of technological innovation in contemporary economies.

And so continue to be the persistence of systematic differences across firms, even within the same lines of activities, in innovative abilities, production efficiencies, profitabilities: that is, what in a shorthand are called elsewhere (Dosi 1988) *asymmetries* across firms. For evidence, see, among many others, Davis, Haltiwanger, and Schuh 1996; Baily, Hulten, and Campbell 1992; Baldwin 1995; and the special issue of *Industrial and Corporate Change*, 1997, volume 6(1). A striking illustration

of a much wider phenomenon is the dispersion of labor productivities even within the same sectors of activity and under roughly the same relative prices. See figure 2 for evidence from Italy to that effect.

Industrial structures and industrial change present a few remarkable regularities, too, shared by most industrialized countries. Variables like capital intensity, advertising expenditures, R & D and patent intensities, concentration, profitability, and firms' entry, exit, and survival rates differ remarkably across sectors while presenting high cross-country similarities. Moreover, specific industries display rather similar characteristics, in terms of industrial dynamics in different countries. Finally, both industrial structures and dynamics appear to be profoundly shaped by the nature of the technologies upon which individual industries draw (Pavitt 1984; Dosi 1988; Dosi et al. 1995; Breschi, Malerba, and Orsenigo 2000; Marsili 2001 and the evidence cited therein).

How does one interpret the bulk of the foregoing evidence? For example, why does technological learning appear, at least at a first look, to be both a driver of economic growth and also a factor of divergence across countries and even across firms? More generally, how does one link any story primarily focused upon the dynamics of knowledge with another one wherein the primary actors are business firms, products, markets, and so on, and with yet another one primarily featuring nonmarket institutions?

In order to begin to address these questions, let us try to characterize the nature of technology and technological innovation, as we see it.

KNOWLEDGE, TECHNOLOGY, AND INNOVATION: SOME BASIC FEATURES

Technological Paradigms and Trajectories

A variety of concepts have been put forward over the last couple of decades to define the nature of innovative activities:[2] *technological regimes, paradigms, trajectories, salients, guideposts, dominant design,* and so on. The names are not so important (although some standardization could make the diffusion of ideas easier!). More crucially, these concepts are highly overlapping in that they try to capture a few common features of the procedures and direction of technical change. Let us consider some of them.

The notion of *technological paradigm* that shall be for the time being our yardstick is based on a

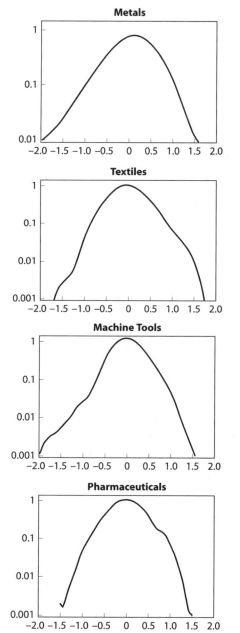

FIGURE 2. Kernel estimation of the empirical density of mean normalized labor productivities in four sectors of the Italian manufacturing industry: (*a*) metals, (*b*) textiles, (*c*) machine tools, (*d*) pharmaceuticals. Note that such distributions imply quite big productivity differences. So, for example, the ratio of the top to the bottom decile is 1.7 in metals, 1.7 in textiles, 1.6 in machine tools, and 2.3 in pharmaceuticals. Source: Bottazzi et al. 2003.

view of technology grounded on the following three fundamental ideas.

First, it suggests that any satisfactory description of "what is technology" and how it changes must also embody the representation of the specific forms of knowledge on which a particular activity is based, and cannot be reduced to a set of well-defined blueprints. It primarily concerns problem-solving activities involving—to varying degrees—also tacit forms of knowledge embodied in individuals and organizational procedures.

Second, paradigms entail specific heuristic and visions on "how to do things" and how to improve them, often shared by the community of practitioners in each particular activity (engineers, firms, technical society, etc.), that is, they entail *collectively shared cognitive frames* (Constant 1980).

Third, paradigms often also define basic templates of artifacts and systems, which over time are progressively modified and improved. These basic artifacts can also be described in terms of some fundamental technological and economic characteristics. For example, in the case of an airplane, their basic attributes are described not only and obviously in terms of inputs and production costs, but also on the basis of some salient technological features such as wing-load, takeoff weight, speed, distance it can cover, and so forth. What is interesting here is that technical progress seems to display patterns and invariances in terms of these product characteristics. Similar examples of technological invariances can be found, for example, in semiconductors, agricultural equipment, automobiles, and a few other microtechnological studies (Sahal 1981; Grupp 1992; Saviotti 1996). Hence the notion of *technological trajectories* associated with the progressive realization of the innovative opportunities underlying each paradigm—which can in principle be measured in terms of the changes in the fundamental techno-economic characteristics of artifacts and production processes.[3] The core ideas involved in this notion of trajectories are the following.

First, each particular body of knowledge (each paradigm) shapes and constrains the rates and direction of technical change, in a first rough approximation, irrespectively of market inducements. Second, technical change is partly driven by repeated attempts to cope with technological imbalances that change itself creates.[4] Third, as a consequence, one should be able to observe regularities and invariances in the pattern of technical change that hold under different market conditions (e.g., under different relative prices) and whose disrup-

TABLE 3. Moore's Law: The Trend in the Number of Transistors per Chip over Time

Microprocessor	Year	Transistors (8000S)	Clock Speed (MHz)
4004	1971	2.3	0.1
8008	1972	3.5	0.2
8080	1974	6	2
8086	1978	29	10
80286	1982	134	12
Intel 386	1985	275	16
Intel 486	1989	1,200	25
Pentium	1993	3,100	60
Pentium Pro	1995	5,500	200
Pentium II	1997	7,500	300
Pentium III	1999	9,500	600

Source: National Science Board 2000.

tion is mainly correlated with radical changes in knowledge bases (in paradigms).[5]

Moore's law (so called)—the steady exponential increase in transistors per chip and clock speed in microprocessors—is just the most famous example among many others (table 3).

Moreover, a rather general property, by now widely acknowledged in the innovation literature, is that learning is *local* and *cumulative*. "Locality" means that the exploration and development of new techniques and product architectures is likely to occur in the neighborhood of the techniques and architectures already in use (Atkinson and Stiglitz 1969; David 1975; Antonelli 1995). "Cumulativeness" stands for the property that current technological developments often build upon past experiences of production and innovation, proceed via sequences of specific problem-solving junctures (Vincenti 1990), and in a few circumstances also lead to microeconomic serial correlations in successes and failures. This is what Paul David, citing Robert Merton (1968, 3) citing the New Testament, calls the "Matthew Effect": "For unto every one that hath shall be given, and he shall have abundance: but from him that hath not shall be taken away even that which he hath" (Matt. 25:29). Note that "cumulativeness" at micro-level provides robust support for those interfirm asymmetries mentioned earlier, while industry-wide, regionwide, and countrywide factors of cumulativeness in learning dynamics are good candidates to the explanation of why industries, region, and countries tend to systematically differ in both technological and economic performances.

The robustness of notions such as technological trajectories is of course a primarily empirical ques-

tion. Come as it may, fundamental issues regard the carriers, the fine-grained processes, and the driving factors underlying the observed patterns of technological change.

Our discussion so far has primarily focused upon some general features of technological knowledge and its revealed techno-economic outcomes (we shall come back to some further properties of knowledge accumulation as such). However, a good deal of "economically useful" technological knowledge is nowadays mastered by business firms, which even undertake in some countries—such as the United States, Nordic European countries, Germany, and a few others—a small but not negligible portion of the effects aimed at more speculative understandings of physical, chemical, and biological properties of our world (i.e., they also undertake "basic science").[6] How does all that relate with the structure and behaviors of firms themselves?

Knowledge, Routines, and Capabilities in Business Organizations

Possibly one of the most exciting, far from over, intellectual enterprises developed over the last decade has involved the interbreeding between the evolutionary economics research program (largely evolutionary inspired), technological innovation studies, and an emerging competence- or capability-based theory of the firm. The roots rest in the pioneering organizational studies by Herbert Simon, James March, and colleagues (Simon 1969; March and Simon 1993; Cyert and March 1992; March 1988) and in the equally pioneering explorations of the nature and economic implications of organizational routines by Nelson and Winter (1982) (with the follow-ups such as those discussed in Cohen et al. 1996; Teece, Pisano, and Schuen 1997; Dosi, Nelson, and Winter 2000; Dosi, Coriat, and Pavitt 2000; the special issue of *Industrial and Corporate Change*, 2000, edited by Mie Augier and James March; Montgomery 1995; and Foss and Mahnke 2000). It is familiar enough to most readers that business firms "know how to do certain things"—things like building automobiles and computers—and know how to do them with different efficacies and revealed performances. In turn, as one discusses in Dosi, Nelson, and Winter 2000 and Dosi, Coriat, and Pavitt 2000, what does "organizational knowledge" mean? What are the mechanisms that govern how it is acquired, maintained, and sometimes lost? As we suggest in the just cited works, organizational knowledge is in fact a fundamental link between the social pool of knowledge, skills, and discovery opportunities, on the one hand, and the rates, direction, and economic effectiveness of their exploration, development, and exploitation on the other.

Distinctive organizational competences and capabilities[7] bear their importance also in that they persistently shape the destiny of individual firms—in terms of, for example, profitability, growth, probability of survival—and, at least equally important, their distribution across firms shapes the patterns of change of broader aggregates such as particular sectors or whole countries.

"Competences" and "capabilities" build on ensembles of organizational routines. In turn, the latter (1) as thoroughly argued by Nelson and Winter (1982), embody a good part of the memory of the problem-solving repertoires of any one organization; (2) entail complementary mechanisms of governance for potentially conflicting interests (for a more detailed discussion see Dosi and Coriat 1998), and, (3) might well involve also some "meta-routines," apt to painstakingly assess and possibly challenge and modify "lower level" organizational practices (R & D activities, often recurrent exercises of "strategic adjustment," are good cases to the point).

In this view, routines and other recurrent organizational practices may be interpreted as a set of problem-solving procedures in turn composed of elementary physical acts (such as moving a drawing from an office to another or doing an operation on a machine tool) and elementary cognitive acts (such as doing a certain calculation).

As one argues in Dosi, Hobday, Marengo, and Prencipe 2002, it is helpful to think of complex problem-solving activities as problems of design: the design of elaborate artifacts and the design of the processes and organizational structures required to produce them. These processes require the design of complex sequences of moves, rules, behaviors, and search heuristics typically involving multiple actors. In turn the patterns of knowledge decomposition contribute to shape (but are far from identical to) the division of labor within and across organization (more in Marengo et al. 2000; Teece et al. 1994; Dosi, Hobday, and Marengo 2000).

The general conjecture of many evolutionary economists is indeed that by opening up, together, the "technological black box" and the "organizational black box," one is likely to find robust mappings between the patterns in the collective distributions of technological knowledge and the properties of organizational structures and behaviors. We shall come back below to some historical examples. Here, in any case, notice a major domain of interaction between (evolutionary) economics, organization theory, and economic sociology—largely waiting to be explored.

The "Anatomy" of Regimes of Knowledge Accumulation and Their Sectoral Dimensions

Another largely unexplored field of inquiry is the exploration of technology-specific patterns of knowledge accumulation—of which an early largely cited prototype is Pavitt 1984—attempting to study the diversity of innovation patterns across industrial sectors and identify taxonomies of *technological regimes*. Such regimes are based on industry-specific properties of search for technological improvements and on specific natures and sources of knowledge bases. In line with taxonomic exercise such as Pavitt 1984, Patel and Pavitt 1997, Breschi, Malerba, and Orsenigo 2000, and Marsili 2001, the inquiry builds on three basic conjectures, namely that, first, notwithstanding the importance of countrywide institutional factors, the properties of innovation processes are, to a significant extent, invariant across countries and specific to technologies or industrial sectors; second, some general properties of innovation processes shared by populations of firms might be identified independently of a variety of idiosyncratic behaviors identifiable at firm level; and third, diverse regimes entail different technological entry barriers, stemming from diverse modes of access to novel opportunities by entrants as opposed to (cumulatively learning) incumbents (see Marsili 2001 for detailed comparative evidence). Again, it could well be at this junction between industrial economics, economic sociology, and the sociology of knowledge that one might fruitfully address a few of the apparent puzzles, briefly mentioned above, concerning the determinants of observed industrial structures and their changes.

Information and Knowledge in Technology and Innovation

That there is more to technology and innovation than sheer "information" is not likely to be big news to social scientists and practitioners alike.

However, one can go a long way by rigorously exploring the economic properties of information as such (and in any case technological activities involve a rich information content). Building on the pioneering works of Arrow (1962), Nelson (1962), Akerlof (1984), Greenwald and Stiglitz (1986), Radner (1992), Aoki (1990) among a few other distinguished authors, it is easy nowadays to acknowledge some fundamental economic specificities of "information" as such.

For example, in many respects similar to that of a "public good"—in many economists' jargon—the use of information is

Nonrival (the fact that one uses it does not prevent the others from using it too)

Nonexcludable (were it not for institutional provisions such as patent-based monopoly rights of exploitation)

Moreover, its generation is subject to

Sunk, up-front, costs of production and basically zero cost of reproduction (in an illustrative caricature, the "cost of production" of Pythagoras's theorem was fully borne by Pythagoras himself, while we can infinitely reuse it at our will; nearer to our concerns, the same applies to, e.g., software)

If anything, *increasing returns* to its use, in the sense that the more we use it, the easier it is, and, dynamically, the higher is the likelihood of learning and producing ourselves "better," "novel," in some sense "innovative" further pieces of information

As already mentioned, far-reaching conclusions can be reached just by seriously exploring the economic implications of different distributions and processes of generation of information. Consider, for example, the pathbreaking works by Masahiko Aoki on the properties of different distributions of information in the comparison between archetypical "Japanese" and "American" firms (Aoki 1990 and 2001).[8] Another example is the painstaking investigation of the conditions for the existence of "markets for technologies" (Arora, Fosfuri, and Gambardella 2001).

More generally, note that the very properties of information mentioned above most often entail phenomena of *market failures* (as marginal prices are of no guidance to efficient market allocation and equilibria might even fail to exist): see Stiglitz 1994 for a through discussion with far-reaching interpretative and political implications.

Having said that, further insights may be gained by distinguishing between sheer information and knowledge. As is discussed at greater length in Dosi, Marengo, and Fagiolo 1996, the former entails well-stated and codified propositions about (*a*)

states of the world (e.g., "It is raining"), (*b*) property of nature (e.g., "A causes B"), (*c*) identities of other agents ("I know Mr. X and he is a crook"), and (*d*) explicit algorithm on how to do things.[9] Conversely, knowledge, in the definition we propose here, includes (*a*) cognitive categories; (*b*) codes of interpretation of the information itself; (*c*) tacit skills; and (*d*) search and problem-solving heuristics irreducible to well-defined algorithms.

So, for example, the few hundred pages of demonstration of the last Fermat theorem would come under the heading of "information." Granted that, only some dozen mathematicians in the world will have the adequate "knowledge" to understand and evaluate it. On the other hand, a chimpanzee facing those same pages of information might just feel like eating them, and the vast majority of human beings would fall somewhere in between these two extremes. Similarly a manual on how to produce microprocessors is "information," while knowledge concerns the preexisting ability of the reader to understand and implement the instruction contained therein.

Moreover, in this definition, knowledge includes tacit and rather automatic skills like operating a particular machine or correctly driving a car to overtake another one (without stopping first in order to solve the appropriate system of differential equations!).

And, finally it includes "visions" and ill-defined rules of search, like those involved in most activities of scientific discovery and in technological and organizational innovation (e.g., proving a new theorem, designing a new kind of car, figuring out the behavioral pattern of a new kind of crook that appeared on the financial market).

In this definition, knowledge is to varying degrees tacit (Polanyi 1966; Nelson and Winter 1982), at the very least in the sense that the agent itself, and even a very sophisticated observer, would find it very hard to explicitly state the sequence of procedures by which information is coded, behavioral patterns are formed, problems are solved, and so on. Note also that even in scientific activities tacit knowledge plays an important role: as recognized by sociologists like Collins (1974) and Callon (1995), the "knowledge" used and diffused cannot be reduced to fully explicit codified statements (i.e., information) but involves personal interactions, observation, and practical experience in specific contexts.

On the ground of these distinctions, one may look again at the puzzles implied by the empirical evidence discussed earlier and ask, with Pavitt, questions such as these:

> If knowledge is costless to transmit and re-use why can't foreigners—who have not paid for research—benefit from it (the free rider problem)? If the cost of obtaining foreign produced knowledge is negligible, why do many small countries in North-Western Europe perform relatively more basic research than the USA itself? Why do firms in science-based industries extensively publish the results of their research when, according to the information based view of knowledge, they should be appropriating them by keeping them secret or protecting them through patents? (Pavitt 2002, 7).

We fully share also Pavitt's answer: the apparent anomalies melt away if one acknowledges the tacit aspect of knowledge, intimately complementary to codified information, person- or organization-embodied, and rather sticky in its transmission (Pavitt 2002).

Not all the analysts of technology, however, share this view. A few scholars argue indeed that the notion of tacitness has been overrated and that the "degrees of tacitness" ultimately depend upon the cost and benefits involved in the process of articulating and codifying knowledge rather than upon some intrinsic properties of knowledge itself (see Cowan, David, and Foray 2000 and the special issue of *Industrial and Corporate Change* [2000] edited by Cohendet and Steinmuller, devoted to the subject). The question, in this alternative view, ultimately boils down to a matter of incentives and availability of new technologies—today, *in primis*, information and communication technologies (ICTs)—apt to facilitate the codification job.

Here of course we are far from denying that a massive process of knowledge codification is in progress, indeed fostered by ICTs and reaching domains previously ruled by tacitness—from artifacts design to a few control and production activities previously unaffected by forms of electromechanical automation (Balconi 1998). However, we maintain that tacit features of knowledge continue to be an intrinsic part of technical change and that they are also essential to the very process of codification and to the attribution of meaning to information itself. Moreover we suggest, quite irrespectively of any incentive, the nature of specific knowledge bases deeply influences the degrees of difficulty in codification (or indeed its sheer impossibility: for example, it can be formally proved that no codified process can be established *ex ante*

in order to prove yet undemonstrated theorems; by the same token, in the technological domain it is hard to think of a codified process able to develop what we do not know yet). Together, our general conjecture here is that the diverse degrees to which knowledge bases can be easily codified contribute to explain also the "uneven development of human know-how"[10] in different fields.

The Tangled Relationships between Sciences and Technologies

There is little question that science plays a crucial role in opening up new possibilities of major technological advances. The linkages between science and technology have been tight ever since the rise of modern science,[11] but, especially in this century, the emergence of major new technological paradigms has frequently been *directly linked* with major scientific breakthroughs. Until the end of the nineteenth century, technological innovations were typically introduced by imaginative craftsmen—typical examples being the development of engines by practical-minded inventors well before the works of Carnot on thermodynamics, or the invention of the chronograph for measuring longitude by the watchmaker John Harrison in 1730 against the opinion of the astronomers including Halley (Sobel 1996). Conversely, in this century, as far as major innovations are concerned, one moves closer to a science-based model of technological innovation. Important instances in this respect are the origin of synthetic chemistry (Freeman 1982) and the transistor (Nelson 1962; Kleiman 1977; Dosi 1984). For example, in the latter case the discovery of certain quantum mechanics properties of semiconductors, yielding a Nobel Prize for physics, and the technological development of the first microelectronics device have been one and the same thing (Nelson 1962; Braun and MacDonald 1978; Dosi 1984). In more recent years, one finds many further examples, the extreme one being probably biotechnology and more generally life sciences (Orsenigo 1988a; Henderson et al. 1999). Other instances include computational chemistry and speech recognition (Koumpis and Pavitt 1999; Mahdi and Pavitt 1997), just to name two.

The increasing role of scientific knowledge in technological advances has gone together with major changes in the overall organization of innovative activities.

The conventional way of representing the impact of science on technological innovation has been often captured by some version of the (improperly called!) "Arrow-Nelson model" (Arrow 1962; Nelson 1959; see also David, Mowery, and Steinmueller 1992), whereby (exogenously determined) science provides the pool of notional opportunities upon which industrial R & D, and more generally "technologically useful" knowledge, draws.

It is indeed a useful first approximation, but we cannot stop there and must acknowledge that the relationship between science and technology goes both ways. As discussed in Rosenberg 1982 and 1994, Freeman and Soete 1997, Pavitt 1999, and Brooks 1994, factors of influence of scientific knowledge on technology include

> Of course, the knowledge of new "properties of nature" upon which technologies can build upon
> The development of new design tools and instruments initially aimed at scientific research that are thereafter applied to commercial uses—examples among many being the scanning electron microscope and the laser (Rosenberg 1990; Brooks 1994)
> Training of applied researchers mastering state-of-the-art scientific knowledge

Conversely, technology has contributed to science

> As a source of new scientific challenges (Brooks 1994)
> With new instrumentation and measurement technologies needed to address novel scientific question more efficiently

Indeed the accumulation of technical knowledge has provided for centuries a base of observations that subsequently stimulated and focused scientific research (see Rosenberg 1982 for a thorough discussion).[12]

Similarly, the development of instrumentation has exerted a major impact on subsequent scientific progress: just think of the microscope, the telescope, x-ray crystallography, and obviously the computer. More generally, the allocation of resources to specific scientific fields is often strongly influenced by prior expectations on technological payoffs as well as by the nature and the interests of the "bridging institutions"[13] that are instrumental in applying theoretical advances to the development of practical devices even under remote or nonexistent direct economic incentives (this is the case of public agencies like the military).[14]

Incidentally note also that in recent years, the increased closeness of scientific research and technological innovation in fields like biotechnology and information technology, jointly with an increasing involvement of scientific institutions in commercial activities, is leading to the concern that scientific research runs the risk of becoming too dependent on immediate and direct economic interests, thereby compromising the ethos of science that has proved so beneficial to society and the economy (Dasgupta and David 1994; Mazzoleni and Nelson 1998; Nelson 2004).[15] We shall briefly come back to this issue below.

In most contemporary developed economies, one typically observes quite a few institutions, together with a multitude of profit-seeking firms, sharing in different combinations the tasks of scientific explorations and search for would-be technological applications.[16] However, the relevance of scientific knowledge and the mechanisms through which such knowledge is transmitted vary greatly across scientific disciplines, technologies, and industries (Rosenberg and Nelson 1994). Various studies (Mansfield 1991; Jaffee 1989; Jaffee, Trajitenberg, and Henderson 1993; Audretsch and Feldman 1996; Klevorick et al. 1995) have shown that science is directly relevant to industrial R & D only in a small number of industries—typically, agriculture, chemicals and pharmaceuticals, electronics, and precision instruments. Some scientific disciplines—like mathematics and physics—are relevant for a very large variety of industries, but mostly in an indirect way. Others—for example, biology—have a more immediate practical impact, which is however concentrated in a small spectrum of industries. In general, however, the evidence seems to support the notion that science is indeed a crucial component of industrial innovation as an ingredient that increases the "general and generic" ability to solve complex technical problems (Mansfield 1991; Klevorick et al. 1995).

Historically, the contemporary symbiotic relationship between activities scientific and technological came about through two converging processes. A first one involved the progressive incorporation of R & D activities within business firms, beginning in the late nineteenth century in a few countries—like Germany, Switzerland, and a bit later the United States—and a few sectors—notably chemicals and heavy electrical engineering. Along with the institutionalization of industrial R & D within "Chandlerian" firms,[17] second, the institutionalization of academic research proceeded too, albeit at a very different pace and with large differences across countries.

In the United States, as Rosenberg and Nelson (1994) have pointed out, before World War II, the linkages between academic and industrial research were frequent but not always systematically organized. Despite some debate among historians, it is usually recognized that the quality of American academic science was by and large lagging behind Europe, with some important exceptions like chemistry and biology (Cohen 1976; Thackray 1982; Mowery and Rosenberg 1998). However, universities developed quickly relatively strong interactions with industry, especially at the local level in response to practical concerns and particularly in practically oriented disciplines—engineering, medicine, agricultural sciences, and so forth. Until World War II, this was actually the main function that—jointly with teaching—universities performed in favor of business firms. Similarly, Mowery and Rosenberg (1998) have argued that the contributions of American university research to economic growth were not the product of a few elite universities, but involved many universities, many of them providing service to local industry and agriculture.

The explosive growth of investment in scientific research—mainly coming from public sources and mainly directed to universities and other public research institutions—marks a distinct feature of the economic development of most industrial countries in the era after War World II. And it also marks the quick emergence of a long-lasting American leadership regarding both quite a few scientific disciplines and most "frontier" technologies.

In a nutshell, all developed contemporary economies—notwithstanding important national specificities—share mechanisms of generation and exploitation of innovative opportunities involving the interaction between

> The continuous accumulation of scientific knowledge (to a good extent exogenous to business firms, but not entirely: to repeat, firms do undertake a significant amount of basic research (Rosenberg 1990; Pavitt 1991)
>
> Multiple learning processes endogenous to individual firms and networks of them entailing (*a*) formal R & D activity, but also more informal processes of (*b*) learning from design, production, and marketing, and (*c*) learning by interacting with customers and suppliers

As already mentioned, the balance between these diverse learning procedures varies across technologies and industrial sectors, highlighting a variegated "anatomy" of the capitalistic innovation engine.[18]

That being said, crucial issues regard the underlying forces driving technological accumulation throughout such a system and in particular the role of economic and social factors.

ECONOMIC AND SOCIAL FACTORS IN THE EMERGENCE OF NEW PARADIGMS

It is useful to separate the genesis of new paradigms from the processes leading to the dominance of some of them. Let us first consider the emergence of new potential paradigms; that is, generation of notional opportunities of radical innovations involving new knowledge bases, new search heuristics, new dominant designs.

Indeed, there are good reasons to believe that one will not be able to find anything like a general theory of the emergence of new technological paradigms. However, what might be possible is (*a*) an analysis of the necessary conditions for such emergence; (*b*) historical taxonomies and also appreciative models of the processes by which it occurs; and (*c*) taxonomies and models of the processes of competition among different paradigms and their diffusions.

Regarding the first heading, one is likely to find that the existence of some unexploited technological opportunities, together with the relevant knowledge base and some minimal appropriability conditions, defines only the boundaries of the set of potential new paradigms: those that are actually explored within this set might crucially depend on particular organizational and social dynamics. So, for example, there is good evidence that the microelectronic paradigm as we know it (silicon-based, etc.) was shaped in its early stages by military requirements (Dosi 1984; Misa 1985). David Noble (1984) argues that the Numerical Control machine-tools paradigm—although he does not use that expression—has been influenced by power consideration regarding labor management. In the history of technologies one finds several examples of this kind. The general point is that various institutions (ranging from incumbent firms to government agencies), social groups, and also individual agents (including of course individual inventors and entrepreneurs) perform as *ex ante* selectors of the avenues of research that are pursued, the techno-economic dimensions upon which research ought to focus, the knowledge base one calls upon. Thus, they ultimately select the new paradigms that are actually explored.

Conversely, there is a much more general theoretical story regarding the development, diffusion, and competition among those (possible alternative) paradigms that are actually explored. It can be told via explicit evolutionary models (as in Nelson and Winter 1982 or in Silverberg, Dosi, and Orsenigo 1988), via path-dependent stochastic models (as in Arthur 1988; Arthur, Ermoliev, and Kaniovski 1987; Dosi and Kaniovski 1994), and also via sociological models of network development (as in Callon 1991). The basic ingredients of the story are (*a*) some forms of dynamics increasing returns (for example in learning); (*b*) positive externalities in the production or the use of technology; (*c*) endogenous expectation formation; (*d*) some market dynamics that select *ex post* among products, and indirectly among technologies and firms; (*e*) the progressive development of standards and relatively inertial institutions that embody and reproduce particular forms of knowledge and also the behavioral norms and incentives to do so (for empirical examples of these phenomena see Dosi 1988 and Freeman 1994).

Economic Influences upon the Patterns of Technological Changes

Economic factors do influence also the rates and direction of "normal" technical change, although within some boundaries set by the nature of each paradigm. The story we propose runs as follows.

Each body of knowledge specific to particular technologies determines in the short term the notional opportunities of "normal" technical advance and also the scope of possible variation in input coefficients, production processes, and characteristics of the artifacts in response to changing economic conditions. So, for example, the semiconductor-based paradigm in microelectronics or the oil-based paradigm in organic chemistry broadly shapes the scope and directions of technical progress—that is, the "trajectories"—in both product and process technologies (for example, miniaturization and increasing chip density in semiconductors, or polymerization techniques in organic chemicals). In turn, *inducement effects* can work basically in four ways, operating through (1) changes in search/problem-solving heuristics induced by relative price changes and supply/demand conditions; (2) effects of demand patterns upon the allocation of search efforts across diverse production activities; (3) the effects of appropriability conditions, again, upon search efforts; and (4) selection dynamics weeding out ever-changing "popula-

tions" of technologies, artifacts, behavioral traits, and firms.

Search Heuristics

Changes in relative price and demand or supply condition may affect search heuristics, acting as *focusing devices* (Rosenberg 1976): historical illustrations are quite a few cases of supply shocks and technological bottlenecks, from the continental blockade during the Napoleonic Wars to technical imbalances in the late-nineteenth-century history of mechanical technologies.

Output Growth and Search Efforts

"Inducement" may take the form of an influence of market conditions upon the relative allocation of search efforts to different technologies or products. In the literature, it has come to be known as the "Schmookler's hypothesis" (Schmookler 1966), suggesting that cross-product differences in the rates of innovation (as measured by patenting) could be explained by differences in the relative rates of growth of demand. Note that, in this respect, while there is no a priori reason why the perception of demand opportunities should not influence the relative allocation of technology efforts, the general idea of "demand-led" innovation has been criticized at its foundations for its theoretical ambiguities (does one talk about observed demand? or expected demand? and how are these expectations formed?) (Mowery and Rosenberg 1979). Moreover, the empirical evidence is mixed. The review in Freeman (1994, 480) concludes that "the majority of innovations characterized as 'demand-led' were actually relatively minor innovation along established trajectories," while, as shown by Walsh (1984) and Fleck (1988), "counter-Schmookler-type pattern was the characteristic of the early stages of innovation in synthetic materials, drugs, dyestuffs [and robotics]" (Freeman 1984, 480).

As emphasized by Freeman himself and by Kline and Rosenberg (1986), the major step forward here is the abandonment of any "linear" model of innovation (no matter whether driven by demand or technological shocks) and the acknowledgment of a coevolutionary view embodying persistent feedback loops between innovation, diffusion, and endogenous generation of further opportunities of advancement.

Appropriability and Rates of Innovation

The properties of innovation and knowledge discussed above also entail a fundamental trade-off powerfully highlighted by Schumpeter (and earlier Marx). Were technological advances (or for that matter technological knowledge) a sheer public good, no incentive would be there for profit-seeking agents to strive for it. Conversely, expected appropriation of some economic benefit from successful technology implies also systematic departures from the mythical "pure competition" yardstick, as defined in most economics textbooks.

In fact, a few appropriability devices are often at work in contemporary economies including patents, secrecy, lead times, costs and time required for duplication, learning-curve effects, and superior sales and service efforts. To these one should add more obvious forms of appropriation of differential technical efficiency related to scale economies and more generally the control of complementary assets and technologies, which are not directly ingredients of the innovation, but allow inventors to extract the profits from it (Teece 1986).[19]

Levin et al. (1984, 33) find that for most industries, "lead times and learning curve advantages, combined with complementary marketing efforts, appear to be the principle mechanisms of appropriating returns for product innovations." Learning curves, secrecy, and lead times are also the major appropriation mechanisms for process innovations. Patenting often appears to be a complementary mechanism that, however, does not seem to be the central one, with some exceptions (e.g., chemicals and pharmaceutical products). Moreover, by comparing the protection of processes and products, one tends to observe that lead times and learning curves are relatively more effective ways of protecting process innovations, while patents are a relatively better protection for product innovations.

Moreover, there appears to be quite significant interindustrial variance in the importance of the various ways of protecting innovations and in the overall degrees of appropriability: Some three-quarters of the industries surveyed by the study reported the existence of at least one effective means of protecting process innovation, and more than 90 percent of the industries reported the same regarding product innovations (Levin, Cohen, and Mowery 1985, 20; these results have been confirmed by a series of other subsequent studies conducted for other countries (see, for example, the PACE study for the European Union, Arundel, van de Paal, and Soete 1995, suggesting that appropriability conditions are rather similar across advanced industrialized countries).

Granted that, highly controversial issues concern the relation between degrees of appropriability, *above some minimal threshold,* and search efforts by private self-seeking agents. Do innovative efforts grow monotonically in the expectations of rents stemming from would-be innovation? And, more specifically, what is the influence of different patenting regimes and other forms of enforcement of intellectual property rights (IPR) upon innovation rates?

One cannot review here a rapidly growing literature whose striking bottom line is, however, the very little evidence supporting the (misplaced) common wisdom that tighter appropriability regimes unambiguously foster innovative activities.

Historical examples, such as those quoted by Merges and Nelson (1994) on the Selden patent around the use of a light gasoline in an internal combustion engine to power an automobile, or the Wright brothers' patent on an efficient stabilizing and steering system for flying machines, are good cases to the point, showing how the IPR regime probably slowed down considerably the subsequent development of automobiles and aircrafts, due to the time and resources consumed by lawsuits against the patents themselves. The current debate on property rights in biotechnology suggests similar problems, whereby granting very broad claims on patents might have a detrimental effect on the rate of technical change, insofar as they preclude the exploration of alternative applications of the patented invention. This is particularly the case when inventions concerning fundamental techniques or knowledge are concerned, for example, genes or the Leder and Stewart patent on the achievement of a genetically engineered mouse that develops cancer. This is clearly a fundamental research tool. To the extent that such techniques and knowledge are critical for further research that proceeds cumulatively on the basis of the original invention, the attribution of broad property rights might severely hamper further developments. This is even more so if the patent protects not only the product the inventors have achieved (the "onco-mouse") but all the class of products that could be produced through that principle, that is, "all transgenic nonhuman mammals," or all the possible uses of a patented invention (say, a gene sequence), even though they are not named in the application.[20]

A further set of problems is exemplified by the celebrated *anticommons tragedy* raised by Heller and Eisenberg (1998): while in the commons problem the lack of proprietary rights is argued to lead to overutilization and depletion of common goods, in biotechnology the risk may be that excessive fragmentation of IPRs among too many owners can slow down research activities because each owner can block the others. (At a more theoretical level, see the insightful discussion in Winter 1993 showing how tight appropriability regimes in evolutionary environments might deter technical progress.)

Finally note that while *some profit expectation* is necessary for economically motivated agents in order to undertake costly activities of innovation search, actual returns often do not bear much link with such expectations. This is so because innovative activities are characterized by an intrinsic uncertainty about both technical and commercial success.[21]

Economic Factors Shaping Selection Process

Evolutionary economists share with evolutionary epistemologists and a few historians of technologies (David 1975; Mokyr 2000; Vincenti 1990; Nelson, forthcoming among others) the view that it is the coupling between some variety-generating mechanism and some selection process that drives technological change. Having said that, more controversial issues regard (*a*) the unit of selection, (*b*) the nature of selection process, and, (*c*) the criteria driving selection itself.

Concerning the unit of selection, good candidates are

Technological paradigms and, at a smaller scale, specific technologies and pieces of knowledge

Artifacts

Organizational routines

Firms

Note that they are not at all mutually exclusive. On the contrary it is plausible to think of diverse processes of selection partially nested into each other and possibly occurring at different time scales. So, for example, products markets typically select upon artifacts, affecting only indirectly—via rewards or penalties in terms of profits and markets shares—the selection among firms. Financial markets, on the contrary, typically operate upon firms as such. In turn, direct or indirect processes of firm selection ultimately involve a selection among routines and among technologies, insofar as firms are their specific carriers. Moreover, techniques and paradigms also undergo, so to speak, *ex-ante* selection processes within firms, communities of practitioners, technical association, universities, and so forth, involving more explicit, even if still mistake-ridden, deliberative procedures. Illustrative examples are

Vincenti's story on aircraft design (Vincenti 1990) and Warglien's account of the hierarchically nested process of project selection within a microelectronic firm (Warglien 2000).

Incidentally, note in this respect that paradigms and dominant designs act at the same time as *sources of variation generation* and also of *blindness reduction* in the generation process itself, without however taking away the intrinsic "stochastic element in what is actually produced, chosen and put to test of use" (Ziman 2000, 6).

Economic criteria clearly shape, in different ways, the selection criteria of all the foregoing processes. For example, prices and users' revealed preferences straightforwardly influence selection over population of artifacts, and so do profitabilities with respect to financial allocation mechanism across firms. And, indirectly, economic influence informs also *ex ante* selection mechanism via the interests and the expectations of all economic actors when "choosing" to explore particular venues of search, particular artifact design, particular problem-solving procedures and not others.

But what about strictly social factors? How do they influence the rates and direction of technical change?

The Scope and Bounds of Social Shaping of Technology

It should be abundantly clear from the foregoing discussion that in our interpretation diverse social and political forces play a crucial role, first, in the dynamic of selection among would-be paradigms, and, second, in the shaping of the actual trajectories explored within each paradigm. If anything, even such a distinction is somewhat artificial: as Constant (1980, 1987) shows, just with a slightly different language, paradigms and trajectories emerge together with a technological community, corporate organizations carriers of such knowledge, and related technological systems. We have briefly mentioned the coevolutionary processes linking the dynamics of knowledge, on the one hand, and the dynamics of business organizations seen as repositories of problem-solving routines, on the other. Yet another, complementary, representation would be in terms of the emergence and establishment of professional communities and related institutions (e.g., the communities of chemical engineers, their journals, professional societies, university departments, etc.), intimately linked with a broadly shared body of knowledge and practices.

In our view, there is indeed little doubt on the importance of the *social shaping of technology,* as MacKenzie and Wajcman (1985) put it (see also Rip, Misa, and Schot 1995). However, important controversies concern (1) the bounds which the nature of specific technical problems and of specific bodies of knowledge put upon the reach of "battling competing interests and more or less effective campaigns to capture the hearts and minds of (different constituencies)" (Nelson 2003, 514), and (2) the degrees of "social renegotiability" of whatever incumbent technological system (i.e., its lack of path dependency).

A rich and diverse literature, stemming primarily from the sociology of science and technology, tackles these issues (see Bijker, Hughes, and Pinch 1997, and the thorough review in Williams and Edge 1996). It is impossible to discuss here this line of studies. Let us just admit that we often find many contributions in this vein a bit too near the second extreme of a continuum having on one side naive forms of "technological determinism" (i.e., search and exploration is always about finding an *objectively better* solution to old and new technical problems) and, on the other, radical forms of *social constructivism* (whereby, in a caricature, with good bargaining skills even gravitation laws may be renegotiated with nature).

A somewhat complementary debate regards possible constraints (or lack of them) posed by specific technological paradigms upon the feasible forms of organization of production. For example, a hypothesis on the emergence of the modern factory system of production is that it has been powerfully fostered by the associated efficiency improvement stemming from the exploitation of inanimate source of energy, an increasing division of labor, and, together, more refined mechanisms of control upon the workforce and more favorable patterns of appropriation of the social products by the capitalist class. An alternative hypothesis is, conversely, that only the latter set of factors was at work—the obvious normative implication being that an alternative organizational history could have been imagined, subject to the collective will of social actors. For a revealing exchange on these questions, see Marglin 1974; Sabel and Zeitlin 1985; Landes 1986.

Similar issues emerge with regard to the efficiency properties of "flexible specialization" as a possible general alternative to mass production (Piore and Sabel 1984; Sabel and Zeitlin 1995).

While it is impossible to enter the debate here, just notice that to a good extent the bottom line has to do with *degrees of plasticity* of technological knowledge. Radical versions of both "economic inducement" and "social construction" theories imply highly malleable features of technologies: "money can buy everything"—in the former—and "society can bargain everything"—in the latter.

Our view is much more cautious, and while fully acknowledging the profound reciprocal influences between technological, economic, and social factors, we maintain that the process of accumulation of technological knowledge entails an inner logic and inner constraints that social or economic drivers can hardly overcome, at least in the short term. A coevolutionary perspective indeed implies a painstaking identification of the subtle intertwining between "windows of opportunity" for social action, on the one hand, and binding constraints inherited from history or from available technologies, on the other.

TECHNO-ECONOMIC PARADIGMS FROM MICROTECHNOLOGIES TO NATIONAL SYSTEMS OF INNOVATION

So far, we have discussed paradigms, trajectories, or equivalent concepts mainly at the microtechnological level. A paradigm-based theory of innovation and production—we have argued—seems to be highly consistent with the evidence on the patterned and cumulative nature of technical change and also with the evidence on microeconomic heterogeneity and technological gaps. Moreover, it directly links with those theories of production in economics that allow for dynamic increasing returns (from Young and Kaldor to recent and more rigorous formalized path-dependent models of innovation diffusion), whereby the interaction between microdecisions and some forms of learning or some externalities produces irreversible technological paths and lock-in effects with respect to technologies that may well be inferior, on any measure, to other notional ones, but still happen to be dominant—loosely speaking—because of the weight of their history (Arthur 1989; David 1985; Bassanini and Dosi 2001).

The upside of the same story is that a world of knowledge-driven increasing returns is much less bleak than conventional economic theory has been preaching: there always are (partly) "free lunches," offered by ever-emerging opportunities for technological, organizational, and institutional innovation. However, there is nothing automatic in the economic fulfillment of the notional promises offered by persistent and widespread learning processes. Indeed the fulfillment of such promise ultimately depends upon matching or mismatching patterns between technological knowledge, the structure and behaviors of business organizations, and broader institutional setups.

The steps leading from a microeconomic theory of innovation and production to more aggregate analyses are clearly numerous and complex. A first obvious question concerns the possibility of identifying relatively coherent structure and dynamics also at broader levels of observation. Indeed, historians of technology—Thomas Hughes and Paul David, among others—highlight the importance of technological systems, that is, in the terminology of this paper, structured combinations of microtechnological paradigms: see, for example, the fascinating reconstruction of the emerging system of electrification and electrical standards in David 1991, taken as an insightful guidance also for contemporary diffusion of ICT systems. One of the messages is that "retardation factors" in the economic realization of the promise are ubiquitous, and they also recurrently explain what contemporaries in various epochs might have identified as an apparent "productivity paradox"—the puzzle emphasized by Robert Solow more than a decade ago—according to which computers show up everywhere but in statistics on productivity. As David points out also, "in 1900 contemporaries might well have said that electric dynamos were to be seen 'everywhere but in the economic statistics'" (1991, 315). The bottom line is that the lag is associated with the requirements of incremental improvements, organizational adaptation, and ultimately "the path dependent nature of the process of transition between one techno-economic regime to the next" (David 1991, 315).

Diverse but overlapping streams of inquiry have recently focused on *systems of innovation* at the levels of sectors, regions, and nations. The analysis of such systems happens to occur, in the literature, from different angles.

A first one focuses upon the specificities of national institutions and policies supporting directly or indirectly innovation, diffusion, and skills accumulation (for sake of illustration, think, for example, of the role of university research and of military or space programs in the U.S. "national system" or of training institutions in the German one). In this vein see especially the contribution of Nelson (1993).

A second approach emphasizes especially the importance of users-producers relations and the asso- ciated development of a collective knowledge base and commonly shared behavioral rules and expectations (see, in particular, the works in Lundvall 1992).

Third, Patel and Pavitt, among others, have stressed the links between national patterns of technological accumulation and the competencies and innovative strategies of a few major national companies. Note that this holds under the hypothesis for which there is rather robust evidence that, with few exceptions, even multinational companies perform most of their innovative activities in the home country (see Patel and Pavitt 1991 and for some qualifications Cantwell 1989, 1997).

Fourth, a few scholars have begun to analyze the institutional and organizational specificities of sectoral systems of innovation, production, and competition (Malerba and Orsenigo 1996; Marsili 2001).

At an even higher level of generality, Freeman and Perez (1988), Freeman and Louçã (2001), and Perez (2002) have used the notion of techno-economic paradigms as a synthetic definition of macro-level systems of production, innovation, political governance, and social relations. So, for example, they identify broad phases of modern industrial development partly isomorphic to the notion of regimes of socioeconomic regulation suggested by the mainly French macroinstitutionalist literature (Aglietta 1976; Boyer 1988a, 1988b; see also Coriat and Dosi 1998).

In an extreme synthesis, both perspectives hold, first, that one can identify rather long periods of capitalist development distinguished according to their specific engines of technological dynamism and their modes of governance of the relationships among the major social actors (e.g., firms, workers, banks, collective political authorities) and, second, that the patterns of technological advancement and those of institutional changes are bound to be coupled in such ways as to yield recognizable invariances for quite long times in most economic and political structures. Just to provide an example, one might roughly identify, over the three decades after World War II, across most developed economies, some "Fordist/Keynesian" regime of socioeconomic "regulation," driven by major innovative opportunities of technological innovation in electromechanical technologies, synthetic chemistry, forms of institutional governance of industrial conflict, income distribution, and aggregate demand management. Analogously, earlier in industrial history, one should be able to detect some sort of archetype of a "classical/Victorian regime" driven in its growth by the full exploitation of tex-

TABLE 4.   A Different Techno-Economic Paradigm for Each Technological Revolution, 1770 to 2000s

Technological Revolution and Country of Initial Development	*Techno-Economic Paradigm ("commonsense" innovation principles)*
"Industrial Revolution" Britain	Factory production Mechanization Productivity/timekeeping and time saving Fluidity of movement (as ideal for machines with water power and for transport through canals and other waterways) Local networks
Age of steam and railways In Britain and spreading to Continent and USA	Economies of agglomeration, industrial cities, national markets Power centers with national networks Scale and progress Standard parts, machine-made machines Energy where needed (steam) Interdependent movement (of machines and of means of transport)
Age of steel, electricity, and heavy engineering USA and Germany overtaking Britain	Giant structures (steel) Economies of scale of plant/vertical integration Distributed power for industry (electricity) Science as a productive force Worldwide networks and empires (including cartels) Universal standardization Cost accounting for control and efficiency Great scale for world market power: "small" is successful, if local
Age of oil, the automobile, and mass production In USA and spreading to Europe	Mass production, mass markets Economies of scale (product and market volume), horizontal integration Standardization of products Energy intensity (oil based) Synthetic materials Functional specialization, hierarchical pyramids Centralization, metropolitan centers-suburbanization National powers, world agreements, and confrontations
Age of information and telecommunications In USA, spreading to Europe and Asia	Information intensity (microelectronics-based ICT) Decentralized integration, network structures Knowledge as capital, intangible value added Heterogeneity, diversity, adaptability Segmentation of markets, proliferation of niches Economies of scope and specialization combined with scale Globalization, interaction between the global and the local Inward and outward cooperation/clusters Instant contact and action, instant global communications

Source: Perez 2002.

tile manufacturing and light engineering mechanization, relatively competitive labor markets, politically-driven effort to expand privileged market outlets, and so on (more on this in Coriat and Dosi 1998).

These general conjectures on historical phases or regimes are grounded on the importance in growth and development of specific combinations among technological systems and forms of socioeconomic governance. Table 4 provides a suggestive taxonomy.

A complementary, somewhat more "cross-sec-tional," exercise concerns the identification of national socioeconomic regimes with distinctive embedding mechanisms of technological learning within national systems of innovation, production, and governance.

So, even if microparadigms present considerable invariances across countries, the ways they are combined in broader national systems of innovation display—we suggest—a considerable variety, shaped by county-specific institutions, policies, and social factors. The hypothesis here is that evolutionary microfoundations are a fruitful starting point for a theory showing how technological gaps and national institutional diversities can jointly reproduce themselves over rather long spans of time in ways that are easily compatible with the patterns of incentives and opportunities facing individual agents, even when they might turn out to be profoundly suboptimal from a collective point of view.

At this level of analyses, inquiries like those undertaken in different veins by Soskice (1997), Boyer and Hollingsworth (1997), Amable, Barré, and Boyer (1997), Hall and Soskice (2001), Crouch and Streek (1997), Kogut (1993), Lazonick (2002), Dore (2000), and Aoki (2001) start where this chapter ends, addressing a few of the macro conditions making up for diverse types of relatively coherent institutional combinatorics (e.g., underlying "Anglo-Saxon" vs. "corporatist" system of innovation and production, etc.).

At this juncture, economic sociology, again, is bound to play a fundamental role, highlighting the social embedding of technological learning and its exploitation at work.

NOTES

The chapter draws upon other works by one of the authors—in particular Cimoli and Dosi 1995; Dosi, Freeman, and Fabiani 1994; and Dosi 1997—to which the reader is referred for more detailed discussions. Comments by Richard Nelson, Keith Pavitt, Woody Powell, Neil J. Smelser, Wolfgang Streeck, and Richard Swedberg have helped along the revision of this work. Support for the research provided by the Sant'Anna School of Advanced Studies is gratefully acknowledged.

1. More generally on long-term international trends in technology, see Landes 1969 and 1998; Freeman 1982; Mokyr 1990.

2. Interpretations of technical change and a number of historical examples can be found in Freeman 1994; Rosenberg 1994; Nelson and Winter 1982; Hughes 1983; David 1975; Mokyr 1990; Saviotti 1996; Pavitt 1999; Dosi 1984; Basalla 1988; Constant 1980; Petroski 1999; Ziman 2000, among others; see, for partial surveys, Dosi 1982, 1988 and Freeman 1994.

3. Incidentally note that the notion of dominant design is well in tune with the general idea technological paradigms, but the latter do not necessarily imply the former. A revealing case to the point is pharmaceuticals technologies, which do involve specific knowledge basis, specific search heuristics, etc.—i.e., the strong mark of paradigms—without, however, any hint at dominant design. Molecules, even when aimed at the same pathology, might have quite different structures: in that space, one is unlikely to find similarities akin to those linking even a Volkswagen Beetle 1937 and a Ferrari 2000. Still, the notion of "paradigm" holds in terms of underlying features of knowledge bases and search processes.

4. This is akin to the notion of reverse salient (Hughes 1983) and technological bottlenecks (Rosenberg 1976): to

illustrate, think of increasing the speed of a machine tool, which in turn demands changes in cutting materials, which leads to changes in other parts of the machine.

5. For more detail and examples see Dosi 1988.

6. See Pavitt 1991; Rosenberg 1990.

7. In the literature, which admittedly includes some of the authors of this work, the two terms have been used quite liberally and interchangeably. In the introduction to Dosi, Nelson, and Winter 2000 and more explicitly in Dosi, Coriat, and Pavitt 2000 one proposes that the notion of capability ought to confined to relatively purposeful, "high level" tasks such as, e.g., "building an automobile" with certain characteristics, while "competences," for sake of clarity might be confined to the ability to master specific knowledge bases (e.g., "mechanical" or "organic chemistry" competences). Clearly, such notion of competences or capabilities largely overlaps with what has come to be known as the "competence view of the firm" (Prahalad and Hamel 1990). Dosi, Nelson, and Winter (2000) attempt to offer also some refinements within a rather germane perspective.

8. Aoki underlines the Japanese firms' ability to flexibly coordinate their operating activities in response to environmental changing conditions. He stresses that this is due to the specific Japanese form of internal organization "in which emergent information is utilized effectively on-site and in which operating activities are coordinated among related operating units on the basis of information sharing" (Aoki 1990, 3). By comparison, traditional model of organizational hierarchies (what he calls the H-mode), resembling classic American organizational practices, assumes hierarchical separation between planning and operational implementation and the exploitation of the economies of specialization. Conversely, the Japanese model (the J-mode) implies horizontal coordination among operating units and sharing of *ex post* on-site information.

9. These four sets correspond quite closely to the codified aspects of Lundvall's taxonomy, distinguishing know-what, know-why, know-who, and know-how (Lundvall and Johnson 1994).

10. This is also the title of an important research, in progress, coordinated by Richard Nelson; for preliminary results, see Nelson 2001 and Nelson and Nelson 2002.

11. The debate among historians about the role of science—or to put it differently—of a positive attitude toward the rational manipulation of the environment and the rational adaptation of means to ends—in the emergence of the Industrial Revolution is highly relevant in this context. See Landes 1969; Needham 1954; Musson and Robinson 1969; among others. Of course, a general underlying issue regards what is science as distinguished from technology. It is an issue that we cannot handle here. For our purposes it suffices to recall the traditional and noble view shared by epistemologists as diverse as Kuhn and Popper, pointing at the distinctions of science in terms of the procedures of discovery, validation, and falsification and at the somewhat overlapping distinction put forward by students of technology such as Vincenti (1990), based on different purposes of science, and aiming at the understanding of "how things are" as opposed to the engineers' focus on "how things ought to be." The distinction mirrors Lundvall's between know-why and know-how. Notice that the foregoing views have been criticized by proponents of the "new economics of science" (see Dasgupta and David 1994), suggesting that science and technology primarily differ in terms of the ethos of the two communities concerning rules of disclosure of results, rules of attribution, etc.

12. A classic example may be found in the aircraft industry. The introduction of the turbojet spurred major advances in aerodynamics, aerothermodynamics, and subsequently magneto thermodynamics, as further technological advances (e.g., higher speed) required a better understanding of underlying properties (Rosenberg 1982; Constant 1980).

13. The expression is due to Freeman (1982).

14. In this respect, it is quite interesting, for example, to read the documents written by academics and government officers to support funding for the emerging field of molecular biology in the 1950s–1960s. Most of them do actually mention the potential benefits that scientific research in this area might have borne in the long run in terms of medical applications. However, in practice those considerations played a very minor role in the decision-making processes on actually funding molecular biology in the various European countries (see Krige 2000; Strasser 2000).

15. Another distinct issue that we cannot address here has to do with the *normative* prescriptions for the relationship between scientific activities and social accountability, including the question whether science as such—in its patterns of search and discovery—should be socially accountable, or whether accountability should refer *in primis* to scientists themselves. The terms of the debate are well illustrated by the comparison between Bush (1945) and Bennal (1971). (For a recent assessment see also Stokes 1997.)

16. For detailed discussions, see Rosenberg 1982; Mowery and Rosenberg 1998; Nelson 1993; Freeman and Soete 1997; Chandler 1977, 1990.

17. By that we mean the organizational setup of typically big firms, extensively analyzed by Alfred Chandler, which emerged first in the United States, typically run by professional management, based on multiple divisions representing also distinct cost/profit entities (cf. Chandler 1977).

18. More on all these points in Freeman and Soete 1997; Freeman 1994; Dosi 1988.

19. The classical example is biotechnology, where inventors—e.g., typically new specialized biotechnology firms (NBFs)—do not control the resources needed to develop the product, to go through the clinical trials and all the procedures needed to have the drug approved by regulatory agencies like the FDA and to market them. Under these circumstances, NBFs are in practice forced to license their invention to big pharmaceutical companies, thereby foregoing a large share of the profits generated by the sales of the drug (Teece 1986).

20. It is not possible to discuss here the underlying theoretical debates, ranging from "patent races models" to more reasonable "markets for technologies" analyses, all the way to evolutionary models of appropriability. Among many others see Stoneman 1995; Arora, Fosfuri, and Gambardella 2001; Winter 1987.

21. Discussions of the evidence are in Dosi 1988; Freeman 1982; Pavitt 1999; and Rosenberg 1976; moreover see Dosi and Lovallo 1997 on the likely cognitive bias displayed by would-be innovators.

REFERENCES

Abernathy, William J., and James M. Utterback. 1978. "Patterns of Industrial Innovation." *Technology Review* 80:41–47.

Aglietta, Michel. 1976. *A Theory of Capitalist Regulation: The US Experience.* Trans. David Fernbach. London: Verso.

Akerlof, George 1984. *An Economic Theorist's Book of Tales.* Cambridge: Cambridge University Press.

Amable Bruno, Remi Barré, and Robert Boyer. 1997. *Les systèmes d'innovation à l'ère de la globalisation.* Paris: Economica.

Antonelli, Cristiano. 1995. *The Economics of Localized Technological Change and Industrial Dynamics.* Boston: Kluwer Academic Publishers.

Aoki, Masahiko. 1990. "Towards an Economic Model of the Japanese Firm." *Journal of Economic Literature* 28:1–27.

———. 2001. *Toward a Comparative Institutional Analysis.* Cambridge: MIT Press.

Archibugi, Daniele, and Jonathan Michie, eds. 1997. *Technology, Globalisation, and Economic Performance.* Cambridge: Cambridge University Press.

Archibugi, Daniele, Jeremy Howells, and Jonathan Michie. 1999. *Innovation Policy in a Global Economy.* Cambridge: Cambridge University Press.

Arora, Ashish, Andrea Fosfuri, and Alfonso Gambardella. 1994. "The Changing Technology of Technical Change: General and Abstract Knowledge and the Division of Innovative Labor." *Research Policy* 23: 523–32.

———. 2001. *Markets for Technology.* Cambridge: MIT Press.

Arrow, Kenneth J. 1962. "Economics of Welfare and the Allocation of Resources for Invention." Pp. 609–25 in *The Rate and Direction of Inventive Activity*, ed. Richard R. Nelson. Princeton: Princeton University Press.

———. 1996. "Technical Information and Industrial Structure." *Industrial and Corporate Change* 5: 645–52.

Arthur, W. Brian. 1988. "Competing Technologies: An Overview." Pp. 590–607 in *Technical Change and Economic Theory*, ed. Giovanni Dosi, Chris Freeman, Richard R. Nelson, Gerald Silverberg, and Luc Soete. London: Pinter.

———. 1989. "Competing Technologies, Increasing Returns, and Lock-in by Historical Events." *Economic Journal* 99:116–46.

Arthur, W. Brian, Yuri M. Ermoliev, and Yuri M. Kaniovski. 1987. "Path-Dependent Processes and the Emergence of Macro-structure." *European Journal of Operational Research* 30:294–303.

Arundel, Anthony, Gert van de Paal, and Luc Soete. 1995. "Innovation Strategies of Europe's Largest Industrial Firms." PACE Final Report, Maastricht Economic Research Institute on Innovation and Technology, University of Limbourg, Maastricht.

Atkinson, Anthony B., and Joseph E. Stiglitz. 1969. "A New View of Technological Change." *Economic Journal* 79:573–78.

Audretsch, David B., and Maryann P. Feldman. 1996. "R&D Spillovers and the Geography of Innovation and Production." *American Economic Review* 86: 630–40.

Baily, Martin Neil, Charles Hulten, and David Campbell. 1992. "Productivity Dynamics in Manufacturing Plants." *Brookings Papers on Economic Activity: Microeconomics* 187–249.

Bairoch, Paul. 1981. "The Main Trends in National Economic Disparities since the Industrial Revolution." Pp. 3–17 in *Disparities in Economic Development since the Industrial Revolution*, ed. Paul Bairoch and Maurice Lévy-Loboyer. London: Macmillan.

Balconi, Margherita. 1998. "Technology, Codification of Knowledge, and Firm Competences." *Revue internationale de systémique* 12(1): 63–82.

Baldwin, John R. 1995. *The Dynamics of Industrial Competition: A North American Perspective*. Cambridge: Cambridge University Press.

Basalla, George. 1988. *The Evolution of Technology*. Cambridge: Cambridge University Press.

Bassanini, Andrea, and Giovanni Dosi. 2001. "When and How Human Will Can Twist the Arms of Clio: An Essay on Path Dependence in a World of Irreversibility." Pp. 41–68 in *Path Dependence and Creation*, ed. Raghu Garud and Peter Karnøe. Mahwah, N.J.: Lawrence Erlbaum Associates.

Bernal, John D. 1971. *Science in History*. Cambridge: MIT Press.

Bijker, Wiebe E., Thomas P. Hughes, and Trevor J. Pinch, eds. 1997. *The Social Construction of Technological Systems: New Directions in the Sociology and History of Technology*. Cambridge: MIT Press.

Bottazzi, Giulio, Elena Cefis, and Giovanni Dosi. 2003. "Corporate Growth and Industrial Structures: Some Evidence from the Italian Manufacturing Industry." *Industrial and Corporate Change* 11:705–23.

Bottazzi, Guilio, Elena Cefis, Giovanni Dosi, and Angelo Secchi. 2003. "Invariances and Diversities in the Evolution of Industries." LEM Papers. Series 2003/21, Laboratory of Economics and Management, Sant'Anna School of Advanced Studies, Pisa.

Boyer, Robert. 1988a. "Technical Change and the Theory of 'Regulation.'" Pp. 67–94 in *Technical Change and Economic Theory*, ed. Giovanni Dosi et al. London: Pinter.

———. 1988b. "Formalizing Growth Regimes within a Regulation Approach: A Method for Assessing the Economic Consequences of Technological Change." Pp. 608–30 in *Technical Change and Economic Theory*, ed. Giovanni Dosi, Chris Freeman, Richard R. Nelson, Gerald Silverberg, and Luc Soete. London: Pinter.

Boyer, Robert, and J. Rogers Hollingsworth. 1997. *Contemporary Capitalism: The Embeddedness of Institutions*. Cambridge: Cambridge University Press.

Braun, Ernest, and Stuart Macdonald. 1978. *Revolution in Miniature: The History and Impact of Semiconductor Electronics*. Cambridge: Cambridge University Press.

Breschi, Stefano, Franco Malerba, and Luigi Orsenigo.

2000. "Technological Regimes and Schumpeterian Patterns of Innovation." *Economic Journal* 110: 388–411.

Brooks, Harvey. 1994. "The Relationship between Science and Technology." *Research Policy* 23:477–86.

Bush, Vannevar. 1945. *Science: The Endless Frontier*. Washington, D.C.: Government Printing Office.

Callon, Michel. 1991. "Techno-economic Networks and Irreversibility." Pp. 132–61 in *A Sociology of Monsters: Essays on Power, Technology, and Domination*, ed. John Law. London: Routledge.

———. 1995. "Is Science a Public Good?" *Science, Technology, and Human Values* 1:395–424.

Cantwell, John A. 1989. *Technological Innovation and Multinational Corporations*. Oxford: Basil Blackwell.

———. 1997. "The Globalization of Technology: What Remains of the Product Cycle Model?" Pp. 215–40 in *Technology, Globalisation, and Economic Performance*, ed. Daniele Archibugi and Jonathan Michie. Cambridge: Cambridge University Press.

Castells, Manuel. 1996. *The Rise of the Network Society: The Information Age: Economy, Society, and Culture*. Oxford: Blackwell.

Chandler, Alfred D., Jr. 1977. *The Visible Hand*. Cambridge: Harvard University Press.

———. 1990. *Scale and Scope: The Dynamics of Modern Capitalism*. Cambridge: Belknap Press of Harvard University Press.

Cimoli, Mario, and Giovanni Dosi. 1995. "Technological Paradigms, Patterns of Learning, and Development: An Introductory Road Map." *Journal of Evolutionary Economics* 5:243–68.

Cipolla, Carlo M. 1965. *Guns and Sails in the Early Phase of European Expansion, 1400–1700*. London: Collins.

Cohen, I. Bernard. 1976. "Science and the Growth of the American Republic." *Review of Politics* 38:359–98.

Cohen, Michael D., Roger Burkhart, Giovanni Dosi, Massimo Egidi, Luigi Marengo, Massimo Warglien, and Sidney G. Winter. 1996. "Routines and Other Recurring Action Patterns of Organizations: Contemporary Research Issues." *Industrial and Corporate Change* 5:653–98.

Cohen, Wesley M., and Daniel A. Levinthal. 1989. "Innovation and Learning: The Two Faces of R&D." *Economic Journal* 99:569–96.

Collins, Harry M. 1974. "The TEA Set: Tacit Knowledge and Scientific Networks." *Science Studies* 4:165–86.

Constant, Edward W., II. 1980. *The Origins of the Turbojet Revolution*. Baltimore: Johns Hopkins University Press.

———. 1987. "The Social Locus of Technological Practice: Community, System, or Organization?" Pp. 223–42 in *The Social Construction of Technological Systems: New Directions in the Sociology and History of Technology*, ed. Wiebe E. Bijker, Thomas P. Hughes, and Trevor J. Pinch. Cambridge: MIT Press.

Coriat, Benjamin, and Giovanni Dosi. 1998. "The Institutional Embeddedness of Economic Change: An Appraisal of the 'Evolutionary' and 'Regulationist' Research Programmes." Pp. 3–32 in *Institutions and Economic Change: New Perspectives on Markets, Firms, and Technology*, ed. Kaus Nielsen and Björn Johnson. Cheltenham, U.K.: Edward Elgar.

Cowan, Robin, Paul A. David, and Dominique Foray. 2000. "The Explicit Economics of Knowledge Codification and Tacitness." *Industrial and Corporate Change* 9(2): 211–54.

Crouch, Colin, and Wolfgang Streeck. 1997. *Political Economy of Modern Capitalism*. London: Sage.

Cyert, Richard M., and James G. March. 1992. *A Behavioral Theory of the Firm*. 2d ed. Oxford: Blackwell Business.

Dasgupta Partha, and Paul A. David. 1994. "The New Economics of Science." *Research Policy* 23:487–521.

David, Paul A. 1975. *Technical Choice, Innovation, and Economic Growth*. Cambridge: Cambridge University Press.

———. 1985. "Clio and the Economics of QWERTY." *American Economic Review* 75:332–37.

———. 1991. "Computer and Dynamo: The Modern Productivity Paradox in a Not Too Distant Mirror." Pp. 315–47 in *Technology and Productivity: The Challenge for Economic Policy*, ed. Organization for Economic Cooperation and Development. Paris: OECD.

David, Paul A., David C. Mowery, and W. Edward Steinmueller. 1992. "Analyzing the Economic Payoffs from Basic Research." *Economic Innovation and New Technologies* 2:73–90.

Davis, Steven J., John C. Haltiwanger, and Scott Schuh. 1996. *Job Creation and Destruction*. Cambridge: MIT Press.

DeLong, J. Bradford. 1988. "Productivity Growth, Convergence, and Welfare." *American Economic Review* 78:1138–54.

DeLong, J. Bradford, and Lawrence H. Summers. 1991. "Equipment Investment and Economic Growth." *Quarterly Journal of Economics* 106:445–502.

Dore, Ronald. 2000. *Stock Market Capitalism: Welfare Capitalism—Japan and Germany versus the Anglo-Saxons*. Oxford: Oxford University Press.

Dosi, Giovanni. 1982. "Technological Paradigms and Technological Trajectories: A Suggested Interpretation." *Research Policy* 11:147–62.

———. 1984. *Technical Change and Industrial Transformation*. London: Macmillan.

———. 1988. "Sources, Procedures, and Microeconomic Effects of Innovation." *Journal of Economic Literature* 26:1120–71.

———. 1997. "Opportunities, Incentives, and the Collective Patterns of Technological Change." *Economic Journal* 107(444): 1530–47.

Dosi, Giovanni, and Benjamin Coriat. 1998. "Learning How to Govern and Learning How to Solve Problems: On the Co-evolution of Competences, Conflicts, and Organizational Routines." Pp. 103–33 in *The Dynamic Firm*, ed. Alfred D. Chandler Jr., Peter Hägstrum, and Örjan Sölvell. Oxford: Oxford University Press.

Dosi, Giovanni, Benjamin Coriat, and Keith Pavitt. 2000. "Competences, Capabilities, and Corporate Performance." Final Report, Dynacom Project, Laboratory of Economics and Management, Sant'Anna School of Advanced Studies, Pisa.

Dosi, Giovanni, Marco Faillo, and Luigi Marengo. 2003. "Organizational Capabilities, Patterns of Knowledge Accumulation, and Governance Structures: An Introduction." Working paper, Laboratory of Economics and Management, Sant'Anna School of Advanced Studies, Pisa.

Dosi, Giovanni, Chris Freeman, and S. Fabiani. 1994. "The Process of Economic Development: Introducing Some Stylized Facts and Theories on Technologies, Firms, and Institutions." *Industrial and Corporate Change* 3(1): 1–45.

Dosi, Giovanni, Christopher Freeman, Richard R. Nelson, Gerald Silverberg, and Luc Soete, eds. 1988. *Technical Change and Economic Theory*. London: Pinter.

Dosi Giovanni, Mike Hobday, and Luigi Marengo. 2000. "Problem-Solving Behaviors, Organizational Forms, and the Complexity of Tasks." LEM Working Paper No. 6, Laboratory of Economics and Management, Sant'Anna School of Advanced Studies, Pisa.

Dosi, Giovanni, Mike Hobday, Luigi Marengo, and Andrea Prencipe. 2002. "The Economics of System Integration: Toward an Evolutionary Interpretation." LEM Working Paper No. 16, Laboratory of Economics and Management, Sant'Anna School of Advanced Studies, Pisa.

Dosi, Giovanni, and Yuri Kaniovski. 1994. "On 'Badly Behaved' Dynamics: Some Applications of Generalized Urn Schemes to Technological and Economic Change." *Journal of Evolutionary Economics* 4(2): 93–123.

Dosi, Giovanni, and Dan Lovallo. 1997. "Rational Entrepreneurs or Optimistic Martyrs? Some Considerations on Technological Regimes, Corporate Entries, and the Evolutionary Role of Decision Biases." Pp. 41–70 in *Technological Innovation: Oversights and Foresights*, ed. Raghu Garud, Praveen Rattan Nayyar, and Zur Baruch Shapira. Cambridge: Cambridge University Press.

Dosi, Giovanni, Luigi Marengo, and Giorgio Fagiolo. 1996. "Learning in Evolutionary Environments." IIASA Working Paper WP-96-124, International Institute for Applied Systems Analysis, Laxenburg, Austria. Forthcoming in *Evolutionary Principles of Economics*, ed. Kurt Dopfer. Cambridge: Cambridge University Press.

Dosi, Giovanni, Orietta Marsili, Luigi Orsenigo, and Roberta Salvatore. 1995. "Learning, Market Selection, and the Evolution of Industrial Structures." *Small Business Economics* 7:411–36.

Dosi, Giovanni, Richard R. Nelson, and Sidney Winter, eds. 2000. *The Nature and Dynamics of Organizational Capabilities*. Oxford: Oxford University Press.

Dosi, Giovanni, Keith Pavitt, and Luc Soete. 1990. *The Economics of Technical Change and International Trade*. Hertfordshire: Harvester Wheatsheaf.

Dosi, Giovanni, and Sidney G. Winter. 2002. "Interpreting Economic Change: Evolution, Structure, and Games." Pp. 337–53 in *The Economics of Choice, Change, and Organizations*, ed. Mie Augier and James G. March. Cheltenham, U.K.: Edward Elgar.

Durlauf, Steven N., and Paul A. Johnson. 1992. "Local versus Global Convergence across National Economies." NBER Working Paper No. 3996.

Easterly, William, Robert King, Ross Levine, and Sergio Rebelo. 1992. "How Do National Policies Affect Long-Run Growth? A Research Agenda." Discussion Papers, World Bank.

Fagerberg, J. 1988. "Why Growth Rates Differ." Pp. 432–57 in *Technical Change and Economic Theory*, ed. Giovanni Dosi, Chris Freeman, Richard R. Nelson, Gerald Silverberg, and Luc Soete. London: Pinter.

Fleck, James. 1988. "Innofusion or Diffusation? The Nature of Technological Developments in Robotics." Working Paper, Programme on Information and Communications Technologies, Edinburgh.

Foss, Nicolai J., and Volker Mahnke, eds. 2000. *Competence, Governance, and Entrepreneurship: Advances in Economic Strategy Research*. Oxford: Oxford University Press.

Freeman, Chris. 1982. *The Economics of Industrial Innovation*. London: Pinter.

———. 1994. "The Economics of Technical Change: A Critical Survey." *Cambridge Journal of Economics* 18:1–50.

———. 1995. "The National System of Innovation in Historical Perspective." *Cambridge Journal of Economics* 19(1): 5–24.

Freeman, Chris, and Francisco Louçã. 2001. *As Time Goes By: The Information Revolution and the Industrial Revolutions in Historical Perspective*. Oxford: Oxford University Press.

Freeman Chris, and Carlota Perez. 1988. "Structural Crises of Adjustment: Business Cycles and Investment Behaviour." Pp. 38–66 in *Technical Change and Economic Theory*, ed. Giovanni Dosi, Chris Freeman, Richard R. Nelson, Gerald Silverberg, and Luc Soete. London: Pinter.

Freeman, Chris, and Luc Soete. 1997. *The Economics of Industrial Innovation*. 3d ed. London: Pinter.

Granovetter, Mark. 1985. "Economic Action and Social Structure: The Problem of Embeddedness." *American Journal of Sociology* 91:481–510.

Greenwald, Bruce, and Joseph E. Stiglitz. 1986. "Externalities in Economics with Imperfect Information and Incomplete Markets." *Quarterly Journal of Economics* 101:229–64.

Grupp, Hariolf, ed. 1992. *Dynamics of Science-Based Innovation*. Berlin: Springer Verlag.

Hall, Peter A., and David Soskice. 2001. *Varieties of Capitalism: The Institutional Foundations of Comparative Advantage*. Oxford: Oxford University Press.

Heller, Michael A., and Rebecca S. Eisenberg. 1998. "Can Patents Deter Innovation? The Anticommons in Biomedical Research." *Science* 280:698–701.

Henderson Rebecca M., and Iain M. Cockburn. 1996. "Scale, Scope, and Spillovers: The Determinants of Research Productivity in Drug Discovery." *Rand Journal of Economics* 27(1): 32–59.

Henderson Rebecca M., Iain M. Cockburn, Luigi Orsenigo, and Gary Pisano. 1999. "Pharmaceuticals and Biotechnology." Pp. 363–98 in *US Industry in 2000: Studies in Competitive Performance*, ed. David C. Mowery. Washington, D.C.: National Academy Press.

Hirschman, Albert O. 1982. "Rival Interpretations of Market Society: Civilizing, Destructive, or Feeble?" *Journal of Economic Literature* 20:1463–84.

Hodgson, Geoffrey M. 1993. *Economics and Evolution: Bringing Life Back into Economics*. Ann Arbor: University of Michigan Press.

Hughes, Thomas P. 1983. *Networks of Power: Electrification in Western Society, 1880–1930*. Baltimore: Johns Hopkins University Press.

Jaffee, Adam B. 1989. "Real Effects of Academic Research." *American Economic Review* 79:957–70.

Jaffee, Adam B., Manuel Trajtenberg, and Rebecca M. Henderson. 1993. "Geographical Localization of Knowledge Spillovers as Evidenced by Patent Citations." *Quarterly Journal of Economics* 63:577–98.

Kleiman, H. S. 1977. *The U.S. Government Role in the Integrated Circuit Innovation*. Paris: Organization for Economic Cooperation and Development.

Klepper, Steven. 1996. "Entry, Exit, Growth, and Innovation over the Product Life Cycle." *American Economic Review* 86:562–83.

Klevorick, Alvin K., Richard Levin, Richard R. Nelson, and Sidney G. Winter. 1995. "On the Sources and Interindustry Differences in Technological Opportunities." *Research Policy* 24:185–205.

Kline, Steven, and Nathan Rosenberg. 1986. "An Overview of Innovation." Pp. 275–306 in *Positive Sum Strategy: Harnessing Technology for Economic Growth*, ed. Ralph Landau and Nathan Rosenberg. Washington, D.C.: National Academy Press.

Kogut, Bruce. 1993. *Country Competitiveness: Technology and Organization of Work*. Oxford: Oxford University Press.

Koumpis, Konstantinos, and Keith Pavitt. 1999. "Corporate Activities in Speech Recognition and Natural Language: Another "New Science"–Based Technology." *International Journal of Innovation Management* 3:335–66.

Krige, J. 2000. "The Birth of EMBO and EMBL." Paper Presented at the conference "Molecular Biology in Postwar Europe," Annecy, France, June 29–July 1.

Landes, David S. 1969. *The Unbound Prometheus.* Cambridge: Cambridge University Press.

———. 1986. "What Do Bosses Really Do?" *Journal of Economic History* 46:585–623.

———. 1998. *The Wealth and Poverty of Nations: Why Are Some So Rich and Others So Poor?* New York: W. W. Norton.

Lazonick, William. 2002. *American Corporate Economy.* London: Routledge.

Levin, Richard C., Wesley M. Cohen, and David C. Mowery. 1985. "R&D Appropriability, Opportunity, and Market Structure: New Evidence on Some Schumpeterian Hypotheses." *American Economic Review Papers and Proceedings* 75(2): 20–24.

Levin, Richard L., Alvin K. Klevorick, Richard R. Nelson, and Sidney G. Winter. 1984. *Survey Research on R & D Appropriability and Technological Opportunity.* Part 1. New Haven: Yale University Press.

Lundvall, Bengt-Åke. 1988. "Innovation as an Interactive Process—from User-Producer Interaction to National Systems of Innovation." Pp. 51–71 in *Technology and Economic Theory*, ed. Giovanni Dosi, Chris Freeman, Richard R. Nelson, Gerald Silverberg, and Luc Soete. London: Pinter.

———. 1992. *National Systems of Innovation: Towards a Theory of Innovation and Interactive Learning.* London: Pinter.

Lundvall, Bengt-Åke, and Björn Johnson. 1994. "The Learning Economy." *Journal of Industry Studies* 1(2): 23–42.

MacKenzie, Donald, and Judy Wajcman. 1985. *The Social Shaping of Technology.* Buckingham: Open University Press.

Mahdi, Surya, and Keith Pavitt. 1997. "Key National Factors in the Emergence of Computational Chemistry Firms." *International Journal of Innovation Management* 1:355–86.

Malerba, Franco, and Luigi Orsenigo. 1996. "The Dynamics and Evolution of Industries." *Industrial and Corporate Change* 5:51–88.

Mansfield, Edwin. 1991. "Academic Research and Industrial Innovation." *Research Policy* 20:1–13.

Mansfield, Edwin, Mark Schwartz, and Samuel Wagner. 1981. "Imitation Costs and Patents: An Empirical Study." *Economic Journal* 91:907–18.

March, James G. 1988. *Decision and Organization.* Oxford: Basil Blackwell.

———. 1991. "Exploration and Exploitation in Organizational Learning." *Organization Science* 1(2): 71–87.

March, James G., and Herbert A. Simon. 1993. "Organizations Revisited." *Industrial and Corporate Change* 2:299–316.

Marengo, Luigi, Giovanni Dosi, Paolo Legrenzi, and Corrado Pasquali. 2000. "The Structure of Problem-Solving Knowledge and the Structure of Organizations." *Industrial and Corporate Change* 9: 757–88.

Marglin, Stephen. 1974. "What Do Bosses Do? The Origins and Functions of Hierarchy in Capitalist Production." *Review of Radical Political Economy* 6:60–112.

Marsili, Orietta. 2001. *The Anatomy and Evolution of Industries: Technological Change and Industrial Dynamics.* Cheltenham, U.K.: Edward Elgar.

Mazzoleni, Roberto, and Richard R. Nelson. 1998. "The Benefits and Costs of Strong Patent Protection: A Contribution to the Current Debate." *Research Policy* 27:273–84.

Merges, Robert P. and Richard R. Nelson. 1994. "On Limiting or Encouraging Rivalry in Technical Progress: The Effects of Patent Scope Decisions." *Journal of Economic Behavior and Organization* 25: 1–24.

Merton, Robert K. 1968. "The Matthew Effect in Science." *Science* 159:59–63.

———. 1973. "The Sociology of Science." in Merton, *The Sociology of Science: Theoretical and Empirical Investigation*, ed. Norman W. Starer. Chicago: University of Chicago Press.

Metcalfe, J. Stanley. 1998. *Evolutionary Economics and Creative Destruction.* London: Routledge.

Misa, Thomas J. 1985. "Military Needs, Commercial Realities, and the Development of the Transistor, 1948–1958." Pp. 253–87 in *Military Enterprise and Technological Change*, ed. Merritt Roe Smith. Cambridge, Mass.: MIT Press.

Mokyr, Joel. 1990. *The Lever of Riches: Technology Creativity and Economic Progress.* Oxford: Oxford University Press.

———. 2000. "Innovation and Selection in Evolutionary Models of Technology: Some Definitional Issues." Pp. 52–65 in *Technological Innovation as an Evolutionary Process*, ed. John Ziman. Cambridge: Cambridge University Press.

Montgomery, Cynthia A., ed. 1995. *Resource-Based and Evolutionary Theories of the Firm.* Dordrecht: Kluwer.

Mowery, David C. 1998. "The Changing Structure of the US National Innovation System: Implications for International Conflict and Cooperation in R&D Policy." *Research Policy* 27:639–54.

Mowery, David C., and Richard R. Nelson, eds. 1999. *Sources of Industrial Leadership.* Cambridge: Cambridge University Press.

Mowery, David C., and Nathan Rosenberg. 1979. "The Influence of Market Demand Upon Innovation: A Critical Review of Some Recent Empirical Studies." *Research Policy* 8:102–53.

———. 1993. "The US National Innovation System." Pp. 29–75 in *National Innovation Systems: A Comparative Analysis*, ed. Richard R. Nelson. Oxford: Oxford University Press.

———. 1998. *Paths of Innovation: Technological Change*

in Twentieth Century America. Cambridge: Cambridge University Press.

Musson A. E., and Eric Robinson. 1969. *Science and Technology in the Industrial Revolution*. Manchester: Manchester University Press.

National Science Board. 2000. *Science and Engineering Indicators—2000*. Arlington, Va.: National Science Foundation.

Needham, J. 1954. *Science and Civilization in China*. Cambridge: Cambridge University Press.

Nelson, Katherine, and Richard R. Nelson. 2002. "On the Nature and Evolution of Human Know-How." *Research Policy* 31:719–33.

Nelson, Richard R. 1959. "The Simple Economics of Basic Scientific Research." *Journal of Political Economy* 67:297–306.

———. 1962. "The Link between Science and Invention: The Case of the Transistor." Pp. 549–83 in *The Rate and Direction of Inventive Activity*. ed. Richard R. Nelson. Princeton: Princeton University Press.

———. 1994. "The Co-evolution of Technology, Industrial Structure, and Supporting Institutions." *Industrial and Corporate Change* 3:47–64.

———. 1995. "Recent Evolutionary Theorizing about Economic Change." *Journal of Economic Literature* 33:48–90.

———. 2001. "On the Uneven Evolution of Human Know-How." *Research Policy* 32:909–22.

———. 2004. "The Market Economy and the Scientific Commons." *Research Policy* 33:455–71.

———. Forthcoming. "Perspectives on Technological Evolution." In *Evolutionary Principles of Economics*, ed. K. Dopfer (Cambridge: Cambridge University Press).

———, ed. 1993. *National Innovation Systems: A Comparative Analysis*. Oxford: Oxford University Press.

Nelson, Richard R., and Sidney G. Winter. 1982. *An Evolutionary Theory of Economic Change*. Cambridge: Belknap Press of Harvard University Press.

———. 2002. "Evolutionary Theorizing in Economics." *Journal of Economic Perspectives* 16(2): 23–46.

Noble, David F. 1984. *Forces of Production*. New York: Alfred A. Knopf.

Nordhaus, William D 1969. *Invention, Growth, and Welfare: A Theoretical Treatment of Technological Change*. Cambridge: MIT Press.

Orsenigo, Luigi. 1989. *The Emergence of Biotechnology*. London: Pinter.

Patel, Pari, and Keith Pavitt. 1991. "Large Firms in the Production of the World's Technology: An Important Case of 'Non-globalization.'" *Journal of International Business Studies* 22(1): 1–21.

———. 1997. "The Technological Competencies of the World's Largest Firms: Complex and Path-Dependent, but Not Much Variety." *Research Policy* 26: 141–56.

Pavitt, Keith. 1984. "Sectoral Patterns of Technical Change: Towards a Taxonomy and a Theory." *Research Policy* 13:343–73.

———. 1991. "What Makes Basic Research Economically Useful?" *Research Policy* 20:109–19.

———. 1999. *Technology Management and Systems of Innovation*. Cheltenham, U.K.: Edward Elgar.

———. 2001. "Public Policies to Support Basic Research: What Can the Rest of the World Learn from US Theory and Practice? (and What They Should Not Learn)." *Industrial and Corporate Change* 10: 761–80.

———. 2002. "Knowledge about Knowledge since Nelson and Winter: A Mixed Record." Electronic Working Paper No. 83, University of Sussex.

Perez, Carlota. 2002. *Technological Revolutions and Financial Capital: The Dynamics of Bubbles and Golden Ages*. Cheltenham, U.K.: Edward Elgar.

Petoski, Henry. 1994. *The Evolution of Useful Things: How Everyday Artifacts—from Forks and Pins to Paper Clips and Zippers—Came to Be as They Are*. New York: Vintage.

Piore, Michael J., and Charles F. Sabel. 1984. *The Second Industrial Divide: Possibilities for Prosperity*. New York: Basic Books.

Polanyi, Karl. 1944. *The Great Transformation: The Political and Economic Origins of Our Time*. Boston: Beacon Press.

Polanyi, Michael. 1958. *Personal Knowledge: Towards a Post-critical Philosophy*. London: Routledge and Kegan Paul.

———. 1966. *The Tacit Dimension*. Garden City, N.Y.: Doubleday.

———. 1967. *The Tacit Dimension*. New York: Doubleday.

Prahalad, C. K., and Gary Hamel. 1990. "The Core Competence of the Corporation." *Harvard Business Review* 68:79–91.

Pritchett, Lant. 1997. "Divergence, Big Time." *Journal of Economic Perspectives* 11(3): 3–17.

Quah, Danny T. 1996. "Twin Peaks: Growth and Convergence in Models of Distribution Dynamics." *Economic Journal* 106:1045–55.

Radner, Roy. 1992. "Hierarchy: The Economics of Managing." *Journal of Economic Literature* 30:1382–415.

Rip, Arie, Thomas J. Misa, and John Schot, eds. 1995. *Managing Technology in Society*. London: Pinter.

Romer, Paul M. 1990. "Endogenous Technical Change." *Journal of Political Economy* 98:71–102.

Rosenberg, Nathan 1976. *Perspectives on Technology*. Cambridge: Cambridge University Press.

———. 1982. *Inside the Black Box: Technology and Economics*. Cambridge: Cambridge University Press.

———. 1990. "Why Do Firms Do Basic Research (with Their Money)?" *Research Policy* 19:165–74.

———. 1994. *Exploring the Black Box: Technology, Economics, and History*. Cambridge: Cambridge University Press.

Rosenberg, Nathan, and Richard R. Nelson. 1994.

"American Universities and Technical Advance in Industry." *Research Policy* 23:323–48.

Sabel, Charles F., and Jonathan Zeitlin. 1985. "Historical Alternatives to Mass Production: Politics, Markets, and Technology in Nineteenth Century Industrialization." *Past and Present* 108:133–76.

———, eds. 1997. *World of Possibilities: Flexibility and Mass Production in Western Industrialization.* Cambridge: Cambridge University Press.

Sahal, Devendra. 1981. *Patterns of Technological Innovation.* Reading, Mass: Addison-Wesley.

Saviotti, Paolo. 1996. *Technological Evolution, Variety, and the Economy.* Cheltenham, U.K.: Edward Elgar.

Scherer, Frederic. M. 1959. *Patents and the Corporation.* Boston: Privately printed.

Schmookler, Jacob. 1966. *Invention and Economic Growth.* Cambridge: Harvard University Press.

Silverberg, Gerald, Giovanni Dosi, and Luigi Orsenigo. 1988. "Innovation, Diversity, and Diffusion: A Self-Organization Model." *Economic Journal* 98:1032–54.

Simon, H. A. 1969. *The Sciences of the Artificial.* Cambridge: MIT Press.

Sobel, Dava. 1996. *Longitude: The True Story of a Lone Genius Who Solved the Greatest Scientific Problem of His Time.* New York: Viking Penguin.

Soete, Luc, and Bart Verspagen. 1993. "Technology and Growth: The Complex Dynamics of Catching Up, Falling Behind, and Taking Over." Pp. 101–27, in *Explaining Economic Growth*, ed. Adam Szirmai, Bart van Ark, and Dirk Pilat. Amsterdam: Elsevier Science Publishers.

Soskice, David. 1997. "German Technology Policy, Innovation, and National Institutional Frameworks." *Industry and Innovation* 4:75–96.

Stephan, Paula E. 1996. "The Economics of Science." *Journal of Economic Literature* 34:1199–235.

Stiglitz, Joseph E. 1985. "Information and Economic Analysis: A Perspective." *Economic Journal* 95:21–41.

———. 1994. *Whither Socialism?* Cambridge: MIT Press.

Stokes, Donald E. 1997. *Pasteur's Quadrant: Basic Science and Technological Innovation.* Washington, D.C.: Brookings Institution Press.

Stoneman, Paul. 1995. *Handbook of the Economics of Innovation and Technological Change.* Oxford: Blackwell.

Strasser, Bruno J. 2000. "Institutionalizing Molecular Biology in Post-war Europe." Paper presented at the conference "Molecular Biology in Postwar Europe," Annecy, France, June 29–July 1.

Teece, David J. 1986. "Profiting from Technological Innovation: Implication for Integration, Collaboration, Licensing, and Public Policy." *Research Policy* 15:185–219.

Teece David J., Gary Pisano, and Amy Shuen. 1997. "Dynamic Capabilities and Strategic Management." *Strategic Management Journal* 18:509–33.

Teece, David J., Richard P. Rumelt, Giovanni Dosi, and Sidney G. Winter. 1994. "Understanding Corporate Coherence: Theory and Evidence." *Journal of Economic Behavior and Organization* 23(1): 1–30.

Thackray, A. 1982. *University-Industry Connections and Chemical Research: A Historical Perspective in University-Industry Research Relationships.* Washington, D.C.: National Science Board.

Verspagen, Bart. 1991. "A New Empirical Approach to Catching Up and Falling Behind." *Structural Change and Economic Dynamics* 2:350–89.

Vincenti, Walter G. 1990. *What Engineers Know and How They Know It: Analytical Studies from Aeronautical History.* Baltimore: Johns Hopkins University Press.

Walsh, Vivien. 1984. "Demand Pull or Discovery Push: Invention and Innovation in the Chemical Industry." *Research Policy* 13:211–34.

Warglien, Massimo. 2000. "The Evolution of Competences in a Population of Projects: A Case Study." Dynacom Working Paper No. 2.

Williams, Robin, and David Edge. 1996. "The Social Shaping of Technology." *Research Policy* 25:865–99.

Winter, Sidney G. 1987. "Knowledge and Competences as Strategic Assets." Pp. 159–84 in *The Competitive Challenge*, ed. David J. Teece. Cambridge, Mass.: Ballinger.

———. 1993. "Patents and Welfare in an Evolutionary Model." *Industrial and Corporate Change* 2: 211–31.

Ziman, John, ed. 2000. *Technological Innovation as an Evolutionary Process.* Cambridge: Cambridge University Press.

30 The Economy and the Environment

Allan Schnaiberg

SOCIAL SCIENTIFIC VERSUS ECOLOGICAL ANALYSES

In many ways, the relationship between "the environment" and "the economy" is straightforward. Nature provides the material support for humans' lives and their production systems. It also removes the unusable waste products of this production, through human dispersal of societal wastes into ecological systems, with some decomposition/absorption inside these systems. *Ecosystems* (Odum 1969) are organized and somewhat stable arrangements of nutrients and living species. For many decades, this nurturing role of nature was taken for granted and viewed as unproblematic. But from at least the early part of the twentieth century to the present (Hays 1969; cf. Mumford [1934] 1963), biological and, later, social scientists became aware of a negative feedback loop from the economy into ecosystems.

As Schnaiberg (1980) conceptualized it, societal production withdrew from ecosystems ever-growing quantities of materials needed for production, and added to ecosystems ever more massive waste products from economic systems. These activities increasingly deplete and pollute, and thus have the potential to disrupt the organized structure and functioning of ecosystems (Odum 1969). Societal efforts to inhibit such disorganization are hampered by the existing political-economic institutional arrangement that the history of economies has generated. Paradoxically, organizations and individuals with the greatest economic, social, and political power are typically those who have utilized depletion and pollution processes for their particular interests. Ecosystems are seen as private assets for many economic organizations, especially with the increased globalization of production. In contrast, environmental movements and community organizations see ecosystems as public goods. These alternative goals for the utilization of ecosystems give rise to the *societal-environmental dialectic*. Essentially, it is a dialectical system of values, because society wants both economic and ecological outcomes, and yet these outcomes are in conflict with one another.

This chapter will first outline the potential and the limits for social scientists who study these interactions. First, the intellectual boundaries of natural versus social scientists are delineated, as are the problematic relationships between these disciplines. In many ways, this chapter is restricted to the analysis of economic (and political) *organizations* and *institutions* (Hoffman and Ventresca 2002). It focuses on the tensions between ecological and economic structures. It notes that reductions of such tensions have either been incorporated into economic systems or deflected by such systems. I outline competing abstract models, showing how previous socioeconomic systems have empirically related to ecosystems, and contrasting this relationship with how competing norms for future *sustainable* socioeconomic systems (IUCN 1980) have emerged. I then sketch distributional tensions of these models of economic/ecological interaction:

> From a sociological perspective, it is never sufficient to *the* environment as having been protected. The question must always be asked, for whom and from whom has it been protected? (Schnaiberg 1980, 5)

Following this theoretical analysis, the chapter offers a concrete case study of contemporary recycling policies in the United States (which are less effective than many European policies). This analysis grounds some of the abstractions of the previous sections. Sections following lay out major dimensions of distributional conflicts about utilizing environmental resources. Who actually gets to use ecosystems, and how? I examine competing social movement organizations and ideologies, in terms of how they deal with existing national inequalities of resource utilization and growing transnational inequalities. Even in a period of *global* warming, "global" policies (as in the Kyoto accords) are greatly influenced by the interests and actions of national and transnational economic organizations (Gould, Schnaiberg, and Weinberg

1995; cf. Canan and Reichman 2002; Buttel and Taylor 1992; Fisher 2003).

This distributional framework is more closely explored in a section dealing with claims about environmentalists' *elitism*, and about the incidence of environmental *injustice* (or *racism*) in the political-economic rule-making for accessing ecosystems and limiting their protection. I also explore some distributional issues in the distinction between local economic organizations and national or transnational ones, in terms of local organizations' sensitivity to environmental problems affecting their communities.

Finally, the chapter concludes by contrasting the more pessimistic theory of the *treadmill of production* (Schnaiberg 1980) with the more optimistic theory of *ecological modernization* (Mol 1995, 1996). In general, the former stresses conflicts between economic growth and environmental protection, while the latter stresses that the social order is incorporating a protection of ecosystems. The analysis points to areas of convergence between the two theories, as well as their more apparent divergence.

This chapter differs substantively from the thoughtful analysis by Johannes Berger in the first *Handbook* edition (1994, chap. 31). To a considerable extent, Berger took on the challenge of evaluating the severity of environmental problems, a task left here to other researchers. Next, Berger only peripherally addressed the distributional features of both environmental problems and environmental protection policies, which I consider the central feature of the economic-environmental relationship. Third, Berger tended to focus on cultural and individual factors affecting this relationship. In contrast, I have chosen to examine the embeddedness (Granovetter 1985) of environmental problems and policies within contemporary political-economic structures. To some extent, then, the two chapters complement each other, with Berger stressing theories of order, this chapter theories of conflict.

One of the first dilemmas of examining the interaction between the economy and its natural systems is the dependence of social science on natural science disciplines for both data and theories. Within the United States, it was natural scientists (Carson 1962; Commoner 1970, 1972; Weinberg 1972; Westman and Gifford 1973) who first called attention to modern U.S. environmental problems. They saw ecosystem disruption as affecting the life of human, animal, and plant populations. In turn, they faced a dilemma that was the mirror image of our own. They sought to create public policies for reducing pollution and depletion, writing proposals for economic and social change. As insightful and informative as these scholars and public intellectuals were, however, they had little expertise in the political-economic functioning of the modern economy. Both of these scientific boundary problems continue to exist. Recently, natural scientists have called for sustainable *biodiversity* (World Commission 1987), while economists have transformed this into a plea for sustainable *development,* and even for sustainable *growth,* expanding the economy while sustaining ecological biodiversity (Daly 1996a, 1996b).

Social scientists have limited expertise in evaluating changes in ecological systems. They are forced to depend on natural science research in universities, as well as on government and industry reports, for assessments of the severity of "environmental problems" (Dietz and Rycroft 1987). Yet there is much dissent among both scientific and technical "experts" (Buttel and Taylor 1992). Few social scientists have enough scientific background to adjudicate such contending claims. Recent examples of disputes include the degree of global warming and the impact of industrial chemicals such as chlorine (Buttel and Taylor 1992; Lomberg 2001; Sonnenfeld 2000). Moreover, these arguments have also been socially framed by a variety of social and economic organizations—whether of environmental movements or of industrial trade associations. Some differences are due to competing scientific data. But these groups also engage in a political competition. They dispute the degree of environmental problems. Economic agents emphasize changes in environmental protection from the *past* economy, while environmentalists stress the gap between present environmental impacts and a sustainable *future* (Schnaiberg and Gould [1994] 2000, x).

ALTERNATIVE MODELING OF THE ECONOMY'S RELATION TO THE ENVIRONMENT

Over the last 40 years, a broad literature has emerged on the economy's impact on the natural environment. Out of the interaction of this literature with the representation of competing economic and social interests, a number of approaches to *protecting the environment* have emerged. The *use-value* of an ecosystem component is a measure of how well the resource can be used to sustain the needs of the human population. In contrast, the *exchange-value* of an ecosystem resource is a measure of how economically profitable will be its processing for markets. Most ecosystem elements cannot be used to simultaneously maximize use-values *and* exchange-values. Yet modern societies desire both kinds of values, creating what was noted earlier as a *dialectical tension* between economic and ecological organizations.

Three distinct syntheses of these dialectical conflicts can be observed: *economic, managed scarcity,* and *ecological* (Schnaiberg 1975; 1980, 422–28). All address the question of how far the state should control use of ecosystems, based on (1) assumptions about the severity of ecological disruptions, and suggesting (2) policies to regulate socioeconomic access to ecological systems. Each model, in short, assumes (1) the mechanism and the degree to which the *economic* structure affects its environment, and (2) the necessity for the state's policy treating such environmental disruption.

Each of these models thus makes assumptions about how *ecological* disruptions affect economic activities. Specifically, they offer evaluations of whether and how: ecological disorganization can

Inflate economic costs
Present hazards to human health
Cause the abandonment of specific economic units
Cause major economic disasters
Threaten the entire political-economic system

Conversely, each model differs in the political-economic norms it suggests for whether and how

Economic activities should utilize natural resources
Economic organizations should relate to the natural resource systems they use
Economic organizations should make decisions about resource utilization
Economic organizations should relate to the state's environmental regulatory system

Economic profits should be allocated to production, to environmental protection, and to influence politically state and nongovernmental environmental organizations

Table 1 outlines the major differences among the three types of syntheses.

Economic Model

All economic activities that are profitable *should* be carried out, so long as there are investors willing to risk capital in the activity. All ecosystems should be made available to *productive* uses, according to this model (Bluestone and Harrison 1982; Logan and Molotch 1987; Logan and Swanstrom 1990; Harrison 1994; Gordon 1996). This is the dominant model in most industrial societies prior to the rise of modern environmental protest.

In this utilization of resources in societal production, little distinction is made with regard to the ecological characteristics of resource systems. Only the ecosystem's utility for creating value is important. In many ways, neoclassical economic theories, and especially the theory of the firm, adhere to this model (Anderson and Leal 2001; Stroup 2003). In recent modifications of this position, market forces add some interest group's definition of environmental values to the decision-making criterion. For example, Anderson and Leal (2001, 6) note, "By linking wealth to good stewardship through private ownership, the market process generates many entrepreneurial experiments." Yet the insistence on an *economic* valuation of environmental externalities ignores many of the firm's efforts to erect economic, legal, and political barriers against internalizing

TABLE 1.   Contrasting Syntheses of the Societal-Environmental Dialectic

	Synthesis		
	Economic	*Managed Scarcity*	*Ecological*
Importance of environmental protection	No policies	Minimal to major policies	Central to policies
Constraints on market forces	None	Minor to substantial	Domination of markets
Political-economic constraints on protection agencies and movements	Total	Near-total to predominating	None (theoretically)

its negative externalities (Mishan 1967; Boulding 1971).

Decisions about resource utilization here are made exclusively by the firm's decision makers, in conjunction with the owners of properties containing resources for *extraction* (e.g., nonsurface land ownership) or *use* (e.g., private land or bodies of water). To some extent, this process follows on Ronald Coase's (1960) theory that negative externalities should first be treated by private negotiation. Political regulation of use of natural and economically useful property is opposed as both inefficient and politically inappropriate. Coase, in contrast, saw such state intervention as necessary when negotiations failed.

Recent court cases have split, for example, on whether environmental regulation of private properties is a *taking* by the government. If so, then governments must reimburse resource owners for all profits foregone, when the state restricts certain forms of development on the lands owned (an opportunity-costs approach). Costs of doing business in the firms affected here include substantial legal and social expenses. Economic organizations thus resist state legislation and the enforcement of environmental protection laws. Resistance may include "public interest advertising" to undermine the arguments of environmental NGOs, appearances by staff at political hearings, and contributions to political candidates who support the firm's position. In recent years, resistance has also included creation of fictive organizations opposing various regulations, including Internet websites for the "wise use movement" and the "balanced energy movement" (e.g., Howard 2002).

Managed Scarcity Models

This model is more complex and substantially more heterogeneous than the other two. It recognizes that economic activity generates ecological disorganization and exchange- and social-use-values. Dialectical tensions between economic growth and ecological protection are most overt in this model. But the problems of commensuration (Levin and Espeland 2002) and the diversity of interests have made political consensus on appropriate state policies difficult to reach. Schnaiberg (1975) argued that the common denominator of all such policies is that the state restricts access by certain categories of users to certain components of ecosystems. Ultimately, ecosystem depletion and disorganization disrupt economic production. Here, the state reduces the risk of this outcome by imposing *antic-*

ipatory restrictions, to create an *imposed scarcity of access* to ecosystems. Policies can also restrict users of want to exploit use-values. Social scientists have primarily studied restrictions imposed on economic organizations that have interests in exchange-values. In part, this is because the latter offer an object of study that is organized, enduring, and analytically accessible through public archives (Schnaiberg 1994).

Coase (1960) outlined a set of neoclassical economic theories about how to manage negative social externalities such as pollution, early in the modern period of environmental concern. He suggested that spillover costs and benefits will not occur, and that government intervention was not necessary when (1) property rights were clearly defined, (2) the number of people involved was small, and (3) bargaining costs were negligible. For most contemporary pollution, however, *none* of these conditions holds. Government's role, he argued, should be, first, to encourage bargaining wherever possible, rather than to get involved in direct restrictions or subsidies. A related bargaining approach is dealing with liability through lawsuits. But this solution is limited to cases in which the damaged parties can afford to initiate the suit, or in the case of many people, can organize to sue (Harr 1996; Brown and Mikkelsen [1990] 1997).

A nonmarket approach is to apply direct government controls or taxes to reduce negative externalities or spillover costs, or to provide subsidies or government provision where spillover benefits exist, using direct controls or specific taxes that can be levied on pollution. This approach marked the early stages of modern environmental protection, after the creation of the U.S. Environmental Protection Agency in 1969. Many states followed this lead, and they often sustained more enforcement than did the EPA itself. But the early modern period of enforcement created substantial economic mobilization against environmental protection legislation and enforcement (Landy, Roberts, and Thomas 1990; Yeager 1992).

In turn, such resistance by economic organizations led to the political creation of new *markets* for externality rights (Meidinger 1986). Pollution control agencies initially decide the amount of pollution acceptable in a region. Then they create *rights* that firms can purchase to allow them to pollute. At high prices, polluters will either stop polluting or buy other firms' rights, rather than acquire expensive equipment to abate pollution. Other firms will sell their rights because they may be able to reduce their pollution at a lower cost. In theory, environmental movements as well as producers can buy rights, although they rarely do, except in the form of the Nature Conservancy buying land for preservation. A market for air pollution rights has thus expanded, along with other forms of *cap and trade* policies (Meidinger 1986; Tietenberg 2002; Rose 2002).

Managed scarcity models acknowledge that the *primary* responsibility for the use of natural resources rests with the market, and this limits state activity (Logan and Swanstrom 1990). However, the state *also* has an enduring responsibility to set sociopolitical limits on use of resources. The state's environmental protection policies should help maintain use-values associated with protected ecosystems. But the state also must be concerned with maintaining the exchange-values controlled by investors, which provide tax revenue. The state must pay attention to the exchange-values of workers—their wages—both to maintain tax revenues and to reduce social expenditures. However, wage labor is also dependent on employment with the firms using natural resources (Logan and Molotch 1987; Logan and Swanstrom 1990). In effect, this model advocates *political* creativity by the state in selectively restricting access to some resources. State regulation may thus exist through rationing by price, if surcharges or fines are used, or by direct command-and-control policies, where access to resources is limited or prohibited outright (as in many conservation policies), or through the more recent cap-and-trade marketing of environmental degradation rights.

Managed scarcity models can be relatively apolitical. Situations are less politicized when ecological problems permit greater economic development. In the early part of the twentieth century (Hays 1969), early *utilitarian* criteria for resource use were highly visible and political. Experts created estimates for maximizing the *sustained yield* of a given local land and water system, and they discouraged less efficient uses. Activists here were professional scientists who assessed ecosystem parameters and provided input to government resource agencies. They often supported more concentrated economic uses, as permitting *sustained yields*. However, in *preservation* conflicts, where little or no economic activity was permitted (Hays 1968), the petitioners were those interested in maintaining use-values of wilderness, often against the interests of major economic entities.

More recent state policies acknowledge a broader need for direct education of political and economic managers. They include training for policies

of environmental protection (preproduction) or of remediation (postproduction). Failures of environmental protection here are often theorized as due to ignorance and misinformation, and scientific studies are encouraged (Lowi 1986). These apolitical research and training approaches seem most validated when new scientific data about human health hazards emerge, since it is harder to ignore these clear hazards (cf. Brown and Mikkelsen [1990] 1997; Sheehan and Wedeen 1990). To some extent, recent models of "ecological modernization" (Mol 1995) follow this pattern (see "Competing Macrostructural Theories" below). Economic agents incorporate *some* ecological concerns in their decision making. In most cases, though, the firms respond only because of the state's increase (or projected increase) in their de facto prices of resource access. Paradoxically, though, many of these firms also attempt to discredit the scientific basis for the state's interventions (Brown and Mikkelsen [1990] 1997; Dietz and Rycroft 1987).

Other forms of managed scarcity models emphasize far more political or contested terrains. Economic organizations protect their exchange-value interests in natural resources, through various forms of political influence. The treadmill of production model (see "Competing Macrostructural Theories" below) explicitly views economic growth as threatening natural resources and ecosystems while accumulating corporate power, which it uses to dampen the state's enforcement of environmental protection. Generally, this pole of the managed scarcity dimension touches on *prohibitions* of access to some resources, and not manageable increases in the prices of accessing these resources.

Ecological Models

Ecological models largely focus on protection of ecosystems, especially on sustaining biodiversity. All are normative, not descriptive of past economies. The *deep ecology* (Evernden 1985; Devall 1980) model views *homo sapiens* as but one species. Its needs and desires are not deemed *more* important than those of other species. Domination of ecosystems by humankind is rejected as philosophically illegitimate. No serious account is taken of the economic or social costs of this position for populations, for political institutions, or for economic organizations. The empirical record for such an approach is invariably drawn from preindustrial societies, especially nomadic groups that are prepastoral. We can argue that deep ecology is politically radical, or that it is apolitical with regard to the political economy of contemporary industrial societies.

Earlier forms of this model have been largely educational and persuasive. But nongovernmental organizations have recently emerged that practice overt political protest and even sabotage. Among them are animal rights movements and those organized to protect wilderness areas. In the United States, sabotage has included actions such as planting nails in trees to be harvested, thereby raising the cost of economic harvesting and lowering the timber's commercial value, and burning experimental forests involved in genetic engineering research. Experiences of terrorism in 2001 led the U.S. government to label these more extreme social movements as *ecoterrorists*. The attorney general viewed direct action against producers, or even the threat of such actions, as a political threat, in contrast with the actions of "mainstream" environmental groups (Jarboe 2002). Presumably, the latter fall well within the economically more benign managed scarcity model.

A more recent evolution of this model is that of *sustainability* (World Commission 1987). Starting from initial concerns about *sustainable biodiversity*, this model has undergone a variety of transitions. Many of its resulting variations, such as sustainable development and especially sustainable growth (Daly 1996a, 1996b), can more properly be classified as managed scarcity models. But the early models advocating *biodiversity* (IUCN 1980) *are* properly included in the ecological model. They focused primarily on the use-value benefits of biodiversity (and some exchange-values, such as natural pharmaceuticals). But they largely avoided discussing the level and social distribution of the costs of environmental regulations (Goldman 1998).

Ecological models tend to promote direct rationing of natural resources, protecting ecosystems and species from exploitation by economic organizations. Such models tend to maximize conflict between environmental advocates and representatives of economic institutions (Redclift 1986, 1987; Baker et al. 1997; Schnaiberg 1997) when the model is introduced to policy debates (European Community 1993; National Commission on the Environment 1993; Weinberg, Schnaiberg, and Gould 1995; President's Council on Sustainable Development 1994, 1997, 1999). Conversely, when the model is discussed in "merely academic" settings, it is treated as an alternative *philosophy*, not a

plan for *action* (Willers 1994). The boundaries between social scientists and philosophers writing about this model are often quite blurred as a result.

DISTRIBUTIONAL DIMENSIONS OF ECONOMIC-ENVIRONMENTAL RELATIONS: INTERNALIZING AND EXTERNALIZING ENVIRONMENTAL COSTS

The three models I have discussed handle the normative issue of distributing the benefits and costs of natural resource usage in different ways. Each proposes different norms for directing economic development. One recent example of the complexities of social control was the Bush administration's proposal (2001) for a new national energy policy, under the direction of Vice President Cheney's National Task Force on Energy. Under managed scarcity, the dominant U.S. policy for controlling economic interests, deliberations on policy should have involved both economic and ecological values. Yet only major energy corporations contributed to the national plan, while environmental groups were "consulted" in brief meetings (Democratic Staff 2002). The politics of the task force seem very close to the economic model, suggesting that the United States has a less than stringent managed scarcity policy. Indeed, the Bush administration advocated an economic model more consistently than did the Clinton administration.

Standard neoclassical economics (Coase 1960) viewed environmental problems in a conceptually clear fashion. Pollution was a negative externality of a firm's operation, and the firm needed to be encouraged to internalize this externality to raise national welfare. Although this approach was logical, it failed the test of political reality. The theory of the firm argued for the firm to maximize its profitability by internalizing positive externalities and evading negative externalities, leading to a clash with the directive to internalize. In social-historical and political-economic history, moreover, it is the latter model that dominates in the United States and, increasingly, in the global market. Left to the dictates of market forces, pollution and depletion would largely be ignored until they reached a critical point at which they threatened market actors and transactions. By then, pollution and depletion would be difficult to control, leading to an "overshoot" model of resource extraction (Catton 1982).

We have an interesting analogue in the case of

computers in the year 2000 (the Y2K problem). Older computer programs were going to deal with the year 2000 as if it were the year 1900. This was because of the earlier use of a two-digit code for year, instead of the four-digit code used in later computer programs. Later machines had higher memory and greater ease of manipulation of data storage. Although much political *attention* was paid to this problem in the very late 1990s, little political *regulation* was achieved. Scenarios were prepared, anticipating a major economic collapse on January 1, 2001. Government agencies were alerted, with emergency operation plans. But little state *control* was mobilized to regulate the private sector. Despite, or more likely *because of*, these dire predictions, firms and computer service organizations muddled through January 1, 2001, with few major problems in any country. The threat of economic collapse of markets stimulated a variety of approaches to deal with the Y2K problem. Market hazards thus created market solutions. In this case, "overshoot" did not materialize.

Some adherents of the economic model see a similar future for resolving problems of resource exhaustion and pollution. When the problems become severe enough, market messages will create incentives for technological innovation in the private sector (cf. Catton 1982). Paradoxically, though, many of these analysts also encourage public subsidies to ease this transition, such as in moving from fossil fuels to renewable energy resources. While they encourage state subsidies, they strongly oppose public disincentives for polluting and depleting. In an example of the paradoxes of the economic model, in 2002 the United States evaded fuel economy legislation while promoting the use of hydrogen fuel cells over the next few decades.

Adherents of the managed scarcity model have a more tolerant view of both the state's incentives and its disincentives. Because these modelers recognize some of the benefits of economic development, as well as the costs of environmental degradation, they accept strategies for state intervention in the market's disruptions of ecosystems. The most conservative of the managed scarcity modelers strongly prefer subsidies: "let the market decide" is a catchword for this group. These adherents favor new markets for trading air pollution permits, and similar principles for dealing with global warming, landfill reduction, and other environmental challenges (Rose 2002; Tietenberg 2002; Levin and Espeland 2002; Meidinger 1986).

The use of permits that encouraged the avoid-

ance of toxic waste through corporate recycling was supposed to be the outcome of the Resource Recovery and Conservation Act (RCRA) of 1976. Later analyses indicated that little recovery of solvents and other chemicals had emerged, except where firms saw them as cost-effective (Yeager 1991; Landy, Roberts, and Thomas 1990). Likewise, cleanup provisions of the Superfund program, built on modest surcharges for waste emitters, have proven woefully inadequate to reclaim most of the polluted areas (Yeager 1991; Weinberg et al. 2000).

Modelers at the more radical end of the managed scarcity continuum show far more support for penalties such as fines, increased taxes, and even prohibition of access to some ecosystems. In addition, these modelers are often more oriented toward social welfare. They thus became key supporters of claims of "environmental injustice" and "environmental racism," which arose in the late 1980s in the United States (see "Competing Macrostructural Theories" below). Mobilization of local and national social movement organizations was largely coordinated and staffed by people of color (Gedicks 1993; Bryant and Mohai 1992; Bullard 1990, 1993, 1994; Hurley 1995; Pellow 1996, 1998a, 1998b, 2001). But they still had to rely on the state apparatus to adjudicate their claims of unequal burdens of environmental degradation. These included high levels of lead concentration and air pollution in dense neighborhoods in the cities, accompanied by rising rates of lead poisoning and asthma. One political achievement of this movement was President Clinton's creation of an Environmental Justice Office within the Environmental Protection Agency (later undermined in the Bush administration).

Finally, ecological modelers tend toward a prohibitive approach by the state. Market forces are the primary engine driving ecological disorganization and species elimination. Ecological modelers thus favor a retreat from modern economic structures, through a "back to the land" or "living off the land" strategy (Devall 1980; Evernden 1985). This strategy can be seen as either radical or retreatist (Merton 1957), depending on whether these actions are intended to politically socialize other social groups, or merely as personal accommodations to the "environmental ethic" (Devall 1980).

In the next section, I trace how environmental policymaking has been shaped in one arena, through the mixture of political will and the political capacity of use-value and exchange-value interest groups.

"INTERNALIZING" NEGATIVE ENVIRONMENTAL EXTERNALITIES: THE CASE OF SOLID WASTE

An extreme illustration of the distributive impacts of environmental problems and solutions noted above is the case of recycling of solid wastes. Weinberg et al. (2000) analyzed urban recycling in the Chicago region in the 1990s. One purpose of the study was to examine whether recycling was an early template for *sustainable development* (as discussed in the section "Alternative Modeling of the Economy's Relation to the Environment," above). Their study followed more than a decade of innovation in urban recycling, and the researchers believed this was an important case study of both *attaining* and *sustaining* better socioenvironmental outcomes of production. It was also a test of theories of *ecological modernization* (Mol 1996; Spaargaren 1997; see "Competing Macrostructural Theories" below), and an arena in which to analyze distributive changes produced by this U.S. "environmental" policy.

In western Europe, the approach of the state has been to (1) encourage the use of returnable containers, wherever possible, and (2) to coerce manufacturers to take responsibility for the solid wastes entailed by the use of their products. For reasons that go beyond this chapter, this approach appears to be working, in contrast to that in the United States. In the United States, while a popular will emerged for strong recycling programs, the capacity of environmentalists to influence recycling organizations was severely limited (Lounsbury, Ventresca, and Hirsch 2003).

In the United States, the disposable container industry and its business customers formed a "public interest" organization in the 1950s, Keep America Beautiful. From the 1960s to the 1980s, this organization promoted the reduction of "litter" on city streets, urging municipalities to have waste containers and citizen consumers to use them for waste containers. With the rise of concern about toxic wastes in the 1970s, many social groups became concerned about having any landfills (solid or liquid waste) near their communities, and an alarm was raised about "running out of landfills" for America's wastes. This led to more state and industry attention to earlier environmentalist pleas to *conserve resources* by recycling waste materials. This was a strong ele-

ment of political will in the early 1980s (Weinberg et al. 2000).

Unlike the case of western Europe, though, American industries sought a different arrangement for solid wastes. Municipalities were encouraged to create curbside recycling, with cities paying the costs for accumulating postconsumer wastes in residential settings. The expectation was that the accumulated wastes would then be sold on the market, as recyclable materials for use as industrial feedstocks. Thus, the state could recapture its expenditures by such revenue generation. This appeared to be a "win-win" game for environmentalists, firms, and the state. Moreover, in cities with diminished labor opportunities for the unskilled, sorting recyclable goods promised to be a new source of stable employment (Weinberg et al. 2000).

Within less than a decade, however, cities discovered that their recyclable material sales garnered limited revenues. In part, this was due to a substantial rise in the supply of recyclable materials, which lowered market prices. In part, it was due to reluctance in many firms to retool, necessary to use recyclable rather than virgin materials in production facilities. Ironically, as prices for recyclables plummeted, some firms adopted recyclable materials because their prices were substantially below those of virgin feedstocks. Thus, it was the economic and political capacity of firms that drove the trajectory of recycling, creating a new recycling industry (Lounsbury, Ventresca, and Hirsch 2003) without a substantial goal of reducing local environmental problems.

If we examine the distributive outcomes of this scheme, it soon becomes clear that local governments were in effect paying subsidies to firms using recyclables, by covering the costs of curbside recycling. Moreover, environmentalists had initially proposed voluntary recycling as a use-value scheme, to preserve natural resources. But the new recycling system increasingly became dominated by transnational waste-handling firms such as Waste Management and Browning-Ferris (themselves later absorbed by other waste disposal firms). For these production intermediaries, the key element was profitability. Capital was widely used to reduce sorting costs, and the laborers involved were often ill-paid and worked in hazardous and uncomfortable environments. As a result, laborers sorting in recycling organizations had very high turnover, reducing the predicted stability of their employment (Pellow 1996, 2001). Since many of these new workers were people of color, it became clear that another form of environmental injustice had been achieved—environmental *solutions* as well as problems entailed disproportionately larger burdens for workers of color (Pellow 1998a, 1998b, 2001).

The outcome of the recycling "boom" has been a curious one. More materials have been diverted from landfills. Yet paper waste, which constitutes the dominant volume of landfill, has been only modestly reduced. Environmentalists' push for resource conservation has been replaced by a commodified view of waste materials. It is the materials' exchange-value, rather than their use-value or the use-value potential of expanding waste dumpsites, that has determined the actual level of recycling and remanufacturing (Lounsbury, Ventresca, and Hirsch 2003). Some modest ecological protection has been achieved, but the system is largely driven by economic rather than ecological criteria. In many ways, then, this is a minimalist form of managed scarcity, bordering on an economic synthesis (Weinberg et al. 2000).

Recycling, in the words of one environmental activist who had earlier started community-development types of recycling programs, "has become an industry" (Lounsbury, Ventresca, and Hirsch 2003). In the process, one may ask, did the waste-handling and remanufacturing firms internalize the negative ecological externalities of disposable products? Or did they externalize many of them, and only arrange for the positive externalities of state subsidies to support this new industry?

THE PARADOX OF ECOLOGICAL EXPLOITATION AND POLITICAL-ECONOMIC CONTROL

The case of recycling illustrates how expansion of a firm's market share and profit facilitates the firm's political capacity to use its economic power to affect legislation protecting the environment. This influence has taken a number of forms:

State organization
   Collaboration with armed forces or police to discourage ecological protest (Goldman 1998)
   Campaign support for favored electoral candidates (Meyer 2002)
   Lobbying against environmental legislation (Meyer 2002)
Regulatory bodies
   Influencing environmental enforcement provisions in administrative committee deliberations (Lowi 1979)

Influencing the public sector's enforcement of environmental laws, for example, by lobbying against adequate funding for agencies, and by administrative resistances (Landy, Roberts, and Thomas 1990)
Labor
   Threatening organized and unorganized labor by using "job blackmail" (Kazis and Grossman 1982) to induce labor's support for the state's permitting more access to natural resources by the firm
   Threatening local and regional officials with job losses and tax base reductions when the firm moves elsewhere, the outcome if environmental regulations are enforced (Longworth 1998, 1999)
Scientific organizations
   Influencing scientific research to ignore environmental problems and focus on expansion of production (Schnaiberg 1980, chap. 6; Sheehan and Wedeen 1993)
   Hiring scientists to attack environmentalist claims (Dietz and Rycroft 1987)
Mass publics
   Creating social support groups for the firm, using traditional media and websites (Howard 2002)
   Directing public relations against environmentalist themes and attacks on the firm (Blumenstyk 1993)
   Conducting campaigns to reassure publics that the firm is "environmentally responsible" (Hoffman and Ventresca 2002; Meyer 2002)

In each of these domains, the economic organization is mobilizing the profits from past utilization of natural resources, allocating them to influence future social policy designed to allow the firm further access to natural resources.

In contrast, the social groups attempting to increase the state's management of scarcity typically have limited resources. While they may have greater public trust, it is frequently under attack (e.g., Lomborg 2001) by firms, trade associations, politicians, and state agencies. The capacity for *economic* mobilization of most of these organizations is far smaller than the economic capacity of firms to engage in political mobilization. It is true that national labor organizations can mobilize substantial campaign contributions (Schnaiberg and Weinberg 2002). But they are usually unable to participate in all the backstage work of regulatory committees, and committees shaping the scientific agenda (Lowi 1979). They lack both the legitimacy and the capacity to match the aggregate political and economic capacity of successful firms. Finally, they lack the power to create (or promise to create) new capital outlays and new jobs, as well as future tax revenues.

ENVIRONMENTALIST ELITISM, ENVIRONMENTAL RACISM AND INJUSTICE, AND SOCIAL INEQUALITIES IN ENVIRONMENTAL PROTECTION

Yet another strategy of the firm has been to discredit organizations in the environmental movement and regulatory agencies by claiming that they are insensitive to the needs of "workers and the poor" (Gould, Weinberg, and Schnaiberg 1993). The core approach of many environmental movements and regulators is to create and manage some form of scarcity. The 1990s was an era of rising profits, increasing inequalities of wealth, *and* rising wage inequalities. Given this situation, many less-affluent groups saw their future as heavily tied to an ever-expanding economy, built around increased capital investment and profits. This "corporate-centered" form of development (Logan and Swanstrom 1990) was thus supported by many of the socially disadvantaged. It was also supported by state officials, who face responsibility for growing social welfare demands.

Since the bulk of the membership and leadership of national U.S. environmental organizations is white and middle to upper middle class (Dunlap and Mertig 1992), the charge of "elitism" is quite credible. The absence of a durable labor-environmental coalition has contributed to this charge (Kazis and Grossman 1982). Indeed, unlike many of the mainstream environmental groups' professional-class members, minority group workers only gained livelihoods in the modern technological production process by a kind of trickle-down economics. They were the very last group to benefit from the unusual expansion of the Clinton era, in contrast to the information-age professionals and dot-com owners and workers. Many minority group workers continued to eke out low wages and welfare benefits. They suffered from increased rates of asthma, lead poisoning, and other urban outcroppings of toxic waste production (Brown and Mikkelsen [1990] 1997). Paradoxically, they also found similar inequalities in the *environmental protection industry* that was emerging. The clearest example is in recycling, where skilled workers were mainly white and middle class. The most degrading work, sorting raw and partly sorted garbage, fell to workers of color (Weinberg et

al. 2000; Pellow 2001). Many such inequalities were also reproduced throughout the pollution-control industry, as discussed below.

Hence, environmental injustice and racism groups were available for mobilization against the national environmental movement organizations. Economic interests emphasized "environmentalist elitism" charges as a divide-and-conquer strategy. Firms most involved in such fragmenting strategies had disproportionately engaged in creating inequalities in exposure to all forms of pollution, including toxic waste. This raised a challenge for mainstream environmental groups to adapt their agenda to address *social* as well as *ecological* distributional outcomes (Szasz 1994). They needed to enlist the support of both environmental justice and labor groups (these latter groups themselves often at loggerheads).

Interestingly, there have actually been few studies of the sociopolitical orientations of members of mainstream environmental organizations. It is difficult to evaluate just how sensitive environmentalists are to social distributional concerns (Ehrenreich 1990). This is the case despite the many social surveys of public opinion about environmental problems (Dunlap and Mertig 1992). One of the early studies (Mitchell 1980) was most instructive, however. It sampled the membership of five national environmental organizations in the late 1970s. One significant finding was that few had previously been involved in social movements, including those that had emphasized social equity: civil rights struggles, antipoverty campaigns, efforts at creating equal opportunity and treatment for women, and the movement against the Vietnam War. This last was concerned with both *international* equity and domestic equity. It noted that the minority population was disproportionately exposed to the hazards of battle in Vietnam, including exposure to the toxic herbicide Agent Orange.

In the United States, the charge of "environmental racism" and "environmental injustice" was raised formally in the late 1980s (United Church of Christ Commission on Racial Justice 1987). Data from the United Church of Christ study showed that polluting facilities were with disproportionate frequency located in areas where people of color and impoverished populations were concentrated. Initially, movements against "environmental racism," as such maldistributions came to be labeled (Bullard 1990, 1993, 1994; Bryant and Mohai 1992), focused on the injuries done to people of color. Later, some of these approaches were broadened to incorporate victims from nonminority low-income populations, leading to a broader concept of *environmental injustice* (Pellow, Weinberg, and Schnaiberg 2001). Some scholars and politicians denied that environmental *racism* was a driving force for the skewed distribution of hazardous wastes. They argued this was an issue of social class and led to environmental *injustice* (Pellow 2001).

Reports such as the one by the United Church of Christ became a foundation for increasing local organizing by minority groups, and the creation of a national coordinating center (Bullard 1994). To some extent, these groups focused attention on the polluting and profiting firms, adding a social and health perspective to the ecological arguments of environmental organizations. Yet they also critiqued mainstream environmental movements, arguing that the plight of minorities and the poor had largely been ignored (Bullard 1993, 1994; Pellow 1998a, 1998b, 2001). These low-income groups suffered both from the health and recreational limitations imposed by expanding firms, using local air, water, and land resources, and also from a lack of economic subsistence. Thus, they experienced an extreme outcome of the economic-environmental dialectic (Pellow 2000, 2002; Pellow and Park 2003; Pellow, Weinberg, and Schnaiberg 2001).

At a minimum, the preceding evidence suggests that many members of environmentalist organizations eschewed "political" action and discourse (Eliasoph 1998), especially before their involvement in environmental movements. Moreover, with the rise of environmental regulation in the 1970s, it is also likely that environmental activists had economic opportunities within the regulatory process. They could work in government agencies applying rules, or in firms attempting to minimize the costs of compliance. Ehrenreich (1990) noted that middle-class professional groups experienced little tension between their "liberalism" and their occupational security. In contrast, for workers facing factory shutdowns or diversions of investment in their communities, environmental protection had direct immediate and opportunity costs. "Job blackmail" (Kazis and Grossman 1982), whereby managers mobilized workers to either resist environmental enforcement or lose their jobs, was quite potent. Workers did have use-value interests in clean air and water in their *communities*. But, as noted below, they also have exchange-value interests in their *jobs*, pulling them into advocating economic activities that entailed pollution and deple-

tion (Brown and Mikkelsen [1990] 1997). Unlike middle-class workers, moreover, their jobs and their homes were often in the same polluted community.

Another way of examining the distributional conflicts over environmental protection is to broadly contrast the powers and orientations of *local* groups of citizens with the *national* and *global* range of firms (Barnet and Cavanagh 1994; Longworth 1998, 1999). The tensions in mediating these conflicts is also apparent in the ambiguous and ambivalent role of *national* environmental movement organizations.

LOCALISM: "NOT IN MY BACKYARD" VERSUS "NOT ANYWHERE"

The following dialogue represents many of the distributional insensitivities of national movement organizations to local working-class citizen workers. It is a dialogue between a Caucasian, upper-middle-class representative of a national environment organization (NEMO), and a working-class African American representative of a nearby poor deindustrialized African American community (LMC). Note that it devolves into two monologues:

NEMO: We'd be delighted to work with you in solving your community's problems.
LMC: Great! What we really need are funds to help stop the rat migration from the riverbanks into the neighborhoods.
NEMO: Well, what I would suggest is that we send over some of our experts on community environmental problems.
LMC: We *know* what our major problem is: but we don't have money to solve it.
NEMO: I think we should really send you some experts . . .
LMC: But that's *not* what we need.[1]

As is true with many human service organizations, the environmentalist organization was responding according to its capacity (Hasenfeld and English 1975). In contrast, the local organizer was setting forth his community's needs (Silver 1998). In this case, NEMO eventually sent its experts, and LMC then withdrew from contact with NEMO. The vignette can be seen as one example of environmental racism. Or it may be viewed as showing the contrast between national environmental organizations with *some* power and resources, and local workers with *little* power and resources (Weinberg 1997a, 1997b, 1997c; cf. Shuman 1998).

From the 1970s onward, this discrepancy created a dilemma for environmental organizations. Much of the initial local mobilization of environmentalists (Weinberg 1994) was of more educated and more affluent nonminority groups. It tended to be in suburban areas, typically resisting new development of economic activities that threatened the quality of the local environment (Portney 1991). Economic agents began to label this a "not in my backyard" movement, in effect accusing these groups of self-interested behavior, and of not taking their "fair share" of environmental hazards. In response, many national environmental groups feared being labeled as "elitist" if they supported the local protest groups, and as insensitive to "local development needs" for employment and an increased tax base. Others covertly formed coalitions with local groups, helping to train and educate local activists (Weinberg 1994; Gould, Schnaiberg, and Weinberg 1996, chap. 10).

However, even without support from the national environmental movement, many community organizations did prevent new polluters from coming into their communities. Portney (1991) concluded that there was nowhere a toxic waste incinerator firm could find a welcoming community. Many of the resisting communities were upper-middle-class suburbs, capable of raising effective barriers against polluting industries. It is important to note that in such cases the conflicts between *local* use-values and exchange-values were often minimal. Residents of these bedroom suburbs earned their income *outside* the community. Hence, they could focus primarily on the environmental use-value qualities of their residential environments (paradoxically, they often also increased the exchange-value of their property, since prices were often enhanced by preservation of environmental amenities).

In contrast, many cases of environmental racism, and environmental inequalities more broadly, deal with *existing production facilities*. Most workers mobilized were responding to direct health hazards from these plants (Brown and Mikkelsen [1990] 1997). Most of the participants were working class, and some faced economic losses if the plant closed down—ostensibly because of the costs of environmental compliance (Gibbs and Levine 1982; Levine 1982). Yet the health dangers, especially when their children were potential victims, were powerful enough to threaten their most basic use-values (Szasz 1994). We have data on only a limited range of protests of this sort, available because a national environmental movement arrived on the scene and thus brought national media (and scholarly) attention. Love Canal is one example.

After years of struggle, more than 800 families were eventually evacuated, and cleanup of Love Canal began. National press coverage made Lois Gibbs a household name. Her efforts also led to the creation of the U.S. Environmental Protection Agency's "Superfund," which is used to locate and clean up toxic sites throughout the United States.

After her successful struggle Gibbs received 3,000 letters from people all over the country, requesting information on how they could solve the toxic waste problems in their area. In response to their pleas, Gibbs formed the Citizens Clearinghouse for Hazardous Waste in 1980 (later renamed Center for Health, Environment, and Justice). CHEJ is a grassroots environmental crisis center that has provided information, resources, technical assistance and training to more than 8,000 community groups around the nation. CHEJ seeks to form strong local organizations in order to protect neighborhoods from exposure to hazardous wastes. Gibbs works extensively with diverse ethnic communities and is strengthening the environmental justice movement.

A central component of CHEJ's work is connecting local leaders by providing a forum for creating collaborative strategies, alliances and coalitions for meeting shared objectives. ("Lois Gibbs" 1999)

Nonetheless, even with sporadic assistance from the national environmental movement, many of these protests achieved little. Working-class protests are undermined because they do not take place in bedroom suburbs, where environmental protection is more affordable. In most cases the local laborers are working in the plants located in their community of residence. Protestors are either living near the production facilities, or near the toxic dumpsites used by the firms (Melosi 1981; Pellow 2001). Sociologically, we can infer that most of these employees are working class. Few have had political experience dealing with local, national, and transnational agencies of government and the private sector (Weinberg 1994). Both Caucasian and minority populations lack power, connection, and influence over the political-economic system (Levine 1982; Brown and Mikkelsen [1990] 1997; Weinberg 1994).

One dismal assessment of these local protests is that they are a "lose-lose" game. Mobilized workers are attacked by their neighbors, who are working for the polluting firms. Settlements of the cases are deferred for many years, and even then are not sufficient to compensate local victims (Szasz

1994). Brown and Mikkelsen ([1990] 1997) celebrate the successes of local groups who create "popular epidemiology" and use it to generate industrial changes. But few have been able to create an effective form of local environmental protection. Moreover, they have often lost employment. This is, in part, what led to new legal regulation of industrial "brownfields," toxic waste sites that had been abandoned by previous investors, and in which potential investors feared being charged with a cleanup (EPA 2002; Reisch and Bearden 2003, under Comprehensive Environmental Response, Compensation and Liability Act [CERCLA or Superfund]). New regulations forced some internalization of exiting costs on previous owners. It is too early to tell how effective this regulation has been, however, and many cities instead supported cleanups from local public funds.

Portney (1991, 138), in reflecting on the NIMBY movements' resistance to siting toxic waste incinerators, proposed a model of risk-substitution for selected communities.

> The focus of substitution is on acknowledging that siting the hypothetical facility (at least as practiced to date) can and often does, indeed, represent new, often unfamiliar and unpredictable, risks to people who live in nearby communities. In risk substitution, the emphasis is on finding sites in communities where people are already living with what they consider (or perceive) to be very high, perhaps even unacceptably high, risks. The foundation of risk substitution strategies is the idea that people may well be willing to trade uncertainty about new risks if these risks are substituted for risks they know or believe to be very high.

While Portney formally includes only existing environmental risks, this same model could be used for social or economic risks. It is almost certain that the communities referred to are precisely those where environmental inequality is evident. In them live immigrants, people of color, low-income populations, and politically marginal groups who tend to bear such hazards. Pellow (2001) has outlined the case of Robbins, Illinois, a desperately poor African American community. Under Illinois law, toxic waste incinerators received subsidies, making Illinois an attractive state in which to operate. But most local movements opposed such incinerators. Robbins was willing to accept one, because of the jobs and taxes it promised. In stark contrast, most of the middle-class communities around Robbins strongly protested both the incinerator and Robbins's acceptance of it. After a relatively short period of operation, moreover, the in-

cinerator closed when Illinois withdrew its subsidies. Robbins argued that its neighboring communities were racist and insensitive. Opponents argued that Robbins's local government had been suborned by the developers.

National environmental organizations have not universally withdrawn from these existing-plant conflicts, but neither have they mobilized around working-class populations. Local mobilization by politically marginalized populations seems energized only where the families are subject to severe *health* risks. Yet these same risks should be part of the agenda of national environmental organizations. It is ironic that many epidemiological hazards of plant wastes are actually easier to document scientifically than more complex environmental and social impact assessments (Schnaiberg 1986; Meidinger and Schnaiberg 1980). For residents who live where they work, scientific assessments of local health hazards may approximate occupational safety and health research. Such more predictable and larger impacts can be more readily measured than ecosystem impacts in diffused geographic settings. Furthermore, these impacts are more measurable than are the potential *future* impacts of unbuilt production facilities, as in the future investment situations characteristic of NIMBY groups. Thus, there is a broader scientific basis for claims about these localized "environmental problems" (Spector and Kitsuse 1977). Hence, the absence of major environmental movement participation in local protests may be more political than scientific (cf. Weinberg 1997c).

At the local level, then, we see local economic inequalities translated into political ineffectiveness of environmental protection movements.

> Lower-income groups suffer more local hazards from nearby production (and extraction).
> They have more difficulty in mounting political campaigns opposing these sources, because of their conflicts between negative use-values of much of this production, and positive exchange-values from associated jobs.
> They are further hampered by both technical and political obstacles to creating epidemiological studies of their hazardous conditions.
> They draw little support from national environmental organizations.
> They have a limited voice in local, regional, and national governance.

Lois Gibbs was an early working-class activist in the Love Canal conflict over toxic waste dumps that appeared to have had health impacts on nearby families (Levine 1982; Gibbs and Levine 1982). Her mobilization arose in the context she describes:

> I read a report that was done in 1976, two years before I got involved. It was a cost-benefit analysis of Love Canal. Its hazards and risk to community were estimated at $20 million versus who would benefit. It put a dollar amount on my head and my children's heads—I was not thinking about my neighbors yet. And because my husband only made $10,000 and my children were only likely to make $10,000, we were not very important. I guess the families there had an average income of $12,000. I read that and said, "What the hell does this mean? How can you do a cost benefit analysis on people's lives and their health? You gotta be kidding. Somebody is deciding what our suffering and what we are worth." I was blown away by that. (Redd, n.d.)

Perhaps the most articulate expression of the frustration of less powerful groups with their representation in "environmental" forums was the argument put forth against the World Summit for Sustainable Development in Johannesburg in 2002. This critique was addressed against domestic and transnational environmental protection procedures, including those in state agencies and even in many nongovernmental organizations (NGOs). The indigenous actors' protests were an extension of the frustrations and complaints by U.S. environmental justice groups, summarized in the following declaration:

> [T]he time seems to be near, when again the deprived "stick-holders" team up and provide some serious lessons to those who divide the earth among themselves only and to those, whose NGOs stand for: Nothing Goes On! . . . the global bandwagon has left the people behind again. (ECOTERRA email, August 17, 2002)

Such angry and anguished responses to environmental NGOs reflect the despair of powerless communities (Goldman 1998). Yet all environmental problems have *localized* impacts, although they may also have a dispersal that can be global. The "stick-holders," or local *stakeholders*, are affected by these negative externalities of production. This is especially painful and poignant when health hazards from toxic wastes from plants or their dumpsites materialize—even more so when the diseases are fatal, and the victims are children (Brown and Mikkelsen [1990] 1997). Children are deemed "innocent" victims. Unlike their parents, they have no direct exchange interests in the production that negatively affects them.[2]

Political concern about U.S. environmental racism has thus been raised by minority organizations, not environmental movements. Similarly, much of the protest in Third World countries arose from indigenous groups there (Goldman 1998). In the United States, minority groups that organized around health risks achieved some direct political influence during the Clinton regime. A presidential order required all federal agencies in their permits, rulings, and activities to screen for environmental racism or injustice. This is testimony to the potential voting influence of minorities, including both African American and Hispanic voters in recent elections. As with the earlier passage of Low-Income Home Energy Assistance (LIHEAP) after 1974 (U.S. Office of Community Services 2004), the major influences on regimes have been *social equity* movements, rather than *environmental* movements (National Energy Assistance Directors' Association 2002).

COMPETING MACROSTRUCTURAL THEORIES: THE TREADMILL OF PRODUCTION VERSUS ECOLOGICAL MODERNIZATION

Although social science has made substantial contributions to analyzing environment-economic interfaces and their social consequences, they are not theoretically rich. Two of the more significant theoretical approaches are reviewed here, and others are mentioned in passing.

The Treadmill of Production

Schnaiberg (1980) argued that environmental problems emerged from a newly emergent *treadmill of production*. At its core, this system was built around a strong drive to expand production and markets.[3] Within the treadmill's logic, capital both displaced workers and required growing amounts of natural resources as feedstocks, to drive new machinery (energy, water), and as waste sites. As the treadmill expanded in the 1950s and beyond, it became strongly supported by the state, and by some unions within "the aristocracy of labor," such as autoworkers and steelworkers. But the growth of the treadmill created a dilemma for both state and labor unions. The state had a growing burden of the social expenses of displaced workers, as emerging ecological disruptions. And union membership declined with the displacement of workers in direct production roles (Harrison 1994; Bluestone and Harrison 1982).

As the logic of the treadmill came to dominate investment in the United States and some other industrial societies, the state supported ever-larger private capital investments. It protected private profits in order to offer jobs for more workers and to raise more taxes to cover rising social and environmental expenses. Hence the label of "treadmill" was associated with this theory: the political economy was running faster (in terms of ecological withdrawals and additions) but staying in one place (in terms of social welfare gains achieved by this resource utilization). The central logic of the treadmill is that its economic organizations sought an unlimited expansion of markets and production. This was a mechanism to generate ever-larger profits for shareholders and managers. The corollary of the treadmill of production is that profitability shifted the benefits of the expansion of production away from most workers, as well as from state social welfare programs. More of the benefits of private investors went to their shareholders, rather than the stakeholders in local communities, living in local ecosystems. Additional components of the treadmill are briefly outlined below.

First, modern factories generally needed higher natural resource inputs. The modern factory was capital intense, and hence, more energy was needed to run the machinery. Likewise, the increase in production meant that more raw materials were needed as feedstocks. This feature of the new production system helped explain why ever greater levels of ecosystem withdrawals were required. Expansion in production required more inputs. This led to environmental problems resulting from natural resource *depletion.*

Second, modern factories used ever growing levels of chemicals in production processes. The modern factory essentially used new "efficient" energy- and chemical-intensive technologies to transform raw materials into products. Workers were increasingly engaged in managing energy and chemical flows, and directing them into the complex machinery that makes marketable products. This feature leads to a set of environmental problems of *pollution,* which disorganized local and regional ecosystems.

Two types of impacts of the treadmill emerged in this new system. As firms made more products using more efficient technologies, they also saw rising profits. These could be invested in still-more productive technologies. This suggested a kind of *ecological treadmill.* Profits were invested in new technologies that would support still greater ex-

pansion of production. This expansion required ever-greater *withdrawals* from ecosystems (raw materials and energy) and hence generated more natural resource depletion. The expansion also led to greater *additions* to ecosystems (toxic chemical pollution and other forms of solid waste dumping). Thus, ecosystems were increasingly used as sources of raw materials and sinks for toxic wastes, and thereby were increasingly degraded, while profit levels rose.

The second form of treadmill was *social.* After each cycle of production, a growing share of profits was allocated to upgrading the technological efficiencies of the firm. Workers, similar to ecosystem elements, were growing the seeds of their own work-life disruption. By helping to generate profits in one cycle, workers would help set in motion a new level of investment in labor-saving technology. This could ultimately lead to their removal from the firm's production process (Harrison 1994; Longworth 1998).[4] A graphic cartoon illustrating both forms of the treadmill shows a logger who is reporting to his boss that he has "felled the last tree." The boss responds, "You're fired."

As this treadmill of production expanded, it created new sources of revenue for governments. Some of this revenue was used to give displaced workers social and economic compensations for loss of livelihoods. Governments provided more services to workers and families, as they lost their jobs, through new "safety nets" of income supplementation. In addition, government agencies themselves expanded, absorbing some displaced workers and providing alternative employment opportunities (Ehrenreich 1990).

Because of these rising investments in capital-intensive technologies, many blue-collar workers found themselves displaced or downgraded in factories. The retained workers formed a new "aristocracy of labor." Such high-technology workers often supported the patterns of investment in their own firms. Displaced workers, in contrast, saw the need for still more investments in *new* plants, as did communities around the world. Industrial society communities faced increasing losses of employment and revenues as factories consolidated, modernized, and then later, moved abroad under new globalization freedoms (Barnet and Cavanagh 1994; Longworth 1998). Labor movements, local political constituencies, and local governments thus all supported this form of "corporate-centered development" (Logan and Swanstrom 1990). This new push eventuated in rapidly increasing demands on ecosystems, for each new job or additional tax payment.

Overall, the effect of these dynamics of shareholder values is that the treadmill's corporate planners struggle to withhold funds from the nation-state. The exception is when these funds further enhance corporate profitability in the short to medium term. Hence, states seek to reduce social welfare expenditures, while raising depreciation allowances and tax exemptions for private sector firms. Firms are less supportive of public education, except where programs will produce highly skilled workers, whose training has been funded by the state (technical schools and colleges). Thus, the treadmill accelerates in two related ways. More capital is allocated to high-technology capital-intensive production (including business services). And capital is diverted from the public sector and social expenses (including environmental protection), into support for expanded private investment and profits.

Ecological Modernization Theory

While the treadmill theory was developed in the United States before 1980 (Schnaiberg 1980), its major competing theory emerged over a decade later (Spaargaren and Mol 1992; Mol 1995, 1996; Spaargaren 1997; Mol and Sonnenfeld 2000). Its origins were in western European analyses, and with a somewhat different set of states and political-economic structures. *Ecological modernization* theorists have postulated a growing independence, or "emancipation," of the ecological sphere from the political and economic spheres in state and industry policymaking (Mol 1995; Spaargaren and Mol 1992). In effect, old forms of social cleavages caused by political-economic allocations were less relevant in this new shared concern about environmental problems.

Thus, within each of the spheres, significant institutional transformations are induced by objective changes in the physical environment, along with new managerial consciousness about these risks—the essence of *reflexive modernization* (Giddens 1991; Beck 1992; Beck, Giddens, and Lash 1995; Mol 1996). Here all parties—industry, the state, environmentalists, and the public—are motivated to deal responsibly with global environmental risks. Firms employ new technologies to reduce the environmental impacts of their production. Central to ecological modernization theory is the argument that environmental considerations have emerged as corporate concerns, as well as state concerns. The domain of "environmental planning" is thus seen as somewhat independent of conventional political, economic, and social conflicts (Beck 1992). However, Meyer (2002) notes that many economic organizations still resist most forms of environmental regulation (as evidenced in a number of the chapters in Hoffman and Ventresca 2002). In the decade since this theory emerged, then, it has been subjected to considerable criticism in social science, focusing on social and political stratification issues missing from the theory, and on the vagueness of some of its propositions. At times it seemed to be grand theory (Mills 1959), rather than empirically falsifiable theory.

But the theory nonetheless migrated to the United States, where some younger scholars have incorporated its positions (e.g., Sonnenfeld 2000). One factor making this transition more feasible was that the leading ecological modernization theorists accepted certain "neo-Marxist" (or structuralist) critiques (e.g., Pellow, Schnaiberg, and Weinberg 2000). They portrayed ecological modernization as much less widespread, and as much more contingent on political contexts, than its proponents had claimed (Mol and Spaargaren 2000; Sonnenfeld 2000). In fact, these theorists incorporated such changes much more extensively and quickly than did theorists of the treadmill of production. The latter has changed primarily to incorporate globalization factors, but has not accommodated other critiques (e.g., Schnaiberg and Gould [1994] 2000, 2001). Unlike ecological consumption theory, however, the treadmill of production has not garnered many adherents (or sustained critiques), other than from a handful of younger scholars (e.g., Weinberg et al. 2000; Gould, Schnaiberg, and Weinberg 1996; Schnaiberg and Gould [1994] 2000).

The relatively high diffusion of the ecological modernization theory among Western scholars may reflect several factors. First, environmental politics in most Western societies has become a series of accommodations between states, environmental NGOs, and private sector leaders (Hoffman and Ventresca 2002). Ecological modernization theory, which is a form of neoliberal political-economic model, fits this history better than does the treadmill. The thrust of the treadmill is, as Mol and Spaargaren argue (2000), *dematerialistic*. Treadmill theorists see the necessity for change from energy- or chemical-intensive production into more labor-intensive production, to solve both social and environmental problems. This change would entail substantial political and social ferment (Stretton 1976). It suggests an intensely conflictual future, building on existing class differences, along with racial, gender, and other societal cleavages. In contrast, the core argument of ecological modernization is that firms have their own interests in anticipating environmental problems arising from their activities, and will seek to find pragmatic solutions. In short, it is an "order," not a "conflict," model.

The future structure of production will be *hypermaterialistic,* ecological modernists argue. That is, both chemical use and energy use will be reduced. New electronic and biological agents will be substituted in production, reducing both ecological withdrawals and additions (as suggested in nanotechnology, which creates biological "machines"). Such changes will only be in the technological sphere, or the forces of production.

In contrast, treadmill theorists argue that in order to decelerate the treadmill, greater attention will need to be paid to the relations of production. More broadly, ecological modernization theorists see the role of the state as enabling and facilitating this transformation of firms. Treadmill theorists see the state as engaging in an internal struggle between its interests in economic expansion, and the need to externally control the forces and relations of production for ecological and social enhancement (Pellow et al. 2000; Schnaiberg et al. 2002).

In ecological modernization theory, the allocation of corporate surplus is to be assigned to corporate leadership and stockholders—a triumph of markets over politics (Lindblom 1977). By contrast, treadmill theorists see a growing need for a redirection of corporate surplus, into new forms of economic organization that will decrease natural resource utilization and disposal into ecosystems, *and* increase labor utilization. Interestingly, one of the examples offered by ecological modernization theorists has been new forms of corporate recycling. Closed production systems will replace open production systems, which both waste potential resources and result in pollution from waste products. Treadmill analysts (Weinberg et al. 2000) have empirically examined postconsumer waste recycling, a related policy. They found that a bottom-line approach was being taken by cities and their contractors, built around market considerations alone. There was minimal state intervention, and no shadow pricing, as used in other public services (Pellow, Schnaiberg, and Weinberg 2000). If this is true in the public sector—which is more susceptible to the triumph of politics over markets—it seems reasonable to be cautious about the extent to which restructuring by industrial managers will generate the hypermaterialism that will protect ecosystems.

Ecological modernization theory is more compatible with neoliberal economic policies, which have increasingly been forced onto both industrial and less-developed societies (Schnaiberg and Gould [1994] 2000, introduction). More powers of the nation-state have been transferred to multinational organizations such as the World Bank and the World Trade Organization, which extol "free trade" and neoliberal government policies (Pezzy 1989). These are designed to enhance the exchange values of private sector investors, at the cost of reducing environmental and social expenses (Longworth 1998, 1999), by decreasing state social expenditures and supporting foreign capital ventures.

An early analysis of environmental protection policies by Hugh Stretton (1976) noted that problems could be variably addressed, with quite different social-distributive outcomes. He argued that by not paying specific attention to the distributive issue, such policies created conditions in which either "the rich rob the poor" (i.e., increasingly negative income distribution), or "business as usual" is maintained (i.e., current stratification levels are sustained). In the United States at least, the "rich rob the poor" model has dominated policies of the last 25 years (Phillips 1989, 1993). Most of this negative redistribution has not been directly related to environmental policies.[5] Yet environmental policies have also increased environmental injustice and environmental racism (Bullard 1990, 1993, 1994; Pellow 1996, 1998a, 1998b, 2001). Benefits of production expansion have been distributed upwards in the stratification system. Environmental and social costs have increasingly been distributed downwards (Brown and Mikkelsen [1990] 1997).

Reflections on the Two Theories

With the recent synthesis of critics' responses to early ecological modernization theory (Mol and Spaargaren 2000), there seem to be new grounds for a more complex integration of the two theories. Ecological modernization theorists measure the *changes* in corporate responsiveness to past ecological destruction. Given firms' historical economic synthesis, ecological modernization theorists see any production reforms as representing a new path to change (Schnaiberg and Gould [1994] 2000, chap. 10). In contrast, treadmill theorists, with extensive management of scarcity as a *goal,* see the firms as complying only to the minimum that they can negotiate.

Recycling policy in the United States (Weinberg et al. 2000) illustrates this difference in evaluation. Environmental organizations helped place recycling on the urban and national agenda, addressing a variety of environmental protections, including closure of highly polluting urban incinerators (Pellow and Park 2003). However, detailed recycling plans increasingly came to reflect the exchange-value interests of both waste-hauling firms and manufacturers using recyclable feedstocks (Lowi 1979). Use-value interests did not totally disappear under these political economic pressures, but forms and prices of recyclables increasingly were mediated by the new "recycling industry" (Lounsbury, Ventresca, and Hirsch 2003). Compared to the prerecycling period (before 1985), some ecological gains were indeed made by cities. But they were far less significant than the ecological objectives of environmental activists and analysts, and the promises of municipal leaders.

Sonnenfeld's (2000) analysis of pulp and paper operations in Indonesia serves as an interesting integration of the two theories. Indonesian mills adopted new technologies that dramatically reduced the use of chlorine in production. They were able to respond because Sweden and other Western societies had produced efficient technologies and made them available to other producers. They were willing to respond in this way because of substantial political and social mobilization by stakeholders in the areas near proposed plants, who feared losing their extractive roles through projected increases in the discharge of chlorine into nearby bodies of water. These stakeholders had political sway (cf. Goldman 1998) in the Indonesian state, which sought alternative solutions. Thus, Indonesian producers had both motives and means to make changes.

Sonnenfeld (2000) also notes that the resulting forces of production were not hypermaterialistic. New plants threatened to denude huge areas of Indonesia in order to feed these "efficient" pulp and paper manufacturing facilities. Sonnenfeld treats this case as a success story for ecological modernization's predictions of pollution reduction. But treadmill theorists also view this outcome as a validation of their predictions. The expansionary ecological impact of the treadmill was accelerated, not diminished, by the new technology. While per unit chlorine pollution was reduced, increased volumes of units were needed to sustain the new technology, accelerating forest depletion (Weinberg, Pellow, and Schnaiberg 1996; Schnaiberg, Pellow, and Weinberg 2002).

This suggests that one reconciliation of the two theories may be a reformulated dialectical approach. Absent other interventions, the treadmill predicts business as usual (Stretton 1976), with continued depletion and pollution. But the results of treadmill action also generate social and political protest, which can impede production plans. When these sociopolitical resistances are high and predictable, firms feel it prudent to make revisions in production in order to placate stakeholders and their state representatives, as a form of the social costs of production (Coase 1960). If these revisions also enhance profitability, then they are even more likely to be adopted quickly and diffused over more firms and states.

This process represents a complex relationship between markets and politics. It is neither a direct internalization of the negative environmental externalities of production, nor a dismissal of environmental problems. The dialectical approach also applies to those raising environmental protection challenges in the state and to firms. Ehrenreich (1990) noted that middle-class professionals often supported liberal social policies, since their employment was precisely in these areas of political intervention in markets. These self-interests are part of the complex dynamics of environmental resistance movements. Even within the private sector, there are segmented responses to production expansion and production control. A large environmental protection industry has emerged (Lounsbury, Ventresca, and Hirsch 2003), generating both new capital products and new professional services,[6] as from engineers and lawyers. For example, the EPA employs far more lawyers than ecological analysts. Even when the former leave public service to provide consulting to the private sector, they are often dependent on the existence of strong regulations to enhance their careers. Yet if these regulations are too stringent and too well enforced, the negotiating ability of private environmental lawyers may be diminished, and their careers truncated.

In like manner, other groupings of workers also have a dialectical relationship to the forces of production. Where employment is diverse and plentiful (Gould 1991), citizens may oppose corporate policies that diminish ecosystem integrity. However, in company towns, such resistance is unlikely to be emergent or sustained (cf. Brown and Mikkelsen [1990] 1997). We might speculate that business cycles produce similar variability of NGO responses to corporate threats to the environment. Where employment and wages are stable or growing, resistance to these threats is likely to be enhanced.

NOTES

I gratefully acknowledge the assistance of my colleagues sharing the treadmill: Ken Gould, David Pellow, and Adam Weinberg. Their critical evaluations and helpful suggestions have immeasurably improved this chapter, as have the comments of the editors.

1. Personal communication from Adam S. Weinberg.

2. In some cases, parents returning from work may transport hazardous particles on their work clothes, and thus their employment is hazardous for their children.

3. Several reviewers of the first formulation of the treadmill noted its parallels to Marx's comments on the organic composition of capital. Recent reviewers have concurred. But this was a case of my induction from observed socioeconomic and environmental degradation trends, and in no way a deduction from Marxist theory. Moreover, the treadmill outlines the system at the level of economic organizations, as well as the level of the national economy.

4. Some workers gained opportunities in this process, becoming more skilled technological workers (Wellin 1997). Others gained other opportunities as their firms expanded, creating new job prospects more remote from direct production. Still other workers in smaller firms gained something, as the production system expanded, requiring new inputs from supplier firms.

5. Many of these critiques parallel those offered a precursor of ecological modernization, the model of "appropriate technology" (or intermediate technology) proposed by Schumacher (1973). In 1934, Lewis Mumford noted that new technological forces in industrial societies were essential *neotechnical* means, which sustained *paleotechnic* ends. He was differentiating the forces of production from the social relations of production, in terms of both social and environmental outcomes of these changes. After Schumacher's proposals, a spate of similar environmental critiques followed (e.g., Schnaiberg 1982, 1983a, 1983b; Lele 1991; Weinberg, Pellow, and Schnaiberg 1996; Willers 1994). Other analyses indicated that changes in technology (e.g., Wellin 1997) and in philanthropy (Silver 1998) similarly failed to address continuing inequalities in the workplace and the community.

6. It has been argued that investment in environmental protection technologies can create both jobs and profits. This may be the case, but there still remains substantial economic organizational resistance to such technologies, in part because of the redistribution of jobs and profits entailed in the application of "greener" technologies. Pollution abatement firms gain profits from environmental enforcement, but producing firms face more costs. What are the political outcomes of this situation?

Consider a simple example. Assume that there are five firms with $100 million in environmental protection revenue: they will support further regulation. In contrast, assume 20 firms with $5 million in environmental protection costs, plus additional labor costs: they will be antiregulatory. The latter likely have far more employees, and more consumers, than the former. Their economic power and social visibility enable them to mobilize political contributions and public relations against environmental protection.

REFERENCES

Anderson, Terry L., and Donald R. Leal. 2001. *Free Market Environmentalism.* Rev. ed. New York: Palgrave Macmillan.

Baker, Susan, Maria Kousis, Dick Richardson, and Stephen Young, eds. 1997. *The Politics of Sustainable Development: Theory: Policy and Practice within the European Union.* London: Routledge.

Barnet, Richard J., and John Cavanagh. 1994. *Global Dreams: Imperial Corporations and the New World Order.* New York: Simon and Schuster.

Beck, Ulrich. 1992. *Risk Society: Towards a New Modernity.* Trans. Mark Ritter. Thousand Oaks, Calif.: Sage.

Beck, Ulrich, Anthony Giddens, and Scott Lash. 1995. *Reflexive Modernization: Politics, Tradition, and Aesthetics in the Modern Social Order.* Stanford, Calif.: Stanford University Press.

Berger, Johannes. "The Economy and the Environment." Pp. 766–97 in *The Handbook of Economic Sociology,* ed. Neil J. Smelser and Richard Swedberg. New York: Russell Sage Foundation; Princeton: Princeton University Press.

Bluestone, Barry, and Bennett Harrison. 1982. *The Deindustrialization of America: Plant Closings, Community Abandonment, and the Dismantling of Basic Industry.* New York: Basic Books.

Blumenstyk, Goldie 1993. "Greening the World or 'Greenwashing' a Reputation? Exxon's Role in Stanford's Huge Environmental-Research Project Attracts Attention and Questions." *Chronicle of Higher Education,* January 10, A22–26.

Boulding, Kenneth E. 1971. "The Economics of the Coming Spaceship Earth." Pp. 180–87 in *Global Ecology: Readings toward a Rational Strategy for Man,* ed. John P. Holdren and Paul R. Ehrlich. New York: Harcourt Brace Jovanich.

Brown, Phil, and Edwin J. Mikkelsen. [1990] 1997. *No Safe Place: Toxic Waste, Leukemia, and Community Action.* Berkeley and Los Angeles: University Of California Press.

Bryant, Bunyan, and Paul Mohai, eds. 1992. *Race and the Incidence of Environmental Hazards: A Time for Discourse.* Boulder, Colo.: Westview Press.

Bullard, Robert D. 1990. *Dumping in Dixie: Race, Class, and Environmental Quality.* Boulder, Colo.: Westview Press.

———, ed. 1993. *Confronting Environmental Racism: Voices from the Crossroads.* Boston: South End Press.

———, ed. 1994. *Unequal Protection: Environmental Justice and Communities of Color.* San Francisco: Sierra Club Books.

Buttel, Frederick H., and P. J. Taylor. 1992. "Environmental Sociology and Global Environmental Change: A Critical Assessment." *Society and Natural Resources* 5(3): 211–30.

Canan, Penelope, and Nancy Reichman. 2002. *Ozone Connections: Expert Networks in Global Environmental Governance.* Sheffield, U.K.: Greenleaf.

Carson, Rachel. 1962. *Silent Spring.* Boston: Houghton Mifflin.

Catton, William R. 1982. *Overshoot: The Ecological Basis of Revolutionary Change.* Urbana: University of Illinois Press.

Coase, Ronald H. 1960. "The Problem of Social Cost." *Journal of Law and Economics* 3:1–44.

Commoner, Barry. 1970. *Science and Survival.* New York: Ballantine.

———. 1972. *The Closing Circle: Nature, Man, and Technology.* New York: Knopf.

Daly, Herman E. 1996a. "Sustainable Growth? No, Thank You." Pp. 192–96 in *The Case against the Global Economy,* ed. Jerry Mander and Edward Goldsmith. San Francisco: Sierra Club Books.

———. 1996b. *Beyond Growth: The Economics of Sustainable Development.* Boston: Beacon Press.

Democratic Staff of the Committee on Energy and Commerce. 2002. "Investigation of the Energy Task Force." Washington, D.C. Email file.

Devall, Bill. 1980. "The Deep Ecology Movement." *Natural Resources Journal* 20 (April): 299–322.

Dietz, Thomas, and Robert W. Rycroft. 1987. *The Risk Professionals.* New York: Russell Sage Foundation.

Dunlap, Riley E., and Angela G. Mertig, eds. 1992. *American Environmentalism: The U.S. Environmental Movement, 1970–1990.* Bristol, Pa.: Crane Russak.

Ehrenreich, Barbara. 1990. *Fear of Falling: The Inner Life of the Middle Class.* New York: Harper Perennial.

Eliasoph, Nina. 1998. *Avoiding Politics: How Americans Produce Apathy in Everyday Life.* Cambridge: Cambridge University Press.

Environmental Protection Agency (EPA). 2002. "Summary of the Small Business Liability Relief and Brownfields Revitalization Act." http://www.epa .gov./swerosps/bf/html-doc/2869sum.htm.

European Community. 1993. *Toward Sustainability: A European Community Programme of Policy and Action in Relation to the Environment and Sustainable Development.* Luxembourg: Commission of the European Communities.

Evernden, Neil. 1985. *The Natural Alien.* Toronto: University of Toronto Press.

Fisher, Dana R. 2003. "Beyond Kyoto: The Formation of a Japanese Climate Change Regime." In *Global Warming and East Asia: The Domestic and International Politics of Climate Change,* ed. Paul G. Harris. London: Routledge.

Gedicks, Al. 1993. *The New Resource Wars: Native and Environmental Struggle against Multinational Corporations.* Boston: South End Press.

Gibbs, Lois M., and Murray Levine. 1982. *Love Canal: My Story.* New York: Grove Press.

Giddens, Anthony. 1991. *The Consequences of Modernity.* Stanford, Calif.: Stanford University Press.

Goldman, Michael, ed. 1998. *Privatizing Nature: Political Struggles for the Global Commons.* New Brunswick, N.J.: Rutgers University Press; London: Pluto Press.

Gordon, David. 1996. *Fat and Mean: The Corporate Squeezing of Working Americans and the Myth of Managerial "Downsizing."* New York: Martin Kessler Books.

Gould, Kenneth A. 1991. "The Sweet Smell of Money: Economic Dependence and Local Environmental Political Mobilization." *Society and Natural Resources* 4:133–50.

Gould, Kenneth A., Allan Schnaiberg, and Adam S. Weinberg. 1995. "Natural Resource Use in a Transnational Treadmill: International Agreements, National Citizenship Practices, and Sustainable Development." *Humboldt Journal of Social Relations* 21(1): 61–94.

———. 1996. *Local Environmental Struggles: Citizen Activism in the Treadmill of Production.* Cambridge: Cambridge University Press.

Gould, Kenneth A., Adam S. Weinberg, and Allan Schnaiberg. 1993. "Legitimating Impotence: Pyrrhic Victories of the Environmental Movement." *Qualitative Sociology* 16(3): 207–46.

Granovetter, Mark. 1985. "Economic Action and Social Structure: The Problem of Embeddedness." *American Journal Of Sociology* 91:481–510.

Harr, Jonathan. 1996. *A Civil Action.* New York: Vintage.

Harrison, Bennett. 1994. *Lean and Mean: The Changing Landscape of Corporate Power in the Age of Flexibility.* New York: Basic Books.

Hasenfeld, Yeheskel, and Richard A. English. 1974. *Human Service Organizations: A Book of Readings.* Ann Arbor: University of Michigan Press.

Hays, Samuel. 1969. *Conservation and the Gospel of Efficiency: The Progressive Conservation Movement, 1890–1920.* New York: Atheneum.

Hoffman, Andrew J., and Marc J. Ventresca, eds. 2002. *Organizations, Policy, and the Natural Environment.* Stanford, Calif.: Stanford University Press.

Howard, Phillip E. N. 2002. "Privatizing the Citizen." Ph.D. diss., Department of Sociology, Northwestern University.

Hurley, Andrew. 1995. *Environmental Inequalities: Class, Race, and Industrial Pollution in Gary, Indiana, 1945–1980.* Chapel Hill: University of North Carolina Press.

International Union for Conservation of Nature and Natural Resources (IUCN). 1980. *World Conservation Strategy: Living Resource Conservation and Sustainable Development.* New York: IUCN, United Nations Environment Programme.

Jarboe, James F. 2002. "The Threat of Eco-terrorism." Testimony by the Domestic Terrorism Section

Chief, Counterterrorism Division, Federal Bureau of Investigation, before the House Resources Committee Subcommittee on Forests and Forest Health. February 12. http://www.fbi.gov/congress/congress02/jarboe021202.htm.

Kazis, Richard, and Richard Grossman. 1982. *Fear at Work: Job Blackmail, Labor, and the Environment.* New York: Pilgrim Press.

Landy, Marc K., Marc J. Roberts, and Stephen R. Thomas. 1990. *The Environmental Protection Agency: Asking the Wrong Questions.* Oxford: Oxford University Press.

Lele, Sharachchandra M. 1991. "Sustainable Development: A Critical Review." *World Development* 19: 607–21.

Levin, Peter, and Wendy N. Espeland. 2002. "Pollution Futures: Commensuration, Commodification, and the Market for Air." Pp. 119–47 in *Organizations, Policy, and the Natural Environment,* ed. Andrew J. Hoffman and Marc J. Ventresca. Stanford, Calif.: Stanford University Press; Lexington, Mass.: Lexington Books.

Levine, Adeline G. 1982. *Love Canal: Science, Politics, and People.* Lexington, Mass.: Lexington Books.

Lindblom, Charles E. 1977. *Politics and Markets: The World's Political-Economic Systems.* New York: Basic Books.

Logan, John R., and Harvey Molotch. 1987. *Urban Fortunes: The Political Economy of Place.* Berkeley and Los Angeles: University of California Press.

Logan, John, and Todd Swanstrom, eds. 1990. *Beyond the City Limits: Urban Policy and Economic Restructuring in Comparative Perspective.* Philadelphia: Temple University Press.

"Lois Gibbs." 1999. http://www.goldmanprize.org/recipients/recipients.html. Accessed May 1, 2004.

Lomborg, Bjorn. 2001. *The Skeptical Environmentalist: Measuring the Real State of the World.* Cambridge: Cambridge University Press.

Longworth, Richard C. 1998. *Global Squeeze: The Coming Crisis for First-World Nations.* Chicago: Contemporary Books.

———. 1999. "Behind Closed Doors: Crafting the Economic Rules of the New Century." *Northwestern Journal of International Affairs* 1 (spring): 4–11.

Lounsbury, Michael, Marc J. Ventresca, and Paul M. Hirsch. 2003. "Social Movements, Field Frames, and Industry Emergence: A Cultural-Political Perspective on U.S. Recycling." *Socio-economic Review* 1:71–104.

Lowi, Theodore. 1979. *The End of Liberalism.* 2d ed. New York: W. W. Norton.

———. 1986. "The Welfare State, the New Regulation, and the Rule of Law." Pp. 109–49 in *Distributional Conflicts in Environmental-Resource Policy,* ed. Allan Schnaiberg, Nicholas Watts, and Klaus Zimmermann. Aldershot: Gower Press.

Meidinger, Errol. 1986. "Discussion: The Politics of 'Market Mechanisms' in US Air Pollution Regulation—Social Structure and Regulatory Culture." Pp. 150–75 in *Distributional Conflicts in Environmental-Resource Policy,* ed. Allan Schnaiberg, Nicholas Watts, and Klaus Zimmermann. Aldershot: Gower Press.

Meidinger, Errol, and Allan Schnaiberg. 1980. "Social Impact Assessment as Evaluation Research: Claimants and Claims." *Evaluation Review* 4:507–35.

Melosi, Martin. 1981. *Garbage in the Cities: Refuse, Reform, and the Environment, 1880–1980.* College Station: Texas A&M University Press.

Merton, Robert K. 1957. "Social Structure and Anomie." In *Social Theory and Social Structure.* Rev. ed. New York: Free Press.

Meyer, John W. 2002. Foreward. Pp. xiii–xvii in *Organizations, Policy, and the Natural Environment,* ed. Andrew J. Hoffman and Marc J. Ventresca. Stanford, Calif.: Stanford University Press.

Mills, C. Wright. 1959. *The Sociological Imagination.* Oxford: Oxford University Press.

Mishan, Ezra J. 1967. *The Costs of Economic Growth.* New York: Praeger.

Mitchell, Robert C. 1980. "How 'Soft,' 'Deep,' or 'Left'? Present Constituencies in the Environmental Movement." *Natural Resources Journal* 20:345–58.

Mol, Arthur P. J. 1995. *The Refinement of Production: Ecological Modernization Theory and the Dutch Chemical Industry.* Ultrecht: Jan van Arkel/International Books.

———. 1996. "Ecological Modernisation and Institutional Reflexivity." *Environmental Politics* 5:302–23.

Mol, Arthur P. J., and Frederick H. Buttel, eds. 2002. *The Environmental State under Pressure.* Amsterdam: Elsevier Science.

Mol, Arthur P. J., and David A. Sonnenfeld, eds. 2000. *Ecological Modernization around the World.* London: Frank Cass.

Mol, Arthur P. J., and Gert Spaargaren. 2000. "Ecological Modernization Theory in Debate: A Review." Pp. 17–49 in *Ecological Modernization around the World,* ed. Arthur P. J. Mol and David A. Sonnenfeld. London: Frank Cass.

Mumford, Lewis. [1934] 1963. *Technics and Civilization.* New York: Harcourt, Brace and World.

National Commission on the Environment. 1993. *Choosing a Sustainable Future: The Report of the National Commission on the Environment.* Washington, D.C.: Island Press.

National Energy Assistance Directors' Association. 2002. "Unemployment Increases and LIHEAP Needs." Press release, February 20.

Odum, Eugene P. 1969. "The Strategy of Ecosystem Development." *Science* 164:262–70.

Pellow, David N. 1996. "Recycling Waste, Throwing Away Labor." *Environment, Technology, and Society* 83:1, 4.

———. 1998a. "Bodies on the Line: Environmental Inequalities and Hazardous Work in the U.S. Recycling Industry." *Race, Gender and Class* 6:124–51.

———. 1998b. "Black Workers in Green Industries: The Hidden Infrastructure of Environmental Racism." Ph.D. diss., Department of Sociology, Northwestern University.

———. 2001. *Garbage Wars: Environmental Justice Struggles in Chicago, 1880–2000.* Cambridge: MIT Press.

Pellow, David N., and Lisa Sun-Hee Park. 2003. *The Silicon Valley of Dreams: Environmental Injustice, Immigrant Workers, and the High-Tech Global Economy.* New York: New York University Press.

Pellow, David N., Allan Schnaiberg, and Adam S. Weinberg. 2000. "Putting the Ecological Modernisation Thesis to the Test: The Promises and Pitfalls of Urban Recycling." Pp. 109–37 in *Ecological Modernization around the World,* ed. Arthur P. J. Mol and David A. Sonnenfeld. London: Frank Cass.

Pellow, David N., Adam S. Weinberg, and Allan Schnaiberg. 2001. "The Environmental Justice Movement: Equitable Allocation of the Costs and Benefits of Environmental Management Outcomes." *Social Justice Research* 14:423–39.

Pezzy, John. 1989. "Economic Analysis of Sustainable Growth and Sustainable Development." World Bank Environment Department Working Paper No. 15. Washington, D.C.

Phillips, Kevin. 1989. *The Politics of Rich and Poor: Wealth and the American Electorate in the Reagan Aftermath.* New York: Random House.

———. 1993. *Boiling Point: Democrats, Republicans, and the Decline of Middle-Class Prosperity.* New York: Random House.

Portney, Kent E. 1991. *Siting Hazardous Waste Treatment Facilities: The Nimby Syndrome.* New York: Auburn House.

President's Council on Sustainable Development. 1994. *Education for Sustainability.* Washington, D.C.: United States Government Printing Office.

———. 1997. *Sustainable Communities Task Force Report.* Washington, D.C.

———. 1999. *Towards a Sustainable America: Advancing Prosperity, Opportunity, and a Healthy Environment for the Twenty-first Century.* Washington, D.C.

Redclift, Michael. 1986. "Redefining the Environmental 'Crisis' in the South." In *Red and Green: The New Politics of the Environment,* ed. J. Weston. London: Pluto Press.

———. 1987. *Sustainable Development: Exploring the Contradictions.* New York: Methuen.

Redd, Adrienne. N.d. "Lois Gibbs, Champion of Love Canal, Working to Rebuild Democracy." http://www.netaxs.com/~adredd/gibbstext.html. Accessed May 1, 2004.

Reisch, Mark, and David M. Bearden. 2003. *Superfund and the Brownfields Issue.* Hauppage, N.Y.: Nova Science Publishers.

Rose, Carol. 2002. "Common Property, Regulatory Property, and Environmental Protection: Comparing Community-Based Management to Tradable Environmental Allowances." Pp. 233–57 in *The Drama of the Commons,* ed. Elinor Ostrom, Thomas Dietz, Nives Dolsak, Paul C. Stern, Susan Stonich, and Elke Weber. Washington, D.C.: National Academy Press.

Schnaiberg, Allan. 1975. "Social Syntheses of the Societal-Environmental Dialectic: The Role of Distributional Impacts." *Social Science Quarterly* 56 (June): 5–20.

———. 1980. *The Environment: From Surplus to Scarcity.* Oxford: Oxford University Press.

———. 1982. "Did You Ever Meet a Payroll? Contradictions in the Structure of the Appropriate Technology Movement." *Humboldt Journal of Social Relations* 9(2): 38–62.

———. 1983a. "Soft Energy and Hard Labor? Structural Restraints on the Transition to Appropriate Technology." Pp. 217–34 in *Technology and Social Change in Rural Areas,* ed. Gene F. Summers. Boulder, Colo.: Westview Press.

———. 1983b. "Redistributive Goals versus Distributive Politics: Social Equity Limits in Environmental and Appropriate Technology Movements." *Sociological Inquiry* 53:200–219.

———. 1986. "The Role of Experts and Mediators in the Channeling of Distributional Conflict." Pp. 363–79 in *Distributional Conflicts in Environmental-Resource Policy,* ed. Allan Schnaiberg, Nicholas Watts, and Klaus Zimmermann. Aldershot, England: Gower Press.

———. 1994. "The Political Economy of Environmental Problems and Policies: Consciousness, Conflict, and Control Capacity." Pp. 23–64 in vol. 3 of *Advances in Human Ecology,* ed. Lee Freese. Greenwich, Conn.: JAI Press.

———. 1997. "Sustainable Development and the Treadmill of Production." Pp. 72–88 in *The Politics of Sustainable Development: Theory, Policy, and Practice within the European Union,* ed. Susan Baker, Maria Kousis, Dick Richardson, and Stephen Young. London: Routledge.

Schnaiberg, Allan, and Kenneth A. Gould. [1994] 2000. *Environment and Society: The Enduring Conflict.* West Caldwell, N.J.: Blackburn Press.

———. 2001. "Reflections on the 1994 Text." *Environment, Technology, and Society Newsletter* (American Sociological Association) 101:5–6.

Schnaiberg, Allan, David N. Pellow, and Adam Weinberg. 2002. "The Treadmill of Production and the Environmental State." Pp. 15–32 in *The Environmental State under Pressure,* ed. Arthur P. J. Mol and Frederick H. Buttel. Amsterdam: Elsevier Science.

Schnaiberg, Allan, and Adam S. Weinberg. 2002. "Globalization and Energy Policy: The Critical Role of the State and Its Constituencies." Working Paper 02-12, Institute for Policy Research, Northwestern University.

Schumacher, E. F. 1973. *Small Is Beautiful: Economics as if People Mattered.* New York: Harper and Row.

Sheehan, Helen E., and Richard P. Wedeen, eds. 1993. *Toxic Circles: Environmental Hazards from the Workplace into the Community*. New Brunswick, N.J.: Rutgers University Press.

Shuman, Michael. 1998. *Going Local: Creating Self-Reliant Communities in a Global Age*. New York: Free Press.

Silver, Ira Daniel. 1998. "Preventing Fires while Feeling the Heat: Philanthropists and Community Organizations Collaborating to Address Urban Poverty." Ph.D. diss., Department of Sociology, Northwestern University.

Sonnenfeld, David A. 2000. "Contradictions in Ecological Modernization: Pulp and Paper Manufacturing in South-east Asia." Pp. 235–56 in *Ecological Modernization around the World*, ed. Arthur P. J. Mol and David A. Sonnenfeld. London: Frank Cass.

Spaargaren, Gert. 1997. "The Ecological Modernization of Production and Consumption." Doctoral thesis, Landbouw University, The Netherlands.

Spaargaren, Gert, and Arthur P. J. Mol. 1992. "Sociology, Environment, and Modernity: Ecological Modernisation as a Theory of Social Change." *Society and Natural Resources* 5(4): 323–44.

Spector, Malcolm, and John I. Kitsuse. 1977. *Constructing Social Problems*. Menlo Park, Calif.: Cummings.

Stroup, Richard L. 2003. *Eco-nomics: What Everyone Should Know about Economics and the Environment*. Washington, D.C.: Cato Institute.

Stretton, Hugh. 1976. *Capitalism, Socialism, and the Environment*. Cambridge: Cambridge University Press.

Szasz, Andrew. 1994. *Ecopopulism: Toxic Waste and the Movement for Environmental Justice*. Minneapolis: University of Minnesota Press.

Tietenberg, Tom. 2002. "The Tradable Permits Approach to Protecting the Commons: What Have We Learned?" Pp. 197–232 in *The Drama of the Commons*, ed. Elinor Ostrom, Thomas Dietz, Nives Dolsak, Paul C. Stern, Susan Stonich, and Elke Weber. Washington, D.C.: National Academy Press.

United Church of Christ Commission on Racial Justice. 1987. *Toxic Wastes and Race in the United States*. New York: United Church of Christ.

U.S. Office of Community Services. Administration for Children and Families. 2004. "Low Income Home Energy Assistance Program." http://www.acf.dhhs.gov/programs/liheap.

Weinberg, Adam S. 1994. "Citizenship and Natural Resources: Paradoxes of the Treadmill." Ph.D. diss., Northwestern University.

———. 1997a. "Legal Reform and Local Environmental Mobilization." Pp. 293–323 in vol. 6 of *Advances in Human Ecology*, ed. Lee Freese. Westport, Conn.: JAI Press.

———. 1997b. "Local Organizing for Environmental Conflict: Explaining Differences between Cases of Participation and Non-participation." *Organization and Environment* 10(2): 194–216.

———. 1997c. "Power and Public Policy: Community Right-to-Know and the Empowerment of People, Places, and Producers." *Humanity and Society* 21(3): 241–56.

Weinberg, Adam S., David N. Pellow, and Allan Schnaiberg. 1996. "Sustainable Development as a Sociologically Defensible Concept: From Foxes and Rovers to Citizen-Workers." Pp. 261–302 in vol. 5 of *Advances in Human Ecology*, ed. Lee Freese. Westport, Conn.: JAI Press.

———. *Urban Recycling and the Search for Sustainable Community Development*. Princeton: Princeton University Press.

Weinberg, Adam, Allan Schnaiberg, and Kenneth A. Gould. 1995. "Recycling: Conserving Resources or Accelerating the Treadmill of Production?" Pp. 173–205 in vol. 4 of *Advances in Human Ecology*, ed. Lee Freese. Westport, Conn.: JAI Press.

Weinberg, Alvin. 1972. "Social Institutions and Nuclear Energy." *Science* 177:27–34.

Wellin, Christopher. 1997. "Liberation Technology? Workers' Knowledge and the Micro-politics of Adopting Computer-Automation in Industry." Ph.D. diss., Department of Sociology, Northwestern University.

Westman, Walter, and R. M. Gifford. 1973. "Environmental Impact: Controlling the Overall Level." *Science* 181:819–25.

Willers, Bill. 1994. "Sustainable Development: A New World Deception." *Conservation Biology* 8:1146–48.

World Commission on Environment and Development. 1987. *Our Common Future*. Oxford: Oxford University Press.

Yeager, Peter. 1991. *The Limits of Law: The Public Regulation of Private Pollution*. Cambridge: Cambridge University Press.

Contributors

NEIL J. SMELSER is director of the Center for Advanced Study in the Behavioral Sciences, emeritus and university professor of sociology at the University of California, Berkeley.

RICHARD SWEDBERG is professor of sociology at Cornell University.

ANDREW ABBOTT is Gustavus F. and Ann M. Swift Distinguished Service Professor in the Department of Sociology and the College at the University of Chicago.

HOWARD E. ALDRICH is Kenan Professor of Sociology and chair of the Department of Sociology at the University of North Carolina, Chapel Hill.

MABEL BEREZIN is associate professor of sociology at Cornell University.

FRED BLOCK is professor of sociology at the University of California, Davis.

The late PIERRE BOURDIEU was professor of sociology at the Collège de France, Paris.

MARY C. BRINTON is professor of sociology at Harvard University.

BRUCE G. CARRUTHERS is professor of sociology at Northwestern University.

GERALD F. DAVIS is the Sparks/Whirlpool Corporation Research Professor, chair of organizational behavior and human resource management, and professor of sociology at the University of Michigan.

ROBYN DAWES is the Charles J. Queenan, Jr. University Professor of Psychology at Carnegie Mellon University.

FRANK DOBBIN is professor of sociology at Harvard University.

GIOVANNI DOSI is professor of economics at the Sant' Anna School of Advanced Studies, Pisa.

LAUREN B. EDELMAN is professor of law and sociology at the University of California, Berkeley.

PAULA ENGLAND is professor of sociology at Stanford University.

PETER EVANS is Marjorie Meyer Eliaser Professor of International Studies and professor of sociology at the University of California, Berkeley.

NEIL FLIGSTEIN is Class of 1939 Chancellor's Professor in the Department of Sociology at the University of California, Berkeley.

NANCY FOLBRE is professor of economics at the University of Massachusetts, Amherst.

GARY GEREFFI is professor of sociology at Duke University.

MARK GRANOVETTER is professor of sociology at Stanford University.

WILLIAM HALLER is professor of sociology at Princeton University.

EVELYNE HUBER is Morehead Alumni Distinguished Professor of Political Science at the University of North Carolina, Chapel Hill.

LAWRENCE P. KING is associate professor of sociology at Yale University.

MAURO SYLOS LABINI is a doctoral candidate in economics at the Sant'Anna School of Advanced Studies, Pisa.

IVAN LIGHT is professor of sociology at the University of California, Los Angeles.

J. G. MANNING is associate professor of ancient history at Stanford University.

MARK S. MIZRUCHI is professor of sociology and business administration at the University of Michigan.

IAN MORRIS is Jean and Rebecca Willard Professor of Classics and professor of history at Stanford University.

VICTOR NEE is Goldwin Smith Professor of Sociology and Director of the Center for the Study of Economy and Society at Cornell University.

LUIGI ORSENIGO is professor of economics at Bocconi University, Milan.

ALEJANDRO PORTES is Howard Harrison and Gabrielle Snyder Beck Professor of Sociology and director of the Center for Migration and Development at Princeton University.

WALTER W. POWELL is professor of education and sociology at Stanford University.

ALLAN SCHNAIBERG is professor of sociology at Northwestern University.

LAUREL SMITH-DOERR is assistant professor of sociology at Boston University.

LINDA BREWSTER STEARNS is professor of sociology at Southern Methodist University.

JOHN D STEPHENS is Gerhard E. Lenski, Jr. Distinguished Professor of Political Science and Sociology at the University of North Carolina, Chapel Hill.

WOLFGANG STREECK is professor of sociology and director at the Max Planck Institute for the Study of Societies in Cologne.

ROBIN STRYKER is professor of sociology at the University of Minnesota.

IVÁN SZELÉNYI is William Graham Sumner Professor of Sociology at Yale University.

ROBERTO WEBER is assistant professor of economics at Carnegie Mellon University.

ROBERT WUTHNOW is Gerhard R. Andlinger '52 Professor of Sociology and director of the Center for the Study of Religion at Princeton University.

VIVIANA ZELIZER is professor of sociology at Princeton University.

Index